Oxford University Press, Ely House, London W. 1

GLASGOW NEW YORK TORONTO MELBOURNE WELLINGTON
CAPE TOWN SALISBURY IBADAN NAIROBI LUSAKA ADDIS ABABA
BOMBAY CALCUTTA MADRAS KARACHI LAHORE DACCA
KUALA LUMPUR HONG KONG TOKYO

LONGFELLOW
POETICAL WORKS

LONDON
OXFORD UNIVERSITY PRESS
NEW YORK   TORONTO

Henry Wadsworth Longfellow

Born, Portland, Maine, U.S.A.　　•　　27 February 1807
Died, Cambridge, Massachusetts, U.S.A. • 24 March 1882

This edition of The Poetical Works of Longfellow *was first
published in 1904, and reprinted in 1905, 1906, 1907, 1908,
1910, 1912, 1913, 1916 (twice), 1919, 1921, 1925, 1928, 1934,
1944, 1946, 1948, 1951, 1953, 1957, 1961, 1965 and 1968*

*Printed in Great Britain by
The Camelot Press Ltd., London and Southampton*

O.S.A.

Contents

Contents.

Contents.

Voices of the Night.

—+—

Πότνια, πότνια νύξ,
ὑπνοδότειρα τῶν πολυπόνων βροτῶν,
Ἐρεβόθεν ἴθι· μόλε μόλε κατάπτερος
Ἀγαμεμνόνιον ἐπὶ δόμον·
ὑπὸ γὰρ ἀλγέων, ὑπό τε συμφορᾶς
διοιχόμεθ᾽, οἰχόμεθα.

EURIPIDES.

—+—

PRELUDE.

PLEASANT it was, when woods were
    green,
And winds were soft and low,
To lie amid some sylvan scene,
Where, the long drooping boughs
    between,
Shadows dark and sunlight sheen
    Alternate come and go;

Or where the denser grove re-
    ceives
No sunlight from above,
But the dark foliage interweaves
In one unbroken roof of leaves,
Underneath whose sloping eaves
    The shadows hardly move.

Beneath some patriarchal tree
    I lay upon the ground;
His hoary arms uplifted he,
And all the broad leaves over
    me
Clapped their little hands in glee,
    With one continuous sound;—

A slumbrous sound, a sound that
    brings
    The feelings of a dream,
As of innumerable wings,
As, when a bell no longer swings,
Faint the hollow murmur rings
    O'er meadow, lake, and stream.

And dreams of that which cannot
    die,
    Bright visions, came to me,
As lapped in thought I used to lie,
And gaze into the summer sky,
Where the sailing clouds went by,
    Like ships upon the sea;

Dreams that the soul of youth en-
    gage
Ere Fancy has been quelled;
Old legends of the monkish page,
Traditions of the saint and sage,
Tales that have the rime of age,
    And chronicles of Eld.

And, loving still these quaint old
    themes,
    Even in the city's throng
I feel the freshness of the streams,
That, crossed by shades and sunny
    gleams,
Water the green land of dreams,
    The holy land of song.

Therefore, at Pentecost, which
    brings
    The Spring, clothed like a bride,
When nestling buds unfold their
    wings,
And bishop's-caps have golden
    rings,
Musing upon many things,
    I sought the woodlands wide.

I

The green trees whispered low and
    mild :
    It was a sound of joy !
They were my playmates when a
    child,
And rocked me in their arms so
    wild :
Still they looked at me and smiled,
    As if I were a boy ;

And ever whispered, mild and low,
    ' Come, be a child once more !'
And waved their long arms to and
    fro,
And beckoned solemnly and slow ;
O, I could not choose but go
    Into the woodlands hoar,—

Into the blithe and breathing air,
    Into the solemn wood,
Solemn and silent everywhere !
Nature with folded hands seemed
    there,
Kneeling at her evening prayer !
    Like one in prayer I stood.

Before me rose an avenue
    Of tall and sombrous pines ;
Abroad their fan-like branches
    grew,
And, where the sunshine darted
    through,
Spread a vapour soft and blue,
    In long and sloping lines.

And, falling on my weary brain,
    Like a fast-falling shower,
The dreams of youth came back
    again,
Low lispings of the summer rain,
Dropping on the ripened grain,
    As once upon the flower.

Visions of childhood ! Stay, O
    stay !
    Ye were so sweet and wild !
And distant voices seemed to say,

' It cannot be !   They pass away !
Other themes demand thy lay ;
    Thou art no more a child !

' The land of Song within thee
    lies,
    Watered by living springs ;
The lids of Fancy's sleepless eyes
Are gates unto that Paradise,
Holy thoughts, like stars, arise,
    Its clouds are angels' wings.

' Learn, that henceforth thy song
    shall be,
    Not mountains capped with snow,
Nor forests sounding like the sea,
Nor rivers flowing ceaselessly,
Where the woodlands bend to
    see
    The bending heavens below.

' There is a forest where the din
    Of iron branches sounds !
A mighty river roars between,
And whosoever looks therein
Sees the heavens all black with
    sin,
    Sees not its depths, nor bounds.

' Athwart the swinging branches
    cast,
    Soft rays of sunshine pour ;
Then comes the fearful wintry
    blast ;
Our hopes, like withered leaves,
    fall fast ;
Pallid lips say, " It is past !
    We can return no more !"

' Look, then, into thine heart, and
    write !
    Yes, into Life's deep stream !
All forms of sorrow and delight,
All solemn Voices of the Night,
That can soothe thee, or affright,—
    Be these henceforth thy theme.'

HYMN TO THE NIGHT.

’Ασπασίη, τρίλλιστος.

I HEARD the trailing garments of
　　the Night
　　　Sweep through her marble
　　　　halls !
I saw her sable skirts all fringed
　　with light
　　　From the celestial walls !

I felt her presence, by its spell of
　　might,
　　　Stoop o’er me from above ;
The calm, majestic presence of the
　　Night,
　　　As of the one I love.

I heard the sounds of sorrow and
　　delight,
　　　The manifold, soft chimes,
That fill the haunted chambers of
　　the Night,
　　　Like some old poet’s rhymes.

From the cool cisterns of the mid-
　　night air
　　　My spirit drank repose ;
The fountain of perpetual peace
　　flows there,—
　　　From those deep cisterns flows.

O holy Night ! from thee I learn
　　to bear
　　　What man has borne before !
Thou layest thy finger on the lips
　　of Care,
　　　And they complain no more.

Peace ! Peace ! Orestes-like I
　　breathe this prayer !
　　　Descend with broad-winged
　　　　flight,
The welcome, the thrice-prayed-
　　for, the most fair,
　　　The best-beloved Night !

A PSALM OF LIFE.

WHAT THE HEART OF THE YOUNG
MAN SAID TO THE PSALMIST.

TELL me not, in mournful numbers,
　　Life is but an empty dream !
For the soul is dead that slumbers,
　　And things are not what they
　　　seem.

Life is real ! Life is earnest !
　　And the grave is not its goal ;
Dust thou art, to dust returnest,
　　Was not spoken of the soul.

Not enjoyment, and not sorrow,
　　Is our destined end or way ;
But to act, that each to-morrow
　　Find us farther than to-day.

Art is long, and Time is fleeting,
　　And our hearts, though stout
　　　and brave,
Still, like muffled drums, are beating
　　Funeral marches to the grave.

In the world’s broad field of battle,
　　In the bivouac of Life,
Be not like dumb, driven cattle !
　　Be a hero in the strife !

Trust no Future, howe’er pleasant !
　　Let the dead Past bury its dead !
Act,—act in the living Present !
　　Heart within, and God o’erhead !

Lives of great men all remind us
　　We can make our lives sublime,
And, departing, leave behind us
　　Footprints on the sands of
　　　time ; —

Footprints, that perhaps another,
　　Sailing o’er life’s solemn main,
A forlorn and shipwrecked brother,
　　Seeing, shall take heart again.

Let us, then, be up and doing,
　　With a heart for any fate ;
Still achieving, still pursuing,
　　Learn to labour and to wait.

3

THE REAPER AND THE FLOWERS.

THERE is a Reaper whose name is
    Death,
  And, with his sickle keen,
He reaps the bearded grain at a
    breath,
  And the flowers that grow be-
    tween.

'Shall I have naught that is fair?'
    saith he;
  'Have naught but the bearded
    grain?
Though the breath of these flowers
    is sweet to me,
  I will give them all back again.'

He gazed at the flowers with tearful
    eyes,
  He kissed their drooping leaves;
It was for the Lord of Paradise
  He bound them in his sheaves.

'My Lord has need of these
    flowerets gay,'
  The Reaper said, and smiled;
'Dear tokens of the earth are they,
  Where He was once a child.

'They shall all bloom in fields of
    light,
  Transplanted by my care,
And saints, upon their garments
    white,
  These sacred blossoms wear.'

And the mother gave, in tears and
    pain,
  The flowers she most did love;
She knew she should find them all
    again
  In the fields of light above.

O, not in cruelty, not in wrath,
  The Reaper came that day;
'Twas an angel visited the green
    earth,
  And took the flowers away.

THE LIGHT OF STARS.

THE night is come, but not too
    soon;
  And sinking silently,
All silently, the little moon
  Drops down behind the sky.

There is no light in earth or heaven
  But the cold light of stars;
And the first watch of night is
    given
  To the red planet Mars.

Is it the tender star of love?
  The star of love and dreams?
O no! from that blue tent above,
  A hero's armour gleams.

And earnest thoughts within me
    rise,
  When I behold afar,
Suspended in the evening skies,
  The shield of that red star.

O star of strength! I see thee stand
  And smile upon my pain;
Thou beckonest with thy mailed
    hand,
  And I am strong again.

Within my breast there is no light
  But the cold light of stars;
I give the first watch of the night
  To the red planet Mars.

The star of the unconquered will,
  He rises in my breast,
Serene, and resolute, and still,
  And calm, and self-possessed.

And thou, too, whosoe'er thou art,
  That readest this brief psalm,
As one by one thy hopes depart,
  Be resolute and calm.

O fear not in a world like this,
  And thou shalt know erelong,
Know how sublime a thing it is
  To suffer and be strong.

FOOTSTEPS OF ANGELS.

WHEN the hours of Day are num-
    bered,
    And the voices of the Night
Wake the better soul, that slum-
    bered,
    To a holy, calm delight;

Ere the evening lamps are lighted,
    And, like phantoms grim and
    tall,
Shadows from the fitful firelight
    Dance upon the parlour wall;

Then the forms of the departed
    Enter at the open door;
The beloved, the true-hearted,
    Come to visit me once more;

He, the young and strong, who
    cherished
Noble longings for the strife,
By the roadside fell and perished,
    Weary with the march of life!

They, the holy ones and weakly,
    Who the cross of suffering bore,
Folded their pale hands so meekly,
    Spake with us on earth no more!

And with them the Being Beau-
    teous,
    Who unto my youth was given,
More than all things else to love
    me,
    And is now a saint in heaven.

With a slow and noiseless footstep
    Comes that messenger divine,
Takes the vacant chair beside me,
    Lays her gentle hand in mine.

And she sits and gazes at me
    With those deep and tender eyes,
Like the stars, so still and saint-
    like,
    Looking downward from the
    skies.

Uttered not, yet comprehended,
    Is the spirit's voiceless prayer,
Soft rebukes, in blessings ended,
    Breathing from her lips of air.

O, though oft depressed and lonely,
    All my fears are laid aside,
If I but remember only
    Such as these have lived and
    died!

FLOWERS.

SPAKE full well, in language quaint
    and olden,
    One who dwelleth by the castled
    Rhine,
When he called the flowers, so blue
    and golden,
    Stars, that in earth's firmament
    do shine.

Stars they are, wherein we read
    our history,
    As astrologers and seers of eld;
Yet not wrapped about with awful
    mystery,
    Like the burning stars, which
    they beheld.

Wondrous truths, and manifold as
    wondrous,
    God hath written in those stars
    above;
But not less in the bright flowerets
    under us
    Stands the revelation of His
    love.

Bright and glorious is that revela-
    tion,
    Written all over this great world
    of ours;
Making evident our own creation,
    In these stars of earth, these
    golden flowers.

And the Poet, faithful and far-
seeing,
    Sees, alike in stars and flowers,
      a part
Of the self-same, universal being,
    Which is throbbing in his brain
      and heart.

Gorgeous flowerets in the sunlight
    shining,
    Blossoms flaunting in the eye of
      day,
Tremulous leaves, with soft and
    silver lining,
    Buds that open only to decay ;

Brilliant hopes, all woven in gor-
    geous tissues,
    Flaunting gaily in the golden
      light,
Large desires, with most uncertain
    issues,
    Tender wishes, blossoming at
      night !

These in flowers and men are more
    than seeming ;
    Workings are they of the self-
      same powers,
Which the Poet, in no idle dream-
    ing,
    Seeth in himself and in the
      flowers.

Everywhere about us are they
    glowing,
    Some like stars, to tell us Spring
      is born ;
Others, their blue eyes with tears
    o'erflowing,
    Stand like Ruth amid the golden
      corn ;

Not alone in Spring's armorial
    bearing,
    And in Summer's green-em-
      blazoned field,

But in arms of brave old Autumn's
    wearing,
    In the centre of his brazen shield ;

Not alone in meadows and green
    alleys,
    On the mountain-top, and by
      the brink
Of sequestered pools in woodland
    valleys,
    Where the slaves of nature stoop
      to drink ;

Not alone in her vast dome of
    glory,
    Not on graves of bird and beast
      alone,
But in old cathedrals, high and
    hoary,
    On the tombs of heroes, carved
      in stone ;

In the cottage of the rudest peasant,
    In ancestral homes, whose
      crumbling towers,
Speaking of the Past unto the
    Present,
    Tell us of the ancient Games of
      Flowers ;

In all places, then, and in all sea-
    sons,
    Flowers expand their light and
      soul-like wings,
Teaching us, by most persuasive
    reasons,
    How akin they are to human
      things.

And with childlike, credulous af-
    fection
    We behold their tender buds ex-
      pand ;
Emblems of our own great resur-
    rection,
    Emblems of the bright and better
      land.

THE BELEAGUERED CITY.

I HAVE read, in some old, marvel-
    lous tale,
  Some legend strange and vague,
That a midnight host of spectres
    pale
  Beleaguered the walls of Prague.

Beside the Moldau's rushing
    stream,
  With the wan moon overhead,
There stood, as in an awful dream,
  The army of the dead.

White as a sea - fog landward
    bound,
  The spectral camp was seen,
And, with a sorrowful, deep sound,
  The river flowed between.

No other voice nor sound was
    there,
  No drum, nor sentry's pace;
The mist-like banners clasped the
    air,
  As clouds with clouds embrace.

But when the old cathedral bell
  Proclaimed the morning prayer,
The white pavilions rose and fell
  On the alarmed air.

Down the broad valley fast and far
  The troubled army fled;
Up rose the glorious morning star,
  The ghastly host was dead.

I have read, in the marvellous
    heart of man,
  That strange and mystic scroll,
That an army of phantoms vast
    and wan
  Beleaguer the human soul.

Encamped beside Life's rushing
    stream,
  In Fancy's misty light,
Gigantic shapes and shadows gleam
  Portentous through the night.

Upon its midnight battle-ground
  The spectral camp is seen,
And, with a sorrowful, deep sound,
  Flows the River of Life between.

No other voice nor sound is there,
  In the army of the grave;
No other challenge breaks the air,
  But the rushing of Life's wave.

And when the solemn and deep
    church-bell
  Entreats the soul to pray,
The midnight phantoms feel the
    spell,
  The shadows sweep away.

Down the broad Vale of Tears afar
  The spectral camp is fled;
Faith shineth as a morning star,
  Our ghastly fears are dead.

-->--

MIDNIGHT MASS FOR THE DYING YEAR.

YES, the Year is growing old,
  And his eye is pale and bleared!
Death, with frosty hand and cold,
  Plucks the old man by the beard,
    Sorely, sorely!

The leaves are falling, falling,
  Solemnly and slow;
Caw! caw! the rooks are calling,
  It is a sound of woe,
    A sound of woe!

Through woods and mountain
    passes
  The winds, like anthems, roll;
They are chanting solemn masses,
  Singing, 'Pray for this poor soul,
    Pray, pray!'

And the hooded clouds, like friars,
  Tell their beads in drops of rain,
And patter their doleful prayers;
  But their prayers are all in vain,
    All in vain!

7

There he stands in the foul weather,
　The foolish, fond Old Year,
Crowned with wild flowers and
　　with heather,
　Like weak, despised Lear,
　　A king, a king!

Then comes the summer-like day,
　Bids the old man rejoice!
His joy! his last! O, the old man
　　gray
Loveth that ever-soft voice,
　　Gentle and low.

To the crimson woods he saith,
　To the voice gentle and low
Of the soft air, like a daughter's
　　breath,
　'Pray do not mock me so!
　　Do not laugh at me!'

And now the sweet day is dead;
　Cold in his arms it lies;
No stain from its breath is spread
　Over the glassy skies,
　　No mist or stain!

Then, too, the Old Year dieth,
　And the forests utter a moan,
Like the voice of one who crieth
　In the wilderness alone,
　　'Vex not his ghost!'

Then comes, with an awful roar,
　Gathering and sounding on,
The storm-wind from Labrador,
　The wind Euroclydon,
　　The storm-wind!

Howl! howl! and from the forest
　Sweep the red leaves away!
Would, the sins that thou abhorrest,
　O Soul! could thus decay,
　　And be swept away!

For there shall come a mightier
　　blast,
　There shall be a darker day;
And the stars, from heaven down-
　　cast
　Like red leaves be swept away!
　　Kyrie, eleyson!
　　Christe, eleyson!

L'ENVOI.

YE voices, that arose
After the Evening's close,
And whispered to my restless heart
　repose!

Go, breathe it in the ear
Of all who doubt and fear,
And say to them, 'Be of good
　cheer!'

Ye sounds, so low and calm,
That in the groves of balm
Seemed to me like an angel's
　psalm!

Go, mingle yet once more
With the perpetual roar
Of the pine forest, dark and hoar!

Tongues of the dead, not lost,
But speaking from death's frost,
Like fiery tongues at Pentecost!

Glimmer, as funeral lamps,
Amid the chills and damps
Of the vast plain where Death
　encamps!

8

Earlier Poems.

[These poems were written for the most part during my college life, and all of them before the age of nineteen. Some have found their way into schools, and seem to be successful. Others lead a vagabond and precarious existence in the corners of newspapers; or have changed their names and run away to seek their fortunes beyond the sea. I say, with the Bishop of Avranches on a similar occasion: 'I cannot be displeased to see these children of mine, which I have neglected, and almost exposed, brought from their wanderings in lanes and alleys, and safely lodged, in order to go forth into the world together in a more decorous garb.']

AN APRIL DAY.

WHEN the warm sun, that brings
Seed-time and harvest, has re-
    turned again,
'Tis sweet to visit the still wood,
    where springs
The first flower of the plain.

I love the season well,
When forest glades are teeming
    with bright forms,
Nor dark and many-folded clouds
    foretell
The coming-on of storms.

From the earth's loosened mould
The sapling draws its sustenance,
    and thrives;
Though stricken to the heart with
    winter's cold,
The drooping tree revives.

The softly-warbled song
Comes from the pleasant woods,
    and coloured wings
Glance quick in the bright sun, that
    moves along
The forest openings.

When the bright sunset fills
The silver woods with light, the
    green slope throws
Its shadows in the hollows of the
    hills,
And wide the upland glows.

And when the eve is born,
In the blue lake the sky, o'er-reach-
    ing far,
Is hollowed out, and the moon dips
    her horn,
And twinkles many a star.

Inverted in the tide
Stand the gray rocks, and trem-
    bling shadows throw,
And the fair trees look over, side
    by side,
And see themselves below.

Sweet April! many a thought
Is wedded unto thee, as hearts are
    wed;
Nor shall they fail, till, to its autumn
    brought,
Life's golden fruit is shed.

AUTUMN.

WITH what a glory comes and
    goes the year!
The buds of spring, those beautiful
    harbingers
Of sunny skies and cloudless times,
    enjoy
Life's newness, and earth's garni-
    ture spread out;
And when the silver habit of the
    clouds

Comes down upon the autumn sun,
and with
A sober gladness the old year takes
up
His bright inheritance of golden
fruits,
A pomp and pageant fill the splendid scene.

There is a beautiful spirit breathing now
Its mellow richness on the clustered
trees,
And, from a beaker full of richest
dyes,
Pouring new glory on the autumn
woods,
And dipping in warm light the
pillared clouds.
Morn on the mountain, like a summer bird,
Lifts up her purple wing, and in the
vales
The gentle wind, a sweet and passionate wooer,
Kisses the blushing leaf, and stirs
up life
Within the solemn woods of ash
deep-crimsoned,
And silver beech, and maple
yellow-leaved,
Where Autumn, like a faint old
man, sits down
By the wayside a-weary. Through
the trees
The golden robin moves. The purple finch,
That on wild cherry and red cedar
feeds,
A winter bird, comes with its plaintive whistle,
And pecks by the witch-hazel,
whilst aloud
From cottage roofs the warbling
blue-bird sings,
And merrily, with oft-repeated
stroke,
Sounds from the threshing-floor the
busy flail.

O what a glory doth this world
put on
For him who, with a fervent heart,
goes forth
Under the bright and glorious sky,
and looks
On duties well performed, and days
well spent !
For him the wind, ay, and the
yellow leaves,
Shall have a voice, and give him
eloquent teachings.
He shall so hear the solemn hymn
that Death
Has lifted up for all, that he shall go
To his long resting-place without a
tear.

———◆———

WOODS IN WINTER.

WHEN winter winds are piercing
chill,
    And through the hawthorn blows
the gale,
With solemn feet I tread the hill,
    That overbrows the lonely vale.

O'er the bare upland, and away
    Through the long reach of desert
woods,
The embracing sunbeams chastely
play,
    And gladden these deep soli-
tudes.

Where, twisted round the barren
oak,
    The summer vine in beauty
clung,
And summer winds the stillness
broke,
    The crystal icicle is hung.

Where, from their frozen urns,
mute springs
    Pour out the river's gradual tide,
Shrilly the skater's iron rings,
    And voices fill the woodland side.

Juvenile Poems.

WRITTEN BETWEEN 1824 AND 1826.

THANKSGIVING.

WHEN first in ancient time from
Jubal's tongue
The tuneful anthem filled the morn-
ing air,
To sacred hymnings and Elysian
song
His music-breathing shell the
minstrel woke.
Devotion breathed aloud from
every chord :
The voice of praise was heard in
every tone,
And prayer, and thanks to Him the
Eternal One,
To Him, that with bright inspira-
tion touched
The high and gifted lyre of heavenly
song,
And warmed the soul with new
vitality.
A stirring energy through Nature
breathed :
The voice of adoration from her
broke,
Swelling aloud in every breeze, and
heard
Long in the sullen waterfall,—what
time
Soft Spring or hoary Autumn threw
on earth
Its bloom or blighting,—when the
Summer smiled,
Or Winter o'er the year's sepulchre
mourned.
The Deity was there !—a nameless
spirit
Moved in the breasts of men to do
Him homage ;

And when the morning smiled, or
evening pale
Hung weeping o'er the melancholy
urn,
They came beneath the broad o'er-
arching trees,
And in their tremulous shadow wor-
shipped oft,
Where pale the vine clung round
their simple altars,
And gray moss mantling hung.
Above was heard
The melody of winds, breathed out
as the green trees
Bowed to their quivering touch in
living beauty,
And birds sang forth their cheerful
hymns. Below
The bright and widely wandering
rivulet
Struggled and gushed amongst the
tangled roots
That choked its reedy fountain, and
dark rocks
Worn smooth by the constant cur-
rent. Even there
The listless wave, that stole with
mellow voice
Where reeds grew rank on the
rushy-fringed brink,
And the green sedge bent to the
wandering wind,
Sang with a cheerful song of sweet
tranquillity.
Men felt the heavenly influence,
and it stole
Like balm into their hearts, till all
was peace ;
And even the air they breathed,
the light they saw,

15

Became religion; for the ethereal
spirit
That to soft music wakes the chords
of feeling,
And mellows everything to beauty,
moved
With cheering energy within their
breasts,
And made all holy there,—for all
was love.
The morning stars, that sweetly
sang together,
The moon, that hung at night in
the mid-sky,
Dayspring, and eventide, and all
the fair
And beautiful forms of nature, had
a voice
Of eloquent worship. Ocean with
its tides
Swelling and deep, where low the
infant storm
Hung on his dun, dark cloud, and
heavily beat
The pulses of the sea, sent forth a
voice
Of awful adoration to the spirit
That, wrapt in darkness, moved
upon its face.
And when the bow of evening
arched the east,
Or, in the moonlight pale, the
curling wave
Kissed with a sweet embrace the
sea-worn beach,
And soft the song of winds came
o'er the waters,
The mingled melody of wind and
wave
Touched like a heavenly anthem
on the ear;
For it arose a tuneful hymn of wor-
ship.
And have *our* hearts grown cold?
Are there on earth
No pure reflections caught from
heavenly light?
Have our mute lips no hymn,—our
souls no song?

Let him that in the summer day of
youth
Keeps pure the holy fount of youthful feeling,
And him that in the nightfall of his
years
Lies down in his last sleep, and
shuts in peace
His dim pale eyes on life's short
wayfaring,
Praise Him that rules the destiny of
man.

—————

AUTUMNAL NIGHTFALL.

ROUND Autumn's mouldering
urn,
Loud mourns the chill and cheerless gale,
When nightfall shades the quiet
vale,
And stars in beauty burn.

'T is the year's eventide.
The wind,—like one that sighs in
pain
O'er joys that ne'er will bloom
again,
Mourns on the far hillside.

And yet my pensive eye
Rests on the faint blue mountain
long,
And for the fairy-land of song,
That lies beyond, I sigh.

The moon unveils her brow;
In the mid-sky her urn glows
bright,
And in her sad and mellowing light
The valley sleeps below.

Upon the hazel gray
The lyre of Autumn hangs unstrung,
And o'er its tremulous chords are
flung
The fringes of decay.

I stand deep musing here,
Beneath the dark and motionless
　　beech,
Whilst wandering winds of nightfall
　　reach
　　My melancholy ear.

The air breathes chill and free ;
A Spirit in soft music calls
From Autumn's gray and moss-
　　grown halls,
　　And round her withered tree.

The hoar and mantled oak,
With moss and twisted ivy brown,
Bends in its lifeless beauty down
　　Where weeds the fountain choke.

That fountain's hollow voice
Echoes the sound of precious
　　things ;—
Of early feeling's tuneful springs
　　Choked with our blighted joys.

Leaves, that the night-wind
　　bears
To earth's cold bosom with a sigh,
Are types of our mortality,
　　And of our fading years.

The tree that shades the plain,
Wasting and hoar as time decays,
Spring shall renew with cheerful
　　days,—
　　But not my joys again.

———⋆———

ITALIAN SCENERY.

——Night rests in beauty on Mont
　　Alto.
Beneath its shade the beauteous
　　Arno sleeps
In Vallombrosa's bosom, and dark
　　trees
Bend with a calm and quiet shadow
　　down
Upon the beauty of that silent river.
Still in the west, a melancholy smile
Mantles the lips of day, and twilight
　　pale

Moves like a spectre in the dusky
　　sky ;
While eve's sweet star on the fast-
　　fading year
Smiles calmly :—Music steals at
　　intervals
Across the water, with a tremulous
　　swell,
From out the upland dingle of tall
　　firs,
And a faint footfall sounds, where
　　dim and dark
Hangs the gray willow from the
　　river's brink,
O'ershadowing its current. Slowly
　　there
The lover's gondola drops down
　　the stream,
Silent,—save when its dipping oar
　　is heard,
Or in its eddy sighs the rippling
　　wave.
Mouldering and moss - grown
　　through the lapse of years,
In motionless beauty stands the
　　giant oak,
Whilst those that saw its green and
　　flourishing youth
Are gone and are forgotten. Soft
　　the fount,
Whose secret springs the star-light
　　pale discloses,
Gushes in hollow music, and be-
　　yond
The broader river sweeps its silent
　　way,
Mingling a silver current with that
　　sea,
Whose waters have no tides, com-
　　ing nor going.
On noiseless wing along that fair
　　blue sea
The halcyon flits,—and where the
　　wearied storm
Left a loud moaning, all is peace
　　again.

A calm is on the deep ! The
　　winds that came

17

O'er the dark sea-surge with a
tremulous breathing,
And mourned on the dark cliff
where weeds grew rank,
And to the autumnal death-dirge
the deep sea
Heaved its long billows,—with a
cheerless song
Have passed away to the cold earth
again,
Like a wayfaring mourner. Silently
Up from the calm sea's dim and
distant verge,
Full and unveiled the moon's broad
disk emerges.
On Tivoli, and where the fairy hues
Of autumn glow upon Abruzzi's
woods,
The silver light is spreading. Far
above,
Encompassed with their thin, cold
atmosphere,
The Apennines uplift their snowy
brows,
Glowing with colder beauty, where
unheard
The eagle screams in the fathom-
less ether,
And stays his wearied wing.
Here let us pause !
The spirit of these solitudes—the
soul
That dwells within these steep and
difficult places—
Speaks a mysterious language to
mine own,
And brings unutterable musings.
Earth
Sleeps in the shades of nightfall,
and the sea
Spreads like a thin blue haze be-
neath my feet,
Whilst the gray columns and the
mouldering tombs
Of the Imperial City, hidden deep
Beneath the mantle of their
shadows, rest.
My spirit looks on earth !—A
heavenly voice

Comes silently : 'Dreamer, is earth
thy dwelling !—
Lo ! nursed within that fair and
fruitful bosom
Which has sustained thy being,
and within
The coller breast of Ocean, lie the
germs
Of thine own dissolution ! E'en
the air,
That fans the clear blue sky and
gives thee strength—
Up from the sullen lake of mouldering reeds,
And the wide waste of forest,
where the osier
Thrives in the damp and motionless atmosphere,—
Shall bring the dire and wasting
pestilence
And blight thy cheek. Dream thou
of higher things ;—
This world is not thy home !' And
yet my eye
Rests upon earth again ! How
beautiful,
Where wild Velino heaves its sullen
waves
Down the high cliff of gray and
shapeless granite,—
Hung on the curling mist, the
moonlight bow
Arches the perilous river. A soft
light
Silvers the Albanian mountains,
and the haze
That rests upon their summits,
mellows down
The austerer features of their
beauty. Faint
And dim-discovered glow the
Sabine hills,
And listening to the sea's monoto-
nous shell,
High on the cliffs of Terracina
stands
The castle of the royal Goth[1] in
ruins.

[1] Theodoric.

But night is in her wane :—day's early flush
Glows like a hectic on her fading cheek,
Wasting its beauty. And the opening dawn
With cheerful lustre lights the royal city,
Where, with its proud tiara of dark towers,
It sleeps upon its own romantic bay.

—◆—

THE LUNATIC GIRL.

MOST beautiful, most gentle! Yet how lost
To all that gladdens the fair earth ; the eye
That watched her being ; the maternal care
That kept and nourished her ; and the calm light
That steals from our own thoughts, and softly rests
On youth's green valleys and smooth-sliding waters!
Alas! few suns ot life, and fewer winds,
Had withered or had wasted the fresh rose
That bloomed upon her cheek ; but one chill frost
Came in that early Autumn, when ripe thought
Is rich and beautiful, and blighted it;
And the fair stalk grew languid day by day,
And drooped, and drooped, and shed its many leaves.
'Tis said that some have died of love, and some,
That once from beauty's high romance had caught
Love's passionate feelings and heart-wasting cares,

Have spurned life's threshold with a desperate foot :
And others have gone mad,—and she was one!
Her lover died at sea ; and they had felt
A coldness for each other when they parted ;
But love returned again, and to her ear
Came tidings that the ship which bore her lover
Had suddenly gone down at sea, and all were lost.
I saw her in her native vale, when high
The aspiring lark up from the reedy river
Mounted on cheerful pinion ; and she sat
Casting smooth pebbles into a clear fountain,
And marking how they sunk ; and oft she sighed
For him that perished thus in the vast deep.
She had a sea-shell, that her lover brought
From the far-distant ocean, and she pressed
Its smooth cold lips unto her ear, and thought
It whispered tidings of the dark blue sea ;
And sad she cried, ' The tides are out !—and now
I see his corse upon the stormy beach !'
Around her neck a string of rose-lipped shells,
And coral, and white pearl, was loosely hung,
And close beside her lay a delicate [fan,
Made of the halcyon's blue wing ; and when
She looked upon it, it would calm her thoughts
As that bird calms the ocean,—for it gave

Mournful, yet pleasant memory.
Once I marked
When through the mountain
hollows and green woods
That bent beneath its footsteps
the loud wind
Came with a voice as of the rest-
less deep,
She raised her head, and on her
pale cold cheek
A beauty of diviner seeming came:
And then she spread her hands,
and smiled, as if
She welcomed a long-absent friend,
—and then
Shrunk timorously back again,
and wept.
I turned away: a multitude of
thoughts,
Mournful and dark, were crowding
on my mind,
And as I left that lost and ruined
one,—
A living monument that still on
earth
There is warm love and deep
sincerity,—
She gazed upon the west, where
the blue sky
Held, like an ocean, in its wide
embrace
Those fairy islands of bright cloud
that lay
So calm and quietly in the thin
ether.
And then she pointed where, alone
and high,
One little cloud sailed onward, like
a lost
And wandering bark, and fainter
grew, and fainter,
And soon was swallowed up in the
blue depths.
And when it sunk away, she
turned again
With sad despondency and tears
to earth.
Three long and weary months,
—yet not a whisper

Of stern reproach for that cold
parting ! Then
She sat no longer by her favourite
fountain !
She was at rest for ever.

THE VENETIAN GON-DOLIER.

HERE rest the weary oar ! soft
airs
Breathe out in the o'erarching
sky ;
And Night—sweet Night—serenely
wears
A smile of peace ; her noon is
nigh.

Where the tall fir in quiet stands,
And waves, embracing the
chaste shores,
Move o'er sea-shells and bright
sands,
Is heard the sound of dipping
oars.

Swift o'er the wave the light bark
springs,
Love's midnight hour draws
lingering near :
And list !—his tuneful viol strings
The young Venetian Gondolier.

Lo ! on the silver-mirrored deep,
On earth and her embosomed
lakes,
And where the silent rivers sweep,
From the thin cloud fair moon-
light breaks.

Soft music breathes around, and
dies
On the calm bosom of the sea;
Whilst in her cell the novice
sighs
Her vespers to her rosary.

At their dim altars bow fair forms,
In tender charity for those
That, helpless left to life's rude
    storms,
    Have never found this calm
    repose.

The bell swings to its midnight
    chime,
    Relieved against the deep blue
    sky!
Haste!—dip the oar again!—'tis
    time
    To seek Genevra's balcony.

—◦—◦—

DIRGE OVER A NAMELESS GRAVE.

By yon still river, where the wave
    Is winding slow at evening's
    close,
The beech upon a nameless grave
    Its sadly-moving shadow throws.

O'er the fair woods the sun looks
    down
    Upon the many-twinkling leaves,
And twilight's mellow shades are
    brown,
    Where darkly the green turf
    upheaves.

The river glides in silence there,
    And hardly waves the sapling
    tree :
Sweet flowers are springing, and
    the air
    Is full of balm,—but where is
    she ?

They bade her wed a son of pride,
    And leave the hopes she
    cherished long ;
She loved but one,—and would
    not hide
    A love which knew no wrong.

And months went sadly on, and
    years ;
    And she was wasting day by day :

At length she died ; and many
    tears
    Were shed, that she should pass
    away.

Then came a gray old man, and
    knelt
    With bitter weeping by her
    tomb ;
And others mourned for him, who
    felt
    That he had sealed a daughter's
    doom,

The funeral train has long passed
    on,
    And time wiped dry the father's
    tear !
Farewell, lost maiden ! there is one
    That mourns thee yet,—and he
    is here.

—◦—◦—

A SONG OF SAVOY.

As the dim twilight shrouds
    The mountains' purple crest,
And Summer's white and folded
    clouds
    Are glowing in the west,
Loud shouts come up the rocky
    dell,
And voices hail the evening bell.

Faint is the goatherd's song,
    And sighing comes the breeze :
The silent river sweeps along
    Amid its bending trees,
And the full moon shines faintly
    there,
And music fills the evening air.

Beneath the waving firs
    The tinkling cymbals sound ;
And as the wind the foliage stirs,
    I feel the dancers bound
Where the green branches, arched
    above,
Bend over this fair scene of love.

And he is there that sought
   My young heart long ago !
But he has left me,—though I
      thought
He ne'er could leave me so.
Ah ! lovers' vows,—how frail are
      they !
And his were made but yesterday.

Why comes he not ? I call
   In tears upon him yet ;
'Twere better ne'er to love at all,
   Than love, and then forget !
Why comes he not ? Alas ! I
      should
Reclaim him still, if weeping could.

But see,—he leaves the glade,
   And beckons me away :
He comes to seek his mountain
      maid ;
   I cannot chide his stay.
Glad sounds along the valley swell,
And voices hail the evening bell.

—◆—

THE INDIAN HUNTER.

When the summer harvest was
      gathered in,
And the sheaf of the gleaner grew
      white and thin,
And the ploughshare was in its fur-
      row left,
Where the stubble land had been
      lately cleft,
An Indian hunter, with unstrung
      bow,
Looked down where the valley lay
      stretched below.

He was a stranger there, and all
      that day
Had been out on the hills, a peril-
      ous way,
But the foot of the deer was far
      and fleet,
And the wolf kept aloof from the
      hunter's feet.

And bitter feelings passed o'er him
      then,
As he stood by the populous haunts
      of men.

The winds of Autumn came over
      the woods
As the sun stole out from their
      solitudes ;
The moss was white on the maple's
      trunk,
And dead from its arms the pale
      vine shrunk,
And ripened the mellow fruit hung,
      and red
Were the trees' withered leaves
      around it shed.

The foot of the reaper moved slow
      on the lawn,
And the sickle cut down the yellow
      corn ;
The mower sung loud by the
      meadow-side,
Where the mists of evening were
      spreading wide,
And the voice of the herdsman
      came up the lea,
And the dance went round by the
      greenwood tree.

Then the hunter turned away from
      that scene,
Where the home of his fathers
      once had been,
And heard by the distant and
      measured stroke
That the woodman hewed down
      the giant oak,
And burning thoughts flashed over
      his mind
Of the white man's faith and love
      unkind.

The moon of the harvest grew high
      and bright,
As her golden horn pierced the
      cloud of white ;
A footstep was heard in the rus-
      tling brake

Where the beech overshadowed
   the misty lake,
And a mourning voice, and a
   plunge from shore.
And the hunter was seen on the
   hills no more.

When years had passed on, by
   that still lake-side
The fisher looked down through
   the silver tide,
And there, on the smooth, yellow
   sand displayed,
A skeleton wasted and white was
   laid,
And 'twas seen, as the waters
   moved deep and slow,
That the hand was still grasping a
   hunter's bow.

—◦◦—

JECKOYVA.

The Indian chief, Jeckoyva, as tradition
says, perished alone on the mountain which
now bears his name. Night overtook him
whilst hunting among the cliffs, and he was
not heard of till after a long time, when his
half-decayed corpse was found at the foot of
a high rock, over which he must have fallen.
Mount Jeckoyva is near the White Hills.

THEY made the warrior's grave
   beside
The dashing of his native tide;
And there was mourning in the
   glen—
The strong wail of a thousand
   men—
  O'er him thus fallen in his pride,
Ere mist of age, or blight, or blast,
Had o'er his mighty spirit past.

They made the warrior's grave
   beneath
The bending of the wild elm's
   wreath,
When the dark hunter's piercing
   eye

Had found that mo...
   high,
  Where, scattered by...
   wind's breath,
Beneath the rugged cl...
   thrown
The strong belt and the moul...
   bone.

Where was the warrior's foot, when
   first
The red sun on the mountain burst?
Where, when the sultry noontime
   came
On the green vales with scorching
   flame,
  And made the woodlands faint
   with thirst?
'Twas where the wind is keen and
   loud,
And the gray eagle breasts the
   cloud.

Where was the warrior's foot when
   night
Veiled in thick cloud the mountain
   height?
None heard the loud and sudden
   crash,—
None saw the fallen warrior dash
  Down the bare rock so high and
   white!
But he that drooped not in the
   chase
Made on the hills his burial-place.

They found him there, when the
   long day
Of cold desertion passed away,
And traces on that barren cleft
Of struggling hard with death were
   left,—
  Deep marks and footprints in
   the clay!
And they have laid this feathery
   helm
By the dark river and green elm.

THE SEA DIVER.

My way is on the bright blue sea,
  My sleep upon its rocking tide;
And many an eye has followed me
  Where billows clasp the worn
    seaside.

My plumage bears the crimson
    blush,
  When ocean by the sun is kissed;
When fades the evening's purple
    flush,
  My dark wing cleaves the silver
    mist.

Full many a fathom down beneath
  The bright arch of the splendid
    deep,
My ear has heard the sea-shell
    breathe
  O'er living myriads in their sleep.

They rested by the coral throne,
  And by the pearly diadem;
Where the pale sea-grape had o'er-
    grown
  The glorious dwellings made for
    them.

At night upon my storm-drenched
    wing,
  I poised above a helmless bark,
And soon I saw the shattered thing
  Had passed away and left no
    mark.

And when the wind and storm
    were done,
  A ship, that had rode out the
    gale,
Sunk down without a signal gun,
  And none was left to tell the
    tale.

I saw the pomp of day depart,
  The cloud resign its golden
    crown,
When to the ocean's beating heart
  The sailor's wasted corse went
    down.

Peace be to those whose graves
    are made
  Beneath the bright and silver
    sea!
Peace, that their relics there were
    laid
  With no vain pride and pa-
    geantry.

MUSINGS.

I sat by my window one night,
  And watched how the stars grew
    high,
And the earth and skies were a
    splendid sight
  To a sober and musing eye.

From heaven the silver moon
    shone down
  With gentle and mellow ray,
And beneath the crowded roofs
    of the town
  In broad light and shadow lay.

A glory was on the silent sea,
  And mainland and island too,
Till a haze came over the lowland
    lea,
  And shrouded that beautiful blue.

Bright in the moon the autumn
    wood
  Its crimson scarf unrolled,
And the trees like a splendid army
    stood
  In a panoply of gold!

I saw them waving their banners
    high,
  As their crests to the night wind
    bowed,
And a distant sound on the air went
    by,
  Like the whispering of a crowd.

24

Then I watched from my window
  how fast
The lights all around me fled,
As the wearied man to his slumber
  passed,
And the sick one to his bed.

All faded save one, that burned
  With distant and steady light ;
But that, too, went out,—and I
  turned
Where my own lamp within
  shone bright !

Thus, thought I, our joys must
  die ;
Yes, the brightest from earth we
  win ;
Till each turns away, with a sigh,
To the lamp that burns brightly
  within.

—◆◆—

SONG.

Where, from the eye of day,
  The dark and silent river
Pursues through tangled woods a
  way
  O'er which the tall trees quiver,—

The silver mist, that breaks
  From out that woodland cover,
Betrays the hidden path it takes,
  And hangs the current over !

So oft the thoughts that burst
  From hidden springs of feeling,
Like silent streams, unseen at first,
  From our cold hearts are stealing.

But soon the clouds that veil
  The eye of Love, when glowing,
Betray the long unwhispered tale
  Of thoughts in darkness flow-
  ing.

TWO SONNETS FROM THE SPANISH OF FRANCISCO DE MEDRANO.

I.

ART AND NATURE.

*Causa la vista el artificio humano,
  etc.*

The works of human artifice soon
  tire
  The curious eye ; the fountain's
  sparkling rill,
  And gardens, when adorned by
  human skill,
Reproach the feeble hand, the vain
  desire.
But oh ! the free and wild magnificence
Of Nature in her lavish hours doth
  steal,
  In admiration silent and intense,
The soul of him who hath a soul to
  feel.
  The river moving on its ceaseless
  way,
The verdant reach of meadows fair
  and green,
And the blue hills that bound the
  sylvan scene,—
  These speak of grandeur that
  defies decay,—
Proclaim the Eternal Architect on
  high,
Who stamps on all his works his
  own eternity.

II.

THE TWO HARVESTS.

*Yo vi romper aquestas vegas
  llanas, etc.*

But yesterday those few and hoary
  sheaves
  Waved in the golden harvest ;
  from the plain
  I saw the blade shoot upward,
  and the grain

Put forth the unripe ear and tender
leaves.
Then the glad upland smiled
upon the view,
And to the air the broad green
leaves unrolled,
A peerless emerald in each silken
fold,
And on its palm a pearl of morning dew.
And thus sprang up and ripened
in brief space
All that beneath the reaper's
sickle died,
All that smiled beauteous in the
summer-tide.
And what are we ? a copy of that
race,
The later harvest of a longer
year !
And oh ! how many fall before
the ripened ear.

COLUMBUS.

A TRANSLATION FROM SCHILLER.

STEER, bold mariner, on ! albeit
witlings deride thee,
And the steersman drop idly his
hand at the helm ;
Ever, ever to westward ! There
must the coast be discovered,
If it but lie distinct, luminous lie in
thy mind.
Trust to the God that leads thee,
and follow the sea that is
silent ;
Did it not yet exist, now would it
rise from the flood.
Nature with Genius stands united
in league everlasting ;
What is promised to one, surely the
other performs.

INSCRIPTION ON THE SHANKLIN FOUNTAIN.

O TRAVELLER, stay thy weary feet ;
Drink of this fountain, pure and sweet ;
It flows for rich and poor the same.
Then go thy way, remembering still
The wayside well beneath the hill,
The cup of water in His name.

Translations.

[Don Jorge Manrique, the author of the following poem, flourished in the last half of the fifteenth century. He followed the profession of arms, and died on the field of battle. Mariana, in his History of Spain, makes honourable mention of him as being present at the siege of Uclés; and speaks of him as 'a youth of estimable qualities, who in this war gave brilliant proofs of his valour. He died young; and was thus cut off from long exercising his great virtues, and exhibiting to the world the light of his genius, which was already known to fame.' He was mortally wounded in a skirmish near Cañavete, in the year 1479.

The name of Rodrigo Manrique, the father of the poet, Conde de Paredes and Maestre de Santiago, is well known in Spanish history and song. He died in 1476; according to Mariana, in the town of Uclés; but, according to the poem of his son, in Ocaña. It was his death that called forth the poem upon which rests the literary reputation of the younger Manrique. In the language of his historian, 'Don Jorge Manrique, in an elegant Ode, full of poetic beauties, rich embellishments of genius, and high moral reflections, mourned the death of his father as with a funeral hymn.' This praise is not exaggerated. The poem is a model in its kind. Its conception is solemn and beautiful; and, in accordance with it, the style moves on,—calm, dignified, and majestic.]

COPLAS DE MANRIQUE.

FROM THE SPANISH.

O LET the soul her slumbers break,
Let thought be quickened, and
   awake;
Awake to see
How soon this life is past and gone,
And death comes softly stealing on,
How silently!

Swiftly our pleasures glide away,
Our hearts recall the distant day
With many sighs;
The moments that are speeding
   fast
We heed not, but the past,—the
   past,
More highly prize.

Onward its course the present
   keeps,
Onward the constant current
   sweeps,
Till life is done;
And, did we judge of time aright,
The past and future in their flight
Would be as one.

Let no one fondly dream again,
That Hope and all her shadowy
   train
Will not decay;
Fleeting as were the dreams of old,
Remembered like a tale that's told,
They pass away.

Our lives are rivers, gliding free
To that unfathomed, boundless sea,
The silent grave!
Thither all earthly pomp and boast
Roll, to be swallowed up and lost
In one dark wave.

Thither the mighty torrents stray,
Thither the brook pursues its way,
And tinkling rill.
There all are equal; side by side
The poor man and the son of pride
Lie calm and still.

I will not here invoke the throng
Of orators and sons of song,
The deathless few;
Fiction entices and deceives,
And, sprinkled o'er her fragrant
   leaves,
Lies poisonous dew.

27

To One alone my thoughts arise,
The Eternal Truth, the Good and
    Wise,
To Him I cry,
Who shared on earth our common
    lot,
But the world comprehended not
His deity.

This world is but the rugged road
Which leads us to the bright abode
Of peace above ;
So let us choose that narrow way,
Which leads no traveller's foot
    astray
From realms of love.

Our cradle is the starting-place,
Life is the running of the race,
We reach the goal
When, in the mansions of the blest,
Death leaves to its eternal rest
The weary soul.

Did we but use it as we ought,
This world would school each
    wandering thought
To its high state.
Faith wings the soul beyond the
    sky,
Up to that better world on high,
For which we wait.

Yes, the glad messenger of love,
To guide us to our home above,
The Saviour came ;
Born amid mortal cares and fears,
He suffered in this vale of tears
A death of shame.

Behold of what delusive worth
The bubbles we pursue on earth,
The shapes we chase,
Amid a world of treachery !
They vanish ere death shuts the
    eye,
And leave no trace.

Time steals them from us, chances
    strange,
Disastrous accident, and change,
That come to all ;
Even in the most exalted state,
Relentless sweeps the stroke of
    fate ;
The strongest fall.

Tell me, the charms that lovers
    seek
In the clear eye and blushing cheek,
The hues that play
O'er rosy lip and brow of snow,
When hoary age approaches slow,
Ah, where are they ?

The cunning skill, the curious arts,
The glorious strength that youth
    imparts
In life's first stage ;
These shall become a heavy weight,
When Time swings wide his out-
    ward gate
To weary age.

The noble blood of Gothic name,
Heroes emblazoned high to fame,
In long array ;
How, in the onward course of time,
The landmarks of that race sublime
Were swept away !

Some, the degraded slaves of lust,
Prostrate and trampled in the dust,
Shall rise no more ;
Others, by guilt and crime, main-
    tain
The 'scutcheon, that, without a
    stain,
Their fathers bore.

Wealth and the high estate of pride,
With what untimely speed they
    glide,
How soon depart !
Bid not the shadowy phantoms
    stay,
The vassals of a mistress they,
Of fickle heart.

These gifts in Fortune's hands are found ;
Her swift revolving wheel turns round,
And they are gone !
No rest the inconstant goddess knows,
But changing, and without repose,
Still hurries on.

Even could the hand of avarice save
Its gilded baubles, till the grave
Reclaimed its prey,
Let none on such poor hopes rely ;
Life, like an empty dream, flits by,
And where are they ?

Earthly desires and sensual lust
Are passions springing from the dust,
They fade and die ;
But, in the life beyond the tomb,
They seal the immortal spirit's doom
Eternally !

The pleasures and delights which mask
In treacherous smiles life's serious task,
What are they, all,
But the fleet coursers of the chase,
And death an ambush in the race,
Wherein we fall ?

No foe, no dangerous pass, we heed,
Brook no delay, but onward speed
With loosened rein ;
And, when the fatal snare is near,
We strive to check our mad career,
But strive in vain.

Could we new charms to age impart,
And fashion with a cunning art
The human face,
As we can clothe the soul with light,
And make the glorious spirit bright
With heavenly grace,

How busily each passing hour
Shou'd we exert that magic power,
What ardour show,
To deck the sensual slave of sin,
Yet leave the freeborn soul within,
In weeds of woe !

Monarchs, the powerful and the strong,
Famous in history and in song
Of olden time,
Saw, by the stern decrees of fate,
Their kingdoms lost, and desolate
Their race sublime.

Who is the champion ? who the strong ?
Pontiff and priest, and sceptred throng ?
On these shall fall
As heavily the hand of Death,
As when it stays the shepherd's breath
Beside his stall.

I speak not of the Trojan name,
Neither its glory nor its shame
Has met our eyes ;
Nor of Rome's great and glorious dead,
Though we have heard so oft, and read,
Their histories.

Little avails it now to know
Of ages passed so long ago,
Nor how they rolled ;
Our theme shall be of yesterday,
Which to oblivion sweeps away,
Like days of old.

Where is the King, Don Juan ?
Where
Each royal prince and noble heir
Of Aragon ?
Where are the courtly gallantries ?
The deeds of love and high emprise,
In battle done ?

29

Tourney and joust, that charmed
    the eye,
And scarf, and gorgeous panoply,
And nodding plume,
What were they but a pageant
    scene?
What but the garlands, gay and
    green,
That deck the tomb?

Where are the high-born dames,
    and where
Their gay attire, and jewelled hair,
And odours sweet?
Where are the gentle knights, that
    came
To kneel, and breathe love's ardent
    flame,
Low at their feet?

Where is the song of Troubadour?
Where are the lute and gay tambour
They loved of yore?
Where is the mazy dance of old,
The flowing robes, inwrought with
    gold,
The dancers wore?

And he who next the sceptre
    swayed,
Henry, whose royal court displayed
Such power and pride;
O, in what winning smiles arrayed,
The world its various pleasures laid
His throne beside!

But O, how false and full of guile
That world, which wore so soft a
    smile
But to betray!
She, that had been his friend before,
Now from the fated monarch tore
Her charms away.

The countless gifts, the stately
    walls,
The royal palaces, and halls
All filled with gold;

Plate with armorial bearings
    wrought,
Chambers with ample treasures
    fraught
Of wealth untold;
The noble steeds, and harness
    bright,
And gallant lord, and stalwart
    knight,
In rich array,
Where shall we seek them now?
    Alas!
Like the bright dewdrops on the
    grass,
They passed away.

His brother, too, whose factious
    zeal
Usurped the sceptre of Castile,
Unskilled to reign;
What a gay, brilliant court had he,
When all the flower of chivalry
Was in his train!

But he was mortal; and the breath,
That flamed from the hot forge of
    Death
Blasted his years;
Judgment of God! that flame by
    Thee,
When raging fierce and fearfully,
Was quenched in tears!

Spain's haughty Constable, the true
And gallant Master, whom we
    knew
Most loved of all;
Breathe not a whisper of his pride,
He on the gloomy scaffold died,
Ignoble fall!

The countless treasures of his care,
His villages and villas fair,
His mighty power,
What were they all but grief and
    shame,
Tears and a broken heart, when
    came
The parting hour?

Translations.

His other brothers, proud and high,
Masters, who, in prosperity,
Might rival kings;
Who made the bravest and the best
The bondsmen of their high behest,
Their underlings;

What was their prosperous estate,
When high exalted and elate
With power and pride?
What, but a transient gleam of light,
A flame, which, glaring at its height,
Grew dim and died?

So many a duke of royal name,
Marquis and count of spotless fame,
And baron brave,
That might the sword of empire wield,
All these, O Death, hast thou concealed
In the dark grave!

Their deeds of mercy and of arms,
In peaceful days, or war's alarms,
When thou dost show,
O Death, thy stern and angry face,
One stroke of thy all-powerful mace
Can overthrow.

Unnumbered hosts, that threaten nigh,
Pennon and standard flaunting high,
And flag displayed;
High battlements intrenched around,
Bastion, and moated wall, and mound,
And palisade,

And covered trench, secure and deep,
All these cannot one victim keep,
O Death, from thee,

When thou dost battle in thy wrath,
And thy strong shafts pursue their path
Unerringly.

O World! so few the years we live,
Would that the life which thou dost give
Were life indeed!
Alas! thy sorrows fall so fast,
Our happiest hour is when at last
The soul is freed.

Our days are covered o'er with grief,
And sorrows neither few nor brief
Veil all in gloom;
Left desolate of real good,
Within this cheerless solitude
No pleasures bloom.

Thy pilgrimage begins in tears,
And ends in bitter doubts and fears,
Or dark despair;
Midway so many toils appear,
That he who lingers longest here
Knows most of care.

Thy goods are bought with many a groan,
By the hot sweat of toil alone,
And weary hearts;
Fleet-footed is the approach of woe,
But with a lingering step and slow
Its form departs.

And he, the good man's shield and shade,
To whom all hearts their homage paid
As Virtue's son,
Roderic Manrique, he whose name
Is written on the scroll of Fame,
Spain's champion;

31

His signal deeds and prowess high
Demand no pompous eulogy.
Ye saw his deeds!
Why should their praise in verse be
    sung?
The name, that dwells on every
    tongue,
No minstrel needs.

To friends a friend; how kind to
    all
The vassals of this ancient hall
And feudal fief!
To foes how stern a foe was he!
And to the valiant and the free
How brave a chief!

What prudence with the old and
    wise:
What grace in youthful gaieties;
In all how sage!
Benignant to the serf and slave,
He showed the base and falsely
    brave
A lion's rage.

His was Octavian's prosperous star,
The rush of Cæsar's conquering car
At battle's call;
His Scipio's virtue; his the skill
And the indomitable will
Of Hannibal.

His was a Trajan's goodness, his
A Titus' noble charities
And righteous laws;
The arm of Hector, and the might
Of Tully, to maintain the right
In truth's just cause;

The clemency of Antonine,
Aurelius' countenance divine,
Firm, gentle, still;
The eloquence of Adrian,
And Theodosius' love to man,
And generous will;

In tented field and bloody fray,
An Alexander's vigorous sway
And stern command;

The faith of Constantine; ay, more,
The fervent love Camillus bore
His native land.

He left no well-filled treasury,
He heaped no pile of riches high,
Nor massive plate;
He fought the Moors, and, in their
    fall,
City and tower and castled wall
Were his estate.

Upon the hard-fought battle-
    ground,
Brave steeds and gallant riders
    found
A common grave;
And there the warrior's hand did
    gain
The rents, and the long vassal train,
That conquest gave.

And if, of old, his halls displayed
The honoured and exalted grade
His worth had gained,
So, in the dark, disastrous hour,
Brothers and bondsmen of his power
His hand sustained.

After high deeds, not left untold,
In the stern warfare, which of old
'Twas his to share,
Such noble leagues he made, that
    more
And fairer regions, than before,
His guerdon were.

These are the records, half effaced,
Which, with the hand of youth, he
    traced
On history's page;
But with fresh victories he drew
Each fading character anew
In his old age.

By his unrivalled skill, by great
And veteran service to the state,
By worth adored,
He stood, in his high dignity,
The proudest knight of chivalry,
Knight of the Sword.

He found his cities and domains
Beneath a tyrant's galling chains
And cruel power;
But, by fierce battle and blockade,
Soon his own banner was displayed
From every tower.

By the tried valour of his hand,
His monarch and his native land
Were nobly served;
Let Portugal repeat the story,
And proud Castile, who shared the
glory
His arms deserved.

And when so oft, for weal or woe,
His life upon the fatal throw
Had been cast down;
When he had served, with patriot
zeal,
Beneath the banner of Castile,
His sovereign's crown;

And done such deeds of valour
strong,
That neither history nor song
Can count them all;
Then, on Ocaña's castled rock,
Death at his portal came to knock,
With sudden call,

Saying, 'Good Cavalier, prepare
To leave this world of toil and care
With joyful mien;
Let thy strong heart of steel this
day
Put on its armour for the fray,
The closing scene.

'Since thou hast been, in battle-
strife,
So prodigal of health and life,
For earthly fame,
Let virtue nerve thy heart again;
Loud on the last stern battle-plain
They call thy name.

'Think not the struggle that draws
near
Too terrible for man, nor fear
To meet the foe;

Nor let thy noble spirit grieve,
Its life of glorious fame to leave
On earth below.

'A life of honour and of worth
Has no eternity on earth,
'Tis but a name;
And yet its glory far exceeds
That base and sensual life, which
leads
To want and shame.

'The eternal life, beyond the sky,
Wealth cannot purchase, nor the
high
And proud estate;
The soul in dalliance laid, the
spirit
Corrupt with sin, shall not inherit
A joy so great.

'But the good monk, in cloistered
cell,
Shall gain it by his book and bell,
His prayers and tears;
And the brave knight, whose arm
endures
Fierce battles, and against the
Moors
His standard rears.

'And thou, brave knight, whose
hand has poured
The life-blood of the Pagan horde
O'er all the land,
In heaven shalt thou receive, at
length,
The guerdon of thine earthly
strength
And dauntless hand.

'Cheered onward by this promise
sure,
Strong in the faith entire and pure
Thou dost profess,
Depart, thy hope is certainty,
The third, the better life on high
Shalt thou possess.'

33

'O Death, no more, no more de-
lay;
My spirit longs to flee away,
And be at rest ;
The will of Heaven my will shall
be,
I bow to the divine decree,
To God's behest.

' My soul is ready to depart,
No thought rebels, the obedient
heart
Breathes forth no sigh ;
The wish on earth to linger still
Were vain, when 'tis God's sove-
reign will
That we shall die.

' O thou, that for our sins didst
take
A human form, and humbly make
Thy home on earth ;
Thou, that to thy divinity
A human nature didst ally
By mortal birth,

' And in that form didst suffer here
Torment, and agony, and fear,
So patiently ;
By thy redeeming grace alone,
And not for merits of my own,
O, pardon me ! '

As thus the dying warrior prayed,
Without one gathering mist or
shade
Upon his mind ;
Encircled by his family,
Watched by affection's gentle eye
So soft and kind,

His soul to Him who gave it rose ;
God lead it to its long repose,
Its glorious rest !
And, though the warrior's sun has
set,
Its light shall linger round us yet,
Bright, radiant, blest.

THE GOOD SHEPHERD.

FROM THE SPANISH OF LOPE DE
VEGA.

SHEPHERD ! who with thine amor-
ous, sylvan song
 Hast broken the slumber that
 encompassed me,
Who mad'st thy crook from the
accursed tree,
 On which thy powerful arms
 were stretched so long !
Lead me to mercy's ever-flowing
fountains ;
 For thou my shepherd, guard,
 and guide shalt be ;
 I will obey thy voice, and wait to
 see
Thy feet all beautiful upon the
mountains.
Hear, Shepherd ! thou who for thy
flock art dying,
 O, wash away these scarlet sins,
 for thou
Rejoicest at the contrite sinner's
vow.
O, wait ! to thee my weary soul is
crying,
 Wait for me ! Yet why ask it,
 when I see,
With feet nailed to the cross,
thou 'rt waiting still for me !

TO-MORROW.

FROM THE SPANISH OF LOPE DE
VEGA.

LORD, what am I, that with unceasing care
 Thou didst seek after me, that
 thou didst wait,
 Wet with unhealthy dews, before
 my gate,

34

And pass the gloomy nights of winter there?

O strange delusion! that I did not greet
Thy blest approach, and O, to Heaven how lost,
If my ingratitude's unkindly frost
Has chilled the bleeding wounds upon thy feet.

How oft my guardian angel gently cried,
'Soul, from thy casement look, and thou shalt see
How he persists to knock and wait for thee!'

And, O! how often to that voice of sorrow,
'To-morrow we will open,' I replied,
And when the morrow came I answered still, 'To-morrow.'

THE NATIVE LAND.

FROM THE SPANISH OF FRAN-
CISCO DE ALDANA.

CLEAR fount of light! my native land on high,
Bright with a glory that shall never fade!
Mansion of truth! without a veil or shade,
Thy holy quiet meets the spirit's eye.

There dwells the soul in its ethereal essence,
Gasping no longer for life's feeble breath;
But, sentinelled in heaven, its glorious presence
With pitying eye beholds, yet fears not, death.

Beloved country! banished from thy shore,

A stranger in this prison-house of clay,
The exiled spirit weeps and sighs for thee!
Heavenward the bright perfections I adore
Direct, and the sure promise cheers the way,
That, whither love aspires, there shall my dwelling be.

THE IMAGE OF GOD.

FROM THE SPANISH OF FRAN-
CISCO DE ALDANA.

O LORD! who seest, from yon starry height,
Centred in one the future and the past,
Fashioned in thine own image, see how fast
The world obscures in me what once was bright!

Eternal Sun! the warmth which thou hast given,
To cheer life's flowery April, fast decays;
Yet, in the hoary winter of my days,
For ever green shall be my trust in Heaven.

Celestial King! O let thy presence pass
Before my spirit, and an image fair
Shall meet that look of mercy from on high,
As the reflected image in a glass
Doth meet the look of him who seeks it there,
And owes its being to the gazer's eye.

35

THE BROOK.

FROM THE SPANISH.

LAUGH of the mountain!—lyre of
    bird and tree!
  Pomp of the meadow! mirror of
    the morn!
  The soul of April, unto whom
    are born
  The rose and jessamine, leaps
    wild in thee!
Although, where'er thy devious
    current strays,
  The lap of earth with gold and
    silver teems,
  To me thy clear proceeding
    brighter seems
  Than golden sands that charm
    each shepherd's gaze.
How without guile thy bosom, all
    transparent
  As the pure crystal, lets the
    curious eye
  Thy secrets scan, thy smooth,
    round pebbles count!
How, without malice murmuring,
    glides thy current!
  O sweet simplicity of days gone
    by!
  Thou shun'st the haunts of man,
    to dwell in limpid fount!

THE CELESTIAL PILOT.

FROM DANTE. PURGATORIO, II.

AND now, behold! as at the ap-
    proach of morning,
  Through the gross vapours, Mars
    grows fiery red
  Down in the west upon the
    ocean floor,
Appeared to me,—may I again
    behold it!—

A light along the sea, so swiftly
    coming,
  Its motion by no flight of wing is
    equalled.
And when therefrom I had with-
    drawn a little
  Mine eyes, that I might question
    my conductor,
  Again I saw it brighter grown
    and larger.
Thereafter, on all sides of it, appeared
  I knew not what of white, and
    underneath,
  Little by little, there came forth
    another.
My master yet had uttered not a
    word,
  While the first whiteness into
    wings unfolded;
  But, when he clearly recognised
    the pilot,
He cried aloud: 'Quick, quick,
    and bow the knee!
  Behold the Angel of God! fold
    up thy hands!
  Henceforward shalt thou see
    such officers!
See, how he scorns all human
    arguments,
  So that no oar he wants, nor
    other sail
  Than his own wings, between so
    distant shores!
See, how he holds them, pointed
    straight to heaven,
  Fanning the air with the eternal
    pinions,
  That do not moult themselves
    like mortal hair!'
And then, as nearer and more
    near us came
  The Bird of Heaven, more
    glorious he appeared,
  So that the eye could not sustain
    his presence,
But down I cast it; and he came
    to shore
  With a small vessel, gliding
    swift and light,

So that the water swallowed
   naught thereof.
Upon the stern stood the Celestial
   Pilot !
Beatitude seemed written in
   his face !
And more than a hundred spirits
   sat within.
'*In exitu Israel de Ægypto !*'
   Thus sang they all together in
   one voice,
   With whatso in that Psalm is
   after written.
Then made he sign of holy rood
   upon them,
   Whereat all cast themselves
   upon the shore,
   And he departed swiftly as he
   came.

—◆—

THE TERRESTRIAL.
PARADISE.

FROM DANTE. PURGATORIO,
   XXVIII.

LONGING already to search in and
   round
   The heavenly forest, dense and
   living-green,
   Which tempered to the eyes the
   new-born day,
Withouten more delay I left the
   bank,
   Crossing the level country slowly,
   slowly,
   Over the soil, that everywhere
   breathed fragrance.
A gently-breathing air, that no
   mutation
   Had in itself, smote me upon the
   forehead,
   No heavier blow than of a
   pleasant breeze,

Whereat the tremulous branches
   readily
   Did all of them bow downward
   towards that side
   Where its first shadow casts the
   Holy Mountain ;
Yet not from their upright direc-
   tion bent
   So that the little birds upon
   their tops
   Should cease the practice of
   their tuneful art ;
But, with full-throated joy, the
   hours of prime
   Singing received they in the
   midst of foliage
   That made monotonous burden
   to their rhymes,
Even as from branch to branch it
   gathering swells
   Through the pine forests on the
   shore of Chiassi,
   When Æolus unlooses the
   Sirocco.
Already my slow steps had led me
   on
   Into the ancient wood so far,
   that I
   Could see no more the place
   where I had entered.
And lo ! my further course cut off
   a river,
   Which, towards the left hand,
   with its little waves,
   Bent down the grass that on its
   margin sprang.
All waters that on earth most
   limpid are,
   Would seem to have within
   themselves some mixture,
   Compared with that, which no-
   thing doth conceal,
Although it moves on with a brown,
   brown current,
   Under the shade perpetual, that
   never
   Ray of the sun lets in, nor of the
   moon.

BEATRICE.

FROM DANTE. PURGATORIO,
XXX, XXXI.

EVEN as the Blessed, at the final
summons,
    Shall rise up quickened, each
one from his grave,
    Wearing again the garments of
the flesh,
So, upon that celestial chariot,
    A hundred rose *ad vocem tanti
senis,*
    Ministers and messengers of life
eternal.
They all were saying, ' *Benedictus
qui venis,*'
    And scattering flowers above
and round about,
' *Manibus o date lilia plenis.*'
Oft have I seen, at the approach of
day,
    The orient sky all stained with
roseate hues,
    And the other heaven with light
serene adorned,
And the sun's face uprising, overshadowed,
    So that, by temperate influence
of vapours,
    The eye sustained his aspect for
long while ;
Thus in the bosom of a cloud of
flowers,
    Which from those hands angelic
were thrown up,
    And down descended inside and
without,
With crown of olive o'er a snow-
white veil,
    Appeared a lady, under a green
mantle,
    Vested in colours of the living
flame.

.   .   .   .   .   .

Even as the snow, among the living
rafters

Upon the back of Italy, congeals,
Blown on and beaten by Scla-
vonian winds,
And then, dissolving, filters through
itself,
    Whene'er the land, that loses
shadow, breathes,
    Like as a taper melts before a
fire,
Even such I was, without a sigh or
tear,
    Before the song of those who
chime for ever
    After the chiming of the eternal
spheres ;
But, when I heard in those sweet
melodies
    Compassion for me, more than
had they said,
    ' O wherefore, lady, dost thou
thus consume him ? '
The ice, that was about my heart
congealed,
    To air and water changed, and,
in my anguish,
    Through lips and eyes came
gushing from my breast.

.   .   .   .   .   .

Confusion and dismay, together
mingled,
    Forced such a feeble ' Yes ! ' out
of my mouth,
    To understand it one had need
of sight.
Even as a cross-bow breaks, when
'tis discharged,
    Too tensely drawn the bow-string
and the bow,
    And with less force the arrow hits
the mark ;
So I gave way beneath this heavy
burden,
    Gushing forth into bitter tears
and sighs,
    And the voice, fainting, flagged
upon its passage.

SPRING.

FROM THE FRENCH OF CHARLES
D'ORLEANS.

XV CENTURY.

GENTLE Spring ! in sunshine clad,
  Well dost thou thy power dis-
    play !
For Winter maketh the light heart
  sad,
  And thou, thou makest the sad
    heart gay.
He sees thee, and calls to his
  gloomy train,

The sleet, and the snow, and the
  wind, and the rain ;
And they shrink away, and they
  flee in fear,
  When thy merry step draws
    near.

Winter giveth the fields and the
  trees, so old,
  Their beards of icicles and snow ;
And the rain, it raineth so fast and
  cold,
  We must cower over the embers
    low ;
And, snugly housed from the wind
  and weather,
Mope like birds that are changing
  feather.
But the storm retires, and the sky
  grows clear,
  When thy merry step draws
    near.

Winter maketh the sun in the
  gloomy sky
  Wrap him round with a mantle
    of cloud ;
But, Heaven be praised, thy step
  is nigh ;
  Thou tearest away the mournful
    shroud,

And the earth looks bright, and
  Winter surly,
Who has toiled for naught both
  late and early,
Is banished afar by the new-born
  year,
  When thy merry step draws near.

—◆—

THE CHILD ASLEEP.

FROM THE FRENCH.

SWEET babe ! true portrait of thy
  father's face,
  Sleep on the bosom that thy lips
    have pressed !
Sleep, little one ; and closely,
  gently place
  Thy drowsy eyelid on thy
    mother's breast.

Upon that tender eye, my little
  friend,
  Soft sleep shall come, that
    cometh not to me !
I watch to see thee, nourish thee,
  defend ;
  'Tis sweet to watch for thee,
    alone for thee !

His arms fall down ; sleep sits
  upon his brow ;
  His eye is closed ; he sleeps, nor
    dreams of harm.
Wore not his cheek the apple's
  ruddy glow,
  Would you not say he slept on
    Death's cold arm ?

Awake, my boy ! I tremble with
  affright !
  Awake, and chase this fatal
    thought ! Unclose
Thine eye but for one moment on
  the light !
  Even at the price of thine, give
    me repose !

Sweet error! he but slept, I
    breathe again ;
Come, gentle dreams, the hour
    of sleep beguile !
O, when shall he, for whom I sigh
    in vain,
    Beside me watch to see thy
      waking smile ?

THE GRAVE.

FROM THE ANGLO-SAXON.

For thee was a house built
Ere thou wast born,
For thee was a mould meant
Ere thou of mother camest.
But it is not made ready,
Nor its depth measured,
Nor is it seen
How long it shall be.
Now I bring thee
Where thou shalt be ;
Now I shall measure thee,
And the mould afterwards.

Thy house is not
Highly timbered,
It is unhigh and low ;
When thou art therein,
The heel-ways are low,
The side-ways unhigh.
The roof is built
Thy breast full nigh,
So thou shalt in mould
Dwell full cold,
Dimly and dark.

Doorless is that house,
And dark it is within ;
There thou art fast detained
And Death hath the key.
Loathsome is that earth-house,
And grim within to dwell.
There thou shalt dwell,
And worms shall divide thee.

Thus thou art laid,
And leavest thy friends ;
Thou hast no friend,
Who will come to thee,
Who will ever see
How that house pleaseth thee ;
Who will ever open
The door for thee,
And descend after thee ;
For soon thou art loathsome
And hateful to see.

KING CHRISTIAN.

A NATIONAL SONG OF DENMARK.

FROM THE DANISH OF JOHANNES EWALD.

King Christian stood by the
    lofty mast
    In mist and smoke ;
His sword was hammering so fast,
Through Gothic helm and brain it
    passed ;
Then sank each hostile hulk and
    mast,
    In mist and smoke.
'Fly !' shouted they, 'fly he who
    can !
Who braves of Denmark's Chris-
    tian
    The stroke?'

Nils Juel gave heed to the tempest's
    roar,
    Now is the hour !
He hoisted his blood-red flag once
    more,
And smote upon the foe full sore,
And shouted loud, through the
    tempest's roar,
    ' Now is the hour!'
'Fly !' shouted they, 'for shelter
    fly !
Of Denmark's Juel who can defy
    The power?'

North Sea! a glimpse of Wessel
    rent
    Thy murky sky!
Then champions to thine arms were
    sent;
Terror and Death glared where he
    went;
From the waves was heard a wail,
    that rent
    Thy murky sky!
From Denmark, thunders Torden-
    skiol',
Let each to Heaven commend his
    soul,
    And fly!

Path of the Dane to fame and might!
    Dark-rolling wave!
Receive thy friend, who, scorning
    flight,
Goes to meet danger with despite,
Proudly as thou the tempest's
    might,
    Dark-rolling wave!
And amid pleasures and alarms,
And war and victory, be thine arms
    My grave!

THE HAPPIEST LAND.

FROM THE GERMAN.

THERE sat one day in quiet,
    By an alehouse on the Rhine,
Four hale and hearty fellows,
    And drank the precious wine.

The landlord's daughter filled their
    cups
    Around the rustic board;
Then sat they all so calm and still,
    And spake not one rude word.

But, when the maid departed,
    A Swabian raised his hand,
And cried, all hot and flushed with
    wine,
    'Long live the Swabian land!

'The greatest kingdom upon earth
    Cannot with that compare;
With all the stout and hardy men
    And the nut-brown maidens
    there.'

'Ha!' cried a Saxon, laughing,
    And dashed his beard with wine;
'I had rather live in Lapland,
    Than that Swabian land of thine!

'The goodliest land on all this
    earth,
    It is the Saxon land!
There have I as many maidens
    As fingers on this hand!'

'Hold your tongues! both Swabian
    and Saxon!'
    A bold Bohemian cries;
'If there's a heaven upon this earth,
    In Bohemia it lies.

'There the tailor blows the flute,
    And the cobbler blows the horn,
And the miner blows the bugle,
    Over mountain gorge and bourn.'

And then the landlord's daughter
    Up to Heaven raised her hand,
And said, 'Ye may no more con-
    tend,—
    There lies the happiest land!'

THE WAVE.

FROM THE GERMAN OF TIEDGE.

'WHITHER, thou turbid wave?
Whither, with so much haste,
As if a thief wert thou?'

  'I am the Wave of Life,
Stained with my margin's dust;
From the struggle and the strife
Of the narrow stream I fly
To the Sea's immensity,
To wash from me the slime
Of the muddy banks of Time.'

10#

THE DEAD.

FROM THE GERMAN OF STOCK-MANN.

How they so softly rest,
All they the holy ones,
Unto whose dwelling-place
Now doth my soul draw near!
How they so softly rest,
All in their silent graves,
Deep to corruption
Slowly down-sinking!

And they no longer weep,
Here, where complaint is still!
And they no longer feel,
Here, where all gladness flies!
And, by the cypresses
Softly o'ershadowed,
Until the Angel
Calls them, they slumber!

THE BIRD AND THE SHIP.

FROM THE GERMAN OF MÜLLER.

'THE rivers rush into the sea,
By castle and town they go;
The winds behind them merrily
Their noisy trumpets blow.

'The clouds are passing far and
high,
We little birds in them play;
And everything, that can sing and
fly,
Goes with us, and far away.

'I greet thee, bonny boat! Whither,
or whence,
With thy fluttering golden
band?'—
'I greet thee, little bird! To the
wide sea
I haste from the narrow land.

'Full and swollen is every sail;
I see no longer a hill,
I have trusted all to the sounding gale,
And it will not let me stand still.

'And wilt thou, little bird, go with us?
Thou mayest stand on the main-mast tall,
For full to sinking is my house
With merry companions all.'—

'I need not and seek not company,
Bonny boat, I can sing all alone;
For the mainmast tall too heavy
am I,
Bonny boat, I have wings of my
own.

'High over the sails, high over the
mast,
Who shall gainsay these joys?
When thy merry companions are
still, at last,
Thou shalt hear the sound of my
voice.

'Who neither may rest, nor listen
may,
God bless them every one!
I dart away, in the bright blue day,
And the golden fields of the sun.

'Thus do I sing my weary song,
Wherever the four winds blow;
And this same song, my whole life
long,
Neither Poet nor Printer may
know.'

WHITHER.

FROM THE GERMAN OF MÜLLER.

I HEARD a brooklet gushing
From its rocky fountain near,
Down into the valley rushing,
So fresh and wondrous clear.

I know not what came o'er me,
Nor who the counsel gave;
But I must hasten downward,
All with my pilgrim-stave;

Downward, and ever farther,
    And ever the brook beside ;
And ever fresher murmured,
    And ever clearer, the tide.

Is this the way I was going ?
    Whither ? O brooklet, say !
Thou hast, with thy soft murmur,
    Murmured my senses away.

What do I say of a murmur ?
    That can no murmur be ;
'Tis the water-nymphs, that are
        singing
    Their roundelays under me.

Let them sing, my friend, let them
        murmur,
    And wander merrily near ;
The wheels of a mill are going
    In every brooklet clear.

———

BEWARE.

FROM THE GERMAN.

I KNOW a maiden fair to see,
    Take care !
She can both false and friendly be,
    Beware ! Beware !
    Trust her not,
She is fooling thee !

She has two eyes, so soft and
        brown,
    Take care !
She gives a side-glance and looks
        down,
    Beware ! Beware !
    Trust her not,
She is fooling thee !

And she has hair of a golden hue,
    Take care !
And what she says, it is not true,
    Beware ! Beware !
    Trust her not,
She is fooling thee !

She has a bosom as white as snow,
    Take care !
She knows how much it is best to
        show,
        Beware ! Beware !
        Trust her not,
She is fooling thee !

She gives thee a garland woven fair,
    Take care !
It is a fool's-cap for thee to wear,
        Beware ! Beware !
        Trust her not,
She is fooling thee !

———

SONG OF THE BELL.

FROM THE GERMAN.

BELL ! thou soundest merrily,
When the bridal party
    To the church doth hie !
Bell ! thou soundest solemnly,
When, on Sabbath morning,
    Fields deserted lie !

Bell ! thou soundest merrily ;
Tellest thou at evening,
    Bed-time draweth nigh !
Bell ! thou soundest mournfully,
Tellest thou the bitter
    Parting hath gone by !

Say ! how canst thou mourn ?
How canst thou rejoice ?
    Thou art but metal dull !
And yet all our sorrowings,
And all our rejoicings,
    Thou dost feel them all !

God hath wonders many,
Which we cannot fathom,
    Placed within thy form !
When the heart is sinking,
Thou alone canst raise it,
    Trembling in the storm !

43

THE CASTLE BY THE SEA.

FROM THE GERMAN OF UHLAND.

'Hast thou seen that lordly
    castle,
    That Castle by the Sea?
Golden and red above it
    The clouds float gorgeously.

'And fain it would stoop down-
    ward
    To the mirrored wave below;
And fain it would soar upward
    In the evening's crimson glow.'

'Well have I seen that castle,
    That Castle by the Sea,
And the moon above it standing,
    And the mist rise solemnly.'

'The winds and the waves of
    ocean,
    Had they a merry chime?
Didst thou hear, from those lofty
    chambers,
    The harp and the minstrel's
    rhyme?'

'The winds and the waves of
    ocean,
    They rested quietly,
But I heard on the gale a sound of
    wail,
    And tears came to mine eye.'

'And sawest thou on the turrets
    The King and his royal bride?
And the wave of their crimson
    mantles?
    And the golden crown of pride?

'Led they not forth, in rapture,
    A beauteous maiden there?
Resplendent as the morning sun,
    Beaming with golden hair?'

'Well saw I the ancient parents,
    Without the crown of pride;
They were moving slow, in weeds
    of woe,
    No maiden was by their side!'

THE BLACK KNIGHT.

FROM THE GERMAN OF UHLAND.

'Twas Pentecost, the Feast of
    Gladness,
When woods and fields put off all
    sadness.
    Thus began the King and spake:
' So from the halls
Of ancient Hofburg's walls,
    A luxuriant Spring shall break.'

Drums and trumpets echo loudly,
Wave the crimson banners proudly,
    From balcony the King looked
    on;
In the play of spears,
Fell all the cavaliers,
    Before the monarch's stalwart
    son.

To the barrier of the fight
Rode at last a sable Knight.
    'Sir Knight! your name and
    'scutcheon, say!'
' Should I speak it here,
Ye would stand aghast with fear;
    I am a Prince of mighty sway!'

When he rode into the lists,
The arch of heaven grew black
    with mists,
    And the castle 'gan to rock;
At the first blow,
Fell the youth from saddle-bow,
    Hardly rises from the shock.

Pipe and viol call the dances,
Torch-light through the high halls
    glances;
    Waves a mighty shadow in;
With manner bland
Doth ask the maiden's hand,
    Doth with her the dance begin.

Danced in sable iron sark,
Danced a measure weird and dark,
    Coldly clasped her limbs around;
From breast and hair
Down fall from her the fair
    Flowerets, faded, to the ground.

44

To the sumptuous banquet came
Every Knight and every Dame ;
  'Twixt son and daughter all dis-
    traught,
With mournful mind
The ancient King reclined,
  Gazed at them in silent thought.

Pale the children both did look,
But the guest a beaker took :
  ' Golden wine will make you
    whole !'
The children drank,
Gave many a courteous thank :
  ' O, that draught was very
    cool !'

Each the father's breast em-
    braces,
Son and daughter ; and their
    faces
Colourless grow utterly ;
Whichever way
Looks the fear-struck father gray,
He beholds his children die.

' Woe ! the blessed children both
Takest thou in the joy of youth ;
  Take me, too, the joyless
    father !'
Spake the grim Guest,
From his hollow, cavernous breast :
  ' Roses in the spring I gather !'

SONG OF THE SILENT LAND.

FROM THE GERMAN OF SALIS.

INTO the Silent Land !
Ah ! who shall lead us thither ?
Clouds in the evening sky more
    darkly gather,
And shattered wrecks lie thicker
    on the strand.
Who leads us with a gentle hand
Thither, O thither,
Into the Silent Land ?

Into the Silent Land !
To you, ye boundless regions
Of all perfection ! Tender morn-
    ing visions
Of beauteous souls ! The Future's
    pledge and band !
Who in Life's battle firm doth
    stand,
Shall bear Hope's tender blossoms
Into the Silent Land !

O Land ! O Land !
For all the broken-hearted
The mildest herald by our fate
    allotted,
Beckons, and with inverted torch
    doth stand
To lead us with a gentle hand
To the land of the great Departed,
Into the Silent Land !

45

Ballads.

THE SKELETON IN ARMOUR.

'SPEAK! speak! thou fearful
     guest!
Who, with thy hollow breast
Still in rude armour drest,
     Comest to daunt me!
Wrapt not in Eastern balms,
But with thy fleshless palms
Stretched, as if asking alms,
     Why dost thou haunt me?'

Then, from those cavernous eyes
Pale flashes seemed to rise,
As when the Northern skies
     Gleam in December;
And, like the water's flow
Under December's snow,
Came a dull voice of woe
     From the heart's chamber.

'I was a Viking old!
My deeds, though manifold,
No Skald in song has told,
     No Saga taught thee!
Take heed, that in thy verse
Thou dost the tale rehearse,
Else dread a dead man's curse;
     For this I sought thee.

'Far in the Northern Land,
By the wild Baltic's strand,
I, with my childish hand,
     Tamed the gerfalcon;
And, with my skates fast-bound,
Skimmed the half-frozen Sound,
That the poor whimpering hound
     Trembled to walk on.

'Oft to his frozen lair
Tracked I the grisly bear,
While from my path the hare
     Fled like a shadow;

Oft through the forest dark
Followed the were-wolf's bark,
Until the soaring lark
     Sang from the meadow.

'But when I older grew,
Joining a corsair's crew,
O'er the dark sea I flew
     With the marauders.
Wild was the life we led;
Many the souls that sped,
Many the hearts that bled,
     By our stern orders.

'Many a wassail-bout
Wore the long Winter out;
Often our midnight shout
     Set the cocks crowing,
As we the Berserk's tale
Measured in cups of ale,
Draining the oaken pail,
     Filled to o'erflowing.

'Once as I told in glee
Tales of the stormy sea,
Soft eyes did gaze on me,
     Burning yet tender;
And as the white stars shine
On the dark Norway pine,
On that dark heart of mine
     Fell their soft splendour.

'I wooed the blue-eyed maid,
Yielding, yet half afraid,
And in the forest's shade
     Our vows were plighted.
Under its loosened vest
Fluttered her little breast,
Like birds within their nest
     By the hawk frighted.

46

'Bright in her father's hall
Shields gleamed upon the wall,
Loud sang the minstrels all,
  Chanting his glory;
When of old Hildebrand
I asked his daughter's hand,
Mute did the minstrels stand
  To hear my story.

'While the brown ale he quaffed,
Loud then the champion laughed,
And as the wind-gusts waft
  The sea-foam brightly,
So the loud laugh of scorn,
Out of those lips unshorn,
From the deep drinking-horn
  Blew the foam lightly.

'She was a Prince's child,
I but a Viking wild,
And though she blushed and
    smiled,
  I was discarded!
Should not the dove so white
Follow the sea-mew's flight,
Why did they leave that night
  Her nest unguarded?

'Scarce had I put to sea,
Bearing the maid with me,
Fairest of all was she
  Among the Norsemen!
When on the white sea-strand,
Waving his armed hand,
Saw we old Hildebrand,
  With twenty horsemen.

'Then launched they to the blast,
Bent like a reed each mast,
Yet we were gaining fast,
  When the wind failed us;
And with a sudden flaw
Came round the gusty Skaw,
So that our foe we saw
  Laugh as he hailed us.

'And as to catch the gale
Round veered the flapping sail,
Death! was the helmsman's hail,
  Death without quarter!

Mid-ships with iron keel
Struck we her ribs of steel;
Down her black hulk did reel
  Through the black water!

'As with his wings aslant,
Sails the fierce cormorant,
Seeking some rocky haunt,
  With his prey laden,
So toward the open main,
Beating to sea again,
Through the wild hurricane,
  Bore I the maiden.

'Three weeks we westward bore,
And when the storm was o'er,
Cloud-like we saw the shore
  Stretching to leeward;
There for my lady's bower
Built I the lofty tower,
Which, to this very hour,
  Stands looking seaward.

'There lived we many years;
Time dried the maiden's tears;
She had forgot her fears,
  She was a mother;
Death closed her mild blue eyes,
Under that tower she lies;
Ne'er shall the sun arise
  On such another!

'Still grew my bosom then,
Still as a stagnant fen!
Hateful to me were men,
  The sunlight hateful!
In the vast forest here,
Clad in my warlike gear,
Fell I upon my spear,
  O, death was grateful!

'Thus, seamed with many scars,
Bursting these prison bars,
Up to its native stars
  My soul ascended!
There from the flowing bowl
Deep drinks the warrior's soul,
Skoal! to the Northland! *skoal!*'
  —Thus the tale ended.

THE WRECK OF THE HESPERUS.

It was the schooner Hesperus,
  That sailed the wintry sea;
And the skipper had taken his
    little daughter,
  To bear him company.

Blue were her eyes as the fairy-flax,
  Her cheeks like the dawn of
    day,
And her bosom white as the haw-
    thorn buds
  That ope in the month of May.

The skipper he stood beside the
    helm,
  His pipe was in his mouth,
And he watched how the veering
    flaw did blow
  The smoke now West, now
    South.

Then up and spake an old Sailor,
  Had sailed the Spanish
    Main,
'I pray thee, put into yonder port,
  For I fear a hurricane.

'Last night the moon had a golden
    ring,
  And to-night no moon we see!'
The skipper he blew a whiff from
    his pipe,
  And a scornful laugh laughed
    he.

Colder and louder blew the wind,
  A gale from the North-east,
The snow fell hissing in the brine,
  And the billows frothed like
    yeast.

Down came the storm, and smote
    amain
  The vessel in its strength;
She shuddered and paused, like a
    frighted steed,
  Then leaped her cable's
    length.

'Come hither! come hither! my
    little daughter,
  And do not tremble so;
For I can weather the roughest
    gale
  That ever wind did blow.'

He wrapped her warm in his sea-
    man's coat
  Against the stinging blast;
He cut a rope from a broken spar,
  And bound her to the mast.

'O father! I hear the church-bells
    ring,
  O say, what may it be?'
''Tis a fog-bell on a rock-bound
    coast!'—
  And he steered for the open
    sea.

'O father! I hear the sound of
    guns,
  O say, what may it be?'
'Some ship in distress, that cannot
    live
  In such an angry sea!'

'O father! I see a gleaming light,
  O say, what may it be?'
But the father answered never a
    word,
  A frozen corpse was he.

Lashed to the helm, all stiff and
    stark,
  With his face turned to the
    skies,
The lantern gleamed through the
    gleaming snow
  On his fixed and glassy eyes.

Then the maiden clasped her
    hands and prayed
  That savèd she might be;
And she thought of Christ, who
    stilled the wave
  On the Lake of Galilee.

And fast through the midnight
dark and drear,
Through the whistling sleet and
snow,
Like a sheeted ghost the vessel
swept
Towards the reef of Norman's
Woe.

And ever the fitful gusts between
A sound came from the land;
It was the sound of the trampling
surf
On the rocks and the hard
sea-sand.

The breakers were right beneath
her bows,
She drifted a dreary wreck,
And a whooping billow swept the
crew
Like icicles from her deck.

She struck where the white and
fleecy waves
Looked soft as carded wool,
But the cruel rocks they gored her
side
Like the horns of an angry bull.

Her rattling shrouds, all sheathed
in ice,
With the masts went by the
board;
Like a vessel of glass she stove
and sank,—
Ho! ho! the breakers roared!

At daybreak on the bleak sea-
beach
A fisherman stood aghast,
To see the form of a maiden fair
Lashed close to a drifting
mast.

The salt sea was frozen on her
breast,
The salt tears in her eyes;
And he saw her hair, like the brown
sea-weed,
On the billows fall and rise.

Such was the wreck of the Hes-
perus,
In the midnight and the snow!
Christ save us all from a death like
this,
On the reef of Norman's Woe!

——⧫——

THE LUCK OF EDENHALL.

FROM THE GERMAN OF UHLAND.

Of Edenhall the youthful Lord
Bids sound the festal trumpet's
call;
He rises at the banquet board,
And cries, 'mid the drunken revel-
lers all,
'Now bring me the Luck of Eden-
hall!'

The butler hears the words with
pain,
The house's oldest seneschal,
Takes slow from its silken cloth
again
The drinking-glass of crystal tall:
They call it The Luck of Edenhall.

Then said the Lord: 'This glass to
praise,
Fill with red wine from Portugal!'
The graybeard with trembling
hand obeys;
A purple light shines over all,
It beams from the Luck of Eden-
hall.

Then speaks the Lord, and waves
it light:
'This glass of flashing crystal tall
Gave to my sires the Fountain-
Sprite;
She wrote in it, *If this glass doth
fall,
Farewell then, O Luck of Eden-
hall!*

49

"'Twas right a goblet the fate
should be
Of the joyous race of Edenhall!
Deep draughts drink we right
willingly;
And willingly ring, with merry call,
Kling! klang! to the Luck of
Edenhall!'

First rings it deep, and full, and
mild,
Like to the song of a nightingale;
Then like the roar of a torrent
wild;
Then mutters at last like the
thunder's fall,
The glorious Luck of Edenhall.

'For its keeper takes a race of
might,
The fragile goblet of crystal tall;
It has lasted longer than is right;
Kling! klang!—with a harder blow
than all
Will I try the Luck of Edenhall!'

As the goblet ringing flies apart,
Suddenly cracks the vaulted hall;
And through the rift the wild
flames start;
The guests in dust are scattered all,
With the breaking Luck of Eden-
hall!

In storms the foe with fire and
sword;
He in the night had scaled the wall,
Slain by the sword lies the youth-
ful Lord,
But holds in his hand the crystal
tall,
The shattered Luck of Edenhall.

On the morrow the butler gropes
alone,
The graybeard in the desert hall,
He seeks his Lord's burnt skeleton,
He seeks in the dismal ruin's fall
The shards of the Luck of Eden-
hall.

'The stone wall,' saith he, 'doth
fall aside,
Down must the stately columns fall;
Glass is this earth's Luck and
Pride;
In atoms shall fall this earthly ball
One day like the Luck of Eden-
hall!'

THE ELECTED KNIGHT.

FROM THE DANISH.

SIR OLUF he rideth over the plain,
Full seven miles broad and seven
miles wide,
But never, ah never, can meet with
the man
A tilt with him dare ride.

He saw under the hillside
A Knight full well equipped;
His steed was black, his helm was
barred;
He was riding at full speed.

He wore upon his spurs
Twelve little golden birds;
Anon he spurred his steed with a
clang,
And there sat all the birds and
sang.

He wore upon his mail
Twelve little golden wheels;
Anon in eddies the wild wind blew,
And round and round the wheels
they flew.

He wore before his breast
A lance that was poised in rest;
And it was sharper than diamond-
stone—
It made Sir Oluf's heart to groan.

He wore upon his helm
A wreath of ruddy gold;
And that gave him the Maidens
Three—
The youngest was fair to behold.

Sir Oluf questioned the Knight eftsoon
  If he were come from Heaven down;
'Art thou Christ of Heaven?' quoth he,
  'So will I yield me unto thee.'

'I am not Christ the Great,
  Thou shalt not yield thee yet;
I am an Unknown Knight,
  Three modest Maidens have me bedight.'

'Art thou a Knight elected,
  And have three Maidens thee bedight;
So shalt thou ride a tilt this day,
  For all the Maidens' honour!'

The first tilt they together rode
  They put their steeds to the test;
The second tilt they together rode
  They proved their manhood best.

The third tilt they together rode,
  Neither of them would yield;
The fourth tilt they together rode
  They both fell on the field.

Now lie the lords upon the plain,
  And their blood runs unto death;
Now sit the Maidens in the high tower,
  The youngest sorrows till death.

The Children of the Lord's Supper.

FROM THE SWEDISH OF BISHOP TEGNÉR.

PENTECOST, day of rejoicing, had come.   The church of the village
Gleaming stood in the morning's sheen.   On the spire of the belfry,
Decked with a brazen cock, the friendly flames of the Spring-sun
Glanced like the tongues of fire beheld by Apostles aforetime.
Clear was the heaven and blue, and May, with her cap crowned with
  roses,
Stood in her holiday dress in the fields, and the wind and the brooklet
Murmured gladness and peace, God's-peace !   With lips rosy-tinted
Whispered the race of the flowers, and merry on balancing branches
Birds were singing their carol, a jubilant hymn to the Highest.
Swept and clean was the churchyard.   Adorned like a leaf-woven arbour
Stood its old-fashioned gate ; and within upon each cross of iron
Hung was a fragrant garland, new twined by the hands of affection.
Even the dial, that stood on a mound among the departed,
(There full a hundred years had it stood,) was embellished with
  blossoms.
Like to the patriarch hoary, the sage of his kith and the hamlet,
Who on his birthday is crowned by children and children's children,
So stood the ancient prophet, and mute with his pencil of iron
Marked on the tablet of stone, and measured the time and its changes,
While all around at his feet an eternity slumbered in quiet.
Also the church within was adorned, for this was the season
When the young, their parents' hope, and the loved-ones of heaven,
Should at the foot of the altar renew the vows of their baptism.
Therefore each nook and corner was swept and cleaned, and the dust
  was
Blown from the walls and ceiling, and from the oil-painted benches.
There stood the church like a garden ; the Feast of the Leafy Pavilions
Saw we in living presentment.   From noble arms on the church wall
Grew forth a cluster of leaves, and the preacher's pulpit of oak-wood
Budded once more anew, as aforetime the rod before Aaron.
Wreathed thereon was the Bible with leaves, and the dove, washed with
  silver,
Under its canopy fastened, had on it a necklace of wind-flowers.
But in front of the choir, round the altar-piece painted by Hörberg,

Crept a garland gigantic; and bright-curling tresses of angels
Peeped, like the sun from a cloud, from out of the shadowy leaf-work.
Likewise the lustre of brass new-polished blinked from the ceiling,
And for lights there were lilies of Pentecost set in the sockets.

Loud rang the bells already; the thronging crowd was assembled
Far from valleys and hills, to list to the holy preaching.
Hark! then roll forth at once the mighty tones of the organ,
Hover like voices from God, aloft like invisible spirits.
Like as Elias in heaven, when he cast from off him his mantle,
So cast off the soul its garments of earth; and with one voice
Chimed in the congregation, and sang an anthem immortal
Of the sublime Wallin, of David's harp in the North-land
Tuned to the choral of Luther. The song on its mighty pinions
Took every living soul, and lifted it gently to heaven,
And each face did shine like the Holy One's face upon Tabor.
Lo! there entered then into the church the Reverend Teacher
Father he hight and he was in the parish; a Christianly plainness
Clothed from his head to his feet the old man of seventy winters.
Friendly was he to behold, and glad as the heralding angel
Walked he among the crowds; but still a contemplative grandeur
Lay on his forehead as clear as on moss-covered gravestone a sunbeam.
As in his inspiration (an evening twilight that faintly
Gleams in the human soul, even now, from the day of creation)
Th' Artist, the friend of heaven, imagines Saint John when in Patmos,
Gray, with his eyes uplifted to heaven, so seemed then the old man;
Such was the glance of his eye, and such were his tresses of silver.
All the congregation arose in the pews that were numbered.
But with a cordial look, to the right and the left hand, the old man
Nodding all hail and peace, disappeared in the innermost chancel.

Simply and solemnly now proceeded the Christian service,
Singing and prayer, and at last an ardent discourse from the old man.
Many a moving word and warning, that out of the heart came,
Fell like the dew of the morning, like manna on those in the desert.
Then, when all was finished, the Teacher re-entered the chancel,
Followed therein by the young. The boys on the right had their places,
Delicate figures, with close-curling hair and cheeks rosy-blooming
But on the left of these there stood the tremulous lilies,
Tinged with the blushing light of the dawn, the diffident maidens,—
Folding their hands in prayer, and their eyes cast down on the pavement.
Now came, with question and answer, the catechism. In the beginning
Answered the children with troubled and faltering voice, but the old man's
Glances of kindness encouraged them soon, and the doctrines eternal
Flowed, like the waters of fountains, so clear from lips unpolluted.
Each time the answer was closed, and as oft as they named the Redeemer,
Lowly louted the boys, and lowly the maidens all courtesied.

Friendly the Teacher stood, like an angel of light there among them,
And to the children explained the holy, the highest, in few words,
Thorough, yet simple and clear—for sublimity always is simple,
Both in sermon and song, a child can seize on its meaning.
E'en as the green-growing bud unfolds when Springtide approaches,
Leaf by leaf puts forth, and warmed by the radiant sunshine
Blushes with purple and gold, till at last the perfected blossom
Opens its odorous chalice, and rocks with its crown in the breezes,
So was unfolded here the Christian lore of salvation,
Line by line from the soul of childhood. The fathers and mothers
Stood behind them in tears, and were glad at the well-worded answer.

Now went the old man up to the altar;—and straightway transfigured
(So did it seem unto me) was then the affectionate Teacher.
Like the Lord's Prophet sublime, and awful as Death and as Judgment
Stood he, the God-commissioned, the soul-searcher; earthward descending
Glances, sharp as a sword, into hearts that to him were transparent
Shot he; his voice was deep, was low like the thunder afar off.
So on a sudden transfigured he stood there, he spake and he questioned.

'This is the faith of the Fathers, the faith the Apostles delivered,
This is moreover the faith whereunto I baptized you, while still ye
Lay on your mothers' breasts, and nearer the portals of heaven.
Slumbering received you then the Holy Church in its bosom;
Wakened from sleep are ye now, and the light in its radiant splendour
Downward rains from the heaven;—to-day on the threshold of childhood
Kindly she frees you again, to examine and make your election,
For she knows naught of compulsion, and only conviction desireth.
This is the hour of your trial, the turning-point of existence,
Seed for the coming days; without revocation departeth
Now from your lips the confession; bethink ye, before ye make answer!
Think not, O think not with guile to deceive the questioning Teacher.
Sharp is his eye to-day, and a curse ever rests upon falsehood.
Enter not with a lie on Life's journey; the multitude hears you,
Brothers and sisters and parents, what dear upon earth is and holy
Standeth before your sight as a witness; the Judge everlasting
Looks from the sun down upon you, and angels in waiting beside Him
Grave your confession in letters of fire upon tablets eternal.
Thus, then,—believe ye in God, in the Father who this world created?
Him who redeemed it, the Son, and the Spirit where both are united?
Will ye promise me here, (a holy promise!) to cherish
God more than all things earthly, and every man as a brother?
Will ye promise me here, to confirm your faith by your living,
Th' heavenly faith of affection! to hope, to forgive, and to suffer,
Be what it may your condition, and walk before God in uprightness?
Will ye promise me this before God and man?'—With a clear voice
Answered the young men Yes!—and Yes! with lips softly-breathing

Answered the maidens eke. Then dissolved from the brow of the
    Teacher
Clouds with the lightnings therein, and he spake in accents more gentle,
Soft as the evening's breath, as harps by Babylon's rivers.

'Hail, then, hail to you all! To the heirdom of heaven be ye welcome;
Children no more from this day, but by covenant brothers and sisters!
Yet,—for what reason not children? Of such is the kingdom of heaven.
Here upon earth an assemblage of children, in heaven one Father,
Ruling them all as his Household,—forgiving in turn and chastising,
That is of human life a picture, as Scripture has taught us.
Blest are the pure before God! Upon purity and upon virtue
Resteth the Christian Faith; she herself from on high is descended.
Strong as a man and pure as a child, is the sum of the doctrine
Which the Divine One taught, and suffered and died on the cross for.
O, as ye wander this day from childhood's sacred asylum
Downward and ever downward, and deeper in Age's chill valley,
O, how soon will ye come,—too soon!—and long to turn backward
Up to its hill-tops again, to the sun-illumined, where Judgment
Stood like a father before you, and Pardon, clad like a mother,
Gave you her hand to kiss, and the loving heart was forgiven,
Life was a play and your hands grasped after the roses of heaven!
Seventy years have I lived already; the Father eternal
Gave me gladness and care; but the loveliest hours of existence,
When I have steadfastly gazed in their eyes, I have instantly known them,
Known them all again;—they were my childhood's acquaintance.
Therefore take from henceforth, as guides in the paths of existence,
Prayer, with her eyes raised to heaven, and Innocence, bride of man's
    childhood.
Innocence, child beloved, is a guest from the world of the blessed,
Beautiful, and in her hand a lily; on life's roaring billows
Swings she in safety, she heedeth them not, in the ship she is sleeping.
Calmly she gazes around in the turmoil of men; in the desert
Angels descend and minister unto her; she herself knoweth
Naught of her glorious attendance; but follows faithful and humble,
Follows so long as she may her friend; O do not reject her,
For she cometh from God and she holdeth the keys of the heavens.—
Prayer is Innocence' friend; and willingly flieth incessant
'Twixt the earth and the sky, the carrier-pigeon of heaven.
Son of Eternity, fettered in Time, and an exile, the Spirit
Tugs at his chains evermore, and struggles like flame ever upward.
Still he recalls with emotion his Father's manifold mansions,
Thinks of the land of his fathers, where blossomed more freshly the
    flowerets,
Shone a more beautiful sun, and he played with the wingèd angels.
Then grows the earth too narrow, too close; and homesick for heaven
Longs the wanderer again; and the Spirit's longings are worship;
Worship is called his most beautiful hour, and its tongue is entreaty.

Ah ! when the infinite burden of life descendeth upon us,
Crushes to earth our hope, and, under the earth, in the graveyard,
Then it is good to pray unto God ; for His sorrowing children
Turns He ne'er from His door, but He heals and helps and consoles them.
Yet it is better to pray when all things are prosperous with us,
Pray in fortunate days, for life's most beautiful Fortune
Kneels before the Eternal's throne ; and with hands interfolded,
Praises thankful and moved the only Giver of blessings.
Or do ye know, ye children, one blessing that comes not from Heaven ?
What has mankind forsooth, the poor ! that it has not received ?
Therefore, fall in the dust and pray ! The seraphs adoring
Cover with pinions six their face in the glory of Him who
Hung His masonry pendent on naught, when the world He created.
Earth declareth His might, and the firmament utters His glory.
Races blossom and die, and stars fall downward from heaven,
Downward like withered leaves ; at the last stroke of midnight, millen-
    niums
Lay themselves down at His feet, and He sees them, but counts them as
    nothing.
Who shall stand in His presence ? The wrath of the Judge is terrific,
Casting the insolent down at a glance. When He speaks in His anger
Hillocks skip like the kid, and mountains leap like the roebuck.
Yet,—why are ye afraid, ye children ? This awful avenger,
Ah ! is a merciful God ! God's voice was not in the earthquake,
Not in the fire, nor the storm, but it was in the whispering breezes.
Love is the root of creation ; God's essence ; worlds without number
Lie in His bosom like children ; He made them for this purpose only.
Only to love and to be loved again, He breathed forth His spirit
Into the slumbering dust, and upright standing, it laid its
Hand on its heart, and felt it was warm with a flame out of heaven.
Quench, O quench not that flame ! It is the breath of your being.
Love is life, but hatred is death. Not father, nor mother
Loved you, as God has loved you ; for 'twas that you may be happy
Gave He His only Son. When He bowed down His head in the death-
    hour
Solemnized Love its triumph ; the sacrifice then was completed.
Lo ! then was rent on a sudden the veil of the temple, dividing
Earth and heaven apart, and the dead from their sepulchres rising
Whispered with pallid lips and low in the ears of each other
Th' answer, but dreamed of before, to creation's enigma,—Atonement !
Depths of Love are Atonement's depths, for Love is Atonement.
Therefore, child of mortality, love thou the merciful Father ;
Wish what the Holy One wishes, and not from fear, but affection ;
Fear is the virtue of slaves ; but the heart that loveth is willing ;
Perfect was before God, and perfect is Love, and Love only.
Lovest thou God as thou oughtest, then lovest thou likewise thy
    brethren ;
One is the sun in heaven, and one, only one, is Love also.

Bears not each human figure the godlike stamp on his forehead?
Readest thou not in his face thine origin? Is he not sailing
Lost like thyself on an ocean unknown, and is he not guided
By the same stars that guide thee? Why shouldst thou hate then thy
    brother?
Hateth he thee, forgive! For 'tis sweet to stammer one letter
Of the Eternal's language;—on earth it is called Forgiveness!
Knowest thou Him who forgave with the crown of thorns on His
    temples?
Earnestly prayed for His foes, for His murderers? Say, dost thou know
    Him?
Ah! thou confessest His name, so follow likewise His example,
Think of thy brother no ill, but throw a veil over his failings,
Guide the erring aright; for the good, the heavenly Shepherd
Took the lost lamb in His arms, and bore it back to its mother.
This is the fruit of Love, and it is by its fruits that we know it.
Love is the creature's welfare, with God; but Love among mortals
Is but an endless sigh! He longs, and endures, and stands waiting,
Suffers and yet rejoices, and smiles with tears on his eyelids.
Hope,—so is called upon earth his recompense,—Hope, the befriending,
Does what she can, for she points evermore up to heaven, and faithful
Plunges her anchor's peak in the depths of the grave, and beneath it
Paints a more beautiful world, a dim, but a sweet play of shadows!
Races, better than we, have leaned on her wavering promise,
Having naught else but Hope. Then praise we our Father in heaven,
Him who has given us more; for to us has Hope been transfigured,
Groping no longer in night; she is Faith, she is living assurance.
Faith is enlightened Hope; she is light, is the eye of affection,
Dreams of the longing interprets, and carves their visions in marble.
Faith is the sun of life; and her countenance shines like the Hebrew's,
For she has looked upon God; the heaven on its stable foundation
Draws she with chains down to earth, and the New Jerusalem sinketh
Splendid with portals twelve in golden vapours descending.
There enraptured she wanders, and looks at the figures majestic,
Fears not the wingèd crowd, in the midst of them all is her homestead.
Therefore love and believe; for works will follow spontaneous
Even as day does the sun; the Right from the Good is an offspring,
Love in a bodily shape; and Christian works are no more than
Animate Love and Faith, as flowers are the animate Springtide.
Works do follow us all unto God; there stand and bear witness
Not what they seemed,—but what they were only. Blessed is he who
Hears their confession secure; they are mute upon earth until Death's
    hand
Opens the mouth of the silent. Ye children, does Death e'er alarm you?
Death is the brother of Love, twin-brother is he, and is only
More austere to behold. With a kiss upon lips that are fading
Takes he the soul and departs, and, rocked in the arms of affection,
Places the ransomed child, new born, 'fore the face of its Father.

Sounds of his coming already I hear,—see dimly his pinions,
Swart as the night, but with stars strewn upon them ! I fear not before
    him.
Death is only release, and in mercy is mute. On his bosom
Freer breathes, in its coolness, my breast ; and face to face standing
Look I on God as He is, a sun unpolluted by vapours ;
Look on the light of the ages I loved, the spirits majestic,
Nobler, better than I ; they stand by the throne all transfigured,
Vested in white, and with harps of gold, and are singing an anthem,
Writ in the climate of heaven, in the language spoken by angels.
You, in like manner, ye children beloved, he one day shall gather,
Never forgets he the weary ;—then welcome, ye loved ones, hereafter !
Meanwhile forget not the keeping of vows, forget not the promise,
Wander from holiness onward to holiness ; earth shall ye heed not ;
Earth is but dust and heaven is light ; I have pledged you to heaven.
God of the universe, hear me ! thou fountain of Love everlasting,
Hark to the voice of thy servant ! I send up my prayer to thy heaven.
Let me hereafter not miss at thy throne one spirit of all these,
Whom thou hast given me here ! I have loved them all like a father.
May they bear witness for me, that I taught them the way of salvation,
Faithful, so far as I knew, of thy word ; again may they know me,
Fall on their Teacher's breast, and before thy face may I place them,
Pure as they now are, but only more tried, and exclaiming with gladness,
Father, lo ! I am here, and the children, whom thou hast given me !'

Weeping he spake in these words ; and now at the beck of the old man
Knee against knee they knitted a wreath round the altar's enclosure.
Kneeling he read then the prayers of the consecration, and softly
With him the children read ; at the close, with tremulous accents,
Asked he the peace of Heaven, a benediction upon them.
Now should have ended his task for the day ; the following Sunday
Was for the young appointed to eat of the Lord's holy Supper.
Sudden, as struck from the clouds, stood the Teacher silent and laid his
Hand on his forehead, and cast his looks upward ; while thoughts high
    and holy
Flew through the midst of his soul, and his eyes glanced with wonderful
    brightness.
' On the next Sunday, who knows ! perhaps I shall rest in the grave-
    yard !
Some one perhaps of yourselves, a lily broken untimely,
Bow down his head to the earth ; why delay I ? the hour is accom-
    plished.
Warm is the heart ;—I will ! for to-day grows the harvest of heaven.
What I began accomplish I now ; what failing therein is
I, the old man, will answer to God and the reverend father.
Say to me only, ye children, ye denizens new-come in heaven.
Are ye ready this day to eat of the bread of Atonement ?
What it denoteth, that know ye full well, I have told it you often.

Of the new covenant symbol it is, of Atonement a token,
Stablished between earth and heaven. Man by his sins and trans-
gressions
Far has wandered from God, from his essence. 'Twas in the beginning
Fast by the Tree of Knowledge he fell, and it hangs its crown o'er the
Fall to this day; in the Thought is the Fall; in the Heart the Atonement.
Infinite is the fall,—the Atonement infinite likewise.
See! behind me, as far as the old man remembers, and forward,
Far as Hope in her flight can reach with her wearied pinions,
Sin and Atonement incessant go through the lifetime of mortals.
Sin is brought forth full-grown; but Atonement sleeps in our bosoms
Still as the cradled babe; and dreams of heaven and of angels,
Cannot awake to sensation; is like the tones in the harp's strings,
Spirits imprisoned, that wait evermore the deliverer's finger.
Therefore, ye children beloved, descended the Prince of Atonement,
Woke the slumberer from sleep, and she stands now with eyes all
resplendent,
Bright as the vault of the sky, and battles with Sin and o'ercomes her.
Downward to earth He came and, transfigured, thence reascended;
Not from the heart in like wise, for there He still lives in the Spirit,
Loves and atones evermore. So long as Time is, is Atonement.
Therefore with reverence take this day her visible token.
Tokens are dead if the things live not. The light everlasting
Unto the blind is not, but is born of the eye that has vision.
Neither in bread nor in wine, but in the heart that is hallowed
Lieth forgiveness enshrined; the intention alone of amendment
Fruits of the earth ennobles to heavenly things, and removes all
Sin and guerdon of sin. Only Love with his arms wide extended,
Penitence weeping and praying; the Will that is tried, and whose gold
flows
Purified forth from the flames; in a word, mankind by Atonement
Breaketh Atonement's bread, and drinketh Atonement's wine-cup.
But he who cometh up hither, unworthy, with hate in his bosom,
Scoffing at men and at God, is guilty of Christ's blessed body,
And the Redeemer's blood! To himself he eateth and drinketh
Death and doom! And from this, preserve us, thou heavenly Father!
Are ye ready, ye children, to eat of the bread of Atonement?'
Thus with emotion he asked, and together answered the children,
'Yes!' with deep sobs interrupted. Then read he the due supplications,
Read the Form of Communion, and in chimed the organ and anthem:
'O Holy Lamb of God, who takest away our transgressions,
Hear us! give us thy peace! have mercy, have mercy upon us!'
Th' old man, with trembling hand, and heavenly pearls on his eyelids,
Filled now the chalice and paten, and dealt round the mystical symbols.
O, then seemed it to me as if God, with the broad eye of midday,
Clearer looked in at the windows, and all the trees in the churchyard
Bowed down their summits of green, and the grass on the graves 'gan
to shiver.

But in the children (I noted it well; I knew it) there ran a
Tremor of holy rapture along through their ice-cold members.
Decked like an altar before them, there stood the green earth, and
above it
Heaven opened itself, as of old before Stephen; they saw there
Radiant in glory the Father, and on His right hand the Redeemer.
Under them hear they the clang of harpstrings, and angels from gold
clouds
Beckon to them like brothers, and fan with their pinions of purple.

Closed was the Teacher's task, and with heaven in their hearts and
their faces,
Up rose the children all, and each bowed him, weeping full sorely,
Downward to kiss that reverend hand, but all of them pressed he
Moved to his bosom, and laid, with a prayer, his hands full of blessings,
Now on the holy breast, and now on the innocent tresses.

Miscellaneous Poems.

THE VILLAGE BLACK-SMITH.

UNDER a spreading chestnut-tree
  The village smithy stands ;
The smith, a mighty man is he,
  With large and sinewy hands ;
And the muscles of his brawny arms
  Are strong as iron bands.

His hair is crisp, and black, and
    long ;
  His face is like the tan ;
His brow is wet with honest sweat,
  He earns whate'er he can,
And looks the whole world in the
    face,
  For he owes not any man.

Week in, week out, from morn till
    night,
  You can hear his bellows blow ;
You can hear him swing his heavy
    sledge,
  With measured beat and slow,
Like a sexton ringing the village bell,
  When the evening sun is low.

And children coming home from
    school
  Look in at the open door ;
They love to see the flaming forge,
  And hear the bellows roar,
And catch the burning sparks that
    fly
  Like chaff from a threshing-floor.

He goes on Sunday to the church,
  And sits among his boys ;
He hears the parson pray and
    preach,
  He hears his daughter's voice
Singing in the village choir,
  And it makes his heart rejoice.

It sounds to him like her mother's
    voice
  Singing in Paradise !
He needs must think of her once
    more,
  How in the grave she lies ;
And with his hard, rough hand he
    wipes
  A tear out of his eyes.

Toiling, — rejoicing, — sorrowing,
  Onward through life he goes ;
Each morning sees some task
    begin,
  Each evening sees it close ;
Something attempted, something
    done,
  Has earned a night's repose.

Thanks, thanks to thee, my worthy
    friend,
  For the lesson thou hast taught !
Thus at the flaming forge of life
  Our fortunes must be wrought ;
Thus on its sounding anvil shaped
  Each burning deed and thought.

ENDYMION.

THE rising moon has hid the stars ;
Her level rays, like golden bars,
  Lie on the landscape green,
  With shadows brown between.

And silver white the river gleams
As if Diana, in her dreams,
  Had dropt her silver bow
  Upon the meadows low.

On such a tranquil night as this,
She woke Endymion with a kiss,
  When, sleeping in the grove,
  He dreamed not of her love.

61

Like Dian's kiss, unasked, un-
sought,
Love gives itself, but is not bought;
  Nor voice, nor sound betrays
  Its deep, impassioned gaze.

It comes, — the beautiful, the free,
The crown of all humanity, —
  In silence and alone
  To seek the elected one.

It lifts the boughs, whose shadows
  deep
Are Life's oblivion, the soul's sleep,
  And kisses the closed eyes
  Of him who slumbering lies.

O weary hearts! O slumbering
  eyes!
O drooping souls, whose destinies
  Are fraught with fear and pain,
  Ye shall be loved again!

No one is so accursed by fate,
No one so utterly desolate,
  But some heart, though un-
    known,
  Responds unto his own.

Responds, — as if with unseen wings,
An angel touched its quivering
  strings;
  And whispers, in its song,
  'Where hast thou stayed so
    long?'

THE TWO LOCKS OF HAIR.

FROM THE GERMAN OF PFIZER.

A YOUTH, light-hearted and con-
  tent,
  I wander through the world;
Here, Arab-like, is pitched my tent,
  And straight again is furled.

Yet oft I dream, that once a wife
  Close in my heart was locked,
And in the sweet repose of life
  A blessed child I rocked.

I wake! Away that dream, —
  away!
  Too long did it remain!
So long, that both by night and
  day
  It ever comes again.

The end lies ever in my thought;
  To a grave so cold and deep
The mother beautiful was brought;
  Then dropt the child asleep.

But now the dream is wholly o'er,
  I bathe my eyes and see;
And wander through the world
  once more,
  A youth so light and free.

Two locks—and they are wondrous
  fair—
  Left me that vision mild;
The brown is from the mother's
  hair,
  The blond is from the child.

And when I see that lock of gold,
  Pale grows the evening-red;
And when the dark lock I behold,
  I wish that I were dead.

IT IS NOT ALWAYS MAY.

No hay pájaros en los nidos de antaño.
            Spanish Proverb.

THE sun is bright,—the air is
  clear,
  The darting swallows soar and
    sing,
And from the stately elms I hear
  The bluebird prophesying
    Spring.

So blue yon winding river flows,
  It seems an outlet from the sky,
Where waiting till the west-wind
  blows,
  The freighted clouds at anchor
    lie.

All things are new ;—the buds, the leaves,
  That gild the elm-tree's nodding crest,
And even the nest beneath the eaves ;—
  There are no birds in last year's nest !

All things rejoice in youth and love,
  The fulness of their first delight !
And learn from the soft heavens above
  The melting tenderness of night.

Maiden, that read'st this simple rhyme,
  Enjoy thy youth, it will not stay;
Enjoy the fragrance of thy prime,
  For O, it is not always May!

Enjoy the Spring of Love and Youth,
  To some good angel leave the rest;
For Time will teach thee soon the truth,
  There are no birds in last year's nest !

—⊷—

THE RAINY DAY.

THE day is cold, and dark, and dreary;
It rains, and the wind is never weary;
The vine still clings to the mouldering wall,
But at every gust the dead leaves fall,
  And the day is dark and dreary.

My life is cold, and dark, and dreary;
It rains, and the wind is never weary;

My thoughts still cling to the mouldering Past,
But the hopes of youth fall thick in the blast,
  And the days are dark and dreary.

Be still, sad heart ! and cease repining ;
Behind the clouds is the sun still shining ;
Thy fate is the common fate of all,
Into each life some rain must fall,
  Some days must be dark and dreary.

—⊷—

GOD'S-ACRE.

I LIKE that ancient Saxon phrase, which calls
  The burial-ground God's-Acre ! It is just ;
It consecrates each grave within its walls,
  And breathes a benison o'er the sleeping dust.

God's-Acre ! Yes, that blessed name imparts
  Comfort to those who in the grave have sown
The seed that they had garnered in their hearts,
  Their bread of life, alas ! no more their own.

Into its furrows shall we all be cast,
  In the sure faith that we shall rise again
At the great harvest, when the archangel's blast
  Shall winnow, like a fan, the chaff and grain.

Then shall the good stand in immortal bloom
  In the fair gardens of that second birth,

And each bright blossom mingle its perfume
With that of flowers which never bloomed on earth.

With thy rude ploughshare, Death, turn up the sod,
And spread the furrow for the seed we sow;
This is the field and Acre of our God,
This is the place where human harvests grow!

TO THE RIVER CHARLES.

RIVER! that in silence windest
Through the meadows, bright and free,
Till at length thy rest thou findest
In the bosom of the sea!

Four long years of mingled feeling
Half in rest, and half in strife,
I have seen thy waters stealing
Onward, like the stream of life.

Thou hast taught me, Silent River!
Many a lesson, deep and long;
Thou hast been a generous giver;
I can give thee but a song.

Oft in sadness and in illness
I have watched thy current glide,
Till the beauty of its stillness
Overflowed me like a tide.

And in better hours and brighter,
When I saw thy waters gleam,
I have felt my heart beat lighter,
And leap onward with thy stream.

Not for this alone I love thee,
Nor because thy waves of blue
From celestial seas above thee
Take their own celestial hue.

Where yon shadowy woodlands hide thee,
And thy waters disappear,
Friends I love have dwelt beside thee,
And have made thy margin dear.

More than this;—thy name reminds me
Of three friends, all true and tried;
And that name, like magic, binds me
Closer, closer to thy side.

Friends my soul with joy remembers!
How like quivering flames they start,
When I fan the living embers
On the hearth-stone of my heart!

'Tis for this, thou Silent River!
That my spirit leans to thee;
Thou hast been a generous giver,
Take this idle song from me.

BLIND BARTIMEUS.

BLIND Bartimeus at the gates
Of Jericho in darkness waits;
He hears the crowd;—he hears a breath
Say, 'It is Christ of Nazareth!'
And calls, in tones of agony,
Ἰησοῦ, ἐλέησόν με!

The thronging multitudes increase;
Blind Bartimeus, hold thy peace!
But still, above the noisy crowd,
The beggar's cry is shrill and loud;
Until they say, 'He calleth thee!'
Θάρσει, ἔγειραι, φωνεῖ σε!

Then saith the Christ, as silent stands
The crowd, 'What wilt thou at my hands?'

64

And he replies, 'O give me light!
Rabbi, restore the blind man's
    sight.'
And Jesus answers Ὕπαγε·
Ἡ πίστις σου σέσωκέ σε !

Ye that have eyes, yet cannot see,
In darkness and in misery,
Recall those mighty Voices Three,
Ἰησοῦ, ἐλέησόν με !
Θάρσει, ἔγειραι, ὕπαγε !
Ἡ πίστις σου σέσωκέ σε !

THE GOBLET OF LIFE.

FILLED is Life's goblet to the
    brim ;
And though my eyes with tears are
    dim,
I see its sparkling bubbles swim,
And chant a melancholy hymn
    With solemn voice and slow.

No purple flowers,—no garlands
    green,
Conceal the goblet's shade or
    sheen,
Nor maddening draughts of Hip-
    pocrene,
Like gleams of sunshine, flash be-
    tween
    Thick leaves of mistletoe.

This goblet, wrought with curious
    art,
Is filled with waters, that upstart
When the deep fountains of the
    heart,
By strong convulsions rent apart,
    Are running all to waste.

And as it mantling passes round,
With fennel is it wreathed and
    crowned,
Whose seed and foliage sun-im-
    browned
Are in its waters steeped and
    drowned,
    And give a bitter taste.

Above the lowly plants it towers,
The fennel, with its yellow flowers,
And in an earlier age than ours
Was gifted with the wondrous
    powers,
    Lost vision to restore.

It gave new strength, and fearless
    mood ;
And gladiators, fierce and rude,
Mingled it in their daily food ;
And he who battled and subdued,
    A wreath of fennel wore.

Then in Life's goblet freely press
The leaves that give it bitterness,
Nor prize the coloured waters less,
For in thy darkness and distress
    New light and strength they
        give !

And he who has not learned to
    know
How false its sparkling bubbles
    show,
How bitter are the drops of woe
With which its brim may overflow,
    He has not learned to live.

The prayer of Ajax was for light ;
Through all that dark and desper-
    ate fight,
The blackness of that noonday
    night,
He asked but the return of sight,
    To see his foeman's face.

Let our unceasing, earnest prayer
Be, too, for light,—for strength to
    bear
Our portion of the weight of care
That crushes into dumb despair
    One half the human race.

O suffering, sad humanity !
O ye afflicted ones, who lie
Steeped to the lips in misery,
Longing, and yet afraid to die,
    Patient, though sorely tried !

65

I pledge you in this cup of grief,
Where floats the fennel's bitter
     leaf!
The Battle of our Life is brief,
The alarm,—the struggle,—the
     relief,
     Then sleep we side by side.

MAIDENHOOD.

MAIDEN! with the meek brown
     eyes,
In whose orbs a shadow lies
Like the dusk in evening skies!

Thou whose locks outshine the sun,
Golden tresses, wreathed in one,
As the braided streamlets run!

Standing, with reluctant feet,
Where the brook and river meet,
Womanhood and childhood fleet!

Gazing, with a timid glance,
On the brooklet's swift advance,
On the river's broad expanse!

Deep and still, that gliding stream
Beautiful to thee must seem
As the river of a dream.

Then why pause with indecision,
When bright angels in thy vision
Beckon thee to fields Elysian?

Seest thou shadows sailing by,
As the dove, with startled eye,
Sees the falcon's shadow fly?

Hearest thou voices on the shore,
That our ears perceive no more,
Deafened by the cataract's roar?

O, thou child of many prayers!
Life hath quicksands,—Life hath
     snares!
Care and age come unawares!

Like the swell of some sweet tune,
Morning rises into noon,
May glides onward into June.

Childhood is the bough, where
     slumbered
Birds and blossoms many-num-
     bered;—
Age, that bough with snows en-
     cumbered.

Gather, then, each flower that
     grows,
When the young heart overflows,
To embalm that tent of snows.

Bear a lily in thy hand;
Gates of brass cannot withstand
One touch of that magic wand.

Bear through sorrow, wrong, and
     ruth,
In thy heart the dew of youth,
On thy lips the smile of truth.

O, that dew, like balm, shall steal
Into wounds that cannot heal,
Even as sleep our eyes doth seal;

And that smile, like sunshine, dart
Into many a sunless heart,
For a smile of God thou art.

EXCELSIOR.

THE shades of night were falling
     fast,
As through an Alpine village
     passed
A youth, who bore, 'mid snow and
     ice,
A banner with the strange device,
     Excelsior!

His brow was sad; his eye be-
     neath
Flashed like a falchion from its
     sheath,
And like a silver clarion rung
The accents of that unknown
     tongue,
     Excelsior!

In happy homes he saw the light
Of household fires gleam warm and
bright ;
Above, the spectral glaciers shone,
And from his lips escaped a groan,
    Excelsior !

'Try not the Pass!' the old man
    said ;
'Dark lowers the tempest over-
head,
The roaring torrent is deep and
    wide!'
And loud that clarion voice re-
plied,
    Excelsior !

'O stay,' the maiden said, 'and
    rest
Thy weary head upon this breast !'
A tear stood in his bright blue eye,
But still he answered, with a sigh,
    Excelsior !

' Beware the pine-tree's withered
    branch !
Beware the awful avalanche !'
This was the peasant's last Good-
night.
A voice replied, far up the height,
    Excelsior !

At break of day, as heavenward
The pious monks of Saint Bernard
Uttered the oft-repeated prayer,
A voice cried through the startled
    air,
    Excelsior !

A traveller, by the faithful hound,
Half-buried in the snow was found,
Still grasping in his hand of ice
That banner with the strange de-
    vice,
    Excelsior !

There in the twilight cold and
    gray,
Lifeless, but beautiful, he lay,
And from the sky, serene and far,
A voice fell, like a falling star,
    Excelsior !

MEZZO CAMMIN.

*Written at Boppard, on the Rhine, August
25, 1842, just before leaving for home.*

HALF of my life is gone, and I have
    let
    The years slip from me and have
      not fulfilled
    The aspiration of my youth, to
      build
    Some tower of song with lofty
      parapet.
Not indolence, nor pleasure, nor
    the fret
    Of restless passions that would
      not be stilled,
    But sorrow, and a care that
      almost killed,
    Kept me from what I may ac-
      complish yet ;
Though, half-way up the hill, I see
    the Past
    Lying beneath me with its sounds
      and sights,—
    A city in the twilight dim and
      vast,
With smoking roofs, soft bells, and
    gleaming lights,—
    And hear above me on the
      autumnal blast
    The cataract of Death far thun-
      dering from the heights.

Poems on Slavery.

[The following poems, with one exception, were written at sea, in the latter part of October, 1842. I had not then heard of Dr. Channing's death. Since that event, the poem addressed to him is no longer appropriate. I have decided, however, to let it remain as it was written, in testimony of my admiration for a great and good man.]

TO WILLIAM E. CHANNING.

THE pages of thy book I read,
　And as I closed each one,
My heart, responding, ever said,
　'Servant of God! well done!'

Well done! Thy words are great
　　and bold;
　At times they seem to me,
Like Luther's, in the days of old,
　Half-battles for the free.

Go on, until this land revokes
　The old and chartered Lie,
The feudal curse, whose whips and
　　yokes
　Insult humanity.

A voice is ever at thy side
　Speaking in tones of might,
Like the prophetic voice that cried
　To John in Patmos, 'Write!'

Write! and tell out this bloody tale;
　Record this dire eclipse,
This Day of Wrath, this Endless
　　Wail,
　This dread Apocalypse!

THE SLAVE'S DREAM.

BESIDE the ungathered rice he lay,
　His sickle in his hand;
His breast was bare, his matted
　　hair
　Was buried in the sand.

Again, in the mist and shadow of
　　sleep,
　He saw his Native Land.

Wide through the landscape of his
　　dreams
　The lordly Niger flowed;
Beneath the palm-trees on the plain
　Once more a king he strode;
And heard the tinkling caravans
　Descend the mountain-road.

He saw once more his dark-eyed
　　queen
　Among her children stand;
They clasped his neck, they kissed
　　his cheeks,
　They held him by the hand!—
A tear burst from the sleeper's lids
　And fell into the sand.

And then at furious speed he rode
　Along the Niger's bank;
His bridle-reins were golden chains,
　And, with a martial clank,
At each leap he could feel his
　　scabbard of steel
　Smiting his stallion's flank.

Before him, like a blood-red flag,
　The bright flamingoes flew;
From morn till night he followed
　　their flight,
　O'er plains where the tamarind
　　grew,
Till he saw the roofs of Caffre huts,
　And the ocean rose to view.

68

At night he heard the lion roar,
 And the hyena scream,
And the river-horse, as he crushed
  the reeds
 Beside some hidden stream ;
And it passed, like a glorious roll
  of drums,
 Through the triumph of his
  dream.

The forests, with their myriad
  tongues,
 Shouted of liberty ;
And the Blast of the Desert cried
  aloud,
 With a voice so wild and free,
That he started in his sleep and
  smiled
 At their tempestuous glee.

He did not feel the driver's whip,
 Nor the burning heat of day ;
For Death had illumined the Land
  of Sleep,
 And his lifeless body lay
A worn-out fetter, that the soul
 Had broken and thrown away !

THE GOOD PART THAT SHALL NOT BE TAKEN AWAY.

SHE dwells by Great Kenhawa's
  side,
 In valleys green and cool ;
And all her hope and all her pride
 Are in the village school.

Her soul, like the transparent air
 That robes the hills above,
Though not of earth, encircles there
 All things with arms of love.

And thus she walks among her
  girls
 With praise and mild rebukes ;
Subduing e'en rude village churls
 By her angelic looks.

She reads to them at eventide
 Of One who came to save ;
To cast the captive's chains aside
 And liberate the slave.

And oft the blessed time foretells
 When all men shall be free,
And musical as silver bells
 Their falling chains shall be.

And following her beloved Lord
 In decent poverty,
She makes her life one sweet record
 And deed of charity.

For she was rich, and gave up all
 To break the iron bands
Of those who waited in her hall
 And laboured in her lands.

Long since beyond the Southern
  Sea
 Their outbound sails have sped,
While she, in meek humility,
 Now earns her daily bread.

It is their prayers, which never
  cease,
 That clothe her with such grace ;
Their blessing is the light of peace
 That shines upon her face.

THE SLAVE IN THE DISMAL SWAMP.

IN dark fens of the Dismal Swamp
 The hunted Negro lay ;
He saw the fire of the midnight
  camp,
 And heard at times a horse's tramp
 And a bloodhound's distant bay.

Where will-o'-the-wisps and glow
  worms shine,
 In bulrush and in brake ;
Where waving mosses shroud the
  pine,
And the cedar grows, and the
  poisonous vine
 Is spotted like the snake ;

Where hardly a human foot could
    pass,
  Or a human heart would dare,
On the quaking turf of the green
    morass
He crouched in the rank and
    tangled grass,
  Like a wild beast in his lair.

A poor old slave, infirm and
    lame;
  Great scars deformed his face;
On his forehead he bore the brand
    of shame,
And the rags, that hid his mangled
    frame,
  Were the livery of disgrace.

All things above were bright and
    fair,
  All things were glad and free;
Lithe squirrels darted here and
    there,
And wild birds filled the echoing
    air
  With songs of Liberty!

On him alone was the doom of
    pain,
  From the morning of his birth;
On him alone the curse of Cain
Fell, like a flail on the garnered
    grain,
  And struck him to the earth!

THE SLAVE SINGING AT
MIDNIGHT.

LOUD he sang the psalm of
    David!
He, a Negro and enslaved,
Sang of Israel's victory,
Sang of Zion, bright and free.

In that hour when night is calmest,
Sang he from the Hebrew Psalmist,
In a voice so sweet and clear
That I could not choose but hear.

Songs of triumph, and ascriptions,
Such as reached the swart Egypt
    ians,
When upon the Red Sea coast
Perished Pharaoh and his host.

And the voice of his devotion
Filled my soul with strange emotion;
For its tones by turns were glad,
Sweetly solemn, wildly sad.

Paul and Silas in their prison
Sang of Christ, the Lord arisen,
And an earthquake's arm of might
Broke their dungeon-gates at night.

But, alas! what holy angel
Brings the Slave this glad evangel?
And what earthquake's arm of
    might
Breaks his dungeon-gates at night?

THE WITNESSES.

IN Ocean's wide domains,
  Half buried in the sands,
Lie skeletons in chains,
  With shackled feet and hands.

Beyond the fall of dews,
  Deeper than plummet lies,
Float ships, with all their crews,
  No more to sink nor rise.

There the black Slave-ship swims,
  Freighted with human forms,
Whose fettered, fleshless limbs
  Are not the sport of storms.

These are the bones of Slaves;
  They gleam from the abyss;
They cry from yawning waves,
  'We are the Witnesses!'

Within Earth's wide domains
  Are markets for men's lives;
Their necks are galled with chains,
  Their wrists are cramped with
    gyves.

Dead bodies, that the kite
  In deserts makes its prey;
Murders, that with affright
  Scare school-boys from their
    play!

All evil thoughts and deeds;
  Anger, and lust, and pride;
The foulest, rankest weeds,
  That choke Life's groaning tide!

These are the woes of Slaves;
  They glare from the abyss;
They cry from unknown graves,
  'We are the Witnesses!'

———

THE QUADROON GIRL.

THE Slaver in the broad lagoon
  Lay moored with idle sail;
He waited for the rising moon
  And for the evening gale.

Under the shore his boat was
    tied,
  And all her listless crew
Watched the gray alligator slide
  Into the still bayou.

Odours of orange-flowers and
    spice
  Reached them from time to
    time,
Like airs that breathe from Para-
    dise
  Upon a world of crime.

The Planter, under his roof of
    thatch,
  Smoked thoughtfully and slow;
The Slaver's thumb was on the
    latch,
  He seemed in haste to go.

He said, ' My ship at anchor rides
  In yonder broad lagoon;
I only wait the evening tides
  And the rising of the moon.'

Before them, with her face up-
    raised,
  In timid attitude,
Like one half curious, half amazed,
  A Quadroon maiden stood.

Her eyes were large and full of
    light,
  Her arms and neck were bare;
No garment she wore save a kirtle
    bright,
  And her own long, raven hair.

And on her lips there played a
    smile
  As holy, meek, and faint,
As lights in some cathedral aisle
  The features of a saint.

' The soil is barren,—the farm is
    old,'
  The thoughtful planter said;
Then looked upon the Slaver's gold,
  And then upon the maid.

His heart within him was at strife
  With such accursed gains:
For he knew whose passions gave
    her life,
  Whose blood ran in her veins.

But the voice of nature was too
    weak;
  He took the glittering gold!
Then pale as death grew the
    maiden's cheek,
  Her hands as icy cold.

The Slaver led her from the door,
  He led her by the hand,
To be his slave and paramour
  In a strange and distant land!

THE WARNING.

BEWARE! The Israelite of old, who tore
  The lion in his path,—when, poor and blind,
He saw the blessed light of heaven no more,
  Shorn of his noble strength and forced to grind
In prison, and at last led forth to be
A pander to Philistine revelry,—

Upon the pillars of the temple laid
  His desperate hands, and in its overthrow
Destroyed himself, and with him those who made
  A cruel mockery of his sightless woe;
The poor, blind Slave, the scoff and jest of all,
Expired, and thousands perished in the fall!

There is a poor, blind Samson in this land,
  Shorn of his strength and bound in bonds of steel,
Who may, in some grim revel, raise his hand,
  And shake the pillars of this Commonweal,
Till the vast Temple of our liberties
A shapeless mass of wreck and rubbish lies.

The Spanish Student.

DRAMATIS PERSONÆ.

VICTORIAN }
HYPOLITO } . . . . *Students of Alcalá.*

THE COUNT OF LARA }
DON CARLOS } . . . *Gentlemen of Madrid.*

THE ARCHBISHOP OF TOLEDO.
A CARDINAL.
BELTRAN CRUZADO . . . . *Count of the Gipsies.*
BARTOLOMÉ ROMAN . . . . *A young Gipsy.*
THE PADRE CURA OF GUADARRAMA.
PEDRO CRESPO . . . . . *Alcalde.*
PANCHO . . . . . . *Alguacil.*
FRANCISCO . . . . . *Lara's Servant.*
CHISPA . . . . . . *Victorian's Servant.*
BALTASAR . . . . . *Innkeeper.*
PRECIOSA . . . . . *A Gipsy Girl.*
ANGELICA . . . . . *A poor Girl.*
MARTINA . . . . . *The Padre Cura's Niece.*
DOLORES . . . . . *Preciosa's Maid.*

Gipsies, Musicians, &c.

ACT I.

SCENE I.—*The* COUNT OF LARA'S *chambers. Night. The* COUNT *in his dressing-gown, smoking, and conversing with* DON CARLOS.

Lara. You were not at the play to-night, Don Carlos;
How happened it?
Don C. I had engagements else-
where.
Pray who was there?
Lara. Why, all the town and court.
The house was crowded; and the busy fans
Among the gaily dressed and per-
fumed ladies
Fluttered like butterflies among the flowers.
There was the Countess of Medina Celi;
The Goblin Lady with her Phan-
tom Lover,
Her Lindo Don Diego; Doña Sol,

And Doña Serafina, and her cousins.
Don C. What was the play?
Lara. It was a dull affair;
One of those comedies in which you see,
As Lope says, the history of the world
Brought down from Genesis to the Day of Judgment.
There were three duels fought in the first act,
Three gentlemen receiving deadly wounds,
Laying their hands upon their hearts, and saying,
'O, I am dead!' a lover in a closet,
An old hidalgo, and a gay Don Juan,
A Doña Inez with a black mantilla,
Followed at twilight by an un-
known lover,
Who looks intently where he knows she is not!
Don C. Of course, the Preciosa danced to-night?

73

Lara. And never better. Every footstep fell
As lightly as a sunbeam on the water.
I think the girl extremely beautiful.

Don C. Almost beyond the privilege of woman!
I saw her in the Prado yesterday.
Her step was royal,—queen-like,—and her face
As beautiful as a saint's in Paradise.

Lara. May not a saint fall from her Paradise,
And be no more a saint?

Don C. Why do you ask?

Lara. Because I have heard it said this angel fell,
And though she is a virgin outwardly,
Within she is a sinner; like those panels
Of doors and altar-pieces the old monks
Painted in convents, with the Virgin Mary
On the outside, and on the inside Venus!

Don C. You do her wrong; indeed, you do her wrong!
She is as virtuous as she is fair.

Lara. How credulous you are!
Why look you, friend,
There's not a virtuous woman in Madrid,
In this whole city! And would you persuade me
That a mere dancing-girl, who shows herself,
Nightly, half naked, on the stage, for money,
And with voluptuous motions fires the blood
Of inconsiderate youth, is to be held
A model for her virtue?

Don C. You forget
She is a Gipsy girl.

Lara. And therefore won
The easier.

Don C. Nay, not to be won at all!
The only virtue that a Gipsy prizes
Is chastity. That is her only virtue.
Dearer than life she holds it. I remember
A Gipsy woman, a vile, shameless bawd,
Whose craft was to betray the young and fair;
And yet this woman was above all bribes.
And when a noble lord, touched by her beauty,
The wild and wizard beauty of her race,
Offered her gold to be what she made others,
She turned upon him with a look of scorn,
And smote him in the face!

Lara. And does that prove
That Preciosa is above suspicion?

Don C. It proves a nobleman may be repulsed
When he thinks conquest easy. I believe
That woman, in her deepest degradation,
Holds something sacred, something undefiled,
Some pledge and keepsake of her higher nature,
And, like the diamond in the dark, retains
Some quenchless gleam of the celestial light!

Lara. Yet Preciosa would have taken the gold.

Don C. (*rising*). I do not think so.

Lara. I am sure of it.
But why this haste? Stay yet a little longer,
And fight the battles of your Dulcinea.

Don C. 'Tis late. I must be-gone; for if I stay
You will not be persuaded.

Lara. Yes; persuade me.

Don C. No one so deaf as he
who will not hear!
Lara. No one so blind as he
who will not see!
Don C. And so good night. I
wish you pleasant dreams,
And greater faith in woman. [*Exit.*
Lara. Greater faith!
I have the greatest faith; for I
believe
Victorian is her lover. I believe
That I shall be to-morrow; and
thereafter
Another, and another, and another,
Chasing each other through her
zodiac,
As Taurus chases Aries.

(*Enter* FRANCISCO *with a casket.*)

Well, Francisco,
What speed with Preciosa?
Fran. None, my lord.
She sends your jewels back, and
bids me tell you
She is not to be purchased by your
gold.
Lara. Then I will try some
other way to win her.
Pray, dost thou know Victorian?
Fran. Yes, my lord;
I saw him at the jeweller's to-day.
Lara. What was he doing there?
Fran. I saw him buy
A golden ring, that had a ruby in it.
Lara. Was there another like it?
Fran. One so like it
I could not choose between them.
Lara. It is well.
To-morrow morning bring that
ring to me.
Do not forget. Now light me to
my bed. [*Exeunt.*

SCENE II.—*A street in Madrid.*
Enter CHISPA, *followed by mu-*
sicians, with a bagpipe, guitars,
and other instruments.

Chispa. Abernuncio Satanas!
and a plague on all lovers who
ramble about at night, drinking the
elements, instead of sleeping quietly
in their beds. Every dead man to
his cemetery, say I; and every
friar to his monastery. Now, here's
my master, Victorian, yesterday a
cowkeeper, and to-day a gentleman; yesterday a student, and to-
day a lover; and I must be up later
than the nightingale, for as the
abbot sings so must the sacristan
respond. God grant he may soon
be married, for then shall all this
serenading cease. Ay, marry!
marry! marry! Mother, what does
marry mean? It means to spin, to
bear children, and to weep, my
daughter! And, of a truth, there is
something more in matrimony than
the wedding-ring. (*To the musi-*
cians.) And now, gentlemen, Pax
vobiscum! as the ass said to the
cabbages. Pray, walk this way;
and don't hang down your heads.
It is no disgrace to have an old
father and a ragged shirt. Now,
look you, you are gentlemen who
lead the life of crickets; you enjoy
hunger by day and noise by night.
Yet, I beseech you, for this once be
not loud, but pathetic; for it is a
serenade to a damsel in bed, and
not to the Man in the Moon.
Your object is not to arouse and
terrify, but to soothe and bring
lulling dreams. Therefore, each
shall not play upon his instrument
as if it were the only one in the
universe, but gently, and with a
certain modesty, according with
the others. Pray, how may I call
thy name, friend?

75

First Mus. Gerónimo Gil, at your service.

Chispa. Every tub smells of the wine that is in it. Pray, Gerónimo, is not Saturday an unpleasant day with thee?

First Mus. Why so?

Chispa. Because I have heard it said that Saturday is an unpleasant day with those who have but one shirt. Moreover, I have seen thee at the tavern, and if thou canst run as fast as thou canst drink, I should like to hunt hares with thee. What instrument is that?

First Mus. An Aragonese bagpipe.

Chispa. Pray, art thou related to the bagpiper of Bujalance, who asked a maravedí for playing, and ten for leaving off?

First Mus. No, your honour.

Chispa. I am glad of it. What other instruments have we?

Second and Third Musicians. We play the bandurria.

Chispa. A pleasing instrument. And thou?

Fourth Mus. The fife.

Chispa. I like it; it has a cheerful, soul-stirring sound, that soars up to my lady's window like the song of a swallow. And you others?

Other Mus. We are the singers, please your honour.

Chispa. You are too many. Do you think we are going to sing mass in the cathedral of Córdova? Four men can make but little use of one shoe, and I see not how you can all sing in one song. But follow me along the garden wall. That is the way my master climbs to the lady's window. It is by the Vicar's skirts that the Devil climbs into the belfry. Come, follow me, and make no noise.   [*Exeunt.*

Scene III.—Preciosa's *chamber.*
She stands at the open window.

Prec. How slowly through the lilac-scented air
Descends the tranquil moon! Like thistle-down
The vapoury clouds float in the peaceful sky;
And sweetly from yon hollow vaults of shade
The nightingales breathe out their souls in song.
And hark! what songs of love, what soul-like sounds,
Answer them from below!

SERENADE.

Stars of the summer night!
　　Far in yon azure deeps,
Hide, hide your golden light!
　　She sleeps!
My lady sleeps!
　　Sleeps!

Moon of the summer night!
　　Far down yon western steeps,
Sink, sink in silver light!
　　She sleeps!
My lady sleeps!
　　Sleeps!

Wind of the summer night!
　　Where yonder woodbine creeps,
Fold, fold thy pinions light!
　　She sleeps!
My lady sleeps!
　　Sleeps!

Dreams of the summer night!
　　Tell her, her lover keeps
Watch! while in slumbers light
　　She sleeps!
My lady sleeps!
　　Sleeps!

(*Enter* Victorian *by the balcony.*)

Vict. Poor little dove! Thou tremblest like a leaf!

Prec. I am so frightened! 'Tis for thee I tremble!
I hate to have thee climb that wall by night!

Did no one see thee?

Vict. None, my love, but thou.

Prec. 'Tis very dangerous; and
when thou art gone
I chide myself for letting thee come
here
Thus stealthily by night. Where
hast thou been?
Since yesterday I have no news
from thee.

Vict. Since yesterday I have
been in Alcalá.
Ere long the time will come, sweet
Preciosa,
When that dull distance shall no
more divide us;
And I no more shall scale thy wall
by night
To steal a kiss from thee, as I do now.

Prec. An honest thief, to steal
but what thou givest.

Vict. And we shall sit together
unmolested,
And words of true love pass from
tongue to tongue,
As singing birds from one bough
to another.

Prec. That were a life to make
time envious!
I knew that thou wouldst come to
me to-night.
I saw thee at the play.

Vict. Sweet child of air!
Never did I behold thee so attired
And garmented in beauty as to-
night!
What hast thou done to make thee
look so fair?

Prec. Am I not always fair?

Vict. Ay, and so fair
That I am jealous of all eyes that
see thee,
And wish that they were blind.

Prec. I heed them not;
When thou art present, I see none
but thee!

Vict. There's nothing fair nor
beautiful, but takes

Something from thee, that makes it
beautiful.

Prec. And yet thou leavest me
for those dusty books.

Vict. Thou comest between me
and those books too often!
I see thy face in everything I see!
The paintings in the chapel wear
thy looks,
The canticles are changed to sara-
bands,
And with the learned doctors of the
schools
I see thee dance cachuchas.

Prec. In good sooth,
I dance with learned doctors of the
schools
To-morrow morning.

Vict. And with whom, I pray?

Prec. A grave and reverend
Cardinal, and his Grace
The Archbishop of Toledo.

Vict. What mad jest
Is this?

Prec. It is no jest; indeed it is
not.

Vict. Prithee, explain thyself.

Prec. Why, simply thus.
Thou knowest the Pope has sent
here into Spain
To put a stop to dances on the stage.

Vict. I have heard it whispered.

Prec. Now the Cardinal,
Who for this purpose comes, would
fain behold
With his own eyes these dances;
and the Archbishop
Has sent for me —

Vict. That thou mayst dance
before them!
Now viva la cachucha! It will
breathe
The fire of youth into these gray old
men!
'Twill be thy proudest conquest!

Prec. Saving one.
And yet I fear these dances will be
stopped,

77

And Preciosa be once more a beggar.

Vict. The sweetest beggar that e'er asked for alms;
With such beseeching eyes, that when I saw thee
I gave my heart away!

Prec. Dost thou remember When first we met?

Vict. It was at Córdova, In the cathedral garden. Thou wast sitting
Under the orange-trees, beside a fountain.

Prec. 'Twas Easter-Sunday. The full-blossomed trees
Filled all the air with fragrance and with joy.
The priests were singing, and the organ sounded,
And then anon the great cathedral bell.
It was the elevation of the Host.
We both of us fell down upon our knees.
Under the orange-boughs, and prayed together.
I never had been happy till that moment.

Vict. Thou blessed angel!

Prec. And when thou wast gone
I felt an aching here. I did not speak
To any one that day. But from that day
Bartolomé grew hateful unto me.

Vict. Remember him no more. Let not his shadow
Come between thee and me. Sweet Preciosa!
I loved thee even then, though I was silent!

Prec. I thought I ne'er should see thy face again.
Thy farewell had a sound of sorrow in it.

Vict. That was the first sound in the song of love!

Scarce more than silence is, and yet a sound.
Hands of invisible spirits touch the strings
Of that mysterious instrument, the soul,
And play the prelude of our fate. We hear
The voice prophetic, and are not alone.

Prec. That is my faith. Dost thou believe these warnings?

Vict. So far as this. Our feelings and our thoughts
Tend ever on, and rest not in the Present.
As drops of rain fall into some dark well,
And from below comes a scarce audible sound,
So fall our thoughts into the dark Hereafter,
And their mysterious echo reaches us.

Prec. I have felt it so, but found no words to say it!
I cannot reason; I can only feel!
But thou hast language for all thoughts and feelings.
Thou art a scholar; and sometimes I think
We cannot walk together in this world!
The distance that divides us is too great!
Henceforth thy pathway lies among the stars;
I must not hold thee back.

Vict. Thou little sceptic!
Dost thou still doubt? What I most prize in woman
Is her affections, not her intellect!
The intellect is finite; but the affections
Are infinite, and cannot be exhausted.
Compare me with the great men of the earth;

78

What am I? Why, a pigmy among
  giants!
But if thou lovest,—mark me! I say
  lovest,—
The greatest of thy sex excels thee
  not!
The world of the affections is thy
  world,
Not that of man's ambition. In
  that stillness
Which most becomes a woman,
  calm and holy,
Thou sittest by the fireside of the
  heart,
Feeding its flame. The element
  of fire
Is pure. It cannot change nor
  hide its nature,
But burns as brightly in a Gipsy
  camp
As in a palace hall. Art thou con-
  vinced?
Prec. Yes, that I love thee, as
  the good love heaven;
But not that I am worthy of that
  heaven.
How shall I more deserve it?
Vict.   Loving more.
Prec. I cannot love thee more;
  my heart is full.
Vict. Then let it overflow, and I
  will drink it,
As in the summer-time the thirsty
  sands
Drink the swift waters of the
  Manzanares,
And still do thirst for more.
  A Watchman (in the street). Ave
  Maria
Purissima! 'Tis midnight and
  serene!
Vict. Hear'st thou that cry?
Prec.   It is a hateful sound,
To scare thee from me!
Vict.   As the hunter's horn
Doth scare the timid stag, or bark
  of hounds

The moor-fowl from his mate.
Prec.   Pray, do not go!
Vict. I must away to Alcalá to-
  night.
Think of me when I am away.
Prec.   Fear not!
I have no thoughts that do not
  think of thee.
Vict. (giving her a ring). And to
  remind thee of my love, take this,
A serpent, emblem of Eternity;
A ruby,—say, a drop of my heart's
  blood.
Prec. It is an ancient saying,
  that the ruby
Brings gladness to the wearer, and
  preserves
The heart pure, and, if laid beneath
  the pillow,
Drives away evil dreams. But
  then, alas!
It was a serpent tempted Eve to sin.
Vict. What convent of bare-
  footed Carmelites
Taught thee so much theology?
*Prec. (laying her hand upon his
  mouth).*   Hush! hush!
Good night! and may all holy
  angels guard thee!
Vict. Good night! good night!
  Thou art my guardian angel!
I have no other saint than thou to
  pray to!

(*He descends by the balcony.*)

Prec. Take care, and do not hurt
  thee. Art thou safe?
Vict. (from the garden). Safe as
  my love for thee! But art
  thou safe?
Others can climb a balcony by
  moonlight
As well as I. Pray shut thy window
  close;
I am jealous of the perfumed air of
  night
That from this garden climbs to kiss
  thy lips.

Prec. (*throwing down her hand-*
kerchief). Thou silly child!
Take this to blind thine eyes.
It is my benison!

Vict. And brings to me
Sweet fragrance from thy lips, as
the soft wind
Wafts to the out-bound mariner the
breath
Of the beloved land he leaves
behind.

Prec. Make not thy voyage long.

Vict. To-morrow night
Shall see me safe returned. Thou
art the star
To guide me to an anchorage.
Good night!
My beauteous star! My star of
love, good night!

Prec. Good night!

Watchman (*at a distance*). Ave
Maria Purissima!

SCENE IV.—*An inn on the road to*
Alcalá. BALTASAR *asleep on a*
bench. Enter CHISPA.

Chispa. And here we are, half-
way to Alcalá, between cocks and
midnight. Body o' me! what an
inn this is! The lights out, and
the landlord asleep. Holá! ancient Baltasar!

Bal. (*waking*). Here I am.

Chispa. Yes, there you are, like
a one-eyed Alcalde in a town without inhabitants. Bring a light, and
let me have supper.

Bal. Where is your master?

Chispa. Do not trouble yourself
about him. We have stopped a
moment to breathe our horses;
and, if he chooses to walk up and
down in the open air, looking into
the sky as one who hears it rain,
that does not satisfy my hunger,
you know. But be quick, for I am

in a hurry, and every man stretches
his legs according to the length of
his coverlet. What have we here?

Bal. (*setting a light on the table*).
Stewed rabbit.

Chispa (*eating*). Conscience of
Portalegre! Stewed kitten, you
mean!

Bal. And a pitcher of Pedro
Ximenes, with a roasted pear in it.

Chispa (*drinking*). Ancient Baltasar, amigo! You know how to
cry wine and sell vinegar. I tell
you this is nothing but Vino Tinto
of La Mancha, with a tang of the
swine-skin.

Bal. I swear to you by Saint
Simon and Judas, it is all as I say.

Chispa. And I swear to you by
Saint Peter and Saint Paul, that it
is no such thing. Moreover, your
supper is like the hidalgo's dinner,
very little meat and a great deal of
tablecloth.

Bal. Ha! ha! ha!

Chispa. And more noise than
nuts.

Bal. Ha! ha! ha! You must
have your joke, Master Chispa.
But shall I not ask Don Victorian
in, to take a draught of the Pedro
Ximenes?

Chispa. No; you might as well
say, 'Don't-you-want-some?' to a
dead man.

Bal. Why does he go so often to
Madrid?

Chispa. For the same reason
that he eats no supper. He is in
love. Were you ever in love,
Baltasar?

Bal. I was never out of it, good
Chispa. It has been the torment
of my life.

Chispa. What! are you on fire,
too, old hay-stack? Why, we shall
never be able to put you out.

Vict. (*without*). Chispa!

Chispa. Go to bed, Pero Grullo, for the cocks are crowing.

Vict. Ea! Chispa! Chispa!

Chispa. Ea! Señor. Come with me, ancient Baltasar, and bring water for the horses. I will pay for the supper to-morrow. [*Exeunt.*

SCENE V.—VICTORIAN'S *chambers at Alcalá.* HYPOLITO *asleep in an armchair. He awakes slowly.*

Hyp. I must have been asleep! ay, sound asleep!
And it was all a dream. O sleep, sweet sleep!
Whatever form thou takest, thou art fair,
Holding unto our lips thy goblet filled
Out of Oblivion's well, a healing draught!
The candles have burned low; it must be late.
Where can Victorian be? Like Fray Carrillo,
The only place in which one cannot find him
Is his own cell. Here's his guitar, that seldom
Feels the caresses of its master's hand.
Open thy silent lips, sweet instrument,
And make dull midnight merry with a song!

(*He plays and sings.*)

Padre Francisco!
Padre Francisco!
What do you want of Padre Francisco?
Here is a pretty young maiden
Who wants to confess her sins!
Open the door and let her come in,
I will shrive her from every sin.

(*Enter* VICTORIAN.)

Vict. Padre Hypolito! Padre Hypolito!

Hyp. What do you want of Padre Hypolito?

Vict. Come, shrive me straight; for, if love be a sin,
I am the greatest sinner that doth live.
I will confess the sweetest of all crimes,
A maiden wooed and won.

Hyp.   The same old tale
Of the old woman in the chimney-corner,
Who, while the pot boils, says,
'Come here, my child;
I'll tell thee a story of my wedding-day.'

Vict. Nay, listen, for my heart is full; so full
That I must speak.

Hyp.   Alas! that heart of thine
Is like a scene in the old play; the curtain
Rises to solemn music, and lo! enter
The eleven thousand virgins of Cologne!

Vict. Nay, like the Sibyl's volumes, thou shouldst say;
Those that remained, after the six were burned,
Being held more precious than the nine together.
But listen to my tale. Dost thou remember
The Gipsy girl we saw at Córdova
Dance the Romalis in the market-place?

Hyp. Thou meanest Preciosa.

Vict.   Ay, the same.
Thou knowest how her image haunted me
Long after we returned to Alcalá.
She's in Madrid.

Hyp.   I know it.

Vict.   And I'm in love.

Hyp. And therefore in Madrid when thou shouldst be
In Alcalá.

Vict. O pardon me, my friend,
If I so long have kept this secret
  from thee;
But silence is the charm that guards
  such treasures,
And, if a word be spoken ere the
  time,
They sink again, they were not
  meant for us.

Hyp. Alas! alas! I see thou art
  in love.
Love keeps the cold out better than
  a cloak.
It serves for food and raiment.
  Give a Spaniard
His mass, his olla, and his Doña
  Luisa—
Thou knowest the proverb. But
  pray tell me, lover,
How speeds thy wooing? Is the
  maiden coy?
Write her a song, beginning with
  an *Ave*;
Sing as the monk sang to the
  Virgin Mary,

> *Ave! cujus calcem clare*
> *Nec centenni commendare*
> *Sciret Seraph studio!*

Vict. Pray, do not jest! This is
  no time for it!
I am in earnest!

Hyp. Seriously enamoured?
What, ho! The Primus of great
  Alcalá
Enamoured of a Gipsy? Tell me
  frankly,
How meanest thou?

Vict. I mean it honestly.

Hyp. Surely thou wilt not marry
  her!

Vict. Why not?

Hyp. She was betrothed to one
  Bartolomé,
If I remember rightly, a young
  Gipsy
Who danced with her at Córdova.

Vict. They quarrelled,
And so the matter ended.

Hyp. But in truth
Thou wilt not marry her.

Vict. In truth I will.
The angels sang in Heaven when
  she was born!
She is a precious jewel I have
  found
Among the filth and rubbish of the
  world.
I 'll stoop for it; but when I wear
  it here,
Set on my forehead like the morning star,
The world may wonder, but it will
  not laugh.

Hyp. If thou wear'st nothing
  else upon thy forehead,
'Twill be indeed a wonder.

Vict. Out upon thee
With thy unseasonable jests! Pray
  tell me,
Is there no virtue in the world?

Hyp. Not much.
What, think'st thou, is she doing
  at this moment;
Now, while we speak of her?

Vict. She lies asleep,
And from her parted lips her gentle
  breath
Comes like the fragrance from the
  lips of flowers.
Her tender limbs are still, and on
  her breast
The cross she prayed to, ere she
  fell asleep,
Rises and falls with the soft tide of
  dreams,
Like a light barge safe moored.

Hyp. Which means, in prose,
She 's sleeping with her mouth a
  little open!

Vict. O, would I had the old
  magician's glass
To see her as she lies in childlike
  sleep!

82

Hyp. And would'st thou venture?

Vict. Ay, indeed I would!

Hyp. Thou art courageous. Hast thou e'er reflected
How much lies hidden in that one word, *now*?

Vict. Yes; all the awful mystery of Life!
I oft have thought, my dear Hypolito,
That could we, by some spell of magic, change
The world and its inhabitants to stone,
In the same attitudes they now are in,
What fearful glances downward might we cast
Into the hollow chasms of human life!
What groups should we behold about the death-bed,
Putting to shame the group of Niobe!
What joyful welcomes, and what sad farewells!
What stony tears in those congealed eyes!
What visible joy or anguish in those cheeks!
What bridal pomps, and what funereal shows!
What foes, like gladiators, fierce and struggling!
What lovers with their marble lips together!

Hyp. Ay, there it is! and, if I were in love,
That is the very point I most should dread.
This magic glass, these magic spells of thine,
Might tell a tale were better left untold.
For instance, they might show us thy fair cousin,
The Lady Violante, bathed in tears

Of love and anger, like the maid of Colchis,
Whom thou, another faithless Argonaut,
Having won that golden fleece, a woman's love,
Desertest for this Glaucè.

Vict. Hold thy peace!
She cares not for me. She may wed another,
Or go into a convent, and, thus dying,
Marry Achilles in the Elysian Fields.

Hyp. (*rising*). And so, good night! Good morning, I should say.

(*Clock strikes three.*)

Hark! how the loud and ponderous mace of Time
Knocks at the golden portals of the day!
And so, once more, good night! We'll speak more largely
Of Preciosa when we meet again.
Get thee to bed, and the magician, Sleep,
Shall show her to thee in his magic glass,
In all her loveliness. Good night!
                                    [*Exit.*

Vict. Good night!
But not to bed; for I must read awhile.

(*Throws himself into the arm-chair which* HYPOLITO *has left, and lays a large book open upon his knees.*)

Must read, or sit in reverie and watch
The changing colour of the waves that break
Upon the idle sea-shore of the mind!
Visions of Fame! that once did visit me,

Making night glorious with your smile, where are ye?

O, who shall give me, now that ye are gone,

Juices of those immortal plants that bloom

Upon Olympus, making us immortal?

Or teach me where that wondrous mandrake grows,

Whose magic root, torn from the earth with groans

At midnight hour, can scare the fiends away,

And make the mind prolific in its fancies!

I have the wish, but want the will, to act!

Souls of great men departed! Ye whose words

Have come to light from the swift river of Time,

Like Roman swords found in the Tagus' bed,

Where is the strength to wield the arms ye bore?

From the barred visor of Antiquity

Reflected shines the eternal light of Truth,

As from a mirror! All the means of action—

The shapeless masses, the materials—

Lie everywhere about us. What we need

Is the celestial fire to change the flint

Into transparent crystal, bright and clear.

That fire is genius! The rude peasant sits

At evening in his smoky cot, and draws

With charcoal uncouth figures on the wall.

The son of genius comes, foot-sore with travel,

And begs a shelter from the inclement night.

He takes the charcoal from the peasant's hand,

And, by the magic of his touch at once

Transfigured, all its hidden virtues shine,

And, in the eyes of the astonished clown

It gleams a diamond! Even thus transformed

Rude popular traditions and old tales

Shine as immortal poems, at the touch

Of some poor, houseless, homeless, wandering bard,

Who had but a night's lodging for his pains.

But there are brighter dreams than those of Fame,

Which are the dreams of Love! Out of the heart

Rises the bright ideal of these dreams,

As from some woodland fount a spirit rises

And sinks again into its silent deeps

Ere the enamoured knight can touch her robe!

'Tis this ideal that the soul of man,

Like the enamoured knight beside the fountain,

Waits for upon the margin of Life's stream;

Waits to behold her rise from the dark waters

Clad in a mortal shape! Alas! how many

Must wait in vain! The stream flows evermore,

But from its silent deeps no spirit rises!

Yet I, born under a propitious star,

Have found the bright ideal of my dreams.

Yes! she is ever with me. I can feel,

84

Here, as I sit at midnight and alone,
Her gentle breathing! on my
    breast can feel
The pressure of her head! God's
    benison
Rest ever on it! Close those beau-
    teous eyes,

Sweet Sleep! and all the flowers
    that bloom at night
With balmy lips breathe in her
    ears my name!

(*Gradually sinks asleep.*)

ACT II.

SCENE I.—PRECIOSA'S *chamber.*
Morning. PRECIOSA *and* AN-
GELICA.

Prec. Why will you go so soon?
    Stay yet a while.
The poor too often turn away un-
    heard
From hearts they shut against
    them with a sound
That will be heard in Heaven.
    Pray, tell me more
Of your adversities. Keep nothing
    from me.
What is your landlord's name?
    Ang.   The Count of Lara.
    Prec. The Count of Lara? O,
    beware that man!
Mistrust his pity,—hold no parley
    with him!
And rather die an outcast in the
    streets
Than touch his gold.
    Ang.   You know him, then!
    Prec.   As much
As any woman may, and yet be
    pure.
As you would keep your name
    without a blemish,
Beware of him!
    Ang.   Alas! what can I do?
I cannot choose my friends. Each
    word of kindness,
Come whence it may, is welcome
    to the poor.
    Prec. Make me your friend. A
    girl so young and fair
Should have no friends but those
    of her own sex.

What is your name?
    Ang.   Angelica.
    Prec.   That name
Was given you, that you might be
    an angel
To her who bore you! When
    your infant smile
Made her home Paradise, you
    were her angel.
O, be an angel still! She needs
    that smile.
So long as you are innocent, fear
    nothing.
No one can harm you! I am a
    poor girl,
Whom chance has taken from the
    public streets.
I have no other shield than mine
    own virtue.
That is the charm which has pro-
    tected me!
Amid a thousand perils I have
    worn it
Here on my heart! It is my guar-
    dian angel.
    Ang. (*rising*). I thank you for
    this counsel, dearest lady.
    Prec. Thank me by following it.
    Ang.   Indeed I will.
    Prec. Pray, do not go. I have
    much more to say.
    Ang. My mother is alone. I
    dare not leave her.
    Prec. Some other time, then,
    when we meet again.
You must not go away with words
    alone.   (*Gives her a purse.*)
Take this. Would it were more.
    Ang.   I thank you, lady.

85

Prec. No thanks. To-morrow
come to me again.
I dance to-night,—perhaps for the
last time.
But what I gain, I promise shall be
yours,
If that can save you from the Count
of Lara.
Ang. O, my dear lady! how
shall I be grateful
For so much kindness?
Prec.   I deserve no thanks;
Thank Heaven, not me.
Ang.   Both Heaven and you.
Prec.   Farewell.
Remember that you come again
to-morrow.
Ang. I will. And may the
Blessed Virgin guard you,
And all good angels.   [*Exit.*
Prec. May they guard thee too,
And all the poor; for they have
need of angels.
Now bring me, dear Dolores, my
basquiña,
My richest maja dress,—my danc-
ing dress,
And my most precious jewels!
Make me look
Fairer than night e'er saw me!
I 've a prize
To win this day, worthy of Preciosa!

(*Enter* BELTRAN CRUZADO.)

Cruz. Ave Maria!
Prec. O God! my evil genius!
What seekest thou here to-day?
Cruz.   Thyself,—my child.
Prec. What is thy will with me?
Cruz.   Gold! gold!
Prec. I gave thee yesterday; I
have no more.
Cruz. The gold of the Busné,—
give me his gold!
Prec. I gave the last in charity
to-day.
Cruz. That is a foolish lie.
Prec.   It is the truth.

Cruz. Curses upon thee! Thou
art not my child!
Hast thou given gold away, and
not to me?
Not to thy father? To whom, then?
Prec.   To one
Who needs it more.
Cruz. No one can need it more.
Prec. Thou art not poor.
Cruz.   What, I, who lurk about
In dismal suburbs and unwhole-
some lanes;
I, who am housed worse than the
galley slave;
I, who am fed worse than the ken-
nelled hound;
I, who am clothed in rags—Bel-
tran Cruzado,—
Not poor!
Prec. Thou hast a stout heart
and strong hands.
Thou canst supply thy wants; what
wouldst thou more?
Cruz. The gold of the Busné!
give me his gold!
Prec. Beltran Cruzado! hear
me once for all.
I speak the truth. So long as I
had gold,
I gave it to thee freely, at all
times,
Never denied thee; never had a
wish
But to fulfil thine own. Now go
in peace!
Be merciful, be patient, and ere long
Thou shalt have more.
Cruz.   And if I have it not,
Thou shalt no longer dwell here in
rich chambers,
Wear silken dresses, feed on dainty
food,
And live in idleness; but go with
me,
Dance the Romalis in the public
streets,
And wander wild again o'er field
and fell;

For here we stay not long.

Prec. What ! march again ?

Cruz. Ay, with all speed. I hate the crowded town ! I cannot breathe shut up within its gates !

Air,—I want air, and sunshine, and blue sky,

The feeling of the breeze upon my face,

The feeling of the turf beneath my feet,

And no walls but the far-off mountain tops.

Then I am free and strong,—once more myself,

Beltran Cruzado, Count of the Calés !

Prec. God speed thee on thy march !—I cannot go.

Cruz. Remember who I am, and who thou art !

Be silent and obey ! Yet one thing more.

Bartolomé Román—

Prec. (*with emotion*). O, I beseech thee !

If my obedience and blameless life,

If my humility and meek submission

In all things hitherto, can move in thee

One feeling of compassion ; if thou art

Indeed my father, and canst trace in me

One look of her who bore me, or one tone

That doth remind thee of her, let it plead

In my behalf, who am a feeble girl,

Too feeble to resist, and do not force me

To wed that man ! I am afraid of him !

I do not love him ! On my knees I beg thee

To use no violence, nor do in haste What cannot be undone !

Cruz. O child, child, child ! Thou hast betrayed thy secret, as a bird

Betrays her nest, by striving to conceal it.

I will not leave thee here in the great city

To be a grandee's mistress. Make thee ready

To go with us ; and until then remember

A watchful eye is on thee.   [*Exit*.

Prec. Woe is me !

I have a strange misgiving in my heart !

But that one deed of charity I 'll do,

Befall what may ; they cannot take that from me.

SCENE II.—*A room in the* ARCHBISHOP'S *Palace. The* ARCHBISHOP *and a* CARDINAL *seated*.

Arch. Knowing how near it touched the public morals,

And that our age is grown corrupt and rotten

By such excesses, we have sent to Rome,

Beseeching that his Holiness would aid

In curing the gross surfeit of the time,

By seasonable stop put here in Spain

To bull-fights and lewd dances on the stage.

All this you know.

Card. Know and approve.

Arch. And further,

That, by a mandate from his Holiness,

The first have been suppressed.

Card. I trust for ever.

It was a cruel sport.

Arch. A barbarous pastime,
Disgraceful to the land that calls
    itself
Most Catholic and Christian.
    Card. Yet the people
Murmur at this ; and, if the public
    dances
Should be condemned upon too
    slight occasion,
Worse ills might follow than the
    ills we cure.
As *Panem et Circenses* was the cry
Among the Roman populace of old,
So *Pan y Toros* is the cry in Spain.
Hence I would act advisedly here-
    in ;
And therefore have induced your
    Grace to see
These national dances, ere we
    interdict them.

(*Enter a Servant.*)

Serv. The dancing-girl, and with
    her the musicians
Your Grace was pleased to order,
    wait without.
    Arch. Bid them come in. Now
        shall your eyes behold
In what angelic, yet voluptuous
    shape
The Devil came to tempt Saint
    Anthony.

(*Enter* PRECIOSA, *with a mantle
    thrown over her head. She
    advances slowly, in modest, half-
    timid attitude.*)

Card. (*aside*). O, what a fair
    and ministering angel
Was lost to Heaven when this sweet
    woman fell !
    Prec. (*kneeling before the* ARCH-
    BISHOP). I have obeyed the
    order of your Grace.
If I intrude upon your better hours,
I proffer this excuse, and here
    beseech
Your holy benediction.

Arch. May God bless thee,
And lead thee to a better life. Arise.
    Card. (*aside*). Her acts are
    modest, and her words discreet!
I did not look for this ! Come
    hither, child.
Is thy name Preciosa ?
    Prec. Thus I am called.
    Card. That is a Gipsy name.
    Who is thy father ?
    Prec. Beltran Cruzado, Count of
    the Calés.
    Arch. I have a dim remem-
    brance of that man ;
He was a bold and reckless char-
    acter,
A sun-burnt Ishmael !
    Card. Dost thou remember
Thy earlier days ?
    Prec. Yes ; by the Darro's side
My childhood passed. I can re-
    member still
The river, and the mountains
    capped with snow ;
The villages, where, yet a little
    child,
I told the traveller's fortune in the
    street :
The smuggler's horse, the brigand
    and the shepherd ;
The march across the moor ; the
    halt at noon ;
The red fire of the evening camp,
    that lighted
The forest where we slept ; and,
    further back,
As in a dream or in some former
    life,
Gardens and palace walls.
    Arch. 'Tis the Alhambra,
Under whose towers the Gipsy
    camp was pitched.
But the time wears ; and we would
    see thee dance.
    Prec. Your Grace shall be
        obeyed.
(*She lays aside her mantilla. The
    music of the cachucha is played,*

and the dance begins. The
ARCHBISHOP *and the* CARDINAL
*look on with gravity and an oc-
casional frown; then make signs
to each other; and, as the dance
continues, become more and more
pleased and excited; and at
length rise from their seats,
throw their caps in the air, and
applaud vehemently as the scene
closes.*)

SCENE III.—*The Prado. A long
avenue of trees leading to the
gate of Atocha. On the right
the dome and spires of a convent.
A fountain. Evening.* DON
CARLOS *and* HYPOLITO *meeting.*

Don C. Holá! good evening,
Don Hypolito.
Hyp. And a good evening to my
friend Don Carlos.
Some lucky star has led my steps
this way.
I was in search of you.
Don C. Command me always.
Hyp. Do you remember, in
Quevedo's Dreams,
The miser, who, upon the Day of
Judgment,
Asks if his money-bags would rise?
Don C. I do;
But what of that?
Hyp. I am that wretched man.
Don C. You mean to tell me
yours have risen empty?
Hyp. And amen! said my Cid
the Campeador.
Don C. Pray, how much need
you?
Hyp. Some half-dozen ounces,
Which, with due interest—
Don C. (giving his purse). What,
am I a Jew
To put my moneys out at usury?
Here is my purse.

Hyp. Thank you. A pretty
purse,
Made by the hand of some fair
Madrilena;
Perhaps a keepsake.
Don C. No, 'tis at your service.
Hyp. Thank you again. Lie
there, good Chrysostom,
And with thy golden mouth remind
me often,
I am the debtor of my friend.
Don C. But tell me,
Come you to-day from Alcalá?
Hyp. This moment.
Don C. And pray, how fares the
brave Victorian?
Hyp. Indifferent well; that is to
say, not well.
A damsel has ensnared him with
the glances
Of her dark roving eyes, as herds-
men catch
A steer of Andalusia with a lazo.
He is in love.
Don C. And is it faring ill
To be in love?
Hyp. In his case very ill.
Don C. Why so?
Hyp. For many rea-
sons. First and foremost,
Because he is in love with an ideal;
A creature of his own imagination;
A child of air; an echo of his heart;
And, like a lily on a river floating,
She floats upon the river of his
thoughts!
Don C. A common thing with
poets. But who is
This floating lily? For, in fine,
some woman,
Some living woman,—not a mere
ideal,—
Must wear the outward semblance
of his thought.
Who is it? Tell me.
Hyp. Well, it is a woman!
But, look you, from the coffer of
his heart

He brings forth precious jewels to
    adorn her,
As pious priests adorn some
    favourite saint
With gems and gold, until at length
    she gleams
One blaze of glory. Without these,
    you know,
And the priest's benediction, 'tis
    a doll.
  Don C. Well, well! who is this
    doll?
  Hyp.   Why, who do you
    think?
  Don C. His cousin Violante.
  Hyp.   Guess again.
To ease his labouring heart, in the
    last storm
He threw her overboard, with all
    her ingots.
  Don C. I cannot guess; so tell
    me who it is.
  Hyp. Not I.
  Don C.   Why not?
  Hyp. (*mysteriously*).   Why?
Because Mari Franca
Was married four leagues out of
    Salamanca!
  Don C. Jesting aside, who is
    it?
  Hyp.   Preciosa.
  Don C. Impossible! The Count
    of Lara tells me
She is not virtuous.
  Hyp.   Did I say she was?
The Roman Emperor Claudius had
    a wife
Whose name was Messalina, as I
    think;
Valeria Messalina was her name.
But hist! I see him yonder through
    the trees,
Walking as in a dream.
  Don C.   He comes this way.
  Hyp. It has been truly said by
    some wise man,
That money, grief, and love cannot
    be hidden.

  (*Enter* VICTORIAN *in front.*)

  Vict. Where'er thy step has
    passed is holy ground!
These groves are sacred! I behold
    thee walking
Under these shadowy trees, where
    we have walked
At evening, and I feel thy presence
    now;
Feel that the place has taken a
    charm from thee,
And is for ever hallowed.
  Hyp.   Mark him well!
See how he strides away with
    lordly air,
Like that odd guest of stone, that
    grim Commander
Who comes to sup with Juan in the
    play.
  Don C. What ho! Victorian!
  Hyp.   Wilt thou sup with us?
  Vict. Holá! amigos! Faith, I
    did not see you.
How fares Don Carlos?
  Don C.   At your service ever.
  Vict. How is that young and
    green-eyed Gaditana
That you both wot of?
  Don C. Ay, soft, emerald eyes!
She has gone back to Cadiz.
  Hyp.   Ay de mí!
  Vict. You are much to blame for
    letting her go back.
A pretty girl; and in her tender
    eyes
Just that soft shade of green we
    sometimes see
In evening skies.
  Hyp. But, speaking of green
    eyes,
Are thine green?
  Vict.   Not a whit. Why so?
  Hyp.   I think
The slightest shade of green would
    be becoming,
For thou art jealous.
  Vict.   No, I am not jealous

Hyp. Thou shouldst be.
Vict. Why?
Hyp. Because thou art in love,
And they who are in love are
    always jealous.
Therefore thou shouldst be.
Vict. Marry, is that all?
Farewell; I am in haste. Farewell,
    Don Carlos.
Thou sayest I should be jealous?
Hyp. Ay, in truth
I fear there is reason. Be upon
    thy guard.
I hear it whispered that the Count
    of Lara
Lays siege to the same citadel.
Vict. Indeed!
Then he will have his labour for his
    pains.
Hyp. He does not think so, and
    Don Carlos tells me
He boasts of his success.
Vict. How's this, Don Carlos?
Don C. Some hints of it I heard
    from his own lips.
He spoke but lightly of the lady's
    virtue,
As a gay man might speak.
Vict. Death and damnation!
I'll cut his lying tongue out of his
    mouth,
And throw it to my dog! But no,
    no, no!
This cannot be. You jest, indeed
    you jest.
Trifle with me no more. For other-
    wise
We are no longer friends. And so,
    farewell!   [*Exit.*
Hyp. Now what a coil is here!
    The Avenging Child
Hunting the traitor Quadros to his
    death,
And the great Moor Calaynos,
    when he rode
To Paris for the ears of Oliver,
Were nothing to him! O hot-
    headed youth!

But come; we will not follow.
    Let us join
The crowd that pours into the
    Prado. There
We shall find merrier company; I
    see
The Marialonzos and the Alma-
    vivas,
And fifty fans, that beckon me
    already.   [*Exeunt.*

SCENE IV.—PRECIOSA'S *chamber.*
*She is sitting, with a book in her
hand, near a table, on which are
flowers. A bird singing in its
cage. The* COUNT OF LARA
enters behind unperceived.

Prec. (*reads*).

    All are sleeping, weary heart!
    Thou, thou only sleepless art!

Heigho! I wish Victorian were here.
I know not what it is makes me so
    restless!

(*The bird sings.*)

Thou little prisoner with thy motley
    coat,
That from thy vaulted, wiry
    dungeon singest,
Like thee I am a captive, and, like
    thee,
I have a gentle jailer. Lack-a-day!

    All are sleeping weary heart!
    Thou, thou only sleepless art!
    All this throbbing, all this aching,
    Evermore shall keep thee waking,
    For a heart in sorrow breaking
    Thinketh ever of its smart!

Thou speakest truly, poet! and
    methinks
More hearts are breaking in this
    world of ours
Than one would say. In distant
    villages
And solitudes remote, where winds
    have wafted

The barbed seeds of love, or birds
　of passage
Scattered them in their flight, do
　they take root,
And grow in silence, and in silence
　perish.
Who hears the falling of the forest
　leaf?
Or who takes note of every flower
　that dies?
Heigho! I wish Victorian would
　come.
Dolores!

(*Turns to lay down her book, and
　perceives the* COUNT.)
　　　　Ha!
Lara.　　　Señora, pardon me!
Prec. How's this? Dolores!
Lara.　　　　Pardon me—
Prec.　　　　　　Dolores!
Lara. Be not alarmed; I found
no one in waiting.
If I have been too bold—
Prec. (*turning her back upon
　him*).　　You are too bold!
Retire! retire, and leave me!
Lara.　　　My dear lady,
First hear me! I beseech you, let
　me speak!
'Tis for your good I come.
Prec. (*turning toward him with
　indignation*). Begone! be-
gone!
You are the Count of Lara, but
　your deeds
Would make the statues of your
　ancestors
Blush on their tombs! Is it
　Castilian honour,
Is it Castilian pride, to steal in
　here
Upon a friendless girl, to do her
　wrong?
O shame! shame! shame! that
　you, a nobleman,
Should be so little noble in your
　thoughts

As to send jewels here to win my
　love,
And think to buy my honour with
　your gold!
I have no words to tell you how I
　scorn you!
Begone! The sight of you is hate-
　ful to me!
Begone, I say!
Lara. Be calm; I will not harm
　you.
Prec. Because you dare not.
Lara.　　　I dare anything!
Therefore beware! You are de-
　ceived in me.
In this false world we do not
　always know
Who are our friends and who our
　enemies.
We all have enemies, and all need
　friends.
Even you, fair Preciosa, here at
　court
Have foes, who seek to wrong you.
Prec.　　　　If to this
I owe the honour of the present
　visit,
You might have spared the coming.
　Having spoken,
Once more I beg you, leave me to
　myself.
Lara. I thought it but a friendly
　part to tell you
What strange reports are current
　here in town.
For my own self, I do not credit
　them;
But there are many who, not
　knowing you,
Will lend a readier ear.
Prec.　　　There was no need
That you should take upon yourself
　the duty
Of telling me these tales.
Lara.　　　Malicious tongues
Are ever busy with your name.
Prec.　　　　　Alas!
I've no protectors. I am a poor girl,

Exposed to insults and unfeeling jests.
They wound me, yet I cannot shield myself.
I give no cause for these reports. I live
Retired ; am visited by none.

Lara.   By none ?
O, then, indeed, you are much wronged !

Prec.   How mean you ?

Lara. Nay, nay ; I will not wound your gentle soul
By the report of idle tales.

Prec.   Speak out !
What are these idle tales ? You need not spare me.

Lara. I will deal frankly with you. Pardon me ;
This window, as I think, looks toward the street,
And this into the Prado, does it not ?
In yon high house, beyond the garden wall,—
You see the roof there just above the trees,—
There lives a friend, who told me yesterday,
That on a certain night,—be not offended
If I too plainly speak,—he saw a man
Climb to your chamber window. You are silent !
I would not blame you, being young and fair—

(He tries to embrace her. She starts back, and draws a dagger from her bosom.)

Prec. Beware ! beware ! I am a Gipsy girl !
Lay not your hand upon me. One step nearer
And I will strike !

Lara.   Pray you, put up that dagger.
Fear not.

Prec.   I do not fear. I have a heart
In whose strength I can trust.

Lara.   Listen to me.
I come here as your friend,—I am your friend,—
And by a single word can put a stop
To all those idle tales, and make your name
Spotless as lilies are. Here on my knees,
Fair Preciosa ! on my knees I swear,
I love you even to madness, and that love
Has driven me to break the rules of custom,
And force myself unasked into your presence.

(VICTORIAN enters behind.)

Prec. Rise, Count of Lara ! That is not the place
For such as you are. It becomes you not
To kneel before me. I am strangely moved
To see one of your rank thus low and humbled ;
For your sake I will put aside all anger,
All unkind feeling, all dislike, and speak
In gentleness, as most becomes a woman,
And as my heart now prompts me. I no more
Will hate you, for all hate is painful to me.
But if, without offending modesty
And that reserve which is a woman's glory,
I may speak freely, I will teach my heart
To love you.

Lara.   O sweet angel !

Prec.   Ay, in truth,

93

Far better than you love yourself
    or me.
    Lara. Give me some sign of
this,—the slightest token.
Let me but kiss your hand !
    Prec.   Nay, come no nearer.
The words I utter are its sign and
    token.
Misunderstand me not ! Be not
    deceived !
The love wherewith I love you is
    not such
As you would offer me. For you
    come here
To take from me the only thing I
    have,
My honour. You are wealthy, you
    have friends
And kindred, and a thousand plea-
    sant hopes
That fill your heart with happiness;
    but I
Am poor, and friendless, having
    but one treasure,
And you would take that from me,
    and for what ?
To flatter your own vanity, and
    make me
What you would most despise. O
    sir, such love,
That seeks to harm me, cannot be
    true love.
Indeed it cannot. But my love for you
Is of a different kind. It seeks
    your good.
It is a holier feeling. It rebukes
Your earthly passion, your unchaste
    desires,
And bids you look into your heart,
    and see
How you do wrong that better
    nature in you,
And grieve your soul with sin.
    Lara.   I swear to you,
I would not harm you ; I would
    only love you.
I would not take **your** honour, but
    restore it,

And in return I ask but some slight
    mark
Of your affection. If indeed you
    love me,
As you confess you do, O let me thus
With this embrace—
    Vict. (rushing forward). Hold !
    hold ! This is too much.
What means this outrage ?
    Lara.   First, what right have
    you
To question thus a nobleman of
    Spain ?
    Vict. I too am noble, and you
    are no more !
Out of my sight !
    Lara. Are you the master here ?
    Vict. Ay, here and elsewhere,
    when the wrong of others
Gives me the right !
    Prec. (to LARA*).* Go! I beseech
    you, go !
    Vict. I shall have business with
    you, Count, anon !
    Lara. You cannot come too
    soon !   *[Exit.*
    Prec.   Victorian !
O, we have been betrayed !
    Vict.   Ha ! ha ! betrayed !
'Tis I have been betrayed, not
    we !—not we !
    Prec. Dost thou imagine—
    Vict.   I imagine nothing ;
I see how 'tis thou whilest the
    time away
When I am gone !
    Prec. O speak not in that tone !
It wounds me deeply.
    Vict. 'Twas not meant to flatter.
    Prec. Too well thou knowest the
    presence of that man
Is hateful to me !
    Vict.   Yet I saw thee stand
And listen to him, when he told his
    love.
    Prec. I did not heed his words.
    Vict.   Indeed thou didst,
And answeredst them with love.

Prec. Hadst thou heard all—
Vict. I heard enough.
Prec. Be not so angry with me.
Vict. I am not angry; I am very
    calm.
Prec. If thou wilt let me speak—
Vict.   Nay, say no more.
I know too much already. Thou
    art false!
I do not like these Gipsy marriages!
Where is the ring I gave thee?
    Prec.   In my casket.
    Vict. There let it rest! I would
    not have thee wear it:
I thought thee spotless, and thou
    art polluted!
    Prec. I call the Heavens to
    witness—
Vict.   Nay, nay, nay!
Take not the name of Heaven upon
    thy lips!
They are forsworn!
    Prec. Victorian! dear Victorian!
    Vict. I gave up all for thee;
    myself, my fame,
My hopes of fortune, ay, my very
    soul!
And thou hast been my ruin! Now,
    go on!
Laugh at my folly with thy para-
    mour,
And, sitting on the Count of Lara's
    knee,
Say what a poor, fond fool Victorian
    was!
(*He casts her from him and rushes
out.*)

    Prec. And this from thee!

    (*Scene closes.*)

SCENE V.—*The* COUNT OF LARA'S
   rooms. Enter the COUNT.

    Lara. There's nothing in this
    world so sweet as love,
And next to love the sweetest thing
    is hate!

I've learned to hate, and therefore
    am revenged.
A silly girl to play the prude with
    me!
The fire that I have kindled—

    (*Enter* FRANCISCO.)

            Well, Francisco,
What tidings from Don Juan?
    Fran.   Good, my lord;
He will be present.
    Lara.   And the Duke of
    Lermos?
    Fran. Was not at home.
    Lara.   How with the rest?
    Fran.   I've found
The men you wanted. They will
    all be there,
And at the given signal raise a
    whirlwind
Of such discordant noises, that the
    dance
Must cease for lack of music.
    Lara.   Bravely done.
Ah! little dost thou dream, sweet
    Preciosa,
What lies in wait for thee. Sleep
    shall not close
Thine eyes this night! Give me
    my cloak and sword.
               [*Exeunt.*

SCENE VI.—*A retired spot beyond
   the city gates. Enter* VICTORIAN
   and HYPOLITO.

    Vict. O shame! O shame!
    Why do I walk abroad
By daylight, when the very sun-
    shine mocks me,
And voices, and familiar sights and
    sounds
Cry 'Hide thyself!' O what a
    thin partition
Doth shut out from the curious
    world the knowledge

Of evil deeds that have been done
in darkness!
Disgrace has many tongues. My
fears are windows,
Through which all eyes seem
gazing. Every face
Expresses some suspicion of my
shame,
And in derision seems to smile at
me!
  Hyp. Did I not caution thee?
Did I not tell thee
I was but half persuaded of her
virtue?
  Vict. And yet, Hypolito, we
may be wrong,
We may be over-hasty in con-
demning!
The Count of Lara is a cursed
villain.
  Hyp. And therefore is she
cursed, loving him.
  Vict. She does not love him!
'Tis for gold! for gold!
  Hyp. Ay, but remember, in the
public streets
He shows a golden ring the Gipsy
gave him,
A serpent with a ruby in its mouth.
  Vict. She had that ring from
me! God! she is false!
But I will be revenged! The hour
is passed.
Where stays the coward?
  Hyp. Nay, he is no coward;
A villain, if thou wilt, but not a
coward.
I 've seen him play with swords; it
is his pastime.
And therefore be not over-con-
fident,
He 'll task thy skill anon. Look,
here he comes.

(*Enter* LARA *followed by* FRAN-
CISCO.)

  Lara. Good evening, gentlemen.
  Hyp. Good evening, Count.

  Lara. I trust I have not kept
you long in waiting.
  Vict. Not long, and yet too
long. Are you prepared?
  Lara. I am.
  Hyp. It grieves me much
to see this quarrel
Between you, gentlemen. Is there
no way
Left open to accord this difference,
But you must make one with your
swords?
  Vict. No! none!
I do entreat thee, dear Hypolito,
Stand not between me and my foe.
Too long
Our tongues have spoken. Let
these tongues of steel
End our debate. Upon your guard,
Sir Count!

(*They fight.* VICTORIAN *disarms
the* COUNT.)

Your life is mine; and what shall
now withhold me
From sending your vile soul to its
account?
  Lara. Strike! strike!
  Vict. You are disarmed.
I will not kill you.
I will not murder you. Take up
your sword.

(FRANCISCO *hands the* COUNT *his
sword, and* HYPOLITO *interposes.*)

  Hyp. Enough! Let it end here!
The Count of Lara
Has shown himself a brave man,
and Victorian
A generous one, as ever. Now be
friends.
Put up your swords; for, to speak
frankly to you,
Your cause of quarrel is too slight
a thing
To move you to extremes.
  Lara. I am content.

I sought no quarrel. A few hasty words,
Spoken in the heat of blood, have led to this.

Vict. Nay, something more than that.

Lara. I understand you.
Therein I did not mean to cross your path.
To me the door stood open, as to others.
But, had I known the girl belonged to you,
Never would I have sought to win her from you.
The truth stands now revealed; she has been false
To both of us.

Vict. Ay, false as hell itself!

Lara. In truth, I did not seek her; she sought me;
And told me how to win her, telling me
The hours when she was oftenest left alone.

Vict. Say, can you prove this to me? O, pluck out
These awful doubts, that goad me into madness!
Let me know all! all! all!

Lara. You shall know all.
Here is my page, who was the messenger
Between us. Question him. Was it not so,
Francisco?

Fran. Ay, my lord.

Lara. If further proof
Is needful, I have here a ring she gave me.

Vict. Pray let me see that ring! It is the same!

(*Throws it upon the ground, and tramples upon it.*)

Thus may she perish who once wore that ring!
Thus do I spurn her from me; do thus trample

Her memory in the dust! O Count of Lara,
We both have been abused, been much abused!
I thank you for your courtesy and frankness.
Though, like the surgeon's hand, yours gave me pain,
Yet it has cured my blindness, and I thank you.
I now can see the folly I have done,
Though 'tis, alas! too late. So fare you well!
To-night I leave this hateful town for ever.
Regard me as your friend. Once more farewell!

Hyp. Farewell, Sir Count.

[*Exeunt* VICTORIAN *and*
HYPOLITO.

Lara. Farewell! farewell! farewell!
Thus have I cleared the field of my worst foe!
I have none else to fear; the fight is done,
The citadel is stormed, the victory won! [*Exit with* FRANCISCO.

SCENE VII.—*A lane in the suburbs.
Night. Enter* CRUZADO *and*
BARTOLOMÉ.

Cruz. And so, Bartolomé, the expedition failed. But where wast thou for the most part?

Bart. In the Guadarrama mountains, near San Ildefonso.

Cruz. And thou bringest nothing back with thee? Didst thou rob no one?

Bart. There was no one to rob, save a party of students from Segovia, who looked as if they would rob us; and a jolly little friar, who had nothing in his pockets but a missal and a loaf of bread.

Cruz. Pray, then, what brings thee back to Madrid ?

Bart. First tell me what keeps thee here ?

Cruz. Preciosa.

Bart. And she brings me back. Hast thou forgotten thy promise !

Cruz. The two years are not passed yet. Wait patiently. The girl shall be thine.

Bart. I hear she has a Busné lover.

Cruz. That is nothing.

Bart. I do not like it. I hate him,—the son of a Busné harlot. He goes in and out, and speaks with her alone, and I must stand aside, and wait his pleasure.

Cruz. Be patient, I say. Thou shalt have thy revenge. When the time comes, thou shalt waylay him.

Bart. Meanwhile, show me her house.

Cruz. Come this way. But thou wilt not find her. She dances at the play to-night.

Bart. No matter. Show me the house. [*Exeunt.*

SCENE VIII.—*The Theatre. The orchestra plays the cachucha. Sound of castanets behind the scenes. The curtain rises, and discovers* PRECIOSA *in the attitude of commencing the dance. The cachucha. Tumult; hisses; cries of 'Brava!' and 'Afuera!' She falters and pauses. The music stops. General confusion.* PRECIOSA *faints.*

SCENE IX.—*The* COUNT OF LARA'S *chambers.* LARA *and his friends at supper.*

Lara. So, Caballeros, once more many thanks !
You have stood by me bravely in this matter.
Pray fill your glasses.

Don J. Did you mark, Don Luis, How pale she looked, when first the noise began,
And then stood still, with her large eyes dilated !
Her nostrils spread ! her lips apart ! her bosom
Tumultuous as the sea !

Don L. 	I pitied her.

Lara. Her pride is humbled ; and this very night
I mean to visit her.

Don J. 	Will you serenade her ?

Lara. No music ! no more music !

Don L. 	Why not music ?
It softens many hearts.

Lara. 	Not in the humour
She now is in. Music would madden her.

Don J. Try golden cymbals.

Don L. 	Yes, try Don Dinero ;
A mighty wooer is your Don Dinero.

Lara. To tell the truth, then, I have bribed her maid.
But, Caballeros, you dislike this wine.
A bumper and away ; for the night wears.
A health to Preciosa.

		(*They rise and drink.*)

All. 		Preciosa !

Lara (*holding up his glass*). Thou bright and flaming minister of Love !
Thou wonderful magician ! who hast stolen
My secret from me, and 'mid sighs of passion

Caught from my lips, with red and
fiery tongue,
Her precious name ! O never more
henceforth
Shall mortal lips press thine ; and
never more
A mortal name be whispered in
thine ear.
Go ! keep my secret !

(*Drinks and dashes the goblet
down.*)

Don J.   Ite ! missa est !

(*Scene closes.*)

SCENE X.—*Street and garden wall.
Night.* *Enter* CRUZADO *and*
BARTOLOMÉ.

Cruz. This is the garden wall,
and above it, yonder, is her house.
The window in which thou seest
the light is her window. But we
will not go in now.

Bart. Why not ?

Cruz. Because she is not at
home.

Bart. No matter ; we can wait.
But how is this ? The gate is
bolted. (*Sound of guitars and
voices in a neighbouring street.*)
Hark ! There comes her lover with
his infernal serenade ! Hark !

SONG.

Good night ! Good night, beloved !
    I come to watch o'er thee !
To be near thee,—to be near thee,
    Alone is peace for me.

Thine eyes are stars of morning,
    Thy lips are crimson flowers !
Good night ! Good night, beloved,
    While I count the weary hours.

Cruz. They are not coming this
way.

Bart. Wait, they begin again.

SONG (*coming nearer*).

Ah ! thou moon that shinest
    Argent-clear above !
All night long enlighten
    My sweet lady-love !
    Moon that shinest,
All night long enlighten !

Bart. Woe be to him, if he
comes this way !

Cruz. Be quiet, they are
passing down the street.

SONG (*dying away*).

The nuns in the cloister
    Sang to each other ;
For so many sisters
    Is there not one brother !
Ay, for the partridge, mother !
    The cat has run away with the
        partridge !
Puss ! puss ! puss !

Bart. Follow that ! follow that !
Come with me. Puss ! puss !

(*Exeunt. On the opposite side
enter the* COUNT OF LARA *and
gentlemen, with* FRANCISCO.)

Lara. The gate is fast. Over
    the wall, Francisco,
And draw the bolt. There, so, and
    so, and over.
Now, gentlemen, come in, and help
    me scale
Yon balcony. How now ? Her
    light still burns.
Move warily. Make fast the gate,
    Francisco.

(*Exeunt.   Re-enter* CRUZADO *and*
BARTOLOMÉ.)

Bart. They went in at the gate.
Hark ! I hear them in the garden
(*Tries the gate.*) Bolted again !
Vive Cristo ! Follow me over the
wall.   (*They climb the wall.*)

SCENE XI.—PRECIOSA'S *bedchamber. Midnight. She is sleeping in an armchair, in an undress.* DOLORES *watching her.*

Dol. She sleeps at last!

(*Opens the window, and listens.*)
                    All silent in the street,
And in the garden. Hark!
    Prec. (*in her sleep*). I must go hence!
Give me my cloak!
    Dol. He comes! I hear his footsteps.
    Prec. Go tell them that I cannot dance to-night;
I am too ill! Look at me! See the fever
That burns upon my cheek! I must go hence.
I am too weak to dance.

(*Signal from the garden.*)

Dol. (*from the window*). Who's there?
    Voice (*from below*). A friend.
    Dol. I will undo the door. Wait till I come.
    Prec. I must go hence. I pray you do not harm me!

Shame! shame! to treat a feeble woman thus!
Be you but kind, I will do all things for you.
I'm ready now,—give me my castanets.
Where is Victorian? Oh, those hateful lamps!
They glare upon me like an evil eye.
I cannot stay. Hark! how they mock at me!
They hiss at me like serpents! Save me! save me!

(*She wakes.*)

How late is it, Dolores?
    Dol.   It is midnight.
    Prec. We must be patient. Smooth this pillow for me.

(*She sleeps again. Noise from the garden, and voices.*)

Voice. Muera!
    Another Voice. O villains! villains!
    Lara.   So! have at you!
    Voice. Take that!
    Lara.   O, I am wounded!
    Dol. (*shutting the window*). Jesu Maria!

ACT III.

SCENE I.—*A cross-road through a wood. In the background a distant village spire.* VICTORIAN *and* HYPOLITO, *as travelling students, with guitars, sitting under the trees.* HYPOLITO *plays and sings.*

SONG.

Ah, Love!
Perjured, false, treacherous Love!
            Enemy
Of all that mankind may not rue!
    Most untrue
To him who keeps most faith with thee.
    Woe is me!

The falcon has the eyes of the dove.
            Ah, Love!
Perjured, false, treacherous Love!

Vict. Yes, Love is ever busy with his shuttle,
Is ever weaving into life's dull warp
Bright, gorgeous flowers and scenes Arcadian;
Hanging our gloomy prison-house about
With tapestries, that make its walls dilate
In never-ending vistas of delight.
    Hyp. Thinking to walk in those Arcadian pastures,
Thou hast run thy noble head against the wall.

SONG (*continued*).

Thy deceits
Give us clearly to comprehend
Whither tend
All thy pleasures, all thy sweets!
They are cheats,
Thorns below and flowers above.
Ah, Love!
Perjured, false, treacherous Love!

Vict. A very pretty song. I thank thee for it.

Hyp. It suits thy case.

Vict. Indeed, I think it does. What wise man wrote it?

Hyp. Lopez Maldonado.

Vict. In truth, a pretty song.

Hyp. With much truth in it. I hope thou wilt profit by it; and in earnest Try to forget this lady of thy love.

Vict. I will forget her! All dear recollections Pressed in my heart, like flowers within a book, Shall be torn out, and scattered to the winds! I will forget her! But perhaps hereafter, When she shall learn how heartless is the world, A voice within her will repeat my name, And she will say, ' He was indeed my friend!' O, would I were a soldier, not a scholar, That the loud march, the deafening beat of drums, The shattering blast of the brass-throated trumpet, The din of arms, the onslaught and the storm, And a swift death, might make me deaf for ever To the upbraidings of this foolish heart!

Hyp. Then let that foolish heart upbraid no more! To conquer love, one need but will to conquer.

Vict. Yet, good Hypolito, it is in vain I throw into Oblivion's sea the sword That pierces me; for, like Excalibar, With gemmed and flashing hilt, it will not sink. There rises from below a hand that grasps it, And waves it in the air; and wailing voices Are heard along the shore.

Hyp. And yet at last Down sank Excalibar to rise no more. This is not well. In truth, it vexes me. Instead of whistling to the steeds of Time, To make them jog on merrily with life's burden, Like a dead weight thou hangest on the wheels. Thou art too young, too full of lusty health To talk of dying.

Vict. Yet I fain would die! To go through life, unloving and unloved; To feel that thirst and hunger of the soul We cannot still; that longing, that wild impulse, And struggle after something we have not And cannot have; the effort to be strong; And, like the Spartan boy, to smile, and smile, While secret wounds do bleed beneath our cloaks; All this the dead feel not,—the dead alone! Would I were with them!

Hyp. We shall all be soon.

Vict. It cannot be too soon ; for
I am weary
Of the bewildering masquerade of
Life,
Where strangers walk as friends,
and friends as strangers ;
Where whispers overheard betray
false hearts ;
And through the mazes of the
crowd we chase
Some form of loveliness, that
smiles, and beckons,
And cheats us with fair words,
only to leave us
A mockery and a jest ; maddened,
—confused,—
Not knowing friend from foe.

Hyp. Why seek to know ?
Enjoy the merry shrove-tide of thy
youth !
Take each fair mask for what it
gives itself,
Nor strive to look beneath it.

Vict. I confess,
That were the wiser part. But
Hope no longer
Comforts my soul. I am a wretched
man,
Much like a poor and shipwrecked
mariner,
Who, struggling to climb up into
the boat,
Has both his bruised and bleeding
hands cut off,
And sinks again into the weltering
sea
Helpless and hopeless !

Hyp. Yet thou shalt not perish.
The strength of thine own arm is
thy salvation.
Above thy head, through rifted
clouds, there shines
A glorious star. Be patient. Trust
thy star !

(*Sound of a village bell in the
distance.*)

Vict. Ave Maria ! I hear the
sacristan
Ringing the chimes from yonder
village belfry !
A solemn sound, that echoes far
and wide
Over the red roofs of the cottages,
And bids the labouring hind a-field,
the shepherd,
Guarding his flock, the lonely
muleteer,
And all the crowd in village streets,
stand still,
And breathe a prayer unto the
blessed Virgin !

Hyp. Amen ! amen ! Not half
a league from hence
The village lies.

Vict. This path will lead us to it,
Over the wheat-fields, where the
shadows sail
Across the running sea, now green,
now blue,
And, like an idle mariner on the
main,
Whistles the quail. Come, let us
hasten on. [*Exeunt.*

SCENE II.—*Public square in the
village of Guadarrama. The Ave
Maria still tolling. A crowd
of villagers, with their hats in
their hands, as if in prayer. In
front, a group of Gipsies. The
bell rings a merrier peal. A
Gipsy dance. Enter* PANCHO,
followed by PEDRO CRESPO.

Pancho. Make room, ye vagabonds and Gipsy thieves !
Make room for the Alcalde and for
me !

Pedro C. Keep silence all ! I
have an edict here
From our most gracious lord, the
King of Spain,
Jerusalem, and the Canary Islands,

Which I shall publish in the market-place.
Open your ears and listen!

(*Enter the* PADRE CURA *at the door of his cottage.*)

Padre Cura,
Good day! and, pray you, hear this edict read.
Padre C. Good day, and God be with you! Pray, what is it?
Pedro C. An act of banishment against the Gipsies!

(*Agitation and murmurs in the crowd.*)

Pancho. Silence!
Pedro C. (reads). 'I hereby order and command,
That the Egyptian and Chaldean strangers,
Known by the name of Gipsies, shall henceforth
Be banished from the realm, as vagabonds
And beggars; and if, after seventy days,
Any be found within our kingdom's bounds,
They shall receive a hundred lashes each;
The second time, shall have their ears cut off;
The third, be slaves for life to him who takes them,
Or burnt as heretics. Signed, I, the King.'

Vile miscreants and creatures unbaptized!
You hear the law! Obey and disappear!
Pancho. And if in seventy days you are not gone,
Dead or alive I make you all my slaves.

(*The Gipsies go out in confusion, showing signs of fear and discontent.* PANCHO *follows.*)

Padre C. A righteous law! A very righteous law!
Pray you, sit down.
Pedro C. I thank you heartily.

(*They seat themselves on a bench at the* PADRE CURA'S *door. Sound of guitars heard at a distance, approaching during the dialogue which follows.*)

A very righteous judgment, as you say.
Now tell me, Padre Cura,—you know all things,—
How came these Gipsies into Spain?
Padre C. Why, look you;
They came with Hercules from Palestine,
And hence are thieves and vagrants, Sir Alcalde,
As the Simoniacs from Simon Magus.
And, look you, as Fray Jayme Bleda says,
There are a hundred marks to prove a Moor
Is not a Christian, so 'tis with the Gipsies.
They never marry, never go to mass,
Never baptize their children, nor keep Lent,
Nor see the inside of a church,— nor—nor—
Pedro C. Good reasons, good, substantial reasons all!
No matter for the other ninety-five.
They should be burnt, I see it plain enough,—
They should be burnt.

(*Enter* VICTORIAN *and* HYPOLITO *playing.*)

Padre C. And pray, whom have we here?
Pedro C. More vagrants! By Saint Lazarus, more vagrants!

Hyp. Good evening, gentlemen!
Is this Guadarrama?

Padre C. Yes, Guadarrama, and
good evening to you.

Hyp. We seek the Padre Cura
of the village ;
And, judging from your dress and
reverend mien,
You must be he.

Padre C. I am. Pray, what's
your pleasure?

Hyp. We are poor students,
travelling in vacation.
You know this mark?
(*Touching the wooden spoon in his
hat-band.*)

Padre C. (*joyfully*). Ay, know
it, and have worn it.

Pedro C. (*aside*). Soup-eaters!
by the mass! The worst of
vagrants !
And there's no law against them.
Sir, your servant.   [*Exit.*

Padre C. Your servant, Pedro
Crespo.

Hyp.   Padre Cura,
From the first moment I beheld
your face,
I said within myself, 'This is the
man!'
There is a certain something in
your looks,
A certain scholar-like and studious
something,—
You understand,—which cannot be
mistaken ;
Which marks you as a very learned
man,
In fine, as one of us.

Vict. (*aside*). What impudence !

Hyp. As we approached, I said
to my companion,
'That is the Padre Cura ; mark my
words!'
Meaning your Grace. 'The other
man,' said I,
'Who sits so awkwardly upon the
bench,

Must be the sacristan.'

Padre C.   Ah! said you so?
Why, that was Pedro Crespo, the
alcalde !

Hyp. Indeed ! you much as-
tonish me ! His air
Was not so full of dignity and grace
As an alcalde's should be.

Padre C.   That is true.
He's out of humour with some
vagrant Gipsies,
Who have their camp here in the
neighbourhood.
There's nothing so undignified as
anger.

Hyp. The Padre Cura will ex-
cuse our boldness,
If, from his well-known hospitality,
We crave a lodging for the night.

Padre C.   I pray you !
You do me honour ! I am but too
happy
To have such guests beneath my
humble roof.
It is not often that I have occasion
To speak with scholars ; and
Emollit mores,
Nec sinit esse feros, Cicero says.

Hyp. 'Tis Ovid, is it not?

Padre C.   No, Cicero.

Hyp. Your Grace is right. You
are the better scholar.
Now what a dunce was I to think
it Ovid !
But hang me if it is not ! (*Aside.*)

Padre C.   Pass this way.
He was a very great man, was
Cicero !
Pray you, go in, go in ! no cere-
mony.   [*Exeunt.*

SCENE III.—*A room in the* PADRE
CURA'S *house. Enter the* PADRE
and HYPOLITO.

Padre C. So then, Señor, you
come from Alcalá.

I am glad to hear it. It was there
  I studied.
   Hyp. And left behind an hon-
    oured name, no doubt.
How may I call your Grace?
   Padre C.   Gerónimo
De Santillana, at your Honour's
  service.
   Hyp. Descended from the Mar-
    quis Santillana?
From the distinguished poet?
   Padre C.   From the Marquis,
Not from the poet.
   Hyp. Why, they were the same.
Let me embrace you! O some
  lucky star
Has brought me hither! Yet once
  more!—once more!
Your name is ever green in Alcalá,
And our professor, when we are
  unruly,
Will shake his hoary head, and say,
  'Alas!
It was not so in Santillana's
  time!'
   Padre C. I did not think my
    name remembered there.
   Hyp. More than remembered;
    it is idolized.
   Padre C. Of what professor
    speak you?
   Hyp.   Timoneda.
   Padre C. I don't remember any
    Timoneda.
   Hyp. A grave and sombre man,
    whose beetling brow
O'erhangs the rushing current of
  his speech
As rocks o'er rivers hang. Have
  you forgotten?
   Padre C. Indeed, I have. O,
    those were pleasant days,
Those college days! I ne'er shall
  see the like!
I had not buried then so many
  hopes!
I had not buried then so many
  friends!

I 've turned my back on what was
  then before me;
And the bright faces of my young
  companions
Are wrinkled like my own, or are
  no more.
Do you remember Cueva?
   Hyp.   Cueva? Cueva?
   Padre C. Fool that I am! He
    was before your time.
You 're a mere boy, and I am an
  old man.
   Hyp. I should not like to try
    my strength with you.
   Padre C. Well, well. But I
    forget; you must be hungry.
Martina! ho! Martina! 'Tis my
  niece.

  (*Enter* MARTINA.)

   Hyp. You may be proud of such
    a niece as that.
I wish I had a niece. *Emollit
  mores.* (*Aside.*)
He was a very great man, was
  Cicero!
Your servant, fair Martina.
   Mart.   Servant, sir.
   Padre C. This gentleman is
    hungry. See thou to it.
Let us have supper.
   Mart.   'Twill be ready soon.
   Padre C. And bring a bottle of
    my Val-de-Peñas
Out of the cellar. Stay; I'll go
  myself.
Pray you, Señor, excuse me.
                        [*Exit.*
   Hyp.   Hist! Martina!
One word with you. Bless me!
  what handsome eyes!
To-day there have been Gipsies in
  the village.
Is it not so?
   Mart. There have been Gipsies
    here.
   Hyp. Yes, and have told your
    fortune.

Mart. (*embarrassed*). Told my fortune?

Hyp. Yes, yes; I know they did. Give me your hand.
I 'll tell you what they said. They said,—they said,
The shepherd boy that loved you was a clown,
And him you should not marry. Was it not?

Mart. (*surprised*). How know you that?

Hyp. O, I know more than that.
What a soft little hand! And then they said,
A cavalier from court, handsome, and tall
And rich, should come one day to marry you,
And you should be a lady. Was it not?
He has arrived, the handsome cavalier.

(*Tries to kiss her. She runs off.
Enter* VICTORIAN, *with a letter.*)

Vict. The muleteer has come.

Hyp. So soon?

Vict. I found him
Sitting at supper by the tavern door,
And, from a pitcher that he held aloft
His whole arm's length, drinking the blood-red wine.

Hyp. What news from Court?

Vict. He brought this letter only.

(*Reads.*)

O cursed perfidy! Why did I let
That lying tongue deceive me!
Preciosa,
Sweet Preciosa! how art thou avenged!

Hyp. What news is this, that makes thy cheek turn pale,

And thy hand tremble?

Vict. O, most infamous!
The Count of Lara is a worthless villain!

Hyp. That is no news, forsooth.

Vict. He strove in vain
To steal from me the jewel of my soul,
The love of Preciosa. Not succeeding,
He swore to be revenged; and set on foot
A plot to ruin her, which has succeeded.
She has been hissed and hooted from the stage,
Her reputation stained by slanderous lies
Too foul to speak of; and, once more a beggar,
She roams a wanderer over God's green earth,
Housing with Gipsies!

Hyp. To renew again
The Age of Gold, and make the shepherd swains
Desperate with love, like Gasper Gil's Diana.
Redit et Virgo!

Vict. Dear Hypolito,
How have I wronged that meek, confiding heart!
I will go seek for her; and with my tears
Wash out the wrong I 've done her!

Hyp. O beware!
Act not that folly o'er again.

Vict. Ay, folly,
Delusion, madness, call it what thou wilt,
I will confess my weakness,—I still love her!
Still fondly love her!

(*Enter the* PADRE CURA.)

Hyp. Tell us, Padre Cura,
Who are these Gipsies in the neighbourhood?

Padre C. Beltran Cruzado and his crew.

Vict.   Kind Heaven,
I thank thee! She is found! is found again!

Hyp. And have they with them a pale, beautiful girl,
Called Preciosa?

Padre C.   Ay, a pretty girl.
The gentleman seems moved.

Hyp. Yes, moved with hunger,
He is half famished with this long day's journey.

Padre C. Then, pray you, come this way. The supper waits.
[*Exeunt.*

SCENE IV.—*A post-house on the road to Segovia, not far from the village of Guadarrama. Enter* CHISPA, *cracking a whip, and singing the cachucha.*

Chispa. Halloo! Don Fulano! Let us have horses, and quickly. Alas, poor Chispa! what a dog's life dost thou lead! I thought, when I left my old master Victorian, the student, to serve my new master Don Carlos, the gentleman, that I too should lead the life of a gentleman; should go to bed early, and get up late. For when the abbot plays cards, what can you expect of the friars? But, in running away from the thunder, I have run into the lightning. Here I am in hot chase after my master and his Gipsy girl. And a good beginning of the week it is, as he said who was hanged on Monday morning.

(*Enter* DON CARLOS.)

Don C. Are not the horses ready yet?

Chispa. I should think not, for the hostler seems to be asleep. Ho! within there! Horses!

horses! horses! (*He knocks at the gate with his whip, and enter* MOSQUITO, *putting on his jacket.*)

Mosq. Pray, have a little patience. I'm not a musket.

Chispa. Health and pistareens! I'm glad to see you come on dancing, padre! Pray, what's the news?

Mosq. You cannot have fresh horses; because there are none.

Chispa. Cachiporra! Throw that bone to another dog. Do I look like your aunt?

Mosq. No; she has a beard.

Chispa. Go to! go to!

Mosq. Are you from Madrid?

Chispa. Yes; and going to Estramadura. Get us horses.

Mosq. What's the news at Court?

Chispa. Why, the latest news is, that I am going to set up a coach, and I have already bought the whip. (*Strikes him round the legs.*)

Mosq. Oh! oh! you hurt me!

Don C. Enough of this folly. Let us have horses. (*Gives money to* MOSQUITO.) It is almost dark; and we are in haste. But tell me, has a band of Gipsies passed this way of late?

Mosq. Yes; and they are still in the neighbourhood.

Don C. And where?

Mosq. Across the fields yonder, in the woods near Guadarrama.
[*Exit.*

Don C. Now this is lucky. We will visit the Gipsy camp.

Chispa. Are you not afraid of the evil eye? Have you a stag's horn with you?

Don C. Fear not. We will pass the night at the village.

Chispa. And sleep like the Squires of Hernan Daza, nine under one blanket.

Don C. I hope we may find the Preciosa among them.

Chispa. Among the Squires?

Don C. No; among the Gipsies, blockhead!

Chispa. I hope we may; for we are giving ourselves trouble enough on her account. Don't you think so? However, there is no catching trout without wetting one's trousers. Yonder come the horses.

[*Exeunt.*

SCENE V.—*The Gipsy camp in the forest. Night. Gipsies working at a forge. Others playing cards by the firelight.*

Gipsies (*at the forge sing*).

On the top of a mountain I stand,
With a crown of red gold in my hand,
Wild Moors come trooping over the lea,
O how from their fury shall I flee, flee, flee?
O how from their fury shall I flee?

First Gipsy (*playing*). Down with your John-Dorados, my pigeon. Down with your John-Dorados, and let us make an end.

Gipsies (*at the forge sing*).

Loud sang the Spanish cavalier,
And thus his ditty ran;
God send the Gipsy lassie here,
And not the Gipsy man.

First Gipsy (*playing*). There you are in your morocco!

Second Gipsy. One more game. The Alcalde's doves against the Padre Cura's new moon.

First Gipsy. Have at you, Chirelin.

Gipsies (*at the forge sing*).

At midnight, when the moon began
To show her silver flame,
There came to him no Gipsy man,
The Gipsy lassie came.

(*Enter* BELTRAN CRUZADO.)

Cruz. Come hither, Murcigalleros and Rastilleros; leave work, leave play; listen to your orders for the night. (*Speaking to the right.*) You will get you to the village, mark you, by the stone cross.

Gipsies. Ay!

Cruz. (*to the left*). And you, by the pole with the hermit's head upon it.

Gipsies. Ay!

Cruz. As soon as you see the planets are out, in with you, and be busy with the ten commandments, under the sly, and Saint Martin asleep. D'ye hear?

Gipsies. Ay!

Cruz. Keep your lanterns open, and, if you see a goblin or a papagayo, take to your trampers. Vineyards and Dancing John is the word. Am I comprehended?

Gipsies. Ay! ay!

Cruz. Away, then!

(*Exeunt severally.* CRUZADO *walks up the stage, and disappears among the trees. Enter* PRECIOSA.)

Prec. How strangely gleams through the gigantic trees
The red light of the forge! Wild, beckoning shadows
Stalk through the forest, ever and anon
Rising and bending with the flickering flame,
Then flitting into darkness! So within me

Strange hopes and fears do beckon
  to each other,
My brightest hopes giving dark
  fears a being
As the light does the shadow. Woe
  is me!
How still it is about me, and how
  lonely!

(BARTOLOMÉ *rushes in.*)

  Bart. Ho! Preciosa!
  Prec.   O Bartolomé!
Thou here?
  Bart. Lo! I am here.
  Prec. Whence comest thou?
  Bart. From the rough ridges of
  the wild Sierra,
From caverns in the rocks, from
  hunger, thirst,
And fever! Like a wild wolf to the
  sheepfold
Come I for thee, my lamb.
  Prec.   O touch me not!
The Count of Lara's blood is on
  thy hands!
The Count of Lara's curse is on
  thy soul!
Do not come near me! Pray, be-
  gone from here!
Thou art in danger! They have
  set a price
Upon thy head!
  Bart. Ay, and I've wandered
  long
Among the mountains; and for
  many days
Have seen no human face, save
  the rough swineherd's.
The wind and rain have been my
  sole companions.
I shouted to them from the rocks
  thy name,
And the loud echo sent it back to
  me,
Till I grew mad. I could not stay
  from thee,
And I am here! Betray me, if thou
  wilt.

  Prec. Betray thee? I betray
  thee?
  Bart.   Preciosa!
I come for thee! for thee I thus
  brave death!
Fly with me o'er the borders of
  this realm!
Fly with me!
  Prec. Speak of that no more.
  I cannot.
I'm thine no longer.
  Bart.   O, recall the time
When we were children! how we
  played together,
How we grew up together; how
  we plighted
Our hearts unto each other, even
  in childhood!
Fulfil thy promise, for the hour has
  come.
I'm hunted from the kingdom, like
  a wolf!
Fulfil thy promise.
  Prec. 'Twas my father's promise,
Not mine. I never gave my heart
  to thee,
Nor promised thee my hand!
  Bart. False tongue of woman!
And heart more false!
  Prec.   Nay, listen unto me.
I will speak frankly. I have never
  loved thee;
I cannot love thee. This is not
  my fault,
It is my destiny. Thou art a man
Restless and violent. What wouldst
  thou with me,
A feeble girl, who have not long to
  live,
Whose heart is broken? Seek
  another wife,
Better than I, and fairer; and let not
Thy rash and headlong moods
  estrange her from thee.
Thou art unhappy in this hopeless
  passion.
I never sought thy love; never did
  aught

To make thee love me. Yet I pity
  thee,
And most of all I pity thy wild
  heart,
That hurries thee to crimes and
  deeds of blood.
Beware, beware of that.

Bart. For thy dear sake
I will be gentle. Thou shalt teach
  me patience.

Prec. Then take this farewell,
  and depart in peace.
Thou must not linger here.

Bart. Come, come with me.

Prec. Hark! I hear footsteps.

Bart. I entreat thee, come!

Prec. Away! It is in vain.

Bart. Wilt thou not come?

Prec. Never!

Bart. Then woe, eternal woe,
  upon thee!
Thou shalt not be another's. Thou
  shalt die. [*Exit.*

Prec. All holy angels keep me in
  this hour!
Spirit of her who bore me, look
  upon me!
Mother of God, the glorified, pro-
  tect me!
Christ and the saints, be merciful
  unto me!
Yet why should I fear death?
  What is it to die?
To leave all disappointment, care,
  and sorrow,
To leave all falsehood, treachery,
  and unkindness,
All ignominy, suffering, and de-
  spair,
And be at rest for ever! O dull
  heart,
Be of good cheer When thou
  shalt cease to beat,
Then shalt thou cease to suffer and
  complain!

(*Enter* VICTORIAN *and* HYPOLITO
  behind.)

Vict. 'Tis she! Behold, how
  beautiful she stands
Under the tent-like trees!

Hyp. A woodland nymph!

Vict. I pray thee, stand aside.
  Leave me.

Hyp. Be wary.
Do not betray thyself too soon.

Vict. (*disguising his voice*). Hist!
  Gipsy!

Prec. (*aside, with emotion*). That
  voice! that voice from
  heaven! O speak again!
Who is it calls?

Vict. A friend.

Prec. (*aside*). 'Tis he! 'Tis he!
I thank thee, Heaven, that thou
  hast heard my prayer,
And sent me this protector! Now
  be strong,
Be strong, my heart! I must
  dissemble here.
False friend or true?

Vict. A true friend to the true;
Fear not; come hither. So; can
  you tell fortunes?

Prec. Not in the dark. Come
  nearer to the fire.
Give me your hand. It is not
  crossed, I see.

Vict. (*putting a piece of gold into
  her hand*). There is the cross.

Prec. Is 't silver?

Vict. No, 'tis gold.

Prec. There's a fair lady at the
  Court, who loves you,
And for yourself alone.

Vict. Fie! the old story!
Tell me a better fortune for my
  money;
Not this old woman's tale!

Prec. You are passion-
  ate;
And this same passionate humour
  in your blood
Has marred your fortune. Yes; I
  see it now;

The line of life is crossed by many
  marks.
Shame! shame! O you have
  wronged the maid who loved
  you!
How could you do it?
  Vict. I never loved a maid;
For she I loved was then a maid
  no more.
  Prec. How know you that?
  Vict. A little bird in the air
Whispered the secret.
  Prec. There, take back your
  gold!
Your hand is cold, like a deceiver's
  hand!
There is no blessing in its charity!
Make her your wife, for you have
  been abused;
And you shall mend your fortunes,
  mending hers.
  Vict. (*aside*). How like an angel's
  speaks the tongue of woman,
When pleading in another's cause
  her own!
That is a pretty ring upon your
  finger.
Pray give it me.
        (*Tries to take the ring.*)
  Prec. No; never from my hand
Shall it be taken!
  Vict. Why, 'tis but a ring.
I'll give it back to you; or, if I
  keep it,
Will give you gold to buy you
  twenty such.
  Prec. Why would you have this
  ring?
  Vict. A traveller's fancy,
A whim, and nothing more. I
  would fain keep it
As a memento of the Gipsy camp
In Guadarrama, and the fortune-
  teller
Who sent me back to wed a
  widowed maid.
Pray, let me have the ring.
  Prec. No, never! never!

I will not part with it, even when
  I die;
But bid my nurse fold my pale
  fingers thus,
That it may not fall from them.
  'Tis a token
Of a beloved friend who is no
  more.
  Vict. How? dead?
  Prec. Yes; dead to me; and
  worse than dead.
He is estranged! And yet I keep
  this ring.
I will rise with it from my grave
  hereafter,
To prove to him that I was never
  false.
  Vict. (*aside*). Be still, my swell-
  ing heart! one moment, still!
Why, 'tis the folly of a love-sick girl.
Come, give it me, or I will say 'tis
  mine,
And that you stole it.
  Prec. O, you will not dare
To utter such a falsehood!
  Vict. I not dare?
Look in my face, and say if there
  is aught
I have not dared, I would not dare
  for thee!

        (*She rushes into his arms.*)

  Prec. 'Tis thou! 'tis thou! Yes;
  yes; my heart's elected! Yes;
My dearest dear Victorian! my
  soul's heaven!
Where hast thou been so long?
  Why didst thou leave me?
  Vict. Ask me not now, my
  dearest Preciosa.
Let me forget we ever have been
  parted!
  Prec. Hadst thou not come—
  Vict. I pray thee, do not chide
  me!
  Prec. I should have perished
  here among these Gipsies.

Vict. Forgive me, sweet ! for what I made thee suffer.
Think'st thou this heart could feel a moment's joy,
Thou being absent ? O, believe it not !
Indeed, since that sad hour I have not slept,
For thinking of the wrong I did to thee !
Dost thou forgive me ? Say, wilt thou forgive me ?
Prec. I have forgiven thee. Ere those words of anger
Were in the book of Heaven writ down against thee,
I had forgiven thee.
Vict. I 'm the veriest fool
That walks the earth, to have believed thee false.
It was the Count of Lara—
Prec. That bad man
Has worked me harm enough.
Hast thou not heard—
Vict. I have heard all. And yet speak on, speak on !
Let me but hear thy voice, and I am happy ;
For every tone, like some sweet incantation,
Calls up the buried past to plead for me.
Speak, my beloved, speak into my heart,
Whatever fills and agitates thine own.

(*They walk aside.*)

Hyp. All gentle quarrels in the pastoral poets,
All passionate love scenes in the best romances,
All chaste embraces on the public stage,
All soft adventures, which the liberal stars
Have winked at, as the natural course of things,

Have been surpassed here by my friend the student,
And this sweet Gipsy lass, fair Preciosa !
Prec. Señor Hypolito ! I kiss your hand.
Pray, shall I tell your fortune ?
Hyp. Not to-night ;
For, should you treat me as you did Victorian,
And send me back to marry maids forlorn,
My wedding day would last from now till Christmas.
Chispa (*within*). What ho ! the Gipsies, ho ! Beltran Cruzado !
Halloo ! halloo ! halloo ! halloo !

(*Enters booted, with a whip and lantern.*)

Vict. What now ?
Why such a fearful din ? Hast thou been robbed ?
Chispa. Ay, robbed and murdered ; and good evening to you,
My worthy masters.
Vict. Speak ; what brings thee here ?
Chispa (*to* PRECIOSA). Good news from Court ; good news ! Beltran Cruzado,
The Count of the Calés, is not your father,
But your true father has returned to Spain
Laden with wealth. You are no more a Gipsy.
Vict. Strange as a Moorish tale !
Chispa. And we have all
Been drinking at the tavern to your health,
As wells drink in November, when it rains.
Vict. Where is the gentleman ?

Chispa. As the old song says,
  His body is in Segovia,
  His soul is in Madrid.

Prec. Is this a dream? O, if it
 be a dream,
Let me sleep on, and do not wake
 me yet!
Repeat thy story! Say I'm not
 deceived!
Say that I do not dream! I am
 awake;
This is the Gipsy camp; this is
 Victorian,
And this his friend, Hypolito!
 Speak! speak!
Let me not wake and find it all a
 dream!

 Vict. It is a dream, sweet child!
 a waking dream,
A blissful certainty, a vision
 bright
Of that rare happiness, which even
 on earth
Heaven gives to those it loves.
 Now art thou rich,
As thou wast ever beautiful and
 good;
And I am now the beggar.

 Prec. (*giving him her hand*). I
 have still
A hand to give.

 Chispa (*aside*). And I have two
 to take.
I've heard my grandmother say,
 that Heaven gives almonds
To those who have no teeth. That's
 nuts to crack.
I've teeth to spare, but where shall
 I find almonds?

 Vict. What more of this strange
 story?

 Chispa. Nothing more.
Your friend, Don Carlos, is now at
 the village
Showing to Pedro Crespo, the
 Alcalde,
The proofs of what I tell you.
The old hag

Who stole you in your childhood
 has confessed;
And probably they'll hang her for
 the crime,
To make the celebration more
 complete.

 Vict. No; let it be a day of
 general joy;
Fortune comes well to all, that
 comes not late.
Now let us join Don Carlos.

 Hyp. So farewell
The student's wandering life!
 Sweet serenades
Sung under ladies' windows in the
 night,
And all that makes vacation beau-
 tiful!
To you, ye cloistered shades of
 Alcalá,
To you, ye radiant visions of ro-
 mance,
Written in books, but here sur-
 passed by truth,
The Bachelor Hypolito returns,
And leaves the Gipsy with the
 Spanish Student.

SCENE VI. — *A pass in the
Guadarrama mountains. Early
morning. A muleteer crosses the
stage, sitting sideways on his
mule, and lighting a paper cigar
with flint and steel.*

SONG.

If thou art sleeping, maiden,
 Awake and open thy door,
'Tis the break of day, and we must away,
 O'er meadow, and mount, and moor.

Wait not to find thy slippers,
 But come with thy naked feet;
We shall have to pass through the dewy
 grass,
 And waters wide and fleet.

(*Disappears down the pass. Enter
a Monk. A shepherd appears on
the rocks above.*)

Monk. Ave Maria, gratia plena. Olá! good man!

Shep. Olá!

Monk. Is this the road to Segovia?

Shep. It is, your reverence.

Monk. How far is it?

Shep. I do not know.

Monk. What is that yonder in the valley?

Shep. San Ildefonso.

Monk. A long way to breakfast.

Shep. Ay, marry.

Monk. Are there robbers in these mountains?

Shep. Yes, and worse than that.

Monk. What?

Shep. Wolves.

Monk. Santa Maria! Come with me to San Ildefonso, and thou shalt be well rewarded.

Shep. What wilt thou give me?

Monk. An Agnus Dei and my benediction.

(*They disappear. A mounted Contrabandista passes, wrapped in his cloak, and a gun at his saddle-bow. He goes down the pass singing.*)

SONG.

Worn with speed is my good steed,
And I march me hurried, worried;
Onward, caballito mio,
With the white star in thy forehead!
Onward, for here comes the Ronda,
And I hear their rifles crack!
Ay, jaléo! Ay, ay, jaléo!
Ay, jaléo! They cross our track.

(*Song dies away. Enter* PRECIOSA, *on horseback, attended by* VICTORIAN, HYPOLITO, DON CARLOS, *and* CHISPA, *on foot, and armed.*)

Vict. This is the highest point. Here let us rest.
See, Preciosa, see how all about us

Kneeling, like hooded friars, the misty mountains
Receive the benediction of the sun!
O glorious sight!

Prec. Most beautiful indeed!

Hyp. Most wonderful!

Vict. And in the vale below,
Where yonder steeples flash like lifted halberds,
San Ildefonso, from its noisy belfries,
Sends up a salutation to the morn,
As if an army smote their brazen shields,
And shouted victory!

Prec. And which way lies Segovia?

Vict. At a great distance yonder. Dost thou not see it?

Prec. No. I do not see it.

Vict. The merest flaw that dents the horizon's edge.
There, yonder!

Hyp. 'Tis a notable old town,
Boasting an ancient Roman aqueduct,
And an Alcázar, builded by the Moors,
Wherein, you may remember, poor Gil Blas
Was fed on *Pan del Rey*. O, many a time
Out of its grated windows have I looked
Hundreds of feet plumb down to the Eresma,
That, like a serpent through the valley creeping,
Glides at its foot.

Prec. O yes! I see it now,
Yet rather with my heart than with mine eyes,
So faint it is. And all my thoughts sail thither,
Freighted with prayers and hopes and forward urged
Against all stress of accident, as in

114

The Eastern tale, against the wind and tide
Great ships were drawn to the Magnetic Mountains,
And there were wrecked, and perished in the sea ! (*She weeps.*)

   Vict. O gentle spirit ! Thou didst bear unmoved
Blasts of adversity and frosts of fate !
But the first ray of sunshine that falls on thee
Melts thee to tears ! O, let thy weary heart
Lean upon mine ! and it shall faint no more,
Nor thirst, nor hunger ; but be comforted
And filled with my affection.

   Prec. Stay no longer !
My father waits. Methinks I see him there,
Now looking from the window, and now watching
Each sound of wheels or footfall in the street,
And saying, 'Hark ! she comes !'
   O father ! father !

(*They descend the pass.* CHISPA *remains behind.*)

   Chispa. I have a father, too, but he is a dead one. Alas and alack-a-day ! Poor was I born, and poor do I remain. I neither win nor lose. Thus I wag through the world, half the time on foot, and the other half walking ; and always as merry as a thunderstorm in the night. And so we plough along, as the fly said to the ox. Who knows what may happen ? Patience, and shuffle the cards ! I am not yet so bald that you can see my brains ; and perhaps, after all, I shall some day go to Rome, and come back Saint Peter. Benedicite ! [*Exit.*

(*A pause. Then enter* BARTOLOMÉ *wildly, as if in pursuit, with a carbine in his hand.*)

   Bart. They passed this way ! I hear their horses' hoofs !
Yonder I see them ! Come, sweet caramillo,
This serenade shall be the Gipsy's last !

   (*Fires down the pass.*)

Ha ! ha ! Well whistled, my sweet caramillo !
Well whistled ! — I have missed her ! — O my God !

(*The shot is returned.* BARTOLOMÉ *falls.*)

The Belfry of Bruges.

CARILLON.

In the ancient town of Bruges,
In the quaint old Flemish city,
As the evening shades descended,
Low and loud and sweetly blended,
Low at times and loud at times,
And changing like a poet's rhymes,
Rang the beautiful wild chimes
From the Belfry in the market
Of the ancient town of Bruges.

Then, with deep sonorous clangour
Calmly answering their sweet anger,
When the wrangling bells had ended,
Slowly struck the clock eleven,
And, from out the silent heaven,
Silence on the town descended.
Silence, silence everywhere,
On the earth and in the air,
Save that footsteps here and there
Of some burgher home returning,
By the street lamps faintly burning,
For a moment woke the echoes
Of the ancient town of Bruges.

But amid my broken slumbers
Still I heard those magic numbers,
As they loud proclaimed the flight
And stolen marches of the night;
Till their chimes in sweet collision
Mingled with each wandering vision,
Mingled with the fortune-telling
Gipsy-bands of dreams and fancies,
Which amid the waste expanses
Of the silent land of trances
Have their solitary dwelling;
All else seemed asleep in Bruges,
In the quaint old Flemish city.

And I thought how like these chimes
Are the poet's airy rhymes,
All his rhymes and roundelays,
His conceits, and songs, and ditties,
From the belfry of his brain,
Scattered downward, though in vain,
On the roofs and stones of cities!
For by night the drowsy ear
Under its curtains cannot hear,
And by day men go their ways,
Hearing the music as they pass,
But deeming it no more, alas!
Than the hollow sound of brass.

Yet perchance a sleepless wight,
Lodging at some humble inn
In the narrow lanes of life,
When the dusk and hush of night
Shut out the incessant din
Of daylight and its toil and strife,
May listen with a calm delight
To the poet's melodies,
Till he hears, or dreams he hears,
Intermingled with the song,
Thoughts that he has cherished long;
Hears amid the chime and singing
The bells of his own village ringing,
And wakes, and finds his slumbrous eyes
Wet with most delicious tears.

Thus dreamed I, as by night I lay
In Bruges, at the Fleur-de-Blé,
Listening with a wild delight
To the chimes that, through the night,
Rang their changes from the Belfry
Of that quaint old Flemish city.

THE BELFRY OF BRUGES.

In the market-place of Bruges stands the belfry old and brown;
Thrice consumed and thrice rebuilded, still it watches o'er the town.

As the summer morn was breaking, on that lofty tower I stood,
And the world threw off the darkness, like the weeds of widowhood.

Thick with towns and hamlets studded, and with streams and vapours gray,
Like a shield embossed with silver, round and vast the landscape lay.

At my feet the city slumbered. From its chimneys, here and there,
Wreaths of snow-white smoke ascending, vanished, ghost-like, into air.

Not a sound rose from the city at that early morning hour,
But I heard a heart of iron beating in the ancient tower.

From their nests beneath the rafters sang the swallows wild and high;
And the world, beneath me sleeping, seemed more distant than the sky.

Then most musical and solemn, bringing back the olden times,
With their strange unearthly changes rang the melancholy chimes,

Like the psalms from some old cloister, when the nuns sing in the choir;
And the great bell tolled among them, like the chanting of a friar.

Visions of the days departed, shadowy phantoms filled my brain;
They who live in history only seemed to walk the earth again;

All the Foresters of Flanders,—mighty Baldwin Bras de Fer,
Lyderick du Bucq and Cressy Philip, Guy de Dampierre.

I beheld the pageants splendid that adorned those days of old;
Stately dames, like queens attended, knights who bore the Fleece of Gold.

Lombard and Venetian merchants with deep-laden argosies;
Ministers from twenty nations; more than royal pomp and ease.

I beheld proud Maximilian, kneeling humbly on the ground;
I beheld the gentle Mary, hunting with her hawk and hound;

And her lighted bridal-chamber, where a duke slept with the queen,
And the armed guard around them, and the sword unsheathed between.

I beheld the Flemish weavers, with Namur and Juliers bold,
Marching homeward from the bloody battle of the Spurs of Gold;

Saw the fight at Minnewater, saw the White Hoods moving west,
Saw great Artevelde victorious scale the Golden Dragon's nest.

And again the whiskered Spaniard all the land with terror smote;
And again the wild alarum sounded from the tocsin's throat;

Till the bell of Ghent responded o'er lagoon and dike of sand,
'I am Roland! I am Roland! there is victory in the land!'

Then the sound of drums aroused me. The awakened city's roar
Chased the phantoms I had summoned back into their graves once more.

Hours had passed away like minutes; and, before I was aware,
Lo! the shadow of the belfry crossed the sun-illumined square.

Miscellaneous Poems.

A GLEAM OF SUNSHINE.

This is the place. Stand still, my
    steed,
  Let me review the scene,
And summon from the shadowy
    Past
  The forms that once have been.

The Past and Present here unite
  Beneath Time's flowing tide,
Like footprints hidden by a brook,
  But seen on either side.

Here runs the highway to the
    town ;
There the green lane descends,
Through which I walked to church
    with thee,
  O gentlest of my friends!

The shadow of the linden-trees
  Lay moving on the grass ;
Between them and the moving
    boughs,
  A shadow, thou didst pass.

Thy dress was like the lilies,
  And thy heart as pure as they ;
One of God's holy messengers
  Did walk with me that day.

I saw the branches of the trees
  Bend down thy touch to meet,
The clover-blossoms in the grass
  Rise up to kiss thy feet.

'Sleep, sleep to-day, tormenting
    cares,
  Of earth and folly born !'
Solemnly sang the village choir
  On that sweet Sabbath morn.

Through the closed blinds the
    golden sun
  Poured in a dusty beam,
Like the celestial ladder seen
  By Jacob in his dream.

And ever and anon the wind,
  Sweet-scented with the hay,
Turned o'er the hymn-book's
    fluttering leaves
  That on the window lay.

Long was the good man's sermon,
  Yet it seemed not so to me ;
For he spake of Ruth the beautiful,
  And still I thought of thee.

Long was the prayer he uttered,
  Yet it seemed not so to me ;
For in my heart I prayed with
    him,
  And still I thought of thee.

But now, alas ! the place seems
    changed ;
  Thou art no longer here :
Part of the sunshine of the scene
  With thee did disappear.

Though thoughts, deep-rooted in
    my heart,
  Like pine-trees dark and high,
Subdue the light of noon, and
    breathe
  A low and ceaseless sigh ;

This memory brightens o'er the
    past,
  As when the sun, concealed
Behind some cloud that near us
    hangs
  Shines on a distant field.

THE ARSENAL AT SPRING-
FIELD.

THIS is the Arsenal. From floor
to ceiling,
Like a huge organ, rise the
burnished arms;
But from their silent pipes no
anthem pealing
Startles the villages with strange
alarms.

Ah! what a sound will rise, how
wild and dreary,
When the death-angel touches
those swift keys!
What loud lament and dismal
Miserere
Will mingle with their awful
symphonies!

I hear even now the infinite fierce
chorus,
The cries of agony, the endless
groan,
Which, through the ages that have
gone before us,
In long reverberations reach our
own.

On helm and harness rings the
Saxon hammer,
Through Cimbric forest roars
the Norseman's song,
And loud, amid the universal
clamour,
O'er distant deserts sounds the
Tartar gong.

I hear the Florentine, who from
his palace
Wheels out his battle-bell with
dreadful din,

And Aztec priests upon their teo-
callis
Beat the wild war-drums made
of serpent's skin;

The tumult of each sacked and
burning village;
The shout that every prayer for
mercy drowns;
The soldiers' revels in the midst of
pillage;
The wail of famine in beleaguered towns;

The bursting shell, the gateway
wrenched asunder,
The rattling musketry, the clashing blade;
And ever and anon, in tones of
thunder,
The diapason of the cannonade.

Is it, O man, with such discordant
noises,
With such accursed instruments
as these,
Thou drownest Nature's sweet and
kindly voices,
And jarrest the celestial harmonies?

Were half the power that fills the
world with terror,
Were half the wealth bestowed
on camps and courts,
Given to redeem the human mind
from error,
There were no need of arsenals
or forts:

The warrior's name would be a
name abhorred!
And every nation that should
lift again
Its hand against a brother, on its
forehead
Would wear for evermore the
curse of Cain!

Down the dark future, through long generations,
The echoing sounds grow fainter and then cease ;
And like a bell, with solemn, sweet vibrations,
  I hear once more the voice of Christ say, ‘ Peace !’

Peace ! and no longer from its brazen portals
  The blast of War’s great organ shakes the skies !
But beautiful as songs of the immortals,
  The holy melodies of love arise.

NUREMBERG.

IN the valley of the Pegnitz, where across broad meadow-lands
Rise the blue Franconian mountains, Nuremberg, the ancient, stands.

Quaint old town of toil and traffic, quaint old town of art and song,
Memories haunt thy pointed gables, like the rooks that round them throng :

Memories of the Middle Ages, when the emperors, rough and bold,
Had their dwelling in thy castle, time-defying, centuries old ;

And thy brave and thrifty burghers boasted, in their uncouth rhyme,
That their great imperial city stretched its hand through every clime.

In the court-yard of the castle, bound with many an iron band,
Stands the mighty linden planted by Queen Cunigunde’s hand ;

On the square the oriel window, where in old heroic days
Sat the poet Melchior singing Kaiser Maximilian’s praise.

Everywhere I see around me rise the wondrous world of Art :
Fountains wrought with richest sculpture standing in the common mart ;

And above cathedral doorways saints and bishops carved in stone,
By a former age commissioned as apostles to our own.

In the church of sainted Sebald sleeps enshrined his holy dust,
And in bronze the Twelve Apostles guard from age to age their trust :

In the church of sainted Lawrence stands a pix of sculpture rare,
Like the foamy sheaf of fountains, rising through the painted air.

Here, when Art was still religion, with a simple, reverent heart,
Lived and laboured Albrecht Dürer, the Evangelist of Art ;

Hence in silence and in sorrow, toiling still with busy hand,
Like an emigrant he wandered, seeking for the Better Land.

Emigravit is the inscription on the tombstone where he lies ;
Dead he is not, but departed,—for the artist never dies.

Fairer seems the ancient city, and the sunshine seems more fair,
That he once has trod its pavement, that he once has breathed its air !

Through these streets so broad and stately, these obscure and dismal
   lanes,
Walked of yore the Master-singers, chanting rude poetic strains.

From remote and sunless suburbs came they to the friendly guild,
Building nests in Fame's great temple, as in spouts the swallows build.

As the weaver plied the shuttle, wove he too the mystic rhyme,
And the smith his iron measures hammered to the anvil's chime ;

Thanking God, whose boundless wisdom makes the flowers of poesy
   bloom
In the forge's dust and cinders, in the tissues of the loom.

Here Hans Sachs, the cobbler-poet, laureate of the gentle craft,
Wisest of the Twelve Wise Masters, in huge folios sang and laughed.

But his house is now an ale-house, with a nicely sanded floor,
And a garland in the window, and his face above the door ;

Painted by some humble artist, as in Adam Puschman's song,
As the old man gray and dove-like, with his great beard white and long.

And at night the swart mechanic comes to drown his cark and care,
Quaffing ale from pewter tankards, in the master's antique chair.

Vanished is the ancient splendour, and before my dreamy eye
Wave these mingled shapes and figures, like a faded tapestry.

Not thy Councils, not thy Kaisers, win for thee the world's regard ;
But thy painter, Albrecht Dürer, and Hans Sachs thy cobbler-bard.

Thus, O Nuremberg, a wanderer from a region far away,
As he paced thy streets and court-yards, sang in thought his careless lay :

Gathering from the pavement's crevice, as a floweret of the soil,
The nobility of labour,—the long pedigree of toil.

121

THE NORMAN BARON.

Dans les moments de la vie où la réflexion devient plus calme et plus profonde, où l'intérêt et l'avarice parlent moins haut que la raison, dans les instants de chagrin domestique, de maladie, et de péril de mort, les nobles se repentirent de posséder des serfs, comme d'une chose peu agréable à Dieu, qui avait créé tous les hommes à son image.
THIERRY, *Conquête de l'Angleterre.*

IN his chamber, weak and dying,
Was the Norman baron lying;
Loud, without, the tempest thun-
    dered,
    And the castle-turret shook.

In this fight was Death the gainer,
Spite of vassal and retainer,
And the lands his sires had plun-
    dered,
    Written in the Doomsday Book.

By his bed a monk was seated,
Who in humble voice repeated
Many a prayer and pater-noster,
    From the missal on his knee;

And, amid the tempest pealing,
Sounds of bells came faintly steal-
    ing,
Bells, that from the neighbouring
    kloster
    Rang for the Nativity.

In the hall the serf and vassal
Held, that night, their Christmas
    wassail;
Many a carol, old and saintly,
    Sang the minstrels and the
        waits;

And so loud these Saxon gleemen
Sang to slaves the songs of freemen,
That the storm was heard but
    faintly,
    Knocking at the castle-gates.

Till at length the lays they chanted
Reached the chamber terror-
    haunted,
Where the monk, with accents holy,
    Whispered at the baron's ear.

Tears upon his eyelids glistened,
As he paused awhile and listened,
And the dying baron slowly
    Turned his weary head to hear.

'Wassail for the kingly stranger
Born and cradled in a manger!
King like David, priest like Aaron,
    Christ is born to set us free!'

And the lightning showed the
    sainted
Figures on the casement painted,
And exclaimed the shuddering
    baron,
    'Miserere, Domine!'

In that hour of deep contrition
He beheld, with clearer vision,
Through all outward show and
    fashion,
    Justice, the Avenger, rise.

All the pomp of earth had vanished,
Falsehood and deceit were ban-
    ished,
Reason spake more loud than
    passion,
    And the truth wore no disguise.

Every vassal of his banner,
Every serf born to his manor,
All those wronged and wretched
    creatures,
    By his hand were freed again.

And, as on the sacred missal
He recorded their dismissal,
Death relaxed his iron features,
    And the monk replied, 'Amen!'

Many centuries have been num-
    bered
Since in death the baron slumbered
By the convent's sculptured portal,
    Mingling with the common dust:

But the good deed, through the ages
Living in historic pages,
Brighter grows and gleams im-
    mortal,
    Unconsumed by moth or rust.

RAIN IN SUMMER.

How beautiful is the rain!
After the dust and heat,
In the broad and fiery street,
In the narrow lane,
How beautiful is the rain!

How it clatters along the roofs,
Like the tramp of hoofs!
How it gushes and struggles out
From the throat of the overflowing
    spout!

Across the window-pane
It pours and pours;
And swift and wide,
With a muddy tide,
Like a river down the gutter roars
The rain, the welcome rain!

The sick man from his chamber
    looks
At the twisted brooks;
He can feel the cool
Breath of each little pool;
His fevered brain
Grows calm again,
And he breathes a blessing on the
    rain.

From the neighbouring school
Come the boys,
With more than their wonted noise
And commotion;
And down the wet streets
Sail their mimic fleets,
Till the treacherous pool
Ingulfs them in its whirling
And turbulent ocean.

In the country, on every side,
Where far and wide,
Like a leopard's tawny and spotted
    hide,
Stretches the plain,
To the dry grass and the drier grain
How welcome is the rain!

In the furrowed land
The toilsome and patient oxen
    stand;
Lifting the yoke-encumbered head,
With their dilated nostrils spread,
They silently inhale
The clover-scented gale,
And the vapours that arise
From the well-watered and smok-
    ing soil
For this rest in the furrow after toil
Their large and lustrous eyes
Seem to thank the Lord,
More than man's spoken word.

Near at hand,
From under the sheltering trees,
The farmer sees
His pastures, and his fields of grain,
As they bend their tops
To the numberless beating drops
Of the incessant rain.
He counts it as no sin
That he sees therein
Only his own thrift and gain.

These, and far more than these,
The Poet sees!
He can behold
Aquarius old
Walking the fenceless fields of air;
And from each ample fold
Of the clouds about him rolled
Scattering everywhere
The showery rain,
As the farmer scatters his grain.

He can behold
Things manifold
That have not yet been wholly
    told,—
Have not been wholly sung nor said.
For his thought, that never stops,
Follows the water-drops
Down to the graves of the dead,
Down through chasms and gulfs
    profound,
To the dreary fountain-head
Of lakes and rivers under ground;

And sees them, when the rain is
  done,
On the bridge of colours seven
Climbing up once more to heaven,
Opposite the setting sun.

Thus the Seer,
With vision clear,
Sees forms appear and disappear
In the perpetual round of strange
Mysterious change
From birth to death, from death to
  birth,
From earth to heaven, from heaven
  to earth ;
Till glimpses more sublime
Of things, unseen before,
Unto his wondering eyes reveal
The Universe, as an immeasurable
  wheel
Turning for evermore
In the rapid and rushing river of
  Time.

TO A CHILD.

DEAR child ! how radiant on thy
  mother's knee,
With merry-making eyes and
  jocund smiles,
Thou gazest at the painted tiles,
Whose figures grace,
With many a grotesque form and
  face,
The ancient chimney of thy nursery !
The lady with the gay macaw,
The dancing girl, the grave bashaw
With bearded lip and chin ;
And, leaning idly o'er his gate,
Beneath the imperial fan of state,
The Chinese mandarin.

With what a look of proud com-
  mand
Thou shakest in thy little hand
The coral rattle with its silver bells,
Making a merry tune !

Thousands of years in Indian seas
That coral grew, by slow degrees,
Until some deadly and wild mon-
  soon
Dashed it on Coromandel's sand !

Those silver bells
Reposed of yore,
As shapeless ore,
Far down in the deep-sunken wells
Of darksome mines,
In some obscure and sunless place
Beneath huge Chimborazo's base,
Or Potosí's o'erhanging pines !

And thus for thee, O little child,
Through many a danger and
  escape,
The tall ships passed the stormy
  cape ;
For thee in foreign lands remote,
Beneath a burning tropic clime,
The Indian peasant, chasing the
  wild goat,
Himself as swift and wild,
In falling clutched the frail arbute,
The fibres of whose shallow root,
Uplifted from the soil, betrayed
The silver veins beneath it laid,
The buried treasures of the miser
  Time.

But, lo ! thy door is left ajar !
Thou hearest footsteps from afar !
And, at the sound,
Thou turnest round
With quick and questioning eyes,
Like one who, in a foreign land,
Beholds on every hand
Some source of wonder and sur-
  prise !
And, restlessly, impatiently,
Thou strivest, strugglest, to be free.
The four walls of thy nursery
Are now like prison walls to thee.
No more thy mother's smiles,
No more the painted tiles,
Delight thee, nor the playthings
  on the floor,

That won thy little beating heart
before ;
Thou strugglest for the open door.

Through these once solitary halls
Thy pattering footstep falls.
The sound of thy merry voice
Makes the old walls
Jubilant, and they rejoice
With the joy of thy young heart,
O'er the light of whose gladness
No shadows of sadness
From the sombre background of
memory start.

Once, ah, once, within these walls,
One whom memory oft recalls,
The Father of his Country, dwelt.
And yonder meadows broad and
damp
The fires of the besieging camp
Encircled with a burning belt.
Up and down these echoing stairs,
Heavy with the weight of cares,
Sounded his majestic tread ;
Yes, within this very room
Sat he in those hours of gloom,
Weary both in heart and head.

But what are these grave thoughts
to thee ?
Out, out ! into the open air !
Thy only dream is liberty,
Thou carest little how or where.
I see thee eager at thy play,
Now shouting to the apples on the
tree,
With cheeks as round and red as
they ;
And now among the yellow stalks,
Among the flowering shrubs and
plants,
As restless as the bee.
Along the garden walks
The tracks of thy small carriage-
wheels I trace ;
And see at every turn how they
efface

Whole villages of sand-roofed
tents,
That rise like golden domes
Above the cavernous and secret
homes
Of wandering and nomadic tribes
of ants.
Ah, cruel little Tamerlane,
Who, with thy dreadful reign,
Dost persecute and overwhelm
These hapless Troglodytes of thy
realm !

What ! tired already ! with those
suppliant looks,
And voice more beautiful than a
poet's books,
Or murmuring sound of water as
it flows,
Thou comest back to parley with
repose !
This rustic seat in the old apple-tree,
With its o'erhanging golden
canopy
Of leaves illuminate with autumnal
hues,
And shining with the argent light
of dews,
Shall for a season be our place of
rest.
Beneath us, like an oriole's pendent
nest,
From which the laughing birds
have taken wing,
By thee abandoned, hangs thy
vacant swing.
Dream-like the waters of the river
gleam ;
A sailless vessel drops adown the
stream,
And like it, to a sea as wide and
deep,
Thou driftest gently down the tides
of sleep.

O child ! O new-born denizen
Of life's great city ! on thy head
The glory of the morn is shed,
Like a celestial benison !

Here at the portal thou dost
    stand,
And with thy little hand
Thou openest the mysterious gate
Into the future's undiscovered
    land.
I see its valves expand,
As at the touch of Fate !
Into those realms of love and
    hate,
Into that darkness blank and
    drear,
By some prophetic feeling taught,
I launch the bold, adventurous
    thought,
Freighted with hope and fear ;
As upon subterranean streams,
In caverns unexplored and dark,
Men sometimes launch a fragile
    bark,
Laden with flickering fire,
And watch its swift-receding beams,
Until at length they disappear,
And in the distant dark expire.

By what astrology of fear or
    hope
Dare I to cast thy horoscope !
Like the new moon thy life ap-
    pears ;
A little strip of silver light,
And widening outward into night
The shadowy disk of future years ;
And yet upon its outer rim,
A luminous circle, faint and dim,
And scarcely visible to us here,
Rounds and completes the perfect
    sphere ;
A prophecy and intimation,
A pale and feeble adumbration,
Of the great world of light that lies
Behind all human destinies.

Ah ! if thy fate, with anguish
    fraught,
Should be to wet the dusty soil
With the hot tears and sweat of
    toil,—

To struggle with imperious thought,
Until the overburdened brain,
Weary with labour, faint with pain,
Like a jarred pendulum, retain
Only its motion, not its power,—
Remember, in that perilous hour,
When most afflicted and oppressed,
From labour there shall come forth
    rest.

And if a more auspicious fate
On thy advancing steps await,
Still let it ever be thy pride
To linger by the labourer's side ;
With words of sympathy or song
To cheer the dreary march along
Of the great army of the poor,
O'er desert sand, o'er dangerous
    moor,
Nor to thyself the task shall be
Without reward ; for thou shalt
    learn
The wisdom early to discern
True beauty in utility ;
As great Pythagoras of yore,
Standing beside the blacksmith's
    door,
And hearing the hammers, as they
    smote
The anvils with a different note,
Stole from the varying tones that
    hung
Vibrant on every iron tongue,
The secret of the sounding wire,
And formed the seven-chorded
    lyre.

Enough ! I will not play the Seer ;
I will no longer strive to ope
The mystic volume, where appear
The herald Hope, forerunning
    Fear,
And Fear, the pursuivant of Hope.
Thy destiny remains untold ;
For, like Acestes' shaft of old,
The swift thought kindles as it
    flies,
And burns to ashes in the skies.

THE OCCULTATION OF ORION[1].

I SAW, as in a dream sublime,
The balance in the hand of Time.
O'er East and West its beam impended ;
And day, with all its hours of light,
Was slowly sinking out of sight,
While, opposite, the scale of night
Silently with the stars ascended.

Like the astrologers of eld,
In that bright vision I beheld
Greater and deeper mysteries.
I saw, with its celestial keys,
Its chords of air, its frets of fire,
The Samian's great Æolian lyre,
Rising through all its sevenfold bars,
From earth unto the fixed stars.
And through the dewy atmosphere
Not only could I see, but hear,
Its wondrous and harmonious strings,
In sweet vibration, sphere by sphere,
From Dian's circle light and near,
Onward to vaster and wider rings,
Where, chanting through his beard of snows,
Majestic, mournful, Saturn goes,
And down the sunless realms of space
Reverberates the thunder of his bass.

Beneath the sky's triumphal arch
This music sounded like a march,
And with its chorus seemed to be
Preluding some great tragedy.
Sirius was rising in the east ;
And slow ascending one by one
The kindling constellations shone.

Begirt with many a blazing star
Stood the great giant Algebar,
Orion, hunter of the beast !
His sword hung gleaming by his side,
And on his arm the lion's hide
Scattered across the midnight air
The golden radiance of its hair.

The moon was pallid, but not faint ;
And beautiful as some fair saint,
Serenely moving on her way
In hours of trial and dismay.
As if she heard the voice of God,
Unharmed with naked feet she trod
Upon the hot and burning stars,
As on the glowing coals and bars,
That were to prove her strength, and try
Her holiness and her purity.

Thus moving on, with silent pace,
And triumph in her sweet pale face,
She reached the station of Orion.
Aghast he stood in strange alarm !
And suddenly from his outstretched arm
Down fell the red skin of the lion
Into the river at his feet.
His mighty club no longer beat
The forehead of the bull ; but he
Reeled as of yore beside the sea,
When, blinded by Œnopion,
He sought the blacksmith at his forge,
And, climbing up the mountain gorge,
Fixed his blank eyes upon the sun.

Then, through the silence overhead,
An angel with a trumpet said,
'For evermore, for evermore,
The reign of violence is o'er !'
And, like an instrument that flings
Its music on another's strings,
The trumpet of the angel cast
Upon the heavenly lyre its blast,

[1] Astronomically speaking, this title is incorrect, as I apply to a constellation what can properly be applied to some of its stars only. But my observation is made from the hill of song, and not from that of science, and will, I trust, be found sufficiently accurate for the present purpose.

And on from sphere to sphere the
    words
Re-echoed down the burning
    chords,—
' For evermore, for evermore,
The reign of violence is o'er !'

THE BRIDGE.

I STOOD on the bridge at midnight,
    As the clocks were striking the
      hour,
And the moon rose o'er the city
    Behind the dark church-tower.

I saw her bright reflection
    In the waters under me,
Like a golden goblet falling
    And sinking into the sea.

And far in the hazy distance
    Of that lovely night in June,
The blaze of the flaming furnace
    Gleamed redder than the moon.

Among the long black rafters
    The wavering shadows lay,
And the current that came from
    the ocean
    Seemed to lift and bear them
      away,

As, sweeping and eddying through
    them,
    Rose the belated tide,
And, streaming into the moonlight,
    The seaweed floated wide.

And like those waters rushing
    Among the wooden piers
A flood of thoughts came o'er me
    That filled my eyes with tears.

How often, O how often,
    In the days that had gone by,
I had stood on that bridge at mid-
    night
    And gazed on that wave and sky !

How often, O how often,
    I had wished that the ebbing
      tide
Would bear me away on its bosom
    O'er the ocean wild and wide !

For my heart was hot and rest-
    less,
    And my life was full of care,
And the burden laid upon me
    Seemed greater than I could
      bear.

But now it has fallen from me,
    It is buried in the sea ;
And only the sorrow of others
    Throws its shadow over me.

Yet whenever I cross the river
    On its bridge with wooden piers,
Like the odour of brine from the
    ocean
    Comes the thought of other years.

And I think how many thousands
    Of care-encumbered men,
Each bearing his burden of sor-
    row,
    Have crossed the bridge since
      then.

I see the long procession
    Still passing to and fro,
The young heart hot and rest-
    less,
    And the old subdued and slow !

And for ever and for ever,
    As long as the river flows,
As long as the heart has passions,
    As long as life has woes,

The moon and its broken reflec-
    tion
    And its shadows shall appear,
As the symbol of love in heaven,
    And its wavering image here.

TO THE DRIVING CLOUD.

GLOOMY and dark art thou, O chief of the mighty Omahas;
Gloomy and dark as the driving cloud, whose name thou hast taken!
Wrapt in thy scarlet blanket, I see thee stalk through the city's
Narrow and populous streets, as once by the margin of rivers
Stalked those birds unknown, that have left us only their footprints.
What, in a few short years, will remain of thy race but the footprints?
How canst thou walk these streets, who hast trod the green turf of the
  prairies?
How canst thou breathe this air, who hast breathed the sweet air of the
  mountains?
Ah! 'tis in vain that with lordly looks of disdain thou dost challenge
Looks of disdain in return, and question these walls and these pavements,
Claiming the soil for thy hunting-grounds, while down-trodden millions
Starve in the garrets of Europe, and cry from its caverns that they, too,
Have been created heirs of the earth, and claim its division!

Back, then, back to thy woods in the regions west of the Wabash!
There as a monarch thou reignest. In autumn the leaves of the maple
Pave the floors of thy palace-halls with gold, and in summer
Pine-trees waft through its chambers the odorous breath of their branches.
There thou art strong and great, a hero, a tamer of horses!
There thou chasest the stately stag on the banks of the Elkhorn,
Or by the roar of the Running-Water, or where the Omaha
Calls thee, and leaps through the wild ravine like a brave of the Blackfeet!

Hark! what murmurs arise from the heart of those mountainous deserts?
Is it the cry of the Foxes and Crows, or the mighty Behemoth,
Who, unharmed, on his tusks once caught the bolts of the thunder,
And now lurks in his lair to destroy the race of the red man?
Far more fatal to thee and thy race than the Crows and the Foxes,
Far more fatal to thee and thy race than the tread of Behemoth,
Lo! the big thunder-canoe, that steadily breasts the Missouri's
Merciless current! and yonder, afar on the prairies, the camp-fires
Gleam through the night; and the cloud of dust in the gray of the day-
  break
Marks not the buffalo's track, nor the Mandan's dexterous horse-race;
It is a caravan, whitening the desert where dwell the Camanches!
Ha! how the breath of these Saxons and Celts, like the blast of the
  east-wind,
Drifts evermore to the west the scanty smokes of thy wigwams!

Songs and Sonnets.

SEAWEED.

WHEN descends on the Atlantic
 The gigantic
Storm-wind of the equinox,
Landward in his wrath he scourges
 The toiling surges,
Laden with seaweed from the rocks:

From Bermuda's reefs; from edges
 Of sunken ledges,
In some far-off, bright Azore;
From Bahama, and the dashing,
 Silver-flashing
Surges of San Salvador;

From the tumbling surf, that buries
 The Orkneyan skerries,
Answering the hoarse Hebrides;
And from wrecks of ships, and drifting
 Spars, uplifting
On the desolate, rainy seas;—

Ever drifting, drifting, drifting
 On the shifting
Currents of the restless main;
Till in sheltered coves, and reaches
 Of sandy beaches,
All have found repose again.

So when storms of wild emotion
 Strike the ocean
Of the poet's soul, ere long
From each cave and rocky fastness,
 In its vastness,
Floats some fragment of a song:

From the far-off isles enchanted,
 Heaven has planted
With the golden fruit of Truth;

From the flashing surf, whose vision
 Gleams Elysian
In the tropic clime of Youth;

From the strong Will, and the Endeavour
 That for ever
Wrestle with the tides of Fate;
From the wreck of Hopes far-scattered,
 Tempest-shattered,
Floating waste and desolate;—

Ever drifting, drifting, drifting
 On the shifting
Currents of the restless heart;
Till at length in books recorded,
 They, like hoarded
Household words, no more depart.

THE DAY IS DONE.

THE day is done, and the darkness
 Falls from the wings of Night,
As a feather is wafted downward
 From an eagle in his flight.

I see the lights of the village
 Gleam through the rain and the mist,
And a feeling of sadness comes o'er me
 That my soul cannot resist:

A feeling of sadness and longing,
That is not akin to pain.
And resembles sorrow only
As the mist resembles the rain.

Come, read to me some poem,
Some simple and heartfelt lay,
That shall soothe this restless feeling,
And banish the thoughts of day.

Not from the grand old masters,
Not from the bards sublime,
Whose distant footsteps echo
Through the corridors of Time.

For, like strains of martial music,
Their mighty thoughts suggest
Life's endless toil and endeavour;
And to-night I long for rest.

Read from some humbler poet,
Whose songs gushed from his heart,
As showers from the clouds of summer,
Or tears from the eyelids start;

Who, through long days of labour,
And nights devoid of ease,
Still heard in his soul the music
Of wonderful melodies.

Such songs have power to quiet
The restless pulse of care,
And come like the benediction
That follows after prayer.

Then read from the treasured volume
The poem of thy choice,
And lend to the rhyme of the poet
The beauty of thy voice.

And the night shall be filled with music,
And the cares that infest the day
Shall fold their tents, like the Arabs,
And as silently steal away.

AFTERNOON IN FEBRUARY.

THE day is ending,
The night is descending;
The marsh is frozen,
The river dead.

Through clouds like ashes
The red sun flashes
On village windows
That glimmer red.

The snow recommences;
The buried fences
Mark no longer
The road o'er the plain;

While through the meadows,
Like fearful shadows,
Slowly passes
A funeral train.

The bell is pealing,
And every feeling
Within me responds
To the dismal knell;

Shadows are trailing,
My heart is bewailing
And toiling within
Like a funeral bell.

TO AN OLD DANISH SONG-BOOK.

WELCOME, my old friend,
Welcome to a foreign fireside,
While the sullen gales of autumn
Shake the windows.

The ungrateful world
Has, it seems, dealt harshly with thee,
Since, beneath the skies of Denmark,
First I met thee.

There are marks of age,
There are thumb-marks on thy
    margin,
Made by hands that clasped thee
    rudely,
At the alehouse.

Soiled and dull thou art;
Yellow are thy time-worn pages,
As the russet, rain-molested
Leaves of autumn.

Thou art stained with wine
Scattered from hilarious goblets,
As the leaves with the libations
Of Olympus.

Yet dost thou recall
Days departed, half-forgotten,
When in dreamy youth I wandered
By the Baltic,—

When I paused to hear
The old ballad of King Christian
Shouted from suburban taverns
In the twilight.

Thou recallest bards,
Who, in solitary chambers,
And with hearts by passion wasted,
Wrote thy pages.

Thou recallest homes
Where thy songs of love and
    friendship
Made the gloomy Northern winter
Bright as summer.

Once some ancient Scald,
In his bleak, ancestral Iceland,
Chanted staves of these old ballads
To the Vikings.

Once in Elsinore,
At the court of old King Hamlet,
Yorick and his boon companions
Sang these ditties.

Once Prince Frederick's Guard
Sang them in their smoky bar-
    racks;—
Suddenly the English cannon
Joined the chorus!

Peasants in the field,
Sailors on the roaring ocean,
Students, tradesmen, pale me-
    chanics,
All have sung them.

Thou hast been their friend;
They, alas! have left thee friend-
    less!
Yet at least by one warm fireside
Art thou welcome.

And, as swallows build
In these wide, old-fashioned chim-
    neys,
So thy twittering songs shall
    nestle
In my bosom,—

Quiet, close, and warm,
Sheltered from all molestation,
And recalling by their voices
Youth and travel.

WALTER VON DER VOGEL-WEID.

VOGELWEID the Minnesinger,
    When he left this world of
      ours,
Laid his body in the cloister,
    Under Würtzburg's minster
      towers.

And he gave the monks his
    treasures,
    Gave them all with this behest:
They should feed the birds at
    noontide
    Daily on his place of rest;

Saying 'From these wandering minstrels
   I have learned the art of song;
Let me now repay the lessons
   They have taught so well and long.'

Thus the bard of love departed;
   And, fulfilling his desire,
On his tomb the birds were feasted
   By the children of the choir.

Day by day, o'er tower and turret,
   In foul weather and in fair,
Day by day, in vaster numbers,
   Flocked the poets of the air.

On the tree whose heavy branches
   Overshadowed all the place,
On the pavement, on the tomb-
   stone,
   On the poet's sculptured face.

On the cross-bars of each window,
   On the lintel of each door,
They renewed the War of Wart-
   burg,
   Which the bard had fought before.

There they sang their merry carols,
   Sang their lauds on every side;
And the name their voices uttered
   Was the name of Vogelweid.

Till at length the portly abbot
   Murmured, 'Why this waste of food?
Be it changed to loaves hencefor-
   ward
   For our fasting brotherhood.'

Then in vain o'er tower and turret,
   From the walls and woodland nests,
When the minster bells rang noontide,
   Gathered the unwelcome guests.

Then in vain, with cries discordant,
   Clamorous round the Gothic spire
Screamed the feathered Minne-
   singers
   For the children of the choir.

Time has long effaced the inscrip-
   tions
   On the cloister's funeral stones,
And tradition only tells us
   Where repose the poet's bones.

But around the vast cathedral,
   By sweet echoes multiplied,
Still the birds repeat the legend,
   And the name of Vogelweid.

DRINKING SONG.

INSCRIPTION FOR AN ANTIQUE PITCHER.

COME, old friend! sit down and listen!
   From the pitcher, placed between us,
How the waters laugh and glisten
   In the head of old Silenus!

Old Silenus, bloated, drunken,
   Led by his inebriate Satyrs;
On his breast his head is sunken,
   Vacantly he leers and chatters.

Fauns with youthful Bacchus follow;
   Ivy crowns that brow supernal
As the forehead of Apollo,
   And possessing youth eternal.

Round about him, fair Bacchantes,
   Bearing cymbals, flutes, and thyrses,
Wild from Naxian groves, or Zante's
   Vineyards, sing delirious verses.

Thus he won, through all the nations,
  Bloodless victories, and the farmer
Bore, as trophies and oblations,
  Vines for banners, ploughs for armour.

Judged by no o'erzealous rigour,
  Much this mystic throng expresses :
Bacchus was the type of vigour,
  And Silenus of excesses.

These are ancient ethnic revels,
  Of a faith long since forsaken ;
Now the Satyrs, changed to devils,
  Frighten mortals wine-o'ertaken.

Now to rivulets from the mountains
  Point the rods of fortune-tellers ;
Youth perpetual dwells in fountains,—
  Not in flasks, and casks, and cellars.

Claudius, though he sang of flagons
  And huge tankards filled with Rhenish,
From that fiery blood of dragons
  Never would his own replenish.

Even Redi, though he chaunted
  Bacchus in the Tuscan valleys,
Never drank the wine he vaunted
  In his dithyrambic sallies.

Then with water fill the pitcher
  Wreathed about with classic fables ;
Ne'er Falernian threw a richer
  Light upon Lucullus' tables.

Come, old friend, sit down and listen
  As it passes thus between us,
How its wavelets laugh and glisten
  In the head of old Silenus !

THE OLD CLOCK ON THE STAIRS.

L'éternité est une pendule, dont le balancier dit et redit sans cesse ces deux mots seulement, dans le silence des tombeaux :
'Toujours! jamais! Jamais! toujours!'
JACQUES BRIDAINE.

SOMEWHAT back from the village street
Stands the old-fashioned country-seat.
Across its antique portico
Tall poplar-trees their shadows throw ;
And from its station in the hall
An ancient timepiece says to all,—
    'For ever—never !
    Never—for ever !'

Half-way up the stairs it stands,
And points and beckons with its hands
From its case of massive oak,
Like a monk, who, under his cloak,
Crosses himself, and sighs, alas !
With sorrowful voice to all who pass,—
    'For ever—never !
    Never—for ever !'

By day its voice is low and light ;
But in the silent dead of night,
Distinct as a passing footstep's fall,
It echoes along the vacant hall,
Along the ceiling, along the floor,
And seems to say, at each chamber-door,—
    'For ever—never !
    Never—for ever !'

Through days of sorrow and of mirth,
Through days of death and days of birth,

134

Through every swift vicissitude
Of changeful time, unchanged it
  has stood,
And as if, like God, it all things
  saw,
It calmly repeats those words of
  awe,—
    'For ever—never !
    Never—for ever ! '

In that mansion used to be
Free-hearted Hospitality ;
His great fires up the chimney
  roared ;
The stranger feasted at his board ;
But, like the skeleton at the feast,
That warning timepiece never
  ceased,—
    'For ever—never !
    Never—for ever ! '

There groups of merry children
  played,
There youths and maidens dream-
  ing strayed ;
O precious hours ! O golden prime,
And affluence of love and time !
Even as a miser counts his gold,
Those hours the ancient timepiece
  told,—
    'For ever—never !
    Never—for ever ! '

From that chamber, clothed in
  white,
The bride came forth on her wedding night ;
There, in that silent room below,
The dead lay in his shroud of
  snow ;
And in the hush that followed the
  prayer,
Was heard the old clock on the
  stair,—
    'For ever—never !
    Never—for ever ! '

All are scattered now and fled,
Some are married, some are
  dead ;
And when I ask, with throbs of
  pain,
'Ah ! when shall they all meet
  again ? '
As in the days long since gone
  by,
The ancient timepiece makes reply,—
    'For ever—never !
    Never—for ever ! '

Never here, for ever there,
Where all parting, pain, and care,
And death, and time shall disap-
  pear,—
For ever there, but never here !
The horologe of Eternity
Sayeth this incessantly,—
    'For ever—never !
    Never—for ever ! '

THE ARROW AND THE SONG.

I SHOT an arrow into the air,
It fell to earth, I knew not where ;
For, so swiftly it flew, the sight
Could not follow it in its flight.

I breathed a song into the air,
It fell to earth, I knew not where ;
For who has sight so keen and
  strong
That it can follow the flight of
  song ?

Long, long afterward, in an oak
I found the arrow, still unbroke ;
And the song, from beginning to
  end,
I found again in the heart of a
  friend.

SONNETS.

THE EVENING STAR.

Lo! in the painted oriel of the West,
    Whose panes the sunken sun incarnadines,
    Like a fair lady at her casement, shines
    The evening star, the star of love and rest!
And then anon she doth herself divest
    Of all her radiant garments, and reclines
    Behind the sombre screen of yonder pines,
    With slumber and soft dreams of love oppressed.
O my beloved, my sweet Hesperus!
    My morning and my evening star of love!
    My best and gentlest lady! even thus,
As that fair planet in the sky above,
    Dost thou retire unto thy rest at night,
    And from thy darkened window fades the light.

AUTUMN.

Thou comest, Autumn, heralded by the rain,
    With banners, by great gales incessant fanned,
    Brighter than brightest silks of Samarcand,
    And stately oxen harnessed to thy wain!
Thou standest, like imperial Charlemagne,
    Upon thy bridge of gold; thy royal hand
    Outstretched with benedictions o'er the land,
    Blessing the farms through all thy vast domain!
Thy shield is the red harvest moon, suspended
    So long beneath the heaven's o'erhanging eaves;
    Thy steps are by the farmer's prayers attended;
Like flames upon an altar shine the sheaves;
    And, following thee, in thy ovation splendid,
    Thine almoner, the wind, scatters the golden leaves!

DANTE.

Tuscan, that wanderest through the realms of gloom
    With thoughtful pace, and sad, majestic eyes,
    Stern thoughts and awful from thy soul arise,
    Like Farinata from his fiery tomb.
Thy sacred song is like the trump of doom;

Yet in thy heart what human sympathies,
What soft compassion glows, as in the skies
The tender stars their clouded lamps relume!
Methinks I see thee stand, with pallid cheeks,
By Fra Hilario in his diocese,
As up the convent-walls, in golden streaks,
The ascending sunbeams mark the day's decrease;
And, as he asks what there the stranger seeks,
Thy voice along the cloister whispers, 'Peace!'

THE CROSS OF SNOW.

In the long, sleepless watches of the night,
A gentle face—the face of one long dead—
Looks at me from the wall, where round its head
The night-lamp casts a halo of pale light.
Here in this room she died; and soul more white
Never through martyrdom of fire was led
To its repose; nor can in books be read
The legend of a life more benedight.
There is a mountain in the distant West
That, sun-defying, in its deep ravines
Displays a cross of snow upon its side.
Such is the cross I wear upon my breast
These eighteen years, through all the changing scenes
And seasons, changeless since the day she died.

Translations.

THE HEMLOCK TREE.

FROM THE GERMAN.

O HEMLOCK tree! O hemlock tree!
　　how faithful are thy branches!
Green not alone in summer
　　time,
But in the winter's frost and
　　rime!
O hemlock tree! O hemlock tree!
　　how faithful are thy branches!

O maiden fair! O maiden fair! how
　　faithless is thy bosom!
To love me in prosperity,
And leave me in adversity!
O maiden fair! O maiden fair! how
　　faithless is thy bosom!

The nightingale, the nightingale,
　　thou tak'st for thine example!
So long as summer laughs she
　　sings,
But in the autumn spreads her
　　wings.
The nightingale, the nightingale,
　　thou tak'st for thine example!

The meadow brook, the meadow
　　brook, is mirror of thy false-
　　hood!
It flows so long as falls the rain,
In drought its springs soon dry
　　again.
The meadow brook, the meadow
　　brook, is mirror of thy false-
　　hood!

ANNIE OF THARAW.

FROM THE LOW GERMAN OF SIMON
DACH.

ANNIE of Tharaw, my true love of
　　old,
She is my life, and my goods, and
　　my gold.

Annie of Tharaw, her heart once
　　again
To me has surrendered in joy and
　　in pain.

Annie of Tharaw, my riches, my
　　good,
Thou, O my soul, my flesh, and my
　　blood!

Then come the wild weather, come
　　sleet or come snow,
We will stand by each other, how-
　　ever it blow.

Oppression, and sickness, and
　　sorrow, and pain
Shall be to our true love as links to
　　the chain.

As the palm-tree standeth so
　　straight and so tall,
The more the hail beats, and the
　　more the rains fall,—

So love in our hearts shall grow
　　mighty and strong,
Through crosses, through sorrows,
　　through manifold wrong.

Shouldst thou be torn from me to
 wander alone
In a desolate land where the sun is
 scarce known,—

Through forests I 'll follow, and
 where the sea flows,
Through ice, and through iron,
 through armies of foes.

Annie of Tharaw, my light and my
 sun,
The threads of our two lives are
 woven in one.

Whate'er I have bidden thee thou
 hast obeyed,
Whatever forbidden thou hast not
 gainsaid.

How in the turmoil of life can love
 stand,
Where there is not one heart, and
 one mouth, and one hand?

Some seek for dissension, and
 trouble, and strife;
Like a dog and a cat live such man
 and wife.

Annie of Tharaw, such is not our
 love;
Thou art my lambkin, my chick,
 and my dove.

Whate'er my desire is, in thine
 may be seen;
I am king of the household, and
 thou art its queen.

It is this, O my Annie, my heart's
 sweetest rest,
That makes of us twain but one
 soul in one breast.

This turns to a heaven the hut
 where we dwell;
While wrangling soon changes a
 home to a hell.

THE STATUE OVER THE CATHEDRAL DOOR.

FROM THE GERMAN OF JULIUS
MOSEN.

FORMS of saints and kings are
 standing
 The cathedral door above;
Yet I saw but one among them
 Who had soothed my soul with
 love.

In his mantle, wound about him
 As their robes the sowers
 wind,
Bore he swallows and their fledg-
 lings,
 Flowers and weeds of every kind.

And so stands he calm and child-
 like,
 High in wind and tempest wild;
O, were I like him exalted,
 I would be like him, a child!

And my songs—green leaves and
 blossoms—
 To the doors of heaven would
 bear,
Calling even in storm and tempest,
 Round me still these birds of
 air.

THE LEGEND OF THE CROSSBILL.

FROM THE GERMAN OF JULIUS
MOSEN.

ON the cross the dying Saviour
 Heavenward lifts his eyelids
 calm,
Feels, but scarcely feels, a trembling
 In his pierced and bleeding
 palm.

And by all the world forsaken,
  Sees he how with zealous care
At the ruthless nail of iron
  A little bird is striving there.

Stained with blood and never
    tiring,
  With its beak it doth not cease,
From the cross 't would free the
    Saviour,
  Its Creator's Son release.

And the Saviour speaks in mild-
    ness :
  'Blest be thou of all the good !
Bear, as token of this moment,
  Marks of blood and holy rood !'

And that bird is called the cross-
    bill ;
  Covered all with blood so clear,
In the groves of pine it singeth
  Songs, like legends, strange to
    hear.

—++—

THE SEA HATH ITS PEARLS.

FROM THE GERMAN OF HEIN-
RICH HEINE.

THE sea hath its pearls,
  The heaven hath its stars ;
But my heart, my heart,
  My heart hath its love.

Great are the sea and the heaven ;
  Yet greater is my heart,
And fairer than pearls and stars
  Flashes and beams my love.

Thou little, youthful maiden,
  Come unto my great heart ;
My heart, and the sea, and the
    heaven
  Are melting away with love !

POETIC APHORISMS.

FROM THE SINNGEDICHTE OF
FRIEDRICH VON LOGAU.

SEVENTEENTH CENTURY.

MONEY.

WHEREUNTO is money good ?
Who has it not wants hardihood,
Who has it has much trouble and
    care,
Who once has had it has despair.

THE BEST MEDICINES.

JOY and Temperance and Repose
Slam the door on the doctor's nose.

SIN.

MAN-LIKE is it to fall into sin,
Fiend-like is it to dwell therein,
Christ-like is it for sin to grieve,
God-like is it all sin to leave.

POVERTY AND BLINDNESS.

A BLIND man is a poor man, and
    blind a poor man is ;
For the former seeth no man, and
    the latter no man sees.

LAW OF LIFE.

LIVE I, so live I,
To my Lord heartily,
To my Prince faithfully,
To my Neighbour honestly.
Die I, so die I.

CREEDS.

LUTHERAN, Popish, Calvinistic,
    all these creeds and doctrines
    three
Extant are ; but still the doubt is,
    where Christianity may be.

THE RESTLESS HEART.

A MILLSTONE and the human heart
    are driven ever round ;
If they have nothing else to grind,
    they must themselves be
    ground.

CHRISTIAN LOVE.

WHILOM Love was like a fire, and
warmth and comfort it bespoke;
But, alas ! it now is quenched, and
only bites us, like the smoke.

ART AND TACT.

INTELLIGENCE and courtesy not
always are combined ;
Often in a wooden house a golden
room we find.

RETRIBUTION.

THOUGH the mills of God grind
slowly, yet they grind exceeding small ;
Though with patience he stands
waiting, with exactness grinds
he all.

TRUTH.

WHEN by night the frogs are
croaking, kindle but a torch's
fire,
Ha ! how soon they all are silent !
Thus Truth silences the liar.

RHYMES.

IF perhaps these rhymes of mine
should sound not well in
strangers' ears,
They have only to bethink them
that it happens so with theirs ;
For so long as words, like mortals,
call a fatherland their own,
They will be most highly valued
where they are best and
longest known.

Evangeline.

A TALE OF ACADIE.

——•◦•——

THIS is the forest primeval. The murmuring pines and the hemlocks,
Bearded with moss, and in garments green, indistinct in the twilight,
Stand like Druids of eld, with voices sad and prophetic,
Stand like harpers hoar, with beards that rest on their bosoms.
Loud from its rocky caverns, the deep-voiced neighbouring ocean
Speaks, and in accents disconsolate answers the wail of the forest.

This is the forest primeval; but where are the hearts that beneath it
Leaped like the roe, when he hears in the woodland the voice of the
    huntsman?
Where is the thatch-roofed village, the home of Acadian farmers,—
Men whose lives glided on like rivers that water the woodlands,
Darkened by shadows of earth, but reflecting an image of heaven?
Waste are those pleasant farms, and the farmers for ever departed!
Scattered like dust and leaves, when the mighty blasts of October
Seize them, and whirl them aloft, and sprinkle them far o'er the ocean;
Naught but tradition remains of the beautiful village of Grand-Pré.

Ye who believe in affection that hopes, and endures, and is patient,
Ye who believe in the beauty and strength of woman's devotion,
List to the mournful tradition still sung by the pines of the forest;
List to a Tale of Love in Acadie, home of the happy.

PART THE FIRST.

I.

IN the Acadian land, on the shores of the Basin of Minas,
Distant, secluded, still, the little village of Grand-Pré
Lay in the fruitful valley. Vast meadows stretched to the eastward,
Giving the village its name, and pasture to flocks without number.
Dikes, that the hands of the farmers had raised with labour incessant,
Shut out the turbulent tides; but at stated seasons the flood-gates
Opened, and welcomed the sea to wander at will o'er the meadows.
West and south there were fields of flax, and orchards and cornfields
Spreading afar and unfenced o'er the plain; and away to the northward
Blomidon rose, and the forests old, and aloft on the mountains
Sea-fogs pitched their tents, and mists from the mighty Atlantic
Looked on the happy valley, but ne'er from their station descended.
There, in the midst of its farms, reposed the Acadian village.

Strongly built were the houses, with frames of oak and of hemlock,
Such as the peasants of Normandy built in the reign of the Henries.
Thatched were the roofs, with dormer-windows; and gables projecting
Over the basement below protected and shaded the doorway.
There in the tranquil evenings of summer, when brightly the sunset
Lighted the village street and gilded the vanes on the chimneys,
Matrons and maidens sat in snow-white caps and in kirtles
Scarlet and blue and green, with distaffs spinning the golden
Flax for the gossiping looms, whose noisy shuttles within doors
Mingled their sound with the whir of the wheels and the songs of the
    maidens.
Solemnly down the street came the parish priest, and the children
Paused in their play to kiss the hand he extended to bless them.
Reverend walked he among them; and up rose matrons and maidens,
Hailing his slow approach with words of affectionate welcome.
Then came the labourers home from the field, and serenely the sun sank
Down to his rest, and twilight prevailed. Anon from the belfry
Softly the Angelus sounded, and over the roofs of the village
Columns of pale blue smoke, like clouds of incense ascending,
Rose from a hundred hearths, the homes of peace and contentment.
Thus dwelt together in love these simple Acadian farmers,—
Dwelt in the love of God and of man. Alike were they free from
Fear, that reigns with the tyrant, and envy, the vice of republics.
Neither locks had they to their doors, nor bars to their windows;
But their dwellings were open as day and the hearts of their owners;
There the richest was poor, and the poorest lived in abundance.

  Somewhat apart from the village, and nearer the Basin of Minas,
Benedict Bellefontaine, the wealthiest farmer of Grand-Pré,
Dwelt on his goodly acres; and with him, directing his household,
Gentle Evangeline lived, his child, and the pride of the village.
Stalworth and stately in form was the man of seventy winters;
Hearty and hale was he, an oak that is covered with snow-flakes;
White as the snow were his locks, and his cheeks as brown as the oak-
    leaves.
Fair was she to behold, that maiden of seventeen summers.
Black were her eyes as the berry that grows on the thorn by the wayside,
Black, yet how softly they gleamed beneath the brown shade of her tresses!
Sweet was her breath as the breath of kine that feed in the meadows.
When in the harvest heat she bore to the reapers at noontide
Flagons of home-brewed ale, ah! fair in sooth was the maiden.
Fairer was she when, on Sunday morn, while the bell from its turret
Sprinkled with holy sounds the air, as the priest with his hyssop
Sprinkles the congregation and scatters blessings upon them,
Down the long street she passed, with her chaplet of beads and her missal
Wearing her Norman cap and her kirtle of blue, and her ear-rings,
Brought in the olden time from France, and since, as an heirloom,
Handed down from mother to child, through long generations.

But a celestial brightness—a more ethereal beauty—
Shone on her face and encircled her form, when, after confession,
Homeward serenely she walked with God's benediction upon her.
When she had passed, it seemed like the ceasing of exquisite music.

Firmly builded with rafters of oak, the house of the farmer
Stood on the side of a hill commanding the sea; and a shady
Sycamore grew by the door, with a woodbine wreathing around it.
Rudely carved was the porch, with seats beneath; and a footpath
Led through an orchard wide, and disappeared in the meadow.
Under the sycamore-tree were hives overhung by a penthouse,
Such as the traveller sees in regions remote by the roadside,
Built o'er a box for the poor, or the blessed image of Mary.
Farther down, on the slope of the hill, was the well with its moss-grown
Bucket, fastened with iron, and near it a trough for the horses.
Shielding the house from storms, on the north, were the barns and the
    farm-yard.
There stood the broad-wheeled wains and the antique ploughs and the
    harrows;
There were the folds for the sheep; and there, in his feathered seraglio,
Strutted the lordly turkey, and crowed the cock, with the selfsame
Voice that in ages of old had startled the penitent Peter.
Bursting with hay were the barns, themselves a village. In each one
Far o'er the gable projected a roof of thatch; and a staircase,
Under the sheltering eaves, led up to the odorous corn-loft.
There too the dove-cot stood, with its meek and innocent inmates
Murmuring ever of love; while above in the variant breezes
Numberless noisy weathercocks rattled and sang of mutation.

Thus, at peace with God and the world, the farmer of Grand-Pré
Lived on his sunny farm, and Evangeline governed his household.
Many a youth, as he knelt in the church and opened his missal,
Fixed his eyes upon her as the saint of his deepest devotion;
Happy was he who might touch her hand or the hem of her garment!
Many a suitor came to her door, by the darkness befriended,
And, as he knocked and waited to hear the sound of her footsteps,
Knew not which beat the louder, his heart or the knocker of iron;
Or at the joyous feast of the Patron Saint of the village,
Bolder grew, and pressed her hand in the dance as he whispered
Hurried words of love, that seemed a part of the music.
But, among all who came, young Gabriel only was welcome;
Gabriel Lajeunesse, the son of Basil the blacksmith,
Who was a mighty man in the village, and honoured of all men;
For, since the birth of time, throughout all ages and nations,
Has the craft of the smith been held in repute by the people.
Basil was Benedict's friend. Their children from earliest childhood
Grew up together as brother and sister; and Father Felician,
Priest and pedagogue both in the village, had taught them their letters

Out of the self-same book, with the hymns of the church and the plain-
song.
But when the hymn was sung, and the daily lesson completed,
Swiftly they hurried away to the forge of Basil the blacksmith.
There at the door they stood, with wondering eyes to behold him
Take in his leathern lap the hoof of the horse as a plaything,
Nailing the shoe in its place ; while near him the tire of the cart-wheel
Lay like a fiery snake, coiled round in a circle of cinders.
Oft on autumnal eves, when without in the gathering darkness
Bursting with light seemed the smithy, through every cranny and crevice,
Warm by the forge within they watched the labouring bellows,
And as its panting ceased, and the sparks expired in the ashes,
Merrily laughed, and said they were nuns going into the chapel.
Oft on sledges in winter, as swift as the swoop of the eagle,
Down the hillside bounding, they glided away o'er the meadow.
Oft in the barns they climbed to the populous nests on the rafters,
Seeking with eager eyes that wondrous stone, which the swallow
Brings from the shore of the sea to restore the sight of its fledglings :
Lucky was he who found that stone in the nest of the swallow !
Thus passed a few swift years, and they no longer were children.
He was a valiant youth, and his face, like the face of the morning,
Gladdened the earth with its light, and ripened thought into action.
She was a woman now, with the heart and hopes of a woman.
'Sunshine of Saint Eulalie' was she called ; for that was the sunshine
Which, as the farmers believed, would load their orchards with apples :
She, too, would bring to her husband's house delight and abundance,
Filling it full of love and the ruddy faces of children.

II.

Now had the season returned, when the nights grow colder and longer,
And the retreating sun the sign of the Scorpion enters.
Birds of passage sailed through the leaden air, from the ice-bound,
Desolate northern bays to the shores of tropical islands.
Harvests were gathered in ; and wild with the winds of September
Wrestled the trees of the forest, as Jacob of old with the angel.
All the signs foretold a winter long and inclement.
Bees, with prophetic instinct of want, had hoarded their honey
Till the hives overflowed ; and the Indian hunters asserted
Cold would the winter be, for thick was the fur of the foxes.
Such was the advent of autumn. Then followed that beautiful season,
Called by the pious Acadian peasants the Summer of All-Saints !
Filled was the air with a dreamy and magical light ; and the landscape
Lay as if new-created in all the freshness of childhood.
Peace seemed to reign upon earth, and the restless heart of the ocean
Was for a moment consoled. All sounds were in harmony blended.
Voices of children at play, the crowing of cocks in the farmyards,
Whir of wings in the drowsy air, and the cooing of pigeons,

All were subdued and low as the murmurs of love, and the great sun
Looked with the eye of love through the golden vapours around him ;
While arrayed in its robes of russet and scarlet and yellow,
Bright with the sheen of the dew, each glittering tree of the forest
Flashed like the plane-tree the Persian adorned with mantles and jewels.

Now recommenced the reign of rest and affection and stillness.
Day with its burden and heat had departed, and twilight descending
Brought back the evening star to the sky, and the herds to the homestead.
Pawing the ground they came, and resting their necks on each other,
And with their nostrils distended inhaling the freshness of evening.
Foremost, bearing the bell, Evangeline's beautiful heifer,
Proud of her snow-white hide, and the ribbon that waved from her collar,
Quietly paced and slow, as if conscious of human affection.
Then came the shepherd back with his bleating flocks from the seaside,
Where was their favourite pasture. Behind them followed the watch-dog,
Patient, full of importance, and grand in the pride of his instinct,
Walking from side to side with a lordly air, and superbly
Waving his bushy tail, and urging forward the stragglers ;
Regent of flocks was he when the shepherd slept ; their protector,
When from the forest at night, through the starry silence, the wolves
    howled.
Late, with the rising moon, returned the wains from the marshes,
Laden with briny hay, that filled the air with its odour.
Cheerily neighed the steeds, with dew on their manes and their fetlocks,
While aloft on their shoulders the wooden and ponderous saddles,
Painted with brilliant dyes, and adorned with tassels of crimson,
Nodded in bright array, like hollyhocks heavy with blossoms.
Patiently stood the cows meanwhile, and yielded their udders
Unto the milkmaid's hand ; whilst loud and in regular cadence
Into the sounding pails the foaming streamlets descended.
Lowing of cattle and peals of laughter were heard in the farmyard,
Echoed back by the barns. Anon they sank into stillness ;
Heavily closed, with a jarring sound, the valves of the barn-doors,
Rattled the wooden bars, and all for a season was silent.

Indoors, warm by the wide-mouthed fireplace, idly the farmer
Sat in his elbow-chair, and watched how the flames and the smoke-
    wreaths
Struggled together like foes in a burning city. Behind him,
Nodding and mocking along the wall, with gestures fantastic,
Darted his own huge shadow, and vanished away into darkness.
Faces, clumsily carved in oak, on the back of his arm-chair
Laughed in the flickering light, and the pewter plates on the dresser
Caught and reflected the flame, as shields of armies the sunshine.
Fragments of song the old man sang, and carols of Christmas,
Such as at home, in the olden time, his fathers before him
Sang in their Norman orchards and bright Burgundian vineyards.

Close at her father's side was the gentle Evangeline seated,
Spinning flax for the loom, that stood in the corner behind her.
Silent awhile were its treadles, at rest was its diligent shuttle,
While the monotonous drone of the wheel, like the drone of a bagpipe,
Followed the old man's song, and united the fragments together.
As in a church, when the chant of the choir at intervals ceases,
Footfalls are heard in the aisles, or words of the priest at the altar,
So, in each pause of the song, with measured motion the clock clicked.

Thus as they sat, there were footsteps heard, and, suddenly lifted,
Sounded the wooden latch, and the door swung back on its hinges.
Benedict knew by the hob-nailed shoes it was Basil the blacksmith,
And by her beating heart Evangeline knew who was with him.
'Welcome!' the farmer exclaimed, as their footsteps paused on the
      threshold,
'Welcome, Basil, my friend! Come, take thy place on the settle
Close by the chimney-side, which is always empty without thee;
Take from the shelf overhead thy pipe and the box of tobacco;
Never so much thyself art thou as when through the curling
Smoke of the pipe or the forge thy friendly and jovial face gleams
Round and red as the harvest moon through the mist of the marshes.'
Then, with a smile of content, thus answered Basil the blacksmith,
Taking with easy air the accustomed seat by the fireside :—
'Benedict Bellefontaine, thou hast ever thy jest and thy ballad!
Ever in cheerfullest mood art thou, when others are filled with
Gloomy forebodings of ill, and see only ruin before them.
Happy art thou, as if every day thou hadst picked up a horseshoe.'
Pausing a moment, to take the pipe that Evangeline brought him,
And with a coal from the embers had lighted, he slowly continued :—
'Four days now are passed since the English ships at their anchors
Ride in the Gaspereau's mouth, with their cannon pointed against us.
What their design may be is unknown; but all are commanded
On the morrow to meet in the church, where his Majesty's mandate
Will be proclaimed as law in the land. Alas! in the meantime
Many surmises of evil alarm the hearts of the people.'
Then made answer the farmer :—' Perhaps some friendlier purpose
Brings these ships to our shores. Perhaps the harvests in England
By untimely rains or untimelier heat have been blighted,
And from our bursting barns they would feed their cattle and children.'
'Not so thinketh the folk in the village,' said, warmly, the blacksmith,
Shaking his head, as in doubt; then, heaving a sigh, he continued :—
'Louisburg is not forgotten, nor Beau Séjour, nor Port Royal.
Many already have fled to the forest, and lurk on its outskirts,
Waiting with anxious hearts the dubious fate of to-morrow.
Arms have been taken from us, and warlike weapons of all kinds;
Nothing is left but the blacksmith's sledge and the scythe of the mower.'
Then with a pleasant smile made answer the jovial farmer :—
'Safer are we unarmed, in the midst of our flocks and our cornfields,

Safer within these peaceful dikes, besieged by the ocean,
Than our fathers in forts, besieged by the enemy's cannon.
Fear no evil, my friend, and to-night may no shadow of sorrow
Fall on this house and hearth; for this is the night of the contract.
Built are the house and the barn. The merry lads of the village
Strongly have built them and well; and, breaking the glebe round about
    them,
Filled the barn with hay, and the house with food for a twelvemonth.
René Leblanc will be here anon, with his papers and inkhorn.
Shall we not then be glad, and rejoice in the joy of our children?'
As apart by the window she stood, with her hand in her lover's,
Blushing Evangeline heard the words that her father had spoken,
And, as they died on his lips, the worthy notary entered.

III.

Bent like a labouring oar, that toils in the surf of the ocean,
Bent, but not broken, by age was the form of the notary public;
Shocks of yellow hair, like the silken floss of the maize, hung
Over his shoulders; his forehead was high; and glasses with horn bows
Sat astride on his nose, with a look of wisdom supernal.
Father of twenty children was he, and more than a hundred
Children's children rode on his knee, and heard his great watch tick.
Four long years in the times of the war had he languished a captive,
Suffering much in an old French fort as the friend of the English.
Now, though warier grown, without all guile or suspicion,
Ripe in wisdom was he, but patient, and simple, and childlike.
He was beloved by all, and most of all by the children;
For he told them tales of the Loup-garou in the forest,
And of the goblin that came in the night to water the horses,
And of the white Létiche, the ghost of a child who unchristened
Died, and was doomed to haunt unseen the chambers of children;
And how on Christmas eve the oxen talked in the stable,
And how the fever was cured by a spider shut up in a nutshell,
And of the marvellous powers of four-leaved clover and horseshoes,
With whatsoever else was writ in the lore of the village.
Then up rose from his seat by the fireside Basil the blacksmith,
Knocked from his pipe the ashes, and slowly extending his right hand,
'Father Leblanc,' he exclaimed, 'thou hast heard the talk in the village,
And, perchance, canst tell us some news of these ships and their errand.'
Then with modest demeanour made answer the notary public,—
'Gossip enough have I heard, in sooth, yet am never the wiser;
And what their errand may be I know not better than others.
Yet am I not of those who imagine some evil intention
Brings them here, for we are at peace; and why then molest us?'
'God's name!' shouted the hasty and somewhat irascible blacksmith;
'Must we in all things look for the how, and the why, and the wherefore?
Daily injustice is done, and might is the right of the strongest!'

But, without heeding his warmth, continued the notary public,—
'Man is unjust, but God is just ; and finally justice
Triumphs ; and well I remember a story, that often consoled me,
When as a captive I lay in the old French fort at Port Royal.'
This was the old man's favourite tale, and he loved to repeat it
When his neighbours complained that any injustice was done them.
'Once in an ancient city, whose name I no longer remember,
Raised aloft on a column, a brazen statue of Justice
Stood in the public square, upholding the scales in its left hand,
And in its right a sword, as an emblem that justice presided
Over the laws of the land, and the hearts and homes of the people.
Even the birds had built their nests in the scales of the balance,
Having no fear of the sword that flashed in the sunshine above them.
But in the course of time the laws of the land were corrupted ;
Might took the place of right, and the weak were oppressed, and the
       mighty
Ruled with an iron rod. Then it chanced in a nobleman's palace
That a necklace of pearls was lost, and ere long a suspicion
Fell on an orphan girl who lived as maid in the household.
She, after form of trial condemned to die on the scaffold,
Patiently met her doom at the foot of the statue of Justice.
As to her Father in heaven her innocent spirit ascended,
Lo ! o'er the city a tempest rose ; and the bolts of the thunder
Smote the statue of bronze, and hurled in wrath from its left hand
Down on the pavement below the clattering scales of the balance,
And in the hollow thereof was found the nest of a magpie,
Into whose clay-built walls the necklace of pearls was inwoven.'
Silenced, but not convinced, when the story was ended, the blacksmith
Stood like a man who fain would speak, but findeth no language ;
All his thoughts were congealed into lines in his face, as the vapours
Freeze in fantastic shapes on the window-panes in the winter.

    Then Evangeline lighted the brazen lamp on the table,
Filled, till it overflowed, the pewter tankard with home-brewed
Nut-brown ale, that was famed for its strength in the village of Grand-
       Pré :
While from his pocket the notary drew his papers and inkhorn,
Wrote with a steady hand the date and the age of the parties,
Naming the dower of the bride in flocks of sheep and in cattle.
Orderly all things proceeded, and duly and well were completed,
And the great seal of the law was set like a sun on the margin.
Then from his leathern pouch the farmer threw on the table
Three times the old man's fee in solid pieces of silver ;
And the notary rising, and blessing the bride and the bridegroom,
Lifted aloft the tankard of ale and drank to their welfare.
Wiping the foam from his lip, he solemnly bowed and departed,
While in silence the others sat and mused by the fireside,
Till Evangeline brought the draught-board out of its corner.

Soon was the game begun. In friendly contention the old men
Laughed at each lucky hit, or unsuccessful manœuvre,
Laughed when a man was crowned, or a breach was made in the king-row.
Meanwhile apart, in the twilight gloom of a window's embrasure,
Sat the lovers, and whispered together, beholding the moon rise
Over the pallid sea and the silvery mist of the meadows.
Silently one by one, in the infinite meadows of heaven,
Blossomed the lovely stars, the forget-me-nots of the angels.

Thus was the evening passed. Anon the bell from the belfry
Rang out the hour of nine, the village curfew, and straightway
Rose the guests and departed; and silence reigned in the household.
Many a farewell word and sweet good-night on the doorstep
Lingered long in Evangeline's heart, and filled it with gladness.
Carefully then were covered the embers that glowed on the hearthstone,
And on the oaken stairs resounded the tread of the farmer.
Soon with a soundless step the foot of Evangeline followed.
Up the staircase moved a luminous space in the darkness,
Lighted less by the lamp than the shining face of the maiden.
Silent she passed the hall, and entered the door of her chamber.
Simple that chamber was, with its curtains of white, and its clothes-press
Ample and high, on whose spacious shelves were carefully folded
Linen and woollen stuffs, by the hand of Evangeline woven.
This was the precious dower she would bring to her husband in marriage,
Better than flocks and herds, being proofs of her skill as a housewife.
Soon she extinguished her lamp, for the mellow and radiant moonlight
Streamed through the windows, and lighted the room, till the heart of
    the maiden
Swelled and obeyed its power, like the tremulous tides of the ocean.
Ah! she was fair, exceeding fair to behold, as she stood with
Naked snow-white feet on the gleaming floor of her chamber!
Little she dreamed that below, among the trees of the orchard,
Waited her lover and watched for the gleam of her lamp and her shadow.
Yet were her thoughts of him, and at times a feeling of sadness
Passed o'er her soul, as the sailing shade of clouds in the moonlight
Flitted across the floor and darkened the room for a moment.
And, as she gazed from the window, she saw serenely the moon pass
Forth from the folds of a cloud, and one star follow her footsteps,
As out of Abraham's tent young Ishmael wandered with Hagar!

IV.

Pleasantly rose next morn the sun on the village of Grand-Pré.
Pleasantly gleamed in the soft, sweet air the Basin of Minas,
Where the ships, with their wavering shadows, were riding at anchor.
Life had long been astir in the village, and clamorous labour
Knocked with its hundred hands at the golden gates of the morning.
Now from the country around, from the farms and neighbouring hamlets,
Came in their holiday dresses the blithe Acadian peasants.

Many a glad good-morrow and jocund laugh from the young folk
Made the bright air brighter, as up from the numerous meadows,
Where no path could be seen but the track of wheels in the greensward,
Group after group appeared, and joined, or passed on the highway.
Long ere noon, in the village all sounds of labour were silenced.
Thronged were the streets with people ; and noisy groups at the house-
  doors
Sat in the cheerful sun, and rejoiced and gossiped together.
Every house was an inn, where all were welcomed and feasted ;
For with this simple people, who lived like brothers together,
All things were held in common, and what one had was another's.
Yet under Benedict's roof hospitality seemed more abundant :
For Evangeline stood among the guests of her father ;
Bright was her face with smiles, and words of welcome and gladness
Fell from her beautiful lips, and blessed the cup as she gave it.

Under the open sky, in the odorous air of the orchard,
Stript of its golden fruit, was spread the feast of betrothal.
There in the shade of the porch were the priest and the notary seated ;
There good Benedict sat, and sturdy Basil the blacksmith.
Not far withdrawn from these, by the cider-press and the beehives,
Michael the fiddler was placed, with the gayest of hearts and of waist-
  coats.
Shadow and light from the leaves alternately played on his snow-white
Hair, as it waved in the wind ; and the jolly face of the fiddler
Glowed like a living coal when the ashes are blown from the embers.
Gaily the old man sang to the vibrant sound of his fiddle,
Tous les Bourgeois de Chartres, and *Le Carillon de Dunkerque*,
And anon with his wooden shoes beat time to the music.
Merrily, merrily whirled the wheels of the dizzying dances
Under the orchard-trees and down the path to the meadows ;
Old folk and young together, and children mingled among them.
Fairest of all the maids was Evangeline, Benedict's daughter !
Noblest of all the youths was Gabriel, son of the blacksmith !

So passed the morning away. And lo ! with a summons sonorous
Sounded the bell from its tower, and over the meadows a drum beat.
Thronged ere long was the church with men. Without, in the churchyard,
Waited the women. They stood by the graves, and hung on the head-
  stones
Garlands of autumn-leaves and evergreens fresh from the forest.
Then came the guard from the ships, and marching proudly among them
Entered the sacred portal. With loud and dissonant clangour
Echoed the sound of their brazen drums from ceiling and casement,—
Echoed a moment only, and slowly the ponderous portal
Closed, and in silence the crowd awaited the will of the soldiers.
Then uprose their commander, and spake from the steps of the altar,
Holding aloft in his hands, with its seals, the royal commission.

'You are convened this day,' he said, 'by his Majesty's orders.
Clement and kind has he been ; but how you have answered his kindness,
Let your own hearts reply ! To my natural make and my temper
Painful the task is I do, which to you I know must be grievous.
Yet must I bow and obey, and deliver the will of our monarch ;
Namely, that all your lands, and dwellings, and cattle of all kinds
Forfeited be to the crown ; and that you yourselves from this province
Be transported to other lands. God grant you may dwell there
Ever as faithful subjects, a happy and peaceable people !
Prisoners now I declare you ; for such is his Majesty's pleasure !'
As, when the air is serene in the sultry solstice of summer,
Suddenly gathers a storm, and the deadly sling of the hailstones
Beats down the farmer's corn in the field and shatters his windows,
Hiding the sun, and strewing the ground with thatch from the house-
    roofs,
Bellowing fly the herds, and seek to break their enclosures ;
So on the hearts of the people descended the words of the speaker.
Silent a moment they stood in speechless wonder, and then rose
Louder and ever louder a wail of sorrow and anger,
And, by one impulse moved, they madly rushed to the doorway.
Vain was the hope of escape ; and cries and fierce imprecations
Rang through the house of prayer ; and high o'er the heads of the others
Rose, with his arms uplifted, the figure of Basil the blacksmith,
As, on a stormy sea, a spar is tossed by the billows.
Flushed was his face and distorted with passion ; and wildly he shouted,—
'Down with the tyrants of England ! we never have sworn them
    allegiance !
Death to these foreign soldiers, who seize on our homes and our
    harvests !'
More he fain would have said, but the merciless hand of a soldier
Smote him upon the mouth, and dragged him down to the pavement.

    In the midst of the strife and tumult of angry contention,
Lo ! the door of the chancel opened, and Father Felician
Entered, with serious mien, and ascended the steps of the altar.
Raising his reverend hand, with a gesture he awed into silence
All that clamorous throng ; and thus he spake to his people ;
Deep were his tones and solemn ; in accents measured and mournful
Spake he, as, after the tocsin's alarum, distinctly the clock strikes.
'What is this that ye do, my children ? what madness has seized you ?
Forty years of my life have I laboured among you, and taught you,
Not in word alone, but in deed, to love one another !
Is this the fruit of my toils, of my vigils and prayers and privations ?
Have you so soon forgotten all lessons of love and forgiveness ?
This is the house of the Prince of Peace, and would you profane it
Thus with violent deeds and hearts overflowing with hatred ?
Lo ! where the crucified Christ from His cross is gazing upon you !
See ! in those sorrowful eyes what meekness and holy compassion !

Hark! how those lips still repeat the prayer, "O Father, forgive them!"
Let us repeat that prayer in the hour when the wicked assail us,
Let us repeat it now, and say, "O Father, forgive them!"
Few were his words of rebuke, but deep in the hearts of his people
Sank they, and sobs of contrition succeeded the passionate outbreak,
While they repeated his prayer, and said, 'O Father, forgive them!'

Then came the evening service. The tapers gleamed from the altar.
Fervent and deep was the voice of the priest, and the people responded,
Not with their lips alone, but their hearts; and the Ave Maria
Sang they, and fell on their knees, and their souls, with devotion translated
Rose on the ardour of prayer, like Elijah ascending to heaven.

Meanwhile had spread in the village the tidings of ill, and on all sides
Wandered, wailing, from house to house the women and children.
Long at her father's door Evangeline stood, with her right hand
Shielding her eyes from the level rays of the sun, that, descending,
Lighted the village street with mysterious splendour, and roofed each
Peasant's cottage with golden thatch, and emblazoned its windows.
Long within had been spread the snow-white cloth on the table;
There stood the wheaten loaf, and the honey fragrant with wild-flowers;
There stood the tankard of ale, and the cheese fresh brought from the dairy;
And, at the head of the board, the great arm-chair of the farmer.
Thus did Evangeline wait at her father's door, as the sunset
Threw the long shadows of trees o'er the broad ambrosial meadows.
Ah! on her spirit within a deeper shadow had fallen,
And from the fields of her soul a fragrance celestial ascended,—
Charity, meekness, love, and hope, and forgiveness, and patience!
Then, all-forgetful of self, she wandered into the village,
Cheering with looks and words the mournful hearts of the women,
As o'er the darkening fields with lingering steps they departed,
Urged by their household cares, and the weary feet of their children.
Down sank the great red sun, and in golden, glimmering vapours
Veiled the light of his face, like the Prophet descending from Sinai.
Sweetly over the village the bell of the Angelus sounded.

Meanwhile, amid the gloom, by the church Evangeline lingered.
All was silent within; and in vain at the door and the windows
Stood she, and listened and looked, till, overcome by emotion,
'Gabriel!' cried she aloud with tremulous voice; but no answer
Came from the graves of the dead, nor the gloomier grave of the living.
Slowly at length she returned to the tenantless house of her father.
Smouldered the fire on the hearth, on the board was the supper untasted,
Empty and drear was each room, and haunted with phantoms of terror.
Sadly echoed her step on the stair and the floor of her chamber.
In the dead of the night she heard the disconsolate rain fall
Loud on the withered leaves of the sycamore-tree by the window.

Keenly the lightning flashed; and the voice of the echoing thunder
Told her that God was in heaven, and governed the world He created!
Then she remembered the tale she had heard of the justice of Heaven;
Soothed was her troubled soul, and she peacefully slumbered till morning.

V.

Four times the sun had risen and set; and now on the fifth day
Cheerily called the cock to the sleeping maids of the farm-house.
Soon o'er the yellow fields, in silent and mournful procession,
Came from the neighbouring hamlets and farms the Acadian women,
Driving in ponderous wains their household goods to the sea-shore,
Pausing and looking back to gaze once more on their dwellings,
Ere they were shut from sight by the winding road and the woodland.
Close at their sides their children ran, and urged on the oxen,
While in their little hands they clasped some fragments of playthings.

   Thus to the Gaspereau's mouth they hurried; and there on the sea-
      beach
Piled in confusion lay the household goods of the peasants.
All day long between the shore and the ships did the boats ply;
All day long the wains came labouring down from the village.
Late in the afternoon, when the sun was near to his setting,
Echoed far o'er the fields came the roll of drums from the churchyard.
Thither the women and children thronged. On a sudden the church-
      doors
Opened, and forth came the guard, and marching in gloomy procession
Followed the long-imprisoned but patient Acadian farmers.
Even as pilgrims, who journey afar from their homes and their country,
Sing as they go, and in singing forget they are weary and wayworn,
So with songs on their lips the Acadian peasants descended
Down from the church to the shore, amid their wives and their daughters.
Foremost the young men came; and, raising together their voices,
Sang with tremulous lips a chant of the Catholic Missions:—
'Sacred heart of the Saviour! O inexhaustible fountain!
Fill our hearts this day with strength and submission and patience!'
Then the old men, as they marched, and the women that stood by the
      wayside,
Joined in the sacred psalm, and the birds in the sunshine above them
Mingled their notes therewith, like voices of spirits departed.

   Half-way down to the shore Evangeline waited in silence,
Not overcome with grief, but strong in the hour of affliction,—
Calmly and sadly she waited, until the procession approached her,
And she beheld the face of Gabriel pale with emotion.
Tears then filled her eyes, and, eagerly running to meet him,
Clasped she his hands, and laid her head on his shoulder, and whispered—

'Gabriel! be of good cheer! for if we love one another
Nothing, in truth, can harm us, whatever mischances may happen!'
Smiling she spake these words; then suddenly paused, for her father
Saw she slowly advancing. Alas! how changed was his aspect!
Gone was the glow from his cheek, and the fire from his eye, and his
    footstep
Heavier seemed with the weight of the heavy heart in his bosom.
But with a smile and a sigh, she clasped his neck and embraced him,
Speaking words of endearment where words of comfort availed not.
Thus to the Gaspereau's mouth moved on that mournful procession.

There disorder prevailed, and the tumult and stir of embarking.
Busily plied the freighted boats; and in the confusion
Wives were torn from their husbands, and mothers, too late, saw their
    children
Left on the land, extending their arms, with wildest entreaties.
So unto separate ships were Basil and Gabriel carried,
While in despair on the shore Evangeline stood with her father.
Half the task was not done when the sun went down, and the twilight
Deepened and darkened around; and in haste the refluent ocean
Fled away from the shore, and left the line of the sand-beach
Covered with waifs of the tide, with kelp and the slippery sea-weed.
Farther back in the midst of the household goods and the wagons,
Like to a gipsy camp, or a leaguer after a battle,
All escape cut off by the sea, and the sentinels near them,
Lay encamped for the night the houseless Acadian farmers.
Back to its nethermost caves retreated the bellowing ocean,
Dragging adown the beach the rattling pebbles, and leaving
Inland and far up the shore the stranded boats of the sailors.
Then, as the night descended, the herds returned from their pastures;
Sweet was the moist still air with the odour of milk from their udders;
Lowing they waited, and long, at the well-known bars of the farmyard,—
Waited and looked in vain for the voice and the hand of the milkmaid.
Silence reigned in the streets; from the church no Angelus sounded,
Rose no smoke from the roofs, and gleamed no lights from the windows.

But on the shores meanwhile the evening fires had been kindled,
Built of the drift-wood thrown on the sands from wrecks in the tempest.
Round them shapes of gloom and sorrowful faces were gathered,
Voices of women were heard, and of men, and the crying of children.
Onward from fire to fire, as from hearth to hearth in his parish,
Wandered the faithful priest, consoling and blessing and cheering,
Like unto shipwrecked Paul on Melita's desolate sea-shore.
Thus he approached the place where Evangeline sat with her father,
And in the flickering light beheld the face of the old man,
Haggard and hollow and wan, and without either thought or emotion,
E'en as the face of a clock from which the hands have been taken.
Vainly Evangeline strove with words and caresses to cheer him,
Vainly offered him food; yet he moved not, he looked not, he spake not,

But, with a vacant stare, ever gazed at the flickering firelight.
'*Benedicite!*' murmured the priest, in tones of compassion.
More he fain would have said, but his heart was full, and his accents
Faltered and paused on his lips, as the feet of a child on a threshold,
Hushed by the scene he beholds, and the awful presence of sorrow.
Silently, therefore, he laid his hand on the head of the maiden,
Raising his tearful eyes to the silent stars that above them
Moved on their way, unperturbed by the wrongs and sorrows of mortals.
Then sat he down at her side, and they wept together in silence.

Suddenly rose from the south a light, as in autumn the blood-red
Moon climbs the crystal walls of heaven, and o'er the horizon
Titan-like stretches its hundred hands upon mountain and meadow,
Seizing the rocks and the rivers, and piling huge shadows together.
Broader and ever broader it gleamed on the roofs of the village,
Gleamed on the sky and the sea, and the ships that lay in the roadstead.
Columns of shining smoke uprose, and flashes of flame were
Thrust through their folds and withdrawn, like the quivering hands of
   a martyr.
Then as the wind seized the gleeds and the burning thatch, and, uplifting,
Whirled them aloft through the air, at once from a hundred housetops
Started the sheeted smoke with flashes of flame intermingled.

These things beheld in dismay the crowd on the shore and on ship-
      board.
Speechless at first they stood, then cried aloud in their anguish,
'We shall behold no more our homes in the village of Grand-Pré!'
Loud on a sudden the cocks began to crow in the farmyards,
Thinking the day had dawned; and anon the lowing of cattle
Came on the evening breeze, by the barking of dogs interrupted.
Then rose a sound of dread, such as startles the sleeping encampments
Far in the western prairies or forests that skirt the Nebraska,
When the wild horses affrighted sweep by with the speed of the whirlwind,
Or the loud bellowing herds of buffaloes rush to the river.
Such was the sound that arose on the night, as the herds and the horses
Broke through their folds and fences, and madly rushed o'er the meadows.

Overwhelmed with the sight, yet speechless, the priest and the maiden
Gazed on the scene of terror that reddened and widened before them;
And as they turned at length to speak to their silent companion,
Lo! from his seat he had fallen, and stretched abroad on the sea-shore
Motionless lay his form, from which the soul had departed.
Slowly the priest uplifted the lifeless head, and the maiden
Knelt at her father's side, and wailed aloud in her terror.
Then in a swoon she sank, and lay with her head on his bosom.
Through the long night she lay in deep, oblivious slumber:
And when she woke from the trance, she beheld a multitude near her.
Faces of friends she beheld, that were mournfully gazing upon her,
Pallid, with tearful eyes, and looks of saddest compassion.

Still the blaze of the burning village illumined the landscape,
Reddened the sky overhead, and gleamed on the faces around her,
And like the day of doom it seemed to her wavering senses.
Then a familiar voice she heard, as it said to the people,—
'Let us bury him here by the sea. When a happier season
Brings us again to our homes from the unknown land of our exile,
Then shall his sacred dust be piously laid in the churchyard.'
Such were the words of the priest. And there in haste by the seaside,
Having the glare of the burning village for funeral torches,
But without bell or book, they buried the farmer of Grand-Pré.
And as the voice of the priest repeated the service of sorrow,
Lo! with a mournful sound, like the voice of a vast congregation,
Solemnly answered the sea, and mingled its roar with the dirges.
'Twas the returning tide, that afar from the waste of the ocean,
With the first dawn of the day, came heaving and hurrying landward.
Then recommenced once more the stir and noise of embarking;
And with the ebb of the tide the ships sailed out of the harbour,
Leaving behind them the dead on the shore, and the village in ruins.

PART THE SECOND.

I.

MANY a weary year had passed since the burning of Grand-Pré,
When on the falling tide the freighted vessels departed,
Bearing a nation, with all its household gods, into exile,
Exile without an end, and without an example in story.
Far asunder, on separate coasts, the Acadians landed;
Scattered were they, like flakes of snow, when the wind from the north-
   east
Strikes aslant through the fogs that darken the Banks of Newfoundland.
Friendless, homeless, hopeless, they wandered from city to city,
From the cold lakes of the North to sultry Southern savannas,—
From the bleak shores of the sea to the lands where the Father of Waters
Seizes the hills in his hands, and drags them down to the ocean,
Deep in their sands to bury the scattered bones of the mammoth.
Friends they sought and homes; and many, despairing, heart-broken,
Asked of the earth but a grave, and no longer a friend nor a fireside.
Written their history stands on tablets of stone in the churchyards.
Long among them was seen a maiden who waited and wandered,
Lowly and meek in spirit, and patiently suffering all things.
Fair was she and young; but, alas! before her extended,
Dreary and vast and silent, the desert of life, with its pathway
Marked by the graves of those who had sorrowed and suffered before her,
Passions long extinguished, and hopes long dead and abandoned,
As the emigrant's way o'er the Western desert is marked by

Camp-fires long consumed, and bones that bleach in the sunshine.
Something there was in her life incomplete, imperfect, unfinished;
As if a morning of June, with all its music and sunshine,
Suddenly paused in the sky, and, fading, slowly descended
Into the east again, from whence it late had arisen.
Sometimes she lingered in towns, till, urged by the fever within her,
Urged by a restless longing, the hunger and thirst of the spirit,
She would commence again her endless search and endeavour;
Sometimes in churchyards strayed, and gazed on the crosses and tomb-
stones,
Sat by some nameless grave, and thought that perhaps in its bosom
He was already at rest, and she longed to slumber beside him.
Sometimes a rumour, a hearsay, an inarticulate whisper,
Came with its airy hand to point and beckon her forward.
Sometimes she spake with those who had seen her beloved and known
him,
But it was long ago, in some far-off place or forgotten.
'Gabriel Lajeunesse!' said they; 'O yes! we have seen him.
He was with Basil the blacksmith, and both have gone to the prairies;
Coureurs-des-Bois are they, and famous hunters and trappers.'
'Gabriel Lajeunesse!' said others; 'O yes! we have seen him.
He is a Voyageur in the lowlands of Louisiana.'
Then would they say, 'Dear child! why dream and wait for him longer?
Are there not other youths as fair as Gabriel? others
Who have hearts as tender and true, and spirits as loyal?
Here is Baptiste Leblanc, the notary's son, who has loved thee
Many a tedious year; come, give him thy hand and be happy!
Thou art too fair to be left to braid St. Catherine's tresses.'
Then would Evangeline answer, serenely but sadly, 'I cannot!
Whither my heart has gone, there follows my hand, and not elsewhere.
For when the heart goes before, like a lamp, and illumines the pathway,
Many things are made clear, that else lie hidden in darkness.'
Thereupon the priest, her friend and father-confessor,
Said, with a smile, 'O daughter! thy God thus speaketh within thee!
Talk not of wasted affection, affection never was wasted;
If it enrich not the heart of another, its waters, returning
Back to their springs, like the rain, shall fill them full of refreshment;
That which the fountain sends forth returns again to the fountain.
Patience; accomplish thy labour; accomplish thy work of affection!
Sorrow and silence are strong, and patient endurance is godlike.
Therefore accomplish thy labour of love, till the heart is made godlike,
Purified, strengthened, perfected, and rendered more worthy of heaven!
Cheered by the good man's words, Evangeline laboured and waited.
Still in her heart she heard the funeral dirge of the ocean,
But with its sound there was mingled a voice that whispered, 'Despair
not!'
Thus did that poor soul wander in want and cheerless discomfort,
Bleeding, barefooted, over the shards and thorns of existence.

Let me essay, O Muse! to follow the wanderer's footsteps;—
Not through each devious path, each changeful year of existence;
But as a traveller follows a streamlet's course through the valley:
Far from its margin at times, and seeing the gleam of its water
Here and there, in some open space, and at intervals only;
Then drawing nearer its banks, through sylvan glooms that conceal it,
Though he behold it not, he can hear its continuous murmur;
Happy, at length, if he find the spot where it reaches an outlet.

II.

It was the month of May. Far down the Beautiful River,
Past the Ohio shore and past the mouth of the Wabash,
Into the golden stream of the broad and swift Mississippi,
Floated a cumbrous boat, that was rowed by Acadian boatmen.
It was a band of exiles: a raft, as it were, from the shipwrecked
Nation, scattered along the coast, now floating together,
Bound by the bonds of a common belief and a common misfortune;
Men and women and children, who, guided by hope or by hearsay,
Sought for their kith and their kin among the few-acred farmers
On the Acadian coast, and the prairies of fair Opelousas.
With them Evangeline went, and her guide, the Father Felician.
Onward o'er sunken sands, through a wilderness sombre with forests,
Day after day they glided adown the turbulent river;
Night after night, by their blazing fires, encamped on its borders.
Now through rushing chutes, among green islands, where plumelike
Cotton-trees nodded their shadowy crests, they swept with the current,
Then emerged into broad lagoons, where silvery sand-bars
Lay in the stream, and along the wimpling waves of their margin,
Shining with snow-white plumes, large flocks of pelicans waded.
Level the landscape grew, and along the shores of the river,
Shaded by china-trees, in the midst of luxuriant gardens,
Stood the houses of planters, with negro-cabins and dove-cots.
They were approaching the region where reigns perpetual summer,
Where through the Golden Coast, and groves of orange and citron,
Sweeps with majestic curve the river away to the eastward.
They, too, swerved from their course; and, entering the Bayou of
    Plaquemine,
Soon were lost in a maze of sluggish and devious waters,
Which, like a network of steel, extended in every direction.
Over their heads the towering and tenebrous boughs of the cypress
Met in a dusky arch, and trailing mosses in mid-air
Waved like banners that hang on the walls of ancient cathedrals.
Deathlike the silence seemed, and unbroken, save by the herons
Home to their roosts in the cedar-trees returning at sunset,
Or by the owl, as he greeted the moon with demoniac laughter.
Lovely the moonlight was as it glanced and gleamed on the water,
Gleamed on the columns of cypress and cedar sustaining the arches,

Down through whose broken vaults it fell as through chinks in a ruin.
Dreamlike, and indistinct, and strange were all things around them;
And o'er their spirits there came a feeling of wonder and sadness,—
Strange forebodings of ill, unseen and that cannot be compassed.
As, at the tramp of a horse's hoof on the turf of the prairies,
Far in advance are closed the leaves of the shrinking mimosa,
So, at the hoof-beats of fate, with sad forebodings of evil,
Shrinks and closes the heart, ere the stroke of doom has attained it.
But Evangeline's heart was sustained by a vision, that faintly
Floated before her eyes, and beckoned her on through the moonlight.
It was the thought of her brain that assumed the shape of a phantom.
Through those shadowy aisles had Gabriel wandered before her,
And every stroke of the oar now brought him nearer and nearer.

Then in his place, at the prow of the boat, rose one of the oarsmen,
And, as a signal sound, if others like them peradventure
Sailed on those gloomy and midnight streams, blew a blast on his bugle,
Wild through the dark colonnades and corridors leafy the blast rang,
Breaking the seal of silence, and giving tongues to the forest.
Soundless above them the banners of moss just stirred to the music.
Multitudinous echoes awoke and died in the distance,
Over the watery floor, and beneath the reverberant branches:
But not a voice replied; no answer came from the darkness;
And, when the echoes had ceased, like a sense of pain was the silence.
Then Evangeline slept; but the boatmen rowed through the midnight,
Silent at times, then singing familiar Canadian boat-songs,
Such as they sang of old on their own Acadian rivers,
While through the night were heard the mysterious sounds of the desert,
Far off,—indistinct,—as of wave or wind in the forest,
Mixed with the whoop of the crane and the roar of the grim alligator.

Thus ere another noon they emerged from the shades; and before them
Lay, in the golden sun, the lakes of the Atchafalaya.
Water-lilies in myriads rocked on the slight undulations
Made by the passing oars, and, resplendent in beauty, the lotus
Lifted her golden crown above the heads of the boatmen.
Faint was the air with the odorous breath of magnolia blossoms,
And with the heat of noon; and numberless sylvan islands,
Fragrant and thickly embowered with blossoming hedges of roses,
Near to whose shores they glided along, invited to slumber.
Soon by the fairest of these their weary oars were suspended.
Under the boughs of Wachita willows, that grew by the margin,
Safely their boat was moored; and scattered about on the greensward,
Tired with their midnight toil, the weary travellers slumbered.
Over them vast and high extended the cope of a cedar.
Swinging from its great arms, the trumpet-flower and the grape-vine
Hung their ladder of ropes aloft like the ladder of Jacob,
On whose pendulous stairs the angels ascending, descending,
Were the swift humming-birds, that flitted from blossom to blossom.

Such was the vision Evangeline saw as she slumbered beneath it.
Filled was her heart with love, and the dawn of an opening heaven
Lighted her soul in sleep with the glory of regions celestial.

Nearer, ever nearer, among the numberless islands,
Darted a light, swift boat, that sped away o'er the water,
Urged on its course by the sinewy arms of hunters and trappers.
Northward its prow was turned, to the land of the bison and beaver.
At the helm sat a youth, with countenance thoughtful and careworn.
Dark and neglected locks overshadowed his brow, and a sadness
Somewhat beyond his years on his face was legibly written.
Gabriel was it, who, weary with waiting, unhappy and restless,
Sought in the Western wilds oblivion of self and of sorrow.
Swiftly they glided along, close under the lee of the island;
But by the opposite bank, and behind a screen of palmettos,
So that they saw not the boat, where it lay concealed in the willows,
All undisturbed by the dash of their oars, and unseen, were the sleepers;
Angel of God was there none to awaken the slumbering maiden.
Swiftly they glided away, like the shade of a cloud on the prairie.
After the sound of their oars on the tholes had died in the distance,
As from a magic trance the sleepers awoke, and the maiden
Said with a sigh to the friendly priest, 'O Father Felician!
Something says in my heart that near me Gabriel wanders.
Is it a foolish dream, an idle and vague superstition?
Or has an angel passed, and revealed the truth to my spirit?'
Then, with a blush, she added, 'Alas for my credulous fancy!
Unto ears like thine such words as these have no meaning.'
But made answer the reverend man, and he smiled as he answered,—
'Daughter, thy words are not idle; nor are they to me without meaning.
Feeling is deep and still; and the word that floats on the surface
Is as the tossing buoy, that betrays where the anchor is hidden.
Therefore trust to thy heart, and to what the world calls illusions.
Gabriel truly is near thee; for not far away to the southward,
On the banks of the Têche, are the towns of St. Maur and St. Martin.
There the long-wandering bride shall be given again to her bridegroom,
There the long-absent pastor regain his flock and his sheepfold.
Beautiful is the land, with its prairies and forests of fruit-trees;
Under the feet a garden of flowers, and the bluest of heavens
Bending above, and resting its dome on the walls of the forest.
They who dwell there have named it the Eden of Louisiana.'

With these words of cheer they arose and continued their journey.
Softly the evening came. The sun from the western horizon
Like a magician extended his golden wand o'er the landscape;
Twinkling vapours arose; and sky and water and forest
Seemed all on fire at the touch, and melted and mingled together.
Hanging between two skies, a cloud with edges of silver,
Floated the boat, with its dripping oars, on the motionless water
Filled was Evangeline's heart with inexpressible sweetness.

Touched by the magic spell, the sacred fountains of feeling
Glowed with the light of love, as the skies and waters around her.
Then from a neighbouring thicket the mocking-bird, wildest of singers,
Swinging aloft on a willow spray that hung o'er the water,
Shook from his little throat such floods of delirious music,
That the whole air and the woods and the waves seemed silent to listen.
Plaintive at first were the tones and sad ; then soaring to madness
Seemed they to follow or guide the revel of frenzied Bacchantes.
Single notes were then heard, in sorrowful, low lamentation ;
Till, having gathered them all, he flung them abroad in derision,
As when, after a storm, a gust of wind through the tree-tops
Shakes down the rattling rain in a crystal shower on the branches.
With such a prelude as this, and hearts that throbbed with emotion,
Slowly they entered the Têche, where it flows through the green Ope-
    lousas,
And, through the amber air, above the crest of the woodland,
Saw the column of smoke that arose from a neighbouring dwelling ;—
Sounds of a horn they heard, and the distant lowing of cattle.

III.

Near to the bank of the river, o'ershadowed by oaks, from whose
    branches
Garlands of Spanish moss and of mystic mistletoe flaunted,
Such as the Druids cut down with golden hatchets at Yule-tide,
Stood, secluded and still, the house of the herdsman.   A garden
Girded it round about with a belt of luxuriant blossoms,
Filling the air with fragrance.   The house itself was of timbers
Hewn from the cypress-tree, and carefully fitted together.
Large and low was the roof ; and on slender columns supported,
Rose-wreathed, vine-encircled, a broad and spacious veranda,
Haunt of the humming-bird and the bee, extended around it.
At each end of the house, amid the flowers of the garden,
Stationed the dove-cots were, as love's perpetual symbol,
Scenes of endless wooing, and endless contentions of rivals.
Silence reigned o'er the place.   The line of shadow and sunshine
Ran near the tops of the trees ; but the house itself was in shadow,
And from its chimney-top, ascending and slowly expanding
Into the evening air, a thin blue column of smoke rose.
In the rear of the house, from the garden gate, ran a pathway
Through the great groves of oak to the skirts of the limitless prairie,
Into whose sea of flowers the sun was slowly descending.
Full in his track of light, like ships with shadowy canvas
Hanging loose from their spars in a motionless calm in the tropics,
Stood a cluster of trees, with tangled cordage of grape-vines.

Just where the woodlands met the flowery surf of the prairie,
Mounted upon his horse, with Spanish saddle and stirrups,
Sat a herdsman, arrayed in gaiters and doublet of deerskin.

Broad and brown was the face that from under the Spanish sombrero
Gazed on the peaceful scene, with the lordly look of its master.
Round about him were numberless herds of kine, that were grazing
Quietly in the meadows, and breathing the vapoury freshness
That uprose from the river, and spread itself over the landscape.
Slowly lifting the horn that hung at his side, and expanding
Fully his broad, deep chest, he blew a blast, that resounded
Wildly and sweet and far, through the still damp air of the evening.
Suddenly out of the grass the long white horns of the cattle
Rose like flakes of foam on the adverse currents of ocean.
Silent a moment they gazed, then bellowing rushed o'er the prairie,
And the whole mass became a cloud, a shade in the distance.
Then, as the herdsman turned to the house, through the gate of the garden
Saw he the forms of the priest and the maiden advancing to meet him.
Suddenly down from his horse he sprang in amazement, and forward
Rushed with extended arms and exclamations of wonder.
When they beheld his face, they recognised Basil the blacksmith.
Hearty his welcome was, as he led his guests to the garden.
There in an arbour of roses with endless question and answer
Gave they vent to their hearts, and renewed their friendly embraces,
Laughing and weeping by turns, or sitting silent and thoughtful.
Thoughtful, for Gabriel came not ; and now dark doubts and misgivings
Stole o'er the maiden's heart ; and Basil, somewhat embarrassed,
Broke the silence and said, 'If you came by the Atchafalaya,
How have you nowhere encountered my Gabriel's boat on the bayous?'
Over Evangeline's face at the words of Basil a shade passed.
Tears came into her eyes, and she said, with a tremulous accent,
'Gone? is Gabriel gone?' and, concealing her face on his shoulder,
All her o'erburdened heart gave way, and she wept and lamented.
Then the good Basil said,—and his voice grew blithe as he said it,—
'Be of good cheer, my child ; it is only to-day he departed.
Foolish boy ! he has left me alone with my herds and my horses.
Moody and restless grown, and tried and troubled, his spirit
Could no longer endure the calm of this quiet existence.
Thinking ever of thee, uncertain and sorrowful ever,
Ever silent, or speaking only of thee and his troubles,
He at length had become so tedious to men and to maidens,
Tedious even to me, that at length I bethought me, and sent him
Unto the town of Adayes to trade for mules with the Spaniards.
Thence he will follow the Indian trails to the Ozark Mountains,
Hunting for furs in the forests, on rivers trapping the beaver.
Therefore be of good cheer ; we will follow the fugitive lover ;
He is not far on his way, and the Fates and the streams are against him.
Up and away to-morrow, and through the red dew of the morning
We will follow him fast, and bring him back to his prison.'

Then glad voices were heard, and up from the banks of the river,
Borne aloft on his comrades' arms, came Michael the fiddler.

Long under Basil's roof had he lived like a god on Olympus,
Having no other care than dispensing music to mortals.
Far renowned was he for his silver locks and his fiddle.
' Long live Michael,' they cried, ' our brave Acadian minstrel ! '
As they bore him aloft in triumphal procession ; and straightway
Father Felician advanced with Evangeline, greeting the old man
Kindly and oft, and recalling the past, while Basil, enraptured,
Hailed with hilarious joy his old companions and gossips,
Laughing loud and long, and embracing mothers and daughters.
Much they marvelled to see the wealth of the cidevant blacksmith,
All his domains and his herds, and his patriarchal demeanour ;
Much they marvelled to hear his tales of the soil and the climate,
And of the prairies, whose numberless herds were his who would take
    them ;
Each one thought in his heart, that he, too, would go and do likewise.
Thus they ascended the steps, and, crossing the breezy veranda,
Entered the hall of the house, where already the supper of Basil
Waited his late return ; and they rested and feasted together.

Over the joyous feast the sudden darkness descended.
All was silent without, and, illuming the landscape with silver,
Fair rose the dewy moon and the myriad stars ; but within doors,
Brighter than these, shone the faces of friends in the glimmering lamplight.
Then from his station aloft, at the head of the table, the herdsman
Poured forth his heart and his wine together in endless profusion.
Lighting his pipe, that was filled with sweet Natchitoches tobacco,
Thus he spake to his guests, who listened, and smiled as they listened :—
' Welcome once more, my friends, who long have been friendless and
    homeless,
Welcome once more to a home, that is better perchance than the old one !
Here no hungry winter congeals our blood like the rivers ;
Here no stony ground provokes the wrath of the farmer.
Smoothly the ploughshare runs through the soil, as a keel through the
    water.
All the year round the orange-groves are in blossom ; and grass grows
More in a single night than a whole Canadian summer.
Here, too, numberless herds run wild and unclaimed in the prairies ;
Here, too, lands may be had for the asking, and forests of timber
With a few blows of the axe are hewn and framed into houses.
After your houses are built, and your fields are yellow with harvests,
No King George of England shall drive you away from your homesteads,
Burning your dwellings and barns, and stealing your farms and your cattle.'
Speaking these words, he blew a wrathful cloud from his nostrils,
While his huge, brown hand came thundering down on the table,
So that the guests all started ; and Father Felician, astounded,
Suddenly paused, with a pinch of snuff half way to his nostrils.
But the brave Basil resumed, and his words were milder and gayer :—
' Only beware of the fever, my friends, beware of the fever !

For it is not like that of our cold Acadian climate,
Cured by wearing a spider hung round one's neck in a nutshell!'
Then there were voices heard at the door, and footsteps approaching
Sounded upon the stairs and the floor of the breezy veranda.
It was the neighbouring Creoles and small Acadian planters,
Who had been summoned all to the house of Basil the herdsman.
Merry the meeting was of ancient comrades and neighbours:
Friend clasped friend in his arms; and they who before were as strangers,
Meeting in exile, became straightway as friends to each other,
Drawn by the gentle bond of a common country together.
But in the neighbouring hall a strain of music, proceeding
From the accordant strings of Michael's melodious fiddle,
Broke up all further speech. Away, like children delighted,
All things forgotten beside, they gave themselves to the maddening
Whirl of the dizzy dance, as it swept and swayed to the music,
Dreamlike, with beaming eyes and the rush of fluttering garments.

Meanwhile, apart, at the head of the hall, the priest and the herdsman
Sat, conversing together of past and present and future;
While Evangeline stood like one entranced, for within her
Olden memories rose, and loud in the midst of the music
Heard she the sound of the sea, and an irrepressible sadness
Came o'er her heart, and unseen she stole forth into the garden.
Beautiful was the night. Behind the black wall of the forest,
Tipping its summit with silver, arose the moon. On the river
Fell here and there through the branches a tremulous gleam of the
  moonlight,
Like the sweet thoughts of love on a darkened and devious spirit.
Nearer and round about her, the manifold flowers of the garden
Poured out their souls in odours, that were their prayers and confessions
Unto the night, as it went its way, like a silent Carthusian.
Fuller of fragrance than they, and as heavy with shadows and night-dews,
Hung the heart of the maiden. The calm and the magical moonlight
Seemed to inundate her soul with indefinable longings,
As, through the garden gate, and beneath the shade of the oak-trees,
Passed she along the path to the edge of the measureless prairie.
Silent it lay, with a silvery haze upon it, and fire-flies
Gleaming and floating away in mingled and infinite numbers.
Over her head the stars, the thoughts of God in the heavens,
Shone on the eyes of man, who had ceased to marvel and worship,
Save when a blazing comet was seen on the walls of that temple,
As if a hand had appeared and written upon them, 'Upharsin.'
And the soul of the maiden, between the stars and the fire-flies,
Wandered alone, and she cried, 'O Gabriel! O my beloved!
Art thou so near unto me, and yet I cannot behold thee?
Art thou so near unto me, and yet thy voice does not reach me?
Ah! how often thy feet have trod this path to the prairie!
Ah! how often thine eyes have looked on the woodlands around me!

Ah! how often beneath this oak, returning from labour,
Thou hast lain down to rest, and to dream of me in thy slumbers!
When shall these eyes behold, these arms be folded about thee?'
Loud and sudden and near the note of a whippoorwill sounded
Like a flute in the woods; and anon, through the neighbouring thickets,
Farther and farther away it floated and dropped into silence.
'Patience!' whispered the oaks from oracular caverns of darkness:
And, from the moonlit meadow, a sigh responded, 'To-morrow!'

Bright rose the sun next day; and all the flowers of the garden
Bathed his shining feet with their tears, and anointed his tresses
With the delicious balm that they bore in their vases of crystal.
'Farewell!' said the priest, as he stood at the shadowy threshold;
'See that you bring us the Prodigal Son from his fasting and famine,
And, too, the Foolish Virgin, who slept when the bridegroom was
coming.'
'Farewell!' answered the maiden, and, smiling, with Basil descended
Down to the river's brink, where the boatmen already were waiting.
Thus beginning their journey with morning, and sunshine, and gladness,
Swiftly they followed the flight of him who was speeding before them,
Blown by the blast of fate like a dead leaf over the desert.
Not that day, nor the next, nor yet the day that succeeded,
Found they trace of his course, in lake or forest or river,
Nor, after many days, had they found him; but vague and uncertain
Rumours alone were their guides through a wild and desolate country;
Till, at the little inn of the Spanish town of Adayes,
Weary and worn, they alighted, and learned from the garrulous landlord,
That on the day before, with horses and guides and companions,
Gabriel left the village, and took the road of the prairies.

IV.

Far in the West there lies a desert land, where the mountains
Lift, through perpetual snows, their lofty and luminous summits.
Down from their jagged, deep ravines, where the gorge, like a gateway,
Opens a passage rude to the wheels of the emigrant's wagon,
Westward the Oregon flows and the Walleway and Owyhee.
Eastward, with devious course, among the Wind-river Mountains,
Through the Sweet-water Valley precipitate leaps the Nebraska;
And to the south, from Fontaine-qui-bout and the Spanish sierras,
Fretted with sands and rocks, and swept by the wind of the desert,
Numberless torrents, with ceaseless sound, descend to the ocean,
Like the great chords of a harp, in loud and solemn vibrations.
Spreading between these streams are the wondrous, beautiful prairies,
Billowy bays of grass ever rolling in shadow and sunshine,
Bright with luxuriant clusters of roses and purple amorphas.
Over them wandered the buffalo herds, and the elk and the roebuck;
Over them wandered the wolves, and herds of riderless horses;

Fires that blast and blight, and winds that are weary with travel;
Over them wander the scattered tribes of Ishmael's children,
Staining the desert with blood; and above their terrible war-trails
Circles and sails aloft, on pinions majestic, the vulture,
Like the implacable soul of a chieftain slaughtered in battle,
By invisible stairs ascending and scaling the heavens.
Here and there rise smokes from the camps of these savage marauders;
Here and there rise groves from the margins of swift-running rivers;
And the grim, taciturn bear, the anchorite monk of the desert,
Climbs down their dark ravines to dig for roots by the brook-side,
And over all is the sky, the clear and crystalline heaven,
Like the protecting hand of God inverted above them.

Into this wonderful land, at the base of the Ozark Mountains,
Gabriel far had entered, with hunters and trappers behind him.
Day after day, with their Indian guides, the maiden and Basil
Followed his flying steps, and thought each day to o'ertake him.
Sometimes they saw, or thought they saw, the smoke of his camp-fire
Rise in the morning air from the distant plain; but at nightfall,
When they had reached the place, they found only embers and ashes.
And, though their hearts were sad at times and their bodies were weary,
Hope still guided them on, as the magic Fata Morgana
Showed them her lakes of light, that retreated and vanished before them.

Once, as they sat by their evening fire, there silently entered
Into the little camp an Indian woman, whose features
Wore deep traces of sorrow, and patience as great as her sorrow.
She was a Shawnee woman returning home to her people,
From the far-off hunting-grounds of the cruel Camanches,
Where her Canadian husband, a Coureur-des-Bois, had been murdered.
Touched were their hearts at her story, and warmest and friendliest
     welcome
Gave they, with words of cheer, and she sat and feasted among them
On the buffalo-meat and the venison cooked on the embers.
But when their meal was done, and Basil and all his companions,
Worn with the long day's march and the chase of the deer and the bison,
Stretched themselves on the ground, and slept where the quivering fire-
     light
Flashed on their swarthy cheeks, and their forms wrapped up in their
     blankets,
Then at the door of Evangeline's tent she sat and repeated
Slowly, with soft, low voice, and the charm of her Indian accent,
All the tale of her love, with its pleasures, and pains, and reverses.
Much Evangeline wept at the tale, and to know that another
Hapless heart like her own had loved and had been disappointed.
Moved to the depths of her soul by pity and woman's compassion,
Yet in her sorrow pleased that one who had suffered was near her,
She in turn related her love and all its disasters.
Mute with wonder the Shawnee sat, and when she had ended

Still was mute; but at length, as if a mysterious horror
Passed through her brain, she spake, and repeated the tale of the Mowis;
Mowis, the bridegroom of snow, who won and wedded a maiden,
But, when the morning came, arose and passed from the wigwam,
Fading and melting away and dissolving into the sunshine,
Till she beheld him no more, though she followed far into the forest.
Then, in those sweet, low tones, that seemed like a weird incantation,
Told she the tale of the fair Lilinau, who was wooed by a phantom,
That, through the pines o'er her father's lodge, in the hush of the twilight,
Breathed like the evening wind, and whispered love to the maiden,
Till she followed his green and waving plume through the forest,
And never more returned, nor was seen again by her people.
Silent with wonder and strange surprise, Evangeline listened
To the soft flow of her magical words, till the region around her
Seemed like enchanted ground, and her swarthy guest the enchantress.
Slowly over the tops of the Ozark Mountains the moon rose,
Lighting the little tent, and with a mysterious splendour
Touching the sombre leaves, and embracing and filling the woodland.
With a delicious sound the brook rushed by, and the branches
Swayed and sighed overhead in scarcely audible whispers.
Filled with the thoughts of love was Evangeline's heart, but a secret,
Subtile sense crept in of pain and indefinite terror,
As the cold, poisonous snake creeps into the nest of the swallow.
It was no earthly fear. A breath from the region of spirits
Seemed to float in the air of night; and she felt for a moment
That, like the Indian maid, she, too, was pursuing a phantom.
With this thought she slept, and the fear and the phantom had vanished.

Early upon the morrow the march was resumed; and the Shawnee
Said, as they journeyed along, 'On the western slope of these mountains
Dwells in his little village the Black Robe chief of the Mission.
Much he teaches the people, and tells them of Mary and Jesus;
Loud laugh their hearts with joy, and weep with pain, as they hear him.'
Then, with a sudden and secret emotion, Evangeline answered,
'Let us go to the Mission, for there good tidings await us!'
Thither they turned their steeds; and behind a spur of the mountains,
Just as the sun went down, they heard a murmur of voices,
And in a meadow green and broad, by the bank of a river,
Saw the tents of the Christians, the tents of the Jesuit Mission.
Under a towering oak, that stood in the midst of the village,
Knelt the Black Robe chief with his children. A crucifix fastened
High on the trunk of the tree, and overshadowed by grape-vines,
Looked with its agonized face on the multitude kneeling beneath it.
This was their rural chapel. Aloft, through the intricate arches
Of its aerial roof, arose the chant of their vespers,
Mingling its notes with the soft susurrus and sighs of the branches.
Silent, with heads uncovered, the travellers, nearer approaching,
Knelt on the swarded floor, and joined in the evening devotions.

But when the service was done, and the benediction had fallen
Forth from the hands of the priest, like seed from the hands of the sower,
Slowly the reverend man advanced to the strangers, and bade them
Welcome; and when they replied, he smiled with benignant expression,
Hearing the homelike sounds of his mother-tongue in the forest,
And, with words of kindness, conducted them into his wigwam.
There upon mats and skins they reposed, and on cakes of the maize-ear
Feasted, and slaked their thirst from the water-gourd of the teacher.
Soon was their story told; and the priest with solemnity answered :—
'Not six suns have risen and set since Gabriel, seated
On this mat by my side, where now the maiden reposes,
Told me this same sad tale; then arose and continued his journey!'
Soft was the voice of the priest, and he spake with an accent of kindness;
But on Evangeline's heart fell his words as in winter the snow-flakes
Fall into some lone nest from which the birds have departed.
'Far to the north he has gone,' continued the priest; 'but in autumn,
When the chase is done, will return again to the Mission.'
Then Evangeline said, and her voice was meek and submissive,
'Let me remain with thee, for my soul is sad and afflicted.'
So seemed it wise and well unto all; and betimes on the morrow,
Mounting his Mexican steed, with his Indian guides and companions,
Homeward Basil returned, and Evangeline stayed at the Mission.

Slowly, slowly, slowly the days succeeded each other,—
Days and weeks and months; and the fields of maize that were springing
Green from the ground when a stranger she came, now waving above her,
Lifted their slender shafts, with leaves interlacing, and forming
Cloisters for mendicant crows and granaries pillaged by squirrels.
Then in the golden weather the maize was husked, and the maidens
Blushed at each blood-red ear, for that betokened a lover,
But at the crooked laughed, and called it a thief in the corn-field.
Even the blood-red ear to Evangeline brought not her lover.
'Patience!' the priest would say; 'have faith, and thy prayer will be
    answered!
Look at this vigorous plant that lifts its head from the meadow,
See how its leaves are turned to the north, as true as the magnet;
This is the compass-flower, that the finger of God has planted
Here in the houseless wild, to direct the traveller's journey
Over the sea-like, pathless, limitless waste of the desert.
Such in the soul of man is faith. The blossoms of passion,
Gay and luxuriant flowers, are brighter and fuller of fragrance,
But they beguile us, and lead us astray, and their odour is deadly.
Only this humble plant can guide us here, and hereafter
Crown us with asphodel flowers, that are wet with the dews of nepenthe.'

So came the autumn, and passed, and the winter,—yet Gabriel came
    not:
Blossomed the opening spring, and the notes of the robin and bluebird

Sounded sweet upon wold and in wood, yet Gabriel came not.
But on the breath of the summer winds a rumour was wafted
Sweeter than song of bird, or hue or odour of blossom.
Far to the north and east, it said, in the Michigan forests,
Gabriel had his lodge by the banks of the Saginaw River.
And, with returning guides, that sought the lakes of St. Lawrence,
Saying a sad farewell, Evangeline went from the Mission.
When over weary ways, by long and perilous marches,
She had attained at length the depths of the Michigan forests,
Found she the hunter's lodge deserted and fallen to ruin !

  Thus did the long sad years glide on, and in seasons and places
Divers and distant far was seen the wandering maiden ;—
Now in the Tents of Grace of the meek Moravian Missions,
Now in the noisy camps and the battlefields of the army,
Now in secluded hamlets, in towns and populous cities.
Like a phantom she came, and passed away unremembered.
Fair was she and young, when in hope began the long journey ;
Faded was she and old, when in disappointment it ended.
Each succeeding year stole something away from her beauty,
Leaving behind it, broader and deeper, the gloom and the shadow.
Then there appeared and spread faint streaks of gray o'er her forehead,
Dawn of another life, that broke o'er her earthly horizon,
As in the eastern sky the first faint streaks of the morning.

V.

In that delightful land which is washed by the Delaware's waters,
Guarding in sylvan shades the name of Penn the apostle,
Stands on the banks of its beautiful stream the city he founded.
There all the air is balm, and the peach is the emblem of beauty,
And the streets still re-echo the names of the trees of the forest,
As if they fain would appease the Dryads whose haunts they molested.
There from the troubled sea had Evangeline landed, an exile,
Finding among the children of Penn a home and a country.
There old René Leblanc had died ; and when he departed,
Saw at his side only one of all his hundred descendants.
Something at least there was in the friendly streets of the city,
Something that spake to her heart, and made her no longer a stranger ·
And her ear was pleased with the Thee and Thou of the Quakers,
For it recalled the past, the old Acadian country,
Where all men were equal, and all were brothers and sisters.
So, when the fruitless search, the disappointed endeavour,
Ended, to recommence no more upon earth, uncomplaining,
Thither, as leaves to the light, were turned her thoughts and her footsteps.
As from a mountain's top the rainy mists of the morning
Roll away, and afar we behold the landscape below us,
Sun-illumined, with shining rivers and cities and hamlets,

So fell the mists from her mind, and she saw the world far below her,
Dark no longer, but all illumined with love; and the pathway
Which she had climbed so far, lying smooth and fair in the distance.
Gabriel was not forgotten. Within her heart was his image,
Clothed in the beauty of love and youth, as last she beheld him,
Only more beautiful made by his deathlike silence and absence.
Into her thoughts of him time entered not, for it was not.
Over him years had no power; he was not changed, but transfigured;
He had become to her heart as one who is dead, and not absent;
Patience and abnegation of self, and devotion to others,—
This was the lesson a life of trial and sorrow had taught her.
So was her love diffused, but, like to some odorous spices,
Suffered no waste nor loss, though filling the air with aroma.
Other hope had she none, nor wish in life, but to follow
Meekly, with reverent steps, the sacred feet of her Saviour.
Thus many years she lived as a Sister of Mercy; frequenting
Lonely and wretched roofs in the crowded lanes of the city,
Where distress and want concealed themselves from the sunlight,
Where disease and sorrow in garrets languished neglected.
Night after night, when the world was asleep, as the watchman repeated
Loud, through the gusty streets, that all was well in the city,
High at some lonely window he saw the light of her taper.
Day after day, in the gray of the dawn, as slow through the suburbs
Plodded the German farmer, with flowers and fruits for the market,
Met he that meek, pale face, returning home from its watchings.

Then it came to pass that a pestilence fell on the city,
Presaged by wondrous signs, and mostly by flocks of wild pigeons,
Darkening the sun in their flight, with naught in their craws but an acorn.
And, as the tides of the sea arise in the month of September,
Flooding some silver stream, till it spreads to a lake in the meadow,
So death flooded life, and, o'erflowing its natural margin,
Spread to a brackish lake, the silver stream of existence.
Wealth had no power to bribe, nor beauty to charm, the oppressor;
But all perished alike beneath the scourge of his anger;—
Only, alas! the poor, who had neither friends nor attendants,
Crept away to die in the almshouse, home of the homeless.
Then in the suburbs it stood, in the midst of meadows and woodlands;—
Now the city surrounds it; but still, with its gateway and wicket
Meek, in the midst of splendour, its humble walls seem to echo
Softly the words of the Lord:—'The poor ye always have with you.'
Thither, by night and by day, came the Sister of Mercy. The dying
Looked up into her face, and thought, indeed, to behold there
Gleams of celestial light encircle her forehead with splendour,
Such as the artist paints o'er the brows of saints and apostles,
Or such as hangs by night o'er a city seen at a distance.
Unto their eyes it seemed the lamps of the city celestial,
Into whose shining gates ere long their spirits would enter.

Thus, on a Sabbath morn, through the streets deserted and silent,
Wending her quiet way, she entered the door of the almshouse.
Sweet on the summer air was the odour of flowers in the garden ;
And she paused on her way to gather the fairest among them,
That the dying once more might rejoice in their fragrance and beauty.
Then, as she mounted the stairs to the corridors, cooled by the east wind,
Distant and soft on her ear fell the chimes from the belfry of Christ
Church,
While, intermingled with these, across the meadows were wafted
Sounds of psalms, that were sung by the Swedes in their church at Wicaco.
Soft as descending wings fell the calm of the hour on her spirit ;
Something within her said, 'At length thy trials are ended' ;
And, with light in her looks, she entered the chambers of sickness.
Noiselessly moved about the assiduous, careful attendants,
Moistening the feverish lip, and the aching brow, and in silence
Closing the sightless eyes of the dead, and concealing their faces,
Where on their pallets they lay, like drifts of snow by the roadside.
Many a languid head, upraised as Evangeline entered,
Turned on its pillow of pain to gaze while she passed, for her presence
Fell on their hearts like a ray of the sun on the walls of a prison.
And, as she looked around, she saw how Death, the consoler,
Laying his hand upon many a heart, had healed it for ever.
Many familiar forms had disappeared in the night time ;
Vacant their places were, or filled already by strangers.

Suddenly, as if arrested by fear or a feeling of wonder,
Still she stood, with her colourless lips apart, while a shudder
Ran through her frame, and, forgotten, the flowerets dropped from her
fingers,
And from her eyes and cheeks the light and bloom of the morning.
Then there escaped from her lips a cry of such terrible anguish,
That the dying heard it, and started up from their pillows.
On the pallet before her was stretched the form of an old man.
Long, and thin, and gray were the locks that shaded his temples ;
But, as he lay in the morning light, his face for a moment
Seemed to assume once more the forms of its earlier manhood ;
So are wont to be changed the faces of those who are dying.
Hot and red on his lips still burned the flush of the fever,
As if life, like the Hebrew, with blood had besprinkled its portals,
That the Angel of Death might see the sign, and pass over.
Motionless, senseless, dying, he lay, and his spirit exhausted
Seemed to be sinking down through infinite depths in the darkness,
Darkness of slumber and death, for ever sinking and sinking.
Then through those realms of shade, in multiplied reverberations,
Heard he that cry of pain, and through the hush that succeeded
Whispered a gentle voice, in accents tender and saint-like,
'Gabriel ! O my beloved !' and died away into silence.
Then he beheld, in a dream, once more the home of his childhood ;

Green Acadian meadows, with sylvan rivers among them,
Village, and mountain, and woodlands; and, walking under their shadow,
As in the days of her youth, Evangeline rose in his vision.
Tears came into his eyes; and as slowly he lifted his eyelids,
Vanished the vision away, but Evangeline knelt by his bedside.
Vainly he strove to whisper her name, for the accents unuttered
Died on his lips, and their motion revealed what his tongue would have
    spoken.
Vainly he strove to rise; and Evangeline, kneeling beside him,
Kissed his dying lips, and laid his head on her bosom.
Sweet was the light of his eyes; but it suddenly sank into darkness,
As when a lamp is blown out by a gust of wind at a casement.

All was ended now,—the hope, and the fear, and the sorrow,
All the aching of heart, the restless, unsatisfied longing,
All the dull, deep pain, and constant anguish of patience!
And, as she pressed once more the lifeless head to her bosom,
Meekly she bowed her own, and murmured, 'Father, I thank thee!'

———

Still stands the forest primeval; but far away from its shadow,
Side by side, in their nameless graves, the lovers are sleeping.
Under the humble walls of the little Catholic churchyard,
In the heart of the city, they lie, unknown and unnoticed.
Daily the tides of life go ebbing and flowing beside them,—
Thousands of throbbing hearts, where theirs are at rest and for ever,
Thousands of aching brains, where theirs no longer are busy,
Thousands of toiling hands, where theirs have ceased from their labours,
Thousands of weary feet, where theirs have completed their journey!

Still stands the forest primeval; but under the shade of its branches
Dwells another race, with other customs and language.
Only along the shore of the mournful and misty Atlantic
Linger a few Acadian peasants, whose fathers from exile
Wandered back to their native land to die in its bosom.
In the fisherman's cot the wheel and the loom are still busy;
Maidens still wear their Norman caps and their kirtles of homespun,
And by the evening fire repeat Evangeline's story,
While from its rocky caverns the deep-voiced, neighbouring ocean
Speaks, and in accents disconsolate answers the wail of the forest.

The Seaside and the Fireside.

DEDICATION.

As one who, walking in the twilight
    gloom,
  Hears round about him voices as
    it darkens,
And seeing not the forms from
    which they come,
  Pauses from time to time, and
    turns and hearkens;

So walking here in twilight, O my
    friends!
  I hear your voices, softened by
    the distance,
And pause, and turn to listen, as
    each sends
  His words of friendship, comfort,
    and assistance.

If any thought of mine, or sung or
    told,
  Has ever given delight or con-
    solation,
Ye have repaid me back a thou-
    sandfold
  By every friendly sign and salu-
    tation.

Thanks for the sympathies that ye
    have shown!
  Thanks for each kindly word,
    each silent token,
That teaches me, when seeming
    most alone,
  Friends are around us, though
    no word be spoken.

Kind messages, that pass from land
    to land;
  Kind letters, that betray the
    heart's deep history,
In which we feel the pressure of a
    hand,—
  One touch of fire,—and all the
    rest is mystery!

The pleasant books, that silently
    among
  Our household treasures take
    familiar places,
And are to us as if a living
    tongue
  Spake from the printed leaves or
    pictured faces!

Perhaps on earth I never shall be-
    hold,
  With eye of sense, your outward
    form and semblance;
Therefore to me ye never will grow
    old,
  But live for ever young in my
    remembrance.

Never grow old, nor change, nor
    pass away!
  Your gentle voices will flow on
    for ever,
When life grows bare and tarnished
    with decay,
  As through a leafless landscape
    flows a river.

Not chance of birth or place has
   made us friends,
Being oftentimes of different
   tongues and nations,
But the endeavour for the selfsame
   ends,
   With the same hopes, and fears,
   and aspirations.

Therefore I hope to join your seaside walk,
   Saddened, and mostly silent,
   with emotion ·

Not interrupting with intrusive
   talk
   The grand, majestic symphonies
   of ocean.

Therefore I hope, as no unwelcome
   guest,
   At your warm fireside, when the
   lamps are lighted,
To have my place reserved among
   the rest,
   Nor stand as one unsought and
   uninvited !

BY THE SEASIDE.

THE BUILDING OF THE SHIP.

'BUILD me straight, O worthy
   Master !
   Staunch and strong, a goodly
   vessel,
That shall laugh at all disaster,
   And with wave and whirlwind
   wrestle ! '

The merchant's word
Delighted the Master heard ;
For his heart was in his work, and
   the heart
Giveth grace unto every Art.

A quiet smile played round his lips,
As the eddies and dimples of the
   tide
Play round the bows of ships
That steadily at anchor ride.
And with a voice that was full of glee,
He answered, 'Ere long we will
   launch
A vessel as goodly, and strong, and
   staunch,
As ever weathered a wintry sea ! '
And first with nicest skill and art,
Perfect and finished in every part,

A little model the Master wrought,
Which should be to the larger plan
What the child is to the man,
Its counterpart in miniature ;
That with a hand more swift and
   sure
The greater labour might be
   brought
To answer to his inward thought.
And as he laboured, his mind ran
   o'er
The various ships that were built
   of yore,
And above them all, and strangest
   of all,
Towered the Great Harry, crank
   and tall,
Whose picture was hanging on the
   wall,
With bows and stern raised high
   in air,
And balconies hanging here and
   there,
And signal lanterns and flags afloat,
And eight round towers, like those
   that frown
From some old castle, looking down
Upon the drawbridge and the moat.
And he said with a smile, 'Our
   ship, I wis,
Shall be of another form than this ! '

It was of another form, indeed;
Built for freight, and yet for speed,
A beautiful and gallant craft;
Broad in the beam, that the stress
    of the blast,
Pressing down upon sail and mast,
Might not the sharp bows over-
    whelm;
Broad in the beam, but sloping aft
With graceful curve and slow
    degrees,
That she might be docile to the
    helm,
And that the currents of parted
    seas,
Closing behind, with mighty force,
Might aid and not impede her
    course.

In the ship-yard stood the Master,
    With the model of the vessel,
That should laugh at all disaster,
    And with wave and whirlwind
        wrestle!

Covering many a rood of ground,
Lay the timber piled around;
Timber of chestnut, and elm, and
    oak,
And scattered here and there, with
    these,
The knarred and crooked cedar
    knees;
Brought from regions far away,
From Pascagoula's sunny bay,
And the banks of the roaring
    Roanoke!
Ah! what a wondrous thing it is
To note how many wheels of toil
One thought, one word, can set in
    motion!
There's not a ship that sails the
    ocean,
But every climate, every soil,
Must bring its tribute, great or
    small,
And help to build the wooden
    wall!

The sun was rising o'er the sea,
And long the level shadows lay,
As if they, too, the beams would be
Of some great, airy argosy,
Framed and launched in a single
    day.
That silent architect, the sun,
Had hewn and laid them every
    one,
Ere the work of man was yet
    begun.
Beside the Master, when he spoke,
A youth, against an anchor leaning,
Listened, to catch his slightest
    meaning.
Only the long waves, as they broke
In ripples on the pebbly beach,
Interrupted the old man's speech.

Beautiful they were, in sooth,
The old man and the fiery youth!
The old man, in whose busy brain
Many a ship that sailed the main
Was modelled o'er and o'er again;—
The fiery youth, who was to be
The heir of his dexterity,
The heir of his house, and his
    daughter's hand,
When he had built and launched
    from land
What the elder head had planned.

'Thus,' said he, 'will we build this
    ship!
Lay square the blocks upon the slip,
And follow well this plan of mine.
Choose the timbers with greatest
    care;
Of all that is unsound beware;
For only what is sound and strong
To this vessel shall belong.
Cedar of Maine and Georgia pine
Here together shall combine.
A goodly frame, and a goodly fame,
And the UNION be her name!
For the day that gives her to the
    sea
Shall give my daughter unto thee!'

The Master's word
Enraptured the young man heard ;
And as he turned his face aside,
With a look of joy and a thrill of
    pride,
Standing before
Her father's door,
He saw the form of his promised
    bride.
The sun shone on her golden hair,
And her cheek was glowing fresh
    and fair
With the breath of morn and the
    soft sea air.
Like a beauteous barge was she,
Still at rest on the sandy beach,
Just beyond the billow's reach ;
But he
Was the restless, seething, stormy
    sea!

Ah, how skilful grows the hand
That obeyeth Love's command !
It is the heart, and not the brain,
That to the highest doth attain,
And he who followeth Love's behest
Far excelleth all the rest !

Thus with the rising of the sun
Was the noble task begun,
And soon throughout the ship-
    yard's bounds
Were heard the intermingled sounds
Of axes and of mallets, plied
With vigorous arms on every side ;
Plied so deftly and so well,
That, ere the shadows of evening
    fell,
The keel of oak for a noble ship,
Scarfed and bolted, straight and
    strong,
Was lying ready, and stretched
    along
The blocks, well placed upon the
    slip.
Happy, thrice happy, every one
Who sees his labour well begun,
And not perplexed and multiplied
By idly waiting for time and tide !

And when the hot, long day was
    o'er,
The young man at the Master's door
Sat with the maiden calm and still,
And within the porch, a little more
Removed beyond the evening chill,
The father sat, and told them tales
Of wrecks in the great September
    gales,
Of pirates coasting the Spanish
    Main,
And ships that never came back
    again,
The chance and change of a sailor's
    life,
Want and plenty, rest and strife,
His roving fancy, like the wind,
That nothing can stay, and nothing
    can bind,
And the magic charm of foreign
    lands,
With shadows of palms, and
    shining sands,
Where the tumbling surf,
O'er the coral reefs of Madagascar,
Washes the feet of the swarthy
    Lascar
As he lies alone and asleep on the
    turf.
And the trembling maiden held
    her breath
At the tales of that awful, pitiless
    sea,
With all its terror and mystery,
The dim, dark sea, so like unto
    Death,
That divides and yet unites man-
    kind !
And whenever the old man paused,
    a gleam
From the bowl of his pipe would
    awhile illume
The silent group in the twilight
    gloom,
And thoughtful faces, as in a dream ;
And for a moment one might mark
What had been hidden by the
    dark,

177

That the head of the maiden lay at rest,
Tenderly, on the young man's breast!

Day by day the vessel grew,
With timbers fashioned strong and true,
Stemson and keelson and sternson-knee,
Till, framed with perfect symmetry,
A skeleton ship rose up to view!
And around the bows and along the side
The heavy hammers and mallets plied,
Till after many a week, at length,
Wonderful for form and strength,
Sublime in its enormous bulk,
Loomed aloft the shadowy hulk!
And around it columns of smoke, up-wreathing,
Rose from the boiling, bubbling, seething
Caldron, that glowed,
And overflowed
With the black tar, heated for the sheathing.
And amid the clamours
Of clattering hammers,
He who listened heard now and then
The song of the Master and his men :—
'Build me straight, O worthy Master,
    Staunch and strong, a goodly vessel,
That shall laugh at all disaster,
    And with wave and whirlwind wrestle!'

With oaken brace and copper band,
Lay the rudder on the sand,
That, like a thought, should have control
Over the movement of the whole;
And near it the anchor, whose giant hand

Would reach down and grapple with the land,
And immovable and fast
Hold the great ship against the bellowing blast!
And at the bows an image stood,
By a cunning artist carved in wood,
With robes of white, that far behind
Seemed to be fluttering in the wind.
It was not shaped in a classic mould,
Not like a Nymph or Goddess of old,
Or Naiad rising from the water,
But modelled from the Master's daughter!
On many a dreary and misty night,
'Twill be seen by the rays of the signal light,
Speeding along through the rain and the dark,
Like a ghost in its snow-white sark,
The pilot of some phantom bark,
Guiding the vessel, in its flight,
By a path none other knows aright!
Behold, at last,
Each tall and tapering mast
Is swung into its place;
Shrouds and stays
Holding it firm and fast!

Long ago,
In the deer-haunted forests of Maine,
When upon mountain and plain
Lay the snow,
They fell,—those lordly pines!
Those grand, majestic pines!
'Mid shouts and cheers
The jaded steers,
Panting beneath the goad,
Dragged down the weary, winding road
Those captive kings so straight and tall,
To be shorn of their streaming hair,
And, naked and bare,
To feel the stress and the strain
Of the wind and the reeling main,
Whose roar

Would remind them for evermore
Of their native forests they should
   not see again.

And everywhere
The slender, graceful spars
Poise aloft in the air,
And at the mast-head,
White, blue, and red,
A flag unrolls the stripes and
   stars.
Ah! when the wanderer, lonely,
   friendless,
In foreign harbours shall behold
That flag unrolled,
'Twill be as a friendly hand
Stretched out from his native land,
Filling his heart with memories
   sweet and endless!

All is finished! and at length
Has come the bridal day
Of beauty and of strength.
To-day the vessel shall be
   launched!
With fleecy clouds the sky is
   blanched,
And o'er the bay,
Slowly, in all his splendours dight,
The great sun rises to behold the
   sight.

The ocean old,
Centuries old,
Strong as youth, and as uncon-
   trolled,
Paces restless to and fro,
Up and down the sands of gold.
His beating heart is not at rest;
And far and wide,
With ceaseless flow,
His beard of snow
Heaves with the heaving of his
   breast.
He waits impatient for his bride.
There she stands,
With her foot upon the sands,
Decked with flags and streamers
   gay,

In honour of her marriage day,
Her snow-white signals fluttering,
   blending,
Round her like a veil descending,
Ready to be
The bride of the gray old sea.

On the deck another bride
Is standing by her lover's side.
Shadows from the flags and shrouds,
Like the shadows cast by clouds,
Broken by many a sunny fleck,
Fall around them on the deck.

The prayer is said,
The service read,
The joyous bridegroom bows his
   head;
And in tears the good old Master
Shakes the brown hand of his son,
Kisses his daughter's glowing cheek
In silence, for he cannot speak,
And ever faster
Down his own the tears begin to
   run.
The worthy pastor—
The shepherd of that wandering
   flock,
That has the ocean for its wold,
That has the vessel for its fold,
Leaping ever from rock to rock—
Spake, with accents mild and clear
Words of warning, words of cheer,
But tedious to the bridegroom's ear.
He knew the chart
Of the sailor's heart,
All its pleasures and its griefs,
All its shallows and rocky reefs,
All those secret currents, that flow
With such resistless undertow,
And lift and drift, with terrible
   force,
The will from its moorings and its
   course.
Therefore he spake, and thus said
   he :—
' Like unto ships far off at sea,
Outward or homeward bound, are
   we.

Before, behind, and all around,
Floats and swings the horizon's
    bound,
Seems at its distant rim to rise
And climb the crystal wall of the
    skies,
And then again to turn and sink,
As if we could slide from its outer
    brink.
Ah! it is not the sea,
It is not the sea that sinks and
    shelves,
But ourselves
That rock and rise
With endless and uneasy motion,
Now touching the very skies,
Now sinking into the depths of
    ocean.
Ah! if our souls but poise and
    swing
Like the compass in its brazen
    ring,
Ever level and ever true
To the toil and the task we have
    to do,
We shall sail securely, and safely
    reach
The Fortunate Isles, on whose
    shining beach
The sights we see, and the sounds
    we hear,
Will be those of joy and not of
    fear!'

Then the Master,
With a gesture of command,
Waved his hand;
And at the word,
Loud and sudden there was heard,
All around them and below,
The sound of hammers, blow on
    blow,
Knocking away the shores and
    spurs.
And see! she stirs!
She starts,—she moves,—she
    seems to feel
The thrill of life along her keel,

And, spurning with her foot the
    ground,
With one exulting, joyous bound,
She leaps into the ocean's arms!

And lo! from the assembled crowd
There rose a shout, prolonged and
    loud,
That to the ocean seemed to say,
'Take her, O bridegroom, old and
    gray,
Take her to thy protecting arms,
With all her youth and all her
    charms!'

How beautiful she is! How fair
She lies within those arms, that
    press
Her form with many a soft caress
Of tenderness and watchful care!
Sail forth into the sea, O ship!
Through wind and wave, right on-
    ward steer!
The moistened eye, the trembling
    lip,
Are not the signs of doubt or fear.

Sail forth into the sea of life,
O gentle, loving, trusting wife,
And safe from all adversity
Upon the bosom of that sea
Thy comings and thy goings be!
For gentleness and love and trust
Prevail o'er angry wave and gust;
And in the wreck of noble lives
Something immortal still survives!

Thou, too, sail on, O Ship of State!
Sail on, O UNION, strong and
    great!
Humanity with all its fears,
With all the hopes of future years,
Is hanging breathless on thy fate!
We know what Master laid thy
    keel,
What Workmen wrought thy ribs
    of steel,
Who made each mast, and sail,
    and rope,

180

What anvils rang, what hammers
    beat,
In what a forge and what a heat
Were shaped the anchors of thy
    hope !
Fear not each sudden sound and
    shock,
'Tis of the wave and not the rock ;
'Tis but the flapping of the sail,
And not a rent made by the gale !
In spite of rock and tempest's roar,
In spite of false lights on the shore,
Sail on, nor fear to breast the sea !
Our hearts, our hopes, are all with
    thee,
Our hearts, our hopes, our prayers,
    our tears,
Our faith triumphant o'er our fears,
Are all with thee,—are all with
    thee !

CHRYSAOR.

JUST above yon sandy bar,
    As the day grows fainter and
    dimmer,
Lonely and lovely, a single star
    Lights the air with a dusky
    glimmer.

Into the ocean faint and far
    Falls the trail of its golden
    splendour,
And the gleam of that single star
    Is ever refulgent, soft, and tender.

Chrysaor, rising out of the sea,
    Showed thus glorious and thus
    emulous,
Leaving the arms of Callirrhoe,
    For ever tender, soft, and tremu-
    lous.

Thus o'er the ocean faint and far
    Trailed the gleam of his falchion
    brightly ;
Is it a God, or is it a star
    That, entranced, I gaze on
    nightly !

THE SECRET OF THE SEA.

AH ! what pleasant visions haunt me
    As I gaze upon the sea !
All the old romantic legends,
    All my dreams, come back to me.

Sails of silk and ropes of sandal,
    Such as gleam in ancient lore ;
And the singing of the sailors,
    And the answer from the shore !

Most of all, the Spanish ballad
    Haunts me oft, and tarries long,
Of the noble Count Arnaldos
    And the sailor's mystic song.

Like the long waves on a sea-beach,
    Where the sand as silver shines,
With a soft, monotonous cadence,
    Flow its unrhymed lyric lines ;—

Telling how the Count Arnaldos,
    With his hawk upon his hand,
Saw a fair and stately galley,
    Steering onward to the land ;—

How he heard the ancient helmsman
    Chant a song so wild and clear,
That the sailing sea-bird slowly
    Poised upon the mast to hear,

Till his soul was full of longing,
    And he cried, with impulse
    strong,—
'Helmsman ! for the love of heaven,
    Teach me, too, that wondrous
    song !'

' Wouldst thou,'—so the helmsman
    answered,—
    ' Learn the secret of the sea ?
Only those who brave its dangers
    Comprehend its mystery !'

In each sail that skims the horizon,
    In each landward-blowing breeze,
I behold that stately galley,
    Hear those mournful melodies ;

Till my soul is full of longing
    For the secret of the sea,
And the heart of the great ocean
    Sends a thrilling pulse through me.

TWILIGHT.

THE twilight is sad and cloudy,
  The wind blows wild and free,
And like the wings of sea-birds
  Flash the white caps of the sea.

But in the fisherman's cottage
  There shines a ruddier light,
And a little face at the window
  Peers out into the night.

Close, close it is pressed to the
    window,
  As if those childish eyes
Were looking into the darkness,
  To see some form arise.

And a woman's waving shadow
  Is passing to and fro,
Now rising to the ceiling,
  Now bowing and bending low.

What tale do the roaring ocean,
  And the night-wind, bleak and
    wild,
As they beat at the crazy casement,
  Tell to that little child?

And why do the roaring ocean,
  And the night-wind, wild and
    bleak,
As they beat at the heart of the
    mother,
  Drive the colour from her cheek?

----•◦----

SIR HUMPHREY GILBERT.

SOUTHWARD with fleet of ice
  Sailed the corsair Death ;
Wild and fast blew the blast,
  And the east-wind was his breath.

His lordly ships of ice
  Glisten in the sun ;
On each side, like pennons wide,
  Flashing crystal streamlets run.

His sails of white sea-mist
  Dripped with silver rain ;
But where he passed there were cast
  Leaden shadows o'er the main.

Eastward from Campobello
  Sir Humphrey Gilbert sailed ;
Three days or more seaward he
    bore,
  Then, alas ! the land-wind failed.

Alas ! the land-wind failed,
  And ice-cold grew the night ;
And never more, on sea or shore,
  Should Sir Humphrey see the
    light.

He sat upon the deck,
  The Book was in his hand ;
' Do not fear ! Heaven is as near,'
  He said, ' by water as by land !'

In the first watch of the night,
  Without a signal's sound,
Out of the sea, mysteriously,
  The fleet of Death rose all around.

The moon and the evening star
  Were hanging in the shrouds ;
Every mast, as it passed,
  Seemed to rake the passing
    clouds.

They grappled with their prize,
  At midnight black and cold !
As of a rock was the shock ;
  Heavily the ground-swell rolled.

Southward through day and dark
  They drift in close embrace,
With mist and rain o'er the open
    main ;
  Yet there seems no change of
    place.

Southward, for ever southward,
  They drift through dark and day ;
And like a dream, in the Gulf-
    Stream
  Sinking, vanish all away.

THE LIGHTHOUSE.

THE rocky ledge runs far into the
    sea,
And on its outer point, some
    miles away,
The Lighthouse lifts its massive
    masonry,
    A pillar of fire by night, of cloud
    by day.

Even at this distance I can see the
    tides,
    Upheaving, break unheard along
    its base,
A speechless wrath, that rises and
    subsides
    In the white lip and tremor of
    the face.

And as the evening darkens, lo!
    how bright,
    Through the deep purple of the
    twilight air,
Beams forth the sudden radiance
    of its light
    With strange, unearthly splen-
    dour in the glare!

Not one alone; from each pro-
    jecting cape
    And perilous reef along the
    ocean's verge,
Starts into life a dim, gigantic
    shape,
    Holding its lantern o'er the rest-
    less surge.

Like the great giant Christopher
    it stands
    Upon the brink of the tempes-
    tuous wave,
Wading far out among the rocks
    and sands,
    The night-o'ertaken mariner to
    save.

And the great ships sail outward
    and return,
    Bending and bowing o'er the
    billowy swells,
And ever joyful, as they see it burn,
    They wave their silent welcomes
    and farewells.

They come forth from the darkness,
    and their sails
    Gleam for a moment only in the
    blaze,
And eager faces, as the light un-
    veils,
    Gaze at the tower, and vanish
    while they gaze.

The mariner remembers when a
    child,
    On his first voyage, he saw it
    fade and sink;
And when, returning from adven-
    tures wild,
    He saw it rise again o'er ocean's
    brink.

Steadfast, serene, immovable, the
    same
    Year after year, through all the
    silent night
Burns on for evermore that quench-
    less flame,
    Shines on that inextinguishable
    light!

It sees the ocean to its bosom clasp
    The rocks and sea-sand with the
    kiss of peace;
It sees the wild winds lift it in their
    grasp,
    And hold it up, and shake it like
    a fleece.

The startled waves leap over it;
    the storm
    Smites it with all the scourges of
    the rain,
And steadily against its solid form
    Press the great shoulders of the
    hurricane.

The sea-bird wheeling round it,
    with the din
Of wings and winds and solitary
    cries,
Blinded and maddened by the light
    within,
    Dashes himself against the glare,
    and dies.

A new Prometheus, chained upon
    the rock,
    Still grasping in his hand the fire
    of Jove,
It does not hear the cry, nor heed
    the shock,
    But hails the mariner with words
    of love.

'Sail on!' it says, 'sail on, ye
    stately ships!
    And with your floating bridge
    the ocean span;
Be mine to guard this light from
    all eclipse,
    Be yours to bring man nearer
    unto man!'

THE FIRE OF DRIFT-WOOD.

DEVEREUX FARM, NEAR MARBLE-
HEAD.

WE sat within the farmhouse old,
    Whose windows, looking o'er the
    bay,
Gave to the sea-breeze, damp and
    cold,
    An easy entrance, night and day.

Not far away we saw the port,
    The strange, old-fashioned, silent
    town,
The lighthouse, the dismantled fort,
    The wooden houses, quaint and
    brown.

We sat and talked until the night,
    Descending, filled the little room;
Our faces faded from the sight,
    Our voices only broke the gloom.

We spake of many a vanished scene,
    Of what we once had thought
    and said,
Of what had been, and might have
    been,
    And who was changed, and who
    was dead;

And all that fills the hearts of
    friends,
    When first they feel, with secret
    pain,
Their lives thenceforth have sepa-
    rate ends,
    And never can be one again;

The first slight swerving of the
    heart,
    That words are powerless to
    express,
And leave it still unsaid in part,
    Or say it in too great excess.

The very tones in which we spake
    Had something strange, I could
    but mark;
The leaves of memory seemed to
    make
    A mournful rustling in the dark.

Oft died the words upon our lips,
    As suddenly, from out the fire
Built of the wreck of stranded ships,
    The flames would leap and then
    expire.

And, as their splendour flashed and
    failed,
    We thought of wrecks upon the
    main,
Of ships dismasted, that were hailed
    And sent no answer back again.

The windows, rattling in their frames,
The ocean, roaring up the beach,
The gusty blast, the bickering flames,
   All mingled vaguely in our speech ;

Until they made themselves a part
   Of fancies floating through the brain,—

The long-lost ventures of the heart,
   That send no answers back again.

O flames that glowed ! O hearts that yearned !
They were indeed too much akin,
The drift-wood fire without that burned,
   The thoughts that burned and glowed within.

BY THE FIRESIDE.

RESIGNATION.

THERE is no flock, however watched and tended,
   But one dead lamb is there !
There is no fireside, howsoe'er defended,
   But has one vacant chair !

The air is full of farewells to the dying,
   And mournings for the dead ;
The heart of Rachel, for her children crying,
   Will not be comforted !

Let us be patient ! These severe afflictions
   Not from the ground arise,
But oftentimes celestial benedictions
   Assume this dark disguise.

We see but dimly through the mists and vapours ;
   Amid these earthly damps
What seem to us but sad, funereal tapers
   May be heaven's distant lamps.

There is no Death ! What seems so is transition ;
   This life of mortal breath
Is but a suburb of the life elysian,
   Whose portal we call Death.

She is not dead, the child of our affection,
   But gone unto that school
Where she no longer needs our poor protection,
   And Christ himself doth rule.

In that great cloister's stillness and seclusion,
   By guardian angels led,
Safe from temptation, safe from sin's pollution,
   She lives, whom we call dead.

Day after day we think what she is doing
   In those bright realms of air ;
Year after year, her tender steps pursuing,
   Behold her grown more fair.

Thus do we walk with her, and keep unbroken
   The bond which nature gives,
Thinking that our remembrance, though unspoken,
   May reach her where she lives.

Not as a child shall we again behold her ;
   For when with raptures wild
In our embraces we again enfold her,
   She will not be a child ;

But a fair maiden, in her Father's
  mansion,
Clothed with celestial grace ;
And beautiful with all the soul's
  expansion
Shall we behold her face.

And though at times impetuous
  with emotion
And anguish long suppressed,
The swelling heart heaves moaning
  like the ocean,
That cannot be at rest,—

We will be patient, and assuage
  the feeling
We may not wholly stay ;
By silence sanctifying, not con-
  cealing,
The grief that must have way.

THE BUILDERS.

ALL are architects of Fate,
  Working in these walls of Time ;
Some with massive deeds and great,
  Some with ornaments of rhyme.

Nothing useless is, or low ;
  Each thing in its place is best ;
And what seems but idle show
  Strengthens and supports the
    rest.

For the structure that we raise,
  Time is with materials filled ;
Our to-days and yesterdays
  Are the blocks with which we
    build.

Truly shape and fashion these ;
  Leave no yawning gaps between ;
Think not, because no man sees,
  Such things will remain unseen.

In the elder days of Art,
  Builders wrought with greatest
    care
Each minute and unseen part ;
  For the Gods see everywhere.

Let us do our work as well,
  Both the unseen and the seen ;
Make the house, where Gods may
  dwell,
  Beautiful, entire, and clean.

Else our lives are incomplete,
  Standing in these walls of Time,
Broken stairways, where the feet
  Stumble as they seek to climb.

Build to-day, then, strong and sure,
  With a firm and ample base ;
And ascending and secure
  Shall to-morrow find its place.

Thus alone can we attain
  To those turrets, where the eye
Sees the world as one vast plain,
  And one boundless reach of sky.

SAND OF THE DESERT IN AN HOUR-GLASS.

A HANDFUL of red sand, from the
  hot clime
Of Arab deserts brought,
Within this glass becomes the spy
  of Time,
  The minister of Thought.

How many weary centuries has it
  been
  About those deserts blown !
How many strange vicissitudes has
  seen,
  How many histories known !

Perhaps the camels of the Ish-
  maelite
  Trampled and passed it o'er,
When into Egypt from the patri-
  arch's sight
  His favourite son they bore.

Perhaps the feet of Moses, burnt
and bare,
  Crushed it beneath their tread;
Or Pharaoh's flashing wheels into
the air
  Scattered it as they sped;

Or Mary, with the Christ of
Nazareth
  Held close in her caress,
Whose pilgrimage of hope and love
and faith
  Illumed the wilderness;

Or anchorites beneath Engaddi's
palms
  Pacing the Dead Sea beach,
And singing slow their old Ar-
menian psalms
  In half-articulate speech;

Or caravans, that from Bassora's
gate
  With westward steps depart;
Or Mecca's pilgrims, confident of
Fate,
  And resolute in heart!

These have passed over it, or may
have passed!
  Now in this crystal tower
Imprisoned by some curious hand
at last,
  It counts the passing hour.

And as I gaze, these narrow walls
expand;
  Before my dreamy eye
Stretches the desert with its shifting
sand,
  Its unimpeded sky.

And borne aloft by the sustaining
blast,
  This little golden thread
Dilates into a column high and vast,
  A form of fear and dread.

And onward, and across the setting
sun,
  Across the boundless plain,
The column and its broader shadow
run,
  Till thought pursues in vain.

The vision vanishes! These walls
again
  Shut out the lurid sun,
Shut out the hot, immeasurable
plain;
  The half-hour's sand is run!

BIRDS OF PASSAGE.

BLACK shadows fall
From the lindens tall,
That lift aloft their massive wall
  Against the southern sky;

And from the realms
Of the shadowy elms
A tide-like darkness overwhelms
  The fields that round us lie.

But the night is fair,
And everywhere
A warm, soft vapour fills the air,
  And distant sounds seem near;

And above, in the light
Of the star-lit night,
Swift birds of passage wing their
flight
  Through the dewy atmosphere.

I hear the beat
Of their pinions fleet,
As from the land of snow and sleet
  They seek a southern lea.

I hear the cry
Of their voices high
Falling dreamily through the sky,
  But their forms I cannot see.

O, say not so!
Those sounds that flow
In murmurs of delight and woe
  Come not from wings of birds.

187

They are the throngs
Of the poet's songs,
Murmurs of pleasures, and pains,
and wrongs,
The sound of winged words.

This is the cry
Of souls, that high
On toiling, beating pinions, fly,
Seeking a warmer clime.

From their distant flight
Through realms of light
It falls into our world of night,
With the murmuring sound of
rhyme.

THE OPEN WINDOW.

THE old house by the lindens
Stood silent in the shade,
And on the gravelled pathway
The light and shadow played.

I saw the nursery windows
Wide open to the air;
But the faces of the children,
They are no longer there.

The large Newfoundland house-dog
Was standing by the door;
He looked for his little playmates,
Who would return no more.

They walked not under the lindens,
They played not in the hall;
But shadow, and silence, and sad-
ness
Were hanging over all.

The birds sang in the branches,
With sweet, familiar tone;
But the voices of the children
Will be heard in dreams alone!

And the boy that walked beside me,
He could not understand
Why closer in mine, ah! closer,
I pressed his warm, soft hand!

KING WITLAF'S DRINKING-HORN.

WITLAF, a king of the Saxons,
Ere yet his last he breathed,
To the merry monks of Croyland
His drinking-horn bequeathed,—

That, whenever they sat at their
revels,
And drank from the golden bowl,
They might remember the donor,
And breathe a prayer for his soul.

So sat they once at Christmas,
And bade the goblet pass;
In their beards the red wine
glistened
Like dew-drops in the grass.

They drank to the soul of Witlaf,
They drank to Christ the Lord,
And to each of the Twelve Apostles,
Who had preached his holy word.

They drank to the Saints and
Martyrs
Of the dismal days of yore,
And as soon as the horn was empty
They remembered one Saint
more.

And the reader droned from the
pulpit,
Like the murmur of many bees,
The legend of good Saint Guthlac,
And Saint Basil's homilies;

Till the great bells of the convent,
From their prison in the tower,
Guthlac and Bartholomæus,
Proclaimed the midnight hour.

And the Yule-log cracked in the
chimney,
And the Abbot bowed his head,
And the flamelets flapped and
flickered,
But the Abbot was stark and
dead.

Yet still in his pallid fingers
  He clutched the golden bowl,
In which, like a pearl dissolving,
  Had sunk and dissolved his soul.

But not for this their revels
  The jovial monks forbore,
For they cried, 'Fill high the
    goblet!
  We must drink to one Saint
    more!'

GASPAR BECERRA.

By his evening fire the artist
  Pondered o'er his secret shame;
Baffled, weary, and disheartened,
  Still he mused, and dreamed of
    fame.

'Twas an image of the Virgin
  That had tasked his utmost skill;
But, alas! his fair ideal
  Vanished and escaped him still.

From a distant Eastern island
  Had the precious wood been
    brought;
Day and night the anxious master
  At his toil untiring wrought;

Till, discouraged and desponding,
  Sat he now in shadows deep,
And the day's humiliation
  Found oblivion in sleep.

Then a voice cried, 'Rise, O
    master!
  From the burning brand of oak
Shape the thought that stirs within
    thee!'
  And the startled artist woke,—

Woke, and from the smoking embers
  Seized and quenched the glowing
    wood;
And therefrom he carved an image,
  And he saw that it was good.

O thou sculptor, painter, poet!
  Take this lesson to thy heart:
That is best which lieth nearest;
  Shape from that thy work of art.

PEGASUS IN POUND.

ONCE into a quiet village,
  Without haste and without heed,
In the golden prime of morning,
  Strayed the poet's winged steed.

It was Autumn, and incessant
  Piped the quails from shocks and
    sheaves,
And, like living coals, the apples
  Burned among the withering
    leaves.

Loud the clamorous bell was ring-
    ing
  From its belfry gaunt and grim;
'Twas the daily call to labour,
  Not a triumph meant for him.

Not the less he saw the landscape,
  In its gleaming vapour veiled;
Not the less he breathed the odours
  That the dying leaves exhaled.

Thus, upon the village common,
  By the schoolboys he was found;
And the wise men, in their wisdom,
  Put him straightway into pound.

Then the sombre village crier,
  Ringing loud his brazen bell,
Wandered down the street pro-
    claiming
  There was an estray to sell.

And the curious country people,
  Rich and poor, and young and
    old,
Came in haste to see this wondrous
  Winged steed, with mane of
    gold.

Thus the day passed, and the
    evening
  Fell, with vapours cold and dim;
But it brought no food nor shelter,
  Brought no straw nor stall, for
    him.

Patiently, and still expectant,
  Looked he through the wooden
    bars,
Saw the moon rise o'er the land-
    scape,
  Saw the tranquil, patient stars;

Till at length the bell at midnight
  Sounded from its dark abode,
And, from out a neighbouring
    farmyard
  Loud the cock Alectryon crowed.

Then, with nostrils wide distended,
  Breaking from his iron chain,
And unfolding far his pinions,
  To those stars he soared again.

On the morrow, when the village
  Woke to all its toil and care,
Lo! the strange steed had departed,
  And they knew not when nor
    where.

But they found, upon the green-
    sward
  Where his struggling hoofs had
    trod,
Pure and bright, a fountain flowing
  From the hoof-marks in the sod.

From that hour, the fount unfailing
  Gladdens the whole region round,
Strengthening all who drink its
    waters,
  While it soothes them with its
    sound.

TEGNÉR'S DRAPA.

I HEARD a voice, that cried,
  'Balder the Beautiful
Is dead, is dead!'
  And through the misty air
Passed like the mournful cry
  Of sunward sailing cranes.

I saw the pallid corpse
  Of the dead sun
Borne through the Northern sky.
  Blasts from Niffelheim
Lifted the sheeted mists
  Around him as he passed.

And the voice for ever cried,
  'Balder the Beautiful
Is dead, is dead!'
  And died away
Through the dreary night,
  In accents of despair.

Balder the Beautiful,
  God of the summer sun,
Fairest of all the Gods!
  Light from his forehead beamed,
Runes were upon his tongue,
  As on the warrior's sword.

All things in earth and air
  Bound were by magic spell
Never to do him harm;
  Even the plants and stones;
All save the mistletoe,
  The sacred mistletoe!

Hœder, the blind old God,
  Whose feet are shod with silence,
Pierced through that gentle breast
  With his sharp spear, by fraud
Made of the mistletoe,
  The accursed mistletoe!

They laid him in his ship,
  With horse and harness,
As on a funeral pyre.
  Odin placed
A ring upon his finger,
  And whispered in his ear.

They launched the burning ship!
  It floated far away
Over the misty sea,
  Till like the sun it seemed,
Sinking beneath the waves.
  Balder returned no more!

So perish the old Gods!
But out of the sea of Time
Rises a new land of song
Fairer than the old.
Over its meadows green
Walk the young bards and sing.

Build it again,
O ye bards,
Fairer than before!
Ye fathers of the new race,
Feed upon morning dew,
Sing the new Song of Love!

The law of force is dead!
The law of love prevails!
Thor, the thunderer,
Shall rule the earth no more,
No more, with threats,
Challenge the meek Christ.

Sing no more,
O ye bards of the North,
Of Vikings and of Jarls!
Of the days of Eld
Preserve the freedom only,
Not the deeds of blood!

SONNET.

ON MRS. KEMBLE'S READINGS
FROM SHAKESPEARE.

O PRECIOUS evenings! all too
    swiftly sped!
Leaving us heirs to amplest
    heritages
Of all the best thoughts of the
    greatest sages,
And giving tongues unto the
    silent dead!
How our hearts glowed and trem-
    bled as she read,
Interpreting by tones the won-
    drous pages
Of the great poet who foreruns
    the ages,
Anticipating all that shall be
    said!

O happy Reader! having for thy
    text
The magic book, whose Sibylline
    leaves have caught
The rarest essence of all human
    thought!
O happy Poet! by no critic vext!
How must thy listening spirit
    now rejoice
To be interpreted by such a
    voice!

THE SINGERS.

GOD sent his Singers upon earth
With songs of sadness and of mirth,
That they might touch the hearts
    of men,
And bring them back to heaven
    again.

The first, a youth, with soul of fire,
Held in his hand a golden lyre;
Through groves he wandered, and
    by streams,
Playing the music of our dreams.

The second, with a bearded face,
Stood singing in the market-place,
And stirred with accents deep and
    loud
The hearts of all the listening
    crowd.

A gray old man, the third and last,
Sang in cathedrals dim and vast,
While the majestic organ rolled
Contrition from its mouths of gold.

And those who heard the Singers
    three
Disputed which the best might be;
For still their music seemed to
    start
Discordant echoes in each heart.

But the great Master said, 'I see
No best in kind, but in degree;
I gave a various gift to each,
To charm, to strengthen, and to
    teach.

'These are the three great chords
    of might,
And he whose ear is tuned aright
Will hear no discord in the three,
But the most perfect harmony.'

SUSPIRIA.

TAKE them, O Death! and bear
    away
  Whatever thou canst call thine
    own!
Thine image, stamped upon this
    clay,
  Doth give thee that, but that
    alone!

Take them, O Grave! and let them
    lie
  Folded upon thy narrow shelves,
As garments by the soul laid by,
  And precious only to ourselves!

Take them, O great Eternity!
  Our little life is but a gust
That bends the branches of thy
    tree,
  And trails its blossoms in the
    dust!

HYMN

FOR MY BROTHER'S ORDINATION.

CHRIST to the young man said:
  'Yet one thing more;
If thou wouldst perfect be,
Sell all thou hast and give it to the
    poor,
  And come and follow me!'

Within this temple Christ again,
    unseen,
  Those sacred words hath said,
And his invisible hands to-day have
    been
  Laid on a young man's head.

And evermore beside him on his
    way
  The unseen Christ shall move,
That he may lean upon his arm and
    say,
  'Dost thou, dear Lord, approve?'

Beside him at the marriage feast
    shall be,
  To make the scene more fair;
Beside him in the dark Gethsemane
  Of pain and midnight prayer.

O holy trust! O endless sense of
    rest!
  Like the beloved John
To lay his head upon the Saviour's
    breast,
  And thus to journey on!

A CHRISTMAS CAROL.

FROM THE NOËL BOURGUIGNON
DE GUI BARÔZAI.

I HEAR along our street
  Pass the minstrel throngs;
Hark! they play so sweet,
On their hautboys, Christmas
    songs!
    Let us by the fire
    Ever higher
Sing them till the night expire!

In December ring
  Every day the chimes;
Loud the gleemen sing
In the streets their merry rhymes.
    Let us by the fire
    Ever higher
Sing them till the night expire!

Shepherds at the grange,
Where the Babe was born,
Sang, with many a change,
Christmas carols until morn.
    Let us by the fire
    Ever higher
Sing them till the night expire!

These good people sang
Songs devout and sweet;
While the rafters rang,
There they stood with freezing feet.
    Let us by the fire
    Ever higher
Sing them till the night expire.

Nuns in frigid cells
At this holy tide,
For want of something else,
Christmas songs at times have
        tried.

Let us by the fire
Ever higher
Sing them till the night expire!

Washerwomen old,
To the sound they beat,
Sing by rivers cold,
With uncovered heads and feet.
    Let us by the fire
    Ever higher
Sing them till the night expire.

Who by the fireside stands
Stamps his feet and sings;
But he who blows his hands
Not so gay a carol brings.
    Let us by the fire
    Ever higher
Sing them till the night expire!

The Blind Girl of Castèl-Cuillè.

FROM THE GASCON OF JASMIN.

Only the Lowland tongue of Scotland might
Rehearse this little tragedy aright ;
Let me attempt it with an English quill ;
And take, O Reader, for the deed the will.

I.

At the foot of the mountain height
Where is perched Castèl-Cuillè,
When the apple, the plum, and the almond tree
In the plain below were growing white,
This is the song one might perceive
On a Wednesday morn of Saint Joseph's Eve :

'The roads should blossom, the roads should bloom,
So fair a bride shall leave her home !
Should blossom and bloom with garlands gay,
So fair a bride shall pass to-day !'

This old Te Deum, rustic rites attending,
Seemed from the clouds descending ;
When lo ! a merry company
Of rosy village girls, clean as the eye,
Each one with her attendant swain,
Came to the cliff, all singing the same strain ;

Resembling there, so near unto the sky,
Rejoicing angels, that kind Heaven has sent
For their delight and our encouragement.
Together blending,
And soon descending
The narrow sweep
Of the hillside steep,
They wind aslant
Towards Saint Amant,
Through leafy alleys
Of verdurous valleys
With merry sallies
Singing their chant :

'The roads should blossom, the roads should bloom,
So fair a bride shall leave her home !
Should blossom and bloom with garlands gay,
So fair a bride shall pass to-day !'

It is Baptiste, and his affianced maiden,
With garlands for the bridal laden !

The sky was blue ; without one cloud of gloom,
The sun of March was shining brightly,

194

And to the air the freshening wind
gave lightly
Its breathings of perfume.

When one beholds the dusky hedges
blossom,
A rustic bridal, ah ! how sweet it is !
To sounds of joyous melodies,
That touch with tenderness the
trembling bosom,
A band of maidens
Gaily frolicking,
A band of youngsters
Wildly rollicking !
Kissing,
Caressing,
With fingers pressing,
Till in the veriest
Madness of mirth, as they
dance,
They retreat and advance,
Trying whose laugh shall be
loudest and merriest ;
While the bride, with roguish
eyes,
Sporting with them, now escapes
and cries :
‘ Those who catch me
Married verily
This year shall be !’

And all pursue with eager haste,
And all attain what they pursue,
And touch her pretty apron fresh
and new,
And the linen kirtle round her
waist.

Meanwhile, whence comes it
that among
These youthful maidens fresh
and fair,
So joyous, with such laughing
air,
Baptiste stands sighing, with
silent tongue ?
And yet the bride is fair and
young !

Is it Saint Joseph would say to us
all,
That love, o’er-hasty, precedeth a
fall ?
O no ! for a maiden frail, I trow,
Never bore so lofty a brow !
What lovers ! they give not a single
caress !
To see them so careless and cold
to-day,
These are grand people, one
would say.
What ails Baptiste ? what grief
doth him oppress ?

It is, that, half-way up the hill,
In yon cottage, by whose walls
Stand the cart-house and the
stalls,
Dwelleth the blind orphan still,
Daughter of a veteran old ;
And you must know, one year
ago,
That Margaret, the young and
tender,
Was the village pride and
splendour,
And Baptiste her lover bold.
Love, the deceiver, them en-
snared ;
For them the altar was pre-
pared ;
But alas ! the summer’s blight,
The dread disease that none can
stay,
The pestilence that walks by
night,
Took the young bride’s sight
away.

All at the father’s stern command
was changed ;
Their peace was gone, but not their
love estranged.
Wearied at home, ere long the lover
fled ;
Returned but three short days
ago,

The golden chain they round him throw,
He is enticed, and onward led
To marry Angela, and yet
Is thinking ever of Margaret.

Then suddenly a maiden cried,
'Anna, Theresa, Mary, Kate!
Here comes the cripple Jane!'
And by a fountain's side
A woman, bent and gray with years,
Under the mulberry-trees appears,
And all towards her run, as fleet
As had they wings upon their feet.

It is that Jane, the cripple Jane,
Is a soothsayer, wary and kind.
She telleth fortunes, and none complain.
She promises one a village swain,
Another a happy wedding-day,
And the bride a lovely boy straightway.
All comes to pass as she avers;
She never deceives, she never errs.

But for this once the village seer
Wears a countenance severe,
And from beneath her eyebrows thin and white
Her two eyes flash like cannons bright
Aimed at the bridegroom in waistcoat blue,
Who, like a statue, stands in view;
Changing colour, as well he might,
When the beldame wrinkled and gray
Takes the young bride by the hand,
And, with the tip of her reedy wand

Making the sign of the cross, doth say :—
'Thoughtless Angela, beware!
Lest, when thou weddest this false bridegroom,
Thou diggest for thyself a tomb!'

And she was silent; and the maidens fair
Saw from each eye escape a swollen tear;
But on a little streamlet silver-clear,
What are two drops of turbid rain?
Saddened a moment, the bridal train
Resumed the dance and song again;
The bridegroom only was pale with fear;—
And down green alleys
Of verdurous valleys,
With merry sallies,
They sang the refrain :—

'The roads should blossom, the roads should bloom,
So fair a bride shall leave her home!
Should blossom and bloom with garlands gay,
So fair a bride shall pass to-day!'

II.

AND by suffering worn and weary,
But beautiful as some fair angel yet,
Thus lamented Margaret,
In her cottage lone and dreary :—

' He has arrived! arrived at last!
Yet Jane has named him not these three days past;
Arrived! yet keeps aloof so far!
And knows that of my night he is the star!
Knows that long months I wait alone, benighted,
And count the moments since he went away!

Come! keep the promise of that
happier day,
That I may keep the faith to thee
I plighted!
What joy have I without thee?
what delight?
Grief wastes my life, and makes it
misery;
Day for the others ever, but for me
For ever night! for ever night!
When he is gone 'tis dark! my
soul is sad!
I suffer! O my God! come, make
me glad.
When he is near, no thoughts of
day intrude;
Day has blue heavens, but Bap-
tiste has blue eyes!
Within them shines for me a heaven
of love,
A heaven all happiness, like that
above,
No more of grief! no more of
lassitude!
Earth I forget,—and heaven, and
all distresses,
When seated by my side my hand
he presses;
But when alone, remember all!
Where is Baptiste? he hears not
when I call!
A branch of ivy, dying on the
ground,
I need some bough to twine
around!
In pity come! be to my suffering
kind!
True love, they say, in grief doth
more abound!
What then—when one is blind?

'Who knows? perhaps I am
forsaken!
Ah! woe is me! then bear me to
my grave!
O God! what thoughts within
me waken!
Away! he will return! I do but
rave!

He will return! I need not
fear!
He swore it by our Saviour dear;
He could not come at his own
will;
Is weary, or perhaps is ill!
Perhaps his heart, in this dis-
guise,
Prepares for me some sweet
surprise!
But some one comes! Though
blind, my heart can see!
And that deceives me not! 'tis he!
'tis he!'

And the door ajar is set,
And poor confiding Margaret
Rises, with outstretched arms, but
sightless eyes;
'Tis only Paul, her brother, who
thus cries:—
'Angela the bride has passed!
I saw the wedding guests go
by;
Tell me, my sister, why were we
not asked?
For all are there but you and I!'

'Angela married! and not send
To tell her secret unto me!
O, speak! who may the bride-
groom be?'
'My sister, 'tis Baptiste, thy
friend!'

A cry the blind girl gave, but no-
thing said;
A milky whiteness spreads upon
her cheeks;
An icy hand, as heavy as lead,
Descending, as her brother
speaks,
Upon her heart, that has ceased
to beat,
Suspends awhile its life and heat.
She stands beside the boy, now
sore distressed,
A wax Madonna as a peasant
dressed.

197

At length the bridal song again
Brings her back to her sorrow
  and pain.

'Hark! the joyous airs are
  ringing!
Sister, dost thou hear them
  singing?
How merrily they laugh and
  jest!
Would we were bidden with
  the rest!
I would don my hose of home-
  spun gray,
And my doublet of linen striped
  and gay;
Perhaps they will come; for they
  do not wed
Till to-morrow at seven o'clock,
  it is said!'
'I know it!' answered Margaret;
Whom the vision, with aspect black
  as jet,
Mastered again; and its hand of
  ice
Held her heart crushed, as in a
  vice!
'Paul, be not sad! 'Tis a holiday;
To-morrow put on thy doublet
  gay!
But leave me now for a while
  alone.'
Away, with a hop and a jump,
  went Paul,
And, as he whistled along the
  hall,
Entered Jane, the crippled crone.

'Holy Virgin! what dreadful
  heat!
I am faint, and weary, and out
  of breath!
But thou art cold—art chill as
  death;
My little friend! what ails thee,
  sweet?'
'Nothing! I hear them singing
  home the bride;
And, as I listened to the song,

I thought my turn would come
  ere long,—
Thou knowest it is at Whitsun-
  tide.
Thy cards forsooth can never lie,
To me such joy they prophesy;
Thy skill shall be vaunted far
  and wide
When they behold him at my
  side.
And poor Baptiste, what sayest
  thou?
It must seem long to him;—me-
  thinks I see him now!'
Jane, shuddering, her hand doth
  press:
'Thy love I cannot all approve;
We must not trust too much to hap-
  piness;—
Go, pray to God, that thou mayst
  love him less!'
'The more I pray, the more I
  love!
It is no sin, for God is on my side!'
It was enough; and Jane no more
  replied.

Now to all hope her heart is barred
  and cold;
But to deceive the beldame old
She takes a sweet, contented air;
Speak of foul weather or of fair,
At every word the maiden
  smiles!
Thus the beguiler she beguiles;
So that, departing at the evening's
  close,
She says, 'She may be saved!
  she nothing knows!'

Poor Jane, the cunning sorceress!
Now that thou wouldst, thou art no
  prophetess!
This morning, in the fulness of thy
  heart,
Thou wast so, far beyond thine
  art!

III.

Now rings the bell, nine times re-
verberating,
And the white daybreak, stealing
up the sky,
Sees in two cottages two maidens
waiting.
How differently!

Queen of a day, by flatterers caressed,
The one puts on her cross and
crown,
Decks with a huge bouquet her
breast,
And flaunting, fluttering up and
down,
Looks at herself, and cannot
rest.

The other, blind, within her little
room,
Has neither crown nor flower's
perfume;
But in their stead for something
gropes apart,
That in a drawer's recess doth lie,
And, 'neath her bodice of bright
scarlet dye,
Convulsive clasps it to her
heart.

The one, fantastic, light as air,
'Mid kisses ringing,
And joyous singing,
Forgets to say her morning
prayer!

The other, with cold drops upon
her brow,
Joins her two hands, and kneels
upon the floor,
And whispers, as her brother opes
the door,
'O God! forgive me now!'

And then the orphan, young and
blind,

Conducted by her brother's
hand,
Towards the church, through
paths unscanned,
With tranquil air, her way doth
wind.
Odours of laurel, making her faint
and pale,
Round her at times exhale,
And in the sky as yet no sunny
ray,
But brumal vapours gray.

Near that castle, fair to see,
Crowded with sculptures old, in
every part,
Marvels of nature and of art,
And proud of its name of high
degree,
A little chapel, almost bare
At the base of the rock, is
builded there;
All glorious that it lifts aloof,
Above each jealous cottage roof,
Its sacred summit, swept by autumn
gales,
And its blackened steeple high
in air,
Round which the osprey screams
and sails.

'Paul, lay thy noisy rattle by!'
Thus Margaret said. 'Where are
we? we ascend!'
'Yes; seest thou not our journey's end?
Hearest not the osprey from the
belfry cry?
The hideous bird, that brings ill
luck, we know!
Dost thou remember when our
father said,
The night we watched beside
his bed,
"O daughter, I am weak and
low;
Take care of Paul; I feel that I
am dying!"

199

And thou, and he, and I, all fell to
crying?
Then on the roof the osprey
screamed aloud;
And here they brought our father
in his shroud.
There is his grave; there stands
the cross we set;
Why dost thou clasp me so, dear
Margaret?
Come in! The bride will be
here soon:
Thou tremblest! O my God! thou
art going to swoon!'

She could no more,—the blind girl,
weak and weary!
A voice seemed crying from that
grave so dreary,
'What wouldst thou do, my daugh-
ter?'—and she started,
And quick recoiled, aghast,
faint-hearted;
But Paul, impatient, urges evermore
Her steps towards the open
door;
And when, beneath her feet, the
unhappy maid
Crushes the laurel near the house
immortal,
And with her head, as Paul talks
on again,
Touches the crown of filigrane
Suspended from the low-arched
portal,
No more restrained, no more
afraid,
She walks, as for a feast arrayed,
And in the ancient chapel's sombre
night
They both are lost to sight.

At length the bell,
With booming sound,
Sends forth, resounding round,
Its hymeneal peal o'er rock and
down the dell.
It is broad day, with sunshine
and with rain;

And yet the guests delay not
long,
For soon arrives the bridal train,
And with it brings the village
throng.

In sooth, deceit maketh no mortal
gay,
For lo! Baptiste on this triumphant
day,
Mute as an idiot, sad as yester-
morning,
Thinks only of the beldame's words
of warning.

And Angela thinks of her cross, I
wis;
To be a bride is all! The pretty
lisper
Feels her heart swell to hear all
round her whisper,
'How beautiful! how beautiful she
is!'

But she must calm that giddy
head,
For already the Mass is said;
At the holy table stands the
priest;
The wedding ring is blessed; Baptiste receives it;
Ere on the finger of the bride he
leaves it,
He must pronounce one word
at least!
'Tis spoken; and sudden at the
groomsman's side
''Tis he!' a well-known voice has
cried.
And while the wedding guests all
hold their breath,
Opes the confessional, and the blind
girl, see!
'Baptiste,' she said, 'since thou
hast wished my death,
As holy water be my blood for
thee!'
And calmly in the air a knife suspended!

200

Doubtless her guardian angel near
    attended,
  For anguish did its work so well,
That, ere the fatal stroke de-
    scended,
    Lifeless she fell!

At eve, instead of bridal verse,
The De Profundis filled the air;
Decked with flowers a simple
    hearse
To the churchyard forth they
    bear;

Village girls in robes of snow
Follow, weeping as they go;
Nowhere was a smile that day,
No, ah no! for each one seemed
    to say:—

'The road should mourn and be
    veiled in gloom,
So fair a corpse shall leave its home!
Should mourn and should weep,
    ah, well-away!
So fair a corpse shall pass to-
    day!'

The Song of Hiawatha.

INTRODUCTION.

SHOULD you ask me, whence these
      stories?
Whence these legends and tra-
      ditions,
With the odours of the forest,
With the dew and damp of meadows,
With the curling smoke of wigwams,
With the rushing of great rivers,
With their frequent repetitions,
And their wild reverberations,
As of thunder in the mountains?

   I should answer, I should tell you,
'From the forests and the prairies,
From the great lakes of the North-
      land,
From the land of the Ojibways,
From the land of the Dacotahs,
From the mountains, moors, and
      fenlands,
Where the heron, the Shuh-shuh-
      gah,
Feeds among the reeds and rushes.
I repeat them as I heard them
From the lips of Nawadaha,
The musician, the sweet singer.'

   Should you ask where Nawadaha
Found these songs, so wild and
      wayward,
Found these legends and traditions,
I should answer, I should tell you,
'In the birds'-nests of the forest,
In the lodges of the beaver,
In the hoof-prints of the bison,
In the eyrie of the eagle!

   'All the wild-fowl sang them to
      him,
In the moorlands and the fenlands,
In the melancholy marshes;

Chetowaik, the plover, sang them,
Mahng, the loon, the wild-goose,
      Wawa,
The blue heron, the Shuh-shuh-
      gah,
And the grouse, the Mushkodasa!'

   If still further you should ask me,
Saying, 'Who was Nawadaha?
Tell us of this Nawadaha,'
I should answer your inquiries
Straightway in such words as
      follow.

   'In the Vale of Tawasentha,
In the green and silent valley,
By the pleasant water-courses,
Dwelt the singer Nawadaha.
Round about the Indian village
Spread the meadows and the corn-
      fields,
And beyond them stood the forest,
Stood the groves of singing pine-
      trees,
Green in Summer, white in Winter,
Ever sighing, ever singing.

   'And the pleasant water-courses,
You could trace them through the
      valley,
By the rushing in the Spring-time,
By the alders in the Summer,
By the white fog in the Autumn,
By the black line in the Winter;
And beside them dwelt the singer,
In the Vale of Tawasentha,
In the green and silent valley.

   'There he sang of Hiawatha,
Sang the Song of Hiawatha,
Sang his wondrous birth and being,
How he prayed and how he fasted,
How he lived, and toiled, and
      suffered,

That the tribes of men might
    prosper,
That he might advance his people!'
Ye who love the haunts of Nature,
Love the sunshine of the meadow,
Love the shadow of the forest,
Love the wind among the branches,
And the rain-shower and the snow-
    storm,
And the rushing of great rivers
Through their palisades of pine-
    trees,
And the thunder in the mountains,
Whose innumerable echoes
Flap like eagles in their eyries;—
Listen to these wild traditions,
To this Song of Hiawatha!

Ye who love a nation's legends,
Love the ballads of a people,
That like voices from afar off
Call to us to pause and listen,
Speak in tones so plain and child-
    like,
Scarcely can the ear distinguish
Whether they are sung or spoken;—
Listen to this Indian Legend,
To this Song of Hiawatha!

Ye whose hearts are fresh and
    simple,
Who have faith in God and Nature,
Who believe, that in all ages
Every human heart is human,
That in even savage bosoms
There are longings, yearnings,
    strivings
For the good they comprehend not,
That the feeble hands and helpless,
Groping blindly in the darkness,
Touch God's right hand in that
    darkness
And are lifted up and strength-
    ened;—
Listen to this simple story,
To this Song of Hiawatha!

Ye, who sometimes, in your
    rambles
Through the green lanes of the
    country,
Where the tangled barberry-bushes
Hang their tufts of crimson berries
Over stone walls gray with mosses,
Pause by some neglected graveyard,
For a while to muse, and ponder
On a half-effaced inscription,
Written with little skill of song-
    craft,—
Homely phrases, but each letter
Full of hope and yet of heart-break,
Full of all the tender pathos
Of the Here and the Hereafter;—
Stay and read this rude inscription,
Read this Song of Hiawatha!

I.

THE PEACE-PIPE.

ON the Mountains of the Prairie,
On the great Red Pipe-stone
    Quarry,
Gitche Manito, the mighty,
He the Master of Life, descending,
On the red crags of the quarry
Stood erect, and called the nations,
Called the tribes of men together.

From his footprints flowed a river,
Leaped into the light of morning,
O'er the precipice plunging down-
    ward
Gleamed like Ishkoodah, the comet.
And the Spirit, stooping earthward,
With his finger on the meadow
Traced a winding pathway for it,
Saying to it, ' Run in this way!'
From the red stone of the quarry
With his hand he broke a fragment,
Moulded it into a pipe-head,
Shaped and fashioned it with
    figures;
From the margin of the river
Took a long reed for a pipe-stem,
With its dark green leaves upon it;
Filled the pipe with bark of willow,
With the bark of the red willow;
Breathed upon the neighbouring
    forest,

Made its great boughs chafe to-
gether,
Till in flame they burst and
kindled;
And erect upon the mountains,
Gitche Manito, the mighty,
Smoked the calumet, the Peace-
Pipe,
As a signal to the nations.

And the smoke rose slowly,
slowly,
Through the tranquil air of morn-
ing,—
First a single line of darkness,
Then a denser, bluer vapour,
Then a snow-white cloud unfolding,
Like the tree-tops of the forest,
Ever rising, rising, rising,
Till it touched the top of heaven,
Till it broke against the heaven,
And rolled outward all around it.

From the Vale of Tawasentha,
From the Valley of Wyoming,
From the groves of Tuscaloosa,
From the far-off Rocky Mountains,
From the Northern lakes and
rivers
All the tribes beheld the signal,
Saw the distant smoke ascending,
The Pukwana of the Peace-Pipe.

And the Prophets of the nations
Said: 'Behold it, the Pukwana!
By this signal from afar off,
Bending like a wand of willow,
Waving like a hand that beckons,
Gitche Manito, the mighty,
Calls the tribes of men together,
Calls the warriors to his council!'

Down the rivers, o'er the prairies,
Came the warriors of the nations,
Came the Delawares and Mohawks,
Came the Choctaws and Caman-
ches,
Came the Shoshonies and Black-
feet,
Came the Pawnees and Omahas,
Came the Mandans and Dacotahs,
Came the Hurons and Ojibways,

All the warriors drawn together
By the signal of the Peace-Pipe,
To the Mountains of the Prairie,
To the great Red Pipe-stone
Quarry.

And they stood there on the
meadow,
With their weapons and their war-
gear,
Painted like the leaves of Autumn,
Painted like the sky of morning,
Wildly glaring at each other;
In their faces stern defiance,
In their hearts the feuds of ages,
The hereditary hatred,
The ancestral thirst of vengeance.

Gitche Manito, the mighty,
The creator of the nations,
Looked upon them with compas-
sion,
With paternal love and pity;
Looked upon their wrath and
wrangling
But as quarrels among children,
But as feuds and fights of children!

Over them he stretched his right
hand,
To subdue their stubborn natures,
To allay their thirst and fever,
By the shadow of his right hand;
Spake to them with voice majestic
As the sound of far-off waters,
Falling into deep abysses,
Warning, chiding, spake in this
wise:—

'O my children! my poor chil-
dren!
Listen to the words of wisdom,
Listen to the words of warning,
From the lips of the Great Spirit,
From the Master of Life, who made
you.

'I have given you lands to hunt
in,
I have given you streams to fish in,
I have given you bear and bison,
I have given you roe and reindeer,
I have given you brant and beaver,

Filled the marshes full of wild-fowl,
Filled the rivers full of fishes;
Why then are you not contented?
Why then will you hunt each
  other?
  'I am weary of your quarrels,
Weary of your wars and bloodshed,
Weary of your prayers for ven-
  geance,
Of your wranglings and dissen-
  sions;
All your strength is in your union,
All your danger is in discord;
Therefore be at peace hencefor-
  ward,
And as brothers live together.
  'I will send a Prophet to you,
A Deliverer of the nations,
Who shall guide you and shall teach
  you,
Who shall toil and suffer with you.
If you listen to his counsels,
You will multiply and prosper;
If his warnings pass unheeded,
You will fade away and perish!
  'Bathe now in the stream before
  you,
Wash the war-paint from your
  faces,
Wash the blood-stains from your
  fingers,
Bury your war-clubs and your
  weapons,
Break the red stone from this
  quarry,
Mould and make it into Peace-
  Pipes,
Take the reeds that grow beside
  you,
Deck them with your brightest
  feathers,
Smoke the calumet together,
And as brothers live hencefor-
  ward!'
  Then upon the ground the war-
  riors
Threw their cloaks and shirts of
  deerskin,

Threw their weapons and their
  war-gear,
Leaped into the rushing river,
Washed the war-paint from their
  faces.
Clear above them flowed the water,
Clear and limpid from the foot-
  prints
Of the Master of Life descending;
Dark below them flowed the water,
Soiled and stained with streaks of
  crimson,
As if blood were mingled with it!
  From the river came the war-
  riors,
Clean and washed from all their
  war-paint;
On the banks their clubs they
  buried,
Buried all their warlike weapons.
Gitche Manito, the mighty,
The Great Spirit, the creator,
Smiled upon his helpless children!
  And in silence all the warriors
Broke the red stone of the quarry,
Smoothed and formed it into Peace-
  Pipes,
Broke the long reeds by the river,
Decked them with their brightest
  feathers,
And departed each one homeward,
While the Master of Life, ascend-
  ing,
Through the opening of cloud-
  curtains,
Through the doorways of the
  heaven,
Vanished from before their faces,
In the smoke that rolled around
  him,
The Pukwana of the Peace-Pipe!

II.

THE FOUR WINDS.

'HONOUR be to Mudjekeewis!'
Cried the warriors, cried the old
  men,

When he came in triumph home-
ward
With the sacred Belt of Wampum,
From the regions of the North-
Wind,
From the kingdom of Wabasso,
From the land of the White Rabbit.

He had stolen the Belt of Wam-
pum
From the neck of Mishe-Mokwa,
From the Great Bear of the moun-
tains,
From the terror of the nations,
As he lay asleep and cumbrous
On the summit of the mountains,
Like a rock with mosses on it,
Spotted brown and gray with
mosses.

Silently he stole upon him,
Till the red nails of the monster
Almost touched him, almost scared
him,
Till the hot breath of his nostrils
Warmed the hands of Mudjekeewis,
As he drew the Belt of Wampum
Over the round ears, that heard
not,
Over the small eyes, that saw
not,
Over the long nose and nostrils,
The black muffle of the nostrils,
Out of which the heavy breathing
Warmed the hands of Mudjekee-
wis.

Then he swung aloft his war-
club,
Shouted loud and long his war-
cry,
Smote the mighty Mishe-Mokwa
In the middle of the forehead,
Right between the eyes he smote
him.

With the heavy blow bewildered,
Rose the Great Bear of the moun-
tains;
But his knees beneath him trem-
bled,
And he whimpered like a woman,

As he reeled and staggered for-
ward,
As he sat upon his haunches;
And the mighty Mudjekeewis,
Standing fearlessly before him,
Taunted him in loud derision,
Spake disdainfully in this wise:—

'Hark you, Bear! you are a
coward,
And no Brave, as you pretended;
Else you would not cry and whim-
per
Like a miserable woman!
Bear! you know our tribes are
hostile,
Long have been at war together;
Now you find that we are strongest,
You go sneaking in the forest,
You go hiding in the mountains!
Had you conquered me in battle
Not a groan would I have uttered;
But you, Bear! sit here and whim-
per,
And disgrace your tribe by crying,
Like a wretched Shaugodaya,
Like a cowardly old woman!'

Then again he raised his war-
club,
Smote again the Mishe-Mokwa
In the middle of his forehead,
Broke his skull, as ice is broken
When one goes to fish in Winter.
Thus was slain the Mishe-Mokwa,
He the Great Bear of the moun-
tains,
He the terror of the nations.

'Honour be to Mudjekeewis!'
With a shout exclaimed the people,
'Honour be to Mudjekeewis!
Henceforth he shall be the West-
Wind,
And hereafter and for ever
Shall he hold supreme dominion
Over all the winds of heaven.
Call him no more Mudjekeewis,
Call him Kabeyun, the West-
Wind!'
Thus was Mudjekeewis chosen

Father of the Winds of Heaven.
For himself he kept the West-
	Wind,
Gave the others to his children;
Unto Wabun gave the East-Wind,
Gave the South to Shawondasee,
And the North-Wind, wild and
	cruel,
To the fierce Kabibonokka.

Young and beautiful was Wabun;
He it was who brought the morn-
	ing,
He it was whose silver arrows
Chased the dark o'er hill and
	valley;
He it was whose cheeks were
	painted
With the brightest streaks of
	crimson,
And whose voice awoke the village,
Called the deer, and called the
	hunter.

Lonely in the sky was Wabun;
Though the birds sang gaily to
	him,
Though the wild-flowers of the
	meadow
Filled the air with odours for him,
Though the forests and the rivers
Sang and shouted at his coming,
Still his heart was sad within him,
For he was alone in heaven.

But one morning, gazing earth-
	ward,
While the village still was sleeping,
And the fog lay on the river,
Like a ghost, that goes at sunrise,
He beheld a maiden walking
All alone upon a meadow,
Gathering water-flags and rushes
By a river in the meadow.

Every morning, gazing earth-
	ward,
Still the first thing he beheld there
Was her blue eyes looking at him,
Two blue lakes among the rushes.
And he loved the lonely maiden,
Who thus waited for his coming;

For they both were solitary,
She on earth and he in heaven.

And he wooed her with caresses,
Wooed her with his smile of sun-
	shine,
With his flattering words he wooed
	her,
With his sighing and his singing,
Gentlest whispers in the branches,
Softest music, sweetest odours,
Till he drew her to his bosom,
Folded in his robes of crimson,
Till into a star he changed her,
Trembling still upon his bosom;
And for ever in the heavens
They are seen together walking,
Wabun and the Wabun-Annung,
Wabun and the Star of Morning.

But the fierce Kabibonokka
Had his dwelling among icebergs,
In the everlasting snow-drifts,
In the kingdom of Wabasso,
In the land of the White Rabbit.
He it was whose hand in Autumn
Painted all the trees with scarlet,
Stained the leaves with red and
	yellow;
He it was who sent the snow-flakes,
Sifting, hissing through the forest,
Froze the ponds, the lakes, the
	rivers,
Drove the loon and sea-gull south-
	ward,
Drove the cormorant and curlew
To their nests of sedge and sea-
	tang
In the realms of Shawondasee.

Once the fierce Kabibonokka
Issued from his lodge of snow-
	drifts,
From his home among the icebergs,
And his hair, with snow besprin-
	kled,
Streamed behind him like a river,
Like a black and wintry river,
As he howled and hurried south-
	ward,
Over frozen lakes and moorlands.

There among the reeds and
  rushes
Found he Shingebis, the diver,
Trailing strings of fish behind
  him,
O'er the frozen fens and moorlands,
Lingering still among the moor-
  lands,
Though his tribe had long departed
To the land of Shawondasee.

  Cried the fierce Kabibonokka,
'Who is this that dares to brave
  me?
Dares to stay in my dominions,
When the Wawa has departed,
When the wild-goose has gone
  southward,
And the heron, the Shuh-shuh-gah,
Long ago departed southward?
I will go into his wigwam,
I will put his smouldering fire
  out!'

  And at night Kabibonokka
To the lodge came wild and wail-
  ing,
Heaped the snow in drifts about it,
Shouted down into the smoke-flue,
Shook the lodge-poles in his fury,
Flapped the curtain of the door-
  way.
Shingebis, the diver, feared not,
Shingebis, the diver, cared not;
Four great logs had he for fire-
  wood,
One for each moon of the winter,
And for food the fishes served him.
By his blazing fire he sat there,
Warm and merry, eating, laughing,
Singing, 'O Kabibonokka,
You are but my fellow-mortal!'

  Then Kabibonokka entered,
And though Shingebis, the diver,
Felt his presence by the coldness,
Felt his icy breath upon him,
Still he did not cease his singing,
Still he did not leave his laughing,
Only turned the log a little,
Only made the fire burn brighter,

Made the sparks fly up the smoke-
  flue.
From Kabibonokka's forehead,
From his snow-besprinkled tresses,
Drops of sweat fell fast and heavy,
Making dints upon the ashes,
As along the eaves of lodges,
As from drooping boughs of hem-
  lock,
Drips the melting snow in spring-
  time,
Making hollows in the snow-drifts.

  Till at last he rose defeated,
Could not bear the heat and
  laughter,
Could not bear the merry singing,
But rushed headlong through the
  doorway,
Stamped upon the crusted snow-
  drifts,
Stamped upon the lakes and rivers,
Made the snow upon them harder,
Made the ice upon them thicker,
Challenged Shingebis, the diver,
To come forth and wrestle with him,
To come forth and wrestle naked
On the frozen fens and moorlands.

  Forth went Shingebis, the diver,
Wrestled all night with the North-
  Wind,
Wrestled naked on the moorlands
With the fierce Kabibonokka,
Till his panting breath grew
  fainter,
Till his frozen grasp grew feebler,
Till he reeled and staggered back-
  ward,
And retreated, baffled, beaten,
To the kingdom of Wabasso,
To the land of the White Rabbit,
Hearing still the gusty laughter,
Hearing Shingebis, the diver,
Singing, 'O Kabibonokka,
You are but my fellow-mortal!'

  Shawondasee, fat and lazy,
Had his dwelling far to southward,
In the drowsy, dreamy sunshine,
In the never-ending Summer.

He it was who sent the wood-
  birds,
Sent the robin, the Opechee,
Sent the bluebird, the Owaissa,
Sent the Shawshaw, sent the
  swallow,
Sent the wild-goose, Wawa, north-
  ward,
Sent the melons and tobacco,
And the grapes in purple clusters.
From his pipe the smoke as-
  cending
Filled the sky with haze and vapour,
Filled the air with dreamy softness,
Gave a twinkle to the water,
Touched the rugged hills with
  smoothness,
Brought the tender Indian Summer
To the melancholy North-land,
In the dreary Moon of Snow-
  shoes.

Listless, careless Shawondasee!
In his life he had one shadow,
In his heart one sorrow had he.
Once, as he was gazing northward,
Far away upon a prairie
He beheld a maiden standing,
Saw a tall and slender maiden
All alone upon a prairie;
Brightest green were all her gar-
  ments,
And her hair was like the sunshine.

Day by day he gazed upon her,
Day by day he sighed with passion,
Day by day his heart within him
Grew more hot with love and
  longing
For the maid with yellow tresses.
But he was too fat and lazy
To bestir himself and woo her;
Yes, too indolent and easy
To pursue her and persuade her.
So he only gazed upon her,
Only sat and sighed with passion
For the maiden of the prairie.

Till one morning, looking northward,
He beheld her yellow tresses

Changed and covered o'er with
  whiteness,
Covered as with whitest snow-
  flakes.
'Ah! my brother from the North-
  land,
From the kingdom of Wabasso,
From the land of the White
  Rabbit!
You have stolen the maiden from
  me,
You have laid your hand upon her,
You have wooed and won my
  maiden,
With your stories of the North-
  land!'

Thus the wretched Shawondasee
Breathed into the air his sorrow;
And the South-Wind o'er the
  prairie
Wandered warm with sighs of
  passion,
With the sighs of Shawondasee,
Till the air seemed full of snow-
  flakes,
Full of thistle-down the prairie,
And the maid with hair like sun-
  shine
Vanished from his sight for ever;
Never more did Shawondasee
See the maid with yellow tresses!

Poor, deluded Shawondasee!
'Twas no woman that you gazed
  at,
'Twas no maiden that you sighed
  for,
'Twas the prairie dandelion
That through all the dreamy
  Summer
You had gazed at with such
  longing,
You had sighed for with such
  passion,
And had puffed away for ever,
Blown into the air with sighing.
Ah! deluded Shawondasee!

Thus the Four Winds were
  divided;

Thus the sons of Mudjekeewis
Had their stations in the heavens,
At the corners of the heavens ;
For himself the West-Wind only
Kept the mighty Mudjekeewis.

III.

HIAWATHA'S CHILDHOOD.

DOWNWARD through the evening
    twilight,
In the days that are forgotten,
In the unremembered ages,
From the full moon fell Nokomis,
Fell the beautiful Nokomis,
She a wife, but not a mother.

She was sporting with her women
Swinging in a swing of grape-vines,
When her rival, the rejected,
Full of jealousy and hatred,
Cut the leafy swing asunder,
Cut in twain the twisted grape-
    vines,
And Nokomis fell affrighted
Downward through the evening
    twilight,
On the Muskoday, the meadow,
On the prairie full of blossoms,
'See ! a star falls !' said the people ;
'From the sky a star is falling !'
    There among the ferns and
    mosses,
There among the prairie lilies,
On the Muskoday, the meadow,
In the moonlight and the starlight,
Fair Nokomis bore a daughter.
And she called her name Wenonah,
As the first-born of her daughters.
And the daughter of Nokomis
Grew up like the prairie lilies,
Grew a tall and slender maiden,
With the beauty of the moonlight,
With the beauty of the starlight.

And Nokomis warned her often,
Saying oft, and oft repeating,
'O, beware of Mudjekeewis,
Of the West-Wind, Mudjekeewis ;

Listen not to what he tells you ;
Lie not down upon the meadow,
Stoop not down among the lilies,
Lest the West-Wind come and
    harm you !'

But she heeded not the warning,
Heeded not those words of wisdom,
And the West-Wind came at even-
    ing,
Walking lightly o'er the prairie,
Whispering to the leaves and blos-
    soms,
Bending low the flowers and
    grasses,
Found the beautiful Wenonah,
Lying there among the lilies,
Wooed her with his words of sweet-
    ness,
Wooed her with his soft caresses,
Till she bore a son in sorrow,
Bore a son of love and sorrow.

Thus was born my Hiawatha,
Thus was born the child of wonder;
But the daughter of Nokomis,
Hiawatha's gentle mother,
In her anguish died deserted
By the West-Wind, false and faith-
    less,
By the heartless Mudjekeewis.

For her daughter, long and loudly
Wailed and wept the sad Nokomis ;
'O that I were dead !' she mur-
    mured,
'O that I were dead, as thou art !
No more work, and no more weep-
    ing,
Wahonowin ! Wahonowin !'

By the shores of Gitche Gumee
By the shining Big-Sea-Water,
Stood the wigwam of Nokomis,
Daughter of the Moon, Nokomis.
Dark behind it rose the forest,
Rose the black and gloomy pine-
    trees,
Rose the firs with cones upon them;
Bright before it beat the water,
Beat the clear and sunny water,
Beat the shining Big-Sea-Water.

There the wrinkled, old Nokomis
Nursed the little Hiawatha,
Rocked him in his linden cradle,
Bedded soft in moss and rushes,
Safely bound with reindeer sinews;
Stilled his fretful wail by saying,
'Hush! the Naked Bear will hear
    thee!'
Lulled him into slumber, singing,
'Ewa-yea! my little owlet!
Who is this, that lights the wig-
    wam?
With his great eyes lights the wig-
    wam?
Ewa-yea! my little owlet!'

Many things Nokomis taught
    him
Of the stars that shine in heaven;
Showed him Ishkoodah, the comet,
Ishkoodah, with fiery tresses;
Showed the Death-Dance of the
    spirits,
Warriors with their plumes and
    war-clubs,
Flaring far away to northward
In the frosty nights of Winter;
Showed the broad, white road in
    heaven,
Pathway of the ghosts, the shadows,
Running straight across the hea-
    vens,
Crowded with the ghosts, the
    shadows.

At the door on summer evenings
Sat the little Hiawatha;
Heard the whispering of the pine-
    trees,
Heard the lapping of the water,
Sounds of music, words of wonder;
'Minne-wawa!' said the pine-trees,
'Mudway-aushka!' said the water.

Saw the fire-fly, Wah-wah-tay-
    see,
Flitting through the dusk of even-
    ing,
With the twinkle of its candle
Lighting up the brakes and bushes;
And he sang the song of children,

Sang the song Nokomis taught
    him:
'Wah-wah-taysee, little fire-fly,
Little, flitting, white-fire insect,
Little, dancing, white-fire creature,
Light me with your little candle,
Ere upon my bed I lay me,
Ere in sleep I close my eyelids!'

Saw the moon rise from the water
Rippling, rounding from the water,
Saw the flecks and shadows on it,
Whispered, 'What is that, Noko-
    mis?'
And the good Nokomis answered:
'Once a warrior, very angry,
Seized his grandmother, and threw
    her
Up into the sky at midnight;
Right against the moon he threw
    her;
'Tis her body that you see there.'

Saw the rainbow in the heaven,
In the eastern sky, the rainbow,
Whispered, 'What is that, Noko-
    mis?'
And the good Nokomis answered:
''Tis the heaven of flowers you see
    there;
All the wild-flowers of the forest,
All the lilies of the prairie,
When on earth they fade and
    perish,
Blossom in that heaven above us.'

When he heard the owls at mid-
    night,
Hooting, laughing in the forest,
'What is that?' he cried in terror;
'What is that?' he said, 'Noko-
    mis?'
And the good Nokomis answered:
'That is but the owl and owlet,
Talking in their native language,
Talking, scolding at each other.'

Then the little Hiawatha
Learned of every bird its lan-
    guage,
Learned their names and all their
    secrets,

How they built their nests in Summer,
Where they hid themselves in Winter,
Talked with them whene'er he met them,
Called them 'Hiawatha's Chickens.'
Of all beasts he learned the language,
Learned their names and all their secrets,
How the beavers built their lodges,
Where the squirrels hid their acorns,
How the reindeer ran so swiftly,
Why the rabbit was so timid,
Talked with them whene'er he met them,
Called them 'Hiawatha's Brothers.'

Then Iagoo, the great boaster,
He the marvellous story-teller,
He the traveller and the talker,
He the friend of old Nokomis,
Made a bow for Hiawatha;
From a branch of ash he made it,
From an oak-bough made the arrows,
Tipped with flint, and winged with feathers,
And the cord he made of deer-skin.

Then he said to Hiawatha:
'Go, my son, into the forest,
Where the red deer herd together,
Kill for us a famous roebuck,
Kill for us a deer with antlers!'

Forth into the forest straightway
All alone walked Hiawatha
Proudly, with his bow and arrows;
And the birds sang round him, o'er him,
'Do not shoot us, Hiawatha!'
Sang the robin, the Opechee,
Sang the bluebird, the Owaissa,
'Do not shoot us, Hiawatha!'

Up the oak-tree, close beside him,
Sprang the squirrel, Adjidaumo,
In and out among the branches,

Coughed and chattered from the oak-tree,
Laughed, and said between his laughing,
'Do not shoot me, Hiawatha!'
And the rabbit from his pathway
Leaped aside, and at a distance
Sat erect upon his haunches,
Half in fear and half in frolic,
Saying to the little hunter,
'Do not shoot me, Hiawatha!'

But he heeded not, nor heard them,
For his thoughts were with the red deer;
On their tracks his eyes were fastened,
Leading downward to the river,
To the ford across the river,
And as one in slumber walked he.

Hidden in the alder-bushes,
There he waited till the deer came,
Till he saw two antlers lifted,
Saw two eyes look from the thicket,
Saw two nostrils point to windward,
And a deer came down the pathway,
Flecked with leafy light and shadow.
And his heart within him fluttered,
Trembled like the leaves above him,
Like the birch-leaf palpitated,
As the deer came down the pathway.

Then, upon one knee uprising,
Hiawatha aimed an arrow;
Scarce a twig moved with his motion,
Scarce a leaf was stirred or rustled;
But the wary roebuck started,
Stamped with all his hoofs together,
Listened with one foot uplifted,
Leaped as if to meet the arrow;
Ah! the singing, fatal arrow,
Like a wasp it buzzed and stung him!

Dead he lay there in the forest,

By the ford across the river ;
Beat his timid heart no longer,
But the heart of Hiawatha
Throbbed and shouted and exulted,
As he bore the red deer homeward,
And Iagoo and Nokomis
Hailed his coming with applauses.

From the red deer's hide Nokomis
Made a cloak for Hiawatha,
From the red deer's flesh Nokomis
Made a banquet in his honour.
All the village came and feasted,
All the guests praised Hiawatha,
Called him Strong-Heart, Soan-ge-
taha !
Called him Loon-Heart, Mahn-go-
taysee !

IV.

HIAWATHA AND MUDJEKEEWIS.

OUT of childhood into manhood
Now had grown my Hiawatha,
Skilled in all the craft of hunters,
Learned in all the lore of old men,
In all youthful sports and pastimes,
In all manly arts and labours.
Swift of foot was Hiawatha ;
He could shoot an arrow from him,
And run forward with such fleetness,
That the arrow fell behind him !
Strong of arm was Hiawatha ;
He could shoot ten arrows upward,
Shoot them with such strength and
swiftness,
That the tenth had left the bow-
string
Ere the first to earth had fallen !

He had mittens, Minjekahwun,
Magic mittens made of deerskin ;
When upon his hands he wore them,
He could smite the rocks asunder,
He could grind them into powder.
He had moccasins enchanted,
Magic moccasins of deerskin ;

When he bound them round his
ankles,
When upon his feet he tied them,
At each stride a mile he measured !

Much he questioned old Nokomis
Of his father Mudjekeewis ;
Learned from her the fatal secret
Of the beauty of his mother,
Of the falsehood of his father ;
And his heart was hot within him,
Like a living coal his heart was.

Then he said to old Nokomis,
' I will go to Mudjekeewis,
See how fares it with my father,
At the doorways of the West-
Wind,
At the portals of the Sunset !'

From his lodge went Hiawatha,
Dressed for travel, armed for hunt-
ing ;
Dressed in deerskin shirt and
leggings,
Richly wrought with quills and
wampum ;
On his head his eagle-feathers,
Round his waist his belt of
wampum,
In his hand his bow of ash-wood,
Strung with sinews of the reindeer ;
In his quiver oaken arrows,
Tipped with jasper, winged with
feathers ;
With his mittens, Minjekahwun,
With his moccasins enchanted.

Warning said the old Nokomis,
' Go not forth, O Hiawatha !
To the kingdom of the West-Wind,
To the realms of Mudjekeewis,
Lest he harm you with his magic,
Lest he kill you with his cunning !'

But the fearless Hiawatha
Heeded not her woman's warning ;
Forth he strode into the forest,
At each stride a mile he measured ;
Lurid seemed the sky above him,
Lurid seemed the earth beneath him,
Hot and close the air around him,
Filled with smoke and fiery vapours,

As of burning woods and prairies,
For his heart was hot within him,
Like a living coal his heart was.

So he journeyed westward, west-
ward,
Left the fleetest deer behind him,
Left the antelope and bison ;
Crossed the rushing Esconaba,
Crossed the mighty Mississippi,
Passed the Mountains of the Prairie,
Passed the land of Crows and
Foxes,
Passed the dwellings of the Black-
feet,
Came unto the Rocky Mountains,
To the kingdom of the West-Wind,
Where upon the gusty summits
Sat the ancient Mudjekeewis,
Ruler of the winds of heaven.

Filled with awe was Hiawatha
At the aspect of his father.
On the air about him wildly
Tossed and streamed his cloudy
tresses,
Gleamed like drifting snow his
tresses,
Glared like Ishkoodah, the comet,
Like the star with fiery tresses.

Filled with joy was Mudjekeewis
When he looked on Hiawatha,
Saw his youth rise up before him
In the face of Hiawatha,
Saw the beauty of Wenonah
From the grave rise up before him.

'Welcome!' said he, 'Hiawatha,
To the kingdom of the West-Wind!
Long have I been waiting for you !
Youth is lovely, age is lonely,
Youth is fiery, age is frosty ;
You bring back the days departed,
You bring back my youth of
passion,
And the beautiful Wenonah !'

Many days they talked together,
Questioned, listened, waited, an-
swered ;
Much the mighty Mudjekeewis
Boasted of his ancient prowess,

Of his perilous adventures,
His indomitable courage,
His invulnerable body.

Patiently sat Hiawatha,
Listening to his father's boasting ;
With a smile he sat and listened,
Uttered neither threat nor menace,
Neither word nor look betrayed him ;
But his heart was hot within him,
Like a living coal his heart was.

Then he said, 'O Mudjekeewis,
Is there nothing that can harm you?
Nothing that you are afraid of ?'
And the mighty Mudjekeewis,
Grand and gracious in his boasting,
Answered, saying, 'There is no-
thing,
Nothing but the black rock yonder,
Nothing but the fatal Wawbeek !'

And he looked at Hiawatha
With a wise look and benignant,
With a countenance paternal,
Looked with pride upon the beauty
Of his tall and graceful figure,
Saying, 'O my Hiawatha !
Is there anything can harm you ?
Anything you are afraid of ?'

But the wary Hiawatha
Paused awhile, as if uncertain,
Held his peace, as if resolving,
And then answered, 'There is no-
thing,
Nothing but the bulrush yonder,
Nothing but the great Apukwa !'

And as Mudjekeewis, rising,
Stretched his hand to pluck the
bulrush,
Hiawatha cried in terror,
Cried in well-dissembled terror,
'Kago ! kago ! do not touch it !'
'Ah, kaween !' said Mudjekeewis,
'No indeed, I will not touch it !'

Then they talked of other
matters ;
First of Hiawatha's brothers,
First of Wabun, of the East-Wind,
Of the South-Wind, Shawondasee,
Of the North, Kabibonokka ;

Then of Hiawatha's mother,
Of the beautiful Wenonah,
Of her birth upon the meadow,
Of her death, as old Nokomis
Had remembered and related.

And he cried, 'O Mudjekeewis,
It was you who killed Wenonah,
Took her young life and her beauty,
Broke the Lily of the Prairie,
Trampled it beneath your footsteps;
You confess it! you confess it!'
And the mighty Mudjekeewis
Tossed upon the wind his tresses,
Bowed his hoary head in anguish,
With a silent nod assented.

Then upstarted Hiawatha,
And with threatening look and
    gesture
Laid his hand upon the black rock,
On the fatal Wawbeek laid it,
With his mittens, Minjekahwun,
Rent the jutting crag asunder,
Smote and crushed it into frag-
    ments,
Hurled them madly at his father,
The remorseful Mudjekeewis;
For his heart was hot within him,
Like a living coal his heart was.

But the ruler of the West-Wind
Blew the fragments backward from
    him,
With the breathing of his nostrils,
With the tempest of his anger,
Blew them back at his assailant;
Seized the bulrush, the Apukwa,
Dragged it with its roots and fibres
From the margin of the meadow,
From its ooze, the giant bulrush;
Long and loud laughed Hiawatha!

Then began the deadly conflict,
Hand to hand among the moun-
    tains;
From his eyrie screamed the eagle,
The Keneu, the great war-eagle;
Sat upon the crags around them,
Wheeling flapped his wings above
    them.
Like a tall tree in the tempest

Bent and lashed the giant bulrush;
And in masses huge and heavy
Crashing fell the fatal Wawbeek;
Till the earth shook with the
    tumult
And confusion of the battle,
And the air was full of shoutings,
And the thunder of the mountains,
Starting, answered, 'Baim-wawa!'

Back retreated Mudjekeewis,
Rushing westward o'er the moun-
    tains,
Stumbling westward down the
    mountains,
Three whole days retreated fighting,
Still pursued by Hiawatha
To the doorways of the West-Wind,
To the portals of the Sunset,
To the earth's remotest border,
Where into the empty spaces
Sinks the sun, as a flamingo
Drops into her nest at nightfall,
In the melancholy marshes.

'Hold!' at length cried Mud-
    jekeewis,
'Hold, my son, my Hiawatha!
'Tis impossible to kill me,
For you cannot kill the immortal.
I have put you to this trial,
But to know and prove your courage;
Now receive the prize of valour!

'Go back to your home and
    people,
Live among them, toil among them,
Cleanse the earth from all that
    harms it,
Clear the fishing-grounds and
    rivers,
Slay all monsters and magicians,
All the Wendigoes, the giants,
All the serpents, the Kenabeeks,
As I slew the Mishe-Mokwa,
Slew the Great Bear of the moun-
    tains.

'And at last when Death draws
    near you,
When the awful eyes of Pauguk
Glare upon you in the darkness,

H

I will share my kingdom with you;
Ruler shall you be thenceforward
Of the Northwest-Wind, Keeway-
  din,
Of the home-wind, the Keewaydin.'
  Thus was fought that famous
    battle
In the dreadful days of Shah-shah,
In the days long since departed,
In the kingdom of the West-Wind.
Still the hunter sees its traces
Scattered far o'er hill and valley;
Sees the giant bulrush growing
By the ponds and water-courses,
Sees the masses of the Wawbeek
Lying still in every valley.

  Homeward now went Hiawatha;
Pleasant was the landscape round
  him,
Pleasant was the air above him,
For the bitterness of anger
Had departed wholly from him,
From his brain the thought of ven-
  geance,
From his heart the burning fever.

  Only once his pace he slackened,
Only once he paused or halted,
Paused to purchase heads of arrows
Of the ancient Arrow-maker,
In the land of the Dacotahs,
Where the Falls of Minnehaha
Flash and gleam among the oak-
  trees,
Laugh and leap into the valley.

  There the ancient Arrow-maker
Made his arrow-heads of sand-
  stone,
Arrow-heads of chalcedony,
Arrow-heads of flint and jasper,
Smoothed and sharpened at the
  edges,
Hard and polished, keen and
  costly.
  With him dwelt his dark-eyed
    daughter,
Wayward as the Minnehaha,
With her moods of shade and sun-
  shine,

Eyes that smiled and frowned al-
  ternate,
Feet as rapid as the river,
Tresses flowing like the water,
And as musical a laughter;
And he named her from the river,
From the waterfall he named her,
Minnehaha, Laughing Water.

  Was it then for heads of arrows,
Arrow-heads of chalcedony,
Arrow-heads of flint and jasper,
That my Hiawatha halted
In the land of the Dacotahs?

  Was it not to see the maiden,
See the face of Laughing Water
Peeping from behind the curtain,
Hear the rustling of her garments
From behind the waving curtain,
As one sees the Minnehaha
Gleaming, glancing through the
  branches,
As one hears the Laughing Water
From behind its screen of branches?

  Who shall say what thoughts
    and visions
Fill the fiery brains of young men?
Who shall say what dreams of
  beauty
Filled the heart of Hiawatha?
All he told to old Nokomis,
When he reached the lodge at
  sunset,
Was the meeting with his father,
Was his fight with Mudjekeewis;
Not a word he said of arrows,
Not a word of Laughing Water.

V.

HIAWATHA'S FASTING.

YOU shall hear how Hiawatha
Prayed and fasted in the forest,
Not for greater skill in hunting,
Not for greater craft in fishing,
Not for triumphs in the battle,
And renown among the warriors,

But for profit of the people,
For advantage of the nations.

First he built a lodge for fasting,
Built a wigwam in the forest,
By the shining Big-Sea-Water,
In the blithe and pleasant Spring-
    time,
In the Moon of Leaves he built it,
And, with dreams and visions
    many,
Seven whole days and nights he
    fasted.

On the first day of his fasting
Through the leafy woods he wan-
    dered;
Saw the deer start from the thicket,
Saw the rabbit in his burrow,
Heard the pheasant, Bena, drum-
    ming,
Heard the squirrel, Adjidaumo,
Rattling in his hoard of acorns,
Saw the pigeon, the Omeme,
Building nests among the pine-
    trees,
And in flocks the wildgoose, Wawa,
Flying to the fenlands northward,
Whirring, wailing far above him.
'Master of Life!' he cried, de-
    sponding,
'Must our lives depend on these
    things?'

On the next day of his fasting
By the river's brink he wandered,
Through the Muskoday, the
    meadow,
Saw the wild rice, Mahnomonee,
Saw the blueberry, Meenahga,
And the strawberry, Odahmin,
And the gooseberry, Shahbomin,
And the grape-vine, the Bemahgut,
Trailing o'er the alder-branches,
Filling all the air with fragrance!
'Master of Life!' he cried, de-
    sponding,
'Must our lives depend on these
    things?'

On the third day of his fasting
By the lake he sat and pondered,

By the still, transparent water;
Saw the sturgeon, Nahma, leaping,
Scattering drops like beads of
    wampum,
Saw the yellow perch, the Sahwa,
Like a sunbeam in the water,
Saw the pike, the Maskenozha,
And the herring, Okahahwis,
And the Shawgashee, the crawfish!
'Master of Life!' he cried, de-
    sponding,
'Must our lives depend on these
    things?'

On the fourth day of his fasting
In his lodge he lay exhausted;
From his couch of leaves and
    branches
Gazing with half-open eyelids,
Full of shadowy dreams and
    visions,
On the dizzy, swimming landscape,
On the gleaming of the water,
On the splendour of the sunset.
And he saw a youth approaching,
Dressed in garments green and
    yellow,
Coming through the purple twilight,
Through the splendour of the
    sunset;
Plumes of green bent o'er his fore-
    head,
And his hair was soft and golden.

Standing at the open doorway,
Long he looked at Hiawatha,
Looked with pity and compassion
On his wasted form and features,
And, in accents like the sighing
Of the South-Wind in the tree-tops,
Said he, 'O my Hiawatha!
All your prayers are heard in
    heaven,
For you pray not like the others;
Not for greater skill in hunting,
Not for greater craft in fishing,
Not for triumph in the battle,
Nor renown among the warriors,
But for profit of the people,
For advantage of the nations.

The Song of Hiawatha.

'From the Master of Life descending,
I, the friend of man, Mondamin,
Come to warn you and instruct you,
How by struggle and by labour
You shall gain what you have prayed for.
Rise up from your bed of branches,
Rise, O youth, and wrestle with me!'
Faint with famine, Hiawatha
Started from his bed of branches,
From the twilight of his wigwam
Forth into the flush of sunset
Came, and wrestled with Mondamin;
At his touch he felt new courage
Throbbing in his brain and bosom,
Felt new life and hope and vigour
Run through every nerve and fibre.
So they wrestled there together
In the glory of the sunset,
And the more they strove and struggled,
Stronger still grew Hiawatha;
Till the darkness fell around them,
And the heron, the Shuh-shuh-gah,
From her nest among the pine-trees,
Gave a cry of lamentation,
Gave a scream of pain and famine.
''Tis enough!' then said Mondamin,
Smiling upon Hiawatha,
'But to-morrow, when the sun sets,
I will come again to try you.'
And he vanished, and was seen not;
Whether sinking as the rain sinks,
Whether rising as the mists rise,
Hiawatha saw not, knew not,
Only saw that he had vanished,
Leaving him alone and fainting,
With the misty lake below him,
And the reeling stars above him.

On the morrow and the next day,
When the sun through heaven descending,
Like a red and burning cinder
From the hearth of the Great Spirit,
Fell into the western waters,
Came Mondamin for the trial,
For the strife with Hiawatha;
Came as silent as the dew comes,
From the empty air appearing,
Into empty air returning,
Taking shape when earth it touches,
But invisible to all men
In its coming and its going.
Thrice they wrestled there together
In the glory of the sunset,
Till the darkness fell around them,
Till the heron, the Shuh-shuh-gah,
From her nest among the pine-trees,
Uttered her loud cry of famine,
And Mondamin paused to listen.
Tall and beautiful he stood there,
In his garments green and yellow;
To and fro his plumes above him
Waved and nodded with his breathing,
And the sweat of the encounter
Stood like drops of dew upon him.
And he cried, 'O Hiawatha!
Bravely have you wrestled with me,
Thrice have wrestled stoutly with me,
And the Master of Life, who sees us,
He will give to you the triumph!'
Then he smiled, and said: 'To-morrow
Is the last day of your conflict,
Is the last day of your fasting.
You will conquer and o'ercome me;
Make a bed for me to lie in,
Where the rain may fall upon me,
Where the sun may come and warm me;

218

Strip these garments, green and
    yellow,
Strip this nodding plumage from
    me,
Lay me in the earth, and make it
Soft and loose and light above me.
'Let no hand disturb my slumber,
Let no weed nor worm molest me,
Let not Kahgahgee, the raven,
Come to haunt me and molest me,
Only come yourself to watch me,
Till I wake, and start, and quicken,
Till I leap into the sunshine.'
    And thus saying, he departed;
Peacefully slept Hiawatha,
But he heard the Wawonaissa,
Heard the whippoorwill complain-
    ing,
Perched upon his lonely wigwam;
Heard the rushing Sebowisha,
Heard the rivulet rippling near
    him,
Talking to the darksome forest;
Heard the sighing of the branches,
As they lifted and subsided
At the passing of the night-wind,
Heard them, as one hears in slum-
    ber
Far-off murmurs, dreamy whispers:
Peacefully slept Hiawatha.
    On the morrow came Nokomis,
On the seventh day of his fasting,
Came with food for Hiawatha,
Came imploring and bewailing,
Lest his hunger should o'ercome
    him,
Lest his fasting should be fatal.
    But he tasted not, and touched
    not,
Only said to her, 'Nokomis,
Wait until the sun is setting,
Till the darkness falls around us,
Till the heron, the Shuh-shuh-gah,
Crying from the desolate marshes,
Tells us that the day is ended.'
    Homeward weeping went Noko-
    mis,
Sorrowing for her Hiawatha,

Fearing lest his strength should fail
    him,
Lest his fasting should be fatal.
He meanwhile sat weary waiting
For the coming of Mondamin,
Till the shadows, pointing east-
    ward,
Lengthened over field and forest,
Till the sun dropped from the hea-
    ven,
Floating on the waters westward,
As a red leaf in the Autumn
Falls and floats upon the water,
Falls and sinks into its bosom.
    And behold! the young Monda-
    min,
With his soft and shining tresses,
With his garments green and yellow,
With his long and glossy plumage,
Stood and beckoned at the door-
    way.
And as one in slumber walking,
Pale and haggard, but undaunted,
From the wigwam Hiawatha
Came and wrestled with Monda-
    min.
    Round about him spun the land-
    scape,
Sky and forest reeled together,
And his strong heart leaped within
    him,
As the sturgeon leaps and struggles
In a net to break its meshes.
Like a ring of fire around him
Blazed and flared the red horizon,
And a hundred suns seemed look-
    ing
At the combat of the wrestlers.
    Suddenly upon the greensward
All alone stood Hiawatha,
Panting with his wild exertion,
Palpitating with the struggle;
And before him, breathless, lifeless,
Lay the youth, with hair dishe-
    velled,
Plumage torn, and garments tat-
    tered,
Dead he lay there in the sunset.

And victorious Hiawatha
Made the grave as he commanded,
Stripped the garments from Mon-
damin,
Stripped his tattered plumage from
him,
Laid him in the earth, and made it
Soft and loose and light above
him;
And the heron, the Shuh-shuh-gah,
From the melancholy moorlands,
Gave a cry of lamentation,
Gave a cry of pain and anguish!
  Homeward then went Hiawatha
To the lodge of old Nokomis,
And the seven days of his fasting
Were accomplished and completed.
But the place was not forgotten
Where he wrestled with Monda-
min;
Nor forgotten nor neglected
Was the grave where lay Monda-
min,
Sleeping in the rain and sunshine,
Where his scattered plumes and
garments
Faded in the rain and sunshine.
  Day by day did Hiawatha
Go to wait and watch beside it;
Kept the dark mould soft above it,
Kept it clean from weeds and insects,
Drove away, with scoffs and shout-
ings,
Kahgahgee, the king of ravens.
  Till at length a small green fea-
ther
From the earth shot slowly upward,
Then another and another,
And before the Summer ended
Stood the maize in all its beauty,
With its shining robes about it,
And its long, soft, yellow tresses;
And in rapture Hiawatha
Cried aloud, 'It is Mondamin!
Yes, the friend of man, Monda-
min!'
  Then he called to old Nokomis
And Iagoo, the great boaster,

Showed them where the maize was
growing,
Told them of his wondrous vision,
Of his wrestling and his triumph,
Of this new gift to the nations,
Which should be their food for ever.
  And still later, when the Autumn
Changed the long green leaves to
yellow,
And the soft and juicy kernels
Grew like wampum hard and yel-
low,
Then the ripened ears he gathered,
Stripped the withered husks from
off them,
As he once had stripped the
wrestler,
Gave the first Feast of Mondamin,
And made known unto the people
This new gift of the Great Spirit.

VI.

HIAWATHA'S FRIENDS.

Two good friends had Hiawatha,
Singled out from all the others,
Bound to him in closest union,
And to whom he gave the right
hand
Of his heart, in joy and sorrow;
Chibiabos, the musician,
And the very strong man, Kwasind.
  Straight between them ran the
pathway,
Never grew the grass upon it;
Singing birds, that utter falsehoods,
Story-tellers, mischief-makers,
Found no eager ear to listen,
Could not breed ill-will between
them,
For they kept each other's counsel,
Spake with naked hearts together,
Pondering much and much con-
triving
How the tribes of men might pros-
per.

Most beloved by Hiawatha
Was the gentle Chibiabos,
He the best of all musicians,
He the sweetest of all singers.
Beautiful and childlike was he,
Brave as man is, soft as woman,
Pliant as a wand of willow,
Stately as a deer with antlers.

When he sang, the village listened;
All the warriors gathered round him,
All the women came to hear him;
Now he stirred their souls to passion,
Now he melted them to pity.
From the hollow reeds he fashioned
Flutes so musical and mellow,
That the brook, the Sebowisha,
Ceased to murmur in the woodland,
That the wood-birds ceased from singing,
And the squirrel, Adjidaumo,
Ceased his chatter in the oak-tree,
And the rabbit, the Wabasso,
Sat upright to look and listen.

Yes, the brook, the Sebowisha,
Pausing, said, 'O Chibiabos,
Teach my waves to flow in music,
Softly as your words in singing!'

Yes, the bluebird, the Owaissa,
Envious, said, 'O Chibiabos,
Teach me tones as wild and wayward,
Teach me songs as full of frenzy!'

Yes, the robin, the Opechee,
Joyous, said, 'O Chibiabos,
Teach me tones as sweet and tender,
Teach me songs as full of gladness!'

And the whippoorwill, Wawonaissa,
Sobbing, said, 'O Chibiabos,
Teach me tones as melancholy,
Teach me songs as full of sadness!'

All the many sounds of nature
Borrowed sweetness from his singing;
All the hearts of men were softened
By the pathos of his music;
For he sang of peace and freedom,
Sang of beauty, love, and longing;
Sang of death, and life undying
In the Islands of the Blessed,
In the kingdom of Ponemah,
In the land of the Hereafter.

Very dear to Hiawatha
Was the gentle Chibiabos,
He the best of all musicians,
He the sweetest of all singers;
For his gentleness he loved him,
And the magic of his singing.

Dear, too, unto Hiawatha
Was the very strong man, Kwasind,
He the strongest of all mortals,
He the mightiest among many;
For his very strength he loved him,
For his strength allied to goodness.

Idle in his youth was Kwasind,
Very listless, dull, and dreamy,
Never played with other children,
Never fished and never hunted,
Not like other children was he;
But they saw that much he fasted,
Much his Manito entreated,
Much besought his Guardian Spirit.

'Lazy Kwasind!' said his mother,
'In my work you never help me!
In the Summer you are roaming
Idly in the fields and forests;
In the Winter you are cowering
O'er the firebrands in the wigwam!
In the coldest days of Winter
I must break the ice for fishing;
With my nets you never help me!
At the door my nets are hanging,
Dripping, freezing with the water;
Go and wring them, Yenadizze!
Go and dry them in the sunshine!'

Slowly from the ashes Kwasind
Rose, but made no angry answer;

From the lodge went forth in
   silence,
Took the nets, that hung together,
Dripping, freezing at the doorway,
Like a wisp of straw he wrung them,
Like a wisp of straw he broke them,
Could not wring them without
   breaking,
Such the strength was in his fingers.

'Lazy Kwasind!' said his father,
'In the hunt you never help me;
Every bow you touch is broken,
Snapped asunder every arrow;
Yet come with me to the forest,
You shall bring the hunting home-
   ward.'

Down a narrow pass they wan-
   dered,
Where a brooklet led them onward,
Where the trail of deer and bison
Marked the soft mud on the margin,
Till they found all further passage
Shut against them, barred securely
By the trunks of trees uprooted,
Lying lengthwise, lying crosswise,
And forbidding further passage.

'We must go back,' said the old
   man,
'O'er these logs we cannot clamber;
Not a woodchuck could get through
   them,
Not a squirrel clamber o'er them!'
And straightway his pipe he lighted,
And sat down to smoke and ponder.
But before his pipe was finished,
Lo! the path was cleared before
   him;
All the trunks had Kwasind lifted,
To the right hand, to the left hand,
Shot the pine-trees swift as arrows,
Hurled the cedars light as lances.

'Lazy Kwasind!' said the young
   men,
As they sported in the meadow:
'Why stand idly looking at us,
Leaning on the rock behind you?
Come and wrestle with the others,
Let us pitch the quoit together!'

Lazy Kwasind made no answer,
To their challenge made no answer,
Only rose, and, slowly turning,
Seized the huge rock in his fingers,
Tore it from its deep foundation,
Poised it in the air a moment,
Pitched it sheer into the river,
Sheer into the swift Pauwating,
Where it still is seen in Summer.

Once as down that foaming
   river,
Down the rapids of Pauwating,
Kwasind sailed with his compan-
   ions,
In the stream he saw a beaver,
Saw Ahmeek, the King of Beavers,
Struggling with the rushing
   currents,
Rising, sinking in the water.

Without speaking, without paus-
   ing,
Kwasind leaped into the river,
Plunged beneath the bubbling sur-
   face,
Through the whirlpools chased
   the beaver,
Followed him among the islands,
Stayed so long beneath the water,
That his terrified companions
Cried, 'Alas! good-bye to Kwasind!
We shall never more see Kwa-
   sind!'
But he reappeared triumphant,
And upon his shining shoulders
Brought the beaver, dead and
   dripping,
Brought the King of all the Beavers.

And these two, as I have told
   you,
Were the friends of Hiawatha,
Chibiabos, the musician,
And the very strong man, Kwasind.
Long they lived in peace together,
Spake with naked hearts together,
Pondering much and much con-
   triving
How the tribes of men might pros-
   per.

VII.

HIAWATHA'S SAILING.

'GIVE me of your bark, O Birch-
Tree!
Of your yellow bark, O Birch-Tree!
Growing by the rushing river,
Tall and stately in the valley!
I a light canoe will build me,
Build a swift Cheemaun for sailing,
That shall float upon the river,
Like a yellow leaf in Autumn,
Like a yellow water-lily!

'Lay aside your cloak, O Birch-
Tree!
Lay aside your white-skin wrapper,
For the Summer-time is coming,
And the sun is warm in heaven,
And you need no white-skin
wrapper!'

Thus aloud cried Hiawatha
In the solitary forest,
By the rushing Taquamenaw,
When the birds were singing gaily,
In the Moon of Leaves were sing-
ing;
And the sun, from sleep awaking,
Started up and said, 'Behold me!
Geezis, the great Sun, behold me!'

And the tree with all its branches
Rustled in the breeze of morning,
Saying, with a sigh of patience,
'Take my cloak, O Hiawatha!'

With his knife the tree he girdled;
Just beneath its lowest branches,
Just above the roots, he cut it,
Till the sap came oozing outward;
Down the trunk, from top to bottom,
Sheer he cleft the bark asunder,
With a wooden wedge he raised it,
Stripped it from the trunk unbroken.

'Give me of your boughs, O
Cedar!
Of your strong and pliant branches,
My canoe to make more steady,
Make more strong and firm be-
neath me!'

Through the summit of the Cedar
Went a sound, a cry of horror,
Went a murmur of resistance;
But it whispered, bending down-
ward,
'Take my boughs, O Hiawatha!'

Down he hewed the boughs of
cedar,
Shaped them straightway to a
framework,
Like two bows he formed and
shaped them,
Like two bended bows together.

'Give me of your roots, O Tama-
rack!
Of your fibrous roots, O Larch-
Tree!
My canoe to bind together,
So to bind the ends together
That the water may not enter,
That the river may not wet me!'

And the Larch, with all its fibres,
Shivered in the air of morning,
Touched his forehead with its
tassels,
Said, with one long sigh of sorrow,
'Take them all, O Hiawatha!'

From the earth he tore the fibres,
Tore the tough roots of the Larch
Tree,
Closely sewed the bark together,
Bound it closely to the framework.

'Give me of your balm, O Fir-Tree!
Of your balsam and your resin,
So to close the seams together
That the water may not enter,
That the river may not wet me!'

And the Fir-Tree, tall and sombre,
Sobbed through all its robes of
darkness,
Rattled like a shore with pebbles,
Answered wailing, answered weep-
ing,
'Take my balm, O Hiawatha!'

And he took the tears of balsam,
Took the resin of the Fir-Tree,
Smeared therewith each seam and
fissure,
Made each crevice safe from water.

'Give me of your quills, O
   Hedgehog!
All your quills, O Kagh, the Hedge-
   hog!
I will make a necklace of them,
Make a girdle for my beauty,
And two stars to deck her bosom!'
   From a hollow tree the Hedgehog
With his sleepy eyes looked at him,
Shot his shining quills, like arrows,
Saying, with a drowsy murmur,
Through the tangle of his whiskers,
'Take my quills, O Hiawatha!'
   From the ground the quills he
   gathered,
All the little shining arrows,
Stained them red and blue and
   yellow,
With the juice of roots and berries;
Into his canoe he wrought them,
Round its waist a shining girdle,
Round its bows a gleaming neck-
   lace,
On its breast two stars resplendent.
   Thus the Birch Canoe was builded
In the valley, by the river,
In the bosom of the forest;
And the forest's life was in it,
All its mystery and its magic,
All the lightness of the birch-tree,
All the toughness of the cedar,
All the larch's supple sinews;
And it floated on the river
Like a yellow leaf in Autumn,
Like a yellow water-lily.
   Paddles none had Hiawatha,
Paddles none he had or needed,
For his thoughts as paddles served
   him,
And his wishes served to guide
   him;
Swift or slow at will he glided,
Veered to right or left at pleasure.
   Then he called aloud to Kwasind,
To his friend, the strong man,
   Kwasind,
Saying, 'Help me clear this river
Of its sunken logs and sand-bars.'

Straight into the river Kwasind
Plunged as if he were an otter,
Dived as if he were a beaver,
Stood up to his waist in water,
To his arm-pits in the river,
Swam and shouted in the river,
Tugged at sunken logs and branches,
With his hands he scooped the
   sand-bars,
With his feet the ooze and tangle.
   And thus sailed my Hiawatha
Down the rushing Taquamenaw,
Sailed through all its bends and
   windings,
Sailed through all its deeps and
   shallows,
While his friend, the strong man,
   Kwasind,
Swam the deeps, the shallows
   waded.
   Up and down the river went
   they,
In and out among its islands,
Cleared its bed of root and sand-
   bar,
Dragged the dead trees from its
   channel,
Made its passage safe and certain,
Made a pathway for the people,
From its springs among the moun-
   tains,
To the waters of Pauwating,
To the bay of Taquamenaw.

VIII.

HIAWATHA'S FISHING.

FORTH upon the Gitche Gumee,
On the shining Big-Sea-Water,
With his fishing-line of cedar,
Of the twisted bark of cedar,
Forth to catch the sturgeon Nah-
   ma,
Mishe-Nahma, King of Fishes,

In his birch-canoe exulting
All alone went Hiawatha.
  Through the clear, transparent
    water
He could see the fishes swimming
Far down in the depths below
  him ;
See the yellow perch, the Sahwa,
Like a sunbeam in the water,
See the Shawgashee, the crawfish,
Like a spider on the bottom,
On the white and sandy bottom.
  At the stern sat Hiawatha,
With his fishing-line of cedar ;
In his plumes the breeze of morning
Played as in the hemlock branches ;
On the bows, with tail erected,
Sat the squirrel, Adjidaumo ;
In his fur the breeze of morning
Played as in the prairie grasses.
  On the white sand of the bottom
Lay the monster Mishe-Nahma,
Lay the sturgeon, King of Fishes ;
Through his gills he breathed the
  water,
With his fins he fanned and win-
  nowed,
With his tail he swept the sand-
  floor.
  There he lay in all his armour ;
On each side a shield to guard
  him,
Plates of bone upon his forehead,
Down his sides and back and
  shoulders
Plates of bone with spines pro-
  jecting.
Painted was he with his war-
  paints,
Stripes of yellow, red, and azure,
Spots of brown and spots of sable ;
And he lay there on the bottom,
Fanning with his fins of purple,
As above him Hiawatha
In his birch-canoe came sailing,
With his fishing-line of cedar.
  ' Take my bait,' cried Hiawatha,
Down into the depths beneath him,

' Take my bait, O Sturgeon,
  Nahma !
Come up from below the water,
Let us see which is the stronger !'
And he dropped his line of cedar
Through the clear, transparent
  water,
Waited vainly for an answer,
Long sat waiting for an answer,
And repeating loud and louder,
' Take my bait, O King of Fishes !'
  Quiet lay the sturgeon, Nahma,
Fanning slowly in the water,
Looking up at Hiawatha,
Listening to his call and clamour,
His unnecessary tumult,
Till he wearied of the shouting ;
And he said to the Kenozha,
To the pike, the Maskenozha,
' Take the bait of this rude fellow,
Break the line of Hiawatha !'
  In his fingers Hiawatha
Felt the loose line jerk and tighten ;
As he drew it in, it tugged so
That the birch-canoe stood end-
  wise,
Like a birch-log in the water,
With the squirrel, Adjidaumo,
Perched and frisking on the sum-
  mit.
  Full of scorn was Hiawatha
When he saw the fish rise upward,
Saw the pike, the Maskenozha,
Coming nearer, nearer to him,
And he shouted through the water,
' Esa ! esa ! shame upon you !
You are but the pike, Kenozha,
You are not the fish I wanted,
You are not the King of Fishes !'
  Reeling downward to the bottom
Sank the pike in great confusion,
And the mighty sturgeon, Nahma,
Said to Ugudwash, the sun-fish,
To the bream, with scales of crimson,
' Take the bait of this great boaster,
Break the line of Hiawatha !
  Slowly upward, wavering, gleam-
  ing,

Rose the Ugudwash, the sun-fish,
Seized the line of Hiawatha,
Swung with all his weight upon it,
Made a whirlpool in the water,
Whirled the birch-canoe in circles,
Round and round in gurgling
    eddies,
Till the circles in the water
Reached the far-off sandy beaches,
Till the water-flags and rushes
Nodded on the distant margins.

But when Hiawatha saw him
Slowly rising through the water,
Lifting up his disc refulgent,
Loud he shouted in derision,
'Esa! esa! shame upon you!
You are Ugudwash, the sun-fish,
You are not the fish I wanted,
You are not the King of Fishes!'

Slowly downward, wavering,
    gleaming,
Sank the Ugudwash, the sun-fish,
And again the sturgeon, Nahma,
Heard the shout of Hiawatha,
Heard his challenge of defiance,
The unnecessary tumult,
Ringing far across the water.

From the white sand of the
    bottom
Up he rose with angry gesture,
Quivering in each nerve and fibre,
Clashing all his plates of armour,
Gleaming bright with all his war-
    paint;
In his wrath he darted upward,
Flashing leaped into the sunshine,
Opened his great jaws, and swal-
    lowed
Both canoe and Hiawatha.

Down into that darksome cavern
Plunged the headlong Hiawatha,
As a log on some black river
Shoots and plunges down the
    rapids,
Found himself in utter darkness,
Groped about in helpless wonder,
Till he felt a great heart beating,
Throbbing in that utter darkness.

And he smote it in his anger,
With his fist, the heart of Nahma,
Felt the mighty King of Fishes
Shudder through each nerve and
    fibre,
Heard the water gurgle round him
As he leaped and staggered
    through it,
Sick at heart, and faint and weary.

Crosswise then did Hiawatha
Drag his birch-canoe for safety,
Lest from out the jaws of Nahma,
In the turmoil and confusion,
Forth he might be hurled and
    perish.
And the squirrel, Adjidaumo,
Frisked and chattered very gaily,
Toiled and tugged with Hiawatha
Till the labour was completed.

Then said Hiawatha to him,
'O my little friend, the squirrel,
Bravely have you toiled to help
    me;
Take the thanks of Hiawatha,
And the name which now he gives
    you;
For hereafter and for ever
Boys shall call you Adjidaumo,
Tail-in-air the boys shall call you!'

And again the sturgeon, Nahma,
Gasped and quivered in the water,
Then was still, and drifted land-
    ward
Till he grated on the pebbles,
Till the listening Hiawatha
Heard him grate upon the margin,
Felt him strand upon the pebbles,
Knew that Nahma, King of Fishes,
Lay there dead upon the margin.

Then he heard a clang and flap-
    ping,
As of many wings assembling,
Heard a screaming and confusion,
As of birds of prey contending,
Saw a gleam of light above him,
Shining through the ribs of Nahma,
Saw the glittering eyes of sea-gulls,
Of Kayoshk, the sea-gulls, peering,

Gazing at him through the opening,
Heard them saying to each other,
''Tis our brother, Hiawatha!'
And he shouted from below them,
Cried exulting from the caverns:
'O ye sea-gulls! O my brothers!
I have slain the sturgeon, Nahma;
Make the rifts a little larger,
With your claws the openings
   widen,
Set me free from this dark prison,
And henceforward and for ever
Men shall speak of your achieve-
   ments,
Calling you Kayoshk, the sea-gulls,
Yes, Kayoshk, the Noble Scratch-
   ers!'

And the wild and clamorous sea-
   gulls
Toiled with beak and claws together,
Made the rifts and openings wider
In the mighty ribs of Nahma,
And from peril and from prison,
From the body of the sturgeon,
From the peril of the water,
They released my Hiawatha.

He was standing near his wig-
   wam,
On the margin of the water,
And he called to old Nokomis,
Called and beckoned to Nokomis,
Pointed to the sturgeon, Nahma,
Lying lifeless on the pebbles,
With the sea-gulls feeding on him.
'I have slain the Mishe-Nahma,
Slain the King of Fishes!' said he;
'Look! the sea-gulls feed upon him,
Yes, my friends Kayoshk, the sea-
   gulls;
Drive them not away, Nokomis,
They have saved me from great
   peril
In the body of the sturgeon,
Wait until their meal is ended,
Till their craws are full with feast-
   ing,
Till they homeward fly, at sunset,
To their nests among the marshes;

Then bring all your pots and kettles.
And make oil for us in Winter.'
And she waited till the sun set,
Till the pallid moon, the Night-sun,
Rose above the tranquil water,
Till Kayoshk, the sated sea-gulls,
From their banquet rose with
   clamour,
And across the fiery sunset
Winged their way to far-off islands,
To their nests among the rushes.

To his sleep went Hiawatha,
And Nokomis to her labour,
Toiling patient in the moonlight,
Till the sun and moon changed
   places,
Till the sky was red with sunrise,
And Kayoshk, the hungry sea-gulls,
Came back from the reedy islands,
Clamorous for their morning ban-
   quet.

Three whole days and nights
   alternate
Old Nokomis and the sea-gulls
Stripped the oily flesh of Nahma,
Till the waves washed through the
   rib-bones,
Till the sea-gulls came no longer,
And upon the sands lay nothing
But the skeleton of Nahma.

IX.

HIAWATHA AND THE PEARL-FEATHER.

ON the shores of Gitche Gumee,
Of the shining Big-Sea-Water,
Stood Nokomis, the old woman,
Pointing with her finger westward,
O'er the water pointing westward,
To the purple clouds of sunset.

Fiercely the red sun descending
Burned his way along the heavens,
Set the sky on fire behind him,
As war-parties, when retreating,
Burn the prairies on their war-trail;
And the moon, the Night-sun,
   eastward

Suddenly starting from his ambush,
Followed fast those bloody foot-
  prints,
Followed in that fiery war-trail,
With its glare upon his features.

And Nokomis, the old woman,
Pointing with her finger westward,
Spake these words to Hiawatha :
' Yonder dwells the great Pearl-
  Feather,
Megissogwon, the Magician,
Manito of Wealth and Wampum,
Guarded by his fiery serpents,
Guarded by the black pitch-water.
You can see his fiery serpents,
The Kenabeek, the great serpents,
Coiling, playing in the water ;
You can see the black pitch-water
Stretching far away beyond them,
To the purple clouds of sunset !

' He it was who slew my father,
By his wicked wiles and cunning,
When he from the moon descended,
When he came on earth to seek me,
He, the mightiest of Magicians,
Sends the fever from the marshes,
Sends the pestilential vapours,
Sends the poisonous exhalations,
Sends the white fog from the fen-
  lands,
Sends disease and death among us !

' Take your bow, O Hiawatha,
Take your arrows, jasper-headed,
Take your war-club, Puggawaugun,
And your mittens, Minjekahwun,
And your birch-canoe for sailing,
And the oil of Mishe-Nahma,
So to smear its sides, that swiftly
You may pass the black pitch-
  water ;
Slay this merciless magician,
Save the people from the fever
That he breathes across the fen-
  lands,
And avenge my father's murder !'

Straightway then my Hiawatha
Armed himself with all his war-
  gear,

Launched his birch-canoe for sail-
  ing ;
With his palm its sides he patted,
Said with glee, ' Cheemaun, my
  darling,
O my Birch-Canoe ! leap forward,
Where you see the fiery serpents,
Where you see the black pitch-
  water !'

Forward leaped Cheemaun exult-
  ing,
And the noble Hiawatha
Sang his war-song wild and woeful,
And above him the war-eagle,
The Keneu, the great war-eagle,
Master of all fowls with feathers,
Screamed and hurtled through the
  heavens.

Soon he reached the fiery ser-
  pents,
The Kenabeek, the great serpents,
Lying huge upon the water,
Sparkling, rippling in the water,
Lying coiled across the passage,
With their blazing crests uplifted,
Breathing fiery fogs and vapours,
So that none could pass beyond
  them.

But the fearless Hiawatha
Cried aloud, and spake in this wise :
' Let me pass my way, Kenabeek,
Let me go upon my journey !'
And they answered, hissing fiercely,
With their fiery breath made
  answer :
' Back, go back ! O Shaugodaya !
Back to old Nokomis, Faint-heart !'

Then the angry Hiawatha
Raised his mighty bow of ash-tree,
Seized his arrows, jasper-headed,
Shot them fast among the serpents ;
Every twanging of the bow-string
Was a war-cry and a death-cry,
Every whizzing of an arrow
Was a death-song of Kenabeek.

Weltering in the bloody water,
Dead lay all the fiery serpents,
And among them Hiawatha

Harmless sailed, and cried exulting:
'Onward, O Cheemaun, my darling!
Onward to the black pitch-water!'
Then he took the oil of Nahma,
And the bows and sides anointed,
Smeared them well with oil, that swiftly
He might pass the black pitch-water.

All night long he sailed upon it,
Sailed upon that sluggish water,
Covered with its mould of ages,
Black with rotting water-rushes,
Rank with flags and leaves of lilies,
Stagnant, lifeless, dreary, dismal,
Lighted by the shimmering moonlight,
And by will-o'-the-wisps illumined,
Fires by ghosts of dead men kindled
In their weary night-encampments.

All the air was white with moonlight,
All the water black with shadow,
And around him the Suggema,
The mosquito, sang his war-song,
And the fire-flies, Wah-wah-taysee,
Waved their torches to mislead him;
And the bull-frog, the Dahinda,
Thrust his head into the moonlight,
Fixed his yellow eyes upon him,
Sobbed and sank beneath the surface;
And anon a thousand whistles,
Answered over all the fenlands,
And the heron, the Shuh-shuh-gah,
Far off on the reedy margin,
Heralded the hero's coming.

Westward thus fared Hiawatha,
Toward the realm of Megissogwon,
Toward the land of the Pearl-Feather,
Till the level moon stared at him,
In his face stared pale and haggard,
Till the sun was hot behind him,

Till it burned upon his shoulders,
And before him on the upland
He could see the Shining Wigwam
Of the Manito of Wampum,
Of the mightiest of Magicians.

Then once more Cheemaun he patted,
To his birch-canoe said, 'Onward!'
And it stirred in all its fibres,
And with one great bound of triumph
Leaped across the water-lilies,
Leaped through tangled flags and rushes,
And upon the beach beyond them
Dry-shod landed Hiawatha.

Straight he took his bow of ash-tree,
On the sand one end he rested,
With his knee he pressed the middle,
Stretched the faithful bow-string tighter,
Took an arrow, jasper-headed,
Shot it at the Shining Wigwam,
Sent it singing as a herald,
As a bearer of his message,
Of his challenge loud and lofty:
'Come forth from your lodge, Pearl-Feather!
Hiawatha waits your coming!'

Straightway from the Shining Wigwam
Came the mighty Megissogwon,
Tall of stature, broad of shoulder,
Dark and terrible in aspect,
Clad from head to foot in wampum,
Armed with all his warlike weapons,
Painted like the sky of morning,
Streaked with crimson, blue, and yellow,
Crested with great eagle-feathers,
Streaming upward, streaming outward.

'Well I know you, Hiawatha!'
Cried he in a voice of thunder,
In a tone of loud derision.
'Hasten back, O Shaugodaya!
Hasten back among the women,

Back to old Nokomis, Faint-heart!
I will slay you as you stand there,
As of old I slew her father!'
    But my Hiawatha answered,
Nothing daunted, fearing nothing:
'Big words do not smite like war-
    clubs,
Boastful breath is not a bow-
    string,
Taunts are not so sharp as arrows,
Deeds are better things than words
    are,
Actions mightier than boastings!'
    Then began the greatest battle
That the sun had ever looked on,
That the war-birds ever witnessed.
All a summer's day it lasted,
From the sunrise to the sunset;
For the shafts of Hiawatha
Harmless hit the shirt of wampum,
Harmless fell the blows he dealt it
With his mittens, Minjekahwun,
Harmless fell the heavy war-club;
It could dash the rocks asunder,
But it could not break the meshes
Of that magic shirt of wampum.
    Till at sunset Hiawatha,
Leaning on his bow of ash-tree,
Wounded, weary, and desponding,
With his mighty war-club broken,
With his mittens torn and tattered,
And three useless arrows only,
Paused to rest beneath a pine-tree,
From whose branches trailed the
    mosses,
And whose trunk was coated over
With the Dead-man's Moccasin-
    leather,
With the fungus white and yellow.
    Suddenly from the boughs above
    him
Sang the Mama, the woodpecker:
'Aim your arrows, Hiawatha,
At the head of Megissogwon,
Strike the tuft of hair upon it,
At their roots the long black
    tresses;
There alone can he be wounded!'

Winged with feathers, tipped
    with jasper,
Swift flew Hiawatha's arrow,
Just as Megissogwon, stooping,
Raised a heavy stone to throw it.
Full upon the crown it struck him,
At the roots of his long tresses,
And he reeled and staggered for-
    ward,
Plunging like a wounded bison,
Yes, like Pezhekee, the bison,
When the snow is on the prairie.
    Swifter flew the second arrow,
In the pathway of the other,
Piercing deeper than the other,
Wounding sorer than the other;
And the knees of Megissogwon
Shook like windy reeds beneath
    him,
Bent and trembled like the rushes.
    But the third and latest arrow
Swiftest flew, and wounded sorest,
And the mighty Megissogwon
Saw the fiery eyes of Pauguk,
Saw the eyes of Death glare at
    him,
Heard his voice call in the dark-
    ness;
At the feet of Hiawatha
Lifeless lay the great Pearl-Feather,
Lay the mightiest of Magicians.
    Then the grateful Hiawatha
Called the Mama, the woodpecker,
From his perch among the branches
Of the melancholy pine-tree,
And, in honour of his service,
Stained with blood the tuft of
    feathers
On the little head of Mama;
Even to this day he wears it,
Wears the tuft of crimson feathers,
As a symbol of his service.
    Then he stripped the shirt of
    wampum
From the back of Megissogwon,
As a trophy of the battle,
As a signal of his conquest.
On the shore he left the body,

Half on land and half in water,
In the sand his feet were buried,
And his face was in the water,
And above him, wheeled and
    clamoured
The Keneu, the great war-eagle,
Sailing round in narrower circles,
Hovering nearer, nearer, nearer.

From the wigwam Hiawatha
Bore the wealth of Megissogwon,
All his wealth of skins and wam-
    pum,
Furs of bison and of beaver,
Furs of sable and of ermine,
Wampum belts and strings and
    pouches,
Quivers wrought with beads of
    wampum,
Filled with arrows, silver-headed.

Homeward then he sailed exult-
    ing,
Homeward through the black pitch-
    water,
Homeward through the weltering
    serpents,
With the trophies of the battle,
With a shout and song of triumph.

On the shore stood old Nokomis,
On the shore stood Chibiabos,
And the very strong man, Kwa-
    sind,
Waiting for the hero's coming,
Listening to his song of triumph.
And the people of the village
Welcomed him with songs and
    dances,
Made a joyous feast, and shouted:
'Honour be to Hiawatha!
He has slain the great Pearl-
    Feather,
Slain the mightiest of Magicians,
Him, who sent the fiery fever,
Sent the white fog from the fen-
    lands,
Sent disease and death among us!'

Ever dear to Hiawatha
Was the memory of Mama!
And in token of his friendship,

As a mark of his remembrance,
He adorned and decked his pipe-
    stem
With the crimson tuft of feathers,
With the blood-red crest of Mama.
But the wealth of Megissogwon,
All the trophies of the battle,
He divided with his people,
Shared it equally among them.

X.

HIAWATHA'S WOOING.

'As unto the bow the cord is,
So unto the man is woman,
Though she bends him, she obeys
    him,
Though she draws him, yet she
    follows,
Useless each without the other!'

Thus the youthful Hiawatha
Said within himself and pondered,
Much perplexed by various feelings,
Listless, longing, hoping, fearing,
Dreaming still of Minnehaha,
Of the lovely Laughing Water,
In the land of the Dacotahs.

'Wed a maiden of your people,'
Warning said the old Nokomis;
'Go not eastward, go not westward,
For a stranger, whom we know
    not!
Like a fire upon the hearthstone
Is a neighbour's homely daughter;
Like the starlight or the moonlight
Is the handsomest of strangers!'

Thus dissuading spake Nokomis,
And my Hiawatha answered
Only this: 'Dear old Nokomis,
Very pleasant is the firelight,
But I like the starlight better,
Better do I like the moonlight!'

Gravely then said old Nokomis:
'Bring not here an idle maiden,
Bring not here a useless woman,
Hands unskilful, feet unwilling;
Bring a wife with nimble fingers.

Heart and hand that move to-
gether,
Feet that run on willing errands!'
Smiling answered Hiawatha:
'In the land of the Dacotahs
Lives the Arrow-maker's daughter,
Minnehaha, Laughing Water,
Handsomest of all the women.
I will bring her to your wigwam,
She shall run upon your errands,
Be your starlight, moonlight, fire-
light,
Be the sunlight of my people!'
Still dissuading said Nokomis:
'Bring not to my lodge a stranger
From the land of the Dacotahs!
Very fierce are the Dacotahs,
Often is there war between us,
There are feuds yet unforgotten,
Wounds that ache and still may
open!'
Laughing answered Hiawatha:
'For that reason, if no other,
Would I wed the fair Dacotah,
That our tribes might be united,
That old feuds might be forgotten,
And old wounds be healed for
ever!'
Thus departed Hiawatha
To the land of the Dacotahs,
To the land of handsome women;
Striding over moor and meadow,
Through interminable forests,
Through uninterrupted silence.
With his moccasins of magic,
At each stride a mile he measured;
Yet the way seemed long before
him,
And his heart outran his footsteps;
And he journeyed without resting,
Till he heard the cataract's laugh-
ter,
Heard the Falls of Minnehaha
Calling to him through the silence.
'Pleasant is the sound!' he mur-
mured,
'Pleasant is the voice that calls
me!'

On the outskirts of the forest,
'Twixt the shadow and the sun-
shine,
Herds of fallow deer were feeding,
But they saw not Hiawatha;
To his bow he whispered, 'Fail
not!'
To his arrow whispered, 'Swerve
not!'
Sent it singing on its errand,
To the red heart of the roebuck;
Threw the deer across his shoulder,
And sped forward without pausing.
At the doorway of his wigwam
Sat the ancient Arrow-maker,
In the land of the Dacotahs,
Making arrow-heads of jasper,
Arrow-heads of chalcedony.
At his side, in all her beauty,
Sat the lovely Minnehaha,
Sat his daughter, Laughing Water,
Plaiting mats of flags and rushes;
Of the past the old man's thoughts
were,
And the maiden's of the future.
He was thinking, as he sat there,
Of the days when with such arrows
He had struck the deer and bison,
On the Muskoday, the meadow;
Shot the wildgoose, flying south-
ward,
On the wing, the clamorous Wawa;
Thinking of the great war-parties,
How they came to buy his arrows,
Could not fight without his arrows.
Ah, no more such noble warriors
Could be found on earth as they
were!
Now the men were all like women,
Only used their tongues for wea-
pons!
She was thinking of a hunter,
From another tribe and country,
Young and tall and very handsome,
Who one morning in the Spring-
time
Came to buy her father's arrows,
Sat and rested in the wigwam,

Lingered long about the doorway,
Looking back as he departed.
She had heard her father praise him,
Praise his courage and his wisdom;
Would he come again for arrows
To the Falls of Minnehaha?
On the mat her hands lay idle,
And her eyes were very dreamy.

Through their thoughts they
  heard a footstep,
Heard a rustling in the branches,
And with glowing cheek and fore-
  head,
With the deer upon his shoulders,
Suddenly from out the woodlands
Hiawatha stood before them.

Straight the ancient Arrow-
  maker
Looked up gravely from his labour,
Laid aside the unfinished arrow,
Bade him enter at the doorway,
Saying, as he rose to meet him,
'Hiawatha, you are welcome!'

At the feet of Laughing Water
Hiawatha laid his burden,
Threw the red deer from his shoul-
  ders;
And the maiden looked up at him,
Looked up from her mat of rushes,
Said with gentle look and accent,
'You are welcome, Hiawatha!'

Very spacious was the wigwam,
Made of deerskin dressed and
  whitened,
With the Gods of the Dacotahs
Drawn and painted on its curtains,
And so tall the doorway, hardly
Hiawatha stooped to enter,
Hardly touched his eagle-feathers
As he entered at the doorway.

Then uprose the Laughing Water,
From the ground fair Minnehaha,
Laid aside her mat unfinished,
Brought forth food and set before
  them,
Water brought them from the
  brooklet,
Gave them food in earthen vessels,

Gave them drink in bowls of bass-
  wood,
Listened while the guest was speak-
  ing,
Listened while her father answered;
But not once her lips she opened,
Not a single word she uttered.

Yes, as in a dream she listened
To the words of Hiawatha,
As he talked of old Nokomis,
Who had nursed him in his child-
  hood,
As he told of his companions,
Chibiabos, the musician,
And the very strong man, Kwasind,
And of happiness and plenty
In the land of the Ojibways,
In the pleasant land and peaceful.

'After many years of warfare,
Many years of strife and bloodshed,
There is peace between the Ojibways
And the tribe of the Dacotahs.'
Thus continued Hiawatha,
And then added, speaking slowly,
'That this peace may last for ever,
And our hands be clasped more
  closely,
And our hearts be more united,
Give me as my wife this maiden,
Minnehaha, Laughing Water,
Loveliest of Dacotah women!'

And the ancient Arrow-maker
Paused a moment ere he answered,
Smoked a little while in silence,
Looked at Hiawatha proudly,
Fondly looked at Laughing Water,
And made answer very gravely:
'Yes, if Minnehaha wishes;
Let your heart speak, Minnehaha!'

And the lovely Laughing Water
Seemed more lovely, as she stood
  there,
Neither willing nor reluctant,
As she went to Hiawatha,
Softly took the seat beside him,
While she said, and blushed to
  say it,
'I will follow you, my husband!'

This was Hiawatha's wooing!
Thus it was he won the daughter
Of the ancient Arrow-maker,
In the land of the Dacotahs!
    From the wigwam he departed,
Leading with him Laughing Water;
Hand in hand they went together,
Through the woodland and the
    meadow,
Left the old man standing lonely
At the doorway of his wigwam,
Heard the Falls of Minnehaha
Calling to them from the distance,
Crying to them from afar off,
'Fare thee well, O Minnehaha!'
    And the ancient Arrow-maker
Turned again unto his labour,
Sat down by his sunny doorway,
Murmuring to himself, and saying:
'Thus it is our daughters leave us,
Those we love, and those who love
    us!
Just when they have learned to
    help us,
When we are old and lean upon
    them,
Comes a youth with flaunting
    feathers,
With his flute of reeds, a stranger
Wanders piping through the village,
Beckons to the fairest maiden,
And she follows where he leads her,
Leaving all things for the stranger!'
    Pleasant was the journey home-
    ward,
Through interminable forests,
Over meadow, over mountain,
Over river, hill, and hollow.
Short it seemed to Hiawatha,
Though they journeyed very slowly,
Though his pace he checked and
    slackened
To the steps of Laughing Water.
    Over wide and rushing rivers
In his arms he bore the maiden;
Light he thought her as a feather,
As the plume upon his head-gear;
Cleared the tangled pathway for her,

Bent aside the swaying branches,
Made at night a lodge of branches,
And a bed with boughs of hemlock,
And a fire before the doorway
With the dry cones of the pine-tree.
    All the travelling winds went
    with them,
O'er the meadow, through the
    forest;
All the stars of night looked at
    them,
Watched with sleepless eyes their
    slumber;
From his ambush in the oak-tree
Peeped the squirrel, Adjidaumo,
Watched with eager eyes the lovers;
And the rabbit, the Wabasso,
Scampered from the path before
    them,
Peering, peeping from his burrow,
Sat erect upon his haunches,
Watched with curious eyes the
    lovers.
    Pleasant was the journey home-
    ward!
All the birds sang loud and sweetly
Songs of happiness and heart's-
    ease;
Sang the bluebird, the Owaissa,
'Happy are you, Hiawatha,
Having such a wife to love you!'
Sang the robin, the Opechee,
'Happy are you, Laughing Water,
Having such a noble husband!'
    From the sky the sun benignant
Looked upon them through the
    branches,
Saying to them, 'O my children,
Love is sunshine, hate is shadow,
Life is checkered shade and sun-
    shine,
Rule by love, O Hiawatha!'
    From the sky the moon looked
    at them,
Filled the lodge with mystic splen-
    dours,
Whispered to them, 'O my chil-
    dren,

Day is restless, night is quiet,
Man imperious, woman feeble ;
Half is mine, although I follow ;
Rule by patience, Laughing Water!'
    Thus it was they journeyed home-
        ward ;
Thus it was that Hiawatha
To the lodge of old Nokomis
Brought the moonlight, starlight,
    firelight,
Brought the sunshine of his people,
Minnehaha, Laughing Water,
Handsomest of all the women
In the land of the Dacotahs,
In the land of handsome women.

XI.

HIAWATHA'S WEDDING-FEAST.

YOU shall hear how Pau-Puk-
    Keewis,
How the handsome Yenadizze
Danced at Hiawatha's wedding ;
How the gentle Chibiabos,
He the sweetest of musicians,
Sang his songs of love and longing ;
How Iagoo, the great boaster,
He the marvellous story-teller,
Told his tales of strange adventure,
That the feast might be more joyous,
That the time might pass more
    gaily,
And the guests be more contented.
    Sumptuous was the feast Noko-
        mis
Made at Hiawatha's wedding ;
All the bowls were made of bass-
    wood,
White and polished very smoothly,
All the spoons of horn of bison,
Black and polished very smoothly.
    She had sent through all the
        village
Messengers with wands of willow,
As a sign of invitation,
As a token of the feasting ;
And the wedding guests assembled

Clad in all their richest raiment,
Robes of fur and belts of wampum,
Splendid with their paint and
    plumage,
Beautiful with beads and tassels.
    First they ate the sturgeon,
        Nahma,
And the pike, the Maskenozha,
Caught and cooked by old Noko-
        mis ;
Then on pemican they feasted,
Pemican and buffalo marrow,
Haunch of deer and hump of bison,
Yellow cakes of the Mondamin,
And the wild rice of the river.
    But the gracious Hiawatha,
And the lovely Laughing Water,
And the careful old Nokomis,
Tasted not the food before them,
Only waited on the others,
Only served their guests in silence.
    And when all the guests had
        finished,
Old Nokomis, brisk and busy,
From an ample pouch of otter,
Filled the red-stone pipes for
    smoking
With tobacco from the South-land,
Mixed with bark of the red willow,
And with herbs and leaves of
    fragrance.
    Then she said, 'O Pau-Puk-
        Keewis,
Dance for us your merry dances,
Dance the Beggar's Dance to please
    us,
That the feast may be more joyous,
That the time may pass more gaily,
And our guests be more contented!'
    Then the handsome Pau-Puk-
        Keewis,
He the idle Yenadizze,
He the merry mischief-maker,
Whom the people called the Storm-
    Fool,
Rose among the guests assembled.
    Skilled was he in sports and
        pastimes,

In the merry dance of snow-shoes,
In the play of quoits and ball-
play;
Skilled was he in games of hazard,
In all games of skill and hazard,
Pugasaing, the Bowl and Counters,
Kuntassoo, the Game of Plum-
stones.

Though the warriors called him
Faint-heart,
Called him coward, Shaugodaya,
Idler, gambler, Yenadizze,
Little heeded he their jesting,
Little cared he for their insults,
For the women and the maidens
Loved the handsome Pau-Puk-
Keewis.

He was dressed in shirt of doe-
skin,
White and soft, and fringed with
ermine,
All inwrought with beads of wam-
pum;
He was dressed in deerskin leg-
gings,
Fringed with hedgehog quills and
ermine,
And in moccasins of buckskin,
Thick with quills and beads em-
broidered.
On his head were plumes of swan's
down,
On his heels were tails of foxes,
In one hand a fan of feathers,
And a pipe was in the other.

Barred with streaks of red and
yellow,
Streaks of blue and bright ver-
milion,
Shone the face of Pau-Puk-Keewis.
From his forehead fell his tresses,
Smooth, and parted like a woman's,
Shining bright with oil, and plaited,
Hung with braids of scented
grasses,
As among the guests assembled,
To the sound of flutes and singing,
To the sound of drums and voices,

Rose the handsome Pau-Puk-
Keewis,
And began his mystic dances.

First he danced a solemn mea-
sure,
Very slow in step and gesture,
In and out among the pine-trees,
Through the shadows and the
sunshine,
Treading softly like a panther.
Then more swiftly and still swifter,
Whirling, spinning round in circles,
Leaping o'er the guests assembled,
Eddying round and round the
wigwam,
Till the leaves went whirling with
him,
Till the dust and wind together
Swept in eddies round about him.

Then along the sandy margin
Of the lake, the Big-Sea-Water,
On he sped with frenzied gestures,
Stamped upon the sand, and tossed
it
Wildly in the air around him;
Till the wind became a whirlwind,
Till the sand was blown and sifted
Like great snowdrifts o'er the
landscape,
Heaping all the shores with Sand
Dunes,
Sand Hills of the Nagow Wudjoo!

Thus the merry Pau-Puk-Keewis
Danced his Beggar's Dance to
please them,
And, returning, sat down laughing
There among the guests assembled,
Sat and fanned himself serenely
With his fan of turkey-feathers.

Then they said to Chibiabos,
To the friend of Hiawatha,
To the sweetest of all singers,
To the best of all musicians,
'Sing to us, O Chibiabos!
Songs of love and songs of longing,
That the feast may be more joyous,
That the time may pass more gaily,
And our guests be more contented!'

And the gentle Chibiabos
Sang in accents sweet and tender,
Sang in tones of deep emotion,
Songs of love and songs of longing ;
Looking still at Hiawatha,
Looking at fair Laughing Water,
Sang he softly, sang in this wise :

'Onaway ! Awake, beloved !
Thou the wild-flower of the forest !
Thou the wild-bird of the prairie !
Thou with eyes so soft and fawn-
    like !

'If thou only lookest at me,
I am happy, I am happy,
As the lilies of the prairie,
When they feel the dew upon them !

'Sweet thy breath is as the fra-
    grance
Of the wild-flowers in the morning,
As their fragrance is at evening,
In the Moon when leaves are
    falling.

'Does not all the blood within me
Leap to meet thee, leap to meet
    thee,
As the springs to meet the sunshine,
In the Moon when nights are
    brightest ?

'Onaway ! my heart sings to
    thee,
Sings with joy when thou art near
    me,
As the sighing, singing branches
In the pleasant Moon of Straw-
    berries !

'When thou art not pleased,
    beloved,
Then my heart is sad and darkened,
As the shining river darkens
When the clouds drop shadows
    on it !

'When thou smilest, my beloved,
Then my troubled heart is
    brightened,
As in sunshine gleam the ripples
That the cold wind makes in rivers.

'Smiles the earth, and smile the
    waters,
Smile the cloudless skies above us,
But I lose the way of smiling
When thou art no longer near me !

'I myself, myself ! behold me !
Blood of my beating heart, behold
    me !
O awake, awake, beloved !
Onaway ! awake, beloved !'

Thus the gentle Chibiabos
Sang his song of love and longing ;
And Iagoo, the great boaster,
He the marvellous story-teller,
He the friend of old Nokomis,
Jealous of the sweet musician,
Jealous of the applause they gave
    him,
Saw in all the eyes around him,
Saw in all their looks and gestures,
That the wedding guests assembled
Longed to hear his pleasant stories,
His immeasurable falsehoods.

Very boastful was Iagoo ;
Never heard he an adventure
But himself had met a greater ;
Never any deed of daring
But himself had done a bolder ;
Never any marvellous story
But himself could tell a stranger.

Would you listen to his boasting,
Would you only give him credence,
No one ever shot an arrow
Half so far and high as he had ;
Ever caught so many fishes,
Ever killed so many reindeer,
Ever trapped so many beaver !

None could run so fast as he
    could,
None could dive so deep as he
    could,
None could swim so far as he
    could ;
None had made so many journeys,
None had seen so many wonders,
As this wonderful Iagoo,
As this marvellous story-teller !

Thus his name became a by-word
And a jest among the people;
And whene'er a boastful hunter
Praised his own address too highly,
Or a warrior, home returning,
Talked too much of his achievements,
All his hearers cried, 'Iagoo!
Here's Iagoo come among us!'

He it was who carved the cradle
Of the little Hiawatha,
Carved its framework out of linden,
Bound it strong with reindeer
sinews;
He it was who taught him later
How to make his bows and arrows,
How to make the bows of ash-tree,
And the arrows of the oak-tree.
So among the guests assembled
At my Hiawatha's wedding
Sat Iagoo, old and ugly,
Sat the marvellous story-teller.

And they said, 'O good Iagoo,
Tell us now a tale of wonder,
Tell us of some strange adventure,
That the feast may be more joyous,
That the time may pass more
gaily,
And our guests be more contented!'

And Iagoo answered straightway,
'You shall hear a tale of wonder,
You shall hear the strange adventures
Of Osseo, the Magician,
From the Evening Star descended.'

XII.

THE SON OF THE EVENING STAR.

CAN it be the sun descending
O'er the level plain of water?
Or the Red Swan floating, flying,
Wounded by the magic arrow,
Staining all the waves with crimson,
With the crimson of its life-blood,

Filling all the air with splendour,
With the splendour of its plumage?

Yes; it is the sun descending,
Sinking down into the water;
All the sky is stained with purple,
All the water flushed with crimson!
No; it is the Red Swan floating,
Diving down beneath the water;
To the sky its wings are lifted,
With its blood the waves are reddened!

Over it the Star of Evening
Melts and trembles through the
purple,
Hangs suspended in the twilight.
No; it is a bead of wampum
On the robes of the Great Spirit,
As he passes through the twilight,
Walks in silence through the
heavens.

This with joy beheld Iagoo
And he said in haste: 'Behold it!
See the sacred Star of Evening!
You shall hear a tale of wonder,
Hear the story of Osseo,
Son of the Evening Star, Osseo!

'Once, in days no more remembered,
Ages nearer the beginning,
When the heavens were closer to
us,
And the Gods were more familiar,
In the North-land lived a hunter,
With ten young and comely daughters,
Tall and lithe as wands of willow;
Only Oweenee, the youngest,
She the wilful and the wayward,
She the silent, dreamy maiden,
Was the fairest of the sisters.

'All these women married warriors,
Married brave and haughty husbands;
Only Oweenee, the youngest,
Laughed and flouted all her lovers,
All her young and handsome suitors,
And then married old Osseo,

Old Osseo, poor and ugly,
Broken with age and weak with
coughing,
Always coughing like a squirrel.
'Ah, but beautiful within him
Was the spirit of Osseo,
From the Evening Star descended,
Star of Evening, Star of Woman,
Star of tenderness and passion !
All its fire was in his bosom,
All its beauty in his spirit,
All its mystery in his being,
All its splendour in his language !
'And her lovers, the rejected,
Handsome men with belts of wam-
pum,
Handsome men with paint and
feathers,
Pointed at her in derision,
Followed her with jest and laughter.
But she said : "I care not for you,
Care not for your belts of wampum,
Care not for your paint and feathers,
Care not for your jests and laughter;
I am happy with Osseo ! "
'Once to some great feast invited,
Through the damp and dusk of
evening
Walked together the ten sisters,
Walked together with their hus-
bands ;
Slowly followed old Osseo,
With fair Oweenee beside him ;
All the others chatted gaily,
These two only walked in silence.
'At the western sky Osseo
Gazed intent, as if imploring,
Often stopped and gazed imploring
At the trembling Star of Evening,
At the tender Star of Woman ;
And they heard him murmur softly,
"*Ah, showain nemeshin, Nosa !*
Pity, pity me, my father ! "
'"Listen ! " said the eldest
sister,
"He is praying to his father !
What a pity that the old man
Does not stumble in the pathway,

Does not break his neck by falling ! "
And they laughed till all the forest
Rang with their unseemly laughter.
'On their pathway through the
woodlands
Lay an oak, by storms uprooted,
Lay the great trunk of an oak-tree,
Buried half in leaves and mosses,
Mouldering, crumbling, huge and
hollow.
And Osseo, when he saw it,
Gave a shout, a cry of anguish,
Leaped into its yawning cavern—
At one end went in an old man,
Wasted, wrinkled, old, and ugly ;
From the other came a young man,
Tall and straight and strong and
handsome.
'Thus Osseo was transfigured,
Thus restored to youth and beauty ;
But, alas for good Osseo,
And for Oweenee, the faithful !
Strangely, too, was she transfigured.
Changed into a weak old woman,
With a staff she tottered onward,
Wasted, wrinkled, old, and ugly !
And the sisters and their husbands
Laughed until the echoing forest
Rang with their unseemly laughter.
'But Osseo turned not from her,
Walked with slower step beside her,
Took her hand, as brown and
withered
As an oak-leaf is in Winter,
Called her sweetheart, Nenemoo-
sha,
Soothed her with soft words of
kindness,
Till they reached the lodge of feast-
ing,
Till they sat down in the wigwam,
Sacred to the Star of Evening,
To the tender Star of Woman.
'Wrapt in visions, lost in dream-
ing,
At the banquet sat Osseo ;
All were merry, all were happy,
All were joyous but Osseo.

Neither food nor drink he tasted,
Neither did he speak nor listen,
But as one bewildered sat he,
Looking dreamily and sadly,
First at Oweenee, then upward
At the gleaming sky above them.

'Then a voice was heard, a whisper,
Coming from the starry distance,
Coming from the empty vastness,
Low, and musical, and tender;
And the voice said: "O Osseo!
O my son, my best beloved!
Broken are the spells that bound you,
All the charms of the magicians,
All the magic powers of evil;
Come to me; ascend, Osseo!

'"Taste the food that stands before you:
It is blessed and enchanted,
It has magic virtues in it,
It will change you to a spirit.
All your bowls and all your kettles
Shall be wood and clay no longer;
But the bowls be changed to wampum,
And the kettles shall be silver;
They shall shine like shells of scarlet,
Like the fire shall gleam and glimmer.

'"And the women shall no longer
Bear the dreary doom of labour,
But be changed to birds, and glisten
With the beauty of the starlight,
Painted with the dusky splendours
Of the skies and clouds of evening!"'

'What Osseo heard as whispers,
What as words he comprehended,
Was but music to the others,
Music as of birds afar off,
Of the whippoorwill afar off,
Of the lonely Wawonaissa
Singing in the darksome forest.

'Then the lodge began to tremble,
Straight began to shake and tremble,
And they felt it rising, rising,

Slowly through the air ascending,
From the darkness of the tree-tops,
Forth into the dewy starlight,
Till it passed the topmost branches;
And behold! the wooden dishes
All were changed to shells of scarlet!
And behold! the earthen kettles
All were changed to bowls of silver!
And the roof-poles of the wigwam
Were as glittering rods of silver,
And the roof of bark upon them
As the shining shards of beetles.

'Then Osseo gazed around him,
And he saw the nine fair sisters,
All the sisters and their husbands,
Changed to birds of various plumage.
Some were jays and some were magpies,
Others thrushes, others blackbirds;
And they hopped, and sang, and twittered,
Perked and fluttered all their feathers,
Strutted in their shining plumage,
And their tails like fans unfolded.

'Only Oweenee, the youngest,
Was not changed, but sat in silence,
Wasted, wrinkled, old, and ugly,
Looking sadly at the others;
Till Osseo, gazing upward,
Gave another cry of anguish,
Such a cry as he had uttered
By the oak-tree in the forest.

'Then returned her youth and beauty,
And her soiled and tattered garments
Were transformed to robes of ermine,
And her staff became a feather,
Yes, a shining silver feather!

'And again the wigwam trembled,
Swayed and rushed through airy currents,
Through transparent cloud and vapour,

And amid celestial splendours
On the Evening Star alighted,
As a snow-flake falls on snow-
flake,
As a leaf drops on a river,
As the thistle-down on water.

  'Forth with cheerful words of
    welcome
Came the father of Osseo,
He with radiant locks of silver,
He with eyes serene and tender.
And he said : "My son, Osseo,
Hang the cage of birds you bring
    there,
Hang the cage with rods of silver,
And the birds with glistening
    feathers,
At the doorway of my wigwam."

  'At the door he hung the bird-
    cage,
And they entered in and gladly
Listened to Osseo's father,
Ruler of the Star of Evening,
As he said : "O my Osseo !
I have had compassion on you,
Given you back your youth and
    beauty,
Into birds of various plumage
Changed your sisters and their
    husbands ;
Changed them thus because they
    mocked you
In the figure of the old man,
In that aspect sad and wrinkled,
Could not see your heart of passion,
Could not see your youth immortal;
Only Oweenee, the faithful,
Saw your naked heart and loved
    you.

  '"In the lodge that glimmers
    yonder,
In the little star that twinkles
Through the vapours, on the left
    hand,
Lives the envious Evil Spirit,
The Wabeno, the magician,
Who transformed you to an old
    man.

Take heed lest his beams fall on you,
For the rays he darts around him
Are the power of his enchantment,
Are the arrows that he uses."

  'Many years, in peace and quiet,
On the peaceful Star of Evening
Dwelt Osseo with his father ;
Many years, in song and flutter,
At the doorway of the wigwam
Hung the cage with rods of silver,
And fair Oweenee, the faithful,
Bore a son unto Osseo,
With the beauty of his mother,
With the courage of his father.

  'And the boy grew up and
    prospered,
And Osseo, to delight him,
Made him little bows and arrows,
Opened the great cage of silver,
And let loose his aunts and uncles,
All those birds with glossy feathers,
For his little son to shoot at.

  'Round and round they wheeled
    and darted,
Filled the Evening Star with music,
With their songs of joy and free-
    dom ;
Filled the Evening Star with
    splendour,
With the fluttering of their plum-
    age ;
Till the boy, the little hunter,
Bent his bow and shot an arrow,
Shot a swift and fatal arrow,
And a bird, with shining feathers,
At his feet fell wounded sorely.

  'But, O wondrous transforma-
    tion !
'Twas no bird he saw before him,
'Twas a beautiful young woman,
With the arrow in her bosom !

  'When her blood fell on the
    planet,
On the sacred Star of Evening,
Broken was the spell of magic,
Powerless was the strange enchant-
    ment,
And the youth, the fearless bowman,

Suddenly felt himself descending,
Held by unseen hands, but sinking
Downward through the empty
  spaces,
Downward through the clouds and
  vapours,
Till he rested on an island,
On an island, green and grassy,
Yonder in the Big-Sea-Water.
  'After him he saw descending
All the birds with shining feathers,
Fluttering, falling, wafted down-
  ward,
Like the painted leaves of Autumn;
And the lodge with poles of silver,
With its roof like wings of beetles,
Like the shining shards of beetles,
By the winds of heaven uplifted,
Slowly sank upon the island,
Bringing back the good Osseo,
Bringing Oweenee, the faithful.
  'Then the birds, again trans-
  figured,
Reassumed the shape of mortals,
Took their shape, but not their
  stature;
They remained as Little People,
Like the pigmies, the Puk-Wudjies,
And on pleasant nights of Summer,
When the Evening Star was shining,
Hand in hand they danced together
On the island's craggy headlands,
On the sand-beach low and level.
  'Still their glittering lodge is seen
  there
On the tranquil Summer evenings,
And upon the shore the fisher
Sometimes hears their happy
  voices,
Sees them dancing in the starlight!'
  When the story was completed,
When the wondrous tale was ended,
Looking round upon his listeners,
Solemnly Iagoo added:
'There are great men, I have known
  such,
Whom their people understand not,
Whom they even make a jest of,

Scoff and jeer at in derision.
From the story of Osseo
Let us learn the fate of jesters!'
  All the wedding guests delighted
Listened to the marvellous story,
Listened laughing and applauding,
And they whispered to each other:
'Does he mean himself, I wonder?
And are we the aunts and uncles?'
  Then again sang Chibiabos,
Sang a song of love and longing,
In those accents sweet and tender,
In those tones of pensive sadness,
Sang a maiden's lamentation
For her lover, her Algonquin.
  'When I think of my beloved,
Ah me! think of my beloved,
When my heart is thinking of him,
O my sweetheart, my Algonquin!
  'Ah me! when I parted from him,
Round my neck he hung the
  wampum,
As a pledge, the snow-white
  wampum,
O my sweetheart, my Algonquin!
  'I will go with you, he whispered,
Ah me! to your native country;
Let me go with you, he whispered,
O my sweetheart, my Algonquin!
  'Far away, away, I answered,
Very far away, I answered,
Ah me! is my native country,
O my sweetheart, my Algonquin!
  'When I looked back to behold
  him,
Where we parted, to behold him,
After me he still was gazing,
O my sweetheart, my Algonquin!
  'By the tree he still was standing,
By the fallen tree was standing,
That had dropped into the water,
O my sweetheart, my Algonquin!
  'When I think of my beloved,
Ah me! think of my beloved,
When my heart is thinking of him,
O my sweetheart, my Algonquin!'
  Such was Hiawatha's Wedding,
Such the dance of Pau-Puk-Keewis,

Such the story of Iagoo,
Such the songs of Chibiabos;
Thus the wedding banquet ended,
And the wedding guests departed,
Leaving Hiawatha happy
With the night and Minnehaha.

XIII.

BLESSING THE CORNFIELDS.

SING, O Song of Hiawatha,
Of the happy days that followed,
In the land of the Ojibways,
In the pleasant land and peaceful!
Sing the mysteries of Mondamin,
Sing the Blessing of the Cornfields!

Buried was the bloody hatchet,
Buried was the dreadful war-club,
Buried were all warlike weapons,
And the war-cry was forgotten.
There was peace among the nations;
Unmolested roved the hunters,
Built the birch-canoe for sailing,
Caught the fish in lake and river,
Shot the deer and trapped the
beaver;
Unmolested worked the women,
Made their sugar from the maple,
Gathered wild rice in the meadows,
Dressed the skins of deer and
beaver.

All around the happy village
Stood the maize-fields, green and
shining,
Waved the green plumes of Mon-
damin,
Waved his soft and sunny tresses,
Filling all the land with plenty.
'Twas the women who in Spring-
time
Planted the broad fields and fruitful,
Buried in the earth Mondamin;
'Twas the women who in Autumn
Stripped the yellow husks of harvest,
Stripped the garments from Mon-
damin,
Even as Hiawatha taught them.

Once, when all the maize was
planted,
Hiawatha, wise and thoughtful,
Spake and said to Minnehaha,
To his wife, the Laughing Water:
'You shall bless to-night the corn-
fields,
Draw a magic circle round them,
To protect them from destruction,
Blast of mildew, blight of insect,
Wagemin, the thief of cornfields,
Paimosaid, who steals the maize-
ear!

'In the night, when all is silence,
In the night, when all is darkness,
When the Spirit of Sleep, Nepah-
win,
Shuts the doors of all the wigwams,
So that not an ear can hear you,
So that not an eye can see you,
Rise up from your bed in silence,
Lay aside your garments wholly,
Walk around the fields you planted,
Round the borders of the corn-
fields,
Covered by your tresses only,
Robed with darkness as a garment.

'Thus the fields shall be more
fruitful,
And the passing of your footsteps
Draw a magic circle round them,
So that neither blight nor mildew,
Neither burrowing worm nor insect,
Shall pass o'er the magic circle;
Not the dragon-fly, Kwo-ne-she,
Nor the spider, Subbekashe,
Nor the grasshopper, Pah-puk-
keena,
Nor the mighty caterpillar,
Way-muk-kwana, with the bear-
skin,
King of all the caterpillars!'

On the tree-tops near the corn-
fields
Sat the hungry crows and ravens,
Kahgahgee, the King of Ravens,
With his band of black marauders.
And they laughed at Hiawatha,

Till the tree-tops shook with
   laughter,
With their melancholy laughter,
At the words of Hiawatha.
'Hear him!' said they; 'hear the
   Wise Man,
Hear the plots of Hiawatha!'

   When the noiseless night de-
   scended
Broad and dark o'er field and forest,
When the mournful Wawonaissa,
Sorrowing sang among the hem-
   locks,
And the Spirit of Sleep, Nepahwin,
Shut the doors of all the wigwams,
From her bed rose Laughing Water,
Laid aside her garments wholly,
And with darkness clothed and
   guarded,
Unashamed and unaffrighted,
Walked securely round the corn-
   fields,
Drew the sacred magic circle
Of her footprints round the corn-
   fields.

   No one but the Midnight only
Saw her beauty in the darkness;
No one but the Wawonaissa
Heard the panting of her bosom;
Guskewau, the darkness, wrapped
   her
Closely in his sacred mantle,
So that none might see her beauty,
So that none might boast, 'I saw
   her!'

   On the morrow, as the day
   dawned,
Kahgahgee, the King of Ravens,
Gathered all his black marauders,
Crows and blackbirds, jays and
   ravens,
Clamorous on the dusky tree-tops,
And descended, fast and fearless,
On the fields of Hiawatha,
On the grave of the Mondamin.
'We will drag Mondamin,' said
   they,
'From the grave where he is buried,

Spite of all the magic circles
Laughing Water draws around it,
Spite of all the sacred footprints
Minnehaha stamps upon it!'

   But the wary Hiawatha,
Ever thoughtful, careful, watchful,
Had o'erheard the scornful laughter
When they mocked him from the
   tree-tops.
'Kaw!' he said, 'my friends the
   ravens!
Kahgahgee, my King of Ravens!
I will teach you all a lesson
That shall not be soon forgotten!'

   He had risen before the day-
   break,
He had spread o'er all the corn-
   fields
Snares to catch the black marau-
   ders,
And was lying now in ambush
In the neighbouring grove of pine-
   trees,
Waiting for the crows and black-
   birds,
Waiting for the jays and ravens.

   Soon they came with caw and
   clamour,
Rush of wings and cry of voices,
To their work of devastation,
Settling down upon the cornfields,
Delving deep with beak and talon,
For the body of Mondamin.
And with all their craft and cunning,
All their skill in wiles of warfare,
They perceived no danger near
   them,
Till their claws became entangled,
Till they found themselves im-
   prisoned
In the snares of Hiawatha.

   From his place of ambush came
   he,
Striding terrible among them,
And so awful was his aspect
That the bravest quailed with terror.
Without mercy he destroyed them
Right and left, by tens and twenties,

244

And their wretched, lifeless bodies
Hung aloft on poles for scarecrows
Round the consecrated cornfields,
As a signal of his vengeance,
As a warning to marauders.

Only Kahgahgee, the leader,
Kahgahgee, the King of Ravens,
He alone was spared among them
As a hostage for his people.
With his prisoner-string he bound
    him,
Led him captive to his wigwam,
Tied him fast with cords of elm-
    bark
To the ridge-pole of his wigwam.

'Kahgahgee, my raven!' said he,
'You the leader of the robbers,
You the plotter of this mischief,
The contriver of this outrage,
I will keep you, I will hold you,
As a hostage for your people,
As a pledge of good behaviour!'

And he left him, grim and sulky,
Sitting in the morning sunshine
On the summit of the wigwam,
Croaking fiercely his displeasure,
Flapping his great sable pinions,
Vainly struggling for his freedom,
Vainly calling on his people!

Summer passed, and Shawon-
    dasee
Breathed his sighs o'er all the
    landscape,
From the South-land sent his
    ardours,
Wafted kisses warm and tender;
And the maize-field grew and
    ripened,
Till it stood in all the splendour
Of its garments green and yellow,
Of its tassels and its plumage,
And the maize-ears full and shining
Gleamed from bursting sheaths of
    verdure.

Then Nokomis, the old woman,
Spake, and said to Minnehaha:
'Tis the Moon when leaves are
    falling;

All the wild-rice has been gathered,
And the maize is ripe and ready;
Let us gather in the harvest,
Let us wrestle with Mondamin,
Strip him of his plumes and tassels,
Of his garments green and yellow!'

And the merry Laughing Water
Went rejoicing from the wigwam,
With Nokomis, old and wrinkled,
And they called the women round
    them,
Called the young men and the
    maidens,
To the harvest of the cornfields,
To the husking of the maize-ear.

On the border of the forest,
Underneath the fragrant pine-trees,
Sat the old men and the warriors
Smoking in the pleasant shadow.
In uninterrupted silence
Looked they at the gamesome
    labour
Of the young men and the women;
Listened to their noisy talking,
To their laughter and their singing,
Heard them chattering like the
    magpies,
Heard them laughing like the blue-
    jays,
Heard them singing like the robins.

And whene'er some lucky maiden
Found a red ear in the husking,
Found a maize-ear red as blood
    is,
'Nushka!' cried they all together,
'Nushka! you shall have a sweet-
    heart,
You shall have a handsome hus-
    band!'
'Ugh!' the old men all responded
From their seats beneath the pine-
    trees.

And whene'er a youth or maiden
Found a crooked ear in husking,
Found a maize-ear in the husking
Blighted, mildewed, or misshapen,
Then they laughed and sang to-
    gether.

Crept and limped about the corn-
  fields,
Mimicked in their gait and gestures
Some old man, bent almost double,
Singing singly or together:
'Wagemin, the thief of cornfields!
Paimosaid, who steals the maize-
  ear!'
  Till the cornfields rang with
  laughter,
Till from Hiawatha's wigwam
Kahgahgee, the King of Ravens,
Screamed and quivered in his
  anger,
And from all the neighbouring
  tree-tops
Cawed and croaked the black
  marauders.
'Ugh!' the old men all responded,
From their seats beneath the pine-
  trees!

XIV.

PICTURE-WRITING.

In those days said Hiawatha,
'Lo! how all things fade and
  perish!
From the memory of the old men
Pass away the great traditions,
The achievements of the warriors,
The adventures of the hunters,
All the wisdom of the Medas,
All the craft of the Wabenos,
All the marvellous dreams and
  visions
Of the Jossakeeds, the Prophets!
  'Great men die and are for-
  gotten,
Wise men speak; their words of
  wisdom
Perish in the ears that hear them,
Do not reach the generations
That, as yet unborn, are waiting
In the great, mysterious darkness
Of the speechless days that shall
  be!

'On the grave-posts of our fathers
Are no signs, no figures painted;
Who are in those graves we know
  not,
Only know they are our fathers.
Of what kith they are and kindred,
From what old, ancestral Totem,
Be it Eagle, Bear, or Beaver,
They descended, this we know not,
Only know they are our fathers.
  'Face to face we speak together,
But we cannot speak when absent,
Cannot send our voices from us
To the friends that dwell afar off;
Cannot send a secret message,
But the bearer learns our secret,
May pervert it, may betray it,
May reveal it unto others.'
  Thus said Hiawatha, walking
In the solitary forest,
Pondering, musing in the forest,
On the welfare of his people.
  From his pouch he took his
  colours,
Took his paints of different colours,
On the smooth bark of a birch-tree
Painted many shapes and figures,
Wonderful and mystic figures,
And each figure had a meaning,
Each some word or thought sug-
  gested.
  Gitche Manito the Mighty,
He, the Master of Life, was painted
As an egg, with points projecting
To the four winds of the heavens.
Everywhere is the Great Spirit,
Was the meaning of this symbol.
  Mitche Manito the Mighty,
He the dreadful Spirit of Evil,
As a serpent was depicted,
As Kenabeek, the great serpent.
Very crafty, very cunning,
Is the creeping Spirit of Evil,
Was the meaning of this symbol.
  Life and Death he drew as
  circles,
Life was white, but Death was
  darkened;

Sun and moon and stars he painted,
Man and beast, and fish and reptile,
Forests, mountains, lakes, and
  rivers.
  For the earth he drew a straight
  line,
For the sky a bow above it;
White the space between for day-
  time,
Filled with little stars for night-
  time;
On the left a point for sunrise,
On the right a point for sunset,
On the top a point for noontide,
And for rain and cloudy weather
Waving lines descending from it.
  Footprints pointing towards a
  wigwam
Were a sign of invitation,
Were a sign of guests assembling;
Bloody hands with palms uplifted
Were a symbol of destruction,
Were a hostile sign and symbol.
  All these things did Hiawatha
Show unto his wondering people,
And interpreted their meaning,
And he said: 'Behold, your grave-
  posts
Have no mark, no sign, nor symbol.
Go and paint them all with figures;
Each one with its household sym-
  bol,
With its own ancestral Totem;
So that those who follow after
May distinguish them and know
  them.'
  And they painted on the grave-
  posts,
On the graves yet unforgotten,
Each his own ancestral Totem,
Each the symbol of his house-
  hold;
Figures of the Bear and Reindeer,
Of the Turtle, Crane, and Beaver,
Each inverted as a token
That the owner was departed,
That the chief who bore the symbol
Lay beneath in dust and ashes.

And the Jossakeeds, the Pro-
  phets,
The Wabenos, the Magicians,
And the Medicine-men, the Medas,
Painted upon bark and deerskin
Figures for the songs they chanted,
For each song a separate symbol,
Figures mystical and awful,
Figures strange and brightly
  coloured;
And each figure had its meaning,
Each some magic song suggested.
  The Great Spirit, the Creator,
Flashing light through all the
  heaven;
The Great Serpent, the Kenabeek,
With his bloody crest erected,
Creeping, looking into heaven;
In the sky the sun, that listens,
And the moon eclipsed and dying;
Owl and eagle, crane and hen-
  hawk,
And the cormorant, bird of magic;
Headless men, that walk the
  heavens,
Bodies lying pierced with arrows,
Bloody hands of death uplifted,
Flags on graves, and great war-
  captains
Grasping both the earth and
  heaven!
  Such as these the shapes they
  painted
On the birch-bark and the deer-
  skin;
Songs of war and songs of hunting,
Songs of medicine and of magic,
All were written in these figures,
For each figure had its meaning,
Each its separate song recorded.
  Nor forgotten was the Love-
  Song,
The most subtle of all medicines,
The most potent spell of magic,
Dangerous more than war or hunt-
  ing!
Thus the Love-Song was recorded,
Symbol and interpretation.

First a human figure standing,
Painted in the brightest scarlet;
'Tis the lover, the musician,
And the meaning is, 'My painting
Makes me powerful over others.'

Then the figure seated, singing,
Playing on a drum of magic,
And the interpretation, 'Listen!
'Tis my voice you hear, my sing-
ing!'

Then the same red figure seated
In the shelter of a wigwam,
And the meaning of the symbol,
'I will come and sit beside you
In the mystery of my passion!'

Then two figures, man and
woman,
Standing hand in hand together
With their hands so clasped to-
gether
That they seem in one united,
And the words thus represented
Are, 'I see your heart within
you,
And your cheeks are red with
blushes!'

Next the maiden on an island,
In the centre of an island;
And the song this shape suggested
Was, 'Though you were at a dis-
tance,
Were upon some far-off island,
Such the spell I cast upon you,
Such the magic power of passion,
I could straightway draw you to
me!'

Then the figure of the maiden
Sleeping, and the lover near her,
Whispering to her in her slumbers,
Saying, 'Though you were far from
me
In the land of Sleep and Silence,
Still the voice of love would reach
you!'

And the last of all the figures
Was a heart within a circle,
Drawn within a magic circle;
And the image had this meaning:

'Naked lies your heart before me,
To your naked heart I whisper!'
Thus it was that Hiawatha,
In his wisdom, taught the people
All the mysteries of painting,
All the art of Picture-Writing,
On the smooth bark of the birch-
tree,
On the white skin of the reindeer,
On the grave-posts of the village.

XV.

HIAWATHA'S LAMENTATION.

IN those days the Evil Spirits,
All the Manitos of mischief,
Fearing Hiawatha's wisdom,
And his love for Chibiabos,
Jealous of their faithful friendship,
And their noble words and actions,
Made at length a league against
them,
To molest them and destroy them.

Hiawatha, wise and wary,
Often said to Chibiabos,
'O my brother! do not leave me,
Lest the Evil Spirits harm you!'
Chibiabos, young and heedless,
Laughing shook his coal-black
tresses,
Answered ever sweet and childlike,
'Do not fear for me, O brother!
Harm and evil come not near me!'

Once when Peboan, the Winter,
Roofed with ice the Big-Sea-
Water,
When the snow-flakes, whirling
downward,
Hissed among the withered oak-
leaves,
Changed the pine-trees into wig-
wams,
Covered all the earth with silence,—
Armed with arrows, shod with
snow-shoes,
Heeding not his brother's warning,

Fearing not the Evil Spirits,
Forth to hunt the deer with antlers
All alone went Chibiabos.
Right across the Big-Sea-Water
Sprang with speed the deer before
    him.
With the wind and snow he
    followed,
O'er the treacherous ice he followed,
Wild with all the fierce commotion
And the rapture of the hunting.
But beneath, the Evil Spirits
Lay in ambush, waiting for him,
Broke the treacherous ice beneath
    him,
Dragged him downward to the
    bottom,
Buried in the sand his body.
Unktahee, the god of water,
He the god of the Dacotahs,
Drowned him in the deep abysses
Of the lake of Gitche Gumee.

From the headlands Hiawatha
Sent forth such a wail of anguish,
Such a fearful lamentation,
That the bison paused to listen,
And the wolves howled from the
    prairies,
And the thunder in the distance
Starting answered ' Baim-wawa ! '
Then his face with black he
    painted,
With his robe his head he covered,
In his wigwam sat lamenting,
Seven long weeks he sat lamenting,
Uttering still this moan of
    sorrow :—
' He is dead, the sweet musician !
He the sweetest of all singers !
He has gone from us for ever,
He has moved a little nearer
To the Master of all music,
To the Master of all singing !
O my brother, Chibiabos ! '
And the melancholy fir-trees
Waved their dark green fans above
    him,
Waved their purple cones above him,

Sighing with him to console him,
Mingling with his lamentation
Their complaining, their lamenting.
Came the Spring, and all the
    forest
Looked in vain for Chibiabos ;
Sighed the rivulet, Sebowisha,
Sighed the rushes in the meadow.
From the tree-tops sang the
    bluebird,
Sang the bluebird, the Owaissa,
' Chibiabos ! Chibiabos !
He is dead, the sweet musician ! '
From the wigwam sang the
    robin,
Sang the robin, the Opechee,
' Chibiabos ! Chibiabos !
He is dead, the sweetest singer ! '
And at night through all the
    forest
Went the whippoorwill complain-
    ing,
Wailing went the Wawonaissa,
' Chibiabos ! Chibiabos !
He is dead, the sweet musician !
He the sweetest of all singers ! '
Then the medicine-men, the
    Medas,
The magicians, the Wabenos,
And the Jossakeeds, the prophets,
Came to visit Hiawatha ;
Built a Sacred Lodge beside him,
To appease him, to console him,
Walked in silent grave procession,
Bearing each a pouch of healing,
Skin of beaver, lynx, or otter,
Filled with magic roots and sim-
    ples,
Filled with very potent medicines.
When he heard their steps ap-
    proaching,
Hiawatha ceased lamenting,
Called no more on Chibiabos ;
Naught he questioned, naught he
    answered,
But his mournful head uncovered,
From his face the mourning colours
Washed he slowly and in silence,

Slowly and in silence followed
Onward to the Sacred Wigwam.
  There a magic drink they gave
    him,
Made of Nahma-wusk, the spear-
    mint,
And Wabeno-wusk, the yarrow,
Roots of power, and herbs of heal-
    ing;
Beat their drums, and shook their
    rattles;
Chanted singly and in chorus,
Mystic songs like these, they
    chanted.
  'I myself, myself! behold me!
'Tis the great Gray Eagle talk-
    ing;
Come, ye white crows, come and
    hear him!
The loud-speaking thunder helps
    me;
All the unseen spirits help me;
I can hear their voices calling,
All around the sky I hear them!
I can blow you strong, my brother,
I can heal you, Hiawatha!'
  'Hi-au-ha!' replied the chorus,
'Way-ha-way!' the mystic chorus.
  'Friends of mine are all the
    serpents!
Hear me shake my skin of hen-
    hawk!
Mahng, the white loon, I can kill
    him;
I can shoot your heart and kill it!
I can blow you strong, my brother,
I can heal you, Hiawatha!'
  'Hi-au-ha!' replied the chorus,
'Way-ha-way!' the mystic chorus.
  'I myself, myself! the prophet!
When I speak the wigwam trem-
    bles,
Shakes the Sacred Lodge with
    terror,
Hands unseen begin to shake it!
When I walk, the sky I tread on
Bends and makes a noise beneath
    me!

I can blow you strong, my brother!
Rise and speak, O Hiawatha!'
  'Hi-au-ha!' replied the chorus,
'Way-ha-way!' the mystic chorus.
  Then they shook their medicine-
    pouches
O'er the head of Hiawatha,
Danced their medicine-dance
    around him;
And upstarting wild and haggard,
Like a man from dreams awakened,
He was healed of all his madness.
As the clouds are swept from
    heaven,
Straightway from his brain de-
    parted
All his moody melancholy;
As the ice is swept from rivers,
Straightway from his heart de-
    parted
All his sorrow and affliction.
  Then they summoned Chibiabos
From his grave beneath the waters,
From the sands of Gitche Gumee
Summoned Hiawatha's brother.
And so mighty was the magic
Of that cry and invocation,
That he heard it as he lay there
Underneath the Big-Sea-Water;
From the sand he rose and listened,
Heard the music and the singing,
Came, obedient to the summons,
To the doorway of the wigwam,
But to enter they forbade him.
  Through a chink a coal they gave
    him,
Through the door a burning fire-
    brand;
Ruler in the Land of Spirits,
Ruler o'er the dead, they made
    him,
Telling him a fire to kindle
For all those that died thereafter,
Camp-fires for their night encamp-
    ments
On their solitary journey
To the kingdom of Ponemah,
To the land of the Hereafter.

From the village of his childhood,
From the homes of those who knew him,
Passing silent through the forest,
Like a smoke-wreath wafted sideways,
Slowly vanished Chibiabos!
Where he passed, the branches moved not,
Where he trod, the grasses bent not,
And the fallen leaves of last year
Made no sound beneath his footsteps.
  Four whole days he journeyed onward
Down the pathway of the dead men;
On the dead-man's strawberry feasted,
Crossed the melancholy river,
On the swinging log he crossed it,
Came unto the Lake of Silver,
In the Stone Canoe was carried
To the Islands of the Blessed,
To the land of ghosts and shadows.
  On that journey, moving slowly,
Many weary spirits saw he,
Panting under heavy burdens,
Laden with war-clubs, bows and arrows,
Robes of fur, and pots and kettles,
And with food that friends had given
For that solitary journey.
  'Ay! why do the living,' said they,
'Lay such heavy burdens on us!
Better were it to go naked,
Better were it to go fasting,
Than to bear such heavy burdens
On our long and weary journey!'
  Forth then issued Hiawatha,
Wandered eastward, wandered westward,
Teaching men the use of simples
And the antidotes for poisons,

And the cure of all diseases.
Thus was first made known to mortals
All the mystery of Medamin,
All the sacred art of healing.

XVI.

PAU-PUK-KEEWIS.

YOU shall hear how Pau-Puk-Keewis,
He, the handsome Yenadizze,
Whom the people called the Storm Fool,
Vexed the village with disturbance;
You shall hear of all his mischief,
And his flight from Hiawatha,
And his wondrous transmigrations,
And the end of his adventures.
  On the shores of Gitche Gumee,
On the dunes of Nagow Wudjoo,
By the shining Big-Sea-Water
Stood the lodge of Pau-Puk-Keewis.
It was he who in his frenzy
Whirled these drifting sands together,
On the dunes of Nagow Wudjoo,
When, among the guests assembled,
He so merrily and madly
Danced at Hiawatha's wedding,
Danced the Beggar's Dance to please them.
  Now, in search of new adventures,
From his lodge went Pau-Puk-Keewis,
Came with speed into the village,
Found the young men all assembled
In the lodge of old Iagoo,
Listening to his monstrous stories,
To his wonderful adventures.
  He was telling them the story
Of Ojeeg, the Summer-Maker,
How he made a hole in heaven,

How he climbed up into heaven,
And let out the summer-weather,
The perpetual, pleasant Summer ;
How the Otter first essayed it ;
How the Beaver, Lynx, and Badger
Tried in turn the great achievement,
From the summit of the mountain
Smote their fists against the heavens,
Smote against the sky their foreheads,
Cracked the sky, but could not break it ;
How the Wolverine, uprising,
Made him ready for the encounter,
Bent his knees down, like a squirrel,
Drew his arms back, like a cricket.

' Once he leaped,' said old Iagoo,
' Once he leaped, and lo ! above him
Bent the sky, as ice in rivers
When the waters rise beneath it ;
Twice he leaped, and lo ! above him
Cracked the sky, as ice in rivers
When the freshet is at highest !
Thrice he leaped, and lo ! above him
Broke the shattered sky asunder,
And he disappeared within it,
And Ojeeg, the Fisher Weasel,
With a bound went in behind him ! '

' Hark you ! ' shouted Pau-Puk-Keewis
As he entered at the doorway ;
' I am tired of all this talking,
Tired of old Iagoo's stories,
Tired of Hiawatha's wisdom.
Here is something to amuse you,
Better than this endless talking.'

Then from out his pouch of wolf-skin
Forth he drew, with solemn manner,

All the game of Bowl and Counters,
Pugasaing, with thirteen pieces.
White on one side were they painted,
And vermilion on the other ;
Two Kenabeeks or great serpents,
Two Ininewug or wedge-men,
One great war-club, Pugamaugun,
And one slender fish, the Keego,
Four round pieces, Ozawabeeks,
And three Sheshebwug or ducklings.
All were made of bone and painted,
All except the Ozawabeeks ;
These were brass, on one side burnished,
And were black upon the other.

In a wooden bowl he placed them,
Shook and jostled them together,
Threw them on the ground before him.
Thus exclaiming and explaining :
' Red side up are all the pieces,
And one great Kenabeek standing
On the bright side of a brass-piece,
On a burnished Ozawabeek ;
Thirteen tens and eight are counted.'

Then again he shook the pieces,
Shook and jostled them together,
Threw them on the ground before him,
Still exclaiming and explaining :
' White are both the great Kenabeeks,
White the Ininewug, the wedge-men,
Red are all the other pieces ;
Five tens and an eight are counted.'

Thus he taught the game of hazard,
Thus displayed it and explained it,
Running through its various chances,
Various changes, various meanings :
Twenty curious eyes stared at him,
Full of eagerness stared at him.

'Many games,' said old Iagoo,
'Many games of skill and hazard
Have I seen in different nations,
Have I played in different countries.
He who plays with old Iagoo
Must have very nimble fingers;
Though you think yourself so skilful
I can beat you, Pau-Puk-Keewis,
I can even give you lessons
In your game of Bowl and
    Counters!'
    So they sat and played together,
All the old men and the young
    men,
Played for dresses, weapons, wam-
    pum,
Played till midnight, played till
    morning,
Played until the Yenadizze,
Till the cunning Pau-Puk-Keewis,
Of their treasures had despoiled
    them,
Of the best of all their dresses,
Shirts of deerskin, robes of ermine,
Belts of wampum, crests of feathers,
Warlike weapons, pipes and
    pouches.
Twenty eyes glared wildly at him,
Like the eyes of wolves glared at
    him.
    Said the lucky Pau-Puk-Keewis:
'In my wigwam I am lonely,
In my wanderings and adventures
I have need of a companion,
Fain would have a Meshinauwa,
An attendant and pipe-bearer.
I will venture all these winnings,
All these garments heaped about
    me,
All this wampum, all these feathers,
On a single throw will venture
All against the young man yonder!'
'Twas a youth of sixteen summers,
'Twas a nephew of Iagoo;
Face-in-a-Mist, the people called
    him.
    As the fire burns in a pipe-head
Dusky red beneath the ashes,

So beneath his shaggy eyebrows
Glowed the eyes of old Iagoo.
'Ugh!' he answered very fiercely;
'Ugh!' they answered all and each
    one.
    Seized the wooden bowl the old
    man,
Closely in his bony fingers
Clutched the fatal bowl, Onagon,
Shook it fiercely and with fury,
Made the pieces ring together
As he threw them down before
    him.
Red were both the great Kena-
    beeks,
Red the Ininewug, the wedge-
    men,
Red the Sheshebwug, the duck-
    lings,
Black the four brass Ozawabeeks,
White alone the fish, the Keego;
Only five the pieces counted!
    Then the smiling Pau-Puk-
    Keewis
Shook the bowl and threw the
    pieces;
Lightly in the air he tossed them,
And they fell about him scattered;
Dark and bright the Ozawabeeks,
Red and white the other pieces,
And upright among the others
One Ininewug was standing,
Even as crafty Pau-Puk-Keewis
Stood alone among the players,
Saying, 'Five tens! mine the game
    is!'
    Twenty eyes glared at him
    fiercely,
Like the eyes of wolves glared at
    him,
As he turned and left the wigwam,
Followed by his Meshinauwa,
By the nephew of Iagoo,
By the tall and graceful stripling,
Bearing in his arms the winnings,
Shirts of deerskin, robes of ermine,
Belts of wampum, pipes and
    weapons.

253

'Carry them,' said Pau-Puk-
Keewis,
Pointing with his fan of feathers,
'To my wigwam far to eastward,
On the dunes of Nagow Wudjoo!'

Hot and red with smoke and
gambling
Were the eyes of Pau-Puk-Keewis
As he came forth to the freshness
Of the pleasant Summer morning.
All the birds were singing gaily,
All the streamlets flowing swiftly,
And the heart of Pau-Puk-Keewis
Sang with pleasure as the birds sing,
Beat with triumph like the stream-
lets,
As he wandered through the village,
In the early gray of morning,
With his fan of turkey-feathers,
With his plumes and tufts of swan's-
down,
Till he reached the farthest wigwam,
Reached the lodge of Hiawatha.

Silent was it and deserted;
No one met him at the doorway,
No one came to bid him welcome;
But the birds were singing round it,
In and out and round the doorway,
Hopping, singing, fluttering, feed-
ing,
And aloft upon the ridge-pole
Kahgahgee, the King of Ravens,
Sat with fiery eyes, and, screaming,
Flapped his wings at Pau-Puk-
Keewis.

'All are gone! the lodge is
empty!'
Thus it was spake Pau-Puk-
Keewis,
In his heart resolving mischief;—
'Gone is wary Hiawatha,
Gone the silly Laughing Water,
Gone Nokomis, the old woman,
And the lodge is left unguarded!'

By the neck he seized the raven,
Whirled it round him like a rattle,
Like a medicine-pouch he shook it,
Strangled Kahgahgee, the raven,

From the ridge-pole of the wigwam
Left its lifeless body hanging,
As an insult to its master,
As a taunt to Hiawatha.

With a stealthy step he entered,
Round the lodge in wild disorder
Threw the household things about
him,
Piled together in confusion
Bowls of wood and earthen kettles,
Robes of buffalo and beaver,
Skins of otter, lynx, and ermine,
As an insult to Nokomis,
As a taunt to Minnehaha.

Then departed Pau-Puk-Keewis,
Whistling, singing through the
forest,
Whistling gaily to the squirrels,
Who from hollow boughs above him
Dropped their acorn-shells upon
him,
Singing gaily to the wood-birds,
Who from out the leafy darkness
Answered with a song as merry.

Then he climbed the rocky head-
lands,
Looking o'er the Gitche Gumee,
Perched himself upon their summit,
Waiting full of mirth and mischief
The return of Hiawatha.

Stretched upon his back he lay
there;
Far below him plashed the waters,
Plashed and washed the dreamy
waters;
Far above him swam the heavens,
Swam the dizzy, dreamy heavens;
Round him hovered, fluttered,
rustled,
Hiawatha's mountain chickens,
Flock-wise swept and wheeled
about him,
Almost brushed him with their
pinions.

And he killed them as he lay
there,
Slaughtered them by tens and
twenties,

Threw their bodies down the head-
land,
Threw them on the beach below
him,
Till at length Kayoshk, the sea-gull,
Perched upon a crag above them,
Shouted: 'It is Pau-Puk-Keewis!
He is slaying us by hundreds!
Send a message to our brother,
Tidings send to Hiawatha!'

XVII.

THE HUNTING OF PAU-PUK-KEEWIS.

FULL of wrath was Hiawatha
When he came into the village,
Found the people in confusion,
Heard of all the misdemeanours,
All the malice and the mischief,
Of the cunning Pau-Puk-Keewis.

  Hard his breath came through
his nostrils,
Through his teeth he buzzed and
muttered
Words of anger and resentment,
Hot and humming, like a hornet.
'I will slay this Pau-Puk-Keewis,
Slay this mischief-maker!' said he.
'Not so long and wide the world is,
Not so rude and rough the way is,
That my wrath shall not attain him,
That my vengeance shall not reach
him!'

  Then in swift pursuit departed
Hiawatha and the hunters
On the trail of Pau-Puk-Keewis,
Through the forest, where he passed
it,
To the headlands where he rested;
But they found not Pau-Puk-
Keewis,
Only in the trampled grasses,
In the whortleberry-bushes,
Found the couch where he had
rested,
Found the impress of his body.

  From the lowlands far beneath
them,
From the Muskoday, the meadow,
Pau-Puk-Keewis, turning back-
ward,
Made a gesture of defiance,
Made a gesture of derision;
And aloud cried Hiawatha,
From the summit of the mountain:
'Not so long and wide the world
is,
Not so rude and rough the way is,
But my wrath shall overtake you,
And my vengeance shall attain
you!'

  Over rock and over river,
Thorough bush, and brake, and
forest,
Ran the cunning Pau-Puk-Keewis;
Like an antelope he bounded,
Till he came unto a streamlet
In the middle of the forest,
To a streamlet still and tranquil,
That had overflowed its margin,
To a dam made by the beavers,
To a pond of quiet water,
Where knee-deep the trees were
standing,
Where the water-lilies floated,
Where the rushes waved and
whispered.

  On the dam stood Pau-Puk-
Keewis,
On the dam of trunks and
branches,
Through whose chinks the water
spouted,
O'er whose summit flowed the
streamlet.
From the bottom rose the beaver,
Looked with two great eyes of
wonder,
Eyes that seemed to ask a question,
At the stranger, Pau-Puk-Keewis.

  On the dam stood Pau-Puk-
Keewis,
O'er his ankles flowed the stream-
let,

Flowed the bright and silvery
water,
And he spake unto the beaver,
With a smile he spake in this wise :
'O my friend Ahmeek, the
beaver,
Cool and pleasant is the water ;
Let me dive into the water,
Let me rest there in your lodges ;
Change me, too, into a beaver !'
Cautiously replied the beaver,
With reserve he thus made answer :
'Let me first consult the others.
Let me ask the other beavers.'
Down he sank into the water,
Heavily sank he, as a stone sinks,
Down among the leaves and
branches,
Brown and matted at the bottom.
On the dam stood Pau-Puk-
Keewis,
O'er his ankles flowed the stream-
let,
Spouted through the chinks below
him,
Dashed upon the stones beneath
him,
Spread serene and calm before him;
And the sunshine and the shadows
Fell in flecks and gleams upon him,
Fell in little shining patches,
Through the waving, rustling
branches.
From the bottom rose the
beavers,
Silently above the surface
Rose one head and then another,
Till the pond seemed full of
beavers,
Full of black and shining faces.
To the beavers Pau-Puk-Keewis
Spake entreating, said in this wise:
'Very pleasant is your dwelling,
O my friends ! and safe from
danger ;
Can you not with all your cunning,
All your wisdom and contrivance,
Change me, too, into a beaver ?'

'Yes!' replied Ahmeek, the
beaver,
He the King of all the beavers,
'Let yourself slide down among us,
Down into the tranquil water.'
Down into the pond among them
Silently sank Pau-Puk-Keewis ;
Black became his shirt of deerskin,
Black his moccasins and leggings,
In a broad black tail behind him
Spread his fox-tails and his fringes ;
He was changed into a beaver.
'Make me large,' said Pau-Puk-
Keewis,
'Make me large and make me
larger,
Larger than the other beavers.'
'Yes,' the beaver chief responded,
'When our lodge below you enter,
In our wigwam we will make you
Ten times larger than the others.'
Thus into the clear brown water
Silently sank Pau-Puk-Keewis :
Found the bottom covered over
With the trunks of trees and
branches,
Hoards of food against the winter,
Piles and heaps against the famine ;
Found the lodge with arching door-
way,
Leading into spacious chambers.
Here they made him large and
larger,
Made him largest of the beavers,
Ten times larger than the others.
'You shall be our ruler,' said they ;
'Chief and King of all the beavers.'
But not long had Pau-Puk-
Keewis
Sat in state among the beavers,
When there came a voice of warning
From the watchman at his station
In the water-flags and lilies,
Saying, 'Here is Hiawatha !
Hiawatha with his hunters !'
Then they heard a cry above
them,
Heard a shouting and a tramping,

Heard a crashing and a rushing,
And the water round and o'er them
Sank and sucked away in eddies,
And they knew their dam was
    broken.
    On the lodge's roof the hunters
Leaped, and broke it all asunder ;
Streamed the sunshine through the
    crevice,
Sprang the beavers through the
    doorway,
Hid themselves in deeper water,
In the channel of the streamlet ;
But the mighty Pau-Puk-Keewis
Could not pass beneath the door-
    way ;
He was puffed with pride and
    feeding,
He was swollen like a bladder.
    Through the roof looked Hia-
    watha,
Cried aloud, ' O Pau-Puk-Keewis !
Vain are all your craft and cunning,
Vain your manifold disguises !
Well I know you, Pau-Puk-Keewis !'
    With their clubs they beat and
    bruised him,
Beat to death poor Pau-Puk-
    Keewis,
Pounded him as maize is pounded,
Till his skull was crushed to pieces.
    Six tall hunters, lithe and limber,
Bore him home on poles and
    branches,
Bore the body of the beaver ;
But the ghost, the Jeebi in him,
Thought and felt as Pau-Puk-
    Keewis,
Still lived on as Pau-Puk-Keewis.
    And it fluttered, strove, and
    struggled,
Waving hither, waving thither,
As the curtains of a wigwam
Struggle with their thongs of deer-
    skin,
When the wintry wind is blowing ;
Till it drew itself together,
Till it rose up from the body,

Till it took the form and features
Of the cunning Pau-Puk-Keewis
Vanishing into the forest.
    But the wary Hiawatha
Saw the figure ere it vanished,
Saw the form of Pau-Puk-Keewis
Glide into the soft blue shadow
Of the pine-trees of the forest ;
Toward the squares of white be-
    yond it,
Toward an opening in the forest,
Like a wind it rushed and panted,
Bending all the boughs before it,
And behind it, as the rain comes,
Came the steps of Hiawatha.
    To a lake with many islands
Came the breathless Pau-Puk-
    Keewis,
Where among the water-lilies
Pishnekuh, the brant, were sailing ;
Through the tufts of rushes floating,
Steering through the reedy islands.
Now their broad black beaks they
    lifted,
Now they plunged beneath the
    water,
Now they darkened in the shadow,
Now they brightened in the sun-
    shine.
    ' Pishnekuh !' cried Pau-Puk-
    Keewis,
' Pishnekuh ! my brother !' said he,
' Change me to a brant with plum-
    age,
With a shining neck and feathers,
Make me large, and make me larger,
Ten times larger than the others.'
    Straightway to a brant they
    changed him,
With two huge and dusky pinions,
With a bosom smooth and rounded,
With a bill like two great paddles,
Made him larger than the others,
Ten times larger than the largest,
Just as, shouting from the forest,
On the shore stood Hiawatha.
    Up they rose with cry and
    clamour,

257

With a whir and beat of pinions,
Rose up from the reedy islands,
From the water-flags and lilies.
And they said to Pau-Puk-Keewis:
' In your flying, look not downward,
Take good heed, and look not
    downward,
Lest some strange mischance
    should happen,
Lest some great mishap befall you!'
    Fast and far they fled to north-
        ward,
Fast and far through mist and sun-
    shine,
Fed among the moors and fenlands,
Slept among the reeds and rushes.
    On the morrow as they journeyed,
Buoyed and lifted by the South-
    wind,
Wafted onward by the South-wind,
Blowing fresh and strong behind
    them,
Rose a sound of human voices,
Rose a clamour from beneath them,
From the lodges of a village,
From the people miles beneath
    them.
    For the people of the village
Saw the flock of brant with wonder,
Saw the wings of Pau-Puk-Keewis
Flapping far up in the ether,
Broader than two doorway curtains.
    Pau-Puk-Keewis heard the
        shouting,
Knew the voice of Hiawatha,
Knew the outcry of Iagoo,
And, forgetful of the warning,
Drew his neck in, and looked
    downward,
And the wind that blew behind him
Caught his mighty fan of feathers,
Sent him wheeling, whirling down-
    ward!
    All in vain did Pau-Puk-Keewis
Struggle to regain his balance!
Whirling round and round and
    downward,
He beheld in turn the village

And in turn the flock above him,
Saw the village coming nearer,
And the flock receding farther,
Heard the voices growing louder,
Heard the shouting and the laugh-
    ter;
Saw no more the flock above him,
Only saw the earth beneath him;
Dead out of the empty heaven,
Dead among the shouting people,
With a heavy sound and sullen,
Fell the brant with broken pinions.
    But his soul, his ghost, his
        shadow,
Still survived as Pau-Puk-Keewis,
Took again the form and features
Of the handsome Yenadizze,
And again went rushing onward,
Followed fast by Hiawatha,
Crying: ' Not so wide the world is,
Not so long and rough the way is,
But my wrath shall overtake you,
But my vengeance shall attain you!'
And so near he came, so near him,
That his hand was stretched to
    seize him,
His right hand to seize and hold him,
When the cunning Pau-Puk-Kee-
    wis
Whirled and spun about in circles,
Fanned the air into a whirlwind,
Danced the dust and leaves about
    him,
And amid the whirling eddies
Sprang into a hollow oak-tree,
Changed himself into a serpent,
Gliding out through root and rub-
    bish.
    With his right hand Hiawatha
Smote amain the hollow oak-tree,
Rent it into shreds and splinters,
Left it lying there in fragments.
But in vain; for Pau-Puk-Keewis
Once again in human figure,
Full in sight ran on before him,
Sped away in gust and whirlwind,
On the shores of Gitche Gumee,
Westward by the Big-Sea-Water,

Came unto the rocky headlands,
To the Pictured Rocks of sand-
stone,
Looking over lake and landscape.
And the Old Man of the Moun-
tain,
He the Manito of Mountains,
Opened wide his rocky doorways,
Opened wide his deep abysses,
Giving Pau-Puk-Keewis shelter
In his caverns dark and dreary,
Bidding Pau-Puk-Keewis welcome
To his gloomy lodge of sandstone.
There without stood Hiawatha,
Found the doorways closed against
him,
With his mittens, Minjekahwun,
Smote great caverns in the sand-
stone,
Cried aloud in tones of thunder,
'Open! I am Hiawatha!'
But the Old Man of the Mountain
Opened not, and made no answer
From the silent crags of sandstone,
From the gloomy rock abysses.
Then he raised his hands to
heaven,
Called imploring on the tempest,
Called Waywassimo, the lightning,
And the thunder, Annemeekee;
And they came with night and
darkness,
Sweeping down the Big-Sea-Water
From the distant Thunder Moun-
tains;
And the trembling Pau-Puk-
Keewis
Heard the footsteps of the thunder,
Saw the red eyes of the lightning,
Was afraid, and crouched and
trembled.
Then Waywassimo, the light-
ning,
Smote the doorways of the caverns,
With his war-club smote the door-
ways,
Smote the jutting crags of sand-
stone,

And the thunder, Annemeekee,
Shouted down into the caverns,
Saying, 'Where is Pau-Puk-Kee-
wis?'
And the crags fell, and beneath
them
Dead among the rocky ruins
Lay the cunning Pau-Puk-Keewis,
Lay the handsome Yenadizze,
Slain in his own human figure.
Ended were his wild adventures,
Ended were his tricks and gambols,
Ended all his craft and cunning,
Ended all his mischief-making,
All his gambling and his dancing,
All his wooing of the maidens.
Then the noble Hiawatha
Took his soul, his ghost, his
shadow,
Spake and said: 'O Pau-Puk-
Keewis,
Never more in human figure
Shall you search for new adven-
tures;
Never more with jest and laughter
Dance the dust and leaves in
whirlwinds;
But above there in the heavens
You shall soar and sail in circles;
I will change you to an eagle,
To Keneu, the great war-eagle,
Chief of all the fowl with feathers,
Chief of Hiawatha's chickens.'
And the name of Pau-Puk-
Keewis
Lingers still among the people,
Lingers still among the singers,
And among the story-tellers;
And in Winter, when the snow-
flakes
Whirl in eddies round the lodges,
When the wind in gusty tumult
O'er the smoke-flue pipes and
whistles,
'There,' they cry, 'comes Pau-Puk-
Keewis;
He is dancing through the village,
He is gathering in his harvest!'

259

XVIII.

THE DEATH OF KWASIND.

FAR and wide among the nations
Spread the name and fame of
  Kwasind;
No man dared to strive with
  Kwasind,
No man could compete with
  Kwasind.
But the mischievous Puk-Wudjies,
They the envious Little People,
They the fairies and the pigmies,
Plotted and conspired against him.
'If this hateful Kwasind,' said
  they,
'If this great, outrageous fellow
Goes on thus a little longer,
Tearing everything he touches,
Rending everything to pieces,
Filling all the world with wonder,
What becomes of the Puk-Wudjies?
Who will care for the Puk-Wud-
  jies?
He will tread us down like mush-
  rooms,
Drive us all into the water,
Give our bodies to be eaten
By the wicked Nee-ba-naw-baigs,
By the Spirits of the water!'
  So the angry Little People
All conspired against the Strong
  Man,
All conspired to murder Kwasind,
Yes, to rid the world of Kwasind,
The audacious, overbearing,
Heartless, haughty, dangerous
  Kwasind!
  Now this wondrous strength of
  Kwasind
In his crown alone was seated;
In his crown too was his weakness;
There alone could he be wounded,
Nowhere else could weapon pierce
  him,
Nowhere else could weapon harm
  him.

Even there the only weapon
That could wound him, that could
  slay him,
Was the seed-cone of the pine-tree,
Was the blue cone of the fir-tree.
This was Kwasind's fatal secret,
Known to no man among mortals;
But the cunning Little People,
The Puk-Wudjies, knew the secret,
Knew the only way to kill him.
  So they gathered cones together,
Gathered seed-cones of the pine-
  tree,
Gathered blue cones of the fir-tree,
In the woods by Taquamenaw,
Brought them to the river's margin,
Heaped them in great piles together,
Where the red rocks from the
  margin
Jutting overhang the river.
There they lay in wait for Kwasind,
The malicious Little People.
  'Twas an afternoon in Summer;
Very hot and still the air was,
Very smooth the gliding river,
Motionless the sleeping shadows:
Insects glistened in the sunshine,
Insects skated on the water,
Filled the drowsy air with buzzing,
With a far resounding war-cry.
  Down the river came the Strong
  Man,
In his birch-canoe came Kwasind,
Floating slowly down the current
Of the sluggish Taquamenaw,
Very languid with the weather
Very sleepy with the silence.
  From the overhanging branches,
From the tassels of the birch-trees,
Soft the Spirit of Sleep descended;
By his airy hosts surrounded,
His invisible attendants,
Came the Spirit of Sleep, Nepah-
  win;
Like the burnished Dush-kwo-ne-
  she,
Like a dragon-fly, he hovered
O'er the drowsy head of Kwasind.

To his ear there came a murmur
As of waves upon a sea-shore,
As of far-off tumbling waters,
As of winds among the pine-trees ;
And he felt upon his forehead
Blows of little airy war-clubs,
Wielded by the slumbrous legions
Of the Spirit of Sleep, Nepahwin,
As of some one breathing on him.

At the first blow of their war-
clubs,
Fell a drowsiness on Kwasind ;
At the second blow they smote him,
Motionless his paddle rested ;
At the third, before his vision
Reeled the landscape into darkness,
Very sound asleep was Kwasind.

So he floated down the river,
Like a blind man seated upright,
Floated down the Taquamenaw,
Underneath the trembling birch-
trees,
Underneath the wooded headlands,
Underneath the war encampment
Of the pigmies, the Puk-Wudjies.

There they stood, all armed and
waiting,
Hurled the pine-cones down upon
him,
Struck him on his brawny shoulders,
On his crown defenceless struck
him.
'Death to Kwasind !' was the
sudden
War-cry of the Little People.

And he sideways swayed and
tumbled,
Sideways fell into the river,
Plunged beneath the sluggish water
Headlong, as an otter plunges ;
And the birch-canoe, abandoned,
Drifted empty down the river,
Bottom upward swerved and drifted :
Nothing more was seen of Kwasind.

But the memory of the Strong
Man
Lingered long among the people,
And whenever through the forest

Raged and roared the wintry
tempest,
And the branches, tossed and
troubled,
Creaked and groaned and split
asunder,
'Kwasind !' cried they ; 'that is
Kwasind !
He is gathering in his firewood !'

XIX.

THE GHOSTS.

NEVER stoops the soaring vulture
On his quarry in the desert,
On the sick or wounded bison,
But another vulture, watching
From his high aerial look-out,
Sees the downward plunge, and
follows ;
And a third pursues the second,
Coming from the invisible ether,
First a speck, and then a vulture,
Till the air is dark with pinions.

So disasters come not singly ;
But as if they watched and waited,
Scanning one another's motions,
When the first descends, the others
Follow, follow, gathering flockwise
Round their victim, sick and
wounded,
First a shadow, then a sorrow,
Till the air is dark with anguish.

Now, o'er all the dreary North-
land,
Mighty Peboan, the Winter,
Breathing on the lakes and rivers,
Into stone had changed their waters.
From his hair he shook the snow-
flakes,
Till the plains were strewn with
whiteness,
One uninterrupted level,
As if, stooping, the Creator
With his hand had smoothed them
over.

Through the forest, wide and
wailing,

Roamed the hunter on his snow-
shoes;
In the village worked the women,
Pounded maize, or dressed the
deerskin;
And the young men played together
On the ice the noisy ball-play,
On the plain the dance of snow-
shoes.

One dark evening, after sundown,
In her wigwam Laughing Water
Sat with old Nokomis, waiting
For the steps of Hiawatha
Homeward from the hunt returning.

On their faces gleamed the fire-
light,
Painting them with streaks of crim-
son,
In the eyes of old Nokomis
Glimmered like the watery moon-
light,
In the eyes of Laughing Water
Glistened like the sun in water;
And behind them crouched their
shadows
In the corners of the wigwam,
And the smoke in wreaths above
them
Climbed and crowded through the
smoke-flue.

Then the curtain of the doorway
From without was slowly lifted;
Brighter glowed the fire a moment,
And a moment swerved the smoke-
wreath,
As two women entered softly,
Passed the doorway uninvited,
Without word of salutation,
Without sign of recognition,
Sat down in the farthest corner,
Crouching low among the shadows.

From their aspect and their gar-
ments,
Strangers seemed they in the village;
Very pale and haggard were they,
As they sat there sad and silent,
Trembling, cowering with the
shadows.

Was it the wind above the smoke-
flue,
Muttering down into the wigwam?
Was it the owl, the Koko-koho,
Hooting from the dismal forest?
Sure a voice said in the silence:
'These are corpses clad in gar-
ments,
These are ghosts that come to
haunt you,
From the kingdom of Ponemah,
From the land of the Hereafter!'

Homeward now came Hiawatha
From his hunting in the forest,
With the snow upon his tresses,
And the red deer on his shoulders.
At the feet of Laughing Water
Down he threw his lifeless burden;
Nobler, handsomer she thought him,
Than when first he came to woo her,
First threw down the deer before
her,
As a token of his wishes,
As a promise of the future.

Then he turned and saw the
strangers,
Cowering, crouching with the
shadows;
Said within himself, 'Who are they?
What strange guests has Minne-
haha?'
But he questioned not the strangers,
Only spake to bid them welcome
To his lodge, his food, his fireside.

When the evening meal was
ready,
And the deer had been divided,
Both the pallid guests, the stran-
gers,
Springing from among the shadows,
Seized upon the choicest portions,
Seized the white fat of the roebuck,
Set apart for Laughing Water,
For the wife of Hiawatha;
Without asking, without thanking,
Eagerly devoured the morsels,
Flitted back among the shadows
In the corner of the wigwam.

Not a word spake Hiawatha,
Not a motion made Nokomis,
Not a gesture Laughing Water;
Not a change came o'er their
  features;
Only Minnehaha softly
Whispered, saying, 'They are
  famished;
Let them do what best delights
  them;
Let them eat, for they are famished.'

Many a daylight dawned and
  darkened,
Many a night shook off the daylight
As the pine shakes off the snow-
  flakes
From the midnight of its branches;
Day by day the guests unmoving
Sat there silent in the wigwam;
But by night, in storm or starlight,
Forth they went into the forest,
Bringing firewood to the wigwam,
Bringing pine-cones for the burning,
Always sad and always silent.

And whenever Hiawatha
Came from fishing or from hunting,
When the evening meal was ready,
And the food had been divided,
Gliding from their darksome corner,
Came the pallid guests, the stran-
  gers,
Seized upon the choicest portions
Set aside for Laughing Water,
And without rebuke or question
Flitted back among the shadows.

Never once had Hiawatha
By a word or look reproved them;
Never once had old Nokomis
Made a gesture of impatience;
Never once had Laughing Water
Shown resentment at the outrage.
All had they endured in silence,
That the rights of guests and
  stranger,
That the virtue of free-giving,
By a look might not be lessened,
By a word might not be broken.

Once at midnight Hiawatha,
Ever wakeful, ever watchful,
In the wigwam, dimly lighted
By the brands that still were
  burning,
By the glimmering, flickering fire-
  light,
Heard a sighing, oft repeated,
Heard a sobbing, as of sorrow.

From his couch rose Hiawatha,
From his shaggy hides of bison,
Pushed aside the deerskin curtain,
Saw the pallid guests, the shadows,
Sitting upright on their couches,
Weeping in the silent midnight.

And he said: 'O guests! why is it
That your hearts are so afflicted,
That you sob so in the midnight?
Has perchance the old Nokomis,
Has my wife, my Minnehaha,
Wronged or grieved you by unkind-
  ness,
Failed in hospitable duties?'

Then the shadows ceased from
  weeping,
Ceased from sobbing and lamenting,
And they said, with gentle voices:
'We are ghosts of the departed,
Souls of those who once were with
  you.
From the realms of Chibiabos
Hither have we come to try you,
Hither have we come to warn you.

'Cries of grief and lamentation
Reach us in the Blessed Islands;
Cries of anguish from the living,
Calling back their friends departed,
Sadden us with useless sorrow.
Therefore have we come to try you;
No one knows us, no one heeds us.
We are but a burden to you,
And we see that the departed
Have no place among the living.

'Think of this, O Hiawatha!
Speak of it to all the people,
That henceforward and for ever
They no more with lamentations
Sadden the souls of the departed
In the Islands of the Blessed.

'Do not lay such heavy burdens
In the graves of those you bury,
Not such weight of furs and wam-
pum,
Not such weight of pots and kettles,
For the spirits faint beneath them,
Only give them food to carry,
Only give them fire to light them.

'Four days is the spirit's journey
To the land of ghosts and shadows,
Four its lonely night encampments;
Four times must their fires be
lighted.
Therefore, when the dead are
buried,
Let a fire, as night approaches,
Four times on the grave be kindled,
That the soul upon its journey
May not lack the cheerful firelight,
May not grope about in darkness.
'Farewell, noble Hiawatha!
We have put you to the trial,
To the proof have put your patience,
By the insult of our presence,
By the outrage of our actions.
We have found you great and noble.
Fail not in the greater trial,
Faint not in the harder struggle.'
When they ceased, a sudden
darkness
Fell and filled the silent wigwam.
Hiawatha heard a rustle
As of garments trailing by him,
Heard the curtain of the doorway
Lifted by a hand he saw not,
Felt the cold breath of the night air,
For a moment saw the starlight;
But he saw the ghosts no longer,
Saw no more the wandering spirits
From the kingdom of Ponemah,
From the land of the Hereafter.

XX.

THE FAMINE.

O THE long and dreary Winter!
O the cold and cruel Winter!

Ever thicker, thicker, thicker
Froze the ice on lake and river,
Ever deeper, deeper, deeper
Fell the snow o'er all the landscape,
Fell the covering snow, and drifted
Through the forest, round the
village.

Hardly from his buried wigwam
Could the hunter force a passage;
With his mittens and his snow-
shoes
Vainly walked he through the forest,
Sought for bird or beast and found
none,
Saw no track of deer or rabbit,
In the snow beheld no footprints,
In the ghastly, gleaming forest
Fell, and could not rise from weak-
ness,
Perished there from cold and
hunger.
O the famine and the fever!
O the wasting of the famine!
O the blasting of the fever!
O the wailing of the children!
O the anguish of the women!
All the earth was sick and fam-
ished;
Hungry was the air around them,
Hungry was the sky above them,
And the hungry stars in heaven
Like the eyes of wolves glared at
them!
Into Hiawatha's wigwam
Came two other guests, as silent
As the ghosts were, and as gloomy,
Waited not to be invited,
Did not parley at the doorway,
Sat there without word of welcome
In the seat of Laughing Water;
Looked with haggard eyes and hol-
low
At the face of Laughing Water.
And the foremost said: 'Behold
me!
I am Famine, Bukadawin!'
And the other said: 'Behold me!
I am Fever, Ahkosewin!'

264

And the lovely Minnehaha
Shuddered as they looked upon
    her,
Shuddered at the words they ut-
    tered,
Lay down on her bed in silence,
Hid her face, but made no answer;
Lay there trembling, freezing, burn-
    ing
At the looks they cast upon her,
At the fearful words they uttered.

Forth into the empty forest
Rushed the maddened Hiawatha;
In his heart was deadly sorrow,
In his face a stony firmness;
On his brow the sweat of anguish
Started, but it froze and fell not.

Wrapped in furs and armed for
    hunting,
With his mighty bow of ash-tree,
With his quiver full of arrows,
With his mittens, Minjekahwun,
Into the vast and vacant forest
On his snow-shoes strode he for-
    ward.

'Gitche Manito, the Mighty!'
Cried he with his face uplifted
In that bitter hour of anguish,
'Give your children food, O father!
Give us food, or we must perish!
Give me food for Minnehaha,
For my dying Minnehaha!'

Through the far-resounding
    forest,
Through the forest vast and vacant
Rang that cry of desolation,
But there came no other answer
Than the echo of his crying,
Than the echo of the woodlands,
'Minnehaha! Minnehaha!'

All day long roved Hiawatha
In that melancholy forest,
Through the shadow of whose
    thickets,
In the pleasant days of Summer,
Of that ne'er forgotten Summer,
He had brought his young wife
    homeward

From the land of the Dacotahs;
When the birds sang in the thickets,
And the streamlets laughed and
    glistened,
And the air was full of fragrance,
And the lovely Laughing Water
Said with voice that did not tremble
'I will follow you my husband!'

In the wigwam with Nokomis,
With those gloomy guests, that
    watched her,
With the Famine and the Fever,
She was lying, the Beloved,
She the dying Minnehaha.
'Hark!' she said; 'I hear a
    rushing,
Hear a roaring and a rushing,
Hear the Falls of Minnehaha
Calling to me from a distance!'
'No, my child!' said old Nokomis,
''Tis the night-wind in the pine-
    trees!'
'Look!' she said; 'I see my
    father
Standing lonely at his doorway,
Beckoning to me from his wigwam
In the land of the Dacotahs!'
'No, my child!' said old Nokomis,
''Tis the smoke, that waves and
    beckons!'
'Ah!' said she, 'the eyes of Pauguk
Glare upon me in the darkness,
I can feel his icy fingers
Clasping mine amid the darkness!
Hiawatha! Hiawatha!'

And the desolate Hiawatha,
Far away amid the forest,
Miles away among the mountains,
Heard that sudden cry of anguish,
Heard the voice of Minnehaha
Calling to him in the darkness,
'Hiawatha! Hiawatha!'

Over snow-fields waste and path-
    less,
Under snow-encumbered branches,
Homeward hurried Hiawatha,
Empty-handed, heavy-hearted.
Heard Nokomis moaning, wailing,

'Wahonowin! Wahonowin!
Would that I had perished for you,
Would that I were dead as you are!
Wahonowin! Wahonowin!'

And he rushed into the wigwam,
Saw the old Nokomis slowly
Rocking to and fro and moaning,
Saw his lovely Minnehaha
Lying dead and cold before him,
And his bursting heart within him
Uttered such a cry of anguish,
That the forest moaned and shud-
dered,
That the very stars in heaven
Shook and trembled with his an-
guish.

Then he sat down still and
speechless,
On the bed of Minnehaha,
At the feet of Laughing Water,
At those willing feet, that never
More would lightly run to meet him,
Never more would lightly follow.

With both hands his face he
covered,
Seven long days and nights he sat
there,
As if in a swoon he sat there,
Speechless, motionless, unconscious
Of the daylight or the darkness.

Then they buried Minnehaha;
In the snow a grave they made her,
In the forest deep and darksome,
Underneath the moaning hem-
locks;
Clothed her in her richest gar-
ments,
Wrapped her in her robes of er-
mine;
Covered her with snow, like ermine,
Thus they buried Minnehaha.

And at night a fire was lighted,
On her grave four times was kin-
dled,
For her soul upon its journey
To the Islands of the Blessed.
From his doorway Hiawatha
Saw it burning in the forest,

Lighting up the gloomy hemlocks;
From his sleepless bed uprising,
From the bed of Minnehaha,
Stood and watched it at the door-
way,
That it might not be extinguished,
Might not leave her in the darkness.

'Farewell!' said he, 'Minnehaha!
Farewell, O my Laughing Water!
All my heart is buried with you,
All my thoughts go onward with
you!
Come not back again to labour,
Come not back again to suffer,
Where the Famine and the Fever
Wear the heart and waste the body.
Soon my task will be completed,
Soon your footsteps I shall follow
To the Islands of the Blessed,
To the Kingdom of Ponemah,
To the Land of the Hereafter!'

XXI.

THE WHITE MAN'S FOOT.

IN his lodge beside a river,
Close beside a frozen river,
Sat an old man, sad and lonely.
White his hair was as a snow-drift;
Dull and low his fire was burning,
And the old man shook and trem-
bled,
Folded in his Waubewyon,
In his tattered white-skin-wrapper,
Hearing nothing but the tempest
As it roared along the forest,
Seeing nothing but the snow-storm,
As it whirled and hissed and drifted.

All the coals were white with
ashes,
And the fire was slowly dying,
As a young man, walking lightly,
At the open doorway entered.
Red with blood of youth his cheeks
were,
Soft his eyes, as stars in Spring-
time,

266

Bound his forehead was with grasses,
Bound and plumed with scented grasses;
On his lips a smile of beauty,
Filling all the lodge with sunshine,
In his hand a bunch of blossoms
Filling all the lodge with sweetness.
　'Ah, my son!' exclaimed the old man,
'Happy are my eyes to see you.
Sit here on the mat beside me,
Sit here by the dying embers,
Let us pass the night together,
Tell me of your strange adventures,
Of the lands where you have travelled;
I will tell you of my prowess,
Of my many deeds of wonder.'
　From his pouch he drew his peace-pipe,
Very old and strangely fashioned;
Made of red stone was the pipe-head,
And the stem a reed with feathers;
Filled the pipe with bark of willow,
Placed a burning coal upon it,
Gave it to his guest, the stranger,
And began to speak in this wise:
　'When I blow my breath about me,
When I breathe upon the landscape,
Motionless are all the rivers,
Hard as stone becomes the water!'
　And the young man answered, smiling:
'When I blow my breath about me,
When I breathe upon the landscape,
Flowers spring up o'er all the meadows,
Singing onward rush the rivers!'
　'When I shake my hoary tresses,'
Said the old man darkly frowning,
'All the land with snow is covered,
All the leaves from all the branches
Fall and fade and die and wither,
For I breathe, and lo! they are not.

From the waters and the marshes
Rise the wild goose and the heron,
Fly away to distant regions,
For I speak, and lo! they are not.
And where'er my footsteps wander,
All the wild beasts of the forest
Hide themselves in holes and caverns,
And the earth becomes as flint-stone!'
　'When I shake my flowing ringlets,'
Said the young man, softly laughing,
'Showers of rain fall warm and welcome,
Plants lift up their heads rejoicing,
Back unto their lakes and marshes
Come the wild goose and the heron,
Homeward shoots the arrowy swallow,
Sing the bluebird and the robin,
And where'er my footsteps wander,
All the meadows wave with blossoms,
All the woodlands ring with music,
All the trees are dark with foliage!'
　While they spake, the night departed
From the distant realms of Wabun,
From his shining lodge of silver,
Like a warrior robed and painted,
Came the sun, and said, 'Behold me!
Gheezis, the great sun, behold me!'
　Then the old man's tongue was speechless
And the air grew warm and pleasant,
And upon the wigwam sweetly
Sang the bluebird and the robin,
And the stream began to murmur,
And a scent of growing grasses
Through the lodge was gently wafted.
　And Segwun, the youthful stranger,
More distinctly in the daylight
Saw the icy face before him;
It was Peboan, the Winter!

From his eyes the tears were
flowing,
As from melting lakes the stream-
lets,
And his body shrunk and dwindled
As the shouting sun ascended,
Till into the air it faded,
Till into the ground it vanished,
And the young man saw before him,
On the hearthstone of the wigwam,
Where the fire had smoked and
smouldered,
Saw the earliest flower of Spring-
time,
Saw the Beauty of the Spring-time,
Saw the Miskodeed in blossom.

Thus it was that in the North-
land
After that unheard-of coldness,
That intolerable Winter,
Came the Spring with all its splen-
dour,
All its birds and all its blossoms,
All its flowers and leaves and
grasses.

Sailing on the wind to northward,
Flying in great flocks, like arrows,
Like huge arrows shot through
heaven,
Passed the swan, the Mahnahbezee,
Speaking almost as a man speaks;
And in long lines waving, bending
Like a bowstring snapped asunder,
Came the white goose, Waw-be-
wawa;
And in pairs, or singly flying,
Mahng the loon, with clangorous
pinions,
The blue heron, the Shuh-shuh-
gah,
And the grouse, the Mushkodasa.

In the thickets and the meadows
Piped the bluebird, the Owaissa;
On the summit of the lodges
Sang the robin, the Opechee;
In the covert of the pine-trees
Cooed the pigeon, the Omemee;
And the sorrowing Hiawatha,

Speechless in his infinite sorrow,
Heard their voices calling to him,
Went forth from his gloomy door-
way,
Stood and gazed into the heaven,
Gazed upon the earth and waters.

From his wanderings far to east-
ward,
From the regions of the morning,
From the shining land of Wabun,
Homeward now returned Iagoo,
The great traveller, the great
boaster,
Full of new and strange adven-
tures,
Marvels many and many wonders.

And the people of the village
Listened to him as he told them
Of his marvellous adventures,
Laughing answered him in this
wise:
'Ugh! it is indeed Iagoo!
No one else beholds such wonders!

He had seen, he said, a water
Bigger than the Big-Sea-Water,
Broader than the Gitche Gumee.
Bitter so that none could drink it!
At each other looked the warriors,
Looked the women at each other,
Smiled, and said, 'It cannot be so!
Kaw!' they said, 'it cannot be so!'
O'er it, said he, o'er this water
Came a great canoe with pinions,
A canoe with wings came flying,
Bigger than a grove of pine-trees,
Taller than the tallest tree-tops!
And the old men and the women
Looked and tittered at each other;
'Kaw!' they said, 'we don't be-
lieve it!'
From its mouth, he said, to greet
him,
Came Waywassimo, the lightning,
Came the thunder, Annemeekee!
And the warriors and the women
Laughed aloud at poor Iagoo;
'Kaw!' they said, 'what tales you
tell us!'

In it, said he, came a people,
In a great canoe with pinions
Came, he said, a hundred warriors ;
Painted white were all their faces
And with hair their chins were
    covered !
And the warriors and the women
Laughed and shouted in derision,
Like the ravens on the tree-tops,
Like the crows upon the hemlocks.
' Kaw ! ' they said, ' what lies you
    tell us !
Do not think that we believe them ! '

Only Hiawatha laughed not,
But he gravely spake and answered
To their jeering and their jesting :
' True is all Iagoo tells us ;
I have seen it in a vision,
Seen the great canoe with pinions,
Seen the people with white faces,
Seen the coming of this bearded
People of the wooden vessel
From the regions of the morning,
From the shining land of Wabun.

' Gitche Manito, the Mighty,
The Great Spirit, the Creator,
Sends them hither on his errand,
Sends them to us with his message.
Wheresoe'er they move, before
    them
Swarms the stinging fly, the Ahmo,
Swarms the bee, the honey-maker ;
Wheresoe'er they tread, beneath
    them
Springs a flower unknown among
    us,
Springs the White-man's foot in
    blossom.

' Let us welcome, then, the stran-
    gers,
Hail them as our friends and
    brothers,
And the heart's right hand of friend-
    ship
Give them when they come to see
    us.
Gitche Manito, the Mighty,
Said this to me in my vision.

' I beheld, too, in that vision
All the secrets of the future,
Of the distant days that shall be.
I beheld the westward marches
Of the unknown, crowded nations.
All the land was full of people,
Restless, struggling, toiling, striv-
    ing,
Speaking many tongues, yet feeling
But one heart-beat in their bosoms.
In the woodlands rang their axes,
Smoked their town in all the val-
    leys,
Over all the lakes and rivers
Rushed their great canoes of thun-
    der.

' Then a darker, drearier vision
Passed before me vague and cloud-
    like :
I beheld our nation scattered,
All forgetful of my counsels,
Weakened, warring with each
    other :
Saw the remnants of our people
Sweeping westward, wild and woe-
    ful,
Like the cloud-rack of a tempest,
Like the withered leaves of Au-
    tumn ! '

XXII.

HIAWATHA'S DEPARTURE.

By the shore of Gitche Gumee,
By the shining Big-Sea-Water,
At the doorway of his wigwam,
In the pleasant Summer morning,
Hiawatha stood and waited.
  All the air was full of freshness,
All the earth was bright and joyous,
And before him, through the sun-
    shine,
Westward toward the neighbouring
    forest
Passed in golden swarms the Ahmo,
Passed the bees, the honey-makers,
Burning, singing in the sunshine.

Bright above him shone the heavens,
Level spread the lake before him;
From its bosom leaped the sturgeon,
Sparkling, flashing in the sunshine;
On its margin the great forest
Stood reflected in the water,
Every tree-top had its shadow,
Motionless beneath the water.

From the brow of Hiawatha
Gone was every trace of sorrow,
As the fog from off the water,
As the mist from off the meadow.
With a smile of joy and triumph,
With a look of exultation,
As of one who in a vision
Sees what is to be, but is not,
Stood and waited Hiawatha.

Toward the sun his hands were lifted,
Both the palms spread out against it,
And between the parted fingers
Fell the sunshine on his features,
Flecked with light his naked shoulders,
As it falls and flecks an oak-tree
Through the rifted leaves and branches.

O'er the water floating, flying,
Something in the hazy distance,
Something in the mists of morning,
Loomed and lifted from the water,
Now seemed floating, now seemed flying,
Coming nearer, nearer, nearer.

Was it Shingebis the diver?
Or the pelican, the Shada?
Or the heron, the Shuh-shuh-gah?
Or the white goose, Waw-be-wawa,
With the water dripping, flashing,
From its glossy neck and feathers?

It was neither goose nor diver,
Neither pelican nor heron,
O'er the water floating, flying,
Through the shining mist of morning,
But a birch-canoe with paddles,

Rising, sinking on the water,
Dripping, flashing in the sunshine;
And within it came a people
From the distant land of Wabun,
From the farthest realms of morning
Came the Black-Robe chief, the Prophet,
He the Priest of Prayer, the Paleface,
With his guides and his companions.

And the noble Hiawatha,
With his hands aloft extended,
Held aloft in sign of welcome,
Waited, full of exultation,
Till the birch-canoe with paddles
Grated on the shining pebbles,
Stranded on the sandy margin,
Till the Black-Robe chief, the Paleface,
With the cross upon his bosom,
Landed on the sandy margin.

Then the joyous Hiawatha
Cried aloud and spake in this wise:
'Beautiful is the sun, O strangers,
When you come so far to see us!
All our town in peace awaits you,
All our doors stand open for you;
You shall enter all our wigwams,
For the heart's right hand we give you.

'Never bloomed the earth so gaily,
Never shone the sun so brightly,
As to-day they shine and blossom
When you come so far to see us!
Never was our lake so tranquil,
Nor so free from rocks and sandbars;
For your birch-canoe in passing
Has removed both rock and sandbar.

'Never before had our tobacco
Such a sweet and pleasant flavour,
Never the broad leaves of our cornfields
Were so beautiful to look on,
As they seem to us this morning,
When you come so far to see us!'

And the Black-Robe chief made answer,
Stammered in his speech a little,
Speaking words yet unfamiliar :
'Peace be with you, Hiawatha,
Peace be with you and your people,
Peace of prayer, and peace of pardon,
Peace of Christ, and joy of Mary !'
Then the generous Hiawatha
Led the strangers to his wigwam,
Seated them on skins of bison,
Seated them on skins of ermine,
And the careful, old Nokomis
Brought them food in bowls of basswood,
Water brought in birchen dippers,
And the calumet, the peace-pipe,
Filled and lighted for their smoking.
All the old men of the village,
All the warriors of the nation,
All the Jossakeeds, the prophets,
The magicians, the Wabenos,
And the medicine-men, the Medas,
Came to bid the strangers welcome ;
'It is well,' they said, 'O brothers,
That you come so far to see us !'
In a circle round the doorway,
With their pipes they sat in silence,
Waiting to behold the strangers,
Waiting to receive their message ;
Till the Black-Robe chief, the Paleface,
From the wigwam came to greet them,
Stammering in his speech a little,
Speaking words yet unfamiliar ;
'It is well,' they said, 'O brother,
That you come so far to see us !'
Then the Black-Robe chief, the prophet,
Told his message to the people,
Told the purport of his mission,
Told them of the Virgin Mary,
And her blessed Son, the Saviour,
How in distant lands and ages
He had lived on earth as we do ;

How he fasted, prayed, and laboured ;
How the Jews, the tribe accursed,
Mocked him, scourged him, crucified him ;
How he rose from where they laid him,
Walked again with his disciples,
And ascended into heaven.
And the chiefs made answer, saying :
'We have listened to your message,
We have heard your words of wisdom,
We will think on what you tell us.
It is well for us, O brothers,
That you come so far to see us !'
Then they rose up and departed
Each one homeward to his wigwam,
To the young men and the women,
Told the story of the strangers
Whom the Master of Life had sent them
From the shining land of Wabun,
Heavy with the heat and silence
Grew the afternoon of Summer ;
With a drowsy sound the forest
Whispered round the sultry wigwam,
With a sound of sleep the water
Rippled on the beach below it ;
From the cornfields shrill and ceaseless
Sang the grasshopper, Pah-puk-keena ;
And the guests of Hiawatha,
Weary with the heat of Summer,
Slumbered in the sultry wigwam.
Slowly o'er the simmering landscape
Fell the evening's dusk and coolness,
And the long and level sunbeams
Shot their spears into the forest,
Breaking through its shields of shadow,
Rushed into each secret ambush,
Searched each thicket, dingle, hollow ;

Still the guests of Hiawatha
Slumbered in the silent wigwam.
From his place rose Hiawatha,
Bade farewell to old Nokomis,
Spake in whispers, spake in this
    wise,
Did not wake the guests, that slum-
    bered :
  'I am going, O Nokomis,
On a long and distant journey,
To the portals of the Sunset,
To the regions of the home-wind,
Of the Northwest wind, Keewaydin.
But these guests I leave behind me,
In your watch and ward I leave
    them ;
See that never harm comes near
    them,
See that never fear molests them,
Never danger nor suspicion,
Never want of food or shelter,
In the lodge of Hiawatha !'
    Forth into the village went he,
Bade farewell to all the warriors,
Bade farewell to all the young
    men,
Spake persuading, spake in this
    wise :
  'I am going, O my people,
On a long and distant journey ;
Many moons and many winters
Will have come, and will have van-
    ished,
Ere I come again to see you.
But my guests I leave behind me ;
Listen to their words of wisdom,
Listen to the truth they tell you,
For the Master of Life has sent
    them
From the land of light and morn-
    ing !'
    On the shore stood Hiawatha,
Turned and waved his hand at
    parting ;
On the clear and luminous water
Launched his birch-canoe for sail-
    ing,
From the pebbles of the margin

Shoved it forth into the water ;
Whispered to it, 'Westward ! west-
    ward !'
And with speed it darted forward.
    And the evening sun descending
Set the clouds on fire with red-
    ness,
Burned the broad sky like a prairie,
Left upon the level water
One long track and trail of splen-
    dour,
Down whose stream, as down a
    river,
Westward, westward Hiawatha
Sailed into the fiery sunset,
Sailed into the purple vapours,
Sailed into the dusk of evening.
    And the people from the margin
Watched him floating, rising, sink-
    ing,
Till the birch-canoe seemed lifted
High into that sea of splendour,
Till it sank into the vapours
Like the new moon slowly, slowly
Sinking in the purple distance.
    And they said, 'Farewell for
    ever !'
Said, 'Farewell, O Hiawatha !'
And the forests, dark and lonely,
Moved through all their depths of
    darkness,
Sighed, 'Farewell, O Hiawatha !'
And the waves upon the margin
Rising, rippling on the pebbles,
Sobbed, 'Farewell, O Hiawatha !'
And the heron, the Shuh-shuh-gah,
From her haunts among the fen-
    lands,
Screamed, 'Farewell, O Hiawatha !'
    Thus departed Hiawatha,
Hiawatha the Beloved,
In the glory of the sunset,
In the purple mists of evening,
To the regions of the home-wind,
Of the Northwest wind Keewaydin,
To the Islands of the Blessed,
To the kingdom of Ponemah,
To the land of the Hereafter !

The Song of Hiawatha.

VOCABULARY.

Adjidau'mo, *the red squirrel.*
Ahdeek', *the reindeer.*
Ahkose'win, *fever.*
Ahmeek', *the beaver.*
Algon'quin, *Ojibway.*
Annemee'kee, *the thunder.*
Apuk'wa, *a bulrush.*
Baim-wa'wa, *the sound of the thunder.*
Bemah'gut, *the grape-vine.*
Be'na, *the pheasant.* [rior.
Big-Sea-Water, *Lake Supe-*
Bukada'win, *famine.*
Cheemaun', *a birch canoe.*
Chetowaik', *the plover.*
Chibia'bos, *a musician; friend of Hiawatha; ruler in the Land of Spirits.*
Dahin'da, *the bull-frog.*
Dush-kwo-ne'she, *or* Kwo-ne'she, *the dragon-fly.*
Esa, *shame upon you.*
Ewa-yea', *lullaby.*
Gee'zis, *the sun.*
Gitche Gu'mee, *the Big-Sea-Water, Lake Superior.*
Gitche Man'ito, *the Great Spirit, the Master of Life.*
Gushkewau', *the darkness.*
Hiawa'tha, *the Wise Man, the Teacher; son of Mudjekeewis, the West Wind, and Wenonah, daughter of Nokomis.*
Ia'goo, *a great boaster and story-teller.*
Inin'ewug, *men, or pawns in the Game of the Bowl.*
Ishkoodah', *fire; a comet.*
Jee'bi, *a ghost, a spirit.*
Joss'akeed, *a prophet.*
Kabibonok'ka, *the North Wind.*
Kagh, *the hedgehog.*
Ka'go, *do not.*
Kahgahgee', *the raven.*
Kaw, *no.*
Kaween', *no indeed.*
Kayoshk', *the sea-gull.*
Kee'go, *a fish.*
Keeway'din, *the North-West Wind, the Home-Wind.*
Kena'beek, *a serpent.*
Keneu', *the great war-eagle.*
Keno'zha, *the pickerel.*
Ko'ko-ko'ho, *the owl.*
Kuntassoo', *the Game of Plum-stones.*
Kwa'sind, *the Strong Man.*
Kwo-ne'she, *or* Dush-kwo-ne'she, *the dragon-fly.*
Mahnahbe'zee, *the swan.*
Mahng, *the loon.*
Mahn-go-tay'see, *loon-hearted, brave.*
Mahnomo'nee, *wild rice.*

Ma'ma, *the woodpecker.*
Maskeno'zha, *the pike.*
Me'da, *a medicine-man.*
Meenah'ga, *the blueberry.*
Megissog'won, *the great Pearl-Feather, a magician, and the Manito of Wealth.*
Meshinau'wa, *a pipe-bearer.*
Minjekah'wun, *Hiawatha's mittens.*
Minneha'ha, *Laughing Water; a waterfall on a stream running into the Mississippi, between Fort Snelling and the Falls of St. Anthony.*
Minneha'ha, *Laughing Water; wife of Hiawatha.*
Minne-wa'wa, *a pleasant sound, as of the wind in the trees.* [*Bear.*
Mishe-Mo'kwa, *the Great*
Mishe-Nah'ma, *the Great Sturgeon.*
Miskodeed', *the Spring-Beauty, the Claytonia Virginica.*
Monda'min, *Indian corn.*
Moon of Bright Nights, *April.*
Moon of Leaves, *May.*
Moon of Strawberries, *June.*
Moon of the Falling Leaves, *September.*
Moon of Snow-Shoes, *November.*
Mudjekee'wis, *the West Wind; father of Hiawatha.*
Mudway-aush'ka, *sound of waves on a shore.*
Mushkoda'sa, *the grouse.*
Nah'ma, *the sturgeon.*
Nah'ma-wusk, *spearmint.*
Na'gow Wudj'oo, *the Sand Dunes of Lake Superior.*
Nee-ba-naw'baigs, *water-spirits.*
Nenemoo'sha, *sweetheart.*
Nepah'win, *sleep.*
Noko'mis, *a grandmother; mother of Wenonah.*
No'sa, *my father.*
Nush'ka, *look! look!*
Odah'min, *the strawberry.*
Okahah'wis, *the fresh-water herring.*
Ome'me, *the pigeon.*
Ona'gon, *a bowl.*
Onaway', *awake.*
Ope'chee, *the robin.* [*Star.*
Osse'o, *Son of the Evening*
Owais'sa, *the bluebird.*
Oweenee', *wife of Osseo.*
Ozawa'beek, *a round piece of brass or copper in the Game of the Bowl.*

Pah-puk-kee'na, *the grasshopper.*
Pau'guk, *death.*
Pau-Puk-Kee'wis, *the handsome Yenadizze, the Storm Fool.* [*Marie.*
Pauwa'ting, *Saut Sainte*
Pe'boan, *Winter.*
Pem'ican, *meat of the deer or buffalo dried and pounded*
Pezhekee', *the bison.*
Pishnekuh', *the brant.*
Pone'mah, *hereafter.*
Pugasaing', *Game of the Bowl.*
Puggawau'gun, *a war-club.*
Puk-Wudj'ies, *little wild men of the woods; pygmies.*
Sah-sah-je'wun, *rapids.*
Sah'wa, *the perch.*
Segwun', *Spring.*
Sha'da, *the pelican.*
Shahbo'min, *the gooseberry.*
Shah-shah, *long ago.*
Shaugoda'ya, *a coward.*
Shawgashee', *the crawfish.*
Shawonda'see, *the South Wind.*
Shawshaw, *the swallow.*
Shesh'ebwug, *ducks; pieces in the Game of the Bowl.*
Shin'gebis, *the diver or grebe.*
Showain' neme'shin, *pity me.*
Shuh-shuh'-gah, *the blue heron.* [*hearted.*
Soan-ge-ta'ha, *strong-*
Subbeka'she, *the spider.*
Sugge'ma, *the mosquito.*
To'tem, *family coat-of-arms.*
Ugh, *yes.*
Ugudwash', *the sun-fish.*
Unktahee', *the God of Water.*
Wabas'so, *the rabbit; the North.* [*juggler.*
Wabe'no, *a magician, a*
Wabe'no-wusk, *yarrow.*
Wa'bun, *the East Wind.*
Wa'bun An'nung, *the Star of the East, the Morning Star.* [*tation.*
Wahono'win, *a cry of lamen-*
Wah-wah-tay'see, *the fire-fly.*
Wam'pum, *beads of shell.*
Waubewy'on, *a white skin wrapper.*
Wa'wa, *the wild-goose.*
Waw'beek, *a rock.*
Wa-be-wa'wa, *the white goose.*
Wawonais'sa, *the whippoorwill.* [*pillar.*
Way-muk-kwa'na, *the cater-*
Wen'digoes, *giants.*
Weno'nah, *Hiawatha's mother, daughter of Nokomis.*
Yenadiz'ze, *an idler and gambler; an Indian dandy.*

273

The Courtship of Miles Standish.

I.

MILES STANDISH.

In the Old Colony days, in Plymouth the land of the Pilgrims,
To and fro in a room of his simple and primitive dwelling,
Clad in doublet and hose, and boots of Cordovan leather,
Strode, with a martial air, Miles Standish the Puritan Captain.
Buried in thought he seemed, with his hands behind him, and pausing
Ever and anon to behold his glittering weapons of warfare,
Hanging in shining array along the walls of the chamber,—
Cutlass and corselet of steel, and his trusty sword of Damascus,
Curved at the point and inscribed with its mystical Arabic sentence,
While underneath, in a corner, were fowling-piece, musket, and matchlock.
Short of stature he was, but strongly built and athletic,
Broad in the shoulders, deep-chested, with muscles and sinews of iron;
Brown as a nut was his face, but his russet beard was already
Flaked with patches of snow, as hedges sometimes in November.
Near him was seated John Alden, his friend, and household companion,
Writing with diligent speed at a table of pine by the window;
Fair-haired, azure-eyed, with delicate Saxon complexion,
Having the dew of his youth, and the beauty thereof, as the captives
Whom Saint Gregory saw, and exclaimed, ' Not Angles, but Angels.'
Youngest of all was he of the men who came in the May Flower.

Suddenly breaking the silence, the diligent scribe interrupting,
Spake, in the pride of his heart, Miles Standish the Captain of Plymouth.
' Look at these arms,' he said, ' the warlike weapons that hang here
Burnished and bright and clean, as if for parade or inspection!
This is the sword of Damascus I fought with in Flanders; this breast-
plate—
Well I remember the day!—once saved my life in a skirmish;
Here in front you can see the very dint of the bullet
Fired point-blank at my heart by a Spanish arcabucero.
Had it not been of sheer steel, the forgotten bones of Miles Standish
Would at this moment be mould, in their grave in the Flemish morasses.'
Thereupon answered John Alden, but looked not up from his writing:
' Truly the breath of the Lord hath slackened the speed of the bullet;
He in his mercy preserved you, to be our shield and our weapon!'
Still the Captain continued, unheeding the words of the stripling:
' See, how bright they are burnished, as if in an arsenal hanging;
That is because I have done it myself, and not left it to others.
Serve yourself, would you be well served, is an excellent adage;
So I take care of my arms, as you of your pens and your inkhorn.
Then, too, there are my soldiers, my great, invincible army,

274

Twelve men, all equipped, having each his rest and his matchlock,
Eighteen shillings a month, together with diet and pillage,
And, like Cæsar, I know the name of each of my soldiers!'
This he said with a smile, that danced in his eyes, as the sunbeams
Dance on the waves of the sea, and vanish again in a moment.
Alden laughed as he wrote, and still the Captain continued :
'Look! you can see from this window my brazen howitzer planted
High on the roof of the church, a preacher who speaks to the purpose,
Steady, straightforward, and strong, with irresistible logic,
Orthodox, flashing conviction right into the hearts of the heathen.
Now we are ready, I think, for any assault of the Indians;
Let them come, if they like, and the sooner they try it the better,—
Let them come, if they like, be it sagamore, sachem, or pow-wow,
Aspinet, Samoset, Corbitant, Squanto, or Tokamahamon!'

    Long at the window he stood, and wistfully gazed on the landscape,
Washed with a cold gray mist, the vapoury breath of the east-wind,
Forest and meadow and hill, and the steel-blue rim of the ocean,
Lying silent and sad, in the afternoon shadows and sunshine.
Over his countenance flitted a shadow like those on the landscape,
Gloom intermingled with light; and his voice was subdued with emotion,
Tenderness, pity, regret, as after a pause he proceeded :
'Yonder there, on the hill by the sea, lies buried Rose Standish;
Beautiful rose of love, that bloomed for me by the wayside!
She was the first to die of all who came in the May Flower!
Green above her is growing the field of wheat we have sown there,
Better to hide from the Indian scouts the graves of our people,
Lest they should count them and see how many already have perished!'
Sadly his face he averted, and strode up and down, and was thoughtful.

    Fixed to the opposite wall was a shelf of books, and among them
Prominent three, distinguished alike for bulk and for binding;
Bariffe's Artillery Guide, and the Commentaries of Cæsar
Out of the Latin translated by Arthur Goldinge of London,
And, as if guarded by these, between them was standing the Bible.
Musing a moment before them, Miles Standish paused, as if doubtful
Which of the three he should choose for his consolation and comfort,
Whether the wars of the Hebrews, the famous campaigns of the Romans,
Or the Artillery practice, designed for belligerent Christians.
Finally down from its shelf he dragged the ponderous Roman,
Seated himself at the window, and opened the book, and in silence
Turned o'er the well-worn leaves, where thumb-marks thick on the margin,
Like the trample of feet, proclaimed the battle was hottest.
Nothing was heard in the room but the hurrying pen of the stripling,
Busily writing epistles important, to go by the May Flower,
Ready to sail on the morrow, or next day at latest, God willing!
Homeward bound with the tidings of all that terrible winter,
Letters written by Alden, and full of the name of Priscilla,
Full of the name and the fame of the Puritan maiden Priscilla!

II.

LOVE AND FRIENDSHIP.

NOTHING was heard in the room but the hurrying pen of the stripling,
Or an occasional sigh from the labouring heart of the Captain,
Reading the marvellous words and achievements of Julius Cæsar.
After a while he exclaimed, as he smote with his hand, palm downwards,
Heavily on the page : ' A wonderful man was this Cæsar !
You are a writer, and I am a fighter, but here is a fellow
Who could both write and fight, and in both was equally skilful !'
Straightway answered and spake John Alden, the comely, the youthful :
' Yes, he was equally skilled, as you say, with his pen and his weapons.
Somewhere have I read, but where I forget, he could dictate
Seven letters at once, at the same time writing his memoirs.'
' Truly,' continued the Captain, not heeding or hearing the other,
' Truly a wonderful man was Caius Julius Cæsar !
Better be first, he said, in a little Iberian village,
Than be second in Rome, and I think he was right when he said it.
Twice was he married before he was twenty, and many times after ;
Battles five hundred he fought, and a thousand cities he conquered ;
He, too, fought in Flanders, as he himself has recorded ;
Finally he was stabbed by his friend, the orator Brutus !
Now, do you know what he did on a certain occasion in Flanders,
When the rear-guard of his army retreated, the front giving way too,
And the immortal Twelfth Legion was crowded so closely together
There was no room for their swords ? Why, he seized a shield from a
      soldier,
Put himself straight at the head of his troops, and commanded the
      captains,
Calling on each by his name, to order forward the ensigns ;
Then to widen the ranks, and give more room for their weapons ;
So he won the day, the battle of something-or-other.
That's what I always say ; if you wish a thing to be well done,
You must do it yourself, you must not leave it to others !'

All was silent again ; the Captain continued his reading.
Nothing was heard in the room but the hurrying pen of the stripling
Writing epistles important to go next day by the May Flower,
Filled with the name and the fame of the Puritan maiden Priscilla ;
Every sentence began or closed with the name of Priscilla,
Till the treacherous pen, to which he confided the secret,
Strove to betray it by singing and shouting the name of Priscilla !
Finally closing his book, with a bang of the ponderous cover,
Sudden and loud as the sound of a soldier grounding his musket,
Thus to the young man spake Miles Standish the Captain of Plymouth :
' When you have finished your work, I have something important to tell
      you.

Be not however in haste; I can wait; I shall not be impatient!'
Straightway Alden replied, as he folded the last of his letters,
Pushing his papers aside, and giving respectful attention:
'Speak; for whenever you speak, I am always ready to listen,
Always ready to hear whatever pertains to Miles Standish.'
Thereupon answered the Captain, embarrassed, and culling his phrases:
''Tis not good for a man to be alone, say the Scriptures.
This have I said before, and again and again I repeat it;
Every hour in the day, I think it, and feel it, and say it.
Since Rose Standish died, my life has been weary and dreary;
Sick at heart have I been, beyond the healing of friendship.
Oft in my lonely hours have I thought of the maiden Priscilla.
She is alone in the world; her father and mother and brother
Died in the winter together; I saw her going and coming,
Now to the grave of the dead, and now to the bed of the dying,
Patient, courageous, and strong, and said to myself, that if ever
There were angels on earth, as there are angels in heaven,
Two have I seen and known; and the angel whose name is Priscilla
Holds in my desolate life the place which the other abandoned.
Long have I cherished the thought, but never have dared to reveal it,
Being a coward in this, though valiant enough for the most part.
Go to the damsel Priscilla, the loveliest maiden of Plymouth,
Say that a blunt old Captain, a man not of words but of actions,
Offers his hand and his heart, the hand and heart of a soldier.
Not in these words, you know, but this in short is my meaning;
I am a maker of war, and not a maker of phrases.
You, who are bred as a scholar, can say it in elegant language,
Such as you read in your books of the pleadings and wooings of lovers,
Such as you think best adapted to win the heart of a maiden.'

When he had spoken, John Alden, the fair-haired, taciturn stripling,
All aghast at his words, surprised, embarrassed, bewildered,
Trying to mask his dismay by treating the subject with lightness,
Trying to smile, and yet feeling his heart stand still in his bosom,
Just as a timepiece stops in a house that is stricken by lightning,
Thus made answer and spake, or rather stammered than answered:
'Such a message as that, I am sure I should mangle and mar it;
If you would have it well done,—I am only repeating your maxim,—
You must do it yourself, you must not leave it to others!'
But with the air of a man whom nothing can turn from his purpose,
Gravely shaking his head, made answer the Captain of Plymouth:
'Truly the maxim is good, and I do not mean to gainsay it;
But we must use it discreetly, and not waste powder for nothing.
Now, as I said before, I was never a maker of phrases.
I can march up to a fortress and summon the place to surrender,
But march up to a woman with such a proposal, I dare not.
I am not afraid of bullets, nor shot from the mouth of a cannon,
But of a thundering " No ! " point-blank from the mouth of a woman,
That I confess I'm afraid of, nor am I ashamed to confess it !

So you must grant my request, for you are an elegant scholar,
Having the graces of speech, and skill in the turning of phrases.'
Taking the hand of his friend, who still was reluctant and doubtful,
Holding it long in his own, and pressing it kindly, he added:
'Though I have spoken thus lightly, yet deep is the feeling that prompts me,
Surely you cannot refuse what I ask in the name of our friendship!'
Then made answer John Alden: 'The name of friendship is sacred;
What you demand in that name, I have not the power to deny you!'
So the strong will prevailed, subduing and moulding the gentler,
Friendship prevailed over love, and Alden went on his errand.

III.

THE LOVER'S ERRAND.

So the strong will prevailed, and Alden went on his errand.
Out of the street of the village, and into the paths of the forest,
Into the tranquil woods, where bluebirds and robins were building
Towns in the populous trees, with hanging gardens of verdure,
Peaceful, aerial cities of joy and affection and freedom.
All around him was calm, but within him commotion and conflict,
Love contending with friendship, and self with each generous impulse.
To and fro in his breast his thoughts were heaving and dashing,
As in a foundering ship, with every roll of the vessel,
Washes the bitter sea, the merciless surge of the ocean!
'Must I relinquish it all,' he cried with a wild lamentation,—
'Must I relinquish it all, the joy, the hope, the illusion?
Was it for this I have loved, and waited, and worshipped in silence?
Was it for this I have followed the flying feet and the shadow
Over the wintry sea, to the desolate shores of New England?
Truly the heart is deceitful, and out of its depths of corruption
Rise, like an exhalation, the misty phantoms of passion;
Angels of light they seem, but are only delusions of Satan.
All is clear to me now; I feel it, I see it distinctly!
This is the hand of the Lord; it is laid upon me in anger,
For I have followed too much the heart's desires and devices,
Worshipping Astaroth blindly, and impious idols of Baal.
This is the cross I must bear; the sin and the swift retribution.'

So through the Plymouth woods John Alden went on his errand;
Crossing the brook at the ford, where it brawled over pebble and shallow,
Gathering still, as he went, the May-flowers blooming around him,
Fragrant, filling the air with a strange and wonderful sweetness,
Children lost in the woods, and covered with leaves in their slumber.
'Puritan flowers,' he said, 'and the type of Puritan maidens,
Modest and simple and sweet, the very type of Priscilla!
So I will take them to her; to Priscilla the May-flower of Plymouth,
Modest and simple and sweet, as a parting gift will I take them;

278

Breathing their silent farewells, as they fade and wither and perish,
Soon to be thrown away as is the heart of the giver.'
So through the Plymouth wooas John Alden went on his errand ;
Came to an open space, and saw the disc of the ocean,
Sailless, sombre and cold with the comfortless breath of the east-wind ;
Saw the new-built house, and the people at work in the meadow ;
Heard, as he drew near the door, the musical voice of Priscilla
Singing the hundredth Psalm, the grand old Puritan anthem,
Music that Luther sang to the sacred words of the Psalmist,
Full of the breath of the Lord, consoling and comforting many.
Then, as he opened the door, he beheld the form of the maiden
Seated beside her wheel, and the carded wool like a snowdrift
Piled at her knee, her white hands feeding the ravenous spindle,
While with her foot on the treadle she guided the wheel in its motion.
Open wide on her lap lay the well-worn psalm-book of Ainsworth,
Printed in Amsterdam, the words and the music together,
Rough-hewn, angular notes, like stones in the wall of a churchyard,
Darkened and overhung by the running vine of the verses.
Such was the book from whose pages she sang the old Puritan anthem,
She, the Puritan girl, in the solitude of the forest,
Making the humble house and the modest apparel of homespun
Beautiful with her beauty, and rich with the wealth of her being !
Over him rushed, like a wind that is keen and cold and relentless,
Thoughts of what might have been, and the weight and woe of his errand ;
All the dreams that had faded, and all the hopes that had vanished,
All his life henceforth a dreary and tenantless mansion,
Haunted by vain regrets, and pallid, sorrowful faces.
Still he said to himself, and almost fiercely he said it,
' Let not him that putteth his hand to the plough look backwards ;
Though the ploughshare cut through the flowers of life to its fountains,
Though it pass o'er the graves of the dead and the hearths of the living,
It is the will of the Lord ; and his mercy endureth for ever ! '

So he entered the house : and the hum of the wheel and the singing
Suddenly ceased ; for Priscilla, aroused by his step on the threshold,
Rose as he entered, and gave him her hand, in signal of welcome,
Say'ng, ' I knew it was you when I heard your step in the passage ;
For I was thinking of you, as I sat there singing and spinning.'
Awkward and dumb with delight, that a thought of him had been mingled
Thus in the sacred psalm, that came from the heart of the maiden,
Silent before her he stood, and gave her the flowers for an answer,
Finding no words for his thought. He remembered that day in the winter,
After the first great snow, when he broke a path from the village,
Reeling and plunging along through the drifts that encumbered the
    doorway,
Stamping the snow from his feet as he entered the house, and Priscilla
Laughed at his snowy locks, and gave him a seat by the fireside,
Grateful and pleased to know he had thought of her in the snowstorm.
Had he but spoken then ! perhaps not in vain had he spoken ;

K

Now it was all too late; the golden moment had vanished !
So he stood there abashed, and gave her the flowers for an answer.

Then they sat down and talked of the birds and the beautiful Spring-
time,
Talked of their friends at home, and the May Flower that sailed on the
morrow.
'I have been thinking all day,' said gently the Puritan maiden,
'Dreaming all night, and thinking all day, of the hedgerows of Eng-
land,—
They are in blossom now, and the country is all like a garden;
Thinking of lanes and fields, and the song of the lark and the linnet,
Seeing the village street, and familiar faces of neighbours
Going about as of old, and stopping to gossip together,
And, at the end of the street, the village church, with the ivy
Climbing the old gray tower, and the quiet graves in the churchyard.
Kind are the people I live with, and dear to me my religion ;
Still my heart is so sad, that I wish myself back in Old England.
You will say it is wrong, but I cannot help it : I almost
Wish myself back in Old England, I feel so lonely and wretched.'

Thereupon answered the youth : 'Indeed I do not condemn you ;
Stouter hearts than a woman's have quailed in this terrible winter.
Yours is tender and trusting, and needs a stronger to lean on ;
So I have come to you now, with an offer and proffer of marriage
Made by a good man and true, Miles Standish the Captain of Plymouth !'

Thus he delivered his message, the dexterous writer of letters,—
Did not embellish the theme, nor array it in beautiful phrases,
But came straight to the point, and blurted it out like a schoolboy ;
Even the Captain himself could hardly have said it more bluntly.
Mute with amazement and sorrow, Priscilla the Puritan maiden
Looked into Alden's face, her eyes dilated with wonder,
Feeling his words like a blow, that stunned her and rendered her speechless;
Till at length she exclaimed, interrupting the ominous silence :
'If the great Captain of Plymouth is so very eager to wed me,
Why does he not come himself, and take the trouble to woo me ?
If I am not worth the wooing, I surely am not worth the winning !'
Then John Alden began explaining and smoothing the matter,
Making it worse as he went, by saying the Captain was busy,—
Had no time for such things ;—such things ! the words grating harshly
Fell on the ear of Priscilla ; and swift as a flash she made answer :
'Has no time for such things, as you call it, before he is married,
Would he be likely to find it, or make it after the wedding ?
That is the way with you men ; you don't understand us, you cannot.
When you have made up your minds, after thinking of this one and that
one,
Choosing, selecting, rejecting, comparing one with another,
Then you make known your desire, with abrupt and sudden avowal,

And are offended and hurt, and indignant perhaps, that a woman
Does not respond at once to a love that she never suspected,
Does not attain at a bound the height to which you have been climbing.
This is not right nor just : for surely a woman's affection
Is not a thing to be asked for, and had for only the asking.
When one is truly in love, one not only says it, but shows it.
Had he but waited awhile, had he only showed that he loved me,
Even this Captain of yours—who knows?—at last might have won me,
Old and rough as he is ; but now it never can happen.'

Still John Alden went on, unheeding the words of Priscilla,
Urging the suit of his friend, explaining, persuading, expanding ;
Spoke of his courage and skill, and of all his battles in Flanders,
How with the people of God he had chosen to suffer affliction,
How, in return for his zeal, they had made him Captain of Plymouth ;
He was a gentleman born, could trace his pedigree plainly
Back to Hugh Standish of Duxbury Hall, in Lancashire, England,
Who was the son of Ralph, and the grandson of Thurston de Standish :
Heir unto vast estates, of which he was basely defrauded,
Still bore the family arms, and had for his crest a cock argent
Combed and wattled gules, and all the rest of the blazon.
He was a man of honour, of noble and generous nature ;
Though he was rough, he was kindly ; she knew how during the winter
He had attended the sick, with a hand as gentle as woman's ;
Somewhat hasty and hot, he could not deny it, and headstrong,
Stern as a soldier might be, but hearty, and placable always,
Not to be laughed at and scorned, because he was little of stature ;
For he was great of heart, magnanimous, courtly, courageous ;
Any woman in Plymouth, nay, any woman in England,
Might be happy and proud to be called the wife of Miles Standish !

But as he warmed and glowed, in his simple and eloquent language,
Quite forgetful of self, and full of the praise of his rival,
Archly the maiden smiled, and, with eyes overrunning with laughter,
Said, in a tremulous voice, 'Why don't you speak for yourself, John ?'

IV.

JOHN ALDEN.

INTO the open air John Alden, perplexed and bewildered,
Rushed like a man insane, and wandered alone by the seaside ;
Paced up and down the sands, and bared his head to the east-wind,
Cooling his heated brow, and the fire and fever within him.
Slowly as out of the heavens, with apocalyptical splendours,
Sank the City of God, in the vision of John the Apostle,
So, with its cloudy walls of chrysolite, jasper, and sapphire,
Sank the broad red sun, and over its turrets uplifted
Glimmered the golden reed of the angel who measured the city

'Welcome, O wind of the East!' he exclaimed in his wild exultation,
'Welcome, O wind of the East, from the caves of the misty Atlantic!
Blowing o'er fields of dulse, and measureless meadows of sea-grass,
Blowing o'er rocky wastes, and the grottoes and gardens of ocean!
Lay thy cold, moist hand on my burning forehead, and wrap me
Close in thy garments of mist, to allay the fever within me!'

Like an awakened conscience, the sea was moaning and tossing,
Beating remorseful and loud the mutable sands of the sea-shore.
Fierce in his soul was the struggle and tumult of passions contending;
Love triumphant and crowned, and friendship wounded and bleeding,
Passionate cries of desire, and importunate pleadings of duty!
'Is it my fault,' he said, 'that the maiden has chosen between us?
Is it my fault that he failed,—my fault that I am the victor?'
Then within him there thundered a voice, like the voice of the Prophet:
'It hath displeased the Lord!'—and he thought of David's trans-
        gression,
Bathsheba's beautiful face, and his friend in the front of the battle!
Shame and confusion of guilt, and abasement and self-condemnation,
Overwhelmed him at once; and he cried in the deepest contrition:
'It hath displeased the Lord! It is the temptation of Satan!'

Then uplifting his head, he looked at the sea, and beheld there
Dimly the shadowy form of the May Flower riding at anchor,
Rocked on the rising tide, and ready to sail on the morrow;
Heard the voices of men through the mist, the rattle of cordage
Thrown on the deck, the shouts of the mate, and the sailors' 'Ay, ay,
        Sir!'
Clear and distinct, but not loud, in the dripping air of the twilight.
Still for a moment he stood, and listened, and stared at the vessel,
Then went hurriedly on, as one who, seeing a phantom,
Stops, then quickens his pace, and follows the beckoning shadow.
'Yes, it is plain to me now,' he murmured; 'the hand of the Lord is
Leading me out of the land of darkness, the bondage of error,
Through the sea, that shall lift the walls of its waters around me,
Hiding me, cutting me off, from the cruel thoughts that pursue me.
Back will I go o'er the ocean, this dreary land will abandon,
Her whom I may not love, and him whom my heart has offended.
Better to be in my grave in the green old churchyard in England,
Close by my mother's side, and among the dust of my kindred;
Better be dead and forgotten, than living in shame and dishonour!
Sacred and safe and unseen, in the dark of the narrow chamber
With me my secret shall lie, like a buried jewel that glimmers
Bright on the hand that is dust, in the chambers of silence and darkness,—
Yes, as the marriage ring of the great espousal hereafter!'

Thus as he spake, he turned, in the strength of his strong resolution,
Leaving behind him the shore, and hurried along in the twilight,

Through the congenial gloom of the forest silent and sombre,
Till he beheld the lights in the seven houses of Plymouth,
Shining like seven stars in the dusk and mist of the evening.
Soon he entered his door, and found the redoubtable Captain
Sitting alone, and absorbed in the martial pages of Cæsar,
Fighting some great campaign in Hainault or Brabant or Flanders.
'Long have you been on your errand,' he said with a cheery demeanour,
Even as one who is waiting an answer, and fears not the issue.
'Not far off is the house, although the woods are between us;
But you have lingered so long, that while you were going and coming
I have fought ten battles and sacked and demolished a city.
Come, sit down, and in order relate to me all that has happened.'

Then John Alden spake, and related the wondrous adventure,
From beginning to end, minutely, just as it happened;
How he had seen Priscilla, and how he had sped in his courtship,
Only smoothing a little, and softening down her refusal.
But when he came at length to the words Priscilla had spoken,
Words so tender and cruel: 'Why don't you speak for yourself, John?'
Up leaped the Captain of Plymouth, and stamped on the floor, till his
      armour
Clanged on the wall, where it hung, with a sound of sinister omen.
All his pent-up wrath burst forth in a sudden explosion,
E'en as a hand-grenade, that scatters destruction around it.
Wildly he shouted, and loud: 'John Alden! you have betrayed me!
Me, Miles Standish, your friend! have supplanted, defrauded, betrayed
      me!
One of my ancestors ran his sword through the heart of Wat Tyler;
Who shall prevent me from running my own through the heart of a
      traitor?
Yours is the greater treason, for yours is a treason to friendship!
You, who lived under my roof, whom I cherished and loved as a brother;
You, who have fed at my board, and drunk at my cup, to whose keeping
I have intrusted my honour, my thoughts the most sacred and secret,—
You too, Brutus! ah woe to the name of friendship hereafter!
Brutus was Cæsar's friend, and you were mine, but henceforward
Let there be nothing between us save war, and implacable hatred!'

So spake the Captain of Plymouth, and strode about in the chamber,
Chafing and choking with rage; like cords were the veins on his temples.
But in the midst of his anger a man appeared at the doorway,
Bringing in uttermost haste a message of urgent importance,
Rumours of danger and war and hostile incursions of Indians!
Straightway the Captain paused, and, without further question or parley,
Took from the nail on the wall his sword with its scabbard of iron,
Buckled the belt round his waist, and, frowning fiercely, departed.
Alden was left alone. He heard the clank of the scabbard
Growing fainter and fainter, and dying away in the distance.
Then he arose from his seat, and looked forth into the darkness,

Felt the cool air blow on his cheek, that was hot with the insult,
Lifted his eyes to the heavens, and, folding his hands as in childhood,
Prayed in the silence of night to the Father who seeth in secret.

Meanwhile the choleric Captain strode wrathful away to the council,
Found it already assembled, impatiently waiting his coming;
Men in the middle of life, austere and grave in deportment,
Only one of them old, the hill that was nearest to heaven,
Covered with snow, but erect, the excellent Elder of Plymouth.
God had sifted three kingdoms to find the wheat for this planting,
Then had sifted the wheat, as the living seed of a nation;
So say the chronicles old, and such is the faith of the people!
Near them was standing an Indian, in attitude stern and defiant,
Naked down to the waist, and grim and ferocious in aspect;
While on the table before them was lying unopened a Bible,
Ponderous, bound in leather, brass-studded, printed in Holland,
And beside it outstretched the skin of a rattlesnake glittered,
Filled, like a quiver, with arrows; a signal and challenge of warfare,
Brought by the Indian, and speaking with arrowy tongues of defiance.
This Miles Standish beheld, as he entered, and heard them debating
What were an answer befitting the hostile message and menace,
Talking of this and of that, contriving, suggesting, objecting;
One voice only for peace, and that the voice of the Elder,
Judging it wise and well that some at least were converted,
Rather than any were slain, for this was but Christian behaviour!
Then out spake Miles Standish, the stalwart Captain of Plymouth,
Muttering deep in his throat, for his voice was husky with anger,
'What! do you mean to make war with milk and the water of roses?
Is it to shoot red squirrels you have your howitzer planted
There on the roof of the church, or is it to shoot red devils?
Truly the only tongue that is understood by a savage
Must be the tongue of fire that speaks from the mouth of the cannon!'
Thereupon answered and said the excellent Elder of Plymouth,
Somewhat amazed and alarmed at this irreverent language:
'Not so thought Saint Paul, nor yet the other Apostles;
Not from the cannon's mouth were the tongues of fire they spake with!'
But unheeded fell this mild rebuke on the Captain,
Who had advanced to the table, and thus continued discoursing:
'Leave this matter to me, for to me by right it pertaineth.
War is a terrible trade; but in the cause that is righteous,
Sweet is the smell of powder; and thus I answer the challenge!'

Then from the rattlesnake's skin, with a sudden, contemptuous gesture,
jerking the Indian arrows, he filled it with powder and bullets
Full to the very jaws, and handed it back to the savage,
Saying, in thundering tones: 'Here, take it! this is your answer!'
Silently out of the room then glided the glistening savage,
Bearing the serpent's skin, and seeming himself like a serpent,
Winding his sinuous way in the dark to the depths of the forest.

V.

THE SAILING OF THE MAY FLOWER.

JUST in the gray of the dawn, as the mists uprose from the meadows,
There was a stir and a sound in the slumbering village of Plymouth;
Clanging and clicking of arms, and the order imperative, 'Forward!'
Given in tone suppressed, a tramp of feet, and then silence.
Figures ten, in the mist, marched slowly out of the village.
Standish the stalwart it was, with eight of his valorous army,
Led by their Indian guide, by Hobomok, friend of the white men,
Northward marching to quell the sudden revolt of the savage.
Giants they seemed in the mist, or the mighty men of King David;
Giants in heart they were, who believed in God and the Bible,—
Ay, who believed in the smiting of Midianites and Philistines.
Over them gleamed far off the crimson banners of morning;
Under them loud on the sands, the serried billows, advancing
Fired along the line, and in regular order retreated.

Many a mile had they marched, when at length the village of Plymouth
Woke from its sleep, and arose, intent on its manifold labours.
Sweet was the air and soft; and slowly the smoke from the chimneys
Rose over roofs of thatch, and pointed steadily eastward;
Men came forth from the doors, and paused and talked of the weather,
Said that the wind had changed, and was blowing fair for the May Flower;
Talked of their Captain's departure, and all the dangers that menaced,
He being gone, the town, and what should be done in his absence.
Merrily sang the birds, and the tender voices of women
Consecrated with hymns the common cares of the household.
Out on the sea rose the sun, and the billows rejoiced at his coming;
Beautiful were his feet on the purple tops of the mountains;
Beautiful on the sails of the May Flower riding at anchor,
Battered and blackened and worn by all the storms of the winter.
Loosely against her masts was hanging and flapping her canvas,
Rent by so many gales, and patched by the hands of the sailors.
Suddenly from her side, as the sun rose over the ocean,
Darted a puff of smoke, and floated seaward; anon rang
Loud over field and forest the cannon's roar, and the echoes
Heard and repeated the sound, the signal-gun of departure!
Ah! but with louder echoes replied the hearts of the people!
Meekly, in voices subdued, the chapter was read from the Bible,
Meekly the prayer was begun, but ended in fervent entreaty!
Then from their houses in haste came forth the Pilgrims of Plymouth,
Men and women and children, all hurrying down to the sea-shore,
Eager, with tearful eyes, to say farewell to the May Flower,
Homeward bound o'er the sea, and leaving them here in the desert.

Foremost among them was Alden. All night he had lain without slumber,

Turning and tossing about in the heat and unrest of his fever.
He had beheld Miles Standish, who came back late from the council,
Stalking into the room, and heard him mutter and murmur,
Sometimes it seemed a prayer, and sometimes it sounded like swearing.
Once he had come to the bed, and stood there a moment in silence ;
Then he had turned away, and said : ' I will not awake him ;
Let him sleep on, it is best ; for what is the use of more talking ! '
Then he extinguished the light, and threw himself down on his pallet,
Dressed as he was, and ready to start at the break of the morning,—
Covered himself with the cloak he had worn in his campaigns in Flanders,
Slept as a soldier sleeps in his bivouac, ready for action.
But with the dawn he arose ; in the twilight Alden beheld him
Put on his corselet of steel, and all the rest of his armour,
Buckle about his waist his trusty blade of Damascus,
Take from the corner his musket, and so stride out of the chamber.
Often the heart of the youth had burned and yearned to embrace him,
Often his lips had essayed to speak, imploring for pardon ;
All the old friendship came back, with its tender and grateful emotions;
But his pride overmastered the nobler nature within him,—
Pride, and the sense of his wrong, and the burning fire of the insult.
So he beheld his friend departing in anger, but spake not,
Saw him go forth to danger, perhaps to death, and he spake not !
Then he arose from his bed, and heard what the people were saying,
Joined in the talk at the door, with Stephen and Richard and Gilbert
Joined in the morning prayer, and in the reading of Scripture,
And, with the others, in haste went hurrying down to the sea-shore,
Down to the Plymouth Rock, that had been to their feet as a doorstep
Into a world unknown,—the corner-stone of a nation !

There with his boat was the Master, already a little impatient
Lest he should lose the tide, or the wind might shift to the eastward,
Square-built, hearty, and strong, with an odour of ocean about him,
Speaking with this one and that, and cramming letters and parcels
Into his pockets capacious, and messages mingled together
Into his narrow brain, till at last he was wholly bewildered.
Nearer the boat stood Alden, with one foot placed on the gunwale,
One still firm on the rock, and talking at times with the sailors,
Seated erect on the thwarts, all ready and eager for starting.
He too was eager to go, and thus put an end to his anguish,
Thinking to fly from despair, that swifter than keel is or canvas,
Thinking to drown in the sea the ghost that would rise and pursue him.
But as he gazed on the crowd, he beheld the form of Priscilla
Standing dejected among them, unconscious of all that was passing.
Fixed were her eyes upon his, as if she divined his intention,
Fixed with a look so sad, so reproachful, imploring, and patient,
That with a sudden revulsion his heart recoiled from its purpose,
As from the verge of a crag, where one step more is destruction.
Strange is the heart of man, with its quick, mysterious instincts !

Strange is the life of man, and fatal or fated are moments,
Whereupon turn, as on hinges, the gates of the wall adamantine!
'Here I remain!' he exclaimed, as he looked at the heavens above him,
Thanking the Lord whose breath had scattered the mist and the madness,
Wherein, blind and lost, to death he was staggering headlong.
'Yonder snow-white cloud, that floats in the ether above me,
Seems like a hand that is pointing and beckoning over the ocean.
There is another hand, that is not so spectral and ghostlike,
Holding me, drawing me back, and clasping mine for protection.
Float, O hand of cloud, and vanish away in the ether!
Roll thyself up like a fist, to threaten and daunt me ; I heed not
Either your warning or menace, or any omen of evil!
There is no land so sacred, no air so pure and so wholesome,
As is the air she breathes, and the soil that is pressed by her footsteps.
Here for her sake will I stay, and like an invisible presence
Hover around her for ever, protecting, supporting her weakness ;
Yes! as my foot was the first that stepped on this rock at the landing,
So, with the blessing of God, shall it be the last at the leaving!'

Meanwhile the Master alert, but with dignified air and important,
Scanning with watchful eye the tide and the wind and the weather,
Walked about on the sands, and the people crowded around him
Saying a few last words, and enforcing his careful remembrance.
Then, taking each by the hand, as if he were grasping a tiller,
Into the boat he sprang, and in haste shoved off to his vessel,
Glad in his heart to get rid of all this worry and flurry,
Glad to be gone from a land of sand and sickness and sorrow,
Short allowance of victual, and plenty of nothing but Gospel!
Lost in the sound of the oars was the last farewell of the Pilgrims.
O strong hearts and true! not one went back in the May Flower!
No, not one looked back, who had set his hand to this ploughing!

Soon were heard on board the shouts and songs of the sailors
Heaving the windlass round, and hoisting the ponderous anchor.
Then the yards were braced, and all sails set to the west-wind,
Blowing steady and strong ; and the May Flower sailed from the harbour,
Rounded the point of the Gurnet, and leaving far to the southward
Island and cape of sand, and the Field of the First Encounter,
Took the wind on her quarter, and stood for the open Atlantic,
Borne on the send of the sea, and the swelling hearts of the Pilgrims.

Long in silence they watched the receding sail of the vessel,
Much endeared to them all, as something living and human ;
Then as if filled with the spirit, and wrapt in a vision prophetic,
Baring his hoary head, the excellent Elder of Plymouth
Said, 'Let us pray!' and they prayed, and thanked the Lord and took
    courage.
Mournfully sobbed the waves at the base of the rock, and above them
Bowed and whispered the wheat on the hill of death, and their kindred

287

Seemed to awake in their graves, and to join in the prayer that they
uttered.
Sun-illumined and white, on the eastern verge of the ocean
Gleamed the departing sail, like a marble slab in a graveyard;
Buried beneath it lay for ever all hope of escaping.
Lo! as they turned to depart, they saw the form of an Indian,
Watching them from the hill; but while they spake with each other,
Pointing with outstretched hands, and saying, ' Look!' he had vanished.
So they returned to their homes ; but Alden lingered a little,
Musing alone on the shore, and watching the wash of the billows
Round the base of the rock, and the sparkle and flash of the sunshine,
Like the spirit of God, moving visibly over the waters.

VI.

PRISCILLA.

THUS for a while he stood, and mused by the shore of the ocean,
Thinking of many things, and most of all of Priscilla ;
And as if thought had the power to draw to itself, like the loadstone,
Whatsoever it touches, by subtile laws of its nature,
Lo! as he turned to depart, Priscilla was standing beside him.

'Are you so much offended, you will not speak to me?' said she.
'Am I so much to blame, that yesterday when you were pleading
Warmly the cause of another, my heart, impulsive and wayward,
Pleaded your own, and spake out, forgetful perhaps of decorum?
Certainly you can forgive me for speaking so frankly, for saying
What I ought not to have said, yet now I can never unsay it;
For there are moments in life, when the heart is so full of emotion,
That if by chance it be shaken, or into its depths like a pebble
Drops some careless word, it overflows, and its secret,
Spilt on the ground like water, can never be gathered together.
Yesterday I was shocked, when I heard you speak of Miles Standish,
Praising his virtues, transforming his very defects into virtues,
Praising his courage and strength, and even his fighting in Flanders,
As if by fighting alone you could win the heart of a woman,
Quite overlooking yourself and the rest, in exalting your hero.
Therefore I spake as I did, by an irresistible impulse.
You will forgive me, I hope, for the sake of the friendship between us,
Which is too true and too sacred to be so easily broken!'
Thereupon answered John Alden, the scholar, the friend of Miles Standish:
'I am not angry with you, with myself alone I was angry,
Seeing how badly I managed the matter I had in my keeping.'
'No!' interrupted the maiden, with answer prompt and decisive;
'No ; you were angry with me, for speaking so frankly and freely.
It was wrong, I acknowledge ; for it is the fate of a woman
Long to be patient and silent, to wait like a ghost that is speechless,

288

Till some questioning voice dissolves the spell of its silence.
Hence is the inner life of so many suffering women
Sunless and silent and deep, like subterranean rivers
Running through caverns of darkness, unheard, unseen, and unfruitful,
Chafing their channels of stone with endless and profitless murmurs.'
Thereupon answered John Alden, the young man, the lover of women :
' Heaven forbid it, Priscilla ; and truly they seem to me always
More like the beautiful rivers that watered the garden of Eden,
More like the river Euphrates, through deserts of Havilah flowing,
Filling the land with delight, and memories sweet of the garden !'
' Ah, by these words, I can see,' again interrupted the maiden,
' How very little you prize me, or care for what I am saying.
When from the depths of my heart, in pain and with secret misgiving,
Frankly I speak to you, asking for sympathy only and kindness,
Straightway you take up my words, that are plain and direct and in earnest,
Turn them away from their meaning, and answer with flattering phrases.
This is not right, is not just, is not true to the best that is in you ;
For I know and esteem you, and feel that your nature is noble,
Lifting mine up to a higher, a more ethereal level.
Therefore I value your friendship, and feel it perhaps the more keenly
If you say aught that implies I am only as one among many,
If you make use of those common and complimentary phrases
Most men think so fine, in dealing and speaking with women,
But which women reject as insipid, if not as insulting.'

Mute and amazed was Alden ; and listened and looked at Priscilla,
Thinking he never had seen her more fair, more divine in her beauty.
He who but yesterday pleaded so glibly the cause of another,
Stood there embarrassed and silent, and seeking in vain for an answer.
So the maiden went on, and little divined or imagined
What was at work in his heart, that made him so awkward and speechless.
' Let us, then, be what we are, and speak what we think, and in all things
Keep ourselves loyal to truth, and the sacred professions of friendship.
It is no secret I tell you, nor am I ashamed to declare it :
I have liked to be with you, to see you, to speak with you always.
So I was hurt at your words, and a little affronted to hear you
Urge me to marry your friend, though he were the Captain Miles Standish.
For I must tell you the truth ; much more to me is your friendship
Than all the love he could give, were he twice the hero you think him.'
Then she extended her hand, and Alden, who eagerly grasped it,
Felt all the wounds in his heart, that were aching and bleeding so sorely,
Healed by the touch of that hand, and he said, with a voice full of feeling :
' Yes, we must ever be friends ; and of all who offer you friendship
Let me be ever the first, the truest, the nearest and dearest !'

Casting a farewell look at the glimmering sail of the May Flower,
Distant, but still in sight, and sinking below the horizon,
Homeward together they walked, with a strange indefinite feeling,

That all the rest had departed and left them alone in the desert.
But, as they went through the fields in the blessing and smile of the sun-
    shine,
Lighter grew their hearts, and Priscilla said very archly :
'Now that our terrible Captain has gone in pursuit of the Indians,
Where he is happier far than he would be commanding a household,
You may speak boldly, and tell me of all that happened between you,
When you returned last night, and said how ungrateful you found me.'
Thereupon answered John Alden, and told her the whole of the story,—
Told her his own despair, and the direful wrath of Miles Standish.
Whereat the maiden smiled, and said between laughing and earnest,
'He is a little chimney, and heated hot in a moment!'
But as he gently rebuked her, and told her how he had suffered,—
How he had even determined to sail that day in the May Flower,
And had remained for her sake, on hearing the dangers that threatened,—
All her manner was changed, and she said with a faltering accent,
'Truly I thank you for this : how good you have been to me always!'

    Thus, as a pilgrim devout, who toward Jerusalem journeys,
Taking three steps in advance, and one reluctantly backward,
Urged by importunate zeal, and withheld by pangs of contrition ;
Slowly but steadily onward, receding yet ever advancing,
Journeyed this Puritan youth to the Holy Land of his longings,
Urged by the fervour of love, and withheld by remorseful misgivings.

VII.

THE MARCH OF MILES STANDISH.

MEANWHILE the stalwart Miles Standish was marching steadily north-
    ward,
Winding through forest and swamp, and along the trend of the seashore,
All day long, with hardly a halt, the fire of his anger
Burning and crackling within, and the sulphurous odour of powder
Seeming more sweet to his nostrils than all the scents of the forest.
Silent and moody he went, and much he revolved his discomfort ;
He who was used to success, and to easy victories always,
Thus to be flouted, rejected, and laughed to scorn by a maiden,
Thus to be mocked and betrayed by the friend whom most he had trusted!
Ah! 'twas too much to be borne, and he fretted and chafed in his armour!

    'I alone am to blame,' he muttered, 'for mine was the folly.
What has a rough old soldier, grown grim and gray in the harness,
Used to the camp and its ways, to do with the wooing of maidens?
'Twas but a dream,—let it pass,—let it vanish like so many others!
What I thought was a flower, is only a weed, and is worthless!
Out of my heart will I pluck it, and throw it away, and henceforward

Be but a fighter of battles, a lover and wooer of dangers!'
Thus he revolved in his mind his sorry defeat and discomfort,
While he was marching by day or lying at night in the forest,
Looking up at the trees, and the constellations beyond them.

After a three days' march he came to an Indian encampment
Pitched on the edge of a meadow, between the sea and the forest;
Women at work by the tents, and the warriors, horrid with war-paint,
Seated about a fire, and smoking and talking together;
Who, when they saw from afar the sudden approach of the white men,
Saw the flash of the sun on breastplate and sabre and musket,
Straightway leaped to their feet, and two, from among them advancing,
Came to parley with Standish, and offer him furs as a present;
Friendship was in their looks, but in their hearts there was hatred.
Braves of the tribe were these, and brothers gigantic in stature,
Huge as Goliath of Gath, or the terrible Og, king of Bashan;
One was Pecksuot named, and the other was called Wattawamat.
Round their necks were suspended their knives in scabbards of wampum,
Two-edged, trenchant knives, with points as sharp as a needle.
Other arms had they none, for they were cunning and crafty.
'Welcome, English!' they said,—these words they had learned from the
     traders
Touching at times on the coast, to barter and chaffer for peltries.
Then in their native tongue they began to parley with Standish,
Through his guide and interpreter, Hobomok, friend of the white man,
Begging for blankets and knives, but mostly for muskets and powder,
Kept by the white man, they said, concealed, with the plague, in his
     cellars,
Ready to be let loose, and destroy his brother the red man!
But when Standish refused, and said he would give them the Bible,
Suddenly changing their tone, they began to boast and to bluster.
Then Wattawamat advanced with a stride in front of the other,
And, with a lofty demeanour, thus vauntingly spake to the Captain:
'Now Wattawamat can see, by the fiery eyes of the Captain,
Angry is he in his heart; but the heart of the brave Wattawamat
Is not afraid at the sight. He was not born of a woman,
But on a mountain, at night, from an oak-tree riven by lightning,
Forth he sprang at a bound, with all his weapons about him,
Shouting, " Who is there here to fight with the brave Wattawamat? "'
Then he unsheathed his knife, and, whetting the blade on his left hand,
Held it aloft and displayed a woman's face on the handle,
Saying, with bitter expression and look of sinister meaning:
' I have another at home, with the face of a man on the handle;
By and by they shall marry; and there will be plenty of children!'

Then stood Pecksuot forth, self-vaunting, insulting Miles Standish:
While with his fingers he patted the knife that hung at his bosom,
Drawing it half from its sheath, and plunging it back, as he muttered,

'By and by it shall see; it shall eat; ah, ha! but shall speak not!
This is the mighty Captain the white men have sent to destroy us!
He is a little man; let him go and work with the women!'

Meanwhile Standish had noted the faces and figures of Indians
Peeping and creeping about from bush to tree in the forest,
Feigning to look for game, with arrows set on their bow-strings,
Drawing about him still closer and closer the net of their ambush.
But undaunted he stood, and dissembled and treated them smoothly;
So the old chronicles say, that were writ in the days of the fathers.
But when he heard their defiance, the boast, the taunt, and the insult,
All the hot blood of his race, of Sir Hugh and of Thurston de Standish,
Boiled and beat in his heart, and swelled in the veins of his temples.
Headlong he leaped on the boaster, and, snatching his knife from its
    scabbard,
Plunged it into his heart, and, reeling backward, the savage
Fell with his face to the sky, and a fiendlike fierceness upon it.
Straight there arose from the forest the awful sound of the war-whoop,
And, like a flurry of snow on the whistling wind of December,
Swift and sudden and keen came a flight of feathery arrows.
Then came a cloud of smoke, and out of the cloud came the lightning,
Out of the lightning thunder; and death unseen ran before it.
Frightened the savages fled for shelter in swamp and in thicket,
Hotly pursued and beset: but their sachem, the brave Wattawamat,
Fled not; he was dead. Unswerving and swift had a bullet
Passed through his brain, and he fell with both hands clutching the
    greensward,
Seeming in death to hold back from his foe the land of his fathers.

There on the flowers of the meadow the warriors lay, and above them,
Silent, with folded arms, stood Hobomok, friend of the white man.
Smiling at length he exclaimed to the stalwart Captain of Plymouth:
Pecksuot bragged very loud, of his courage, his strength, and his
    stature,—
Mocked the great Captain, and called him a little man; but I see now
Big enough have you been to lay him speechless before you!'

Thus the first battle was fought and won by the stalwart Miles Standish.
When the tidings thereof were brought to the village of Plymouth,
And as a trophy of war the head of the brave Wattawamat
Scowled from the roof of the fort, which at once was a church and
    a fortress,
All who beheld it rejoiced, and praised the Lord, and took courage.
Only Priscilla averted her face from this spectre of terror,
Thanking God in her heart that she had not married Miles Standish;
Shrinking, fearing almost, lest, coming home from his battles,
He should lay claim to her hand, as the prize and reward of his valour.

VIII.

THE SPINNING-WHEEL.

MONTH after month passed away, and in Autumn the ships of the
merchants
Came with kindred and friends, with cattle and corn for the Pilgrims
All in the village was peace ; the men were intent on their labours,
Busy with hewing and building, with garden-plot and with merestead,
Busy with breaking the glebe, and mowing the grass in the meadows,
Searching the sea for its fish, and hunting the deer in the forest.
All in the village was peace ; but at times the rumour of warfare
Filled the air with alarm, and the apprehension of danger.
Bravely the stalwart Standish was scouring the land with his forces,
Waxing valiant in fight and defeating the alien armies,
Till his name had become a sound of fear to the nations.
Anger was still in his heart, but at times the remorse and contrition
Which in all noble natures succeed the passionate outbreak,
Came like a rising tide, that encounters the rush of a river,
Staying its current awhile, but making it bitter and brackish.

Meanwhile Alden at home had built him a new habitation,
Solid, substantial, of timber rough-hewn from the firs of the forest.
Wooden-barred was the door, and the roof was covered with rushes ;
Latticed the windows were, and the window-panes were of paper,
Oiled to admit the light, while wind and rain were excluded.
There too he dug a well, and around it planted an orchard :
Still may be seen to this day some trace of the well and the orchard.
Close to the house was the stall, where, safe and secure from annoyance,
Raghorn, the snow-white bull, that had fallen to Alden's allotment
In the division of cattle, might ruminate in the night-time
Over the pastures he cropped, made fragrant by sweet pennyroyal.

Oft when his labour was finished, with eager feet would the dreamer
Follow the pathway that ran through the woods to the house of Priscilla,
Led by illusions romantic and subtile deceptions of fancy,
Pleasure disguised as duty, and love in the semblance of friendship.
Ever of her he thought, when he fashioned the walls of his dwelling ;
Ever of her he thought, when he delved in the soil of his garden ;
Ever of her he thought, when he read in his Bible on Sunday
Praise of the virtuous woman, as she is described in the Proverbs,—
How the heart of her husband doth safely trust in her always,
How all the days of her life she will do him good, and not evil,
How she seeketh the wool and the flax and worketh with gladness,
How she layeth her hand to the spindle and holdeth the distaff,
How she is not afraid of the snow for herself or her household,
Knowing her household are clothed with the scarlet cloth of her weaving !

So as she sat at her wheel one afternoon in the Autumn,
Alden, who opposite sat, and was watching her dexterous fingers,
As if the thread she was spinning were that of his life and his fortune,
After a pause in their talk, thus spake to the sound of the spindle.
'Truly, Priscilla,' he said, 'when I see you spinning and spinning,
Never idle a moment, but thrifty and thoughtful of others,
Suddenly you are transformed, are visibly changed in a moment;
You are no longer Priscilla, but Bertha the Beautiful Spinner.'
Here the light foot on the treadle grew swifter and swifter; the spindle
Uttered an angry snarl, and the thread snapped short in her fingers;
While the impetuous speaker, not heeding the mischief, continued:
'You are the beautiful Bertha, the spinner, the queen of Helvetia;
She whose story I read at a stall in the streets of Southampton,
Who, as she rode on her palfrey, o'er valley and meadow and mountain,
Ever was spinning her thread from a distaff fixed to her saddle.
She was so thrifty and good, that her name passed into a proverb.
So shall it be with your own, when the spinning-wheel shall no longer
Hum in the house of the farmer, and fill its chambers with music.
Then shall the mothers, reproving, relate how it was in their childhood,
Praising the good old times, and the days of Priscilla the spinner!'
Straight uprose from her wheel the beautiful Puritan maiden,
Pleased with the praise of her thrift from him whose praise was the
        sweetest,
Drew from the reel on the table a snowy skein of her spinning,
Thus making answer, meanwhile, to the flattering phrases of Alden:
'Come, you must not be idle; if I am a pattern for housewives,
Show yourself equally worthy of being the model of husbands.
Hold this skein on your hands, while I wind it, ready for knitting;
Then who knows but hereafter, when fashions have changed and the
        manners,
Fathers may talk to their sons of the good old times of John Alden!'
Thus, with a jest and a laugh, the skein on his hands she adjusted,
He sitting awkwardly there, with his arms extended before him,
She standing graceful, erect, and winding the thread from his fingers,
Sometimes chiding a little his clumsy manner of holding,
Sometimes touching his hands, as she disentangled expertly
Twist or knot in the yarn, unawares—for how could she help it?—
Sending electrical thrills through every nerve in his body.

Lo! in the midst of this scene, a breathless messenger entered,
Bringing in hurry and heat the terrible news from the village.
Yes; Miles Standish was dead!—an Indian had brought them the
        tidings,
Slain by a poisoned arrow, shot down in the front of the battle,
Into an ambush beguiled, cut off with the whole of his forces;
All the town would be burned, and all the people be murdered!
Such were the tidings of evil that burst on the hearts of the hearers.
Silent and statue-like stood Priscilla, her face looking backward

Still at the face of the speaker, her arms uplifted in horror ;
But John Alden, upstarting, as if the barb of the arrow
Piercing the heart of his friend had struck his own, and had sundered
Once and for ever the bonds that held him bound as a captive,
Wild with excess of sensation, the awful delight of his freedom,
Mingled with pain and regret, unconscious of what he was doing,
Clasped, almost with a groan, the motionless form of Priscilla,
Pressing her close to his heart, as for ever his own, and exclaiming :
' Those whom the Lord hath united, let no man put them asunder !'

Even as rivulets twain, from distant and separate sources,
Seeing each other afar, as they leap from the rocks, and pursuing
Each one its devious path, but drawing nearer and nearer,
Rush together at last, at their trysting-place in the forest ;
So these lives that had run thus far in separate channels,
Coming in sight of each other, then swerving and flowing asunder,
Parted by barriers strong, but drawing nearer and nearer,
Rushed together at last, and one was lost in the other.

IX.

THE WEDDING-DAY.

FORTH from the curtain of clouds, from the tent of purple and scarlet,
Issued the sun, the great High-Priest, in his garments resplendent,
Holiness unto the Lord, in letters of light, on his forehead,
Round the hem of his robe the golden bells and pomegranates.
Blessing the world he came, and the bars of vapour beneath him
Gleamed like a grate of brass, and the sea at his feet was a laver !

This was the wedding morn of Priscilla the Puritan maiden.
Friends were assembled together ; the Elder and Magistrate also
Graced the scene with their presence, and stood like the Law and the
     Gospel,
One with the sanction of earth and one with the blessing of heaven.
Simple and brief was the wedding, as that of Ruth and of Boaz.
Softly the youth and the maiden repeated the words of betrothal,
Taking each other for husband and wife in the Magistrate's presence,
After the Puritan way, and the laudable custom of Holland.
Fervently then, and devoutly, the excellent Elder of Plymouth
Prayed for the hearth and the home, that were founded that day in
     affection,
Speaking of life and of death, and imploring Divine benedictions.

Lo ! when the service was ended, a form appeared on the threshold,
Clad in armour of steel, a sombre and sorrowful figure !
Why does the bridegroom start and stare at the strange apparition ?

Why does the bride turn pale, and hide her face on his shoulder?
Is it a phantom of air,—a bodiless, spectral illusion?
Is it a ghost from the grave, that has come to forbid the betrothal?
Long had it stood there unseen, a guest uninvited, unwelcomed;
Over its clouded eyes there had passed at times an expression
Softening the gloom and revealing the warm heart hidden beneath them,
As when across the sky the driving rack of the rain-cloud
Grows for a moment thin, and betrays the sun by its brightness.
Once it had lifted its hand, and moved its lips, but was silent,
As if an iron will had mastered the fleeting intention.
But when were ended the troth and the prayer and the last benediction,
Into the room it strode, and the people beheld with amazement
Bodily there in his armour Miles Standish, the Captain of Plymouth!
Grasping the bridegroom's hand, he said with emotion, 'Forgive me!
I have been angry and hurt,—too long have I cherished the feeling;
I have been cruel and hard, but now, thank God! it is ended.
Mine is the same hot blood that leaped in the veins of Hugh Standish,
Sensitive, swift to resent, but as swift in atoning for error.
Never so much as now was Miles Standish the friend of John Alden.'
Thereupon answered the bridegroom : ' Let all be forgotten between us,—
All save the dear old friendship, and that shall grow older and dearer !'
Then the Captain advanced, and, bowing, saluted Priscilla,
Gravely, and after the manner of old-fashioned gentry in England,
Something of camp and of court, of town and of country, commingled,
Wishing her joy of her wedding, and loudly lauding her husband.
Then he said with a smile : 'I should have remembered the adage,—
If you would be well served, you must serve yourself; and moreover,
No man can gather cherries in Kent at the season of Christmas !'

Great was the people's amazement, and greater yet their rejoicing,
Thus to behold once more the sunburnt face of their Captain,
Whom they had mourned as dead ; and they gathered and crowded about him,
Eager to see him and hear him, forgetful of bride and of bridegroom,
Questioning, answering, laughing, and each interrupting the other,
Till the good Captain declared, being quite overpowered and bewildered,
He had rather by far break into an Indian encampment,
Than come again to a wedding to which he had not been invited.

Meanwhile the bridegroom went forth and stood with the bride at the doorway,
Breathing the perfumed air of that warm and beautiful morning.
Touched with autumnal tints, but lonely and sad in the sunshine,
Lay extended before them the land of toil and privation ;
There were the graves of the dead, and the barren waste of the seashore,
There the familiar fields, the groves of pine, and the meadows ;
But to their eyes transfigured, it seemed as the Garden of Eden,
Filled with the presence of God, whose voice was the sound of the ocean.

Soon was their vision disturbed by the noise and stir of departure,
Friends coming forth from the house, and impatient of longer delaying,
Each with his plan for the day, and the work that was left uncompleted.
Then from a stall near at hand, amid exclamations of wonder,
Alden the thoughtful, the careful, so happy, so proud of Priscilla,
Brought out his snow-white bull, obeying the hand of its master,
Led by a cord that was tied to an iron ring in its nostrils,
Covered with crimson cloth, and a cushion placed for a saddle.
She should not walk, he said, through the dust and heat of the noonday ;
Nay, she should ride like a queen, not plod along like a peasant.
Somewhat alarmed at first, but reassured by the others,
Placing her hand on the cushion, her foot in the hand of her husband,
Gaily, with joyous laugh, Priscilla mounted her palfrey.
' Nothing is wanting now,' he said with a smile, ' but the distaff ;
Then you would be in truth my queen, my beautiful Bertha !'

Onward the bridal procession now moved to their new habitation,
Happy husband and wife, and friends conversing together.
Pleasantly murmured the brook, as they crossed the ford in the forest,
Pleased with the image that passed, like a dream of love through its bosom,
Tremulous, floating in air, o'er the depths of the azure abysses.
Down through the golden leaves the sun was pouring his splendours,
Gleaming on purple grapes, that, from branches above them suspended,
Mingled their odorous breath with the balm of the pine and the fir-tree,
Wild and sweet as the clusters that grew in the valley of Eshcol.
Like a picture it seemed of the primitive, pastoral ages,
Fresh with the youth of the world, and recalling Rebecca and Isaac,
Old and yet ever new, and simple and beautiful always,
Love immortal and young in the endless succession of lovers.
So through the Plymouth woods passed onward the bridal procession.

. . come i gru van cantando lor lai,
Facendo in aer di sè lunga riga.

Dante.

FLIGHT THE FIRST.

PROMETHEUS,

OR THE POET'S FORETHOUGHT.

Of Prometheus, how undaunted
  On Olympus' shining bastions
His audacious foot he planted,
Myths are told and songs are
    chanted,
    Full of promptings and sugges-
      tions.

Beautiful is the tradition
  Of that flight through heavenly
    portals,
The old classic superstition
Of the theft and the transmission
  Of the fire of the Immortals!

First the deed of noble daring,
  Born of heavenward aspiration,
Then the fire with mortals sharing,
Then the vulture,—the despairing
  Cry of pain on crags Caucasian.

All is but a symbol painted
  Of the Poet, Prophet, Seer;
Only those are crowned and sainted
Who with grief have been ac-
    quainted,
  Making nations nobler, freer.

In their feverish exultations,
  In their triumph and their yearn-
    ing,
In their passionate pulsations,
In their words among the nations,
  The Promethean fire is burning.

Shall it, then, be unavailing,
  All this toil for human culture?
Through the cloud-rack, dark and
    trailing
Must they see above them sailing
  O'er life's barren crags the vul-
    ture?

Such a fate as this was Dante's,
  By defeat and exile maddened;
Thus were Milton and Cervantes,
Nature's priests and Corybantes,
  By affliction touched and sad-
    dened.

But the glories so transcendent
  That around their memories
    cluster,
And, on all their steps attendant,
Make their darkened lives resplen-
    dent
  With such gleams of inward
    lustre!

All the melodies mysterious
  Through the dreary darkness
    chanted;
Thoughts in attitudes imperious,
Voices soft, and deep, and serious,
  Words that whispered, songs
    that haunted!

All the soul in rapt suspension,
  All the quivering, palpitating
Chords of life in utmost tension,
With the fervour of invention,
  With the rapture of creating!

Ah, Prometheus! heaven-scaling!
  In such hours of exultation
Even the faintest heart, unquailing,
Might behold the vulture sailing
  Round the cloudy crags Caucasian!

Though to all there is not given
  Strength for such sublime endeavour,
Thus to scale the walls of heaven,
And to leaven with fiery leaven
  All the hearts of men for ever;

Yet all bards, whose hearts unblighted
  Honour and believe the presage,
Hold aloft their torches lighted,
Gleaming through the realms benighted,
  As they onward bear the message!

——

THE LADDER OF ST. AUGUSTINE.

SAINT AUGUSTINE! well hast thou said,
  That of our vices we can frame
A ladder, if we will but tread
  Beneath our feet each deed of shame!

All common things, each day's events,
  That with the hour begin and end,
Our pleasures and our discontents,
  Are rounds by which we may ascend.

The low desire, the base design,
  That makes another's virtues less;
The revel of the ruddy wine,
  And all occasions of excess;

The longing for ignoble things;
  The strife for triumph more than truth;
The hardening of the heart, that brings
  Irreverence for the dreams of youth;

All thoughts of ill; all evil deeds,
  That have their root in thoughts of ill;
Whatever hinders or impedes
  The action of the nobler will;—

All these must first be trampled down
  Beneath our feet, if we would gain
In the bright fields of fair renown
  The right of eminent domain.

We have not wings, we cannot soar;
  But we have feet to scale and climb
By slow degrees, by more and more,
  The cloudy summits of our time.

The mighty pyramids of stone
  That wedge-like cleave the desert airs,
When nearer seen, and better known,
  Are but gigantic flights of stairs.

The distant mountains, that uprear
  Their solid bastions to the skies,
Are crossed by pathways, that appear
  As we to higher levels rise.

The heights by great men reached and kept
  Were not attained by sudden flight,
But they, while their companions slept,
  Were toiling upward in the night.

Standing on what too long we bore
  With shoulders bent and down-
    cast eyes,
We may discern—unseen before—
  A path to higher destinies.

Nor deem the irrevocable Past,
  As wholly wasted, wholly vain,
If, rising on its wrecks, at last
  To something nobler we attain.

THE PHANTOM SHIP.

IN Mather's Magnalia Christi,
  Of the old colonial time,
May be found in prose the legend
  That is here set down in rhyme.

A ship sailed from New Haven,
  And the keen and frosty airs,
That filled her sails at parting,
  Were heavy with good men's
    prayers.

' O Lord ! if it be thy pleasure '—
  Thus prayed the old divine—
' To bury our friends in the ocean,
  Take them, for they are thine ! '

But Master Lamberton muttered,
  And under his breath said he,
' This ship is so crank and walty
  I fear our grave she will be ! '

And the ships that came from
  England,
  When the winter months were
    gone,
Brought no tidings of this vessel
  Nor of Master Lamberton.

This put the people to praying
  That the Lord would let them hear
What in his greater wisdom
  He had done with friends so
    dear.

And at last their prayers were an-
  swered :—
  It was in the month of June,
An hour before the sunset
  Of a windy afternoon,

When, steadily steering landward,
  A ship was seen below,
And they knew it was Lamberton,
  Master,
  Who sailed so long ago.

On she came, with a cloud of
  canvas,
  Right against the wind that blew,
Until the eye could distinguish
  The faces of the crew.

Then fell her straining topmasts,
  Hanging tangled in the shrouds,
And her sails were loosened and
  lifted,
  And blown away like clouds.

And the masts, with all their
  rigging,
  Fell slowly, one by one,
And the hulk dilated and vanished,
  As a sea-mist in the sun '

And the people who saw this marvel
  Each said unto his friend,
That this was the mould of their
  vessel,
  And thus her tragic end.

And the pastor of the village
  Gave thanks to God in prayer,
That, to quiet their troubled spirits,
  He had sent this Ship of Air.

THE WARDEN OF THE
CINQUE PORTS.

A MIST was driving down the
  British Channel,
  The day was just begun,
And through the window-panes, on
  floor and panel,
  Streamed the red autumn sun.

It glanced on flowing flag and
  rippling pennon,
And the white sails of ships;
And, from the frowning rampart,
  the black cannon
Hailed it with feverish lips.

Sandwich and Romney, Hastings,
  Hythe, and Dover
Were all alert that day,
To see the French war-steamers
  speeding over,
When the fog cleared away.

Sullen and silent, and like couchant
  lions,
Their cannon, through the night,
Holding their breath, had watched,
  in grim defiance,
The sea-coast opposite.

And now they roared at drum-beat
  from their stations
On every citadel;
Each answering each, with morning
  salutations,
That all was well.

And down the coast, all taking up
  the burden,
Replied the distant forts,
As if to summon from his sleep the
  Warden
And Lord of the Cinque Ports.

Kim shall no sunshine from the
  fields of azure,
No drum-beat from the wall,
No morning gun from the black
  fort's embrasure,
Awaken with its call!

No more, surveying with an eye
  impartial
The long line of the coast,
Shall the gaunt figure of the old
  Field Marshal
Be seen upon his post!

For in the night, unseen, a single
  warrior,
In sombre harness mailed,
Dreaded of man, and surnamed the
  Destroyer,
The rampart wall had scaled.

He passed into the chamber of the
  sleeper,
The dark and silent room,
And as he entered, darker grew,
  and deeper,
The silence and the gloom.

He did not pause to parley or
  dissemble,
But smote the Warden hoar;
Ah! what a blow! that made all
  England tremble
And groan from shore to shore.

Meanwhile, without, the surly
  cannon waited,
The sun rose bright o'erhead;
Nothing in Nature's aspect inti-
  mated
That a great man was dead.

HAUNTED HOUSES.

ALL houses wherein men have
  lived and died
Are haunted houses. Through
  the open doors
The harmless phantoms on their
  errands glide,
With feet that make no sound
  upon the floors.

We meet them at the doorway, on
  the stair,
Along the passages they come
  and go,
Impalpable impressions on the air,
A sense of something moving to
  and fro.

There are more guests at table,
than the hosts
  Invited; the illuminated hall
Is thronged with quiet, inoffensive
ghosts,
  As silent as the pictures on the
wall.

The stranger at my fireside cannot
see
  The forms I see, nor hear the
sounds I hear;
He but perceives what is; while
unto me
  All that has been is visible and
clear.

We have no title-deeds to house or
lands;
  Owners and occupants of earlier
dates
From graves forgotten stretch their
dusty hands,
  And hold in mortmain still their
old estates.

The spirit world around this world
of sense
  Floats like an atmosphere, and
everywhere
Wafts through these earthly mists
and vapours dense
  A vital breath of more ethereal
air.

Our little lives are kept in equipoise
  By opposite attractions and
desires;
The struggle of the instinct that
enjoys,
  And the more noble instinct that
aspires.

These perturbations, this perpetual
jar
  Of earthly wants and aspirations
high,
Come from the influence of an
unseen star,
  An undiscovered planet in our
sky.

And as the moon from some dark
gate of cloud
  Throws o'er the sea a floating
bridge of light,
Across whose trembling planks our
fancies crowd
  Into the realm of mystery and
night,—

So from the world of spirits there
descends
  A bridge of light, connecting it
with this,
O'er whose unsteady floor, that
sways and bends,
  Wander our thoughts above the
dark abyss.

IN THE CHURCHYARD AT CAMBRIDGE.

IN the village churchyard she lies,
Dust is in her beautiful eyes,
  No more she breathes, nor feels,
nor stirs;
At her feet and at her head
Lies a slave to attend the dead,
  But their dust is white as hers.

Was she a lady of high degree,
So much in love with the vanity
  And foolish pomp of this world
of ours?
Or was it Christian charity,
And lowliness and humility,
  The richest and rarest of all
dowers?

Who shall tell us? No one speaks;
No colour shoots into those cheeks,
  Either of anger or of pride,
At the rude question we have
asked;
Nor will the mystery be unmasked
  By those who are sleeping at her
side.

Hereafter?—And do you think to
    look
On the terrible pages of that Book
    To find her failings, faults, and
      errors?
Ah, you will then have other cares,
In your own shortcomings and
    despairs,
    In your own secret sins and
      terrors!

THE EMPEROR'S BIRD'S-
NEST.

ONCE the Emperor Charles of
    Spain,
    With his swarthy, grave com-
      manders,
I forget in what campaign,
Long besieged, in mud and rain,
    Some old frontier town of Flan-
      ders.

Up and down the dreary camp,
    In great boots of Spanish lea-
      ther,
Striding with a measured tramp,
These Hidalgos, dull and damp,
    Cursed the Frenchmen, cursed
      the weather.

Thus as to and fro they went,
    Over upland and through hollow,
Giving their impatience vent,
Perched upon the Emperor's tent,
    In her nest, they spied a swallow.

Yes, it was a swallow's nest,
    Built of clay and hair of horses,
Mane, or tail, or dragoon's crest,
Found on hedgerows east and
    west,
    After skirmish of the forces.

Then an old Hidalgo said,
    As he twirled his gray mustachio,
'Sure this swallow overhead
Thinks the Emperor's tent a shed,
    And the Emperor but a Macho!'

Hearing his imperial name
    Coupled with those words of
      malice,
Half in anger, half in shame,
Forth the great campaigner came
    Slowly from his canvas palace.

'Let no hand the bird molest,'
    Said he solemnly, 'nor hurt her!'
Adding then, by way of jest,
'Golondrina is my guest,
    'Tis the wife of some deserter!'

Swift as bowstring speeds a shaft,
    Through the camp was spread
      the rumour,
And the soldiers, as they quaffed
Flemish beer at dinner, laughed
    At the Emperor's pleasant hu-
      mour.

So unharmed and unafraid
    Sat the swallow still and brood-
      ed,
Till the constant cannonade
Through the walls a breach had
    made
    And the siege was thus con-
      cluded.

Then the army, elsewhere bent,
    Struck its tents as if disbanding,
Only not the Emperor's tent,
For he ordered, ere he went,
    Very curtly, 'Leave it standing!'

So it stood there all alone,
    Loosely flapping, torn and tat-
      tered,
Till the brood was fledged and
    flown,
Singing o'er those walls of stone
    Which the cannon-shot had shat-
      tered.

THE TWO ANGELS.

Two angels, one of Life and one
    of Death,
    Passed o'er our village as the
        morning broke ;
The dawn was on their faces, and
    beneath,
    The sombre houses hearsed with
        plumes of smoke.

Their attitude and aspect were the
    same,
    Alike their features and their
        robes of white ;
But one was crowned with ama-
    ranth, as with flame,
    And one with asphodels, like
        flakes of light.

I saw them pause on their celestial
    way ;
    Then said I, with deep fear and
        doubt oppressed,
'Beat not so loud, my heart, lest
    thou betray
    The place where thy beloved are
        at rest !'

And he who wore the crown of as-
    phodels,
    Descending, at my door began
        to knock,
And my soul sank within me, as in
    wells
    The waters sink before an earth-
        quake's shock.

I recognised the nameless agony,
    The terror and the tremor and
        the pain,
That oft before had filled or haunt-
    ed me,
    And now returned with threefold
        strength again.

The door I opened to my heavenly
    guest,
    And listened, for I thought I
        heard God's voice ;

And, knowing whatsoe'er he sent
    was best,
    Dared neither to lament nor to
        rejoice.

Then with a smile, that filled the
    house with light,
    'My errand is not Death, but
        Life,' he said ;
And ere I answered, passing out
    of sight,
    On his celestial embassy he sped.

'Twas at thy door, O friend ! and
    not at mine,
    The angel with the amaranthine
        wreath,
Pausing, descended, and with voice
    divine,
    Whispered a word that had a
        sound like Death.

Then fell upon the house a sudden
    gloom,
    A shadow on those features fair
        and thin ;
And softly, from that hushed and
    darkened room,
    Two angels issued, where but one
        went in.

All is of God ! If he but wave his
    hand,
    The mists collect, the rain falls
        thick and loud,
Till, with a smile of light on sea
    and land,
    Lo ! he looks back from the de-
        parting cloud.

Angels of Life and Death alike are
    his ;
    Without his leave they pass no
        threshold o'er ;
Who, then, would wish or dare, be-
    lieving this,
    Against his messengers to shut
        the door ?

DAYLIGHT AND MOON-LIGHT.

In broad daylight, and at noon,
Yesterday I saw the moon
Sailing high, but faint and white,
As a schoolboy's paper kite.

In broad daylight, yesterday,
I read a Poet's mystic lay;
And it seemed to me at most
As a phantom, or a ghost.

But at length the feverish day
Like a passion died away,
And the night, serene and still,
Fell on village, vale, and hill.

Then the moon, in all her pride,
Like a spirit glorified,
Filled and overflowed the night
With revelations of her light.

And the Poet's song again
Passed like music through my brain;
Night interpreted to me
All its grace and mystery.

THE JEWISH CEMETERY AT NEWPORT.

How strange it seems! these Hebrews in their graves,
Close by the street of this fair seaport town,
Silent beside the never-silent waves,
At rest in all this moving up and down!

The trees are white with dust, that o'er their sleep
Wave their broad curtains in the south-wind's breath,
While underneath these leafy tents they keep
The long, mysterious Exodus of Death.

And these sepulchral stones, so old and brown,
That pave with level flags their burial-place,
Seem like the tablets of the Law, thrown down
And broken by Moses at the mountain's base.

The very names recorded here are strange,
Of foreign accent, and of different climes;
Alvares and Rivera interchange
With Abraham and Jacob of old times.

'Blessed be God! for he created Death!'
The mourners said, 'and Death is rest and peace;'
Then added, in the certainty of faith,
'And giveth Life that nevermore shall cease.'

Closed are the portals of their Synagogue,
No Psalms of David now the silence break,
No Rabbi reads the ancient Decalogue
In the grand dialect the Prophets spake.

Gone are the living, but the dead remain,
And not neglected; for a hand unseen,
Scattering its bounty, like a summer rain,
Still keeps their graves and their remembrance green.

How came they here? What burst of Christian hate,
What persecution, merciless and blind,
Drove o'er the sea—that desert desolate—
These Ishmaels and Hagars of mankind?

They lived in narrow streets and lanes obscure,
Ghetto and Judenstrass, in mirk and mire;
Taught in the school of patience to endure
The life of anguish and the death of fire.

All their lives long, with the unleavened bread
And bitter herbs of exile and its fears,
The wasting famine of the heart they fed,
And slaked its thirst with marah of their tears.

Anathema maranatha! was the cry
That rang from town to town, from street to street;
At every gate the accursed Mordecai
Was mocked and jeered, and spurned by Christian feet.

Pride and humiliation hand in hand
Walked with them through the world where'er they went;
Trampled and beaten were they as the sand,
And yet unshaken as the continent.

For in the background figures vague and vast
Of patriarchs and of prophets rose sublime,
And all the great traditions of the Past
They saw reflected in the coming time.

And thus for ever with reverted look
The mystic volume of the world they read,
Spelling it backward, like a Hebrew book,
Till life became a Legend of the Dead.

But ah! what once has been shall be no more!
The groaning earth in travail and in pain
Brings forth its races, but does not restore,
And the dead nations never rise again.

OLIVER BASSELIN.

IN the Valley of the Vire
Still is seen an ancient mill,
With its gables quaint and queer,
And beneath the window-sill,
On the stone,
These words alone:
'Oliver Basselin lived here.'

Far above it, on the steep,
Ruined stands the old Chateau;
Nothing but the donjon-keep
Left for shelter or for show.
Its vacant eyes
Stare at the skies,
Stare at the valley green and deep.

Once a convent, old and brown,
Looked, but ah! it looks no more,
From the neighbouring hillside down
On the rushing and the roar
Of the stream
Whose sunny gleam
Cheers the little Norman town.

In that darksome mill of stone,
To the water's dash and din,
Careless, humble, and unknown,
Sang the poet Basselin
Songs that fill
That ancient mill
With a splendour of its own.

Never feeling of unrest
  Broke the pleasant dream he
      dreamed;
Only made to be his nest,
  All the lovely valley seemed;
      No desire
      Of soaring higher
Stirred or fluttered in his breast.

True, his songs were not divine;
  Were not songs of that high art,
Which, as winds do in the pine,
  Find an answer in each heart;
      But the mirth
      Of this green earth
Laughed and revelled in his line.

From the alehouse and the inn,
  Opening on the narrow street,
Came the loud, convivial din,
  Singing and applause of feet,
      The laughing lays
      That in those days
Sang the poet Basselin.

In the castle, cased in steel,
  Knights, who fought at Agin-
      court,
Watched and waited, spur on heel;
  But the poet sang for sport
      Songs that rang
      Another clang,
Songs that lowlier hearts could
  feel.

In the convent, clad in gray,
  Sat the monks in lonely cells,
Paced the cloisters, knelt to pray,
  And the poet heard their bells;
      But his rhymes
      Found other chimes,
Nearer to the earth than they.

Gone are all the barons bold,
  Gone are all the knights and
      squires,
Gone the abbot stern and cold,
  And the brotherhood of friars;

Not a name
  Remains to fame,
From those mouldering days of
  old!

But the poet's memory here
  Of the landscape makes a part;
Like the river, swift and clear,
  Flows his song through many
      a heart;
      Haunting still
      That ancient mill,
In the Valley of the Vire.

VICTOR GALBRAITH.

UNDER the walls of Monterey
At daybreak the bugles began to
    play,
        Victor Galbraith!
In the mist of the morning damp
    and gray,
These were the words they seemed
    to say:
      'Come forth to thy death,
        Victor Galbraith!'

Forth he came, with a martial
    tread;
Firm was his step, erect his head;
        Victor Galbraith,
He who so well the bugle played,
Could not mistake the words it said:
      'Come forth to thy death,
        Victor Galbraith!'

He looked at the earth, he looked
    at the sky,
He looked at the files of musketry,
        Victor Galbraith!
And he said, with a steady voice
    and eye,
'Take good aim; I am ready to
    die!'
      Thus challenges death
        Victor Galbraith.

Twelve fiery tongues flashed straight
   and red,
Six leaden balls on their errand
   sped ;
      Victor Galbraith
Falls to the ground, but he is not
   dead ;
His name was not stamped on those
   balls of lead,
      And they only scathe
      Victor Galbraith.

Three balls are in his breast and
   brain,
But he rises out of the dust again,
      Victor Galbraith !
The water he drinks has a bloody
   stain ;
'O kill me, and put me out of my
   pain !'
      In his agony prayeth
      Victor Galbraith.

Forth dart once more those tongues
   of flame,
And the bugler has died a death of
   shame,
      Victor Galbraith !
His soul has gone back to whence
   it came,
And no one answers to the
   name,
      When the Sergeant saith,
      'Victor Galbraith !'

Under the walls of Monterey
By night a bugle is heard to
   play,
      Victor Galbraith !
Through the mist of the valley
   damp and gray
The sentinels hear the sound, and
   say,
      'That is the wraith
      Of Victor Galbraith !'

MY LOST YOUTH.

OFTEN I think of the beautiful town
   That is seated by the sea ;
Often in thought go up and down
The pleasant streets of that dear
   old town,
   And my youth comes back to me.
     And a verse of a Lapland song
     Is haunting my memory still :
   ' A boy's will is the wind's will,
And the thoughts of youth are long,
   long thoughts.'

I can see the shadowy lines of its
   trees,
   And catch in sudden gleams,
The sheen of the far-surrounding
   seas,
And islands that were the Hesper-
   ides
   Of all my boyish dreams.
     And the burden of that old
     song,
     It murmurs and whispers still :
   ' A boy's will is the wind's will,
And the thoughts of youth are long,
   long thoughts.'

I remember the black wharves and
   the slips,
   And the sea-tides tossing free ;
And Spanish sailors with bearded
   lips,
And the beauty and mystery of the
   ships,
   And the magic of the sea.
     And the voice of that wayward
     song
     Is singing and saying still :
   ' A boy's will is the wind's will,
And the thoughts of youth are long,
   long thoughts.'

I remember the bulwarks by the
   shore,
   And the fort upon the hill ;

The sunrise gun, with its hollow roar,
The drum-beat repeated o'er and o'er,
And the bugle wild and shrill.
  And the music of that old song
  Throbs in my memory still:
' A boy's will is the wind's will,
And the thoughts of youth are long, long thoughts.'

I remember the sea-fight far away,
How it thundered o'er the tide !
And the dead captains, as they lay
In their graves, o'erlooking the tranquil bay,
  Where they in battle died.
  And the sound of that mournful song
  Goes through me with a thrill :
' A boy's will is the wind's will,
And the thoughts of youth are long, long thoughts.'

I can see the breezy dome of groves,
The shadows of Deering's Woods ;
And the friendships old and the early loves
Come back with a sabbath sound, as of doves
  In quiet neighbourhoods.
  And the verse of that sweet old song,
  It flutters and murmurs still :
' A boy's will is the wind's will,
And the thoughts of youth are long, long thoughts.'

I remember the gleams and glooms that dart
Across the schoolboy's brain ;
The song and the silence in the heart,
That in part are prophecies, and in part
Are longings wild and vain.

And the voice of that fitful song
Sings on, and is never still :
' A boy's will is the wind's will,
And the thoughts of youth are long, long thoughts.'

There are things of which I may not speak ;
There are dreams that cannot die ;
There are thoughts that make the strong heart weak,
And bring a pallor into the cheek,
  And a mist before the eye.
  And the words of that fatal song
  Come over me like a chill :
' A boy's will is the wind's will,
And the thoughts of youth are long, long thoughts.'

Strange to me now are the forms I meet
When I visit the dear old town ;
But the native air is pure and sweet,
And the trees that o'ershadow each well-known street,
  As they balance up and down,
  Are singing the beautiful song,
  Are sighing and whispering still :
' A boy's will is the wind's will,
And the thoughts of youth are long, long thoughts.'

And Deering's Woods are fresh and fair,
And with joy that is almost pain
My heart goes back to wander there,
And among the dreams of the days that were,
  I find my lost youth again.
  And the strange and beautiful song,
  The groves are repeating it still :
' A boy's will is the wind's will,
And the thoughts of youth are long, long thoughts.'

THE ROPEWALK.

IN that building, long and low,
With its windows all a-row,
  Like the port-holes of a hulk,
Human spiders spin and spin,
Backward down their threads so
    thin
  Dropping, each a hempen bulk.

At the end an open door ;
Squares of sunshine on the floor
  Light the long and dusky lane ;
And the whirring of a wheel,
Dull and drowsy, makes me feel
  All its spokes are in my brain.

As the spinners to the end
Downward go and reascend,
  Gleam the long threads in the
    sun ;
While within this brain of mine
Cobwebs brighter and more fine
  By the busy wheel are spun.

Two fair maidens in a swing,
Like white doves upon the wing,
  First before my vision pass ;
Laughing, as their gentle hands
Closely clasp the twisted strands,
  At their shadow on the grass.

Then a booth of mountebanks,
With its smell of tan and planks,
  And a girl poised high in air
On a cord, in spangled dress,
With a faded loveliness,
  And a weary look of care.

Then a homestead among farms,
And a woman with bare arms
  Drawing water from a well ;
As the bucket mounts apace,
With it mounts her own fair face,
  As at some magician's spell.

Then an old man in a tower,
Ringing loud the noontide hour,

While the rope coils round and
    round
Like a serpent at his feet,
And again, in swift retreat,
  Nearly lifts him from the ground.

Then within a prison-yard,
Faces fixed, and stern, and hard,
  Laughter and indecent mirth ;
Ah ! it is the gallows-tree !
Breath of Christian charity,
  Blow, and sweep it from the earth !

Then a schoolboy, with his kite
Gleaming in a sky of light,
  And an eager, upward look ;
Steeds pursued through lane and
    field ;
Fowlers with their snares con-
    cealed ;
  And an angler by a brook.

Ships rejoicing in the breeze,
Wrecks that float o'er unknown
    seas,
  Anchors dragged through faith-
    less sand ;
Sea-fog drifting overhead,
And, with lessening line and lead,
  Sailors feeling for the land.

All these scenes do I behold,
These, and many left untold,
  In that building long and low ;
While the wheel goes round and
    round,
With a drowsy, dreamy sound,
  And the spinners backward go.

———◆———

THE GOLDEN MILE-STONE.

LEAFLESS are the trees ; their pur-
    ple branches
Spread themselves abroad, like
    reefs of coral,
    Rising silent
In the Red Sea of the winter sun-
    set.

From the hundred chimneys of the village,
Like the Afreet in the Arabian story,
   Smoky columns
Tower aloft into the air of amber.

At the window winks the flickering fire-light;
Here and there the lamps of evening glimmer,
   Social watch-fires
Answering one another through the darkness.

On the hearth the lighted logs are glowing,
And like Ariel in the cloven pine-tree
   For its freedom
Groans and sighs the air imprisoned in them.

By the fireside there are old men seated,
Seeing ruined cities in the ashes,
   Asking sadly
Of the Past what it can ne'er restore them.

By the fireside there are youthful dreamers,
Building castles fair, with stately stairways,
   Asking blindly
Of the Future what it cannot give them.

By the fireside tragedies are acted
In whose scenes appear two actors only,
   Wife and husband,
And above them God the sole spectator.

By the fireside there are peace and comfort,
Wives and children, with fair, thoughtful faces,
   Waiting, watching
For a well-known footstep in the passage.

Each man's chimney is his Golden Milestone;
Is the central point, from which he measures
   Every distance
Through the gateways of the world around him.

In his farthest wanderings still he sees it;
Hears the talking flame, the answering night-wind,
   As he heard them
When he sat with those who were, but are not.

Happy he whom neither wealth nor fashion,
Nor the march of the encroaching city,
   Drives an exile
From the hearth of his ancestral homestead.

We may build more splendid habitations,
Fill our rooms with paintings and with sculptures,
   But we cannot
Buy with gold the old associations!

CATAWBA WINE.

THIS song of mine
   Is a Song of the Vine,
To be sung by the glowing embers
   Of wayside inns,
   When the rain begins
To darken the drear Novembers.

   It is not a song
   Of the Scuppernong,
From warm Carolinian valleys,
   Nor the Isabel
   And the Muscadel
That bask in our garden alleys.

Nor the red Mustang,
Whose clusters hang
O'er the waves of the Colorado,
And the fiery flood
Of whose purple blood
Has a dash of Spanish bravado.

For richest and best
Is the wine of the West,
That grows by the Beautiful River;
Whose sweet perfume
Fills all the room
With a benison on the giver.

And as hollow trees
Are the haunts of bees,
For ever going and coming;
So this crystal hive
Is all alive
With a swarming and buzzing and
humming.

Very good in its way
Is the Verzenay,
Or the Sillery soft and creamy;
But Catawba wine
Has a taste more divine,
More dulcet, delicious, and dreamy.

There grows no vine
By the haunted Rhine,
By Danube or Guadalquivir,
Nor on island or cape,
That bears such a grape
As grows by the Beautiful River.

Drugged is their juice
For foreign use,
When shipped o'er the reeling
Atlantic,
To rack our brains
With the fever pains,
That have driven the Old World
frantic.

To the sewers and sinks
With all such drinks,
And after them tumble the mixer;
For a poison malign
Is such Borgia wine,
Or at best but a Devil's Elixir.

While pure as a spring
Is the wine I sing,
And to praise it, one needs but
name it;
For Catawba wine
Has need of no sign,
No tavern-bush to proclaim it.

And this Song of the Vine,
This greeting of mine,
The winds and the birds shall
deliver
To the Queen of the West,
In her garlands dressed,
On the banks of the Beautiful
River.

SANTA FILOMENA.

WHENE'ER a noble deed is
wrought,
Whene'er is spoken a noble
thought,
Our hearts, in glad surprise,
To higher levels rise.

The tidal wave of deeper souls
Into our inmost being rolls,
And lifts us unawares
Out of all meaner cares.

Honour to those whose words or
deeds
Thus help us in our daily needs,
And by their overflow
Raise us from what is low!

Thus thought I, as by night I
read
Of the great army of the dead,
The trenches cold and damp,
The starved and frozen camp,—

The wounded from the battle-plain,
In dreary hospitals of pain,
The cheerless corridors,
The cold and stony floors.

Lo! in that house of misery
A lady with a lamp I see
  Pass through the glimmering
    gloom,
And flit from room to room.

And slow, as in a dream of bliss,
The speechless sufferer turns to kiss
  Her shadow, as it falls
  Upon the darkening walls.

As if a door in heaven should be
Opened and then closed suddenly,
  The vision came and went,
  The light shone and was spent.

On England's annals, through the
    long
Hereafter of her speech and song,
  That light its rays shall cast
  From portals of the past.

A Lady with a Lamp shall stand
In the great history of the land,
  A noble type of good,
  Heroic womanhood.

Nor even shall be wanting here
The palm, the lily, and the spear,
  The symbols that of yore
  Saint Filomena bore.

———— ✦ ————

THE DISCOVERER OF THE NORTH CAPE.

A LEAF FROM KING ALFRED'S OROSIUS.

OTHERE, the old sea-captain,
  Who dwelt in Helgoland,
To King Alfred, the Lover of Truth,
Brought a snow-white walrus-tooth,
  Which he held in his brown
    right hand.

His figure was tall and stately,
  Like a boy's his eye appeared;
His hair was yellow as hay,
But threads of a silvery gray
  Gleamed in his tawny beard.

Hearty and hale was Othere,
  His cheek had the colour of oak;
With a kind of laugh in his speech,
Like the sea-tide on a beach,
  As unto the King he spoke.

And Alfred, King of the Saxons,
  Had a book upon his knees,
And wrote down the wondrous tale
Of him who was first to sail
  Into the Arctic seas.

' So far I live to the northward,
  No man lives north of me;
To the east are wild mountain-
    chains,
And beyond them meres and
    plains;
  To the westward all is sea.

' So far I live to the northward,
  From the harbour of Skeringes-
    hale,
If you only sailed by day,
With a fair wind all the way,
  More than a month would you
    sail.

' I own six hundred reindeer,
  With sheep and swine beside;
I have tribute from the Finns,
Whalebone and reindeer-skins,
  And ropes of walrus-hide.

' I ploughed the land with horses,
  But my heart was ill at ease,
For the old seafaring men
Came to me now and then,
  With their sagas of the seas;—

' Of Iceland and of Greenland,
  And the stormy Hebrides,
And the undiscovered deep;—
Oh, I could not eat nor sleep
  For thinking of those seas.

' To the northward stretched the
    desert,
  How far I fain would know;
So at last I sallied forth,
And three days sailed due north,
  As far as the whale-ships go.

'To the west of me was the
    ocean,
 To the right the desolate shore,
But I did not slacken sail
 For the walrus or the whale,
    Till after three days more.

'The days grew longer and longer,
    Till they became as one,
And northward through the haze
 I saw the sullen blaze
    Of the red midnight sun.

'And then uprose before me,
    Upon the water's edge,
The huge and haggard shape
 Of that unknown North Cape,
    Whose form is like a wedge.

'The sea was rough and stormy,
    The tempest howled and wailed,
And the sea-fog, like a ghost,
 Haunted that dreary coast,
    But onward still I sailed.

'Four days I steered to eastward,
    Four days without a night :
Round in a fiery ring
 Went the great sun, O King,
    With red and lurid light.'

Here Alfred, King of the Saxons,
    Ceased writing for a while ;
And raised his eyes from his
    book,
With a strange and puzzled look,
    And an incredulous smile.

But Othere, the old sea-captain,
    He neither paused nor stirred,
Till the King listened and then
Once more took up his pen,
    And wrote down every word.

'And now the land,' said Othere,
    'Bent southward suddenly,
And I followed the curving shore
And ever southward bore
    Into a nameless sea.

'And there we hunted the walrus,
    The narwhale, and the seal ;
Ha ! 'twas a noble game !
And like the lightning's flame
    Flew our harpoons of steel.

'There were six of us all together,
    Norsemen of Helgoland ;
In two days and no more
We killed of them three score,
    And dragged them to the strand !'

Here Alfred the Truth-Teller
    Suddenly closed his book,
And lifted his blue eyes,
With doubt and strange surmise
    Depicted in their look.

And Othere, the old sea-captain,
    Stared at him wild and weird,
Then smiled, till his shining teeth
Gleamed white from underneath
    His tawny, quivering beard.

And to the King of the Saxons,
    In witness of the truth,
Raising his noble head,
He stretched his brown hand, and
    said,
    'Behold this walrus-tooth !'

DAYBREAK.

A WIND came up out of the sea,
    And said, 'O mists, make room for
    me.'

It hailed the ships, and cried, 'Sail
    on,
Ye mariners, the night is gone.'

And hurried landward far away,
Crying, 'Awake ! it is the day.'

It said unto the forest, 'Shout !
Hang all your leafy banners out !'

It touched the wood-bird's folded
  wing,
And said, ' O bird, awake and sing.'

And o'er the farms, ' O chanticleer,
Your clarion blow; the day is near.'

It whispered to the fields of corn,
' Bow down, and hail the coming
  morn.'

It shouted through the belfry-tower,
'Awake, O bell ! proclaim the hour.'

It crossed the churchyard with a
  sigh,
And said, ' Not yet ! in quiet lie.'

THE FIFTIETH BIRTHDAY OF AGASSIZ.

MAY 28, 1857.

IT was fifty years ago
  In the pleasant month of May,
In the beautiful Pays de Vaud,
  A child in its cradle lay.

And Nature, the old nurse, took
  The child upon her knee,
Saying : ' Here is a story-book
  Thy Father has written for thee.'

' Come, wander with me,' she said,
  ' Into regions yet untrod ;
And read what is still unread
  In the manuscripts of God.'

And he wandered away and away
  With Nature, the dear old nurse,
Who sang to him night and day
  The rhymes of the universe.

And whenever the way seemed
  long,
  Or his heart began to fail,
She would sing a more wonderful
  song,
  Or tell a more marvellous tale.

So she keeps him still a child
  And will not let him go,
Though at times his heart beats
  wild
  For the beautiful Pays de Vaud ;

Though at times he hears in his
  dreams
  The Ranz des Vaches of old,
And the rush of mountain streams
  From glaciers clear and cold ;

And the mother at home says,
  ' Hark !
For his voice I listen and yearn ;
It is growing late and dark,
  And my boy does not return !'

CHILDREN.

COME to me, O ye children !
  For I hear you at your play,
And the questions that perplexed
  me
  Have vanished quite away.

Ye open the eastern windows,
  That look towards the sun,
Where thoughts are singing swal-
  lows
  And the brooks of morning run.

In your hearts are the birds and the
  sunshine,
  In your thoughts the brooklet's
  flow,
But in mine is the wind of Autumn.
  And the first fall of the snow.

Ah ! what would the world be
  to us
  If the children were no more ?
We should dread the desert behind
  us
  Worse than the dark before.

What the leaves are to the forest,
  With light and air for food,
Ere their sweet and tender juices
  Have been hardened into wood,

That to the world are children;
  Through them it feels the glow
Of a brighter and sunnier climate
  Than reaches the trunks below.

Come to me, O ye children!
  And whisper in my ear
What the birds and the winds are
    singing
  In your sunny atmosphere.

For what are all our contrivings,
  And the wisdom of our books,
When compared with your caresses,
  And the gladness of your looks?

Ye are better than all the ballads
  That ever were sung or said;
For ye are living poems,
  And all the rest are dead.

SANDALPHON.

HAVE you read in the Talmud of
    old,
In the Legends the Rabbins have
    told
  Of the limitless realms of the air,
Have you read it,—the marvellous
    story
Of Sandalphon, the Angel of Glory,
  Sandalphon, the Angel of
    Prayer?

How, erect, at the outermost gates
Of the City Celestial he waits,
  With his feet on the ladder of
    light,
That, crowded with angels un-
    numbered,
By Jacob was seen, as he slum-
    bered
  Alone in the desert at night?

The Angels of Wind and of Fire
Chant only one hymn, and expire
  With the song's irresistible
    stress;
Expire in their rapture and wonder,
As harp-strings are broken asunder
  By music they throb to express.

But serene in the rapturous throng,
Unmoved by the rush of the song,
  With eyes unimpassioned and
    slow,
Among the dead angels, the death-
    less
Sandalphon stands listening
    breathless
  To sounds that ascend from
    below;—

From the spirits on earth that
    adore,
From the souls that entreat and
    implore
  In the fervour and passion of
    prayer;
From the hearts that are broken
    with losses,
And weary with dragging the
    crosses
  Too heavy for mortals to bear.

And he gathers the prayers as he
    stands,
And they change into flowers in
    his hands,
  Into garlands of purple and red;
And beneath the great arch of the
    portal,
Through the streets of the City
    Immortal
  Is wafted the fragrance they
    shed.

It is but a legend, I know,—
A fable, a phantom, a show,
  Of the ancient Rabbinical lore;
Yet the old mediæval tradition,
The beautiful, strange superstition,
  But haunts me and holds me the
    more.

When I look from my window at night,
And the welkin above is all white,
All throbbing and panting with stars,
Among them majestic is standing
Sandalphon the angel, expanding
His pinions in nebulous bars.

And the legend, I feel, is a part
Of the hunger and thirst of the heart,
The frenzy and fire of the brain,
That grasps at the fruitage forbidden,
The golden pomegranates of Eden,
To quiet its fever and pain.

FLIGHT THE SECOND.

THE CHILDREN'S HOUR.

BETWEEN the dark and the daylight,
When the night is beginning to lower,
Comes a pause in the day's occupations,
That is known as the Children's Hour.

I hear in the chamber above me
The patter of little feet,
The sound of a door that is opened,
And voices soft and sweet.

From my study I see in the lamplight,
Descending the broad hall stair
Grave Alice, and laughing Allegra,
And Edith with golden hair.

A whisper, and then a silence:
Yet I know by their merry eyes
They are plotting and planning together
To take me by surprise.

A sudden rush from the stairway,
A sudden raid from the hall!
By three doors left unguarded
They enter my castle wall!

They climb up into my turret
O'er the arms and back of my chair;
If I try to escape, they surround me;
They seem to be everywhere.

They almost devour me with kisses,
Their arms about me entwine,
Till I think of the Bishop of Bingen
In his Mouse-Tower on the Rhine!

Do you think, O blue-eyed banditti,
Because you have scaled the wall,
Such an old moustache as I am
Is not a match for you all!

I have you fast in my fortress,
And will not let you depart,
But put you down into the dungeon
In the round-tower of my heart.

And there will I keep you for ever,
Yes, for ever and a day,
Till the walls shall crumble to ruin,
And moulder in dust away!

ENCELADUS.

UNDER Mount Etna he lies,
  It is slumber, it is not death;
For he struggles at times to arise,
And above him the lurid skies
  Are hot with his fiery breath.

The crags are piled on his breast,
  The earth is heaped on his
    head;
But the groans of his wild unrest,
Though smothered and half sup-
    pressed,
  Are heard, and he is not dead.

And the nations far away
  Are watching with eager eyes;
They talk together and say,
'To-morrow, perhaps to-day.
  Enceladus will arise!'

And the old gods, the austere
  Oppressors in their strength,
Stand aghast and white with fear
At the ominous sounds they hear,
  And tremble, and mutter, 'At
    length!'

Ah me! for the land that is sown
  With the harvest of despair!
Where the burning cinders, blown
From the lips of the overthrown
  Enceladus, fill the air.

Where ashes are heaped in drifts,
  Over vineyard and field and
    town,
Whenever he starts and lifts
His head through the blackened
    rifts
  Of the crags that keep him down.

See, see! the red light shines!
  'Tis the glare of his awful eyes!
And the storm-wind shouts through
    the pines
Of Alps and of Apennines,
  'Enceladus, arise!'

THE CUMBERLAND.

AT anchor in Hampton Roads we
    lay,
  On board of the Cumberland,
    sloop-of-war;
And at times from the fortress
    across the bay
  The alarum of drums swept
    past,
  Or a bugle blast
From the camp on the shore.

Then far away to the south uprose
  A little feather of snow-white
    smoke,
And we knew that the iron ship of
    our foes
  Was steadily steering its course
  To try the force
Of our ribs of oak.

Down upon us heavily runs,
  Silent and sullen, the floating
    fort;
Then comes a puff of smoke from
    her guns,
  And leaps the terrible death,
  With fiery breath,
From each open port.

We are not idle, but send her
    straight
  Defiance back in a full broad-
    side!
As hail rebounds from a roof of
    slate,
  Rebounds our heavier hail
  From each iron scale
Of the monster's hide.

'Strike your flag!' the rebel cries,
  In his arrogant old plantation
    strain,
'Never!' our gallant Morris
    replies;
  'It is better to sink than to
    yield!'
  And the whole air pealed
With the cheers of our men.

Then, like a kraken huge and
    black,
  She crushed our ribs in her iron
    grasp!
Down went the Cumberland all a
    wrack,
    With a sudden shudder of
      death,
    And the cannon's breath
  For her dying gasp.

Next morn, as the sun rose over the
    bay,
  Still floated our flag at the main-
    mast head.
Lord, how beautiful was Thy day!
  Every waft of the air
    Was a whisper of prayer,
  Or a dirge for the dead.

Ho! brave hearts that went down
    in the seas!
  Ye are at peace in the troubled
    stream;
Ho! brave land! with hearts like
    these,
  Thy flag, that is rent in
    twain,
  Shall be one again,
  And without a seam!

SNOW-FLAKES.

Out of the bosom of the Air,
  Out of the cloud-folds of her
    garments shaken,
Over the woodlands brown and
    bare,
  Over the harvest fields for-
    saken,
  Silent, and soft, and slow
  Descends the snow.

Even as our cloudy fancies take
  Suddenly shape in some divine
    expression,

Even as the troubled heart doth
    make
  In the white countenance con-
    fession,
  The troubled sky reveals
  The grief it feels.

This is the poem of the air,
  Slowly in silent syllables re-
    corded;
This is the secret of despair,
  Long in its cloudy bosom
    hoarded,
  Now whispered and revealed
  To wood and field.

A DAY OF SUNSHINE.

O gift of God! O perfect day:
Whereon shall no man work, but
    play;
Whereon it is enough for me,
Not to be doing, but to be!

Through every fibre of my brain,
Through every nerve, through
    every vein,
I feel the electric thrill, the touch
Of life, that seems almost too
    much.

I hear the wind among the trees
Playing celestial symphonies;
I see the branches downward bent,
Like keys of some great instrument.

And over me unrolls on high
The splendid scenery of the sky,
Where through a sapphire sea the
    sun
Sails like a golden galleon,

Towards yonder cloud-land in the
    West,
Towards yonder Islands of the
    Blest,

Whose steep sierra far uplifts
Its craggy summits white with
drifts.

Blow, winds! and waft through all
the rooms
The snow-flakes of the cherry-
blooms!
Blow, winds! and bend within my
reach
The fiery blossoms of the peach!

O Life and Love! O happy throng
Of thoughts, whose only speech is
song!
O heart of man! canst thou not
be
Blithe as the air is, and as free?

SOMETHING LEFT UNDONE.

LABOUR with what zeal we will,
  Something still remains un-
done,
Something uncompleted still
  Waits the rising of the sun.

By the bedside, on the stair,
  At the threshold, near the gates,
With its menace or its prayer,
  Like a mendicant it waits;

Waits, and will not go away;
  Waits, and will not be gainsaid;
By the cares of yesterday
  Each to-day is heavier made;

Till at length the burden seems
  Greater than our strength can
bear,
Heavy as the weight of dreams,
  Pressing on us everywhere.

And we stand from day to day,
  Like the dwarfs of times gone by,
Who, as northern legends say,
  On their shoulders held the sky.

WEARINESS.

O LITTLE feet! that such long years
Must wander on through hopes and
fears,
  Must ache and bleed beneath
  your load;
I, nearer to the wayside inn
Where toil shall cease and rest
begin,
  Am weary, thinking of your road!

O little hands! that, weak or
strong,
Have still to serve or rule so long,
  Have still so long to give or ask;
I, who so much with book and pen
Have toiled among my fellow-
men,
  Am weary, thinking of your task.

O little hearts! that throb and beat
With such impatient, feverish heat,
  Such limitless and strong
  desires;
Mine that so long has glowed and
burned,
With passions into ashes turned
  Now covers and conceals its fires.

O little souls! as pure and white
And crystalline as rays of light
  Direct from heaven, their source
  divine;
Refracted through the mist of
years,
How red my setting sun appears,
  How lurid looks this soul of
  mine!

FLIGHT THE THIRD.

FATA MORGANA.

O SWEET illusions of Song,
  That tempt me everywhere,
In the lonely fields, and the throng
  Of the crowded thoroughfare!

I approach, and ye vanish away,
  I grasp you, and ye are gone;
But ever by night and by day
  The melody soundeth on.

As the weary traveller sees
  In desert or prairie vast,
Blue lakes, overhung with trees,
  That a pleasant shadow cast;

Fair towns with turrets high,
  And shining roofs of gold,
That vanish as he draws nigh,
  Like mists together rolled,—

So I wander and wander along,
  And for ever before me gleams
The shining city of song,
  In the beautiful land of dreams.

But when I would enter the gate
  Of that golden atmosphere,
It is gone, and I wander and
  wait
For the vision to reappear.

THE HAUNTED CHAMBER.

EACH heart has its haunted
  chamber,
  Where the silent moonlight falls!
On the floor are mysterious footsteps,
  There are whispers along the
  walls!

And mine at times is haunted
  By phantoms of the Past,
As motionless as shadows
  By the silent moonlight cast.

A form sits by the window,
  That is not seen by day,
For as soon as the dawn ap-
  proaches
  It vanishes away.

It sits there in the moonlight,
  Itself as pale and still,
And points with its airy finger
  Across the window-sill.

Without, before the window,
  There stands a gloomy pine,
Whose boughs wave upward and
  downward
  As wave these thoughts of mine.

And underneath its branches
  Is the grave of a little child,
Who died upon life's threshold,
  And never wept nor smiled.

What are ye, O pallid phantoms!
  That haunt my troubled brain?
That vanish when day approaches,
  And at night return again?

What are ye, O pallid phantoms!
  But the statues without breath,
That stand on the bridge over-
  arching
  The silent river of death?

THE MEETING.

AFTER so long an absence
  At last we meet again:
Does the meeting give us pleasure,
  Or does it give us pain?

321

The tree of life has been shaken,
  And but few of us linger now,
Like the Prophet's two or three
    berries
    In the top of the uppermost
    bough.

We cordially greet each other
  In the old, familiar tone;
And we think, though we do not
    say it,
  How old and gray he is grown!

We speak of a Merry Christmas
  And many a Happy New Year;
But each in his heart is thinking
  Of those that are not here.

We speak of friends and their for-
    tunes,
  And of what they did and said,
Till the dead alone seem living,
  And the living alone seem dead.

And at last we hardly distinguish
  Between the ghosts and the
    guests;
And a mist and shadow of sadness
  Steals over our merriest jests.

VOX POPULI.

WHEN Mazárvan the magician
  Journeyed westward through
    Cathay,
Nothing heard he but the praises
  Of Badoura on his way.

But the lessening rumour ended
  When he came to Khaledan,
There the folk were talking only
  Of Prince Camaralzaman.

So it happens with the poets:
  Every province hath its own;
Camaralzaman is famous
  Where Badoura is unknown.

THE CASTLE-BUILDER.

A GENTLE boy, with soft and silken
    locks,
  A dreamy boy, with brown and
    tender eyes,
A castle-builder, with his wooden
    blocks,
  And towers that touch imaginary
    skies.

A fearless rider on his father's
    knee,
  An eager listener unto stories
    told
At the Round Table of the nursery,
  Of heroes and adventures mani-
    fold.

There will be other towers for thee
    to build;
  There will be other steeds for thee
    to ride;
There will be other legends, and
    all filled
  With greater marvels and more
    glorified.

Build on, and make thy castles high
    and fair,
  Rising and reaching upward to
    the skies;
Listen to voices in the upper air,
  Nor lose thy simple faith in mys-
    teries.

CHANGED.

FROM the outskirts of the town,
  Where of old the mile-stone
    stood,
Now a stranger, looking down
  I behold the shadowy crown
    Of the dark and haunted wood.

Is it changed, or am I changed?
  Ah! the oaks are fresh and
    green,
But the friends with whom I ranged
Through their thickets are estranged
  By the years that intervene.

Bright as ever flows the sea,
  Bright as ever shines the sun,
But, alas! they seem to me
Not the sun that used to be,
  Not the tides that used to run.

THE CHALLENGE.

I HAVE a vague remembrance
  Of a story that is told
In some ancient Spanish legend
  Or chronicle of old.

It was when brave King Sanchez
  Was before Zamora slain,
And his great besieging army
  Lay encamped upon the plain.

Don Diego de Ordoñez
  Sallied forth in front of all,
And shouted loud his challenge
  To the warders on the wall.

All the people of Zamora,
  Both the born and the unborn,
As traitors did he challenge
  With taunting words of scorn.

The living, in their houses,
  And in their graves, the dead!
And the waters of their rivers,
  And their wine, and oil, and
    bread!

There is a greater army
  That besets us round with strife,
A starving, numberless army,
  At all the gates of life.

The poverty-stricken millions
  Who challenge our wine and
    bread,
And impeach us all as traitors,
  Both the living and the dead.

And whenever I sit at the banquet,
  Where the feast and song are
    high,
Amid the mirth and the music
  I can hear that fearful cry.

And hollow and haggard faces
  Look into the lighted hall,
And wasted hands are extended
  To catch the crumbs that fall.

For within there is light and plenty,
  And odours fill the air;
But without there is cold and dark-
    ness,
  And hunger and despair.

And there in the camp of famine,
  In wind and cold and rain,
Christ, the great Lord of the army,
  Lies dead upon the plain!

THE BROOK AND THE
WAVE.

THE brooklet came from the moun-
    tain,
  As sang the bard of old,
Running with feet of silver
  Over the sands of gold!

Far away in the briny ocean
  There rolled a turbulent wave,
Now singing along the sea-beach,
  Now howling along the cave.

And the brooklet has found the
    billow,
  Though they flowed so far apart,
And has filled with its freshness
    and sweetness
  That turbulent, bitter heart!

FROM THE SPANISH CAN-CIONEROS.

I.

EYES so tristful, eyes so tristful,
Heart so full of care and cumber,
I was lapped in rest and slumber,
Ye have made me wakeful, wistful!

In this life of labour endless
Who shall comfort my distresses?
Querulous my soul and friendless
In its sorrow shuns caresses.
Ye have made me, ye have made me
Querulous of you, that care not,
Eyes so tristful, yet I dare not
Say to what ye have betrayed me.

II.

Some day, some day,
O troubled breast,
Shalt thou find rest.

If Love in thee
To grief give birth,
Six feet of earth
Can more than he;
There calm and free
And unoppressed
Shalt thou find rest.

The unattained
In life at last,
When life is passed
Shall all be gained;
And no more pained,
No more distressed,
Shalt thou find rest.

III.

Come, O Death, so silent flying
That unheard thy coming be,
Lest the sweet delight of dying
Bring life back again to me.

For thy sure approach perceiving,
In my constancy and pain
I new life should win again,
Thinking that I am not living.
So to me, unconscious lying,
All unknown thy coming be,
Lest the sweet delight of dying
Bring life back again to me.

Unto him who finds thee hateful,
Death, thou art inhuman pain;
But to me, who dying gain,
Life is but a task ungrateful.
Come, then, with my wish comply-
ing,
All unheard thy coming be,
Lest the sweet delight of dying
Bring life back again to me.

IV.

Glove of black in white hand
bare,
And about her forehead pale
Wound a thin, transparent veil,
That doth not conceal her hair;
Sovereign attitude and air,
Cheek and neck alike displayed,
With coquettish charms arrayed,
Laughing eyes and fugitive;—
This is killing men that live,
'Tis not mourning for the dead.

AFTERMATH.

WHEN the Summer fields are
mown,
When the birds are fledged and
flown,
    And the dry leaves strew the
    path;
With the falling of the snow,
With the cawing of the crow,
Once again the fields we mow
    And gather in the aftermath.

324

Not the sweet, new grass with
  flowers
Is this harvesting of ours ;
  Not the upland clover bloom ;
But the rowen mixed with weeds,
Tangled tufts from marsh and
  meads,
Where the poppy drops its seeds
  In the silence and the gloom.

EPIMETHEUS,

OR THE POET'S AFTERTHOUGHT.

HAVE I dreamed ? or was it real,
  What I saw as in a vision,
When to marches hymeneal
In the land of the Ideal
  Moved my thought o'er Fields
    Elysian ?

What ! are these the guests whose
  glances
  Seemed like sunshine gleaming
    round me ?
These the wild, bewildering fancies,
That with dithyrambic dances
  As with magic circles bound me ?

Ah ! how cold are their caresses !
  Pallid cheeks, and haggard
    bosoms !
Spectral gleam their snow-white
  dresses,
And from loose, dishevelled tresses
  Fall the hyacinthine blossoms !

O my songs ! whose winsome
  measures
  Filled my heart with secret
    rapture !
Children of my golden leisures !
Must even your delights and plea-
  sures
  Fade and perish with the cap-
    ture ?

Fair they seemed, those songs
  sonorous,
  When they came to me un-
    bidden ;
Voices single, and in chorus,
Like the wild birds singing o'er us
  In the dark of branches hidden.

Disenchantment ! Disillusion !
  Must each noble aspiration
Come at last to this conclusion,
Jarring discord, wild confusion,
  Lassitude, renunciation ?

Not with steeper fall nor faster,
  From the sun's serene dominions,
Not through brighter realms nor
  vaster,
In swift ruin and disaster,
  Icarus fell with shattered
    pinions !

Sweet Pandora ! dear Pandora !
  Why did mighty Jove create
    thee
Coy as Thetis, fair as Flora,
Beautiful as young Aurora,
  If to win thee is to hate thee ?

No, not hate thee ! for this feeling
  Of unrest and long resistance
Is but passionate appealing,
A prophetic whisper stealing
  O'er the chords of our existence.

Him whom thou dost once enamour
  Thou, beloved, never leavest ;
In life's discord, strife, and clamour
Still he feels thy spell of glamour ;
  Him of Hope thou ne'er bereav-
    est.

Weary hearts by thee are lifted,
  Struggling souls by thee are
    strengthened,
Clouds of fear asunder rifted,
Truth from falsehood cleansed and
  sifted,
  Lives, like days in summer,
    lengthened !

Therefore art thou ever dearer,
O my Sibyl, my deceiver!
For thou makest each mystery
clearer,
And the unattained seems nearer,
When thou fillest my heart with
fever!

Muse of all the Gifts and Graces!
Though the fields around us
wither,
There are ampler realms and
spaces,
Where no foot has left its traces:
Let us turn and wander thither!

FLIGHT THE FOURTH.

CHARLES SUMNER.

GARLANDS upon his grave,
And flowers upon his hearse,
And to the tender heart and brave
The tribute of this verse.

His was the troubled life,
The conflict and the pain,
The grief, the bitterness of strife,
The honour without stain.

Like Winkelried, he took
Into his manly breast
The sheaf of hostile spears, and
broke
A path for the oppressed.

Then from the fatal field,
Upon a nation's heart
Borne like a warrior on his shield!—
So should the brave depart.

Death takes us by surprise,
And stays our hurrying feet;
The great design unfinished lies,
Our lives are incomplete.

But in the dark unknown
Perfect their circles seem,
Even as a bridge's arch of stone
Is rounded in the stream.

Alike are life and death,
When life in death survives,
And the uninterrupted breath
Inspires a thousand lives.

Were a star quenched on high,
For ages would its light,
Still travelling downward from the
sky,
Shine on our mortal sight.

So when a great man dies,
For years beyond our ken
The light he leaves behind him lies
Upon the paths of men.

TRAVELS BY THE FIRE-SIDE.

THE ceaseless rain is falling fast,
And yonder gilded vane,
Immovable for three days past,
Points to the misty main.

It drives me in upon myself
And to the fireside gleams,
To pleasant books that crowd my
shelf,
And still more pleasant dreams.

I read whatever bards have sung
Of lands beyond the sea,
And the bright days when I was
young
Come thronging back to me.

In fancy I can hear again
The Alpine torrent's roar,
The mule-bells on the hills of Spain,
The sea at Elsinore.

I see the convent's gleaming wall
    Rise from its groves of pine,
And towers of old cathedrals tall,
    And castles by the Rhine.

I journey on by park and spire,
    Beneath centennial trees,
Through fields with poppies all on
    fire,
    And gleams of distant seas.

I fear no more the dust and heat,
    No more I fear fatigue,
While journeying with another's
    feet
    O'er many a lengthening league.

Let others traverse sea and land,
    And toil through various climes,
I turn the world round with my
    hand
    Reading these poets' rhymes.

From them I learn whatever lies
    Beneath each changing zone,
And see, when looking with their
    eyes,
    Better than with mine own.

CADENABBIA.

LAKE OF COMO.

No sounds of wheels or hoof-beat
    breaks
    The silence of the summer day,
As by the loveliest of all lakes
    I while the idle hours away.

I pace the leafy colonnade
    Where level branches of the
    plane
Above me weave a roof of shade
    Impervious to the sun and rain.

At times a sudden rush of air
    Flutters the lazy leaves o'erhead,
And gleams of sunshine toss and
    flare
    Like torches down the path I
    tread.

By Somariva's garden gate
    I make the marble stairs my
    seat,
And hear the water, as I wait,
    Lapping the steps beneath my
    feet.

The undulation sinks and swells
    Along the stony parapets,
And far away the floating bells
    Tinkle upon the fisher's nets.

Silent and slow, by tower and town
    The freighted barges come and
    go,
Their pendent shadows gliding
    down
    By town and tower submerged
    below.

The hills sweep upward from the
    shore,
    With villas scattered one by one
Upon their wooded spurs, and
    lower
    Bellagio blazing in the sun.

And dimly seen, a tangled mass
    Of walls and woods, of light and
    shade,
Stands beckoning up the Stelvio
    Pass
    Varenna with its white cascade.

I ask myself, Is this a dream?
    Will it all vanish into air?
Is there a land of such supreme
    And perfect beauty anywhere?

Sweet vision! Do not fade away;
    Linger until my heart shall take
Into itself the summer day,
    And all the beauty of the lake.

Linger until upon my brain
    Is stamped an image of the
    scene,
Then fade into the air again,
    And be as if thou hadst not been.

MONTE CASSINO.

TERRA DI LAVORO.

BEAUTIFUL valley ! through whose
 verdant meads
  Unheard the Garigliano glides
   along ;—
The Liris, nurse of rushes and of
 reeds,
  The river taciturn of classic song.

The Land of Labour and the Land
 of Rest,
  Where mediæval towns are white
   on all
The hillsides, and where every
 mountain's crest
  Is an Etrurian or a Roman wall.

There is Alagna, where Pope Boni-
 face
  Was dragged with contumely
   from his throne ;
Sciarra Colonna, was that day's
 disgrace
  The Pontiff's only, or in part
   thine own ?

There is Ceprano, where a renegade
  Was each Apulian, as great
   Dante saith,
When Manfred, by his men-at-arms
 betrayed,
  Spurred on to Benevento and to
   death.

There is Aquinum, the old Volscian
 town,
  Where Juvenal was born, whose
   lurid light
Still hovers o'er his birthplace like
 the crown
  Of splendour seen o'er cities in
   the night.

Doubled the splendour is, that in
 its streets
  The Angelic Doctor as a schoolboy played,

And dreamed perhaps the dreams
 that he repeats
  In ponderous folios for scholas-
   tics made.

And there, uplifted, like a passing
 cloud
  That pauses on a mountain
   summit high,
Monte Cassino's convent rears its
 proud
  And venerable walls against the
   sky.

Well I remember how on foot I
 climbed
  The stony pathway leading to its
   gate ;
Above, the convent bells for vespers
 chimed,
  Below, the darkening town grew
   desolate.

Well I remember the low arch and
 dark,
  The courtyard with its well, the
   terrace wide,
From which, far down, the valley
 like a park
  Veiled in the evening mists, was
   dim descried.

The day was dying, and with feeble
 hands
  Caressed the mountain tops ; the
   vales between
Darkened ; the river in the
 meadow-lands
  Sheathed itself as a sword, and
   was not seen.

The silence of the place was like a
 sleep,
  So full of rest it seemed ; each
   passing tread
Was a reverberation from the
 deep
  Recesses of the ages that are
   dead.

For, more than thirteen centuries
  ago,
Benedict fleeing from the gates
  of Rome,
A youth disgusted with its vice and
  woe,
Sought in these mountain solitudes a home.

He founded here his Convent and
  his Rule
Of prayer and work, and counted
  work as prayer;
The pen became a clarion, and his
  school
Flamed like a beacon in the
  midnight air.

What though Boccaccio, in his
  reckless way,
Mocking the lazy brotherhood,
  deplores
The illuminated manuscripts, that
  lay
Torn and neglected on the dusty
  floors?

Boccaccio was a novelist, a child
Of fancy and of fiction at the
  best!
This the urbane librarian said, and
  smiled
Incredulous, as at some idle jest.

Upon such themes as these, with
  one young friar
I sat conversing late into the
  night,
Till in its cavernous chimney the
  wood-fire
Had burnt its heart out like an
  anchorite.

And then translated, in my convent
  cell,
Myself yet not myself, in dreams
  I lay,
And, as a monk who hears the
  matin bell,
Started from sleep; already it
  was day.

From the high window I beheld
  the scene
On which Saint Benedict so oft
  had gazed,—
The mountains and the valley in
  the sheen
Of the bright sun,—and stood as
  one amazed.

Gray mists were rolling, rising,
  vanishing;
The woodlands glistened with
  their jewelled crowns;
Far off the mellow bells began to
  ring
For matins in the half-awakened
  towns.

The conflict of the Present and the
  Past,
The ideal and the actual in our
  life,
As on a field of battle held me
  fast,
Where this world and the next
  world were at strife.

For, as the valley from its sleep
  awoke,
I saw the iron horses of the
  steam
Toss to the morning air their plumes
  of smoke,
And woke, as one awaketh from
  a dream.

AMALFI.

SWEET the memory is to me
Of a land beyond the sea,
Where the waves and mountains
  meet,
Where, amid her mulberry-trees
Sits Amalfi in the heat,
Bathing ever her white feet
In the tideless summer seas.

In the middle of the town,
From its fountains in the hills,
Tumbling through the narrow
    gorge,
The Canneto rushes down,
Turns the great wheels of the
    mills,
Lifts the hammers of the forge.

'Tis a stairway, not a street,
That ascends the deep ravine,
Where the torrent leaps between
Rocky walls that almost meet.
Toiling up from stair to stair
Peasant girls their burdens bear;
Sunburnt daughters of the soil,
Stately figures tall and straight,
What inexorable fate
Dooms them to this life of toil?

Lord of vineyards and of lands,
Far above the convent stands.
On its terraced walk aloof
Leans a monk with folded hands,
Placid, satisfied, serene,
Looking down upon the scene
Over wall and red tiled roof;
Wondering unto what good end
All this toil and traffic tend,
And why all men cannot be
Free from care and free from pain,
And the sordid love of gain,
And as indolent as he.

Where are now the freighted barks
From the marts of east and west?
Where the knights in iron sarks
Journeying to the Holy Land,
Glove of steel upon the hand,
Cross of crimson on the breast?
Where the pomp of camp and
    court?
Where the pilgrims with their
    prayers?
Where the merchants with their
    wares,
And their gallant brigantines
Sailing safely into port
Chased by corsair Algerines?

Vanished like a fleet of cloud,
Like a passing trumpet-blast,
Are those splendours of the past,
And the commerce and the crowd!
Fathoms deep beneath the seas
Lie the ancient wharves and quays
Swallowed by the engulfing waves;
Silent streets and vacant halls,
Ruined roofs and towers and walls;
Hidden from all mortal eyes
Deep the sunken city lies:
Even cities have their graves!

This is an enchanted land!
Round the headlands far away
Sweeps the blue Salernian bay
With its sickle of white sand:
Further still and furthermost
On the dim-discovered coast
Paestum with its ruins lies,
And its roses all in bloom
Seem to tinge the fatal skies
Of that lonely land of doom.

On his terrace, high in air,
Nothing doth the good monk care
For such worldly themes as these.
From the garden just below
Little puffs of perfume blow,
And a sound is in his ears
Of the murmur of the bees
In the shining chestnut-trees;
Nothing else he heeds or hears.
All the landscape seems to swoon
In the happy afternoon;
Slowly o'er his senses creep
The encroaching waves of sleep,
And he sinks as sank the town,
Unresisting, fathoms down,
Into caverns cool and deep!

Walled about with drifts of snow,
Hearing the fierce north wind blow,
Seeing all the landscape white,
And the river cased in ice,
Comes this memory of delight,
Comes this vision unto me
Of a long-lost Paradise
In the land beyond the sea.

THE SERMON OF ST. FRANCIS.

UP soared the lark into the air,
A shaft of song, a winged prayer,
As if a soul, released from pain,
Were flying back to heaven again.

St. Francis heard; it was to him
An emblem of the Seraphim;
The upward motion of the fire,
The light, the heat, the heart's de-
        sire.

Around Assisi's convent gate
The birds, God's poor who cannot
        wait,
From moor and mere and dark-
        some wood
Came flocking for their dole of food.

'O brother birds,' St. Francis said,
'Ye come to me and ask for bread,
But not with bread alone to-day
Shall ye be fed and sent away.

'Ye shall be fed, ye happy birds,
With manna of celestial words;
Not mine, though mine they seem
        to be,
Not mine, though they be spoken
        through me.

O, doubly are ye bound to praise
The great Creator in your lays;
He giveth you your plumes of down,
Your crimson hoods, your cloaks
        of brown.

'He giveth you your wings to fly
And breathe a purer air on high,
And careth for you everywhere,
Who for yourselves so little care!'

With flutter of swift wings and songs
Together rose the feathered throngs,
And singing scattered far apart;
Deep peace was in St. Francis'
    heart.

He knew not if the brotherhood
His homily had understood;
He only knew that to one ear
The meaning of his words was clear.

BELISARIUS.

I AM poor and old and blind;
The sun burns me, and the wind
        Blows through the city gate
And covers me with dust
From the wheels of the august
        Justinian the Great.

It was for him I chased
The Persians o'er wild and waste,
        As General of the East;
Night after night I lay
In their camps of yesterday;
        Their forage was my feast.

For him, with sails of red,
And torches at mast-head,
        Piloting the great fleet,
I swept the Afric coasts
And scattered the Vandal hosts,
        Like dust in a windy street.

For him I won again
The Ausonian realm and reign,
        Rome and Parthenope;
And all the land was mine
From the summits of Apennine
        To the shores of either sea.

For him, in my feeble age,
I dared the battle's rage,
        To save Byzantium's state,
When the tents of Zabergan,
Like snowdrifts overran
        The road of the Golden Gate

And for this, for this, behold!
Infirm and blind and old,
        With gray, uncovered head,
Beneath the very arch
Of my triumphal march,
        I stand and beg my bread!

Methinks I still can hear,
Sounding distinct and near,
   The Vandal monarch's cry,
As, captive and disgraced,
With majestic step he paced,—
   'All, all is Vanity!'

Ah! vainest of all things
Is the gratitude of kings;
   The plaudits of the crowd
Are but the clatter of feet
At midnight in the street,
   Hollow and restless and loud.

But the bitterest disgrace
Is to see for ever the face
   Of the Monk of Ephesus!
The unconquerable will
This, too, can bear;—I still
   Am Belisarius!

SONGO RIVER.

NOWHERE such a devious stream,
Save in fancy or in dream,
Winding slow through bush and
   brake,
Links together lake and lake.

Walled with woods or sandy shelf,
Ever doubling on itself,
Flows the stream, so still and slow,
That it hardly seems to flow.

Never errant knight of old,
Lost in woodland or on wold,
Such a winding path pursued
Through the sylvan solitude.

Never schoolboy in his quest
After hazel-nut or nest,
Through the forest in and out
Wandered loitering thus about.

In the mirror of its tide
Tangled thickets on each side
Hang inverted, and between
Floating cloud or sky serene.

Swift or swallow on the wing
Seems the only living thing,
Or the loon, that laughs and flies
Down to those reflected skies.

Silent stream! thy Indian name
Unfamiliar is to fame;
For thou hidest here alone,
Well content to be unknown.

But thy tranquil waters teach
Wisdom deep as human speech,
Moving without haste or noise
In unbroken equipoise.

Though thou turnest no busy
   mill,
And art ever calm and still,
Even thy silence seems to say
To the traveller on his way:—

'Traveller, hurrying from the heat
Of the city, stay thy feet!
Rest a while, no longer waste
Life with inconsiderate haste!

'Be not like a stream that brawls
Loud with shallow waterfalls;
But in quiet self-control
Link together soul and soul.'

FLIGHT THE FIFTH.

THE HERONS OF ELM-WOOD.

WARM and still is the summer night,
  As here by the river's brink I wander ;
White overhead are the stars, and white
  The glimmering lamps on the hillside yonder.

Silent are all the sounds of day ;
  Nothing I hear but the chirp of crickets,
And the cry of the herons winging their way
  O'er the poet's house in the Elm-wood thickets.

Call to him, herons, as slowly you pass
  To your roosts in the haunts of the exiled thrushes,
Sing him the song of the green morass,
  And the tides that water the reeds and rushes.

Sing him the mystical Song of the Hern,
  And the secret that baffles our utmost seeking ;
For only a sound of lament we discern,
  And cannot interpret the words you are speaking.

Sing of the air, and the wild delight
  Of wings that uplift and winds that uphold you,
The joy of freedom, the rapture of flight
  Through the drift of the floating mists that enfold you ;

Of the landscape lying so far below,
  With its towns and rivers and desert places ;
And the splendour of light above, and the glow
  Of the limitless, blue, ethereal spaces.

Ask him if songs of the Troubadours,
  Or of Minnesingers in old black-letter,
Sound in his ears more sweet than yours,
  And if yours are not sweeter and wilder and better.

Sing to him, say to him, here at his gate,
  Where the boughs of the stately elms are meeting,
Some one hath lingered to meditate,
  And send him unseen this friend-ly greeting ;

That many another hath done the same,
  Though not by a sound was the silence broken ;
The surest pledge of a deathless name
  Is the silent homage of thoughts unspoken.

A DUTCH PICTURE.

SIMON DANZ has come home again
  From cruising about with his buccaneers ;
He has singed the beard of the King of Spain,
And carried away the Dean of Jaen
  And sold him in Algiers.

In his house by the Maese, with its roof of tiles,
  And weathercocks flying aloft in air,

333

There are silver tankards of antique
  styles,
Plunder of convent and castle, and
  piles
  Of carpets rich and rare.

In his tulip-garden there by the
  town,
  Overlooking the sluggish stream,
With his Moorish cap and dressing-
  gown,
The old sea-captain, hale and
  brown,
  Walks in a waking dream.

A smile in his gray mustachio lurks
  Whenever he thinks of the King
  of Spain,
And the listed tulips look like
  Turks,
And the silent gardener as he
  works
  Is changed to the Dean of Jaen.

The windmills on the outermost
  Verge of the landscape in the
  haze,
To him are towers on the Spanish
  coast,
With whiskered sentinels at their
  post,
  Though this is the river Maese.

But when the winter rains begin,
  He sits and smokes by the blaz-
  ing brands,
And old seafaring men come in,
Goat-bearded, gray, and with
  double chin,
  And rings upon their hands.

They sit there in the shadow and
  shine
  Of the flickering fire of the winter
  night;
Figures in colour and design
Like those by Rembrandt of the
  Rhine,
  Half darkness and half light.

And they talk of ventures lost or
  won,
  And their talk is ever and ever
  the same,
While they drink the red wine of
  Tarragon,
From the cellars of some Spanish
  Don,
  Or convent set on flame.

Restless at times with heavy strides
  He paces his parlour to and fro;
He is like a ship that at anchor
  rides,
And swings with the rising and
  falling tides,
  And tugs at her anchor-tow.

Voices mysterious far and near,
  Sound of the wind and sound of
  the sea,
Are calling and whispering in his
  ear,
'Simon Danz! Why stayest thou
  here?
  Come forth and follow me!'

So he thinks he shall take to the
  sea again
  For one more cruise with his
  buccaneers,
To singe the beard of the King of
  Spain,
And capture another Dean of Jaen
  And sell him in Algiers.

CASTLES IN SPAIN.

How much of my young heart, O
  Spain,
  Went out to thee in days of yore!
What dreams romantic filled my
  brain,
And summoned back to life again
The Paladins of Charlemagne,
  The Cid Campeador!

And shapes more shadowy than
these,
  In the dim twilight half revealed ;
Phœnician galleys on the seas,
The Roman camps like hives of
bees,
The Goth uplifting from his knees
  Pelayo on his shield.

It was these memories perchance,
From annals of remotest eld,
That lent the colours of romance
To every trivial circumstance,
And changed the form and coun-
tenance
  Of all that I beheld.

Old towns, whose history lies hid
  In monkish chronicle or rhyme,
Burgos, the birthplace of the Cid,
Zamora and Valladolid,
Toledo, built and walled amid
  The wars of Wamba's time ;

The long, straight line of the high-
way,
  The distant town that seems so
near,
The peasants in the fields, that
stay
Their toil to cross themselves and
pray,
When from the belfry at midday
  The Angelus they hear ;

White crosses in the mountain
pass,
  Mules gay with tassels, the loud
din
Of muleteers, the tethered ass
That crops the dusty wayside
grass,
And cavaliers with spurs of brass
  Alighting at the inn ;

White hamlets hidden in fields of
wheat,
  White cities slumbering by the
sea,

White sunshine flooding square
and street,
Dark mountain-ranges, at whose
feet
The river-beds are dry with heat,—
  All was a dream to me.

Yet something sombre and severe
  O'er the enchanted landscape
reigned ;
A terror in the atmosphere,
As if King Philip listened near,
Or Torquemada, the austere,
  His ghostly sway maintained.

The softer Andalusian skies
  Dispelled the sadness and the
gloom ;
There Cadiz by the seaside lies,
And Seville's orange-orchards rise,
Making the land a paradise
  Of beauty and of bloom.

There Cordova is hidden among
  The palm, the olive, and the
vine ;
Gem of the South, by poets sung,
And in whose Mosque Almanzor
hung
As lamps the bells that once had
rung
  At Compostella's shrine.

But over all the rest supreme,
  The star of stars, the cynosure,
The artist's and the poet's theme,
The young man's vision, the old
man's dream,—
Granada by its winding stream,
  The city of the Moor !

And there the Alhambra still re-
calls
  Aladdin's palace of delight :
Allah il Allah ! through its halls
Whispers the fountain as it falls,
The Darro darts beneath its
walls,
  The hills with snow are white.

Ah yes, the hills are white with
snow,
And cold with blasts that bite
and freeze ;
But in the happy vale below
The orange and pomegranate grow,
And wafts of air toss to and fro
The blossoming almond-trees.

The Vega cleft by the Xenil,
The fascination and allure
Of the sweet landscape chains the
will ;
The traveller lingers on the hill,
His parted lips are breathing still
The last sigh of the Moor.

How like a ruin overgrown
With flowers that hide the rents
of time,
Stands now the Past that I have
known,
Castles in Spain, not built of stone
But of white summer clouds, and
blown
Into this little mist of rhyme !

————

VITTORIA COLONNA.

Vittoria Colonna, on the death of her
husband, the Marchese di Pescara, retired
to her castle at Ischia (Inarimé), and there
wrote the Ode upon his death, which gained
her the title of Divine.

ONCE more, once more, Inarimé,
I see thy purple hills !—once
more
I hear the billows of the bay
Wash the white pebbles on thy
shore.

High o'er the sea-surge and the
sands,
Like a great galleon wrecked and
cast
Ashore by storms, thy castle stands,
A mouldering landmark of the
Past.

Upon its terrace-walk I see
A phantom gliding to and fro ;
It is Colonna,—it is she
Who lived and loved so long ago.

Pescara's beautiful young wife,
The type of perfect womanhood,
Whose life was love, the life of
life,
That time and change and death
withstood.

For death, that breaks the marriage
band
In others, only closer pressed
The wedding-ring upon her hand
And closer locked and barred
her breast.

She knew the life-long martyrdom,
The weariness, the endless pain
Of waiting for some one to come
Who never more would come
again.

The shadows of the chestnut-trees,
The odour of the orange-blooms,
The song of birds, and, more than
these,
The silence of deserted rooms ;

The respiration of the sea,
The soft caresses of the air,
All things in nature seemed to be
But ministers of her despair ;

Till the o'erburdened heart, so
long
Imprisoned in itself, found vent
And voice in one impassioned song
Of inconsolable lament.

Then as the sun, though hidden
from sight,
Transmutes to gold the leaden
mist,
Her life was interfused with light,
From realms that, though unseen,
exist.

336

Inarimé! Inarimé!
  Thy castle on the crags above
In dust shall crumble and decay,
  But not the memory of her
    love.

THE REVENGE OF RAIN-
IN-THE-FACE.

IN that desolate land and lone,
Where the Big Horn and Yellow-
    stone
  Roar down their mountain path,
By their fires the Sioux Chiefs
Muttered their woes and griefs
  And the menace of their wrath.

'Revenge!' cried Rain-in-the-
    Face,
'Revenge upon all the race
  Of the White Chief with yellow
    hair!'
And the mountains dark and high
From their crags re-echoed the
    cry
  Of his anger and despair.

In the meadow, spreading wide
By woodland and riverside,
  The Indian village stood;
All was silent as a dream,
Save the rushing of the stream
  And the blue-jay in the wood.

In his war-paint and his beads,
Like a bison among the reeds,
  In ambush the Sitting Bull
Lay with three thousand braves
Crouched in the clefts and caves,
  Savage, unmerciful!

Into the fatal snare
The White Chief with yellow hair
  And his three hundred men
Dashed headlong, sword in hand;
But of that gallant band
  Not one returned again.

The sudden darkness of death
Overwhelmed them like the breath
  And smoke of a furnace fire:
By the river's bank, and between
The rocks of the ravine,
  They lay in their bloody attire.

But the foemen fled in the night,
And Rain-in-the-Face, in his flight
  Uplifted high in air
As a ghastly trophy, bore
The brave heart, that beat no more,
  Of the White Chief with yellow
    hair.

Whose was the right and the wrong?
Sing it, O funeral song,
  With a voice that is full of tears,
And say that our broken faith
Wrought all this ruin and scathe,
  In the Year of a Hundred Years.

TO THE RIVER YVETTE.

O LOVELY river of Yvette!
  O darling river! like a bride,
Some dimpled, bashful, fair Lisette,
  Thou goest to wed the Orge's
    tide.

Maincourt, and lordly Dampierre,
  See and salute thee on thy way,
And, with a blessing and a prayer,
  Ring the sweet bells of St. Forget.

The valley of Chevreuse in vain
  Would hold thee in its fond em-
    brace;
Thou glidest from its arms again
  And hurriest on with swifter pace.

Thou wilt not stay; with restless
    feet
  Pursuing still thine onward flight,
Thou goest as one in haste to meet
  Her sole desire, her heart's de-
    light.

O lovely river of Yvette !
  O darling stream ! on balanced
    wings
The wood-birds sang the chanson-
  nette
    That here a wandering poet sings.

THE EMPEROR'S GLOVE.

'Combien faudrait-il de peaux d'Espagne
pour faire un gant de cette grandeur?' A play
upon the words *gant*, a glove, and *Gand*, the
French for Ghent.

ON St. Bavon's tower, commanding
  Half of Flanders, his domain,
Charles the Emperor once was
    standing,
While beneath him on the landing
  Stood Duke Alva and his train.

Like a print in books of fables,
  Or a model made for show,
With its pointed roofs and gables,
Dormer windows, scrolls and la-
  bels,
    Lay the city far below.

Through its squares and streets
    and alleys
Poured the populace of Ghent ;
As a routed army rallies,
Or as rivers run through valleys,
  Hurrying to their homes they
    went.

'Nest of Lutheran misbelievers ! '
  Cried Duke Alva as he gazed ;
' Haunt of traitors and deceivers,
Stronghold of insurgent weavers,
  Let it to the ground be razed ! '

On the Emperor's cap the feather
  Nods, as laughing he replies :
'How many skins of Spanish
    leather,
Think you, would, if stitched to-
  gether,
    Make a glove of such a size ?'

A BALLAD OF THE FRENCH FLEET.

OCTOBER, 1746.

MR. THOMAS PRINCE *loquitur*.

A FLEET with flags arrayed
  Sailed from the port of Brest,
And the Admiral's ship displayed
  The signal : ' Steer southwest.'
For this Admiral D'Anville
  Had sworn by cross and crown
To ravage with fire and steel
  Our helpless Boston Town.

There were rumours in the street,
  In the houses there was fear
Of the coming of the fleet,
  And the danger hovering near.
And while from mouth to mouth
  Spread the tidings of dismay,
I stood in the Old South,
  Saying humbly : ' Let us pray !

' O Lord ! we would not advise ;
  But if in thy Providence
A tempest should arise
  To drive the French Fleet hence,
And scatter it far and wide,
  Or sink it in the sea,
We should be satisfied,
  And thine the glory be.'

This was the prayer I made,
  For my soul was all on flame,
And even as I prayed
  The answering tempest came ;
It came with a mighty power,
  Shaking the windows and walls,
And tolling the bell in the tower,
  As it tolls at funerals.

The lightning suddenly
  Unsheathed its flaming sword,
And I cried : ' Stand still, and see
  The salvation of the Lord ! '
The heavens were black with cloud,
  The sea was white with hail,
And ever more fierce and loud
  Blew the October gale.

The fleet it overtook,
  And the broad sails in the van
Like the tents of Cushan shook,
  Or the curtains of Midian.
Down on the reeling decks
  Crashed the o'erwhelming seas ;
Ah, never were there wrecks
  So pitiful as these !

Like a potter's vessel broke
  The great ships of the line ;
They were carried away as a
    smoke,
  Or sank like lead in the brine.
O Lord ! before thy path
  They vanished and ceased to be,
When thou didst walk in wrath
  With thine horses through the
    sea !

—◆—

THE LEAP OF ROUSHAN BEG.

MOUNTED on Kyrat strong and
    fleet,
His chestnut steed with four white
    feet,
  Roushan Beg, called Kurroglou,
Son of the road and bandit chief,
Seeking refuge and relief,
  Up the mountain pathway flew.

Such was Kyrat's wondrous speed,
Never yet could any steed
  Reach the dust-cloud in his
    course.
More than maiden, more than wife,
More than gold and next to life
  Roushan the Robber loved his
    horse.

In the land that lies beyond
Erzeroum and Trebizond,
  Garden-girt his fortress stood ;
Plundered khan, or caravan
Journeying north from Koordistan,
  Gave him wealth and wine and
    food.

Seven hundred and fourscore
Men at arms his livery wore,
  Did his bidding night and day.
Now, through regions all unknown,
He was wandering, lost, alone,
  Seeking without guide his way.

Suddenly the pathway ends,
Sheer the precipice descends,
  Loud the torrent roars unseen ;
Thirty feet from side to side
Yawns the chasm; on air must
    ride
  He who crosses this ravine.

Following close in his pursuit,
At the precipice's foot,
  Reyhan the Arab of Orfah
Halted with his hundred men,
Shouting upward from the glen,
  'La Illáh illa Alláh !'

Gently Roushan Beg caressed
Kyrat's forehead, neck, and breast ;
  Kissed him upon both his eyes ;
Sang to him in his wild way,
As upon the topmost spray
  Sings a bird before it flies.

' O my Kyrat, O my steed,
Round and slender as a reed,
  Carry me this peril through !
Satin housings shall be thine,
Shoes of gold, O Kyrat mine,
  O thou soul of Kurroglou !

' Soft thy skin as silken skein,
Soft as woman's hair thy mane,
  Tender are thine eyes and true;
All thy hoofs like ivory shine,
Polished bright ; O, life of mine,
  Leap, and rescue Kurroglou ! '

Kyrat, then, the strong and fleet,
Drew together his four white feet,
  Paused a moment on the verge,
Measured with his eye the space,
And into the air's embrace
  Leaped as leaps the ocean surge.

As the ocean surge o'er sand
Bears a swimmer safe to land,
  Kyrat safe his rider bore;
Rattling down the deep abyss
Fragments of the precipice
  Rolled like pebbles on a shore.

Roushan's tasselled cap of red
Trembled not upon his head,
  Careless sat he and upright;
Neither hand nor bridle shook,
Nor his head he turned to look,
  As he galloped out of sight.

Flash of harness in the air,
Seen a moment like the glare
  Of a sword drawn from its sheath;
Thus the phantom horseman
    passed,
And the shadow that he cast
  Leaped the cataract underneath.

Reyhan the Arab held his breath
While this vision of life and death
  Passed above him. 'Allahu!'
Cried he. 'In all Koordistan
Lives there not so brave a man
  As this Robber Kurroglou!'

HAROUN AL RASCHID.

ONE day, Haroun Al Raschid read
A book wherein the poet said :—

'Where are the kings, and where
  the rest
Of those who once the world possessed?

'They're gone with all their pomp
  and show,
They're gone the way that thou
  shalt go.

'O thou who choosest for thy share
The world, and what the world
  calls fair,

'Take all that it can give or lend,
But know that death is at the end!'

Haroun Al Raschid bowed his head:
Tears fell upon the page he read.

KING TRISANKU.

VISWAMITRA the Magician,
  By his spells and incantations,
Up to Indra's realms elysian
  Raised Trisanku, king of nations.

Indra and the gods offended
  Hurled him downward, and de-
    scending
In the air he hung suspended,
  With these equal powers con-
    tending.

Thus by aspirations lifted,
  By misgivings downward driven,
Human hearts are tossed and
    drifted
  Midway between earth and
    heaven.

A WRAITH IN THE MIST.

'Sir, I should build me a fortification, if
I came to live here.'—BOSWELL'S *Johnson*.

ON the green little isle of Inch-
  kenneth,
  Who is it that walks by the shore,
So gay with his Highland blue
  bonnet,
  So brave with his targe and
    claymore?

His form is the form of a giant,
  But his face wears an aspect of
    pain;
Can this be the Laird of Inch-
  kenneth?
  Can this be Sir Allan McLean?

Ah, no! It is only the Rambler,
  The Idler, who lives in Bolt
    Court,
And who says, were he Laird of
  Inchkenneth,
  He would wall himself round
    with a fort.

THE THREE KINGS.

Three Kings came riding from far
 away,
 Melchior and Gaspar and Baltasar ;
Three Wise Men out of the East
 were they,
And they travelled by night and
 they slept by day,
 For their guide was a beautiful,
  wonderful star.

The star was so beautiful, large,
 and clear,
 That all the other stars of the sky
Became a white mist in the atmosphere,
And by this they knew that the
 coming was near
 Of the Prince foretold in the
  prophecy.

Three caskets they bore on their
 saddle-bows,
 Three caskets of gold with golden
  keys ;
Their robes were of crimson silk
 with rows
Of bells and pomegranates and
 furbelows,
 Their turbans like blossoming
  almond-trees.

And so the Three Kings rode into
 the West,
 Through the dusk of night, over
  hill and dell,
And sometimes they nodded with
 beard on breast,
And sometimes talked, as they
 paused to rest,
 With the people they met at some
  wayside well.

'Of the child that is born,' said
 Baltasar,
 'Good people, I pray you, tell us
 the news ;

For we in the East have seen his
 star,
And have ridden fast, and have
 ridden far,
 To find and worship the King of
  the Jews.'

And the people answered, 'You
 ask in vain ;
 We know of no king but Herod
  the Great !'
They thought the Wise Men were
 men insane,
As they spurred their horses across
 the plain,
 Like riders in haste, and who
  cannot wait.

And when they came to Jerusalem,
 Herod the Great, who had heard
  this thing,
Sent for the Wise Men and questioned them ;
And said, 'Go down unto Bethlehem,
 And bring me tidings of this new
  king.'

So they rode away ; and the star
 stood still,
 The only one in the gray of
  morn ;
Yes, it stopped, it stood still of its
 own free will,
Right over Bethlehem on the hill,
 The city of David where Christ
  was born.

And the Three Kings rode through
 the gate and the guard,
 Through the silent street, till
  their horses turned
And neighed as they entered the
 great inn-yard ;
But the windows were closed, and
 the doors were barred,
 And only a light in the stable
  burned.

And cradled there in the scented hay,
   In the air made sweet by the breath of kine,
The little child in the manger lay,
The child, that would be king one day
   Of a kingdom not human but divine.

His mother Mary of Nazareth
   Sat watching beside his place of rest,
Watching the even flow of his breath,
For the joy of life and the terror of death
   Were mingled together in her breast.

They laid their offerings at his feet:
   The gold was their tribute to a King,
The frankincense, with its odour sweet,
Was for the Priest, the Paraclete,
   The myrrh for the body's burying.

And the mother wondered and bowed her head,
   And sat as still as a statue of stone;
Her heart was troubled yet comforted,
Remembering what the Angel had said
   Of an endless reign and of David's throne.

Then the Kings rode out of the city gate,
   With a clatter of hoofs in proud array;
But they went not back to Herod the Great,
For they knew his malice and feared his hate,
   And returned to their homes by another way.

SONG.

STAY, stay at home, my heart, and rest;
Home-keeping hearts are happiest,
For those that wander they know not where
Are full of trouble and full of care;
   To stay at home is best.

Weary and homesick and distressed,
They wander east, they wander west,
And are baffled and beaten and blown about
By the winds of the wilderness of doubt;
   To stay at home is best.

Then stay at home, my heart, and rest;
The bird is safest in its nest;
O'er all that flutter their wings and fly
A hawk is hovering in the sky;
   To stay at home is best.

———

THE WHITE CZAR.

The White Czar is Peter the Great. Batyushka, *Father dear*, and Gosudar, *Sovereign*, are titles the Russian people are fond of giving to the Czar in their popular songs.

DOST thou see on the rampart's height
That wreath of mist, in the light
Of the midnight moon? O, hist!
It is not a wreath of mist;
It is the Czar, the White Czar,
   Batyushka! Gosudar!

He has heard, among the dead,
The artillery roll o'erhead;
The drums and the tramp of feet
Of his soldiery in the street;
He is awake! the White Czar,
   Batyushka! Gosudar!

He has heard in the grave the cries
Of his people : ' Awake ! arise !'
He has rent the gold brocade
Whereof his shroud was made ;
He is risen ! the White Czar,
    Batyushka ! Gosudar !

From the Volga and the Don
He has led his armies on,
Over river and morass,
Over desert and mountain pass ;
The Czar, the Orthodox Czar,
    Batyushka ! Gosudar !

He looks from the mountain-chain
Toward the seas, that cleave in
    twain
The continents ; his hand
Points southward o'er the land
Of Roumili ! O Czar,
    Batyushka ! Gosudar !

And the words break from his lips:
'I am the builder of ships,
And my ships shall sail these seas
To the Pillars of Hercules !
I say it ; the White Czar,
    Batyushka ! Gosudar !

' The Bosphorus shall be free ;
It shall make room for me ;
And the gates of its water-streets
Be unbarred before my fleets.
I say it ; the White Czar,
    Batyushka ! Gosudar !

' And the Christian shall no more
Be crushed, as heretofore,
Beneath thine iron rule,
O Sultan of Istamboul !
I swear it ; I the Czar,
    Batyushka ! Gosudar !

DELIA.

SWEET as the tender fragrance that
    survives,
When martyred flowers breathe
    out their little lives,
Sweet as a song that once consoled
    our pain,
But never will be sung to us again,
Is thy remembrance. Now the
    hour of rest
Hath come to thee. Sleep, darling,
    it is best.

Tales of a Wayside Inn.

PART I.

PRELUDE.

THE WAYSIDE INN.

ONE Autumn night, in Sudbury town,
Across the meadows bare and brown,
The windows of the wayside inn
Gleamed red with firelight through the leaves
Of woodbine, hanging from the eaves
Their crimson curtains rent and thin.

As ancient is this hostelry
As any in the land may be,
Built in the old Colonial day,
When men lived in a grander way,
With ampler hospitality;
A kind of old Hobgoblin Hall,
Now somewhat fallen to decay,
With weather-stains upon the wall,
And stairways worn, and crazy doors,
And creaking and uneven floors,
And chimneys huge, and tiled and tall.
A region of repose it seems,
A place of slumber and of dreams,
Remote among the wooded hills!
For there no noisy railway speeds,
Its torch-race scattering smoke and gleeds;
But noon and night, the panting teams
Stop under the great oaks, that throw
Tangles of light and shade below,
On roofs and doors and window-sills.
Across the road the barns display
Their lines of stalls, their mows of hay;
Through the wide doors the breezes blow,
The wattled cocks strut to and fro,
And, half effaced by rain and shine,
The Red Horse prances on the sign.

Round this old-fashioned, quaint abode
Deep silence reigned, save when a gust
Went rushing down the country road,
And skeletons of leaves, and dust,
A moment quickened by its breath,
Shuddered and danced their dance of death,
And through the ancient oaks o'erhead
Mysterious voices moaned and fled.

But from the parlour of the inn
A pleasant murmur smote the ear,
Like water rushing through a weir;
Oft interrupted by the din
Of laughter and of loud applause,
And, in each intervening pause,
The music of a violin.
The firelight, shedding over all
The splendour of its ruddy glow,
Filled the whole parlour large and low;
It gleamed on wainscot and on wall,
It touched with more than wonted grace
Fair Princess Mary's pictured face;

344

It bronzed the rafters overhead,
On the old spinet's ivory keys
It played inaudible melodies,
It crowned the sombre clock with
    flame,
The hands, the hours, the maker's
    name,
And painted with a livelier red
The Landlord's coat-of-arms again;
And, flashing on the window-pane,
Emblazoned with its light and shade
The jovial rhymes, that still remain,
Writ near a century ago,
By the great Major Molineaux,
Whom Hawthorne has immortal
    made.

Before the blazing fire of wood
Erect the rapt musician stood;
And ever and anon he bent
His head upon his instrument,
And seemed to listen, till he caught
Confessions of its secret thought,—
The joy, the triumph, the lament,
The exultation and the pain;
Then, by the magic of his art,
He soothed the throbbings of its
    heart,
And lulled it into peace again.

Around the fireside at their ease
There sat a group of friends, en-
    tranced
With the delicious melodies;
Who from the far-off noisy town
Had to the wayside inn come
    down,
To rest beneath its old oak-trees.
The firelight on their faces glanced,
Their shadows on the wainscot
    danced,
And, though of different lands and
    speech,
Each had his tale to tell, and each
Was anxious to be pleased and
    please.
And while the sweet musician plays,
Let me in outline sketch them all,
Perchance uncouthly as the blaze

With its uncertain touch portrays
Their shadowy semblance on the
    wall.

But first the Landlord will I trace:
Grave in his aspect and attire;
A man of ancient pedigree,
A Justice of the Peace was he,
Known in all Sudbury as 'The
    Squire.'
Proud was he of his name and
    race,
Of old Sir William and Sir Hugh,
And in the parlour, full in view,
His coat-of-arms, well framed and
    glazed,
Upon the wall in colours blazed;
He beareth gules upon his shield,
A chevron argent in the field,
With three wolf's-heads, and for
    the crest
A Wyvern part-per-pale addressed
Upon a helmet barred; below
The scroll reads, 'By the name of
    Howe.'
And over this, no longer bright,
Though glimmering with a latent
    light,
Was hung the sword his grandsire
    bore
In the rebellious days of yore,
Down there at Concord in the fight.

A youth was there, of quiet ways,
A Student of old books and days,
To whom all tongues and lands
    were known,
And yet a lover of his own;
With many a social virtue graced,
And yet a friend of solitude;
A man of such a genial mood
The heart of all things he em-
    braced,
And yet of such fastidious taste,
He never found the best too good.
Books were his passion and delight,
And in his upper room at home
Stood many a rare and sumptuous
    tome,

In vellum bound, with gold bedight,
Great volumes garmented in white,
Recalling Florence, Pisa, Rome.
He loved the twilight that surrounds
The borderland of old romance;
Where glitter hauberk, helm, and
lance,
And banner waves, and trumpet
sounds,
And ladies ride with hawk on wrist,
And mighty warriors sweep along,
Magnified by the purple mist,
The dusk of centuries and of song.
The chronicles of Charlemagne,
Of Merlin and the Mort d'Arthure,
Mingled together in his brain
With tales of Flores and Blanche-
fleur,
Sir Ferumbras, Sir Eglamour,
Sir Launcelot, Sir Morgadour,
Sir Guy, Sir Bevis, Sir Gawain.

A young Sicilian, too, was there;
In sight of Etna born and bred,
Some breath of its volcanic air
Was glowing in his heart and brain,
And, being rebellious to his liege,
After Palermo's fatal siege,
Across the western seas he fled,
In good King Bomba's happy reign.
His face was like a summer night,
All flooded with a dusky light;
His hands were small; his teeth
shone white
As sea-shells, when he smiled or
spoke;
His sinews supple and strong as
oak;
Clean shaven was he as a priest
Who at the mass on Sunday sings,
Save that upon his upper lip
His beard, a good palm's length at
least,
Level and pointed at the tip,
Shot sideways, like a swallow's
wings.
The poets read he o'er and o'er,
And most of all the Immortal Four
Of Italy; and next to those,

The story-telling bard of prose,
Who wrote the joyous Tuscan
tales
Of the Decameron, that make
Fiesole's green hills and vales
Remembered for Boccaccio's sake.
Much too of music was his thought;
The melodies and measures fraught
With sunshine and the open air,
Of vineyards and the singing sea
Of his beloved Sicily;
And much it pleased him to peruse
The songs of the Sicilian muse,—
Bucolic songs by Meli sung
In the familiar peasant tongue,
That made men say, 'Behold!
once more
The pitying gods to earth restore
Theocritus of Syracuse!'

A Spanish Jew from Alicant
With aspect grand and grave was
there;
Vender of silks and fabrics rare,
And attar of rose from the Levant.
Like an old Patriarch he appeared,
Abraham or Isaac, or at least
Some later Prophet or High Priest;
With lustrous eyes, and olive skin,
And, wildly tossed from cheeks and
chin,
The tumbling cataract of his beard.
His garments breathed a spicy
scent
Of cinnamon and sandal blent,
Like the soft aromatic gales
That meet the mariner, who sails
Through the Moluccas, and the
seas
That wash the shores of Celebes.
All stories that recorded are
By Pierre Alphonse he knew by
heart,
And it was rumoured he could say
The Parables of Sandabar,
And all the Fables of Pilpay,—
Or if not all, the greater part!
Well versed was he in Hebrew
books,

346

Talmud and Targum, and the lore
Of Kabala; and evermore
There was a mystery in his looks;
His eyes seemed gazing far away,
As if in vision or in trance
He heard the solemn sackbut play,
And saw the Jewish maidens dance.

A Theologian, from the school
Of Cambridge on the Charles, was
    there;
Skilful alike with tongue and pen,
He preached to all men everywhere
The Gospel of the Golden Rule,
The New Commandment given to
    men,
Thinking the deed, and not the
    creed,
Would help us in our utmost need.
With reverent feet the earth he
    trod,
Nor banished nature from his plan,
But studied still with deep research
To build the Universal Church,
Lofty as is the love of God,
And ample as the wants of man.

A Poet, too, was there, whose verse
Was tender, musical, and terse;
The inspiration, the delight,
The gleam, the glory, the swift
    flight,
Of thoughts so sudden, that they
    seem
The revelations of a dream,
All these were his; but with them
    came
No envy of another's fame;
He did not find his sleep less sweet
For music in some neighbouring
    street,
Nor rustling hear in every breeze
The laurels of Miltiades.
Honour and blessings on his head
While living, good report when
    dead,
Who, not too eager for renown,
Accepts, but does not clutch, the
    crown!

Last the Musician, as he stood
Illumined by that fire of wood;
Fair-haired, blue-eyed, his aspect
    blithe,
His figure tall and straight and
    lithe,
And every feature of his face
Revealing his Norwegian race;
A radiance, streaming from within,
Around his eyes and forehead
    beamed,
The Angel with the violin,
Painted by Raphael, he seemed.
He lived in that ideal world
Whose language is not speech, but
    song;
Around him evermore the throng
Of elves and sprites their dances
    whirled;
The Strömkarl sang, the cataract
    hurled
Its headlong waters from the height;
And mingled in the wild delight
The scream of sea-birds in their
    flight,
The rumour of the forest trees,
The plunge of the implacable
    seas,
The tumult of the wind at night,
Voices of eld, like trumpets blow-
    ing,
Old ballads, and wild melodies
Through mist and darkness pour-
    ing forth,
Like Elivagar's river flowing
Out of the glaciers of the North.

The instrument on which he
    played
Was in Cremona's workshops made,
By a great master of the past,
Ere yet was lost the art divine;
Fashioned of maple and of pine,
That in Tyrolian forests vast
Had rocked and wrestled with the
    blast.
Exquisite was it in design,
Perfect in each minutest part,
A marvel of the lutist's art;

And in its hollow chamber, thus,
The maker from whose hands it
came
Had written his unrivalled name,—
'Antonius Stradivarius.'

And when he played, the at-
mosphere
Was filled with magic, and the ear
Caught echoes of that Harp of
Gold,
Whose music had so weird a
sound,
The hunted stag forgot to bound,
The leaping rivulet backward
rolled,
The birds came down from bush
and tree,
The dead came from beneath the
sea,
The maiden to the harper's knee !

The music ceased ; the applause
was loud,
The pleased musician smiled and
bowed ;
The wood-fire clapped its hands of
flame,
The shadows on the wainscot
stirred,
And from the harpsichord there
came
A ghostly murmur of acclaim,
A sound like that sent down at
night
By birds of passage in their flight,
From the remotest distance heard.

Then silence followed ; then began
A clamour for the Landlord's
tale,—
The story promised them of old,
They said, but always left un-
told ;
And he, although a bashful man,
And all his courage seemed to
fail,
Finding excuse of no avail,
Yielded ; and thus the story ran.

THE LANDLORD'S TALE.

PAUL REVERE'S RIDE.

LISTEN, my children, and you shall
hear
Of the midnight ride of Paul
Revere,
On the eighteenth of April, in
Seventy-five ;
Hardly a man is now alive
Who remembers that famous day
and year.

He said to his friend, 'If the British
march
By land or sea from the town to-
night,
Hang a lantern aloft in the belfry
arch
Of the North Church tower as a
signal light,—
One, if by land, and two, if by sea ;
And I on the opposite shore will be,
Ready to ride and spread the alarm
Through every Middlesex village
and farm,
For the country folk to be up and
to arm.'

Then he said, 'Good night !' and
with muffled oar
Silently rowed to the Charlestown
shore,
Just as the moon rose over the bay,
Where swinging wide at her moor-
ings lay
The Somerset, British man-of-war ;
A phantom ship, with each mast
and spar
Across the moon like a prison bar,
And a huge black hulk, that was
magnified
By its own reflection in the tide.

Meanwhile, his friend, through
alley and street,
Wanders and watches with eager
ears,

Till in the silence around him he
    hears
The muster of men at the barrack
    door,
The sound of arms, and the tramp
    of feet,
And the measured tread of the
    grenadiers,
Marching down to their boats on
    the shore.

Then he climbed the tower of the
    Old North Church,
By the wooden stairs, with stealthy
    tread,
To the belfry-chamber overhead,
And startled the pigeons from their
    perch
On the sombre rafters, that round
    him made
Masses and moving shapes of
    shade,—
By the trembling ladder, steep and
    tall,
To the highest window in the
    wall,
Where he paused to listen and look
    down
A moment on the roofs of the
    town,
And the moonlight flowing over
    all.

Beneath, in the churchyard, lay the
    dead,
In their night-encampment on the
    hill,
Wrapped in silence so deep and
    still
That he could hear, like a sentinel's
    tread,
The watchful night-wind, as it went
Creeping along from tent to tent,
And seeming to whisper, ' All is
    well ! '
A moment only he feels the spell
Of the place and the hour, and the
    secret dread
Of the lonely belfry and the dead ;

For suddenly all his thoughts are
    bent
On a shadowy something far away,
Where the river widens to meet the
    bay,—
A line of black that bends and
    floats
On the rising tide, like a bridge of
    boats.

Meanwhile, impatient to mount and
    ride,
Booted and spurred, with a heavy
    stride
On the opposite shore walked Paul
    Revere.
Now he patted his horse's side,
Now gazed at the landscape far
    and near,
Then, impetuous, stamped the
    earth,
And turned and tightened his
    saddle-girth ;
But mostly he watched with eager
    search
The belfry-tower of the Old North
    Church,
As it rose above the graves on the
    hill,
Lonely and spectral and sombre
    and still.
And lo ! as he looks, on the belfry's
    height
A glimmer, and then a gleam of
    light !
He springs to the saddle, the bridle
    he turns,
But lingers and gazes, till full on his
    sight
A second lamp in the belfry burns !

A hurry of hoofs in a village
    street,
A shape in the moonlight, a bulk
    in the dark,
And beneath, from the pebbles, in
    passing, a spark
Struck out by a steed flying fearless
    and fleet :

That was all! And yet, through
the gloom and the light,
The fate of a nation was riding that
night ;
And the spark struck out by that
steed, in his flight,
Kindled the land into flame with
its heat.

He has left the village and mounted
the steep,
And beneath him, tranquil and
broad and deep,
Is the Mystic, meeting the ocean
tides ;
And under the alders, that skirt its
edge,
Now soft on the sand, now loud on
the ledge,
Is heard the tramp of his steed as
he rides.

It was twelve by the village clock
When he crossed the bridge into
Medford town.
He heard the crowing of the cock,
And the barking of the farmer's
dog,
And felt the damp of the river fog,
That rises after the sun goes
down.

It was one by the village clock,
When he galloped into Lexington.
He saw the gilded weathercock
Swim in the moonlight as he
passed,
And the meeting-house windows,
blank and bare,
Gaze at him with a spectral glare,
As if they already stood aghast
At the bloody work they would
look upon.

It was two by the village clock,
When he came to the bridge in
Concord town.
He heard the bleating of the flock,
And the twitter of birds among the
trees,

And felt the breath of the morning
breeze
Blowing over the meadows brown.
And one was safe and asleep in his
bed
Who at the bridge would be first to
fall,
Who that day would be lying
dead,
Pierced by a British musket-ball.

You know the rest. In the books
you have read,
How the British Regulars fired and
fled,—
How the farmers gave them ball for
ball,
From behind each fence and farmyard wall,
Chasing the red-coats down the
lane,
Then crossing the fields to emerge
again
Under the trees at the turn of the
road,
And only pausing to fire and load.

So through the night rode Paul
Revere ;
And so through the night went his
cry of alarm
To every Middlesex village and
farm,—
A cry of defiance and not of fear,
A voice in the darkness, a knock
at the door,
And a word that shall echo for ever-
more !
For, borne on a night-wind of the
Past,
Through all our history, to the last,
In the hour of darkness and peril
and need,
The people will waken and listen
to hear
The hurrying hoof-beats of that
steed,
And the midnight message of Paul
Revere.

INTERLUDE.

THE Landlord ended thus his tale,
Then rising took down from its nail
The sword that hung there, dim
    with dust,
And cleaving to its sheath with rust,
And said, 'This sword was in the
    fight.'
The Poet seized it, and exclaimed,
'It is the sword of a good knight,
Though homespun was his coat-of-
    mail;
What matter if it be not named
Joyeuse, Colado, Durindale,
Excalibar, or Aroundight,
Or other name the books record?
Your ancestor, who bore this sword
As Colonel of the Volunteers,
Mounted upon his old gray mare,
Seen here and there and every-
    where,
To me a grander shape appears
Than old Sir William, or what not,
Clinking about in foreign lands
With iron gauntlets on his hands,
And on his head an iron pot!

All laughed; the Landlord's face
    grew red
As his escutcheon on the wall;
He could not comprehend at all
The drift of what the Poet said;
For those who had been longest
    dead
Were always greatest in his eyes;
And he was speechless with surprise
To see Sir William's plumed head
Brought to a level with the rest,
And made the subject of a jest.
And this perceiving, to appease
The Landlord's wrath, the others'
    fears,
The Student said, with careless
    ease,
'The ladies and the cavaliers,
The arms, the loves, the courtesies,
The deeds of high emprise, I sing!

Thus Ariosto says, in words
That have the stately stride and ring
Of armed knights and clashing
    swords.
Now listen to the tale I bring;
Listen! though not to me belong
The flowing draperies of his song,
The words that rouse, the voice that
    charms.
The Landlord's tale was one of
    arms,
Only a tale of love is mine,
Blending the human and divine,
A tale of the Decameron, told
In Palmieri's garden old,
By Fiametta, laurel-crowned,
While her companions lay around,
And heard the intermingled sound
Of airs that on their errands sped,
And wild birds gossiping overhead,
And lisp of leaves, and fountain's
    fall,
And her own voice more sweet than
    all,
Telling the tale, which, wanting
    these,
Perchance may lose its power to
    please.'

THE STUDENT'S TALE.

THE FALCON OF SER FEDERIGO.

ONE summer morning, when the
    sun was hot,
Weary with labour in his garden-
    plot,
On a rude bench beneath his cottage
    eaves,
Ser Federigo sat among the leaves
Of a huge vine, that, with its arms
    outspread,
Hung its delicious clusters over-
    head.
Below him, through the lovely
    valley flowed
The river Arno, like a winding road,

And from its banks were lifted high
  in air
The spires and roofs of Florence
  called the Fair ;
To him a marble tomb, that rose
  above
His wasted fortunes and his buried
  love.
For there, in banquet and in tournament,
His wealth had lavished been, his
  substance spent,
To woo and lose, since ill his
  wooing sped,
Monna Giovanna, who his rival
  wed,
Yet ever in his fancy reigned supreme,
The ideal woman of a young man's
  dream.

Then he withdrew, in poverty and
  pain,
To this small farm, the last of his
  domain,
His only comfort and his only care
To prune his vines, and plant the
  fig and pear ;
His only forester and only guest
His falcon, faithful to him, when
  the rest,
Whose willing hands had found so
  light of yore
The brazen knocker of his palace
  door,
Had now no strength to lift the
  wooden latch,
That entrance gave beneath a roof
  of thatch.
Companion of his solitary ways,
Purveyor of his feasts on holidays,
On him this melancholy man be-
  stowed
The love with which his nature
  overflowed.

And so the empty-handed years
  went round,

Vacant, though voiceful with prophetic sound,
And so, that summer morn, he sat
  and mused
With folded, patient hands, as he
  was used,
And dreamily before his half-closed
  sight
Floated the vision of his lost
  delight.
Beside him motionless the drowsy
  bird
Dreamed of the chase, and in his
  slumbering heard
The sudden, scythe-like sweep of
  wings, that dare
The headlong plunge thro' eddying
  gulfs of air,
Then, starting broad awake upon
  his perch,
Tinkled his bells, like mass-bells in
  a church,
And, looking at his master, seemed
  to say,
' Ser Federigo, shall we hunt to-
  day ? '

Ser Federigo thought not of the
  chase ;
The tender vision of her lovely
  face,
I will not say he seems to see, he
  sees
In the leaf-shadows of the trellises,
Herself, yet not herself ; a lovely
  child
With flowing tresses, and eyes wide
  and wild,
Coming undaunted up the garden
  walk,
And looking not at him, but at the
  hawk.
' Beautiful falcon ! ' said he, ' would
  that I
Might hold thee on my wrist, or see
  thee fly ! '
The voice was hers, and made
  strange echoes start

352

Through all the haunted chambers
    of his heart,
As an Æolian harp through gusty
    doors
Of some old ruin its wild music
    pours.

' Who is thy mother, my fair boy?'
    he said,
His hand laid softly on that shining
    head.
' Monna Giovanna. Will you let
    me stay
A little while, and with your falcon
    play?
We live there, just beyond your
    garden wall,
In the great house behind the
    poplars tall.'

So he spake on; and Federigo
    heard
As from afar each softly uttered
    word,
And drifted onward through the
    golden gleams
And shadows of the misty sea of
    dreams,
As mariners becalmed through
    vapours drift,
And feel the sea beneath them
    sink and lift,
And hear far off the mournful
    breakers roar,
And voices calling faintly from the
    shore!
Then, waking from his pleasant
    reveries,
He took the little boy upon his
    knees,
And told him stories of his gallant
    bird,
Till in their friendship he became a
    third.

Monna Giovanna, widowed in her
    prime,
Had come with friends to pass the
    summer time

In her grand villa, half-way up the
    hill,
O'erlooking Florence, but retired
    and still;
With iron gates, that opened
    through long lines
Of sacred ilex and centennial pines,
And terraced gardens, and broad
    steps of stone,
And sylvan deities, with moss o'er-
    grown,
And fountains palpitating in the
    heat,
And all Val d'Arno stretched be-
    neath its feet.

Here in seclusion, as a widow may,
The lovely lady whiled the hours
    away,
Pacing in sable robes the statued
    hall,
Herself the stateliest statue among
    all,
And seeing more and more, with
    secret joy,
Her husband risen and living in
    her boy,
Till the lost sense of life returned
    again,
Not as delight, but as relief from
    pain.
Meanwhile the boy, rejoicing in his
    strength,
Stormed down the terraces from
    length to length;
The screaming peacock chased in
    hot pursuit,
And climbed the garden trellises
    for fruit.
But his chief pastime was to watch
    the flight
Of a gerfalcon, soaring into sight,
Beyond the trees that fringed the
    garden wall,
Then downward stooping at some
    distant call;
And as he gazed full often wondered
    he
Who might the master of the falcon
    be,

Until that happy morning, when
   he found
Master and falcon in the cottage
   ground.

And now a shadow and a terror fell
On the great house, as if a passing-
   bell
Tolled from the tower, and filled
   each spacious room
With secret awe, and preternatural
   gloom ;
The petted boy grew ill, and day
   by day
Pined with mysterious malady
   away.
The mother's heart would not be
   comforted ;
Her darling seemed to her already
   dead,
And often, sitting by the sufferer's
   side,
'What can I do to comfort thee?'
   she cried.
At first the silent lips made no reply,
But, moved at length by her im-
   portunate cry,
'Give me,' he answered, with
   imploring tone,
'Ser Federigo's falcon for my own !'

No answer could the astonished
   mother make ;
How could she ask, e'en for her
   darling's sake,
Such favour at a luckless lover's
   hand,
Well knowing that to ask was to
   command ?
Well knowing, what all falconers
   confessed,
In all the land that falcon was the
   best,
The master's pride and passion
   and delight,
And the sole pursuivant of this
   poor knight.
But yet, for her child's sake, she
   could no less

Than give assent, to soothe his
   restlessness,
So promised, and then promising
   to keep
Her promise sacred, saw him fall
   asleep.

The morrow was a bright September morn ;
The earth was beautiful as if new-
   born ;
There was that nameless splendour
   everywhere,
That wild exhilaration in the air,
Which makes the passers in the
   city street
Congratulate each other as they
   meet.
Two lovely ladies, clothed in cloak
   and hood,
Passed through the garden gate
   into the wood,
Under the lustrous leaves, and
   through the sheen
Of dewy sunshine showering down
   between.

The one, close-hooded, had the
   attractive grace
Which sorrow sometimes lends a
   woman's face ;
Her dark eyes moistened with the
   mists that roll
From the gulf-stream of passion in
   the soul ;
The other with her hood thrown
   back, her hair
Making a golden glory in the air,
Her cheeks suffused with an auroral
   blush,
Her young heart singing louder
   than the thrush.
So walked, that morn, through
   mingled light and shade,
Each by the other's presence
   lovelier made,
Monna Giovanna and her bosom
   friend,
Intent upon their errand and its end.

They found Ser Federigo at his toil,
Like banished Adam, delving in the soil;
And when he looked and these fair women spied,
The garden suddenly was glorified;
His long-lost Eden was restored again,
And the strange river winding through the plain
No longer was the Arno to his eyes,
But the Euphrates watering Paradise!

Monna Giovanna raised her stately head,
And with fair words of salutation said:
'Ser Federigo, we come here as friends,
Hoping in this to make some poor amends
For past unkindness. I who ne'er before
Would even cross the threshold of your door,
I who in happier days such pride maintained,
Refused your banquets, and your gifts disdained,
This morning come, a self-invited guest,
To put your generous nature to the test,
And breakfast with you under your own vine.'
To which he answered: 'Poor desert of mine,
Not your unkindness call it, for if aught
Is good in me of feeling or of thought,
From you it comes, and this last grace outweighs
All sorrows, all regrets of other days.'

And after further compliment and talk,
Among the asters in the garden walk
He left his guests; and to his cottage turned,
And as he entered for a moment yearned
For the lost splendours of the days of old,
The ruby glass, the silver and the gold,
And felt how piercing is the sting of pride,
By want embittered and intensified.
He looked about him for some means or way
To keep this unexpected holiday;
Searched every cupboard, and then searched again,
Summoned the maid, who came, but came in vain;
'The Signor did not hunt to-day,' she said,
'There's nothing in the house but wine and bread.'

Then suddenly the drowsy falcon shook
His little bells, with that sagacious look,
Which said, as plain as language to the ear,
'If anything is wanting, I am here!'
Yes, everything is wanting, gallant bird!
The master seized thee without further word.
Like thine own lure, he whirled thee round; ah me!
The pomp and flutter of brave falconry,
The bells, the jesses, the bright scarlet hood,
The flight and the pursuit o'er field and wood,
All these for evermore are ended now;
No longer victor, but the victim thou!

355

Then on the board a snow-white
cloth he spread,
Laid on its wooden dish the loaf of
bread,
Brought purple grapes with autumn
sunshine hot,
The fragrant peach, the juicy ber-
gamot;
Then in the midst a flask of wine
he placed,
And with autumnal flowers the
banquet graced.
Ser Federigo, would not these suffice
Without thy falcon stuffed with
cloves and spice?

When all was ready, and the courtly
dame
With her companion to the cottage
came,
Upon Ser Federigo's brain there
fell
The wild enchantment of a magic
spell!
The room they entered, mean and
low and small,
Was changed into a sumptuous
banquet-hall,
With fanfares by aerial trumpets
blown;
The rustic chair she sat on was a
throne;
He ate celestial food, and a divine
Flavour was given to his country
wine,
And the poor falcon, fragrant with
his spice,
A peacock was, or bird of paradise!

When the repast was ended, they
arose
And passed again into the garden-
close.
Then said the lady, 'Far too well
I know,
Remembering still the days of long
ago,

Though you betray it not, with
what surprise
You see me here in this familiar
wise.
You have no children, and you cannot guess
What anguish, what unspeakable
distress
A mother feels, whose child is lying
ill,
Nor how her heart anticipates his
will.
And yet for this, you see me lay
aside
All womanly reserve and check of
pride,
And ask the thing most precious
in your sight,
Your falcon, your sole comfort and
delight,
Which if you find it in your heart
to give,
My poor, unhappy boy perchance
may live.'

Ser Federigo listens, and replies,
With tears of love and pity in his
eyes:
'Alas, dear lady! there can be no
task
So sweet to me as giving when you
ask.
One little hour ago, if I had
known
This wish of yours, it would have
been my own.
But thinking in what manner I
could best
Do honour to the presence of my
guest,
I deemed that nothing worthier
could be
Than what most dear and precious
was to me,
And so my gallant falcon breathed
his last
To furnish forth this morning our
repast.'

In mute contrition, mingled with
    dismay,
The gentle lady turned her eyes
    away,
Grieving that he such sacrifice
    should make,
And kill his falcon for a woman's
    sake,
Yet feeling in her heart a woman's
    pride,
That nothing she could ask for was
    denied;
Then took her leave, and passed
    out at the gate
With footstep slow and soul dis-
    consolate.

Three days went by, and lo! a
    passing bell
Tolled from the little chapel in the
    dell;
Ten strokes Ser Federigo heard,
    and said,
Breathing a prayer, 'Alas! her child
    is dead!'
Three months went by; and lo! a
    merrier chime
Rang from the chapel bells at
    Christmas time;
The cottage was deserted, and no
    more
Ser Federigo sat beside its door,
But now, with servitors to do his will,
In the grand villa, half-way up the
    hill,
Sat at the Christmas feast, and at
    his side
Monna Giovanna, his beloved bride,
Never so beautiful, so kind, so fair,
Enthroned once more in the old
    rustic chair,
High-perched upon the back of
    which there stood
The image of a falcon carved in
    wood,
And underneath the inscription,
    with a date,
'All things come round to him who
    will but wait.'

INTERLUDE.

SOON as the story reached its end,
One, over eager to commend,
Crowned it with injudicious praise;
And then the voice of blame found
    vent,
And fanned the embers of dissent
Into a somewhat lively blaze.

The Theologian shook his head;
'These old Italian tales,' he said,
'From the much-praised Decame-
    ron down
Through all the rabble of the rest,
Are either trifling, dull, or lewd;
The gossip of a neighbourhood
In some remote provincial town,
A scandalous chronicle at best!
They seem to me a stagnant fen,
Grown rank with rushes and with
    reeds,
Where a white lily, now and then,
Blooms in the midst of noxious
    weeds
And deadly nightshade on its
    banks.'

To this the Student straight replied,
'For the white lily, many thanks!
One should not say, with too much
    pride,
Fountain I will not drink of thee!
Nor were it grateful to forget,
That from these reservoirs and tanks
Even imperial Shakespeare drew
His Moor of Venice, and the Jew,
And Romeo and Juliet,
And many a famous comedy.'

Then a long pause; till some one
    said,
'An Angel is flying overhead!'
At these words spake the Spanish
    Jew,
And murmured with an inward
    breath:
'God grant, if what you say be true,
It may not be the Angel of Death!'

And then another pause ; and then,
Stroking his beard, he said again :
'This brings back to my memory
A story in the Talmud told,
That book of gems, that book of gold,
Of wonders many and manifold,
A tale that often comes to me,
And fills my heart, and haunts my brain,
And never wearies nor grows old.'

THE SPANISH JEW'S TALE.

THE LEGEND OF RABBI BEN LEVI.

RABBI Ben Levi, on the Sabbath, read
A volume of the Law, in which it said,
'No man shall look upon my face and live.'
And as he read, he prayed that God would give
His faithful servant grace with mortal eye
To look upon His face and yet not die.

Then fell a sudden shadow on the page,
And, lifting up his eyes, grown dim with age,
He saw the Angel of Death before him stand,
Holding a naked sword in his right hand.

Rabbi Ben Levi was a righteous man,
Yet through his veins a chill of terror ran.
With trembling voice he said, 'What wilt thou here ?'
The Angel answered, 'Lo ! the time draws near

When thou must die ; yet first, by God's decree,
Whate'er thou askest shall be granted thee.'
Replied the Rabbi, 'Let these living eyes
First look upon my place in Paradise.'

Then said the Angel, 'Come with me and look.'
Rabbi Ben Levi closed the sacred book,
And rising, and uplifting his gray head,
'Give me thy sword,' he to the Angel said,
'Lest thou shouldst fall upon me by the way.'
The Angel smiled and hastened to obey,
Then led him forth to the Celestial Town,
And set him on the wall, whence, gazing down,
Rabbi Ben Levi, with his living eyes,
Might look upon his place in Paradise.

Then straight into the city of the Lord
The Rabbi leaped with the Death-Angel's sword,
And through the streets there swept a sudden breath
Of something there unknown, which men call death.

Meanwhile the Angel stayed without, and cried,
'Come back !' To which the Rabbi's voice replied,
'No ! in the name of God, whom I adore,
I swear that hence I will depart no more !'

Then all the Angels cried, 'O Holy One,

See what the son of Levi here hath
    done !
The kingdom of Heaven he takes
    by violence,
And in Thy name refuses to go
    hence ! '
The Lord replied, ' My Angels, be
    not wroth ;
Did e'er the son of Levi break his
    oath ?
Let him remain ; for he with mor-
    tal eye
Shall look upon my face and yet
    not die.'

Beyond the outer wall the Angel
    of Death
Heard the great voice, and said,
    with panting breath,
' Give back the sword, and let me
    go my way.'
Whereat the Rabbi paused, and
    answered, ' Nay !
Anguish enough already hath it
    caused
Among the sons of men.' And
    while he paused
He heard the awful mandate of
    the Lord
Resounding through the air, ' Give
    back the sword ! '

The Rabbi bowed his head in silent
    prayer ;
Then said he to the dreadful Angel,
    ' Swear,
No human eye shall look on it
    again ;
But when thou takest away the
    souls of men,
Thyself unseen, and with an un-
    seen sword,
Thou wilt perform the bidding of
    the Lord.'

The Angel took the sword again,
    and swore,
And walks on earth unseen for ever-
    more.

INTERLUDE.

HE ended : and a kind of spell
Upon the silent listeners fell.
His solemn manner and his words
Had touched the deep, mysterious
    chords,
That vibrate in each human breast
Alike, but not alike confessed.
The spiritual world seemed near ;
And close above them, full of fear,
Its awful adumbration passed,
A luminous shadow, vague and
    vast.
They almost feared to look, lest
    there,
Embodied from the impalpable air,
They might behold the Angel stand,
Holding the sword in his right
    hand.

At last, but in a voice subdued,
Not to disturb their dreamy mood,
Said the Sicilian : ' While you
    spoke,
Telling your legend marvellous,
Suddenly in my memory woke
The thought of one, now gone from
    us,—
An old Abate, meek and mild,
My friend and teacher, when a
    child,
Who sometimes in those days of
    old
The legend of an Angel told,
Which ran, as I remember, thus.'

—◆—

THE SICILIAN'S TALE.

KING ROBERT OF SICILY.

ROBERT of Sicily, brother of Pope
    Urbane
And Valmond, Emperor of Alle-
    maine,
Apparelled in magnificent attire,
With retinue of many a knight
    and squire,

On St. John's eve, at vespers, proud-
ly sat
And heard the priests chant the
Magnificat.
And as he listened, o'er and o'er
again
Repeated, like a burden or refrain,
He caught the words, '*Deposuit
potentes
De sede, et exaltavit humiles*';
And slowly lifting up his kingly
head
He to a learned clerk beside him
said,
'What mean these words?' The
clerk made answer meet,
'He has put down the mighty
from their seat,
And has exalted them of low de-
gree.'
Thereat King Robert muttered
scornfully,
''Tis well that such seditious words
are sung
Only by priests and in the Latin
tongue;
For unto priests and people be it
known,
There is no power can push me
from my throne!'
And leaning back, he yawned and
fell asleep,
Lulled by the chant monotonous
and deep.

When he awoke, it was already
night;
The church was empty, and there
was no light,
Save where the lamps, that glimmered few and faint,
Lighted a little space before some
saint.
He started from his seat and gazed
around,
But saw no living thing and heard
no sound.
He groped towards the door, but it
was locked;

He cried aloud, and listened, and
then knocked,
And uttered awful threatenings
and complaints,
And imprecations upon men and
saints.
The sounds re-echoed from the
roof and walls
As if dead priests were laughing in
their stalls.

At length the sexton, hearing from
without
The tumult of the knocking and
the shout,
And thinking thieves were in the
house of prayer,
Came with his lantern, asking,
'Who is there?'
Half-choked with rage, King
Robert fiercely said,
'Open: 'tis I, the King! Art thou
afraid?'
The frightened sexton, muttering,
with a curse,
'This is some drunken vagabond,
or worse!'
Turned the great key and flung the
portal wide;
A man rushed by him at a single
stride,
Haggard, half-naked, without hat
or cloak,
Who neither turned, nor looked at
him, nor spoke,
But leaped into the blackness of
the night,
And vanished like a spectre from
his sight.

Robert of Sicily, brother of Pope
Urbane
And Valmond, Emperor of Alle-
maine,
Despoiled of his magnificent attire,
Bareheaded, breathless, and be-
sprent with mire,
With sense of wrong and outrage
desperate,

Strode on and thundered at the
  palace gate ;
Rushed through the courtyard,
  thrusting in his rage
To right and left each seneschal
  and page,
And hurried up the broad and
  sounding stair,
His white face ghastly in the
  torches' glare.
From hall to hall he passed with
  breathless speed ;
Voices and cries he heard, but did
  not heed,
Until at last he reached the ban-
  quet-room,
Blazing with light, and breathing
  with perfume.

There on the dais sat another
  king,
Wearing his robes, his crown, his
  signet-ring,
King Robert's self in features, form,
  and height,
But all transfigured with angelic
  light !
It was an Angel ; and his presence
  there
With a divine effulgence filled the
  air,
An exaltation, piercing the disguise,
Though none the hidden Angel
  recognize.

A moment speechless, motionless,
  amazed,
The throneless monarch on the
  Angel gazed,
Who met his look of anger and
  surprise
With the divine compassion of his
  eyes,
Then said, ' Who art thou ? and
  why com'st thou here ?'
To which King Robert answered,
  with a sneer,
' I am the King, and come to claim
  my own

From an impostor, who usurps my
  throne !'
And suddenly, at these audacious
  words,
Up sprang the angry guests, and
  drew their swords ;
The Angel answered, with unruffled
  brow,
' Nay, not the King, but the King's
  Jester, thou
Henceforth shall wear the bells and
  scalloped cape,
And for thy counsellor shalt lead
  an ape ;
Thou shalt obey my servants when
  they call,
And wait upon my henchmen in
  the hall !'

Deaf to King Robert's threats and
  cries and prayers,
They thrust him from the hall and
  down the stairs ;
A group of tittering pages ran
  before,
And as they opened wide the folding door,
His heart failed, for he heard, with
  strange alarms,
The boisterous laughter of the men-
  at-arms,
And all the vaulted chamber roar
  and ring
With the mock plaudits of ' Long
  live the King !'

Next morning, waking with the
  day's first beam,
He said within himself, ' It was a
  dream !'
But the straw rustled as he turned
  his head,
There were the cap and bells beside his bed,
Around him rose the bare, dis-
  coloured walls,
Close by, the steeds were champing
  in their stalls,

And in the corner, a revolting
shape,
Shivering and chattering sat the
wretched ape.
It was no dream; the world he
loved so much
Had turned to dust and ashes at
his touch!

Days came and went; and now
returned again
To Sicily the old Saturnian reign;
Under the Angel's governance
benign
The happy island danced with corn
and wine,
And deep within the mountain's
burning breast
Enceladus, the giant, was at rest.
Meanwhile King Robert yielded to
his fate,
Sullen and silent and disconsolate.
Dressed in the motley garb that
Jesters wear,
With look bewildered and a vacant
stare,
Close shaven above the ears, as
monks are shorn,
By courtiers mocked, by pages
laughed to scorn,
His only friend the ape, his only
food
What others left,—he still was un-
subdued.
And when the Angel met him on
his way,
And half in earnest, half in jest,
would say,
Sternly, though tenderly, that he
might feel
The velvet scabbard held a sword
of steel,
'Art thou the King?' the passion
of his woe
Burst from him in resistless over-
flow,
And, lifting high his forehead, he
would fling

The haughty answer back, 'I am,
I am the King!'

Almost three years were ended;
when there came
Ambassadors of great repute and
name
From Valmond, Emperor of Alle-
maine,
Unto King Robert, saying that
Pope Urbane
By letter summoned them forthwith
to come
On Holy Thursday to his city of
Rome.
The Angel with great joy received
his guests,
And gave them presents of em-
broidered vests,
And velvet mantles with rich er-
mine lined,
And rings and jewels of the rarest
kind.
Then he departed with them o'er
the sea
Into the lovely land of Italy,
Whose loveliness was more re-
splendent made
By the mere passing of that caval-
cade,
With plumes, and cloaks, and
housings, and the stir
Of jewelled bridle and of golden spur.

And lo! among the menials, in
mock state,
Upon a piebald steed, with sham-
bling gait,
His cloak of fox-tails flapping in
the wind,
The solemn ape demurely perched
behind,
King Robert rode, making huge
merriment
In all the country towns through
which they went.

The Pope received them with great
pomp and blare

362

Of bannered trumpets, on Saint
    Peter's square,
Giving his benediction and embrace,
Fervent, and full of apostolic grace.
While with congratulations and
    with prayers
He entertained the Angel unawares,
Robert, the Jester, bursting through
    the crowd,
Into their presence rushed, and
    cried aloud,
'I am the King! Look, and behold
    in me
Robert, your brother, King of
    Sicily!
This man, who wears my semblance
    to your eyes,
Is an impostor in a king's disguise.
Do you not know me? does no
    voice within
Answer my cry, and say we are
    akin?'
The Pope in silence, but with
    troubled mien,
Gazed at the Angel's countenance
    serene;
The Emperor, laughing, said, 'It
    is strange sport
To keep a madman for thy Fool at
    court!'
And the poor, baffled Jester in
    disgrace
Was hustled back among the popu-
    lace.

In solemn state the Holy Week
    went by,
And Easter Sunday gleamed upon
    the sky;
The presence of the Angel, with its
    light,
Before the sun rose, made the city
    bright,
And with new fervour filled the
    hearts of men,
Who felt that Christ indeed had
    risen again.
Even the Jester, on his bed of straw,

With haggard eyes the unwonted
    splendour saw;
He felt within a power unfelt before,
And, kneeling humbly on his
    chamber floor,
He heard the rushing garments of
    the Lord
Sweep through the silent air, as-
    cending heavenward.

And now the visit ending, and once
    more
Valmond returning to the Danube's
    shore,
Homeward the Angel journeyed,
    and again
The land was made resplendent
    with his train,
Flashing along the towns of Italy
Unto Salerno, and from thence by
    sea.
And when once more within Paler-
    mo's wall,
And, seated on the throne in his
    great hall,
He heard the Angelus from convent
    towers,
As if the better world conversed
    with ours,
He beckoned to King Robert to
    draw nigher,
And with a gesture bade the rest
    retire;
And when they were alone, the
    Angel said,
'Art thou the King?' Then, bow-
    ing down his head,
King Robert crossed both hands
    upon his breast,
And meekly answered him: 'Thou
    knowest best!
My sins as scarlet are; let me go
    hence,
And in some cloister's school of
    penitence,
Across those stones, that pave the
    way to heaven,
Walk barefoot, till my guilty soul
    be shriven!'

The Angel smiled, and from his
    radiant face
A holy light illumined all the place,
And through the open window, loud
    and clear,
They heard the monks chant in
    the chapel near,
Above the stir and tumult of the
    street :
'He has put down the mighty from
    their seat,
And has exalted them of low de-
    gree!'
And through the chant a second
    melody
Rose like the throbbing of a single
    string :
'I am an Angel, and thou art the
    King!'

King Robert, who was standing
    near the throne,
Lifted his eyes, and lo! he was
    alone !
But all apparelled as in days of old,
With ermined mantle and with cloth
    of gold ;
And when his courtiers came, they
    found him there
Kneeling upon the floor, absorbed
    in silent prayer.

INTERLUDE.

AND then the blue-eyed Norseman
    told
A Saga of the days of old.
'There is,' said he, 'a wondrous
    book
Of Legends in the old Norse tongue,
Of the dead kings of Norroway,—
Legends that once were told or
    sung
In many a smoky fireside nook
Of Iceland, in the ancient day,
By wandering Saga-man or Scald ;

Heimskringla is the volume called ;
And he who looks may find therein
The story that I now begin.'

And in each pause the story made
Upon his violin he played,
As an appropriate interlude,
Fragments of old Norwegian tunes
That bound in one the separate
    runes,
And held the mind in perfect mood,
Entwining and encircling all
The strange and antiquated rhymes
With melodies of olden times ;
As over some half-ruined wall,
Disjointed and about to fall,
Fresh woodbines climb and inter-
    lace,
And keep the loosened stones in
    place.

THE MUSICIAN'S TALE.

THE SAGA OF KING OLAF.

I.

THE CHALLENGE OF THOR.

I AM the God Thor,
I am the War God,
I am the Thunderer !
Here in my Northland,
My fastness and fortress,
Reign I for ever !

Here amid icebergs
Rule I the nations ;
This is my hammer,
Miölner the mighty ;
Giants and sorcerers
Cannot withstand it !

These are the gauntlets
Wherewith I wield it,
And hurl it afar off ;
This is my girdle ;
Whenever I brace it,
Strength is redoubled !

The light thou beholdest
Stream through the heavens,
  In flashes of crimson,
Is but my red beard
Blown by the night-wind,
  Affrighting the nations!

Jove is my brother;
  Mine eyes are the lightning;
The wheels of my chariot
  Roll in the thunder,
The blows of my hammer
  Ring in the earthquake!

Force rules the world still,
Has ruled it, shall rule it;
  Meekness is weakness,
Strength is triumphant,
Over the whole earth
  Still is it Thor's-Day!

Thou art a God too,
  O Galilean!
And thus single-handed
  Unto the combat,
Gauntlet or Gospel,
  Here I defy thee!

II.

KING OLAF'S RETURN.

AND King Olaf heard the cry,
Saw the red light in the sky,
  Laid his hand upon his sword,
As he leaned upon the railing,
And his ships went sailing, sailing
  Northward into Drontheim fiord.

There he stood as one who dreamed;
And the red light glanced and
    gleamed
  On the armour that he wore;
And he shouted, as the rifted
Streamers o'er him shook and
    shifted,
  'I accept thy challenge, Thor!'

To avenge his father slain,
And reconquer realm and reign,
  Came the youthful Olaf home,
Through the midnight sailing, sail-
    ing,
Listening to the wild wind's wailing,
  And the dashing of the foam.

To his thoughts the sacred name
Of his mother Astrid came,
  And the tale she oft had told
Of her flight by secret passes
Through the mountains and mo-
    rasses,
  To the home of Hakon old.

Then strange memories crowded
    back
Of Queen Gunhild's wrath and
    wrack,
  And a hurried flight by sea;
Of grim Vikings, and the rapture
Of the sea-fight, and the capture,
  And the life of slavery.

How a stranger watched his face
In the Esthonian market-place,
  Scanned his features one by one,
Saying, 'We should know each
    other;
I am Sigurd, Astrid's brother,
  Thou art Olaf, Astrid's son!'

Then as Queen Allogia's page,
Old in honours, young in age,
  Chief of all her men-at-arms;
Till vague whispers, and mys-
    terious,
Reached King Valdemar, the im-
    perious,
  Filling him with strange alarms.

Then his cruisings o'er the seas,
Westward to the Hebrides,
  And to Scilly's rocky shore;
And the hermit's cavern dismal,
Christ's great name and rites bap-
    tismal
  In the ocean's rush and roar.

365

All these thoughts of love and
   strife
Glimmered through his lurid life,
   As the stars' intenser light
Through the red flames o'er him
   trailing,
As his ships went sailing, sailing,
   Northward in the summer night.

Trained for either camp or court,
Skilful in each manly sport,
   Young and beautiful and tall ;
Art of warfare, craft of chases,
Swimming, skating, snow-shoe
   races,
   Excellent alike in all.

When at sea, with all his rowers,
He along the bending oars
   Outside of his ship could run.
He the Smalsor Horn ascended,
And his shining shield suspended
   On its summit, like a sun.

On the ship-rails he could stand,
Wield his sword with either hand,
   And at once two javelins throw ;
At all feasts where ale was
   strongest
Sat the merry monarch longest,
   First to come and last to go.

Norway never yet had seen
One so beautiful of mien,
   One so royal in attire,
When in arms completely fur-
   nished,
Harness gold-inlaid and burnished,
   Mantle like a flame of fire.

Thus came Olaf to his own,
When upon the night-wind blown
   Passed that cry along the shore ;
And he answered, while the rifted
Streamers o'er him shook and
   shifted,
   ' I accept thy challenge, Thor ! '

III.
THORA OF RIMOL.

' THORA of Rimol ! hide me ! hide
   me !
Danger and shame and death be-
   tide me !
For Olaf the King is hunting me
   down
Through field and forest, through
   thorp and town ! '
   Thus cried Jarl Hakon
   To Thora, the fairest of women.

' Hakon Jarl ! for the love I bear
   thee
Neither shall shame nor death come
   near thee !
But the hiding-place wherein thou
   must lie
Is the cave underneath the swine
   in the sty.'
   Thus to Jarl Hakon
   Said Thora, the fairest of women.

So Hakon Jarl and his base thrall
   Karker
Crouched in the cave, than a dun-
   geon darker,
As Olaf came riding, with men in
   mail,
Through the forest roads into Or-
   kadale,
   Demanding Jarl Hakon
   Of Thora, the fairest of women.

' Rich and honoured shall be whoever
The head of Hakon Jarl shall dis-
   sever ! '
Hakon heard him, and Karker the
   slave,
Through the breathing-holes of the
   darksome cave.
   Alone in her chamber
   Wept Thora, the fairest of women.

Said Karker, the crafty, 'I will not
　　slay thee !
For all the king's gold I will never
　　betray thee !'
'Then why dost thou turn so pale,
　　O churl,
And then again black as the earth?'
　　said the Earl.
　　More pale and more faithful
　　Was Thora, the fairest of wo-
　　men.

From a dream in the night the
　　thrall started, saying,
'Round my neck a gold ring King
　　Olaf was laying !'
And Hakon answered, 'Beware of
　　the King !
He will lay round thy neck a blood-
　　red ring.'
　　At the ring on her finger
　　Gazed Thora, the fairest of wo-
　　men.

At daybreak slept Hakon, with
　　sorrows encumbered,
But screamed and drew up his feet
　　as he slumbered ;
The thrall in the darkness plunged
　　with his knife,
And the Earl awakened no more
　　in this life.
　　But wakeful and weeping
　　Sat Thora, the fairest of wo-
　　men.

At Nidarholm the priests are all
　　singing,
Two ghastly heads on the gibbet
　　are swinging ;
One is Jarl Hakon's and one is his
　　thrall's,
And the people are shouting from
　　windows and walls ;
　　While alone in her chamber
　　Swoons Thora, the fairest of wo-
　　men.

IV.

QUEEN SIGRID THE HAUGHTY.

QUEEN Sigrid the Haughty sat
　　proud and aloft
In her chamber, that looked over
　　meadow and croft.
　　Heart's dearest,
　　Why dost thou sorrow so?

The floor with tassels of fir was
　　besprent,
Filling the room with their fragrant
　　scent.

She heard the birds sing, she saw
　　the sun shine,
The air of summer was sweeter than
　　wine.

Like a sword without scabbard the
　　bright river lay
Between her own kingdom and
　　Norroway.

But Olaf the King had sued for her
　　hand,
The sword would be sheathed, the
　　river be spanned.

Her maidens were seated around
　　her knee,
Working bright figures in tapestry.

And one was singing the ancient
　　rune
Of Brynhilda's love and the wrath
　　of Gudrun.

And through it, and round it, and
　　over it all
Sounded incessant the waterfall.

The Queen in her hand held a ring
　　of gold,
From the door of Ladé's Temple old.

King Olaf had sent her this wedding
　　gift,
But her thoughts as arrows were
　　keen and swift.

367

She had given the ring to her gold-
    smiths twain,
Who smiled, as they handed it
    back again.

And Sigrid the Queen, in her
    haughty way,
Said, 'Why do you smile, my gold-
    smiths, say?'

And they answered: 'O Queen!
    if the truth must be told,
The ring is of copper, and not of
    gold!'

The lightning flashed o'er her fore-
    head and cheek,
She only murmured, she did not
    speak:

'If in his gifts he can faithless be,
There will be no gold in his love to
    me.'

A footstep was heard on the outer
    stair,
And in strode King Olaf with royal
    air.

He kissed the Queen's hand, and he
    whispered of love,
And swore to be true as the stars
    are above.

But she smiled with contempt as she
    answered: 'O King,
Will you swear it, as Odin once
    swore, on the ring?'

And the King: 'O speak not of
    Odin to me,
The wife of King Olaf a Christian
    must be.'

Looking straight at the King, with
    her level brows,
She said, 'I keep true to my faith
    and my vows.'

Then the face of King Olaf was
    darkened with gloom,
He rose in his anger and strode
    through the room.

'Why, then, should I care to have
    thee?' he said,—
'A faded old woman, a heathenish
    jade!'

His zeal was stronger than fear or
    love,
And he struck the Queen in the face
    with his glove.

Then forth from the chamber in
    anger he fled,
And the wooden stairway shook
    with his tread.

Queen Sigrid the Haughty said
    under her breath,
'This insult, King Olaf, shall be
    thy death!'
    Heart's dearest,
    Why dost thou sorrow so?

v.
THE SKERRY OF SHRIEKS.

Now from all King Olaf's farms
    His men-at-arms
Gathered on the Eve of Easter;
To his house at Angvalds-ness
    Fast they press,
Drinking with the royal feaster.

Loudly through the wide-flung door
    Came the roar
Of the sea upon the Skerry;
And its thunder loud and near
    Reached the ear,
Mingling with their voices merry.

'Hark!' said Olaf to his Scald,
    Halfred the Bald,
'Listen to that song, and learn it!
Half my kingdom would I give,
    As I live,
If by such songs you would earn it!

'For of all the runes and rhymes
    Of all times,
Best I like the ocean's dirges,
When the old harper heaves and
    rocks,
    His hoary locks
Flowing and flashing in the surges!'

Halfred answered : 'I am called
    The Unappalled!
Nothing hinders me or daunts me.
Hearken to me, then, O King,
    While I sing
The great Ocean Song that haunts
    me.'

'I will hear your song sublime
    Some other time,'
Says the drowsy monarch, yawning,
And retires ; each laughing guest
    Applauds the jest ;
Then they sleep till day is dawning.

Pacing up and down the yard,
    King Olaf's guard
Saw the sea-mist slowly creeping
O'er the sands, and up the hill,
    Gathering still
Round the house where they were
    sleeping.

It was not the fog he saw,
    Nor misty flaw,
That above the landscape brooded ;
It was Eyvind Kallda's crew
    Of warlocks blue
With their caps of darkness hooded!

Round and round the house they go,
    Weaving slow
Magic circles to encumber
And imprison in their ring
    Olaf the King,
As he helpless lies in slumber.

Then athwart the vapours dun
    The Easter sun
Streamed with one broad track of
    splendour !

In their real forms appeared
    The warlocks weird,
Awful as the Witch of Endor.

Blinded by the light that glared,
    They groped and stared
Round about with steps unsteady ;
From his window Olaf gazed,
    And, amazed,
'Who are these strange people ?'
    said he.

'Eyvind Kallda and his men !'
    Answered then
From the yard a sturdy farmer ;
While the men-at-arms apace
    Filled the place,
Busily buckling on their armour.

From the gates they sallied forth,
    South and north,
Scoured the island coast around
    them,
Seizing all the warlock band,
    Foot and hand
On the Skerry's rocks they bound
    them.

And at eve the King again
    Called his train,
And, with all the candles burning,
Silent sat and heard once more
    The sullen roar
Of the ocean tides returning.

Shrieks and cries of wild despair
    Filled the air,
Growing fainter as they listened ;
Then the bursting surge alone
    Sounded on ;—
Thus the sorcerers were christened!

'Sing, O Scald, your song sublime,
    Your ocean-rhyme,'
Cried King Olaf : 'it will cheer me !'
Said the Scald, with pallid cheeks,
    'The Skerry of Shrieks
Sings too loud for you to hear me !'

VI.

THE WRAITH OF ODIN.

THE guests were loud, the ale was
    strong,
King Olaf feasted late and long;
The hoary Scalds together sang;
O'erhead the smoky rafters rang.
    Dead rides Sir Morten of Fogel-
      sang.

The door swung wide, with creak
    and din;
A blast of cold night-air came in,
And on the threshold shivering
    stood
A one-eyed guest, with cloak and
    hood.
    Dead rides Sir Morten of Fogel-
      sang.

The King exclaimed, 'O graybeard
    pale!
Come warm thee with this cup of
    ale.'
The foaming draught the old man
    quaffed,
The noisy guests looked on and
    laughed.
    Dead rides Sir Morten of Fogel-
      sang.

Then spake the King: 'Be not
    afraid;
Sit here by me.' The guest obeyed,
And, seated at the table, told
Tales of the sea, and Sagas old.
    Dead rides Sir Morten of Fogel-
      sang.

And ever, when the tale was o'er,
The King demanded yet one
    more;
Till Sigurd the Bishop smiling
    said,
''Tis late, O King, and time for
    bed.'
    Dead rides Sir Morten of Fogel-
      sang.

The King retired; the stranger
    guest
Followed and entered with the rest;
The lights were out, the pages gone,
But still the garrulous guest spake
    on.
    Dead rides Sir Morten of Fogel-
      sang.

As one who from a volume reads,
He spake of heroes and their deeds,
Of lands and cities he had seen,
And stormy gulfs that tossed
    between.
    Dead rides Sir Morten of Fogel-
      sang.

Then from his lips in music rolled
The Havamal of Odin old,
With sounds mysterious as the roar
Of billows on a distant shore.
    Dead rides Sir Morten of Fogel-
      sang.

'Do we not learn from runes and
    rhymes
Made by the gods in elder times,
And do not still the great Scalds
    teach
That silence better is than speech?'
    Dead rides Sir Morten of Fogel-
      sang.

Smiling at this, the King replied,
'Thy lore is by thy tongue belied;
For never was I so enthralled
Either by Saga-man or Scald.'
    Dead rides Sir Morten of Fogel-
      sang.

The Bishop said, 'Late hours we
    keep!
Night wanes, O King! 'tis time
    for sleep!'
Then slept the King, and when he
    woke
The guest was gone, the morning
    broke.
    Dead rides Sir Morten of Fogel-
      sang.

They found the doors securely barred,
They found the watch-dog in the yard,
There was no footprint in the grass,
And none had seen the stranger pass.
  Dead rides Sir Morten of Fogelsang.

King Olaf crossed himself and said:
'I know that Odin the Great is dead;
Sure is the triumph of our Faith,
The one-eyed stranger was his wraith.'
  Dead rides Sir Morten of Fogelsang.

VII.

IRON-BEARD.

OLAF the King, one summer morn,
Blew a blast on his bugle-horn,
Sending his signal through the land of Drontheim.

And to the Hus-Ting held at Mere
Gathered the farmers far and near,
With their war weapons ready to confront him.

Ploughing under the morning star,
Old Iron-Beard in Yriar
Heard the summons, chuckling with a low laugh.

He wiped the sweat-drops from his brow,
Unharnessed his horses from the plough,
And clattering came on horseback to King Olaf.

He was the churliest of the churls;
Little he cared for king or earls;
Bitter as home-brewed ale were his foaming passions.

Hodden-gray was the garb he wore,
And by the Hammer of Thor he swore;
He hated the narrow town, and all its fashions.

But he loved the freedom of his farm,
His ale at night, by the fireside warm,
Gudrun his daughter, with her flaxen tresses.

He loved his horses and his herds,
The smell of the earth, and the song of birds,
His well-filled barns, his brook with its water-cresses.

Huge and cumbersome was his frame;
His beard, from which he took his name,
Frosty and fierce, like that of Hymer the Giant.

So at the Hus-Ting he appeared,
The farmer of Yriar, Iron-Beard,
On horseback, in an attitude defiant.

And to King Olaf he cried aloud,
Out of the middle of the crowd,
That tossed about him like a stormy ocean:

'Such sacrifices shalt thou bring;
To Odin and to Thor, O King,
As other kings have done in their devotion!'

King Olaf answered : 'I command
This land to be a Christian land ;
Here is my Bishop who the folk baptizes !

'But if you ask me to restore
Your sacrifices, stained with gore,
Then will I offer human sacrifices !

'Not slaves and peasants shall they be,
But men of note and high degree,
Such men as Orm of Lyra and Kar of Gryting !'

Then to their Temple strode he in,
And loud behind him heard the din
Of his men-at-arms and the peasants fiercely fighting.

There in the Temple, carved in wood,
The image of great Odin stood,
And other gods, with Thor supreme among them.

King Olaf smote them with the blade
Of his huge war-axe, gold-inlaid,
And downward shattered to the pavement flung them.

At the same moment rose without,
From the contending crowd, a shout,
A mingled sound of triumph and of wailing.

And there upon the trampled plain
The farmer Iron-Beard lay slain,
Midway between the assailed and the assailing.

King Olaf from the doorway spoke :
'Choose ye between two things, my folk,
To be baptized or given up to slaughter !'

And seeing their leader stark and dead,
The people with a murmur said,
'O King, baptize us with thy holy water.'

So all the Drontheim land became
A Christian land in name and fame,
In the old gods no more believing and trusting.

And as a blood-atonement, soon
King Olaf wed the fair Gudrun ;
And thus in peace ended the Drontheim Hus-Ting !

VIII.

GUDRUN.

ON King Olaf's bridal night
Shines the moon with tender light,
And across the chamber streams
Its tide of dreams.

At the fatal midnight hour,
When all evil things have power,
In the glimmer of the moon
Stands Gudrun.

Close against her heaving breast,
Something in her hand is pressed ;
Like an icicle, its sheen
Is cold and keen.

On the cairn are fixed her eyes
Where her murdered father lies,
And a voice remote and drear
She seems to hear.

What a bridal night is this !
Cold will be the dagger's kiss ;
Laden with the chill of death
Is its breath.

Like the drifting snow she sweeps
To the couch where Olaf sleeps;
Suddenly he wakes and stirs,
    His eyes meet hers.

'What is that,' King Olaf said,
'Gleams so bright above thy
    head?
Wherefore standest thou so white
    In pale moonlight?'

'''Tis the bodkin that I wear
When at night I bind my hair;
It woke me falling on the floor;
    'Tis nothing more.'

'Forests have ears, and fields have
    eyes;
Often treachery lurking lies
Underneath the fairest hair!
    Gudrun beware!'

Ere the earliest peep of morn
Blew King Olaf's bugle-horn;
And for ever sundered ride
    Bridegroom and bride!

IX.

THANGBRAND THE PRIEST.

SHORT of stature, large of limb,
Burly face and russet beard,
All the women stared at him,
    When in Iceland he appeared.
'Look!' they said,
    With nodding head,
'There goes Thangbrand, Olaf's
    Priest.'

All the prayers he knew by rote,
He could preach like Chrysos-
    tome,
From the Fathers he could quote,
He had even been at Rome.
    A learned clerk,
    A man of mark,
Was this Thangbrand, Olaf's Priest.

He was quarrelsome and loud,
    And impatient of control,
Boisterous in the market crowd,
    Boisterous at the wassail-bowl,
    Everywhere
    Would drink and swear,
Swaggering Thangbrand, Olaf's
    Priest.

In his house this malcontent
    Could the King no longer bear,
So to Iceland he was sent
    To convert the heathen there,
    And away
    One summer day
Sailed this Thangbrand, Olaf's
    Priest.

There in Iceland, o'er their books
    Pored the people day and
    night,
But he did not like their looks,
    Nor the songs they used to
    write.
    'All this rhyme
    Is waste of time!'
Grumbled Thangbrand, Olaf's
    Priest.

To the alehouse, where he sat,
    Came the Scalds and Saga-
    men;
Is it to be wondered at
    That they quarrelled now and
    then,
    When o'er his beer
    Began to leer
Drunken Thangbrand, Olaf's
    Priest?

All the folk in Altafiord
    Boasted of their island grand;
Saying in a single word,
    'Iceland is the finest land
    That the sun
    Doth shine upon!'
Loud laughed Thangbrand, Olaf's
    Priest.

And he answered : 'What's the use
Of this bragging up and down,
When three women and one goose
Make a market in your town !'
    Every Scald
    Satires scrawled
On poor Thangbrand, Olaf's Priest.

Something worse they did than
    that ;
    And what vexed him most of all
Was a figure in shovel hat,
    Drawn in charcoal on the wall ;
      With words that go
      Sprawling below,
'This is Thangbrand, Olaf's Priest.'

Hardly knowing what he did,
    Then he smote them might and
    main,
Thorvald Veile and Veterlid
    Lay there in the alehouse slain.
      ' To-day we are gold,
      To-morrow mould !'
Muttered Thangbrand, Olaf's
    Priest.

Much in fear of axe and rope,
    Back to Norway sailed he then.
' O, King Olaf ! little hope
    Is there of these Iceland men !'
      Meekly said,
      With bending head,
Pious Thangbrand, Olaf's Priest.

x.

RAUD THE STRONG.

' ALL the old gods are dead,
    All the wild warlocks fled ;
But the White Christ lives and
    reigns,
And throughout my wide domains
His Gospel shall be spread !'
      On the Evangelists
    Thus swore King Olaf.

But still in dreams of the night
Beheld he the crimson light,
And heard the voice that defied
Him who was crucified,
And challenged him to the fight.
      To Sigurd the Bishop
    King Olaf confessed it.

And Sigurd the Bishop said,
' The old gods are not dead,
For the great Thor still reigns,
And among the Jarls and Thanes
The old witchcraft still is spread.'
      Thus to King Olaf
    Said Sigurd the Bishop.

' Far north in the Salten Fiord,
By rapine, fire, and sword,
Lives the Viking, Raud the Strong ;
All the Godoe Isles belong
To him and his heathen horde.'
      Thus went on speaking
    Sigurd the Bishop.

' A warlock, a wizard is he,
And lord of the wind and the
    sea ;
And whichever way he sails,
He has ever favouring gales,
By his craft in sorcery.'
      Here the sign of the cross
    Made devoutly King Olaf.

' With rites that we both abhor,
He worships Odin and Thor ;
So it cannot yet be said,
That all the old gods are dead,
And the warlocks are no more,'
      Flushing with anger
    Said Sigurd the Bishop.

Then King Olaf cried aloud :
' I will talk with this mighty Raud,
And along the Salten Fiord
Preach the Gospel with my sword,
Or be brought back in my shroud !'
      So northward from Dron-
      theim
    Sailed King Olaf !

BISHOP SIGURD AT SALTEN FIORD.

LOUD the angry wind was wailing
As King Olaf's ships came sailing
Northward out of Drontheim haven
  To the mouth of Salten Fiord.

Though the flying sea-spray
    drenches
Fore and aft the rowers' benches,
Not a single heart is craven
  Of the champions there on
    board.

All without the Fiord was quiet,
But within it storm and riot,
Such as on his Viking cruises
  Raud the Strong was wont to
    ride.

And the sea through all its tide-
    ways
Swept the reeling vessels sideways,
As the leaves are swept through
    sluices,
  When the flood-gates open
    wide.

''Tis the warlock ! 'tis the demon
Raud !' cried Sigurd to the seamen;
' But the Lord is not affrighted
  By the witchcraft of his foes.'

To the ship's bow he ascended,
By his choristers attended,
Round him were the tapers lighted,
  And the sacred incense rose.

On the bow stood Bishop Sigurd,
In his robes, as one transfigured,
And the Crucifix he planted
  High amid the rain and mist.

Then with holy water sprinkled
All the ship; the mass-bells tinkled;
Loud the monks around him
    chanted,
  Loud he read the Evangelist.

As into the Fiord they darted,
On each side the water parted;
Down a path like silver molten
  Steadily rowed King Olaf's
    ships ;

Steadily burned all night the tapers,
And the White Christ through the
    vapours
Gleamed across the Fiord of Salten,
  As through John's Apocalypse,—

Till at last they reached Raud's
    dwelling
On the little isle of Gelling ;
Not a guard was at the doorway,
  Not a glimmer of light was seen.

But at anchor, carved and gilded,
Lay the dragon-ship he builded ;
'Twas the grandest ship in Norway,
  With its crest and scales of
    green.

Up the stairway, softly creeping,
To the loft where Raud was sleep-
    ing,
With their fists they burst asunder
  Bolt and bar that held the door.

Drunken with sleep and ale they
    found him,
Dragged him from his bed and
    bound him,
While he stared with stupid wonder,
  At the look and garb they
    wore.

Then King Olaf said : ' O Sea-
    King !
Little time have we for speaking,
Choose between the good and
    evil ;
  Be baptized, or thou shalt die !'

But in scorn the heathen scoffer
Answered : ' I disdain thine offer ;
Neither fear I God nor Devil ;
  Thee and thy Gospel I defy !'

Then between his jaws distended,
When his frantic struggles ended,
Through King Olaf's horn an adder,
    Touched by fire, they forced to
        glide.

Sharp his tooth was as an arrow,
As he gnawed through bone and
    marrow ;
But without a groan or shudder,
Raud the Strong blaspheming
    died.

Then baptized they all that re-
    gion,
Swarthy Lap and fair Norwegian,
Far as swims the salmon, leaping,
    Up the streams of Salten Fiord.

In their temples Thor and Odin
Lay in dust and ashes trodden,
As King Olaf, onward sweeping,
    Preached the Gospel with his
        sword.

Then he took the carved and
    gilded
Dragon-ship that Raud had build-
    ed,
And the tiller single-handed,
    Grasping, steered into the main.

Southward sailed the sea-gulls o'er
    him,
Southward sailed the ship that bore
    him,
Till at Drontheim haven landed
    Olaf and his crew again.

XII.

KING OLAF'S CHRISTMAS.

At Drontheim, Olaf the King
Heard the bells of Yule-tide ring,
    As he sat in his banquet-hall,
Drinking the nut-brown ale,
With his bearded Berserks hale
    And tall.

Three days his Yule-tide feasts
He held with Bishops and Priests,
    And his horn filled up to the
        brim ;
But the ale was never too strong,
Nor the Saga-man's tale too long,
    For him.

O'er his drinking-horn, the sign
He made of the cross divine,
    As he drank, and muttered his
        prayers ;
But the Berserks evermore
Made the sign of the Hammer of
    Thor
    Over theirs.

The gleams of the firelight dance
Upon helmet and hauberk and
    lance,
    And laugh in the eyes of the
        King ;
And he cries to Halfred the Scald,
Gray-bearded, wrinkled, and bald,
    'Sing !'

'Sing me a song divine,
With a sword in every line,
    And this shall be thy reward.'
And he loosened the belt at his
    waist,
And in front of the singer placed
    His sword.

'Quern-biter of Hakon the Good,
Wherewith at a stroke he hewed
    The millstone through and
        through,
And Foot-breadth of Thoralf the
    Strong,
Were neither so broad nor so long,
    Nor so true.'

Then the Scald took his harp and
    sang,
And loud through the music rang
    The sound of that shining
        word

And the harp-strings a clangour
made,
As if they were struck with the
blade
Of a sword.

And the Berserks round about
Broke forth into a shout
That made the rafters ring.
They smote with their fists on the
board,
And shouted, ' Long live the Sword,
And the King ! '

But the King said, ' O my son,
I miss the bright word in one
Of thy measures and thy rhymes.'
And Halfred the Scald replied,
' In another 'twas multiplied
Three times.'

Then King Olaf raised the hilt
Of iron, cross-shaped and gilt,
And said,' Do not refuse ;
Count well the gain and the loss,
Thor's hammer or Christ's cross :
Choose ! '

And Halfred the Scald said, ' This
In the name of the Lord I kiss,
Who on it was crucified ! '
And a shout went round the board,
' In the name of Christ the Lord,
Who died ! '

Then over the waste of snows
The noonday sun uprose,
Through the driving mists re-
vealed,
Like the lifting of the Host,
By incense-clouds almost
Concealed.

On the shining wall a vast
And shadowy cross was cast
From the hilt of the lifted sword,
And in foaming cups of ale
The Berserks drank ' Was-hael !
To the Lord ! '

XIII.

THE BUILDING OF THE LONG
SERPENT.

THORBERG SKAFTING, master-
builder,
In his ship-yard by the sea,
Whistling, said, ' It would bewilder
Any man but Thorberg Skafting,
Any man but me ! '

Near him lay the Dragon stranded,
Built of old by Raud the Strong,
And King Olaf had commanded
He should build another Dragon,
Twice as large and long.

Therefore whistled Thorberg Skaft-
ing,
As he sat with half-closed eyes,
And his head turned sideways,
drafting
That new vessel for King Olaf
Twice the Dragon's size.

Round him busily hewed and ham-
mered
Mallet huge and heavy axe ;
Workmen laughed and sang and
clamoured ;
Whirred the wheels, that into rig-
ging
Spun the shining flax !

All this tumult heard the master,—
It was music to his ear ;
Fancy whispered all the faster,
' Men shall hear of Thorberg Skaft-
ing
For a hundred year ! '

Workmen sweating at the forges
Fashioned iron bolt and bar,
Like a warlock's midnight orgies
Smoked and bubbled the black
caldron
With the boiling tar.

377

Did the warlocks mingle in it,
  Thorberg Skafting, any curse ?
Could you not be gone a minute
But some mischief must be doing,
  Turning bad to worse ?

'Twas an ill wind that came waft-
  ing
  From his homestead words of
    woe ;
To his farm went Thorberg Skaft-
  ing,
Oft repeating to his workmen,
  Build ye thus and so.

After long delays returning
  Came the master back by night ;
To his ship-yard longing, yearning,
Hurried he, and did not leave it
  Till the morning's light.

'Come and see my ship, my dar-
  ling,'
  On the morrow said the King ;
'Finished now from keel to carling ;
Never yet was seen in Norway
  Such a wondrous thing !'

In the ship-yard, idly talking,
  At the ship the workmen stared :
Some one, all their labour balking,
Down her sides had cut deep
  gashes,
  Not a plank was spared !

'Death be to the evil-doer !'
  With an oath King Olaf spoke ;
'But rewards to his pursuer !'
And with wrath his face grew redder
  Than his scarlet cloak.

Straight the master-builder, smil-
  ing,
  Answered thus the angry King :
'Cease blaspheming and reviling,
Olaf, it was Thorberg Skafting
  Who has done this thing !'

Then he chipped and smoothed the
  planking,
  Till the King, delighted, swore,
With much lauding and much
  thanking,
'Handsomer is now my Dragon
  Than she was before !'

Seventy ells and four extended
  On the grass the vessel's keel ;
High above it, gilt and splendid,
Rose the figure-head ferocious
  With its crest of steel.

Then they launched her from the
  tressels,
  In the ship-yard by the sea ;
She was the grandest of all vessels,
Never ship was built in Norway
  Half so fine as she !

The Long Serpent was she
  christened,
  'Mid the roar of cheer on cheer !
They who to the Saga listened
Heard the name of Thorberg
  Skafting
  For a hundred year !

XIV.

THE CREW OF THE LONG SERPENT.

SAFE at anchor in Drontheim
  bay
King Olaf's fleet assembled lay,
  And, striped with white and
    blue,
Downward fluttered sail and
  banner,
As alights the screaming lanner ;
Lustily cheered, in their wild
  manner,
  The Long Serpent's crew.

Her forecastle man was Ulf the
  Red ;
Like a wolf's was his shaggy head,
  His teeth as large and white ;

His beard, of gray and russet
blended,
Round as a swallow's nest de-
scended ;
As standard-bearer he defended
Olaf's flag in the fight.

Near him Kolbiorn had his place,
Like the King in garb and face,
So gallant and so hale ;
Every cabin-boy and varlet
Wondered at his cloak of scarlet ;
Like a river, frozen and star-lit,
Gleamed his coat of mail.

By the bulkhead, tall and dark,
Stood Thrand Rame of Thelemark,
A figure gaunt and grand ;
On his hairy arm imprinted
Was an anchor, azure-tinted ;
Like Thor's hammer, huge and
dinted
Was his brawny hand.

Einar Tamberskelver, bare
To the winds his golden hair,
By the mainmast stood ;
Graceful was his form, and slender,
And his eyes were deep and tender
As a woman's in the splendour
Of her maidenhood.

In the fore-hold Biorn and Bork
Watched the sailors at their work :
Heavens ! how they swore !
Thirty men they each commanded,
Iron-sinewed, horny-handed,
Shoulders broad, and chests ex-
panded,
Tugging at the oar.

These, and many more like these,
With King Olaf sailed the seas,
Till the waters vast
Filled them with a vague devo-
tion,
With the freedom and the motion,
With the roll and roar of ocean
And the sounding blast.

When they landed from the fleet,
How they roared through Dron-
theim's street,
Boisterous as the gale !
How they laughed and stamped
and pounded,
Till the tavern roof resounded,
And the host looked on astounded
As they drank the ale !

Never saw the wild North Sea
Such a gallant company
Sail its billows blue !
Never, while they cruised and
quarrelled,
Old King Gorm, or Blue-Tooth
Harald,
Owned a ship so well apparelled,
Boasted such a crew !

xv.

A LITTLE BIRD IN THE AIR.

A LITTLE bird in the air
Is singing of Thyri the fair,
The sister of Svend the Dane ;
And the song of the garrulous
bird
In the streets of the town is heard,
And repeated again and again.
Hoist up your sails of silk,
And flee away from each other.

To King Burislaf, it is said,
Was the beautiful Thyri wed,
And a sorrowful bride went she ;
And after a week and a day,
She has fled away and away,
From his town by the stormy
sea.
Hoist up your sails of silk,
And flee away from each other.

They say, that through heat and
through cold,
Through weald, they say, and
through wold,
By day and by night, they say,

379

She has fled; and the gossips report
She has come to King Olaf's court,
  And the town is all in dismay.
    Hoist up your sails of silk,
    And flee away from each other.

It is whispered King Olaf has seen,
Has talked with the beautiful
    Queen;
  And they wonder how it will end;
For surely, if here she remain,
It is war with King Svend the Dane,
  And King Burislaf the Vend!
    Hoist up your sails of silk,
    And flee away from each other.

O, greatest wonder of all!
It is published in hamlet and hall,
  It roars like a flame that is
    fanned!
The King—yes, Olaf the King—
Has wedded her with his ring,
  And Thyri is Queen in the land!
    Hoist up your sails of silk,
    And flee away from each other.

XVI.

QUEEN THYRI AND THE ANGELICA
STALKS.

NORTHWARD over Drontheim
Flew the clamorous sea-gulls,
Sang the lark and linnet
  From the meadows green;

Weeping in her chamber,
Lonely and unhappy,
Sat the Drottning Thyri,
  Sat King Olaf's Queen.

In at all the windows
Streamed the pleasant sunshine,
On the roof above her
  Softly cooed the dove;

But the sound she heard not,
Nor the sunshine heeded,
For the thoughts of Thyri
  Were not thoughts of love.

Then King Olaf entered,
Beautiful as morning,
Like the sun at Easter
  Shone his happy face;

In his hand he carried
Angelicas uprooted,
With delicious fragrance
  Filling all the place.

Like a rainy midnight
Sat the Drottning Thyri,
Even the smile of Olaf
  Could not cheer her gloom;

Nor the stalks he gave her
With a gracious gesture,
And with words as pleasant
  As their own perfume.

In her hands he placed them,
And her jewelled fingers
Through the green leaves glistened
  Like the dews of morn;

But she cast them from her,
Haughty and indignant,
On the floor she threw them
  With a look of scorn.

' Richer presents,' said she,
' Gave King Harald Gormson
To the Queen, my mother,
  Than such worthless weeds;

' When he ravaged Norway,
Laying waste the kingdom,
Seizing scatt and treasure
  For her royal needs.

' But thou darest not venture
Through the Sound to Vendland,
My domains to rescue
  From King Burislaf;

' Lest King Svend of Denmark,
Forked Beard, my brother,
Scatter all thy vessels
  As the wind the chaff.'

Then up sprang King Olaf,
Like a reindeer bounding,
With an oath he answered
  Thus the luckless Queen :

' Never yet did Olaf
Fear King Svend of Denmark ;
This right hand shall hale him
  By his forked chin ! '

Then he left the chamber,
Thundering through the doorway,
Loud his steps resounded
  Down the outer stair.

Smarting with the insult,
Through the streets of Drontheim
Strode he red and wrathful,
  With his stately air.

All his ships he gathered,
Summoned all his forces,
Making his war levy
  In the region round ;

Down the coast of Norway,
Like a flock of sea-gulls,
Sailed the fleet of Olaf
  Through the Danish Sound.

With his own hand fearless,
Steered he the Long Serpent,
Strained the creaking cordage,
  Bent each boom and gaff ;

Till in Vendland landing,
The domains of Thyri
He redeemed and rescued
  From King Burislaf.

Then said Olaf, laughing,
' Not ten yoke of oxen
Have the power to draw us
  Like a woman's hair !

' Now will I confess it,
Better things are jewels
Than angelica stalks are
  For a Queen to wear.'

XVII.

KING SVEND OF THE FORKED BEARD.

LOUDLY the sailors cheered
Svend of the Forkèd Beard,
As with his fleet he steered
  Southward to Vendland ;
Where with their courses hauled
All were together called,
Under the Isle of Svald
  Near to the mainland.

After Queen Gunhild's death,
So the old Saga saith,
Plighted King Svend his faith
  To Sigrid the Haughty ;
And to avenge his bride,
Soothing her wounded pride,
Over the waters wide
  King Olaf sought he.

Still on her scornful face,
Blushing with deep disgrace,
Bore she the crimson trace
  Of Olaf's gauntlet ;
Like a malignant star,
Blazing in heaven afar,
Red shone the angry scar
  Under her frontlet.

Oft to King Svend she spake,
' For thine own honour's sake
Shalt thou swift vengeance take
  On the vile coward ! '
Until the King at last,
Gusty and overcast,
Like a tempestuous blast
  Threatened and lowered.

Soon as the Spring appeared,
Svend of the Forkèd Beard
High his red standard reared,
  Eager for battle ;
While every warlike Dane,
Seizing his arms again,
Left all unsown the grain,
  Unhoused the cattle.

Likewise the Swedish King
Summoned in haste a Thing,
Weapons and men to bring
   In aid of Denmark ;
Eric the Norseman, too,
As the war-tidings flew,
Sailed with a chosen crew
   From Lapland and Finmark.

So upon Easter day
Sailed the three kings away,
Out of the sheltered bay,
   In the bright season ;
With them Earl Sigvald came,
Eager for spoil and fame ;
Pity that such a name
   Stooped to such treason !

Safe under Svald at last,
Now were their anchors cast,
Safe from the sea and blast,
   Plotted the three kings ;
While, with a base intent,
Southward Earl Sigvald went,
On a foul errand bent,
   Unto the Sea-kings.

Thence to hold on his course,
Unto King Olaf's force,
Lying within the hoarse
   Mouths of Stet-haven ;
Him to ensnare and bring
Unto the Danish king,
Who his dead corse would fling
   Forth to the raven !

XVIII.

KING OLAF AND EARL SIGVALD.

On the gray sea-sands
King Olaf stands,
Northward and seaward
He points with his hands.

With eddy and whirl
The sea-tides curl,
Washing the sandals
Of Sigvald the Earl.

The mariners shout,
The ships swing about,
The yards are all hoisted,
The sails flutter out.

The war-horns are played,
The anchors are weighed,
Like moths in the distance
The sails flit and fade.

The sea is like lead,
The harbour lies dead,
As a corse on the sea-shore,
Whose spirit has fled !

On that fatal day,
The histories say,
Seventy vessels
Sailed out of the bay.

But soon scattered wide
O'er the billows they ride,
While Sigvald and Olaf
Sail side by side.

Cried the Earl : ' Follow me !
I your pilot will be,
For I know all the channels
Where flows the deep sea ! '

So into the strait
Where his foes lie in wait,
Gallant King Olaf
Sails to his fate !

Then the sea-fog veils
The ships and their sails ;
Queen Sigrid the Haughty,
Thy vengeance prevails !

XIX.

KING OLAF'S WAR-HORNS.

' Strike the sails ! ' King Olaf said ;
' Never shall men of mine take
    flight ;
Never away from battle I fled,
Never away from my foes !
   Let God dispose
Of my life in the fight ! '

'Sound the horns!' said Olaf the
  King;
And suddenly through the drifting
  brume
The blare of the horns began to ring,
Like the terrible trumpet shock
  Of Regnarock,
On the Day of Doom!

Louder and louder the war-horns
  sang
Over the level floor of the flood;
All the sails came down with a
  clang,
And there in the mist overhead
  The sun hung red
As a drop of blood.

Drifting down on the Danish fleet
Three together the ships were lashed,
So that neither should turn and re-
  treat;
In the midst, but in front of the
  rest
  The burnished crest
Of the Serpent flashed.

King Olaf stood on the quarter-
  deck,
With bow of ash and arrows of oak,
His gilded shield was without a
  fleck,
His helmet inlaid with gold,
  And in many a fold
Hung his crimson cloak.

On the forecastle Ulf the Red
Watched the lashing of the ships;
'If the Serpent lie so far ahead,
We shall have hard work of it here,
  Said he with a sneer
On his bearded lips.

King Olaf laid an arrow on string,
'Have I a coward on board?' said
  he.
'Shoot it another way, O King!'
Sullenly answered Ulf,
  The old sea-wolf;
'You have need of me!'

In front came Svend, the King of
  the Danes,
Sweeping down with his fifty row-
  ers;
To the right, the Swedish king with
  his thanes;
And on board of the Iron Beard
  Earl Eric steered
To the left with his oars.

'These soft Danes and Swedes'
  said the King,
'At home with their wives had
  better stay,
Than come within reach of my Ser-
  pent's sting:
But where Eric the Norseman leads
  Heroic deeds
Will be done to-day!'

Then as together the vessels crash-
  ed,
Eric severed the cables of hide,
With which King Olaf's ships were
  lashed,
And left them to drive and drift
  With the currents swift
Of the outward tide.

Louder the war-horns growl and
  snarl,
Sharper the dragons bite and sting!
Eric the son of Hakon Jarl
A death-drink salt as the sea
  Pledges to thee,
Olaf the King!

XX.
EINAR TAMBERSKELVER.

IT was Einar Tamberskelver
  Stood beside the mast;
From his yew-bow, tipped with
  silver,
  Flew the arrows fast;
Aimed at Eric unavailing,
  As he sat concealed,
Half behind the quarter-railing,
  Half behind his shield.

First an arrow struck the tiller,
  Just above his head;
'Sing, O Eyvind Skaldaspiller,'
  Then Earl Eric said.
'Sing the song of Hakon dying,
  Sing his funeral wail!'
And another arrow flying
  Grazed his coat of mail.

Turning to a Lapland yeoman,
  As the arrow passed,
Said Earl Eric, 'Shoot that bow-
    man
  Standing by the mast.'
Sooner than the word was spoken
  Flew the yeoman's shaft;
Einar's bow in twain was broken,
  Einar only laughed.

'What was that?' said Olaf, stand-
    ing
  On the quarter-deck.
'Something heard I like the strand-
    ing
  Of a shattered wreck.'
Einar then, the arrow taking
  From the loosened string,
Answered, 'That was Norway
    breaking
  From thy hand, O King!'

'Thou art but a poor diviner,'
  Straightway Olaf said;
'Take my bow, and swifter, Einar,
  Let thy shafts be sped.'
Of his bows the fairest choosing,
  Reached he from above;
Einar saw the blood-drops oozing
  Through his iron glove.

But the bow was thin and narrow;
  At the first assay,
O'er its head he drew the arrow,
  Flung the bow away;
Said, with hot and angry temper
  Flushing in his cheek,
'Olaf! for so great a Kämper
  Are thy bows too weak!'

Then, with smile of joy defiant
  On his beardless lip,
Scaled he, light and self-reliant,
  Eric's dragon-ship.
Loose his golden locks were flow-
    ing,
  Bright his armour gleamed;
Like Saint Michael overthrowing
  Lucifer he seemed.

XXI.
KING OLAF'S DEATH-DRINK.

ALL day has the battle raged,
All day have the ships engaged,
But not yet is assuaged
  The vengeance of Eric the Earl.

The decks with blood are red,
The arrows of death are sped,
The ships are filled with the dead,
  And the spears the champions
    hurl.

They drift as wrecks on the tide,
The grappling irons are plied,
The boarders climb up the side,
  The shouts are feeble and few.

Ah! never shall Norway again
See her sailors come back o'er the
    main;
They all lie wounded or slain,
  Or asleep in the billows blue!

On the deck stands Olaf the
    King,
Around him whistle and sing
The spears that the foemen fling,
  And the stones they hurl with
    their hands.

In the midst of the stones and the
    spears,
Kolbiorn, the marshal, appears,
His shield in the air he uprears,
  By the side of King Olaf he
    stands.

384

Over the slippery wreck
Of the Long Serpent's deck
Sweeps Eric with hardly a check,
  His lips with anger are pale;

He hews with his axe at the mast,
Till it falls, with the sails overcast,
Like a snow-covered pine in the vast
  Dim forests of Orkadale.

Seeking King Olaf then,
He rushes aft with his men,
As a hunter into the den
  Of the bear, when he stands at bay.

'Remember Jarl Hakon!' he cries;
When lo! on his wondering eyes,
Two kingly figures arise,
  Two Olafs in warlike array!

Then Kolbiorn speaks in the ear
Of King Olaf a word of cheer,
In a whisper that none may hear,
  With a smile on his tremulous lip;

Two shields raised high in the air,
Two flashes of golden hair,
Two scarlet meteors' glare,
  And both have leaped from the ship.

Earl Eric's men in the boats
Seize Kolbiorn's shield as it floats,
And cry, from their hairy throats,
  'See! it is Olaf the King!'

While far on the opposite side
Floats another shield on the tide,
Like a jewel set in the wide
  Sea-current's eddying ring.

There is told a wonderful tale,
How the King stripped off his mail,
Like leaves of the brown sea-kale,
  As he swam beneath the main;

But the young grew old and gray,
And never, by night or by day,
In his kingdom of Norroway
  Was King Olaf seen again!

XXII.

THE NUN OF NIDAROS.

IN the convent of Drontheim,
Alone in her chamber
Knelt Astrid the Abbess,
At midnight, adoring,
Beseeching, entreating
The Virgin and Mother.

She heard in the silence
The voice of one speaking,
Without in the darkness,
In gusts of the night-wind
Now louder, now nearer,
Now lost in the distance.

The voice of a stranger
It seemed as she listened,
Of some one who answered,
Beseeching, imploring,
A cry from afar off
She could not distinguish.

The voice of Saint John,
The beloved disciple,
Who wandered and waited
The Master's appearance,
Alone in the darkness,
Unsheltered and friendless.

'It is accepted
The angry defiance,
The challenge of battle!
It is accepted,
But not with the weapons
Of war that thou wieldest!

'Cross against corselet,
Love against hatred,
Peace-cry for war-cry!
Patience is powerful;
He that o'ercometh
Hath power o'er the nations!

'As torrents in summer,
Half dried in their channels,
Suddenly rise, though the
Sky is still cloudless,
For rain has been falling
Far off at their fountains;

'So hearts that are fainting
Grow full to o'erflowing,
And they that behold it
Marvel, and know not
That God at their fountains
Far off has been raining!

'Stronger than steel
Is the sword of the Spirit;
Swifter than arrows
The light of the truth is,
Greater than anger
Is love, and subdueth!

'Thou art a phantom,
A shape of the sea-mist,
A shape of the brumal
Rain, and the darkness
Fearful and formless;
Day dawns and thou art not!

'The dawn is not distant,
Nor is the night starless;
Love is eternal!
God is still God, and
His faith shall not fail us;
Christ is eternal!'

——+——

INTERLUDE.

A STRAIN of music closed the tale,
A low, monotonous, funeral wail,
That with its cadence, wild and
    sweet,
Made the long Saga more com-
    plete.

'Thank God,' the Theologian said,
'The reign of violence is dead,
Or dying surely from the world;
While Love triumphant reigns in-
    stead,
And in a brighter sky o'erhead
His blessed banners are unfurled.
And most of all thank God for
    this:
The war and waste of clashing
    creeds

Now end in words, and not in
    deeds,
And no one suffers loss, or bleeds,
For thoughts that men call heresies.

'I stand without here in the porch,
I hear the bell's melodious din,
I hear the organ peal within,
I hear the prayer, with words that
    scorch
Like sparks from an inverted torch,
I hear the sermon upon sin,
With threatenings of the last ac-
    count.
And all, translated in the air,
Reach me but as our dear Lord's
    Prayer,
And as the Sermon on the Mount.

'Must it be Calvin, and not Christ?
Must it be Athanasian creeds,
Or holy water, books, and beads?
Must struggling souls remain con-
    tent
With councils and decrees of Trent?
And can it be enough for these
The Christian Church the year
    embalms
With evergreens and boughs of
    palms,
And fills the air with litanies?

'I know that yonder Pharisee
Thanks God that he is not like me;
In my humiliation dressed,
I only stand and beat my breast,
And pray for human charity.

'Not to one church alone, but
    seven,
The voice prophetic spake from
    heaven;
And unto each the promise came,
Diversified, but still the same;
For him that overcometh are
The new name written on the stone,
The raiment white, the crown, the
    throne,
And I will give him the Morning
    Star!

386

'Ah! to how many Faith has been
No evidence of things unseen,
But a dim shadow, that recasts
The creed of the Phantasiasts,
For whom no Man of Sorrows died,
For whom the Tragedy Divine
Was but a symbol and a sign,
And Christ a phantom crucified!

'For others a diviner creed
Is living in the life they lead.
The passing of their beautiful feet
Blesses the pavement of the street,
And all their looks and words re-
    peat
Old Fuller's saying, wise and sweet,
Not as a vulture, but a dove,
The Holy Ghost came from above.

'And this brings back to me a tale
So sad the hearer well may quail,
And question if such things can be;
Yet in the chronicles of Spain
Down the dark pages runs this
    stain,
And naught can wash them white
    again,
So fearful is the tragedy.'

—◆—

THE THEOLOGIAN'S TALE.

TORQUEMADA.

IN the heroic days when Ferdinand
And Isabella ruled the Spanish
    land,
And Torquemada, with his subtle
    brain,
Ruled them, as Grand Inquisitor
    of Spain,
In a great castle near Valladolid,
Moated and high and by fair wood-
    lands hid,
There dwelt, as from the chronicles
    we learn,
An old Hidalgo proud and taci-
    turn,

Whose name has perished, with
    his towers of stone,
And all his actions save this one
    alone;
This one, so terrible, perhaps
    'twere best
If it, too, were forgotten with the
    rest;
Unless, perchance, our eyes can
    see therein
The martyrdom triumphant o'er the
    sin;
A double picture, with its gloom
    and glow,
The splendour overhead, the death
    below.

This sombre man counted each
    day as lost
On which his feet no sacred thres-
    hold crossed;
And when he chanced the passing
    Host to meet,
He knelt and prayed devoutly in
    the street;
Oft he confessed; and with each
    mutinous thought,
As with wild beasts at Ephesus,
    he fought.
In deep contrition scourged him-
    self in Lent,
Walked in processions, with his
    head down bent,
At plays of Corpus Christi oft was
    seen,
And on Palm Sunday bore his
    bough of green.

His sole diversion was to hunt the
    boar
Through tangled thickets of the
    forest hoar,
Or with his jingling mules to hurry
    down
To some grand bull-fight in the
    neighbouring town,
Or in the crowd with lighted taper
    stand,

When Jews were burned, or banished from the land.
Then stirred within him a tumultuous joy ;
The demon whose delight is to
destroy
Shook him, and shouted with a
trumpet tone,
Kill ! kill ! and let the Lord find
out his own !'

And now, in that old castle in the
wood,
His daughters, in the dawn of
womanhood,
Returning from their convent
school, had made
Resplendent with their bloom the
forest shade,
Reminding him of their dead
mother's face,
When first she came into that
gloomy place,—
A memory in his heart as dim and
sweet
As moonlight in a solitary street,
Where the same rays, that lift the
sea, are thrown
Lovely but powerless upon walls of
stone.
These two fair daughters of a
mother dead
Were all the dream had left him
as it fled.
A joy at first, and then a growing
care,
As if a voice within him cried,
'Beware !'
A vague presentiment of impend-
ing doom,
Like ghostly footsteps in a vacant
room,
Haunted him day and night ; a
formless fear
That death to some one of his
house was near,
With dark surmises of a hidden
crime,

Made life itself a death before its
time.
Jealous, suspicious, with no sense
of shame,
A spy upon his daughters he became ;
With velvet slippers, noiseless on
the floors,
He glided softly through half-
open doors ;
Now in the room, and now upon
the stair,
He stood beside them ere they
were aware ;
He listened in the passage when
they talked,
He watched them from the casement when they walked,
He saw the gipsy haunt the river's
side,
He saw the monk among the cork-
trees glide ;
And, tortured by the mystery and
the doubt
Of some dark secret, past his finding out,
Baffled he paused ; then reassured
again
Pursued the flying phantom of his
brain.
He watched them even when they
knelt in church ;
And then, descending lower in his
search,
Questioned the servants, and with
eager eyes
Listened incredulous to their replies ;
The gipsy ? none had seen her in
the wood !
The monk ? a mendicant in search
of food !
At length the awful revelation
came,
Crushing at once his pride of birth
and name ;
The hopes his yearning bosom
forward cast,

And the ancestral glories of the past,
All fell together, crumbling in disgrace,
A turret rent from battlement to base.
His daughters talking in the dead of night
In their own chamber, and without a light,
Listening, as he was wont, he overheard,
And learned the dreadful secret, word by word;
And hurrying from his castle, with a cry
He raised his hands to the unpitying sky,
Repeating one dread word, till bush and tree
Caught it, and shuddering answered, 'Heresy!'

Wrapped in his cloak, his hat drawn o'er his face,
Now hurrying forward, now with lingering pace,
He walked all night the alleys of his park,
With one unseen companion in the dark,
The Demon who within him lay in wait,
And by his presence turned his love to hate,
For ever muttering in an undertone,
'Kill! kill! and let the Lord find out his own!'

Upon the morrow, after early Mass,
While yet the dew was glistening on the grass,
And all the woods were musical with birds,
The old Hidalgo, uttering fearful words,
Walked homeward with the Priest, and in his room

Summoned his trembling daughters to their doom.
When questioned, with brief answers they replied,
Nor when accused evaded or denied;
Expostulations, passionate appeals,
All that the human heart most fears or feels,
In vain the Priest with earnest voice essayed;
In vain the father threatened, wept, and prayed;
Until at last he said, with haughty mien,
'The Holy Office, then, must intervene!'

And now the Grand Inquisitor of Spain,
With all the fifty horsemen of his train,
His awful name resounding, like the blast
Of funeral trumpets, as he onward passed,
Came to Valladolid, and there began
To harry the rich Jews with fire and ban.
To him the Hidalgo went, and at the gate
Demanded audience on affairs of state,
And in a secret chamber stood before
A venerable graybeard of fourscore,
Dressed in the hood and habit of a friar;
Out of his eyes flashed a consuming fire,
And in his hand the mystic horn he held,
Which poison and all noxious charms dispelled.
He heard in silence the Hidalgo's tale,
Then answered in a voice that made him quail:

389

'Son of the Church! when Abraham of old
To sacrifice his only son was told,
He did not pause to parley nor protest,
But hastened to obey the Lord's behest.
In him it was accounted righteousness;
The Holy Church expects of thee no less!'

A sacred frenzy seized the father's brain,
And Mercy from that hour implored in vain.
Ah! who will e'er believe the words I say?
His daughters he accused, and the same day
They both were cast into the dungeon's gloom,
That dismal antechamber of the tomb,
Arraigned, condemned, and sentenced to the flame,
The secret torture and the public shame.

Then to the Grand Inquisitor once more
The Hidalgo went, more eager than before,
And said: 'When Abraham offered up his son,
He clave the wood wherewith it might be done.
By his example taught, let me too bring
Wood from the forest for my offering!'
And the deep voice, without a pause, replied:
'Son of the Church! by faith now justified,
Complete thy sacrifice, even as thou wilt;
The Church absolves thy conscience from all guilt!'

Then this most wretched father went his way
Into the woods, that round his castle lay,
Where once his daughters in their childhood played
With their young mother in the sun and shade.
Now all the leaves had fallen; the branches bare
Made a perpetual moaning in the air,
And screaming from their eyries overhead
The ravens sailed athwart the sky of lead.
With his own hands he lopped the boughs and bound
Fagots, that crackled with foreboding sound,
And on his mules, caparisoned and gay
With bells and tassels, sent them on their way.

Then with his mind on one dark purpose bent,
Again to the Inquisitor he went,
And said: 'Behold, the fagots I have brought,
And now, lest my atonement be as naught,
Grant me one more request, one last desire,—
With my own hand to light the funeral fire!'
And Torquemada answered from his seat,
'Son of the Church! Thine offering is complete;
Her servants through all ages shall not cease
To magnify thy deed. Depart in peace!'

Upon the market-place, builded of stone
The scaffold rose, whereon Death claimed his own.

At the four corners, in stern attitude,
Four statues of the Hebrew Prophets stood,
Gazing with calm indifference in their eyes
Upon this place of human sacrifice,
Round which was gathering fast the eager crowd,
With clamour of voices, dissonant and loud,
And every roof and window was alive
With restless gazers, swarming like a hive.

The church-bells tolled, the chant of monks drew near,
Loud trumpets stammered forth their notes of fear,
A line of torches smoked along the street,
There was a stir, a rush, a tramp of feet,
And, with its banners floating in the air,
Slowly the long procession crossed the square,
And, to the statues of the Prophets bound,
The victims stood, with fagots piled around.
Then all the air a blast of trumpets shook,
And louder sang the monks with bell and book,
And the Hidalgo, lofty, stern, and proud,
Lifted his torch, and, bursting through the crowd,
Lighted in haste the fagots, and then fled,
Lest those imploring eyes should strike him dead!

O pitiless skies! why did your clouds retain
For peasants' fields their floods of hoarded rain?
O pitiless earth! why open no abyss
To bury in its chasm a crime like this?

That night, a mingled column of fire and smoke
From the dark thickets of the forest broke,
And, glaring o'er the landscape leagues away,
Made all the fields and hamlets bright as day.
Wrapped in a sheet of flame the castle blazed,
And as the villagers in terror gazed,
They saw the figure of that cruel knight
Lean from a window in the turret's height,
His ghastly face illumined with the glare,
His hands upraised above his head in prayer,
Till the floor sank beneath him, and he fell
Down the black hollow of that burning well.

Three centuries and more above his bones
Have piled the oblivious years like funeral stones;
His name has perished with him, and no trace
Remains on earth of his afflicted race;
But Torquemada's name, with clouds o'ercast,
Looms in the distant landscape of the Past,
Like a burnt tower upon a blackened heath,
Lit by the fires of burning woods beneath!

INTERLUDE.

THUS closed the tale of guilt and
  gloom,
That cast upon each listener's face
Its shadow, and for some brief
  space
Unbroken silence filled the room.
The Jew was thoughtful and dis-
  tressed;
Upon his memory thronged and
  pressed
The persecution of his race,
Their wrongs and sufferings and
  disgrace;
His head was sunk upon his breast,
And from his eyes alternate came
Flashes of wrath and tears of
  shame.

The Student first the silence broke,
As one who long has lain in wait,
With purpose to retaliate,
And thus he dealt the avenging
  stroke.
'In such a company as this,
A tale so tragic seems amiss,
That by its terrible control
O'ermasters and drags down the
  soul
Into a fathomless abyss.
The Italian Tales that you disdain,
Some merry Night of Straparole,
Or Machiavelli's Belphagor,
Would cheer us and delight us
  more,
Give greater pleasure and less
  pain
Than your grim tragedies of
  Spain!'

And here the Poet raised his hand,
With such entreaty and command,
It stopped discussion at its birth,
And said: 'The story I shall tell
Has meaning in it, if not mirth;
Listen, and hear what once befell
The merry birds of Killingworth!'

THE POET'S TALE.

THE BIRDS OF KILLINGWORTH.

IT was the season, when through
  all the land
  The merle and mavis build, and
    building sing
Those lovely lyrics, written by His
  hand,
  Whom Saxon Cædmon calls the
    Blitheheart King;
When on the boughs the purple
  buds expand,
  The banners of the vanguard of
    the Spring,
And rivulets, rejoicing, rush and
  leap,
And wave their fluttering signals
  from the steep.

The robin and the bluebird, piping
  loud,
  Filled all the blossoming orchards
    with their glee;
The sparrows chirped as if they
  still were proud
  Their race in Holy Writ should
    mentioned be;
And hungry crows assembled in a
  crowd,
  Clamoured their piteous prayer
    incessantly,
Knowing who hears the ravens cry,
  and said:
'Give us, O Lord, this day our
  daily bread!'

Across the Sound the birds of pas-
  sage sailed,
  Speaking some unknown lan-
    guage strange and sweet
Of tropic isle remote, and passing
  hailed
  The village with the cheers of all
    their fleet;
Or quarrelling together, laughed
  and railed

Like foreign sailors, landed in the street
Of seaport town, and with outlandish noise
Of oaths and gibberish frightening girls and boys.

Thus came the jocund Spring in Killingworth,
In fabulous days, some hundred years ago;
And thrifty farmers, as they tilled the earth,
Heard with alarm the cawing of the crow,
That mingled with the universal mirth,
Cassandra-like, prognosticating woe;
They shook their heads, and doomed with dreadful words
To swift destruction the whole race of birds.

And a town-meeting was convened straightway
To set a price upon the guilty heads
Of these marauders, who, in lieu of pay,
Levied blackmail upon the garden beds
And cornfields, and beheld without dismay
The awful scarecrow, with his fluttering shreds;
The skeleton that waited at their feast,
Whereby their sinful pleasure was increased.

Then from his house, a temple painted white,
With fluted columns, and a roof of red,
The Squire came forth, august and splendid sight!
Slowly descending, with majestic tread,

Three flights of steps, nor looking left nor right,
Down the long street he walked, as one who said,
'A town that boasts inhabitants like me
Can have no lack of good society!'

The Parson, too, appeared, a man austere,
The instinct of whose nature was to kill;
The wrath of God he preached from year to year,
And read, with fervour, Edwards on the Will;
His favourite pastime was to slay the deer
In summer on some Adirondac hill;
E'en now, while walking down the rural lane,
He lopped the wayside lilies with his cane.

From the Academy, whose belfry crowned
The hill of Science with its vane of brass,
Came the Preceptor, gazing idly round,
Now at the clouds, and now at the green grass,
And all absorbed in reveries profound
Of fair Almira in the upper class,
Who was, as in a sonnet he had said,
As pure as water, and as good as bread.

And next the Deacon issued from his door,
In his voluminous neckcloth white as snow;
A suit of sable bombazine he wore;
His form was ponderous, and his step was slow;

There never was so wise a man
  before;
  He seemed the incarnate 'Well,
    I told you so!'
And to perpetuate his great renown
There was a street named after
  him in town.

These came together in the new
  town-hall,
  With sundry farmers from the
    region round.
The Squire presided, dignified and
  tall,
  His air impressive and his rea-
    soning sound:
Ill fared it with the birds, both
  great and small;
  Hardly a friend in all that crowd
    they found,
But enemies enough, who every one
Charged them with all the crimes
  beneath the sun.

When they had ended, from his
  place apart,
  Rose the Preceptor, to redress
    the wrong,
And, trembling like a steed before
  the start,
  Looked round bewildered on the
    expectant throng;
Then thought of fair Almira, and
  took heart
  To speak out what was in him,
    clear and strong,
Alike regardless of their smile or
  frown,
And quite determined not to be
  laughed down.

'Plato, anticipating the Reviewers,
  From his Republic banished
    without pity
The Poets; in this little town of
  yours,
  You put to death, by means of a
    Committee,

The ballad-singers and the Troubadours,
  The street-musicians of the hea-
    venly city,—
The birds,—who make sweet music
  for us all
In our dark hours, as David did
  for Saul.

'The thrush that carols at the dawn
  of day
  From the green steeples of the
    piny wood;
The oriole in the elm; the noisy jay,
  Jargoning like a foreigner at his
    food;
The bluebird balanced on some
  topmost spray,
  Flooding with melody the neigh-
    bourhood;
Linnet and meadow-lark, and all
  the throng
That dwell in nests, and have the
  gift of song.

'You slay them all! and wherefore?
  for the gain
  Of a scant handful more or less
    of wheat,
Or rye, or barley, or some other grain,
  Scratched up at random by in-
    dustrious feet,
Searching for worm or weevil after
  rain!
Or a few cherries, that are not
  so sweet
As are the songs these uninvited
  guests
Sing at their feast with comfortable
  breasts.

'Do you ne'er think what wondrous
  beings these?
  Do you ne'er think who made
    them, and who taught
The dialect they speak, where
  melodies
  Alone are the interpreters of
    thought?

Whose household words are songs
    in many keys,
  Sweeter than instrument of man
    e'er caught !
Whose habitations in the tree-tops
    even
Are half-way houses on the road to
    heaven !

' Think, every morning when the
    sun peeps through
  The dim, leaf-latticed windows
    of the grove,
How jubilant the happy birds renew
  Their old, melodious madrigals
    of love !
And when you think of this, re-
    member too
'Tis always morning somewhere,
    and above
The awakening continents, from
    shore to shore,
Somewhere the birds are singing
    evermore.

' Think of your woods and orchards
    without birds !
  Of empty nests that cling to
    boughs and beams
As in an idiot's brain remembered
    words
  Hang empty 'mid the cobwebs
    of his dreams !
Will bleat of flocks or bellowing of
    herds
  Make up for the lost music, when
    your teams
Drag home the stingy harvest, and
    no more
The feathered gleaners follow to
    your door ?

' What ! would you rather see the
    incessant stir
  Of insects in the windrows of the
    hay,
And hear the locust and the grass-
    hopper
  Their melancholy hurdy-gurdies
    play ?

Is this more pleasant to you than
    the whir
  Of meadow-lark, and her sweet
    roundelay,
Or twitter of little field-fares, as
    you take
Your nooning in the shade of bush
    and brake ?

' You call them thieves and pil-
    lagers ; but know,
  They are the winged wardens of
    your farms,
Who from the cornfields drive the
    insidious foe,
  And from your harvests keep a
    hundred harms ;
Even the blackest of them all, the
    crow,
  Renders good service as your
    man-at-arms,
Crushing the beetle in his coat of
    mail,
And crying havoc on the slug and
    snail.

' How can I teach your children
    gentleness,
  And mercy to the weak, and re-
    verence
For Life, which, in its weakness or
    excess,
  Is still a gleam of God's omni-
    potence,
Or Death, which, seeming dark-
    ness, is no less
  The self-same light, although
    averted hence,
When by your laws, your actions,
    and your speech,
You contradict the very things I
    teach ?'

With this he closed ; and through
    the audience went
  A murmur, like the rustle of dead
    leaves ;

The farmers laughed and nodded,
and some bent
  Their yellow heads together like
  their sheaves ;
Men have no faith in fine-spun
sentiment
  Who put their trust in bullocks
  and in beeves.
The birds were doomed ; and, as
the record shows,
A bounty offered for the heads of
crows.

There was another audience out
of reach,
  Who had no voice nor vote in
  making laws,
But in the papers read his little
speech,
  And crowned his modest temples
  with applause ;
They made him conscious, each
one more than each,
  He still was victor, vanquished
  in their cause.
Sweetest of all the applause he won
from thee,
O fair Almira at the Academy !

And so the dreadful massacre
began ;
  O'er fields and orchards, and
  o'er woodland crests,
The ceaseless fusillade of terror ran.
  Dead fell the birds, with blood-
  stains on their breasts,
Or wounded crept away from sight
of man,
  While the young died of famine
  in their nests ;
A slaughter to be told in groans,
not words,
The very St. Bartholomew of
Birds !

The Summer came, and all the
birds were dead ;
  The days were like hot coals ;
  the very ground

Was burned to ashes ; in the
orchards fed
  Myriads of caterpillars, and
  around
The cultivated fields and garden beds
  Hosts of devouring insects
  crawled, and found
No foe to check their march, till
they had made
The land a desert without leaf or
shade.

Devoured by worms, like Herod,
was the town,
  Because, like Herod, it had ruth-
  lessly
Slaughtered the Innocents. From
the trees spun down
  The cankerworms upon the
  passers-by,
Upon each woman's bonnet, shawl,
and gown,
  Who shook them off with just a
  little cry ;
They were the terror of each
favourite walk,
The endless theme of all the village
talk.

The farmers grew impatient, but a
few
  Confessed their error, and would
  not complain,
For after all, the best thing one can
do
  When it is raining, is to let it rain.
Then they repealed the law,
although they knew
  It would not call the dead to life
  again ;
As schoolboys, finding their mistake too late,
Draw a wet sponge across the
accusing slate.

That year in Killingworth the
Autumn came
  Without the light of his majestic
  look,

The wonder of the falling tongues
of flame,
The illumined pages of his
Doomsday book.
A few lost leaves blushed crimson
with their shame,
And drowned themselves de-
spairing in the brook,
While the wild wind went moaning
everywhere,
Lamenting the dead children of
the air!

But the next Spring, a stranger sight
was seen,
A sight that never yet by bard
was sung,
As great a wonder as it would have
been
If some dumb animal had found
a tongue!
A wagon, overarched with ever-
green,
Upon whose boughs were wicker
cages hung,
All full of singing birds, came down
the street,
Filling the air with music wild and
sweet.

From all the country round these
birds were brought,
By order of the town, with
anxious quest,
And, loosened from their wicker
prisons, sought
In woods and fields the places
they loved best,
Singing loud canticles, which many
thought
Were satires to the authorities
addressed,
While others, listening in green
lanes, averred
Such lovely music never had been
heard!

But blither still and louder carolled
they

Upon the morrow, for they
seemed to know
It was the fair Almira's wedding-day,
And everywhere, around, above,
below,
When the Preceptor bore his bride
away,
Their songs burst forth in joyous
overflow,
And a new heaven bent over a new
earth
Amid the sunny farms of Killingworth.

———

FINALE.

THE hour was late; the fire burned
low,
The Landlord's eyes were closed in
sleep,
And near the story's end a deep
Sonorous sound at times was heard,
As when the distant bagpipes blow.
At this all laughed; the Landlord
stirred,
As one awaking from a swound,
And, gazing anxiously around,
Protested that he had not slept,
But only shut his eyes, and kept
His ears attentive to each word.

Then all arose, and said 'Good
Night.'
Alone remained the drowsy Squire
To rake the embers of the fire,
And quench the waning parlour
light;
While from the windows, here and
there,
The scattered lamps a moment
gleamed,
And the illumined hostel seemed
The constellation of the Bear,
Downward, athwart the misty air,
Sinking and setting toward the sun.
Far off the village clock struck one.

PART II.

PRELUDE.

A COLD, uninterrupted rain,
That washed each southern win-
    dow-pane,
And made a river of the road ;
A sea of mist that overflowed
The house, the barns, the gilded
    vane,
And drowned the upland and the
    plain,
Through which the oak-trees,
    broad and high,
Like phantom ships went drifting
    by ;
And, hidden behind a watery
    screen,
The sun unseen, or only seen
As a faint pallor in the sky ;—
Thus cold and colourless and gray,
The morn of that autumnal day,
As if reluctant to begin,
Dawned on the silent Sudbury Inn,
And all the guests that in it lay.

Full late they slept. They did not
    hear
The challenge of Sir Chanticleer,
Who on the empty threshing-floor,
Disdainful of the rain outside,
Was strutting with a martial stride,
As if upon his thigh he wore
The famous broadsword of the
    Squire,
And said, 'Behold me, and
    admire !'

Only the Poet seemed to hear,
In drowse or dream, more near and
    near
Across the border-land of sleep
The blowing of a blithesome horn,
That laughed the dismal day to
    scorn ;
A splash of hoofs and rush of
    wheels

Through sand and mire like strand-
    ing keels,
As from the road with sudden
    sweep
The Mail drove up the little steep,
And stopped beside the tavern
    door ;
A moment stopped, and then again
With crack of whip and bark of dog
Plunged forward through the sea
    of fog,
And all was silent as before,—
All silent save the dripping rain.

Then one by one the guests came
    down,
And greeted with a smile the Squire,
Who sat before the parlour fire,
Reading the paper fresh from town.
First the Sicilian, like a bird,
Before his form appeared, was heard
Whistling and singing down the
    stair ;
Then came the Student, with a look
As placid as a meadow-brook ;
The Theologian, still perplexed
With thoughts of this world and
    the next ;
The Poet then, as one who seems
Walking in visions and in dreams,
Then the Musician, like a fair
Hyperion from whose golden hair
The radiance of the morning
    streams ;
And last the aromatic Jew
Of Alicant, who, as he threw
The door wide open, on the air
Breathed round about him a per-
    fume
Of damask roses in full bloom,
Making a garden of the room.

The breakfast ended, each pursued
The promptings of his various
    mood ;

398

Beside the fire in silence smoked
The taciturn, impassive Jew,
Lost in a pleasant reverie ;
While, by his gravity provoked,
His portrait the Sicilian drew,
And wrote beneath it ' Edrehi,
At the Red Horse in Sudbury.'

By far the busiest of them all,
The Theologian in the hall
Was feeding robins in a cage,—
Two corpulent and lazy birds,
Vagrants and pilferers at best,
If one might trust the hostler's
      words,
Chief instrument of their arrest ;
Two poets of the Golden Age,
Heirs of a boundless heritage
Of fields and orchards, east and
      west,
And sunshine of long summer days,
Though outlawed now and dispos-
      sessed ! —
Such was the Theologian's phrase.

Meanwhile the Student held dis-
      course
With the Musician, on the source
Of all the legendary lore
Among the nations, scattered wide
Like silt and seaweed by the force
And fluctuation of the tide ;
The tale repeated o'er and o'er,
With change of place and change
      of name,
Disguised, transformed, and yet
      the same
We 've heard a hundred times be-
      fore.

The Poet at the window mused,
And saw, as in a dream confused,
The countenance of the Sun, dis-
      crowned,
And haggard with a pale despair,
And saw the cloud-rack trail and
      drift
Before it, and the trees uplift
Their leafless branches, and the air

Filled with the arrows of the rain,
And heard amid the mist below,
Like voices of distress and pain,
That haunt the thoughts of men
      insane,
The fateful cawings of the crow.

Then down the road, with mud be-
      sprent,
And drenched with rain from head
      to hoof,
The raindrops dripping from his
      mane
And tail as from a pent-house roof,
A jaded horse, his head down bent,
Passed slowly, limping as he went.

The young Sicilian — who had
      grown
Impatient longer to abide
A prisoner, greatly mortified
To see completely overthrown
His plans for angling in the brook,
And, leaning o'er the bridge of
      stone,
To watch the speckled trout glide
      by,
And float through the inverted sky,
Still round and round the baited
      hook—
Now paced the room with rapid
      stride,
And, pausing at the Poet's side,
Looked forth, and saw the wretched
      steed,
And said : 'Alas for human greed,
That with cold hand and stony eye
Thus turns an old friend out to die,
Or beg his food from gate to gate !
This brings a tale into my mind,
Which, if you are not disinclined
To listen, I will now relate.'

All gave assent ; all wished to hear,
Not without many a jest and jeer,
The story of a spavined steed ;
And even the Student with the rest
Put in his pleasant little jest

Out of Malherbe, that Pegasus
Is but a horse that with all speed
Bears poets to the hospital;
While the Sicilian, self-possessed,
After a moment's interval
Began his simple story thus.

———

THE SICILIAN'S TALE.

THE BELL OF ATRI.

AT Atri in Abruzzo, a small town
Of ancient Roman date, but scant
    renown,
One of those little places that have
    run
Half up the hill, beneath a blazing
    sun,
And then sat down to rest, as if to
    say,
'I climb no farther upward, come
    what may,'—
The Re Giovanni, now unknown to
    fame,
So many monarchs since have
    borne the name,
Had a great bell hung in the
    market-place
Beneath a roof, projecting some
    small space,
By way of shelter from the sun and
    rain.
Then rode he through the streets
    with all his train,
And, with a blast of trumpets loud
    and long,
Made proclamation, that whenever
    wrong
Was done to any man, he should
    but ring
The great bell in the square, and
    he, the King,
Would cause the Syndic to decide
    thereon.
Such was the proclamation of King
    John.

How swift the happy days in Atri
    sped,
What wrongs were righted, need
    not here be said.
Suffice it that, as all things must
    decay,
The hempen rope at length was
    worn away,
Unravelled at the end, and, strand
    by strand,
Loosened and wasted in the ring-
    er's hand,
Till one, who noted this in passing
    by,
Mended the rope with braids of
    briony,
So that the leaves and tendrils of
    the vine
Hung like a votive garland at a
    shrine.

By chance it happened that in Atri
    dwelt
A knight, with spur on heel and
    sword in belt,
Who loved to hunt the wild-boar
    in the woods,
Who loved his falcons with their
    crimson hoods,
Who loved his hounds and horses,
    and all sports
And prodigalities of camps and
    courts ;—
Loved, or had loved them ; for at
    last, grown old,
His only passion was the love of
    gold.

He sold his horses, sold his hawks
    and hounds,
Rented his vineyards and his
    garden-grounds,
Kept but one steed, his favourite
    steed of all,
To starve and shiver in a naked stall,
And day by day sat brooding in
    his chair,
Devising plans how best to hoard
    and spare.

At length he said : 'What is the use or need
To keep at my own cost this lazy steed,
Eating his head off in my stables here,
When rents are low and provender is dear ?
Let him go feed upon the public ways ;
I want him only for the holidays.'
So the old steed was turned into the heat
Of the long, lonely, silent, shadeless street ;
And wandered in suburban lanes forlorn,
Barked at by dogs, and torn by brier and thorn.

One afternoon, as in that sultry clime
It is the custom in the summer time,
With bolted doors and window-shutters closed,
The inhabitants of Atri slept or dozed ;
When suddenly upon their senses fell
The loud alarum of the accusing bell !
The Syndic started from his deep repose,
Turned on his couch, and listened, and then rose
And donned his robes, and with reluctant pace
Went panting forth into the market-place,
Where the great bell upon its cross-beam swung
Reiterating with persistent tongue,
In half-articulate jargon, the old song :
'Some one hath done a wrong, hath done a wrong !'

But ere he reached the belfry's light arcade
He saw, or thought he saw, beneath its shade,
No shape of human form of woman born,
But a poor steed dejected and forlorn,
Who with uplifted head and eager eye
Was tugging at the vines of briony.
'Domeneddio !' cried the Syndic straight,
'This is the Knight of Atri's steed of state !
He calls for justice, being sore distressed,
And pleads his cause as loudly as the best.'

Meanwhile from street and lane a noisy crowd
Had rolled together like a summer cloud,
And told the story of the wretched beast
In five-and-twenty different ways at least,
With much gesticulation and appeal
To heathen gods, in their excessive zeal.
The Knight was called and questioned ; in reply
Did not confess the fact, did not deny ;
Treated the matter as a pleasant jest,
And set at naught the Syndic and the rest,
Maintaining, in an angry undertone,
That he should do what pleased him with his own.

And thereupon the Syndic gravely read
The proclamation of the King ; then said :

'Pride goeth forth on horseback
  grand and gay,
But cometh back on foot, and begs
  its way;
Fame is the fragrance of heroic
  deeds,
Of flowers of chivalry and not of
  weeds!
These are familiar proverbs; but I
  fear
They never yet have reached your
  knightly ear.
What fair renown, what honour,
  what repute
Can come to you from starving this
  poor brute?
He who serves well and speaks not,
  merits more
Than they who clamour loudest at
  the door.
Therefore the law decrees that as
  this steed
Served you in youth, henceforth
  you shall take heed
To comfort his old age, and to
  provide
Shelter in stall, and food and field
  beside.'

The Knight withdrew abashed;
  the people all
Led home the steed in triumph to
  his stall.
The King heard and approved, and
  laughed in glee,
And cried aloud: 'Right well it
  pleaseth me!
Church-bells at best but ring us to
  the door;
But go not in to mass; my bell
  doth more:
It cometh into court and pleads the
  cause
Of creatures dumb and unknown
  to the laws;
And this shall make, in every
  Christian clime,
The Bell of Atri famous for all
  time.'

INTERLUDE.

'Yes, well your story pleads the
  cause
Of those dumb mouths that have
  no speech,
Only a cry from each to each
In its own kind, with its own laws;
Something that is beyond the reach
Of human power to learn or teach,—
An inarticulate moan of pain,
Like the immeasurable main
Breaking upon an unknown beach.'

Thus spake the Poet with a sigh;
Then added, with impassioned cry,
As one who feels the words he
  speaks,
The colour flushing in his cheeks,
The fervour burning in his eye:
'Among the noblest in the land,
Though he may count himself the
  least,
That man I honour and revere
Who without favour, without fear,
In the great city dares to stand
The friend of every friendless beast,
And tames with his unflinching
  hand
The brutes that wear our form and
  face,
The were-wolves of the human
  race!'

Then paused, and waited with a
  frown,
Like some old champion of romance,
Who, having thrown his gauntlet
  down,
Expectant leans upon his lance;
But neither Knight nor Squire is
  found
To raise the gauntlet from the
  ground,
And try with him the battle's chance.

'Wake from your dreams, O Edrehi!
Or dreaming speak to us, and make
A feint of being half awake,

And tell us what your dreams may
    be.
Out of the hazy atmosphere
Of cloud-land deign to reappear
Among us in this Wayside Inn ;
Tell us what visions and what
    scenes
Illuminate the dark ravines
In which you grope your way.
    Begin ! '

Thus the Sicilian spake. The Jew
Made no reply, but only smiled,
As men unto a wayward child,
Not knowing what to answer, do.
As from a cavern's mouth, o'ergrown
With moss and intertangled vines,
A streamlet leaps into the light
And murmurs over root and stone
In a melodious undertone ;
Or as amid the noonday night
Of sombre and wind-haunted pines,
There runs a sound as of the sea ;
So from his bearded lips there came
A melody without a name,
A song, a tale, a history,
Or whatsoever it may be,
Writ and recorded in these lines.

─♦─

THE SPANISH JEW'S TALE.

KAMBALU.

INTO the city of Kambalu,
By the road that leadeth to Is-
    pahan,
At the head of his dusty caravan,
Laden with treasure from realms
    afar,
Baldacca and Kelat and Kandahar,
Rode the great captain Alau.
The Khan from his palace-window
    gazed,
And saw in the thronging street
    beneath,

In the light of the setting sun, that
    blazed
Through the clouds of dust by the
    caravan raised,
The flash of harness and jewelled
    sheath,
And the shining scymitars of the
    guard,
And the weary camels that bared
    their teeth,
As they passed and passed through
    the gates unbarred
Into the shade of the palace-yard.

Thus into the city of Kambalu
Rode the great captain Alau ;
And he stood before the Khan, and
    said :
' The enemies of my lord are dead ;
All the Kalifs of all the West
Bow and obey thy least behest ;
The plains are dark with the mul-
    berry-trees,
The weavers are busy in Samarcand,
The miners are sifting the golden
    sand,
The divers plunging for pearls in
    the seas,
And peace and plenty are in the
    land.

' Baldacca's Kalif, and he alone,
Rose in revolt against thy throne :
His treasures are at thy palace-
    door,
With the swords and the shawls and
    the jewels he wore ;
His body is dust o'er the desert
    blown.

' A mile outside of Baldacca's gate
I left my forces to lie in wait,
Concealed by forests and hillocks
    of sand,
And forward dashed with a handful
    of men,
To lure the old tiger from his den
Into the ambush I had planned.

Ere we reached the town the alarm
    was spread,
For we heard the sound of gongs
    from within ;
And with clash of cymbals and
    warlike din
The gates swung wide ; and we
    turned and fled ;
And the garrison sallied forth and
    pursued,
With the gray old Kalif at their
    head,
And above them the banner of
    Mohammed :
So we snared them all, and the
    town was subdued.

'As in at the gate we rode, behold,
A tower that is called the Tower of
    Gold !
For there the Kalif had hidden his
    wealth,
Heaped and hoarded and piled on
    high,
Like sacks of wheat in a granary ;
And thither the miser crept in
    stealth
To feel of the gold that gave him
    health,
And to gaze and gloat with his
    hungry eye
On jewels that gleamed like a glow-
    worm's spark,
Or the eyes of a panther in the
    dark.

'I said to the Kalif : "Thou art
    old,
Thou hast no need of so much
    gold.
Thou shouldst not have heaped
    and hidden it here,
Till the breath of battle was hot
    and near,
But have sown through the land
    these useless hoards
To spring into shining blades of
    swords,

And keep thine honour sweet and
    clear.
These grains of gold are not grains
    of wheat ;
These bars of silver thou canst not
    eat ;
These jewels and pearls and pre-
    cious stones
Cannot cure the aches in thy bones,
Nor keep the feet of Death one
    hour
From climbing the stairways of thy
    tower ! "

'Then into his dungeon I locked
    the drone,
And left him to feed there all alone
In the honey-cells of his golden
    hive :
Never a prayer, nor a cry, nor a
    groan
Was heard from those massive
    walls of stone,
Nor again was the Kalif seen
    alive !

'When at last we unlocked the
    door,
We found him dead upon the floor ;
The rings had dropped from his
    withered hands,
His teeth were like bones in the
    desert sands :
Still clutching his treasure he had
    died ;
And as he lay there, he appeared
A statue of gold with a silver beard,
His arms outstretched as if cruci-
    fied.'

This is the story, strange and true,
That the great captain Alau
Told to his brother the Tartar
    Khan,
When he rode that day into Kam-
    balu
By the road that leadeth to Ispa-
    han.

INTERLUDE.

'I THOUGHT before your tale began,'
The Student murmured, ' we should
      have
Some legend written by Judah Rav
In his Gemara of Babylon ;
Or something from the Gulistan,—
The tale of the Cazy of Hamadan,
Or of that King of Khorasan
Who saw in dreams the eyes of one
That had a hundred years been
      dead
Still moving restless in his head,
Undimmed, and gleaming with the
      lust
Of power, though all the rest was
      dust.

'But lo ! your glittering caravan
On the road that leadeth to Ispahan
Hath led us farther to the East
Into the regions of Cathay.
Spite of your Kalif and his gold,
Pleasant has been the tale you told,
And full of colour ; that at least
No one will question or gainsay.
And yet on such a dismal day
We need a merrier tale to clear
The dark and heavy atmosphere.
So listen, Lordlings, while I tell,
Without a preface, what befell
A simple cobbler, in the year—
No matter ; it was long ago ;
And that is all we need to know.'

THE STUDENT'S TALE.

THE COBBLER OF HAGENAU.

I TRUST that somewhere and some-
      how
You all have heard of Hagenau,
A quiet, quaint, and ancient town
Among the green Alsatian hills,
A place of valleys, streams, and
      mills,

Where Barbarossa's castle, brown
With rust of centuries, still looks
      down
On the broad, drowsy land below,—
On shadowy forests filled with
      game,
And the blue river winding slow
Through meadows, where the
      hedges grow
That give this little town its name.

It happened in the good old times,
While yet the Master-singers filled
The noisy workshop and the guild
With various melodies and rhymes,
That here in Hagenau there dwelt
A cobbler,—one who loved debate,
And, arguing from a postulate,
Would say what others only felt ;
A man of forecast and of thrift,
And of a shrewd and careful mind
In this world's business, but in-
      clined
Somewhat to let the next world
      drift.

Hans Sachs with vast delight he
      read,
And Regenbogen's rhymes of love,
For their poetic fame had spread
Even to the town of Hagenau ;
And some Quick Melody of the
      Plough,
Or Double Harmony of the Dove,
Was always running in his head.
He kept, moreover, at his side,
Among his leathers and his tools,
Reynard the Fox, the Ship of Fools,
Or Eulenspiegel, open wide ;
With these he was much edified :
He thought them wiser than the
      Schools.

His good wife, full of godly fear,
Liked not these worldly themes to
      hear ;
The Psalter was her book of
      songs ;

405

The only music to her ear
Was that which to the Church be-
longs,
When the loud choir on Sunday
chanted,
And the two angels carved in wood,
That by the windy organ stood,
Blew on their trumpets loud and
clear,
And all the echoes, far and near,
Gibbered as if the church were
haunted.
Outside his door, one afternoon,
This humble votary of the muse
Sat in the narrow strip of shade
By a projecting cornice made,
Mending the Burgomaster's shoes,
And singing a familiar tune :—

'Our ingress into the world
Was naked and bare ;
Our progress through the world
Is trouble and care ;
Our egress from the world
Will be nobody knows where ;
But if we do well here
We shall do well there ;
And I could tell you no more,
Should I preach a whole year !'

Thus sang the cobbler at his work ;
And with his gestures marked the
time,
Closing together with a jerk
Of his waxed thread the stitch and
rhyme.
Meanwhile his quiet little dame
Was leaning o'er the window-sill,
Eager, excited, but mouse-still,
Gazing impatiently to see
What the great throng of folk might
be
That onward in procession came,
Along the unfrequented street,
With horns that blew, and drums
that beat,
And banners flying, and the flame
Of tapers, and, at times, the sweet
Voices of nuns ; and as they sang
Suddenly all the church-bells rang.

In a gay coach, above the crowd,
There sat a monk in ample hood,
Who with his right hand held aloft
A red and ponderous cross of wood,
To which at times he meekly
bowed.
In front three horsemen rode, and
oft,
With voice and air importunate,
A boisterous herald cried aloud :
'The grace of God is at your gate !'
So onward to the church they
passed.

The cobbler slowly turned his last,
And, wagging his sagacious head,
Unto his kneeling housewife said :
' 'Tis the monk Tetzel. I have
heard
The cawings of that reverend bird.
Don't let him cheat you of your
gold ;
Indulgence is not bought and sold.'

The church of Hagenau, that night,
Was full of people, full of light ;
An odour of incense filled the
air,
The priest intoned, the organ
groaned
Its inarticulate despair ;
The candles on the altar blazed,
And full in front of it upraised
The red cross stood against the
glare.
Below, upon the altar-rail
Indulgences were set to sale,
Like ballads at a country fair.
A heavy strong-box, iron-bound
And carved with many a quaint
device,
Received, with a melodious sound,
The coin that purchased Paradise.

Then from the pulpit overhead,
Tetzel the monk, with fiery glow,
Thundered upon the crowd below.
'Good people all, draw near !' he
said ;

'Purchase these letters, signed and
      sealed,
By which all sins, though un-
      revealed
And unrepented, are forgiven!
Count but the gain, count not the
      loss!
Your gold and silver are but dross,
And yet they pave the way to
      heaven.
I hear your mothers and your sires
Cry from their purgatorial fires,
And will ye not their ransom pay?
O senseless people! when the gate
Of heaven is open, will ye wait?
Will ye not enter in to-day?
To-morrow it will be too late;
I shall be gone upon my way.
Make haste! bring money while ye
      may!'

The women shuddered, and turned
      pale;
Allured by hope or driven by fear,
With many a sob and many a tear,
All crowded to the altar-rail.
Pieces of silver and of gold
Into the tinkling strong-box fell
Like pebbles dropped into a well;
And soon the ballads were all sold.
The cobbler's wife among the rest
Slipped into the capacious chest
A golden florin; then withdrew,
Hiding the paper in her breast;
And homeward through the dark-
      ness went
Comforted, quieted, content;
She did not walk, she rather flew,
A dove that settles to her nest,
When some appalling bird of prey
That scared her has been driven
      away.

The days went by, the monk was
      gone,
The summer passed, the winter
      came;
Though seasons changed, yet still
      the same

The daily round of life went on;
The daily round of household care,
The narrow life of toil and prayer.
But in her heart the cobbler's dame
Had now a treasure beyond price,
A secret joy without a name,
The certainty of Paradise.
Alas, alas! Dust unto dust!
Before the winter wore away,
Her body in the churchyard lay,
Her patient soul was with the Just!
After her death, among the things
That even the poor preserve with
      care,—
Some little trinkets and cheap
      rings,
A locket with her mother's hair,
Her wedding gown, the faded
      flowers
She wore upon her wedding day,—
Among these memories of past
      hours,
That so much of the heart reveal,
Carefully kept and put away,
The Letter of Indulgence lay
Folded, with signature and seal.

Meanwhile the Priest, aggrieved
      and pained,
Waited and wondered that no word
Of mass or requiem he heard,
As by the Holy Church ordained:
Then to the Magistrate com-
      plained,
That as this woman had been dead
A week or more, and no mass said,
It was rank heresy, or at least
Contempt of Church; thus said the
      Priest;
And straight the cobbler was ar-
      raigned.

He came, confiding in his cause,
But rather doubtful of the laws.
The Justice from his elbow-chair
Gave him a look that seemed to
      say:
'Thou standest before a Magis-
      trate,

Therefore do not prevaricate!'
Then asked him in a business
    way,
Kindly but cold: 'Is thy wife
    dead?'
The cobbler meekly bowed his
    head;
'She is,' came struggling from his
    throat
Scarce audibly. The Justice wrote
The words down in a book, and
    then
Continued, as he raised his pen:
'She is; and hath a mass been said
For the salvation of her soul?
Come, speak the truth! confess
    the whole!'
The cobbler without pause replied:
'Of mass or prayer there was no
    need;
For at the moment when she died
Her soul was with the glorified!'
And from his pocket with all speed
He drew the priestly title-deed,
And prayed the Justice he would
    read.

The Justice read, amused, amazed;
And as he read his mirth increased;
At times his shaggy brows he
    raised,
Now wondering at the cobbler
    gazed,
Now archly at the angry Priest.
'From all excesses, sins, and
    crimes
Thou hast committed in past times
Thee I absolve! And furthermore,
Purified from all earthly taints,
To the communion of the Saints
And to the sacraments restore!
All stains of weakness, and all
    trace
Of shame and censure I efface;
Remit the pains thou shouldst
    endure,
And make thee innocent and pure,
So that in dying, unto thee
The gates of heaven shall open be!

Though long thou livest, yet this
    grace
Until the moment of thy death
Unchangeable continueth!'

Then said he to the Priest: 'I find
This document is duly signed
Brother John Tetzel, his own hand.
At all tribunals in the land
In evidence it may be used;
Therefore acquitted is the accused.'
Then to the cobbler turned: 'My
    friend,
Pray tell me, didst thou ever read
Reynard the Fox?'—'O yes, in-
    deed!'—
'I thought so. Don't forget the
    end.'

INTERLUDE.

'WHAT was the end? I am
    ashamed
Not to remember Reynard's fate;
I have not read the book of late;
Was he not hanged?' the Poet said.
The Student gravely shook his
    head,
And answered: 'You exaggerate.
There was a tournament pro-
    claimed,
And Reynard fought with Isegrim
The Wolf, and having vanquished
    him,
Rose to high honour in the State,
And Keeper of the Seals was
    named!'

At this the gay Sicilian laughed:
'Fight fire with fire, and craft with
    craft;
Successful cunning seems to be
The moral of your tale,' said he.
'Mine had a better, and the Jew's
Had none at all, that I could see,
His aim was only to amuse.'

Meanwhile from out its ebon case
His violin the Minstrel drew,
And having tuned its strings anew,
Now held it close in his embrace,
And poising in his outstretched
    hand
The bow, like a magician's wand,
He paused, and said, with beaming
    face :
' Last night my story was too long ;
To-day I give you but a song,
An old tradition of the North ;
But first, to put you in the mood,
I will a little while prelude,
And from this instrument draw
    forth
Something by way of overture.'

He played ; at first the tones were
    pure
And tender as a summer night,
The full moon climbing to her
    height,
The sob and ripple of the seas,
The flapping of an idle sail ;
And then by sudden and sharp
    degrees
The multiplied, wild harmonies
Freshened and burst into a gale ;
A tempest howling through the
    dark,
A crash as of some shipwrecked
    bark,
A loud and melancholy wail.

Such was the prelude to the tale
Told by the Minstrel ; and at
    times
He paused amid its varying
    rhymes,
And at each pause again broke in
The music of his violin,
With tones of sweetness or of fear,
Movements of trouble or of calm,
Creating their own atmosphere ;
As sitting in a church we hear
Between the verses of the psalm
The organ playing soft and clear,
Or thundering on the startled ear.

THE MUSICIAN'S TALE.

THE BALLAD OF CARMILHAN.

I.

AT Stralsund, by the Baltic Sea,
    Within the sandy bar,
At sunset of a summer's day,
Ready for sea, at anchor lay
    The good ship Valdemar.

The sunbeams danced upon the
    waves,
    And played along her side ;
And through the cabin windows
    streamed
In ripples of golden light, that
    seemed
    The ripple of the tide.

There sat the captain with his
    friends,
    Old skippers brown and hale,
Who smoked and grumbled o'er
    their grog,
And talked of iceberg and of fog,
    Of calm and storm and gale.

And one was spinning a sailor's yarn
    About Klaboterman,
The Kobold of the sea ; a spright
Invisible to mortal sight,
    Who o'er the rigging ran.

Sometimes he hammered in the
    hold,
    Sometimes upon the mast,
Sometimes abeam, sometimes
    abaft,
Or at the bows he sang and laughed,
    And made all tight and fast.

He helped the sailors at their work,
    And toiled with jovial din ;
He helped them hoist and reef the
    sails,
He helped them stow the casks
    and bales,
    And heave the anchor in.

But woe unto the lazy louts,
  The idlers of the crew;
Them to torment was his delight,
And worry them by day and
    night,
  And pinch them black and blue.

And woe to him whose mortal eyes
  Klaboterman behold.
It is a certain sign of death!—
The cabin-boy here held his breath,
  He felt his blood run cold.

II.

THE jolly skipper paused awhile,
  And then again began;
'There is a Spectre Ship,' quoth
    he,
'A ship of the Dead that sails the
    sea,
  And is called the Carmilhan.

'A ghostly ship, with a ghostly
    crew,
  In tempests she appears;
And before the gale, or against the
    gale,
She sails without a rag of sail,
  Without a helmsman steers.

'She haunts the Atlantic north and
    south,
  But mostly the mid-sea,
Where three great rocks rise bleak
    and bare
Like furnace-chimneys in the air,
  And are called the Chimneys
    Three.

'And ill betide the luckless ship
  That meets the Carmilhan;
Over her decks the seas will leap,
She must go down into the deep,
  And perish mouse and man.'

The captain of the Valdemar
  Laughed loud with merry heart.
'I should like to see this ship,'
    said he;
'I should like to find these Chim-
    neys Three,
  That are marked down in the
    chart.

'I have sailed right over the spot,'
    he said,
  'With a good stiff breeze behind,
When the sea was blue, and the
    sky was clear,—
You can follow my course by these
    pin-holes here,—
  And never a rock could find.'

And then he swore a dreadful oath,
  He swore by the Kingdoms
    Three,
That, should he meet the Carmil-
    han,
He would run her down, although
    he ran
  Right into Eternity!

All this, while passing to and fro,
  The cabin-boy had heard;
He lingered at the door to hear,
And drank in all with greedy
    ear,
  And pondered every word.

He was a simple country lad,
  But of a roving mind.
'O, it must be like heaven,' thought
    he,
'Those far-off foreign lands to
    see,
  And fortune seek and find!'

But in the fo'castle, when he heard
  The mariners blaspheme,
He thought of home, he thought of
    God,
And his mother under the church-
    yard sod,
  And wished it were a dream.

One friend on board that ship had
  he;
'Twas the Klaboterman,
Who saw the Bible in his chest,
And made a sign upon his breast,
  All evil things to ban.

III.

THE cabin windows have grown
  blank
As eyeballs of the dead;
No more the glancing sunbeams
  burn
On the gilt letters of the stern,
  But on the figure-head;

On Valdemar Victorious,
  Who looketh with disdain
To see his image in the tide
Dismembered float from side to
  side,
  And reunite again.

'It is the wind,' those skippers
  said,
  'That swings the vessel so;
It is the wind; it freshens fast,
'Tis time to say farewell at last,
  'Tis time for us to go.'

They shook the captain by the
  hand,
  'Good luck! good luck!' they
    cried;
Each face was like the setting sun,
As, broad and red, they one by one
  Went o'er the vessel's side.

The sun went down, the full moon
  rose,
  Serene o'er field and flood;
And all the winding creeks and
  bays
And broad sea-meadows seemed
  ablaze,—
  The sky was red as blood.

The southwest wind blew fresh and
  fair,
As fair as wind could be;
Bound for Odessa, o'er the bar,
With all sail set, the Valdemar
  Went proudly out to sea.

The lovely moon climbs up the sky
  As one who walks in dreams;
A tower of marble in her light,
A wall of black, a wall of white,
  The stately vessel seems.

Low down upon the sandy coast
  The lights begin to burn;
And now, uplifted high in air,
They kindle with a fiercer glare,
  And now drop far astern.

The dawn appears, the land is gone,
  The sea is all around;
Then on each hand low hills of sand
Emerge and form another land;
  She steereth through the Sound.

Through Kattegat and Skager-rack
  She flitteth like a ghost;
By day and night, by night and day,
She bounds, she flies upon her way
  Along the English coast.

Cape Finisterre is drawing near,
  Cape Finisterre is past;
Into the open ocean stream
She floats, the vision of a dream
  Too beautiful to last.

Suns rise and set, and rise, and yet
  There is no land in sight;
The liquid planets overhead
Burn brighter now the moon is dead,
  And longer stays the night.

IV.

AND now along the horizon's edge
  Mountains of cloud uprose,
Black as with forests underneath,
Above their sharp and jagged teeth
  Were white as drifted snows.

411

Unseen behind them sank the sun,
  But flushed each snowy peak
A little while with rosy light
That faded slowly from the sight
  As blushes from the cheek.

Black grew the sky,—all black, all
    black;
  The clouds were everywhere;
There was a feeling of suspense
In nature, a mysterious sense
  Of terror in the air.

And all on board the Valdemar
  Was still as still could be;
Save when the dismal ship-bell
    tolled,
As ever and anon she rolled,
  And lurched into the sea.

The captain up and down the deck
  Went striding to and fro;
Now watched the compass at the
    wheel,
Now lifted up his hand to feel
  Which way the wind might blow.

And now he looked up at the sails,
  And now upon the deep;
In every fibre of his frame
He felt the storm before it came,
  He had no thought of sleep.

Eight bells! and suddenly abaft,
  With a great rush of rain,
Making the ocean white with
    spume,
In darkness like the day of doom,
  On came the hurricane.

The lightning flashed from cloud
    to cloud,
  And rent the sky in two;
A jagged flame, a single jet
Of white fire, like a bayonet,
  That pierced the eyeballs through.

Then all around was dark again,
  And blacker than before;
But in that single flash of light
He had beheld a fearful sight,
  And thought of the oath he swore.

For right ahead lay the Ship of the
    Dead,
  The ghostly Carmilhan!
Her masts were stripped, her yards
    were bare,
And on her bowsprit, poised in air,
  Sat the Klaboterman.

Her crew of ghosts was all on deck
  Or clambering up the shrouds;
The boatswain's whistle, the cap-
    tain's hail,
Were like the piping of the gale,
  And thunder in the clouds.

And close behind the Carmilhan
  There rose up from the sea,
As from a foundered ship of stone,
Three bare and splintered masts
    alone:
  They were the Chimneys Three.

And onward dashed the Valdemar
  And leaped into the dark;
A denser mist, a colder blast,
A little shudder, and she had passed
  Right through the Phantom
    Bark.

She cleft in twain the shadowy
    hulk,
  But cleft it unaware;
As when, careering to her nest,
The sea-gull severs with her breast
  The unresisting air.

Again the lightning flashed; again
  They saw the Carmilhan,
Whole as before in hull and spar;
But now on board of the Valdemar
  Stood the Klaboterman.

And they all knew their doom was
    sealed;
  They knew that death was near;
Some prayed who never prayed
    before,
And some they wept, and some
    they swore,
  And some were mute with fear.

Then suddenly there came a shock,
And louder than wind or sea
A cry burst from the crew on deck,
As she dashed and crashed, a
hopeless wreck,
Upon the Chimneys Three.

The storm and night were passed,
the light
To streak the east began;
The cabin-boy, picked up at sea,
Survived the wreck, and only he,
To tell of the Carmilhan.

---++---

INTERLUDE.

WHEN the long murmur of applause
That greeted the Musician's lay
Had slowly buzzed itself away,
And the long talk of Spectre Ships
That followed died upon their lips
And came unto a natural pause,
'These tales you tell are one and
all
Of the Old World,' the Poet said,
'Flowers gathered from a crumbling
wall,
Dead leaves that rustle as they
fall;
Let me present you in their stead
Something of our New England
earth,
A tale which, though of no great
worth,
Has still this merit, that it yields
A certain freshness of the fields,
A sweetness as of home-made
bread.'

The Student answered: 'Be dis-
creet;
For if the flour be fresh and sound,
And if the bread be light and
sweet,
Who careth in what mill 'twas
ground,
Or of what oven felt the heat.

Unless, as old Cervantes said,
You are looking after better bread
Than any that is made of wheat?
You know that people nowadays
To what is old give little praise;
All must be new in prose and verse:
They want hot bread, or something
worse,
Fresh every morning, and half
baked;
The wholesome bread of yesterday,
Too stale for them, is thrown away,
Nor is their thirst with water slaked.'

As oft we see the sky in May
Threaten to rain, and yet not rain,
The Poet's face, before so gay,
Was clouded with a look of pain,
But suddenly brightened up again;
And without further let or stay
He told his tale of yesterday.

---++---

THE POET'S TALE.

LADY WENTWORTH.

ONE hundred years ago, and some-
thing more,
In Queen Street, Portsmouth, at
her tavern door,
Neat as a pin, and blooming as a
rose,
Stood Mistress Stavers in her
furbelows,
Just as her cuckoo-clock was striking
nine,
Above her head, resplendent on
the sign,
The portrait of the Earl of Halifax,
In scarlet coat and periwig of flax,
Surveyed at leisure all her varied
charms,
Her cap, her bodice, her white
folded arms,
And half resolved, though he was
past his prime,

413

And rather damaged by the lapse
of time,
To fall down at her feet, and to
declare
The passion that had driven him
to despair.
For from his lofty station he had
seen
Stavers, her husband, dressed in
bottle-green,
Drive his new Flying Stage-coach,
four in hand,
Down the long lane, and out into
the land,
And knew that he was far upon
the way
To Ipswich and to Boston on the
Bay!

Just then the meditations of the
Earl
Were interrupted by a little girl,
Barefooted, ragged, with neglected
hair,
Eyes full of laughter, neck and
shoulders bare,
A thin slip of a girl, like a new
moon,
Sure to be rounded into beauty
soon,
A creature men would worship and
adore,
Though now in mean habiliments
she bore
A pail of water, dripping, through
the street,
And bathing, as she went, her naked
feet.

It was a pretty picture, full of
grace,—
The slender form, the delicate, thin
face ;
The swaying motion, as she hurried
by ;
The shining feet, the laughter in
her eye,
That o'er her face in ripples gleamed
and glanced,

As in her pail the shifting sunbeam
danced :
And with uncommon feelings of
delight
The Earl of Halifax beheld the
sight.
Not so Dame Stavers, for he heard
her say
These words, or thought he did, as
plain as day :
' O Martha Hilton ! Fie ! how dare
you go
About the town half dressed, and
looking so ! '
At which the gipsy laughed, and
straight replied :
' No matter how I look ; I yet shall
ride
In my own chariot, ma'am.' And
on the child
The Earl of Halifax benignly smiled,
As with her heavy burden she
passed on,
Looked back, then turned the corner,
and was gone.

What next, upon that memorable
day,
Arrested his attention was a gay
And brilliant equipage, that flashed
and spun,
The silver harness glittering in the
sun,
Outriders with red jackets, lithe and
lank,
Pounding the saddles as they rose
and sank,
While all alone within the chariot
sat
A portly person with three-cornered
hat,
A crimson velvet coat, head high
in air,
Gold-headed cane, and nicely powdered hair,
And diamond buckles sparkling at
his knees,
Dignified, stately, florid, much at
ease.

Onward the pageant swept, and as
it passed,
Fair Mistress Stavers courtesied
low and fast ;
For this was Governor Wentworth,
driving down
To Little Harbour, just beyond the
town,
Where his Great House stood
looking out to sea,
A goodly place, where it was good
to be.

It was a pleasant mansion, an abode
Near and yet hidden from the great
high-road,
Sequestered among trees, a noble
pile,
Baronial and colonial in its style ;
Gables and dormer-windows every-
where,
And stacks of chimneys rising high
in air,—
Pandæan pipes, on which all winds
that blew
Made mournful music the whole
winter through.
Within, unwonted splendours met
the eye,
Panels, and floors of oak, and
tapestry ;
Carved chimney-pieces, where on
brazen dogs
Revelled and roared the Christmas
fires of logs ;
Doors opening into darkness un-
awares,
Mysterious passages, and flights of
stairs ;
And on the walls, in heavy gilded
frames,
The ancestral Wentworths with
Old-Scripture names.

Such was the mansion where the
great man dwelt,
A widower and childless ; and he
felt

The loneliness, the uncongenial
gloom,
That like a presence haunted every
room ;
For though not given to weakness,
he could feel
The pain of wounds, that ache
because they heal.

The years came and the years
went,—seven in all,
And passed in cloud and sunshine
o'er the Hall ;
The dawns their splendour through
its chambers shed,
The sunsets flushed its western
windows red ;
The snow was on its roofs, the
wind, the rain ;
Its woodlands were in leaf and bare
again ;
Moons waxed and waned, the lilacs
bloomed and died,
In the broad river ebbed and flowed
the tide,
Ships went to sea, and ships came
home from sea,
And the slow years sailed by and
ceased to be.

And all these years had Martha
Hilton served
In the Great House, not wholly un-
observed :
By day, by night, the silver crescent
grew,
Though hidden by clouds, her
light still shining through ;
A maid of all work, whether coarse
or fine,
A servant who made service seem
divine !
Through her each room was fair to
look upon ;
The mirrors glistened, and the
brasses shone,
The very knocker on the outer door,
If she but passed, was brighter
than before.

And now the ceaseless turning of
the mill
Of Time, that never for an hour
stands still,
Ground out the Governor's sixtieth
birthday,
And powdered his brown hair with
silver-gray.
The robin, the forerunner of the
spring,
The bluebird with his jocund carol-
ling,
The restless swallows building in
the eaves,
The golden buttercups, the grass,
the leaves,
The lilacs tossing in the winds of
May,
All welcomed this majestic holi-
day!
He gave a splendid banquet, served
on plate,
Such as became the Governor of
the State,
Who represented England and the
King,
And was magnificent in every-
thing.
He had invited all his friends and
peers, —
The Pepperels, the Langdons, and
the Lears,
The Sparhawks, the Penhallows,
and the rest;
For why repeat the name of every
guest?
But I must mention one, in bands
and gown,
The rector there, the Reverend
Arthur Brown
Of the Established Church; with
smiling face
He sat beside the Governor and
said grace;
And then the feast went on, as
others do,
But ended as none other I e'er
knew.

When they had drunk the King,
with many a cheer,
The Governor whispered in a ser-
vant's ear,
Who disappeared, and presently
there stood
Within the room, in perfect woman-
hood,
A maiden, modest and yet self-
possessed,
Youthful and beautiful, and simply
dressed.
Can this be Martha Hilton? It
must be!
Yes, Martha Hilton, and no other
she!
Dowered with the beauty of her
twenty years,
How ladylike, how queenlike she
appears;
The pale, thin crescent of the days
gone by
Is Dian now in all her majesty!
Yet scarce a guest perceived that
she was there,
Until the Governor, rising from his
chair,
Played slightly with his ruffles, then
looked down,
And said unto the Reverend Arthur
Brown:
'This is my birthday: it shall like-
wise be
My wedding-day; and you shall
marry me!'

The listening guests were greatly
mystified,
None more so than the rector, who
replied:
'Marry you? Yes, that were a
pleasant task,
Your Excellency; but to whom? I
ask.'
The Governor answered: 'To this
lady here;'
And beckoned Martha Hilton to
draw near.

She came and stood, all blushes, at
   his side.
The rector paused. The impatient
   Governor cried :
'This is the lady; do you hesitate?
Then I command you as Chief
   Magistrate.'
The rector read the service loud
   and clear :
'Dearly beloved, we are gathered
   here,'
And so on to the end. At his com-
   mand
On the fourth finger of her fair left
   hand
The Governor placed the ring ; and
   that was all :
Martha was Lady Wentworth of
   the Hall !

INTERLUDE.

WELL pleased the audience heard
   the tale.
The Theologian said : ' Indeed,
To praise you there is little need ;
One almost hears the farmer's flail
Thresh out your wheat, nor does
   there fail
A certain freshness, as you said,
And sweetness as of home-made
   bread.
But not less sweet and not less fresh
Are many legends that I know,
Writ by the monks of long-ago,
Who loved to mortify the flesh,
So that the soul might purer grow,
And rise to a diviner state ;
And one of these—perhaps of all
Most beautiful—I now recall,
And with permission will narrate ;
Hoping thereby to make amends
For that grim tragedy of mine,
As strong and black as Spanish
   wine,

I told last night, and wish almost
It had remained untold, my friends ;
For Torquemada's awful ghost
Came to me in the dreams I
   dreamed ;
And in the darkness glared and
   gleamed
Like a great lighthouse on the
   coast.'

The Student laughing said : ' Far
   more
Like to some dismal fire of bale
Flaring portentous on a hill ;
Or torches lighted on a shore
By wreckers in a midnight gale.
No matter ; be it as you will,
Only go forward with your tale.'

THE THEOLOGIAN'S TALE

THE LEGEND BEAUTIFUL.

' HADST thou stayed, I must have
   fled ! '
That is what the Vision said.

In his chamber all alone,
Kneeling on the floor of stone,
Prayed the Monk in deep contrition
For his sins of indecision,
Prayed for greater self-denial
In temptation and in trial ;
It was noonday by the dial,
And the Monk was all alone.

Suddenly, as if it lightened,
An unwonted splendour brightened
All within him and without him
In that narrow cell of stone ;
And he saw the Blessed Vision
Of our Lord, with light Elysian
Like a vesture wrapped about him,
Like a garment round him thrown.
Not as crucified and slain,
Not in agonies of pain,

Not with bleeding hands and feet,
Did the Monk his Master see;
But as in the village street,
In the house or harvest-field,
Halt and lame and blind he healed,
When he walked in Galilee.

In an attitude imploring,
Hands upon his bosom crossed,
Wondering, worshipping, adoring,
Knelt the Monk in rapture lost.
Lord, he thought, in heaven that
   reignest,
Who am I, that thus thou deignest
To reveal thyself to me?
Who am I, that from the centre
Of thy glory thou shouldst enter
This poor cell, my guest to be?

Then amid his exaltation,
Loud the convent bell appalling,
From its belfry calling, calling,
Rang through court and corridor
With persistent iteration
He had never heard before.
It was now the appointed hour
When alike in shine or shower,
Winter's cold or summer's heat,
To the convent portals came
All the blind and halt and lame,
All the beggars of the street,
For their daily dole of food
Dealt them by the brotherhood;
And their almoner was he
Who upon his bended knee,
Rapt in silent ecstasy
Of divinest self-surrender,
Saw the Vision and the Splendour.

Deep distress and hesitation
Mingled with his adoration;
Should he go, or should he stay?
Should he leave the poor to wait
Hungry at the convent gate,
Till the Vision passed away?
Should he slight his radiant guest,
Slight this visitant celestial,
For a crowd of ragged, bestial

Beggars at the convent gate?
Would the Vision there remain?
Would the Vision come again?
Then a voice within his breast
Whispered, audible and clear
As if to the outward ear:
'Do thy duty; that is best;
Leave unto thy Lord the rest!'

Straightway to his feet he started,
And with longing look intent
On the Blessed Vision bent,
Slowly from his cell departed,
Slowly on his errand went.

At the gate the poor were waiting,
Looking through the iron grating,
With that terror in the eye
That is only seen in those
Who amid their wants and woes
Hear the sound of doors that close,
And of feet that pass them by;
Grown familiar with disfavour,
Grown familiar with the savour
Of the bread by which men die!
But to-day, they knew not why,
Like the gate of Paradise
Seemed the convent gate to rise,
Like a sacrament divine
Seemed to them the bread and wine.
In his heart the Monk was praying,
Thinking of the homeless poor,
What they suffer and endure;
What we see not, what we see;
And the inward voice was saying:
'Whatsoever thing thou doest
To the least of mine and lowest,
That thou doest unto me!'

Unto me! but had the Vision
Come to him in beggar's clothing,
Come a mendicant imploring,
Would he then have knelt adoring,
Or have listened with derision,
And have turned away with loathing?

Thus his conscience put the question,
Full of troublesome suggestion,

As at length, with hurried pace,
Towards his cell he turned his face,
And beheld the convent bright
With a supernatural light,
Like a luminous cloud expanding
Over floor and wall and ceiling.

But he paused with awe-struck
feeling
At the threshold of his door,
For the Vision still was standing
As he left it there before,
When the convent bell appalling,
From its belfry calling, calling,
Summoned him to feed the poor.
Through the long hour intervening
It had waited his return,
And he felt his bosom burn,
Comprehending all the meaning,
When the Blessed Vision said,
' Hadst thou stayed, I must have
fled !'

—••—

INTERLUDE.

ALL praised the Legend more or
less ;
Some liked the moral, some the
verse ;
Some thought it better, and some
worse
Than other legends of the past ;
Until, with ill-concealed distress
At all their cavilling, at last
The Theologian gravely said :
' The Spanish proverb, then, is
right ;
Consult your friends on what you do,
And one will say that it is white,
And others say that it is red.'
And ' Amen !' quoth the Spanish
Jew.

' Six stories told ! We must have
seven,
A cluster like the Pleiades,
And lo ! it happens, as with these,
That one is missing from our
heaven.

Where is the Landlord ? Bring
him here ;
Let the Lost Pleiad reappear.'

Thus the Sicilian cried, and went
Forthwith to seek his missing star,
But did not find him in the bar,
A place that landlords most fre-
quent,
Nor yet beside the kitchen fire,
Nor up the stairs, nor in the hall ;
It was in vain to ask or call,
There were no tidings of the Squire.

So he came back with downcast
head,
Exclaiming : ' Well, our bashful
host
Hath surely given up the ghost.
Another proverb says the dead
Can tell no tales ; and that is true.
It follows, then, that one of you
Must tell a story in his stead.
You must,' he to the Student said,
' Who know so many of the best,
And tell them better than the rest.'

Straight, by these flattering words
beguiled,
The Student, happy as a child
When he is called a little man,
Assumed the double task imposed,
And without more ado unclosed
His smiling lips, and thus began.

—••—

THE STUDENT'S SECOND
TALE.

THE BARON OF ST. CASTINE.

BARON CASTINE of St. Castine
Has left his château in the Pyrenees,
And sailed across the western seas,
When he went away from his fair
demesne
The birds were building, the woods
were green ;

And now the winds of winter blow
Round the turrets of the old château,
The birds are silent and unseen,
The leaves lie dead in the ravine,
And the Pyrenees are white with
snow.

His father, lonely, old, and gray,
Sits by the fireside day by day,
Thinking ever one thought of care;
Through the southern windows,
narrow and tall,
The sun shines into the ancient
hall,
And makes a glory round his hair.
The house-dog, stretched beneath
his chair,
Groans in his sleep as if in pain,
Then wakes, and yawns, and sleeps
again,
So silent is it everywhere,—
So silent you can hear the mouse
Run and rummage along the beams
Behind the wainscot of the wall;
And the old man rouses from his
dreams,
And wanders restless through the
house,
As if he heard strange voices call.

His footsteps echo along the floor
Of a distant passage, and pause
awhile;
He is standing by an open door
Looking long, with a sad, sweet
smile,
Into the room of his absent son.
There is the bed on which he lay,
There are the pictures bright and
gay,
Horses and hounds and sun-lit seas;
There are his powder-flask and gun,
And his hunting-knives in shape of
a fan;
The chair by the window where he
sat,
With the clouded tiger-skin for a
mat,

Looking out on the Pyrenees,
Looking out on Mount Marboré
And the Seven Valleys of Lavedan.
Ah me! he turns away and sighs;
There is a mist before his eyes.

At night, whatever the weather be,
Wind or rain or starry heaven,
Just as the clock is striking seven,
Those who look from the windows
see
The village Curate, with lantern
and maid,
Come through the gateway from
the park
And cross the courtyard damp and
dark,—
A ring of light in a ring of shade.

And now at the old man's side he
stands,
His voice is cheery, his heart ex-
pands,
He gossips pleasantly, by the blaze
Of the fire of fagots, about old days,
And Cardinal Mazarin and the
Fronde,
And the Cardinal's nieces fair and
fond,
And what they did, and what they
said,
When they heard his Eminence was
dead.

And after a pause the old man
says,
His mind still coming back again
To the one sad thought that haunts
his brain,
'Are there any tidings from over
sea?
Ah, why has that wild boy gone
from me?'
And the Curate answers, looking
down,
Harmless and docile as a lamb,
'Young blood! young blood! It
must so be!'

420

And draws from the pocket of his
  gown
A handkerchief like an oriflamb,
And wipes his spectacles, and they
  play
Their little game of lansquenet
In silence for an hour or so,
Till the clock at nine strikes loud
  and clear
From the village lying asleep below,
And across the courtyard, into the
  dark
Of the winding pathway in the
  park,
Curate and lantern disappear,
And darkness reigns in the old
  château.

The ship has come back from over
  sea,
She has been signalled from below,
And into the harbour of Bordeaux
She sails with her gallant company.
But among them is nowhere seen
The brave young Baron of St.
  Castine;
He hath tarried behind, I ween,
In the beautiful land of Acadie!

And the father paces to and fro
Through the chambers of the old
  château,
Waiting, waiting to hear the hum
Of wheels on the road that runs
  below,
Of servants hurrying here and
  there,
The voice in the courtyard, the step
  on the stair,
Waiting for some one who doth not
  come!
But letters there are, which the old
  man reads
To the Curate, when he comes at
  night,
Word by word, as an acolyte
Repeats his prayers and tells his
  beads;

Letters full of the rolling sea,
Full of a young man's joy to be
Abroad in the world, alone and free;
Full of adventures and wonderful
  scenes,
Of hunting the deer through forests
  vast
In the royal grant of Pierre du
  Gast;
Of nights in the tents of the
  Tarratines;
Of Madocawando the Indian chief,
And his daughters, glorious as
  queens,
And beautiful beyond belief;
And so soft the tones of their native
  tongue,
The words are not spoken, they are
  sung!

And the Curate listens, and smiling
  says:
'Ah yes, dear friend! in our young
  days
We should have liked to hunt the
  deer
All day amid those forest scenes,
And to sleep in the tents of the
  Tarratines;
But now it is better sitting here
Within four walls, and without the
  fear
Of losing our hearts to Indian
  queens;
For man is fire and woman is tow,
And the Somebody comes and
  begins to blow.'
Then a gleam of distrust and vague
  surmise
Shines in the father's gentle eyes,
As firelight on a window-pane
Glimmers and vanishes again;
But naught he answers; he only
  sighs,
And for a moment bows his head;
Then, as their custom is, they play
Their little game of lansquenet,
And another day is with the dead.

Another day, and many a day
And many a week and month
depart,
When a fatal letter wings its way
Across the sea, like a bird of prey,
And strikes and tears the old man's
heart.
Lo! the young Baron of St. Castine,
Swift as the wind is, and as wild,
Has married a dusky Tarratine,
Has married Madocawando's child!

The letter drops from the father's
hand;
Though the sinews of his heart are
wrung,
He utters no cry, he breathes no
prayer,
No malediction falls from his
tongue;
But his stately figure, erect and
grand,
Bends and sinks like a column of
sand
In the whirlwind of his great
despair.
Dying, yes, dying! His latest
breath
Of parley at the door of death
Is a blessing on his wayward son.
Lower and lower on his breast
Sinks his gray head; he is at rest;
No longer he waits for any one.

For many a year the old château
Lies tenantless and desolate;
Rank grasses in the courtyard grow,
About its gables caws the crow;
Only the porter at the gate
Is left to guard it, and to wait
The coming of the rightful heir;
No other life or sound is there;
No more the Curate comes at
night,
No more is seen the unsteady light,
Threading the alleys of the park;
The windows of the hall are dark,
The chambers dreary, cold, and
bare!

At length, at last, when the winter
is past,
And birds are building, and woods
are green,
With flying skirts is the Curate
seen
Speeding along the woodland way,
Humming gaily, 'No day is so
long
But it comes at last to vesper-song.'
He stops at the porter's lodge to
say
That at last the Baron of St.
Castine
Is coming home with his Indian
queen,
Is coming without a week's delay;
And all the house must be swept
and clean,
And all things set in good array!
And the solemn porter shakes his
head;
And the answer he makes is:
'Lackaday!
We will see, as the blind man
said!'

Alert since first the day began,
The cock upon the village church
Looks northward from his airy
perch,
As if beyond the ken of man
To see the ships come sailing on,
And pass the Isle of Oléron,
And pass the Tower of Cordouan.

In the church below is cold in clay
The heart that would have leaped
for joy—
O tender heart of truth and trust!—
To see the coming of that day;
In the church below the lips are
dust;
Dust are the hands, and dust the
feet,
That would have been so swift to
meet
The coming of that wayward boy.

At night the front of the old château
Is a blaze of light above and below;
There 's a sound of wheels and
  hoofs in the street,
A cracking of whips, and scamper
  of feet,
Bells are ringing, and horns are
  blown,
And the Baron hath come again to
  his own.

The Curate is waiting in the hall,
Most eager and alive of all
To welcome the Baron and
  Baroness;
But his mind is full of vague
  distress,
For he hath read in Jesuit books
Of those children of the wilderness,
And now, good, simple man! he
  looks
To see a painted savage stride
Into the room, with shoulders bare,
And eagle feathers in her hair,
And around her a robe of panther's
  hide.

Instead, he beholds with secret
  shame
A form of beauty undefined,
A loveliness without a name,
Not of degree, but more of kind;
Nor bold nor shy, nor short nor tall,
But a new mingling of them all.
Yes, beautiful beyond belief,
Transfigured and transfused, he
  sees
The lady of the Pyrenees,
The daughter of the Indian chief.

Beneath the shadow of her hair
The gold-bronze colour of the skin
Seems lighted by a fire within,
As when a burst of sunlight shines
Beneath a sombre grove of pines,—
A dusky splendour in the air.
The two small hands, that now are
  pressed
In his, seem made to be caressed,

They lie so warm and soft and still,
Like birds half hidden in a nest,
Trustful, and innocent of ill.
And ah! he cannot believe his ears
When her melodious voice he hears
Speaking his native Gascon tongue;
The words she utters seem to be
Part of some poem of Goudouli,
They are not spoken, they are sung!
And the Baron smiles, and says,
  'You see,
I told you but the simple truth;
Ah, you may trust the eyes of
  youth!'

Down in the village day by day
The people gossip in their way,
And stare to see the Baroness pass
On Sunday morning to early Mass;
And when she kneeleth down to
  pray,
They wonder, and whisper to-
  gether, and say,
'Surely this is no heathen lass!'
And in course of time they learn to
  bless
The Baron and the Baroness.

And in course of time the Curate
  learns
A secret so dreadful, that by turns
He is ice and fire, he freezes and
  burns.
The Baron at confession hath said,
That though this woman be his
  wife,
He hath wed her as the Indians
  wed,
He hath bought her for a gun and
  a knife!
And the Curate replies: 'O pro-
  fligate,
O Prodigal Son! return once more
To the open arms and the open
  door
Of the Church, or ever it be too late.
Thank God, thy father did not live
To see what he could not forgive;

423

On thee, so reckless and perverse,
He left his blessing, not his curse.
But the nearer the dawn the darker
the night,
And by going wrong all things come
right;
Things have been mended that
were worse,
And the worse, the nearer they are
to mend.
For the sake of the living and the
dead,
Thou shalt be wed as Christians
wed,
And all things come to a happy
end.'

O sun, that followest the night,
In yon blue sky, serene and pure,
And pourest thine impartial light
Alike on mountain and on moor,
Pause for a moment in thy course,
And bless the bridegroom and the
bride!
O Gave, that from thy hidden
source
In yon mysterious mountain-side
Pursuest thy wandering way alone,
And leaping down its steps of
stone,
Along the meadow-lands demure
Stealest away to the Adour,
Pause for a moment in thy course
To bless the bridegroom and the
bride!

The choir is singing the matin song,
The doors of the church are opened
wide,
The people crowd, and press, and
throng
To see the bridegroom and the
bride.
They enter and pass along the
nave;
They stand upon the father's
grave;
The bells are ringing soft and
slow;

The living above and the dead
below
Give their blessing on one and
twain;
The warm wind blows from the
hills of Spain,
The birds are building, the leaves
are green,
And Baron Castine of St. Castine
Hath come at last to his own again.

FINALE.

'*Nunc plaudite!*' the Student
cried,
When he had finished; 'now ap-
plaud,
As Roman actors used to say
At the conclusion of a play;'
And rose, and spread his hands
abroad,
And smiling bowed from side to
side,
As one who bears the palm away.
And generous was the applause and
loud,
But less for him than for the sun,
That even as the tale was done
Burst from its canopy of cloud,
And lit the landscape with the blaze
Of afternoon on autumn days,
And filled the room with light, and
made
The fire of logs a painted shade.

A sudden wind from out the west
Blew all its trumpets loud and
shrill;
The windows rattled with the blast,
The oak-trees shouted as it passed,
And straight, as if by fear
possessed,
The cloud encampment on the hill
Broke up, and fluttering flag and
tent
Vanished into the firmament,

424

And down the valley fled amain
The rear of the retreating rain.

Only far up in the blue sky
A mass of clouds, like drifted snow
Suffused with a faint Alpine glow,
Was heaped together, vast and
    high,
On which a shattered rainbow hung,
Not rising like the ruined arch
Of some aerial aqueduct,
But like a roseate garland plucked

From an Olympian god, and flung
Aside in his triumphal march.

Like prisoners from their dungeon
    gloom,
Like birds escaping from a snare,
Like schoolboys at the hour of
    play,
All left at once the pent-up room,
And rushed into the open air ;
And no more tales were told that
    day.

PART III.

PRELUDE.

THE evening came ; the golden
    vane
A moment in the sunset glanced,
Then darkened, and then gleamed
    again,
As from the east the moon
    advanced
And touched it with a softer light ;
While underneath, with flowing
    mane,
Upon the sign the Red Horse
    pranced,
And galloped forth into the night.

But brighter than the afternoon
That followed the dark day of rain,
And brighter than the golden vane
That glistened in the rising moon,
Within the ruddy firelight
    gleamed ;
And every separate window-pane,
Backed by the outer darkness,
    showed
A mirror, where the flamelets
    gleamed
And flickered to and fro, and
    seemed
A bonfire lighted in the road.

Amid the hospitable glow,
Like an old actor on the stage,
With the uncertain voice of age,
The singing chimney chanted low
The homely songs of long ago.

The voice that Ossian heard of
    yore,
When midnight winds were in his
    hall ;
A ghostly and appealing call,
A sound of days that are no more !
And dark as Ossian sat the Jew,
And listened to the sound, and
    knew
The passing of the airy hosts,
The gray and misty cloud of ghosts
In their interminable flight ;
And listening muttered in his
    beard,
With accent indistinct and weird,
'Who are ye, children of the
    Night ?'

Beholding his mysterious face,
'Tell me,' the gay Sicilian said,
'Why was it that in breaking bread
At supper, you bent down your head
And, musing, paused a little space,
As one who says a silent grace?'

The Jew replied, with solemn air,
'I said the Manichæan's prayer.
It was his faith,—perhaps is mine,—
That life in all its forms is one,
And that its secret conduits run
Unseen, but in unbroken line,
From the great fountain-head divine,
Through man and beast, through grain and grass.
Howe'er we struggle, strive, and cry,
From death there can be no escape,
And no escape from life, alas!
Because we cannot die, but pass
From one into another shape:
It is but into life we die.

'Therefore the Manichæan said
This simple prayer on breaking bread,
Lest he with hasty hand or knife
Might wound the incarcerated life,
The soul in things that we call dead:
"I did not reap thee, did not bind thee,
I did not thrash thee, did not grind thee,
Nor did I in the oven bake thee!
It was not I, it was another
Did these things unto thee, O brother;
I only have thee, hold thee, break thee!"'

'That birds have souls I can concede,'
The poet cried, with glowing cheeks;
'The flocks that from their beds of reed
Uprising north or southward fly,
And flying write upon the sky
The biforked letter of the Greeks,
As hath been said by Rucellai;
All birds that sing or chirp or cry,
Even those migratory bands,
The minor poets of the air,

The plover, peep, and sanderling,
That hardly can be said to sing,
But pipe along the barren sands,—
All these have souls akin to ours;
So hath the lovely race of flowers:
Thus much I grant, but nothing more.
The rusty hinges of a door
Are not alive because they creak;
This chimney, with its dreary roar,
These rattling windows, do not speak!'
'To me they speak,' the Jew replied;
'And in the sounds that sink and soar,
I hear the voices of a tide
That breaks upon an unknown shore!'

Here the Sicilian interfered:
'That was your dream, then, as you dozed
A moment since, with eyes half-closed,
And murmured something in your beard.'
The Hebrew smiled, and answered,
'Nay;
Not that, but something very near;
Like, and yet not the same, may seem
The vision of my waking dream;
Before it wholly dies away,
Listen to me, and you shall hear.'

THE SPANISH JEW'S TALE.

AZRAEL.

KING SOLOMON, before his palace gate
At evening, on the pavement tessellate
Was walking with a stranger from the East,
Arrayed in rich attire as for a feast,

The mighty Runjeet-Sing, a learned
man,
And Rajah of the realms of Hin-
dostan.
And as they walked the guest
became aware
Of a white figure in the twilight air,
Gazing intent, as one who with
surprise
His form and features seemed to
recognise ;
And in a whisper to the king he
said :
'What is yon shape, that, pallid as
the dead,
Is watching me, as if he sought to
trace
In the dim light the features of my
face ?'

The king looked, and replied : ' I
know him well ;
It is the Angel men call Azrael,
'Tis the Death Angel ; what hast
thou to fear ?'
And the guest answered : ' Lest he
should come near,
And speak to me, and take away
my breath !
Save me from Azrael, save me from
death !
O king, that hast dominion o'er the
wind,
Bid it arise and bear me hence to
Ind.'

The king gazed upward at the
cloudless sky,
Whispered a word, and raised his
hand on high,
And lo ! the signet-ring of chryso-
prase
On his uplifted finger seemed to
blaze
With hidden fire, and rushing from
the west
There came a mighty wind, and
seized the guest

And lifted him from earth, and on
they passed,
His shining garments streaming in
the blast,
A silken banner o'er the walls up-
reared,
A purple cloud, that gleamed and
disappeared.
Then said the Angel, smiling : ' If
this man
Be Rajah Runjeet-Sing of Hindo-
stan,
Thou hast done well in listening to
his prayer ;
I was upon my way to seek him
there.'

—••—

INTERLUDE.

' O EDREHI, forbear to-night
Your ghostly legends of affright,
And let the Talmud rest in peace ;
Spare us your dismal tales of death
That almost take away one's breath ;
So doing, may your tribe increase.'

Thus the Sicilian said ; then went
And on the spinet's rattling keys
Played Marianina, like a breeze
From Naples and the Southern
seas,
That brings us the delicious scent
Of citron and of orange trees,
And memories of soft days of ease
At Capri and Amalfi spent.

' Not so,' the eager Poet said ;
' At least, not so before I tell
The story of my Azrael,
An angel mortal as ourselves,
Which in an ancient tome I found
Upon a convent's dusty shelves,
Chained with an iron chain, and
bound
In parchment, and with clasps of
brass,

Lest from its prison, some dark day,
It might be stolen or steal away,
While the good friars were singing
    mass.

'It is a tale of Charlemagne,
When like a thunder-cloud, that
    lowers
And sweeps from mountain-crest
    to coast,
With lightning flaming through its
    showers,
He swept across the Lombard plain,
Beleaguering with his warlike train
Pavía, the country's pride and
    boast,
The City of the Hundred Towers.'
Thus heralded the tale began,
And thus in sober measure ran.

---◆---

THE POET'S TALE.

CHARLEMAGNE.

OLGER the Dane and Desiderio,
King of the Lombards, on a lofty
    tower
Stood gazing northward o'er the
    rolling plains,
League after league of harvests, to
    the foot
Of the snow-crested Alps, and saw
    approach
A mighty army, thronging all the
    roads
That led into the city. And the
    King
Said unto Olger, who had passed
    his youth
As hostage at the court of France,
    and knew
The Emperor's form and face :
'Is Charlemagne
Among that host?' And Olger
answered : 'No.'

And still the innumerable multitude
Flowed onward and increased, until
    the King
Cried in amazement : 'Surely
    Charlemagne
Is coming in the midst of all these
    knights ! '
And Olger answered slowly : 'No;
    not yet ;
He will not come so soon.' Then
    much disturbed
King Desiderio asked : 'What
    shall we do,
If he approach with a still greater
    army ? '
And Olger answered : 'When he
    shall appear,
You will behold what manner of
    man he is ;
But what will then befall us I know
    not.'

Then came the guard that never
    knew repose,
The Paladins of France ; and at
    the sight
The Lombard King o'ercome with
    terror cried :
'This must be Charlemagne ! ' and
    as before
Did Olger answer : 'No ; not yet,
    not yet.'

And then appeared in panoply
    complete
The Bishops and the Abbots and
    the Priests
Of the imperial chapel, and the
    Counts ;
And Desiderio could no more en-
    dure
The light of day, nor yet encounter
    death,
But sobbed aloud and said : 'Let
    us go down
And hide us in the bosom of the
    earth,
Far from the sight and anger of
    a foe

So terrible as this!' And Olger
said:
'When you behold the harvests in
the fields
Shaking with fear, the Po and the
Ticino
Lashing the city walls with iron
waves,
Then may you know that Charle-
magne is come.'
And even as he spake, in the north-
west,
Lo! there uprose a black and
threatening cloud,
Out of whose bosom flashed the
light of arms
Upon the people pent up in the city;
A light more terrible than any dark-
ness;
And Charlemagne appeared;—a
Man of Iron!

His helmet was of iron, and his
gloves
Of iron, and his breastplate and
his greaves
And tassets were of iron, and his
shield.
In his left hand he held an iron
spear,
In his right hand his sword invincible.
The horse he rode on had the
strength of iron,
And colour of iron. All who went
before him,
Beside him and behind him, his
whole host,
Were armed with iron, and their
hearts within them
Were stronger than the armour
that they wore.
The fields and all the roads were
filled with iron,
And points of iron glistened in the
sun
And shed a terror through the city
streets.

This at a single glance Olger the
Dane
Saw from the tower, and turning to
the King
Exclaimed in haste: 'Behold! this
is the man
You looked for with such eager-
ness!' and then
Fell as one dead at Desiderio's feet.

———

INTERLUDE.

WELL pleased all listened to the
tale,
That drew, the Student said, its
pith
And marrow from the ancient myth
Of some one with an iron flail;
Or that portentous Man of Brass
Hephæstus made in days of yore,
Who stalked about the Cretan
shore,
And saw the ships appear and pass,
And threw stones at the Argonauts,
Being filled with indiscriminate ire
That tangled and perplexed his
thoughts;
But, like a hospitable host,
When strangers landed on the coast,
Heated himself red-hot with fire,
And hugged them in his arms, and
pressed
Their bodies to his burning breast.

The Poet answered: 'No, not thus
The legend rose; it sprang at first
Out of the hunger and the thirst
In all men for the marvellous.
And thus it filled and satisfied
The imagination of mankind,
And this ideal to the mind
Was truer than historic fact.
Fancy enlarged and multiplied
The terrors of the awful name
Of Charlemagne, till he became
Armipotent in every act,

429

And, clothed in mystery, appeared
Not what men saw, but what they
feared.
Besides, unless my memory fail,
Your some one with an iron flail
Is not an ancient myth at all,
But comes much later on the
scene
As Talus in the Faerie Queene,
The iron groom of Artegall,
Who threshed out falsehood and
deceit,
And truth upheld, and righted
wrong,
As was, as is the swallow, fleet,
And as the lion is, was strong.'

The Theologian said : ' Perchance
Your chronicler in writing this
Had in his mind the Anabasis,
Where Xenophon describes the
advance
Of Artaxerxes to the fight ;
At first the low gray cloud of dust,
And then a blackness o'er the fields
As of a passing thunder-gust,
Then flash of brazen armour bright,
And ranks of men, and spears up-
thrust,
Bowmen and troops with wicker
shields,
And cavalry equipped in white,
And chariots ranged in front of
these
With scythes upon their axle-trees.'

To this the Student answered :
'Well,
I also have a tale to tell
Of Charlemagne ; a tale that throws
A softer light, more tinged with
rose,
Than your grim apparition cast
Upon the darkness of the past.
Listen, and hear in English rhyme
What the good Monk of Lauresheim
Gives as the gossip of his time,
In mediæval Latin prose.'

THE STUDENT'S TALE.

EMMA AND EGINHARD.

WHEN Alcuin taught the sons of
Charlemagne,
In the free schools of Aix, how
kings should reign,
And with them taught the children
of the poor
How subjects should be patient and
endure,
He touched the lips of some, as
best befit,
With honey from the hives of Holy
Writ ;
Others intoxicated with the wine
Of ancient history, sweet but less
divine ;
Some with the wholesome fruits of
grammar fed ;
Others with mysteries of the stars
o'erhead,
That hang suspended in the vaulted
sky
Like lamps in some fair palace vast
and high.

In sooth, it was a pleasant sight to
see
That Saxon monk, with hood and
rosary,
With inkhorn at his belt, and pen
and book,
And mingled love and reverence
in his look,
Or hear the cloister and the court
repeat
The measured footfalls of his sandalled feet,
Or watch him with the pupils of
his school,
Gentle of speech, but absolute of
rule.

Among them, always earliest in
his place,
Was Eginhard, a youth of Frankish
race,

430

Whose face was bright with flashes
  that forerun
The splendours of a yet unrisen
  sun.
To him all things were possible,
  and seemed
Not what he had accomplished,
  but had dreamed,
And what were tasks to others were
  his play,
The pastime of an idle holiday.

Smaragdo, Abbot of St. Michael's,
  said,
With many a shrug and shaking of
  the head,
Surely some demon must possess
  the lad,
Who showed more wit than ever
  schoolboy had,
And learned his Trivium thus with-
  out the rod ;
But Alcuin said it was the grace of
  God.

Thus he grew up, in Logic point-
  device,
Perfect in Grammar, and in Rhe-
  toric nice ;
Science of Numbers, Geometric
  art,
And lore of Stars, and Music knew
  by heart ;
A Minnesinger, long before the
  times
Of those who sang their love in
  Suabian rhymes.

The Emperor, when he heard this
  good report
Of Eginhard much buzzed about
  the court,
Said to himself, 'This stripling
  seems to be
Purposely sent into the world for
  me ;
He shall become my scribe, and
  shall be schooled

In all the arts whereby the world
  is ruled.'
Thus did the gentle Eginhard attain
To honour in the court of Charlemagne ;
Became the sovereign's favourite,
  his right hand,
So that his fame was great in all
  the land,
And all men loved him for his
  modest grace
And comeliness of figure and of
  face.
An inmate of the palace, yet recluse,
A man of books, yet sacred from
  abuse
Among the armed knights with spur
  on heel,
The tramp of horses and the clang
  of steel ;
And as the Emperor promised he
  was schooled
In all the arts by which the world
  is ruled.
But the one art supreme, whose
  law is fate,
The Emperor never dreamed of
  till too late.

Home from her convent to the
  palace came
The lovely Princess Emma, whose
  sweet name,
Whispered by seneschal or sung by
  bard,
Had often touched the soul of
  Eginhard.
He saw her from his window, as in
  state
She came, by knights attended
  through the gate ;
He saw her at the banquet of that
  day,
Fresh as the morn, and beautiful
  as May ;
He saw her in the garden, as she
  strayed

431

Among the flowers of summer with
   her maid,
And said to him, 'O Eginhard,
   disclose
The meaning and the mystery of
   the rose ;'
And trembling he made answer :
   'In good sooth,
Its mystery is love, its meaning
   youth !'

How can I tell the signals and the
   signs
By which one heart another heart
   divines ?
How can I tell the many thousand
   ways
By which it keeps the secret it
   betrays ?

O mystery of love ! O strange
   romance !
Among the Peers and Paladins of
   France,
Shining in steel, and prancing on
   gay steeds,
Noble by birth, yet nobler by great
   deeds,
The Princess Emma had no words
   nor looks
But for this clerk, this man of
   thought and books.

The summer passed, the autumn
   came ; the stalks
Of lilies blackened in the garden
   walks ;
The leaves fell, russet-golden and
   blood-red,
Love-letters thought the poet
   fancy-led,
Or Jove descending in a shower of
   gold
Into the lap of Danae of old ;
For poets cherish many a strange
   conceit,
And love transmutes all nature by
   its heat.

No more the garden lessons, nor
   the dark
And hurried meetings in the
   twilight park ;
But now the studious lamp, and
   the delights
Of firesides in the silent winter
   nights,
And watching from his window
   hour by hour
The light that burned in Princess
   Emma's tower.

At length one night, while musing
   by the fire,
O'ercome at last by his insane
   desire,—
For what will reckless love not do
   and dare ?—
He crossed the court, and climbed
   the winding stair,
With some feigned message in the
   Emperor's name ;
But when he to the lady's presence
   came
He knelt down at her feet, until
   she laid
Her hand upon him, like a naked
   blade,
And whispered in his ear : 'Arise,
   Sir Knight,
To my heart's level, O my heart's
   delight.'

And there he lingered till the
   crowing cock,
The Alectryon of the farmyard and
   the flock,
Sang his aubade with lusty voice
   and clear,
To tell the sleeping world that
   dawn was near.
And then they parted ; but at
   parting, lo !
They saw the palace courtyard
   white with snow,
And, placid as a nun, the moon on
   high

Gazing from cloudy cloisters of the sky.
'Alas!' he said, 'how hide the fatal line
Of footprints leading from thy door to mine,
And none returning!' Ah, he little knew
What woman's wit, when put to proof, can do!

That night the Emperor, sleepless with the cares
And troubles that attend on state affairs,
Had risen before the dawn, and musing gazed
Into the silent night, as one amazed
To see the calm that reigned o'er all supreme,
When his own reign was but a troubled dream.
The moon lit up the gables capped with snow,
And the white roofs, and half the court below,
And he beheld a form, that seemed to cower
Beneath a burden, come from Emma's tower,—
A woman, who upon her shoulders bore
Clerk Eginhard to his own private door,
And then returned in haste, but still essayed
To tread the footprints she herself had made;
And as she passed across the lighted space,
The Emperor saw his daughter Emma's face!

He started not; he did not speak or moan,
But seemed as one who hath been turned to stone;
And stood there like a statue, nor awoke

Out of his trance of pain, till morning broke,
Till the stars faded, and the moon went down,
And o'er the towers and steeples of the town
Came the gray daylight; then the sun, who took
The empire of the world with sovereign look,
Suffusing with a soft and golden glow
All the dead landscape in its shroud of snow,
Touching with flame the tapering chapel spires,
Windows and roofs, and smoke of household fires,
And kindling park and palace as he came;
The stork's nest on the chimney seemed in flame.
And thus he stood till Eginhard appeared,
Demure and modest with his comely beard
And flowing flaxen tresses, come to ask,
As was his wont, the day's appointed task.

The Emperor looked upon him with a smile,
And gently said: 'My son, wait yet a while;
This hour my council meets upon some great
And very urgent business of the state.
Come back within the hour. On thy return
The work appointed for thee shalt thou learn.'

Having dismissed this gallant Troubadour,
He summoned straight his council, and secure

433

And steadfast in his purpose, from
    the throne
All the adventure of the night made
    known ;
Then asked for sentence ; and with
    eager breath
Some answered banishment, and
    others death.

Then spake the king : 'Your
    sentence is not mine ;
Life is the gift of God, and is
    divine ;
Nor from these palace walls shall
    one depart
Who carries such a secret in his
    heart ;
My better judgment points another
    way.
Good Alcuin, I remember how one
    day
When my Pepino asked you, "What
    are men ? "
You wrote upon his tablets with
    your pen,
" Guests of the grave and travellers
    that pass ! "
This being true of all men, we, alas !
Being all fashioned of the selfsame
    dust,
Let us be merciful as well as just ;
This passing traveller, who hath
    stolen away
The brightest jewel of my crown
    to-day,
Shall of himself the precious gem
    restore ;
By giving it, I make it mine once
    more.
Over those fatal footprints I will
    throw
My ermine mantle like another
    snow.'

Then Eginhard was summoned to
    the hall,
And entered, and in presence of
    them all,

The Emperor said : ' My son, for
    thou to me
Hast been a son, and evermore
    shalt be,
Long hast thou served thy
    sovereign, and thy zeal
Pleads to me with importunate
    appeal,
While I have been forgetful to
    requite
Thy service and affection as was
    right.
But now the hour is come, when I,
    thy Lord,
Will crown thy love with such
    supreme reward,
A gift so precious kings have
    striven in vain
To win it from the hands of
    Charlemagne.'

Then sprang the portals of the
    chamber wide,
And Princess Emma entered, in
    the pride
Of birth and beauty, that in part
    o'ercame
The conscious terror and the blush
    of shame.
And the good Emperor rose up
    from his throne,
And taking her white hand within
    his own
Placed it in Eginhard's, and said :
    ' My son,
This is the gift thy constant zeal
    hath won ;
Thus I repay the royal debt I owe,
And cover up the footprints in the
    snow.'

INTERLUDE.

THUS ran the Student's pleasant
    rhyme
Of Eginhard and love and youth ;
Some doubted its historic truth,

434

But while they doubted, ne'er-
    theless
Saw in it gleams of truthfulness,
And thanked the Monk of Laures-
    heim.

This they discussed in various
    mood ;
Then in the silence that ensued
Was heard a sharp and sudden
    sound
As of a bowstring snapped in air ;
And the Musician with a bound
Sprang up in terror from his chair,
And for a moment listening stood,
Then strode across the room, and
    found
His dear, his darling violin
Still lying safe asleep within
Its little cradle, like a child
That gives a sudden cry of pain,
And wakes to fall asleep again ;
And as he looked at it and smiled,
By the uncertain light beguiled,
Despair ! two strings were broken
    in twain.

While all lamented and made moan,
With many a sympathetic word
As if the loss had been their own,
Deeming the tones they might have
    heard
Sweeter than they had heard before,
They saw the Landlord at the door,
The missing man, the portly Squire !
He had not entered, but he stood
With both arms full of seasoned
    wood,
To feed the much-devouring fire,
That like a lion in a cage
Lashed its long tail and roared with
    rage.

The missing man ! Ah, yes, they
    said,
Missing, but whither had he fled ?
Where had he hidden himself
    away ?
No farther than the barn or shed ;

He had not hidden himself, nor
    fled ;
How should he pass the rainy day
But in his barn with hens and hay,
Or mending harness, cart, or sled?
Now, having come, he needs must
    stay
And tell his tale as well as they.

The Landlord answered only :
    ' These
Are logs from the dead apple-trees
Of the old orchard planted here
By the first Howe of Sudbury.
Nor oak nor maple has so clear
A flame, or burns so quietly,
Or leaves an ash so clean and
    white ;'
Thinking by this to put aside
The impending tale that terrified ;
When suddenly, to his delight,
The Theologian interposed,
Saying that when the door was
    closed,
And they had stopped that draft of
    cold,
Unpleasant night air, he proposed
To tell a tale world-wide apart
From that the Student had just
    told ;
World-wide apart, and yet akin,
As showing that the human heart
Beats on for ever as of old,
As well beneath the snow-white
    fold
Of Quaker kerchief, as within
Sendal or silk or cloth of gold,
And without preface would begin.

And then the clamorous clock
    struck eight,
Deliberate, with sonorous chime
Slow measuring out the march of
    time,
Like some grave Consul of old
    Rome
In Jupiter's temple driving home
The nails that marked the year and
    date.

Thus interrupted in his rhyme,
The Theologian needs must wait;
But quoted Horace, where he sings
The dire Necessity of things,
That drives into the roofs sublime
Of new-built houses of the great
The adamantine nails of Fate.

When ceased the little carillon
To herald from its wooden tower
The important transit of the
   hour,
The Theologian hastened on,
Content to be allowed at last
To sing his Idyl of the Past.

THE THEOLOGIAN'S TALE.

ELIZABETH.

I.

'Ah, how short are the days! How soon the night overtakes us!
In the old country the twilight is longer; but here in the forest
Suddenly comes the dark, with hardly a pause in its coming,
Hardly a moment between the two lights, the day and the lamplight;
Yet how grand is the winter! How spotless the snow is, and perfect!'

Thus spake Elizabeth Haddon at nightfall to Hannah the housemaid,
As in the farmhouse kitchen, that served for kitchen and parlour,
By the window she sat with her work, and looked on a landscape
White as the great white sheet that Peter saw in his vision,
By the four corners let down and descending out of the heavens.
Covered with snow were the forests of pine, and the fields and the
   meadows.
Nothing was dark but the sky, and the distant Delaware flowing
Down from its native hills, a peaceful and bountiful river.

Then with a smile on her lips made answer Hannah the housemaid:
'Beautiful winter! yea, the winter is beautiful, surely,
If one could only walk like a fly with one's feet on the ceiling.
But the great Delaware River is not like the Thames, as we saw it
Out of our upper windows in Rotherhithe Street in the Borough,
Crowded with masts and sails of vessels coming and going;
Here there is nothing but pines, with patches of snow on their branches.
There is snow in the air, and see! it is falling already;
All the roads will be blocked, and I pity Joseph to-morrow,
Breaking his way through the drifts, with his sled and oxen; and then,
   too,
How in all the world shall we get to Meeting on First-Day?'

But Elizabeth checked her, and answered, mildly reproving:
'Surely the Lord will provide; for unto the snow he sayeth,
Be thou on the earth, the good Lord sayeth; he is it
Giveth snow like wool, like ashes scatters the hoar-frost.'
So she folded her work and laid it away in her basket.

Meanwhile Hannah the housemaid had closed and fastened the
    shutters,
Spread the cloth, and lighted the lamp on the table, and placed there
Plates and cups from the dresser, the brown rye loaf, and the butter
Fresh from the dairy, and then, protecting her hand with a holder,
Took from the crane in the chimney the steaming and simmering kettle,
Poised it aloft in the air, and filled up the earthen teapot,
Made in Delft, and adorned with quaint and wonderful figures.

Then Elizabeth said, 'Lo! Joseph is long on his errand.
I have sent him away with a hamper of food and of clothing
For the poor in the village. A good lad and cheerful is Joseph;
In the right place is his heart, and his hand is ready and willing.'

Thus in praise of her servant she spake, and Hannah the housemaid
Laughed with her eyes, as she listened, but governed her tongue, and
    was silent,
While her mistress went on : 'The house is far from the village ;
We should be lonely here, were it not for friends that in passing
Sometimes tarry o'ernight, and make us glad by their coming.'

Thereupon answered Hannah the housemaid, the thrifty, the frugal :
'Yea, they come and they tarry, as if thy house were a tavern ;
Open to all are its doors, and they come and go like the pigeons
In and out of the holes of the pigeon-house over the hayloft,
Cooing and smoothing their feathers and basking themselves in the
    sunshine.'

But in meekness of spirit, and calmly, Elizabeth answered :
'All I have is the Lord's, not mine to give or withhold it ;
I but distribute his gifts to the poor, and to those of his people
Who in journeyings often surrender their lives to his service.
His, not mine, are the gifts, and only so far can I make them
Mine, as in giving I add my heart to whatever is given.
Therefore my excellent father first built this house in the clearing ;
Though he came not himself, I came ; for the Lord was my guidance,
Leading me here for this service. We must not grudge, then, to others
Ever the cup of cold water, or crumbs that fall from our table.'

Thus rebuked, for a season was silent the penitent housemaid ;
And Elizabeth said in tones even sweeter and softer :
'Dost thou remember, Hannah, the great May-Meeting in London,
When I was still a child, how we sat in the silent assembly,
Waiting upon the Lord in patient and passive submission ?
No one spake, till at length a young man, a stranger, John Estaugh,
Moved by the Spirit, rose, as if he were John the Apostle,
Speaking such words of power that they bowed our hearts, as a strong
    wind
Bends the grass of the fields, or grain that is ripe for the sickle.

Thoughts of him to-day have been oft borne inward upon me,
Wherefore I do not know; but strong is the feeling within me
That once more I shall see a face I have never forgotten.'

II.

E'en as she spake they heard the musical jangle of sleigh-bells,
First far off, with a dreamy sound and faint in the distance,
Then growing nearer and louder, and turning into the farmyard,
Till it stopped at the door, with sudden creaking of runners.
Then there were voices heard as of two men talking together,
And to herself, as she listened, upbraiding said Hannah the housemaid,
'It is Joseph come back, and I wonder what stranger is with him.'

Down from its nail she took and lighted the great tin lantern
Pierced with holes, and round, and roofed like the top of a lighthouse,
And went forth to receive the coming guest at the doorway,
Casting into the dark a network of glimmer and shadow
Over the falling snow, the yellow sleigh, and the horses,
And the forms of men, snow-covered, looming gigantic.
Then giving Joseph the lantern, she entered the house with the stranger.
Youthful he was and tall, and his cheeks aglow with the night air;
And as he entered, Elizabeth rose, and, going to meet him,
As if an unseen power had announced, and preceded his presence,
And he had come as one whose coming had long been expected,
Quietly gave him her hand, and said, 'Thou art welcome, John Estaugh.'
And the stranger replied, with staid and quiet behaviour,
'Dost thou remember me still, Elizabeth? After so many
Years have passed, it seemeth a wonderful thing that I find thee.
Surely the hand of the Lord conducted me here to thy threshold.
For as I journeyed along, and pondered alone and in silence
On His ways, that are past finding out, I saw in the snow-mist,
Seemingly weary with travel, a wayfarer, who by the wayside
Paused and waited. Forthwith I remembered Queen Candace's eunuch,
How on the way that goes down from Jerusalem unto Gaza,
Reading Esaias the Prophet, he journeyed, and spake unto Philip,
Praying him to come up and sit in his chariot with him.
So I greeted the man, and he mounted the sledge beside me,
And as we talked on the way he told me of thee and thy homestead,
How, being led by the light of the Spirit, that never deceiveth,
Full of zeal for the work of the Lord, thou hadst come to this country.
And I remembered thy name, and thy father and mother in England,
And on my journey have stopped to see thee, Elizabeth Haddon,
Wishing to strengthen thy hand in the labours of love thou art doing.'

And Elizabeth answered with confident voice, and serenely
Looking into his face with her innocent eyes as she answered,
'Surely the hand of the Lord is in it; His Spirit hath led thee
Out of the darkness and storm to the light and peace of my fireside.'

Then, with stamping of feet, the door was opened, and Joseph
Entered, bearing the lantern, and, carefully blowing the light out,
Hung it up on its nail, and all sat down to their supper;
For underneath that roof was no distinction of persons,
But one family only, one heart, one hearth, and one household.

When the supper was ended they drew their chairs to the fireplace,
Spacious, open-hearted, profuse of flame and of firewood,
Lord of forests unfelled, and not a gleaner of fagots,
Spreading its arms to embrace with inexhaustible bounty
All who fled from the cold, exultant, laughing at winter !
Only Hannah the housemaid was busy in clearing the table,
Coming and going, and bustling about in closet and chamber.

Then Elizabeth told her story again to John Estaugh,
Going far back to the past, to the early days of her childhood ;
How she had waited and watched, in all her doubts and besetments
Comforted with the extendings and holy, sweet inflowings
Of the spirit of love, till the voice imperative sounded,
And she obeyed the voice, and cast in her lot with her people
Here in the desert land, and God would provide for the issue.

Meanwhile Joseph sat with folded hands, and demurely
Listened, or seemed to listen, and in the silence that followed
Nothing was heard for a while but the step of Hannah the housemaid
Walking the floor overhead, and setting the chambers in order.
And Elizabeth said, with a smile of compassion, ' The maiden
Hath a light heart in her breast, but her feet are heavy and awkward.'
Inwardly Joseph laughed, but governed his tongue, and was silent.

Then came the hour of sleep, death's counterfeit, nightly rehearsal
Of the great Silent Assembly, the Meeting of shadows, where no man
Speaketh, but all are still, and the peace and rest are unbroken !
Silently over that house the blessing of slumber descended.
But when the morning dawned, and the sun uprose in his splendour,
Breaking his way through clouds that encumbered his path in the
    heavens,
Joseph was seen with his sled and oxen breaking a pathway
Through the drifts of snow ; the horses already were harnessed,
And John Estaugh was standing and taking leave at the threshold,
Saying that he should return at the Meeting in May ; while above them
Hannah the housemaid, the homely, was looking out of the attic,
Laughing aloud at Joseph, then suddenly closing the casement,
As the bird in a cuckoo-clock peeps out of its window,
Then disappears again, and closes the shutter behind it.

III.

Now was the winter gone, and the snow; and Robin the Redbreast
Boasted on bush and tree it was he, it was he and no other,
That had covered with leaves the Babes in the Wood, and blithely
All the birds sang with him, and little cared for his boasting,
Or for his Babes in the Wood, or the cruel Uncle, and only
Sang for the mates they had chosen, and cared for the nests they were
      building.
With them, but more sedately and meekly, Elizabeth Haddon
Sang in her inmost heart, but her lips were silent and songless.
Thus came the lovely spring with a rush of blossoms and music,
Flooding the earth with flowers, and the air with melodies vernal.

Then it came to pass, one pleasant morning, that slowly
Up the road there came a cavalcade, as of pilgrims,
Men and women, wending their way to the Quarterly Meeting
In the neighbouring town; and with them came riding John Estaugh.
At Elizabeth's door they stopped to rest, and alighting
Tasted the currant wine, and the bread of rye, and the honey
Brought from the hives, that stood by the sunny wall of the garden;
Then remounted their horses, refreshed, and continued their journey,
And Elizabeth with them, and Joseph, and Hannah the housemaid.
But, as they started, Elizabeth lingered a little, and leaning
Over her horse's neck, in a whisper said to John Estaugh:
'Tarry awhile behind, for I have something to tell thee,
Not to be spoken lightly, nor in the presence of others;
Them it concerneth not, only thee and me it concerneth.'
And they rode slowly along through the woods, conversing together.
It was a pleasure to breathe the fragrant air of the forest;
It was a pleasure to live on that bright and happy May morning!

Then Elizabeth said, though still with a certain reluctance,
As if impelled to reveal a secret she fain would have guarded:
'I will no longer conceal what is laid upon me to tell thee;
I have received from the Lord a charge to love thee, John Estaugh.'

And John Estaugh made answer, surprised by the words she had
      spoken,
'Pleasant to me are thy converse, thy ways, thy meekness of spirit;
Pleasant thy frankness of speech, and thy soul's immaculate white-
      ness,
Love without dissimulation, a holy and inward adorning.
But I have yet no light to lead me, no voice to direct me.
When the Lord's work is done, and the toil and the labour completed
He hath appointed to me, I will gather into the stillness
Of my own heart awhile, and listen and wait for his guidance.'

446

Then Elizabeth said, not troubled nor wounded in spirit,
'So is it best, John Estaugh. We will not speak of it further.
It hath been laid upon me to tell thee this, for to-morrow
Thou art going away, across the sea, and I know not
When I shall see thee more; but if the Lord hath decreed it,
Thou wilt return again to seek me here and to find me.'
And they rode onward in silence, and entered the town with the others.

IV.

Ships that pass in the night, and speak each other in passing,
Only a signal shown and a distant voice in the darkness;
So on the ocean of life we pass and speak one another,
Only a look and a voice, then darkness again and a silence.

Now went on as of old the quiet life of the homestead.
Patient and unrepining Elizabeth laboured, in all things
Mindful not of herself, but bearing the burdens of others,
Always thoughtful and kind and untroubled; and Hannah the housemaid,
Diligent early and late, and rosy with washing and scouring,
Still as of old disparaged the eminent merits of Joseph,
And was at times reproved for her light and frothy behaviour,
For her shy looks, and her careless words, and her evil surmisings,
Being pressed down somewhat, like a cart with sheaves overladen,
As she would sometimes say to Joseph, quoting the Scriptures.

Meanwhile John Estaugh departed across the sea, and departing
Carried hid in his heart a secret sacred and precious,
Filling its chambers with fragrance, and seeming to him in its sweetness
Mary's ointment of spikenard, that filled all the house with its odour.
O lost days of delight, that are wasted in doubting and waiting!
O lost hours and days in which we might have been happy!
But the light shone at last, and guided his wavering footsteps,
And at last came the voice, imperative, questionless, certain.

Then John Estaugh came back o'er the sea for the gift that was
    offered,
Better than houses and lands, the gift of a woman's affection.
And on the First-Day that followed, he rose in the Silent Assembly,
Holding in his strong hand a hand that trembled a little,
Promising to be kind and true and faithful in all things.
Such were the marriage-rites of John and Elizabeth Estaugh.

And not otherwise Joseph, the honest, the diligent servant,
Sped in his bashful wooing with homely Hannah the housemaid;
For when he asked her the question, she answered, 'Nay'; and then
    added,
'But thee may make believe, and see what will come of it, Joseph.'

441

INTERLUDE.

'A PLEASANT and a winsome tale,'
The Student said, 'though some-
    what pale
And quiet in its colouring,
As if it caught its tone and air
From the gray suits that Quakers
    wear ;
Yet worthy of some German bard,
Hebel, or Voss, or Eberhard,
Who love of humble themes to sing,
In humble verse ; but no more true
Than was the tale I told to you.'

The Theologian made reply,
And with some warmth, 'That I
    deny ;
'Tis no invention of my own,
But something well and widely
    known
To readers of a riper age,
Writ by the skilful hand that wrote
The Indian tale of Hobomok,
And Philothea's classic page.
I found it like a waif afloat,
Or dulse uprooted from its rock,
On the swift tides that ebb and flow
In daily papers, and at flood
Bear freighted vessels to and fro,
But later, when the ebb is low,
Leave a long waste of sand and
    mud.'

'It matters little,' quoth the Jew ;
'The cloak of truth is lined with
    lies,
Sayeth some proverb old and wise ;
And Love is master of all arts,
And puts it into human hearts
The strangest things to say and do.'

And here the controversy closed
Abruptly, ere 'twas well begun ;
For the Sicilian interposed
With, 'Lordlings, listen, every one
That listen may, unto a tale
That's merrier than the nightingale ;

A tale that cannot boast, forsooth,
A single rag or shred of truth ;
That does not leave the mind in
    doubt
As to the with it or without ;
A naked falsehood and absurd
As mortal ever told or heard.
Therefore I tell it ; or, maybe,
Simply because it pleases me.'

THE SICILIAN'S TALE.

THE MONK OF CASAL-MAGGIORE.

ONCE on a time, some centuries
    ago,
  In the hot sunshine two Fran-
    ciscan friars
Wended their weary way with foot-
    steps slow
  Back to their convent, whose
    white walls and spires
Gleamed on the hillside like a patch
    of snow ;
  Covered with dust they were, and
    torn by briers,
And bore like sumpter-mules upon
    their backs
The badge of poverty, their beggar's
    sacks.

The first was Brother Anthony, a
    spare
  And silent man, with pallid
    cheeks and thin,
Much given to vigils, penance,
    fasting, prayer,
  Solemn and gray, and worn with
    discipline,
As if his body but white ashes were,
  Heaped on the living coals that
    glowed within ;
A simple monk, like many of his
    day,
Whose instinct was to listen and
    obey.

442

A different man was Brother
Timothy,
Of larger mould and of a coarser
paste;
A rubicund and stalwart monk was
he,
Broad in the shoulders, broader
in the waist,
Who often filled the dull refectory
With noise by which the convent
was disgraced,
But to the mass-book gave but
little heed,
By reason he had never learned to
read.

Now, as they passed the outskirts
of a wood,
They saw, with mingled pleasure
and surprise,
Fast tethered to a tree an ass, that
stood
Lazily winking his large, limpid
eyes.
The farmer Gilbert of that neighbourhood
His owner was; who, looking for
supplies
Of fagots, deeper in the wood had
strayed,
Leaving his beast to ponder in the
shade.

As soon as Brother Timothy espied
The patient animal, he said:
'Good-lack!
Thus for our needs doth Providence
provide;
We'll lay our wallets on the
creature's back.'
This being done, he leisurely untied
From head and neck the halter
of the jack,
And put it round his own, and to
the tree
Stood tethered fast as if the ass
were he.

And, bursting forth into a merry
laugh,

He cried to Brother Anthony:
'Away!
And drive the ass before you with
your staff;
And when you reach the convent
you may say
You left me at a farm, half tired
and half
Ill with a fever, for a night and day,
And that the farmer lent this ass to
bear
Our wallets, that are heavy with
good fare.'

Now Brother Anthony, who knew
the pranks
Of Brother Timothy, would not
persuade
Or reason with him on his quirks
and cranks,
But, being obedient, silently
obeyed;
And, smiting with his staff the ass's
flanks,
Drove him before him over hill
and glade,
Safe with his provend to the convent gate,
Leaving poor Brother Timothy to
his fate.

Then Gilbert, laden with fagots
for his fire,
Forth issued from the wood, and
stood aghast
To see the ponderous body of the
friar
Standing where he had left his
donkey last.
Trembling he stood, and dared not
venture nigher,
But stared, and gaped, and
crossed himself full fast;
For, being credulous and of little
wit,
He thought it was some demon
from the pit.

While speechless and bewildered
thus he gazed,

And dropped his load of fagots
on the ground,
Quoth Brother Timothy : ' Be not
amazed
That where you left a donkey
should be found
A poor Franciscan friar, half-
starved and crazed,
Standing demure and with a
halter bound ;
But set me free, and hear the
piteous story
Of Brother Timothy of Casal-
Maggiore.

' I am a sinful man, although you
see
I wear the consecrated cowl and
cape ;
You never owned an ass, but you
owned me,
Changed and transformed from
my own natural shape
All for the deadly sin of gluttony,
From which I could not otherwise escape,
Than by this penance, dieting on
grass,
And being worked and beaten as
an ass.

' Think of the ignominy I endured ;
Think of the miserable life I led,
The toil and blows to which I was
inured,
My wretched lodging in a windy
shed,
My scanty fare so grudgingly pro-
cured,
The damp and musty straw that
formed my bed !
But, having done this penance for
my sins,
My life as man and monk again
begins.'

The simple Gilbert, hearing words
like these,
Was conscience-stricken, and fell
down apace

Before the friar upon his bended
knees,
And with a suppliant voice implored his grace ;
And the good monk, now very much
at ease,
Granted him pardon with a
smiling face,
Nor could refuse to be that night
his guest,
It being late, and he in need of rest.

Upon a hillside, where the olive
thrives,
With figures painted on its whitewashed walls,
The cottage stood ; and near the
humming hives
Made murmurs as of far-off
waterfalls ;
A place where those who love secluded lives
Might live content, and, free
from noise and brawls,
Like Claudian's Old Man of Verona
here
Measure by fruits the slow-revolv-
ing year.

And, coming to this cottage of
content,
They found his children, and the
buxom wench
His wife, Dame Cicely, and his
father, bent
With years and labour, seated on
a bench,
Repeating over some obscure event
In the old wars of Milanese and
French ;
All welcomed the Franciscan, with
a sense
Of sacred awe and humble reve-
rence.

When Gilbert told them what had
come to pass,
How beyond question, cavil, or
surmise,

Good Brother Timothy had been
  their ass,
  You should have seen the wonder
  in their eyes ;
You should have heard them cry,
  'Alas ! alas !'
  Have heard their lamentations
  and their sighs !
For all believed the story, and began
To see a saint in this afflicted man.

Forthwith there was prepared a
  grand repast,
  To satisfy the craving of the friar
After so rigid and prolonged a fast ;
  The bustling housewife stirred
  the kitchen fire ;
Then her two barnyard fowls, her
  best and last,
  Were put to death, at her express
  desire,
And served up with a salad in a
  bowl,
And flasks of country wine to crown
  the whole.

It would not be believed should I
  repeat
  How hungry Brother Timothy
  appeared ;
It was a pleasure but to see him eat,
  His white teeth flashing through
  his russet beard,
His face aglow and flushed with
  wine and meat,
  His roguish eyes that rolled and
  laughed and leered !
Lord ! how he drank the blood-red
  country wine
As if the village vintage were divine !

And all the while he talked without
  surcease,
  And told his merry tales with
  jovial glee
That never flagged, but rather did
  increase,
  And laughed aloud as if insane
  were he,

And wagged his red beard, matted
  like a fleece,
  And cast such glances at Dame
  Cicely
That Gilbert now grew angry with
  his guest,
And thus in words his rising wrath
  expressed.

'Good father,' said he, 'easily we
  see
  How needful in some persons,
  and how right,
Mortification of the flesh may be.
  The indulgence you have given
  it to-night,
After long penance, clearly proves
  to me
  Your strength against temptation
  is but slight,
And shows the dreadful peril you
  are in
Of a relapse into your deadly sin.

'To-morrow morning, with the
  rising sun,
  Go back unto your convent, nor
  refrain
From fasting and from scourging,
  for you run
  Great danger to become an ass
  again,
Since monkish flesh and asinine
  are one ;
  Therefore be wise, nor longer
  here remain,
Unless you wish the scourge
  should be applied
By other hands, that will not spare
  your hide.'

When this the monk had heard, his
  colour fled
  And then returned, like lightning
  in the air,
Till he was all one blush from foot
  to head,
  And even the bald spot in his
  russet hair

Turned from its usual pallor to
   bright red !
The old man was asleep upon
   his chair.
Then all retired, and sank into the
   deep
And helpless imbecility of sleep.

They slept until the dawn of day
   drew near,
   Till the cock should have crowed,
   but did not crow,
For they had slain the shining
   chanticleer
   And eaten him for supper, as you
   know.
The monk was up betimes and of
   good cheer,
   And, having breakfasted, made
   haste to go,
As if he heard the distant matin
   bell,
And had but little time to say
   farewell.

Fresh was the morning as the
   breath of kine ;
   Odours of herbs commingled with
   the sweet
Balsamic exhalations of the pine ;
   A haze was in the air presaging
   heat ;
Uprose the sun above the Apennine,
   And all the misty valleys at its
   feet
Were full of the delirious song of
   birds,
Voices of men, and bells, and low
   of herds.

All this to Brother Timothy was
   naught ;
   He did not care for scenery, nor
   here
His busy fancy found the thing it
   sought ;
   But when he saw the convent
   walls appear,

And smoke from kitchen chimneys upward caught
And whirled aloft into the atmosphere,
He quickened his slow footsteps,
   like a beast
That scents the stable a league off
   at least.

And as he entered through the
   convent gate
   He saw there in the court the
   ass, who stood
Twirling his ears about, and
   seemed to wait,
   Just as he found him waiting in
   the wood ;
And told the Prior that, to alle-
   viate
   The daily labours of the brotherhood,
The owner, being a man of means
   and thrift,
Bestowed him on the convent as
   a gift.

And thereupon the Prior for many
   days
   Revolved this serious matter in
   his mind,
And turned it over many different
   ways,
   Hoping that some safe issue he
   might find ;
But stood in fear of what the
   world would say,
   If he accepted presents of this
   kind,
Employing beasts of burden for
   the packs,
That lazy monks should carry on
   their backs.

Then, to avoid all scandal of the
   sort,
   And stop the mouth of cavil, he
   decreed
That he would cut the tedious
   matter short,

And sell the ass with all con-
venient speed,
Thus saving the expense of his
support,
And hoarding something for a
time of need.
So he despatched him to the neighbouring Fair,
And freed himself from cumber
and from care.

It happened now by chance, as
some might say,
Others perhaps would call it
destiny,
Gilbert was at the Fair; and heard
a bray,
And nearer came, and saw that
it was he,
And whispered in his ear, 'Ah,
lackaday!
Good father, the rebellious flesh,
I see,
Has changed you back into an ass
again,
And all my admonitions were in
vain.'

The ass, who felt this breathing in
his ear,
Did not turn round to look, but
shook his head,
As if he were not pleased these
words to hear,
And contradicted all that had
been said.
And this made Gilbert cry in voice
more clear,
'I know you well; your hair is
russet-red;
Do not deny it; for you are the
same
Franciscan friar, and Timothy by
name.'

The ass, though now the secret
had come out,
Was obstinate, and shook his
head again;

Until a crowd was gathered round
about
To hear this dialogue between
the twain;
And raised their voices in a noisy
shout
When Gilbert tried to make the
matter plain,
And flouted him and mocked him
all day long
With laughter and with jibes and
scraps of song.

'If this be Brother Timothy,' they
cried,
'Buy him, and feed him on the
tenderest grass;
Thou canst not do too much for
one so tried
As to be twice transformed into
an ass.'
So simple Gilbert bought him, and
untied
His halter, and o'er mountain
and morass
He led him homeward, talking as
he went
Of good behaviour and a mind
content.

The children saw them coming,
and advanced,
Shouting with joy, and hung
about his neck,—
Not Gilbert's, but the ass's,—round
him danced,
And wove green garlands where-
withal to deck
His sacred person; for again it
chanced
Their childish feelings, without
rein or check,
Could not discriminate in any way
A donkey from a friar of Orders
Gray.

'O Brother Timothy,' the children
said,
'You have come back to us just
as before;

447

We were afraid, and thought that
    you were dead,
And we should never see you
    any more.'
And then they kissed the white
    star on his head,
That like a birth-mark or a
    badge he wore,
And patted him upon the neck and
    face,
And said a thousand things with
    childish grace.

Thenceforward and for ever he was
    known
    As Brother Timothy, and led
      alway
A life of luxury, till he had grown
    Ungrateful, being stuffed with
      corn and hay,
And very vicious. Then in angry
    tone,
    Rousing himself, poor Gilbert
      said one day,
'When simple kindness is mis-
    understood
A little flagellation may do good.'

His many vices need not here be
    told;
    Among them was a habit that
      he had
Of flinging up his heels at young
    and old,
    Breaking his halter, running off
      like mad
O'er pasture-lands and meadow,
    wood and wold,
    And other misdemeanours quite
      as bad;
But worst of all was breaking from
    his shed
At night, and ravaging the cabbage-
    bed.

So Brother Timothy went back
    once more
    To his old life of labour and dis-
      tress;

Was beaten worse than he had
    been before.
And now, instead of comfort and
    caress,
Came labours manifold and trials
    sore;
    And as his toils increased his
      food grew less,
Until at last the great consoler,
    Death,
Ended his many sufferings with his
    breath.

Great was the lamentation when
    he died;
    And mainly that he died im-
      penitent;
Dame Cicely bewailed, the children
    cried,
    The old man still remembered
      the event
In the French war, and Gilbert
    magnified
    His many virtues, as he came
      and went,
And said: 'Heaven pardon Brother
    Timothy,
And keep us from the sin of
    gluttony.'

INTERLUDE.

'SIGNOR LUIGI,' said the Jew,
When the Sicilian's tale was told,
'The were-wolf is a legend old,
But the were-ass is something new,
And yet for one I think it true.
The days of wonder have not
    ceased;
If there are beasts in forms of
    men,
As sure it happens now and then,
Why may not man become a beast,
In way of punishment at least?

' But this I will not now discuss:
I leave the theme, that we may
    thus

Remain within the realm of song.
The story that I told before,
Though not acceptable to all,
At least you did not find too long.
I beg you, let me try again,
With something in a different vein,
Before you bid the curtain fall.
Meanwhile keep watch upon the
    door,
Nor let the Landlord leave his
    chair,
Lest he should vanish into air,
And thus elude our search once
    more.'

Thus saying, from his lips he blew
A little cloud of perfumed breath,
And then, as if it were a clew
To lead his footsteps safely through,
Began his tale as followeth.

THE SPANISH JEW'S SECOND TALE.

SCANDERBEG.

THE battle is fought and won
By King Ladislaus the Hun,
In fire of hell and death's frost,
On the day of Pentecost.
And in rout before his path
From the field of battle red
Flee all that are not dead
Of the army of Amurath.

In the darkness of the night
Iskander, the pride and boast
Of that mighty Othman host,
With his routed Turks, takes flight
From the battle fought and lost
On the day of Pentecost;
Leaving behind him dead
The army of Amurath,
The vanguard as it led,
The rearguard as it fled,
Mown down in the bloody swath
Of the battle's aftermath.

But he cared not for Hospodars,
Nor for Baron or Voivode,
As on through the night he rode
And gazed at the fateful stars,
That were shining overhead ;
But smote his steed with his staff,
And smiled to himself, and said :
'This is the time to laugh.'

In the middle of the night,
In a halt of the hurrying flight,
There came a Scribe of the King
Wearing his signet ring,
And said in a voice severe:
'This is the first dark blot
On thy name, George Castriot !
Alas ! why art thou here,
And the army of Amurath slain,
And left on the battle plain ?'

And Iskander answered and said :
'They lie on the bloody sod
By the hoofs of horses trod ;
But this was the decree
Of the watchers overhead ;
For the war belongeth to God,
And in battle who are we,
Who are we, that shall withstand
The wind of his lifted hand ?'

Then he bade them bind with
    chains
This man of books and brains ;
And the Scribe said : 'What mis-
    deed
Have I done, that, without need,
Thou doest to me this thing ?'
And Iskander answering
Said unto him : 'Not one
Misdeed to me hast thou done ;
But for fear that thou shouldst run
And hide thyself from me,
Have I done this unto thee.

'Now write me a writing, O Scribe,
And a blessing be on thy tribe !
A writing sealed with thy ring,
To King Amurath's Pasha
In the city of Croia,

449

The city moated and walled,
That he surrender the same
In the name of my master, the
King;
For what is writ in his name
Can never be recalled.'

And the Scribe bowed low in
dread,
And unto Iskander said:
'Allah is great and just,
But we are as ashes and dust;
How shall I do this thing,
When I know that my guilty head
Will be forfeit to the King?'

Then swift as a shooting star
The curved and shining blade
Of Iskander's scimitar
From its sheath, with jewels bright,
Shot, as he thundered: 'Write!'
And the trembling Scribe obeyed,
And wrote in the fitful glare
Of the bivouac fire apart,
With the chill of the midnight air
On his forehead white and bare,
And the chill of death in his heart.

Then again Iskander cried:
'Now follow whither I ride,
For here thou must not stay.
Thou shalt be as my dearest friend,
And honours without end
Shall surround thee on every side,
And attend thee night and day.'
But the sullen Scribe replied:
'Our pathways here divide;
Mine leadeth not thy way.'

And even as he spoke
Fell a sudden scimitar-stroke,
When no one else was near;
And the Scribe sank to the ground,
As a stone, pushed from the brink
Of a black pool, might sink
With a sob and disappear;
And no one saw the deed;

And in the stillness around
No sound was heard but the sound
Of the hoofs of Iskander's steed,
As forward he sprang with a
bound.

Then onward he rode and afar,
With scarce three hundred men,
Through river and forest and fen,
O'er the mountains of Argentar;
And his heart was merry within,
When he crossed the river Drin,
And saw in the gleam of the morn
The White Castle Ak-Hissar,
The city Croia called,
The city moated and walled,
The city where he was born,—
And above it the morning star.

Then his trumpeters in the van
On their silver bugles blew,
And in crowds about him ran
Albanian and Turkoman,
That the sound together drew.
And he feasted with his friends,
And when they were warm with
wine,
He said: 'O friends of mine,
Behold what fortune sends,
And what the fates design!
King Amurath commands
That my father's wide domain,
This city and all its lands,
Shall be given to me again.'

Then to the Castle White
He rode in regal state,
And entered in at the gate
In all his arms bedight,
And gave to the Pasha
Who ruled in Croia
The writing of the King,
Sealed with his signet ring.
And the Pasha bowed his head,
And after a silence said:
'Allah is just and great!
I yield to the will divine,
The city and lands are thine;
Who shall contend with fate?'

Anon from the castle walls
The crescent banner falls,
And the crowd beholds instead,
Like a portent in the sky,
Iskander's banner fly,
The Black Eagle with double
   head ;
And a shout ascends on high,
For men's souls are tired of the
   Turks,
And their wicked ways and works,
That have made of Ak-Hissar
A city of the plague ;
And the loud, exultant cry
That echoes wide and far
Is : ' Long live Scanderbeg ! '

It was thus Iskander came
Once more unto his own ;
And the tidings, like the flame
Of a conflagration blown
By the winds of summer, ran,
Till the land was in a blaze,
And the cities far and near,
Sayeth Ben Joshua Ben Meir,
In his Book of the Words of the
   Days,
' Were taken as a man
Would take the tip of his ear.'

———✦———

INTERLUDE.

' Now that is after my own heart,'
The Poet cried ; ' one understands
Your swarthy hero Scanderbeg,
Gauntlet on hand and boot on
   leg,
And skilled in every warlike art,
Riding through his Albanian lands,
And following the auspicious star
That shone for him o'er Ak-Hissar.'

The Theologian added here
His word of praise not less sincere,
Although he ended with a jibe ;

' The hero of romance and song
Was born,' he said, ' to right the
   wrong ;
And I approve ; but all the same
That bit of treason with the Scribe
Adds nothing to your hero's fame.'

The Student praised the good old
   times,
And liked the canter of the rhymes,
That had a hoofbeat in their sound ;
But longed some further word to
   hear
Of the old chronicler Ben Meir,
And where his volume might be
   found.
The tall Musician walked the room
With folded arms and gleaming
   eyes,
As if he saw the Vikings rise,
Gigantic shadows in the gloom ;
And much he talked of their
   emprise,
And meteors seen in Northern
   skies,
And Heimdal's horn, and day of
   doom.
But the Sicilian laughed again ;
' This is the time to laugh,' he
   said.
For the whole story he well knew
Was an invention of the Jew,
Spun from the cobwebs in his
   brain,
And of the same bright scarlet
   thread
As was the Tale of Kambalu.

Only the Landlord spake no word ;
'Twas doubtful whether he had
   heard
The tale at all, so full of care
Was he of his impending fate,
That, like the sword of Damocles,
Above his head hung blank and
   bare,
Suspended by a single hair,
So that he could not sit at ease,

451

But sighed and looked disconso-
  late,
And shifted restless in his chair,
Revolving how he might evade
The blow of the descending blade.

The Student came to his relief
By saying in his easy way
To the Musician: 'Calm your
    grief,
My fair Apollo of the North,
Balder the Beautiful and so forth;
Although your magic lyre or lute
With broken strings is lying mute,
Still you can tell some doleful tale
Of shipwreck in a midnight gale,
Or something of the kind to suit
The mood that we are in to-night
For what is marvellous and strange;
So give your nimble fancy range,
And we will follow in its flight.'

But the Musician shook his head;
'No tale I tell to-night,' he said,
'While my poor instrument lies
    there,
Even as a child with vacant stare
Lies in its little coffin dead.'

Yet, being urged, he said at last:
'There comes to me out of the
    Past
A voice, whose tones are sweet and
    wild,
Singing a song almost divine,
And with a tear in every line;
An ancient ballad, that my nurse
Sang to me when I was a child,
In accents tender as the verse;
And sometimes wept, and some-
    times smiled
While singing it, to see arise
The look of wonder in my eyes,
And feel my heart with terror
    beat.
This simple ballad I retain
Clearly imprinted on my brain,
And as a tale will now repeat.'

THE MUSICIAN'S TALE.

THE MOTHER'S GHOST.

SVEND DYRING he rideth adown
    the glade;
  I myself was young!
There he hath wooed him so win-
    some a maid;
  *Fair words gladden so many a
    heart.*

Together were they for seven years,
And together children six were
    theirs.

Then came Death abroad through
    the land,
And blighted the beautiful lily-
    wand.

Svend Dyring he rideth adown the
    glade,
And again hath he wooed him
    another maid.

He hath wooed him a maid and
    brought home a bride,
But she was bitter and full of pride.

When she came driving into the
    yard,
There stood the six children weep-
    ing so hard.

There stood the small children
    with sorrowful heart;
From before her feet she thrust
    them apart.

She gave to them neither ale nor
    bread;
'Ye shall suffer hunger and hate,'
    she said.

She took from them their quilts of
    blue,
And said: 'Ye shall lie on the straw
    we strew.'

452

She took from them the great wax-
light;
'Now ye shall lie in the dark at
night.'

In the evening late they cried with
cold;
The mother heard it under the
mould.

The woman heard it the earth
below:
'To my little children I must go.'

She standeth before the Lord of
all:
'And may I go to my children
small?'

She prayed him so long, and would
not cease,
Until he bade her depart in peace.

'At cock-crow thou shalt return
again;
Longer thou shalt not there remain!'

She girded up her sorrowful bones,
And rifted the walls and the marble
stones.

As through the village she flitted
by,
The watch-dogs howled aloud to
the sky.

When she came to the castle gate,
There stood her eldest daughter in
wait.

'Why standest thou here, dear
daughter mine?
How fares it with brothers and
sisters thine?'

'Never art thou mother of mine,
For my mother was both fair and
fine.

'My mother was white, with cheeks
of red,
But thou art pale, and like to the
dead.'

'How should I be fair and fine?
I have been dead; pale cheeks are
mine.

'How should I be white and red,
So long, so long have I been
dead?'

When she came in at the chamber
door,
There stood the small children
weeping sore.

One she braided, another she
brushed,
The third she lifted, the fourth she
hushed.

The fifth she took on her lap and
pressed,
As if she would suckle it at her
breast.

Then to her eldest daughter said
she,
'Do thou bid Svend Dyring come
hither to me.'

Into the chamber when he came
She spake to him in anger and
shame.

'I left behind me both ale and
bread;
My children hunger and are not
fed.

'I left behind me quilts of blue;
My children lie on the straw ye
strew.

'I left behind me the great wax-
light;
My children lie in the dark at
night.

'If I come again unto your hall,
As cruel a fate shall you befall!

'Now crows the cock with feathers
    red;
Back to the earth must all the dead.

'Now crows the cock with feathers
    swart;
The gates of heaven fly wide apart.

'Now crows the cock with feathers
    white;
I can abide no longer to-night.'

Whenever they heard the watch-
    dogs wail,
They gave the children bread and
    ale.

Whenever they heard the watch-
    dogs bay,
They feared lest the dead were on
    their way.

Whenever they heard the watch-
    dogs bark;
    I myself was young!
They feared the dead out there in
    the dark.
    *Fair words gladden so many a
    heart.*

—◆—

INTERLUDE.

TOUCHED by the pathos of these
    rhymes,
The Theologian said: 'All praise
Be to the ballads of old times
And to the bards of simple ways,
Who walked with Nature hand in
    hand,
Whose country was their Holy
    Land,
Whose singing robes were home-
    spun brown
From looms of their own native
    town,

Which they were not ashamed to
    wear,
And not of silk or sendal gay,
Nor decked with fanciful array
Of cockle-shells from Outre-Mer.'

To whom the Student answered:
    'Yes;
All praise and honour! I confess
That bread and ale, home-baked,
    home-brewed,
Are wholesome and nutritious
    food,
But not enough for all our needs;
Poets—the best of them—are birds
Of passage; where their instinct
    leads
They range abroad for thoughts
    and words,
And from all climes bring home
    the seeds
That germinate in flowers or weeds.
They are not fowls in barnyards
    born
To cackle o'er a grain of corn;
And, if you shut the horizon down
To the small limits of their town,
What do you but degrade your bard
Till he at last becomes as one
Who thinks the all-encircling sun
Rises and sets in his back yard?'

The Theologian said again:
'It may be so; yet I maintain
That what is native still is best,
And little care I for the rest.
'Tis a long story; time would fail
To tell it, and the hour is late;
We will not waste it in debate,
But listen to our Landlord's tale.'

And thus the sword of Damocles
Descending not by slow degrees,
But suddenly, on the Landlord fell,
Who blushing, and with much
    demur
And many vain apologies,
Plucking up heart, began to tell
The Rhyme of one Sir Christopher.

THE LANDLORD'S TALE.

THE RHYME OF SIR CHRISTOPHER.

IT was Sir Christopher Gardiner,
Knight of the Holy Sepulchre,
From Merry England over the sea,
Who stepped upon this continent
As if his august presence lent
A glory to the colony.

You should have seen him in the
    street
Of the little Boston of Winthrop's
    time,
His rapier dangling at his feet,
Doublet and hose and boots com-
    plete,
Prince Rupert hat with ostrich
    plume,
Gloves that exhaled a faint per-
    fume,
Luxuriant curls and air sublime,
And superior manners now obso-
    lete!

He had a way of saying things
That made one think of courts and
    kings,
And lords and ladies of high de-
    gree;
So that not having been at court
Seemed something very little short
Of treason or lese-majesty,
Such an accomplished knight was
    he.

His dwelling was just beyond the
    town,
At what he called his country-seat;
For, careless of Fortune's smile or
    frown,
And weary grown of the world and
    its ways,
He wished to pass the rest of his
    days
In a private life and a calm retreat.

But a double life was the life he led,
And, while professing to be in
    search
Of a godly course, and willing, he
    said,
Nay, anxious to join the Puritan
    church,
He made of all this but small
    account,
And passed his idle hours instead
With roystering Morton of Merry
    Mount,
That pettifogger from Furnival's
    Inn,
Lord of misrule and riot and sin,
Who looked on the wine when it
    was red.

This country-seat was little more
Than a cabin of logs; but in front
    of the door
A modest flower-bed thickly sown
With sweet alyssum and columbine
Made those who saw it at once
    divine
The touch of some other hand
    than his own.
At first it was whispered, and then
    it was known,
That he in secret was harbouring
    there
A little lady with golden hair,
Whom he called his cousin, but
    whom he had wed
In the Italian manner, as men said,
And great was the scandal every-
    where.

But worse than this was the vague
    surmise,
Though none could vouch for it or
    aver,
That the Knight of the Holy
    Sepulchre
Was only a Papist in disguise;
And the more to embitter their
    bitter lives,
And the more to trouble the public
    mind,

Came letters from England, from
two other wives,
Whom he had carelessly left be-
hind ;
Both of them letters of such a kind
As made the governor hold his
breath ;
The one imploring him straight to
send
The husband home, that he might
amend ;
The other asking his instant death,
As the only way to make an end.

The wary governor deemed it
right,
When all this wickedness was
revealed,
To send his warrant signed and
sealed,
And take the body of the knight.
Armed with this mighty instrument,
The marshal, mounting his gallant
steed,
Rode forth from town at the top of
his speed,
And followed by all his bailiffs bold,
As if on high achievement bent,
To storm some castle or stronghold,
Challenge the warders on the wall,
And seize in his ancestral hall
A robber-baron grim and old.

But when through all the dust and
heat
He came to Sir Christopher's
country-seat,
No knight he found, nor warder
there,
But the little lady with golden hair,
Who was gathering in the bright
sunshine
The sweet alyssum and columbine ;
While gallant Sir Christopher, all
so gay,
Being forewarned, through the
postern gate
Of his castle wall had tripped away,

And was keeping a little holiday
In the forests, that bounded his
estate.

Then as a trusty squire and true
The marshal searched the castle
through,
Not crediting what the lady said ;
Searched from cellar to garret in
vain,
And, finding no knight, came out
again
And arrested the golden damsel
instead,
And bore her in triumph into the
town,
While from her eyes the tears rolled
down
On the sweet alyssum and colum-
bine,
That she held in her fingers white
and fine.

The governor's heart was moved to
see
So fair a creature caught within
The snares of Satan and of sin,
And he read her a little homily
On the folly and wickedness of the
lives
Of women, half cousins and half
wives ;
But, seeing that naught his words
availed,
He sent her away in a ship that
sailed
For Merry England over the sea,
To the other two wives in the old
countree,
To search her further, since he had
failed
To come at the heart of the mystery.

Meanwhile Sir Christopher wandered away
Through pathless woods for a month
and a day,
Shooting pigeons, and sleeping at
night

With the noble savage, who took
  delight
In his feathered hat and his velvet
  vest,
His gun and his rapier and the rest.
But as soon as the noble savage
  heard
That a bounty was offered for this
  gay bird,
He wanted to slay him out of hand,
And bring in his beautiful scalp for
  a show,
Like the glossy head of a kite or
  crow,
Until he was made to understand
They wanted the bird alive, not
  dead;
Then he followed him whither-
  soever he fled,
Through forest and field, and
  hunted him down,
And brought him prisoner into the
  town.

Alas! it was a rueful sight,
To see this melancholy knight
In such a dismal and hapless case;
His hat deformed by stain and
  dent,
His plumage broken, his doublet
  rent,
His beard and flowing locks for-
  lorn,
Matted, dishevelled, and unshorn,
His boots with dust and mire
  besprent;
But dignified in his disgrace,
And wearing an unblushing face.
And thus before the magistrate
He stood to hear the doom of fate.
In vain he strove with wonted ease
To modify and extenuate
His evil deeds in church and state,
For gone was now his power to
  please;
And his pompous words had no
  more weight
Than feathers flying in the breeze.

With suavity equal to his own
The governor lent a patient ear
To the speech evasive and high-
  flown,
In which he endeavoured to make
  clear
That colonial laws were too severe
When applied to a gallant cavalier,
A gentleman born, and so well
  known,
And accustomed to move in a
  higher sphere.

All this the Puritan governor heard,
And deigned in answer never a
  word;
But in summary manner shipped
  away,
In a vessel that sailed from Salem
  Bay,
This splendid and famous cavalier,
With his Rupert hat and his
  popery,
To Merry England over the sea,
As being unmeet to inhabit here.

Thus endeth the Rhyme of Sir
  Christopher,
Knight of the Holy Sepulchre,
The first who furnished this barren
  land
With Apples of Sodom and ropes
  of sand.

———

FINALE.

THESE are the tales those merry
  guests
Told to each other, well or ill;
Like summer birds that lift their
  crests
Above the borders of their nests
And twitter, and again are still.

These are the tales, or new or old,
In idle moments idly told;
Flowers of the field with petals
  thin,

Lilies that neither toil nor spin,
And tufts of wayside weeds and
    gorse
Hung in the parlour of the inn
Beneath the sign of the Red Horse.

And still, reluctant to retire,
The friends sat talking by the fire
And watched the smouldering
    embers burn
To ashes, and flash up again
Into a momentary glow,
Lingering like them when forced
    to go,
And going when they would re-
    main ;
For on the morrow they must turn
Their faces homeward, and the pain
Of parting touched with its unrest
A tender nerve in every breast.

But sleep at last the victory won ;
They must be stirring with the sun,
And drowsily good night they said,
And went still gossiping to bed,
And left the parlour wrapped in
    gloom.
The only live thing in the room
Was the old clock, that in its pace
Kept time with the revolving
    spheres
And constellations in their flight,
And struck with its uplifted mace
The dark, unconscious hours of
    night,
To senseless and unlistening ears.

Uprose the sun ; and every guest,
Uprisen, was soon equipped and
    dressed
For journeying home and city-
    ward ;

The old stage-coach was at the
    door,
With horses harnessed, long before
The sunshine reached the withered
    sward
Beneath the oaks, whose branches
    hoar
Murmured : ' Farewell for ever-
    more.'

' Farewell ! ' the portly Landlord
    cried ;
' Farewell ! ' the parting guests
    replied,
But little thought that nevermore
Their feet would pass that threshold
    o'er ;
That nevermore together there
Would they assemble, free from
    care,
To hear the oaks' mysterious roar,
And breathe the wholesome
    country air.

Where are they now ? What lands
    and skies
Paint pictures in their friendly
    eyes ?
What hope deludes, what promise
    cheers,
What pleasant voices fill their ears?
Two are beyond the salt sea waves,
And three already in their graves.
Perchance the living still may look
Into the pages of this book,
And see the days of long ago
Floating and fleeting to and fro,
As in the well-remembered brook
They saw the inverted landscape
    gleam.
And their own faces like a dream
Look up upon them from below.

The Golden Legend.

PROLOGUE.

The spire of Strasburg Cathedral. Night and storm. LUCIFER, *with the Powers of the Air, trying to tear down the Cross.*

Lucifer. Hasten! hasten!
O ye spirits!
From its station drag the ponderous
Cross of iron, that to mock us
Is uplifted high in air!

Voices. O, we cannot!
For around it
All the Saints and Guardian Angels
Throng in legions to protect it;
They defeat us everywhere!

The Bells.

Laudo Deum verum!
Plebem voco!
Congrego clerum!

Lucifer. Lower! lower!
Hover downward!
Seize the loud, vociferous bells, and
Clashing, clanging, to the pavement
Hurl them from their windy tower!

Voices. All thy thunders
Here are harmless!
For these bells have been anointed,
And baptized with holy water!
They defy our utmost power.

The Bells.

Defunctos ploro!
Pestem fugo!
Festa decoro!

Lucifer. Shake the casements!
Break the painted
Panes, that flame with gold and
crimson;
Scatter them like leaves of Autumn,
Swept away before the blast!

Voices. O, we cannot!
The Archangel
Michael flames from every window,
With the sword of fire that drove us
Headlong, out of heaven, aghast!

The Bells.

Funera plango!
Fulgura frango!
Sabbata pango!

Lucifer. Aim your lightnings
At the oaken,
Massive, iron-studded portals!
Sack the house of God, and scatter
Wide the ashes cf the dead!

Voices. O, we cannot!
The Apostles
And the Martyrs, wrapped in mantles,
Stand as warders at the entrance,
Stand as sentinels o'erhead!

The Bells.

Excito lentos!
Dissipo ventos!
Paco cruentos!

Lucifer. Baffled! baffled!
Inefficient,
Craven spirits! leave this labour
Unto Time, the great Destroyer!
Come away, ere night is gone!

Voices. Onward! onward!
With the night-wind,
Over field and farm and forest,
Lonely homestead, darksome hamlet,
Blighting all we breathe upon!

(*They sweep away. Organ and Gregorian Chant.*)

Choir.

Nocte surgentes
Vigilemus omnes.

459

I.

The Castle of Vautsberg on the Rhine. A chamber in a tower. PRINCE HENRY, *sitting alone, ill and restless. Midnight.*

Pr. Henry. I cannot sleep! my fervid brain
Calls up the vanished Past again,
And throws its misty splendours deep
Into the pallid realms of sleep!
A breath from that far-distant shore
Comes freshening ever more and more,
And wafts o'er intervening seas
Sweet odours from the Hesperides!
A wind, that through the corridor
Just stirs the curtain, and no more,
And, touching the æolian strings,
Faints with the burden that it brings!
Come back! ye friendships long departed!
That like o'erflowing streamlets started,
And now are dwindled, one by one,
To stony channels in the sun!
Come back! ye friends, whose lives are ended,
Come back, with all that light attended,
Which seemed to darken and decay
When ye arose and went away!

They come, the shapes of joy and woe,
The airy crowds of long ago,
The dreams and fancies known of yore,
That have been, and shall be no more.
They change the cloisters of the night
Into a garden of delight;
They make the dark and dreary hours
Open and blossom into flowers!
I would not sleep! I love to be
Again in their fair company;
But ere my lips can bid them stay,
They pass and vanish quite away!
Alas! our memories may retrace
Each circumstance of time and place,
Season and scene come back again,
And outward things unchanged remain;
The rest we cannot reinstate;
Ourselves we cannot re-create,
Nor set our souls to the same key
Of the remembered harmony!

Rest! rest! O, give me rest and peace!
The thought of life that ne'er shall cease
Has something in it like despair,
A weight I am too weak to bear!
Sweeter to this afflicted breast
The thought of never-ending rest!
Sweeter the undisturbed and deep
Tranquillity of endless sleep!

(*A flash of lightning, out of which* LUCIFER *appears, in the garb of a travelling Physician.*)

Lucifer. All hail, Prince Henry!
Pr. Henry (*starting*). Who is it speaks?
Who and what are you?
Lucifer. One who seeks
A moment's audience with the Prince.
Pr. Henry. When came you in?
Lucifer. A moment since.
I found your study door unlocked,
And thought you answered when I knocked.
Pr. Henry. I did not hear you.
Lucifer. You heard the thunder;
It was loud enough to waken the dead.
And it is not a matter of special wonder
That, when God is walking overhead,
You should not hear my feeble tread.

Pr. Henry. What may your wish or purpose be?

Lucifer. Nothing or everything, as it pleases Your Highness. You behold in me Only a travelling Physician; One of the few who have a mission To cure incurable diseases, Or those that are called so.

Pr. Henry.　　　Can you bring The dead to life?

Lucifer.　　　Yes; very nearly. And, what is a wiser and better thing, Can keep the living from ever needing Such an unnatural, strange proceeding, By showing conclusively and clearly That death is a stupid blunder merely, And not a necessity of our lives. My being here is accidental; The storm, that against your casement drives, In the little village below waylaid me. And there I heard, with a secret delight, Of your maladies physical and mental, Which neither astonished nor dismayed me. And I hastened hither, though late in the night, To proffer my aid!

Pr. Henry (*ironically*). For this you came! Ah, how can I ever hope to requite This honour from one so erudite?

Lucifer. The honour is mine, or will be, when I have cured your disease.

Pr. Henry.　　　But not till then.

Lucifer. What is your illness?

Pr. Henry.　　　It has no name. A smouldering, dull, perpetual flame,

As in a kiln, burns in my veins, Sending up vapours to the head; My heart has become a dull lagoon, Which a kind of leprosy drinks and drains; I am accounted as one who is dead, And, indeed, I think that I shall be soon.

Lucifer. And has Gordonius the Divine, In his famous Lily of Medicine,— I see the book lies open before you,— No remedy potent enough to restore you?

Pr. Henry. None whatever!

Lucifer. The dead are dead, And their oracles dumb, when questioned Of the new diseases that human life Evolves in its progress, rank and rife. Consult the dead upon things that were, But the living only on things that are. Have you done this, by the appliance And aid of doctors?

Pr. Henry. Ay, whole schools Of doctors, with their learned rules; But the case is quite beyond their science. Even the doctors of Salern Send me back word they can discern No cure for a malady like this, Save one which in its nature is Impossible, and cannot be!

Lucifer. That sounds oracular!

Pr. Henry. Unendurable!

Lucifer. What is their remedy?

Pr. Henry. You shall see; Writ in this scroll is the mystery.

Lucifer (*reading*). 'Not to be cured, yet not incurable! The only remedy that remains Is the blood that flows from a maiden's veins,

Who of her own free will shall die,
And give her life as the price of
    yours !'
That is the strangest of all cures,
And one, I think, you will never try;
The prescription you may well put
    by,
As something impossible to find
Before the world itself shall end !
And yet who knows ? One cannot
    say
That into some maiden's brain that
    kind
Of madness will not find its way.
Meanwhile permit me to recom-
    mend,
As the matter admits of no delay,
My wonderful Catholicon,
Of very subtile and magical powers !
    Pr. Henry. Purge with your nos-
        trums and drugs infernal
The spouts and gargoyles of these
    towers,
Not me. My faith is utterly gone
In every power but the Power
    Supernal !
Pray tell me, of what school are you ?
    Lucifer. Both of the Old and of
        the New !
The school of Hermes Trisme-
        gistus,
Who uttered his oracles sublime
Before the Olympiads, in the dew
Of the early dusk and dawn of
    Time,
The reign of dateless old He-
    phæstus !
As northward, from its Nubian
    springs,
The Nile, for ever new and old,
Among the living and the dead,
Its mighty, mystic stream has
    rolled ;
So, starting from its fountain-head
Under the lotus-leaves of Isis,
From the dead demigods of eld,
Through long, unbroken lines of
    kings

Its course the sacred art has held,
Unchecked, unchanged by man's
    devices.
This art the Arabian Geber taught,
And in alembics, finely wrought,
Distilling herbs and flowers, dis-
    covered
The secret that so long had hovered
Upon the misty verge of Truth,
The Elixir of Perpetual Youth,
Called Alcohol, in the Arab speech!
Like him, this wondrous lore I teach !
    Pr. Henry. What ! an adept ?
    Lucifer.   Nor less, nor more !
    Pr. Henry. I am a reader of your
        books,
A lover of that mystic lore !
With such a piercing glance it looks
Into great Nature's open eye,
And sees within it trembling lie
The portrait of the Deity !
And yet, alas ! with all my pains,
The secret and the mystery
Have baffled and eluded me,
Unseen the grand result remains !
    Lucifer (*showing a flask*). Behold
        it here ! this little flask
Contains the wonderful quintes-
    sence,
The perfect flower and efflores-
    cence,
Of all the knowledge man can ask !
Hold it up thus against the light !
    Pr. Henry. How limpid, pure, and
        crystalline,
How quick, and tremulous, and
    bright
The little wavelets dance and shine,
As were it the Water of Life in
    sooth !
    Lucifer. It is ! It assuages every
        pain,
Cures all disease, and gives again
To age the swift delights of youth.
Inhale its fragrance.
    Pr. Henry.   It is sweet,
A thousand different odours meet
And mingle in its rare perfume,

462

Such as the winds of summer waft
At open windows through a room!
Lucifer. Will you not taste it?
Pr. Henry. Will one draught suf-
fice?
Lucifer. If not, you can drink
more.
Pr. Henry. Into this crystal gob-
let pour
So much as safely I may drink.
Lucifer (pouring). Let not the
quantity alarm you;
You may drink all; it will not harm
you.
Pr. Henry. I am as one who on
the brink
Of a dark river stands and sees
The waters flow, the landscape dim
Around him waver, wheel, and
swim,
And, ere he plunges, stops to
think
Into what whirlpools he may sink;
One moment pauses, and no more,
Then madly plunges from the
shore!
Headlong into the mysteries
Of life and death I boldly leap,
Nor fear the fateful current's sweep,
Nor what in ambush lurks below!
For death is better than disease!

(*An* ANGEL *with an æolian harp
hovers in the air.*)

Angel. Woe! woe! eternal woe!
Not only the whispered prayer
Of love,
But the imprecations of hate,
Reverberate
For ever and ever through the air
Above!
This fearful curse
Shakes the great universe!
Lucifer (disappearing). Drink!
drink!
And thy soul shall sink
Down into the dark abyss
Into the infinite abyss,

From which no plummet nor rope
Ever drew up the silver sand of
hope!
Pr. Henry (drinking). It is like
a draught of fire!
Through every vein
I feel again
The fever of youth, the soft desire;
A rapture that is almost pain
Throbs in my heart and fills my
brain!
O joy! O joy! I feel
The band of steel
That so long and heavily has
pressed
Upon my breast
Uplifted, and the malediction
Of my affliction
Is taken from me, and my weary
breast
At length finds rest.
The Angel. It is but the rest of
the fire, from which the air has
been taken!
It is but the rest of the sand, when
the hour-glass is not shaken!
It is but the rest of the tide between
the ebb and the flow!
It is but the rest of the wind between
the flaws that blow!
With fiendish laughter,
Hereafter,
This false physician
Will mock thee in thy perdition.
Pr. Henry. Speak! speak!
Who says that I am ill?
I am not ill! I am not weak!
The trance, the swoon, the dream,
is o'er!
I feel the chill of death no more!
At length,
I stand renewed in all my strength!
Beneath me I can feel
The great earth stagger and reel,
As if the feet of a descending God
Upon its surface trod,
And like a pebble it rolled beneath
his heel!

463

This, O brave physician ! this
Is thy great Palingenesis !

(Drinks again.)

The Angel. Touch the goblet no
    more !
It will make thy heart sore
To its very core !
Its perfume is the breath
Of the Angel of Death,
And the light that within it lies
Is the flash of his evil eyes.
Beware ! O, beware !
For sickness, sorrow, and care
All are there !

Pr. Henry (sinking back). O thou
    voice within my breast !
Why entreat me, why upbraid me,
When the steadfast tongues of truth
And the flattering hopes of youth
Have all deceived me and betrayed
    me ?
Give me, give me rest, O rest !
Golden visions wave and hover,
Golden vapours, waters streaming,
Landscapes moving, changing,
    gleaming !
I am like a happy lover
Who illumines life with dreaming !
Brave physician ! Rare physician !
Well hast thou fulfilled thy mission !

(His head falls on his book.)

The Angel (receding). Alas ! alas !
Like a vapour the golden vision
Shall fade and pass,
And thou wilt find in thy heart
    again
Only the blight of pain,
And bitter, bitter, bitter contrition !

Court-yard of the Castle. HUBERT
    standing by the gateway.

Hubert. How sad the grand old
    castle looks !
O'erhead, the unmolested rooks
Upon the turret's windy top
Sit, talking of the farmer's crop ;

Here in the courtyard springs the
    grass,
So few are now the feet that pass ;
The stately peacocks, bolder grown,
Come hopping down the steps of
    stone,
As if the castle were their own ;
And I, the poor old seneschal,
Haunt, like a ghost, the banquet-
    hall.
Alas ! the merry guests no more
Crowd through the hospitable door ;
No eyes with youth and passion
    shine,
No cheeks grow redder than the
    wine ;
No song, no laugh, no jovial din
Of drinking wassail to the pin ;
But all is silent, sad, and drear,
And now the only sounds I hear
Are the hoarse rooks upon the walls,
And horses stamping in their stalls !

(A horn sounds.)

What ho ! that merry, sudden blast
Reminds me of the days long past !
And, as of old resounding, grate
The heavy hinges of the gate,
And, clattering loud, with iron
    clank,
Down goes the sounding bridge of
    plank,
As if it were in haste to greet
The pressure of a traveller's feet.

(Enter WALTER *the Minnesinger.)*

Walter. How now, my friend !
    This looks quite lonely !
No banner flying from the walls,
No pages and no seneschals,
No warders, and one porter only !
Is it you, Hubert ?
Hubert. Ah ! Master Walter !
Walter. Alas ! how forms and
    faces alter !
I did not know you. You look
    older !
Your hair has grown much grayer
    and thinner,

And you stoop a little in the
shoulder !

Hubert. Alack ! I am a poor old
sinner,

And, like these towers, begin to
moulder ;

And you have been absent many a
year !

Walter. How is the Prince ?

Hubert. He is not here ;
He has been ill : and now has fled.

Walter. Speak it out frankly :
say he's dead !
Is it not so ?

Hubert. No ; if you please,
A strange, mysterious disease
Fell on him with a sudden blight.
Whole hours together he would
stand
Upon the terrace, in a dream,
Resting his head upon his hand,
Best pleased when he was most
alone,
Like Saint John Nepomuck in stone,
Looking down into a stream.
In the Round Tower, night after
night,
He sat, and bleared his eyes with
books ;
Until one morning we found him
there
Stretched on the floor, as if in a
swoon
He had fallen from his chair.
We hardly recognised his sweet
looks !

Walter. Poor Prince !

Hubert. I think he might have
mended ;
And he did mend ; but very soon
The priests came flocking in, like
rooks,
With all their crosiers and their
crooks,
And so at last the matter ended.

Walter. How did it end ?

Hubert. Why, in
Saint Rochus

They made him stand, and wait
his doom ;
And, as if he were condemned to
the tomb,
Began to mutter their hocus-pocus.
First, the Mass for the Dead they
chanted,
Then three times laid upon his
head
A shovelful of churchyard clay,
Saying to him, as he stood un-
daunted,
' This is a sign that thou art dead,
So in thy heart be penitent ! '
And forth from the chapel door he
went
Into disgrace and banishment,
Clothed in a cloak of hodden gray,
And bearing a wallet, and a bell,
Whose sound should be a perpetual
knell
To keep all travellers away.

Walter. O, horrible fate ! Outcast, rejected,
As one with pestilence infected !

Hubert. Then was the family
tomb unsealed,
And broken helmet, sword, and
shield,
Buried together in common wreck,
As is the custom, when the last
Of any princely house has passed ;
And thrice, as with a trumpet-
blast,
A herald shouted down the stair
The words of warning and de-
spair,—
' O Hoheneck ! O Hoheneck ! '

Walter. Still in my soul that
cry goes on,—
For ever gone ! for ever gone !
Ah, what a cruel sense of loss,
Like a black shadow, would fall
across
The hearts of all, if he should die !
His gracious presence upon earth
Was as a fire upon a hearth ;
As pleasant songs, at morning sung,

The words that dropped from his
   sweet tongue
Strengthened our hearts ; or, heard
   at night,
Made all our slumbers soft and light.
Where is he ?
   Hubert.   In the Odenwald.
Some of his tenants, unappalled
By fear of death, or priestly word,—
A holy family, that make
Each meal a Supper of the Lord,—
Have him beneath their watch and
   ward,
For love of him, and Jesus' sake !
Pray you come in. For why should I
With out-door hospitality
My prince's friend thus entertain ?
   Walter.   I would a moment here
   remain.
But you, good Hubert, go before,
Fill me a goblet of May-drink,
As aromatic as the May
From which it steals the breath
   away,
And which he loved so well of yore ;
It is of him that I would think.
You shall attend me, when I call,
In the ancestral banquet-hall.
Unseen companions, guests of air,
You cannot wait on, will be there ;
They taste not food, they drink not
   wine,
But their soft eyes look into mine,
And their lips speak to me, and all
The vast and shadowy banquet-hall
Is full of looks and words divine !

(*Leaning over the parapet.*)

The day is done ; and slowly from
   the scene
The stooping sun upgathers his
   spent shafts,
And puts them back into his golden
   . quiver !
Below me in the valley, deep and
   green
As goblets are, from which in
   thirsty draughts

We drink its wine, the swift and
   mantling river
Flows on triumphant through these
   lovely regions,
Etched with the shadows of its
   sombre margent,
And soft, reflected clouds of gold
   and argent !
Yes, there it flows, for ever, broad
   and still,
As when the vanguard of the
   Roman legions
First saw it from the top of yonder
   hill !
How beautiful it is !   Fresh fields
   of wheat,
Vineyard, and town, and tower with
   fluttering flag,
The consecrated chapel on the crag,
And the white hamlet gathered
   round its base,
Like Mary sitting at her Saviour's
   feet,
And looking up at his beloved face !
O friend ! O best of friends ! Thy
   absence more
Than the impending night darkens
   the landscape o'er !

II.

*A Farm in the Odenwald. A
Garden. Morning.* PRINCE
HENRY *seated, with a book.*
ELSIE, *at a distance, gathering
flowers.*

   Prince Henry (*reading*).   One
   morning, all alone,
Out of his convent of gray stone,
Into the forest older, darker, grayer,
His lips moving as if in prayer,
His head sunken upon his breast
As in a dream of rest,
Walked the Monk Felix. All about
The broad, sweet sunshine lay
   without,
Filling the summer air ;
And within the woodlands as he trod,

466

The dusk was like the Truce of God
With worldly woe and care;
Under him lay the golden moss;
And above him the boughs of
    hoary trees
Waved, and made the sign of the
    cross,
And whispered their Benedicites;
And from the ground
Rose an odour sweet and fragrant
Of the wild-flowers and the vagrant
Vines that wandered,
Seeking the sunshine, round and
    round.

These he heeded not, but pondered
On the volume in his hand,
A volume of Saint Augustine,
Wherein he read of the unseen
Splendours of God's great town
In the unknown land,
And, with his eyes cast down
In humility, he said:
'I believe, O God,
What herein I have read,
But, alas! I do not understand!'

And lo! he heard
The sudden singing of a bird,
A snow-white bird, that from a cloud
Dropped down,
And among the branches brown
Sat singing
So sweet, and clear, and loud,
It seemed a thousand harp-strings
    ringing.

And the Monk Felix closed his book,
And long, long,
With rapturous look,
He listened to the song,
And hardly breathed or stirred,
Until he saw, as in a vision,
The land Elysian,
And in the heavenly city heard
Angelic feet
Fall on the golden flagging of the
    street.
And he would fain
Have caught the wondrous bird,

But strove in vain;
For it flew away, away,
Far over hill and dell,
And instead of its sweet singing
He heard the convent bell
Suddenly in the silence ringing
For the service of noonday.
And he retraced
His pathway homeward sadly and
    in haste.

In the convent there was a change!
He looked for each well-known face,
But the faces were new and strange;
New figures sat in the oaken stalls,
New voices chanted in the choir;
Yet the place was the same place,
The same dusky walls
Of cold, gray stone,
The same cloisters and belfry and
    spire.

A stranger and alone
Among that brotherhood
The Monk Felix stood.
'Forty years,' said a Friar,
'Have I been Prior
Of this convent in the wood,
But for that space
Never have I beheld thy face!'
The heart of the Monk Felix fell:
And he answered, with submissive
    tone,
'This morning, after the hour of
    Prime,
I left my cell,
And wandered forth alone.
Listening all the time
To the melodious singing
Of a beautiful white bird,
Until I heard
The bells of the convent ringing
Noon from their noisy towers.
It was as if I dreamed;
For what to me had seemed
Moments only, had been hours!'

'Years!' said a voice close by.
It was an aged monk who spoke,
From a bench of oak

Fastened against the wall ;—
He was the oldest monk of all.
For a whole century
Had he been there,
Serving God in prayer,
The meekest and humblest of his
    creatures.
He remembered well the features
Of Felix, and he said,
Speaking distinct and slow :
' One hundred years ago,
When I was a novice in this place,
There was here a monk, full of
    God's grace,
Who bore the name
Of Felix, and this man must be the
    same.'

And straightway
They brought forth to the light of
    day
A volume old and brown,
A huge tome, bound
In brass and wild-boar's hide,
Wherein were written down
The names of all who had died
In the convent, since it was edified.
And there they found,
Just as the old monk said,
That on a certain day and date,
One hundred years before,
Had gone forth from the convent
    gate,
The Monk Felix, and never more
Had entered that sacred door.
He had been counted among the
    dead !
And they knew, at last,
That, such had been the power
Of that celestial and immortal song,
A hundred years had passed,
And had not seemed so long
As a single hour !

(ELSIE *comes in with flowers*.)

Elsie. Here are flowers for you,
But they are not all for you.
Some of them are for the Virgin
And for Saint Cecilia.

Prince Henry. As thou standest
    there,
Thou seemest to me like the angel
That brought the immortal roses
To Saint Cecilia's bridal chamber.
Elsie. But these will fade.
Prince Henry. Themselves will
    fade,
But not their memory,
And memory has the power
To re-create them from the dust.
They remind me, too,
Of martyred Dorothea,
Who from celestial gardens sent
Flowers as her witnesses
To him who scoffed and doubted.
Elsie. Do you know the story
Of Christ and the Sultan's
    daughter ?
That is the prettiest legend of them
    all.
Prince Henry. Then tell it to
    me.
But first come hither.
Lay the flowers down beside me,
And put both thy hands in mine.
Now tell me the story.
Elsie. Early in the morning
The Sultan's daughter
Walked in her father's garden,
Gathering the bright flowers,
All full of dew.
Prince Henry. Just as thou hast
    been doing
This morning, dearest Elsie.
Elsie. And as she gathered
    them,
She wondered more and more
Who was the Master of the Flowers,
And made them grow
Out of the cold, dark earth.
' In my heart,' she said,
' I love him ; and for him
Would leave my father's palace,
To labour in his garden.'
Prince Henry. Dear, innocent
    child !
How sweetly thou recallest

The long-forgotten legend,
That in my early childhood
My mother told me!
Upon my brain
It reappears once more,
As a birth-mark on the forehead
When a hand suddenly
Is laid upon it, and removed!

Elsie. And at midnight,
As she lay upon her bed,
She heard a voice
Call to her from the garden,
And, looking forth from her
    window,
She saw a beautiful youth
Standing among the flowers.
It was the Lord Jesus;
And she went down to him,
And opened the door for him;
And he said to her, 'O maiden!
Thou hast thought of me with
    love,
And for thy sake
Out of my Father's kingdom
Have I come hither:
I am the Master of the Flowers.
My garden is in Paradise,
And if thou wilt go with me,
Thy bridal garland
Shall be of bright red flowers.'
And then he took from his finger
A golden ring,
And asked the Sultan's daughter
If she would be his bride.
And when she answered him with
    love,
His wounds began to bleed,
And she said to him,
'O Love! how red thy heart is,
And thy hands are full of roses.'
'For thy sake,' answered he,
'For thy sake is my heart so red,
For thee I bring these roses;
I gathered them at the cross
Whereon I died for thee!
Come, for my Father calls.
Thou art my elected bride!'
And the Sultan's daughter

Followed him to his Father's
    garden.
Prince Henry. Wouldst thou
    have done so, Elsie?
Elsie. Yes, very gladly.
Prince Henry. Then the Celes-
    tial Bridegroom
Will come for thee also.
Upon thy forehead he will place,
Not his crown of thorns,
But a crown of roses.
In thy bridal chamber,
Like Saint Cecilia,
Thou shalt hear sweet music
And breathe the fragrance
Of flowers immortal!
Go now and place these flowers
Before her picture.

A room in the farm-house.
Twilight. URSULA *spinning.*
GOTTLIEB *asleep in his chair.*

Ursula. Darker and darker!
    Hardly a glimmer
Of light comes in at the window-
    pane;
Or is it my eyes are growing
    dimmer?
I cannot disentangle this skein,
Nor wind it rightly upon the reel.
Elsie!
Gottlieb (*starting*). The stopping
    of thy wheel
Has wakened me out of a pleasant
    dream.
I thought I was sitting beside a
    stream,
And heard the grinding of a mill,
When suddenly the wheels stood
    still,
And a voice cried 'Elsie' in my ear!
It startled me, it seemed so near.
Ursula. I was calling her: I
    want a light.
I cannot see to spin my flax.
Bring the lamp, Elsie. Dost thou
    hear?
Elsie (*within*). In a moment!

Gottlieb. Where are Bertha and Max?

Ursula. They are sitting with Elsie at the door.

She is telling them stories of the wood,

And the Wolf, and little Red Riding-hood.

Gottlieb. And where is the Prince?

Ursula. In his room overhead ;

I heard him walking across the floor,

And he always does, with a heavy tread.

(ELSIE *comes in with a lamp.* MAX *and* BERTHA *follow her ; and they all sing the Evening Song on the lighting of the lamps.*)

EVENING SONG.

O gladsome light
Of the Father Immortal,
And of the celestial
Sacred and blessed
Jesus, our Saviour !

Now to the sunset
Again hast thou brought us ;
And, seeing the evening
Twilight, we bless thee,
Praise thee, adore thee !

Father omnipotent !
Son, the Life-giver !
Spirit, the Comforter !
Worthy at all times
Of worship and wonder.

Prince Henry (*at the door*).
Amen !

Ursula. Who was it said Amen ?

Elsie. It was the Prince : he stood at the door,

And listened a moment, as we chanted

The evening song. He is gone again.

I have often seen him there before.

Ursula. Poor Prince !

Gottlieb. I thought the house was haunted !

Poor Prince, alas ! and yet as mild

And patient as the gentlest child !

Max. I love him because he is so good,

And makes me such fine bows and arrows,

To shoot at the robins and the sparrows,

And the red squirrels in the wood !

Bertha. I love him, too !

Gottlieb. Ah, yes ! we all

Love him, from the bottom of our hearts ;

He gave us the farm, the house, and the grange,

He gave us the horses and the carts,

And the great oxen in the stall,

The vineyard, and the forest range !

We have nothing to give him but our love !

Bertha. Did he give us the beautiful stork above

On the chimney-top, with its large round nest ?

Gottlieb. No, not the stork ; by God in heaven,

As a blessing, the dear white stork was given,

But the Prince has given us all the rest.

God bless him, and make him well again.

Elsie. Would I could do something for his sake,

Something to cure his sorrow and pain !

Gottlieb. That no one can ; neither thou nor I,

Nor any one else.

Elsie. And must he die ?

Ursula. Yes ; if the dear God does not take

Pity upon him, in his distress,

And work a miracle !

Gottlieb. Or unless
Some maiden, of her own accord,
Offers her life for that of her lord,
And is willing to die in his stead.

Elsie. I will!

Ursula. Prithee, thou foolish
 child, be still!
Thou shouldst not say what thou
 dost not mean!

Elsie. I mean it truly!

Max. O father! this morning,
Down by the mill, in the ravine,
Hans killed a wolf, the very same
That in the night to the sheepfold
 came,
And ate up my lamb, that was left
 outside.

Gottlieb. I am glad he is dead.
 It will be a warning
To the wolves in the forest, far
 and wide.

Max. And I am going to have
 his hide!

Bertha. I wonder if this is the
 wolf that ate
Little Red Riding-hood!

Ursula. O no!
That wolf was killed a long while
 ago.
Come, children, it is growing late.

Max. Ah, how I wish I were a
 man,
As stout as Hans is, and as
 strong!
I would do nothing else, the whole
 day long,
But just kill wolves.

Gottlieb. Then go to bed,
And grow as fast as a little boy
 can.
Bertha is half asleep already.
See how she nods her heavy head,
And her sleepy feet are so un-
 steady
She will hardly be able to creep
 up-stairs.

Ursula. Good night, my children.
 Here's the light.

And do not forget to say your
 prayers
Before you sleep.

Gottlieb. Good night!

Max and Bertha. Good night!

(*They go out with* ELSIE.)

Ursula (*spinning*). She is a
 strange and wayward child,
That Elsie of ours. She looks so
 old,
And thoughts and fancies weird
 and wild
Seem of late to have taken hold
Of her heart, that was once so
 docile and mild!

Gottlieb. She is like all girls.

Ursula. Ah no, forsooth!
Unlike all I have ever seen.
For she has visions and strange
 dreams,
And in all her words and ways,
 she seems
Much older than she is in truth.
Who would think her but fifteen?
And there has been of late such a
 change!
My heart is heavy with fear and
 doubt
That she may not live till the year
 is out.
She is so strange,—so strange,—
 so strange!

Gottlieb. I am not troubled with
 any such fear;
She will live and thrive for many
 a year.

———

ELSIE'S *chamber. Night.* ELSIE
praying.

Elsie. My Redeemer and my
 Lord,
I beseech thee, I entreat thee,
Guide me in each act and word,
That hereafter I may meet thee,
Watching, waiting, hoping, yearning,
With my lamp well trimmed and
 burning!

Interceding
With these bleeding
Wounds upon thy hands and side,
For all who have lived and erred
Thou hast suffered, thou hast died,
Scourged, and mocked, and cruci-
fied,
And in the grave hast thou been
buried!

If my feeble prayer can reach thee,
O my Saviour, I beseech thee,
Even as thou hast died for me,
More sincerely
Let me follow where thou leadest,
Let me, bleeding as thou bleedest,
Die, if dying I may give
Life to one who asks to live,
And more nearly,
Dying thus, resemble thee!

The chamber of GOTTLIEB _and_
URSULA. _Midnight._ ELSIE
_standing by their bed-side, weep-
ing._

Gottlieb. The wind is roaring;
the rushing rain
Is loud upon roof and window-
pane,
As if the Wild Huntsman of Ro-
denstein,
Boding evil to me and mine,
Were abroad to-night with his
ghostly train!
In the brief lulls of the tempest wild,
The dogs howl in the yard; and
hark!
Some one is sobbing in the dark,
Here in the chamber!
Elsie.   It is I.
Ursula. Elsie! what ails thee,
my poor child?
Elsie. I am disturbed and much
distressed,
In thinking our dear Prince must
die;
I cannot close mine eyes, nor rest.

Gottlieb. What wouldst thou?
In the Power Divine
His healing lies, not in our own;
It is in the hand of God alone.
Elsie. Nay, he has put it into
mine,
And into my heart!
Gottlieb. Thy words are wild!
Ursula. What dost thou mean?
my child! my child!
Elsie. That for our dear Prince
Henry's sake
I will myself the offering make,
And give my life to purchase his.
Ursula. Am I still dreaming, or
awake?
Thou speakest carelessly of death,
And yet thou knowest not what it is.
Elsie. 'Tis the cessation of our
breath.
Silent and motionless we lie;
And no one knoweth more than
this.
I saw our little Gertrude die;
She left off breathing, and no more
I smoothed the pillow beneath her
head.
She was more beautiful than before.
Like violets faded were her eyes;
By this we knew that she was dead.
Through the open window looked
the skies
Into the chamber where she lay,
And the wind was like the sound of
wings,
As if angels came to bear her away.
Ah! when I saw and felt these
things,
I found it difficult to stay;
I longed to die, as she had died,
And go forth with her, side by side.
The Saints are dead, the Martyrs
dead,
And Mary, and our Lord; and I
Would follow in humility
The way by them illumined!
Ursula. My child! my child!
thou must not die!

472

Elsie. Why should I live? Do
I not know
The life of woman is full of woe!
Toiling on and on and on,
With breaking heart, and tearful
  eyes,
And silent lips, and in the soul
The secret longings that arise,
Which this world never satisfies!
Some more, some less, but of the
  whole
Not one quite happy, no, not one!
  Ursula. It is the malediction
  of Eve!
  Elsie. In place of it, let me
  receive
The benediction of Mary, then.
  Gottlieb. Ah, woe is me! Ah,
  woe is me!
Most wretched am I among men!
  Ursula. Alas! that I should
  live to see
Thy death, beloved, and to stand
Above thy grave! Ah, woe the
  day!
  Elsie. Thou wilt not see it. I
  shall lie
Beneath the flowers of another
  land;
For at Salerno, far away
Over the mountains, over the sea,
It is appointed me to die!
And it will seem no more to thee
Than if at the village on market-
  day
I should a little longer stay
Than I am wont.
  Ursula. Even as thou sayest!
And how my heart beats when thou
  stayest!
I cannot rest until my sight
Is satisfied with seeing thee.
What, then, if thou wert dead?
  Gottlieb. Ah me!
Of our old eyes thou art the light!
The joy of our old hearts art thou!
And wilt thou die?
  Ursula. Not now! not now!

Elsie. Christ died for me, and
  shall not I
Be willing for my Prince to die?
You both are silent; you cannot
  speak.
This said I at our Saviour's feast
After confession, to the priest,
And even he made no reply.
Does he not warn us all to seek
The happier, better land on high,
Where flowers immortal never
  wither;
And could he forbid me to go
  thither?
  Gottlieb. In God's own time, my
  heart's delight!
When he shall call thee, not before!
  Elsie. I heard him call. When
  Christ ascended
Triumphantly, from star to star,
He left the gates of heaven ajar.
I had a vision in the night,
And saw him standing at the door
Of his Father's mansion, vast and
  splendid,
And beckoning to me from afar.
I cannot stay!
  Gottlieb. She speaks almost
As if it were the Holy Ghost
Spake through her lips, and in her
  stead!
What if this were of God?
  Ursula. Ah, then
Gainsay it dare we not.
  Gottlieb. Amen!
Elsie! the words that thou hast said
Are strange and new for us to hear,
And fill our hearts with doubt and
  fear.
Whether it be a dark temptation
Of the Evil One, or God's inspira-
  tion,
We in our blindness cannot say.
We must think upon it, and pray;
For evil and good it both resembles.
If it be of God, his will be done!
May he guard us from the Evil
  One!

How hot thy hand is! how it
trembles!
Go to thy bed, and try to sleep.
    Ursula. Kiss me. Good night;
    and do not weep.

(ELSIE *goes out.*)

Ah, what an awful thing is this!
I almost shuddered at her kiss,
As if a ghost had touched my cheek,
I am so childish and so weak!
As soon as I see the earliest gray
Of morning glimmer in the east,
I will go over to the priest,
And hear what the good man has
to say!

---

*A Village Church. A woman
kneeling at the confessional.*

The Parish Priest (from within).
    Go, sin no more! Thy penance
    o'er,
A new and better life begin!
God maketh thee for ever free
From the dominion of thy sin!
Go, sin no more! He will restore
The peace that filled thy heart
before,
And pardon thine iniquity!

(*The woman goes out. The Priest
comes forth, and walks slowly up
and down the church.*)

O blessed Lord! how much I need
Thy light to guide me on my way!
So many hands, that, without heed,
Still touch thy wounds, and make
them bleed!
So many feet, that, day by day,
Still wander from thy fold astray!
Unless thou fill me with thy light,
I cannot lead thy flock aright;
Nor, without thy support, can bear
The burden of so great a care,
But am myself a castaway!

(*A pause.*)

The day is drawing to its close;

And what good deeds, since first it
rose,
Have I presented, Lord, to thee,
As offerings of my ministry?
What wrong repressed, what right
maintained,
What struggle passed, what victory
gained,
What good attempted and attained?
Feeble, at best, is my endeavour!
I see, but cannot reach, the height
That lies for ever in the light,
And yet for ever and for ever,
When seeming just within my
grasp,
I feel my feeble hands unclasp,
And sink discouraged into night!
For thine own purpose thou hast
sent
The strife and the discouragement!

(*A pause.*)

Why stayest thou, Prince of Ho-
heneck?
Why keep me pacing to and fro
Amid these aisles of sacred gloom,
Counting my footsteps as I go,
And marking with each step a
tomb?
Why should the world for thee
make room,
And wait thy leisure and thy beck?
Thou comest in the hope to hear
Some word of comfort and of cheer.
What can I say? I cannot give
The counsel to do this and live;
But rather, firmly to deny
The tempter, though his power be
strong,
And, inaccessible to wrong,
Still like a martyr live and die!

(*A pause.*)

The evening air grows dusk and
brown;
I must go forth into the town,
To visit beds of pain and death,
Of restless limbs, and quivering
breath,

474

And sorrowing hearts, and patient
    eyes
That see, through tears, the sun go
    down,
But nevermore shall see it rise.
The poor in body and estate,
The sick and the disconsolate,
Must not on man's convenience
    wait.

        (Goes out.)

(Enter LUCIFER, *as a Priest.)*

*Lucifer (with a genuflexion,
    mocking).* This is the Black
    Paternoster.
God was my foster,
He fostered me
Under the book of the Palm-tree !
St. Michael was my dame.
He was born at Bethlehem,
He was made of flesh and blood.
God sent me my right food,
My right food, and shelter too,
That I may to yon kirk go,
To read upon yon sweet book
Which the mighty God of heaven
    shook.
Open, open, hell's gates !
Shut, shut, heaven's gates !
All the devils in the air
The stronger be, that hear the
    Black Prayer !

    (Looking round the church.)

What a darksome and dismal place !
I wonder that any man has the face
To call such a hole the House of
    the Lord,
And the Gate of Heaven,—yet such
    is the word.
Ceiling, and walls, and windows old,
Covered with cobwebs, blackened
    with mould ;
Dust on the pulpit, dust on the stairs,
Dust on the benches, and stalls,
    and chairs !
The pulpit, from which such pon-
    derous sermons

Have fallen down on the brains of
    the Germans,
With about as much real edification
As if a great Bible, bound in lead,
Had fallen, and struck them on the
    head ;
And I ought to remember that
    sensation !
Here stands the holy-water stoup !
Holy-water it may be to many,
But to me, the veriest Liquor
    Gehennæ !
It smells like a filthy fast-day soup !
Near it stands the box for the poor ;
With its iron padlock, safe and sure.
I and the priest of the parish know
Whither all these charities go ;
Therefore, to keep up the institution,
I will add my little contribution !

        (He puts in money.)

Underneath this mouldering tomb,
With statue of stone, and scutcheon
    of brass,
Slumbers a great lord of the village.
All his life was riot and pillage,
But at length, to escape the doom
Of the everlasting, penal fire,
He died in the dress of a mendicant
    friar,
And bartered his wealth for a daily
    mass.
But all that afterwards came to
    pass,
And whether he finds it dull or
    pleasant,
Is kept a secret for the present,
At his own particular desire.

And here, in a corner of the wall,
Shadowy, silent, apart from all,
With its awful portal open wide,
And its latticed windows on either
    side,
And its step well worn by the bended
    knees
Of one or two pious centuries,
Stands the village confessional !
Within it, as an honoured guest,

I will sit me down awhile and rest !

(*Seats himself in the confessional.*)

Here sits the priest; and faint and low,
Like the sighing of an evening breeze,
Comes through these painted lattices
The ceaseless sound of human woe;
Here, while her bosom aches and throbs
With deep and agonizing sobs,
That half are passion, half contrition,
The luckless daughter of perdition
Slowly confesses her secret shame !
The time, the place, the lover's name !
Here the grim murderer, with a groan,
From his bruised conscience rolls the stone,
Thinking that thus he can atone
For ravages of sword and flame !
Indeed, I marvel, and marvel greatly,
How a priest can sit here so sedately,
Reading, the whole year out and in,
Naught but the catalogue of sin,
And still keep any faith whatever
In human virtue ! Never ! never !

I cannot repeat a thousandth part
Of the horrors and crimes and sins and woes
That arise, when with palpitating throes
The graveyard in the human heart
Gives up its dead, at the voice of the priest,
As if he were an archangel, at least.
It makes a peculiar atmosphere,
This odour of earthly passions and crimes,
Such as I like to breathe, at times,
And such as often brings me here
In the hottest and most pestilential season.

To-day, I come for another reason;
To foster and ripen an evil thought
In a heart that is almost to madness wrought,
And to make a murderer out of a prince,
A sleight of hand I learned long since !
He comes. In the twilight he will not see
The difference between his priest and me !
In the same net was the mother caught !

Prince Henry (*entering and kneeling at the confessional*).
Remorseful, penitent, and lowly,
I come to crave, O Father holy,
Thy benediction on my head.

Lucifer. The benediction shall be said
After confession, not before !
'Tis a God-speed to the parting guest,
Who stands already at the door,
Sandalled with holiness, and dressed
In garments pure from earthly stain.
Meanwhile, hast thou searched well thy breast ?
Does the same madness fill thy brain ?
Or have thy passion and unrest
Vanished for ever from thy mind ?

Prince Henry. By the same madness still made blind,
By the same passion still possessed,
I come again to the house of prayer,
A man afflicted and distressed !
As in a cloudy atmosphere,
Through unseen sluices of the air,
A sudden and impetuous wind
Strikes the great forest white with fear,
And every branch, and bough, and spray
Points all its quivering leaves one way,

And meadows of grass, and fields of grain,
And the clouds above, and the slanting rain,
And smoke from chimneys of the town,
Yield themselves to it, and bow down,
So does this dreadful purpose press
Onward, with irresistible stress,
And all my thoughts and faculties,
Struck level by the strength of this,
From their true inclination turn,
And all stream forward to Salern!

Lucifer. Alas! we are but eddies of dust,
Uplifted by the blast, and whirled
Along the highway of the world
A moment only, then to fall
Back to a common level all,
At the subsiding of the gust!

Prince Henry. O holy Father!
pardon in me
The oscillation of a mind
Unsteadfast, and that cannot find
Its centre of rest and harmony!
For evermore before mine eyes
This ghastly phantom flits and flies,
And as a madman through a crowd,
With frantic gestures and wild cries,
It hurries onward, and aloud
Repeats its awful prophecies!
Weakness is wretchedness! To be strong
Is to be happy! I am weak,
And cannot find the good I seek,
Because I feel and fear the wrong!

Lucifer. Be not alarmed! The Church is kind,
And in her mercy and her meekness
She meets half-way her children's weakness,
Writes their transgressions in the dust!
Though in the Decalogue we find
The mandate written, 'Thou shalt not kill!'
Yet there are cases when we must.

In war, for instance, or from scathe
To guard and keep the one true Faith!
We must look at the Decalogue in the light
Of an ancient statute, that was meant
For a mild and general application,
To be understood with the reservation,
That, in certain instances, the Right
Must yield to the Expedient!
Thou art a Prince. If thou shouldst die,
What hearts and hopes would prostrate lie!
What noble deeds, what fair renown,
Into the grave with thee go down!
What acts of valour and courtesy
Remain undone, and die with thee!
Thou art the last of all thy race!
With thee a noble name expires,
And vanishes from the earth's face
The glorious memory of thy sires!
She is a peasant. In her veins
Flows common and plebeian blood;
It is such as daily and hourly stains
The dust and the turf of battle-plains,
By vassals shed, in a crimson flood,
Without reserve, and without reward,
At the slightest summons of their lord!
But thine is precious; the fore-appointed
Blood of kings, of God's anointed!
Moreover, what has the world in store
For one like her, but tears and toil?
Daughter of sorrow, serf of the soil,
A peasant's child and a peasant's wife,
And her soul within her sick and sore
With the roughness and barrenness of life!
I marvel not at the heart's recoil
From a fate like this in one so tender,

477

Nor at its eagerness to surrender
All the wretchedness, want, and woe
That await it in this world below,
For the unutterable splendour
Of the world of rest beyond the
    skies.
So the Church sanctions the sacri-
    fice :
Therefore inhale this healing balm,
And breathe this fresh life into thine ;
Accept the comfort and the calm
She offers, as a gift divine ;
Let her fall down and anoint thy feet
With the ointment costly and most
    sweet
Of her young blood, and thou shalt
    live.
   Prince Henry. And will the
    righteous Heaven forgive ?
No action, whether foul or fair,
Is ever done, but it leaves some-
    where
A record, written by fingers ghostly,
As a blessing or a curse, and mostly
In the greater weakness or greater
    strength
Of the acts which follow it, till at
    length
The wrongs of ages are redressed,
And the justice of God made mani-
    fest !
   Lucifer. In ancient records it is
    stated
That, whenever an evil deed is done,
Another devil is created
To scourge and torment the offend-
    ing one !
But the evil is only good perverted,
And Lucifer, the Bearer of Light,
But an angel fallen and deserted,
Thrust from his Father's house
    with a curse
Into the black and endless night.
   Prince Henry. If justice rules the
    universe,
From the good actions of good men
Angels of light should be begotten,
And thus the balance restored again.

   Lucifer. Yes ; if the world were
    not rotten,
And so given over to the Devil !
   Prince Henry. But this deed, is it
    good or evil ?
Have I thine absolution free
To do it, and without restriction ?
   Lucifer. Ay ; and from whatso-
    ever sin
Lieth around it and within,
From all crimes in which it may
    involve thee,
I now release thee and absolve
    thee !
   Prince Henry. Give me thy holy
    benediction.
   *Lucifer (stretching forth his hand
    and muttering).*
     Maledictione perpetua
     Maledicat vos
     Pater eternus !
   *The Angel (with the æolian
    harp).* Take heed ! take heed !
Noble art thou in thy birth,
By the good and the great of earth
Hast thou been taught !
Be noble in every thought
And in every deed !
Let not the illusion of thy senses
Betray thee to deadly offences.
Be strong ! be good ! be pure !
The right only shall endure,
All things else are but false pre-
    tences.
I entreat thee, I implore,
Listen no more
To the suggestions of an evil spirit,
That even now is there,
Making the foul seem fair,
And selfishness itself a virtue and a
    merit !

        A room in the farm-house.

   Gottlieb. It is decided ! For
    many days,
And nights as many, we have had
A nameless terror in our breast,

The Golden Legend.

Making us timid, and afraid
Of God, and his mysterious ways!
We have been sorrowful and sad;
Much have we suffered, much have
    prayed
That he would lead us as is best,
And show us what his will required.
It is decided; and we give
Our child, O Prince, that you may
    live!

Ursula. It is of God. He has
    inspired
This purpose in her; and through
    pain,
Out of a world of sin and woe,
He takes her to himself again.
The mother's heart resists no
    longer;
With the Angel of the Lord in vain
It wrestled, for he was the stronger.

Gottlieb. As Abraham offered
    long ago
His son unto the Lord, and even
The Everlasting Father in heaven
Gave his, as a lamb unto the
    slaughter,
So do I offer up my daughter!

(URSULA *hides her face.*)

Elsie. My life is little,
Only a cup of water,
But pure and limpid.
Take it, O my Prince!
Let it refresh you,
Let it restore you.
It is given willingly,
It is given freely,
May God bless the gift!

Prince Henry. And the giver!
Gottlieb. Amen!
Prince Henry. I accept it!
Gottlieb. Where are the children?
Ursula. They are already asleep.
Gottlieb. What if they were dead?

In the Garden.

Elsie. I have one thing to ask of
    you.

Prince Henry. What is it?
It is already granted.

Elsie. Promise me,
When we are gone from here, and
    on our way
Are journeying to Salerno, you will
    not,
By word or deed, endeavour to
    dissuade me
And turn me from my purpose; but
    remember
That as a pilgrim to the Holy City
Walks unmolested, and with
    thoughts of pardon
Occupied wholly, so would I ap-
    proach
The gates of Heaven, in this great
    jubilee,
With my petition, putting off from me
All thoughts of earth, as shoes from
    off my feet.
Promise me this.

Prince Henry. Thy words fall
    from thy lips
Like roses from the lips of Angelo:
    and angels
Might stoop to pick them up!

Elsie. Will you not promise?
Prince Henry. If ever we depart
    upon this journey,
So long to one or both of us, I
    promise!

Elsie. Shall we not go, then?
    Have you lifted me
Into the air, only to hurl me back
Wounded upon the ground? and
    offered me
The waters of eternal life, to bid me
Drink the polluted puddles of this
    world?

Prince Henry. O Elsie! what a
    lesson thou dost teach me!
The life which is, and that which is
    to come,
Suspended hang in such nice equi-
    poise
A breath disturbs the balance; and
    that scale

479

In which we throw our hearts pre-
    ponderates,
And the other, like an empty one,
    flies up,
And is accounted vanity and air !
To me the thought of death is
    terrible,
Having such hold on life. To thee
    it is not
So much even as the lifting of a
    latch ;
Only a step into the open air
Out of a tent already luminous
With light that shines through its
    transparent walls !
O pure in heart ! from thy sweet
    dust shall grow
Lilies, upon whose petals will be
    written
' Ave Maria' in characters of gold !

III.

A street in Strasburg. Night.
PRINCE HENRY *wandering
alone, wrapped in a cloak.*

Prince Henry. Still is the night.
    The sound of feet
Has died away from the empty
    street,
And like an artisan, bending down
His head on his anvil, the dark town
Sleeps, with a slumber deep and
    sweet.
Sleepless and restless, I alone,
In the dusk and damp of these
    walls of stone,
Wander and weep in my remorse !

Crier of the Dead (ringing a bell).

    Wake ! wake !
    All ye that sleep !
    Pray for the Dead !
    Pray for the Dead !

Prince Henry. Hark ! with what
    accents loud and hoarse
This warder on the walls of death
Sends forth the challenge of his
    breath !

I see the dead that sleep in the
    grave !
They rise up and their garments
    wave,
Dimly and spectral, as they rise,
With the light of another world in
    their eyes !

Crier of the Dead.

    Wake ! wake !
    All ye that sleep !
    Pray for the Dead !
    Pray for the Dead !

Prince Henry. Why for the
    dead, who are at rest ?
Pray for the living, in whose breast
The struggle between right and
    wrong
Is raging terrible and strong,
As when good angels war with
    devils !
This is the Master of the Revels,
Who, at Life's flowing feast, pro-
    poses
The health of absent friends, and
    pledges,
Not in bright goblets crowned with
    roses,
And tinkling as we touch their
    edges,
But with his dismal, tinkling bell,
That mocks and mimics their
    funeral knell !

Crier of the Dead.

    Wake ! wake !
    All ye that sleep !
    Pray for the Dead !
    Pray for the Dead !

Prince Henry. Wake not, be-
    loved ! be thy sleep
Silent as night is, and as deep !
There walks a sentinel at thy gate
Whose heart is heavy and desolate,
And the heavings of whose bosom
    number
The respirations of thy slumber,
As if some strange, mysterious fate

Had linked two hearts in one, and
mine
Went madly wheeling about thine,
Only with wider and wilder sweep!

Crier of the Dead (at a distance).

Wake! wake
All ye that sleep!
Pray for the Dead!
Pray for the Dead!

Prince Henry. Lo! with what
depth of blackness thrown
Against the clouds, far up the skies
The walls of the cathedral rise,
Like a mysterious grove of stone,
With fitful lights and shadows
blending,
As from behind, the moon, ascend-
ing,
Lights its dim aisles and paths
unknown!
The wind is rising; but the boughs
Rise not and fall not with the wind
That through their foliage sobs and
soughs;
Only the cloudy rack behind,
Drifting onward, wild and ragged,
Gives to each spire and buttress
jagged
A seeming motion undefined.
Below on the square, an armed
knight,
Still as a statue and as white,
Sits on his steed, and the moon-
beams quiver
Upon the points of his armour
bright
As on the ripples of a river.
He lifts the visor from his cheek,
And beckons, and makes as he
would speak.
Walter the Minnesinger.
Friend! can you tell me where
alight
Thuringia's horsemen for the
night?
For I have lingered in the rear,
And wander vainly up and down.

Prince Henry. I am a stranger
in the town,
As thou art; but the voice I hear
Is not a stranger to mine ear.
Thou art Walter of the Vogelweid!
Walter. Thou hast guessed
rightly; and thy name
Is Henry of Hoheneck!
Prince Henry. Ay, the same.
Walter (embracing him). Come
closer, closer to my side;
What brings thee hither? What
potent charm
Has drawn thee from thy German
farm
Into the old Alsatian city?
Prince Henry. A tale of wonder
and of pity!
A wretched man, almost by stealth
Dragging my body to Salern,
In the vain hope and search for
health,
And destined never to return.
Already thou hast heard the rest.
But what brings thee, thus armed
and dight
In the equipments of a knight?
Walter. Dost thou not see upon
my breast
The cross of the Crusaders shine?
My pathway leads to Palestine.
Prince Henry. Ah, would that
way were also mine!
O noble poet! thou whose heart
Is like a nest of singing-birds
Rocked on the topmost bough of
life,
Wilt thou, too, from our sky de-
part,
And in the clangour of the strife
Mingle the music of thy words?
Walter. My hopes are high, my
heart is proud,
And like a trumpet long and loud,
Thither my thoughts all clang and
ring!
My life is in my hand, and lo
I grasp and bend it as a bow

And shoot forth from its trembling
string
An arrow, that shall be, perchance,
Like the arrow of the Israelite king
Shot from the window toward the
east,
That of the Lord's deliverance !

Prince Henry.   My life, alas ! is
what thou seest !
O enviable fate ! to be
Strong, beautiful, and armed like
thee
With lyre and sword, with song and
steel ;
A hand to smite, a heart to feel !
Thy heart, thy hand, thy lyre, thy
sword,
Thou givest all unto thy Lord ;
While I, so mean and abject grown,
Am thinking of myself alone.

Walter.   Be patient : Time will
reinstate
Thy health and fortunes.

Prince Henry.   'Tis too late !
I cannot strive against my fate !

Walter.   Come with me ; for
my steed is weary ;
Our journey has been long and
dreary,
And, dreaming of his stall, he dints
With his impatient hoofs the flints.

Prince Henry (aside).   I am
ashamed, in my disgrace,
To look into that noble face !
To-morrow, Walter, let it be.

Walter.   To-morrow, at the dawn
of day,
I shall again be on my way.
Come with me to the hostelry,
For I have many things to say.
Our journey into Italy
Perchance together we may make ;
Wilt thou not do it for my sake ?

Prince Henry.   A sick man's
pace would but impede
Thine eager and impatient speed.
Besides, my pathway leads me
round

To Hirschau, in the forest's bound,
Where I assemble man and steed,
And all things for my journey's
need.

(*They go out.*)

Lucifer (flying over the city).
Sleep, sleep, O city ! till the
light
Wake you to sin and crime again,
Whilst on your dreams, like dismal
rain,
I scatter downward through the
night
My maledictions dark and deep.
I have more martyrs in your walls
Than God has ; and they cannot
sleep ;
They are my bondsmen and my
thralls ;
Their wretched lives are full of
pain,
Wild agonies of nerve and brain ;
And every heart-beat, every breath,
Is a convulsion worse than death !
Sleep, sleep, O city ! though
within
The circuit of your walls there be
No habitation free from sin,
And all its nameless misery ;
The aching heart, the aching head,
Grief for the living and the dead,
And foul corruption of the time,
Disease, distress, and want, and
woe,
And crimes, and passions that may
grow
Until they ripen into crime !

*Square in front of the Cathedral.
Easter Sunday.* FRIAR CUTH-
BERT *preaching to the crowd
from a pulpit in the open air.*
PRINCE HENRY *and* ELSIE
crossing the square.

Prince Henry.   This is the day,
when from the dead
Our Lord arose ; and everywhere,

482

Out of their darkness and despair,
Triumphant over his fears and foes,
The hearts of his disciples rose,
When to the women, standing
    near,
The Angel in shining vesture said,
'The Lord is risen; he is not
    here!'
And, mindful that the day is come,
On all the hearths in Christendom
The fires are quenched, to be
    again
Rekindled from the sun, that high
Is dancing in the cloudless sky.
The churches are all decked with
    flowers,
The salutations among men
Are but the Angel's words divine,
'Christ is arisen!' and the bells
Catch the glad murmur as it
    swells,
And chant together in their towers.
All hearts are glad; and free from
    care
The faces of the people shine.
See what a crowd is in the square,
Gaily and gallantly arrayed!
    Elsie. Let us go back; I am
        afraid!
    Prince Henry. Nay, let us mount
        the church-steps here,
Under the doorway's sacred
        shadow;
We can see all things, and be
    freer
From the crowd that madly heaves
    and presses!
    Elsie. What a gay pageant!
        what bright dresses!
It looks like a flower-besprinkled
    meadow.
What is that yonder on the square?
    Prince Henry. A pulpit in the
        open air,
And a Friar, who is preaching to
    the crowd
In a voice so deep and clear and
    *l*oud,

That, if we listen, and give heed,
His lowest words will reach the
    ear.
    *Friar Cuthbert (gesticulating
        and cracking a postilion's
        whip).* What ho! good
    people! do you not hear?
Dashing along at the top of his
    speed,
Booted and spurred, on his jaded
    steed,
A courier comes with words of
    cheer.
Courier! what is the news, I pray?
'Christ is arisen!' Whence come
    you? 'From court.'
Then I do not believe it; you say
    it in sport.
    (Cracks his whip again.)
Ah, here comes another, riding
    this way:
We soon shall know what he has
    to say.
Courier! what are the tidings to-
    day?
'Christ is arisen!' Whence come
    you? 'From town.'
Then I do not believe it; away
    with you, clown.
    (Cracks his whip more violently.)
And here comes a third, who is
    spurring amain:
What news do you bring, with
    your loose-hanging rein,
Your spurs wet with blood, and
    your bridle with foam?
'Christ is arisen!' Whence come
    you? 'From Rome.'
Ah, now I believe. He is risen,
    indeed.
Ride on with the news, at the top
    of your speed!
    (Great applause among the crowd.)
To come back to my text! When
    the news was first spread
That Christ was arisen indeed
    from the dead,

483

Very great was the joy of the
angels in heaven;
And as great the dispute as to who
should carry
The tidings thereof to the Virgin
Mary,
Pierced to the heart with sorrows
seven.
Old Father Adam was first to
propose,
As being the author of all our woes;
But he was refused, for fear, said
they,
He would stop to eat apples on the
way!
Abel came next, but petitioned in
vain,
Because he might meet with his
brother Cain!
Noah, too, was refused, lest his
weakness for wine
Should delay him at every tavern-
sign;
And John the Baptist could not
get a vote,
On account of his old-fashioned
camel's-hair coat;
And the Penitent Thief, who died
on the cross,
Was reminded that all his bones
were broken!
Till at last, when each in turn had
spoken,
The company being still at a loss,
The Angel, who rolled away the
stone,
Was sent to the sepulchre, all
alone,
And filled with glory that gloomy
prison,
And said to the Virgin, ' The Lord
is arisen!'

(*The Cathedral bells ring.*)

But hark! the bells are beginning
to chime!
And I feel that I am growing
hoarse.

I will put an end to my dis-
course,
And leave the rest for some other
time.
For the bells themselves are the
best of preachers;
Their brazen lips are learned
teachers,
From their pulpits of stone, in the
upper air,
Sounding aloft, without crack or
flaw,
Shriller than trumpets under the
Law,
Now a sermon and now a prayer.
The clangorous hammer is the
tongue,
This way, that way, beaten and
swung,
That from mouth of brass, as from
Mouth of Gold,
May be taught the Testaments,
New and Old.
And above it the great cross-beam
of wood
Representeth the Holy Rood,
Upon which, like the bell, our
hopes are hung.
And the wheel wherewith it is
swayed and rung
Is the mind of man, that round and
round
Sways, and maketh the tongue to
sound!
And the rope, with its twisted
cordage three,
Denoteth the Scriptural Trinity
Of Morals, and Symbols, and
History;
And the upward and downward
motions show
That we touch upon matters high
and low;
And the constant change and
transmutation
Of action and of contemplation,
Downward, the Scripture brought
from on high,

484

Upward, exalted again to the sky:
Downward, the literal interpretation,
Upward, the Vision and Mystery!

And now, my hearers, to make an end,
I have only one word more to say;
In the church, in honour of Easter day,
Will be represented a Miracle Play;
And I hope you will all have the grace to attend.
Christ bring us at last to his felicity!
Pax vobiscum! et Benedicite!

—————

In the Cathedral.

Chant.

Kyrie Eleison!
Christe Eleison!

Elsie. I am at home here in my Father's house!
These paintings of the Saints upon the walls
Have all familiar and benignant faces.
Prince Henry. The portraits of the family of God!
Thine own hereafter shall be placed among them.
Elsie. How very grand it is and wonderful!
Never have I beheld a church so splendid!
Such columns, and such arches, and such windows,
So many tombs and statues in the chapels,
And under them so many confessionals.
They must be for the rich. I should not like
To tell my sins in such a church as this.
Who built it?

Prince Henry. A great master of his craft,
Erwin von Steinbach; but not he alone,
For many generations laboured with him.
Children that came to see these Saints in stone,
As day by day out of the blocks they rose,
Grew old and died, and still the work went on,
And on, and on, and is not yet completed.
The generation that succeeds our own
Perhaps may finish it. The architect
Built his great heart into these sculptured stones,
And with him toiled his children, and their lives
Were builded, with his own, into the walls,
As offerings unto God. You see that statue
Fixing its joyous, but deep-wrinkled eyes
Upon the Pillar of the Angels yonder.
That is the image of the master, carved
By the fair hand of his own child, Sabina.
Elsie. How beautiful is the column that he looks at!
Prince Henry. That, too, she sculptured. At the base of it
Stand the Evangelists; above their heads
Four Angels blowing upon marble trumpets,
And over them the blessed Christ surrounded
By his attendant ministers, upholding
The instruments of his passion.
Elsie. O my Lord!

Would I could leave behind me
    upon earth
Some monument to thy glory, such
    as this !
Prince Henry. A greater monu-
    ment than this thou leavest
In thine own life, all purity and
    love !
See, too, the Rose, above the
    western portal
Resplendent with a thousand gor-
    geous colours,
The perfect flower of Gothic love-
    liness !
Elsie. And, in the gallery, the
    long line of statues,
Christ with his twelve Apostles
    watching us !

(*A Bishop in armour, booted and
spurred, passes with his train.*)

Prince Henry. But come away ;
    we have not time to look.
The crowd already fills the church,
    and yonder
Upon a stage, a herald with a
    trumpet,
Clad like the Angel Gabriel, pro-
    claims
The Mystery that will now be
    represented.

THE NATIVITY.

A MIRACLE-PLAY.

INTROITUS.

Præco. Come, good people, all
    and each,
Come and listen to our speech !
In your presence here I stand,
With a trumpet in my hand,
To announce the Easter Play,
Which we represent to-day !
First of all we shall rehearse,
In our action and our verse,

The Nativity of our Lord,
As written in the old record
Of the Protevangelion,
So that he who reads may run !

(*Blows his trumpet.*)

I. HEAVEN.

Mercy (*at the feet of God*). Have
    pity, Lord ! be not afraid
To save mankind, whom thou hast
    made,
Nor let the souls that were betrayed
    Perish eternally !
Justice. It cannot be, it must not
    be !
When in the garden placed by
    thee,
The fruit of the forbidden tree
    He ate, and he must die !
Mercy. Have pity, Lord ! let
    penitence
Atone for disobedience,
Nor let the fruit of man's offence
    Be endless misery !
Justice. What penitence pro-
    portionate
Can e'er be felt for sin so great ?
Of the forbidden fruit he ate,
    And damned must he be !
God. He shall be saved, if that
    within
The bounds of earth one free from
    sin
Be found, who for his kith and kin
    Will suffer martyrdom.
The Four Virtues. Lord ! we have
    searched the world around,
From centre to the utmost bound,
But no such mortal can be found ;
    Despairing, back we come.
Wisdom. No mortal, but a God
    made man,
Can ever carry out this plan,
Achieving what none other can,
    Salvation unto all !
God. Go, then, O my beloved
    Son !

486

It can by thee alone be done ;
By thee the victory shall be won
 O'er Satan and the Fall !

(*Here the* ANGEL GABRIEL *shall
leave Paradise and fly towards
the earth : the jaws of Hell open
below, and the Devils walk about,
making a great noise.*)

II. MARY AT THE WELL.

Mary. Along the garden walk,
 and thence
Through the wicket in the garden
 fence,
 I steal with quiet pace,
My pitcher at the well to fill,
That lies so deep and cool and still
 In this sequestered place.
These sycamores keep guard
 around ;
I see no face, I hear no sound ;
 Save bubblings of the spring,
And my companions, who within
The threads of gold and scarlet spin,
 And at their labour sing.
 The Angel Gabriel. Hail, Virgin
 Mary, full of grace !

(*Here* MARY *looketh around her,
trembling, and then saith :*)

 Mary. Who is it speaketh in this
 place,
 With such a gentle voice ?
Gabriel. The Lord of heaven is
 with thee now !
Blessed among all women thou,
 Who art his holy choice !
Mary (*setting down the pitcher*).
 What can this mean? No
 one is near,
And yet, such sacred words I hear,
 I almost fear to stay.

(*Here the Angel appearing to
her, shall say :*)

 Gabriel. Fear not, O Mary ! but
 believe !

For thou, a Virgin, shalt conceive
 A child this very day.
Fear not, O Mary ! from the sky
The majesty of the Most High
 Shall overshadow thee !
 Mary. Behold the handmaid of
 the Lord !
According to thy holy word,
 So be it unto me !

(*Here the Devils shall again make
a great noise, under the stage.*)

III. THE ANGELS OF THE SEVEN PLANETS, BEARING THE STAR OF BETHLEHEM.

 The Angels. The Angels of the
 Planets Seven,
Across the shining fields of heaven
 The natal star we bring !
Dropping our sevenfold virtues
 down,
As priceless jewels in the crown
 Of Christ, our new-born King.
 Raphael. I am the Angel of the
 Sun,
Whose flaming wheels began to run
 When God's almighty breath
Said to the darkness and the Night,
Let there be light ! and there was
 light !
 I bring the gift of Faith.
 Gabriel. I am the Angel of the
 Moon,
Darkened, to be rekindled soon
 Beneath the azure cope !
Nearest to earth, it is my ray
That best illumes the midnight way.
 I bring the gift of Hope !
 Anael. The Angel of the Star of
 Love,
The Evening Star, that shines
 above
 The place where lovers be,
Above all happy hearths and
 homes,
On roofs of thatch, or golden domes,
 I give him Charity !

Zobiachel. The Planet Jupiter is
    mine !
The mightiest star of all that shine,
    Except the sun alone !
He is the High Priest of the Dove,
And sends, from his great throne
    above,
    Justice, that shall atone !
Michael. The Planet Mercury,
    whose place
Is nearest to the sun in space
    Is my allotted sphere !
And with celestial ardour swift
I bear upon my hands the gift
    Of heavenly Prudence here !
Uriel. I am the Minister of
    Mars,
The strongest star among the stars !
    My songs of power prelude
The march and battle of man's life,
And for the suffering and the strife,
    I give him Fortitude !
Orifiel. The Angel of the utter-
    most
Of all the shining, heavenly host,
    From the far-off expanse
Of the Saturnian, endless space
I bring the last, the crowning grace,
    The gift of Temperance !

(*A sudden light shines from the
    windows of the stable in the
    village below.*)

IV.   THE WISE MEN OF THE EAST.

The stable of the Inn. The VIRGIN
    and CHILD. *Three Gipsy Kings,*
    GASPAR, MELCHIOR, *and* BEL-
    SHAZZAR, *shall come in.*

    Gaspar. Hail to thee, Jesus of
        Nazareth !
Though in a manger thou draw
        breath,
Thou art greater than Life and
        Death,
        Greater than Joy or Woe !
This cross upon the line of life

Portendeth struggle, toil, and strife,
And through a region with peril rife
    In darkness shalt thou go !
Melchior. Hail to thee, King of
    Jerusalem !
Though humbly born in Bethlehem,
A sceptre and a diadem
    Await thy brow and hand !
The sceptre is a simple reed,
The crown will make thy temples
    bleed,
And in thy hour of greatest need,
    Abashed thy subjects stand !
Belshazzar. Hail to thee, Christ
    of Christendom !
O'er all the earth thy kingdom
    come !
From distant Trebizond to Rome
    Thy name shall men adore !
Peace and good-will among all men,
The Virgin has returned again,
Returned the old Saturnian reign
    And Golden Age once more.
The Child Christ. Jesus, the Son
    of God, am I,
Born here to suffer and to die
According to the prophecy,
    That other men may live !
The Virgin. And now these
    clothes, that wrapped him,
    take,
And keep them precious, for his
    sake ;
Our benediction thus we make,
    Nought else have we to give.

(*She gives them swaddling clothes,
    and they depart.*)

V.   THE FLIGHT INTO EGYPT.

(*Here shall* JOSEPH *come in,
    leading an ass, on which are
    seated* MARY *and the* CHILD.)

    Mary. Here will we rest us,
        under these
O'erhanging branches of the trees,
Where robins chant their litanies
    And canticles of joy.

Joseph. My saddle-girths have
    given way
With trudging through the heat
    to-day;
To you I think it is but play
    To ride and hold the boy.
  Mary. Hark! how the robins
    shout and sing,
As if to hail their infant King!
I will alight at yonder spring
    To wash his little coat.
  Joseph. And I will hobble well
    the ass,
Lest, being loose upon the grass,
He should escape; for, by the
    mass,
    He's nimble as a goat.

(*Here* MARY *shall alight and go to
    the spring.*)

  Mary. O Joseph! I am much
    afraid,
For men are sleeping in the shade;
I fear that we shall be waylaid,
    And robbed and beaten sore!

(*Here a band of robbers shall be
seen sleeping, two of whom shall
rise and come forward.*)

  Dumachus. Cock's soul! deliver
    up your gold!
  Joseph. I pray you, Sirs, let go
    your hold!
You see that I am weak and old,
    Of wealth I have no store.
  Dumachus. Give up your
    money!
  Titus. Prithee cease.
Let these good people go in peace.
  Dumachus. First let them pay
    for their release,
    And then go on their way.
  Titus. These forty groats I give
    in fee,
If thou wilt only silent be.
  Mary. May God be merciful to
    thee,
    Upon the Judgment Day!

Jesus. When thirty years shall
    have gone by,
I at Jerusalem shall die,
By Jewish hands exalted high
    On the accursed tree.
Then on my right and my left side,
These thieves shall both be cruci-
    fied,
And Titus thenceforth shall abide
    In paradise with me.

(*Here a great rumour of trumpets
and horses, like the noise of a
king with his army, and the
robbers shall take flight.*)

VI. THE SLAUGHTER OF THE
    INNOCENTS.

  King Herod. Potz-tausend!
    Himmel-sacrament!
Filled am I with great wonderment
    At this unwelcome news!
Am I not Herod? Who shall dare
My crown to take, my sceptre bear,
    As king among the Jews?

(*Here he shall stride up and down
    and flourish his sword.*)

What ho! I fain would drink a can
Of the strong wine of Canaan!
    The wine of Helbon bring
I purchased at the Fair of Tyre,
As red as blood, as hot as fire,
    And fit for any king!

(*He quaffs great goblets of wine.*)

Now at the window will I stand,
While in the street the armed band
    The little children slay:
The babe just born in Bethlehem
Will surely slaughtered be with
    them,
    Nor live another day!

(*Here a voice of lamentation shall
    be heard in the street.*)

  Rachel. O wicked king! O cruel
    speed!

To do this most unrighteous deed!
  My children all are slain!
Herod. Ho, seneschal! another
  cup!
With wine of Sorek fill it up!
  I would a bumper drain!
Rahab. May maledictions fall
  and blast
Thyself and lineage to the last
  Of all thy kith and kin!
Herod. Another goblet! quick!
  and stir,
Pomegranate juice and drops of
  myrrh
  And calamus therein!
Soldiers (*in the street*). Give up
  thy child into our hands!
It is King Herod who commands
  That he should thus be slain!
The Nurse Medusa. O monstrous
  men!
  What have ye done!
It is King Herod's only son
  That ye have cleft in twain!
Herod. Ah luckless day! What
  words of fear
Are these that smite upon my ear
  With such a doleful sound!
What torments rack my heart and
  head!
Would I were dead! would I were
  dead,
  And buried in the ground!

(*He falls down and writhes as
  though eaten by worms. Hell
  opens, and* SATAN *and* ASTA-
  ROTH *come forth, and drag him
  down.*)

VII. JESUS AT PLAY WITH HIS
  SCHOOLMATES.

Jesus. The shower is over. Let
  us play,
And make some sparrows out of
  clay,
  Down by the river's side.

Judas. See, how the stream has
  overflowed
Its banks, and o'er the meadow
  road
  Is spreading far and wide!

(*They draw water out of the river
  by channels, and form little pools.*
  JESUS *makes twelve sparrows of
  clay, and the other boys do the
  same.*)

Jesus. Look! look! how prettily
  I make
These little sparrows by the lake
  Bend down their necks and
  drink!
Now will I make them sing and
  soar
So far, they shall return no more
  Unto this river's brink.
Judas. That canst thou not!
  They are but clay,
They cannot sing, nor fly away
  Above the meadow lands!
Jesus. Fly, fly! ye sparrows!
  you are free!
And while you live, remember me
  Who made you with my hands.

(*Here* JESUS *shall clap his hands,
  and the sparrows shall fly away,
  chirruping.*)

Judas. Thou art a sorcerer, I
  know;
Oft has my mother told me so,
  I will not play with thee!

(*He strikes* JESUS *on the right
  side.*)

Jesus. Ah, Judas! thou hast
  smote my side,
And when I shall be crucified,
  There shall I pierced be!

(*Here* JOSEPH *shall come in, and
  say :*)

Joseph. Ye wicked boys! why
  do ye play,

And break the holy Sabbath day?
What, think ye, will your mothers say
    To see you in such plight!
In such a sweat, and such a heat,
With all that mud upon your feet!
There's not a beggar in the street
    Makes such a sorry sight!

VIII. THE VILLAGE SCHOOL.

(*The* RABBI BEN ISRAEL, *with a
long beard, sitting on a high
stool, with a rod in his hand.*)

Rabbi. I am the Rabbi Ben Israel,
Throughout this village known full well,
And, as my scholars all will tell,
    Learned in things divine;
The Cabala and Talmud hoar
Than all the prophets prize I more,
For water is all Bible lore,
    But Mishna is strong wine.
My fame extends from West to East,
And always, at the Purim feast,
I am as drunk as any beast,
    That wallows in his sty;
The wine it so elateth me,
That I no difference can see
Between 'Accursed Haman be!'
    And ' Blessed be Mordecai!'

Come hither, Judas Iscariot;
Say, if thy lesson thou hast got
From the Rabbinical Book or not.
    Why howl the dogs at night?
    Judas. In the Rabbinical Book,
      it saith
The dogs howl, when with icy breath
Great Sammaël, the Angel of Death,
    Takes through the town his flight!

Rabbi. Well, boy! now say, if
    thou art wise,
When the Angel of Death, who is
    full of eyes,
Comes where a sick man dying lies,
    What doth he to the wight?
    Judas. He stands beside him,
      dark and tall,
Holding a sword, from which doth fall
Into his mouth a drop of gall,
    And so he turneth white.
    Rabbi. And now, my Judas, say
      to me
What the great Voices Four may be,
That quite across the world do flee,
    And are not heard by men?
    Judas. The Voice of the Sun in
      heaven's dome,
The Voice of the Murmuring of
    Rome,
The Voice of a Soul that goeth
    home,
    And the Angel of the Rain!
    Rabbi. Right are thine answers
      every one!
Now little Jesus, the carpenter's son,
Let us see how thy task is done.
    Canst thou thy letters say?
    Jesus. Aleph.
    Rabbi. What next? Do not stop
      yet!
Go on with all the alphabet.
Come, Aleph, Beth; dost thou forget?
    Cock's soul! thou'dst rather
      play!
    Jesus. What Aleph means I fain
      would know,
Before I any further go!
    Rabbi. O, by Saint Peter!
      wouldst thou so?
    Come hither, boy, to me.

As surely as the letter Jod
Once cried aloud, and spake to
God,
So surely shalt thou feel this rod,
    And punished shalt thou be !

(*Here* RABBI BEN ISRAEL *shall
lift up his rod to strike* JESUS,
*and his right arm shall be para-
lyzed.*)

IX. CROWNED WITH FLOWERS.

(JESUS *sitting among his playmates
crowned with flowers as their
King.*)

Boys. We spread our garments
    on the ground !
With fragrant flowers thy head is
    crowned,
While like a guard we stand
    around,
    And hail thee as our King !
Thou art the new King of the
    Jews !
Nor let the passers-by refuse
To bring that homage which men use
    To majesty to bring.

(*Here a traveller shall go by, and
the boys shall lay hold of his
garments and say:*)

Boys. Come hither ! and all
    reverence pay
Unto our monarch, crowned to-
    day !
Then go rejoicing on your way,
    In all prosperity !
Traveller. Hail to the King of
    Bethlehem,
Who weareth in his diadem
The yellow crocus for the gem
    Of his authority !

(*He passes by ; and others come
in, bearing on a litter a sick
child.*)

Boys. Set down the litter and
    draw near !

The King of Bethlehem is here !
What ails the child, who seems to
    fear
    That we shall do him harm ?
The Bearers. He climbed up to
    the robin's nest,
And out there darted, from his rest
A serpent with a crimson crest,
    And stung him in the arm.
Jesus. Bring him to me, and let
    me feel
The wounded place ; my touch can
    heal
The sting of serpents, and can steal
    The poison from the bite !

(*He touches the wound, and the boy
begins to cry.*)

Cease to lament ! I can foresee
That thou hereafter known shalt be
Among the men who follow me,
    As Simon the Canaanite !

EPILOGUE.

In the after part of the day
Will be represented another play,
Of the Passion of our Blessed Lord,
Beginning directly after Nones !
At the close of which we shall
    accord,
By way of benison and reward,
The sight of a holy Martyr's bones !

IV.

The road to Hirschau. PRINCE
HENRY *and* ELSIE, *with their
attendants, on horseback.*

Elsie. Onward and onward the
    highway runs to the distant
    city, impatiently bearing
Tidings of human joy and disaster,
    of love and of hate, of doing
    and daring !
Prince Henry. This life of ours
    is a wild æolian harp of many
    a joyous strain,

But under them all there runs a loud perpetual wail, as of souls in pain.

Elsie. Faith alone can interpret life, and the heart that aches and bleeds with the stigma

Of pain, alone bears the likeness of Christ, and can comprehend its dark enigma.

Prince Henry. Man is selfish, and seeketh pleasure with little care of what may betide;

Else why am I travelling here beside thee, a demon that rides by an angel's side?

Elsie. All the hedges are white with dust, and the great dog under the creaking wain,

Hangs his head in the lazy heat, while onward the horses toil and strain.

Prince Henry. Now they stop at the wayside inn, and the wagoner laughs with the landlord's daughter,

While out of the dripping trough the horses distend their leathern sides with water.

Elsie. All through life there are wayside inns, where man may refresh his soul with love;

Even the lowest may quench his thirst at rivulets fed by springs from above.

Prince Henry. Yonder, where rises the cross of stone, our journey along the highway ends,

And over the fields, by a bridle path, down into the broad green valley descends.

Elsie. I am not sorry to leave behind the beaten road with its dust and heat;

The air will be sweeter far, and the turf will be softer under our horses' feet.

(They turn down a green lane.)

Elsie. Sweet is the air with the budding haws, and the valley stretching for miles below

Is white with blossoming cherry-trees, as if just covered with lightest snow.

Prince Henry. Over our heads a white cascade is gleaming against the distant hill;

We cannot hear it, nor see it move, but it hangs like a banner when winds are still.

Elsie. Damp and cool is this deep ravine, and cool the sound of the brook by our side!

What is this castle that rises above us, and lords it over a land so wide?

Prince Henry. It is the home of the Counts of Calva; well have I known these scenes of old,

Well I remember each tower and turret, remember the brooklet, the wood, and the wold.

Elsie. Hark! from the little village below us the bells of the church are ringing for rain!

Priests and peasants in long procession come forth and kneel on the arid plain.

Prince Henry. They have not long to wait, for I see in the south uprising a little cloud,

That before the sun shall be set will cover the sky above us as with a shroud.

(They pass on.)

The Convent of Hirschau in the Black Forest. The Convent cellar. FRIAR CLAUS *comes in with a light and a basket of empty flagons.*

Friar Claus. I always enter this sacred place

With a thoughtful, solemn, and reverent pace,

Pausing long enough on each stair
To breathe an ejaculatory prayer,
And a benediction on the vines
That produce these various sorts
    of wines !
For my part, I am well content
That we have got through with the
    tedious Lent !
Fasting is all very well for those
Who have to contend with invisible
    foes ;
But I am quite sure it does not
    agree
With a quiet, peaceable man like
    me,
Who am not of that nervous and
    meagre kind
That are always distressed in body
    and mind !
And at times it really does me
    good
To come down among this brother-
    hood,
Dwelling for ever under ground,
Silent, contemplative, round and
    sound ;
Each one old, and brown with
    mould,
But filled to the lips with the
    ardour of youth,
With the latent power and love of
    truth,
And with virtues fervent and
    manifold.

I have heard it said, that at Easter-
    tide,
When buds are swelling on every
    side,
And the sap begins to move in the
    vine,
Then in all cellars, far and wide,
The oldest, as well as the newest,
    wine
Begins to stir itself, and ferment,
With a kind of revolt and dis-
    content
At being so long in darkness pent,

And fain would burst from its
    sombre tun
To bask on the hillside in the sun ;
As in the bosom of us poor friars,
The tumult of half-subdued de-
    sires
For the world that we have left
    behind
Disturbs at times all peace of
    mind !
And now that we have lived through
    Lent,
My duty it is, as often before,
To open awhile the prison-door,
And give these restless spirits vent.

Now here is a cask that stands
    alone,
And has stood a hundred years or
    more,
Its beard of cobwebs, long and
    hoar,
Trailing and sweeping along the
    floor,
Like Barbarossa, who sits in his
    cave,
Taciturn, sombre, sedate, and
    grave,
Till his beard has grown through
    the table of stone !
It is of the quick and not of the
    dead !
In its veins the blood is hot and
    red,
And a heart still beats in those ribs
    of oak
That time may have tamed, but
    has not broke.
It comes from Bacharach on the
    Rhine,
Is one of the three best kinds of
    wine,
And cost some hundred florins the
    ohm ;
But that I do not consider dear,
When I remember that every year
Four butts are sent to the Pope of
    Rome.

And whenever a goblet thereof I drain,
The old rhyme keeps running in my brain !

At Bacharach on the Rhine,
At Hochheim on the Main,
And at Würzburg on the Stein,
Grow the three best kinds of wine !

They are all good wines, and better far
Than those of the Neckar, or those of the Ahr.
In particular Würzburg well may boast
Of its blessed wine of the Holy Ghost,
Which of all wines I like the most.
This I shall draw for the Abbot's drinking,
Who seems to be much of my way of thinking.

(*Fills a flagon.*)

Ah ! how the streamlet laughs and sings !
What a delicious fragrance springs
From the deep flagon while it fills,
As of hyacinths and daffodils !
Between this cask and the Abbot's lips
Many have been the sips and slips ;
Many have been the draughts of wine,
On their way to his, that have stopped at mine ;
And many a time my soul has hankered
For a deep draught out of his silver tankard,
When it should have been busy with other affairs,
Less with its longings and more with its prayers.
But now there is no such awkward condition,
No danger of death and eternal perdition ;

So here's to the Abbot and Brothers all,
Who dwell in this convent of Peter and Paul !

(*He drinks.*)

O cordial delicious ! O soother of pain !
It flashes like sunshine into my brain !
A benison rest on the Bishop who sends
Such a fudder of wine as this to his friends !
And now a flagon for such as may ask
A draught from the noble Bacharach cask,
And I will be gone, though I know full well
The cellar 's a cheerfuller place than the cell.
Behold where he stands, all sound and good,
Brown and old in his oaken hood ;
Silent he seems externally
As any Carthusian monk may be ;
But within, what a spirit of deep unrest !
What a seething and simmering in his breast !
As if the heaving of his great heart
Would burst his belt of oak apart !
Let me unloose this button of wood,
And quiet a little his turbulent mood.

(*Sets it running.*)

See ! how its currents gleam and shine,
As if they had caught the purple hues
Of autumn sunsets on the Rhine,
Descending and mingling with the dews ;
Or as if the grapes were stained with the blood

495

Of the innocent boy, who, some
    years back,
Was taken and crucified by the
    Jews,
In that ancient town of Bacha-
    rach;
Perdition upon those infidel Jews,
In that ancient town of Bacha-
    rach!
The beautiful town that gives us
    wine
With the fragrant odour of Musca-
    dine!
I should deem it wrong to let this
    pass
Without first touching my lips to
    the glass,
For here in the midst of the current
    I stand,
Like the stone Pfalz in the midst of
    the river,
Taking toll upon either hand,
And much more grateful to the
    giver.

        (*He drinks.*)

Here, now, is a very inferior kind,
Such as in any town you may find,
Such as one might imagine would
    suit
The rascal who drank wine out of
    a boot.
And, after all, it was not a crime,
For he won thereby Dorf Hüffels-
    heim.
A jolly old toper! who at a pull
Could drink a postilion's jack-boot
    full,
And ask with a laugh, when that
    was done,
If the fellow had left the other one!
This wine is as good as we can
    afford
To the friars, who sit at the lower
    board,
And cannot distinguish bad from
    good,
And are far better off than if they
    could,

Being rather the rude disciples of
    beer
Than of anything more refined and
    dear!

    (*Fills the other flagon and departs.*)

The Scriptorium. FRIAR PACI-
FICUS *transcribing and illu-
minating.*

Friar Pacificus. It is growing
    dark! Yet one line more,
And then my work for to-day is o'er.
I come again to the name of the
    Lord!
Ere I that awful name record,
That is spoken so lightly among
    men,
Let me pause a while, and wash my
    pen;
Pure from blemish and blot must it be
When it writes that word of mys-
    tery!

Thus have I laboured on and on,
Nearly through the Gospel of John.
Can it be that from the lips
Of this same gentle Evangelist,
That Christ himself perhaps has
    kissed,
Came the dread Apocalypse!
It has a very awful look,
As it stands there at the end of the
    book,
Like the sun in an eclipse.
Ah me! when I think of that vision
    divine,
Think of writing it, line by line,
I stand in awe of the terrible curse,
Like the trump of doom, in the
    closing verse!
God forgive me! if ever I
Take aught from the book of that
    Prophecy,
Lest my part too should be taken
    away
From the Book of Life on the
    Judgment Day.

This is well written, though I say
    it !
I should not be afraid to display it,
In open day, on the selfsame shelf
With the writings of St. Thecla
    herself,
Or of Theodosius, who of old
Wrote the Gospels in letters of
    gold !
That goodly folio standing yonder,
Without a single blot or blunder,
Would not bear away the palm
    from mine,
If we should compare them line for
    line.

There, now, is an initial letter !
Saint Ulric himself never made a
    better !
Finished down to the leaf and the
    snail,
Down to the eyes on the peacock's
    tail !
And now, as I turn the volume
    over,
And see what lies between cover
    and cover,
What treasures of art these pages
    hold,
All a-blaze with crimson and gold,
God forgive me ! I seem to feel
A certain satisfaction steal
Into my heart, and into my brain,
As if my talent had not lain
Wrapped in a napkin, and all in
    vain.
Yes, I might almost say to the Lord,
Here is a copy of thy Word,
Written out with much toil and
    pain ;
Take it, O Lord, and let it be
As something I have done for thee !

(*He looks from the window.*)

How sweet the air is ! How fair
    the scene !
I wish I had as lovely a green
To paint my landscapes and my
    leaves !

How the swallows twitter under the
    eaves !
There, now, there is one in her
    nest ;
I can just catch a glimpse of her
    head and breast,
And will sketch her thus, in her
    quiet nook,
For the margin of my Gospel book.

(*He makes a sketch.*)

I can see no more. Through the
    valley yonder
A shower is passing ; I hear the
    thunder
Mutter its curses in the air,
The Devil's own and only prayer !
The dusty road is brown with rain,
And, speeding on with might and
    main,
Hitherward rides a gallant train.
They do not parley, they cannot
    wait,
But hurry in at the convent gate.
What a fair lady ! and beside her
What a handsome, graceful, noble
    rider !
Now she gives him her hand to
    alight ;
They will beg a shelter for the
    night.
I will go down to the corridor,
And try to see that face once more ;
It will do for the face of some
    beautiful Saint,
Or for one of the Maries I shall
    paint.

(*Goes out.*)

The Cloisters. The ABBOT
ERNESTUS *pacing to and fro.*

Abbot. Slowly, slowly up the
    wall
Steals the sunshine, steals the
    shade ;
Evening damps begin to fall,
Evening shadows are displayed.
Round me, o'er me, everywhere,
All the sky is grand with clouds,

497

And athwart the evening air
Wheel the swallows home in
    crowds.
Shafts of sunshine from the west
Paint the dusky windows red;
Darker shadows, deeper rest,
Underneath and overhead.
Darker, darker, and more wan,
In my breast the shadows fall;
Upward steals the life of man,
As the sunshine from the wall.
From the wall into the sky,
From the roof along the spire;
Ah, the souls of those that die
Are but sunbeams lifted higher.

(*Enter* PRINCE HENRY.)

Prince Henry. Christ is arisen!
Abbot.   Amen! he is risen!
His peace be with you.
Prince Henry.   Here it reigns
    for ever!
The peace of God, that passeth
    understanding,
Reigns in these cloisters and these
    corridors.
Are you Ernestus, Abbot of the
    convent?
Abbot. I am.
Prince Henry.   And I Prince
    Henry of Hoheneck,
Who crave your hospitality to-
    night.
Abbot. You are thrice welcome
    to our humble walls.
You do us honour; and we shall
    requite it,
I fear, but poorly, entertaining you
With Paschal eggs, and our poor
    convent wine,
The remnants of our Easter
    holidays.
Prince Henry. How fares it with
    the holy monks of Hirschau?
Are all things well with them?
Abbot. All things are well.
Prince Henry. A noble convent!
    I have known it long

By the report of travellers. I now
    see
Their commendations lag behind
    the truth.
You lie here in the valley of the
    Nagold
As in a nest: and the still river,
    gliding
Along its bed, is like an admonition
How all things pass. Your lands
    are rich and ample,
And your revenues large. God's
    benediction
Rests on your convent.
Abbot.   By our charities
We strive to merit it. Our Lord
    and Master,
When he departed, left us in his
    will,
As our best legacy on earth, the
    poor!
These we have always with us;
    had we not,
Our hearts would grow as hard as
    are these stones.
Prince Henry. If I remember
    right, the Counts of Calva
Founded your convent.
Abbot.   Even as you say.
Prince Henry. And, if I err not,
    it is very old.
Abbot. Within these cloisters lie
    already buried
Twelve holy Abbots. Underneath
    the flags
On which we stand, the Abbot
    William lies,
Of blessed memory.
Prince Henry.   And whose
    tomb is that,
Which bears the brass escutcheon?
Abbot.   A benefactor's,
Conrad, a Count of Calva, he who
    stood
Godfather to our bells.
Prince Henry. Your monks are
    learned
And holy men, I trust.

498

Abbot. There are among them
Learned and holy men. Yet in this age
We need another Hildebrand, to shake
And purify us like a mighty wind.
The world is wicked, and sometimes I wonder
God does not lose his patience with it wholly,
And shatter it like glass! Even here, at times,
Within these walls, where all should be at peace,
I have my trials. Time has laid his hand
Upon my heart, gently, not smiting it,
But as a harper lays his open palm
Upon his harp, to deaden its vibrations.
Ashes are on my head, and on my lips
Sackcloth, and in my breast a heaviness
And weariness of life, that makes me ready
To say to the dead Abbots under us,
' Make room for me !' Only I see the dusk
Of evening twilight coming, and have not
Completed half my task ; and so at times
The thought of my shortcomings in this life
Falls like a shadow on the life to come.
Prince Henry. We must all die, and not the old alone ;
The young have no exemption from that doom.
Abbot. Ah, yes ! the young may die, but the old must !
That is the difference.
Prince Henry. I have heard much laud

Of your transcribers. Your Scriptorium
Is famous among all ; your manuscripts
Praised for their beauty and their excellence.
Abbot. That is indeed our boast.
If you desire it,
You shall behold these treasures.
And meanwhile
Shall the Refectorarius bestow
Your horses and attendants for the night.

(*They go in. The Vesper-bell rings.*)

The Chapel. Vespers: after which the monks retire, a chorister leading an old monk who is blind.

Prince Henry. They are all gone, save one who lingers,
Absorbed in deep and silent prayer.
As if his heart could find no rest,
At times he beats his heaving breast
With clenched and convulsive fingers,
Then lifts them trembling in the air.
A chorister, with golden hair,
Guides hitherward his heavy pace.
Can it be so ? Or does my sight
Deceive me in the uncertain light ?
Ah no ! I recognise that face,
Though Time has touched it in his flight,
And changed the auburn hair to white.
It is Count Hugo of the Rhine,
The deadliest foe of all our race,
And hateful unto me and mine !
The Blind Monk. Who is it that doth stand so near
His whispered words I almost hear ?
Prince Henry. I am Prince Henry of Hoheneck,

And you, Count Hugo of the
    Rhine!
I know you, and I see the scar,
The brand upon your forehead,
    shine
And redden like a baleful star!

The Blind Monk. Count Hugo
    once, but now the wreck
Of what I was. O Hoheneck!
The passionate will, the pride, the
    wrath
That bore me headlong on my path,
Stumbled and staggered into fear,
And failed me in my mad career,
As a tired steed some evil-doer,
Alone upon a desolate moor,
Bewildered, lost, deserted, blind,
And hearing loud and close behind
The o'ertaking steps of his pursuer,
Then suddenly from the dark there
    came
A voice that called me by my name,
And said to me, 'Kneel down and
    pray!'
And so my terror passed away,
Passed utterly away for ever.
Contrition, penitence, remorse,
Came on me with o'erwhelming
    force;
A hope, a longing, an endeavour,
By days of penance and nights of
    prayer,
To frustrate and defeat despair!
Calm, deep, and still is now my
    heart,
With tranquil waters overflowed;
A lake whose unseen fountains
    start,
Where once the hot volcano
    glowed.
And you, O prince of Hoheneck!
Have known me in that earlier
    time,
A man of violence and crime,
Whose passions brooked no curb
    nor check.
Behold me now, in gentler mood,
One of this holy brotherhood.

Give me your hand; here let me
    kneel;
Make your reproaches sharp as
    steel;
Spurn me, and smite me on each
    cheek;
No violence can harm the meek,
There is no wound Christ cannot
    heal!
Yes; lift your princely hand, and
    take
Revenge, if 'tis revenge you seek;
Then pardon me, for Jesus' sake!

Prince Henry. Arise, Count
    Hugo! let there be
No further strife nor enmity
Between us twain; we both have
    erred!
Too rash in act, too wroth in word.
From the beginning have we stood
In fierce, defiant attitude,
Each thoughtless of the other's
    right,
And each reliant on his might.
But now our souls are more sub-
    dued;
The hand of God, and not in vain,
Has touched us with the fire of
    pain.
Let us kneel down, and side by
    side
Pray, till our souls are purified,
And pardon will not be denied!

(*They kneel.*)

*The Refectory. Gaudiolum of
    Monks at midnight.* LUCIFER
    disguised as a Friar.

Friar Paul (*sings*).

    Ave! color vini clari,
    Dulcis potus, non amari,
    Tua nos inebriari
    Digneris potentia!

Friar Cuthbert. Not so much
    noise, my worthy freres,
You'll disturb the Abbot at his
    prayers.

Friar Paul (sings).

> O! quam placens in colore!
> O! quam fragrans in odore!
> O! quam sapidum in ore!
> Dulce linguae vinculum!

Friar Cuthbert. I should think your tongue had broken its chain!

Friar Paul (sings).

> Felix venter quem intrabis!
> Felix guttur quod rigabis!
> Felix os quod tu lavabis!
> Et beata labia!

Friar Cuthbert. Peace! I say, peace!
Will you never cease!
You will rouse up the Abbot, I tell you again!

Friar John. No danger! to-night he will let us alone,
As I happen to know he has guests of his own.

Friar Cuthbert. Who are they?

Friar John. A German Prince and his train,
Who arrived here just before the rain.
There is with him a damsel fair to see,
As slender and graceful as a reed!
When she alighted from her steed,
It seemed like a blossom blown from a tree.

Friar Cuthbert. None of your pale-faced girls for me!
None of your damsels of high degree!

Friar John. Come, old fellow, drink down to your peg!
But do not drink any farther, I beg!

Friar Paul (sings).

> In the days of gold!
> The days of old,
> Crosier of wood
> And bishop of gold!

Friar Cuthbert. What an infernal racket and riot!
Can you not drink your wine in quiet!
Why fill the convent with such scandals,
As if we were so many drunken Vandals?

Friar Paul (continues).

> Now we have changed
> That law so good,
> To crosier of gold
> And bishop of wood!

Friar Cuthbert. Well, then, since you are in the mood
To give your noisy humours vent,
Sing and howl to your heart's content!

Chorus of Monks.

> Funde vinum, funde!
> Tanquam sint fluminis undae,
> Nec quaeras unde
> Sed fundas semper abunde!

Friar John. What is the name of yonder friar,
With an eye that glows like a coal of fire,
And such a black mass of tangled hair?

Friar Paul. He who is sitting there,
With a rollicking,
Devil may care,
Free-and-easy look and air,
As if he were used to such feasting and frolicking?

Friar John. The same.

Friar Paul. He's a stranger.
You had better ask his name,
And where he is going, and whence he came.

Friar John. Hallo! Sir Friar!

Friar Paul. You must raise your voice a little higher,
He does not seem to hear what you say.

501

Now, try again! He is looking
   this way.
Friar John. Hallo! Sir Friar.
We wish to inquire
Whence you came, and where you
   are going,
And anything else that is worth the
   knowing.
So be so good as to open your
   head.
   Lucifer. I am a Frenchman
   born and bred,
Going on a pilgrimage to Rome.
My home
Is the convent of St. Gildas de
   Rhuys,
Of which, very like, you never have
   heard.
   Monks. Never a word!
   Lucifer. You must know, then,
   it is in the diocese
Called the diocese of Vannes,
In the province of Brittany.
From the gray rocks of Morbihan
It overlooks the angry sea;
The very sea-shore where,
In his great despair,
Abbot Abelard walked to and fro,
Filling the night with woe,
And wailing aloud to the merciless
   seas
The name of his sweet Heloise!
Whilst overhead
The convent windows gleamed as
   red
As the fiery eyes of the monks within,
Who with jovial din
Gave themselves up to all kinds of
   sin!
Ha! that is a convent! that is an
   abbey!
Over the doors,
None of your death-heads carved
   in wood,
None of your Saints looking pious
   and good,
None of your patriarchs old and
   shabby;

But the heads and tusks of boars,
And the cells
Hung all round with the fells
Of the fallow-deer.
And then what cheer;
What jolly, fat friars,
Sitting round the great roaring fires,
Roaring louder than they,
With their strong wines,
And their concubines,
And never a bell,
With its swagger and swell,
Calling you up with a start of affright
In the dead of night,
To send you grumbling down dark
   stairs,
To mumble your prayers.
But the cheery crow
Of cocks in the yard below,
After daybreak, an hour or so,
And the barking of deep-mouthed
   hounds,—
These are the sounds
That, instead of bells, salute the ear.
And then all day
Up and away
Through the forest, hunting the
   deer!
Ah, my friends! I'm afraid that
   here
You are a little too pious, a little too
   tame,
And the more is the shame.
'Tis the greatest folly
Not to be jolly;
That's what I think!
Come drink, drink,
Drink, and die game!
   Monks. And your Abbot What's-
   his-name?
   Lucifer. Abelard!
   Monks. Did he drink hard?
   Lucifer. O no! Not he!
He was a dry old fellow,
Without juice enough to get
   thoroughly mellow.
There he stood,
Lowering at us in sullen mood,

As if he had come into Brittany
Just to reform our brotherhood!

(*A roar of laughter.*)

But you see
It never would do!
For some of us knew a thing or two,
In the Abbey of St. Gildas de
Rhuys!
For instance, the great ado
With old Fulbert's niece,
The young and lovely Heloise.
Friar John. Stop there, if you
please,
Till we drink to the fair Heloise.
All (*drinking and shouting*).
Heloise! Heloise!

(*The Chapel-bell tolls.*)

Lucifer (*starting*). What is that
bell for? Are you such asses
As to keep up the fashion of mid-
night masses?
Friar Cuthbert. It is only a poor
unfortunate brother,
Who is gifted with most miraculous
powers
Of getting up at all sorts of hours,
And, by way of penance and Chris-
tian meekness,
Of creeping silently out of his cell
To take a pull at that hideous bell;
So that all the monks who are lying
awake
May murmur some kind of prayer
for his sake,
And adapted to his peculiar weak-
ness!
Friar John. From frailty and fall—
All. Good Lord, deliver us all!
Friar Cuthbert. And before the
bell for matins sounds,
He takes his lantern, and goes the
rounds,
Flashing it into our sleepy eyes,
Merely to say it is time to arise.
But enough of that. Go on, if you
please,

With your story about St. Gildas de
Rhuys.
Lucifer. Well, it finally came to
pass
That, half in fun and half in malice,
One Sunday at Mass
We put some poison into the
chalice.
But, either by accident or design,
Peter Abelard kept away
From the chapel that day,
And a poor young friar, who in his
stead
Drank the sacramental wine,
Fell on the steps of the altar, dead!
But look! do you see at the window
there
That face, with a look of grief and
despair,
That ghastly face, as of one in pain?
Monks. Who? where?
Lucifer. As I spoke, it vanished
away again.
Friar Cuthbert. It is that nefarious
Siebald the Refectorarius.
That fellow is always playing the
scout,
Creeping and peeping and prowling
about;
And then he regales
The Abbot with scandalous tales.
Lucifer. A spy in the convent?
One of the brothers
Telling scandalous tales of the
others?
Out upon him, the lazy loon!
I would put a stop to that pretty
soon,
In a way he should rue it.
Monks. How shall we do it?
Lucifer. Do you, brother Paul,
Creep under the window, close to
the wall,
And open it suddenly when I call.
Then seize the villain by the hair,
And hold him there,
And punish him soundly, once for
all.

R

Friar Cuthbert. As St. Dunstan
of old,
We are told,
Once caught the Devil by the nose!

Lucifer. Ha! ha! that story is
very clever,
But has no foundation whatsoever.
Quick! for I see his face again
Glaring in at the window-pane;
Now! now! and do not spare your
blows.

(FRIAR PAUL *opens the window
suddenly, and seizes* SIEBALD.
They beat him.)

Friar Siebald. Help! help! are
you going to slay me?

Friar Paul. That will teach you
again to betray me!

Friar Siebald. Mercy! mercy!

*Friar Paul (shouting and beat-
ing).*
Rumpas bellorum lorum,
Vim confer amorum
Morum verorum rorum
Tu plena polorum!

Lucifer. Who stands in the door-
way yonder,
Stretching out his trembling hand,
Just as Abelard used to stand,
The flash of his keen black eyes
Forerunning the thunder?

The Monks (in confusion). The
Abbot! the Abbot!

Friar Cuthbert. And what is the
wonder!
He seems to have taken you by surprise!

Friar Francis. Hide the great
flagon
From the eyes of the dragon!

Friar Cuthbert. Pull the brown
hood over your face!
This will bring us into disgrace!

Abbot. What means this revel
and carouse?
Is this a tavern and drinking-house?
Are you Christian monks, or
heathen devils,

To pollute this convent with your
revels?
Were Peter Damian still upon
earth,
To be shocked by such ungodly
mirth,
He would write your names, with
pen of gall,
In his Book of Gomorrah, one and
all!
Away, you drunkards! to your
cells,
And pray till you hear the matin-
bells;
You, Brother Francis, and you,
Brother Paul!
And as a penance mark each prayer
With the scourge upon your
shoulders bare;
Nothing atones for such a sin
But the blood that follows the dis-
cipline.
And you, Brother Cuthbert, come
with me
Alone into the sacristy;
You, who should be a guide to your
brothers,
And are ten times worse than all
the others,
For you I've a draught that has
long been brewing,
You shall do a penance worth the
doing!
Away to your prayers, then, one and
all!
I wonder the very convent wall
Does not crumble and crush you in
its fall!

The neighbouring Nunnery. The
ABBESS IRMINGARD *sitting
with* ELSIE *in the moonlight.*

Irmingard. The night is silent,
the wind is still,
The moon is looking from yonder
hill
Down upon convent, and grove, and
garden;

The clouds have passed away from
   her face,
Leaving behind them no sorrowful
   trace,
Only the tender and quiet grace
Of one, whose heart has been healed
   with pardon !

And such am I. My soul within
Was dark with passion and soiled
   with sin.
But now its wounds are healed
   again ;
Gone are the anguish, the terror,
   and pain ;
For across that desolate land of woe,
O'er whose burning sands I was
   forced to go,
A wind from heaven began to blow ;
And all my being trembled and
   shook,
As the leaves of the tree, or the
   grass of the field,
And I was healed, as the sick are
   healed,
When fanned by the leaves of the
   Holy Book !

As thou sittest in the moonlight
   there,
Its glory flooding thy golden
   hair,
And the only darkness that which
   lies
In the haunted chambers of thine
   eyes,
I feel my soul drawn unto thee,
Strangely, and strongly, and more
   and more,
As to one I have known and loved
   before ;
For every soul is akin to me
That dwells in the land of mys-
   tery !
I am the Lady Irmingard,
Born of a noble race and name !
Many a wandering Suabian bard,
Whose life was dreary, and bleak,
   and hard,

Has found through me the way to
   fame.
Brief and bright were those days,
   and the night
Which followed was full of a lurid
   light.
Love, that of every woman's heart
Will have the whole, and not a
   part,
That is to her, in Nature's plan,
More than ambition is to man,
Her light, her life, her very breath,
With no alternative but death,
Found me a maiden soft and young,
Just from the convent's cloistered
   school,
And seated on my lowly stool,
Attentive while the minstrels sung.

Gallant, graceful, gentle, tall,
Fairest, noblest, best of all,
Was Walter of the Vogelweid ;
And, whatsoever may betide,
Still I think of him with pride !
His song was of the summer-time,
The very birds sang in his rhyme ;
The sunshine, the delicious air,
The fragrance of the flowers, were
   there ;
And I grew restless as I heard,
Restless and buoyant as a bird,
Down soft, aerial currents sailing,
O'er blossomed orchards, and
   fields in bloom,
And through the momentary
   gloom
Of shadows o'er the landscape
   trailing,
Yielding and borne I knew not
   where,
But feeling resistance unavailing.

And thus, unnoticed and apart,
And more by accident than choice,
I listened to that single voice
Until the chambers of my heart
Were filled with it by night and
   day.

One night—it was a night in May—
Within the garden, unawares,
Under the blossoms in the gloom,
I heard it utter my own name
With protestations and wild prayers;
And it rang through me, and became
Like the archangel's trump of doom,
Which the soul hears, and must obey;
And mine arose as from a tomb.
My former life now seemed to me
Such as hereafter death may be,
When in the great Eternity
We shall awake and find it day.
It was a dream, and would not stay;
A dream, that in a single night
Faded and vanished out of sight.
My father's anger followed fast
This passion, as a freshening blast
Seeks out and fans the fire, whose rage
It may increase, but not assuage.
And he exclaimed : ' No wandering bard
Shall win thy hand, O Irmingard!
For which Prince Henry of Hoheneck
By messenger and letter sues.'

Gently, but firmly, I replied :
' Henry of Hoheneck I discard !
Never the hand of Irmingard
Shall lie in his as the hand of a bride!'
This said I, Walter, for thy sake;
This said I, for I could not choose.
After a pause, my father spake
In that cold and deliberate tone
Which turns the hearer into stone,
And seems itself the act to be
That follows with such dread certainty;
'This, or the cloister and the veil!'

No other words than these he said,
But they were like a funeral wail;
My life was ended, my heart was dead.
That night from the castle-gate went down,
With silent, slow, and stealthy pace,
Two shadows, mounted on shadowy steeds,
Taking the narrow path that leads
Into the forest dense and brown.
In the leafy darkness of the place,
One could not distinguish form nor face,
Only a bulk without a shape,
A darker shadow in the shade;
One scarce could say it moved or stayed.
Thus it was we made our escape !
A foaming brook, with many a bound,
Followed us like a playful hound;
Then leaped before us, and in the hollow
Paused, and waited for us to follow,
And seemed impatient, and afraid
That our tardy flight should be betrayed
By the sound our horses' hoof-beats made.
And when we reached the plain below,
We paused a moment and drew rein
To look back at the castle again ;
And we saw the windows all aglow
With lights, that were passing to and fro :
Our hearts with terror ceased to beat ;
The brook crept silent to our feet ;
We knew what most we feared to know.

506

Then suddenly horns began to
blow;
And we heard a shout, and a heavy
tramp,
And our horses snorted in the
damp
Night-air of the meadows green
and wide,
And in a moment, side by side,
So close, they must have seemed
but one,
The shadows across the moonlight
run,
And another came, and swept
behind,
Like the shadow of clouds before
the wind!

How I remember that breathless
flight
Across the moors, in the summer
night!
How under our feet the long, white
road
Backward like a river flowed,
Sweeping with it fences and
hedges,
Whilst farther away, and over-
head,
Paler than I, with fear and dread,
The moon fled with us, as we fled
Along the forest's jagged edges!

All this I can remember well;
But of what afterwards befell
I nothing further can recall
Than a blind, desperate, headlong
fall;
The rest is a blank and darkness
all.
When I awoke out of this swoon,
The sun was shining, not the
moon,
Making a cross upon the wall
With the bars of my windows
narrow and tall;
And I prayed to it, as I had been
wont to pray,

From early childhood, day by day,
Each morning, as in bed I lay!
I was lying again in my own
room!
And I thanked God, in my fever
and pain,
That those shadows on the mid-
night plain
Were gone, and could not come
again!
I struggled no longer with my
doom!

This happened many years ago.
I left my father's home to come
Like Catherine to her martyrdom,
For blindly I esteemed it so.
And when I heard the convent door
Behind me close, to ope no more,
I felt it smite me like a blow.
Through all my limbs a shudder
ran,
And on my bruised spirit fell
The dampness of my narrow cell
As night-air on a wounded man,
Giving intolerable pain.

But now a better life began.
I felt the agony decrease
By slow degrees, then wholly
cease,
Ending in perfect rest and peace!
It was not apathy, nor dulness,
That weighed and pressed upon
my brain,
But the same passion I had given
To earth before, now turned to
heaven
With all its overflowing fulness.

Alas! the world is full of peril!
The path that runs through the
fairest meads,
On the sunniest side of the valley,
leads
Into a region bleak and sterile!
Alike in the high-born and the
lowly,

507

The will is feeble, and passion
     strong.
We cannot sever right from wrong;
Some falsehood mingles with all
     truth ;
Nor is it strange the heart of youth
Should waver and comprehend but
     slowly
The things that are holy and
     unholy !
But in this sacred, calm retreat,
We are all well and safely shielded
From winds that blow, and waves
     that beat,
From the cold, and rain, and
     blighting heat,
To which the strongest hearts have
     yielded.
Here we stand as the Virgins
     Seven,
For our celestial bridegroom
     yearning ;
Our hearts are lamps for ever
     burning,
With a steady and unwavering
     flame,
Pointing upward, for ever the
     same,
Steadily upward toward the
     heaven !

The moon is hidden behind a
     cloud ;
A sudden darkness fills the room,
And thy deep eyes, amid the
     gloom,
Shine like jewels in a shroud.
On the leaves is a sound of falling
     rain ;
A bird, awakened in its nest,
Gives a faint twitter of unrest,
Then smooths its plumes and
     sleeps again.
No other sounds than these I hear ;
The hour of midnight must be near.
Thou art o'erspent with the day's
     fatigue
Of riding many a dusty league ;

Sink, then, gently to thy slumber ;
Me so many cares encumber,
So many ghosts, and forms of
     fright,
Have started from their graves to-
     night,
They have driven sleep from mine
     eyes away :
I will go down to the chapel and
     pray.

V.

A covered bridge at Lucerne.

Prince Henry. God's blessing
     on the architects who build
The bridges o'er swift rivers and
     abysses
Before impassable to human feet,
No less than on the builders of
     cathedrals,
Whose massive walls are bridges
     thrown across
The dark and terrible abyss of
     Death.
Well has the name of Pontifex been
     given
Unto the Church's head, as the
     chief builder
And architect of the invisible
     bridge
That leads from earth to heaven.
     Elsie.   How dark it grows ?
What are these paintings on the
     walls around us ?
     Prince Henry.   The Dance
     Macaber !
     Elsie.   What ?
     Prince Henry. The Dance of
     Death !
All that go to and fro must look
     upon it,
Mindful of what they shall be,
     while beneath,
Among the wooden piles, the
     turbulent river
Rushes, impetuous as the river of
     life,

508

With dimpling eddies, ever green
    and bright,
Save where the shadow of this
    bridge falls on it.
    Elsie. O yes! I see it now!
    Prince Henry. The grim
    musician
Leads all men through the mazes
    of that dance,
To different sounds in different
    measures moving;
Sometimes he plays a lute, some-
    times a drum,
To tempt or terrify.
    Elsie. What is this picture?
    Prince Henry. It is a young
    man singing to a nun,
Who kneels at her devotions, but
    in kneeling
Turns round to look at him, and
    Death, meanwhile,
Is putting out the candles on the
    altar!
    Elsie. Ah, what a pity 'tis that
    she should listen
Unto such songs, when in her
    orisons
She might have heard in heaven
    the angels singing!
    Prince Henry. Here he has
    stolen a jester's cap and bells,
And dances with the Queen.
    Elsie. A foolish jest!
    Prince Henry. And here the
    heart of the new-wedded wife,
Coming from church with her
    beloved lord,
He startles with the rattle of his drum.
    Elsie. Ah, that is sad! And yet
    perhaps 'tis best
That she should die, with all the
    sunshine on her,
And all the benedictions of the
    morning,
Before this affluence of golden light
Shall fade into a cold and clouded
    gray,
Then into darkness!

    Prince Henry. Under it is
    written,
'Nothing but death shall separate
    thee and me!'
    Elsie. And what is this, that
    follows close upon it?
    Prince Henry. Death, playing
    on a dulcimer. Behind him,
A poor old woman, with a rosary,
Follows the sound, and seems to
    wish her feet
Were swifter to o'ertake him.
    Underneath,
The inscription reads, 'Better is
    Death than Life.'
    Elsie. Better is Death than
    Life! Ah yes! to thousands
Death plays upon a dulcimer, and
    sings
That song of consolation, till the air
Rings with it, and they cannot
    choose but follow
Whither he leads. And not the old
    alone,
But the young also hear it, and are
    still.
    Prince Henry. Yes, in their
    sadder moments. 'Tis the
    sound
Of their own hearts they hear, half
    full of tears,
Which are like crystal cups, half
    filled with water,
Responding to the pressure of a
    finger
With music sweet and low and
    melancholy.
Let us go forward, and no longer
    stay
In this great picture-gallery of
    Death!
I hate it! ay, the very thought of it!
    Elsie. Why is it hateful to you?
    Prince Henry. For the reason
That life, and all that speaks of
    life, is lovely,
And death, and all that speaks of
    death, is hateful.

Elsie. The grave itself is but a covered bridge,
Leading from light to light, through a brief darkness!
Prince Henry (emerging from the bridge). I breathe again more freely! Ah, how pleasant
To come once more into the light of day,
Out of that shadow of death! To hear again
The hoof-beats of our horses on firm ground,
And not upon those hollow planks, resounding
With a sepulchral echo, like the clods
On coffins in a churchyard! Yonder lies
The Lake of the Four Forest-Towns, apparelled
In light, and lingering, like a village maiden,
Hid in the bosom of her native mountains,
Then pouring all her life into another's,
Changing her name and being! Overhead,
Shaking his cloudy tresses loose in air,
Rises Pilatus, with his windy pines.

(*They pass on.*)

The Devil's Bridge. PRINCE HENRY *and* ELSIE *crossing, with attendants.*

Guide. This bridge is called the Devil's Bridge.
With a single arch, from ridge to ridge,
It leaps across the terrible chasm
Yawning beneath us, black and deep,
As if, in some convulsive spasm,
The summits of the hills had cracked,

And made a road for the cataract,
That raves and rages down the steep!
Lucifer (under the bridge). Ha! ha!
Guide. Never any bridge but this
Could stand across the wild abyss;
All the rest, of wood or stone,
By the Devil's hand were overthrown.
He toppled crags from the precipice,
And whatsoe'er was built by day
In the night was swept away;
None could stand but this alone.
Lucifer (under the bridge). Ha! ha!
Guide. I showed you in the valley a boulder
Marked with the imprint of his shoulder;
As he was bearing it up this way,
A peasant, passing, cried, 'Herr Jé!'
And the Devil dropped it in his fright,
And vanished suddenly out of sight!
Lucifer (under the bridge). Ha! ha!
Guide. Abbot Giraldus of Einsiedel,
For pilgrims on their way to Rome,
Built this at last, with a single arch,
Under which, on its endless march,
Runs the river, white with foam,
Like a thread through the eye of a needle.
And the Devil promised to let it stand,
Under compact and condition
That the first living thing which crossed
Should be surrendered into his hand,
And be beyond redemption lost.
Lucifer (under the bridge). Ha! ha! perdition!
Guide. At length, the bridge being all completed,

The Abbot, standing at its head,
Threw across it a loaf of bread,
Which a hungry dog sprang after,
And the rocks re-echoed with peals
   of laughter
To see the Devil thus defeated!

     (*They pass on.*)

  Lucifer (*under the bridge*). Ha!
   ha! defeated!
For journeys and for crimes like this
I let the bridge stand o'er the abyss!

    The St. Gothard Pass.

  Prince Henry. This is the highest
   point. Two ways the rivers
Leap down to different seas, and as
   they roll
Grow deep and still, and their majes-
   tic presence
Becomes a benefaction to the towns
They visit, wandering silently
   among them,
Like patriarchs old among their
   shining tents.
  Elsie. How bleak and bare it is!
   Nothing but mosses
Grow on these rocks.
  Prince Henry.   Yet are they
   not forgotten;
Beneficent Nature sends the mists
   to feed them.
  Elsie. See yonder little cloud,
   that, borne aloft
So tenderly by the wind, floats fast
   away
Over the snowy peaks! It seems to
   me
The body of St Catherine, borne by
   angels!
  Prince Henry. Thou art St.
   Catherine, and invisible angels
Bear thee across these chasms and
   precipices,
Lest thou shouldst dash thy feet
   against a stone!
  Elsie. Would I were borne unto
   my grave, as she was,

Upon angelic shoulders! Even now
I seem uplifted by them, light as air!
What sound is that?
  Prince Henry. The tumbling ava-
   lanches!
  Elsie. How awful, yet how beau-
   tiful!
  Prince Henry.   These are
The voices of the mountains! Thus
   they ope
Their snowy lips, and speak unto
   each other
In the primeval language, lost to
   man.
  Elsie. What land is this that
   spreads itself beneath us?
  Prince Henry. Italy! Italy!
  Elsie.   Land of the Madonna!
How beautiful it is! It seems a
   garden
Of Paradise!
  Prince Henry. Nay, of Gethse-
   mane
To thee and me, of passion and of
   prayer!
Yet once of Paradise. Long years ago
I wandered as a youth among its
   bowers,
And never from my heart has faded
   quite
Its memory, that, like a summer
   sunset,
Encircles with a ring of purple light
All the horizon of my youth.
  Guide.   O friends!
The days are short, the way before
   us long;
We must not linger, if we think to
   reach
The inn at Belinzona before vespers!

     (*They pass on.*)

---

*At the foot of the Alps. A halt
   under the trees at noon.*

  Prince Henry. Here let us pause
   a moment in the trembling
Shadow and sunshine of the roadside trees,

And, our tired horses in a group
  assembling,
Inhale long draughts of this delicious
  breeze.
Our fleeter steeds have distanced
  our attendants ;
They lag behind us with a slower
  pace ;
We will await them under the green
  pendants
Of the great willows in this shady
  place.
Ho, Barbarossa ! how thy mottled
  haunches
Sweat with this canter over hill and
  glade !
Stand still, and let these overhanging branches
Fan thy hot sides and comfort thee
  with shade !

  Elsie. What a delightful landscape spreads before us,
Marked with a whitewashed cottage
  here and there !
And, in luxuriant garlands drooping
  o'er us,
Blossoms of grape-vines scent the
  sunny air.

  Prince Henry. Hark ! What
  sweet sounds are those, whose
  accents holy
Fill the warm noon with music sad
  and sweet !

  Elsie. It is a band of pilgrims,
  moving slowly
On their long journey, with uncovered feet.

  Pilgrims (chanting the Hymn of
St. Hildebert).

  Me receptet Sion illa,
  Sion David, urbs tranquilla,
  Cujus faber auctor lucis,
  Cujus portae lignum crucis,
  Cujus claves lingua Petri,
  Cujus eives semper laeti,
  Cujus muri lapis vivus,
  Cujus custos Rex festivus !

  Lucifer (as a Friar in the pro-
  cession). Here am I, too, in the
  pious band,
In the garb of a barefooted Car-
  melite dressed !
The soles of my feet are as hard
  and tanned
As the conscience of old Pope Hil-
  debrand,
The Holy Satan, who made the wives
Of the bishops lead such shameful
  lives.
All day long I beat my breast,
And chant with a most particular
  zest
The Latin hymns, which I under-
  stand
Quite as well, I think, as the rest.
And at night such lodging in barns
  and sheds,
Such a hurly-burly in country inns,
Such a clatter of tongues in empty
  heads,
Such a helter-skelter of prayers and
  sins !
Of all the contrivances of the time
For sowing broadcast the seeds of
  crime,
There is none so pleasing to me and
  mine
As a pilgrimage to some far-off
  shrine !

  Prince Henry. If from the outward man we judge the inner,
And cleanliness is godliness, I fear
A hopeless reprobate, a hardened
  sinner,
Must be that Carmelite now passing
  near.

  Lucifer. There is my German
  Prince again,
Thus far on his journey to Salern,
And the lovesick girl, whose heated
  brain,
Is sowing the cloud to reap the rain;
But it's a long road that has no turn !
Let them quietly hold their way,
I have also a part in the play.

But first I must act to my heart's
content
This mummery and this merri-
ment,
And drive this motley flock of
sheep
Into the fold, where drink and sleep
The jolly old friars of Benevent.
Of a truth, it often provokes me to
laugh
To see these beggars hobble along,
Lamed and maimed, and fed upon
chaff,
Chanting their wonderful piff and
paff,
And, to make up for not understand-
ing the song,
Singing it fiercely, and wild, and
strong !
Were it not for my magic garters
and staff,
And the goblets of goodly wine I
quaff,
And the mischief I make in the idle
throng,
I should not continue the business
long.

Pilgrims (*chanting*).

In hâc urbe, lux solennis,
Ver aeternum, pax perennis;
In hâc odor implens caelos,
In hâc semper festum melos !

Prince Henry. Do you observe
that monk among the train,
Who pours from his great throat the
roaring bass,
As a cathedral spout pours out the
rain,
And this way turns his rubicund,
round face ?
Elsie. It is the same who, on
the Strasburg square,
Preached to the people in the open
air.
Prince Henry. And he has
crossed o'er mountain, field,
and fell,

On that good steed, that seems to
bear him well,
The hackney of the Friars of Orders
Gray,
His own stout legs ! He, too, was in
the play,
Both as King Herod and Ben Israel.
Good morrow, Friar !
Friar Cuthbert. Good morrow,
noble sir !
Prince Henry. I speak in Ger-
man, for, unless I err,
You are a German.
Friar Cuthbert. I cannot gain-
say you.
But by what instinct, or what secret
sign,
Meeting me here, do you straight-
way divine
That northward of the Alps my
country lies ?
Prince Henry. Your accent, like
St. Peter's, would betray you,
Did not your yellow beard and your
blue eyes.
Moreover, we have seen your face
before,
And heard you preach at the
cathedral door
On Easter Sunday, in the Strasburg
square.
We were among the crowd that
gathered there,
And saw you play the Rabbi with
great skill,
As if, by leaning o'er so many
years
To walk with little children, your
own will
Had caught a childish attitude from
theirs,
A kind of stooping in its form and
gait,
And could no longer stand erect
and straight.
Whence come you now ?
Friar Cuthbert. From the
old monastery

513

Of Hirschau, in the forest; being sent
Upon a pilgrimage to Benevent,
To see the image of the Virgin Mary,
That moves its holy eyes and sometimes speaks,
And lets the piteous tears run down its cheeks,
To touch the hearts of the impenitent.

Prince Henry. O, had I faith, as in the days gone by,
That knew no doubt, and feared no mystery!

Lucifer (at a distance). Ho, Cuthbert! Friar Cuthbert!

Friar Cuthbert. Farewell, Prince!
I cannot stay to argue and convince.

Prince Henry. This is indeed the blessed Mary's land,
Virgin and Mother of our dear Redeemer!
All hearts are touched and softened at her name;
Alike the bandit, with the bloody hand,
The priest, the prince, the scholar, and the peasant,
The man of deeds, the visionary dreamer,
Pay homage to her as one ever present!
And even as children, who have much offended
A too indulgent father, in great shame,
Penitent, and yet not daring unattended
To go into his presence, at the gate
Speak with their sister, and confiding wait
Till she goes in before and intercedes;
So men, repenting of their evil deeds,

And yet not venturing rashly to draw near
With their requests an angry Father's ear,
Offer to her their prayers and their confession,
And she for them in heaven makes intercession.
And if our Faith had given us nothing more
Than this example of all womanhood,
So mild, so merciful, so strong, so good,
So patient, peaceful, loyal, loving, pure,
This were enough to prove it higher and truer
Than all the creeds the world had known before.

Pilgrims (chanting afar off).

Urbs coelestis, urbs beata,
Supra petram collocata,
Urbs in portu satis tuto
De longinquo te saluto,
Te saluto, te suspiro,
Te affecto, te requiro!

The Inn at Genoa. A terrace overlooking the sea. Night.

Prince Henry. It is the sea, it is the sea,
In all its vague immensity,
Fading and darkening in the distance!
Silent, majestical, and slow,
The white ships haunt it to and fro,
With all their ghostly sails unfurled,
As phantoms from another world
Haunt the dim confines of existence!
But ah! how few can comprehend
Their signals, or to what good end
From land to land they come and go!
Upon a sea more vast and dark
The spirits of the dead embark,
All voyaging to unknown coasts.

We wave our farewells from the
    shore,
And they depart, and come no more,
Or come as phantoms and as ghosts.

Above the darksome sea of death
Looms the great life that is to be,
A land of cloud and mystery,
A dim mirage, with shapes of men
Long dead, and passed beyond our
    ken.
Awe-struck we gaze, and hold our
    breath
Till the fair pageant vanisheth,
Leaving us in perplexity,
And doubtful whether it has been
A vision of the world unseen,
Or a bright image of our own
Against the sky in vapours thrown.
    Lucifer (singing from the sea).
        Thou didst not make it, thou
        canst not mend it,
But thou hast the power to end it !
The sea is silent, the sea is dis-
    creet,
Deep it lies at thy very feet ;
There is no confessor like unto
    Death !
Thou canst not see him, but he is
    near ;
Thou needest not whisper above thy
    breath,
And he will hear ;
He will answer the questions,
The vague surmises and sug-
    gestions,
That fill thy soul with doubt and
    fear !
    Prince Henry. The fisherman,
        who lies afloat,
With shadowy sail, in yonder boat,
Is singing softly to the Night !
But do I comprehend aright
The meaning of the words he sung
So sweetly in his native tongue ?
Ah yes ! the sea is still and deep.
All things within its bosom sleep !
A single step, and all is o'er ;

A plunge, a bubble, and no more ;
And thou, dear Elsie, wilt be free
From martyrdom and agony.
    *Elsie (coming from her chamber
        upon the terrace).* The night
        is calm and cloudless,
And still as still can be,
And the stars come forth to listen
To the music of the sea.
They gather, and gather, and
    gather,
Until they crowd the sky,
And listen, in breathless silence,
To the solemn litany.
It begins in rocky caverns,
As a voice that chants alone
To the pedals of the organ
In monotonous undertone ;
And anon from shelving beaches,
And shallow sands beyond,
In snow-white robes uprising
The ghostly choirs respond.
And sadly and unceasing
The mournful voice sings on,
And the snow-white choirs still
    answer
Christe eleison !
    Prince Henry. Angel of God !
        thy finer sense perceives
Celestial and perpetual harmonies !
Thy purer soul, that trembles and
    believes,
Hears the archangel's trumpet in
    the breeze,
And where the forest rolls, or
    ocean heaves,
Cecilia's organ sounding in the seas,
And tongues of prophets speaking
    in the leaves.
But I hear discord only and
    despair,
And whispers as of demons in the
    air !

At sea.

Il Padrone. The wind upon our
    quarter lies,
And on before the freshening gale,

That fills the snow-white lateen
  sail,
Swiftly our light felucca flies.
Around, the billows burst and
  foam ;
They lift her o'er the sunken
  rock,
They beat her sides with many a
  shock,
And then upon their flowing dome
They poise her, like a weathercock !
Between us and the western skies
The hills of Corsica arise ;
Eastward, in yonder long, blue
  line,
The summits of the Apennine,
And southward, and still far away,
Salerno, on its sunny bay.
You cannot see it, where it lies.
  Prince Henry. Ah, would that
  nevermore mine eyes
Might see its towers by night or
  day !
  Elsie. Behind us, dark and
  awfully,
There comes a cloud out of the
  sea,
That bears the form of a hunted
  deer,
With hide of brown, and hoofs of
  black,
And antlers laid upon its back,
And fleeing fast and wild with
  fear,
As if the hounds were on its
  track !
  Prince Henry. Lo ! while we
  gaze, it breaks and falls
In shapeless masses, like the walls
Of a burnt city. Broad and red
The fires of the descending sun
Glare through the windows, and
  o'erhead,
Athwart the vapours, dense and
  dun,
Long shafts of silvery light arise,
Like rafters that support the
  skies !

  Elsie. See ! from its summit the
  lurid levin
Flashes downward without warn-
  ing,
As Lucifer, son of the morning,
Fell from the battlements of
  heaven !
  Il Padrone. I must entreat you,
  friends, below !
The angry storm begins to blow,
For the weather changes with the
  moon.
All this morning, until noon,
We had baffling winds, and sudden
  flaws
Struck the sea with their cat's-
  paws.
Only a little hour ago
I was whistling to Saint Antonio
For a capful of wind to fill our
  sail,
And instead of a breeze he has sent
  a gale.
Last night I saw Saint Elmo's
  stars,
With their glimmering lanterns, all
  at play
On the tops of the masts and the
  tips of the spars,
And I knew we should have foul
  weather to-day.
Cheerly, my hearties ! yo heave ho !
Brail up the mainsail, and let her
  go
As the winds will and Saint An-
  tonio !

Do you see that Livornese felucca,
That vessel to the windward
  yonder,
Running with her gunwale under ?
I was looking when the wind o'er-
  took her.
She had all sail set, and the only
  wonder
Is, that at once the strength of the
  blast
Did not carry away her mast.

516

She is a galley of the Gran
    Duca,
That, through the fear of the
    Algerines,
Convoys those lazy brigantines,
Laden with wine and oil from
    Lucca.
Now all is ready, high and low ;
Blow, blow, good Saint Antonio !
Ha ! that is the first dash of the
    rain,
With a sprinkle of spray above the
    rails,
Just enough to moisten our sails,
And make them ready for the
    strain.
See how she leaps, as the blasts
    o'ertake her,
And speeds away with a bone in
    her mouth !
Now keep her head toward the
    south,
And there is no danger of bank or
    breaker.
With the breeze behind us, on we
    go ;
Not too much, good Saint An-
    tonio !

VI.

The School of Salerno. A travel-
* ling Scholastic affixing his*
* Theses to the gate of the College.*

  Scholastic. There, that is my
    gauntlet, my banner, my
    shield,
Hung up as a challenge to all the
    field !
One hundred and twenty-five
    propositions,
Which I will maintain with the
    sword of the tongue
Against all disputants, old and
    young.
Let us see if doctors or dia-
    lecticians

Will dare to dispute my definitions,
Or attack any one of my learned
    theses.
Here stand I ; the end shall be as
    God pleases.
I think I have proved, by profound
    researches,
The error of all those doctrines so
    vicious
Of the old Areopagite Dionysius,
That are making such terrible
    work in the churches,
By Michael the Stammerer sent
    from the East,
And done into Latin by that
    Scottish beast,
Johannes Duns Scotus, who dares
    to maintain,
In the face of the truth, and error
    infernal,
That the universe is and must be
    eternal :
At first laying down, as a fact
    fundamental,
That nothing with God can be
    accidental ;
Then asserting that God before
    the creation
Could not have existed, because it
    is plain
That, had he existed, he would
    have created ;
Which is begging the question that
    should be debated,
And moveth me less to anger than
    laughter.
All nature, he holds, is a respira-
    tion
Of the Spirit of God, who, in
    breathing, hereafter
Will inhale it into his bosom
    again,
So that nothing but God alone will
    remain.
And therein he contradicteth him-
    self ;
For he opens the whole discussion
    by stating,

That God can only exist in creating.
That question I think I have laid on the shelf!

(He goes out. Two Doctors come in disputing, and followed by pupils.)

Doctor Serafino. I, with the Doctor Seraphic, maintain,
That a word which is only conceived in the brain
Is a type of eternal Generation;
The spoken word is the Incarnation.
Doctor Cherubino. What do I care for the Doctor Seraphic,
With all his wordy chaffer and traffic?
Doctor Serafino. You make but a paltry show of resistance;
Universals have no real existence!
Doctor Cherubino. Your words are but idle and empty chatter;
Ideas are eternally joined to matter!
Doctor Serafino. May the Lord have mercy on your position,
You wretched, wrangling culler of herbs!
Doctor Cherubino. May he send your soul to eternal perdition,
For your Treatise on the Irregular Verbs.

(They rush out fighting. Two Scholars come in.)

First Scholar. Monte Cassino, then, is your College.
What think you of ours here at Salern?
Second Scholar. To tell the truth, I arrived so lately,
I hardly yet have had time to discern.

So much at least, I am bound to acknowledge:
The air seems healthy, the buildings stately,
And on the whole I like it greatly.
First Scholar. Yes, the air is sweet: the Calabrian hills
Send us down puffs of mountain air;
And in summer-time the sea-breeze fills
With its coolness cloister and court and square.
Then at every season of the year
There are crowds of guests and travellers here;
Pilgrims, and mendicant friars, and traders
From the Levant, with figs and wine,
And bands of wounded and sick Crusaders,
Coming back from Palestine.
Second Scholar. And what are the studies you pursue?
What is the course you here go through?
First Scholar. The first three years of the college course
Are given to Logic alone, as the source
Of all that is noble, and wise, and true.
Second Scholar. That seems rather strange, I must confess,
In a Medical School; yet, nevertheless,
You doubtless have reasons for that.
First Scholar. O yes!
For none but a clever dialectician
Can hope to become a great physician;
That has been settled long ago.
Logic makes an important part
Of the mystery of the healing art;
For without it how could you hope to show

That nobody knows so much as
    you know?
After this there are five years
    more
Devoted wholly to medicine,
With lectures on chirurgical lore,
And dissections of the bodies of
    swine,
As likest the human form divine.

Second Scholar. What are the
    books now most in vogue?

First Scholar. Quite an extensive
    catalogue;
Mostly, however, books of our
    own;
As Gariopontus' Passionarius,
And the writings of Matthew
    Platearius;
And a volume universally known
As the Regimen of the School of
    Salern,
For Robert of Normandy written
    in terse
And very elegant Latin verse.
Each of these writings has its
    turn.
And when at length we have
    finished these,
Then comes the struggle for de-
    grees,
With all the oldest and ablest
    critics;
The public thesis and disputation,
Question, and answer, and explana-
    tion
Of a passage out of Hippocrates,
Or Aristotle's Analytics.
There the triumphant Magister
    stands!
A book is solemnly placed in his
    hands,
On which he swears to follow the
    rule
And ancient forms of the good old
    School;
To report if any confectionarius
Mingles his drugs with matters
    various,

And to visit his patients twice a
    day,
And once in the night, if they live
    in town,
And if they are poor, to take no
    pay.
Having faithfully promised these,
His head is crowned with a laurel
    crown;
A kiss on his cheek, a ring on his
    hand,
The Magister Artium et Physices
Goes forth from the school like a
    lord of the land.
And now, as we have the whole
    morning before us,
Let us go in, if you make no ob-
    jection,
And listen awhile to a learned
    prelection
On Marcus Aurelius Cassiodorus.

(*They go in. Enter* LUCIFER *as a
    Doctor.*)

Lucifer. This is the great School
    of Salern!
A land of wrangling and of quar-
    rels,
Of brains that seethe, and hearts
    that burn,
Where every emulous scholar
    hears,
In every breath that comes to his
    ears,
The rustling of another's laurels!
The air of the place is called salu-
    brious;
The neighbourhood of Vesuvius
    lends it
An odour volcanic, that rather
    mends it,
And the buildings have an aspect
    lugubrious,
That inspires a feeling of awe and
    terror
Into the heart of the beholder,
And befits such an ancient home-
    stead of error,

Where the old falsehoods moulder
and smoulder,
And yearly by many hundred
hands
Are carried away, in the zeal of
youth,
And sown like tares in the field of
truth,
To blossom and ripen in other
lands.

What have we here, affixed to the
gate?
The challenge of some scholastic
wight,
Who wishes to hold a public
debate
On sundry questions wrong or
right!
Ah, now this is my great delight!
For I have often observed of late
That such discussions end in a
fight.
Let us see what the learned wag
maintains
With such a prodigal waste of
brains.

(*Reads.*)

'Whether angels in moving from
place to place
Pass through the intermediate
space;
Whether God himself is the author
of evil,
Or whether that is the work of the
Devil;
When, where, and wherefore Luci-
fer fell,
And whether he now is chained in
hell.'

I think I can answer that question
well!
So long as the boastful human
mind
Consents in such mills as this to
grind,
I sit very firmly upon my throne!

Of a truth it almost makes me
laugh,
To see men leaving the golden
grain
To gather in piles the pitiful chaff
That old Peter Lombard thrashed
with his brain,
To have it caught up and tossed
again
On the horns of the Dumb Ox of
Cologne!

But my guests approach! there is
in the air
A fragrance, like that of the Beau-
tiful Garden
Of Paradise, in the days that were!
An odour of innocence, and of
prayer,
And of love, and faith that never
fails,
Such as the fresh young heart
exhales
Before it begins to wither and
harden!
I cannot breathe such an atmo-
sphere!
My soul is filled with a nameless
fear,
That, after all my trouble and
pain,
After all my restless endeavour,
The youngest, fairest soul of the
twain,
The most ethereal, most divine,
Will escape from my hands for
ever and ever.
But the other is already mine!
Let him live to corrupt his race,
Breathing among them, with every
breath,
Weakness, selfishness, and the
base
And pusillanimous fear of death.
I know his nature, and I know
That of all who in my ministry
Wander the great earth to and fro,
And on my errands come and go,

520

The safest and subtlest are such as he.

(*Enter* PRINCE HENRY *and* ELSIE, *with attendants.*)

Prince Henry. Can you direct us to Friar Angelo?

Lucifer. He stands before you.

Prince Henry. Then you know our purpose.

I am Prince Henry of Hoheneck, and this

The maiden that I spake of in my letters.

Lucifer. It is a very grave and solemn business !

We must not be precipitate. Does she

Without compulsion, of her own free will,

Consent to this?

Prince Henry. Against all opposition,

Against all prayers, entreaties, protestations.

She will not be persuaded.

Lucifer. That is strange !

Have you thought well of it?

Elsie. I come not here

To argue, but to die. Your business is not

To question, but to kill me. I am ready.

I am impatient to be gone from here

Ere any thoughts of earth disturb again

The spirit of tranquillity within me.

Prince Henry. Would I had not come here ! Would I were dead,

And thou wert in thy cottage in the forest,

And hadst not known me ! Why have I done this?

Let me go back and die.

Elsie. It cannot be ;

Not if these cold, flat stones on which we tread

Were coulters heated white, and yonder gateway

Flamed like a furnace with a sevenfold heat.

I must fulfil my purpose.

Prince Henry. I forbid it ;

Not one step farther. For I only meant

To put thus far thy courage to the proof.

It is enough. I, too, have strength to die,

For thou hast taught me !

Elsie. O my Prince ! remember

Your promises. Let me fulfil my errand.

You do not look on life and death as I do.

There are two angels, that attend unseen

Each one of us, and in great books record

Our good and evil deeds. He who writes down

The good ones, after every action closes

His volume, and ascends with it to God.

The other keeps his dreadful daybook open

Till sunset, that we may repent ; which doing,

The record of the action fades away,

And leaves a line of white across the page.

Now if my act be good, as I believe,

It cannot be recalled. It is already

Sealed up in heaven, as a good deed accomplished.

The rest is yours. Why wait you?

I am ready.

(*To her attendants.*)

Weep not, my friends ! rather rejoice with me.

I shall not feel the pain, but shall
be gone,
And you will have another friend
in heaven.
Then start not at the creaking of
the door
Through which I pass. I see what
lies beyond it.

(*To* PRINCE HENRY.)

And you, O Prince! bear back my
benison
Unto my father's house, and all
within it.
This morning in the church I
prayed for them,
After confession, after absolu-
tion,
When my whole soul was white, I
prayed for them.
God will take care of them, they
need me not.
And in your life let my remem-
brance linger,
As something not to trouble and
disturb it,
But to complete it, adding life to
life.
And if at times beside the evening
fire
You see my face among the other
faces,
Let it not be regarded as a ghost
That haunts your house, but as a
guest that loves you,
Nay, even as one of your own
family,
Without whose presence there were
something wanting.
I have no more to say.   Let us go
in.
  Prince Henry. Friar Angelo!
    I charge you on your life,
Believe not what she says, for she
is mad,
And comes here not to die, but to
be healed.
  Elsie. Alas! Prince Henry!

Lucifer.   Come with me;
  this way.

(ELSIE *goes in with* LUCIFER, *who
thrusts* PRINCE HENRY *back
and closes the door.*)

  Prince Henry. Gone! and the
    light of all my life gone with
    her!
A sudden darkness falls upon the
  world!
O, what a vile and abject thing
  am I,
That purchase length of days at
  such a cost!
Not by her death alone, but by the
  death
Of all that's good and true and
  noble in me!
All manhood, excellence, and self-
  respect,
All love, and faith, and hope, and
  heart are dead!
All my divine nobility of nature
By this one act is forfeited for
  ever.
I am a Prince in nothing but in
  name!

(*To the attendants.*)

Why did you let this horrible deed
  be done?
Why did you not lay hold on her,
  and keep her
From self-destruction?   Angelo!
  murderer!

(*Struggles at the door, but cannot
  open it.*)

  Elsie (*within*). Farewell, dear
    Prince! farewell!
  Prince Henry. Unbar the door!
  Lucifer. It is too late!
  Prince Henry.   It shall not
    be too late!

(*They burst the door open and
  rush in.*)

522

The Cottage in the Odenwald.
URSULA *spinning. Summer
afternoon. A table spread.*

Ursula. I have marked it well,—
    it must be true,—
Death never takes one alone, but
    two!
Whenever he enters in at a door,
Under roof of gold or roof of
    thatch,
He always leaves it upon the latch,
And comes again ere the year is
    o'er.
Never one of a household only!
Perhaps it is a mercy of God,
Lest the dead there under the sod,
In the land of strangers, should be
    lonely!
Ah me! I think I am lonelier here!
It is hard to go,—but harder to
    stay!
Were it not for the children, I
    should pray
That Death would take me within
    the year!
And Gottlieb!—he is at work all
    day,
In the sunny field, or the forest
    murk,
But I know that his thoughts are
    far away,
I know that his heart is not in his
    work!
And when he comes home to me at
    night
He is not cheery, but sits and
    sighs,
And I see the great tears in his
    eyes,
And try to be cheerful for his sake.
Only the children's hearts are light.
Mine is weary, and ready to break.
God help us! I hope we have done
    right;
We thought we were acting for the
    best!

(*Looking through the open door.*)

Who is it coming under the trees?
A man, in the Prince's livery
    dressed!
He looks about him with doubtful
    face,
As if uncertain of the place.
He stops at the beehives;—now he
    sees
The garden gate;—he is going
    past!
Can he be afraid of the bees?
No; he is coming in at last!
He fills my heart with strange
    alarm!

(*Enter a Forester.*)

Forester. Is this the tenant
    Gottlieb's farm?
Ursula. This is his farm, and I
    his wife.
Pray sit. What may your business
    be?
Forester. News from the Prince!
Ursula.   Of death or life?
Forester. You put your questions
    eagerly!
Ursula. Answer me, then! How
    is the Prince?
Forester. I left him only two
    hours since
Homeward returning down the
    river,
As strong and well as if God, the
    Giver,
Had given him back his youth
    again.
Ursula (*despairing*). Then
    Elsie, my poor child, is dead!
Forester. That, my good woman,
    I have not said.
Don't cross the bridge till you
    come to it,
Is a proverb old, and of excellent
    wit.
Ursula. Keep me no longer in
    this pain!
Forester. It is true your daughter
    is no more;—

That is, the peasant she was before.

Ursula. Alas! I am simple and
lowly bred,
I am poor, distracted, and forlorn,
And it is not well that you of the
court
Should mock me thus, and make a
sport
Of a joyless mother whose child is
dead,
For you, too, were of mother born!

Forester. Your daughter lives,
and the Prince is well!
You will learn ere long how it all
befell.
Her heart for a moment never
failed;
But when they reached Salerno's
gate,
The Prince's nobler self prevailed,
And saved her for a nobler fate.
And he was healed, in his despair,
By the touch of St. Matthew's sacred
bones;
Though I think the long ride in the
open air,
That pilgrimage over stocks and
stones,
In the miracle must come in for a
share!

Ursula. Virgin! who lovest the
poor and lowly,
If the loud cry of a mother's heart
Can ever ascend to where thou art,
Into thy blessed hands and holy
Receive my prayer of praise and
thanksgiving!
Let the hands that bore our Saviour
bear it
Into the awful presence of God;
For thy feet with holiness are shod,
And if thou bearest it he will
hear it.
Our child who was dead again is
living!

Forester. I did not tell you she
was dead;

If thou thought so 'twas no fault of
mine;
At this very moment, while I speak,
They are sailing homeward down
the Rhine,
In a splendid barge, with golden
prow,
And decked with banners white
and red
As the colours on your daughter's
cheek.
They call her the Lady Alicia now;
For the Prince in Salerno made a
vow
That Elsie only would he wed.

Ursula. Jesu Maria! what a
change,
All seems to me so weird and strange!

Forester. I saw her standing on
the deck,
Beneath an awning cool and shady;
Her cap of velvet could not hold
The tresses of her hair of gold,
That flowed and floated like the
stream,
And fell in masses down her neck.
As fair and lovely did she seem
As in a story or a dream
Some beautiful and foreign lady.
And the Prince looked so grand
and proud,
And waved his hand thus to the
crowd
That gazed and shouted from the
shore,
All down the river, long and loud.

Ursula. We shall behold our
child once more;
She is not dead! She is not dead!
God, listening, must have over-
heard
The prayers, that, without sound or
word,
Our hearts in secrecy have said!
O, bring me to her; for mine eyes
Are hungry to behold her face;
My very soul within me cries;
My very hands seem to caress her,

To see her, gaze at her, and bless
     her ;
Dear Elsie, child of God and grace!

(*Goes out toward the garden.*)

Forester. There goes the good
     woman out of her head ;
And Gottlieb's supper is waiting
     here ;
A very capacious flagon of beer,
And a very portentous loaf of bread.
One would say his grief did not
     much oppress him.
Here's to the health of the Prince,
     God bless him !

(*He drinks.*)

Ha ! it buzzes and stings like a
     hornet !
And what a scene there, through
     the door !
The forest behind and the garden
     before,
And midway an old man of three-
     score,
With a wife and children that
     caress him.
Let me try still further to cheer and
     adorn it
With a merry, echoing blast of my
     cornet !

(*Goes out blowing his horn.*)

*The Castle of Vautsberg on the
Rhine.* PRINCE HENRY *and*
ELSIE *standing on the terrace at
evening. The sound of bells
heard from a distance.*

Prince Henry. We are alone.
     The wedding guests
Ride down the hill, with plumes and
     cloaks,
And the descending dark invests
The Niederwald, and all the nests
Among its hoar and haunted oaks.
Elsie. What bells are those, that
     ring so slow,
So mellow, musical, and low ?

Prince Henry. They are the bells
     of Geisenheim,
That with their melancholy chime
Ring out the curfew of the sun.
Elsie. Listen, beloved.
Prince Henry. They are done.
Dear Elsie ! many years ago
Those same soft bells at eventide
Rang in the ears of Charlemagne,
As, seated by Fastrada's side
At Ingelheim, in all his pride
He heard their sound with secret
     pain.
Elsie. Their voices only speak to
     me
Of peace and deep tranquillity,
And endless confidence in thee.
Prince Henry. Thou knowest
     the story of her ring,
How, when the court went back to
     Aix,
Fastrada died ; and how the king
Sat watching by her night and day
Till into one of the blue lakes,
Which water that delicious land,
They cast the ring drawn from her
     hand ;
And the great monarch sat serene
And sad beside the fated shore,
Nor left the land for evermore.
Elsie. That was true love.
Prince Henry. For him the queen
Ne'er did what thou hast done for
     me.
Elsie. Wilt thou as fond and faith-
     ful be ?
Wilt thou so love me after death ?
Prince Henry. In life's delight,
     in death's dismay,
In storm and sunshine, night and
     day,
In health, in sickness, in decay,
Here and hereafter, I am thine !
Thou hast Fastrada's ring. Beneath
The calm blue waters of thine eyes
Deep in thy steadfast soul it lies,
And, undisturbed by this world's
     breath,

With magic light its jewels shine !
This golden ring, which thou hast
    worn
Upon thy finger since the morn,
Is but a symbol and a semblance,
An outward fashion, a remem-
    brance,
Of what thou wearest within unseen,
O my Fastrada, O my queen !
Behold ! the hill-tops all aglow
With purple and with amethyst ;
While the whole valley deep below
Is filled, and seems to overflow,
With a fast-rising tide of mist.
The evening air grows damp and
    chill ;
Let us go in.
    Elsie.   Ah, not so soon.
See yonder fire ! it is the moon
Slow rising o'er the eastern hill.
It glimmers on the forest tips,
And through the dewy foliage drips
In little rivulets of light,
And makes the heart in love with
    night.
    Prince Henry. Oft on this ter-
race, when the day
Was closing, have I stood and
    gazed,
And seen the landscape fade away,
And the white vapours rise and
    drown
Hamlet and vineyard, tower and
    town,
While far above the hill-tops blazed.
But then another hand than thine
Was gently held and clasped in
    mine ;
Another head upon my breast
Was laid, as thine is now, at rest.
Why dost thou lift those tender eyes
With so much sorrow and surprise?
A minstrel's, not a maiden's hand,
Was that which in my own was
    pressed.
A manly form usurped thy place,
A beautiful, but bearded face,
That now is in the Holy Land,

Yet in my memory from afar
Is shining on us like a star.
But linger not. For while I speak,
A sheeted spectre white and tall,
The cold mist, climbs the castle
    wall,
And lays his hand upon thy cheek !

    (*They go in.*)

EPILOGUE.

THE TWO RECORDING ANGELS
ASCENDING.

The Angel of Good Deeds (*with
    closed book*). God sent his
    messenger the rain,
And said unto the mountain brook,
'Rise up, and from thy caverns look
And leap, with naked, snow-white
    feet,
From the cool hills into the heat
Of the broad, arid plain.'

God sent his messenger of faith,
And whispered in the maiden's
    heart,
'Rise up, and look from where thou
    art,
And scatter with unselfish hands
Thy freshness on the barren sands
And solitudes of Death.'
O beauty of holiness,
Of self-forgetfulness, of lowliness !
O power of meekness,
Whose very gentleness and weak-
    ness
Are like the yielding, but irresistible
    air !
Upon the pages
Of the sealed volume that I bear
The deed divine
Is written in characters of gold,
That never shall grow old,
But through all ages
Burn and shine,

With soft effulgence !
O God ! it is thy indulgence
That fills the world with the bliss
Of a good deed like this !
 The Angel of Evil Deeds (with
  open book). Not yet, not yet
Is the red sun wholly set,
But evermore recedes,
While open still I bear
The Book of Evil Deeds,
To let the breathings of the upper
 air
Visit its pages and erase
The records from its face !
Fainter and fainter as I gaze
In the broad blaze
The glimmering landscape shines,
And below me the black river
Is hidden by wreaths of vapour !
Fainter and fainter the black lines
Begin to quiver
Along the whitening surface of the
 paper ;
Shade after shade
The terrible words grow faint and
 fade,
And in their place
Runs a white space !

Down goes the sun !
But the soul of one,

Who by repentance
Has escaped the dreadful sentence,
Shines bright below me as I look.
It is the end !
With closed book
To God do I ascend.

Lo ! over the mountain steeps
A dark, gigantic shadow sweeps
Beneath my feet ;
A blackness inwardly brightening
With sullen heat,
As a storm-cloud lurid with light-
 ning.
And a cry of lamentation,
Repeated and again repeated,
Deep and loud
As the reverberation
Of cloud answering unto cloud,
Swells and rolls away in the dis-
 tance,
As if the sheeted
Lightning retreated,
Baffled and thwarted by the wind's
 resistance.
It is Lucifer,
The son of mystery ;
And since God suffers him to be,
He, too, is God's minister,
And labours for some good
By us not understood !

The Golden Legend.

Martin Luther.

A Chamber in the Wartburg.
Morning. MARTIN LUTHER,
writing.

Martin Luther. Our God, a
    Tower of Strength is he,
A goodly wall and weapon ;
From all our need he helps us free,
    That now to us doth happen.
    The old evil foe
    Doth in earnest grow,
    In grim armour dight,
    Much guile and great might ;
On earth there is none like him.
O yes ; a tower of strength indeed,
A present help in all our need,
A sword and buckler is our God.
Innocent men have walked unshod
O'er burning ploughshares, and
    have trod
Unharmed on serpents in their path,
And laughed to scorn the Devil's
    wrath !

Safe in this Wartburg tower I stand
Where God hath led me by the hand,
And look down, with a heart at ease,
Over the pleasant neighbourhoods,
Over the vast Thuringian Woods,
With flash of river, and gloom of
    trees,
With castles crowning the dizzy
    heights,
And farms and pastoral delights,
And the morning pouring every-
    where
Its golden glory on the air.

Safe, yes, safe am I here at last,
Safe from the overwhelming blast
Of the mouths of Hell, that followed
    me fast,
And the howling demons of despair,
That hunted me like a beast to his
    lair.
Of our own might we nothing can ;
    We soon are unprotected ;
There fighteth for us the right
    Man,
    Whom God himself elected.
    Who is he ? ye exclaim ;
    Christus is his name,
    Lord of Sabaoth,
    Very God in troth ;
The field he holds for ever.

Nothing can vex the Devil more
Than the name of Him whom we
    adore.
Therefore doth it delight me best
To stand in the choir among the rest,
With the great organ trumpeting
Through its metallic tubes, and
    sing :
Et Verbum caro factum est !
These words the Devil cannot
    endure,
For he knoweth their meaning well !
Him they trouble and repel,
Us they comfort and allure ;
And happy it were, if our delight
Were as great as his affright !
Yea, music is the Prophets' art ;
Among the gifts that God hath sent,

528

One of the most magnificent!
It calms the agitated heart;
Temptations, evil thoughts, and all
The passions that disturb the soul,
Are quelled by its divine control,
As the Evil Spirit fled from Saul,
And his distemper was allayed,
When David took his harp and
    played.

This world may full of Devils be,
    All ready to devour us;
Yet not so sore afraid are we,
    They shall not overpower us.
        This World's Prince, howe'er
        Fierce he may appear,
        He can harm us not,
        He is doomed, God wot!
    One little word can slay him!

Incredible it seems to some
And to myself a mystery,
That such weak flesh and blood
        as we,
Armed with no other shield or
        sword,
Or other weapon than the Word,
Should combat and should over-
        come
A spirit powerful as he!
He summons forth the Pope of
        Rome
With all his diabolic crew,
His shorn and shaven retinue
Of priests and children of the dark;
Kill! kill! they cry, the Heresiarch,
Who rouseth up all Christendom
Against us; and at one fell blow
Seeks the whole Church to over-
        throw!
Not yet; my hour is not yet come.

Yesterday in an idle mood,
Hunting with others in the wood,
I did not pass the hours in vain,
For in the very heart of all
The joyous tumult raised around,
Shouting of men, and baying of
        hound,

And the bugle's blithe and cheery
        call,
And echoes answering back again,
From crags of the distant mountain
        chain,—
In the very heart of this, I found
A mystery of grief and pain.
It was an image of the power
Of Satan, hunting the world about,
With his nets and traps and well-
        trained dogs,
His bishops and priests and theo-
        logues,
And all the rest of the rabble rout,
Seeking whom he may devour!
Enough have I had of hunting
        hares,
Enough of these hours of idle
        mirth,
Enough of nets and traps and
        gins!
The only hunting of any worth
Is where I can pierce with javelins
The cunning foxes and wolves and
        bears,
The whole iniquitous troop of
        beasts,
The Roman Pope and the Roman
        priests
That sorely infest and afflict the
        earth!
Ye nuns, ye singing birds of the
        air!
The fowler hath caught you in his
        snare,
And keeps you safe in his gilded
        cage,
Singing the song that never tires,
To lure down others from their
        nests;
How ye flutter and beat your
        breasts,
Warm and soft with young desires,
Against the cruel pitiless wires,
Reclaiming your lost heritage!
Behold! a hand unbars the door,
Ye shall be captives held no
        more.

The Word they shall perforce let stand,
And little thanks they merit!
For He is with us in the land,
  With gifts of his own Spirit!
    Though they take our life,
    Goods, honours, child and wife,
    Let these pass away,
    Little gain have they;
    The Kingdom still remaineth!

Yea, it remaineth for evermore,
However Satan may rage and roar,
Though often he whispers in my ears:
What if thy doctrines false should be?
And wrings from me a bitter sweat.
Then I put him to flight with jeers,
Saying: Saint Satan! pray for me;
If thou thinkest I am not saved yet!

And my mortal foes that lie in wait
In every avenue and gate!
As to that odious monk, John Tetzel,
Hawking about his hollow wares
Like a huckster at village fairs,
And those mischievous fellows, Wetzel,
Campanus, Carlstadt, Martin Cellarius,
And all the busy, multifarious
Heretics, and disciples of Arius,
Half-learned, dunce-bold, dry and hard,
They are not worthy of my regard,
Poor and humble as I am.
But ah! Erasmus of Rotterdam,
He is the vilest miscreant
That ever walked this world below!

A Momus, making his mock and mow
At Papist and at Protestant,
Sneering at St. John and St. Paul,
At God and Man, at one and all;
And yet as hollow and false and drear,
As a cracked pitcher to the ear,
And ever growing worse and worse!
Whenever I pray, I pray for a curse
On Erasmus, the Insincere!

Philip Melancthon! thou alone
Faithful among the faithless known,
Thee I hail, and only thee!
Behold the record of us three!
  Res et verba Philippus,
  Res sine verbis Lutherus;
  Erasmus verba sine re!
My Philip, prayest thou for me?
Lifted above all earthly care,
From these high regions of the air,
Among the birds that day and night
Upon the branches of tall trees
Sing their lauds and litanies,
Praising God with all their might,
My Philip, unto thee I write.

My Philip! thou who knowest best
All that is passing in this breast;
The spiritual agonies,
The inward deaths, the inward hell,
And the divine new births as well,
That surely follow after these,
As after winter follows spring;
My Philip, in the night-time sing
This song of the Lord I send to thee,
And I will sing it for thy sake,
Until our answering voices make
A glorious antiphony,
And choral chant of victory!

Flower=de=Luce.

FLOWER-DE-LUCE.

BEAUTIFUL lily, dwelling by still
rivers,
  Or solitary mere,
Or where the sluggish meadow-
brook delivers
  Its waters to the weir !

Thou laughest at the mill, the whir
and worry
  Of spindle and of loom,
And the great wheel that toils amid
the hurry
  And rushing of the flume.

Born in the purple, born to joy
and pleasance,
  Thou dost not toil nor spin,
But makest glad and radiant with
thy presence
  The meadow and the lin.

The wind blows, and uplifts thy
drooping banner,
  And round thee throng and run
The rushes, the green yeomen of
thy manor,
  The outlaws of the sun.

The burnished dragon-fly is thine
attendant,
  And tilts against the field,
And down the listed sunbeam rides
resplendent
  With steel-blue mail and shield.

Thou art the Iris, fair among the
fairest,
  Who, armed with golden rod
And winged with the celestial
azure, bearest
  The message of some God.

Thou art the Muse, who far from
crowded cities
  Hauntest the sylvan streams,
Playing on pipes of reed the artless
ditties
  That come to us as dreams.

O flower-de-luce, bloom on, and
let the river
  Linger to kiss thy feet !
O flower of song, bloom on, and
make for ever
  The world more fair and sweet.

PALINGENESIS.

I LAY upon the headland-height,
and listened
To the incessant sobbing of the sea
  In caverns under me,
And watched the waves, that
tossed and fled and glistened,
Until the rolling meadows of ame-
thyst
  Melted away in mist.

Then suddenly, as one from sleep,
I started;
For round about me all the sunny
capes
  Seemed peopled with the shapes
Of those whom I had known in
days departed,
Apparelled in the loveliness which
gleams
  On faces seen in dreams.

531

A moment only, and the light and
glory
Faded away, and the disconsolate
shore
Stood lonely as before;
And the wild-roses of the promon-
tory
Around me shuddered in the wind,
and shed
Their petals of pale red.

There was an old belief that in the
embers
Of all things their primordial form
exists,
And cunning alchemists
Could re-create the rose with all its
members
From its own ashes, but without
the bloom,
Without the lost perfume.

Ah me! what wonder-working,
occult science
Can from the ashes in our hearts
once more
The rose of youth restore?
What craft of alchemy can bid
defiance
To time and change, and for a
single hour
Renew this phantom-flower?

'O, give me back,' I cried, 'the
vanished splendours,
The breath of morn, and the exul-
tant strife,
When the swift stream of life
Bounds o'er its rocky channel, and
surrenders
The pond, with all its lilies, for the
leap
Into the unknown deep!'

And the sea answered, with a
lamentation,
Like some old prophet wailing, and
it said,
'Alas! thy youth is dead!

It breathes no more, its heart has
no pulsation;
In the dark places with the dead
of old
It lies for ever cold!'

Then said I, 'From its consecrated
cerements
I will not drag this sacred dust
again,
Only to give me pain;
But, still remembering all the lost
endearments,
Go on my way, like one who looks
before,
And turns to weep no more.'

Into what land of harvests, what
plantations
Bright with autumnal foliage and
the glow
Of sunsets burning low;
Beneath what midnight skies, whose
constellations
Light up the spacious avenues be-
tween
This world and the unseen!

Amid what friendly greetings and
caresses,
What households, though not alien,
yet not mine,
What bowers of rest divine;
To what temptations in lone wilder-
nesses,
What famine of the heart, what
pain and loss,
The bearing of what cross!

I do not know; nor will I vainly
question
Those pages of the mystic book
which hold
The story still untold,
But without rash conjecture or
suggestion
Turn its last leaves in reverence
and good heed,
Until 'The End' I read.

THE BRIDGE OF CLOUD.

Burn, O evening hearth, and waken
  Pleasant visions as of old !
Though the house by winds be shaken,
  Safe I keep this room of gold !

Ah, no longer wizard Fancy
  Builds her castles in the air,
Luring me by necromancy
  Up the never-ending stair !

But, instead, she builds me bridges
  Over many a dark ravine,
Where beneath the gusty ridges
  Cataracts dash and roar unseen.

And I cross them, little heeding
  Blast of wind or torrent's roar,
As I follow the receding
  Footsteps that have gone before.

Naught avails the imploring gesture,
  Naught avails the cry of pain !
When I touch the flying vesture,
  'Tis the gray robe of the rain.

Baffled I return, and, leaning
  O'er the parapets of cloud,
Watch the mist that intervening
  Wraps the valley in its shroud.

And the sounds of life ascending
  Faintly, vaguely, meet the ear,
Murmur of bells and voices blending
  With the rush of waters near.

Well I know what there lies hidden,
  Every tower and town and farm,
And again the land forbidden
  Reassumes its vanished charm.

Well I know the secret places,
  And the nests in hedge and tree ;
At what doors are friendly faces,
  In what hearts are thoughts of me.

Through the mist and darkness sinking,
  Blown by wind and beaten by shower,
Down I fling the thought I'm thinking,
  Down I toss this Alpine flower.

——◆◆——

HAWTHORNE.

MAY 23, 1864.

How beautiful it was, that one bright day
  In the long week of rain !
Though all its splendour could not chase away
  The omnipresent pain.

The lovely town was white with apple-blooms,
  And the great elms o'erhead
Dark shadows wove on their aerial looms
  Shot through with golden thread.

Across the meadows, by the gray old manse,
  The historic river flowed :
I was as one who wanders in a trance,
  Unconscious of his road.

The faces of familiar friends seemed strange ;
  Their voices I could hear,
And yet the words they uttered seemed to change
  Their meaning to my ear.

For the one face I looked for was not there,
  The one low voice was mute ;
Only an unseen presence filled the air,
  And baffled my pursuit.

Now I look back, and meadow,
    manse, and stream
  Dimly my thought defines;
I only see—a dream within a dream—
  The hill-top hearsed with pines.

I only hear above his place of rest
  Their tender undertone,
The infinite longings of a troubled
    breast,
  The voice so like his own.

There in seclusion and remote from
    men
  The wizard hand lies cold,
Which at its topmost speed let fall
    the pen,
  And left the tale half told.

Ah! who shall lift that wand of
    magic power,
  And the lost clew regain?
The unfinished window in Aladdin's
    tower
  Unfinished must remain!

—◆—

CHRISTMAS BELLS.

I HEARD the bells on Christmas Day
Their old familiar carols play,
    And wild and sweet
    The words repeat
Of peace on earth, good-will to men!

And thought how, as the day had
    come,
The belfries of all Christendom
    Had rolled along
    The unbroken song
Of peace on earth, good-will to men!

Till, ringing, singing on its way,
The world revolved from night to
    day,
    A voice, a chime,
    A chant sublime
Of peace on earth, good-will to men!

Then from each black accursed
    mouth
The cannon thundered in the South,
    And with the sound
    The carols drowned
Of peace on earth, good-will to men!

It was as if an earthquake rent
The hearth-stones of a continent,
    And made forlorn
    The households born
Of peace on earth, good-will to men!

And in despair I bowed my head;
'There is no peace on earth,' I said;
    'For hate is strong,
    And mocks the song
Of peace on earth, good-will to men!'

Then pealed the bells more loud
    and deep:
  'God is not dead; nor doth he
    sleep!
    The Wrong shall fail,
    The Right prevail,
With peace on earth, good-will
    to men!'

—◆—

THE WIND OVER THE CHIMNEY.

SEE, the fire is sinking low,
Dusky red the embers glow,
  While above them still I cower,
While a moment more I linger,
Though the clock, with lifted finger,
  Points beyond the midnight hour.

Sings the blackened log a tune
Learned in some forgotten June
  From a school-boy at his play,
When they both were young to-
    gether,
Heart of youth and summer weather
  Making all their holiday.

And the night-wind rising, hark!
How above there in the dark,
  In the midnight and the snow,
Ever wilder, fiercer, grander,
Like the trumpets of Iskander,
  All the noisy chimneys blow!

Every quivering tongue of flame
Seems to murmur some great
      name,
  Seems to say to me, 'Aspire!'
But the night-wind answers, 'Hol-
      low
Are the visions that you follow,
  Into darkness sinks your fire!'

Then the flicker of the blaze
Gleams on volumes of old days,
  Written by masters of the art,
Loud through whose majestic pages
Rolls the melody of ages,
    Throb the harp-strings of the
      heart.

And again the tongues of flame
Start exulting and exclaim:
  'These are prophets, bards, and
      seers;
In the horoscope of nations,
Like ascendant constellations,
    They control the coming years.'

But the night-wind cries: 'Des-
      pair!
Those who walk with feet of air
  Leave no long-enduring marks;
At God's forges incandescent
Mighty hammers beat incessant,
    These are but the flying sparks.

'Dust are all the hands that
      wrought;
Books are sepulchres of thought;
  The dead laurels of the dead
Rustle for a moment only,
Like the withered leaves in lonely
  Churchyards at some passing
      tread.'

Suddenly the flame sinks down;
Sink the rumours of renown;
  And alone the night-wind drear
Clamours louder, wilder, vaguer,—
''Tis the brand of Meleager
  Dying on the hearth-stone here!'

And I answer, — 'Though it be,
Why should that discomfort me?
  No endeavour is in vain;
Its reward is in the doing,
And the rapture of pursuing
  Is the prize the vanquished gain.

THE BELLS OF LYNN.

HEARD AT NAHANT.

O CURFEW of the setting sun! O
    Bells of Lynn!
O requiem of the dying day! O Bells
    of Lynn!

From the dark belfries of yon cloud-
    cathedral wafted,
Your sounds aerial seem to float,
    O Bells of Lynn!

Borne on the evening wind across
    the crimson twilight,
O'er land and sea they rise and fall,
    O Bells of Lynn!

The fisherman in his boat, far out
    beyond the headland,
Listens, and leisurely rows ashore,
    O Bells of Lynn!

Over the shining sands the wan-
    dering cattle homeward
Follow each other at your call, O
    Bells of Lynn!

The distant lighthouse hears, and
    with his flaming signal
Answers you, passing the watch-
    word on, O Bells of Lynn!

And down the darkening coast run the tumultuous surges,
And clap their hands, and shout to you, O Bells of Lynn!

Till from the shuddering sea, with your wild incantations,
Ye summon up the spectral moon, O Bells of Lynn!

And startled at the sight, like the weird woman of Endor,
Ye cry aloud, and then are still, O Bells of Lynn!

KILLED AT THE FORD.

HE is dead, the beautiful youth,
The heart of honour, the tongue of truth,
He, the life and light of us all,
Whose voice was blithe as a bugle-call,
Whom all eyes followed with one consent,
The cheer of whose laugh, and whose pleasant word,
Hushed all murmurs of discontent.

Only last night, as we rode along,
Down the dark of the mountain gap,
To visit the picket-guard at the ford,
Little dreaming of any mishap,
He was humming the words of some old song:
' Two red roses he had on his cap,
And another he bore at the point of his sword.'

Sudden and swift a whistling ball
Came out of a wood, and the voice was still;
Something I heard in the darkness fall,
And for a moment my blood grew chill;

I spake in a whisper, as he who speaks
In a room where some one is lying dead;
But he made no answer to what I said.

We lifted him up to his saddle again,
And through the mire and the mist and the rain
Carried him back to the silent camp,
And laid him as if asleep on his bed;
And I saw by the light of the surgeon's lamp
Two white roses upon his cheeks,
And one, just over his heart, blood-red!

And I saw in a vision how far and fleet
That fatal bullet went speeding forth,
Till it reached a town in the distant North,
Till it reached a house in a sunny street,
Till it reached a heart that ceased to beat
Without a murmur, without a cry;
And a bell was tolled, in that far-off town,
For one who had passed from cross to crown,
And the neighbours wondered that she should die.

GIOTTO'S TOWER.

HOW many lives, made beautiful and sweet
    By self-devotion and by self-restraint,
    Whose pleasure is to run without complaint
    On unknown errands of the Paraclete,
Wanting the reverence of unshodden feet,

Fail of the nimbus which the
    artists paint
Around the shining forehead of
    the saint,
And are in their completeness
    incomplete!
In the old Tuscan town stands
    Giotto's tower,
The lily of Florence blossoming
    in stone,—
A vision, a delight, and a desire,—
The builder's perfect and centennial
    flower,
    That in the night of ages bloomed
      alone,
    But wanting still the glory of the
      spire.

TO-MORROW.

'TIS late at night, and in the realm
    of sleep
My little lambs are folded like
    the flocks;
From room to room I hear the
    wakeful clocks
Challenge the passing hour, like
    guards that keep
Their solitary watch on tower and
    steep;
Far off I hear the crowing of the
    cocks,
And through the opening door
    that time unlocks
Feel the fresh breathing of To-
    morrow creep.
To-morrow! the mysterious, un-
    known guest,
Who cries to me: 'Remember
    Barmecide,
And tremble to be happy with
    the rest.'
And I make answer: 'I am
    satisfied;
I dare not ask; I know not what
    is best;
God hath already said what shall
    betide.'

DIVINA COMMEDIA.

I.

OFT have I seen at some cathedral
    door
A labourer, pausing in the dust
    and heat,
Lay down his burden, and with
    reverent feet
Enter, and cross himself, and on
    the floor
Kneel to repeat his paternoster o'er;
Far off the noises of the world
    retreat;
The loud vociferations of the
    street
Become an undistinguishable
    roar.
So, as I enter here from day to day,
And leave my burden at this
    minster gate,
Kneeling in prayer, and not
    ashamed to pray,
The tumult of the time disconsolate
To inarticulate murmurs dies
    away,
While the eternal ages watch and
    wait.

II.

How strange the sculptures that
    adorn these towers!
This crowd of statues, in whose
    folded sleeves
Birds build their nests; while
    canopied with leaves
Parvis and portal bloom like
    trellised bowers,
And the vast minster seems a cross
    of flowers!
But fiends and dragons on the
    gargoyled eaves
Watch the dead Christ between
    the living thieves,
And, underneath, the traitor
    Judas lowers!
Ah! from what agonies of heart and
    brain,

What exultations trampling on
despair,
What tenderness, what tears,
what hate of wrong,
What passionate outcry of a soul
in pain,
Uprose this poem of the earth
and air,
This mediaeval miracle of song!

III.

I enter, and I see thee in the gloom
Of the long aisles, O poet satur-
nine!
And strive to make my steps keep
pace with thine.
The air is filled with some un-
known perfume;
The congregation of the dead make
room
For thee to pass; the votive
tapers shine;
Like rooks that haunt Ravenna's
groves of pine
The hovering echoes fly from
tomb to tomb.
From the confessionals I hear arise
Rehearsals of forgotten tragedies,
And lamentations from the crypts
below;
And then a voice celestial, that
begins
With the pathetic words, 'Al-
though your sins
As scarlet be,' and ends with 'as
the snow.'

IV.

With snow-white veil and garments as of flame,
She stands before thee, who so
long ago
Filled thy young heart with
passion and the woe
From which thy song and all its
splendours came;
And while with stern rebuke she
speaks thy name,

The ice about thy heart melts as
the snow
On mountain heights, and in swift
overflow
Comes gushing from thy lips in
sobs of shame.
Thou makest full confession; and
a gleam,
As of the dawn on some dark
forest cast,
Seems on thy lifted forehead to
increase;
Lethe and Eunoe—the remembered
dream
And the forgotten sorrow—bring
at last
That perfect pardon which is
perfect peace.

V.

I lift mine eyes, and all the
windows blaze
With forms of saints and holy
men who died,
Here martyred and hereafter
glorified;
And the great Rose upon its
leaves displays
Christ's Triumph, and the angelic
roundelays,
With splendour upon splendour
multiplied;
And Beatrice again at Dante's
side
No more rebukes, but smiles her
words of praise.
And then the organ sounds, and
unseen choirs
Sing the old Latin hymns of
peace and love,
And benedictions of the Holy
Ghost;
And the melodious bells among
the spires
O'er all the house-tops and
through heaven above
Proclaim the elevation of the
Host!

VI.

O star of morning and of liberty!
O bringer of the light, whose
 splendour shines
Above the darkness of the Apen-
 nines,
Forerunner of the day that is to
 be!
The voices of the city and the sea,
The voices of the mountains and
 the pines,
Repeat thy song, till the familiar
 lines
Are footpaths for the thought of
 Italy!
Thy fame is blown abroad from all
 the heights,
Through all the nations, and a
 sound is heard,
As of a mighty wind, and men
 devout,
Strangers of Rome, and the new
 proselytes,
In their own language hear thy
 wondrous word,
And many are amazed and many
 doubt.

NOËL.

ENVOYÉ À M. AGASSIZ, LA VEILLE
DE NOËL 1864, AVEC UN PANIER
DE VINS DIVERS.

L'Académie en respect,
Nonobstant l'incorrection
A la faveur du sujet,
 Ture-lure,
N'y fera point de rature;
Noël! ture-lure-lure.
 GUI BARÔZAI.

QUAND les astres de Noël
Brillaient, palpitaient au ciel,
Six gaillards, et chacun ivre,
Chantaient gaîment dans le givre,
 'Bons amis
Allons donc chez Agassiz!'

Ces illustres Pèlerins
D'Outre-Mer adroits et fins,
Se donnant des airs de prêtre,
A l'envi se vantaient d'être
 'Bons amis
De Jean Rudolphe Agassiz!'

Œil-de-Perdrix, grand farceur,
Sans reproche et sans pudeur,
Dans son patois de Bourgogne,
Bredouillait comme un ivrogne,
 'Bons amis,
J'ai dansé chez Agassiz!'

Verzenay le Champenois,
Bon Français, point New-Yorquois,
Mais des environs d'Avize,
Fredonne à mainte reprise,
 'Bons amis,
J'ai chanté chez Agassiz!'

A côté marchait un vieux
Hidalgo, mais non mousseux,
Dans le temps de Charlemagne
Fut son père Grand d'Espagne!
 'Bons amis
J'ai dîné chez Agassiz!'

Derrière eux un Bordelais,
Gascon, s'il en fût jamais,
Parfumé de poésie
Riait, chantait, plein de vie,
 'Bons amis,
J'ai soupé chez Agassiz!'

Avec ce beau cadet roux,
Bras dessus et bras dessous,
Mine altière et couleur terne,
Vint le Sire de Sauterne;
 'Bons amis,
J'ai couché chez Agassiz!'

Mais le dernier de ces preux,
Était un pauvre Chartreux,
Qui disait, d'un ton robuste,
'Bénédictions sur le Juste!
 Bons amis
Bénissons Père Agassiz!'

Ils arrivent trois à trois,
Montent l'escalier de bois
Clopin-clopant ! quel gendarme
Peut permettre ce vacarme,
    Bons amis,
A la porte d'Agassiz !

'Ouvrez donc, mon bon Seigneur,
Ouvrez vite et n'ayez peur ;
Ouvrez, ouvrez, car nous sommes

Gens de bien et gentilshommes,
    Bons amis
De la famille Agassiz !'

Chut, ganaches ! taisez-vous !
C'en est trop de vos glouglous ;
Epargnez aux Philosophes
Vos abominables strophes !
    Bons amis,
Respectez mon Agassiz !

Judas Maccabæus.

ACT I.

The Citadel of Antiochus at Jerusalem.

SCENE I.—ANTIOCHUS; JASON.

Antiochus. O Antioch, my
Antioch, my city!
Queen of the East! my solace, my
delight!
The dowry of my sister Cleopatra
When she was wed to Ptolemy,
and now
Won back and made more wonder-
ful by me!
I love thee, and I long to be once
more
Among the players and the dancing
women
Within thy gates, and bathe in the
Orontes,
Thy river and mine. O Jason, my
High-Priest,
For I have made thee so, and thou
art mine,
Hast thou seen Antioch the Beau-
tiful?
Jason. Never, my Lord.
Ant. Then hast
thou never seen
The wonder of the world. This
city of David
Compared with Antioch is but a
village,
And its inhabitants compared with
Greeks
Are mannerless boors.

Jason. They are barbarians,
And mannerless.
Ant. They must be civilised.
They must be made to have more
gods than one;
And goddesses besides.
Jason. They shall have more.
Ant. They must have hippo-
dromes, and games, and baths,
Stage-plays and festivals, and most
of all
The Dionysia.
Jason. They shall have them all.
Ant. By Heracles! but I should
like to see
These Hebrews crowned with ivy,
and arrayed
In skins of fawns, with drums and
flutes and thyrsi,
Revel and riot through the solemn
streets
Of their old town. Ha, ha! It
makes me merry
Only to think of it!—Thou dost
not laugh.
Jason. Yea, I laugh inwardly.
Ant. The new Greek leaven
Works slowly in this Israelitish
dough!
Have I not sacked the Temple,
and on the altar
Set up the statue of Olympian Zeus
To Hellenize it?

541

Jason. Thou hast done all this.

Ant. As thou wast Joshua once
and now art Jason,
And from a Hebrew hast become
a Greek,
So shall this Hebrew nation be
translated,
Their very natures and their names
be changed,
And all be Hellenized.

Jason. It shall be done.

Ant. Their manners and their
laws and way of living
Shall all be Greek. They shall
unlearn their language,
And learn the lovely speech of
Antioch.
Where hast thou been to-day? Thou
comest late.

Jason. Playing at discus with the
other priests
In the Gymnasium.

Ant. Thou hast done well.
There's nothing better for you lazy
priests
Than discus-playing with the
common people.
Now tell me, Jason, what these
Hebrews call me
When they converse together at
their games.

Jason. Antiochus Epiphanes, my
Lord;
Antiochus the Illustrious.

Ant. O, not that;
That is the public cry; I mean the
name
They give me when they talk among
themselves,
And think that no one listens;
what is that?

Jason. Antiochus Epimanes, my
Lord!

Ant. Antiochus the Mad! Ay,
that is it.
And who hath said it? Who hath
set in motion
That sorry jest?

Jason. The Seven Sons insane
Of a weird woman, like themselves
insane.

Ant. I like their courage, but it
shall not save them.
They shall be made to eat the flesh
of swine,
Or they shall die. Where are they?

Jason. In the dungeons
Beneath this tower.

Ant. There let them stay and
starve,
Till I am ready to make Greeks of
them,
After my fashion.

Jason. They shall stay and starve.
My Lord, the Ambassadors of Sa-
maria
Await thy pleasure.

Ant. Why not my displeasure?
Ambassadors are tedious. They
are men
Who work for their own ends, and
not for mine;
There is no furtherance in them.
Let them go
To Apollonius, my governor
There in Samaria, and not trouble
me.
What do they want?

Jason. Only the royal sanction
To give a name unto a nameless
temple
Upon Mount Gerizim.

Ant. Then bid them enter.
This pleases me, and furthers my
designs.
The occasion is auspicious. Bid
them enter.

SCENE II.—ANTIOCHUS; JASON;
the SAMARITAN AMBASSADORS.

Ant. Approach. Come forward;
stand not at the door
Wagging your long beards, but
demean yourselves
As doth become Ambassadors.
What seek ye?

An Ambassador. An audience from the King.

Ant. Speak, and be brief. Waste not the time in useless rhetoric. Words are not things.

Ambassador (*reading*). 'To King Antiochus,

The God, Epiphanes ; a Memorial From the Sidonians, who live at Sichem.'

Ant. Sidonians ?

Ambassador. Ay, my Lord.

Ant. Go on, go on ! And do not tire thyself and me with bowing !

Ambassador (*reading*). ' We are a colony of Medes and Persians.'

Ant. No, ye are Jews from one of the Ten Tribes ;

Whether Sidonians or Samaritans, Or Jews of Jewry, matters not to me; Ye are all Israelites, ye are all Jews. When the Jews prosper, ye claim kindred with them ; When the Jews suffer, ye are Medes and Persians :

I know that in the days of Alexander Ye claimed exemption from the annual tribute In the Sabbatic Year, because, ye said, Your fields had not been planted in that year.

Ambassador (*reading*). ' Our fathers, upon certain frequent plagues,

And following an ancient superstition,

Were long accustomed to observe that day Which by the Israelites is called the Sabbath,

And in a temple on Mount Gerizim Without a name, they offered sacrifice.

Now we, who are Sidonians, beseech thee,

Who art our benefactor and our saviour,

Not to confound us with these wicked Jews,

But to give royal order and injunction To Apollonius in Samaria,

Thy Governor, and likewise to Nicanor,

Thy procurator, no more to molest us ;

And let our nameless temple now be named The Temple of Jupiter Hellenius.'

Ant. This shall be done. Full well it pleaseth me Ye are not Jews, or are no longer Jews,

But Greeks ; if not by birth, yet Greeks by custom.

Your nameless temple shall receive the name Of Jupiter Hellenius. Ye may go !

Scene III.—Antiochus; Jason.

Ant. My task is easier than I dreamed. These people Meet me half-way. Jason, didst thou take note How these Samaritans of Sichem said They were not Jews? that they were Medes and Persians,

They were Sidonians, anything but Jews ?

'Tis of good augury. The rest will follow Till the whole land is Hellenized.

Jason. My Lord, These are Samaritans. The tribe of Judah Is of a different temper, and the task Will be more difficult.

Ant. Dost thou gainsay me ?

Jason. I know the stubborn nature of the Jew.

Yesterday, Eleazer, an old man,
Being fourscore years and ten, chose
    rather death
By torture than to eat the flesh of
    swine.

Ant. The life is in the blood,
    and the whole nation
Shall bleed to death, or it shall
    change its faith !

Jason. Hundreds have fled al-
    ready to the mountains
Of Ephraim, where Judas Macca-
    bæus
Hath raised the standard of revolt
    against thee.

Ant. I will burn down their city,
    and will make it

Waste as a wilderness. Its thorough-
    fares
Shall be but furrows in a field of
    ashes.
It shall be sown with salt as Sodom
    is !
This hundred and fifty-third Olym-
    piad
Shall have a broad and blood-red
    seal upon it,
Stamped with the awful letters of my
    name,
Antiochus the God, Epiphanes !—
Where are those Seven Sons ?

Jason.   My Lord, they wait
Thy royal pleasure.

Ant. They shall wait no longer !

ACT II.

The Dungeons in the Citadel.

SCENE I.—THE MOTHER *of the*
SEVEN SONS *alone, listening.*

The Mother. Be strong, my heart !
    Break not till they are dead,
All, all my Seven Sons ; then burst
    asunder,
And let this tortured and tormented
    soul
Leap and rush out like water through
    the shards
Of earthen vessels broken at a well.
O my dear children, mine in life and
    death,
I know not how ye came into my
    womb ;
I neither gave you breath, nor gave
    you life,
And neither was it I that formed the
    members
Of every one of you. But the Creator,
Who made the world, and made
    the heavens above us,
Who formed the generation of man-
    kind,

And found out the beginning of all
    things,
He gave you breath and life, and
    will again
Of his own mercy, as ye now regard
Not your own selves, but his eternal
    law.
I do not murmur, nay, I thank thee,
    God,
That I and mine have not been
    deemed unworthy
To suffer for thy sake, and for thy
    law,
And for the many sins of Israel.
Hark ! I can hear within the sound
    of scourges !
I feel them more than ye do, O my
    sons !
But cannot come to you. I, who
    was wont
To wake at night at the least cry ye
    made,
To whom ye ran at every slightest
    hurt,—
I cannot take you now into my lap

And soothe your pain, but God will
    take you all
Into his pitying arms, and comfort
    you,
And give you rest.
    A Voice (*within*).   What wouldst
        thou ask of us?
Ready are we to die, but we will
    never
Transgress the law and customs of
    our fathers.
    The Mother.   It is the voice of
        my first-born!   O brave
And noble boy!   Thou hast the
    privilege
Of dying first, as thou wast born the
    first.
    The same Voice (*within*).   God
        looketh on us, and hath comfort
        in us;
As Moses in his song of old de-
    clared,
He in his servants shall be com-
    forted.
    The Mother.   I knew thou wouldst
        not fail! — He speaks no
        more,
He is beyond all pain!
    Ant. (*within*).   If thou eat not
Thou shalt be tortured throughout
    all the members
Of thy whole body.   Wilt thou eat
    then?
    Second Voice (*within*).   No.
    The Mother.   It is Adaiah's voice.
        I tremble for him.
I know his nature, devious as the
    wind,
And swift to change, gentle and
    yielding always.
Be steadfast, O my son!
    The same Voice (*within*).   Thou,
        like a fury,
Takest us from this present life, but
    God,
Who rules the world, shall raise us
    up again
Into life everlasting.

    The Mother.   God, I thank thee
That thou hast breathed into that
    timid heart
Courage to die for thee.   O my
    Adaiah,
Witness of God! if thou for whom
    I feared
Canst thus encounter death, I need
    not fear;
The others will not shrink.
    Third Voice (*within*).   Behold
        these hands
Held out to thee, O King Antiochus,
Not to implore thy mercy, but to
    show
That I despise them.   He who gave
    them to me
Will give them back again.
    The Mother.   O Avilan,
It is thy voice.   For the last time
    I hear it;
For the last time on earth, but not
    the last.
To death it bids defiance and to
    torture.
It sounds to me as from another
    world,
And makes the petty miseries of
    this
Seem unto me as naught, and less
    than naught.
Farewell, my Avilan; nay, I should
    say
Welcome, my Avilan; for I am dead
Before thee.   I am waiting for the
    others.
Why do they linger?
    Fourth Voice (*within*).   It is
        good, O King,
Being put to death by men, to look
    for hope
From God, to be raised up again by
    him.
But thou—no resurrection shalt
    thou have
To life hereafter.
    The Mother.   Four! already
        four!

Three are still living; nay, they all
    are living,
Half here, half there. Make haste,
    Antiochus,
To reunite us; for the sword that
    cleaves
These miserable bodies makes a
    door
Through which our souls, impatient
    of release,
Rush to each other's arms.
    Fifth Voice (within). Thou
    hast the power;
Thou doest what thou wilt. Abide
    awhile,
And thou shalt see the power of
    God, and how
He will torment thee and thy seed.
    The Mother. O hasten;
Why dost thou pause? Thou who
    hast slain already
So many Hebrew women, and hast
    hung
Their murdered infants round their
    necks, slay me,
For I too am a woman, and these
    boys
Are mine. Make haste to slay us
    all,
And hang my lifeless babes about
    my neck.
    Sixth Voice (within). Think
    not, Antiochus, that takest in
    hand
To strive against the God of
    Israel,
Thou shalt escape unpunished, for
    his wrath
Shall overtake thee and thy bloody
    house.
    The Mother. One more, my
    Sirion, and then all is ended.
Having put all to bed, then in my
    turn
I will lie down and sleep as sound
    as they.
My Sirion, my youngest, best be-
    loved!

And those bright golden locks, that
    I so oft
Have curled about these fingers,
    even now
Are foul with blood and dust, like
    a lamb's fleece,
Slain in the shambles.—Not a
    sound I hear.
This silence is more terrible to me
Than any sound, than any cry of
    pain,
That might escape the lips of one
    who dies.
Doth his heart fail him? Doth he
    fall away
In the last hour from God? O
    Sirion, Sirion,
Art thou afraid? I do not hear thy
    voice.
Die as thy brothers died. Thou
    must not live!

SCENE II.—THE MOTHER; ANTI-
OCHUS; SIRION.

    The Mother. Are they all dead?
    Ant. Of all thy Seven Sons
One only lives. Behold them
    where they lie;
How dost thou like this picture?
    The Mother. God in heaven!
Can a man do such deeds, and yet
    not die
By the recoil of his own wickedness?
Ye murdered, bleeding, mutilated
    bodies,
That were my children once, and
    still are mine,
I cannot watch o'er you as Rizpah
    watched
In sackcloth o'er the seven sons of
    Saul,
Till water drop upon you out of
    heaven
And wash this blood away! I can-
    not mourn
As she, the daughter of Aiah,
    mourned the dead,

From the beginning of the barley-
harvest
Until the autumn rains, and suffered
not
The birds of air to rest on them by
day,
Nor the wild beasts by night. For
ye have died
A better death, a death so full of life
That I ought rather to rejoice than
mourn.—
Wherefore art thou not dead, O
Sirion?
Wherefore art thou the only living
thing
Among thy brothers dead? Art
thou afraid?
   Ant. O woman, I have spared
him for thy sake,
For he is fair to look upon and
comely;
And I have sworn to him by all the
gods
That I would crown his life with
joy and honour,
Heap treasures on him, luxuries,
delights,
Make him my friend and keeper of
my secrets,
If he would turn from your Mosaic
Law
And be as we are; but he will not
listen.
   The Mother. My noble Sirion!
   Ant. Therefore I beseech thee,
Who art his mother, thou wouldst
speak with him,
And wouldst persuade him. I am
sick of blood.
   The Mother. Yea, I will speak
with him and will persuade him.
O Sirion, my son! have pity on me,
On me that bare thee, and that
gave thee suck,
And fed and nourished thee, and
brought thee up
With the dear trouble of a mother's
care

Unto this age. Look on the
heavens above thee,
And on the earth and all that is
therein;
Consider that God made them out
of things
That were not; and that likewise
in this manner
Mankind was made. Then fear not
this tormentor;
But, being worthy of thy brethren,
take
Thy death as they did, that I may
receive thee
Again in mercy with them.
   Ant. I am mocked,
Yea, I am laughed to scorn.
   Sirion. Whom wait ye for?
Never will I obey the King's com-
mandment,
But the commandment of the
ancient Law,
That was by Moses given unto our
fathers.
And thou, O godless man, that of
all others
Art the most wicked, be not lifted up,
Nor puffed up with uncertain hopes,
uplifting
Thy hand against the servants of
the Lord,
For thou hast not escaped the
righteous judgment
Of the Almighty God, who seeth
all things!
   Ant. He is no God of mine; I
fear him not.
   Sirion. My brothers, who have
suffered a brief pain,
Are dead; but thou, Antiochus,
shalt suffer
The punishment of pride. I offer
up
My body and my life, beseeching
God
That he would speedily be merciful
Unto our nation, and that thou by
plagues

Mysterious and by torments mayest
confess
That he alone is God.
  Ant.   Ye both shall perish
By torments worse than any that
    your God,
Here or hereafter, hath in store for
    me.
  The Mother. My Sirion, I am
    proud of thee!
  Ant.   Be silent!
Go to thy bed of torture in yon
    chamber,
Where lie so many sleepers, heart-
    less mother!

Thy footsteps will not wake them,
    nor thy voice,
Nor wilt thou hear, amid thy
    troubled dreams,
Thy children crying for thee in the
    night!
  The Mother. O Death, that
    stretchest thy white hands to me,
I fear them not, but press them to
    my lips,
That are as white as thine; for I
    am Death,
Nay, am the Mother of Death,
    seeing these sons
All lying lifeless.—Kiss me, Sirion.

ACT III.

The Battlefield of Beth-horon.

SCENE I.—JUDAS MACCABÆUS *in
    armour before his tent.*

  Judas. The trumpets sound; the
    echoes of the mountains
Answer them, as the Sabbath
    morning breaks
Over Beth-horon and its battle-
    field,
Where the great captain of the
    hosts of God,
A slave brought up in the brick-
    fields of Egypt,
O'ercame the Amorites. There
    was no day
Like that, before or after it, nor
    shall be.
The sun stood still; the hammers
    of the hail
Beat on their harness; and the
    captains set
Their weary feet upon the necks of
    kings,
As I will upon thine, Antiochus,
Thou man of blood!—Behold the
    rising sun
Strikes on the golden letters of my
    banner,

Be Elohim Yehovah! Who is like
To thee, O Lord, among the gods?
  —Alas!
I am not Joshua, I cannot say,
'Sun, stand thou still on Gibeon,
    and thou Moon,
In Ajalon!' Nor am I one who
    wastes
The fateful time in useless lamenta-
    tion;
But one who bears his life upon his
    hand
To lose it or to save it, as may best
Serve the designs of Him who
    giveth life.

SCENE II.—JUDAS MACCABÆUS;
    JEWISH FUGITIVES.

  Judas. Who and what are ye,
    that with furtive steps
Steal in among our tents?
  Fugitives.   O Maccabæus,
Outcasts are we, and fugitives as
    thou art,
Jews of Jerusalem, that have es-
    caped

548

From the polluted city, and from
    death.
    Judas. None can escape from
    death. Say that ye come
To die for Israel, and ye are wel-
    come.
What tidings bring ye?
    Fugitives. Tidings of despair.
The Temple is laid waste; the
    precious vessels,
Censers of gold, vials and veils and
    crowns,
And golden ornaments, and hidden
    treasures,
Have all been taken from it, and
    the Gentiles
With revelling and with riot fill its
    courts,
And dally with harlots in the holy
    places.
    Judas. All this I knew before.
    Fugitives. Upon
the altar
Are things profane, things by the
    law forbidden;
Nor can we keep our Sabbaths or
    our Feasts,
But on the festivals of Dionysus
Must walk in their processions,
    bearing ivy
To crown a drunken god.
    Judas. This too I know.
But tell me of the Jews. How
    fare the Jews?
    Fugitives. The coming of this
    mischief hath been sore
And grievous to the people. All
    the land
Is full of lamentation and of mourn-
    ing.
The Princes and the Elders weep
    and wail;
The young men and the maidens
    are made feeble;
The beauty of the women hath
    been changed.
    Judas. And are there none to die
    for Israel?

'Tis not enough to mourn. Breast-
    plate and harness
Are better things than sackcloth.
    Let the women
Lament for Israel; the men should
    die.
    Fugitives. Both men and women
    die; old men and young:
Old Eleazer died: and Máhala
With all her Seven Sons.
    Judas. Antiochus,
At every step thou takest there is left
A bloody footprint in the street, by
    which
The avenging wrath of God will
    track thee out!
It is enough. Go to the sutler's
    tents:
Those of you who are men, put on
    such armour
As ye may find; those of you who
    are women,
Buckle that armour on; and for a
    watchword
Whisper, or cry aloud, 'The Help
    of God.'

SCENE III.—JUDAS MACCABÆUS;
    NICANOR.

    Nicanor. Hail, Judas Macca-
    bæus!
    Judas. Hail!—Who art thou
That comest here in this mysterious
    guise
Into our camp unheralded?
    Nic. A herald
Sent from Nicanor.
    Judas. Heralds come not thus.
Armed with thy shirt of mail from
    head to heel,
Thou glidest like a serpent silently
Into my presence. Wherefore dost
    thou turn
Thy face from me? A herald
    speaks his errand
With forehead unabashed. Thou
    art a spy
Sent by Nicanor.

Nic. No disguise avails!
Behold my face; I am Nicanor's self.
Judas. Thou art indeed Nicanor.
  I salute thee.
What brings thee hither to this
  hostile camp
Thus unattended?
Nic. Confidence in thee.
Thou hast the nobler virtues of thy
  race,
Without the failings that attend
  those virtues.
Thou canst be strong, and yet not
  tyrannous,
Canst righteous be and not in-
  tolerant.
Let there be peace between us.
Judas. What is peace?
Is it to bow in silence to our
  victors?
Is it to see our cities sacked and
  pillaged,
Our people slain, or sold as slaves,
  or fleeing
At night-time by the blaze of burn-
  ing towns;
Jerusalem laid waste; the Holy
  Temple
Polluted with strange gods? Are
  these things peace?
Nic. These are the dire necessi-
  ties that wait
On war, whose loud and bloody
  enginery
I seek to stay. Let there be peace
  between
Antiochus and thee.
Judas. Antiochus?
What is Antiochus, that he should
  prate
Of peace to me, who am a fugi-
  tive?
To-day he shall be lifted up; to-
  morrow
Shall not be found, because he is
  returned
Unto his dust; his thought has
  come to nothing.

There is no peace between us, nor
  can be,
Until this banner floats upon the
  walls
Of our Jerusalem.
Nic. Between that city
And thee there lies a waving wall
  of tents,
Held by a host of forty thousand
  foot,
And horsemen seven thousand.
  What hast thou
To bring against all these?
Judas. The power of God,
Whose breath shall scatter your
  white tents abroad,
As flakes of snow.
Nic. Your Mighty One in
  heaven
Will not do battle on the Seventh
  Day;
It is his day of rest.
Judas. Silence, blasphemer.
Go to thy tents.
Nic. Shall it be war or peace?
Judas. War, war, and only war.
  Go to thy tents
That shall be scattered, as by you
  were scattered
The torn and trampled pages of
  the Law,
Blown through the windy streets.
Nic. Farewell, brave foe!
Judas. Ho, there, my captains!
  Have safe-conduct given
Unto Nicanor's herald through the
  camp,
And come yourselves to me.—Fare-
  well, Nicanor!

SCENE IV.—JUDAS MACCABÆUS;
  CAPTAINS AND SOLDIERS.

Judas. The hour is come. Gather
  the host together
For battle. Lo, with trumpets and
  with songs
The army of Nicanor comes against
  us.

Judas Maccabæus.

Go forth to meet them, praying in
your hearts,
And fighting with your hands.
   Captains.   Look forth and see!
The morning sun is shining on their
shields
Of gold and brass; the mountains
glisten with them,
And shine like lamps.   And we
who are so few
And poorly armed, and ready to
faint with fasting,
How shall we fight against this
multitude?
   Judas.   The victory of a battle
standeth not
In multitudes, but in the strength
that cometh
From heaven above.   The Lord
forbid that I
Should do this thing, and flee away
from them.
Nay, if our hour be come, then let
us die;
Let us not stain our honour.
   Captains.   'Tis the Sabbath.
Wilt thou fight on the Sabbath,
Maccabæus?
   Judas.   Ay; when I fight the
battles of the Lord,
I fight them on his day, as on all
others.
Have ye forgotten certain fugi-
tives
That fled once to these hills, and
hid themselves
In caves? How their pursuers
camped against them
Upon the Seventh Day, and chal-
lenged them?
And how they answered not, nor
cast a stone,
Nor stopped the places where they
lay concealed,
But meekly perished with their
wives and children,
Even to the number of a thousand
souls?

We who are fighting for our laws
and lives
Will not so perish.
   Captains.   Lead us to the battle!
   Judas.   And let our watchword
be, 'The Help of God!'
Last night I dreamed a dream;
and in my vision
Beheld Onias, our High-Priest of
old,
Who holding up his hands prayed
for the Jews.
This done, in the like manner there
appeared
An old man, and exceeding glorious,
With hoary hair, and of a wonderful
And excellent majesty.   And Onias
said:
'This is a lover of the Jews, who
prayeth
Much for the people and the Holy
City,—
God's prophet Jeremias.'   And the
prophet
Held forth his right hand and gave
unto me
A sword of gold; and giving it he
said:
'Take thou this holy sword, a gift
from God,
And with it thou shalt wound thine
adversaries.'
   Captains.   The Lord is with
us!
   Judas.   Hark! I hear the
trumpets
Sound from Beth-horon; from the
battle-field
Of Joshua, where he smote the
Amorites,
Smote the Five Kings of Eglon and
of Jarmuth,
Of Hebron, Lachish, and Jeru-
salem,
As we to-day will smite Nicanor's
hosts
And leave a memory of great deeds
behind us.

551

Captains and Soldiers. The
Help of God!

Judas. *Be Elohim Yehovah!*
Lord, thou didst send thine Angel
in the time
Of Esekias, King of Israel,
And in the armies of Sennacherib
Didst slay a hundred fourscore and
five thousand.

Wherefore, O Lord of heaven, now
also send
Before us a good angel for a fear,
And through the might of thy right
arm let those
Be stricken with terror that have
come this day
Against thy holy people to blaspheme!

ACT IV.

The outer Courts of the Temple at Jerusalem.

SCENE I.—JUDAS MACCABÆUS;
CAPTAINS; JEWS.

Judas. Behold, our enemies are
discomfited.
Jerusalem is fallen; and our ban-
ners
Float from her battlements, and o'er
her gates
Nicanor's severed head, a sign of
terror,
Blackens in wind and sun.
Captains. O Maccabæus,
The citadel of Antiochus, wherein
The Mother with her Seven Sons
was murdered,
Is still defiant.
Judas. Wait.
Captains. Its hateful aspect
Insults us with the bitter memories
Of other days.
Judas. Wait; it shall disappear
And vanish as a cloud. First let
us cleanse
The Sanctuary. See, it is become
Waste like a wilderness. Its
golden gates
Wrenched from their hinges and
consumed by fire;
Shrubs growing in its courts as in
a forest;
Upon its altars hideous and strange
idols;
And strewn about its pavement at
my feet

Its Sacred Books, half burned and
painted o'er
With images of heathen gods.
Jews. Woe! woe!
Our beauty and our glory are laid
waste!
The Gentiles have profaned our
holy places!
(*Lamentation and alarm of
trumpets.*)
Judas. This sound of trumpets,
and this lamentation,
The heart-cry of a people toward
the heavens,
Stir me to wrath and vengeance.
Go, my captains;
I hold you back no longer. Batter
down
The citadel of Antiochus, while here
We sweep away his altars and his
gods.

SCENE II.—JUDAS MACCABÆUS;
JASON; JEWS.

Jews. Lurking among the ruins
of the Temple,
Deep in its inner courts, we found
this man,
Clad as High-Priest.
Judas. I ask not who thou art.
I know thy face, writ over with
deceit
As are these tattered volumes of
the Law

With heathen images. A priest of
God
Wast thou in other days, but thou
art now
A priest of Satan. Traitor, thou
art Jason.
Jason. I am thy prisoner, Judas
Maccabæus.
And it would ill become me to
conceal
My name or office.
Judas. Over yonder gate
There hangs the head of one who
was a Greek.
What should prevent me now, thou
man of sin,
From hanging at its side the head
of one
Who born a Jew hath made him-
self a Greek?
Jason. Justice prevents thee.
Judas. Justice?
Thou art stained
With every crime 'gainst which the
Decalogue
Thunders with all its thunder.
Jason. If not Justice,
Then Mercy, her handmaiden.
Judas. When hast thou
At any time, to any man or woman,
Or even to any little child, shown
mercy?
Jason. I have but done what
King Antiochus
Commanded me.
Judas. True, thou hast
been the weapon
With which he struck; but hast
been such a weapon,
So flexible, so fitted to his hand,
It tempted him to strike. So thou
hast urged him
To double wickedness, thine own
and his.
Where is this King? Is he in
Antioch
Among his women still, and from
his windows

Throwing down gold by handfuls,
for the rabble
To scramble for?
Jason. Nay, he is gone from
there,
Gone with an army into the far East.
Judas. And wherefore gone?
Jason. I know not.
For the space
Of forty days almost were horsemen
seen
Running in air, in cloth of gold,
and armed
With lances, like a band of soldiery;
It was a sign of triumph.
Judas. Or of death.
Wherefore art thou not with him?
Jason. I was left
For service in the Temple.
Judas. To pollute it,
And to corrupt the Jews; for there
are men
Whose presence is corruption; to
be with them
Degrades us and deforms the
things we do.
Jason. I never made a boast,
as some men do,
Of my superior virtue, nor denied
The weakness of my nature, that
hath made me
Subservient to the will of other men.
Judas. Upon this day, the five
and twentieth day
Of the month Caslan, was the
Temple here
Profaned by strangers,—by Anti-
ochus
And thee, his instrument. Upon
this day
Shall it be cleansed. Thou, who
didst lend thyself
Unto this profanation, canst not be
A witness of these solemn services.
There can be nothing clean where
thou art present.
The people put to death Callis-
thenes,

Judas Maccabæus.

Who burned the Temple gates;
and if they find thee
Will surely slay thee. I will spare
thy life
To punish thee the longer. Thou
shalt wander
Among strange nations. Thou,
that hast cast out
So many from their native land,
shalt perish
In a strange land. Thou, that hast
left so many
Unburied, shalt have none to mourn
for thee,
Nor any solemn funerals at all,
Nor sepulchre with thy fathers.
Get thee hence!

(*Music. Procession of Priests and
people, with citherns, harps, and
cymbals.* JUDAS MACCABÆUS
*puts himself at their head, and
they go into the inner courts.*)

SCENE III.—JASON, *alone.*

Jason. Through the Gate Beau-
tiful I see them come
With branches and green boughs
and leaves of palm,
And pass into the inner courts.
Alas!
I should be with them, should be
one of them,
But in an evil hour, an hour of
weakness,
That cometh unto all, I fell away
From the old faith, and did not
clutch the new,
Only an outward semblance of
belief;
For the new faith I cannot make
mine own,
Not being born to it. It hath no root
Within me. I am neither Jew nor
Greek,

But stand between them both, a
renegade
To each in turn; having no longer
faith
In gods or men. Then what mysterious charm,
What fascination is it chains my
feet,
And keeps me gazing like a curious
child
Into the holy places, where the
priests
Have raised their altar?—Striking
stones together,
They take fire out of them, and
light the lamps
In the great candlestick. They
spread the veils,
And set the loaves of shewbread
on the table.
The incense burns; the well-
remembered odour
Comes wafted unto me, and takes
me back
To other days. I see myself among
them
As I was then; and the old superstition
Creeps over me again!— A childish
fancy!—
And hark! they sing with citherns
and with cymbals,
And all the people fall upon their
faces,
Praying and worshipping!—I will
away
Into the East, to meet Antiochus
Upon his homeward journey,
crowned with triumph.
Alas! to-day I would give everything
To see a friend's face, or to hear a
voice
That had the slightest tone of
comfort in it!

554

Judas Maccabæus.

ACT V.

The Mountains of Ecbatana.

SCENE I.—ANTIOCHUS; PHILIP; ATTENDANTS.

Ant. Here let us rest awhile.
Where are we, Philip?
What place is this?
Philip. Ecbatana, my Lord;
And yonder mountain range is the
Orontes.
Ant. The Orontes is my river
at Antioch.
Why did I leave it? Why have I
been tempted
By coverings of gold and shields
and breastplates
To plunder Elymais, and be driven
From out its gates, as by a fiery
blast
Out of a furnace?
Philip. These are fortune's
changes.
Ant. What a defeat it was!
The Persian horsemen
Came like a mighty wind, the wind
Khamáseen,
And melted us away, and scattered
us
As if we were dead leaves, or desert
sand.
Philip. Be comforted, my Lord;
for thou hast lost
But what thou hadst not.
Ant. I, who made the Jews
Skip like the grasshoppers, am
made myself
To skip among these stones.
Philip. Be not discouraged.
Thy realm of Syria remains to thee;
That is not lost nor marred.
Ant. O, where are now
The splendours of my court, my
baths and banquets?
Where are my players and my
dancing women?
Where are my sweet musicians
with their pipes,

That made me merry in the olden
time?
I am a laughing-stock to man and
brute.
The very camels, with their ugly
faces,
Mock me and laugh at me.
Philip. Alas! my Lord,
It is not so. If thou wouldst sleep
awhile,
All would be well.
Ant. Sleep from mine
eyes is gone,
And my heart faileth me for very
care,
Dost thou remember, Philip, the
old fable
Told us when we were boys, in
which the bear
Going for honey overturns the hive,
And is stung blind by bees? I am
that beast,
Stung by the Persian swarms of
Elymais.
Philip. When thou art come
again to Antioch
These thoughts will be as covered
and forgotten
As are the tracks of Pharaoh's
chariot-wheels
In the Egyptian sands.
Ant. Ah! when I come
Again to Antioch! When will that
be?
Alas! alas!

SCENE II.—ANTIOCHUS; PHILIP; A MESSENGER.

Messenger. May the King live for
ever!
Ant. Who art thou, and whence
comest thou?
Messenger. My Lord,
I am a messenger from Antioch,
Sent here by Lysias.

555

Ant.   A strange foreboding
Of something evil overshadows me.
I am no reader of the Jewish Scrip-
    tures ;
I know not Hebrew ; but my High-
    Priest Jason,
As I remember, told me of a
    Prophet
Who saw a little cloud rise from the
    sea
Like a man's hand, and soon the
    heaven was black
With clouds and rain. Here, Philip,
    read ; I cannot ;
I see that cloud. It makes the
    letters dim
Before mine eyes.
    Philip (reading). 'To King
    Antiochus,
The God, Epiphanes.'
    Ant.   O mockery !
Even Lysias laughs at me ! — Go
    on, go on !
    Philip (reading). 'We pray thee
    hasten thy return. The realm
Is falling from thee. Since thou
    hast gone from us
The victories of Judas Maccabæus
Form all our annals. First he over-
    threw
Thy forces at Beth-horon, and
    passed on,
And took Jerusalem, the Holy City.
And then Emmaus fell ; and then
    Beth-sura ;
Ephron and all the towns of Galaad,
And Maccabæus marched to Car-
    nion.'
    Ant. Enough, enough ! Go call
    my chariot-men ;
We will drive forward, forward,
    without ceasing,
Until we come to Antioch. My
    captains,
My Lysias, Gorgias, Seron, and
    Nicanor
Are babes in battle, and this dread-
    ful Jew

Will rob me of my kingdom and
    my crown.
My elephants shall trample him to
    dust ;
I will wipe out his nation, and will
    make
Jerusalem a common burying-place,
And every home within its walls a
    tomb !

*(Throws up his hands, and sinks
    into the arms of attendants,
    who lay him upon a bank.)*

    Philip. Antiochus ! Antiochus !
    Alas,
The King is ill ! What is it, O
    my Lord ?
    Ant. Nothing. A sudden and
    sharp spasm of pain,
As if the lightning struck me, or
    the knife
Of an assassin smote me to the
    heart.
'Tis passed, even as it came. Let
    us set forward.
    Philip. See that the chariots be
    in readiness ;
We will depart forthwith.
    Ant.   A moment more.
I cannot stand. I am become at
    once
Weak as an infant. Ye will have
    to lead me.
Jove, or Jehovah, or whatever name
Thou wouldst be named,— it is
    alike to me,—
If I knew how to pray, I would en-
    treat
To live a little longer.
    Philip.   O my Lord,
Thou shalt not die ; we will not let
    thee die !
    Ant. How canst thou help it,
    Philip ? O the pain !
Stab after stab. Thou hast no
    shield against
This unseen weapon. God of
    Israel.

Since all the other gods abandon
me,
Help me. I will release the Holy
City,
Garnish with goodly gifts the Holy
Temple.
Thy people, whom I judged to be
unworthy
To be so much as buried, shall be
equal
Unto the citizens of Antioch.
I will become a Jew, and will
declare
Through all the world that is
inhabited
The power of God !

Philip. He faints. It is like
death.
Bring here the royal litter. We
will bear him
Into the camp, while yet he lives.

Ant. O Philip,
Into what tribulation am I come !
Alas ! I now remember all the
evil
That I have done the Jews ; and
for this cause

These troubles are upon me, and
behold
I perish through great grief in a
strange land.

Philip. Antiochus ! my King !

Ant. Nay, King no longer.
Take thou my royal robes, my
signet-ring,
My crown and sceptre, and deliver
them
Unto my son, Antiochus Eupator ;
And unto the good Jews, my
citizens,
In all my towns, say that their
dying monarch
Wisheth them joy, prosperity, and
health.
I who, puffed up with pride and
arrogance,
Thought all the kingdoms of the
earth mine own,
If I would but outstretch my hand
and take them,
Meet face to face a greater poten-
tate,
King Death—Epiphanes—the Il-
lustrious !   [*Dies.*

A Handful of Translations.

THE FUGITIVE.

Tartar Song, from the Prose Version of Chodzko.

I.

'HE is gone to the desert land!
I can see the shining mane
Of his horse on the distant plain,
As he rides with his Kossak band!

'Come back, rebellious one!
Let thy proud heart relent;
Come back to my tall, white tent,
Come back, my only son!

'Thy hand in freedom shall
Cast thy hawks, when morning breaks,
On the swans of the Seven Lakes,
On the lakes of Karajal.

'I will give thee leave to stray
And pasture thy hunting steeds
In the long grass and the reeds
Of the meadows of Karaday.

'I will give thee my coat of mail,
Of softest leather made,
With choicest steel inlaid;
Will not all this prevail?'

II.

'This hand no longer shall
Cast my hawks when morning breaks
On the swans of the Seven Lakes,
On the lakes of Karajal.

'I will no longer stray
And pasture my hunting steeds
In the long grass and the reeds
Of the meadows of Karaday.

'Though thou give me thy coat of mail,
Of softest leather made,
With choicest steel inlaid,
All this cannot prevail.

'What right hast thou, O Khan,
To me, who am mine own,
Who am slave to God alone,
And not to any man?

'God will appoint the day
When I again shall be
By the blue, shallow sea,
Where the steel-bright sturgeons play.

'God, who doth care for me,
In the barren wilderness,
On unknown hills, no less
Will my companion be.

'When I wander lonely and lost
In the wind; when I watch at night
Like a hungry wolf, and am white
And covered with hoar-frost;

'Yea, wheresoever I be,
In the yellow desert sands,
In mountains or unknown lands
Allah will care for me!'

III.

Then Sobra, the old, old man,—
Three hundred and sixty years
Had he lived in this land of tears,
Bowed down and said, 'O Khan!

'If you bid me, I will speak.
There's no sap in dry grass,
No marrow in dry bones! Alas,
The mind of old men is weak!

'I am old, I am very old:
I have seen the primeval man,
I have seen the great Gengis Khan,
Arrayed in his robes of gold.

'What I say to you is the truth;
And I say to you, O Khan,
Pursue not the star-white man,
Pursue not the beautiful youth.

'Him the Almighty made,
And brought him forth of the light,
At the verge and end of the night,
When men on the mountain
prayed.

'He was born at the break of day,
When abroad the angels walk;
He hath listened to their talk,
And he knoweth what they say.

'Gifted with Allah's grace,
Like the moon of Ramazan
When it shines in the skies, O
Khan,
Is the light of his beautiful face.

'When first on earth he trod,
The first words that he said
Were these, as he stood and prayed,
There is no God but God!

'And he shall be king of men,
For Allah hath heard his prayer,
And the Archangel in the air,
Gabriel, hath said, Amen!'

THE SIEGE OF KAZAN.

Tartar Song, from the Prose Version of Chodzko.

BLACK are the moors before Kazan,
And their stagnant waters smell
of blood:
I said in my heart, with horse and
man
I will swim across this shallow
flood.

Under the feet of Argamack,
Like new moons were the shoes
he bare,
Silken trappings hung on his back,
In a talisman on his neck, a
prayer.

My warriors, thought I, are follow-
ing me;
But when I looked behind, alas!
Not one of all the band could I
see,
All had sunk in the black morass!

Where are our shallow fords? and
where
The power of Kazan with its
fourfold gates?
From the prison windows our
maidens fair
Talk of us still through the iron
gates.

We cannot hear them; for horse
and man
Lie buried deep in the dark abyss!
Ah! the black day hath come down
on Kazan!
Ah! was ever a grief like this?

THE BOY AND THE BROOK.

Armenian Popular Song, from the Prose Version of Alishan.

DOWN from yon distant mountain
height
The brooklet flows through the
village street;
A boy comes forth to wash his hands,
Washing, yes washing, there he
stands,
In the water cool and sweet.

Brook, from what mountain dost
thou come?
O my brooklet cool and sweet!

559

I come from yon mountain high
    and cold,
Where lieth the new snow on the old,
    And melts in the summer heat.

Brook, to what river dost thou go?
    O my brooklet cool and sweet!
I go to the river there below
Where in bunches the violets grow,
    And sun and shadow meet.

Brook, to what garden dost thou go?
    O my brooklet cool and sweet!
I go to the garden in the vale
Where all night long the nightingale
    Her love-song doth repeat.

Brook, to what fountain dost thou go?
    O my brooklet cool and sweet!
I go to the fountain at whose brink
The maid that loves thee comes to
    drink,
And whenever she looks therein,
I rise to meet her, and kiss her chin,
    And my joy is then complete.

TO THE STORK.

*Armenian Popular Song, from the
Prose Version of Alishan.*

WELCOME, O Stork! that dost wing
    Thy flight from the far-away!
Thou hast brought us the signs of
    Spring,
Thou hast made our sad hearts gay.

Descend, O Stork! descend
    Upon our roof to rest;
In our ash-tree, O my friend,
    My darling, make thy nest.

To thee, O Stork, I complain,
    O Stork, to thee I impart
The thousand sorrows, the pain
    And aching of my heart.

When thou away didst go,
    Away from this tree of ours,
The withering winds did blow,
    And dried up all the flowers.

Dark grew the brilliant sky,
    Cloudy and dark and drear;
They were breaking the snow on
    high,
    And winter was drawing near.

From Varaca's rocky wall,
    From the rock of Varaca unrolled,
The snow came and covered all,
    And the green meadow was cold.

O Stork, our garden with snow
    Was hidden away and lost,
And the rose-trees that in it grow
    Were withered by snow and frost.

CONSOLATION.

*To M. Duperrier, Gentleman of
Aix in Provence, on the Death of
his Daughter.*

FROM MALHERBE.

WILL then, Duperrier, thy sorrow
    be eternal?
And shall the sad discourse
Whispered within thy heart, by
    tenderness paternal,
    Only augment its force?

Thy daughter's mournful fate, into
    the tomb descending
By death's frequented ways,
Has it become to thee a labyrinth
    never ending,
    Where thy lost reason strays?

I know the charms that made her
    youth a benediction:
    Nor should I be content,
As a censorious friend, to solace
    thine affliction
    By her disparagement.

But she was of the world, which
    fairest things exposes
    To fates the most forlorn;
A rose, she too hath lived as long as
    live the roses,
    The space of one brief morn.

    *   *   *   *

Death has his rigorous laws, un-
    paralleled, unfeeling ;
All prayers to him are vain ;
Cruel, he stops his ears, and, deaf
    to our appealing,
He leaves us to complain.

The poor man in his hut, only thatch
    for cover,
Unto these laws must bend ;
The sentinel that guards the barriers
    of the Louvre
Cannot our kings defend.

To murmur against death, in petu-
    lant defiance,
Is never for the best ;
To will what God doth will, that is
    the only science
That gives us any rest.

TO CARDINAL RICHELIEU.

FROM MALHERBE.

Thou mighty Prince of Church and
    State,
Richelieu ! until the hour of death,
Whatever road man chooses, Fate
Still holds him subject to her breath.
Spun of all silks, our days and nights
Have sorrows woven with delights ;
And of this intermingled shade
Our various destiny appears,
Even as one sees the course of years
Of summers and of winters made.

Sometimes the soft, deceitful hours
Let us enjoy the halcyon wave ;
Sometimes impending peril lowers
Beyond the seaman's skill to save.
The Wisdom, infinitely wise,
That gives to human destinies
Their foreordained necessity,
Has made no law more fixed below
Than the alternate ebb and flow
Of Fortune and Adversity.

THE ANGEL AND THE CHILD.

FROM JEAN REBOUL, THE BAKER OF NISMES.

An angel with a radiant face,
    Above a cradle bent to look,
Seemed his own image there to trace,
    As in the waters of a brook.

'Dear child ! who me resemblest so,'
    It whispered, ' come, O come
    with me !
Happy together let us go,
    The earth unworthy is of thee !

' Here none to perfect bliss attain ;
    The soul in pleasure suffering lies ;
Joy hath an undertone of pain,
    And even the happiest hours
    their sighs.

' Fear doth at every portal knock ;
    Never a day serene and pure
From the o'ershadowing tempest's
    shock
    Hath made the morrow's dawn
    secure.

' What, then, shall sorrows and
    shall fears
    Come to disturb so pure a brow ?
And with the bitterness of tears
    These eyes of azure troubled
    grow ?

' Ah no ! into the fields of space,
    Away shalt thou escape with me ;
And Providence will grant thee
    grace
    Of all the days that were to be.

' Let no one in thy dwelling cower
    In sombre vestments draped and
    veiled ;
But let them welcome thy last hour
    As thy first moments once they
    hailed.

'Without a cloud be there each
    brow;
  There let the grave no shadow
    cast;
When one is pure as thou art now
  The fairest day is still the last.'

And waving wide his wings of white,
  The angel, at these words, had
    sped
Towards the eternal realms of
    light!—
Poor mother! see, thy son is dead!

TO ITALY.

FROM FILICAJA.

ITALY! Italy! thou who 'rt doomed
    to wear
  The fatal gift of beauty, and
    possess
  The dower funest of infinite
    wretchedness
  Written upon thy forehead by
    despair;
Ah! would that thou wert stronger,
    or less fair,
  That they might fear thee more,
    or love thee less,
  Who in the splendour of thy love-
    liness
  Seem wasting, yet to mortal
    combat dare!
Then from the Alps I should not
    see descending
  Such torrents of armed men, nor
    Gallic horde
  Drinking the wave of Po, dis-
    tained with gore,
Nor should I see thee girded with
    a sword
  Not thine, and with the stranger's
    arm contending,
  Victor or vanquished, slave for
    evermore

WANDERER'S NIGHT-SONGS.

FROM GOETHE.

I.

THOU that from the heavens art,
Every pain and sorrow stillest,
And the doubly wretched heart
Doubly with refreshment fillest,
I am weary with contending!
Why this rapture and unrest?
Peace descending
Come, ah, come into my breast!

II.

O'er all the hill-tops
Is quiet now,
In all the tree-tops
Hearest thou
Hardly a breath;
The birds are asleep in the trees:
Wait; soon like these
Thou too shalt rest.

REMORSE.

FROM AUGUST VON PLATEN.

HOW I started up in the night, in
    the night,
  Drawn on without rest or re-
    prieval!
The streets, with their watchmen,
    were lost to my sight,
  As I wandered so light
  In the night, in the night,
Through the gate with the arch
    mediaeval.

The mill-brook rushed from the
    rocky height,
  I leaned o'er the bridge in my
    yearning;
Deep under me watched I the
    waves in their flight,
  As they glided so light
  In the night, in the night,
Yet backward not one was returning.

O'erhead were revolving, so count-
　　less and bright,
　The stars in melodious existence ;
And with them the moon, more
　　serenely bedight ;—
　They sparkled so light
　In the night, in the night,
Through the magical, measureless
　　distance.

And upward I gazed in the night,
　　in the night,
　And again on the waves in their
　　fleeting ;
Ah woe ! thou hast wasted thy
　　days in delight,
　Now silence thou light,
　In the night, in the night,
The remorse in thy heart that is
　　beating.

SANTA TERESA'S BOOK-MARK.

FROM THE SPANISH OF SANTA
TERESA.

　LET nothing disturb thee,
　Nothing affright thee ;
　All things are passing ;
　God never changeth ;
　Patient endurance
　Attaineth to all things ;
　Who God possesseth
　In nothing is wanting ;
　Alone God sufficeth.

The New-England Tragedies.

I. JOHN ENDICOTT.

DRAMATIS PERSONÆ.

JOHN ENDICOTT	.	Governor.
JOHN ENDICOTT	.	His son.
RICHARD BELLINGHAM	.	Deputy Governor.
JOHN NORTON	.	Minister of the Gospel.
EDWARD BUTTER	.	Treasurer.
WALTER MERRY	.	Tithing-man.
NICHOLAS UPSALL	.	An old citizen.
SAMUEL COLE	.	Landlord of the Three Mariners.
SIMON KEMPTHORN } RALPH GOLDSMITH }	.	Sea-Captains.
WENLOCK CHRISTISON } EDITH, his daughter } EDWARD WHARTON }	.	Quakers.

Assistants, Halberdiers, Marshal, &c.

The Scene is in Boston in the year 1665.

PROLOGUE.

TO-NIGHT we strive to read, as we
may best,
This city, like an ancient palimpsest;
And bring to light, upon the blotted
page,
The mournful record of an earlier
age,
That, pale and half effaced, lies
hidden away
Beneath the fresher writing of to-
day.

Rise, then, O buried city that
hast been;
Rise up, rebuilded in the painted
scene,
And let our curious eyes behold
once more

The pointed gable and the pent-
house door,
The Meeting-house with leaden-
latticed panes,
The narrow thoroughfares, the
crooked lanes!

Rise, too, ye shapes and shadows
of the Past,
Rise from your long-forgotten
graves at last;
Let us behold your faces, let us hear
The words ye uttered in those days
of fear!
Revisit your familiar haunts again—
The scenes of triumph, and the
scenes of pain,
And leave the footprints of your
bleeding feet
Once more upon the pavement of
the street!

Nor let the Historian blame the Poet here,
If he perchance misdate the day or year,
And group events together, by his art,
That in the Chronicles lie far apart;
For as the double stars, though sundered far,
Seem to the naked eye a single star,
So facts of history, at a distance seen,
Into one common point of light convene.
' Why touch upon such themes?' perhaps some friend
May ask, incredulous; ' and to what good end?
Why drag again into the light of day
The errors of an age long passed away?'
I answer: ' For the lesson that they teach;
The tolerance of opinion and of speech.

Hope, Faith, and Charity remain,—these three;
And greatest of them all is Charity.'
Let us remember, if these words be true,
That unto all men Charity is due;
Give what we ask; and pity, while we blame,
Lest we become copartners in the shame,—
Lest we condemn, and yet ourselves partake,
And persecute the dead for conscience' sake.
Therefore it is the author seeks and strives
To represent the dead as in their lives,
And lets at times his characters unfold
Their thoughts in their own language, strong and bold:
He only asks of you to do the like;
To hear him first, and, if you will, then strike.

ACT I.

SCENE I.—*Sunday afternoon. The interior of the Meeting-house. On the pulpit, an hour-glass; below, a box for contributions.* JOHN NORTON *in the pulpit.* GOVERNOR ENDICOTT *in a canopied seat, attended by four halberdiers. The congregation singing.*

The Lord descended from above,
    And bowed the heavens high;
And underneath his feet he cast
    The darkness of the sky.

On Cherubim and Seraphim
    Right royally he rode,
And on the wings of mighty winds
    Came flying all abroad.

Norton (rising, and turning the hourglass on the pulpit). I heard a great voice from the temple saying
Unto the Seven Angels, Go your ways;
Pour out the vials of the wrath of God
Upon the earth. And the first Angel went
And poured his vial on the earth; and straight
There fell a noisome and a grievous sore
On them which had the birth-mark of the Beast,
And them which worshipped and adored his image.

On us hath fallen this grievous
    pestilence.
There is a sense of horror in the air ;
And apparitions of things horrible
Are seen by many. From the sky
    above us
The stars fall ; and beneath us the
    earth quakes !
The sound of drums at midnight in
    the air,
The sound of horsemen riding to
    and fro,
As if the gates of the invisible world
Were opened, and the dead came
    forth to warn us,—
All these are omens of some dire
    disaster
Impending over us, and soon to
    fall.
Moreover, in the language of the
    Prophet,
Death is again come up into our
    windows,
To cut off little children from with-
    out,
And young men from the streets.
    And in the midst
Of all these supernatural threats
    and warnings
Doth Heresy uplift its horrid head ;
A vision of Sin more awful and
    appalling
Than any phantasm, ghost, or
    apparition,
As arguing and portending some
    enlargement
Of the mysterious Power of Dark-
    ness !

(EDITH, *barefooted, and clad in
sackcloth, with her hair hanging
loose upon her shoulders, walks
slowly up the aisle, followed by*
WHARTON *and other Quakers.
The congregation starts up in
confusion.*)

    Edith (*to Norton, raising her
    hand*). Peace !

Norton. Anathema maranatha !
    The Lord cometh !
    Edith. Yea, verily he cometh,
    and shall judge
The shepherds of Israel, who do
    feed themselves,
And leave their flocks to eat what
    they have trodden
Beneath their feet.
    Norton.   Be silent, babbling
    woman !
St. Paul commands all women to
    keep silence
Within the churches.
    Edith.   Yet the women prayed
And prophesied at Corinth in his
    day ;
And, among those on whom the
    fiery tongues
Of Pentecost descended, some
    were women !
    Norton. The Elders of the
    Churches, by our law,
Alone have power to open the doors
    of speech
And silence in the Assembly. I
    command you !
    Edith. The law of God is greater
    than your laws !
Ye build your church with blood,
    your town with crime ;
The heads thereof give judgment
    for reward ;
The priests thereof teach only for
    their hire ;
Your laws condemn the innocent
    to death ;
And against this I bear my testi-
    mony.
    Norton. What testimony ?
    Edith.   That of the
    Holy Spirit,
Which, as your Calvin says, sur-
    passeth reason.
    Norton. The labourer is worthy
    of his hire.
    Edith. Yet our great Master
    did not teach for hire,

And the Apostles without purse or
scrip
Went forth to do his work. Behold
this box
Beneath thy pulpit. Is it for the
poor ?
Thou canst not answer. It is for
the Priest ;
And against this I bear my testimony.

Norton. Away with all these
Heretics and Quakers !
Quakers, forsooth ! Because a
quaking fell
On Daniel, at beholding of the
Vision,
Must ye needs shake and quake ?
Because Isaiah
Went stripped and barefoot, must
ye wail and howl ?
Must ye go stripped and naked ?
must ye make
A wailing like the dragons, and a
mourning
As of the owls ? Ye verify the adage
That Satan is God's ape ! Away
with them !

(*Tumult. The Quakers are driven
out with violence*, EDITH *following slowly. The congregation retires in confusion.*)

Thus freely do the Reprobates
commit
Such measure of iniquity as fits
them
For the intended measure of God's
wrath,
And even in violating God's com-
mands
Are they fulfilling the divine de-
cree !
The will of man is but an instru-
ment
Disposed and predetermined to its
action
According unto the decree of God,
Being as much subordinate thereto
As is the axe unto the hewer's hand !

(*He descends from the pulpit, and
joins* GOVERNOR ENDICOTT,
who comes forward to meet him.)

The omens and the wonders of the
time,
Famine, and fire, and shipwreck,
and disease,
The blast of corn, the death of our
young men,
Our sufferings in all precious, plea-
sant things,
Are manifestations of the wrath
divine,
Signs of God's controversy with
New England.
These emissaries of the Evil One,
These servants and ambassadors
of Satan,
Are but commissioned executioners
Of God's vindictive and deserved
displeasure.
We must receive them as the
Roman Bishop
Once received Attila, saying, I
rejoice
You have come safe, whom I esteem
to be
The scourge of God, sent to chas-
tise his people.
This very heresy, perchance, may
serve
The purposes of God to some good
end.
With you I leave it ; but do not
neglect
The holy tactics of the civil sword.

Endicott. And what more can be
done ?

Norton.   The hand that cut
The Red Cross from the colours of
the king
Can cut the red heart from this
heresy.
Fear not. All blasphemies imme-
diate
And heresies turbulent must be
suppressed
By civil power.

Endicott. But in what way suppressed?

Norton. The Book of Deuteronomy declares
That if thy son, thy daughter, or thy wife,
Ay, or the friend which is as thine own soul,
Entice thee secretly, and say to thee,
Let us serve other gods, then shall thine eye
Not pity him, but thou shalt surely kill him,
And thine own hand shall be the first upon him
To slay him.

Endicott. Four already have been slain ;
And others banished upon pain of death.
But they come back again to meet their doom,
Bringing the linen for their winding-sheets.
We must not go too far. In truth, I shrink
From shedding of more blood. The people murmur
At our severity.

Norton. Then let them murmur !
Truth is relentless ! justice never wavers ;
The greatest firmness is the greatest mercy ;
The noble order of the Magistracy
Cometh immediately from God, and yet
This noble order of the Magistracy
Is by these Heretics despised and outraged.

Endicott. To-night they sleep in prison. If they die,
They cannot say that we have caused their death.
We do but guard the passage, with the sword
Pointed towards them ; if they dash upon it,

Their blood will be on their own heads, not ours.

Norton. Enough, I ask no more.
My predecessor
Coped only with the milder heresies
Of Antinomians and of Anabaptists. He was not born to wrestle with these fiends.
Chrysostom in his pulpit ; Augustine
In disputation ; Timothy in his house !
The lantern of St. Botolph's ceased to burn
When from the portals of that church he came
To be a burning and a shining light
Here in the wilderness. And, as he lay
On his death-bed, he saw me in a vision
Ride on a snow-white horse into this town.
His vision was prophetic ; thus I came,
A terror to the impenitent, and Death
On the pale horse of the Apocalypse
To all the accursed race of Heretics !   [*Exeunt.*

SCENE II. — *A street. On one side,* NICHOLAS UPSALL'S *house ; on the other,* WALTER MERRY'S, *with a flock of pigeons on the roof.* UPSALL *seated in the porch of his house.*

Upsall. O day of rest ! How beautiful, how fair,
How welcome to the weary and the old !
Day of the Lord ! and truce to earthly cares !
Day of the Lord, as all our days should be !
Ah, why will man by his austerities

Shut out the blessed sunshine and
the light,
And make of thee a dungeon of
despair!

*Walter Merry (entering, and
looking around him).* All silent
as a graveyard! No one stirring;
No footfall in the street, no sound
of voices!
By righteous punishment and perseverance,
And perseverance in that punishment
At last I've brought this contumacious town
To strict observance of the Sabbath
day.
Those wanton gospellers, the
pigeons yonder,
Are now the only Sabbath-breakers
left.
I cannot put them down. As if to
taunt me,
They gather every Sabbath afternoon
In noisy congregation on my roof,
Billing and cooing. Whir! take
that, ye Quakers.

*(Throws a stone at the pigeons.
Sees* UPSALL.*)*

Ah! Master Nicholas!
Upsall. Good afternoon,
Dear neighbour Walter.
Merry. Master Nicholas,
You have to-day withdrawn your-
self from meeting.
Upsall. Yea, I have chosen rather
to worship God
Sitting in silence here at my own
door.
Merry. Worship the Devil! You
this day have broken
Three of our strictest laws. First,
by abstaining
From public worship. Secondly,
by walking
Profanely on the Sabbath.

Upsall. Not one step.
I have been sitting still here, seeing
the pigeons
Feed in the street and fly about the
roofs.
Merry. You have been in the
street with other intent
Than going to and from the Meet-
ing-house.
And, thirdly, you are harbouring
Quakers here.
I am amazed!
Upsall. Men sometimes, it is said,
Entertain angels unawares.
Merry. Nice angels!
Angels in broad-brimmed hats and
russet cloaks,
The colour of the Devil's nutting-
bag! They came
Into the Meeting-house this after-
noon
More in the shape of devils than of
angels;
The women screamed and fainted;
and the boys
Made such an uproar in the gallery
I could not keep them quiet.
Upsall. Neighbour Walter,
Your persecution is of no avail.
Merry. 'Tis prosecution, as the
Governor says,
Not persecution.
Upsall. Well, your prosecution;
Your hangings do no good.
Merry. The reason is,
We do not hang enough. But, mark
my words,
We'll scour them; yea, I warrant
ye, we'll scour them!
And now go in and entertain your
angels,
And don't be seen here in the street
again
Till after sundown! — There they
are again!

(Exit UPSALL. MERRY *throws
another stone at the pigeons, and
then goes into his house.)*

SCENE III. — *A room in* UPSALL'S *house. Night.* EDITH WHARTON, *and other Quakers, seated at a table.* UPSALL *seated near them. Several books on the table.*

Wharton. William and Marmaduke, our martyred brothers,
Sleep in untimely graves, if aught untimely
Can find place in the providence of God,
Where nothing comes too early or too late.
I saw their noble death. They to the scaffold
Walked hand in hand. Two hundred armed men
And many horsemen guarded them, for fear
Of rescue by the crowd, whose hearts were stirred.
Edith. O holy martyrs!
Wharton. When they tried to speak,
Their voices by the roll of drums were drowned.
When they were dead they still looked fresh and fair,
The terror of death was not upon their faces.
Our sister Mary, likewise, the meek woman,
Has passed through martyrdom to her reward;
Exclaiming, as they led her to her death,
'These many days I 've been in Paradise.'
And, when she died, Priest Wilson threw the hangman
His handkerchief, to cover the pale face
He dared not look upon.
Edith. As persecuted,
Yet not forsaken; as unknown, yet known;
As dying, and behold we are alive;

As sorrowful, and yet rejoicing alway;
As having nothing, yet possessing all!
Wharton. And Leddra, too, is dead. But from his prison,
The day before his death, he sent these words
Unto the little flock of Christ:
'Whatever
May come upon the followers of the Light,—
Distress, affliction, famine, nakedness,
Or perils in the city or the sea,
Or persecution, or even death itself,—
I am persuaded that God's armour of Light,
As it is loved and lived in, will preserve you.
Yea, death itself; through which you will find entrance
Into the pleasant pastures of the fold,
Where you shall feed for ever as the herds
That roam at large in the low valleys of Achor.
And as the flowing of the ocean fills
Each creek and branch thereof, and then retires,
Leaving behind a sweet and wholesome savour;
So doth the virtue and the life of God
Flow evermore into the hearts of those
Whom he hath made partakers of his nature;
And, when it but withdraws itself a little,
Leaves a sweet savour after it, that many
Can say they are made clean by every word
That he hath spoken to them in their silence.'

Edith (*rising, and breaking into a kind of chant*). Truly, we do but grope here in the dark,

Near the partition-wall of Life and Death,

At every moment dreading or desiring

To lay our hands upon the unseen door!

Let us, then, labour for an inward stillness,—

An inward stillness and an inward healing;

That perfect silence where the lips and heart

Are still, and we no longer entertain

Our own imperfect thoughts and vain opinions,

But God alone speaks in us, and we wait

In singleness of heart, that we may know

His will, and in the silence of our spirits,

That we may do His will, and do that only!

(*A long pause, interrupted by the sound of a drum approaching; then shouts in the street, and a loud knocking at the door.*)

Marshal. Within there! Open the door!

Merry. Will no one answer?

Marshal. In the King's name! Within there!

Merry. Open the door!

Upsall (*from the window*). It is not barred. Come in. Nothing prevents you.

The poor man's door is ever on the latch.

He needs no bolt nor bar to shut out thieves;

He fears no enemies, and has no friends

Importunate enough to turn the key upon them!

(*Enter* JOHN ENDICOTT, *the* MARSHAL, MERRY, *and a crowd. Seeing the Quakers silent and unmoved, they pause, awe-struck,* ENDICOTT *opposite* EDITH.)

Marshal. In the King's name do I arrest you all!

Away with them to prison. Master Upsall,

You are again discovered harbouring here

These ranters and disturbers of the peace.

You know the law.

Upsall. I know it, and am ready

To suffer yet again its penalties.

Edith (*to Endicott*). Why dost thou persecute me, Saul of Tarsus?

ACT II.

SCENE I.—JOHN ENDICOTT'S *room. Early morning.*

John Endicott. 'Why dost thou persecute me, Saul of Tarsus?'

All night these words were ringing in mine ears!

A sorrowful sweet face; a look that pierced me

With meek reproach; a voice of resignation

That had a life of suffering in its tone;

And that was all! And yet I could not sleep,

Or, when I slept, I dreamed that awful dream!

I stood beneath the elm-tree on the Common

On which the Quakers have been hanged, and heard

A voice, not hers, that cried amid the darkness,

'This is Aceldama, the field of
  blood!
I will have mercy, and not sacrifice!'

(*Opens the window, and looks out.*)

The sun is up already; and my heart
Sickens and sinks within me when
  I think
How many tragedies will be enacted
Before his setting. As the earth rolls
  round,
It seems to me a huge Ixion's wheel,
Upon whose whirling spokes we are
  bound fast,
And must go with it! Ah, how
  bright the sun
Strikes on the sea and on the masts
  of vessels,
That are uplifted in the morning air,
Like crosses of some peaceable
  crusade!
It makes me long to sail for lands
  unknown,
No matter whither! Under me,
  in shadow,
Gloomy and narrow lies the little
  town,
Still sleeping, but to wake and toil
  awhile,
Then sleep again. How dismal looks
  the prison,
How grim and sombre in the sunless
  street,—
The prison where she sleeps, or
  wakes and waits
For what I dare not think of,—
  death, perhaps!
A word that has been said may be
  unsaid.
It is but air. But when a deed is done
It cannot be undone, nor can our
  thoughts
Reach out to all the mischiefs that
  may follow.
'Tis time for morning prayers. I
  will go down.
My father, though severe, is kind
  and just;

And when his heart is tender with
  devotion,—
When from his lips have fallen the
  words 'Forgive us
As we forgive,'—then will I intercede
For these poor people, and perhaps
  may save them.   [*Exit.*

SCENE II.—*Dock Square. On one
  side, the tavern of the Three
  Mariners. In the background,
  a quaint building with gables;
  and, beyond it, wharves and
  shipping.* CAPTAIN KEMPTHORN
  *and others seated at a table before
  the door.* SAMUEL COLE *standing near them.*

Kempthorn. Come, drink about!
  Remember Parson Melham,
And bless the man who first in-
  vented flip!

(*They drink.*)

Cole. Pray, Master Kempthorn,
  where were you last night?
Kempthorn.   On board the
  Swallow, Simon Kempthorn,
  master,
Up for Barbadoes, and the Wind-
  ward Islands.
Cole. The town was in a tumult.
Kempthorn.   And for what?
Cole. Your Quakers were arrested.
Kempthorn. How my Quakers?
Cole. Those you brought in your
  vessel from Barbadoes.
They made an uproar in the Meet-
  ing-house
Yesterday, and they're now in
  prison for it.
I owe you little thanks for bringing
  them
To the Three Mariners.
Kempthorn.   They have not
  harmed you.

572

I tell you, Goodman Cole, that
    Quaker girl
Is precious as a sea-bream's eye. I
    tell you
It was a lucky day when first she set
Her little foot upon the Swallow's
    deck,
Bringing good luck, fair winds, and
    pleasant weather.
    Cole. I am a law-abiding citizen;
I have a seat in the new Meeting-
    house,
A cow-right on the Common; and,
    besides,
Am corporal in the Great Artillery.
I rid me of the vagabonds at once.
    Kempthorn. Why should you not
have Quakers at your tavern
If you have fiddlers?
    Cole. Never! never! never!
If you want fiddling you must go
    elsewhere,
To the Green Dragon and the
    Admiral Vernon,
And other such disreputable places.
But the Three Mariners is an
    orderly house,
Most orderly, quiet, and respect-
    able.
Lord Leigh said he could be as quiet
    here
As at the Governor's. And have I
    not
King Charles's Twelve Good Rules,
    all framed and glazed,
Hanging in my best parlour?
    Kempthorn. Here's a health
To good King Charles. Will you
    not drink the King?
Then drink confusion to old Parson
    Palmer.
    Cole. And who is Parson Palmer?
I don't know him.
    Kempthorn. He had his cellar
underneath his pulpit,
And so preached o'er his liquor, just
    as you do.
        (*A drum within.*)

    Cole. Here comes the Marshal.
    Merry (*within*).   Make room
    for the Marshal.
    Kempthorn. How pompous and
    imposing he appears;
His great buff doublet bellying like
    a mainsail,
And all his streamers fluttering in
    the wind.
What holds he in his hand?
    Cole.   A Proclamation.

(*Enter the* MARSHAL, *with a pro-
    clamation; and* MERRY, *with
    a halberd. They are preceded by
    a drummer, and followed by the
    hangman, with an armful of
    books, and a crowd of people,
    among whom are* UPSALL *and*
    JOHN ENDICOTT. *A pile is made
    of the books.*)

    Merry. Silence the drum! Good
    citizens, attend
To the new laws enacted by the
    Court.
    Marshal (*reads*). 'Whereas a
    cursed sect of Heretics
Has lately risen, commonly called
    Quakers,
Who take upon themselves to be
    commissioned
Immediately of God, and further-
    more
Infallibly assisted by the Spirit
To write and utter blasphemous
    opinions,
Despising Government and the
    order of God
In Church and Commonwealth,
    and speaking evil
Of Dignities, reproaching and
    reviling
The Magistrates and Ministers, and
    seeking
To turn the people from their faith,
    and thus
Gain proselytes to their pernicious
    ways;—

This Court, considering the premises,
And to prevent like mischief as is wrought
By their means in our land, doth hereby order,
That whatsoever master or commander
Of any ship, bark, pink, or catch shall bring
To any roadstead, harbour, creek, or cove
Within this Jurisdiction any Quakers,
Or other blasphemous Heretics, shall pay
Unto the Treasurer of the Commonwealth
One hundred pounds, and for default thereof
Be put in prison, and continue there
Till the said sum be satisfied and paid.'

Cole. Now, Simon Kempthorn, what say you to that?

Kempthorn. I pray you, Cole, lend me a hundred pound!

Marshal (*reads*). ' If any one within this Jurisdiction
Shall henceforth entertain, or shall conceal,
Quakers, or other blasphemous Heretics,
Knowing them so to be, every such person
Shall forfeit to the country forty shillings
For each hour's entertainment or concealment,
And shall be sent to prison, as aforesaid,
Until the forfeiture be wholly paid.'

(*Murmurs in the crowd.*)

Kempthorn. Now, Goodman Cole, I think your turn has come!

Cole. Knowing them so to be!

Kempthorn. At forty shillings
The hour, your fine will be some forty pound !

Cole. Knowing them so to be! That is the law.

Marshal (*reads*). 'And it is further ordered and enacted,
If any Quaker or Quakers shall presume
To come henceforth into this Jurisdiction,
Every male Quaker for the first offence
Shall have one ear cut off; and shall be kept
At labour in the Workhouse, till such time
As he be sent away at his own charge.
And for the repetition of the offence
Shall have his other ear cut off, and then
Be branded in the palm of his right hand.
And every woman Quaker shall be whipt
Severely in three towns ; and every Quaker,
Or he or she, that shall for a third time
Herein again offend, shall have their tongues
Bored through with a hot iron, and shall be
Sentenced to Banishment on pain of Death.'

(*Loud murmurs. The voice of* CHRISTISON *in the crowd.*
O patience of the Lord ! How long, how long,
Ere Thou avenge the blood of Thine Elect ?*)

Merry. Silence, there, silence ! Do not break the peace !

Marshal (*reads*). 'Every inhabitant of this Jurisdiction
Who shall defend the horrible opinions

Of Quakers, by denying due respect
To equals and superiors, and with-
    drawing
From Church Assemblies, and
    thereby approving
The abusive and destructive prac-
    tices
Of this accursed sect, in opposition
To all the orthodox received opin-
    ions
Of godly men, shall be forthwith
    committed
Unto close prison for one month;
    and then
Refusing to retract and to reform
The opinions as aforesaid, he shall
    be
Sentenced to Banishment on pain
    of Death.
By the Court. Edward Rawson,
    Secretary.'
Now, hangman, do your duty. Burn
    those books.

(*Loud murmurs in the crowd. The
    pile of books is lighted.*)

  Upsall. I testify against these
    cruel laws !
Forerunners are they of some judg-
    ment on us ;
And, in the love and tenderness I
    bear
Unto this town and people, I be-
    seech you,
O Magistrates, take heed, lest ye be
    found
As fighters against God !
  John Endicott (*taking Upsall's
    hand*). Upsall, I thank you
For speaking words such as some
    younger man,
I or another, should have said before
    you.
Such laws as these are cruel and
    oppressive ;
A blot on this fair town, and a dis-
    grace
To any Christian people.

  Merry (*aside, listening behind
    them*). Here 's sedition !
I never thought that any good would
    come
Of this young popinjay, with his long
    hair
And his great boots, fit only for the
    Russians
Or barbarous Indians, as his father
    says !
  The Voice. Woe to the bloody
    town ! And rightfully
Men call it the Lost Town ! The
    blood of Abel
Cries from the ground, and at the
    final judgment
The Lord will say, ' Cain, Cain !
    where is thy brother ? '
  Merry. Silence there in the
    crowd !
  Upsall (*aside*). 'Tis Christison !
  The Voice. O foolish people, ye
    that think to burn
And to consume the truth of God,
    I tell you
That every flame is a loud tongue of
    fire
To publish it abroad to all the world
Louder than tongues of men !
  Kempthorn (*springing to his feet*).
    Well said, my hearty !
There 's a brave fellow ! There 's a
    man of pluck !
A man who 's not afraid to say his
    say,
Though a whole town 's against him.
    Rain, rain, rain,
Bones of St. Botolph, and put out
    this fire !

(*The drum beats. Exeunt all but*
MERRY, KEMPTHORN, *and* COLE.)

  Merry. And now that matter 's
    ended, Goodman Cole,
Fetch me a mug of ale, your
    strongest ale.
  Kempthorn (*sitting down*). And
    me another mug of flip ; and put

Two gills of brandy in it. [*Exit Cole.*
Merry.   No; no more.
Not a drop more, I say. You've
  had enough.
Kempthorn. And who are you, sir?
Merry.   I'm a Tithing-man,
And Merry is my name.
Kempthorn.   A merry name!
I like it; and I'll drink your merry
  health
Till all is blue.
Merry. And then you will be
  clapped
Into the stocks, with the red letter D
Hung round about your neck for
  drunkenness.
You're a free-drinker,—yes, and a
  free-thinker!
Kempthorn. And you are Andrew
  Merry, or Merry Andrew.
Merry. My name is Walter
  Merry, and not Andrew.
Kempthorn. Andrew or Walter,
  you're a merry fellow;
I'll swear to that.
Merry. No swearing, let me tell
  you.
The other day one Shorthose had
  his tongue
Put into a cleft stick for profane
  swearing.

(COLE *brings the ale.*)

Kempthorn. Well, where's my
  flip? As sure as my name's
  Kempthorn—
Merry. Is your name Kempthorn?
Kempthorn. That's the name I
  go by.
Merry. What, Captain Simon
  Kempthorn of the Swallow?
Kempthorn. No other.
Merry (*touching him on the
  shoulder*). Then you're want-
  ed. I arrest you
In the King's name.
Kempthorn. And where's your
  warrant?

Merry (*unfolding a paper, and
  reading*). Here.
Listen to me. 'Hereby you are
  required,
In the King's name, to apprehend
  the body
Of Simon Kempthorn, mariner, and
  him
Safely to bring before me, there to
  answer
All such objections as are laid to him,
Touching the Quakers.' Signed,
  John Endicott.
Kempthorn.   Has it the Gover-
  nor's seal?
Merry.   Ay, here it is.
Kempthorn. Death's head and
  crossbones. That's a pirate's
  flag!
Merry. Beware how you revile
  the Magistrates;
You may be whipped for that.
Kempthorn.   Then mum's
  the word.

(*Exeunt* MERRY *and* KEMP-
  THORN.)

Cole. There's mischief brewing!
  Sure, there's mischief brewing!
I feel like Master Josselyn when he
  found
The hornets' nest, and thought it
  some strange fruit,
Until the seeds came out, and then
  he dropped it.   [*Exit.*

———

SCENE III.—*A room in the Governor's house. Enter* GOVERNOR
ENDICOTT *and* MERRY.

Endicott. My son, you say?
Merry.   Your Worship's
  eldest son.
Endicott. Speaking against the
  laws?
Merry.   Ay, worshipful sir.
Endicott. And in the public
  market-place?

Merry. I saw him
With my own eyes, heard him with
my own ears.

Endicott. Impossible!

Merry. He stood
there in the crowd
With Nicholas Upsall, when the
laws were read
To-day against the Quakers, and I
heard him
Denounce and vilipend them as
unjust,
As cruel, wicked, and abominable.

Endicott. Ungrateful son! O
God! thou layest upon me
A burden heavier than I can
bear!
Surely the power of Satan must be
great
Upon the earth, if even the elect
Are thus deceived and fall away
from grace!

Merry. Worshipful sir! I meant
no harm—

Endicott. 'Tis well.
You've done your duty, though
you've done it roughly,
And every word you've uttered since
you came
Has stabbed me to the heart!

Merry. I do beseech
Your Worship's pardon!

Endicott. He whom I
have nurtured
And brought up in the reverence
of the Lord!
The child of all my hopes and my
affections!
He upon whom I leaned as a sure
staff
For my old age! It is God's chas-
tisement
For leaning upon any arm but His!

Merry. Your Worship!—

Endicott. And this comes from
holding parley
With the delusions and deceits of
Satan.

At once, for ever, must they be
crushed out,
Or all the land will reek with
heresy!
Pray, have you any children?

Merry. No, not any.

Endicott. Thank God for that.
He has delivered you
From a great care. Enough; my
private griefs
Too long have kept me from the
public service.

(*Exit* MERRY. ENDICOTT *seats
himself at the table and arranges
his papers.*)

The hour has come; and I am
eager now
To sit in judgment on these Heretics.

(*A knock.*)

Come in. Who is it? (*Not looking
up.*)

John Endicott. It is I.

Endicott (*restraining himself*).
Sit down!

John Endicott (*sitting down*). I
come to intercede for these
poor people
Who are in prison, and await their
trial.

Endicott. It is of them I wish to
speak with you.
I have been angry with you, but
'tis passed.
For when I hear your footsteps
come or go,
See in your features your dead
mother's face,
And in your voice detect some tone
of hers,
All anger vanishes, and I remember
The days that are no more, and
come no more,
When as a child you sat upon my
knee,
And prattled of your playthings,
and the games

577

You played among the pear-trees
in the orchard !
John Endicott. O, let the memory
of my noble mother
Plead with you to be mild and
merciful !
For mercy more becomes a Magistrate
Than the vindictive wrath which
men call justice !
Endicott. The sin of heresy is a
deadly sin.
'Tis like the falling of the snow,
whose crystals
The traveller plays with, thoughtless of his danger,
Until he sees the air so full of
light
That it is dark ; and blindly staggering onward,
Lost, and bewildered, he sits down
to rest ;
There falls a pleasant drowsiness
upon him,
And what he thinks is sleep, alas !
is death.
John Endicott. And yet who is
there that has never doubted ?
And, doubting and believing, has
not said,
' Lord, I believe ; help thou mine
unbelief ' ?
Endicott. In the same way we
trifle with our doubts,
Whose shining shapes are like the
stars descending ;
Until at last, bewildered and dismayed,
Blinded by that which seemed to
give us light,
We sink to sleep, and find that it
is death,— *(rising)*
Death to the soul through all eternity !
Alas that I should see you growing
up
To man's estate, and in the admonition

And nurture of the Law, to find
you now
Pleading for Heretics !
John Endicott (rising). In the
sight of God,
Perhaps all men are Heretics. Who
dares
To say that he alone has found the
truth ?
We cannot always feel and think
and act
As those who go before us. Had
you done so,
You would not now be here.
Endicott. Have
you forgotten
The doom of Heretics, and the fate
of those
Who aid and comfort them ? Have
you forgotten
That in the market-place this very
day
You trampled on the laws ? What
right have you,
An inexperienced and untravelled
youth,
To sit in judgment here upon the
acts
Of older men and wiser than your-
self,
Thus stirring up sedition in the
streets,
And making me a byword and a
jest ?
John Endicott. Words of an in-
experienced youth like me
Were powerless if the acts of older
men
Went not before them. 'Tis these
laws themselves
Stir up sedition, not my judgment
of them.
Endicott. Take heed, lest I be
called, like Brutus was,
To be the judge of my own son !
Begone !
When you are tired of feeding upon
husks,

Return again to duty and submission,
But not till then.

   John Endicott. I hear and I
     obey!   [*Exit.*
   Endicott. O happy, happy they
     who have no children!

He's gone! I hear the hall door
   shut behind him.
It sends a dismal echo through my
   heart,
As if for ever it had closed between
   us,

And I should look upon his face
   no more!
O, this will drag me down into my
   grave,—
To that eternal resting-place
   wherein
Man lieth down, and riseth not again!
Till the heavens be no more he
   shall not wake,
Nor be roused from his sleep; for
   Thou dost change
His countenance, and sendest him
   away!   [*Exit.*

ACT III.

SCENE I.—*The Court of Assistants.*
  ENDICOTT, BELLINGHAM, ATH-
  ERTON, *and other magistrates.*
  KEMPTHORN, MERRY, *and con-*
  stables. Afterwards WHARTON,
  EDITH, *and* CHRISTISON.

   Endicott. Call Captain Simon
   Kempthorn.
   Merry.   Simon Kempthorn,
Come to the bar!

  (KEMPTHORN *comes forward.*)

   Endicott.   You are accused of
   bringing
Into this Jurisdiction, from Barbadoes,
Some persons of that sort and sect
   of people
Known by the name of Quakers,
   and maintaining
Most dangerous and heretical
   opinions;
Purposely coming here to propa-
   gate
Their heresies and errors; bringing
   with them
And spreading sundry books here,
   which contain
Their doctrines most corrupt and
   blasphemous,

And contrary to the truth professed
   among us.
What say you to this charge?
   Kempthorn.   I do
   acknowledge,
Among the passengers on board
   the Swallow
Were certain persons saying Thee
   and Thou.
They seemed a harmless people,
   mostways silent,
Particularly when they said their
   prayers.
   Endicott. Harmless and silent
   as the pestilence!
You'd better have brought the fever
   or the plague
Among us in your ship! Therefore,
   this Court,
For preservation of the Peace and
   Truth,
Hereby commands you speedily to
   transport,
Or cause to be transported speedily,
The aforesaid persons hence unto
   Barbadoes,
From whence they came; you
   paying all the charges
Of their imprisonment.
   Kempthorn.   Worshipful sir,

No ship e'er prospered that has
    carried Quakers
Against their will! I knew a vessel
    once—
    Endicott.   And for the more
    effectual performance
Hereof you are to give security
In bonds amounting to one hundred
    pounds.
On your refusal, you will be com-
    mitted
To prison till you do it.
    Kempthorn.   But you see
I cannot do it. The law, sir, of
    Barbadoes
Forbids the landing Quakers on
    the island.
    Endicott.   Then you will be
    committed. Who comes next?
    Merry.   There is another charge
    against the Captain.
    Endicott.   What is it?
    Merry.   Profane swearing, please
    your Worship.
He cursed and swore from Dock
    Square to the Court-house.
    Endicott.   Then let him stand in
    the pillory for one hour.

(*Exit* KEMPTHORN *with constable.*)
Who's next?
    Merry.   The Quakers.
    Endicott.   Call them.
    Merry.   Edward Wharton,
Come to the bar!
    Wharton.   Yea, even to the
    bench.
    Endicott.   Take off your hat.
    Wharton.   My hat offendeth not.
If it offendeth any, let him take it;
For I shall not resist.
    Endicott.   Take off his hat.
Let him be fined ten shillings for
    contempt.

(MERRY *takes off* WHARTON'S *hat.*)

    Wharton.   What evil have I
    done?

    Endicott.   Your hair's too long;
And in not putting off your hat to us
You've disobeyed and broken that
    commandment
Which sayeth 'Honour thy father
    and thy mother.'
    Wharton.   John Endicott, thou
    art become too proud;
And lovest him who putteth off the
    hat,
And honoureth thee by bowing of
    the body,
And sayeth 'Worshipful sir!' 'Tis
    time for thee
To give such follies over, for thou
    mayest
Be drawing very near unto thy
    grave.
    Endicott.   Now, sirrah, leave
    your canting. Take the oath.
    Wharton.   Nay, sirrah me no
    sirrahs!
    Endicott.   Will you swear?
    Wharton.   Nay, I will not.
    Endicott.   You made
    a great disturbance
And uproar yesterday in the
    Meeting-house,
Having your hat on.
    Wharton.   I made no dis-
    turbance;
For peacefully I stood, like other
    people.
I spake no words; moved against
    none my hand;
But by the hair they haled me out,
    and dashed
Their books into my face.
    Endicott.   You, Edward
    Wharton,
On pain of death, depart this Juris-
    diction
Within ten days. Such is your
    sentence. Go.
    Wharton.   John Endicott, it had
    been well for thee
If this day's doings thou hadst left
    undone.

But, banish me as far as thou hast
  power,
Beyond the guard and presence of
  my God
Thou canst not banish me!
   Endicott.   Depart the Court;
We have no time to listen to your
  babble.
Who's next?   [*Exit* WHARTON.
   Merry.   This woman, for the
  same offence.
     (EDITH *comes forward.*)
   Endicott. What is your name?
   Edith.   'Tis to the
  world unknown,
But written in the Book of Life.
   Endicott.   Take heed
It be not written in the Book of
  Death!
What is it?
   Edith.   Edith Christison.
   Endicott (*with eagerness*). The
  daughter
Of Wenlock Christison?
   Edith.   I am his daughter.
   Endicott. Your father hath given
  us trouble many times.
A bold man and a violent, who sets
At nought the authority of our
  Church and State,
And is in banishment on pain of
  death.
Where are you living?
   Edith.   In the Lord.
   Endicott.   Make answer
Without evasion. Where?
   Edith.   My outward being
Is in Barbadoes.
   Endicott. Then why come you
  here?
   Edith. I come upon an errand
  of the Lord.
   Endicott. 'Tis not the business
  of the Lord you're doing;
It is the Devil's. Will you take
  the oath?
Give her the book.
    (MERRY *offers the Book.*)

   Edith.   You offer me this
  Book
To swear on; and it saith, 'Swear
  not at all,
Neither by heaven, because it is
  God's Throne,
Nor by the earth, because it is his
  footstool!'
I dare not swear.
   Endicott. You dare not? Yet
  you Quakers
Deny this Book of Holy Writ, the
  Bible,
To be the Word of God.
   Edith (*reverentially*). Christ is
  the Word,
The everlasting oath of God. I
  dare not.
   Endicott. You own yourself a
  Quaker,—do you not?
   Edith. I own that in derision
  and reproach
I am so called.
   Endicott. Then you deny the
  Scripture
To be the rule of life.
   Edith.   Yea, I believe
The Inner Light, and not the
  Written Word,
To be the rule of life.
   Endicott. And you deny
That the Lord's Day is holy.
   Edith.   Every day
Is the Lord's Day. It runs through
  all our lives,
As through the pages of the Holy
  Bible
'Thus saith the Lord.'
   Endicott.   You are accused
  of making
An horrible disturbance, and
  affrighting
The people in the Meeting-house
  on Sunday.
What answer make you?
   Edith.   I do not deny
That I was present in your Steeple-
  house

On the First Day ; but I made no
disturbance.

Endicott. Why came you there ?

Edith. Because the Lord commanded.

His word was in my heart, a burning fire

Shut up within me and consuming
me,

And I was very weary with forbear-
ing ;

I could not stay.

Endicott. 'Twas not the
Lord that sent you ;

As an incarnate devil did you come!

Edith. On the First Day, when,
seated in my chamber,

I heard the bells toll, calling you
together,

The sound struck at my life, as once
at his,

The holy man, our Founder, when
he heard

The far-off bells toll in the Vale of
Beavor.

It sounded like a market bell to call

The folk together, that the Priest
might set

His wares to sale. And the Lord
said within me,

'Thou must go cry aloud against
that Idol,

And all the worshippers thereof.'
I went

Barefooted, clad in sackcloth, and
I stood

And listened at the threshold ; and
I heard

The praying and the singing and
the preaching,

Which were but outward forms, and
without power.

Then rose a cry within me, and my
heart

Was filled with admonitions and
reproofs.

Remembering how the Prophets
and Apostles

Denounced the covetous hirelings
and diviners,

I entered in, and spake the words
the Lord

Commanded me to speak. I could
no less.

Endicott. Are you a Prophetess ?

Edith. Is it not written,
'Upon my handmaidens will I pour
out

My spirit, and they shall prophesy'?

Endicott. Enough ;

For out of your own mouth are you
condemned !

Need we hear further ?

The Judges. We are satisfied.

Endicott. It is sufficient. Edith
Christison,

The sentence of the Court is, that
you be

Scourged in three towns, with forty
stripes save one,

Then banished upon pain of death !

Edith. Your sentence
Is truly no more terrible to me

Than had you blown a feather into
the air,

And, as it fell upon me, you had
said,

'Take heed it hurt thee not !' God's
will be done !

*Wenlock Christison (unseen in
the crowd).* Woe to the city of
blood ! The stone shall cry

Out of the wall : the beam from out
the timber

Shall answer it ! Woe unto him that
buildeth

A town with blood, and stablisheth
a city

By his iniquity !

Endicott. Who is it makes
Such outcry here ?

Christison (coming forward). I,
Wenlock Christison !

Endicott. Banished on pain of
death, why come you here ?

Christison. I come to warn you that you shed no more
The blood of innocent men! It cries aloud
For vengeance to the Lord!
Endicott. Your life is forfeit Unto the law; and you shall surely die,
And shall not live.
Christison. Like unto Eleazer,
Maintaining the excellence of ancient years
And the honour of his gray head, I stand before you;
Like him disdaining all hypocrisy,
Lest, through desire to live a little longer,
I get a stain to my old age and name!
Endicott. Being in banishment on pain of death,
You come now in among us in rebellion.
Christison. I come not in among you in rebellion,
But in obedience to the Lord of Heaven.
Not in contempt to any Magistrate,
But only in the love I bear your souls,
As ye shall know hereafter, when all men
Give an account of deeds done in the body!
God's righteous judgments ye can not escape.
One of the Judges. Those who have gone before you said the same,
And yet no judgment of the Lord hath fallen
Upon us.
Christison. He but waiteth till the measure
Of your iniquities shall be filled up,
And ye have run your race. Then will his wrath
Descend upon you to the uttermost!

For thy part, Humphrey Atherton, it hangs
Over thy head already. It shall come
Suddenly, as a thief doth in the night,
And in the hour when least thou thinkest of it!
Endicott. We have a law, and by that law you die.
Christison. I, a free man of England and free-born,
Appeal unto the laws of mine own nation!
Endicott. There's no appeal to England from this Court!
What! do you think our statutes are but paper?
Are but dead leaves that rustle in the wind?
Or litter to be trampled under foot?
What say ye, Judges of the Court,— what say ye?
Shall this man suffer death? Speak your opinions.
One of the Judges. I am a mortal man, and die I must,
And that ere long; and I must then appear
Before the awful judgment-seat of Christ,
To give account of deeds done in the body.
My greatest glory on that day will be
That I have given my vote against this man.
Christison. If, Thomas Danforth, thou hast nothing more
To glory in upon that dreadful day
Than blood of innocent people, then thy glory
Will be turned into shame! The Lord hath said it!
Another Judge. I cannot give consent, while other men
Who have been banished upon pain of death
Are now in their own houses here among us.

Endicott. Ye that will not consent,
  make record of it.
I thank my God that I am not afraid
To give my judgment. Wenlock
  Christison,
You must be taken back from hence
  to prison,
Thence to the place of public execu-
  tion,
There to be hanged till you be dead
  —dead—dead!

Christison. If ye have power to
  take my life from me,—
Which I do question,—God hath
  power to raise
The principle of life in other men,
And send them here among you.
  There shall be
No peace unto the wicked, saith my
  God.
Listen, ye Magistrates, for the Lord
  hath said it!
The day ye put his servitors to
  death,
That day the Day of your own Visit-
  ation,
The Day of Wrath, shall pass
  above your heads,
And ye shall be accursed for ever-
  more!

(*To* EDITH, *embracing her.*)

Cheer up, dear heart! they have not
  power to harm us

(*Exeunt* CHRISTISON *and* EDITH
  guarded. The scene closes.)

SCENE II.—*A Street. Enter* JOHN
  ENDICOTT *and* UPSALL.

John Endicott. Scourged in three
  towns! and yet the busy people
Go up and down the streets on their
  affairs
Of business or of pleasure, as if
  nothing

Had happened to disturb them or
  their thoughts!
When bloody tragedies like this are
  acted
The pulse of a nation should stand
  still;
The town should be in mourning,
  and the people
Speak only in low whispers to each
  other.

Upsall. I know this people; and
  that underneath
A cold outside there burns a secret
  fire
That will find vent, and will not be
  put out,
Till every remnant of these barbarous laws
Shall be to ashes burned, and blown
  away.

John Endicott. Scourged in three
  towns! It is incredible
Such things can be! I feel the
  blood within me
Fast mounting in rebellion, since in
  vain
Have I implored compassion of my
  father!

Upsall. You know your father
  only as a father;
I know him better as a Magistrate.
He is a man both loving and se-
  vere;
A tender heart; a will inflexible.
None ever loved him more than I
  have loved him.
He is an upright man and a just man
In all things save the treatment of
  the Quakers.

John Endicott. Yet I have found
  him cruel and unjust
Even as a father. He has driven me
  forth
Into the street; has shut his door
  upon me,
With words of bitterness. I am as
  homeless
As these poor Quakers are.

Upsall.   Then come with me.
You shall be welcome for your
  father's sake,
And the old friendship that has
  been between us.
He will relent ere long. A father's
  anger
Is like a sword without a handle,
  piercing
Both ways alike, and wounding him
  that wields it
No less than him that it is pointed at
              [Exeunt.

Scene III.—*The Prison. Night.*
Edith *reading the Bible by a lamp.*

Edith.   'Blessed are ye when
  men shall persecute you,
And shall revile you, and shall say
  against you
All manner of evil falsely for my
  sake !
Rejoice, and be exceeding glad, for
  great
Is your reward in heaven. For so
  the prophets,
Which were before you, have been
  persecuted.'

(*Enter* John Endicott.)

John Endicott. Edith !
  Edith.   Who is it speaketh ?
John Endicott. Saul of Tarsus :
As thou didst call me once.
  Edith (*coming forward*). Yea, I
  remember.
Thou art the Governor's son.
John Endicott.   I am ashamed
Thou shouldst remember me.
  Edith.   Why comest thou
Into this dark guest-chamber in
  the night ?
What seekest thou ?
  John Endicott. Forgiveness !
  Edith.   I forgive
All who have injured me. What
  hast thou done ?

John Endicott. I have betrayed
  thee, thinking that in this
I did God service. Now, in deep
  contrition,
I come to rescue thee.
  Edith.   From what ?
John Endicott. From prison.
  Edith.   I am safe here within
  these gloomy walls.
John Endicott. From scourging
  in the streets, and in three
  towns !
  Edith. Remembering who was
  scourged for me, I shrink not
Nor shudder at the forty stripes
  save one.
  John Endicott. Perhaps from
  death itself !
  Edith.   I fear not death,
Knowing who died for me.
  John Endicott (*aside*). Sure
  some divine
Ambassador is speaking through
  those lips
And looking through those eyes ! I
  cannot answer !
  Edith. If all these prison doors
  stood opened wide
I would not cross the threshold,—
  not one step.
There are invisible bars I cannot
  break ;
There are invisible doors that shut
  me in,
And keep me ever steadfast to my
  purpose.
  John Endicott. Thou hast the
  patience and the faith of Saints !
  Edith. Thy Priest hath been
  with me this day to save me,
Not only from the death that comes
  to all,
But from the second death !
  John Endicott.   The Pharisee !
My heart revolts against him and
  his creed !
Alas ! the coat that was without a
  seam

Is rent asunder by contending
  sects ;
Each bears away a portion of the
  garment,
Blindly believing that he has the
  whole !

  Edith. When Death, the Healer,
  shall have touched our eyes
With moist clay of the grave, then
  shall we see
The truth as we have never yet
  beheld it.
But he that overcometh shall not be
Hurt of the second death. Has he
  forgotten
The many mansions in our Father's
  house ?

  John Endicott. There is no pity
  in his iron heart !
The hands that now bear stamped
  upon their palms
The burning sign of Heresy, hereafter
Shall be uplifted against such
  accusers,
And then the imprinted letter and
  its meaning
Will not be Heresy, but Holiness !

  Edith. Remember thou con-
  demnest thine own father !

  John Endicott. I have no father !
  He has cast me off.
I am as homeless as the wind that
  moans
And wanders through the streets.
  O, come with me !
Do not delay. Thy God shall be my
  God,
And where thou goest I will go.

  Edith. I cannot.
Yet will I not deny it, nor conceal
  it ;
From the first moment I beheld thy
  face

I felt a tenderness in my soul towards
  thee.
My mind has since been inward to
  the Lord,
Waiting his word. It has not yet
  been spoken.

  John Endicott. I cannot wait.
  Trust me. O, come with me !

  Edith. In the next room, my
  father, an old man,
Sitteth imprisoned and condemned
  to death,
Willing to prove his faith by
  martyrdom ;
And thinkest thou his daughter
  would do less ?

  John Endicott. O, life is sweet,
  and death is terrible !

  Edith. I have too long walked
  hand in hand with death
To shudder at that pale familiar
  face.
But leave me now. I wish to be
  alone.

  John Endicott. Not yet. O, let
  me stay.

  Edith.   Urge me no more.

  John Endicott. Alas ! good night.
  I will not say good-bye !

  Edith. Put this temptation under-
  neath thy feet.
To him that overcometh shall be
  given
The white stone with the new name
  written on it,
That no man knows save him that
  doth receive it.
And I will give thee a new name,
  and call thee
Paul of Damascus and not Saul of
  Tarsus.

(*Exit* ENDICOTT. EDITH *sits down
  again to read the Bible.*)

ACT IV.

SCENE I.—*King Street, in front of the town-house.* KEMPTHORN *in the pillory.* MERRY, *and a crowd of lookers-on.*

Kempthorn (sings).

The world is full of care,
  Much like unto a bubble ;
Women and care, and care and women,
  And women and care and trouble.

Good Master Merry, may I say confound ?
    Merry. Ay, that you may.
    Kempthorn. Well, then, with your permission,
Confound the Pillory !
    Merry.   That 's the very thing
The joiner said who made the Shrewsbury stocks.
He said, Confound the stocks, because they put him
Into his own. He was the first man in them.
    Kempthorn. For swearing, was it ?
    Merry.   No, it was for charging ;
He charged the town too much ; and so the town,
To make things square, set him in his own stocks,
And fined him five pound sterling,— just enough
To settle his own bill.
    Kempthorn.   And served him right ;
But, Master Merry, is it not eight bells ?
    Merry. Not quite.
    Kempthorn. For, do you see ? I 'm getting tired
Of being perched up aloft here in this cro' nest
Like the first mate of a whaler, or a Middy

Mast-headed, looking out for land !
  Sail ho !
Here comes a heavy-laden merchantman
With the lee clews eased off, and running free
Before the wind. A solid man of Boston.
A comfortable man, with dividends,
And the first salmon, and the first green peas.

      (*A gentleman passes.*)

He does not even turn his head to look.
He 's gone without a word. Here comes another
A different kind of craft on a taut bowline,—
Deacon Giles Firmin the apothecary,
A pious and a ponderous citizen,
Looking as rubicund and round and splendid
As the great bottle in his own shop window !

    (DEACON FIRMIN *passes.*)

And here 's my host of the Three Mariners,
My creditor and trusty taverner,
My corporal in the Great Artillery !
He 's not a man to pass me without speaking.

    (COLE *looks away and passes.*)

Don't yaw so ; keep your luff, old hypocrite !
Respectable, ah yes, respectable,
You, with your seat in the new Meeting-house,
Your cow-right on the Common !
  But who 's this?
I did not know the Mary Ann was in !
And yet this is my old friend, Captain Goldsmith,

As sure as I stand in the bilboes here.
Why, Ralph, my boy!

(*Enter* RALPH GOLDSMITH.)

Goldsmith.   Why, Simon, is
it you?
See in the bilboes?
Kempthorn. Chock-a-block, you
see,
And without chafing-gear.
Goldsmith. And what's it for?
Kempthorn. Ask that starbowline
with the boat-hook there—
That handsome man.
Merry (*bowing*). For swearing.
Kempthorn.   In this town
They put sea-captains in the stocks
for swearing,
And Quakers for not swearing. So
look out.
Goldsmith. I pray you set him
free; he meant no harm;
'Tis an old habit he picked up afloat.
Merry. Well, as your time is out,
you may come down.
The law allows you now to go at large
Like Elder Oliver's horse upon the
Common.
Kempthorn. Now, hearties, bear
a hand! Let go and haul.

(KEMPTHORN *is set free, and comes
forward, shaking* GOLDSMITH'S
hand.)

Kempthorn. Give me your hand,
Ralph. Ah, how good it feels!
The hand of an old friend.
Goldsmith.   God bless you,
Simon!
Kempthorn. Now let us make
a straight wake for the tavern
Of the Three Mariners, Samuel
Cole commander;
Where we can take our ease, and
see the shipping,
And talk about old times.
Goldsmith.   First I must pay
My duty to the Governor, and take
him

His letters and despatches.   Come
with me.
Kempthorn. I'd rather not.   I
saw him yesterday.
Goldsmith. Then wait for me at
the Three Nuns and Comb.
Kempthorn. I thank you. That's
too near to the town pump.
I will go with you to the Governor's,
And wait outside there, sailing off
and on;
If I am wanted, you can hoist a
signal.
Merry. Shall I go with you and
point out the way?
Goldsmith. O no, I thank you.
I am not a stranger
Here in your crooked little town.
Merry.   How now, sir;
Do you abuse our town?   [*Exit.*
Goldsmith.   O, no offence.
Kempthorn. Ralph, I am under
bonds for a hundred pound.
Goldsmith. Hard lines. What for?
Kempthorn.   To take some
Quakers back
I brought here from Barbadoes in
the Swallow.
And how to do it I don't clearly see,
For one of them is banished, and
another
Is sentenced to be hanged!   What
shall I do?
Goldsmith. Just slip your hawser
on some cloudy night;
Sheer off, and pay it with the top-
sail, Simon!   [*Exeunt.*

———

SCENE II.—*Street in front of the
prison. In the background a
gateway and several flights of
steps leading up terraces to the*
GOVERNOR'S *house. A pump on
one side of the street.* JOHN EN-
DICOTT, MERRY, UPSALL, *and
others.   A drum beats.*

John Endicott. O shame, shame,
shame!

Merry. Yes, it would be a shame
But for the damnable sin of
Heresy !
John Endicott. A woman
scourged and dragged about
our streets !
Merry. Well, Roxbury and
Dorchester must take
Their share of shame. She will be
whipped in each !
Three towns, and forty stripes
save one ; that makes
Thirteen in each.
John Endicott. And are we
Jews or Christians ?
See where she comes, amid a
gaping crowd !
And she a child. O, pitiful ! pitiful !
There's blood upon her clothes, her
hands, her feet !

(*Enter* MARSHAL *and a drummer ;*
EDITH, *stripped to the waist,*
followed by the hangman with a
scourge, and a noisy crowd.)

Edith. Here let me rest one
moment. I am tired.
Will some one give me water ?
Merry. At his peril.
Upsall. Alas ! that I should
live to see this day !
A Woman. Did I forsake my
father and my mother
And come here to New England to
see this ?
Edith. I am athirst. Will no
one give me water ?
John Endicott (*making his way*
through the crowd with water).
In the Lord's name !
Edith (*drinking*). In his name
I receive it !
Sweet as the water of Samaria's
well
This water tastes. I thank thee.
Is it thou ?
I was afraid thou hadst deserted
me.

John Endicott. Never will I
desert thee, nor deny thee.
Be comforted.
Merry. O Master Endicott,
Be careful what you say.
John Endicott. Peace, idle
babbler !
Merry. You'll rue these words !
John Endicott. Art thou
not better now ?
Edith. They've struck me as
with roses.
John Endicott. Ah, these
wounds !
These bloody garments !
Edith. It is granted me
To seal my testimony with my blood.
John Endicott. O blood-red seal
of man's vindictive wrath !
O roses of the garden of the Lord !
I, of the household of Iscariot,
I have betrayed in thee my Lord
and Master !

(WENLOCK CHRISTISON *appears*
above, at the window of the
prison, stretching out his hands
through the bars.)

Christison. Be of good courage,
O my child ! my child !
Blessed art thou when men shall
persecute thee !
Fear not their faces, saith the Lord,
fear not,
For I am with thee to deliver thee.
A Citizen. Who is it crying
from the prison yonder ?
Merry. It is old Wenlock
Christison.
Christison. Remember
Him who was scourged, and
mocked, and crucified !
I see his messengers attending thee.
Be steadfast, O, be steadfast to the
end !
Edith (*with exultation*). I can-
not reach thee with these arms,
O father !

But closely in my soul do I embrace
 thee
And hold thee. In thy dungeon
 and thy death
I will be with thee, and will comfort
 thee!
 Marshal. Come, put an end to
 this. Let the drum beat.

(*The drum beats. Exeunt all but*
JOHN ENDICOTT, UPSALL, *and*
MERRY.)

 Christison. Dear child, farewell!
 Never shall I behold
Thy face again with these bleared
 eyes of flesh ;
And never wast thou fairer, lovelier,
 dearer
Than now, when scourged and
 bleeding, and insulted
For the truth's sake. O pitiless,
 pitiless town !
The wrath of God hangs over thee ;
 and the day
Is near at hand when thou shalt be
 abandoned
To desolation and the breeding of
 nettles.
The bittern and the cormorant shall
 lodge
Upon thine upper lintels, and their
 voice
Sing in thy windows. Yea, thus
 saith the Lord !
 John Endicott. Awake! awake!
 ye sleepers, ere too late,
And wipe these bloody statutes from
 your books !   [*Exit.*
 Merry. Take heed ; the walls
 have ears !
 Upsall. At last, the heart
Of every honest man must speak
 or break !

(*Enter* GOVERNOR ENDICOTT
 with his halberdiers.)

 Endicott. What is this stir and
 tumult in the street ?

 Merry. Worshipful sir, the
 whipping of a girl,
And her old father howling from
 the prison.
 Endicott (*to his halberdiers*). Go
 on.
 Christison. Antiochus ! Antio-
 chus !
O thou that slayest the Maccabees !
 The Lord
Shall smite thee with incurable
 disease,
And no man shall endure to carry
 thee !
 Merry. Peace, old blasphemer !
 Christison. I both
 feel and see
The presence and the waft of death
 go forth
Against thee, and already thou dost
 look
Like one that 's dead !
 Merry (*pointing*). And there is
 your own son,
Worshipful sir, abetting the sedition.
 Endicott. Arrest him. Do not
 spare him.
 Merry (*aside*). His own child !
There is some special providence
 takes care
That none shall be too happy in
 this world !
His own first-born !
 Endicott. O Absalom, my son !

(*Exeunt ; the* GOVERNOR, *with his
 halberdiers, ascending the steps
 of his house.*)

SCENE III.—*The Governor's private room. Papers upon the
 table.* ENDICOTT *and* BELL-
 INGHAM.

 Endicott. There is a ship from
 England has come in,
Bringing despatches and much
 news from home.

His Majesty was at the Abbey crowned ;
And when the coronation was complete
There passed a mighty tempest o'er the city,
Portentous with great thunderings and lightnings.

Bellingham. After his father's, if I well remember,
There was an earthquake, that foreboded evil.

Endicott. Ten of the Regicides have been put to death !
The bodies of Cromwell, Ireton, and Bradshaw
Have been dragged from their graves, and publicly
Hanged in their shrouds at Tyburn.

Bellingham. Horrible !

Endicott. Thus the old tyranny revives again !
Its arm is long enough to reach us here,
As you will see. For, more insulting still
Than flaunting in our faces dead men's shrouds,
Here is the King's Mandamus, taking from us,
From this day forth, all power to punish Quakers.

Bellingham. That takes from us all power ; we are but puppets,
And can no longer execute our laws.

Endicott. His Majesty begins with pleasant words,
' Trusty and well-beloved, we greet you well ' ;
Then with a ruthless hand he strips from me
All that which makes me what I am ; as if
From some old general in the field, grown gray
In service, scarred with many wounds,

Just at the hour of victory, he should strip
His badge of office and his well-gained honours,
And thrust him back into the ranks again.

(*Opens the Mandamus, and hands it to* BELLINGHAM ; *and, while he is reading,* ENDICOTT *walks up and down the room.*)

Here read it for yourself ; you see his words
Are pleasant words—considerate—not reproachful—
Nothing could be more gentle—or more royal ;
But then the meaning underneath the words,
Mark that. He says all people known as Quakers
Among us, now condemned to suffer death
Or any corporal punishment whatever,
Who are imprisoned, or may be obnoxious
To the like condemnation, shall be sent
Forthwith to England, to be dealt with there
In such wise as shall be agreeable
Unto the English law and their demerits.
Is it not so ?

Bellingham (returning the paper). Ay, so the paper says.

Endicott. It means we shall no longer rule the Province ;
It means farewell to law and liberty,
Authority, respect for Magistrates,
The peace and welfare of the Commonwealth.
If all the knaves upon this continent
Can make appeal to England, and so thwart

591

The ends of truth and justice by
delay,
Our power is gone for ever. We
are nothing
But ciphers, valueless save when
we follow
Some unit; and our unit is the
King!
'Tis he that gives us value.
   Bellingham.   I confess
Such seems to be the meaning of
this paper.
But being the King's Mandamus,
signed and sealed,
We must obey, or we are in rebel-
lion.
   Endicott. I tell you, Richard
Bellingham,—I tell you,
That this is the beginning of a
struggle
Of which no mortal can foresee the
end.
I shall not live to fight the battle
for you,
I am a man disgraced in every
way;
This order takes from me my self-
respect
And the respect of others. 'Tis my
doom,
Yes, my death-warrant, but must
be obeyed!
Take it, and see that it is exe-
cuted
So far as this, that all be set at
large;
But see that none of them be sent
to England
To bear false witness, and to spread
reports
That might be prejudicial to ourselves. [*Exit* BELLINGHAM.
There's a dull pain keeps knocking at my heart,
Dolefully saying, 'Set thy house in
order,
For thou shalt surely die, and shalt
not live!'

For me the shadow on the dial-
plate
Goeth not back, but on into the
dark!   [*Exit.*

SCENE IV.—*The street. A crowd,
reading a placard on the door of
the Meeting-house.* NICHOLAS
UPSALL *among them. Enter*
JOHN NORTON.

   Norton. What is this gathering
here?
   Upsall.   One William Brand,
An old man like ourselves, and
weak in body,
Has been so cruelly tortured in his
prison,
The people are excited, and they
threaten
To tear the prison down.
   Norton.   What has been done?
   Upsall. He has been put in irons,
with his neck
And heels tied close together, and
so left
From five in the morning until nine
at night.
   Norton. What more was done?
   Upsall.   He has
been kept five days
In prison without food, and cruelly
beaten,
So that his limbs were cold, his
senses stopped.
   Norton. What more?
   Upsall.   And is this
not enough?
   Norton.   Now hear me.
This William Brand of yours has
tried to beat
Our Gospel Ordinances black and
blue;
And, if he has been beaten in like
manner,
It is but justice, and I will appear
In his behalf that did so. I suppose
That he refused to work.

Upsall.　　　He was too weak.
How could an old man work, when
　　he was starving?
　Norton. And what is this pla-
　　card?
　Upsall.　　　The Magistrates,
To appease the people and prevent
　　a tumult,
Have put up these placards through-
　　out the town,
Declaring that the jailer shall be
　　dealt with
Impartially and sternly by the
　　Court.
　*Norton (tearing down the pla-
　　card).* Down with this weak
　　and cowardly concession,
This flag of truce with Satan and
　　with Sin!
I fling it in his face! I trample it
Under my feet? It is his cunning
　　craft,
The masterpiece of his diplomacy,
To cry and plead for boundless
　　toleration.
But toleration is the first-born child
Of all abominations and deceits.
There is no room in Christ's trium-
　　phant army
For tolerationists. And if an Angel
Preach any other gospel unto you
Than that ye have received, God's
　　malediction
Descend upon him! Let him be
　　accursed!　　　　　　 [*Exit.*
　Upsall. Now, go thy ways, John
　　Norton! go thy ways,
Thou Orthodox Evangelist, as men
　　call thee!
But even now there cometh out of
　　England,
Like an o'ertaking and accusing
　　conscience,
An outraged man, to call thee to
　　account
For the unrighteous murder of his
　　son!　　　　　　　　　 [*Exit.*

SCENE V.—*The Wilderness.*

Enter EDITH.

　Edith. How beautiful are these
　　autumnal woods!
The wilderness doth blossom like
　　the rose,
And change into a garden of the
　　Lord!
How silent everywhere! Alone
　　and lost
Here in the forest, there comes
　　over me
An inward awfulness. I recall the
　　words
Of the Apostle Paul: 'In journey-
　　ings often,
Often in perils in the wilderness,
In weariness, in painfulness, in
　　watchings,
In hunger and thirst, in cold and
　　nakedness;'
And I forget my weariness and pain,
My watchings, and my hunger and
　　my thirst.
The Lord hath said that he will
　　seek his flock
In cloudy and dark days, and they
　　shall dwell
Securely in the wilderness, and
　　sleep
Safe in the woods! Whichever way
　　I turn,
I come back with my face towards
　　the town.
Dimly I see it, and the sea beyond it.
O cruel town! I know what waits
　　me there,
And yet I must go back; for ever
　　louder
I hear the inward calling of the
　　Spirit,
And must obey the voice. O woods,
　　that wear
Your golden crown of martyrdom,
　　bloodstained,
From you I learn a lesson of sub-
　　mission,

And am obedient even unto death,
If God so wills it. [*Exit.*
John Endicott (*within*). Edith!
Edith! Edith!

(*He enters.*)

It is in vain! I call, she answers not!
I follow, but I find no trace of her!
Blood! blood! The leaves above me
and around me
Are red with blood! The pathways
of the forest,
The clouds that canopy the setting
sun,
And even the little river in the
meadows,
Are stained with it! Where'er I
look, I see it!
Away, thou horrible vision! Leave
me! leave me!

Alas! yon winding stream, that
gropes its way
Through mist and shadow, doubling
on itself,
At length will find, by the unerring
law
Of nature, what it seeks. O soul of
man,
Groping through mist and shadow,
and recoiling
Back on thyself, are, too, thy devious
ways
Subject to law? and when thou
seemest to wander
The farthest from thy goal, art thou
still drawing
Nearer and nearer to it, till at length
Thou findest, like the river, what
thou seekest?
[*Exit.*

ACT V.

SCENE I.—*Daybreak. Street in
front of* UPSALL'S *house. A light
in the window. Enter* JOHN
ENDICOTT.

John Endicott. O silent, sombre,
and deserted streets,
To me ye 're peopled with a sad
procession,
And echo only to the voice of sor-
row!
O houses full of peacefulness and
sleep,
Far better were it to awake no more
Than wake to look upon such scenes
again!
There is a light in Master Upsall's
window.
The good man is already risen, for
sleep
Deserts the couches of the old.

(*Knocks at* UPSALL'S *door.*)

Upsall (*at the window*). Who 's
there?

John Endicott. Am I so changed
you do not know my voice?
Upsall. I know you. Have you
heard what things have happened?
John Endicott. I have heard
nothing.
Upsall. Stay; I will come down.
John Endicott. I am afraid some
dreadful news awaits me!
I do not dare to ask, yet am impatient
To know the worst. O, I am very
weary
With waiting and with watching
and pursuing!

(*Enter* UPSALL.)

Upsall. Thank God, you have
come back! I 've much to tell
you.
Where have you been?
John Endicott. You know that
I was seized,

594

Fined, and released again. You know that Edith

After her scourging in three towns, was banished

Into the wilderness, into the land

That is not sown ; and there I followed her,

But found her not. Where is she ?

Upsall. She is here.

John Endicott. O, do not speak that word, for it means death !

Upsall. No, it means life. She sleeps in yonder chamber.

Listen to me. When news of Leddra's death

Reached England, Edward Burroughs, having boldly

Got access to the presence of the King,

Told him there was a vein of innocent blood

Opened in his dominions here, which threatened

To overrun them all. The King replied,

' But I will stop that vein ! ' and he forthwith

Sent his Mandamus to our Magistrates,

That they proceed no further in this business.

So all are pardoned, and all set at large.

John Endicott. Thank God ! This is a victory for truth !

Our thoughts are free. They cannot be shut up

In prison walls, nor put to death on scaffolds !

Upsall. Come in ; the morning air blows sharp and cold

Through the damp streets.

John Endicott. It is the dawn of day

That chases the old darkness from our sky,

And fills the land with liberty and light. [*Exeunt.*

SCENE II.—*The parlour of the Three Mariners. Enter* KEMPTHORN.

Kempthorn. A dull life this,—a dull life anyway !

Ready for sea; the cargo all aboard,

Cleared for Barbadoes, and a fair wind blowing

From nor'-nor'-west; and I, an idle lubber,

Laid neck and heels by that confounded bond !

I said to Ralph, says I, ' What 's to be done ? '

Says he : ' Just slip your hawser in the night ;

Sheer off, and pay it with the topsail, Simon.'

But that won't do ; because, you see, the owners

Somehow or other are mixed up with it.

Here are King Charles's Twelve Good Rules, that Cole

Thinks as important as the Rule of Three. (*Reads.*)

' Make no comparisons ; make no long meals.'

Those are good rules and golden for a landlord

To hang in his best parlour, framed and glazed !

' Maintain no ill opinions ; urge no healths.'

I drink the King's, whatever he may say,

And, as to ill opinions, that depends.

Now of Ralph Goldsmith I 've a good opinion,

And of the bilboes I 've an ill opinion ;

And both of these opinions I 'll maintain

As long as there 's a shot left in the locker.

(*Enter* EDWARD BUTTER *with an ear-trumpet.*)

Butter. Good morning, Captain
   Kempthorn.
Kempthorn.   Sir, to you.
You 've the advantage of me.   I
   don't know you.
What may I call your name ?
Butter. That 's not your name ?
Kempthorn. Yes, that 's my name.
   What 's yours ?
Butter.   My name is Butter.
I am the treasurer of the Common-
   wealth.
Kempthorn. Will you be seated ?
Butter.   What
   say ?   Who 's conceited ?
Kempthorn. Will you sit down ?
Butter.   O, thank you.
Kempthorn.   Spread
   yourself
Upon this chair, sweet Butter.
Butter (sitting down). A fine
   morning.
Kempthorn. Nothing 's the matter
   with it that I know of.
I have seen better, and I have seen
   worse.
The wind 's nor'-west. That 's fair
   for them that sail.
Butter. You need not speak so
   loud ; I understand you.
You sail to-day.
Kempthorn. No, I don't sail to-
   day.
So, be it fair or foul, it matters not.
Say, will you smoke ? There 's choice
   tobacco here.
Butter. No, thank you.   It 's
   against the law to smoke.
Kempthorn. Then, will you drink ?
   There 's good ale at this inn.
Butter. No, thank you.   It 's
   against the law to drink.
Kempthorn. Well, almost every-
   thing 's against the law
In this good town.   Give a wide
   berth to one thing,
You 're sure to fetch up soon on
   something else.

Butter. And so you sail to-day
   for dear Old England.
I am not one of those who think a
   sup
Of this New England air is better
   worth
Than a whole draught of our Old
   England's ale.
Kempthorn. Nor I.   Give me
   the ale and keep the air.
But, as I said, I do not sail to-day.
Butter. Ah yes ; you sail to-day.
Kempthorn. I 'm under bonds
To take some Quakers back to the
   Barbadoes ;
And one of them is banished, and
   another
Is sentenced to be hanged.
Butter.   No, all are pardoned,
All are set free, by order of the
   Court ;
But some of them would fain return
   to England.
You must not take them. Upon that
   condition
Your bond is cancelled.
Kempthorn. Ah, the wind has
   shifted !
I pray you, do you speak officially ?
Butter. I always speak officially.
   To prove it.
Here is the bond.

   (Rising, and giving a paper.)

Kempthorn. And here 's my hand
   upon it.
And, look you, when I say I 'll do a
   thing
The thing is done. Am I now free
   to go ?
Butter. What say ?
Kempthorn.   I say, confound
   the tedious man
With his strange speaking-trumpet !
   Can I go ?
Butter. You 're free to go, by order
   of the Court.
Your servant, sir.   *[Exit*

Kempthorn (*shouting from the window*). Swallow, ahoy! Hallo!

If ever a man was happy to leave Boston,
That man is Simon Kempthorn of the Swallow!

(*Re-enter* BUTTER.)

Butter. Pray, did you call?
Kempthorn.   Call? Yes, I hailed the Swallow.
Butter. That's not my name. My name is Edward Butter.
You need not speak so loud.
Kempthorn (*shaking hands*). Good-bye! Good-bye!
Butter. Your servant, sir.
Kempthorn.   And yours a thousand times!   [*Exeunt.*

SCENE III.—GOVERNOR ENDI-COTT'S *private room. An open window.* ENDICOTT *seated in an arm-chair.* BELLINGHAM *standing near.*

Endicott. O lost, O loved! wilt thou return no more?
O loved and lost, and loved the more when lost!
How many men are dragged into their graves
By their rebellious children! I now feel
The agony of a father's breaking heart
In David's cry, 'O Absalom, my son!'
Bellingham. Can you not turn your thoughts a little while
To public matters? There are papers here
That need attention.
Endicott. Trouble me no more!
My business now is with another world.

Ah, Richard Bellingham! I greatly fear
That in my righteous zeal I have been led
To doing many things which left undone
My mind would now be easier. Did I dream it,
Or has some person told me, that John Norton
Is dead?
Bellingham.   You have not dreamed it. He is dead,
And gone to his reward. It was no dream.
Endicott. Then it was very sudden; for I saw him
Standing where you now stand not long ago.
Bellingham. By his own fireside, in the afternoon
A faintness and a giddiness came o'er him;
And, leaning on the chimney-piece, he cried,
'The hand of God is on me!' and fell dead.
Endicott. And did not some one say, or have I dreamed it,
That Humphrey Atherton is dead?
Bellingham.   Alas!
He is gone, and by a death as sudden,
Returning home one evening, at the place
Where usually the Quakers have been scourged,
His horse took fright, and threw him to the ground,
So that his brains were dashed about the street.
Endicott. I am not superstitious, Bellingham,
And yet I tremble lest it may have been
A judgment on him.
Bellingham.   So the people think.

They say his horse saw standing in
the way
The ghost of William Leddra, and
was frightened.
And furthermore, brave Richard
Davenport,
The captain of the Castle, in the
storm
Has been struck dead by lightning.
Endicott. Speak
no more,
For as I listen to your voice it seems
As if the Seven Thunders uttered
their voices
And the dead bodies lay about the
streets
Of the disconsolate city ! Belling-
ham,
I did not put those wretched men
to death.
I did but guard the passage with
the sword
Pointed towards them, and they
rushed upon it !
Yet now I would that I had taken
no part
In all that bloody work.
Bellingham. The guilt of it
Be on their heads, not ours.
Endicott. Are all set free ?
Bellingham. All are at large.
Endicott. And none have
been sent back
To England to malign us with the
King ?
Bellingham. The ship that brought
them sails this very hour,
But carries no one back.

(*A distant cannon.*)

Endicott. What is that gun ?
Bellingham. Her parting signal.
Through the window there,
Look, you can see her sails, above
the roofs,
Dropping below the Castle, outward
bound.

Endicott. O white, white, white !
Would that my soul had wings
As spotless as those shining sails to
fly with !
Now lay this cushion straight. I
thank you. Hark !
I thought I heard the hall door
open and shut !
I thought I heard the footsteps of
my boy !
Bellingham. It was the wind.
There 's no one in the passage.
Endicott. O Absalom, my son !
I feel the world
Sinking beneath me, sinking, sink-
ing, sinking !
Death knocks ! I go to meet him !
Welcome, Death !

(*Rises, and sinks back dead ; his
head falling aside upon his
shoulder.*)

Bellingham. O ghastly sight !
Like one who has been hanged !
Endicott ! Endicott ! He makes
no answer !

(*Raises* ENDICOTT'S *head.*)

He breathes no more ! How bright
this signet-ring
Glitters upon his hand, where he
has worn it
Through such long years of trouble,
as if Death
Had given him this memento of
affection,
And whispered in his ear, ' Remember me ! '
How placid and how quiet is his
face,
Now that the struggle and the strife
are ended !
Only the acrid spirit of the times
Corroded this true steel. O, rest
in peace,
Courageous heart ! For ever rest in
peace !

II. GILES COREY OF THE SALEM FARMS.

DRAMATIS PERSONÆ.

GILES COREY	*Farmer.*	
JOHN HATHORNE.	*Magistrate.*	
COTTON MATHER.	*Minister of the Gospel.*	
JONATHAN WALCOT	*A youth.*	
RICHARD GARDNER	*Sea-Captain.*	
JOHN GLOYD	*Corey's hired man.*	
MARTHA	*Wife of Giles Corey.*	
TITUBA	*An Indian woman.*	
MARY WALCOT	*One of the Afflicted.*	

The Scene is in Salem in the year 1692.

PROLOGUE.

DELUSIONS of the days that once
    have been,
Witchcraft and wonders of the
    world unseen,
Phantoms of air, and necromantic
    arts
That crushed the weak and awed
    the stoutest hearts,—
These are our theme to-night; and
    vaguely here,
Through the dim mists that crowd
    the atmosphere,
We draw the outlines of weird
    figures cast
In shadow on the background of
    the Past.

Who would believe that in the
    quiet town
Of Salem, and amid the woods that
    crown
The neighbouring hillsides, and
    the sunny farms
That fold it safe in their paternal
    arms,—
Who would believe that in those
    peaceful streets,
Where the great elms shut out the
    summer heats,
Where quiet reigns, and breathes
    through brain and breast

The benediction of unbroken rest,—
Who would believe such deeds could
    find a place
As these whose tragic history we
    retrace?

'Twas but a village then: the
    goodman ploughed
His ample acres under sun or cloud;
The goodwife at her doorstep sat
    and spun,
And gossiped with her neighbours
    in the sun;
The only men of dignity and state
Were then the Minister and the
    Magistrate,
Who ruled their little realm with
    iron rod,
Less in the love than in the fear of
    God;
And who believed devoutly in the
    Powers
Of Darkness, working in this world
    of ours,
In spells of Witchcraft, incantations
    dread,
And shrouded apparitions of the
    dead.

Upon the simple folk 'with fire
    and flame,'
Saith the old Chronicle, 'the Devil
    came;

Scattering his firebrands and his
poisonous darts,
To set on fire of Hell all tongues and
hearts!
And 'tis no wonder; for, with all his
host,
There most he rages where he
hateth most,
And is most hated; soon on us he brings
All these stupendous and portentous things!

Something of this our scene to-
night will show;

And ye who listen to the Tale of
Woe,
Be not too swift in casting the first
stone,
Nor think New England bears the
guilt alone.
This sudden burst of wickedness
and crime
Was but the common madness of
the time,
When in all lands, that lie within
the sound
Of Sabbath bells, a Witch was
burned or drowned.

ACT I.

SCENE I.—*The woods near Salem
Village. Enter* TITUBA, *with a
basket of herbs.*

Tituba. Here's monk's-hood,
that breeds fever in the
blood;
And deadly nightshade, that makes
men see ghosts;
And henbane, that will shake them
with convulsions;
And meadow-saffron and black
hellebore,
That rack the nerves, and puff the
skin with dropsy;
And bitter-sweet, and briony, and
eye-bright,
That cause eruptions, nosebleed,
rheumatisms;
I know them, and the places where
they hide
In field and meadow; and I know
their secrets,
And gather them because they give
me power
Over all men and women. Armed
with these,
I, Tituba, an Indian and a slave,
Am stronger than the captain with
his sword,
Am richer than the merchant with
his money,

Am wiser than the scholar with his
books,
Mightier than Ministers and Magis-
trates,
With all the fear and reverence that
attend them!
For I can fill their bones with aches
and pains,
Can make them cough with asthma,
shake with palsy,
Can make their daughters see and
talk with ghosts;
Or fall into delirium and convulsions.
I have the Evil Eye, the Evil Hand;
A touch from me, and they are
weak with pain;
A look from me, and they consume
and die.
The death of cattle and the blight
of corn,
The shipwreck, the tornado, and
the fire,—
These are my doings, and they know
it not.
Thus I work vengeance on mine
enemies,
Who, while they call me slave, are
slaves to me!

(*Exit* TITUBA. *Enter* MATHER,
*booted and spurred, with a
riding-whip in his hand.*)

Mather. Methinks that I have
come by paths unknown
Into the land and atmosphere of
Witches;
For, meditating as I journeyed on,
Lo! I have lost my way! If I re-
member
Rightly, it is Scribonius the learned
That tells the story of a man who,
praying
For one that was possessed by Evil
Spirits,
Was struck by Evil Spirits in the face;
I, journeying to circumvent the
Witches,
Surely by Witches have been led
astray.
I am persuaded there are few affairs
In which the Devil doth not inter-
fere.
We cannot undertake a journey even,
But Satan will be there to meddle
with it
By hindering or by furthering. He
hath led me
Into this thicket, struck me in the face
With branches of the trees, and so
entangled
The fetlocks of my horse with vines
and brambles,
That I must needs dismount, and
search on foot
For the lost pathway leading to the
village.

(Re-enter TITUBA.*)*

What shape is this? What monstrous apparition,
Exceeding fierce, that none may
pass that way?
Tell me, good woman, if you are a
woman—
Tituba. I am a woman, but I am
not good.
I am a Witch!
Mather. Then tell me, Witch
and woman,
For you must know the pathways
through this wood,

Where lieth Salem Village!
Tituba. Reverend sir,
The village is near by. I'm going
there
With these few herbs. I'll lead you.
Follow me.
Mather. First say, who are you?
I am loath to follow
A stranger in this wilderness, for fear
Of being misled, and left in some
morass.
Who are you?
Tituba. I am Tituba the Witch,
Wife of John Indian.
Mather. You are Tituba?
I know you then. You have re-
nounced the Devil,
And have become a penitent con-
fessor.
The Lord be praised! Go on, I'll
follow you.
Wait only till I fetch my horse, that
stands
Tethered among the trees, not far
from here.
Tituba. Let me get up behind
you, reverend sir.
Mather. The Lord forbid! What
would the people think,
If they should see the Reverend
Cotton Mather
Ride into Salem with a Witch be-
hind him?
The Lord forbid!
Tituba. I do not need a horse;
I can ride through the air upon a
stick;
Above the tree-tops and above the
houses,
And no one see me, no one over-
take me! [*Exeunt.*

SCENE II.—*A room at* JUSTICE
HATHORNE'S. *A clock in the
corner. Enter* HATHORNE *and*
MATHER.

Hathorne. You are welcome, reverend sir, thrice welcome here

Beneath my humble roof.

Mather. I thank your Worship.

Hathorne. Pray you be seated.
You must be fatigued
With your long ride through unfre-
quented woods.

(*They sit down.*)

Mather. You know the purport
of my visit here,—
To be advised by you, and counsel
with you,
And with the Reverend Clergy of
the village,
Touching these witchcrafts that so
much afflict you;
And see with mine own eyes the
wonders told
Of spectres and the shadows of the
dead,
That come back from their graves
to speak with men.

Hathorne. Some men there are,
I have known such, who think
That the two worlds—the seen and
the unseen,
The world of matter and the world
of spirit—
Are like the hemispheres upon our
maps,
And touch each other only at a point.
But these two worlds are not di-
vided thus,
Save for the purposes of common
speech.
They form one globe, in which the
parted seas
All flow together and are inter-
mingled,
While the great continents remain
distinct.

Mather. I doubt it not. The
spiritual world
Lies all about us, and its avenues
Are open to the unseen feet of phantoms
That come and go, and we perceive
them not

Save by their influence, or when at
times
A most mysterious Providence permits them
To manifest themselves to mortal
eyes.

Hathorne. You, who are always
welcome here among us,
Are doubly welcome now. We
need your wisdom,
Your learning in these things, to be
our guide.
The Devil hath come down in wrath
upon us,
And ravages the land with all his
hosts.

Mather. The Unclean Spirit
said, 'My name is Legion!'
Multitudes in the Valley of De-
struction!
But when our fervent, well-directed
prayers,
Which are the great artillery of
Heaven,
Are brought into the field, I see
them scattered
And driven like Autumn leaves be-
fore the wind.

Hathorne. You, as a Minister of
God, can meet them
With spiritual weapons; but, alas!
I, as a Magistrate, must combat them
With weapons from the armoury of
the flesh.

Mather. These wonders of the
world invisible,—
These spectral shapes that haunt
our habitations,—
The multiplied and manifold afflictions
With which the aged and the dying
saints
Have their death prefaced and their
age imbittered,—
Are but prophetic trumpets that
proclaim
The Second Coming of our Lord on
earth.

The evening wolves will be much
   more abroad
When we are near the evening of
   the world.
   Hathorne. When you shall see,
   as I have hourly seen,
The sorceries and the witchcrafts
   that torment us,
See children tortured by invisible
   spirits,
And wasted and consumed by
   powers unseen,
You will confess the half has not
   been told you.
   Mather. It must be so. The
   death-pangs of the Devil
Will make him more a Devil than
   before,
And Nebuchadnezzar's furnace will
   be heated
Seven times more hot before its
   putting out.
   Hathorne. Advise me, reverend
   sir. I look to you
For counsel and for guidance in
   this matter.
What further shall we do?
   Mather.   Remember this,
That as a sparrow falls not to the
   ground
Without the will of God, so not a
   Devil
Can come down from the air with-
   out his leave.
We must inquire.
   Hathorne.   Dear sir, we have
   inquired;
Sifted the matter thoroughly,
   through and through,
And then resifted it.
   Mather.   If God permits
These Evil Spirits from the unseen
   regions
To visit us with surprising infor-
   mations,
We must inquire what cause there
   is for this,
But not receive the testimony borne

By spectres as conclusive proof of
   guilt
In the accused.
   Hathorne.   Upon such evidence
We do not rest our case. The ways
   are many
In which the guilty do betray them-
   selves.
   Mather.   Be careful. Carry the
   knife with such exactness,
That on one side no innocent blood
   be shed
By too excessive zeal, and, on the
   other,
No shelter given to any work of
   darkness.
   Hathorne. For one, I do not
   fear excess of zeal.
What do we gain by parleying with
   the Devil?
You reason, but you hesitate to act!
Ah, reverend sir! believe me, in
   such cases
The only safety is in acting promptly.
'Tis not the part of wisdom to delay
In things where not to do is still to do
A deed more fatal than the deed
   we shrink from.
You are a man of books and medi-
   tation,
But I am one who acts.
   Mather.   God give us wisdom
In the directing of this thorny
   business,
And guide us, lest New England
   should become
Of an unsavoury and sulphurous
   odour
In the opinion of the world abroad!

(The clock strikes.)

I never hear the striking of a clock
Without a warning and an ad-
   monition
That time is on the wing, and we
   must quicken
Our tardy pace in journeying
   Heavenward,

As Israel did in journeying
Canaanward!

(*They rise.*)

Hathorne. Then let us make
all haste; and I will show you
In what disguises and what fearful
shapes
The Unclean Spirits haunt this
neighbourhood,
And you will pardon my excess of
zeal.

Mather. Ah, poor New England!
He who hurricanoed
The house of Job is making now on
thee
One last assault, more deadly and
more snarled
With unintelligible circumstances
Than any thou hast hitherto en-
countered! [*Exeunt.*

SCENE III.—*A room in* WALCOT'S
house. MARY WALCOT *seated
in an arm-chair.* TITUBA *with
a mirror.*

Mary. Tell me another story,
Tituba.
A drowsiness is stealing over me
Which is not sleep; for, though I
close mine eyes,
I am awake, and in another world.
Dim faces of the dead and of the
absent
Come floating up before me,—
floating, fading,
And disappearing.

Tituba. Look into this glass.
What see you?

Mary. Nothing but a golden
vapour,
Yes, something more. An island,
with the sea
Breaking all round it, like a blooming hedge.
What land is this?

Tituba. It is San Salvador,
Where Tituba was born. What
see you now?

Mary. A man all black and fierce.

Tituba. That is my father.
He was an Obi man, and taught me
magic,
Taught me the use of herbs and
images.
What is he doing?

Mary. Holding in his hand
A waxen figure. He is melting it
Slowly before a fire.

Tituba. And now what see you?

Mary. A woman lying on a bed
of leaves,
Wasted and worn away. Ah, she
is dying!

Tituba. That is the way the Obi
men destroy
The people they dislike! That is
the way
Some one is wasting and consuming you.

Mary. You terrify me, Tituba!
O, save me
From those who make me pine and
waste away!
Who are they? Tell me.

Tituba. That I do not know,
But you will see them. They will
come to you.

Mary. No, do not let them come!
I cannot bear it!
I am too weak to bear it! I am
dying.

(*Falls into a trance.*)

Tituba. Hark! there is some
one coming!

(*Enter* HATHORNE, MATHER, *and*
WALCOT.)

Walcot. There she lies,
Wasted and worn by devilish in-
cantations!
O my poor sister!

Mather. Is she always thus?

604

Walcot. Nay, she is sometimes
tortured by convulsions.

Mather. Poor child! How thin
she is! How wan and wasted!

Hathorne. Observe her. She
is troubled in her sleep.

Mather. Some fearful vision
haunts her.

Hathorne. You now see
With your own eyes, and touch
with your own hands,
The mysteries of this Witchcraft.

Mather. One would need
The hands of Briareus and the eyes
of Argus
To see and touch them all.

Hathorne. You now have entered
The realm of ghosts and phantoms
— the vast realm
Of the unknown and the invisible,
Through whose wide-open gates
there blows a wind
From the dark valley of the shadow
of Death,
That freezes us with horror.

Mary (starting). Take her hence!
Take her away from me. I see her
there!
She's coming to torment me!

Walcot (taking her hand). O
my sister!
What frightens you? She neither
hears nor sees me.
She's in a trance.

Mary. Do you not see her
there?

Tituba. My child, who is it?

Mary. Ah, I do not know.
I cannot see her face.

Tituba. How is she clad?

Mary. She wears a crimson
bodice. In her hand
She holds an image, and is pinch-
ing it
Between her fingers. Ah, she
tortures me!
I see her face now. It is Goodwife Bishop!

Why does she torture me? I never
harmed her!
And now she strikes me with an
iron rod!
O, I am beaten!

Mather. This is wonderful!
I can see nothing! Is this apparition
Visibly there, and yet we cannot
see it?

Hathorne. It is. The spectre is
invisible
Unto our grosser senses, but she
sees it.

Mary. Look! look! there is an-
other clad in gray!
She holds a spindle in her hand
and threatens
To stab me with it! It is Goodwife
Corey!
Keep her away! Now she is coming
at me!
O mercy! mercy!

*Walcot (thrusting with his
sword).* There is nothing
there!

Mather (to Hathorne). Do you
see anything?

Hathorne. The laws that
govern
The spiritual world prevent our
seeing
Things palpable and visible to her.
These spectres are to us as if they
were not.
Mark her, she wakes.

(TITUBA *touches her, and she
awakes.*)

Mary. Who are these
gentlemen?

Walcot. They are our friends.
Dear Mary are you better?

Mary. Weak, very weak.

(*Taking a spindle from her lap,
and holding it up.*)

How came this spindle here?

Tituba. You wrenched it from
the hand of Goodwife Corey
When she rushed at you.
   Hathorne.   Mark that,
      reverend sir!
   Mather. It is most marvellous,
      most inexplicable!
   Tituba (*picking up a bit of gray
   cloth from the floor*). And
   here, too is a bit of her gray
   dress,
That the sword cut away.
   Mather.   Beholding this,
It were indeed by far more credu-
   lous

To be incredulous than to believe.
None but a Sadducee, who doubts
   of all
Pertaining to the spiritual world,
Could doubt such manifest and
   damning proofs!
   Hathorne. Are you convinced?
   Mather (*to Mary*). Dear child,
   be comforted!
Only by prayer and fasting can you
   drive
These Unclean Spirits from you.
   An old man
Gives you his blessing. God be
   with you, Mary!

ACT II.

SCENE I.—GILES COREY'S *Farm.
Morning. Enter* COREY *with a
horseshoe and a hammer.*

   Corey. The Lord hath prospered
      me. The rising sun
Shines on my Hundred Acres and
   my woods
As if he loved them. On a morn
   like this
I can forgive mine enemies, and
   thank God
For all his goodness unto me and
   mine.
My orchard groans with russets
   and pearmains;
My ripening corn shines golden in
   the sun;
My barns are crammed with hay,
   my cattle thrive;
The birds sing blithely on the trees
   around me!
And blither than the birds my
   heart within me,
But Satan still goes up and down
   the earth;
And to protect this house from his
   assaults,
And keep the powers of darkness
   from my door,

This horseshoe will I nail upon the
   threshold.
   (*Nails down the horseshoe.*)
There, ye night-hags and witches
   that torment
The neighbourhood, ye shall not
   enter here!—
What is the matter in the field?—
   John Gloyd!
The cattle are all running to the
   woods!—
John Gloyd! Where is the man?
   (*Enter* JOHN GLOYD.)
                     Look here!
What ails the cattle? Are they all
   bewitched?
They run like mad.
   Gloyd.   They have been
   overlooked.
   Corey. The Evil Eye is on them
   sure enough.
Call all the men. Be quick. Go
   after them!
(*Exit* GLOYD *and enter* MARTHA.)
   Martha. What is amiss?
   Corey.   The cattle
   are bewitched.
They are broken loose and making
   for the woods.

606

Martha. Why will you harbour such delusions, Giles?

Bewitched? Well, then it was John Gloyd bewitched them;

I saw him even now take down the bars

And turn them loose! They're only frolicsome.

   Corey. The rascal!

   Martha.   I was standing in the road.

Talking with Goodwife Proctor, and I saw him.

   Corey. With Proctor's wife? And what says Goodwife Proctor?

   Martha. Sad things indeed; the saddest you can hear

Of Bridget Bishop. She's cried out upon!

   Corey. Poor soul! I've known her forty year or more.

She was the widow Wasselby; and then

She married Oliver, and Bishop next.

She's had three husbands. I remember well

My games of shovel-board at Bishop's tavern

In the old merry days, and she so gay

With her red paragon bodice and her ribbons!

Ah, Bridget Bishop always was a Witch!

   Martha. They'll little help her now,—her caps and ribbons

And her red paragon bodice, and her plumes,

With which she flaunted in the Meeting-house!

When next she goes there it will be for trial.

   Corey. When will that be?

   Martha. This very day at ten.

   Corey. Then get you ready. We will go and see it.

Come; you shall ride behind me on the pillion

   Martha. Not I. You know I do not like such things.

I wonder you should. I do not believe

In Witches nor in Witchcraft.

   Corey.   Well, I do.

There's a strange fascination in it all

That draws me on and on. I know not why.

   Martha. What do we know of spirits good or ill,

Or of their power to help us or to harm us?

   Corey. Surely what's in the Bible must be true.

Did not an Evil Spirit come on Saul?

Did not the Witch of Endor bring the ghost

Of Samuel from his grave? The Bible says so.

   Martha. That happened very long ago.

   Corey.   With God

There is no long ago.

   Martha.   There is with us.

   Corey. And Mary Magdalene had seven devils,

And he who dwelt among the tombs a legion!

   Martha. God's power is infinite. I do not doubt it.

If in his providence he once permitted

Such things to be among the Israelites,

It does not follow he permits them now,

And among us who are not Israelites.

But we will not dispute about it, Giles.

Go to the village, if you think it best,

And leave me here; I'll go about my work. [*Exit into the house.*

   Corey. And I will go and saddle the gray mare.

The last word always. That is woman's nature.
If an old man will marry a young wife
He must make up his mind to many things.
It 's putting new cloth into an old garment,
When the strain comes, it is the old gives way.

(*Goes to the door.*)

O Martha! I forgot to tell you something.
I 've had a letter from a friend of mine,
A certain Richard Gardner of Nantucket,
Master and owner of a whaling-vessel;
He writes that he is coming down to see us.
I hope you 'll like him.
 Martha. I will do my best.
 Corey. That 's a good woman.
Now I will be gone.
I 've not seen Gardner for this twenty year;
But there is something of the sea about him,—
Something so open, generous, large, and strong,
It makes me love him better than a brother. [*Exit.*

(Martha *comes to the door.*)

 Martha. O these old friends and cronies of my husband,
These captains from Nantucket and the Cape,
That come and turn my house into a tavern
With their carousing! Still there 's something frank
In these seafaring men that makes me like them.
Why, here 's a horseshoe nailed upon the doorstep!
Giles has done this to keep away the Witches.

I hope this Richard Gardner will bring with him
A gale of good sound common-sense, to blow
The fog of these delusions from his brain!
 Corey (*within*). Ho! Martha! Martha!

(*Enter* COREY.)

 Have you seen my saddle?
 Martha. I saw it yesterday.
 Corey. Where did you see it?
 Martha. On a gray mare, that somebody was riding
Along the village road.
 Corey. Who was it? Tell me.
 Martha. Some one who should have stayed at home.
 Corey (*restraining himself*). I see!
Don't vex me, Martha. Tell me where it is.
 Martha. I 've hidden it away.
 Corey. Go fetch it me.
 Martha. Go find it.
 Corey. No, I 'll ride down to the village
Bare-back; and when the people stare and say,
' Giles Corey, where 's your saddle?'
 I will answer,
' A witch has stolen it.' How shall you like that?
 Martha. I shall not like it.
 Corey. Then go fetch the saddle. [*Exit* MARTHA.
If an old man will marry a young wife,
Why then—why then—why then—he must spell Baker [1]!

(*Enter* MARTHA *with the saddle, which she throws down.*)

 Martha. There! There 's the saddle.

---

[1] A local expression for doing anything difficult. In the old spelling-books, 'Baker' was the first word of two syllables, and when a child came to it he thought he had a hard task before him.

Corey.   Take it up.
Martha.   I won't!
Corey. Then let it lie there. I 'll ride to the village,
And say you are a Witch.
     Martha.   No, not that, Giles.
     (*She takes up the saddle.*)

     Corey. Now come with me, and saddle the gray mare
With your own hands ; and you shall see me ride
Along the village road as is becoming
Giles Corey of the Salem Farms,
    your husband!   [*Exeunt.*

SCENE II.—*The Green in front of the Meeting-house in Salem Village. People coming and going. Enter* GILES COREY.

     Corey. A melancholy end! Who would have thought
That Bridget Bishop e'er would come to this?
Accused, convicted, and condemned to death
For Witchcraft! And so good a woman too!
     A Farmer. Good morrow, neighbour Corey.
     Corey (*not hearing him*). Who is safe?
How do I know but under my own roof
I too may harbour Witches, and some Devil
Be plotting and contriving against me?
     Farmer. He does not hear.
     Good morrow, neighbour Corey!
     Corey. Good morrow.
     Farmer.   Have you seen John Proctor lately?
     Corey. No, I have not.
     Farmer.   Then do not see him, Corey.

     Corey. Why should I not?
     Farmer.   Because he 's angry with you.
So keep out of his way. Avoid a quarrel.
     Corey. Why does he seek to fix a quarrel on me?
     Farmer. He says you burned his house.
     Corey.   I burn his house?
If he says that, John Proctor is a liar!
The night his house was burned I was in bed,
And I can prove it! Why, we are old friends!
He could not say that of me.
     Farmer.   He did say it.
I heard him say it.
     Corey.   Then he shall unsay it.
     Farmer. He said you did it out of spite to him
For taking part against you in the quarrel
You had with your John Gloyd about his wages.
He says you murdered Goodell ; that you trampled
Upon his body till he breathed no more.
And so beware of him ; that 's my advice!   [*Exit.*
     Corey. By Heaven! this is too much! I 'll seek him out,
And make him eat his words, or strangle him.
I 'll not be slandered at a time like this
When every word is made an accusation,
When every whisper kills, and every man
Walks with a halter round his neck!

     (*Enter* GLOYD *in haste.*)

               What now?
     Gloyd. I came to look for you.
The cattle—

Corey.   Well,
What of them? Have you found
    them?
Gloyd.   They are dead.
I followed them through the woods,
    across the meadows;
Then they all leaped into the
    Ipswich River,
And swam across, but could not
    climb the bank,
And so were drowned.
    Corey.   You are to blame
    for this;
For you took down the bars, and
    let them loose.
    Gloyd. That I deny. They broke
    the fences down.
You know they were bewitched.
    Corey.   Ah, my poor cattle!
The Evil Eye was on them; that
    is true.
Day of disaster! Most unlucky day!
Why did I leave my ploughing and
    my reaping
To plough and reap this Sodom
    and Gomorrah?
O, I could drown myself for sheer
    vexation!   [*Exit.*
    Gloyd. He's going for his cattle.
    He won't find them.
By this time they have drifted out
    to sea.
They will not break his fences any
    more,
Though they may break his heart.
And what care I?   [*Exit.*

SCENE III.—COREY'S *Kitchen. A
table with supper.* MARTHA
knitting.

Martha. He's come at last. I
    hear him in the passage.
Something has gone amiss with him
    to-day;
I know it by his step, and by the
    sound
The door made as he shut it. He
    is angry.

(*Enter* COREY *with his riding-
whip. As he speaks, he takes off
his hat and gloves, and throws
them down violently.*)

Corey. I say if Satan ever entered
    man
He's in John Proctor.
    Martha.   Giles, what is the
    matter?
You frighten me.
    Corey.   I say if any man
Can have a devil in him, then that
    man
Is Proctor,—is John Proctor, and
    no other!
    Martha. Why, what has he been
    doing?
    Corey.   Everything!
What do you think I heard there
    in the village?
    Martha. I'm sure I cannot guess.
    What did you hear?
    Corey. He says I burned his
    house!
    Martha.   Does he say that?
    Corey. He says I burned his
    house. I was in bed
And fast asleep that night and I
    can prove it.
    Martha. If he says that, I think
    the Father of Lies
Is surely in the man.
    Corey.   He does say that,
And that I did it to wreak vengeance
    on him
For taking sides against me in the
    quarrel
I had with that John Gloyd about
    his wages.
And God knows that I never bore
    him malice
For that, as I have told him twenty
    times!
    Martha. It is John Gloyd has
    stirred him up to this.
I do not like that Gloyd. I think
    him crafty,

Not to be trusted, sullen, and un-
truthful.
Come, have your supper. You are
tired and hungry.
   Corey. I'm angry, and not hungry.
   Martha.   Do eat something.
You'll be the better for it.
   Corey (*sitting down*). I'm not
hungry.
   Martha. Let not the sun go down
upon your wrath.
   Corey. It has gone down upon it,
and will rise
To-morrow, and go down again
upon it.
They have trumped up against me
the old story
Of causing Goodell's death by
trampling on him.
   Martha. O, that is false. I
know it to be false.
   Corey. He has been dead these
fourteen years or more.
Why can't they let him rest? Why
must they drag him
Out of his grave to give me a bad
name?
I did not kill him. In his bed he
died,
As most men die, because his hour
had come.
I have wronged no man. Why
should Proctor say
Such things about me? I will not
forgive him
Till he confesses he has slandered
me.
Then, I've more trouble. All my
cattle gone.
   Martha. They will come back
again.
   Corey.   Not in this world.
Did I not tell you they were overlooked?
They ran down through the woods,
into the meadows,
And tried to swim the river, and
were drowned.

It is a heavy loss.
   Martha.   I'm sorry for it.
   Corey. All my dear oxen dead.
I loved them, Martha,
Next to yourself. I liked to look
at them,
And watch the breath come out of
their wide nostrils,
And see their patient eyes. Some-
how I thought
It gave me strength only to look at
them.
And how they strained their necks
against the yoke
If I but spoke, or touched them
with the goad!
They were my friends; and when
Gloyd came and told me
They were all drowned, I could
have drowned myself
From sheer vexation; and I said
as much
To Gloyd and others.
   Martha.   Do not trust
John Gloyd
With anything you would not have
repeated.
   Corey. As I came through the
woods this afternoon,
Impatient at my loss, and much
perplexed
With all that I had heard there in
the village,
The yellow leaves lit up the trees
about me,
Like an enchanted palace, and I
wished
I knew enough of magic or of
Witchcraft
To change them into gold. Then
suddenly
A tree shook down some crimson
leaves upon me
Like drops of blood, and in the path
before me
Stood Tituba the Indian, the old
crone.
   Martha. Were you not frightened?

Corey.   No, I do not think
I know the meaning of that word.
    Why frightened?
I am not one of those who think
    the Lord
Is waiting till he catches them some
    day
In the back yard alone! What
    should I fear?
She started from the bushes by the
    path,
And had a basket full of herbs and
    roots
For some witch-broth or other,—
    the old hag!
    Martha. She has been here to-
        day.
    Corey. With hand outstretched
She said: 'Giles Corey, will you
    sign the Book?'
'Avaunt!' I cried: 'Get thee behind
    me, Satan!'
At which she laughed and left me.
    But a voice
Was whispering in my ear con-
    tinually:
'Self-murder is no crime. The
    life of man
Is his, to keep it or to throw away!'
    Martha. 'Twas a temptation of
        the Evil One!
Giles, Giles! why will you harbour
    these dark thoughts?
    Corey (*rising*). I am too tired to
        talk.   I 'll go to bed.
    Martha. First tell me something
        about Bridget Bishop.
How did she look?   You saw her?
    You were there?

ACT III.

SCENE I.—GILES COREY'S *Kitchen.*
    Morning.   COREY *and* MAR-
    THA *sitting at the breakfast
    table.*
    Corey (*rising*). Well, now I 've
    told you all I saw and heard

Corey. I 'll tell you that to-mor-
    row, not to-night.
I 'll go to bed.
    Martha.   First let us pray
        together.
    Corey. I cannot pray to-night.
    Martha. Say the Lord's Prayer,
And that will comfort you.
    Corey.   I cannot say,
'As we forgive those that have
    sinned against us,'
When I do not forgive them.
    Martha (*kneeling on the hearth*).
        God forgive you!
    Corey. I will not make believe!
        I say, to-night
There 's something thwarts me
    when I wish to pray,
And thrusts into my mind, instead
    of prayers,
Hate and revenge, and things that
    are not prayers.
Something of my old self,—my old,
    bad life,—
And the old Adam in me, rises up,
And will not let me pray.   I am
    afraid
The Devil hinders me.   You know
    I say
Just what I think, and nothing more
    nor less,
And, when I pray, my heart is in
    my prayer.
I cannot say one thing and mean
    another.
If I can't pray, I will not make
    believe!
(*Exit* COREY.   MARTHA *continues
        kneeling.*)

Of Bridget Bishop; and I must be
    gone.
    Martha. Don't go into the vil-
        lage, Giles, to-day.
Last night you came back tired and
    out of humour.

Corey. Say, angry; say, right angry. I was never
In a more devilish temper in my life.
All things went wrong with me.

Martha. You were much vexed;
So don't go to the village.

Corey (going). No, I won't,
I won't go near it. We are going to mow
The Ipswich meadows for the aftermath,
The crop of sedge and rowens.

Martha. Stay a moment.
I want to tell you what I dreamed last night.
Do you believe in dreams?

Corey. Why, yes and no.
When they come true, then I believe in them;
When they come false, I don't believe in them.
But let me hear. What did you dream about?

Martha. I dreamed that you and I were both in prison;
That we had fetters on our hands and feet;
That we were taken before the Magistrates,
And tried for Witchcraft, and condemned to death!
I wished to pray; they would not let me pray;
You tried to comfort me, and they forbade it.
But the most dreadful thing in all my dream
Was that they made you testify against me!
And then there came a kind of mist between us;
I could not see you; and I woke in terror.
I never was more thankful in my life
Than when I found you sleeping at my side!

Corey (with tenderness). It was our talk last night that made you dream.
I 'm sorry for it. I 'll control myself
Another time, and keep my temper down!
I do not like such dreams.—Remember, Martha,
I 'm going to mow the Ipswich River meadows;
If Gardner comes, you 'll tell him where to find me. [*Exit.*

Martha. So this delusion grows from bad to worse.
First, a forsaken and forlorn old woman,
Ragged and wretched, and without a friend;
Then something higher. Now it 's Bridget Bishop;
God only knows whose turn it will be next;
The Magistrates are blind, the people mad!
If they would only seize the Afflicted Children,
And put them in the Workhouse, where they should be,
There 'd be an end of all this wickedness. [*Exit.*

SCENE II.—*A street in Salem Village. Enter* MATHER *and* HATHORNE.

Mather. Yet one thing troubles me.

Hathorne. And what is that?

Mather. May not the Devil take the outward shape
Of innocent persons? Are we not in danger,
Perhaps, of punishing some who are not guilty?

Hathorne. As I have said, we do not trust alone
To spectral evidence.

Mather. And then again,

If any shall be put to death for
Witchcraft,
We do but kill the body, not the
soul.
The Unclean Spirits that possessed
them once
Live still, to enter into other bodies.
What have we gained? Surely,
there's nothing gained.

Hathorne. Doth not the Scripture say, 'Thou shalt not suffer
A Witch to live'?

Mather. The Scripture sayeth it,
But speaketh to the Jews; and we
are Christians.
What say the laws of England?

Hathorne. They make Witchcraft
Felony without the benefit of Clergy.
Witches are burned in England.
You have read—
For you read all things, not a book
escapes you—
The famous Demonology of King
James?

Mather. A curious volume. I
remember also
The plot of the Two Hundred, with
one Fian,
The Registrar of the Devil, at their
head,
To drown his Majesty on his return
From Denmark; how they sailed in
sieves or riddles
Unto North Berwick Kirk in Lothian,
And, landing there, danced hand in
hand, and sang,
'Goodwife, go ye before! goodwife,
go ye!
If ye'll not go before, goodwife, let
me!'
While Geilis Duncan played the
Witches' Reel
Upon a jews-harp.

Hathorne. Then you know
full well
The English law, and that in England Witches,

When lawfully convicted and attainted,
Are put to death.

Mather. When lawfully convicted:
That is the point.

Hathorne. You heard the evidence
Produced before us yesterday at the
trial
Of Bridget Bishop.

Mather. One of the Afflicted,
I know, bore witness to the apparition
Of ghosts unto the spectre of this
Bishop,
Saying, 'You murdered us!' of the
truth whereof
There was in matter of fact too
much suspicion.

Hathorne. And when she cast
her eyes on the Afflicted,
They were struck down; and this
in such a manner
There could be no collusion in the
business.
And when the accused but laid her
hand upon them,
As they lay in their swoons, they
straight revived,
Although they stirred not when the
others touched them.

Mather. What most convinced
me of the woman's guilt
Was finding hidden in her cellar wall
Those poppets made of rags, with
headless pins
Stuck into them point outwards,
and whereof
She could not give a reasonable
account.

Hathorne. When you shall read
the testimony given
Before the Court in all the other
cases,
I am persuaded you will find the
proof
No less conclusive than it was in this.
Come, then, with me, and I will
tax your patience

With reading of the documents so
far
As may convince you that these
sorcerers
Are lawfully convicted and attainted.
Like doubting Thomas, you shall
lay your hand
Upon these wounds, and you will
doubt no more.   [*Exeunt.*

SCENE III.—*A room in* COREY'S
house. MARTHA *and two Deacons
of the church.*

  Martha. Be seated. I am glad
to see you here.
I know what you are come for.
You are come
To question me, and learn from my
own lips
If I have any dealings with the Devil;
In short, if I'm a Witch.
  Deacon (*sitting down*). Such is
our purpose.
How could you know beforehand
why we came?
  Martha. 'Twas only a surmise.
  Deacon. We came to ask you,
You being with us in church cove-
nant,
What part you have, if any, in these
matters.
  Martha. And I make answer, No
part whatsoever.
I am a farmer's wife, a working
woman;
You see my spinning-wheel, you see
my loom,
You know the duties of a farmer's
wife,
And are not ignorant that my life
among you
Has been without reproach until
this day.
Is it not true?
  Deacon. So much we're bound
to own;

And say it frankly, and without
reserve.
  Martha. I've heard the idle tales
that are abroad;
I've heard it whispered that I am
a Witch;
I cannot help it. I do not believe
In any Witchcraft. It is a delusion.
  Deacon. How can you say that it
is a delusion,
When all our learned and good
men believe it?—
Our Ministers and worshipful
Magistrates?
  Martha. Their eyes are blinded,
and see not the truth.
Perhaps one day they will be open
to it.
  Deacon. You answer boldly. The
Afflicted Children
Say you appeared to them.
  Martha.   And did they say
What clothes I came in?
  Deacon.   No, they could
not tell.
They said that you foresaw our
visit here,
And blinded them, so that they
could not see
The clothes you wore.
  Martha.   The cunning,
crafty girls!
I say to you, in all sincerity,
I never have appeared to any one
In my own person. If the Devil
takes
My shape to hurt these children, or
afflict them,
I am not guilty of it. And I say
It's all a mere delusion of the senses.
  Deacon. I greatly fear that you
will find too late
It is not so.
  Martha (*rising*). They do accuse
me falsely.
It is delusion, or it is deceit.
There is a story in the ancient
Scriptures

Which much I wonder comes not
to your minds.

Let me repeat it to you.

Deacon. We will hear it.

Martha. It came to pass that
Naboth had a vineyard

Hard by the palace of the King
called Ahab.

And Ahab, King of Israel, spake
to Naboth,

And said to him, Give unto me thy
vineyard,

That I may have it for a garden of
herbs,

And I will give a better vineyard
for it,

Or, if it seemeth good to thee, its
worth

In money. And then Naboth said
to Ahab,

The Lord forbid it me that I should
give

The inheritance of my fathers
unto thee.

And Ahab came into his house
displeased

And heavy at the words which
Naboth spake,

And laid him down upon his bed,
and turned

His face away; and he would eat
no bread.

And Jezebel, the wife of Ahab, came

And said to him, Why is thy spirit
sad?

And he said unto her, Because I
spake

To Naboth, to the Jezreelite, and
said,

Give me thy vineyard; and he
answered, saying,

I will not give my vineyard unto
thee.

And Jezebel, the wife of Ahab, said,

Dost thou not rule the realm of
Israel?

Arise, eat bread, and let thy heart
be merry;

I will give Naboth's vineyard unto
thee.

So she wrote letters in King Ahab's
name,

And sealed them with his seal, and
sent the letters

Unto the elders that were in his
city

Dwelling with Naboth, and unto
the nobles;

And in the letters wrote, Proclaim
a fast;

And set this Naboth high among
the people,

And set two men, the sons of
Belial,

Before him, to bear witness and to
say,

Thou didst blaspheme against God
and the King;

And carry him out and stone him,
that he die!

And the elders and the nobles of
the city

Did even as Jezebel, the wife of
Ahab,

Had sent to them and written in
the letters.

And then it came to pass, when
Ahab heard

Naboth was dead, that Ahab rose
to go

Down unto Naboth's vineyard, and
to take

Possession of it. And the word of
God

Came to Elijah, saying to him, Arise,

Go down to meet the King of Israel

In Naboth's vineyard, whither he
hath gone

To take possession. Thou shalt
speak to him,

Saying, Thus saith the Lord!
What! hast thou killed

And also taken possession? In the
place

Wherein the dogs have licked the
blood of Naboth

616

Shall the dogs lick thy blood,—ay,
even thine !

(*Both of the Deacons start from
their seats.*)

And Ahab then, the King of Israel,
Said, Hast thou found me, O mine
enemy ?
Elijah the Prophet answered, I
have found thee !
So will it be with those who have
stirred up
The sons of Belial here to bear
false witness
And swear away the lives of innocent people ;
Their enemy will find them out at
last,
The Prophet's voice will thunder, I
have found thee !   [*Exeunt.*

SCENE IV.—*Meadows on Ipswich
River.* COREY *and his men
mowing ;* COREY *in advance.*

Corey. Well done, my men. You
see, I lead the field !
I'm an old man, but I can swing a
scythe
Better than most of you, though
you be younger.

(*Hangs his scythe upon a tree.*)

Gloyd (*aside to the others*). How
strong he is ! It's supernatural.
No man so old as he is has such
strength.
The Devil helps him !
Corey (*wiping his forehead*).
Now we'll rest awhile,
And take our nooning. What's the
matter with you ?
You are not angry with me,—are
you, Gloyd ?
Come, come, we will not quarrel.
Let 's be friends.
It's an old story, that the Raven
said,

'Read the Third of Colossians and
fifteenth.'
Gloyd. You're handier at the
scythe, but I can beat you
At wrestling.
Corey.   Well, perhaps so. I
don't know,
I never wrestled with you. Why,
you're vexed !
Come, come, don't bear a grudge.
Gloyd.   You are afraid.
Corey. What should I be afraid
of ? All bear witness
The challenge comes from him.
Now, then, my man.

(*They wrestle, and* GLOYD *is
thrown.*)

One of the Men. That's a fair
fall.
Another. 'Twas nothing but a
foil !
Others. You've hurt him !
Corey (*helping* GLOYD *rise*). No ;
this meadow-land is soft.
You're not hurt,—are you, Gloyd ?
Gloyd (*rising*).   No, not
much hurt !
Corey. Well, then, shake hands ;
and there 's an end of it.
How do you like that Cornish hug,
my lad ?
And now we'll see what's in our
basket here.
Gloyd (*aside*). The Devil and all
his imps are in that man !
The clutch of his ten fingers burns
like fire !
Corey (*reverentially taking off
his hat*). God bless the food
he hath provided for us,
And make us thankful for it, for
Christ's sake !

(*He lifts up a keg of cider, and
drinks from it.*)

Gloyd. Do you see that ? Don't
tell me it's not Witchcraft.

Two of us could not lift that cask as he does !

(COREY *puts down the keg, and opens a basket. A voice is heard calling.*)

Voice. Ho ! Corey, Corey !

Corey. What is that ? I surely Heard some one calling me by name !

Voice. Giles Corey !

(*Enter a boy, running and out of breath.*)

Boy. Is Master Corey here ?

Corey. Yes, here I am.

Boy. O Master Corey !

Corey. Well ?

Boy. Your wife—your wife—

Corey. What 's happened to my wife ?

Boy. She 's sent to prison !

Corey. The dream ! the dream ! O God, be merciful !

Boy. She sent me here to tell you.

Corey (*putting on his jacket*). Where 's my horse ? Don't stand there staring, fellows. Where 's my horse ?

[*Exit* COREY.

Gloyd. Under the trees there. Run, old man, run ! run ! You 've got some one to wrestle with you now Who 'll trip your heels up, with your Cornish hug. If there 's a Devil, he has got you now. Ah, there he goes ! His horse is snorting fire !

One of the Men. John Gloyd, don't talk so ! It 's a shame to talk so ! He 's a good master, though you quarrel with him.

Gloyd. If hard work and low wages make good masters, Then he is one. But I think otherwise.

Come, let us have our dinner and be merry, And talk about the old man and the Witches. I know some stories that will make you laugh.

(*They sit down on the grass and eat.*)

Now there are Goody Cloyse and Goody Good, Who have not got a decent tooth between them, And yet these children—the Afflicted Children— Say that they bite them, and show marks of teeth Upon their arms !

One of the Men. That makes the wonder greater.

That 's Witchcraft. Why, if they had teeth like yours, 'Twould be no wonder if the girls were bitten !

Gloyd. And then those ghosts that come out of their graves And cry, ' You murdered us ! you murdered us !'

One of the Men. And all those Apparitions that stick pins Into the flesh of the Afflicted Children !

Gloyd. O those Afflicted Children ! they know well Where the pins come from. I can tell you that. And there 's old Corey, he has got a horseshoe Nailed on his doorstep to keep off the Witches, And all the same his wife has gone to prison.

One of the Men. O, she 's no Witch. I 'll swear that Goodwife Corey Never did harm to any living creature. She 's a good woman, if there ever was one.

Gloyd. Well, we shall see. As
for that Bridget Bishop,
She has been tried before; some
years ago
A negro testified he saw her shape
Sitting upon the rafters in a barn,
And holding in its hand an egg;
and while
He went to fetch his pitchfork, she
had vanished.
And now be quiet, will you? I am
tired,
And want to sleep here on the grass
a little.

(*They stretch themselves on the
grass.*)

One of the Men. There may be
Witches riding through the
air
Over our heads on broomsticks at
this moment,
Bound for some Satan's Sabbath
in the woods
To be baptized.
Gloyd. I wish they'd take
you with them,
And hold you under water, head
and ears,
Till you were drowned; and that
would stop your talking,
If nothing else will. Let me sleep,
I say.

ACT IV.

SCENE I.—*The Green in front of
the village Meeting-house. An
excited crowd gathering. Enter*
JOHN GLOYD.

A Farmer. Who will be tried to-
day?
A Second. I do not know.
Here is John Gloyd. Ask him;
he knows.
Farmer. John Gloyd,
Whose turn is it to-day?
Gloyd. It's Goodwife Corey's.
Farmer. Giles Corey's wife?
Gloyd. The same.
She is not mine.
It will go hard with her with all her
praying.
The hypocrite! She's always on
her knees;
But she prays to the Devil when
she prays.
Let us go in.

(*A trumpet blows.*)

Farmer. Here come the Magistrates.
Second Farmer. Who's the tall
man in front?

Gloyd. O, that is Hathorne,
A Justice of the Court, and Quarter-
master
In the Three County Troop. He'll
sift the matter.
That's Corwin with him; and the
man in black
Is Cotton Mather, Minister of Boston.

(*Enter* HATHORNE *and other Magistrates on horseback, followed
by the Sheriff, constables, and
attendants on foot. The Magistrates dismount, and enter the
Meeting-house, with the rest.*)

Farmer. The Meeting-house is
full. I never saw
So great a crowd before.
Gloyd. No matter. Come.
We shall find room enough by
elbowing
Our way among them. Put your
shoulder to it.
Farmer. There were not half so
many at the trial
Of Goodwife Bishop.

Gloyd. Keep close after me,
I'll find a place for you. They'll
   want me there.
I am a friend of Corey's, as you
   know,
And he can't do without me just at
   present.   [*Exeunt.*

SCENE II.—*Interior of the Meeting-
house.* MATHER *and the Magistrates seated in front of the pulpit.
Before them a raised platform.*
MARTHA *in chains.* COREY *near
her.* MARY WALCOT *in a chair.
A crowd of spectators, among
them* GLOYD. *Confusion and
murmurs during the scene.*

Hathorne. Call Martha Corey.
Martha.   I am here.
Hathorne.   Come forward.

(*She ascends the platform.*)

The Jurors of our Sovereign Lord
   and Lady
The King and Queen, here present,
   do accuse you
Of having on the tenth of June last
   past,
And divers other times before and
   after,
Wickedly used and practised cer-
   tain arts
Called Witchcrafts, Sorceries, and
   Incantations,
Against one Mary Walcot, single
   woman,
Of Salem Village ; by which wicked
   arts
The aforesaid Mary Walcot was
   tormented,
Tortured, afflicted, pined, con-
   sumed, and wasted,
Against the peace of our Sovereign
   Lord and Lady
The King and Queen, as well as of
   the Statute
Made and provided in that case.
   What say you ?

Martha. Before I answer give
   me leave to pray.
Hathorne. We have not sent for
   you, nor are we here,
To hear you pray, but to examine you
In whatsoever is alleged against you.
Why do you hurt this person ?
Martha.   I do not.
I am not guilty of the charge against
   me.
Mary. Avoid, she-devil ! You
   torment me now !
Avoid, avoid, Witch ?
Martha.   I am innocent.
I never had to do with any witch-
   craft
Since I was born. I am a gospel
   woman.
Mary. You are a Gospel Witch !
Martha (*clasping her hands*).
   Ah me ! ah me ! O, give me
   leave to pray !
Mary (*stretching out her hands*).
   She hurts me now.
See, she has pinched my hands !
Hathorne.   Who
   made these marks
Upon her hands ?
Martha. I do not know. I stand
Apart from her. I did not touch
   her hands.
Hathorne. Who hurt her then ?
Martha.   I know not.
Hathorne.   Do you think
She is bewitched ?
Martha. Indeed I do not think so.
I am no Witch, and have no faith
   in Witches.
Hathorne. Then answer me :
   When certain persons came
To see you yesterday, how did you
   know
Beforehand why they came ?
Martha. I had had speech,
The children said I hurt them, and
   I thought
These people came to question me
   about it.

Hathorne. How did you know
the children had been told
To note the clothes you wore?
Martha. My husband told me
What others said about it.
Hathorne. Goodman Corey,
Say, did you tell her?
Corey. I must speak the truth;
I did not tell her. It was some one
else.
Hathorne. Did you not say your
husband told you so?
How dare you tell a lie in this as-
sembly?
Who told you of the clothes? Con-
fess the truth.

(MARTHA *bites her lips, and is
silent.*)

You bite your lips, but do not an-
swer me!
Mary. Ah, she is biting me!
Avoid, avoid!
Hathorne. You said your hus-
band told you.
Martha. Yes, he told me
The children said I troubled them.
Hathorne. Then tell me,
Why do you trouble them?
Martha. I have denied it.
Mary. She threatened me; stab-
bed at me with her spindle;
And, when my brother thrust her
with his sword,
He tore her gown, and cut a piece
away.
Here are they both, the spindle and
the cloth.

(*Shows them.*)

Hathorne. And there are persons
here who know the truth
Of what has now been said. What
answer make you?
Martha. I make no answer.
Give me leave to pray.
Hathorne. Whom would you
pray to?
Martha. To my God and Father.

Hathorne. Who is your God and
Father?
Martha. The Almighty!
Hathorne. Doth he you pray to
say that he is God?
It is the Prince of Darkness, and
not God.
Mary. There is a dark shape
whispering in her ear.
Hathorne. What does he say to
you?
Martha. I see no shape.
Hathorne. Did you not hear it
whisper?
Martha. I heard nothing.
Mary. What torture! Ah, what
agony I suffer!

(*Falls into a swoon.*)

Hathorne. You see this woman
cannot stand before you.
If you would look for mercy, you
must look
In God's way, by confession of your
guilt.
Why does your spectre haunt and
hurt this person?
Martha. I do not know. He
who appeared of old
In Samuel's shape, a saint and
glorified,
May come in whatsoever shape he
chooses.
I cannot help it. I am sick at
heart!
Corey. O Martha, Martha; let
me hold your hand.
Hathorne. No; stand aside, old
man.
Mary (*starting up*). Look there!
Look there!
I see a little bird, a yellow bird,
Perched on her finger; and it pecks
at me.
Ah, it will tear mine eyes out!
Martha. I see nothing.
Hathorne. 'Tis the Familiar
Spirit that attends her.

Mary. Now it has flown away.
It sits up there
Upon the rafters. It is gone; is
vanished.
   Martha. Giles, wipe these tears
of anger from mine eyes.
Wipe the sweat from my forehead.
I am faint.
   (*She leans against the railing.*)
   Mary. O, she is crushing me
with all her weight!
   Hathorne. Did you not carry
once the Devil's Book
To this young woman?
   Martha.   Never.
   Hathorne. Have you signed it,
Or touched it?
   Martha.   No; I never saw it.
   Hathorne. Did you not scourge
her with an iron rod?
   Martha. No, I did not. If any
Evil Spirit
Has taken my shape to do these
evil deeds,
I cannot help it. I am innocent.
   Hathorne. Did you not say the
Magistrates were blind?
That you would open their eyes?
   Martha (*with a scornful laugh*).
Yes, I said that;
If you call me a sorceress, you are
blind!
If you accuse the innocent, you are
blind!
Can the innocent be guilty?
   Hathorne.   Did you not
On one occasion hide your hus-
band's saddle
To hinder him from coming to the
Sessions?
   Martha. I thought it was a folly
in a farmer
To waste his time pursuing such
illusions.
   Hathorne. What was the bird
that this young woman saw
Just now upon your hand?
   Martha.   I know no bird.

   Hathorne. Have you not dealt
with a Familiar Spirit?
   Martha. No, never, never!
   Hathorne.   What then
was the Book
You showed to this young woman,
and besought her
To write in it?
   Martha. Where should I have
a book?
I showed her none, nor have none.
   Mary.   The next Sabbath
Is the Communion-day, but Martha
Corey
Will not be there!
   Martha.   Ah, you are all
against me.
What can I do or say?
   Hathorne.   You can confess.
   Martha. No, I cannot, for I am
innocent.
   Hathorne. We have the proof of
many witnesses
That you are guilty.
   Martha. Give me leave to speak.
Will you condemn me on such evi-
dence,—
You who have known me for so
many years?
Will you condemn me in this house
of God,
Where I so long have worshipped
with you all?
Where I have eaten the bread and
drunk the wine
So many times at our Lord's Table
with you?
Bear witness, you that hear me;
you all know
That I have led a blameless life
among you,
That never any whisper of suspicion
Was breathed against me till this
accusation.
And shall this count for nothing?
Will you take
My life away from me, because this
girl,

Who is distraught, and not in her
right mind,
Accuses me of things I blush to
name?

Hathorne. What! is it not
enough? Would you hear
more?

Giles Corey!

Corey. I am here.

Hathorne. Come forward, then.

(COREY *ascends the platform.*)

Is it not true, that on a certain night
You were impeded strangely in your
prayers?
That something hindered you? and
that you left
This woman here, your wife, kneel-
ing alone
Upon the hearth?

Corey. Yes; I cannot deny it.

Hathorne. Did you not say the
Devil hindered you?

Corey. I think I said some words
to that effect.

Hathorne. Is it not true, that
fourteen head of cattle,
To you belonging, broke from their
enclosure
And leaped into the river, and were
drowned?

Corey. It is most true.

Hathorne. And did
you not then say
That they were overlooked?

Corey. So much I said.

I see; they 're drawing round me
closer, closer,
A net I cannot break, cannot escape
from! (*Aside.*)

Hathorne. Who did these things?

Corey. I do not
know who did them.

Hathorne. Then I will tell you.
It is some one near you:
You see her now; this woman, your
own wife.

Corey. I call the heavens to
witness, it is false!

She never harmed me, never hindered me
In anything but what I should not
do.
And I bear witness in the sight of
heaven,
And in God's house here, that I
never knew her
As otherwise than patient, brave,
and true,
Faithful, forgiving, full of charity,
A virtuous and industrious and
good wife!

Hathorne. Tut, tut, man; do not
rant so in your speech;
You are a witness, not an advocate!
Here, Sheriff, take this woman back
to prison.

Martha. O Giles, this day
you 've sworn away my life!

Mary. Go, go and join the
Witches at the door.
Do you not hear the drum? Do you
not see them?
Go quick. They 're waiting for you.
You are late.

(*Exit* MARTHA; COREY *following.*)

Corey. The dream! the dream!
the dream!

Hathorne. What does he say?
Giles Corey, go not hence. You are
yourself
Accused of Witchcraft and of
Sorcery
By many witnesses. Say, are you
guilty?

Corey. I know my death is foreordained by you,—
Mine and my wife's. Therefore I
will not answer.

(*During the rest of the scene he
remains silent.*)

Hathorne. Do you refuse to
plead?— 'twere better for you
To make confession, or to plead
Not Guilty.—

Do you not hear me?—Answer, are
  you guilty?
Do you not know a heavier doom
  awaits you,
If you refuse to plead, than if found
  guilty?
Where is John Gloyd?
  Gloyd (coming forward). Here
  am I.
  Hathorne.   Tell the Court;
Have you not seen the supernatural
  power
Of this old man? Have you not
  seen him do
Strange feats of strength?
  Gloyd.   I 've seen
  him lead the field,
On a hot day, in mowing, and
  against
Us younger men; and I have
  wrestled with him.
He threw me like a feather. I have
  seen him
Lift up a barrel with his single hands,
Which two strong men could
  hardly lift together,
And, holding it above his head,
  drink from it.
  Hathorne. That is enough;
  we need not question further.
What answer do you make to this,
  Giles Corey?
  Mary. See there! See there!
  Hathorne.   What is it?
I see nothing.

Mary. Look! look! It is the
  ghost of Robert Goodell,
Whom fifteen years ago this man
  did murder
By stamping on his body! In his
  shroud
He comes here to bear witness to
  the crime!

(*The crowd shrinks back from*
  COREY *in horror.*)

Hathorne. Ghosts of the dead
  and voices of the living
Bear witness to your guilt, and you
  must die!
It might have been an easier death.
  Your doom
Will be on your own head, and not
  on ours.
Twice more will you be questioned
  of these things;
Twice more have you room to plead
  or to confess.
If you are contumacious to the
  Court,
And if, when questioned, you refuse
  to answer,
Then by the Statute you will be
  condemned
To the *peine forte et dure!* To
  have your body
Pressed by great weights until you
  shall be dead!
And may the Lord have mercy on
  your soul!

ACT V.

SCENE I.—COREY'S *Farm, as in*
  Act II, Scene I. *Enter* RICHARD
  GARDNER, *looking round him.*

Gardner. Here stands the house
  as I remember it,
The four tall poplar-trees before
  the door;
The house, the barn, the orchard,
  and the well,

With its moss-covered bucket and
  its trough;
The garden, with its hedge of cur-
  rant-bushes;
The woods, the harvest-fields; and,
  far beyond,
The pleasant landscape stretching
  to the sea.
But everything is silent and deserted!

624

No bleat of flocks, no bellowing of
herds,
No sound of flails, that should be
beating now ;
Nor man nor beast astir. What
can this mean ?

(*Knocks at the door.*)

What ho ! Giles Corey ! Hillo-ho !
Giles Corey !—
No answer but the echo from the
barn,
And the ill-omened cawing of the
crow,
That yonder wings his flight across
the fields,
As if he scented carrion in the air.

(*Enter* TITUBA *with a basket.*)

What woman 's this, that, like an
apparition,
Haunts this deserted homestead in
broad day ?
Woman, who are you ?
Tituba.   I am Tituba.
I am John Indian's wife. I am a
Witch.
Gardner. What are you doing
here ?
Tituba. I 'm gathering herbs,—
Cinquefoil, and saxifrage, and
pennyroyal.
Gardner (*looking at the herbs*).
This is not cinquefoil, it is
deadly nightshade !
This is not saxifrage, but helle-
bore !
This is not pennyroyal, it is hen-
bane !
Do you come here to poison these
good people ?
Tituba. I get these for the
Doctor in the village.
Beware of Tituba. I pinch the
children ;
Make little poppets and stick pins
in them,
And then the children cry out they
are pricked.

The Black Dog came to me, and
said, 'Serve me !'
I was afraid. He made me hurt
the children.
Gardner. Poor soul ! She 's
crazed, with all these Devil's
doings.
Tituba. Will you, sir, sign the
Book ?
Gardner.   No, I 'll not sign it.
Where 's Giles Corey ? Do you
know Giles Corey ?
Tituba. He 's safe enough. He 's
down there in the prison.
Gardner. Corey in prison ?
What is he accused of ?
Tituba. Giles Corey and Martha
Corey are in prison
Down there in Salem Village. Both
are Witches.
She came to me and whispered,
' Kill the children !'
Both signed the Book !
Gardner.   Begone, you
imp of darkness !
You Devil's dam !
Tituba.   Beware of Tituba !
[*Exit.*

Gardner. How often out at sea
on stormy nights,
When the waves thundered round
me, and the wind
Bellowed, and beat the canvas, and
my ship
Clove through the solid darkness,
like a wedge,
I 've thought of him upon his
pleasant farm,
Living in quiet with his thrifty
housewife,
And envied him, and wished his fate
were mine !
And now I find him shipwrecked
utterly
Drifting upon this sea of sorceries,
And lost, perhaps, beyond all aid
of man !

625

SCENE II.—*The Prison.* GILES
COREY *at a table, on which are
some papers.*

Corey. Now I have done with
earth and all its cares ;
I give my worldly goods to my dear
children ;
My body I bequeath to my tor-
mentors,
And my immortal soul to Him who
made it.
O God ! who in thy wisdom dost
afflict me
With an affliction greater than most
men
Have ever yet endured or shall endure,
Suffer me not in this last bitter hour
For any pains of death to fall from
thee !

(MARTHA *is heard singing.*)

Arise, O righteous Lord !
And disappoint my foes ;
They are but thine avenging sword,
Whose wounds are swift to close.

Corey. Hark, hark ! it is her
voice ! She is not dead !
She lives ! I am not utterly forsaken !

(MARTHA, *singing.*)

By thine abounding grace
And mercies multiplied,
I shall awake, and see thy face ;
I shall be satisfied.

(COREY *hides his face in his hands.
Enter the* JAILER, *followed by*
RICHARD GARDNER.)

Jailer. Here's a seafaring man,
one Richard Gardner,
A friend of yours, who asks to
speak with you.

(COREY *rises. They embrace.*)

Corey. I'm glad to see you ; ay,
right glad to see you.
Gardner. And I most sorely
grieved to see you thus.
Corey. Of all the friends I had in
happier days,
You are the first, ay, and the only
one
That comes to seek me out in my
disgrace !
And you but come in time to say
farewell.
They've dug my grave already in
the field.
I thank you. There is something
in your presence,
I know not what it is, that gives me
strength.
Perhaps it is the bearing of the
man
Familiar with all dangers of the
deep,
Familiar with the cries of drowning
men,
With fire, and wreck, and founder-
ing ships at sea !
Gardner. Ah, I have never known
a wreck like yours !
Would I could save you !
Corey. Do not speak of that.
It is too late. I am resolved to
die.
Gardner. Why would you die who
have so much to live for ?—
Your daughters, and—
Corey. You cannot say the word.
My daughters have gone from me.
They are married ;
They have their homes, their
thoughts, apart from me ;
I will not say their hearts,—that
were too cruel.
What would you have me do ?
Gardner. Confess and live.
Corey. That's what they said who
came here yesterday
To lay a heavy weight upon my
conscience

626

By telling me that I was driven forth
As an unworthy member of their
church.
   Gardner. It is an awful death.
   Corey.   'Tis but to drown,
And have the weight of all the seas
   upon you.
   Gardner. Say something; say
   enough to fend off death
Till this tornado of fanaticism
Blows itself out. Let me come in
   between you
And your severer self, with my plain
   sense ;
Do not be obstinate.
   Corey.   I will not plead.
If I deny, I am condemned already,
In courts where ghosts appear as
   witnesses,
And swear men's lives away.   If I
   confess,
Then I confess a lie, to buy a life
Which is not life, but only death in
   life.
I will not bear false witness against
   any,
Not even against myself, whom I
   count least.
   Gardner (*aside*). Ah, what a
   noble character is this !
   Corey. I pray you, do not urge me
   to do that
You would not do yourself. I have
   already
The bitter taste of death upon my
   lips ;
I feel the pressure of the heavy
   weight
That will crush out my life within
   this hour ;
But if a word could save me, and
   that word
Were not the Truth ; nay, if it did
   but swerve
A hair's-breadth from the Truth, I
   would not say it !
   Gardner (*aside*). How mean I
   seem beside a man like this !

   Corey. As for my wife, my Martha
   and my Martyr,—
Whose virtues, like the stars, un-
   seen by day,
Though numberless, do but await
   the dark
To manifest themselves unto all
   eyes,—
She who first won me from my evil
   ways,
And taught me how to live by her
   example,
By her example teaches me to die,
And leads me onward to the better
   life !
   Sheriff (*without*). Giles Corey !
   Come ! The hour has struck !
   Corey.   I come !
Here is my body ; ye may torture
   it,
But the immortal soul ye cannot
   crush !   [*Exeunt*.

———

SCENE III. — *A Street in the
Village. Enter* GLOYD *and
others.*

   Gloyd.   Quick, or we shall be
   late !
   A Man.   That 's not the way.
Come here ; come up this lane.
   Gloyd.   I wonder now
If the old man will die, and will not
   speak ?
He 's obstinate enough and tough
   enough
For anything on earth.

        (*A bell tolls.*)

        Hark ! What is that ?
   A Man. The passing bell. He 's
   dead !
   Gloyd.   We are too late.
        [*Exeunt in haste*.

———

SCENE IV.—*A field near the grave-yard.* GILES COREY *lying dead, with a great stone on his breast. The Sheriff at his head,* RICHARD GARDNER *at his feet. A crowd behind. The bell tolling. Enter* HATHORNE *and* MATHER.

Hathorne. This is the Potter's Field. Behold the fate
Of those who deal in Witchcrafts, and, when questioned,
Refuse to plead their guilt or innocence,
And stubbornly drag death upon themselves.
Mather. O sight most horrible!
In a land like this,
Spangled with Churches Evangelical,
Inwrapped in our salvations, must we seek
In mouldering statute-books of English Courts
Some old forgotten law, to do such deeds?
Those who lie buried in the Potter's Field
Will rise again, as surely as ourselves
That sleep in honoured graves with epitaphs;
And this poor man, whom we have made a victim,
Hereafter will be counted as a martyr!

628

St. John.

SAINT JOHN *wandering over the face of the earth.*

St. John. The Ages come and go,
The Centuries pass as Years;
My hair is white as the snow,
My feet are weary and slow,
The earth is wet with my tears!
The kingdoms crumble, and fall
Apart, like a ruined wall,
Or a bank that is undermined
By a river's ceaseless flow,
And leave no trace behind!
The world itself is old;
The portals of Time unfold
On hinges of iron, that grate
And groan with the rust and the weight,
Like the hinges of a gate
That hath fallen to decay;
But the evil doth not cease;
There is war instead of peace,
Instead of love there is hate;
And still I must wander and wait,
Still I must watch and pray,
Not forgetting in whose sight,
A thousand years in their flight
Are as a single day.

The life of man is a gleam
Of light, that comes and goes
Like the course of the Holy Stream,
The cityless river, that flows
From fountains no one knows,
Through the Lake of Galilee,
Through forests and level lands,
Over rocks, and shallows, and sands
Of a wilderness wild and vast,
Till it findeth its rest at last
In the desolate Dead Sea!
But alas! alas for me,
Not yet this rest shall be!

What, then! doth Charity fail?
Is Faith of no avail?
Is Hope blown out like a light
By a gust of wind in the night?

The clashing of creeds, and the strife
Of the many beliefs, that in vain
Perplex man's heart and brain,
Are nought but the rustle of leaves,
When the breath of God upheaves
The boughs of the Tree of Life,
And they subside again!
And I remember still
The words, and from whom they came,
Not he that repeateth the name,
But he that doeth the will!

And Him evermore I behold
Walking in Galilee,
Through the cornfield's waving gold,
In hamlet, in wood, and in wold,
By the shores of the Beautiful Sea.
He toucheth the sightless eyes;
Before him the demons flee;
To the dead he sayeth: Arise!
To the living: Follow me!
And that voice still soundeth on
From the centuries that are gone,
To the centuries that shall be!
From all vain pomps and shows,
From the pride that overflows,
And the false conceits of men;
From all the narrow rules
And subtleties of Schools,
And the craft of tongue and pen;
Bewildered in its search,
Bewildered with the cry:
Lo, here! lo, there, the Church!
Poor, sad Humanity
Through all the dust and heat
Turns back with bleeding feet,
By the weary road it came,
Unto the simple thought
By the Great Master taught,
And that remaineth still:
Not he that repeateth the name,
But he that doeth the will!

The Divine Tragedy.

INTROITUS.

The ANGEL *bearing the* PROPHET
HABAKKUK *through the air.*

Prophet. Why dost thou bear me
   aloft,
O Angel of God, on thy pinions
O'er realms and dominions?
Softly I float as a cloud
In air, for thy right hand upholds
   me,
Thy garment enfolds me!
   Angel. Lo! as I passed on my
   way
In the harvest-field I beheld thee
When no man compelled thee,
Bearing with thine own hands
This food to the famishing reapers,
A flock without keepers!
The fragrant sheaves of the wheat
Made the air above them sweet;
Sweeter and more divine
Was the scent of the scattered grain,
That the reaper's hand let fall
To be gathered again
By the hand of the gleaner!
Sweetest, divinest of all,
Was the humble deed of thine,
And the meekness of thy demeanour!
   Prophet. Angel of Light,
I cannot gainsay thee,
I can but obey thee!
   Angel. Beautiful was it in the
   Lord's sight,
To behold his Prophet
Feeding those that toil,
The tillers of the soil.
But why should the reapers eat of it

And not the Prophet of Zion
In the den of the lion?
The Prophet should feed the
   Prophet!
Therefore I thee have uplifted,
And bear thee aloft by the hair
Of thy head, like a cloud that is
   drifted
Through the vast unknown of the
   air!
Five days hath the Prophet been
   lying
In Babylon, in the den
Of the lions, death-defying,
Defying hunger and thirst;
But the worst
Is the mockery of men!
Alas! how full of fear
Is the fate of Prophet and Seer!
For evermore, for evermore,
It shall be as it hath been here-
   tofore;
The age in which they live
Will not forgive
The splendour of the everlasting
   light,
That makes their foreheads bright,
Nor the sublime
Forerunning of their time!
   Prophet. O tell me, for thou
   knowest,
Wherefore, and by what grace,
Have I, who am least and lowest,
Been chosen to this place,
To this exalted part?
   Angel. Because thou art
The Struggler; and from thy youth
Thy humble and patient life

Hath been a strife
And battle for the Truth;
Nor hast thou paused nor halted,
Nor ever in thy pride
Turned from the poor aside,
But with deed and word and pen
Hast served thy fellow-men;
Therefore art thou exalted!
Prophet. By thine arrow's light
Thou goest onward through the night,
And by the clear
Sheen of thy glittering spear!
When will our journey end?
Angel. Lo, it is ended!
Yon silver gleam
Is the Euphrates stream.
Let us descend
Into the city splendid,
Into the City of Gold!
Prophet. Behold!
As if the stars had fallen from their places
Into the firmament below,
The streets, the gardens, and the vacant spaces
With light are all aglow;
And hark!
As we draw near,
What sound is it I hear
Ascending through the dark?
Angel. The tumultuous noise of the nations,
Their rejoicings and lamentations,
The pleadings of their prayer,
The groans of their despair,
The cry of their imprecations,
Their wrath, their love, their hate.
Prophet. Surely the world doth wait
The coming of its Redeemer!
Angel. Awake from thy sleep, O dreamer!
The hour is near, though late;
Awake! write the vision sublime,
The vision, that is for a time,
Though it tarry, wait; it is nigh;
In the end it will speak and not lie.

THE FIRST PASSOVER.

I.

VOX CLAMANTIS.

John the Baptist. Repent! repent! repent!
For the kingdom of God is at hand,
And all the land
Full of the knowledge of the Lord shall be
As the waters cover the sea,
And encircle the continent!

Repent! repent! repent!
For lo, the hour appointed,
The hour so long foretold
By the Prophets of old,
Of the coming of the Anointed,
The Messiah, the Paraclete,
The Desire of the Nations, is nigh!
He shall not strive nor cry,
Nor his voice be heard in the street;
Nor the bruised reed shall he break,
Nor quench the smoking flax;
And many of them that sleep
In the dust of earth shall awake,
On that great and terrible day,
And the wicked shall wail and weep,
And be blown like a smoke away,
And be melted away like wax.
Repent! repent! repent!

O Priest, and Pharisee,
Who hath warned you to flee
From the wrath that is to be?
From the coming anguish and ire?
The axe is laid at the root
Of the trees, and every tree
That bringeth not forth good fruit
Is hewn down and cast into the fire!

Ye Scribes, why come ye hither?
In the hour that is uncertain,
In the day of anguish and trouble,
He that stretcheth the heavens as a curtain
And spreadeth them out as a tent,
Shall blow upon you, and ye shall wither,

631   x

And the whirlwind shall take you
    away as stubble!
Repent! repent! repent!
   Priest. Who art thou, O man
    of prayer!
In raiment of camel's hair,
Begirt with leathern thong,
That here in the wilderness,
With a cry as of one in distress,
Preachest unto this throng?
Art thou the Christ?
   John. Priest of Jerusalem,
In meekness and humbleness,
I deny not, I confess
I am not the Christ!
   Priest. What shall we say unto
    them
That sent us here? Reveal
Thy name, and nought conceal!
Art thou Elias?
   John. No!
   Priest. Art thou that Prophet, then,
Of lamentation and woe,
Who, as a symbol and sign
Of impending wrath divine
Upon unbelieving men,
Shattered the vessel of clay
In the Valley of Slaughter?
   John. Nay.
I am not he thou namest!
   Priest. Who art thou, and what
    is the word
That here thou proclaimest?
   John. I am the voice of one
Crying in the wilderness alone:
Prepare ye the way of the Lord;
Make his paths straight
In the land that is desolate!
   Priest. If thou be not the Christ,
Nor yet Elias, nor he
That, in sign of the things to be,
Shattered the vessel of clay
In the Valley of Slaughter,
Then declare unto us, and say
By what authority now
Baptizest thou?
   John. I indeed baptize you with
    water

Unto repentance; but He,
That cometh after me,
Is mightier than I and higher;
The latchet of whose shoes
I am not worthy to unloose;
He shall baptize you with fire,
And with the Holy Ghost!
Whose fan is in his hand;
He will purge to the uttermost
His floor, and garner his wheat,
But will burn the chaff in the brand
And fire of unquenchable heat!
Repent! repent! repent!

II.

MOUNT QUARANTANIA.

I.

   Lucifer. Not in the lightning's
    flash, nor in the thunder,
Not in the tempest, nor the cloudy
    storm,
   Will I array my form;
But part invisible these boughs
    asunder,
And move and murmur, as the wind
    upheaves
   And whispers in the leaves.

Not as a terror and a desolation,
Not in my natural shape, inspiring
    fear
   And dread, will I appear;
But in soft tones of sweetness and
    persuasion,
A sound as of the fall of mountain
    streams,
   Or voices heard in dreams.

He sitteth there in silence, worn
    and wasted
With famine, and uplifts his hollow
    eyes
   To the unpitying skies;
For forty days and nights he hath
    not tasted
Of food or drink, his parted lips are
    pale,
   Surely his strength must fail.

Wherefore dost thou in penitential fasting
Waste and consume the beauty of thy youth?
Ah, if thou be in truth
The Son of the Unnamed, the Everlasting,
Command these stones beneath thy feet to be
Changed into bread for thee!

Christus. 'Tis written: Man shall not live by bread alone,
But by each word that from God's mouth proceedeth!

II.

Lucifer. Too weak, alas! too weak is the temptation
For one whose soul to nobler things aspires
Than sensual desires!
Ah, could I, by some sudden aberration,
Lead and delude to suicidal death
This Christ of Nazareth!

Unto the holy Temple on Moriah,
With its resplendent domes, and manifold
Bright pinnacles of gold,
Where they await thy coming, O Messiah!
Lo, I have brought thee! Let thy glory here
Be manifest and clear.

Reveal thyself by royal act and gesture,
Descending with the bright triumphant host
Of all the highermost
Archangels, and about thee as a vesture
The shining clouds, and all thy splendours show
Unto the world below!

Cast thyself down, it is the hour appointed;

And God hath given his angels charge and care
To keep thee and upbear
Upon their hands his only Son, the Anointed,
Lest he should dash his foot against a stone
And die, and be unknown.

Christus. 'Tis written: Thou shalt not tempt the Lord thy God!

III.

Lucifer. I cannot thus delude him to perdition!
But one temptation still remains untried,
The trial of his pride,
The thirst of power, the fever of ambition!
Surely by these a humble peasant's son
At last may be undone!

Above the yawning chasms and deep abysses,
Across the headlong torrents, I have brought
Thy footsteps, swift as thought;
And from the highest of these precipices,
The Kingdoms of the world thine eyes behold,
Like a great map unrolled.

From far-off Lebanon, with cedars crested,
To where the waters of the Asphalt Lake
On its white pebbles break,
And the vast desert, silent, sand-invested,
These kingdoms are all mine, and thine shall be,
If thou wilt worship me!

Christus. Get thee behind me, Satan! thou shalt worship
The Lord thy God; Him only shalt thou serve!

Angels Ministrant. The sun goes
    down ; the evening shadows
    lengthen,
The fever and the struggle of the day
    Abate and pass away ;
Thine Angels Ministrant, we come
    to strengthen
And comfort thee, and crown thee
    with the palm,
The silence and the calm.

III.

THE MARRIAGE IN CANA.

The Musicians. Rise up, my love,
    my fair one,
Rise up, and come away,
For lo ! the winter is past,
The rain is over and gone,
The flowers appear on the earth,
The time of the singing of birds is
    come,
And the voice of the turtle is heard
    in our land.
    The Bridegroom. Sweetly the
    minstrels sing the Song of
    Songs !
My heart runs forward with it, and
    I say :
O set me as a seal upon thine heart,
And set me as a seal upon thine arm ;
For love is strong as life, and strong
    as death,
And cruel as the grave is jealousy !
    The Musicians. I sleep, but my
    heart awaketh ;
'Tis the voice of my beloved
Who knocketh, saying : Open to me,
My sister, my love, my dove,
For my head is filled with dew,
My locks with the drops of the
    night !
    The Bride. Ah yes, I sleep, and
    yet my heart awaketh,
It is the voice of my beloved who
    knocks.
    The Bridegroom. O beautiful as
    Rebecca at the fountain,

O beautiful as Ruth among the
    sheaves !
O fairest among women ! O unde-
    filed !
Thou art all fair, my love, there 's
    no spot in thee !
    The Musicians. My beloved is
    white and ruddy,
The chiefest among ten thousand ;
His locks are black as a raven,
His eyes are the eyes of doves,
Of doves by the rivers of water,
His lips are like unto lilies,
Dropping   with   sweet-smelling
    myrrh.
    Architriclinus. Who is that
    youth, with the dark azure eyes,
And hair, in colour like unto the
    wine,
Parted upon his forehead, and behind
Falling in flowing locks ?
    Paranymphus. The Nazarene
Who preacheth to the poor in field
    and village
The coming of God's Kingdom.
    Architriclinus. How serene
His aspect is ! manly yet womanly.
    Paranymphus. Most beautiful
    among the sons of men !
Oft known to weep, but never known
    to laugh.
    Architriclinus. And tell me, she
    with eyes of olive tint,
And skin as fair as wheat, and pale
    brown hair,
The woman at his side ?
    Paranymphus. His mother,
    Mary.
    Architriclinus. And the tall
    figure standing close beside
    them,
Clad all in white, with face and
    beard like ashes,
As if he were Elias, the White Wit-
    ness,
Come from his cave on Carmel to
    foretell
The end of all things ?

Paranymphus.   That is
    Manahem
The Essenian, he who dwells among
    the palms
Near the Dead Sea.
    Architriclinus.   He who fore-
    told to Herod
He should one day be King?
    Paranymphus.   The same.
    Architriclinus.   Then why
Doth he come here to sadden with
    his presence
Our marriage feast, belonging to a
    sect
Haters of women, and that taste not
    wine?
    The Musicians. My undefiled is
    but one,
The only one of her mother,
The choice of her that bare her;
The daughters saw her and blessed
    her;
The queens and the concubines
    praised her,
Saying: Lo! who is this
That looketh forth as the morning?
    Manahem (aside). The Ruler of
    the Feast is gazing at me,
As if he asked, why is that old man
    here
Among the revellers? And thou,
    the Anointed!
Why art thou here? I see as in a
    vision
A figure clothed in purple, crowned
    with thorns;
I see a cross uplifted in the dark-
    ness,
And hear a cry of agony, that shall
    echo
For ever and for ever through the
    world!
    Architriclinus. Give us more
    wine. These goblets are all
    empty.
    Mary (to Christus). They have
    no wine!
    Christus. O woman, what have I

To do with thee? Mine hour is
    not yet come.
    Mary (to the servants). What-
    ever he shall say to you, that do.
    Christus. Fill up these pots with
    water.
    The Musicians. Come, my be-
    loved,
Let us go forth into the field,
Let us lodge in the villages;
Let us get up early to the vineyards,
Let us see if the vine flourish,
Whether the tender grape appear,
And the pomegranates bud forth.
    Christus.   Draw out now,
And bear unto the Ruler of the Feast.
    Manahem (aside). O thou
    brought up among the Esse-
    nians,
Nurtured in abstinence, taste not
    the wine!
It is the poison of dragons from
    the vineyards
Of Sodom, and the taste of death
    is in it.
    *Architriclinus (to the Bride-
    groom).* All men set forth good
    wine at the beginning,
And when men have well drunk,
    that which is worse;
But thou hast kept the good wine
    until now.
    Manahem (aside). The things
    that have been and shall be no
    more,
The things that are, and that here-
    after shall be
The things that might have been,
    and yet were not,
The fading twilight of great joys
    departed,
The daybreak of great truths as yet
    unrisen,
The intuition and the expectation
Of something, which, when come,
    is not the same,
But only like its forecast in men's
    dreams,

The longing, the delay, and the
  delight,
Sweeter for the delay; youth, hope,
  love, death,
And disappointment which is also
  death,
All these make up the sum of human
  life;
A dream within a dream, a wind at
  night
Howling across the desert in
  despair,
Seeking for something lost it cannot
  find.
Fate or foreseeing, or whatever
  name
Men call it, matters not; what is
  to be
Hath been forewritten in the
  thought divine
From the beginning. None can
  hide from it,
But it will find him out; nor run
  from it,
But it o'ertaketh him! The Lord
  hath said it.
The Bridegroom (*to the Bride, on
  the balcony*). When Abraham went with Sarah into
  Egypt,
The land was all illumined with her
  beauty;
But thou dost make the very night
  itself
Brighter than day! Behold, in glad
  procession,
Crowding the threshold of the sky
  above us,
The stars come forth to meet thee
  with their lamps;
And the soft winds, the ambassadors
  of flowers,
From neighbouring gardens and
  from fields unseen,
Come laden with odours unto thee,
  my Queen!
The Musicians. Awake, O north-
  wind,

And come, thou wind of the South,
Blow, blow upon my garden,
That the spices thereof may flow
  out.

IV.

IN THE CORNFIELDS.

Philip. Onward through leagues
  of sun-illumined corn,
As if through parted seas, the
  pathway runs,
And crowned with sunshine as the
  Prince of Peace
Walks the beloved Master, leading
  us,
As Moses led our fathers in old
  times
Out of the land of bondage! We
  have found
Him of whom Moses and the
  Prophets wrote,
Jesus of Nazareth, the Son of
  Joseph.
Nathanael. Can any good come
  out of Nazareth?
Can this be the Messiah?
Philip.   Come and see.
Nathanael. The summer sun
  grows hot; I am an hungred.
How cheerily the Sabbath-breaking
  quail
Pipes in the corn, and bids us to his
  Feast
Of Wheat Sheaves! How the
  bearded, ripening ears
Toss in the roofless temple of the
  air;
As if the unseen hand of some High
  Priest
Waved them before Mount Tabor
  as an altar!
It were no harm, if we should pluck
  and eat.
Philip. How wonderful it is to
  walk abroad
With the Good Master! Since the
  miracle

He wrought at Cana, at the marriage feast,
His fame hath gone abroad through
all the land,
And when we come to Nazareth,
thou shalt see
How his own people will receive
their Prophet,
And hail him as Messiah ! See, he
turns
And looks at thee.

Christus. Behold an Israelite
In whom there is no guile.

Nathanael. Whence knowest
thou me ?

Christus. Before that Philip
called thee, when thou wast
Under the fig-tree, I beheld
thee.

Nathanael. Rabbi,
Thou art the Son of God, thou art
the King
Of Israel !

Christus. Because I said I saw
thee
Under the fig-tree, before Philip
called thee,
Believest thou ? Thou shalt see
greater things.
Hereafter thou shalt see the
heavens unclosed,
And angels of God ascending and
descending
Upon the Son of Man !

Pharisees (*passing*). Hail, Rabbi!

Christus. Hail !

Pharisees. Behold how thy disciples do a thing
Which is not lawful on the Sabbath
day,
And thou forbiddest them not !

Christus. Have ye not read
What David did when he an
hungred was,
And all they that were with him ?
How he entered
Into the house of God, and ate the
shew-bread,

Which was not lawful saving for
the priests ?
Have ye not read, how on the Sabbath days
The priests profane the Sabbath in
the Temple,
And yet are blameless ? But I say
to you,
One in this place is greater than
the Temple !
And had ye known the meaning of
the words,
I will have mercy and not sacrifice,
The guiltless ye would not condemn. The Sabbath
Was made for man, and not man
for the Sabbath.

(*Passes on with the disciples.*)

Pharisees. This is, alas ! some
poor demoniac
Wandering about the fields, and
uttering
His unintelligible blasphemies
Among the common people, who
receive
As prophecies the words they com-
prehend not !
Deluded folk ! The incomprehen-
sible
Alone excites their wonder. There
is none
So visionary, or so void of sense,
But he will find a crowd to follow
him !

V.

NAZARETH.

Christus (*reading in the synagogue*). The Spirit of the Lord
God is upon me.
He hath anointed me to preach
good tidings
Unto the poor ; to heal the broken-
hearted ;
To comfort those that mourn, and
to throw open

The prison doors of captives, and proclaim
The Year Acceptable of the Lord our God !

(*He closes the book and sits down.*)

  A Pharisee. Who is this youth ? He hath taken the Teacher's seat !
Will he instruct the Elders ?
  A Priest.   Fifty years
Have I been Priest here in the Synagogue,
And never have I seen so young a man
Sit in the Teacher's seat !
  Christus.   Behold, to-day
This scripture is fulfilled. One is appointed
And hath been sent to them that mourn in Zion,
To give them beauty for ashes, and the oil
Of joy for mourning ! They shall build again
The old waste places ; and again raise up
The former desolations, and repair
The cities that are wasted ! As a bridegroom
Decketh himself with ornaments, as a bride
Adorneth herself with jewels, so the Lord
Hath clothed me with the robe of righteousness.
  A Priest. He speaks the Prophet's words ; but with an air
As if himself had been foreshadowed in them !
  Christus. For Zion's sake I will not hold my peace,
And for Jerusalem's sake I will not rest
Until its righteousness be as a brightness,
And its salvation as a lamp that burneth !

Thou shalt be called no longer the Forsaken,
Nor any more thy land, the Desolate,
The Lord hath sworn, by his right hand hath sworn,
And by his arm of strength : I will no more
Give to thine enemies thy corn as meat ;
The sons of strangers shall not drink thy wine.
Go through, go through the gates ! Prepare a way
Unto the people ! Gather out the stones !
Lift up a standard for the people !
  A Priest.   Ah !
These are seditious words !
  Christus.   And they shall call them
The holy people ; the redeemed of God !
And thou, Jerusalem, shalt be called Sought out,
A city not forsaken !
  A Pharisee.   Is not this
The carpenter Joseph's son ? Is not his mother
Called Mary ? and his brethren and his sisters
Are they not with us ? Doth he make himself
To be a Prophet ?
  Christus. No man is a Prophet
In his own country, and among his kin.
In his own house no Prophet is accepted.
I say to you, in the land of Israel
Were many widows in Elijah's day,
When for three years and more the heavens were shut,
And a great famine was throughout the land ;
But unto no one was Elijah sent
Save to Sarepta, to a city of Sidon,
And to a woman there that was a widow.

And many lepers were there in the
    land
Of Israel, in the time of Eliseus
The Prophet, and yet none of them
    was cleansed,
Save Naaman the Syrian !
  A Priest.   Say no more !
Thou comest here into our syna-
    gogue
And speakest to the Elders and the
    Priests,
As if the very mantle of Elijah
Had fallen upon thee ! Art thou not
    ashamed?
  A Pharisee. We want no Pro-
    phets here ! Let him be driven
From Synagogue and city! Let
    him go
And prophesy to the Samaritans !
  An Elder. The world is changed.
    We elders are as nothing !
We are but yesterdays, that have
    no part
Or portion in to-day ! Dry leaves
    that rustle,
That make a little sound, and then
    are dust !
  A Pharisee. A carpenter's appren-
    tice ! a mechanic,
Whom we have seen at work here
    in the town
Day after day ; a stripling without
    learning,
Shall he pretend to unfold the Word
    of God
To men grown old in study of the
    Law !

    (CHRISTUS *is thrust out.*)

VI.

THE SEA OF GALILEE.

PETER *and* ANDREW, *mending their*
nets.

  Peter. Never was such a marvel-
    lous draught of fishes
Heard of in Galilee ! The market-
    places

Both of Bethsaida and Capernaum
Are full of them ! Yet we had toiled
    all night
And taken nothing, when the Master
    said :
Launch out into the deep, and cast
    your nets ;
And doing this, we caught such
    multitudes
Our nets like spiders' webs were
    snapped asunder,
And with the draught we filled two
    ships so full
That they began to sink. Then I
    knelt down
Amazed, and said : O Lord, depart
    from me,
I am a sinful man. And he made
    answer :
Simon, fear not ; henceforth thou
    shalt catch men !
What was the meaning of those
    words ?
  Andrew.   I know not.
But here is Philip, come from
    Nazareth.
He hath been with the Master. Tell
    us, Philip,
What tidings dost thou bring ?
  Philip.   Most wonderful !
As we drew near to Nain, out of
    the gate
Upon a bier was carried the dead
    body
Of a young man, his mother's only
    son,
And she a widow, who with lamen-
    tation
Bewailed her loss, and the much
    people with her ;
And when the Master saw her he
    was filled
With pity ; and he said to her : Weep
    not !
And came and touched the bier,
    and they that bare it
Stood still ; and then he said : Young
    man, arise !

And he that had been dead sat up,
and soon
Began to speak ; and he delivered
him
Unto his mother ; and there came
a fear
On all the people, and they glori-
fied
The Lord, and said, rejoicing : A
great Prophet
Is risen up among us ! and the Lord
Hath visited his people !
 Peter.   A great Prophet ?
Ay, greater than a Prophet: greater
even
Than John the Baptist !
 Philip. Yet the Nazarenes
Rejected him.
 Peter. The Nazarenes are dogs !
As natural brute beasts, they growl
at things
They do not understand ; and they
shall perish,
Utterly perish in their own corrup-
tion.
The Nazarenes are dogs !
 Philip. They drave him forth
Out of their Synagogue, out of their
city,
And would have cast him down a
precipice,
But passing through the midst of
them he vanished
Out of their hands.
 Peter.   Wells are they
without water,
Clouds carried with a tempest, unto
whom
The mist of darkness is reserved
for ever !
 Philip. Behold, he cometh. There
is one man with him
I am amazed to see !
 Andrew. What man is that ?
 Philip. Judas Iscariot ; he that
cometh last
Girt with a leathern apron. No one
knoweth

His history ; but the rumour of him is
He had an unclean spirit in his
youth.
It hath not left him yet.
 Christus (passing). Come unto
me,
All ye that labour and are heavy
laden,
And I will give you rest ! Come
unto me,
And take my yoke upon you and
learn of me,
For I am meek, and I am lowly in
heart,
And ye shall all find rest unto your
souls !
 Philip. O there is something in
that voice that reaches
The innermost recesses of my spirit !
I feel that it might say unto the
blind :
Receive your sight ! and straight-
way they would see !
I feel that it might say unto the dead,
Arise ! and they would hear it and
obey !
Behold, he beckons to us !
 Christus (to Peter and Andrew).
Follow me !
 Peter. Master, I will leave all and
follow thee.

VII.

THE DEMONIAC OF GADARA.

 A Gadarene. He hath escaped,
hath plucked his chains asunder,
And broken his fetters ; always
night and day
Is in the mountains here, and in
the tombs,
Crying aloud, and cutting himself
with stones,
Exceeding fierce, so that no man
can tame him !
 *The Demoniac (from above,
unseen).* O Aschmedai ! O
Aschmedai, have pity !

A Gadarene. Listen! It is his voice! Go warn the people
Just landing from the lake!

The Demoniac. O Aschmedai! Thou angel of the bottomless pit, have pity!
It was enough to hurl King Solomon,
On whom be peace! two hundred leagues away
Into the country, and to make him scullion
In the kitchen of the King of Maschkemen!
Why dost thou hurl me here among these rocks,
And cut me with these stones?

A Gadarene. He raves and mutters
He knows not what.

The Demoniac (appearing from a tomb among the rocks). The wild cock Tarnegal
Singeth to me, and bids me to the banquet,
Where all the Jews shall come; for they have slain
Behemoth the great ox, who daily cropped
A thousand hills for food, and at a draught
Drank up the river Jordan, and have slain
The huge Leviathan, and stretched his skin
Upon the high walls of Jerusalem,
And made them shine from one end of the world
Unto the other; and the fowl Barjuchne,
Whose outspread wings eclipse the sun, and make
Midnight at noon o'er all the continents!
And we shall drink the wine of Paradise
From Adam's cellars.

A Gadarene. O, thou unclean spirit!

The Demoniac (hurling down a stone). This is the wonderful Barjuchne's egg,
That fell out of her nest, and broke to pieces,
And swept away three hundred cedar-trees,
And threescore villages!—Rabbi Eliezer,
How thou didst sin there in that seaport town,
When thou hadst carried safe thy chest of silver
Over the seven rivers for her sake!
I too have sinned beyond the reach of pardon.
Ye hills and mountains, pray for mercy on me!
Ye stars and planets, pray for mercy on me!
Ye sun and moon, O pray for mercy on me!

(CHRISTUS *and his disciples pass.*)

A Gadarene. There is a man here of Decapolis,
Who hath an unclean spirit; so that none
Can pass this way. He lives among the tombs
Up there upon the cliffs, and hurls down stones
On those who pass beneath.

Christus. Come out of him, Thou unclean spirit!

The Demoniac. What have I to do With thee, thou Son of God? Do not torment us.

Christus. What is thy name?

Demoniac. Legion; for we are many.
Cain, the first murderer; and the King Belshazzar,
And Evil Merodach of Babylon,
And Admatha, the death-cloud, prince of Persia;
And Aschmedai, the angel of the pit,

And many other devils. We are
    Legion.
Send us not forth beyond Decapolis;
Command us not to go into the
    deep!
There is a herd of swine here in
    the pastures,—
Let us go into them.
    Christus.   Come out of him,
Thou unclean spirit!
    A Gadarene. See, how stupefied,
How motionless he stands! He
    cries no more;
He seems bewildered and in silence
    stares
As one who, walking in his sleep,
    awakes
And knows not where he is, and
    looks about him,
And at his nakedness, and is
    ashamed.
    The Demoniac. Why am I here
    alone among the tombs?
What have they done to me, that
    I am naked?
Ah, woe is me!
    Christus.   Go home unto thy
    friends
And tell them how great things the
    Lord hath done
For thee, and how he had com-
    passion on thee!
    A Swineherd (running). The
    herds! the herds! O most
    unlucky day!
They were all feeding quiet in the
    sun,
When suddenly they started, and
    grew savage
As the wild boars of Tabor, and
    together
Rushed down a precipice into the
    sea!
They are all drowned!
    Peter.   Thus righteously
    are punished
The apostate Jews, that eat the
    flesh of swine,

And broth of such abominable
    things!
    Greeks of Gadara. We sacrifice
    a sow unto Demeter
At the beginning of harvest, and
    another
To Dionysus at the vintage-time.
Therefore we prize our herds of
    swine, and count them
Not as unclean, but as things con-
    secrate
To the immortal gods. O great
    magician,
Depart out of our coasts; let us
    alone,—
We are afraid of thee!
    Peter.   Let us depart;
For they that sanctify and purify
Themselves in gardens, eating flesh
    of swine,
And the abomination, and the
    mouse,
Shall be consumed together, saith
    the Lord!

VIII.

TALITHA CUMI.

Jairus (at the feet of Christus).
    O Master! I entreat thee! I
    implore thee!
My daughter lieth at the point of
    death;
I pray thee come and lay thy hands
    upon her,
And she shall live!
    Christus. Who was it touched
    my garments?
    Simon Peter. Thou seest the
    multitude that throng and press
    thee,
And sayest thou: Who touched me?
    'Twas not I.
    Christus. Some one hath touched
    my garments; I perceive
That virtue is gone out of me.
    A Woman. O Master!
Forgive me! For I said within
    myself,

If I so much as touch his garment's hem,
I shall be whole.

    Christus. Be of good comfort, daughter!
Thy faith hath made thee whole. Depart in peace.

    A Messenger from the house. Why troublest thou the Master? Hearest thou not
The flute-players, and the voices of the women
Singing their lamentation? She is dead!

    The Minstrels and Mourners. We have girded ourselves with sackcloth!
We have covered our heads with ashes!
For our young men die, and our maidens
Swoon in the streets of the city;
And into their mother's bosom
They pour out their souls like water!

    Christus (going in). Give place. Why make ye this ado, and weep?
She is not dead, but sleepeth.

    The Mother (from within). Cruel death!
To take away from me this tender blossom!
To take away my dove, my lamb, my darling?

    The Minstrels and Mourners. He hath led me and brought into darkness,
Like the dead of old in dark places!
He hath bent his bow, and hath set me
Apart as a mark for his arrow!
He hath covered himself with a cloud
That our prayer should not pass through and reach him!

    The Crowd. He stands beside her bed! He takes her hand!
Listen, he speaks to her!

    Christus (within). Maiden, arise!

    The Crowd. See, she obeys his voice! She stirs! She lives!
Her mother holds her folded in her arms!
O miracle of miracles! O marvel!

IX.

THE TOWER OF MAGDALA.

    Mary Magdalene. Companionless, unsatisfied, forlorn,
I sit here in this lonely tower, and look
Upon the lake below me, and the hills
That swoon with heat, and see as in a vision
All my past life unroll itself before me.
The princes and the merchants come to me,
Merchants of Tyre and Princes of Damascus,
And pass, and disappear, and are no more;
But leave behind their merchandise and jewels,
Their perfumes, and their gold, and their disgust.
I loathe them, and the very memory of them
Is unto me as thought of food to one
Cloyed with the luscious figs of Dalmanutha!
What if hereafter, in the long hereafter
Of endless joy or pain, or joy in pain,
It were my punishment to be with them
Grown hideous and decrepit in their sins,
And hear them say: Thou that hast brought us here,
Be unto us as thou hast been of old!

I look upon this raiment that I wear,
These silks, and these embroideries, and they seem

Only as cerements wrapped about
my limbs!
I look upon these rings thick set
with pearls
And emerald and amethyst and
jasper,
And they are burning coals upon
my flesh!
This serpent on my wrist becomes
alive!
Away, thou viper! and away, ye
garlands
Whose odours bring the swift remembrance back
Of the unhallowed revels in these
chambers!
But yesterday,—and yet it seems to
me
Something remote, like a pathetic
song
Sung long ago by minstrels in the
street,—
But yesterday, as from this tower I
gazed,
Over the olive and the walnut
trees,
Upon the lake and the white ships,
and wondered
Whither and whence they steered,
and who was in them,
A fisher's boat drew near the land-
ing-place
Under the oleanders, and the
people
Came up from it, and passed beneath the tower,
Close under me. In front of them,
as leader,
Walked one of royal aspect, clothed
in white,
Who lifted up his eyes, and looked
at me,
And all at once the air seemed
filled and living
With a mysterious power, that
streamed from him,
And overflowed me with an atmosphere

Of light and love. As one entranced
I stood,
And when I woke again, lo! he
was gone,
So that I said: Perhaps it is a dream.
But from that very hour the seven
demons
That had their habitation in this
body
Which men call beautiful, departed
from me!

This morning, when the first gleam
of the dawn
Made Lebanon a glory in the air,
And all below was darkness, I beheld
An angel, or a spirit glorified,
With wind-tossed garments walk-
ing on the lake.
The face I could not see, but I
distinguished
The attitude and gesture, and I
knew
'Twas he that healed me. And the
gusty wind
Brought to mine ears a voice,
which seemed to say:
Be of good cheer! 'Tis I! Be not
afraid!
And from the darkness, scarcely
heard, the answer:
If it be thou, bid me come unto thee
Upon the water! And the voice
said: Come!
And then I heard a cry of fear:
Lord, save me!
As of a drowning man. And then
the voice:
Why didst thou doubt, O thou of
little faith!
At this all vanished, and the wind
was hushed,
And the great sun came up above
the hills,
And the swift-flying vapours hid
themselves
In caverns among the rocks! O, I
must find him

And follow him, and be with him for
    ever !
Thou box of alabaster, in whose walls
The souls of flowers lie pent, the
    precious balm
And spikenard of Arabian farms,
    the spirits
Of aromatic herbs, ethereal natures
Nursed by the sun and dew, not all
    unworthy
To bathe his consecrated feet,
    whose step
Makes every threshold holy that he
    crosses ;
Let us go forth upon our pilgrimage,
Thou and I only ! Let us search for
    him
Until we find him, and pour out our
    souls
Before his feet, till all that's left of us
Shall be the broken caskets, that
    once held us !

X.

THE HOUSE OF SIMON THE PHARISEE.

A Guest (at table). Are ye de-
    ceived ? Have any of the Rulers
Believed on him ? or do they know
    indeed
This man to be the very Christ ?
    Howbeit
We know whence this man is, but
    when the Christ
Shall come, none knoweth whence
    he is.
Christus. Whereunto shall I
    liken, then, the men
Of this generation ? and what are
    they like ?
They are like children sitting in the
    markets,
And calling unto one another, say-
    ing :
We have piped unto you, and ye
    have not danced :

We have mourned unto you, and
    ye have not wept !
This say I unto you, for John the
    Baptist
Came neither eating bread nor
    drinking wine ;
Ye say he hath a devil. The Son of
    Man
Eating and drinking cometh, and
    ye say :
Behold a gluttonous man, and a
    wine-bibber ;
Behold a friend of publicans and
    sinners !
    A Guest (aside to Simon). Who
    is that woman yonder, gliding in
So silently behind him ?
    Simon.   It is Mary,
Who dwelleth in the Tower of
    Magdala.
    The Guest. See, how she kneels
    there weeping, and her tears
Fall on his feet ; and her long
    golden hair
Waves to and fro and wipes them
    dry again.
And now she kisses them, and from
    a box
Of alabaster is anointing them
With precious ointment, filling all
    the house
With its sweet odour !
    Simon (aside).   O, this man,
    forsooth,
Were he indeed a Prophet, would
    have known
Who and what manner of woman
    this may be
That toucheth him ! would know
    she is a sinner !
    Christus. Simon, somewhat have
    I to say to thee.
    Simon. Master, say on.
    Christus.   A certain creditor
Had once two debtors ; and the
    one of them
Owed him five hundred pence ; the
    other, fifty.

They having nought to pay withal, he frankly
Forgave them both. Now tell me which of them
Will love him most?
    Simon. He, I suppose, to whom He most forgave.
    Christus.   Yea, thou hast rightly judged.
Seest thou this woman? When thine house I entered,
Thou gavest me no water for my feet,
But she hath washed them with her tears, and wiped them
With her own hair! Thou gavest me no kiss;
This woman hath not ceased, since I came in,
To kiss my feet! My head with oil didst thou
Anoint not; but this woman hath anointed
My feet with ointment. Hence I say to thee,
Her sins, which have been many, are forgiven,
For she loved much.
    The Guests.   O, who, then, is this man
That pardoneth also sins without atonement?
    Christus. Woman, thy faith hath saved thee! Go in peace!

——◆——

THE SECOND PASSOVER.

I.

BEFORE THE GATES OF MACHÆRUS.

Manahem. Welcome, O wilderness, and welcome night
And solitude, and ye swift-flying stars
That drift with golden sands the barren heavens,

Welcome once more! The Angels of the Wind
Hasten across the desert to receive me;
And sweeter than men's voices are to me
The voices of these solitudes; the sound
Of unseen rivulets, and the far-off cry
Of bitterns in the reeds of water-pools.
And lo! above me, like the Prophet's arrow
Shot from the eastern window, high in air
The clamorous cranes go singing through the night.
O ye mysterious pilgrims in the air,
Would I had wings that I might follow you!

I look forth from these mountains, and behold
The omnipotent and omnipresent night,
Mysterious as the future and the fate
That hangs o'er all men's lives! I see beneath me
The desert stretching to the Dead Sea shore,
And westward, faint and far away, the glimmer
Of torches on Mount Olivet, announcing
The rising of the Moon of Passover.
Like a great cross it seems, on which suspended,
With head bowed down in agony, I see
A human figure! Hide, O merciful heaven,
The awful apparition from my sight!

And thou, Machærus, lifting high and black
Thy dreadful walls against the rising moon,
Haunted by demons and by apparitions

646

Lilith, and Jezerhara, and Bedar-
gon,
How grim thou showest in the un-
certain light,
A palace and a prison, where King
Herod
Feasts with Herodias, while the
Baptist John
Fasts, and consumes his unavailing
life !
And in thy court-yard grows the
untithed rue,
Huge as the olives of Gethsemane,
And ancient as the terebinth of
Hebron,
Coeval with the world. Would
that its leaves
Medicinal could purge thee of the
demons
That now possess thee, and the
cunning fox
That burrows in thy walls, contriv-
ing mischief !

(*Music is heard from within.*)

Angels of God ! Sandalphon, thou
that weavest
The prayers of men into immortal
garlands,
And thou, Metatron, who dost
gather up
Their songs, and bear them to the
gates of heaven,
Now gather up together in your
hands
The prayers that fill this prison,
and the songs
That echo from the ceiling of this
palace,
And lay them side by side before
God's feet !

(*He enters the castle.*)

II.

HEROD'S BANQUET-HALL.

Manahem. Thou hast sent for
me, O King, and I am here.
Herod. Who art thou ?

Manahem. Manahem,
the Essenian.
Herod. I recognize thy features,
but what mean
These torn and faded garments ?
On thy road
Have demons crowded thee, and
rubbed against thee,
And given thee weary knees ? A
cup of wine !
Manahem. The Essenians drink
no wine.
Herod. What wilt thou, then ?
Manahem. Nothing.
Herod. Not even a cup
of water ?
Manahem. Nothing.
Why hast thou sent for me ?
Herod. Dost thou remember
One day when I, a schoolboy in
the streets
Of the great city, met thee on my way
To school, and thou didst say to
me : Hereafter
Thou shalt be King ?
Manahem. Yea, I remember it.
Herod. Thinking thou didst not
know me, I replied :
I am of humble birth ; whereat,
thou, smiling,
Didst smite me with thy hand, and
saidst again :
Thou shalt be King ; and let the
friendly blows
That Manahem hath given thee on
this day
Remind thee of the fickleness of
fortune.
Manahem. What more ?
Herod. No more.
Manahem. Yea, for
I said to thee :
It shall be well with thee if thou
love justice
And clemency towards thy fellow-
men.
Hast thou done this, O King ?
Herod. Go, ask my people.

Manahem. And then, foreseeing
all thy life, I added:
But these thou wilt forget; and at
the end
Of life the Lord will punish thee.
  Herod.   The end!
When will that come? For this I
sent to thee.
How long shall I still reign? Thou
dost not answer!
Speak! shall I reign ten years?
  Manahem.   Thou
shalt reign twenty,
Nay, thirty years. I cannot name
the end.
  Herod. Thirty? I thank thee,
good Essenian!
This is my birthday, and a happier
one
Was never mine. We hold a ban-
quet here.
See, yonder are Herodias and her
daughter.
  Manahem (*aside*). 'Tis said that
devils sometimes take the
shape
Of ministering angels, clothed with
air,
That they may be inhabitants of
earth,
And lead man to destruction. Such
are these.
  Herod. Knowest thou John the
Baptist?
  Manahem. Yea, I know him;
Who knows him not?
  Herod.   Know, then,
this John the Baptist
Said that it was not lawful I should
marry
My brother Philip's wife, and John
the Baptist
Is here in prison. In my father's
time
Matthias Margaloth was put to
death
For tearing the golden eagle from
its station

Above the Temple Gate,—a slighter
crime
Than John is guilty of. These things
are warnings
To intermeddlers not to play with
eagles,
Living or dead. I think the Essen-
ians
Are wiser, or more wary, are they
not?
  Manahem. The Essenians do not
marry.
  Herod. Thou hast given
My words a meaning foreign to my
thought.
  Manahem. Let me go hence, O
King!
  Herod.   Stay yet awhile,
And see the daughter of Herodias
dance.
Cleopatra of Jerusalem, my mother,
In her best days was not more
beautiful.

(*Music.* THE DAUGHTER OF
HERODIAS *dances.*)

  Herod. O, what was Miriam
dancing with her timbrel,
Compared to this one?
  Manahem (*aside*). O thou Angel
of Death,
Dancing at funerals among the
women,
When men bear out the dead! The
air is hot
And stifles me! O for a breath of
air!
Bid me depart, O King!
  Herod. Not yet. Come hither,
Salome, thou enchantress! Ask of
me
Whate'er thou wilt; and even unto
the half
Of all my kingdom, I will give it
thee,
As the Lord liveth!
  Daughter of Herodias (*kneeling*).
          Give me here the head

Of John the Baptist on this silver
  charger!

Herod. Not that, dear child! I
  dare not, for the people

Regard John as a prophet.

Daughter of Herodias. Thou
  hast sworn it.

Herod. For mine oath's sake,
  then. Send unto the prison:

Let him die quickly. O accursed
  oath!

Manahem. Bid me depart, O
  King!

Herod. Good Manahem,

Give me thy hand. I love the Essenians.

He's gone and hears me not! The
  guests are dumb,

Awaiting the pale face, the silent
  witness.

The lamps flare; and the curtains
  of the doorways

Wave to and fro as if a ghost were
  passing!

Strengthen my heart, red wine of
  Ascalon!

III.

UNDER THE WALLS OF MACHÆRUS.

Manahem (rushing out). Away
  from this Palace of sin!

The demons, the terrible powers
Of the air, that haunt its towers
And hide in its water-spouts,
Deafen me with the din
Of their laughter and their shouts
For the crimes that are done within!

Sink back into the earth,
Or vanish into the air,
Thou castle of despair!
Let it all be but a dream
Of the things of monstrous birth,
Of the things that only seem!
White Angel of the Moon,
Onafiel! be my guide

Out of this hateful place
Of sin and death, nor hide
In yon black cloud too soon
Thy pale and tranquil face!

(*A trumpet is blown from the walls.*)

Hark! hark! It is the breath
Of the trump of doom and death,
From the battlements overhead
Like a burden of sorrow cast
On the midnight and the blast,
A wailing for the dead,
That the gusts drop and uplift!
O Herod, thy vengeance is swift!
O Herodias, thou hast been
The demon, the evil thing,
That in place of Esther the Queen,
In place of the lawful bride,
Hast lain at night by the side
Of Ahasuerus the king!

(*The trumpet again.*)

The Prophet of God is dead;
At a drunken monarch's call,
At a dancing-woman's beck,
They have severed that stubborn
  neck,
And into the banquet-hall
Are bearing the ghastly head!

(*A body is thrown from the tower.*)

A torch of lurid red
Lights the window with its glow;
And a white mass as of snow
Is hurled into the abyss
Of the black precipice,
That yawns for it below!
O hand of the Most High,
O hand of Adonai!
Bury it, hide it away
From the birds and beasts of prey,
And the eyes of the homicide,
More pitiless than they,
As thou didst bury of yore
The body of him that died
On the mountain of Peor!
Even now I behold a sign,
A threatening of wrath divine,
A watery, wandering star,

Through whose streaming hair, and
 the white
Unfolding garments of light,
That trail behind it afar,
The constellations shine !
And the whiteness and brightness
 appear
Like the Angel bearing the Seer
By the hair of his head, in the might
And rush of his vehement flight.
And I listen until I hear
From fathomless depths of the sky
The voice of his prophecy
Sounding louder and more near !
Malediction ! malediction !
May the lightnings of heaven fall
On palace and prison wall,
And their desolation be
As the day of fear and affliction,
As the day of anguish and ire,
With the burning and fuel of fire,
In the Valley of the Sea !

IV.

NICODEMUS AT NIGHT.

Nicodemus. The streets are silent.
 The dark houses seem
Like sepulchres, in which the
 sleepers lie
Wrapped in their shrouds, and for
 the moment dead.
The lamps are all extinguished ;
 only one
Burns steadily, and from the door
 its light
Lies like a shining gate across the
 street.
He waits for me. Ah, should this
 be at last
The long-expected Christ ! I see
 him there
Sitting alone, deep-buried in his
 thought,
As if the weight of all the world
 were resting

Upon him, and thus bowed him
 down. O Rabbi,
We know thou art a Teacher come
 from God,
For no man can perform the mira-
 cles
Thou dost perform, except the Lord
 be with him.
Thou art a Prophet, sent here to
 proclaim
The Kingdom of the Lord. Behold
 in me
A Ruler of the Jews, who long have
 waited
The coming of that Kingdom. Tell
 me of it.
 Christus. Verily, verily I say
 unto thee
Except a man be born again, he
 cannot
Behold the Kingdom of God !
 Nicodemus. Be born again ?
How can a man be born when he
 is old ?
Say, can he enter for a second time
Into his mother's womb, and so be
 born ?
 Christus. Verily I say unto thee,
 except
A man be born of water and the
 spirit,
He cannot enter into the Kingdom
 of God.
For that which of the flesh is born,
 is flesh ;
And that which of the spirit is born,
 is spirit.
 Nicodemus. We Israelites from
 the Primeval Man
Adam Ahelion derive our bodies ;
Our souls are breathings of the Holy
 Ghost.
No more than this we know, or
 need to know.
 Christus. Then marvel not, that
 I said unto thee
Ye must be born again.
 Nicodemus. The mystery

Of birth and death we cannot comprehend.

Christus. The wind bloweth where it listeth, and we hear

The sound thereof, but know not whence it cometh,

Nor whither it goeth. So is every one

Born of the spirit !

Nicodemus (aside). How can these things be ?

He seems to speak of some vague realm of shadows,

Some unsubstantial kingdom of the air !

It is not this the Jews are waiting for,

Nor can this be the Christ, the Son of David,

Who shall deliver us !

Christus. Art thou a master

Of Israel, and knowest not these things ?

We speak that we do know, and testify

That we have seen, and ye will not receive

Our witness. If I tell you earthly things,

And ye believe not, how shall ye believe

If I should tell you of things heavenly?

And no man hath ascended up to heaven,

But he alone that first came down from heaven,

Even the Son of Man which is in heaven !

Nicodemus (aside). This is a dreamer of dreams ; a visionary,

Whose brain is overtasked, until he deems

The unseen world to be a thing substantial,

And this we live in an unreal vision !

And yet his presence fascinates and fills me

With wonder, and I feel myself exalted

Into a higher region, and become

Myself in part a dreamer of his dreams,

A seer of his visions !

Christus. And as Moses

Uplifted the serpent in the wilderness,

So must the Son of Man be lifted up ;

That whosoever shall believe in him

Shall perish not, but have eternal life.

He that believes in him is not condemned ;

He that believes not, is condemned already.

Nicodemus (aside). He speaketh like a Prophet of the Lord !

Christus. This is the condemnation : that the light

Is come into the world, and men loved darkness

Rather than light, because their deeds are evil !

Nicodemus (aside). Of me he speaketh ! He reproveth me

Because I come by night to question him !

Christus. For every one that doeth evil deeds

Hateth the light, nor cometh to the light,

Lest he should be reproved.

Nicodemus (aside). Alas, how truly

He readeth what is passing in my heart !

Christus. But he that doeth truth comes to the light.

So that his deeds may be made manifest,

That they are wrought in God.

Nicodemus. Alas ! alas !

V.

BLIND BARTIMEUS.

Bartimeus. Be not impatient,
    Chilion ; it is pleasant
To sit here in the shadow of the walls
Under the palms, and hear the hum
    of bees,
And rumour of voices passing to
    and fro,
And drowsy bells of caravans on
    their way
To Sidon or Damascus. This is
    still
The City of Palms, and yet the
    walls thou seest
Are not the old walls, not the walls
    where Rahab
Hid the two spies, and let them
    down by cords
Out of the window, when the gates
    were shut,
And it was dark. Those walls were
    overthrown
When Joshua's army shouted, and
    the priests
Blew with their seven trumpets.
    Chilion.   When was that ?
Bartimeus. O, my sweet rose of
    Jericho, I know not.
Hundreds of years ago. And over
    there
Beyond the river, the great prophet
    Elijah
Was taken by a whirlwind up to
    heaven,
In chariot of fire, with fiery horses.
That is the plain of Moab; and
    beyond it
Rise the blue summits of Mount
    Abarim,
Nebo and Pisgah and Peor, where
    Moses
Died, whom the Lord knew face to
    face, and whom
He buried in a valley, and no man
Knows of his sepulchre unto this
    day.

Chilion. Would thou couldst see
    these places, as I see them.
Bartimeus. I have not seen a
    glimmer of light
Since thou wast born. I never saw
    thy face,
And yet I seem to see it ; and one day
Perhaps shall see it ; for there is a
    Prophet
In Galilee, the Messiah, the Son of
    David,
Who heals the blind—if I could only
    find him.
I hear the sound of many feet
    approaching,
And voices, like the murmur of a
    crowd !
What seest thou ?
    Chilion. A young man clad in
    white
Is coming through the gateway,
    and a crowd
Of people follow.
    Bartimeus. Can it be the Prophet?
O neighbours, tell me who it is
    that passes !
    One of the Crowd. Jesus of
    Nazareth.
    Bartimeus (crying).   O Son of
    David !
Have mercy on me !
    Many of the Crowd. Peace, Blind
    Bartimeus !
Do not disturb the Master.
    Bartimeus (crying more vehe-
    mently).   Son of David,
Have mercy on me !
    One of the Crowd. See, the
    Master stops.
Be of good comfort; rise, he
    calleth thee !
    Bartimeus (casting away his
    cloak). Chilion ! good neigh-
    bours ! lead me on.
    Christus.   What wilt thou
That I should do to thee ?
    Bartimeus.   Good Lord !
    my sight—

That I receive my sight!
   Christus.   Receive thy sight!
Thy faith hath made thee whole!
   The Crowd.   He sees again!

(CHRISTUS *passes on. The crowd*
   gathers round BARTIMEUS.)

   Bartimeus. I see again; but
    sight bewilders me!
Like a remembered dream, familiar
    things
Come back to me. I see the tender
    sky
Above me, see the trees, the city
    walls,
And the old gateway, through
    whose echoing arch
I groped so many years; and you,
    my neighbours;
But know you by your friendly
    voices only.
How beautiful the world is! and
    how wide!
O, I am miles away, if I but look!
Where art thou, Chilion?
   Chilion.   Father, I am here.
   Bartimeus. O let me gaze upon
    thy face, dear child!
For I have only seen thee with my
    hands!
How beautiful thou art! I should
    have known thee;
Thou hast her eyes whom we shall
    see hereafter!
O God of Abraham? Elion! Ado-
    nai!
Who art thyself a Father, pardon
    me
If for a moment I have thee post-
    poned
To the affections and the thoughts
    of earth,
Thee, and the adoration that I owe
    thee,
When by thy power alone these
    darkened eyes
Have been unsealed again to see
    thy light!

VI.

JACOB'S WELL.

   A Samaritan Woman. The sun
    is hot; and the dry east-wind
    blowing
Fills all the air with dust. The
    birds are silent;
Even the little fieldfares in the corn
No longer twitter; only the grass-
    hoppers
Sing their incessant song of sun
    and summer.
I wonder who those strangers were
    I met
Going into the city? Galileans
They seemed to me in speaking,
    when they asked
The short way to the market-place.
    Perhaps
They are fishermen from the lake;
    or travellers,
Looking to find the inn. And here
    is some one
Sitting beside the well; another
    stranger;
A Galilean also by his looks.
What can so many Jews be doing
    here
Together in Samaria? Are they
    going
Up to Jerusalem to the Passover?
Our Passover is better here at
    Sychem,
For here is Ebal; here is Gerizim,
The mountain where our father
    Abraham
Went up to offer Isaac; here the
    tomb
Of Joseph,—for they brought his
    bones from Egypt
And buried them in this land, and
    it is holy.
   Christus. Give me to drink.
   Samaritan Woman. How
    can it be that thou,
Being a Jew, askest to drink of me
Which am a woman of Samaria?

You Jews despise us; have no dealings with us;
Make us a by-word; call us in derision
The silly folk of Sychar. Sir, how is it
Thou askest drink of me?

Christus. If thou hadst known
The gift of God, and who it is that sayeth
Give me to drink, thou wouldst have asked of him;
He would have given thee the living water.

Samaritan Woman. Sir, thou hast nought to draw with, and the well
Is deep! Whence hast thou living water?
Say, art thou greater than our father Jacob,
Which gave this well to us, and drank thereof
Himself, and all his children, and his cattle?

Christus. Ah, whosoever drinketh of this water
Shall thirst again; but whosoever drinketh
The water I shall give him shall not thirst
For evermore, for it shall be within him
A well of living water, springing up
Into life everlasting.

Samaritan Woman. Every day
I must go to and fro, in heat and cold,
And I am weary. Give me of this water,
That I may thirst not, nor come here to draw.

Christus. Go call thy husband, woman, and come hither,

Samaritan Woman. I have no husband, Sir,

Christus. Thou hast well said
I have no husband. Thou hast had five husbands;

And he whom now thou hast is not thy husband.

Samaritan Woman. Surely thou art a Prophet, for thou readest
The hidden things of life! Our fathers worshipped
Upon this mountain Gerizim; and ye say
The only place in which men ought to worship
Is at Jerusalem.

Christus. Believe me, woman,
The hour is coming, when ye neither shall
Upon this mount, nor at Jerusalem,
Worship the Father; for the hour is coming,
And is now come, when the true worshippers
Shall worship the Father in spirit and in truth.
The Father seeketh such to worship him.
God is a Spirit; and they that worship him
Must worship him in spirit and in truth.

Samaritan Woman. Master, I know that the Messiah cometh,
Which is called Christ; and he will tell us all things.

Christus. I that speak unto thee am he!

The Disciples (*returning*). Behold,
The Master sitting by the well, and talking
With a Samaritan woman! With a woman
Of Sychar, the silly people, always boasting
Of their Mount Ebal, and Mount Gerizim,
Their Everlasting Mountain, which they think
Higher and holier than our Mount Moriah!

Why, once upon the Feast of the
New Moon,
When our great Sanhedrim of Jeru-
salem
Had all its watch-fires kindled on
the hills
To warn the distant villages, these
people
Lighted up others to mislead the
Jews,
And make a mockery of their festi-
val!
See, she has left the Master; and
is running
Back to the city!
Samaritan Woman. O, come
see a man
Who hath told me all things that I
ever did!
Say, is not this the Christ?
The Disciples. Lo, Master, here
Is food, that we have brought thee
from the city.
We pray thee eat it.
Christus. I have food to eat
Ye know not of.
The Disciples (*to each other*).
Hath any man been here,
And brought him aught to eat,
while we were gone?
Christus. The food I speak of is
to do the will
Of him that sent me, and to finish
his work.
Do ye not say, Lo! there are yet
four months
And cometh harvest? I say unto
you,
Lift up your eyes, and look upon
the fields,
For they are white already unto
harvest!

VII.

THE COASTS OF CÆSAREA PHILIPPI.

Christus (*going up the mountain*).
Whom do the people say I am?

John. Some say
That thou art John the Baptist;
some, Elias;
And others, Jeremiah.
James. Or that one
Of the old Prophets is risen again.
Christus. But who say ye I am?
Peter. Thou art the Christ!
Thou art the Son of God!
Christus. Blessed art thou,
Simon Barjona! Flesh and blood
hath not
Revealed it unto thee, but even my
Father,
Which is in heaven. And I say
unto thee
That thou art Peter; and upon this
rock
I build my Church, and all the
gates of Hell
Shall not prevail against it. But
take heed
Ye tell to no man that I am the
Christ.
For I must go up to Jerusalem,
And suffer many things, and be re-
jected
Of the Chief Priests, and of the
Scribes and Elders,
And must be crucified, and the
third day
Shall rise again!
Peter. Be it far from thee, Lord!
This shall not be!
Christus. Get thee behind me,
Satan!
Thou savourest not the things that
be of God,
But those that be of men! If any
will
Come after me, let him deny himself,
And daily take his cross, and follow
me.
For whosoever will save his life
shall lose it,
And whosoever will lose his life
shall find it.
For wherein shall a man be profited

655

If he shall gain the whole world,
and shall lose
Himself or be a castaway !

James (*after a long pause*). Why
doth
The Master lead us up into this
mountain ?

Peter. He goeth up to pray.

John. See, where he standeth
Above us on the summit of the hill !
His face shines as the sun ! and all
his raiment
Exceeding white as snow, so as
no fuller
On earth can white them ! He is
not alone ;
There are two with him there ; two
men of eld,
Their white beards blowing on the
mountain air,
Are talking with him.

James. I am sore afraid !

Peter. Who and whence are they ?

John. Moses and Elias !

Peter. O Master ! it is good for
us to be here !
If thou wilt, let us make three
tabernacles ;
For thee one, and for Moses and
Elias !

John. Behold a bright cloud sailing in the sun !
It overshadows us. A golden mist
Now hides them from us, and
envelops us
And all the mountain in a luminous shadow !
I see no more. The nearest rocks
are hidden.

Voice from the cloud. Lo ! this
is my beloved Son ! Hear him !

Peter. It is the voice of God.
He speaketh to us,
As from the burning bush he spake
to Moses !

John. The cloud-wreaths roll
away. The veil is lifted ;
We see again. Behold ! he is alone,

It was a vision that our eyes beheld,
And it hath vanished into the unseen.

Christus (*coming down from the
mountain*). I charge ye, tell
the vision unto no one,
Till the Son of Man be risen from
the dead !

Peter (*aside*). Again he speaks
of it ! What can it mean,
This rising from the dead ?

James. Why say the Scribes
Elias must first come ?

Christus. He cometh first,
Restoring all things. But I say to
you,
That this Elias is already come.
They knew him not, but have done
unto him
Whate'er they listed, as is written
of him.

Peter (*aside*). It is of John the
Baptist he is speaking.

James. As we descend, see, at
the mountain's foot,
A crowd of people ; coming, going,
thronging
Round the disciples, that we left
behind us,
Seeming impatient that we stay so
long.

Peter. It is some blind man, or
some paralytic
That waits the Master's coming to
be healed.

James. I see a boy, who struggles
and demeans him
As if an unclean spirit tormented
him ?

A certain Man (*running forward*). Lord ! I beseech thee,
look upon my son.
He is mine only child ; a lunatic,
And sorely vexed ; for oftentimes
he falleth
Into the fire and oft into the water.
Wherever the dumb spirit taketh
him

He teareth him. He gnasheth
with his teeth,
And pines away. I spake to thy
disciples
That they should cast him out, and
they could not.

Christus. O faithless generation
and perverse!
How long shall I be with you, and
suffer you?
Bring thy son hither.

Bystanders. How the unclean
spirit
Seizes the boy, and tortures him
with pain!
He falleth to the ground and wal-
lows, foaming!
He cannot live.

Christus. How long is it ago
Since this came unto him?

The Father. Even of a child.
O have compassion on us, Lord,
and help us,
If thou canst help us.

Christus. If thou canst believe!
For unto him that verily believeth,
All things are possible.

The Father. Lord, I believe!
Help thou mine unbelief!

Christus. Dumb and deaf spirit,
Come out of him, I charge thee,
and no more
Enter thou into him!

*(The boy utters a loud cry of pain,
and then lies still.)*

Bystanders. How motionless
He lieth there. No life is left in him.
His eyes are like a blind man's,
that see not.
The boy is dead!

Others. Behold, the Master
stoops,
And takes him by the hand, and
lifts him up.
He is not dead.

Disciples. But one word from
those lips

But one touch of that hand, and he
is healed!
Ah, why could we not do it?

The Father. My poor child!
Now thou art mine again. The
unclean spirit
Shall never more torment thee!
Look at me!
Speak unto me! Say that thou
knowest me!

Disciples to Christus (departing).
Good Master, tell us, for what
reason was it
We could not cast him out?

Christus. Because
of your unbelief!

VIII.

THE YOUNG RULER.

Christus. Two men went up into
the Temple to pray.
The one was a self-righteous Phari-
see,
The other a Publican. And the
Pharisee
Stood and prayed thus within him-
self: O God,
I thank thee I am not as other men,
Extortioners, unjust, adulterers,
Or even as this Publican. I fast
Twice in the week, and also I give
tithes
Of all that I possess! The Publican,
Standing afar off, would not lift so
much
Even as his eyes to heaven, but
smote his breast,
Saying: God be merciful to me a
sinner!
I tell you that this man went to his
house
More justified than the other.
Every one
That doth exalt himself shall be
abased,
And he that humbleth himself shall
be exalted!

Children (among themselves).
  Let us go nearer ! He is telling
    stories !
Let us go listen to them.
  An old Jew. Children, children,
What are ye doing here ? Why do
  ye crowd us ?
It was such little vagabonds as you
That followed Elisha, mocking him
  and crying :
Go up, thou bald-head ! But the
  bears—the bears
Came out of the wood, and tare
  them !
  A Mother.   Speak not thus !
We brought them here, that he
  might lay his hands
On them, and bless them.
  Christus. Suffer little children
To come unto me, and forbid them
  not ;
Of such is the kingdom of heaven;
  and their angels
Look always on my Father's face.

(*Takes them in his arms and blesses
them.*)

  A Young Ruler (*running*). Good
  Master !
What good thing shall I do, that
  I may have
Eternal life ?
  Christus. Why callest thou me
  good ?
There is none good but one, and
  that is God.
If thou wilt enter into life eternal,
Keep the commandments.
  Young Ruler. Which of them ?
  Christus.   Thou shalt not
Commit adultery ; thou shalt not
  kill ;
Thou shalt not steal; thou shalt
  not bear false witness ;
Honour thy father and thy mother;
  and love
Thy neighbour as thyself.
  Young Ruler.   From my
  youth up

All these things have I kept.
  What lack I yet ?
  John. With what divine compas-
    sion in his eyes
The Master looks upon this eager
  youth,
As if he loved him !
  Christus.   Wouldst thou
  perfect be,
Sell all thou hast, and give it to
  the poor,
And come, take up thy cross, and
  follow me,
And thou shalt have thy treasure
  in the heavens.
  John. Behold, how sorrowful he
  turns away !
  Christus. Children ! how hard
  it is for them that trust
In riches to enter into the kingdom
  of God !
'Tis easier for a camel to go through
A needle's eye, than for the rich to
  enter
The kingdom of God !
  John.   Ah, who then
  can be saved ?
  Christus. With men this is in-
  deed impossible,
But unto God all things are pos-
  sible !
  Peter. Behold, we have left all,
  and followed thee.
What shall we have therefor ?
  Christus.   Eternal life.

IX.

AT BETHANY.

MARTHA *busy about household
affairs.* MARY *sitting at the feet
of* CHRISTUS.

  Martha. She sitteth idly at the
  Master's feet,
And troubles not herself with
  household cares.
'Tis the old story. When a guest
  arrives

She gives up all to be with him;
while I
Must be the drudge, make ready
the guest-chamber,
Prepare the food, set everything in
order,
And see that nought is wanting in
the house.
She shows her love by words, and
I by works.

Mary. O Master! when thou
comest it is always
A Sabbath in the house. I cannot
work;
I must sit at thy feet; must see
thee, hear thee!
I have a feeble, wayward, doubting
heart,
Incapable of endurance or great
thoughts,
Striving for something that it cannot reach,
Baffled and disappointed, wounded,
hungry;
And only when I hear thee am I
happy,
And only when I see thee am at
peace!

Stronger than I, and wiser, and
far better
In every manner, is my sister
Martha.
You see how well she orders every-
thing
To make thee welcome; how she
comes and goes,
Careful and cumbered ever with
much serving,
While I but welcome thee with
foolish words!
Whene'er thou speakest to me, I
am happy;
When thou art silent, I am satisfied.
Thy presence is enough. I ask no
more.
Only to be with thee, only to see
thee,

Sufficeth me. My heart is then at
rest.
I wonder I am worthy of so much.
Martha. Lord, dost thou care
not that my sister Mary
Hath left me thus to wait on thee
alone?
I pray thee, bid her help me.
Christus. Martha, Martha,
Careful and troubled about many
things
Art thou, and yet one thing alone
is needful!
Thy sister Mary hath chosen that
good part,
Which never shall be taken away
from her!

X.

BORN BLIND.

A Jew. Who is this beggar
blinking in the sun?
Is it not he who used to sit and beg
By the Gate Beautiful?
Another. It is the same.
A Third. It is not he, but like
him, for that beggar
Was blind from birth. It cannot
be the same.
The Beggar. Yea, I am he.
A Jew. How have
thine eyes been opened?
The Beggar. A man that is
called Jesus made a clay
And put it on mine eyes, and said
to me:
Go to Siloam's Pool and wash thy-
self.
I went and washed, and I received
my sight.
A Jew. Where is he?
The Beggar. I know not.
Pharisees. What
is this crowd
Gathered about a beggar? What
has happened?
A Jew. Here is a man who hath
been blind from birth,

And now he sees. He says a man
called Jesus
Hath healed him.

Pharisees.   As God liveth,
the Nazarene!

How was this done?

The Beggar. Rabboni, he put clay
Upon mine eyes; I washed, and
now I see.

Pharisees. When did he this?

The Beggar.   Rabboni,
yesterday.

Pharisees. The Sabbath-day.
This man is not of God
Because he keepeth not the Sab-
bath-day!

A Jew. How can a man that is
a sinner do
Such miracles?

Pharisees. What dost thou say
of him
That hath restored thy sight?

The Beggar. He is a Prophet.

A Jew. This is a wonderful
story, but not true.
A beggar's fiction. He was not
born blind,
And never has been blind!

Others. Here are his parents.
Ask them.

Pharisees. Is this your son?

The Parents. Rabboni, yea;
We know this is our son.

Pharisees. Was he born blind?

The Parents. He was born blind.

Pharisees.   Then
how doth he now see?

The Parents (aside). What answer shall we make? If we
confess
It was the Christ, we shall be
driven forth
Out of the Synagogue! We know,
Rabboni,
This is our son, and that he was
born blind;
But by what means he seeth, we
know not,

Or who his eyes hath opened, we
know not.
He is of age—ask him; we cannot
say;
He shall speak for himself.

Pharisees.   Give God
the praise!
We know the man that healed thee
is a sinner!

The Beggar. Whether he be a
sinner I know not;
One thing I know, that whereas I
was blind,
I now do see.

Pharisees. How opened he thine
eyes?
What did he do?

The Beggar. I have already told
you.
Ye did not hear; why would ye
hear again?
Will ye be his disciples?

Pharisees.   God of Moses!
Are we demoniacs, are we halt or
blind,
Or palsy-stricken, or lepers, or the
like,
That we should join the Synagogue
of Satan,
And follow jugglers? Thou art his
disciple,
But we are disciples of Moses; and
we know
That God spake unto Moses; but
this fellow,
We know not whence he is!

The Beggar.   Why, herein is
A marvellous thing! Ye know not
whence he is,
Yet he hath opened mine eyes!
We know that God
Heareth not sinners; but if any man
Doeth God's will, and is his wor-
shipper,
Him doth he hear. O, since the
world began
It was not heard that any man hath
opened

The eyes of one that was born blind.
If he
Were not of God, surely he could
do nothing !
Pharisees. Thou, who wast alto-
gether born in sins
And in iniquities, dost thou teach us ?
Away with thee out of the holy
places,
Thou reprobate, thou beggar, thou
blasphemer !

(THE BEGGAR *is cast out.*)

XI.

SIMON MAGUS AND HELEN OF
TYRE.

*On the house-top at Endor. Night.
A lighted lantern on a table.*

Simon. Swift are the blessed Im-
mortals to the mortal
That perseveres ! So doth it stand
recorded
In the divine Chaldean Oracles
Of Zoroaster, once Ezekiel's slave,
Who in his native East betook
himself
To lonely meditation, and the writing
On the dried skins of oxen the
Twelve Books
Of the Avesta and the Oracles !
Therefore I persevere ; and I have
brought thee
From the great city of Tyre, where
men deride
The things they comprehend not,
to this plain
Of Esdraelon, in the Hebrew tongue
Called Armageddon, and this town
of Endor,
Where men believe ; where all the
air is full
Of marvellous traditions, and the
Enchantress
That summoned up the ghost of
Samuel

Is still remembered. Thou hast
seen the land :
Is it not fair to look on ?
Helen. It is fair,
Yet not so fair as Tyre.
Simon. Is not Mount Tabor
As beautiful as Carmel by the Sea ?
Helen. It is too silent and too
solitary ;
I miss the tumult of the streets ;
the sounds
Of traffic, and the going to and fro
Of people in gay attire, with cloaks
of purple,
And gold and silver jewelry !
Simon. Inventions
Of Ahriman, the spirit of the dark,
The Evil Spirit !
Helen. I regret the gossip
Of friends and neighbours at the
open door
On summer nights.
Simon. An idle waste of time.
Helen. The singing and the
dancing, the delight
Of music and of motion. Woe is
me,
To give up all these pleasures, and
to lead
The life we lead !
Simon. Thou canst not raise
thyself
Up to the level of my higher
thought,
And though possessing thee, I still
remain
Apart from thee, and with thee, am
alone
In my high dreams.
Helen. Happier was I in Tyre.
O, I remember how the gallant
ships
Came sailing in, with ivory, gold
and silver,
And apes and peacocks ; and the
singing sailors ;
And the gay captains, with their
silken dresses,

Smelling of aloes, myrrh, and cinnamon!

Simon. But the dishonour, Helen! Let the ships
Of Tarshish howl for that!

Helen. And what dishonour?
Remember Rahab, and how she became
The ancestress of the great Psalmist David;
And wherefore should not I, Helen of Tyre,
Attain like honour?

Simon. Thou art Helen of Tyre,
And hast been Helen of Troy, and hast been Rahab,
The Queen of Sheba, and Semiramis,
And Sara of seven husbands, and Jezebel,
And other women of the like allurements;
And now thou art Minerva, the first Æon,
The Mother of Angels!

Helen. And the concubine
Of Simon the Magician! Is it honour
For one who has been all these noble dames,
To tramp about the dirty villages
And cities of Samaria with a juggler—
A charmer of serpents?

Simon. He who knows himself,
Knows all things in himself. I have charmed thee,
Thou beautiful asp; yet am I no magician.
I am the Power of God, and the Beauty of God!
I am the Paraclete, the Comforter!

Helen. Illusions! Thou deceiver, self-deceived!
Thou dost usurp the titles of another;
Thou art not what thou sayest.

Simon. Am I not?
Then feel my power.

Helen. Would I had ne'er left Tyre!

(*He looks at her, and she sinks into a deep sleep.*)

Simon. Go, see it in thy dreams, fair unbeliever!
And leave me unto mine, if they be dreams,
That take such shapes before me, that I see them;
These effable and ineffable impressions
Of the mysterious world, that come to me
From the elements of Fire and Earth and Water,
And the all-nourishing Ether! It is written,
Look not on Nature, for her name is fatal!
Yet there are Principles, that make apparent
The images of unapparent things,
And the impression of vague characters
And visions most divine appear in ether.
So speak the Oracles; then wherefore fatal?
I take this orange-bough, with its five leaves,
Each equidistant on the upright stem;
And I project them on a plane below,
In the circumference of a circle drawn
About a centre where the stem is planted,
And each still equidistant from the other;
As if a thread of gossamer were drawn
Down from each leaf, and fastened with a pin.

Now if from these five points a line
    be traced
To each alternate point, we shall
    obtain
The Pentagram, or Solomon's
    Pentangle,
A charm against all witchcraft, and
    a sign,
Which on the banner of Antiochus
Drove back the fierce barbarians of
    the North,
Demons esteemed, and gave the
    Syrian King
The sacred name of Soter, or of
    Saviour.
Thus Nature works mysteriously
    with man;
And from the Eternal One, as from
    a centre,
All things proceed, in fire, air, earth,
    and water,
And all are subject to one law,
    which broken
Even in a single point, is broken in
    all;
Demons rush in, and chaos comes
    again.

By this will I compel the stubborn
    spirits
That guard the treasures, hid in
    caverns deep
On Gerizim by Uzzi the High-
    Priest,
The ark and holy vessels, to reveal
Their secret unto me, and to restore
These precious things to the Sa-
    maritans.

A mist is rising from the plain below
    me,
And as I look the vapours shape
    themselves
Into strange figures, as if unawares
My lips had breathed the Tetra-
    grammaton,
And from their graves, o'er all the
    battlefields

Of Armageddon, the long-buried
    captains
Had started, with their thousands,
    and ten thousands,
And rushed together to renew their
    wars,
Powerless, and weaponless, and
    without a sound!
Wake, Helen, from thy sleep! The
    air grows cold;
Let us go down.
    Helen (*awaking*). O would I were
      at home!
    Simon. Thou sayest that I usurp
      another's titles.
In youth I saw the Wise Men of the
    East,
Magalath and Pangalath, and Sara-
    cen,
Who followed the bright star, but
    home returned
For fear of Herod by another way.
O shining worlds above me! in what
    deep
Recesses of your realms of mystery
Lies hidden now that star; and
    where are they
That brought the gifts of frank-
    incense and myrrh?
    Helen. The Nazarene still liveth.
    Simon.   We have heard
His name in many towns, but have
    not seen him.
He flits before us; tarries not; is
    gone
When we approach like something
    unsubstantial,
Made of the air, and fading into
    air.
He is at Nazareth, he is at Nain,
Or at the Lovely Village on the
    Lake,
Or sailing on its waters.
    Helen.   So say those
Who do not wish to find him.
    Simon.   Can this be
The King of Israel, whom the Wise
    Men worshipped?

Or does he fear to meet me? It
would seem so.
We should soon learn which of us
twain usurps
The titles of the other, as thou
sayest.

(*They go down.*)

THE THIRD PASSOVER.

I.

THE ENTRY INTO JERUSALEM.

THE SYRO-PHŒNICIAN WOMAN
and her DAUGHTER *on the house-
top at Jerusalem.*

The Daughter (*singing*).

Blind Bartimeus at the gates
Of Jericho in darkness waits;
He hears the crowd; he hears a
breath
Say: It is Christ of Nazareth!
And calls, in tones of agony,
Ἰησοῦ, ἐλέησόν με!

The thronging multitudes increase:
Blind Bartimeus, hold thy peace!
But still, above the noisy crowd,
The beggar's cry is shrill and loud;
Until they say: He calleth thee!
Θάρσει, ἔγειραι, φωνεῖ σε!

Then saith the Christ, as silent
stands
The crowd: What wilt thou at my
hands?
And he replies: O, give me light!
Rabbi, restore the blind man's sight!
And Jesus answers, Ὕπαγε·
Ἡ πίστις σου σέσωκέ σε!

Ye that have eyes, yet cannot see,
In darkness and in misery,
Recall those mighty Voices Three,
Ἰησοῦ, ἐλέησόν με!
Θάρσει, ἔγειραι Ὕπαγε!
Ἡ πίστις σου σέσωκέ σε!

The Mother. Thy faith hath saved
thee! Ah, how true that is!
For I had faith; and when the
Master came
Into the coasts of Tyre and Sidon,
fleeing
From those who sought to slay him,
I went forth
And cried unto him, saying: Have
mercy on me,
O Lord, thou Son of David! for my
daughter
Is grievously tormented with a
devil.
But he passed on, and answered not
a word.
And his disciples said, beseeching
him:
Send her away! She crieth after us!
And then the Master answered them
and said:
I am not sent but unto the lost sheep
Of the House of Israel! Then I
worshipped him,
Saying: Lord, help me! And he
answered me,
It is not meet to take the children's
bread
And cast it unto dogs! Truth, Lord,
I said;
And yet the dogs may eat the crumbs
which fall
From off their master's table; and
he turned,
And answered me; and said to me:
O woman,
Great is thy faith; then be it unto
thee,
Even as thou wilt. And from that
very hour
Thou wast made whole, my darling!
my delight!

The Daughter. There came upon
my dark and troubled mind
A calm, as when the tumult of the city
Suddenly ceases, and I lie and hear
The silver trumpets of the Temple
blowing

Their welcome to the Sabbath. Still
   I wonder
That one who was so far away from
   me,
And could not see me, by his
   thought alone
Had power to heal me. O that I
   could see him!
The Mother. Perhaps thou wilt;
for I have brought thee here
To keep the holy Passover, and lay
Thine offering of thanksgiving on
   the altar.
Thou mayst both see and hear him.
   Hark!
Voices afar off. Hosanna!
The Daughter. A crowd comes
   pouring through the city gate!
O mother, look!
Voices in the street. Hosanna to
   the Son
Of David!
   The Daughter. A great multitude
   of people
Fills all the street; and riding on
   an ass
Comes one of noble aspect, like a
   king!
The people spread their garments
   in the way,
And scatter branches of the palm-
   trees!
Voices. Blessed
Is he that cometh in the name of
   the Lord!
Hosanna in the highest!
   Other Voices. Who is this?
Voices. Jesus of Nazareth!
The Daughter. Mother, it is he!
Voices. He hath called Lazarus
   of Bethany
Out of his grave, and raised him
   from the dead!
Hosanna in the highest!
   Pharisees. Ye perceive
That nothing we prevail. Behold,
   the world
Is all gone after him!

The Daughter. What majesty
What power is in that careworn
   countenance!
What sweetness, what compassion!
   I no longer
Wonder that he hath healed me!
Voices. Peace in heaven,
And glory in the highest!
Pharisees. Rabbi! Rabbi!
Rebuke thy followers!
   Christus. Should they
   hold their peace
The very stones beneath us would
   cry out!
The Daughter. All hath passed
   by me like a dream of wonder!
But I have seen him, and have
   heard his voice,
And I am satisfied! I ask no more!

II.

SOLOMON'S PORCH.

Gamaliel the Scribe. When Rab-
   ban Simeon, upon whom be
   peace!
Taught in these Schools, he boasted
   that his pen
Had written no word that he could
   call his own,
But wholly and always had been
   consecrated
To the transcribing of the Law and
   Prophets.
He used to say, and never tired of
   saying,
The world itself was built upon the
   Law.
And ancient Hillel said, that who-
   soever
Gains a good name, gains something
   for himself,
But he who gains a knowledge of
   the Law
Gains everlasting life. And they
   spake truly.
Great is the Written Law; but
   greater still

The Unwritten, the Traditions of
the Elders,
The lovely words of Levites, spoken
first
To Moses on the Mount, and
handed down
From mouth to mouth, in one
unbroken sound
And sequence of divine authority,
The voice of God resounding
through the ages.

The Written Law is water; the
Unwritten
Is precious wine; the Written Law
is salt,
The Unwritten costly spice; the
Written Law
Is but the body; the Unwritten,
the soul
That quickens it, and makes it
breathe and live.

I can remember, many years ago,
A little bright-eyed schoolboy, a
mere stripling,
Son of a Galilean carpenter,
From Nazareth, I think, who came
one day
And sat here in the Temple with
the Scribes,
Hearing us speak, and asking many
questions,
And we were all astonished at his
quickness.
And when his mother came, and
said: Behold,
Thy father and I have sought thee,
sorrowing;
He looked as one astonished, and
made answer:
How is it that ye sought me? Wist
ye not
That I must be about my Father's
business?
Often since then I see him here
among us,
Or dream I see him, with his up-
raised face

Intent and eager, and I often wonder
Unto what manner of manhood he
hath grown!
Perhaps a poor mechanic, like his
father,
Lost in his little Galilean village
And toiling at his craft, to die un-
known
And be no more remembered among
men.

  Christus (*in the outer court*). The
Scribes and Pharisees sit in
Moses' seat;
All, therefore, whatsoever they
command you,
Observe and do; but follow not
their works;
They say and do not. They bind
heavy burdens
And very grievous to be borne, and
lay them
Upon men's shoulders, but they
move them not
With so much as a finger!

  Gamaliel (*looking forth*). Who is
this
Exhorting in the outer courts so
loudly?
  Christus. Their works they do
for to be seen of men:
They make broad their phylacteries,
and enlarge
The borders of their garments, and
they love
The uppermost rooms at feasts, and
the chief seats
In Synagogues, and greetings in the
markets,
And to be called of all men Rabbi,
Rabbi!
  Gamaliel. It is that loud and
turbulent Galilean,
That came here at the Feast of
Dedication,
And stirred the people up to break
the Law!
  Christus. Woe unto you, ye
Scribes and Pharisees,

Ye hypocrites! for ye shut up the kingdom
Of heaven, and neither go ye in yourselves
Nor suffer them that are entering to go in!

Gamaliel. How eagerly the people throng and listen,
As if his ribald words were words of wisdom!

Christus. Woe unto you, ye Scribes and Pharisees,
Ye hypocrites! for ye devour the houses
Of widows, and for pretence ye make long prayers;
Therefore shall ye receive the more damnation.

Gamaliel. This brawler is no Jew,—he is a vile
Samaritan, and hath an unclean spirit!

Christus. Woe unto you, ye Scribes and Pharisees,
Ye hypocrites! ye compass sea and land
To make one proselyte, and when he is made
Ye make him twofold more the child of hell
Than you yourselves are!

Gamaliel. O my father's father!
Hillel of blessed memory, hear and judge!

Christus. Woe unto you, ye Scribes and Pharisees,
Ye hypocrites! for ye pay tithe of mint,
Of anise and of cumin, and omit
The weightier matters of the law of God,
Judgment and faith and mercy; and all these
Ye ought to have done, nor leave undone the others!

Gamaliel. O Rabban Simeon! how must thy bones

Stir in their grave to hear such blasphemies!

Christus. Woe unto you, ye Scribes and Pharisees,
Ye hypocrites! for ye make clean and sweet
The outside of the cup and of the platter,
But they within are full of all excess!

Gamaliel. Patience of God! canst thou endure so long?
Or art thou deaf, or gone upon a journey?

Christus. Woe unto you, ye Scribes and Pharisees,
Ye hypocrites! for ye are very like
To whited sepulchres, which indeed appear
Beautiful outwardly, but are within
Filled full of dead men's bones and all uncleanness!

Gamaliel. Am I awake? Is this Jerusalem?
And are these Jews that throng and stare and listen?

Christus. Woe unto you, ye Scribes and Pharisees,
Ye hypocrites! because ye build the tombs
Of Prophets, and adorn the sepulchres
Of righteous men, and say: If we had lived
When lived our fathers, we would not have been
Partakers with them in the blood of Prophets.
So ye be witnesses unto yourselves,
That ye are children of them that killed the Prophets!
Fill ye up then the measure of your fathers.
I send unto you Prophets and Wise Men,
And Scribes, and some ye crucify, and some
Scourge in your Synagogues, and persecute

From city to city! that on you may
  come
The righteous blood that hath been
  shed on earth,
From the blood of righteous Abel
  to the blood
Of Zacharias, son of Barachias,
Ye slew between the Temple and
  the altar!

Gamaliel. O, had I here my
  subtle dialectician,
My little Saul of Tarsus, the tent-
  maker,
Whose wit is sharper than his
  needle's point,
He would delight to foil this noisy
  wrangler!

Christus. Jerusalem! Jerusalem! O thou
That killest the Prophets, and that
  stonest them
Which are sent unto thee, how
  often would I
Have gathered together thy children, as a hen
Gathereth her chickens underneath
  her wing,
And ye would not! Behold, your
  house is left
Unto you desolate!

The People. This is a Prophet!
This is the Christ that was to
  come!

Gamaliel. Ye fools!
Think ye, shall Christ come out of
  Galilee?

III.

LORD, IS IT I?

Christus. One of you shall betray
  me.

The Disciples. Is it I?
Lord, is it I?

Christus. One of the Twelve it is
That dippeth with me in this dish
  his hand;

He shall betray me. Lo, the Son
  of Man
Goeth indeed as it is written of
  him;
But woe shall be unto that man by
  whom
He is betrayed! Good were it for
  that man
If he had ne'er been born!

Judas Iscariot. Lord, is it I?
Christus. Ay, thou hast said.
  And that thou doest, do quickly.

Judas Iscariot (going out). Ah,
  woe is me!

Christus. All ye shall be offended
Because of me this night; for it is
  written:
Awake, O sword, against my shep-
  herd! Smite
The shepherd, saith the Lord of
  Hosts, and scattered
Shall be the sheep!—But after I
  am risen
I go before you into Galilee.

Peter. O Master! though all
  men shall be offended
Because of thee, yet will not I be!

Christus. Simon,
Behold how Satan hath desired to
  have you,
That he may sift you as one sifteth
  wheat!
Whither I go thou canst not follow
  me,—
Not now;—but thou shalt follow
  me hereafter.

Peter. Wherefore can I not
  follow thee? I am ready
To go with thee to prison and to
  death.

Christus. Verily say I unto thee,
  this night,
Ere the cock crow, thou shalt deny
  me thrice!

Peter. Though I should die, yet
  will I not deny thee.

Christus. When first I sent you
  forth without a purse,

Or scrip, or shoes, did ye lack any-
thing?
The Disciples. Not anything.
Christus. But he
that hath a purse,
Now let him take it, and likewise
his scrip;
And he that hath no sword, let him
go sell
His clothes and buy one. That
which hath been written
Must be accomplished now: He
hath poured out
His soul even unto death; he hath
been numbered
With the transgressors, and him-
self hath borne
The sin of many, and made inter-
cession
For the transgressors. And here
have an end
The things concerning me.
Peter. Behold, O Lord,
Behold, here are two swords!
Christus. It is enough.

IV.

THE GARDEN OF GETHSEMANE.

Christus. My spirit is exceeding
sorrowful,
Even unto death! Tarry ye here
and watch.

(*He goes apart.*)

Peter. Under this ancient olive-
tree, that spreads
Its broad centennial branches like
a tent,
Let us lie down and rest.
John. What are those torches
That glimmer on Brook Kedron
there below us?
James. It is some marriage-
feast; the joyful maidens
Go out to meet the bridegroom.

Peter. I am weary.
The struggles of this day have overcome me.

(*They sleep.*)

Christus (*falling on his face*).
Father! all things are possible
to thee,—
O let this cup pass from me!
Nevertheless
Not as I will, but as thou wilt, be
done!

(*Returning to the Disciples.*)

What! could ye not watch with me
for one hour?
O watch and pray, that ye may
enter not
Into temptation. For the spirit
indeed
Is willing, but the flesh is weak!
John. Alas!
It is for sorrow that our eyes are
heavy.—
I see again the glimmer of those
torches
Among the olives; they are coming
hither.
James. Outside the garden wall
the path divides;
Surely they come not hither.

(*They sleep again.*)

Christus (*as before*). O my
Father!
If this cup may not pass away from
me,
Except I drink of it, thy will be done.

(*Returning to the Disciples.*)

Sleep on; and take your rest!
John. Beloved Master,
Alas! we know not what to answer
thee!
It is for sorrow that our eyes are
heavy.—
Behold, the torches now encompass
us.
James. They do but go about
the garden wall,

669

Seeking for some one, or for something lost.

(*They sleep again.*)

Christus (*as before*). If this cup may not pass away from me,
Except I drink of it, thy will be done.

(*Returning to the Disciples.*)

It is enough! Behold, the Son of Man
Hath been betrayed into the hands of sinners!
The hour is come. Rise up, let us be going;
For he that shall betray me is at hand.

John. Ah me! See, from his forehead, in the torchlight,
Great drops of blood are falling to the ground!

Peter. What lights are these? What torches glare and glisten
Upon the swords and armour of these men?
And there among them Judas Iscariot!

(*He smites the servant of the High-Priest with his sword.*)

Christus. Put up thy sword into its sheath ; for they
That take the sword shall perish with the sword.
The cup my Father hath given me to drink,
Shall I not drink it? Think'st thou that I cannot
Pray to my Father, and that he shall give me
More than twelve legions of angels presently?

Judas (*to Christus, kissing him*). Hail, Master! hail!

Christus.   Friend, wherefore art thou come?
Whom seek ye?

Captain of the Temple. Jesus of Nazareth.

Christus.   I am he.
Are ye come hither as against a thief,
With swords and staves to take me? When I daily
Was with you in the Temple, ye stretched forth
No hands to take me! But this is your hour,
And this the power of darkness. If ye seek
Me only, let these others go their way.

(*The Disciples depart.* CHRISTUS *is bound and led away. A certain young man follows him, having a linen cloth cast about his body. They lay hold of him, and the young man flees from them naked.*)

V.

THE PALACE OF CAIAPHAS.

Pharisees. What do we? Clearly something must we do,
For this man worketh many miracles.

Caiaphas. I am informed that he is a mechanic;
A carpenter's son; a Galilean peasant,
Keeping disreputable company.

Pharisees. The people say that here in Bethany
He hath raised up a certain Lazarus,
Who had been dead three days.

Caiaphas.   Impossible!
There is no resurrection of the dead;
This Lazarus should be taken, and put to death
As an impostor. If this Galilean
Would be content to stay in Galilee,
And preach in country towns, I should not heed him.

But when he comes up to Jerusalem
Riding in triumph, as I am in-
    formed,
And drives the money-changers
    from the Temple,
That is another matter.
    Pharisees.   If we thus
Let him alone, all will believe on
    him,
And then the Romans come and
    take away
Our place and nation.
    Caiaphas.   Ye know nothing
    at all.
Simon Ben Camith, my great pre-
    decessor,
On whom be peace! would have
    dealt presently
With such a demagogue. I shall
    no less.
The man must die. Do ye consider
    not
It is expedient that one man
    should die,
Not the whole nation perish? What
    is death?
It differeth from sleep but in dura-
    tion.
We sleep and wake again; an hour
    or two
Later or earlier, and it matters not,
And if we never wake it matters not;
When we are in our graves we are
    at peace,—
Nothing can wake us or disturb
    us more.
There is no resurrection.
    Pharisees (*aside*).   O most
    faithful
Disciple of Hyrcanus Maccabæus,
Will nothing but complete annihil-
    ation
Comfort and satisfy thee?
    Caiaphas. While ye are talking
And plotting, and contriving how to
    take him,
Fearing the people, and so doing
    naught,

I, who fear not the people, have
    been acting;
Have taken this Prophet, this
    young Nazarene,
Who by Beelzebub the Prince of
    devils
Casteth out devils, and doth raise
    the dead,
That might as well be dead, and
    left in peace.
Annas my father-in-law hath sent
    him hither.
I hear the guard. Behold your
    Galilean!

(CHRISTUS *is brought in bound.*)

    Servant (*in the vestibule*). Why
    art thou up so late, my pretty
    damsel?
    Damsel. Why art thou up so
    early, pretty man?
It is not cock-crow yet, and art
    thou stirring?
    Servant. What brings thee here?
    Damsel.   What
    brings the rest of you?
    Servant. Come here and warm
    thy hands.
    Damsel (*to Peter*).   Art thou
    not also
One of this man's disciples?
    Peter.   I am not.
    Damsel. Now surely thou art
    also one of them;
Thou art a Galilean, and thy speech
Bewrayeth thee.
    Peter. Woman, I know him not!
    Caiaphas (*to Christus, in the
    Hall*). Who art thou? Tell us
    plainly of thyself
And of thy doctrines, and of thy
    disciples.
    Christus. Lo, I have spoken
    openly to the world;
I have taught ever in the Syna-
    gogue,
And in the Temple, where the Jews
    resort;

In secret have said nothing.
Wherefore then
Askest thou me of this? Ask them
that heard me
What I have said to them. Behold,
they know
What I have said!

Officer (*striking him*). What,
fellow! answerest thou
The High-Priest so?

Christus. If I have spoken evil,
Bear witness of the evil; but if well,
Why smitest thou me?

Caiaphas. Where are the
witnesses?
Let them say what they know.

The two False Witnesses. We
heard him say:
I will destroy this Temple made
with hands,
And will within three days build
up another
Made without hands.

Scribes and Pharisees. He is
o'erwhelmed with shame
And cannot answer!

Caiaphas. Dost thou answer
nothing?
What is this thing they witness
here against thee?

Scribes and Pharisees. He holds
his peace.

Caiaphas. Tell us, art thou the
Christ?
I do adjure thee by the living God,
Tell us, art thou indeed the Christ?

Christus. I am.
Hereafter shall ye see the Son of
Man
Sit on the right hand of the power
of God,
And come in clouds of heaven!

Caiaphas (*rending his clothes*).
It is enough.
He hath spoken blasphemy! What
further need
Have we of witnesses? Now ye
have heard

His blasphemy. What think ye?
Is he guilty?

Scribes and Pharisees. Guilty of
death!

Kinsman of Malchus (*to Peter,
in the vestibule*). Surely I know
thy face;
Did I not see thee in the garden
with him?

Peter. How couldst thou see me?
I swear unto thee
I do not know this man of whom
ye speak!

(*The cock crows.*)

Hark! the cock crows! That
sorrowful pale face
Seeks for me in the crowd, and
looks at me,
As if he would remind me of those
words:
Ere the cock crow thou shalt deny
me thrice!

(*Goes out weeping.* CHRISTUS *is
blindfolded and buffeted.*)

An Officer (*striking him with his
palm*). Prophesy unto us, thou
Christ, thou Prophet!
Who is it smote thee?

Caiaphas. Lead him unto Pilate!

VI.

PONTIUS PILATE.

Pilate. Wholly incomprehensible
to me,
Vainglorious, obstinate, and given
up
To unintelligible old traditions,
And proud and self-conceited are
these Jews!
Not long ago, I marched the legions
down

From Cæsarea to their winter-
quarters
Here in Jerusalem, with the effigies
Of Cæsar on their ensigns, and a
tumult
Arose among these Jews, because
their Law
Forbids the making of all images !
They threw themselves upon the
ground with wild
Expostulations, bared their necks,
and cried
That they would sooner die than
have their Law
Infringed in any manner: as if
Numa
Were not as great as Moses, and
the Laws
Of the Twelve Tables as their Penta-
teuch !
And then, again, when I desired to
span
Their valley with an aqueduct, and
bring
A rushing river in to wash the city
And its inhabitants,—they all re-
belled
As if they had been herds of un-
washed swine !
Thousands and thousands of them
got together
And raised so great a clamour round
my doors,
That, fearing violent outbreak, I
desisted,
And left them to their wallowing in
the mire.

And now here comes the reverend
Sanhedrim
Of lawyers, priests, and Scribes and
Pharisees,
Like old and toothless mastiffs, that
can bark,
But cannot bite, howling their ac-
cusations
Against a mild enthusiast, who hath
preached

I know not what new doctrine, being
King
Of some vague kingdom in the other
world,
That hath no more to do with Rome
and Cæsar
Than I have with the patriarch
Abraham !
Finding this man to be a Gali-
lean,
I sent him straight to Herod, and I
hope
That is the last of it ; but if it be
not,
I still have power to pardon and
release him,
As is the custom at the Passover,
And so accommodate the matter
smoothly,
Seeming to yield to them, yet saving
him ;
A prudent and sagacious policy
For Roman Governors in the
Provinces.

Incomprehensible, fanatic people !
Ye have a God, who seemeth like
yourselves
Incomprehensible, dwelling apart,
Majestic, cloud - encompassed,
clothed in darkness !
One whom ye fear, but love not ;
yet ye have
No Goddesses to soften your stern
lives,
And make you tender unto human
weakness,
While we of Rome have everywhere
around us
Our amiable divinities, that haunt
The woodlands, and the waters,
and frequent
Our households, with their sweet
and gracious presence !
I will go in, and while these Jews
are wrangling,
Read my Ovidius on the Art of
Love.

VII.

BARABBAS IN PRISON.

Barabbas (to his fellow-prisoners).

Barabbas is my name,
Barabbas, the Son of Shame,
  Is the meaning I suppose ;
I 'm no better than the best,
And whether worse than the rest
  Of my fellow-men, who knows ?

I was once, to say it in brief,
A highwayman, a robber chief,
  In the open light of day.
So much I am free to confess ;
But all men, more or less,
  Are robbers in their way.

From my cavern in the crags,
From my lair of leaves and flags,
  I could see, like ants, below,
The camels with their load
Of merchandise, on the road
  That leadeth to Jericho.

And I struck them unaware,
As an eagle from the air
  Drops down upon bird or beast ;
And I had my heart's desire
Of the merchants of Sidon and Tyre,
  And Damascus and the East.

But it is not for that I fear ;
It is not for that I am here
  In these iron fetters bound ;
Sedition ! that is the word
That Pontius Pilate heard,
  And he liketh not the sound.

What, think ye, would he care
For a Jew slain here or there,
  Or a plundered caravan ?
But Cæsar !—ah, that is a crime,
To the uttermost end of time
  Shall not be forgiven to man.

Therefore was Herod wroth
With Matthias Margaloth,
  And burned him for a show !
Therefore his wrath did smite
Judas the Gaulonite,
  And his followers, as ye know.

For that cause, and no more,
Am I here, as I said before ;
  For one unlucky night
Jucundus, the captain of horse,
Was upon us with all his force,
  And I was caught in the fight.

I might have fled with the rest,
But my dagger was in the breast
  Of a Roman equerry ;
As we rolled there in the street,
They bound me, hands and feet ;
  And this is the end of me.

Who cares for death ? Not I !
A thousand times I would die,
  Rather than suffer wrong !
Already those women of mine
Are mixing the myrrh and the wine ;
  I shall not be with you long.

VIII.

ECCE HOMO.

*Pilate (on the Tessellated Pave-
ment in front of his Palace).*
  Ye have brought unto me this
    man, as one
Who doth pervert the people ; and
  behold !
I have examined him, and found no
  fault
Touching the things whereof ye do
  accuse him.
No, nor yet Herod : for I sent you
  to him,
And nothing worthy of death he
  findeth in him.
Ye have a custom at the Passover,
That one condemned to death shall
  be released.

Whom will ye, then, that I release to you?

Jesus Barabbas, called the Son of Shame,

Or Jesus, son of Joseph, called the Christ?

The People (shouting). Not this man, but Barabbas!

Pilate. What then will ye That I should do with him that is called Christ?

The People. Crucify him!

Pilate. Why, what evil hath he done?

Lo, I have found no cause of death in him;

I will chastise him, and then let him go.

The People (more vehemently). Crucify him! crucify him!

A Messenger (to Pilate). Thy wife sends

This message to thee: Have thou nought to do

With that just man; for I this day in dreams

Have suffered many things because of him.

Pilate (aside). The Gods speak to us in our dreams! I tremble

At what I have to do! O Claudia,

How shall I save him? Yet one effort more,

Or he must perish!

(Washes his hands before them.)

           I am innocent

Of the blood of this just person; see ye to it!

The People. Let his blood be on us and on our children!

Voices (within the Palace). Put on thy royal robes; put on thy crown,

And take thy sceptre! Hail, thou King of the Jews!

Pilate. I bring him forth to you, that ye may know

I find no fault in him. Behold the man!

(Christus is led in, with the purple robe and crown of thorns.)

Chief Priests and Officers. Crucify him! crucify him!

Pilate. Take ye him; I find no fault in him.

Chief Priests We have a Law, And by our Law he ought to die; because

He made himself to be the Son of God.

Pilate (aside). Ah! there are Sons of God, and demi-gods

More than ye know, ye ignorant High-Priests!

(To Christus.)

Whence art thou?

Chief Priests. Crucify him! crucify him!

Pilate (to Christus). Dost thou not answer me? Dost thou not know

That I have power enough to crucify thee?

That I have also power to set thee free?

Christus. Thou couldest have no power at all against me

Except that it were given thee from above;

Therefore hath he that sent me unto thee

The greater sin.

Chief Priests. If thou let this man go

Thou art not Cæsar's friend. For whosoever

Maketh himself a King speaks against Cæsar.

Pilate. Ye Jews, behold your King!

Chief Priests. Away with him! Crucify him!

Pilate. Shall I crucify your King?

Chief Priests. We have no King
but Cæsar!
Pilate. Take him, then,
Take him, ye cruel and bloodthirsty
Priests,
More merciless than the plebeian
mob,
Who pity and spare the fainting
gladiator
Blood-stained in Roman amphi-
theatres,—
Take him, and crucify him if ye will;
But if the immortal Gods do ever
mingle
With the affairs of mortals, which
I doubt not,
And hold the attribute of justice
dear,
They will commission the Eu-
menides
To scatter you to the four winds of
heaven,
Exacting tear for tear, and blood
for blood.
Here, take ye this inscription,
Priests, and nail it
Upon the cross, above your victim's
head:
Jesus of Nazareth, King of the Jews.
Chief Priests. Nay, we entreat!
write not, the King of the Jews;
But that he said: I am the King
of the Jews!
Pilate. Enough. What I have
written, I have written!

IX.

ACELDAMA.

Judas Iscariot. Lost! lost! for
ever lost! I have betrayed
The innocent blood! O God! if
thou art love,
Why didst thou leave me naked to
the tempter?
Why didst thou not commission
thy swift lightning

To strike me dead? or why did
I not perish
With those by Herod slain, the
innocent children
Who went with playthings in their
little hands,
Into the darkness of the other world,
As if to bed? Or wherefore was
I born,
If thou in thy foreknowledge didst
perceive
All that I am, and all that I must be?
I know I am not generous, am not
gentle
Like other men; but I have tried
to be,
And I have failed. I thought by
following Him,
I should grow like him; but the
unclean spirit
That from my childhood up hath
tortured me
Hath been too cunning and too
strong for me.
Am I to blame for this? Am I to
blame
Because I cannot love, and ne'er
have known
The love of woman or the love of
children?
It is a curse and a fatality,
A mark, that hath been set upon my
forehead,
That none shall slay me, for it were
a mercy
That I were dead, or never had
been born.

Too late! too late! I shall not see
him more
Among the living. That sweet,
patient face
Will never more rebuke me, nor
those lips
Repeat the words: One of you
shall betray me!
It stung me into madness. How
I loved,

Yet hated him ! But in the other
world !

I will be there before him, and will
wait

Until he comes, and fall down on
my knees

And kiss his feet, imploring pardon,
pardon !

I heard him say : All sins shall be
forgiven,

Except the sin against the Holy
Ghost.

That shall not be forgiven in this
world,

Nor in the world to come. Is that
my sin ?

Have I offended so there is no hope
Here nor hereafter ? That I soon
shall know.

O God, have mercy ! Christ have
mercy on me !

(*Throws himself headlong from
the cliff.*)

X.

THE THREE CROSSES.

Manahem, the Essenian. Three
crosses in this noonday night
uplifted,

Three human figures, that in mortal pain

Gleam white against the supernatural darkness ;

Two thieves, that writhe in torture,
and between them

The suffering Messiah, the son of
Joseph,

Ay, the Messiah Triumphant, son
of David !

A crown of thorns on that dis-
honoured head !

Those hands that healed the sick
now pierced with nails,

Those feet that wandered homeless
through the world

Now crossed and bleeding, and at
rest for ever !

And the three faithful Maries, overwhelmed

By this great sorrow, kneeling,
praying, weeping !

O Joseph Caiaphas, thou great
High-Priest,

How wilt thou answer for this deed
of blood ?

   Scribes and Elders. Thou that
destroyest the Temple, and
dost build it

In three days, save thyself ; and if
thou be

The Son of God, come down now
from the cross.

   Chief Priests. Others he saved,
himself he cannot save !

Let Christ the King of Israel
descend,

That we may see and believe !

   Scribes and Elders. In God he
trusted ;

Let him deliver him, if he will have
him,

And we will then believe.

   Christus. Father ! forgive them ;
They know not what they do.

   The Impenitent Thief. If thou
be Christ,

O save thyself and us !

   The Penitent Thief. Remember
me,

Lord, when thou comest into thine
own kingdom.

   Christus. This day shalt thou be
with me in Paradise.

   Manahem. Golgotha ! Golgotha !
O the pain and darkness !

O the uplifted cross, that shall for
ever

Shine through the darkness, and
shall conquer pain

By the triumphant memory of this
hour !

Simon Magus. O Nazarene! I find thee here at last!
Thou art no more a phantom unto me!
This is the end of one who called himself
The Son of God! Such is the fate of those
Who preach new doctrines. 'Tis not what he did,
But what he said, hath brought him unto this.
I will speak evil of no dignitaries.
This is my hour of triumph, Nazarene!

The Young Ruler. This is the end of him who said to me:
Sell that thou hast, and give unto the poor!
This is the treasure in heaven he promised me!

Christus. Eloi, Eloi, lama sabacthani!

A Soldier (preparing the hyssop). He calleth for Elias!

Another. Nay, let be!
See if Elias now will come to save him!

Christus. I thirst.

A Soldier. Give him the wormwood!

Christus (with a loud cry, bowing his head). It is finished!

XI.

THE TWO MARIES.

Mary Magdalene. We have arisen early, yet the sun
O'ertakes us ere we reach the sepulchre,
To wrap the body of our blessed Lord
With our sweet spices.

Mary, mother of James. Lo, this is the garden,
And yonder is the sepulchre. But who
Shall roll away the stone for us to enter?

Mary Magdalene. It hath been rolled away! The sepulchre
Is open! Ah, who hath been here before us,
When we rose early, wishing to be first?

Mary, mother of James. I am affrighted!

Mary Magalene. Hush! I will stoop down
And look within. There is a young man sitting
On the right side, clothed in a long white garment!
It is an angel!

The Angel. Fear not; ye are seeking
Jesus of Nazareth, which was crucified.
Why do ye seek the living among the dead?
He is no longer here; he is arisen!
Come see the place where the Lord lay! Remember
How he spake unto you in Galilee,
Saying: The Son of Man must be delivered
Into the hands of sinful men; by them
Be crucified, and the third day rise again!
But go your way, and say to his disciples,
He goeth before you into Galilee;
There shall ye see him as he said to you.

Mary, mother of James. I will go swiftly for them.

Mary Magdalene (alone, weeping). They have taken
My Lord away from me, and now I know not
Where they have laid him! Who is there to tell me?

This is the gardener. Surely he must know.

Christus. Woman, why weepest thou? Whom seekest thou?

Mary Magdalene. They have taken my Lord away; I cannot find him.

O Sir, if thou have borne him hence, I pray thee

Tell me where thou hast laid him.

Christus. Mary!

Mary Magdalene. Rabboni!

XII.

THE SEA OF GALILEE.

Nathanael (in the ship). All is now ended.

John. Nay, he is arisen.

I ran unto the tomb, and stooping down

Looked in, and saw the linen grave-clothes lying,

Yet dared not enter.

Peter. I went in, and saw

The napkin that had been about his head,

Not lying with the other linen clothes,

But wrapped together in a separate place.

Thomas. And I have seen him. I have seen the print

Of nails upon his hands, and thrust my hands

Into his side. I know he is arisen;

But where are now the kingdom and the glory

He promised unto us? We have all dreamed

That we were princes, and we wake to find

We are but fishermen.

Peter. Who should have been Fishers of men!

John. We have come back again

To the old life, the peaceful life, among

The white towns of the Galilean lake.

Peter. They seem to me like silent sepulchres

In the gray light of morning! The old life,—

Yea, the old life! for we have toiled all night

And have caught nothing.

John. Do ye see a man

Standing upon the beach and beckoning?

'Tis like an apparition. He hath kindled

A fire of coals, and seems to wait for us.

He calleth.

Christus (from the shore). Children, have ye any meat?

Peter. Alas! we have caught nothing.

Christus. Cast the net

On the right side of the ship, and ye shall find.

Peter. How that reminds me of the days gone by,

And one who said: Launch out into the deep,

And cast your nets!

Nathanael. We have but let them down

And they are filled, so that we cannot draw them!

John. It is the Lord!

Peter (girding his fisher's coat about him). He said: When I am risen

I will go before you into Galilee!

(He casts himself into the lake.)

John. There is no fear in love; for perfect love

Casteth out fear. Now then, if ye are men,

Put forth your strength ; we are not
    far from shore ;
The net is heavy, but breaks not.
    All is safe.
    Peter (on the shore). Dear Lord !
    I heard thy voice and could not
    wait.
Let me behold thy face, and kiss
    thy feet !
Thou art not dead, thou livest !
    Again I see thee.
Pardon, dear Lord ! I am a sinful
    man ;
I have denied thee thrice. Have
    mercy on me !
    The Others (coming to land).
    Dear Lord ! stay with us !
    cheer us ! comfort us !
Lo ! we again have found thee !
    Leave us not !
    Christus. Bring hither the fish
    that ye have caught,
And come and eat.
    John. Behold ! he breaketh bread
As he was wont. From his own
    blessed hands
Again we take it.
    Christus. Simon, son of Jonas,
Lovest thou me more than these
    others ?
    Peter.   Yea,
More, Lord, than all men ; even
    more than these.
Thou knowest that I love thee.
    Christus. Feed my lambs.
    Thomas (aside). How more than
    we do ? He remaineth ever
Self-confident and boastful as be-
    fore.
Nothing will cure him.
    Christus. Simon, son of Jonas,
Lovest thou me ?
    Peter.   Yea, dearest Lord,
    I love thee.
Thou knowest that I love thee.
    Christus. Feed my sheep.
    Thomas (aside). Again, the self-
    same question, and the answer

Repeated with more vehemence
    Can the Master
Doubt if we love him ?
    Christus. Simon, son of Jonas,
Lovest thou me ?
    Peter (grieved). Dear Lord ! thou
    knowest all things.
Thou knowest that I love thee.
    Christus.   Feed my sheep.
When thou wast young thou gird-
    edst thyself, and walkedst
Whither thou wouldst ; but when
    thou shalt be old,
Thou shalt stretch forth thy hands,
    and other men
Shall gird and carry thee whither
    thou wouldst not.
Follow thou me !
    John (aside).   It is a prophecy
Of what death he shall die.
    Peter (pointing to John). Tell
    me, O Lord,
And what shall this man do ?
    Christus.   And if I will
He tarry till I come, what is it to
    thee ?
Follow thou me !
    Peter. Yea, I will follow thee, dear
    Lord and Master !
Will follow thee through fasting
    and temptation,
Through all thine agony and bloody
    sweat,
Thy cross and passion, even unto
    death !

—◆—

EPILOGUE.

SYMBOLUM APOSTOLORUM.

Peter.   I believe in God the
    Father Almighty ;
John.   Maker of Heaven and
    Earth ;
James.   And in Jesus Christ his
    only Son, our Lord ;

Andrew. Who was conceived by the Holy Ghost, born of the Virgin Mary ;

Philip. Suffered under Pontius Pilate, was crucified, dead and buried ;

Thomas. And the third day he rose again from the dead ;

Bartholomew. He ascended into Heaven, and sitteth on the right hand of God, the Father Almighty ;

Matthew. From thence he shall come to judge the quick and the dead.

James, the son of Alpheus. I believe in the Holy Ghost ; the holy Catholic Church ;

Simon Zelotes. The communion of Saints ; the forgiveness of sins ;

Jude. The resurrection of the body ;

Matthias. And the Life Everlasting.

The Abbot Joachim.

A room in the Convent of Flora in Calabria. Night.

Joachim. The wind is rising ; it
    seizes and shakes
The doors and window-blinds, and
    makes
Mysterious moanings in the halls ;
The convent-chimneys seem almost
The trumpets of some heavenly
    host,
Setting its watch upon our walls !
Where it listeth, there it bloweth ;
We hear the sound, but no man
    knoweth
Whence it cometh or whither it
    goeth,
And thus it is with the Holy Ghost.
O breath of God ! O my delight
In many a vigil of the night,
Like the great voice in Patmos
    heard
By John, the Evangelist of the Word,
I hear thee behind me saying : Write
In a book the things that thou hast
    seen,
The things that are, and that have
    been,
And the things that shall hereafter
    be !
This convent, on the rocky crest
Of the Calabrian hills, to me
A Patmos is wherein I rest ;
While round about me like a sea
The white mists roll, and overflow

The world that lies unseen below
In darkness and in mystery.
Here in the Spirit, in the vast
Embrace of God's encircling arm,
Am I uplifted from all harm ;
The world seems something far
    away,
Something belonging to the Past,
A hostelry, a peasant's farm,
That lodged me for a night or day,
In which I care not to remain,
Nor, having left, to see again.

Thus, in the hollow of God's hand
I dwelt on sacred Tabor's height,
When as a simple acolyte
I journeyed to the Holy Land,
A pilgrim for my Master's sake,
And saw the Galilean Lake,
And walked through many a village
    street
That once had echoed to his feet.
There first I heard the great com-
    mand,
The voice behind me saying : Write !
And suddenly my soul became
Illumined by a flash of flame,
That left imprinted on my thought
The image I in vain had sought,
And which for ever shall remain ;
As sometimes from these windows
    high,

Gazing at midnight on the sky
Black with a storm of wind and rain,
I have beheld a sudden glare
Of lightning lay the landscape bare,
With tower and town and hill and
    plain
Distinct, and burnt into my brain,
Never to be effaced again !
And I have written. These volumes
    three,
The Apocalypse, the Harmony
Of the Sacred Scriptures, new and
    old,
And the Psalter with Ten Strings,
    enfold
Within their pages, all and each,
The Eternal Gospel that I teach.
Well I remember the Kingdom of
    Heaven
Hath been likened to a little leaven
Hidden in two measures of meal,
Until it leavened the whole mass ;
So likewise will it come to pass
With the doctrine that I here con-
    ceal.
Open and manifest to me
The truth appears, and must be told:
All sacred mysteries are threefold ;
Three Persons in the Trinity,
Three Ages of Humanity,
And Holy Scriptures likewise Three,
Of Fear, of Wisdom, and of Love ;
For Wisdom that begins in Fear
Endeth in Love ; the atmosphere
In which the soul delights to be,
And finds that perfect liberty
Which cometh only from above.

In the first Age, the early prime
And dawn of all historic time,
The Father reigned ; and face to
    face
He spake with the primeval race.
Bright Angels on his errands sent,
Sat with the patriarch in his tent ;
His prophets thundered in the street;
His lightnings flashed, his hail-
    storms beat :

In tempest and in cloud he came,
In earthquake and in flood and
    flame !
The fear of God is in his Book ;
The pages of the Pentateuch
Are full of the terror of his name.

Then reigned the Son; his Covenant
Was peace on earth, good-will to
    man ;
With him the reign of Law began.
He was the Wisdom and the Word,
And sent his Angels Ministrant,
Unterrified and undeterred,
To rescue souls forlorn and lost.
The troubled, tempted, tempest-
    tost,
To heal, to comfort, and to teach.
The fiery tongues of Pentecost
His symbols were, that they should
    preach
In every form of human speech,
From continent to continent.
He is the Light Divine, whose rays
Across the thousand years unspent
Shine through the darkness of our
    days,
And touch with their celestial fires
Our churches and our convent
    spires.
His Book is the New Testament.
These Ages now are of the Past ;
And the Third Age begins at last.
The coming of the Holy Ghost,
The reign of Grace, the reign of
    Love,
Brightens the mountain-tops above,
And the dark outline of the coast.
Already the whole land is white
With convent walls, as if by night
A snow had fallen on hill and height !
Already from the streets and marts
Of town and traffic, and low cares,
Men climb the consecrated stairs
With weary feet, and bleeding
    hearts ;
And leave the world and its delights,
Its passions, struggles, and de-
    spairs,

683

For contemplation and for prayers
In cloister-cells of Cœnobites.

Eternal benedictions rest
Upon thy name, Saint Benedict !
Founder of convents in the West,
Who built on Mount Cassino's crest,
In the Land of Labour, thine eagle's
    nest !
May I be found not derelict
In aught of faith or godly fear,
If I have written, in many a page,
The Gospel of the coming age,
The Eternal Gospel men shall hear.
O may I live resembling thee,
And die at last as thou hast died ;
So that hereafter men may see,
Within the choir, a form of air,
Standing with arms outstretched in
    prayer,
As one that hath been crucified !

My work is finished ; I am strong
In faith and hope and charity ;
For I have written the things I see,
The things that have been and shall
    be,
Conscious of right, nor fearing
    wrong ;
Because I am in love with Love,
And the sole thing I hate is Hate ;
For Hate is death ; and Love is
    life,
A peace, a splendour from above ;
And Hate, a never-ending strife,
A smoke, a blackness from the
    abyss
Where unclean serpents coil and
    hiss !
Love is the Holy Ghost within ;
Hate, the unpardonable sin !
Who preaches otherwise than this,
Betrays his Master with a kiss !

The Masque of Pandora.

I.

THE WORKSHOP OF HEPHÆSTUS.

Hephæstus (standing before the statue of PANDORA).

Not fashioned out of gold, like
  Hera's throne,
Nor forged of iron like the thunder-
  bolts
Of Zeus omnipotent, or other works
Wrought by my hands at Lemnos
  or Olympus,
But moulded in soft clay, that un-
  resisting
Yields itself to the touch, this lovely
  form
Before me stands, perfect in every
  part.
Not Aphrodite's self appeared more
  fair,
When first upwafted by caressing
  winds
She came to high Olympus, and
  the gods
Paid homage to her beauty. Thus
  her hair
Was cinctured; thus her floating
  drapery
Was like a cloud about her, and her
  face
Was radiant with the sunshine and
  the sea.

The Voice of Zeus.

Is thy work done, Hephæstus?

Heph.   It is finished!

The Voice.

Not finished till I breathe the breath
  of life
Into her nostrils, and she moves
  and speaks.

Heph.

Will she become immortal like ourselves?

The Voice.

The form that thou hast fashioned
  out of clay
Is of the earth and mortal; but the
  spirit,
The life, the exhalation of my
  breath,
Is of diviner essence and immortal.
The gods shall shower on her their
  benefactions,
She shall possess all gifts: the gift
  of song,
The gift of eloquence, the gift of
  beauty,
The fascination and the nameless
  charm
That shall lead all men captive.

Heph. Wherefore? wherefore?

(*A wind shakes the house.*)

I heard the rushing of a mighty
  wind
Through all the halls and chambers
  of my house!
Her parted lips inhale it, and her
  bosom

Heaves with the inspiration. As
  a reed
Beside a river in the rippling current
Bends to and fro, she bows or lifts
  her head.
She gazes round about as if
  amazed ;
She is alive ; she breathes, but yet
  she speaks not !

(PANDORA *descends from the
  pedestal.*)

CHORUS OF THE GRACES.

Aglaia.

In the workshop of Hephæstus
  What is this I see ?
Have the Gods to four increased us
  Who were only three ?
Beautiful in form and feature,
  Lovely as the day,
Can there be so fair a creature
  Formed of common clay ?

Thalia.

O sweet, pale face ! O lovely eyes of
  azure,
  Clear as the waters of a brook
    that run
  Limpid and laughing in the sum-
    mer sun !
  O golden hair that like a miser's
    treasure
In its abundance overflows the
  measure !
  O graceful form, that cloudlike
    floatest on
  With the soft, undulating gait of
    one
Who moveth as if motion were a
  pleasure !
By what name shall I call thee ?
  Nymph or Muse,
  Callirrhoë or Urania ? Some sweet
    name
Whose every syllable is a caress
Would best befit thee ; but I cannot
  choose,

Nor do I care to choose ; for
  still the same,
Nameless or named, will be thy
  loveliness.

Euphrosyne.

Dowered with all celestial gifts,
  Skilled in every art
That ennobles and uplifts
  And delights the heart,
Fair on earth shall be thy fame
  As thy face is fair,
And Pandora be the name
  Thou henceforth shall bear.

II.

OLYMPUS.

Hermes (putting on his sandals).

Much must he toil who serves the
  Immortal Gods,
And I, who am their herald, most
  of all.
No rest have I, nor respite.   I no
  sooner
Unclasp the winged sandals from
  my feet,
Than I again must clasp them, and
  depart
Upon some foolish errand. But to-
  day
The errand is not foolish. Never yet
With greater joy did I obey the
  summons
That sends me earthward.   I will
  fly so swiftly
That my caduceus in the whistling
  air
Shall make a sound like the Pan-
  dæan pipes,
Cheating the shepherds ; for to-day
  I go,
Commissioned by high-thundering
  Zeus, to lead
A maiden to Prometheus, in his
  tower,

And by my cunning arguments persuade him
To marry her.   What mischief lies concealed
In this design I know not ; but I know
Who thinks of marrying hath already taken
One step upon the road to penitence.
Such embassies delight me. Forth I launch
On the sustaining air, nor fear to fall
Like Icarus, nor swerve aside like him
Who drove amiss Hyperion's fiery steeds.
I sink, I fly ! The yielding element
Folds itself round about me like an arm,
And holds me as a mother holds her child.

III.

TOWER OF PROMETHEUS ON MOUNT CAUCASUS.

Prometheus.

I hear the trumpet of Alectryon
Proclaim the dawn. The stars begin to fade,
And all the heavens are full of prophecies
And evil auguries.   Blood-red last night
I saw great Kronos rise ; the crescent moon
Sank through the mist, as if it were the scythe
His parricidal hand had flung far down
The western steeps. O ye Immortal Gods,
What evil are ye plotting and contriving ?

(HERMES *and* PANDORA *at the threshold.*)

Pandora.

I cannot cross the threshold.   An unseen
And icy hand repels me.   These blank walls
Oppress me with their weight !

Prom.   Powerful ye are,
But not omnipotent. Ye cannot fight
Against Necessity. The Fates control you,
As they do us, and so far we are equals !

Pandora.

Motionless,   passionless,   companionless,
He sits there muttering in his beard. His voice
Is like a river flowing underground!

Hermes.

Prometheus, hail !

Prom.   Who calls me ?

Herm.   It is I.
Dost thou not know me ?

Prom.   By thy winged cap
And winged heels I know thee.   Thou art Hermes,
Captain of thieves !   Hast thou again been stealing
The heifers of Admetus in the sweet
Meadows of asphodel ? or Hera's girdle ?
Or the earth-shaking trident of Poseidon ?

Herm.

And thou, Prometheus ; say, hast thou again
Been stealing fire from Helios' chariot-wheels
To light thy furnaces ?

Prom. Why comest thou hither
So early in the dawn ?

Herm.   The Immortal Gods

687

Know naught of late or early. Zeus
   himself
The omnipotent hath sent me.

Prom.   For what purpose?

Herm.

To bring this maiden to thee.

Prom.   I mistrust
The Gods and all their gifts. If
   they have sent her
It is for no good purpose.

Herm.   What disaster
Could she bring on thy house, who
   is a woman?

Prom.

The Gods are not my friends, nor
   am I theirs.
Whatever comes from them, though
   in a shape
As beautiful as this, is evil only.
Who art thou?

Pand.   One who, though
   to thee unknown,
Yet knoweth thee.

Prom.   How shouldst thou
   know me, woman?

Pand.

Who knoweth not Prometheus the
   humane?

Prom.

Prometheus the unfortunate; to
   whom
Both Gods and men have shown
   themselves ungrateful.
When every spark was quenched
   on every hearth
Throughout the earth, I brought to
   man the fire
And all its ministrations. My reward
Hath been the rock and vulture.

Herm.   But the Gods
At last relent and pardon.

Prom.   They relent not;

They pardon not; they are implacable,
Revengeful, unforgiving!

Herm.   As a pledge
Of reconciliation they have sent to
   thee
This divine being, to be thy companion,
And bring into thy melancholy
   house
The sunshine and the fragrance of
   her youth.

Prom.

I need them not. I have within
   myself
All that my heart desires; the ideal
   beauty
Which the creative faculty of mind
Fashions and follows in a thousand
   shapes
More lovely than the real. My
   own thoughts
Are my companions; my designs
   and labours
And aspirations are my only friends.

Herm.

Decide not rashly. The decision
   made
Can never be recalled. The Gods
   implore not,
Plead not, solicit not; they only
   offer
Choice and occasion, which once
   being passed
Return no more. Dost thou accept
   the gift?

Prom.

No gift of theirs, in whatsoever
   shape
It comes to me, with whatsoever
   charm
To fascinate my sense, will I receive.
Leave me.

Pand.   Let us go hence. I will
   not stay.

Herm.

We leave thee to thy vacant dreams,
     and all
The silence and the solitude of
     thought,
The endless bitterness of un-
     belief,
The loneliness of existence without
     love.

CHORUS OF THE FATES.

Clotho.

How the Titan, the defiant,
The self-centred, self-reliant,
Wrapped in visions and illusions
Robs himself of life's best gifts !
Till by all the storm-winds
     shaken,
By the blast of fate o'ertaken,
Hopeless, helpless, and forsaken,
In the mists of his confusions
To the reefs of doom he drifts !

Lachesis.

Sorely tried and sorely tempted,
From no agonies exempted,
In the penance of his trial,
And the discipline of pain ;
Often by illusions cheated,
Often baffled and defeated
In the tasks to be completed,
He, by toil and self-denial,
To the highest shall attain.

Atropos.

Tempt no more the noble schemer ;
Bear unto some idle dreamer
This new toy and fascination,
This new dalliance and delight !
To the garden where reposes
Epimetheus crowned with roses,
To the door that never closes
Upon pleasure and temptation,
Bring this vision of the night !

IV.

THE AIR.

Hermes (returning to Olympus).

As lonely as the tower that he in-
     habits,
As firm and cold as are the crags
     about him,
Prometheus stands. The thunder-
     bolts of Zeus
Alone can move him ; but the
     tender heart
Of Epimetheus, burning at white
     heat,
Hammers and flames like all his
     brother's forges !
Now as an arrow from Hyperion's
     bow,
My errand done, I fly, I float, I soar
Into the air, returning to Olympus.
O joy of motion ! O delight to cleave
The infinite realms of space, the
     liquid ether,
Through the warm sunshine and
     the cooling cloud,
Myself as light as sunbeam or as
     cloud !
With one touch of my swift and
     winged feet,
I spurn the solid earth, and leave it
     rocking
As rocks the bough from which a
     bird takes wing.

V.

THE HOUSE OF EPIME-
THEUS.

Epimetheus.

Beautiful apparition ! go not hence !
Surely thou art a Goddess, for thy
     voice
Is a celestial melody, and thy form
Self-poised as if it floated on the air !

689

Pandora.

No Goddess am I, nor of heavenly
    birth,
But a mere woman fashioned out
    of clay
And mortal as the rest.

    Epim.   Thy face is fair ;
There is a wonder in thine azure
    eyes
That fascinates me. Thy whole
    presence seems
A soft desire, a breathing thought
    of love.
Say, would thy star like Merope's
    grow dim
If thou shouldst wed beneath thee ?

    Pand.   Ask me not ;
I cannot answer thee. I only
    know
The Gods have sent me hither.

    Epim.   I believe,
And thus believing am most for-
    tunate.
It was not Hermes led thee here,
    but Eros,
And swifter than his arrows were
    thine eyes
In wounding me. There was no
    moment's space
Between my seeing thee and loving
    thee.
O, what a tell-tale face thou hast !
    Again
I see the wonder in thy tender
    eyes.

Pand.

They do but answer to the love in
    thine.
Yet secretly I wonder thou shouldst
    love me :
Thou knowest me not.

    Epim.   Perhaps I know
    thee better
Than had I known thee longer.
    Yet it seems
That I have always known thee,
    and but now

Have found thee. Ah, I have been
    waiting long.

    Pand.

How beautiful is this house ! The
    atmosphere
Breathes rest and comfort, and the
    many chambers
Seem full of welcomes.

    Epim.   They not only seem,
But truly are. This dwelling and
    its master
Belong to thee.

    Pand. Here let me stay for ever !
There is a spell upon me.

    Epim.   Thou thyself
Art the enchantress, and I feel thy
    power
Envelop me, and wrap my soul and
    sense
In an Elysian dream.

    Pand.   O, let me stay.
How beautiful are all things round
    about me,
Multiplied by the mirrors on the
    walls !
What treasures hast thou here ! Yon
    oaken chest,
Carven with figures and embossed
    with gold,
Is wonderful to look upon ! What
    choice
And precious things dost thou keep
    hidden in it ?

    Epim.

I know not. 'Tis a mystery.

    Pand.   Hast thou never
Lifted the lid ?

    Epim.   The oracle forbids.
Safely concealed there from all
    mortal eyes
For ever sleeps the secret of the
    Gods.
Seek not to know what they have
    hidden from thee,
Till they themselves reveal it.

    Pand.   As thou wilt.

Epim.

Let us go forth from this mysterious
    place.
The garden walks are pleasant at
    this hour ;
The nightingales among the shel-
    tering boughs
Of populous and many-nested
    trees
Shall teach me how to woo thee,
    and shall tell me
By what resistless charms or in-
    cantations
They won their mates.
   Pand.   Thou dost not
    need a teacher.

       (*They go out.*)

CHORUS OF THE EUMENIDES.

What the Immortals
Confide to thy keeping,
Tell unto no man ;
Waking or sleeping,
Closed be thy portals
To friend as to foeman.

Silence conceals it ;
The word that is spoken
Betrays and reveals it ;
By breath or by token
The charm may be broken.

With shafts of their splendours
The Gods unforgiving
Pursue the offenders,
The dead and the living !
Fortune forsakes them,
Nor earth shall abide them,
Nor Tartarus hide them ;
Swift wrath overtakes them !

With useless endeavour,
For ever, for ever,
Is Sisyphus rolling
His stone up the mountain!
Immersed in the fountain,
Tantalus tastes not
The water that wastes not !

Through ages increasing
The pangs that afflict him,
With motion unceasing
The wheel of Ixion
Shall torture its victim !

VI.

IN THE GARDEN.

Epimetheus.

Yon snow-white cloud that sails
    sublime in ether
Is but the sovereign Zeus, who like
    a swan
Flies to fair-ankled Leda !
   Pandora.   Or perchance
Ixion's cloud, the shadowy shape
    of Hera,
That bore the Centaurs.
   Epim.   The divine and human.

CHORUS OF BIRDS.

Gently swaying to and fro,
Rocked by all the winds that blow,
Bright with sunshine from above
Dark with shadow from below,
Beak to beak and breast to breast
In the cradle of their nest,
Lie the fledglings of our love.
   Echo.   Love ! love !
   Epim.
Hark ! listen ! Hear how sweetly
    overhead
The feathered flute-players pipe
    their songs of love,
And echo answers, love and only
    love.

CHORUS OF BIRDS.

Every flutter of the wing,
Every note of song we sing,
Every murmur, every tone,
Is of love and love alone.
   Echo.   Love alone !
   Epim.
Who would not love, if loving she
    might be

Changed like Callisto to a star in
    heaven?

Pand.

Ah, who would love, if loving she
    might be
Like Semele consumed and burnt to
    ashes?

Epim.

Whence knowest thou these stories?

    Pand.   Hermes taught me;
He told me all the history of the
    Gods.

CHORUS OF REEDS.

Evermore a sound shall be
In the reeds of Arcady,
Evermore a low lament
Of unrest and discontent,
As the story is retold
Of the nymph so coy and cold,
Who with frightened feet outran
The pursuing steps of Pan.

    Epim.

The pipe of Pan out of these reeds
    is made,
And when he plays upon it to the
    shepherds
They pity him, so mournful is the
    sound.
Be thou not coy and cold as Syrinx
    was.

    Pand.

Nor thou as Pan be rude and
    mannerless.

    Prom. (without).

Ho! Epimetheus!

    Epim. 'Tis my brother's voice;
A sound unwelcome and inoppor-
    tune
As was the braying of Silenus' ass,
Once heard in Cybele's garden.

    Pand.   Let me go.
I would not be found here. I would
    not see him.

(*She escapes among the trees.*)

CHORUS OF DRYADES.

Haste and hide thee,
    Ere too late,
In these thickets intricate;
    Lest Prometheus
See and chide thee,
    Lest some hurt
Or harm betide thee,
    Haste and hide thee!

    Prom. (entering).

Who was it fled from here? I saw
    a shape
Flitting among the trees.

    Epim.   It was Pandora.

    Prom.

O Epimetheus? Is it then in vain
That I have warned thee? Let me
    now implore.
Thou harbourest in thy house a
    dangerous guest.

    Epim.

Whom the Gods love they honour
    with such guests.

    Prom.

Whom the Gods would destroy they
    first make mad.

    Epim.

Shall I refuse the gifts they send to
    me!

    Prom.

Reject all gifts that come from
    higher powers.

    Epim.

Such gifts as this are not to be re-
    jected.

    Prom.

Make not thyself the slave of any
    woman.

    Epim.

Make not thyself the judge of any
    man.

    Prom.

I judge thee not; for thou art
    more than man;

Thou art descended from Titanic
race,
And hast a Titan's strength, and
faculties
That make thee godlike ; and thou
sittest here
Like Heracles spinning Omphale's
flax,
And beaten with her sandals.

Epim. O my brother !
Thou drivest me to madness with
thy taunts.

Prom.
And me thou drivest to madness
with thy follies.
Come with me to my tower on
Caucasus :
See there my forges in the roaring
caverns,
Beneficent to man, and taste the
joy
That springs from labour. Read
with me the stars,
And learn the virtues that lie hid-
den in plants,
And all things that are useful.

Epim. O my brother !
I am not as thou art. Thou dost
inherit
Our father's strength, and I our
mother's weakness :
The softness of the Oceanides,
The yielding nature that cannot
resist.

Prom.
Because thou wilt not.

Epim. Nay ; because I cannot.

Prom.
Assert thyself ; rise up to thy full
height ;
Shake from thy soul these dreams
effeminate,
These passions born of indolence
and ease.
Resolve, and thou art free. But
breathe the air

Of mountains, and their unap-
proachable summits
Will lift thee to the level of themselves.

Epim.
The roar of forests and of water-
falls,
The rushing of a mighty wind, with
loud
And undistinguishable voices call-
ing,
Are in my ear !

Prom. O, listen and obey.

Epim.
Thou leadest me as a child. I
follow thee.

(*They go out.*)

CHORUS OF OREADES.

Centuries old are the mountains ;
Their foreheads wrinkled and rifted
Helios crowns by day,
Pallid Selene by night ;
From their bosoms uptossed
The snows are driven and drifted,
Like Tithonus' beard
Streaming dishevelled and white.

Thunder and tempest of wind
Their trumpets blow in the vastness ;
Phantoms of mist and rain,
Cloud and the shadow of cloud,
Pass and repass by the gates
Of their inaccessible fastness ;
Ever unmoved they stand,
Solemn, eternal, and proud.

VOICES OF THE WATERS.

Flooded by rain and snow
In their inexhaustible sources,
Swollen by affluent streams
Hurrying onward and hurled
Headlong over the crags,
The impetuous water-courses
Rush and roar and plunge
Down to the nethermost world.

Say, have the solid rocks
Into streams of silver been melted,
Flowing over the plains,
Spreading to lakes in the fields?
Or have the mountains, the giants,
The ice-helmed, the forest-belted,
Scattered their arms abroad;
Flung in the meadows their shields?

VOICES OF THE WINDS.

High on their turreted cliffs
That bolts of thunder have shattered,
Storm-winds muster and blow
Trumpets of terrible breath;
Then from the gateways rush,
And before them routed and scattered
Sullen the cloud-rack flies,
Pale with the pallor of death.

Onward the hurricane rides,
And flee for shelter the shepherds;
White are the frightened leaves,
Harvests with terror are white;
Panic seizes the herds,
And even the lions and leopards,
Prowling no longer for prey,
Crouch in their caverns with fright.

VOICES OF THE FOREST.

Guarding the mountains around
Majestic the forests are standing,
Bright are their crested helms,
Dark is their armour of leaves;
Filled with the breath of freedom
Each bosom subsiding, expanding,
Now like the ocean sinks,
Now like the ocean upheaves.

Planted firm on the rock,
With foreheads stern and defiant,
Loud they shout to the winds,
Loud to the tempest they call;
Naught but Olympian thunders,
That blasted Titan and Giant,
Them can uproot and o'erthrow,
Shaking the earth with their fall.

CHORUS OF OREADES.

These are the Voices Three
Of winds and forests and fountains,
Voices of earth and of air,
Murmur and rushing of streams,
Making together one sound,
The mysterious voice of the mountains,
Waking the sluggard that sleeps,
Waking the dreamer of dreams.

These are the Voices Three,
That speak of endless endeavour,
Speak of endurance and strength,
Triumph and fulness of fame,
Sounding about the world,
An inspiration for ever,
Stirring the hearts of men,
Shaping their end and their aim.

VII.

THE HOUSE OF EPIMETHEUS.

Pandora.

Left to myself I wander as I will,
And as my fancy leads me, through
this house,
Nor could I ask a dwelling more
complete
Were I indeed the Goddess that
he deems me.
No mansion of Olympus, framed
to be
The habitation of the Immortal
Gods,
Can be more beautiful. And this
is mine,
And more than this, the love wherewith he crowns me.
As if impelled by powers invisible
And irresistible, my steps return
Unto this spacious hall. All corridors
And passages lead hither, and all
doors
But open into it. Yon mysterious
chest

Attracts and fascinates me. Would
    I knew
What there lies hidden! But the
    oracle
Forbids. Ah me! The secret
    then is safe.
So would it be if it were in my
    keeping.
A crowd of shadowy faces from the
    mirrors
That line these walls are watching
    me. I dare not
Lift up the lid. A hundred times
    the act
Would be repeated, and the secret
    seen
By twice a hundred incorporeal eyes.

(*She walks to the other side of the
    hall.*)

My feet are weary, wandering to
    and fro,
My eyes with seeing and my heart
    with waiting.
I will lie here and rest till he returns,
Who is my dawn, my day, my Helios.

(*Throws herself upon a couch, and
    falls asleep.*)

ZEPHYRUS.

Come from thy caverns dark and
    deep,
O son of Erebus and Night;
All sense of hearing and of sight
Enfold in the serene delight
And quietude of sleep!

Set all thy silent sentinels
To bar and guard the Ivory Gate,
And keep the evil dreams of fate
And falsehood and infernal hate
Imprisoned in their cells.

But open wide the Gate of Horn,
Whence, beautiful as planets, rise
The dreams of truth, with starry
    eyes,
And all the wondrous prophecies
And visions of the morn.

CHORUS OF DREAMS FROM THE
IVORY GATE.

Ye sentinels of sleep,
It is in vain ye keep
Your drowsy watch before the
    Ivory Gate;
Though closed the portal seems,
The airy feet of dreams
Ye cannot thus in walls incarcerate.

We phantoms are and dreams
Born by Tartarean streams,
As ministers of the infernal powers;
O son of Erebus
And Night, behold! we thus
Elude your watchful warders on the
    towers!

From gloomy Tartarus
The Fates have summoned us
To whisper in her ear, who lies
    asleep,
A tale to fan the fire
Of her insane desire
To know a secret that the Gods
    would keep.

This passion, in their ire,
The Gods themselves inspire,
To vex mankind with evils mani-
    fold,
So that disease and pain
O'er the whole earth may reign,
And nevermore return the Age of
    Gold.

Pand. (*waking*).

A voice said in my sleep: 'Do
    not delay:
Do not delay; the golden moments
    fly!
The oracle hath forbidden; yet not
    thee
Doth it forbid, but Epimetheus
    only!'
I am alone. These faces in the
    mirrors
Are but the shadows and phantoms
    of myself;

They cannot help nor hinder. No
    one sees me,
Save the all-seeing Gods, who,
    knowing good
And knowing evil, have created me
Such as I am, and filled me with
    desire
Of knowing good and evil like
    themselves.

    (*She approaches the chest.*)

I hesitate no longer. Weal or woe,
Or life or death, the moment shall
    decide.

    (*She lifts the lid. A dense mist
    rises from the chest, and fills the
    room.* PANDORA *falls senseless
    on the floor. Storm without.*)

CHORUS OF DREAMS FROM THE
    GATE OF HORN.

Yes, the moment shall decide !
It already hath decided ;
And the secret once confided
To the keeping of the Titan
Now is flying far and wide,
Whispered, told on every side,
To disquiet and to frighten.

Fever of the heart and brain,
Sorrow, pestilence, and pain,
Moans of anguish, maniac laughter,
All the evils that hereafter
Shall afflict and vex mankind,
All into the air have risen
From the chambers of their prison ;
Only Hope remains behind.

VIII.

IN THE GARDEN.

Epimetheus.

The storm is past, but it hath left
    behind it
Ruin and desolation. All the walks
Are strewn with shattered boughs;
    the birds are silent ;

The flowers, downtrodden by the
    wind, lie dead ;
The swollen rivulet sobs with secret
    pain,
The melancholy reeds whisper
    together
As if some dreadful deed had been
    committed
They dare not name, and all the air
    is heavy
With an unspoken sorrow ! Pre-
    monitions,
Foreshadowings of some terrible
    disaster
Oppress my heart. Ye Gods, avert
    the omen !

    Pandora (*coming from the house*).

O Epimetheus, I no longer dare
To lift mine eyes to thine, nor hear
    thy voice,
Being no longer worthy of thy love.

    Epim.

What hast thou done ?

    Pand.   Forgive me
    not, but kill me.

    Epim.

What hast thou done ?

    Pand.   I pray for death,
    not pardon.

    Epim.

What hast thou done ?

    Pand.   I dare not speak of it.

    Epim.

Thy pallor and thy silence terrify
    me !

    Pand.

I have brought wrath and ruin on
    thy house !
My heart hath braved the oracle
    that guarded
The fatal secret from us, and my
    hand
Lifted the lid of the mysterious
    chest !

Epim.

Then all is lost! I am indeed undone.

Pand.

I pray for punishment, and not for pardon.

Epim.

Mine is the fault, not thine. On me shall fall

The vengeance of the Gods, for I betrayed

Their secret when, in evil hour, I said

It was a secret ; when, in evil hour,

I left thee here alone to this temptation.

Why did I leave thee ?

Pand. Why didst thou return ?

Eternal absence would have been to me

The greatest punishment. To be left alone

And face to face with my own crime, had been

Just retribution. Upon me, ye Gods,

Let all your vengeance fall !

Epim. On thee and me.

I do not love thee less for what is done,

And cannot be undone. Thy very weakness

Hath brought thee nearer to me, and henceforth

My love will have a sense of pity in it,

Making it less a worship than before.

Pand.

Pity me not ; pity is degradation.

Love me and kill me.

Epim. Beautiful Pandora !

Thou art a Goddess still !

Pand. I am a woman ;

And the insurgent demon in my nature,

That made me brave the oracle, revolts

At pity and compassion. Let me die ;

What else remains for me ?

Epim. Youth, hope, and love ;

To build a new life on a ruined life,

To make the future fairer than the past,

And make the past appear a troubled dream.

Even now in passing through the garden walks

Upon the ground I saw a fallen nest

Ruined and full of rain ; and over me

Beheld the uncomplaining birds already

Busy in building a new habitation.

Pand.

Auspicious omen !

Epim. May the Eumenides

Put out their torches and behold us not,

And fling away their whips of scorpions

And touch us not.

Pand. Me let them punish.

Only through punishment of our evil deeds,

Only through suffering, are we reconciled

To the immortal Gods and to ourselves.

CHORUS OF THE EUMENIDES.

Never shall souls like these
Escape the Eumenides,
The daughters dark of Acheron and Night !
Unquenched our torches glare,
Our scourges in the air
Send forth prophetic sounds before they smite.

Never by lapse of time
The soul defaced by crime
Into its former self returns
  again ;
For every guilty deed
Holds in itself the seed
Of retribution and undying
  pain.

Never shall be the loss
Restored, till Helios
Hath purified them with his hea-
  venly fires ;
Then what was lost is won,
And the new life begun,
Kindled with nobler passions and
  desires.

The Hanging of the Crane.

I.

THE lights are out, and gone are all the guests
That thronging came with merriment and jests
  To celebrate the Hanging of the Crane
In the new house,—into the night are gone;
But still the fire upon the hearth burns on,
  And I alone remain.

O fortunate, O happy day,
  When a new household finds its piace
  Among the myriad homes of earth,
  Like a new star just sprung to birth,
  And rolled on its harmonious way
  Into the boundless realms of space !

So said the guests in speech and song,
As in the chimney, burning bright,
We hung the iron crane to-night,
And merry was the feast and long.

II.

And now I sit and muse on what may be,
And in my vision see, or seem to see,
  Through floating vapours interfused with light,
Shapes indeterminate, that gleam and fade,
As shadows passing into deeper shade
  Sink and elude the sight.

For two alone, there in the hall,
Is spread the table round and small;
Upon the polished silver shine
The evening lamps, but, more divine,
The light of love shines over all;
Of love, that says not mine and thine,
But ours,—for ours is thine and mine.

They want no guests, to come between
Their tender glances like a screen,
And tell them tales of land and sea,
And whatsoever may betide
The great, forgotten world outside;
They want no guests; they needs must be
Each other's own best company.

III.

The picture fades; as at a village fair
A showman's views, dissolving into air,
  Again appear transfigured on the screen,
So in my fancy this ; and now once more,

699

In part transfigured, through the
 open door
  Appears the self-same scene.

Seated, I see the two again,
But not alone ; they entertain
A little angel unaware,
With face as round as is the
 moon ;
A royal guest with flaxen hair,
Who, throned upon his lofty
 chair,
Drums on the table with his
 spoon,
Then drops it careless on the floor,
To grasp at things unseen before.

Are these celestial manners ?
 these
The ways that win, the arts that
 please ?
Ah yes ; consider well the guest,
And whatsoe'er he does seems
 best ;
He ruleth by the right divine
Of helplessness, so lately born
In purple chambers of the morn,
As sovereign over thee and thine.
He speaketh not ; and yet there
 lies
A conversation in his eyes ;
The golden silence of the Greek,
The gravest wisdom of the wise,
Not spoken in language, but in
 looks
More legible than printed books,
As if he could but would not
 speak.
And now, O monarch absolute,
Thy power is put to proof ; for,
 lo !
Resistless, fathomless, and slow,
The nurse comes rustling like
 the sea,
And pushes back thy chair and
 thee,
And so good night to King
Canute.

IV.

As one who walking in a forest
 sees
A lovely landscape through the
 parted trees,
 Then sees it not, for boughs that
  intervene ;
Or as we see the moon sometimes
 revealed
Through drifting clouds, and then
 again concealed,
 So I behold the scene.

There are two guests at table
 now ;
 The king, deposed and older
  grown,
No longer occupies the throne,—
The crown is on his sister's
 brow ;
A Princess from the Fairy Isles,
The very pattern girl of girls,
All covered and embowered in
 curls,
Rose-tinted from the Isle of
 Flowers,
And sailing with soft, silken sails
From far-off Dreamland into
 ours.
Above their bowls with rims of
 blue
Four azure eyes of deeper hue
Are looking, dreamy with de-
 light ;
Limpid as planets that emerge
Above the ocean's rounded verge,
Soft-shining through the sum-
 mer night.
Steadfast they gaze, yet nothing
 see
Beyond the horizon of their
 bowls ;
Nor care they for the world that
 rolls
With all its freight of troubled
 souls
Into the days that are to be.

V.

Again the tossing boughs shut out
 the scene,
Again the drifting vapours inter-
 vene,
 And the moon's pallid disc is
 hidden quite ;
And now I see the table wider
 grown,
As round a pebble into water thrown
 Dilates a ring of light.

I see the table wider grown,
I see it garlanded with guests,
As if fair Ariadne's Crown
Out of the sky had fallen down ;
Maidens within whose tender
 breasts
A thousand restless hopes and
 fears,
Forth reaching to the coming
 years,
Flutter awhile, then quiet lie,
Like timid birds that fain would
 fly,
But do not dare to leave their
 nests ;—
And youths, who in their strength
 elate
Challenge the van and front of
 fate,
Eager as champions to be
In the divine knight-errantry
Of youth, that travels sea and
 land
Seeking adventures, or pursues,
Through cities, and through soli-
 tudes
Frequented by the lyric Muse,
The phantom with the beckoning
 hand,
That still allures and still eludes.
O sweet illusions of the brain !
O sudden thrills of fire and frost !
The world is bright while ye re-
 main,
And dark and dead when ye are
 lost !

VI.

The meadow-brook, that seemeth
 to stand still,
Quickens its current as it nears the
 mill;
 And so the stream of Time that
 lingereth
In level places, and so dull appears,
Runs with a swifter current as it
 nears
 The gloomy mills of Death.

And now, like the magician's
 scroll,
That in the owner's keeping
 shrinks
With every wish he speaks or
 thinks,
Till the last wish consumes the
 whole,
The table dwindles, and again
I see the two alone remain.
The crown of stars is broken in
 parts ;
Its jewels, brighter than the day,
Have one by one been stolen
 away
To shine in other homes and
 hearts.
One is a wanderer now afar
In Ceylon or in Zanzibar,
Or sunny regions of Cathay ;
And one is in the boisterous camp
Mid clink of arms and horses'
 tramp,
And battle's terrible array.
I see the patient mother read,
With aching heart, of wrecks that
 float
Disabled on those seas remote,
Or of some great heroic deed
On battlefields, where thousands
 bleed
To lift one hero into fame.
Anxious she bends her graceful
 head
Above these chronicles of pain,

And trembles with a secret dread
Lest there among the drowned
or slain
She find the one beloved name.

VII.

After a day of cloud and wind
and rain
Sometimes the setting sun breaks
out again,
And, touching all the darksome
woods with light,
Smiles on the fields, until they
laugh and sing,
Then like a ruby from the horizon's
ring
Drops down into the night.

What see I now? The night is
fair,
The storm of grief, the clouds of
care,
The wind, the rain, have passed
away;
The lamps are lit, the fires burn
bright,
The house is full of life and light:
It is the Golden Wedding day.
The guests come thronging in
once more,
Quick footsteps sound along the
floor,

The trooping children crowd the
stair,
And in and out and everywhere
Flashes along the corridor
The sunshine of their golden
hair.
On the round table in the hall
Another Ariadne's Crown
Out of the sky hath fallen down;
More than one Monarch of the
Moon
Is drumming with his silver
spoon;
The light of love shines over all.

O fortunate, O happy day!
The people sing, the people say.
The ancient bridegroom and the
bride,
Smiling contented and serene
Upon the blithe, bewildering
scene,
Behold, well pleased, on every
side
Their forms and features multi-
plied,
As the reflection of a light
Between two burnished mirrors
gleams,
Or lamps upon a bridge at night
Stretch on and on before the
sight,
Till the long vista endless seems.

Morituri Salutamus.

POEM FOR THE FIFTIETH ANNIVERSARY OF THE CLASS OF 1825 IN BOWDOIN COLLEGE.

——◆◆——

Tempora labuntur, tacitisque senescimus annis,
Et fugiunt freno non remorante dies.

OVID, *Fastorum*, Lib. vi.

——◆◆——

'O CÆSAR, we who are about to die
Salute you!' was the gladiators' cry
In the arena, standing face to face
With death and with the Roman populace.

O ye familiar scenes,—ye groves of pine,
That once were mine and are no longer mine,—
Thou river, widening through the meadows green
To the vast sea, so near and yet unseen,—
Ye halls, in whose seclusion and repose
Phantoms of fame, like exhalations, rose
And vanished,—we who are about to die
Salute you; earth and air and sea and sky,
And the Imperial Sun that scatters down
His sovereign splendours upon grove and town.

Ye do not answer us! ye do not hear!
We are forgotten; and in your austere
And calm indifference, ye little care
Whether we come or go, or whence or where.

What passing generations fill these halls,
What passing voices echo from these walls,
Ye heed not; we are only as the blast,
A moment heard, and then for ever past.

Not so the teachers who in earlier days
Led our bewildered feet through learning's maze;
They answer us—alas! what have I said?
What greetings come there from the voiceless dead?
What salutation, welcome, or reply?
What pressure from the hands that lifeless lie?
They are no longer here; they all are gone
Into the land of shadows,—all save one.
Honour and reverence, and the good repute
That follows faithful service as its fruit,
Be unto him, whom living we salute.

The great Italian poet, when he made
His dreadful journey to the realms of shade,
Met there the old instructor of his youth,

703

And cried in tones of pity and of
    ruth :
'O, never from the memory of my
    heart
Your dear, paternal image shall
    depart,
Who while on earth, ere yet by
    death surprised,
Taught me how mortals are im-
    mortalized ;
How grateful am I for that patient
    care
All my life long my language shall
    declare.'

To-day we make the poet's words
    our own,
And utter them in plaintive under-
    tone ;
Nor to the living only be they said,
But to the other living called the
    dead,
Whose dear, paternal images appear
Not wrapped in gloom, but robed in
    sunshine here ;
Whose simple lives, complete and
    without flaw,
Were part and parcel of great
    Nature's law ;
Who said not to their Lord, as if
    afraid,
'Here is thy talent in a napkin laid,'
But laboured in their sphere, as men
    who live
In the delight that work alone can
    give.
Peace be to them ; eternal peace
    and rest,
And the fulfilment of the great
    behest :
'Ye have been faithful over a few
    things,
Over ten cities shall ye reign as
    kings.'

And ye who fill the places we once
    filled,
And follow in the furrows that we
    tilled,

Young men, whose generous hearts
    are beating high,
We who are old, and are about to
    die,
Salute you ; hail you ; take your
    hands in ours,
And crown you with our welcome as
    with flowers !

How beautiful is youth ! how bright
    it gleams
With its illusions, aspirations,
    dreams !
Book of Beginnings, Story without
    End,
Each maid a heroine, and each man
    a friend !
Aladdin's Lamp, and Fortunatus'
    Purse,
That holds the treasures of the
    universe !
All possibilities are in its hands,
No danger daunts it, and no foe
    withstands ;
In its sublime audacity of faith,
'Be thou removed !' it to the moun-
    tain saith,
And with ambitious feet, secure and
    proud,
Ascends the ladder leaning on the
    cloud !

As ancient Priam at the Scæan gate
Sat on the walls of Troy in regal
    state
With the old men, too old and
    weak to fight,
Chirping like grasshoppers in their
    delight
To see the embattled hosts, with
    spear and shield,
Of Trojans and Achaians in the
    field ;
So from the snowy summits of our
    years
We see you in the plain, as each
    appears,
And question of you ; asking, 'Who
    is he

That towers above the others?
    Which may be
Atreides, Menelaus, Odysseus,
Ajax the great, or bold Idomeneus?'
Let him not boast who puts his
    armour on
As he who puts it off, the battle done.
Study yourselves; and most of all
    note well
Wherein kind Nature meant you to
    excel.
Not every blossom ripens into fruit;
Minerva, the inventress of the flute,
Flung it aside, when she her face
    surveyed
Distorted in a fountain as she
    played;
The unlucky Marsyas found it, and
    his fate
Was one to make the bravest hesi-
    tate.

Write on your doors the saying
    wise and old,
'Be bold! be bold!' and every-
    where—'Be bold;
Be not too bold!' Yet better the
    excess
Than the defect; better the more
    than less;
Better like Hector in the field to die,
Than like a perfumed Paris turn
    and fly.

And now, my classmates; ye
    remaining few
That number not the half of those
    we knew,
Ye, against whose familiar names
    not yet
The fatal asterisk of death is set,
Ye I salute! The horologe of Time
Strikes the half-century with a
    solemn chime,
And summons us together once
    again,
The joy of meeting not unmixed
    with pain.

Where are the others? Voices
    from the deep
Caverns of darkness answer me:
    'They sleep!'
I name no names; instinctively I feel
Each at some well-remembered
    grave will kneel,
And from the inscription wipe the
    weeds and moss,
For every heart best knoweth its
    own loss.
I see their scattered gravestones
    gleaming white
Through the pale dusk of the im-
    pending night;
O'er all alike the impartial sunset
    throws
Its golden lilies mingled with the
    rose;
We give to each a tender thought,
    and pass
Out of the graveyards with their
    tangled grass,
Unto these scenes frequented by
    our feet
When we were young, and life was
    fresh and sweet.

What shall I say to you? What
    can I say
Better than silence is? When I
    survey
This throng of faces turned to meet
    my own,
Friendly and fair, and yet to me
    unknown,
Transformed the very landscape
    seems to be;
It is the same, yet not the same to
    me.
So many memories crowd upon my
    brain,
So many ghosts are in the wooded
    plain,
I fain would steal away, with noise-
    less tread,
As from a house where some one
    lieth dead.

I cannot go;—I pause;—I hesitate;
My feet reluctant linger at the gate;
As one who struggles in a troubled
    dream
To speak and cannot, to myself I
    seem.

Vanish the dream! Vanish the
    idle fears!
Vanish the rolling mists of fifty
    years!
Whatever time or space may inter-
    vene,
I will not be a stranger in this scene.
Here every doubt, all indecision,
    ends;
Hail, my companions, comrades,
    classmates, friends!

Ah me! the fifty years since last
    we met
Seem to me fifty folios bound and
    set
By Time, the great transcriber, on
    his shelves,
Wherein are written the histories of
    ourselves.
What tragedies, what comedies,
    are there;
What joy and grief, what rapture
    and despair!
What chronicles of triumph and
    defeat,
Of struggle, and temptation, and
    retreat!
What records of regrets, and doubts,
    and fears!
What pages blotted, blistered by
    our tears!
What lovely landscapes on the
    margin shine,
What sweet, angelic faces, what
    divine
And holy images of love and trust,
Undimmed by age, unsoiled by
    damp or dust!

Whose hand shall dare to open and
    explore

These volumes, closed and clasped
    for evermore?
Not mine. With reverential feet I
    pass;
I hear a voice that cries, 'Alas!
    alas!
Whatever hath been written shall
    remain,
Nor be erased nor written o'er again;
The unwritten only still belongs to
    thee:
Take heed, and ponder well what
    that shall be.'

As children frightened by a thun-
    der-cloud
Are reassured if some one reads
    aloud
A tale of wonder, with enchantment
    fraught,
Or wild adventure, that diverts
    their thought,
Let me endeavour with a tale to
    chase
The gathering shadows of the time
    and place,
And banish what we all too deeply
    feel
Wholly to say, or wholly to con-
    ceal.

In mediæval Rome, I know not
    where,
There stood an image with its arm
    in air,
And on its lifted finger, shining
    clear,
A golden ring with the device,
    'Strike here!'
Greatly the people wondered,
    though none guessed
The meaning that these words but
    half expressed,
Until a learned clerk, who at noon-
    day
With downcast eyes was passing
    on his way,
Paused, and observed the spot, and
    marked it well,

Whereon the shadow of the finger fell;
And, coming back at midnight, delved, and found
A secret stairway leading under ground.
Down this he passed into a spacious hall,
Lit by a flaming jewel on the wall;
And opposite, in threatening attitude,
With bow and shaft a brazen statue stood.
Upon its forehead, like a coronet,
Were these mysterious words of menace set:
'That which I am, I am; my fatal aim
None can escape, not even yon luminous flame!'

Midway the hall was a fair table placed,
With cloth of gold, and golden cups enchased
With rubies, and the plates and knives were gold,
And gold the bread and viands manifold.
Around it, silent, motionless, and sad,
Were seated gallant knights in armour clad,
And ladies beautiful with plume and zone,
But they were stone, their hearts within were stone;
And the vast hall was filled in every part
With silent crowds, stony in face and heart.

Long at the scene, bewildered and amazed
The trembling clerk in speechless wonder gazed;
Then from the table, by his greed made bold,
He seized a goblet and a knife of gold,

And suddenly from their seats the guests upsprang,
The vaulted ceiling with loud clamours rang,
The archer sped his arrow, at their call,
Shattering the lambent jewel on the wall,
And all was dark around and overhead;—
Stark on the floor the luckless clerk lay dead!

The writer of this legend then records
Its ghostly application in these words:
The image is the Adversary old,
Whose beckoning finger points to realms of gold;
Our lusts and passions are the downward stair
That leads the soul from a diviner air;
The archer, Death; the flaming jewel, Life;
Terrestrial goods, the goblet and the knife;
The knights and ladies, all whose flesh and bone
By avarice have been hardened into stone;
The clerk, the scholar whom the love of pelf
Tempts from his books and from his nobler self.

The scholar and the world! The endless strife,
The discord in the harmonies of life!
The love of learning, the sequestered nooks,
And all the sweet serenity of books;
The market-place, the eager love of gain,
Whose aim is vanity, and whose end is pain!

But why, you ask me, should this
  tale be told
To men grown old, or who are
  growing old?
It is too late! Ah, nothing is too late
Till the tired heart shall cease to
  palpitate.
Cato learned Greek at eighty;
  Sophocles
Wrote his grand Œdipus, and
  Simonides
Bore off the prize of verse from his
  compeers,
When each had numbered more
  than fourscore years,
And Theophrastus, at fourscore
  and ten,
Had but begun his Characters of
  Men;
Chaucer, at Woodstock with the
  nightingales,
At sixty wrote the Canterbury
  Tales;
Goethe at Weimar, toiling to the
  last,
Completed Faust when eighty
  years were past.
These are indeed exceptions; but
  they show
How far the gulf-stream of our
  youth may flow
Into the arctic regions of our lives,
Where little else than life itself sur-
  vives.

As the barometer foretells the storm
While still the skies are clear, the
  weather warm,
So something in us, as old age
  draws near,
Betrays the pressure of the atmosphere.
The nimble mercury, ere we are
  aware,
Descends the elastic ladder of the
  air;
The tell-tale blood in artery and
  vein

Sinks from its higher levels in the
  brain;
Whatever poet, orator, or sage
May say of it, old age is still old age.
It is the waning, not the crescent
  moon;
The dusk of evening, not the blaze
  of noon:
It is not strength, but weakness;
  not desire,
But its surcease; not the fierce
  heat of fire,
The burning and consuming ele-
  ment,
But that of ashes and of embers
  spent,
In which some living sparks we
  still discern,
Enough to warm, but not enough
  to burn.

What then? Shall we sit idly down
  and say
The night hath come; it is no
  longer day?
The night hath not yet come; we
  are not quite
Cut off from labour by the failing
  light;
Something remains for us to do or
  dare;
Even the oldest tree some fruit
  may bear;
Not Œdipus Coloneus, or Greek
  Ode,
Or tales of pilgrims that one morn-
  ing rode
Out of the gateway of the Tabard
  Inn,
But other something, would we but
  begin;
For age is opportunity no less
Than youth itself, though in another
  dress,
And as the evening twilight fades
  away
The sky is filled with stars, invisible
  by day.

A Book of Sonnets.

PART I.

THREE FRIENDS OF MINE.

I.

WHEN I remember them, those friends of mine,
  Who are no longer here, the noble three,
  Who half my life were more than friends to me,
  And whose discourse was like a generous wine,
I most of all remember the divine
  Something, that shone in them, and made us see
  The archetypal man, and what might be
  The amplitude of Nature's first design.
In vain I stretch my hands to clasp their hands ;
  I cannot find them. Nothing now is left
  But a majestic memory. They meanwhile
Wander together in Elysian lands,
  Perchance remembering me, who am bereft
  Of their dear presence, and, remembering, smile.

II.

In Attica thy birthplace should have been,
  Or the Ionian Isles, or where the seas
  Encircle in their arms the Cyclades,
  So wholly Greek wast thou in thy serene
And childlike joy of life, O Philhellene !
  Around thee would have swarmed the Attic bees ;
  Homer had been thy friend, or Socrates,
  And Plato welcomed thee to his demesne.
For thee old legends breathed historic breath ;
  Thou sawest Poseidon in the purple sea,
  And in the sunset Jason's fleece of gold !
O, what hadst thou to do with cruel Death,
  Who wast so full of life, or Death with thee,
  That thou shouldst die before thou hadst grown old !

III.

I stand again on the familiar shore,
    And hear the waves of the distracted sea
    Piteously calling and lamenting thee,
    And waiting restless at thy cottage door.
The rocks, the sea-weed on the ocean floor,
    The willows in the meadow, and the free
    Wild winds of the Atlantic welcome me ;
    Then why shouldst thou be dead, and come no more ?
Ah, why shouldst thou be dead, when common men
    Are busy with their trivial affairs,
    Having and holding ?   Why, when thou hadst read
Nature's mysterious manuscript, and then
    Wast ready to reveal the truth it bears,
    Why art thou silent ?   Why shouldst thou be dead ?

IV.

River, that stealest with such silent pace
    Around the City of the Dead, where lies
    A friend who bore thy name, and whom these eyes
    Shall see no more in his accustomed place,
Linger and fold him in thy soft embrace
    And say good night, for now the western skies
    Are red with sunset, and gray mists arise
    Like damps that gather on a dead man's face.
Good night ! good night ! as we so oft have said
    Beneath this roof at midnight, in the days
    That are no more, and shall no more return.
Thou hast but taken thy lamp and gone to bed ;
    I stay a little longer, as one stays
    To cover up the embers that still burn.

V.

The doors are all wide open ; at the gate
    The blossomed lilacs counterfeit a blaze,
    And seem to warm the air ; a dreamy haze
    Hangs o'er the Brighton meadows like a fate,
And on their margin, with sea-tides elate,
    The flooded Charles, as in the happier days,
    Writes the last letter of his name, and stays
    His restless steps, as if compelled to wait.
I also wait ; but they will come no more,
    Those friends of mine, whose presence satisfied
    The thirst and hunger of my heart.   Ah me !
They have forgotten the pathway to my door !
    Something is gone from nature since they died,
    And summer is not summer, nor can be.

CHAUCER.

AN old man in a lodge within a park ;
   The chamber walls depicted all around
   With portraitures of huntsman, hawk, and hound,
   And the hurt deer.   He listeneth to the lark,
Whose song comes with the sunshine through the dark
   Of painted glass in leaden lattice bound ;
   He listeneth and he laugheth at the sound,
   Then writeth in a book like any clerk.
He is the poet of the dawn, who wrote
   The Canterbury Tales, and his old age
   Made beautiful with song ; and as I read
I hear the crowing cock, I hear the note
   Of lark and linnet, and from every page
   Rise odours of ploughed field or flowery mead.

SHAKESPEARE.

A VISION as of crowded city streets,
   With human life in endless overflow ;
   Thunder of thoroughfares ; trumpets that blow
   To battle ; clamour, in obscure retreats,
Of sailors landed from their anchored fleets ;
   Tolling of bells in turrets, and below
   Voices of children, and bright flowers that throw
   O'er garden-walls their intermingled sweets !
This vision comes to me when I unfold
   The volume of the Poet paramount,
   Whom all the Muses loved, not one alone ;—
Into his hands they put the lyre of gold,
   And, crowned with sacred laurel at their fount,
   Placed him as Musagetes on their throne.

MILTON.

I PACE the sounding sea-beach and behold
   How the voluminous billows roll and run,
   Upheaving and subsiding, while the sun
   Shines through their sheeted emerald far unrolled,
And the ninth wave, slow gathering fold by fold
   All its loose-flowing garments into one,
   Plunges upon the shore, and floods the dun
   Pale reach of sands, and changes them to gold.
So in majestic cadence rise and fall
   The mighty undulations of thy song,
   O sightless bard, England's Mæonides !

And ever and anon, high over all
    Uplifted, a ninth wave superb and strong,
    Floods all the soul with its melodious seas.

KEATS.

THE young Endymion sleeps Endymion's sleep ;
    The shepherd-boy whose tale was left half told !
    The solemn grove uplifts its shield of gold
    To the red rising moon, and loud and deep
The nightingale is singing from the steep ;
    It is midsummer, but the air is cold ;
    Can it be death ? Alas, beside the fold
    A shepherd's pipe lies shattered near his sheep.
Lo ! in the moonlight gleams a marble white,
    On which I read : ' Here lieth one whose name
    Was writ in water.' And was this the meed
Of his sweet singing ? Rather let me write :
    ' The smoking flax before it burst to flame
    Was quenched by death, and broken the bruised reed.

THE GALAXY.

TORRENT of light and river of the air,
    Along whose bed the glimmering stars are seen
    Like gold and silver sands in some ravine
    Where mountain streams have left their channels bare !
The Spaniard sees in thee the pathway, where
    His patron saint descended in the sheen
    Of his celestial armour, on serene
    And quiet nights, when all the heavens were fair.
Not this I see, nor yet the ancient fable
    Of Phaeton's wild course, that scorched the skies
    Where'er the hoofs of his hot coursers trod ;
But the white drift of worlds o'er chasms of sable,
    The star-dust, that is whirled aloft and flies
    From the invisible chariot-wheels of God.

THE SOUND OF THE SEA.

THE sea awoke at midnight from its sleep,
    And round the pebbly beaches far and wide
    I heard the first wave of the rising tide
    Rush onward with uninterrupted sweep ;
A voice out of the silence of the deep,
    A sound mysteriously multiplied
    As of a cataract from the mountain's side,
    Or roar of winds upon a wooded steep.

So comes to us at times, from the unknown
    And inaccessible solitudes of being,
    The rushing of the sea-tides of the soul;
And inspirations, that we deem our own,
    Are some divine foreshadowing and foreseeing
    Of things beyond our reason or control.

A SUMMER DAY BY THE SEA.

THE sun is set; and in his latest beams
    Yon little cloud of ashen gray and gold,
    Slowly upon the amber air unrolled,
    The falling mantle of the Prophet seems.
From the dim headlands many a lighthouse gleams,
    The street-lamps of the ocean; and behold,
    O'erhead the banners of the night unfold;
    The day hath passed into the land of dreams.
O summer day beside the joyous sea!
    O summer day so wonderful and white,
    So full of gladness and so full of pain!
For ever and for ever shalt thou be
    To some the gravestone of a dead delight,
    To some the landmark of a new domain.

THE TIDES.

I SAW the long line of the vacant shore,
    The sea-weed and the shells upon the sand,
    And the brown rocks left bare on every hand,
    As if the ebbing tide would flow no more.
Then heard I, more distinctly than before,
    The ocean breathe and its great breast expand,
    And hurrying came on the defenceless land
    The insurgent waters with tumultuous roar.
All thought and feeling and desire, I said,
    Love, laughter, and the exultant joy of song
    Have ebbed from me for ever! Suddenly o'er me
They swept again from their deep ocean bed,
    And in a tumult of delight, and strong
    As youth, and beautiful as youth, upbore me.

A SHADOW.

I SAID unto myself, if I were dead,
    What would befall these children? What would be
    Their fate, who now are looking up to me
    For help and furtherance? Their lives, I said,
Would be a volume wherein I have read
    But the first chapters, and no longer see

To read the rest of their dear history,
So full of beauty and so full of dread.
Be comforted ; the world is very old,
And generations pass, as they have passed,
A troop of shadows moving with the sun ;
Thousands of times has the old tale been told ;
The world belongs to those who come the last,
They will find hope and strength as we have done.

A NAMELESS GRAVE.

'A SOLDIER of the Union mustered out,'
Is the inscription on an unknown grave
At Newport News, beside the salt-sea wave,
Nameless and dateless ; sentinel or scout
Shot down in skirmish, or disastrous rout
Of battle, when the loud artillery drave
Its iron wedges through the ranks of brave
And doomed battalions, storming the redoubt.
Thou unknown hero sleeping by the sea
In thy forgotten grave ! with secret shame
I feel my pulses beat, my forehead burn,
When I remember thou hast given for me
All that thou hadst, thy life, thy very name,
And I can give thee nothing in return.

SLEEP.

LULL me to sleep, ye winds, whose fitful sound
Seems from some faint Æolian harp-string caught ;
Seal up the hundred wakeful eyes of thought
As Hermes with his lyre in sleep profound
The hundred wakeful eyes of Argus bound ;
For I am weary, and am overwrought
With too much toil, with too much care distraught,
And with the iron crown of anguish crowned.
Lay thy soft hand upon my brow and cheek,
O peaceful Sleep ! until from pain released
I breathe again uninterrupted breath !
Ah, with what subtile meaning did the Greek
Call thee the lesser mystery at the feast
Whereof the greater mystery is death !

THE OLD BRIDGE AT FLORENCE.

TADDEO GADDI built me. I am old,
Five centuries old. I plant my foot of stone
Upon the Arno, as St. Michael's own
Was planted on the dragon. Fold by fold

Beneath me as it struggles, I behold
    Its glistening scales. Twice hath it overthrown
    My kindred and companions. Me alone
    It moveth not, but is by me controlled.
I can remember when the Medici
    Were driven from Florence; longer still ago
    The final wars of Ghibelline and Guelf.
Florence adorns me with her jewelry;
    And when I think that Michael Angelo
    Hath leaned on me, I glory in myself.

IL PONTE VECCHIO DI FIRENZE.

GADDI mi fece ; il Ponte Vecchio sono ;
    Cinquecent' anni già sull' Arno pianto
    Il piede, come il suo Michele Santo
    Piantò sul draco. Mentre ch' io ragiono
Lo vedo torcere con flebil suono
    Le rilucenti scaglie. Ha questi affranto
    Due volte i miei maggior. Me solo intanto
    Neppure muove, ed io non l' abbandono.
Io mi rammento quando fur cacciati
    I Medici ; pur quando Ghibellino
    E Guelfo fecer pace mi rammento.
Fiorenza i suoi giojelli m' ha prestati ;
    E quando penso ch' Agnolo il divino
    Su me posava, insuperbir mi sento.

PART II.

NATURE.

AS a fond mother, when the day is o'er,
    Leads by the hand her little child to bed,
    Half willing, half reluctant to be led,
    And leave his broken playthings on the floor,
Still gazing at them through the open door,
    Nor wholly reassured and comforted
    By promises of others in their stead,
    Which, though more splendid, may not please him more;
So Nature deals with us, and takes away
    Our playthings one by one, and by the hand
    Leads us to rest so gently, that we go
Scarce knowing if we wished to go or stay,
    Being too full of sleep to understand
    How far the unknown transcends the what we know.

IN THE CHURCHYARD AT TARRYTOWN.

HERE lies the gentle humourist, who died
   In the bright Indian summer of his fame !
   A simple stone, with but a date and name,
   Marks the secluded resting-place beside
The river that he loved and glorified.
   Here in the autumn of his days he came,
   But the dry leaves of life were all aflame
   With tints that brightened and were multiplied.
How sweet a life was his ; how sweet a death !
   Living, to wing with mirth the weary hours,
   Or with romantic tales the heart to cheer ;
Dying, to leave a memory like the breath
   Of summers full of sunshine and of showers,
   A grief and gladness in the atmosphere.

ELIOT'S OAK.

THOU ancient oak ! whose myriad leaves are loud
   With sounds of unintelligible speech,
   Sounds as of surges on a shingly beach,
   Or multitudinous murmurs of a crowd ;
With some mysterious gift of tongues endowed,
   Thou speakest a different dialect to each ;
   To me a language that no man can teach,
   Of a lost race, long vanished like a cloud.
For underneath thy shade, in days remote,
   Seated like Abraham at eventide
   Beneath the oaks of Mamre, the unknown
Apostle of the Indians, Eliot, wrote
   His Bible in a language that hath died
   And is forgotten, save by thee alone.

THE DESCENT OF THE MUSES.

NINE sisters, beautiful in form and face,
   Came from their convent on the shining heights
   Of Pierus, the mountain of delights,
   To dwell among the people at its base.
Then seemed the world to change. All time and space
   Splendour of cloudless days and starry nights,
   And men and manners, and all sounds and sights,
   Had a new meaning, a diviner grace.
Proud were these sisters, but were not too proud
   To teach in schools of little country towns
   Science and song, and all the arts that please ;

So that while housewives span, and farmers ploughed,
 Their comely daughters, clad in homespun gowns,
 Learned the sweet songs of the Pierides.

VENICE.

WHITE swan of cities, slumbering in thy nest
 So wonderfully built among the reeds
 Of the lagoon, that fences thee and feeds,
 As sayeth thy old historian and thy guest!
White water-lily, cradled and caressed
 By ocean streams, and from the silt and weeds
 Lifting thy golden filaments and seeds,
 Thy sun-illumined spires, thy crown and crest!
White phantom city, whose untrodden streets
 Are rivers, and whose pavements are the shifting
 Shadows of palaces and strips of sky;
I wait to see thee vanish like the fleets
 Seen in mirage, or towers of cloud uplifting
 In air their unsubstantial masonry.

THE POETS.

O YE dead Poets, who are living still
 Immortal in your verse, though life be fled,
 And ye, O living Poets, who are dead
 Though ye are living, if neglect can kill,
Tell me if in the darkest hours of ill,
 With drops of anguish falling fast and red
 From the sharp crown of thorns upon your head,
 Ye were not glad your errand to fulfil?
Yes; for the gift and ministry of Song
 Have something in them so divinely sweet,
 It can assuage the bitterness of wrong;
Not in the clamour of the crowded street,
 Not in the shouts and plaudits of the throng,
 But in ourselves, are triumph and defeat.

PARKER CLEAVELAND.

WRITTEN ON REVISITING BRUNSWICK IN THE SUMMER OF 1875.

AMONG the many lives that I have known,
 None I remember more serene and sweet,
 More rounded in itself and more complete,
 Than his, who lies beneath this funeral stone.
These pines, that murmur in low monotone,
 These walks frequented by scholastic feet,

Were all his world ; but in this calm retreat
For him the Teacher's chair became a throne.
With fond affection memory loves to dwell
    On the old days, when his example made
    A pastime of the toil of tongue and pen ;
And now, amid the groves he loved so well
    That naught could lure him from their grateful shade,
    He sleeps, but wakes elsewhere, for God hath said, Amen !

THE HARVEST MOON.

IT is the Harvest Moon ! On gilded vanes
    And roofs of villages, on woodland crests
    And their aerial neighbourhoods of nests
    Deserted, on the curtained window-panes
Of rooms where children sleep, on country lanes
    And harvest-fields, its mystic splendour rests !
    Gone are the birds that were our summer guests,
    With the last sheaves return the labouring wains !
All things are symbols : the external shows
    Of Nature have their image in the mind,
    As flowers and fruits and falling of the leaves ;
The song-birds leave us at the summer's close,
    Only the empty nests are left behind,
    And pipings of the quail among the sheaves.

TO THE RIVER RHONE.

THOU Royal River, born of sun and shower
    In chambers purple with the Alpine glow,
    Wrapped in the spotless ermine of the snow
    And rocked by tempests !—at the appointed hour
Forth, like a steel-clad horseman from a tower,
    With clang and clink of harness dost thou go
    To meet thy vassal torrents, that below
    Rush to receive thee and obey thy power.
And now thou movest in triumphal march,
    A king among the rivers ! On thy way
    A hundred towns await and welcome thee ;
Bridges uplift for thee the stately arch,
    Vineyards encircle thee with garlands gay,
    And fleets attend thy progress to the sea !

THE THREE SILENCES OF MOLINOS.

TO JOHN GREENLEAF WHITTIER.

THREE Silences there are : the first of speech,
    The second of desire, the third of thought ;
    This is the lore a Spanish monk, distraught
    With dreams and visions, was the first to teach.

These Silences, commingling each with each,
   Made up the perfect Silence, that he sought
   And prayed for, and wherein at times he caught
   Mysterious sounds from realms beyond our reach.
O thou, whose daily life anticipates
   The life to come, and in whose thought and word
   The spiritual world preponderates,
Hermit of Amesbury! thou too hast heard
   Voices and melodies from beyond the gates,
   And speakest only when thy soul is stirred!

THE TWO RIVERS.

I.

SLOWLY the hour-hand of the clock moves round;
   So slowly that no human eye hath power
   To see it move! Slowly in shine or shower
   The painted ship above it, homeward bound,
Sails, but seems motionless, as if aground;
   Yet both arrive at last; and in his tower
   The slumbrous watchman wakes and strikes the hour,
   A mellow, measured, melancholy sound.
Midnight! the outpost of advancing day!
   The frontier town and citadel of night!
   The watershed of Time, from which the streams
Of Yesterday and To-morrow take their way,
   One to the land of promise and of light,
   One to the land of darkness and of dreams!

II.

O River of Yesterday, with current swift
   Through chasms descending, and soon lost to sight,
   I do not care to follow in their flight
   The faded leaves, that on thy bosom drift!
O River of To-morrow, I uplift
   Mine eyes, and thee I follow, as the night
   Wanes into morning, and the dawning light
   Broadens, and all the shadows fade and shift!
I follow, follow, where thy waters run
   Through unfrequented, unfamiliar fields,
   Fragrant with flowers and musical with song;
Still follow, follow; sure to meet the sun,
   And confident, that what the future yields
   Will be the right, unless myself be wrong.

III.

Yet not in vain, O River of Yesterday,
   Through chasms of darkness to the deep descending,

I heard thee sobbing in the rain, and blending
  Thy voice with other voices far away.
I called to thee, and yet thou wouldst not stay,
  But turbulent, and with thyself contending,
  And torrent-like thy force on pebbles spending,
  Thou wouldst not listen to a poet's lay.
Thoughts, like a loud and sudden rush of wings,
  Regrets and recollections of things past,
  With hints and prophecies of things to be,
And inspirations, which, could they be things,
  And stay with us, and we could hold them fast,
  Were our good angels,—these I owe to thee.

IV.

And thou, O River of To-morrow, flowing
  Between thy narrow adamantine walls,
  But beautiful, and white with waterfalls,
  And wreaths of mist, like hands the pathway showing;
I hear the trumpets of the morning blowing,
  I hear thy mighty voice, that calls and calls,
  And see, as Ossian saw in Morven's halls,
  Mysterious phantoms, coming, beckoning, going!
It is the mystery of the unknown
  That fascinates us; we are children still,
  Wayward and wistful; with one hand we cling
To the familiar things we call our own,
  And with the other, resolute of will,
  Grope in the dark for what the day will bring.

BOSTON.

St. Botolph's Town! Hither across the plains
  And fens of Lincolnshire, in garb austere,
  There came a Saxon monk, and founded here
  A Priory, pillaged by marauding Danes,
So that thereof no vestige now remains;
  Only a name, that, spoken loud and clear,
  And echoed in another hemisphere,
  Survives the sculptured walls and painted panes.
St. Botolph's Town! Far over leagues of land
  And leagues of sea looks forth its noble tower,
  And far around the chiming bells are heard;
So may that sacred name for ever stand
  A landmark, and a symbol of the power,
  That lies concentred in a single word.

ST. JOHN'S, CAMBRIDGE.

I STAND beneath the tree, whose branches shade
   Thy western window, Chapel of St. John!
   And hear its leaves repeat their benison
   On him, whose hand thy stones memorial laid;
Then I remember one of whom was said
   In the world's darkest hour, 'Behold thy son!'
   And see him living still, and wandering on
   And waiting for the advent long delayed.
Not only tongues of the apostles teach
   Lessons of love and light, but these expanding
   And sheltering boughs with all their leaves implore,
And say in language clear as human speech,
   'The peace of God, that passeth understanding,
   Be and abide with you for evermore!'

MOODS.

O THAT a Song would sing itself to me
   Out of the heart of Nature, or the heart
   Of man, the child of Nature, not of Art,
   Fresh as the morning, salt as the salt sea,
With just enough of bitterness to be
   A medicine to this sluggish mood, and start
   The life-blood in my veins, and so impart
   Healing and help in this dull lethargy!
Alas! not always doth the breath of song
   Breathe on us. It is like the wind that bloweth
   At its own will, not ours, nor tarries long;
We hear the sound thereof, but no man knoweth
   From whence it comes, so sudden and swift and strong,
   Nor whither in its wayward course it goeth.

WOODSTOCK PARK.

HERE in a little rustic hermitage
   Alfred the Saxon King, Alfred the Great,
   Postponed the cares of kingcraft to translate
   The Consolations of the Roman sage.
Here Geoffrey Chaucer in his ripe old age
   Wrote the unrivalled Tales, which soon or late
   The venturous hand that strives to imitate
   Vanquished must fall on the unfinished page.
Two kings were they, who ruled by right divine,
   And both supreme; one in the realm of Truth,
   One in the realm of Fiction and of Song.

What prince hereditary of their line,
   Uprising in the strength and flush of youth,
   Their glory shall inherit and prolong ?

THE FOUR PRINCESSES AT WILNA.

A PHOTOGRAPH.

SWEET faces, that from pictured casements lean
   As from a castle window, looking down
   On some gay pageant passing through a town,
   Yourselves the fairest figures in the scene ;
With what a gentle grace, with what serene
   Unconsciousness ye wear the triple crown
   Of youth and beauty and the fair renown
   Of a great name, that ne'er hath tarnished been !
From your soft eyes, so innocent and sweet,
   Four spirits, sweet and innocent as they,
   Gaze on the world below, the sky above ;
Hark ! there is some one singing in the street ;
   'Faith, Hope, and Love ! these three,' he seems to say ;
   'These three ; and greatest of the three is Love.'

HOLIDAYS.

THE holiest of all holidays are those
   Kept by ourselves in silence and apart ;
   The secret anniversaries of the heart,
   When the full river of feeling overflows ;—
The happy days unclouded to their close ;
   The sudden joys that out of darkness start
   As flames from ashes ; swift desires that dart
   Like swallows singing down each wind that blows !
White as the gleam of a receding sail,
   White as a cloud that floats and fades in air,
   White as the whitest lily on a stream,
These tender memories are ;—a Fairy Tale
   Of some enchanted land we know not where,
   But lovely as a landscape in a dream.

WAPENTAKE.

TO ALFRED TENNYSON.

POET ! I come to touch thy lance with mine ;
   Not as a knight, who on the listed field
   Of tourney touched his adversary's shield
   In token of defiance, but in sign

Of homage to the mastery, which is thine,
  In English song; nor will I keep concealed,
  And voiceless as a rivulet frost-congealed,
  My admiration for thy verse divine.
Not of the howling dervishes of song,
  Who craze the brain with their delirious dance,
  Art thou, O sweet historian of the heart!
Therefore to thee the laurel-leaves belong,
  To thee our love and our allegiance,
  For thy allegiance to the poet's art.

THE BROKEN OAR.

ONCE upon Iceland's solitary strand
  A poet wandered with his book and pen,
  Seeking some final word, some sweet Amen,
  Wherewith to close the volume in his hand.
The billows rolled and plunged upon the sand,
  The circling sea-gulls swept beyond his ken,
  And from the parting cloud-rack now and then
  Flashed the red sunset over sea and land.
Then by the billows at his feet was tossed
  A broken oar; and carved thereon he read,
  'Oft was I weary, when I toiled at thee';
And like a man, who findeth what was lost,
  He wrote the words, then lifted up his head,
  And flung his useless pen into the sea.

Art thou, O sweet historian of the heart!
Therefore to thee the laurel-leaves belong,
To thee our love and our allegiance,

Kéramos.

1878.

TURN, turn, my wheel! Turn
  round and round
Without a pause, without a sound:
  So spins the flying world away!
This clay, well mixed with marl
  and sand,
Follows the motion of my hand;
For some must follow, and some
  command,
  Though all are made of clay!

Thus sang the Potter at his task
Beneath the blossoming hawthorn-
  tree,
While o'er his features, like a mask,
The quilted sunshine and leaf-shade
Moved, as the boughs above him
  swayed,
And clothed him, till he seemed
  to be
A figure woven in tapestry,
So sumptuously was he arrayed
In that magnificent attire
Of sable tissue flaked with fire.
Like a magician he appeared,
A conjurer without book or beard;
And while he plied his magic art—
For it was magical to me—
I stood in silence and apart,
And wondered more and more to
  see
That shapeless, lifeless mass of clay
Rise up to meet the master's hand,
And now contract and now expand,
And even his slightest touch obey;
While ever in a thoughtful mood
He sang his ditty, and at times
Whistled a tune between the rhymes,
As a melodious interlude.

Turn, turn, my wheel! All things
  must change
To something new, to something
  strange;
  Nothing that is can pause or
    stay;
The moon will wax, the moon will
  wane,
The mist and cloud will turn to
  rain,
The rain to mist and cloud again,
  To-morrow be to-day.

Thus still the Potter sang, and still,
By some unconscious act of will,
The melody and even the words
Were intermingled with my thought,
As bits of coloured thread are
  caught
And woven into nests of birds.
And thus to regions far remote,
Beyond the ocean's vast expanse,
This wizard in the motley coat
Transported me on wings of song,
And by the northern shores of
  France
Bore me with restless speed along.

What land is this that seems to be
A mingling of the land and sea?
This land of sluices, dikes, and
  dunes?
This water-net, that tessellates
The landscape? this unending
  maze
Of gardens, through whose latticed
  gates
The imprisoned pinks and tulips
  gaze;

Where in long summer afternoons
The sunshine, softened by the haze,
Comes streaming down as through
    a screen ;
Where over fields and pastures
    green
The painted ships float high in air,
And over all and everywhere
The sails of windmills sink and soar
Like wings of sea-gulls on the
    shore ?

What land is this ? Yon pretty
    town
Is Delft, with all its wares dis-
    played ;
The pride, the market-place, the
    crown
And centre of the Potter's trade.
See ! every house and room is bright
With glimmers of reflected light
From plates that on the dresser
    shine ;
Flagons to foam with Flemish beer,
Or sparkle with the Rhenish wine,
And pilgrim flasks with fleurs-de-
    lis,
And ships upon a rolling sea,
And tankards pewter topped, and
    queer
With comic mask and musketeer !
Each hospitable chimney smiles
A welcome from its painted tiles ;
The parlour walls, the chamber
    floors,
The stairways and the corridors,
The borders of the garden walks,
Are beautiful with fadeless flowers,
That never droop in winds or
    showers,
And never wither on their stalks.

Turn, turn, my wheel ! All life is
    brief ;
What now is bud will soon be leaf,
    What now is leaf will soon
    decay ;
The wind blows east, the wind blows
    west ;

The blue eggs in the robin's nest
Will soon have wings and beak and
    breast,
    And flutter and fly away.

Now southward through the air I
    glide,
The song my only pursuivant,
And see across the landscape wide
The blue Charente, upon whose tide
The belfries and the spires of
    Saintes
Ripple and rock from side to side,
As, when an earthquake rends its
    walls,
A crumbling city reels and falls.

Who is it in the suburbs here,
This Potter, working with such
    cheer,
In this mean house, this mean
    attire,
His manly features bronzed with
    fire,
Whose figulines and rustic wares
Scarce find him bread from day to
    day ?
This madman, as the people say,
Who breaks his tables and his chairs
To feed his furnace fires, nor cares
Who goes unfed if they are fed,
Nor who may live if they are dead ?
This alchemist with hollow cheeks
And sunken, searching eyes, who
    seeks,
By mingled earths and ores com-
    bined
With potency of fire, to find
Some new enamel, hard and bright,
His dream, his passion, his delight ?

O Palissy ! within thy breast
Burned the hot fever of unrest ;
Thine was the prophet's vision, thine
The exultation, the divine
Insanity of noble minds,
That never falters nor abates,
But labours and endures and waits,
Till all that it foresees it finds,
Or what it cannot find creates !

Turn, turn, my wheel! This
earthen jar
A touch can make, a touch can mar ;
And shall it to the Potter say,
What makest thou ? Thou hast no
hand ?
As men who think to understand
A world by their Creator planned,
Who wiser is than they.

Still guided by the dreamy song,
As in a trance I float along
Above the Pyrenean chain,
Above the fields and farms of Spain,
Above the bright Majorcan isle,
That lends its softened name to
art,—
A spot, a dot upon the chart,
Whose little towns, red-roofed with
tile,
Are ruby-lustred with the light
Of blazing furnaces by night,
And crowned by day with wreaths
of smoke.
Then eastward, wafted in my flight
On my enchanter's magic cloak,
I sail across the Tyrrhene Sea
Into the land of Italy,
And o'er the windy Apennines,
Mantled and musical with pines.

The palaces, the princely halls,
The doors of houses and the walls
Of churches and of belfry towers,
Cloister and castle, street and mart,
Are garlanded and gay with flowers
That blossom in the fields of art.
Here Gubbio's workshops gleam
and glow
With brilliant, iridescent dyes,
The dazzling whiteness of the snow,
The cobalt blue of summer skies ;
And vase and scutcheon, cup and
plate,
In perfect finish emulate
Faenza, Florence, Pesaro.

Forth from Urbino's gate there came
A youth with the angelic name
Of Raphael, in form and face

Himself angelic, and divine
In arts of colour and design.
From him Francesco Xanto caught
Something of his transcendent
grace,
And into fictile fabrics wrought
Suggestions of the master's thought.
Nor less Maestro Giorgio shines
With madre-perl and golden lines
Of arabesques, and interweaves
His birds and fruits and flowers and
leaves
About some landscape, shaded
brown,
With olive tints on rock and town.
Behold this cup within whose bowl,
Upon a ground of deepest blue
With yellow-lustred stars o'erlaid,
Colours of every tint and hue
Mingle in one harmonious whole !
With large blue eyes and steadfast
gaze,
Her yellow hair in net and braid,
Necklace and earrings all ablaze
With golden lustre o'er the glaze,
A woman's portrait ; on the scroll,
Cana, the Beautiful ! A name
Forgotten save for such brief fame
As this memorial can bestow,—
A gift some lover long ago
Gave with his heart to this fair
dame.

A nobler title to renown
Is thine, O pleasant Tuscan town,
Seated beside the Arno's stream ;
For Lucca della Robbia there
Created forms so wondrous fair,
They made thy sovereignty su-
preme.
These choristers with lips of stone,
Whose music is not heard, but seen,
Still chant, as from their organ-
screen,
Their Maker's praise ; nor these
alone,
But the more fragile forms of clay,
Hardly less beautiful than they,

726

These saints and angels that adorn
The walls of hospitals, and tell
The story of good deeds so well
That poverty seems less forlorn,
And life more like a holiday.

Here in this old neglected church,
That long eludes the traveller's
    search,
Lies the dead bishop on his tomb ;
Earth upon earth he slumbering lies,
Life-like and death-like in the
    gloom ;
Garlands of fruit and flowers in
    bloom
And foliage deck his resting place ;
A shadow in the sightless eyes,
A pallor on the patient face,
Made perfect by the furnace heat ;
All earthly passions and desires
Burnt out by purgatorial fires ;
Seeming to say, 'Our years are fleet,
And to the weary death is sweet.'

But the most wonderful of all
The ornaments on tomb or wall
That grace the fair Ausonian shores
Are those the faithful earth restores,
Near some Apulian town concealed,
In vineyard or in harvest field,—
Vases and urns and bas-reliefs,
Memorials of forgotten griefs,
Or records of heroic deeds
Of demigods and mighty chiefs :
Figures that almost move and speak,
And, buried amid mould and weeds,
Still in their attitudes attest
The presence of the graceful
    Greek,—
Achilles in his armour dressed,
Alcides with the Cretan bull,
And Aphrodite with her boy,
Or lovely Helena of Troy,
Still living and still beautiful.

Turn, turn, my wheel ! 'Tis Na-
    ture's plan
The child should grow into the man,
    The man grow wrinkled, old, and
    gray ;

In youth the heart exults and sings,
    The pulses leap, the feet have
    wings ;
In age the cricket chirps, and brings
    The harvest home of day.

And now the winds that southward
    blow,
And cool the hot Sicilian isle,
Bear me away. I see below
The long line of the Libyan Nile,
Flooding and feeding the parched
    land
With annual ebb and overflow,
A fallen palm whose branches lie
Beneath the Abyssinian sky,
Whose roots are in Egyptian sands.
On either bank huge water-wheels,
Belted with jars and dripping weeds,
Send forth their melancholy moans,
As if, in their gray mantles hid,
Dead anchorites of the Thebaid
Knelt on the shore and told their
    beads,
Beating their breasts with loud ap-
    peals
And penitential tears and groans.

This city, walled and thickly set
With glittering mosque and mina-
    ret,
Is Cairo, in whose gay bazaars
The dreaming traveller first inhales
The perfume of Arabian gales,
And sees the fabulous earthen jars,
Huge as were those wherein the
    maid
Morgiana found the Forty Thieves
Concealed in midnight ambuscade ;
And seeing, more than half believes
The fascinating tales that run
Through all the Thousand Nights
    and One,
Told by the fair Scheherezade.

More strange and wonderful than
    these
Are the Egyptian deities,
Ammon, and Emeth, and the grand

Osiris, holding in his hand
The lotus; Isis, crowned and veiled;
The sacred Ibis, and the Sphinx;
Bracelets with blue enamelled links;
The Scarabee in emerald mailed,
Or spreading wide his funeral
    wings;
Lamps that perchance their night-
    watch kept
O'er Cleopatra while she slept,—
All plundered from the tombs of
    kings.

Turn, turn, my wheel! The human
    race
Of every tongue, of every place,
    Caucasian, Coptic, or Malay,
All that inhabit this great earth,
Whatever be their rank or worth,
Are kindred and allied by birth,
    And made of the same clay.

O'er desert sands, o'er gulf and bay,
O'er Ganges and o'er Himalay,
Bird-like I fly, and flying sing,
To flowery kingdoms of Cathay,
And bird-like poise on balanced
    wing
Above the town of King-te-tching,
A burning town, or seeming so,—
Three thousand furnaces that glow
Incessantly, and fill the air
With smoke uprising, gyre on gyre,
And painted by the lurid glare,
Of jets and flashes of red fire.

As leaves that in the autumn fall,
Spotted and veined with various
    hues,
Are swept along the avenues,
And lie in heaps by hedge and wall,
So from this grove of chimneys
    whirled
To all the markets of the world,
These porcelain leaves are wafted
    on,—
Light yellow leaves with spots and
    stains
Of violet and of crimson dye,

Or tender azure of a sky
Just washed by gentle April rains,
And beautiful with celadon.

Nor less the coarser household
    wares,—
The willow pattern, that we knew
In childhood, with its bridge of blue
Leading to unknown thoroughfares;
The solitary man who stares
At the white river flowing through
Its arches, the fantastic trees
And wild perspective of the view;
And intermingled among these
The tiles that in our nurseries
Filled us with wonder and delight,
Or haunted us in dreams at night.

And yonder by Nankin, behold!
The Tower of Porcelain, strange
    and old,
Uplifting to the astonished skies
Its ninefold painted balconies,
With balustrades of twining leaves,
And roofs of tile, beneath whose
    eaves
Hang porcelain bells that all the time
Ring with a soft, melodious chime;
While the whole fabric is ablaze
With varied tints, all fused in one
Great mass of colour, like a maze
Of flowers illumined by the sun.

Turn, turn, my wheel!   What is
    begun
At daybreak must at dark be done,
    To-morrow will be another day;
To-morrow the hot furnace flame
Will search the heart and try the
    frame,
And stamp with honour or with
    shame
    These vessels made of clay.

Cradled and rocked in Eastern seas,
The islands of the Japanese
Beneath me lie; o'er lake and plain
The stork, the heron, and the crane
Through the clear realms of azure
    drift;

And on the hillside I can see
The villages of Imari,
Whose thronged and flaming work-
  shops lift
Their twisted columns of smoke on
  high,
Cloud cloisters that in ruins lie,
With sunshine streaming through
  each rift,
And broken arches of blue sky.

All the bright flowers that fill the
  land,
Ripple of waves on rock or sand,
The snow on Fusiyama's cone,
The midnight heaven so thickly
  sown
With constellations of bright stars,
The leaves that rustle, the reeds
  that make
A whisper by each stream and lake,
The saffron dawn, the sunset red,
Are painted on these lovely jars ;
Again the skylark sings, again
The stork, the heron, and the crane
Float through the azure overhead,
The counterfeit and counterpart
Of Nature reproduced in Art.

Art is the child of Nature ; yes,
Her darling child, in whom we trace
The features of the mother's face,
Her aspect and her attitude,
All her majestic loveliness
Chastened and softened and sub-
  dued
Into a more attractive grace,
And with a human sense imbued.

He is the greatest artist, then,
Whether of pencil or of pen,
Who follows Nature. Never man,
As artist or as artisan,
Pursuing his own fantasies,
Can touch the human heart, or
  please,
Or satisfy our nobler needs,
As he who sets his willing feet
In Nature's footprints, light and
  fleet,
And follows fearless where she leads.

Thus mused I on that morn in May,
Wrapped in my visions like the Seer,
Whose eyes behold not what is near,
But only what is far away,
When, suddenly sounding peal on
  peal,
The church-bell from the neighbour-
  ing town
Proclaimed the welcome hour of
  noon.
The Potter heard, and stopped his
  wheel,
His apron on the grass threw down,
Whistled his quiet little tune,
Not overloud nor overlong,
And ended thus his simple song:

Stop, stop, my wheel ! Too soon,
  too soon
The noon will be the afternoon,
  Too soon to-day be yesterday;
Behind us in our path we cast
The broken potsherds of the past,
And all are ground to dust at last,
  And trodden into clay !

Translations.

CANTOS FROM DANTE'S PARADISO.

CANTO XXIII.

EVEN as a bird, 'mid the beloved leaves,
  Quiet upon the nest of her sweet brood
  Throughout the night, that hideth all things from us,
Who, that she may behold their longed-for looks
  And find the food wherewith to nourish them,
  In which, to her, grave labours grateful are,
Anticipates the time on open spray,
  And with an ardent longing waits the sun,
  Gazing intent, as soon as breaks the dawn :
Even thus my Lady standing was, erect
  And vigilant, turned round towards the zone
  Underneath which the sun displays less haste ;
So that beholding her distraught and wistful,
  Such I became as he is who desiring
  For something yearns, and hoping is appeased.

But brief the space from one When to the other ;
  Of my awaiting, say I, and the seeing
  The welkin grow resplendent more and more.
And Beatrice exclaimed : ' Behold the hosts
  Of Christ's triumphal march, and all the fruit
  Harvested by the rolling of these spheres ! '
It seemed to me her face was all aflame ;
  And eyes she had so full of ecstasy
  That I must needs pass on without describing.
As when in nights serene of the full moon
  Smiles Trivia among the nymphs eternal
  Who paint the firmament through all its gulfs,
Saw I, above the myriads of lamps,
  A Sun that one and all of them enkindled,
  E'en as our own doth the supernal sights,
And through the living light transparent shone
  The lucent substance so intensely clear
  Into my sight that I sustained it not.

O Beatrice, thou gentle guide and
dear !
  To me she said : ' What overmasters thee
  A virtue is from which naught
  shields itself.
There are the wisdom and the
omnipotence
  That oped the thoroughfares
  'twixt heaven and earth,
  For which there erst had been
  so long a yearning.'
As fire from out a cloud unlocks
itself,
  Dilating so it finds not room
  therein,
  And down, against its nature,
  falls to earth,
So did my mind, among those
aliments
  Becoming larger, issue from it-
  self,
  And that which it became cannot
  remember.
' Open thine eyes, and look at what
  I am :
  Thou hast beheld such things,
  that strong enough
  Hast thou become to tolerate my
  smile.'
I was as one who still retains the
feeling
  Of a forgotten vision, and en-
  deavours
  In vain to bring it back into his
  mind,
When I this invitation heard, de-
serving
  Of so much gratitude, it never
  fades
  Out of the book that chronicles
  the past.
If at this moment sounded all the
tongues
  That Polyhymnia and her sisters
  made
  Most lubrical with their delicious
  milk,

To aid me, to a thousandth of the
truth
  It would not reach, singing the
  holy smile,
  And how the holy aspect it
  illumed.
And therefore, representing Paradise,
  The sacred poem must perforce
  leap over,
  Even as a man who finds his
  way cut off ;
But whoso thinketh of the pon-
derous theme,
  And of the mortal shoulder laden
  with it,
  Should blame it not, if under this
  it tremble.
It is no passage for a little boat,
  This which goes cleaving the
  audacious prow,
  Nor for a pilot who would spare
  himself.
' Why doth my face so much ena-
  mour thee,
  That to the garden fair thou
  turnest not,
  Which under the rays of Christ
  is blossoming ?
There is the Rose in which the
Word Divine
  Became incarnate ; there the
  lilies are
  By whose perfume the good way
  was discovered.'
Thus Beatrice ; and I, who to her
counsels
  Was wholly ready, once again
  betook me
  Unto the battle of the feeble brows.
As in the sunshine, that unsullied
streams
  Through fractured cloud, ere now
  a meadow of flowers
  Mine eyes with shadow covered
  o'er have seen,
So troops of splendours manifold
I saw

731

Illumined from above with burning rays,
Beholding not the source of the
effulgence.
O power benignant that does so
imprint them !
Thou didst exalt thyself to give
more scope
There to mine eyes, that were
not strong enough.
The name of that fair flower I e'er
invoke
Morning and evening utterly en-
thralled
My soul to gaze upon the greater
fire.
And when in both mine eyes de-
picted were
The glory and greatness of the
living star
Which there excelleth, as it here
excelled,
Athwart the heavens a little torch
descended
Formed in a circle like a coronal,
And cinctured it, and whirled
itself about it.
Whatever melody most sweetly
soundeth
On earth, and to itself most
draws the soul,
Would seem a cloud that, rent
asunder, thunders,
Compared unto the sounding of
that lyre
Wherewith was crowned the
sapphire beautiful,
Which gives the clearest heaven
its sapphire hue.
'I am Angelic Love, that circle round
The joy sublime which breathes
from out the womb
That was the hostelry of our
Desire ;
And I shall circle, Lady of Heaven,
while
Thou followest thy Son, and
mak'st diviner

The sphere supreme, because
thou enterest there. '
Thus did the circulated melody
Seal itself up ; and all the other
lights
Were making to resound the
name of Mary.
The regal mantle of the volumes all
Of that world, which most fervid
is and living
With breath of God and with
his works and ways,
Extended over us its inner border,
So very distant, that the sem-
blance of it
There where I was not yet
appeared to me.
Therefore mine eyes did not possess
the power
Of following the incoronated
flame,
Which mounted upward near to
its own seed.
And as a little child, that towards
its mother
Stretches its arms, when it the
milk has taken,
Through impulse kindled into
outward flame,
Each of those gleams of whiteness
upward reached
So with its summit, that the deep
affection
They had for Mary was revealed
to me.
Thereafter they remained there in
my sight,
Regina coeli singing with such
sweetness,
That ne'er from me has the
delight departed.
O, what exuberance is garnered up
Within those richest coffers, which
had been
Good husbandmen for sowing
here below !
There they enjoy and live upon the
treasure

Which was acquired while weeping in the exile
Of Babylon, wherein the gold was left.
There triumpheth, beneath the exalted Son
Of God and Mary, in his victory,
Both with the ancient council and the new,
He who doth keep the keys of such a glory.

CANTO XXIV.

'O COMPANY elect to the great supper
Of the lamb benedight, who feedeth you,
So that for ever full is your desire,
If by the grace of God this man foretaste
Something of that which falleth from your table,
Or ever death prescribe to him the time,
Direct your mind to his immense desire,
And him somewhat bedew; ye drinking are
For ever at the fount whence comes his thought.'
Thus Beatrice; and those souls beatified
Transformed themselves to spheres on steadfast poles,
Flaming intensely in the guise of comets.
And as the wheels in works of horologes
Revolve so that the first to a beholder
Motionless seems, and the last one to fly,
So in like manner did those carols, dancing
In different measure, of their affluence
Give me the gauge, as they were swift or slow.

From that one which I noted of most beauty
Beheld I issue forth a fire so happy
That none it left there of a greater brightness ;
And around Beatrice three several times
It whirled itself with so divine a song,
My fantasy repeats it not to me ;
Therefore the pen skips, and I write it not,
Since our imagination for such folds,
Much more our speech, is of a tint too glaring.
'O holy sister mine, who us implorest
With such devotion, by thine ardent love
Thou dost unbind me from that beautiful sphere !'
Thereafter, having stopped, the blessed fire
Unto my Lady did direct its breath,
Which spake in fashion, as I here have said.
And she : 'O light eterne of the great man
To whom our Lord delivered up the keys
He carried down of this miraculous joy,
This one examine on points light and grave,
As good beseemeth thee, about the Faith
By means of which thou on the sea didst walk.
If he love well, and hope well, and believe,
From thee 'tis hid not ; for thou hast thy sight
There where depicted everything is seen.
But since this kingdom has made citizens

733

By means of the true Faith, to
glorify it
'Tis well he have the chance to
speak thereof.'
As baccalaureate arms himself, and
speaks not
Until the master doth propose
the question,
To argue it, and not to terminate
it,
So did I arm myself with every
reason,
While she was speaking, that I
might be ready
For such a questioner and such
profession.
'Say, thou good Christian; mani-
fest thyself;
What is the Faith?' Whereat I
raised my brow
Unto that light wherefrom was
this breathed forth.
Then turned I round to Beatrice,
and she
Prompt signals made to me that
I should pour
The water forth from my internal
fountain.
'May grace, that suffers me to
make confession,'
Began I, 'to the great cen-
turion,
Cause my conceptions all to be
explicit!'
And I continued : 'As the truthful
pen,
Father, of thy dear brother wrote
of it,
Who put with thee Rome into
the good way,
Faith is the substance of the things
we hope for,
And evidence of those that are
not seen ;
And this appears to me its
quiddity.'
Then heard I : 'Very rightly thou
perceivest,

If well thou understandest why
he placed it
With substances and then with
evidences.'
And I thereafterward : 'The things
profound,
That here vouchsafe to me their
apparition,
Unto all eyes below are so con-
cealed,
That they exist there only in belief,
Upon the which is founded the
high hope,
And hence it has the nature of a
substance.
And it behoveth us from this belief
To reason without having other
sight,
And hence it has the nature of
evidence.'
Then heard I : 'If whatever is ac-
quired
Below by doctrine were thus
understood,
No sophist's subtlety would there
find place.'
Thus was breathed forth from that
enkindled love ;
Then added : 'Very well has
been gone over
Already of this coin the alloy and
weight ;
But tell me if thou hast it in thy
purse?'
And I : 'Yes, both so shining
and so round,
That in its stamp there is no
peradventure.'
Thereafter issued from the light
profound
That there resplendent was : 'This
precious jewel,
Upon the which is every virtue
founded,
Whence hadst thou it?' And I :
'The large outpouring
Of Holy Spirit, which has been
diffused

Upon the ancient parchments and the new,
A syllogism is, which proved it to me
With such acuteness, that, compared therewith,
All demonstration seems to me obtuse.'
And then I heard : ' The ancient and the new
Postulates, that to thee are so conclusive,
Why dost thou take them for the word divine ? '
And I : ' The proofs which show the truth to me,
Are the works subsequent, whereunto Nature
Ne'er heated iron yet, nor anvil beat.'
'Twas answered me : ' Say, who assureth thee
That those works ever were ? the thing itself
That must be proved, nought else to thee affirms it.'
' Were the world to Christianity converted,'
I said, ' withouten miracles, this one
Is such, the real are not its hundredth part ;
Because that poor and fasting thou didst enter
Into the field to sow there the good plant,
Which was a vine and has become a thorn ! '
This being finished, the high, holy Court
Resounded through the spheres, ' One God we praise ! '
In melody that there above is chanted.
And then that Baron, who from branch to branch,
Examining, had thus conducted me,

Till the extremest leaves we were approaching,
Again began : ' The Grace that dallying
Plays with thine intellect thy mouth has opened,
Up to this point, as it should opened be,
So that I do approve what forth emerged ;
But now thou must express what thou believest,
And whence to thy belief it was presented.'
' O holy father, spirit who beholdest
What thou believedst so that thou o'ercamest,
Towards the sepulchre, more youthful feet,'
Began I, ' thou dost wish me in this place
The form to manifest of my prompt belief,
And likewise thou the cause thereof demandest.
And I respond : In one God I believe,
Sole and eterne, who moveth all the heavens
With love and with desire, himself unmoved ;
And of such faith not only have I proofs
Physical and metaphysical, but gives them
Likewise the truth that from this place rains down
Through Moses, through the Prophets and the Psalms,
Through the Evangel, and through you who wrote
After the fiery Spirit sanctified you ;
In Persons three eterne believe, and these
One essence I believe, so one and trine

They bear conjunction both with *sunt* and *est*.

With the profound condition, and divine

Which now I touch upon, doth stamp my mind

Ofttimes the doctrine evangelical.

This the beginning is, this is the spark

Which afterwards dilates to vivid flame,

And, like a star in heaven, is sparkling in me.

Even as a lord who hears what pleaseth him

His servant straight embraces, gratulating

For the good news as soon as he is silent;

So, giving me its benediction, singing,

Three times encircled me, when I was silent,

The apostolic light, at whose command

I spoken had, in speaking I so pleased him.

CANTO XXV.

If e'er it happen that the Poem Sacred,

To which both heaven and earth have set their hand,

So that it many a year hath made me lean,

O'ercome the cruelty that bars me out

From the fair sheepfold, where a lamb I slumbered,

An enemy to the wolves that war upon it,

With other voice forthwith, with other fleece,

Poet will I return, and at my font

Baptismal will I take the laurel crown;

Because into the Faith that maketh known

All souls to God there entered I, and then

Peter for her sake thus my brow encircled.

Thereafterward towards us moved a light

Out of that band whence issued the first-fruits

Which of his vicars Christ behind him left,

And then my Lady, full of ecstasy,

Said unto me: 'Look, look! behold the Baron

For whom below Galicia is frequented.'

In the same way as, when a dove alights

Near his companion, both of them pour forth,

Circling about and murmuring, their affection,

So one beheld I by the other grand,

Prince glorified to be with welcome greeted

Lauding the food that there above is eaten.

But when their gratulations were complete,

Silently *coram me* each one stood still,

So incandescent it o'ercame my sight.

Smiling thereafterwards, said Beatrice:

'Illustrious life, by whom the benefactions

Of our Basilica have been described,

Make Hope resound within this altitude;

Thou knowest as oft thou dost personify it

As Jesus to the three gave greater clearness.'—

'Lift up thy head, and make thyself assured;

For what comes hither from the mortal world
Must needs be ripened in our radiance.'
This comfort came to me from the second fire;
Wherefore mine eyes I lifted to the hills,
Which bent them down before with too great weight.
'Since, through his grace, our Emperor wills that thou
Shouldst find thee face to face, before thy death,
In the most secret chamber, with his Counts,
So that, the truth beholden of this court,
Hope, which below there rightfully enamours,
Thereby thou strengthen in thyself and others,
Say what it is, and how is flowering with it
Thy mind, and say from whence it came to thee.'
Thus did the second light again continue.
And the Compassionate, who piloted
The plumage of my wings in such high flight,
Did in reply anticipate me thus :
'No child whatever the Church Militant
Of greater hope possesses, as is written
In that Sun which irradiates all our band ;
Therefore it is conceded him from Egypt
To come into Jerusalem to see,
Or ever yet his warfare be completed.
The two remaining points, that not for knowledge
Have been demanded, but that he report

How much this virtue unto thee is pleasing,
To him I leave ; for hard he will not find them,
Nor of self-praise ; and let him answer them ;
And may the grace of God in this assist him !'
As a disciple, who his teacher follows,
Ready and willing, where he is expert,
That his proficiency may be displayed,
'Hope,' said I, 'is the certain expectation
Of future glory, which is the effect
Of grace divine and merit precedent.
From many stars this light comes unto me !
But he instilled it first into my heart
Who was chief singer unto the chief captain.
"*Sperent in te,*" in the high Theody
He sayeth, "those who know thy name ;" and who
Knoweth it not, if he my faith possess ?
Thou didst instil me, then, with his instilling
In the Epistle, so that I am full,
And upon others rain again your rain.'
While I was speaking, in the living bosom
Of that combustion quivered an effulgence,
Sudden and frequent, in the guise of lightning ;
Then breathed : ' The love wherewith I am inflamed
Towards the virtue still which followed me
Unto the palm and issue of the field,
Wills that I breathe to thee that thou delight

In her ; and grateful to me is thy
telling
Whatever things Hope promises
to thee.'
And I : ' The ancient Scriptures
and the new
The mark establish, and this
shows it me,
Of all the souls whom God hath
made his friends.
Isaiah saith, that each one gar-
mented
In his own land shall be with two-
fold garments,
And his own land is this delight-
ful life.
Thy brother, too, far more explicitly,
There where he treateth of the
robes of white,
This revelation manifests to us.'
And first, and near the ending of
these words,
'*Sperent in te*' from over us was
heard,
To which responsive answered all
the carols.
Thereafterward a light among them
brightened,
So that, if Cancer once such
crystal had,
Winter would have a month of
one sole day.
And as uprises, goes, and enters the
dance
A winsome maiden, only to do
honour
To the new bride, and not from any
failing,
Even thus did I behold the brightened splendour
Approach the two, who in a wheel
revolved
As was beseeming to their ardent
love.
Into the song and music there it
entered ;
And fixed on them my Lady kept
her look,

Even as a bride silent and motion-
less.
' This is the one who lay upon the
breast
Of him our Pelican ; and this
is he
To the great office from the cross
elected.'
My Lady thus ; but therefore none
the more
Did move her sight from its atten-
tive gaze
Before or afterward these words
of hers.
Even as a man who gazes, and en-
deavours
To see the eclipsing of the sun a
little,
And who, by seeing, sightless doth
become,
So I became before that latest fire,
While it was said, 'Why dost thou
daze thyself
To see a thing which here hath no
existence ?
Earth in the earth my body is, and
shall be
With all the others there, until
our number
With the eternal proposition
tallies.
With the two garments in the
blessed cloister
Are the two lights alone that have
ascended :
And this shalt thou take back
into your world.'
And at this utterance the flaming
circle
Grew quiet, with the dulcet inter-
mingling
Of sound that by the trinal breath
was made,
As to escape from danger or fatigue
The oars that erst were in the
water beaten
Are all suspended at a whistle's
sound.

Ah, how much in my mind was I
    disturbed,
    When I turned round to look on
    Beatrice,
    That her I could not see, although
    I was
Close at her side and in the Happy
    World !

—◆—

BEOWULF'S EXPEDITION TO HEORT.

FROM THE ANGLO-SAXON.

THUS then, much care-worn,
The son of Healfden
Sorrowed evermore,
Nor might the prudent hero
His woes avert.
The war was too hard,
Too loath and longsome,
That on the people came,
Dire wrath and grim,
Of night-woes the worst.
This from home heard
Higelac's Thane,
Good among the Goths,
Grendel's deeds.
He was of mankind
In might the strongest,
At that day
Of this life,
Noble and stalwart.
He bade him a sea-ship,
A goodly one, prepare.
Quoth he, the war-king,
Over the swan's road,
Seek he would
The mighty monarch,
Since he wanted men.
For him that journey
His prudent fellows
Straight made ready,
Those that loved him.
They excited their souls,
The omen they beheld.
Had the good-man
Of the Gothic people

Champions chosen,
Of those that keenest
He might find,
Some fifteen men.
The sea-wood sought he.
The warrior showed,
Sea-crafty man !
The landmarks,
And first went forth.
The ship was on the waves,
Boat under the cliffs.
The barons ready
To the prow mounted.
The streams they whirled
The sea against the sands.
The chieftains bore
On the naked breast
Bright ornaments,
War-gear, Goth-like.
The men shoved off,
Men on their willing way,
The bounden wood.
    Then went over the sea-waves,
Hurried by the wind,
The ship with foamy neck,
Most like a sea-fowl,
Till about one hour
Of the second day
The curved prow
Had passed onward
So that the sailors
The land saw,
The shore-cliffs shining,
Mountains steep,
And broad sea-noses.
Then was the sea-sailing
Of the earl at an end.
    Then up speedily
The Weather people
On the land went,
The sea-bark moored,
Their mail-sarks shook,
Their war-weeds.
God thanked they,
That to them the sea-journey
Easy had been.
    Then from the wall beheld
The warden of the Scyldings,

He who the sea-cliffs
Had in his keeping.
Bear o'er the balks
The bright shields,
The war-weapons speedily.
Him the doubt disturbed
In his mind's thought,
What these men might be.

Went then to the shore,
On his steed riding,
The Thane of Hrothgar.
Before the host he shook
His warden's staff in hand,
In measured words demanded :
'What men are ye,
War-gear wearing,
Host in harness,
Who thus the brown keel
Over the water-street
Leading come
Hither over the sea ?
I these boundaries
As shore-warden hold ;
That in the Land of the Danes
Nothing loathsome
With a ship-crew
Scathe us might. . . .
Ne'er saw I mightier
Earl upon earth
Than is your own,
Hero in harness.
Not seldom this warrior
Is in weapons distinguished ;
Never his beauty belies him,
His peerless countenance !
Now would I fain
Your origin know,
Ere ye forth
As false spies
Into the Land of the Danes
Farther fare.
Now, ye dwellers afar off !
Ye sailors of the sea !
Listen to my
One-fold thought.
Quickest is best
To make known
Whence your coming may be.'

THE SOUL'S COMPLAINT
AGAINST THE BODY.

FROM THE ANGLO-SAXON.

MUCH it behoveth
Each one of mortals,
That he his soul's journey
In himself ponder,
How deep it may be.
When Death cometh,
The bonds he breaketh
By which united
Were body and soul.

Long it is thenceforth
Ere the soul taketh
From God himself
Its woe or its weal ;
As in the world erst,
Even in its earth-vessel,
It wrought before.

The soul shall come
Wailing with loud voice,
After a sennight,
The soul, to find
The body
That it erst dwelt in ;—
Three hundred winters,
Unless ere that worketh
The eternal Lord,
The Almighty God,
The end of the world.

Crieth then, so care-worn,
With cold utterance,
And speaketh grimly,
The ghost to the dust :
'Dry dust ! thou dreary one !
How little didst thou labour for
me !
In the foulness of earth
Thou all wearest away
Like to the loam !
Little didst thou think
How thy soul's journey
Would be thereafter,
When from the body
It should be led forth.'

740

Then Turpin died in service of
    Charlon,
In battle great and eke great ori-
    son;
'Gainst Pagan host alway strong
    champion;—
God grant to him his holy benison!

—◦—

RONDEL.

FROM FROISSART.

LOVE, love, what wilt thou with
    this heart of mine?
  Naught see I fixed or sure in
    thee!
I do not know thee,—nor what
    deeds are thine:
Love, love, what wilt thou with
    this heart of mine?
  Naught see I fixed or sure in
    thee!

Shall I be mute, or vows with
    prayers combine?
  Ye who are blessed in loving,
    tell it me:
Love, love, what wilt thou with
    this heart of mine?
  Naught see I permanent or sure
    in thee!

—◦—

RONDEL.

FROM CHARLES D'ORLÉANS.

HENCE away, begone, begone,
  Carking care and melancholy!
  Think ye thus to govern me
All my life long, as ye have done?
  That shall ye not, I promise ye;
  Reason shall have the mastery.
So hence away, begone, begone,
  Carking care and melancholy!

If ever ye return this way,
  With your mournful company,
A curse be on ye, and the day
  That brings ye moping back to
    me!
Hence away, begone, I say,
  Carking care and melancholy!

—◦—

RENOUVEAU.

FROM THE FRENCH.

NOW Time throws off his cloak
    again
Of ermined frost, and cold and rain,
And clothes him in the embroidery
Of glittering sun and clear blue sky.

With beast and bird the forest rings,
Each in his jargon cries or sings;
And Time throws off his cloak again
Of ermined frost, and cold and rain.

River, and fount, and tinkling brook
  Wear in their dainty livery
  Drops of silver jewelry;
In new-made suit they merry look;
And Time throws off his cloak again
Of ermined frost, and cold and rain.

—◦—

THE NATURE OF LOVE.

FROM THE ITALIAN.

TO noble heart Love doth for
    shelter fly,
As seeks the bird the forest's leafy
    shade;
Love was not felt till noble heart
    beat high,
Nor before love the noble heart was
    made.
Soon as the sun's broad flame
Was formed, so soon the clear light
    filled the air;
Yet was not till he came:

So love springs up in noble breasts,
and there
Has its appointed space,
As heat in the bright flame finds its
allotted place.

Kindles in noble heart the fire of love,
As hidden virtue in the precious
stone :
This virtue comes not from the
stars above,
Till round it the ennobling sun has
shone ;
But when his powerful blaze
Has drawn forth what was vile, the
stars impart
Strange virtue in their rays :
And thus when Nature doth create
the heart
Noble and pure and high,
Like virtue from the star, love
comes from woman's eye.

FRIAR LUBIN.

FROM THE FRENCH.

To gallop off to town post-haste,
  So oft, the times I cannot tell ;
To do vile deed, nor feel disgraced,—
  Friar Lubin will do it well.
But a sober life to lead,
  To honour virtue, and pursue it,
That's a pious, Christian deed,—
  Friar Lubin cannot do it.

To mingle with a knowing smile,
  The goods of others with his own,
And leave you without cross or pile,
  Friar Lubin stands alone.
To say 'tis yours is all in vain,
  If once he lays his finger to it ;
For as to giving back again,
  Friar Lubin cannot do it.

With flattering words and gentle
tone,
  To woo and win some guileless
maid,

Cunning pander need you none,—
  Friar Lubin knows the trade.
Loud preacheth he sobriety,
  But as for water, doth eschew it ;
Your dog may drink it,—but not he ;
  Friar Lubin cannot do it.

ENVOI.

When an evil deed's to do,
Friar Lubin is stout and true ;
Glimmers a ray of goodness through
it,
Friar Lubin cannot do it.

BLESSED ARE THE DEAD.

FROM THE GERMAN.

O, HOW blest are ye whose toils
  are ended !
Who, through death, have unto God
  ascended !
Ye have arisen
From the cares which keep us still
  in prison.

We are still as in a dungeon living,
Still oppressed with sorrow and
  misgiving ;
Our undertakings
Are but toils, and troubles, and
  heart-breakings.

Ye, meanwhile, are in your chambers sleeping,
Quiet, and set free from all our
  weeping ;
No cross nor trial
Hinders your enjoyments with
  denial.

Christ has wiped away your tears
  for ever ;
Ye have that for which we still
  endeavour.
To you are chanted
Songs which yet no mortal ear
  have haunted.

Ah ! who would not, then, depart
with gladness,
To inherit heaven for earthly sad-
ness ?
Who here would languish
Longer in bewailing and in anguish ?

Come, O Christ, and loose the
chains that bind us !
Lead us forth, and cast this world
behind us !
With thee, the Anointed,
Finds the soul its joy and rest
appointed.

———+——

MY SECRET.

FROM THE FRENCH OF FELIX
ARVERS.

MY soul its secret hath, my life too
hath its mystery,
A love eternal in a moment's space
conceived ;

Hopeless the evil is, I have not told
its history,
And say who was the cause nor
knew it nor believed.
Alas ! I shall have passed close by
her unperceived,
For ever at her side and yet for
ever lonely,
I shall unto the end have made
life's journey, only
Daring to ask for naught and having naught received.

For her, though God hath made
her gentle and endearing,
She will go on her way distraught
and without hearing
These murmurings of love that
round her steps ascend,
Piously faithful still unto her austere duty,
Will say, when she shall read these
lines full of her beauty,
'Who can this woman be ? ' and
will not comprehend.

———+——

VIRGIL'S FIRST ECLOGUE.

MELIBŒUS.

TITYRUS, thou in the shade of a spreading beech-tree reclining,
Meditatest, with slender pipe, the Muse of the woodlands.
We our country's bounds and pleasant pastures relinquish,
We our country fly ; thou, Tityrus, stretched in the shadow,
Teachest the woods to resound with the name of the fair Amaryllis.

TITYRUS.

O Melibœus, a god for us this leisure created,
For he will be unto me a god for ever ; his altar
Oftentimes shall imbue a tender lamb from our sheepfolds.
He, my heifers to wander at large, and myself, as thou seest,
On my rustic reed to play what I will, hath permitted.

MELIBŒUS.

Truly I envy not, I marvel rather ; on all sides
In all the fields is such trouble. Behold, my goats I am driving,
Heartsick, further away ; this one scarce, Tityrus, lead I ;
For having here yeaned twins just now among the dense hazels,
Hope of the flock, ah me ! on the naked flint she hath left them.

Often this evil to me, if my mind had not been insensate,
Oak-trees stricken by heaven predicted, as now I remember;
Often the sinister crow from the hollow ilex predicted.
Nevertheless, who this god may be, O Tityrus, tell me.

TITYRUS.

O Meliboeus, the city that they call Rome, I imagined,
Foolish I! to be like this of ours, where often we shepherds
Wonted are to drive down of our ewes the delicate offspring.
Thus whelps like unto dogs had I known, and kids to their mothers,
Thus to compare great things with small had I been accustomed.
But this among other cities its head as far hath exalted
As the cypresses do among the lissome viburnums.

MELIBOEUS.

And what so great occasion of seeing Rome hath possessed thee?

TITYRUS.

Liberty, which, though late, looked upon me in my inertness,
After the time when my beard fell whiter from me in shaving,—
Yet she looked upon me, and came to me after a long while,
Since Amaryllis possesses and Galatea hath left me.
For I will even confess that while Galatea possessed me
Neither care of my flock nor hope of liberty was there.
Though from my wattled folds there went forth many a victim,
And the unctuous cheese was pressed for the city ungrateful,
Never did my right hand return home heavy with money.

MELIBOEUS.

I have wondered why sad thou invokest the gods, Amaryllis,
And for whom thou didst suffer the apples to hang on the branches!
Tityrus hence was absent! Thee, Tityrus, even the pine-trees,
Thee, the very fountains, the very copses were calling.

TITYRUS.

What could I do? No power had I to escape from my bondage,
Nor had I power elsewhere to recognise gods so propitious.
Here I beheld that youth, to whom each year, Meliboeus,
During twice six days ascends the smoke of our altars.
Here first gave he response to me soliciting favour :
'Feed as before your heifers, ye boys, and yoke up your bullocks.'

MELIBOEUS.

Fortunate old man ! So then thy fields will be left thee,
And large enough for thee, though naked stone and the marish
All thy pasture-lands with the dreggy rush may encompass.
No unaccustomed food thy gravid ewes shall endanger,
Nor of the neighbouring flock the dire contagion infect them.
Fortunate old man ! Here among familiar rivers,
And these sacred founts, shalt thou take the shadowy coolness.
On this side, a hedge along the neighbouring cross-road,

Where Hyblæan bees ever feed on the flower of the willow,
Often with gentle susurrus to fall asleep shall persuade thee.
Yonder, beneath the high rock, the pruner shall sing to the breezes,
Nor meanwhile shall thy heart's delight, the hoarse wood-pigeons,
Nor the turtle-dove cease to mourn from aerial elm-trees.

TITYRUS.

Therefore the agile stags shall sooner feed in the ether,
And the billows leave the fishes bare on the sea-shore,
Sooner, the border-lands of both overpassed, shall the exiled
Parthian drink of the Soane, or the German drink of the Tigris,
Than the face of him shall glide away from my bosom!

MELIBŒUS.

But we hence shall go, a part to the thirsty Africs,
Part to Scythia come, and the rapid Cretan Oaxes,
And to the Britons from all the universe utterly sundered.
Ah, shall I ever, a long time hence, the bounds of my country
And the roof of my lowly cottage covered with greensward
Seeing, with wonder behold,—my kingdoms, a handful of wheat-ears!
Shall an impious soldier possess these lands newly cultured,
And these fields of corn a barbarian? Lo, whither discord
Us wretched people have brought! for whom our fields we have planted!
Graft, Melibœus, thy pear-trees now, put in order thy vineyards.
Go, my goats, go hence, my flocks so happy aforetime.
Never again henceforth outstretched in my verdurous cavern
Shall I behold you afar from the bushy precipice hanging.
Songs no more shall I sing; not with me, ye goats, as your shepherd,
Shall ye browse on the bitter willow or blooming laburnum.

TITYRUS.

Nevertheless, this night together with me canst thou rest thee
Here on the verdant leaves; for us there are mellowing apples,
Chestnuts soft to the touch, and clouted cream in abundance;
And the high roofs now of the villages smoke in the distance,
And from the lofty mountains are falling larger the shadows.

——++——

OVID IN EXILE.

AT TOMIS, IN BESSARABIA, NEAR THE MOUTHS OF THE DANUBE.

TRISTIA, Book III, Elegy X.

SHOULD any one there in Rome remember Ovid the exile,
    And, without me, my name still in the city survive;

Tell him that under stars which never set in the ocean
    I am existing still, here in a barbarous land.

Fierce Sarmatians encompass me round, and the Bessi and Getae;
    Names how unworthy to be sung by a genius like mine!

Yet when the air is warm, intervening Ister defends us :
  He, as he flows, repels inroads of war with his waves.

But when the dismal winter reveals its hideous aspect,
  When all the earth becomes white with a marble-like frost ;

And when Boreas is loosed, and the snow hurled under Arcturus,
  Then these nations, in sooth, shudder and shiver with cold.

Deep lies the snow, and neither the sun nor the rain can dissolve it ;
  Boreas hardens it still, makes it for ever remain.

Hence, ere the first has melted away, another succeeds it,
  And two years it is wont, in many places, to lie.

And so great is the power of the North wind awakened, it levels
  Lofty towers with the ground, roofs uplifted bears off.

Wrapped in skins, and with trousers sewed, they contend with the weather,
  And their faces alone of the whole body are seen.

Often their tresses, when shaken, with pendent icicles tinkle,
  And their whitened beards shine with the gathering frost.

Wines consolidate stand, preserving the form of the vessels :
  No more draughts of wine,—pieces presented they drink.

Why should I tell you how all the rivers are frozen and solid,
  And from out of the lake frangible water is dug ?

Ister,—no narrower stream than the river that bears the papyrus,—
  Which through its many mouths mingles its waves with the deep ;

Ister, with hardening winds, congeals its cerulean waters,
  Under a roof of ice, winding its way to the sea.

There where ships have sailed, men go on foot ; and the billows,
  Solid made by the frost, hoof-beats of horses indent.

Over unwonted bridges, with water gliding beneath them,
  The Sarmatian steers drag their barbarian carts.

Scarcely shall I be believed ; yet when naught is gained by a falsehood,
  Absolute credence then should to a witness be given.

I have beheld the vast Black Sea of ice all compacted,
  And a slippery crust pressing its motionless tides.

'Tis not enough to have seen, I have trodden this indurate ocean ;
  Dry shod passed my foot over its uppermost wave.

If thou hadst had of old such a sea as this is, Leander !
  Then thy death had not been charged as a crime to the Strait.

Nor can the curvéd dolphins uplift themselves from the water;
  All their struggles to rise merciless winter prevents;

And though Boreas sound with roar of wings in commotion,
  In the blockaded gulf never a wave will there be;

And the ships will stand hemmed in by the frost, as in marble,
  Nor will the oar have power through the stiff waters to cleave.

Fast-bound in the ice have I seen the fishes adhering,
  Yet notwithstanding this some of them still were alive.

Hence, if the savage strength of omnipotent Boreas freezes
  Whether the salt-sea wave, whether the refluent stream,—

Straightway,—the Ister made level by arid blasts of the North-wind,—
  Comes the barbaric foe borne on his swift-footed steed;

Foe, that powerful made by his steed and his far-flying arrows,
  All the neighbouring land void of inhabitants makes.

Some take flight, and none being left to defend their possessions,
  Unprotected, their goods pillage and plunder become;

Cattle and creaking carts, the little wealth of the country,
  And what riches beside indigent peasants possess.

Some as captives are driven along, their hands bound behind them,
  Looking backward in vain toward their Lares and lands.

Others, transfixed with barbéd arrows, in agony perish,
  For the swift arrow-heads all have in poison been dipped.

What they cannot carry or lead away they demolish,
  And the hostile flames burn up the innocent cots.

Even when there is peace, the fear of war is impending;
  None, with the ploughshare pressed, furrows the soil any more.

Either this region sees, or fears a foe that it sees not,
  And the sluggish land slumbers in utter neglect.

No sweet grape lies hidden here in the shade of its vine-leaves,
  No fermenting must fills and o'erflows the deep vats.

Apples the region denies; nor would Acontius have found here
  Aught upon which to write words for his mistress to read.

Naked and barren plains without leaves or trees we behold here,—
  Places, alas! unto which no happy man would repair.

Since then this mighty orb lies open so wide upon all sides,
  Has this region been found only my prison to be?

TRISTIA, Book III, Elegy XII.

Now the zephyrs diminish the cold, and the year being ended,
    Winter Mæotian seems longer than ever before;

And the Ram that bore unsafely the burden of Helle,
    Now makes the hours of the day equal with those of the night.

Now the boys and the laughing girls the violet gather,
    Which the fields bring forth, nobody sowing the seed.

Now the meadows are blooming with flowers of various colours,
    And with untaught throats carol the garrulous birds.

Now the swallow, to shun the crime of her merciless mother,
    Under the rafters builds cradles and dear little homes;

And the blade that lay hid, covered up in the furrows of Ceres,
    Now from the tepid ground raises its delicate head.

Where there is ever a vine, the bud shoots forth from the tendrils,
    But from the Getic shore distant afar is the vine!

Where there is ever a tree, on the tree the branches are swelling,
    But from the Getic land distant afar is the tree!

Now it is holiday there in Rome, and to games in due order
    Give place the windy wars of the vociferous bar.

Now they are riding the horses; with light arms now they are playing,
    Now with the ball, and now round rolls the swift-flying hoop:

Now, when the young athlete with flowing oil is anointed,
    He in the Virgin's Fount bathes, overwearied, his limbs.

Thrives the stage; and applause, with voices at variance, thunders,
    And the Theatres three for the three Forums resound.

Four times happy is he, and times without number is happy,
    Who the city of Rome, uninterdicted, enjoys.

But all I see is the snow in the vernal sunshine dissolving,
    And the waters no more delved from the indurate lake.

Nor is the sea now frozen, nor as before o'er the Ister
    Comes the Sarmatian boor driving his stridulous cart.

Hitherward, nevertheless, some keels already are steering,
    And on this Pontic shore alien vessels will be.

Eagerly shall I run to the sailor, and, having saluted,
    Who he may be, I shall ask; wherefore and whence he hath come.

Strange indeed will it be, if he come not from regions adjacent,
    And incautious unless ploughing the neighbouring sea.

Rarely a mariner over the deep from Italy passes,
  Rarely he comes to these shores, wholly of harbours devoid.

Whether he knoweth Greek, or whether in Latin he speaketh,
  Surely on this account he the more welcome will be.

Also perchance from the mouth of the Strait and the waters Propontic,
  Unto the steady South-wind, some one is spreading his sails.

Whosoever he is, the news he can faithfully tell me,
  Which may become a part and an approach to the truth.

He, I pray, may be able to tell me the triumphs of Cæsar,
  Which he has heard of, and vows paid to the Latin Jove;

And that thy sorrowful head, Germania, thou, the rebellious,
  Under the feet, at last, of the Great Captain hast laid.

Whoso shall tell me these things, that not to have seen will afflict me,
  Forthwith unto my house welcomed as guest shall he be.

Woe is me! Is the house of Ovid in Scythian lands now?
  And doth punishment now give me its place for a home?

Grant, ye gods, that Cæsar make this not my house and my homestead,
  But decree it to be only the inn of my pain.

---·---

ON THE TERRACE OF THE AIGALADES.

FROM THE FRENCH OF MÉRY.

FROM this high portal, where up-
    springs
The rose to touch our hands in
    play,
We at a glance behold three
    things,—
The Sea, the Town, and the High-
    way.

And the Sea says: My shipwrecks
    fear;
I drown my best friends in the
    deep;
And those who braved my tempests,
    here
Among my sea-weeds lie asleep!

The Town says: I am filled and
    fraught
With tumult and with smoke and
    care;
My days with toil are overwrought,
And in my nights I gasp for air.

The Highway says: My wheel-
    tracks guide
To the pale climates of the North;
Where my last milestone stands
    abide
The people to their death gone
    forth.

Here, in the shade, this life of
    ours,
Full of delicious air, glides by
Amid a multitude of flowers
As countless as the stars on high;

These red-tiled roofs, this fruitful
   soil,
Bathed with an azure all divine,
Where springs the tree that gives
   us oil,
The grape that giveth us the wine;

Beneath these mountains stripped
   of trees,
Whose tops with flowers are covered
   o'er,
Where springtime of the Hesperides
Begins, but endeth nevermore;

Under these leafy vaults and walls,
That unto gentle sleep persuade;
This rainbow of the waterfalls,
Of mingled mist and sunshine
   made;

Upon these shores, where all invites,
We live our languid life apart;
This air is that of life's delights,
The festival of sense and heart;

This limpid space of time prolong,
Forget to-morrow in to-day,
And leave unto the passing throng
The Sea, the Town, and the High-
   way.

—◆—

TO MY BROOKLET.

FROM THE FRENCH OF DUCIS.

THOU brooklet, all unknown to
   song,
Hid in the covert of the wood!
Ah, yes, like thee I fear the throng,
Like thee I love the solitude.

O brooklet, let my sorrows past
Lie all forgotten in their graves,
Till in my thoughts remain at last
Only thy peace, thy flowers, thy
   waves,

The lily by thy margin waits;—
The nightingale, the marguerite;
In shadow here he meditates
His nest, his love, his music sweet.

Near thee the self-collected soul
Knows naught of error or of crime;
Thy waters, murmuring as they roll,
Transform his musings into rhyme.

Ah, when, on bright autumnal eves,
Pursuing still thy course, shall I
Lisp the soft shudder of the leaves,
And hear the lapwing's plaintive
   cry?

—◆—

BARRÉGES.

FROM THE FRENCH OF LEFRANC
DE POMPIGNAN.

I LEAVE you, ye cold mountain
   chains,
Dwelling of warriors stark and frore!
You, may these eyes behold no
   more,
Save on the horizon of our plains.

Vanish, ye frightful, gloomy views!
Ye rocks that mount up to the
   clouds!
Of skies, enwrapped in misty
   shrouds,
Impracticable avenues!

Ye torrents, that with might and
   main
Break pathways through the rocky
   walls,
With your terrific waterfalls
Fatigue no more my weary brain!

Arise, ye landscapes full of charms,
Arise, ye pictures of delight!
Ye brooks, that water in your flight
The flowers and harvests of our
   farms!

Translations.

You I perceive, ye meadows green,
Where the Garonne the lowland fills,
Not far from that long chain of hills,
With intermingled vales between.

Yon wreath of smoke, that mounts so high,
Methinks from my own hearth must come ;
With speed, to that beloved home,
Fly, ye too lazy coursers, fly !

And bear me thither, where the soul
In quiet may itself possess,
Where all things soothe the mind's distress,
Where all things teach me and console.

—◆—

FORSAKEN.

FROM THE GERMAN.

SOMETHING the heart must have to cherish,
Must love and joy and sorrow learn,
Something with passion clasp, or perish,
And in itself to ashes burn.

So to this child my heart is clinging,
And its frank eyes, with look intense,
Me from a world of sin are bringing
Back to a world of innocence.

Disdain must thou endure for ever ;
Strong may thy heart in danger be !
Thou shalt not fail ! but ah, be never
False as thy father was to me.

Never will I forsake thee, faithless,
And thou thy mother ne'er forsake,
Until her lips are white and breathless,
Until in death her eyes shall break.

—◆—

ALLAH.

FROM THE GERMAN OF MAHLMANN.

ALLAH gives light in darkness,
Allah gives rest in pain,
Cheeks that are white with weeping
Allah paints red again.

The flowers and the blossoms wither,
Years vanish with flying feet ;
But my heart will live on for ever,
That here in sadness beat.

Gladly to Allah's dwelling
Yonder would I take flight ;
There will the darkness vanish,
There will my eyes have sight.

755

Seven Sonnets and a Canzone.

FROM THE ITALIAN OF MICHAEL ANGELO.

[The following translations are from the poems of Michael Angelo as revised by his nephew Michael Angelo the Younger, and were made before the publication of the original text by Guasti.]

I. THE ARTIST.

NOTHING the greatest artist can conceive
    That every marble block doth not confine
    Within itself; and only its design
    The hand that follows intellect can achieve.
The ill I flee, the good that I believe,
    In thee, fair lady, lofty and divine,
    Thus hidden lie; and so that death be mine
    Art, of desired success, doth me bereave.
Love is not guilty, then, nor thy fair face,
    Nor fortune, cruelty, nor great disdain,
    Of my disgrace, nor chance, nor destiny,
If in thy heart both death and love find place
    At the same time, and if my humble brain,
    Burning, can nothing draw but death from thee.

II. FIRE.

NOT without fire can any workman mould
    The iron to his preconceived design,
    Nor can the artist without fire refine
    And purify from all its dross the gold;
Nor can revive the phœnix, we are told,
    Except by fire.   Hence if such death be mine
    I hope to rise again with the divine,
    Whom death augments, and time cannot make old.
O sweet, sweet death! O fortunate fire that burns
    Within me still to renovate my days,
    Though I am almost numbered with the dead!
If by its nature unto heaven returns
    This element, me, kindled in its blaze,
    Will it bear upward when my life is fled.

III.   YOUTH AND AGE.

O GIVE me back the days when loose and free
To my blind passion were the curb and rein,
O give me back the angelic face again,
With which all virtue buried seems to be !
O give my panting footsteps back to me,
That are in age so slow and fraught with pain,
And fire and moisture in the heart and brain,
If thou wouldst have me burn and weep for thee !
If it be true thou livest alone, Amor,
On the sweet-bitter tears of human hearts,
In an old man thou canst not wake desire ;
Souls that have almost reached the other shore
Of a diviner love should feel the darts,
And be as tinder to a holier fire.

IV.   OLD AGE.

THE course of my long life hath reached at last,
In fragile bark o'er a tempestuous sea,
The common harbour, where must rendered be
Account of all the actions of the past.
The impassioned fantasy, that, vague and vast,
Made art an idol and a king to me,
Was an illusion, and but vanity
Were the desires that lured me and harassed.
The dreams of love, that were so sweet of yore,
What are they now, when two deaths may be mine.---
One sure, and one forecasting its alarms ?
Painting and sculpture satisfy no more
The soul now turning to the Love Divine,
That oped, to embrace us, on the cross its arms.

V.   TO VITTORIA COLONNA.

LADY, how can it chance—yet this we see
In long experience—that will longer last
A living image carved from quarries vast
Than its own maker, who dies presently ?
Cause yieldeth to effect if this so be,
And even Nature is by Art surpassed ;
This know I, who to Art have given the past,
But see that Time is breaking faith with me.
Perhaps on both of us long life can I
Either in colour or in stone bestow,
By now portraying each in look and mien ;
So that a thousand years after we die,
How fair thou wast, and I how full of woe,
And wherefore I so loved thee, may be seen.

VI. TO VITTORIA COLONNA.

WHEN the prime mover of my many sighs
  Heaven took through death from out her earthly place,
  Nature, that never made so fair a face,
  Remained ashamed, and tears were in all eyes.
O fate, unheeding my impassioned cries!
  O hopes fallacious! O thou spirit of grace,
  Where art thou now? Earth holds in its embrace
  Thy lovely limbs, thy holy thoughts the skies.
Vainly did cruel death attempt to stay
  The rumour of thy virtuous renown,
  That Lethe's waters could not wash away!
A thousand leaves, since he hath stricken thee down,
  Speak of thee, nor to thee could Heaven convey,
  Except through death, a refuge and a crown.

VII. DANTE.

WHAT should be said of him cannot be said;
  By too great splendour is his name attended;
  To blame is easier those who him offended,
  Than reach the faintest glory round him shed.
This man descended to the doomed and dead
  For our instruction; then to God ascended;
  Heaven opened wide to him its portals splendid,
  Who from his country's, closed against him, fled.
Ungrateful land! To its own prejudice
  Nurse of his fortunes; and this showeth well,
  That the most perfect most of grief shall see.
Among a thousand proofs let one suffice,
  That as his exile hath no parallel,
  Ne'er walked the earth a greater man than he.

———

CANZONE.

AH me! ah me! when thinking of the years,
  The vanished years, alas, I do not find
Among them all one day that was my own!
  Fallacious hopes, desires of the unknown,
Lamenting, loving, burning, and in tears
  (For human passions all have stirred my mind),
Have held me, now I feel and know, confined
  Both from the true and good still far away.
I perish day by day;
  The sunshine fails, the shadows grow more dreary,
And I am near to fall, infirm and weary.

And now some fragments of its
    branches bare,
  Shaped as a stately chair,
Have by my hearthstone found a
    home at last,
  And whisper of the past.

The Danish king could not in all
    his pride
  Repel the ocean tide,
But, seated in this chair, I can in
    rhyme
  Roll back the tide of Time.

I see again, as one in vision sees,
  The blossoms and the bees,
And hear the children's voices shout
    and call,
  And the brown chestnuts fall.

I see the smithy with its fires
    aglow,
  I hear the bellows blow,
And the shrill hammers on the anvil
    beat
  The iron white with heat !

And thus, dear children, have ye
    made for me
  This day a jubilee,
And to my more than three-score
    years and ten
  Brought back my youth again.

The heart hath its own memory,
    like the mind,
  And in it are enshrined
The precious keepsakes, into
    which is wrought
  The giver's loving thought.

Only your love and your remem-
    brance could
  Give life to this dead wood,
And make these branches, leafless
    now so long,
  Blossom again in song.

JUGURTHA.

How cold are thy baths, Apollo !
  Cried the African monarch, the
    splendid,
As down to his death in the hollow
  Dark dungeons of Rome he de-
    scended,
    Uncrowned unthroned, unat-
      tended ;
How cold are thy baths, Apollo !

How cold are thy baths, Apollo !
  Cried the Poet, unknown, unbe-
    friended,
As the vision, that lured him to
    follow,
  With the mist and the darkness
    blended,
  And the dream of his life was
    ended ;
How cold are thy baths, Apollo !

THE IRON PEN.

Made from a fetter of Bonnivard, the Prisoner
of Chillon ; the handle of wood from the
Frigate Constitution, and bound with a
circlet of gold, inset with three precious
stones from Siberia, Ceylon, and Maine.

I THOUGHT this Pen would arise
From the casket where it lies—
  Of itself would arise and write
My thanks and my surprise.

When you gave it me under the
    pines,
I dreamed these gems from the
    mines
  Of Siberia, Ceylon, and Maine
Would glimmer as thoughts in the
    lines ;
That this iron link from the chain
Of Bonnivard might retain
  Some verse of the Poet who sang
Of the prisoner and his pain ;

That this wood from the frigate's
    mast
Might write me a rhyme at last,
    As it used to write on the sky
The song of the sea and the blast.

But motionless as I wait,
Like a Bishop lying in state
    Lies the Pen, with its mitre of
      gold,
And its jewels inviolate.

Then must I speak, and say
That the light of that summer day
    In the garden under the pines
Shall not fade and pass away.

I shall see you standing there,
Caressed by the fragrant air,
    With the shadow on your face,
And the sunshine on your hair.

I shall hear the sweet low tone
Of a voice before unknown,
    Saying, 'This is from me to
      you—
From me, and to you alone.'

And in words not idle and vain
I shall answer and thank you again
    For the gift, and the grace of the
      gift,
O beautiful Helen of Maine!

And for ever this gift will be
As a blessing from you to me,
    As a drop of the dew of your
      youth
On the leaves of an aged tree.

ROBERT BURNS.

I SEE amid the fields of Ayr
A ploughman, who, in foul and fair,
    Sings at his task
So clear, we know not if it is
The laverock's song we hear, or his,
    Nor care to ask.

For him the ploughing of those
    fields
A more ethereal harvest yields
    Than sheaves of grain;
Songs flush with purple bloom the
    rye,
The plover's call, the curlew's cry,
    Sing in his brain.

Touched by his hand, the wayside
    weed
Becomes a flower; the lowliest reed
    Beside the stream
Is clothed with beauty; gorse and
    grass
And heather, where his footsteps
    pass,
    The brighter seem.

He sings of love, whose flame
    illumes
The darkness of lone cottage rooms;
    He feels the force,
The treacherous undertow and stress
Of wayward passions, and no less
    The keen remorse.

At moments, wrestling with his fate,
His voice is harsh, but not with hate;
    The brushwood, hung
Above the tavern door, lets fall
Its bitter leaf, its drop of gall
    Upon his tongue.

But still the music of his song
Rises o'er all elate and strong;
    Its master-chords
Are Manhood, Freedom, Brother-
      hood,
Its discords but an interlude
    Between the words.

And then to die so young and leave
Unfinished what he might achieve!
    Yet better sure
Is this, than wandering up and down
An old man in a country town,
    Infirm and poor.

For now he haunts his native land
As an immortal youth ; his hand
    Guides every plough ;
He sits beside each ingle-nook,
His voice is in each rushing brook,
    Each rustling bough.

His presence haunts this room to-
        night,
A form of mingled mist and light
    From that far coast.
Welcome beneath this roof of mine !
Welcome ! this vacant chair is thine,
    Dear guest and ghost !

——+——

HELEN OF TYRE.

WHAT phantom is this that appears
Through the purple mist of the
        years,
    Itself but a mist like these ?
A woman of cloud and of fire ;
It is she ; it is Helen of Tyre,
    The town in the midst of the seas.

O Tyre ! in thy crowded streets
The phantom appears and retreats,
    And the Israelites that sell
Thy lilies and lions of brass,
Look up as they see her pass,
    And murmur 'Jezebel !'

Then another phantom is seen
At her side, in a gray gabardine,
    With beard that floats to his
        waist ;
It is Simon Magus, the Seer ;
He speaks, and she pauses to hear
    The words he utters in haste.

He says : 'From this evil fame,
From this life of sorrow and shame,
    I will lift thee and make thee
        mine ;
Thou hast been Queen Candace,
And Helen of Troy, and shalt be
    The Intelligence Divine !'

Oh, sweet as the breath of morn,
To the fallen and forlorn
    Are whispered words of praise ;
For the famished heart believes
The falsehood that tempts and de-
        ceives,
    And the promise that betrays.

So she follows from land to land
The wizard's beckoning hand,
    As a leaf is blown by the gust,
Till she vanishes into night.
O reader, stoop down and write
    With thy finger in the dust.

O town in the midst of the seas,
With thy rafts of cedar trees,
    Thy merchandise and thy ships,
Thou, too, art become as naught,
A phantom, a shadow, a thought,
    A name upon men's lips.

——+——

ELEGIAC.

DARK is the morning with mist ; in
    the narrow mouth of the har-
    bour
Motionless lies the sea, under its
    curtain of cloud ;
Dreamily glimmer the sails of ships
    on the distant horizon,
Like to the towers of a town, built
    on the verge of the sea.

Slowly and stately and still, they sail
    forth into the ocean ;
With them sail my thoughts over
    the limitless deep,
Farther and farther away, borne on
    by unsatisfied longings,
    Unto Hesperian isles, unto Au-
    sonian shores.

Now they have vanished away, have
    disappeared in the ocean ;
Sunk are the towers of the town
    into the depths of the sea !

All have vanished but those that,
    moored in the neighbouring
    roadstead,
Sailless at anchor ride, looming so
    large in the mist.

Vanished, too, are the thoughts, the
    dim, unsatisfied longings ;
    Sunk are the turrets of cloud into
    the ocean of dreams ;
While in a haven of rest my heart
    is riding at anchor,
    Held by the chains of love, held
    by the anchors of trust !

OLD ST. DAVID'S AT RADNOR.

WHAT an image of peace and rest
    Is this little church among its
    graves !
All is so quiet ; the troubled breast,
The wounded spirit, the heart op-
    pressed,
    Here may find the repose it craves.

See, how the ivy climbs and expands
    Over this humble hermitage,
And seems to caress with its little
    hands
The rough, gray stones, as a child
    that stands
    Caressing the wrinkled cheeks of
    age !

You cross the threshold ; and dim
    and small
    Is the space that serves for the
    Shepherd's Fold ;

The narrow aisle, the bare, white
    wall,
The pews, and the pulpit quaint and
    tall,
    Whisper and say : 'Alas ! we are
    old.'

Herbert's chapel at Bemerton
    Hardly more spacious is than this ;
But Poet and Pastor, blent in one,
Clothed with a splendour, as of the
    sun,
    That lowly and holy edifice.

It is not the wall of stone without
    That makes the building small
    or great,
But the soul's light shining round
    about,
And the faith that overcometh doubt,
    And the love that stronger is than
    hate.

Were I a pilgrim in search of peace,
    Were I a pastor of Holy Church,
More than a Bishop's diocese
Should I prize this place of rest,
    and release
    From farther longing and farther
    search.

Here would I stay, and let the world
    With its distant thunder roar
    and roll ;
Storms do not rend the sail that is
    furled ;
Nor like a dead leaf, tossed and
    whirled
    In an eddy of wind, is the an-
    chored soul.

Folk-Songs.

THE SIFTING OF PETER.

In Saint Luke's Gospel we are told
How Peter in the days of old
    Was sifted;
And now, though ages intervene,
Sin is the same, while time and scene
    Are shifted.

Satan desires us, great and small,
As wheat to sift us, and we all
    Are tempted;
Not one, however rich or great,
Is by his station or estate
    Exempted.

No house so safely guarded is
But he, by some device of his,
    Can enter;
No heart hath armour so complete
But he can pierce with arrows fleet
    Its centre.

For all at last the cock will crow,
Who hear the warning voice, but go
    Unheeding,
Till thrice and more they have denied
The Man of Sorrows, crucified
    And bleeding.

One look of that pale suffering face
Will make us feel the deep disgrace
    Of weakness;
We shall be sifted till the strength
Of self-conceit be changed at length
    To meekness.

Wounds of the soul, though healed, will ache;
The reddening scars remain, and make
    Confession;
Lost innocence returns no more;
We are not what we were before
    Transgression.

But noble souls, through dust and heat,
Rise from disaster and defeat
    The stronger,
And conscious still of the divine
Within them, lie on earth supine
    No longer.

MAIDEN AND WEATHER-COCK.

MAIDEN.

O Weathercock on the village spire,
With your golden feathers all on fire,
Tell me, what can you see from your perch
Above there over the tower of the church?

WEATHERCOCK.

I can see the roofs and the streets below,
And the people moving to and fro,
And beyond, without either roof or street.
The great salt sea, and the fisherman's fleet.

I can see a ship come sailing in
Beyond the headlands and harbour of Lynn,
And a young man standing on the deck,
With a silken kerchief round his neck.

Now he is pressing it to his lips,
And now he is kissing his finger-tips,
And now he is lifting and waving his hand,
And blowing the kisses toward the land.

MAIDEN.

Ah, that is the ship from over the
  sea,
That is bringing my lover back to
  me,
Bringing my lover so fond and true,
Who does not change with the wind
  like you.

WEATHERCOCK.

If I change with all the winds that
  blow,
It is only because they made me so,
And people would think it wondrous
  strange
If I, a Weathercock, should not
  change.

O pretty Maiden, so fine and fair,
With your dreamy eyes and your
  golden hair,
When you and your lover meet to-
  day
You will thank me for looking some
  other way.

THE WINDMILL.

BEHOLD ! a giant am I !
  Aloft here in my tower,
  With my granite jaws I devour
The maize, and the wheat, and the
  rye,
  And grind them into flour.

I look down over the farms ;
  In the fields of grain I see
  The harvest that is to be,
And I fling to the air my arms,
  For I know it is all for me.

I hear the sound of flails
  Far off, from the threshing-floors
  In barns, with their open doors,
And the wind, the wind in my sails,
  Louder and louder roars.

I stand here in my place,
  With my foot on the rock below,
  And which ever way it may blow
I meet it face to face,
  As a brave man meets his foe.

And while we wrestle and strive,
  My master, the miller, stands
  And feeds me with his hands ;
For he knows who makes him
  thrive,
  Who makes him lord of lands.

On Sundays I take my rest ;
  Church-going bells begin
  Their low, melodious din ;
I cross my arms on my breast,
  And all is peace within.

THE TIDE RISES, THE TIDE
FALLS.

THE tide rises, the tide falls,
The twilight darkens, the curlew
  calls ;
Along the sea-sands damp and
  brown
The traveller hastens toward the
  town,
  And the tide rises, the tide falls.

Darkness settles on roofs and
  walls,
But the sea in the darkness calls
  and calls ;
The little waves, with their soft
  white hands,
Efface the footprints in the sands,
  And the tide rises, the tide falls.

The morning breaks ; the steeds
  in their stalls
Stamp and neigh, as the hostler
  calls ;
The day returns, but nevermore
Returns the traveller to the shore,
  And the tide rises, the tide falls.

Sonnets.

MY CATHEDRAL.

LIKE two cathedral towers these stately pines
  Uplift their fretted summits tipped with cones;
  The arch beneath them is not built with stones—
Not Art but Nature traced these lovely lines,
And carved this graceful arabesque of vines;
  No organ but the wind here sighs and moans,
  No sepulchre conceals a martyr's bones,
  No marble bishop on his tomb reclines.
Enter! the pavement, carpeted with leaves,
  Gives back a softened echo to thy tread!
  Listen! the choir is singing; all the birds,
In leafy galleries beneath the eaves,
  Are singing! listen, ere the sound be fled,
  And learn there may be worship without words.

—♦♦—

THE BURIAL OF THE POET.

RICHARD HENRY DANA.

IN the old churchyard of his native town,
  And in the ancestral tomb beside the wall,
  We laid him in the sleep that comes to all,
  And left him to his rest and his renown.
The snow was falling, as if Heaven dropped down
  White flowers of Paradise to strew his pall;—
  The dead around him seemed to wake, and call
  His name, as worthy of so white a crown.
And now the moon is shining on the scene,
  And the broad sheet of snow is written o'er
  With shadows cruciform of leafless trees,
As once the winding-sheet of Saladin
  With chapters of the Koran; but, ah! more
  Mysterious and triumphant signs are these.

NIGHT.

Into the darkness and the hush of night
    Slowly the landscape sinks, and fades away,
    And with it fade the phantoms of the day,
    The ghosts of men and things, that haunt the light.
The crowd, the clamour, the pursuit, the flight,
    The unprofitable splendour and display,
    The agitations, and the cares that prey
    Upon our hearts, all vanish out of sight.
The better life begins ; the world no more
    Molests us ; all its records we erase
    From the dull commonplace-book of our lives
That like a palimpsest is written o'er
    With trivial incidents of time and place,
    And lo ! the ideal, hidden beneath, revives.

L'Envoi.

THE POET AND HIS SONGS.

As the birds come in the Spring,
  We know not from where;
As the stars come at evening
  From depths of the air;

As the rain comes from the cloud,
  And the brook from the ground;
As suddenly, low or loud,
  Out of silence a sound;

As the grape comes to the vine,
  The fruit to the tree;
As the wind comes to the pine,
  And the tide to the sea;

As come the white sails of ships
  O'er the ocean's verge;
As comes the smile to the lips,
  The foam to the surge:

So come to the Poet his songs,
  All hitherward blown
From the misty realm, that belongs
  To the vast Unknown.

His, and not his, are the lays
  He sings; and their fame
Is his, and not his; and the praise
  And the pride of a name.

For voices pursue him by day,
  And haunt him by night,
And he listens, and needs must obey,
  When the Angel says: 'Write!'

In the Harbour.

BECALMED.

BECALMED upon the sea of Thought,
Still unattained the land it sought,
My mind, with loosely-hanging
    sails,
Lies waiting the auspicious gales.

On either side, behind, before,
The ocean stretches like a floor,—
A level floor of amethyst,
Crowned by a golden dome of mist.

Blow, breath of inspiration, blow!
Shake and uplift this golden glow!
And fill the canvas of the mind
With wafts of thy celestial wind.

Blow, breath of song! until I feel
The straining sail, the lifting keel,
The life of the awakening sea,
Its motion and its mystery!

HERMES TRISMEGISTUS.

As Seleucus narrates, Hermes describes the
principles that rank as wholes in two myriads
of books; or, as we are informed by Manetho,
he perfectly unfolded these principles in three
myriads six thousand five hundred and
twenty-five volumes. . . .
  . . . Our ancestors dedicated the inventions
of their wisdom to this deity, inscribing all
their own writings with the name of Hermes.
— IAMBLICUS.

STILL through Egypt's desert places
    Flows the lordly Nile;
From its banks the great stone faces
    Gaze with patient smile.
Still the pyramids imperious
    Pierce the cloudless skies,
And the Sphinx stares with mys-
    terious,
    Solemn, stony eyes.

But where are the old Egyptian
    Demi-gods and kings?
Nothing left but an inscription
    Graven on stones and rings.
Where are Helios and Hephaestus,
    Gods of eldest eld?
Where is Hermes Trismegistus,
    Who their secrets held?

Where are now the many hundred
    Thousand books he wrote?
By the Thaumaturgists plundered,
    Lost in lands remote;
In oblivion sunk for ever,
    As when o'er the land
Blows a storm-wind, in the river
    Sinks the scattered sand.

Something unsubstantial, ghostly,
    Seems this Theurgist,
In deep meditation mostly
    Wrapped, as in a mist.
Vague, phantasmal, and unreal
    To our thought he seems,
Walking in a world ideal,
    In a land of dreams.

Was he one, or many, merging
    Name and fame in one,
Like a stream, to which, converging,
    Many streamlets run?
Till, with gathered power proceed-
    ing
    Ampler sweep it takes,
Downward the sweet waters leading
    From unnumbered lakes.

By the Nile I see him wandering,
    Pausing now and then,
On the mystic union pondering
    Between gods and men;

Half believing, wholly feeling,
  With supreme delight,
How the gods, themselves conceal-
    ing,
  Lift men to their height.
Or in Thebes, the hundred-gated,
  In the thoroughfare
Breathing, as if consecrated,
  A diviner air;
And amid discordant noises,
  In the jostling throng,
Hearing far, celestial voices
  Of Olympian song.

Who shall call his dreams fallacious?
  Who has searched or sought
All the unexplored and spacious
  Universe of thought?
Who, in his own skill confiding,
  Shall with rule and line
Mark the border-land dividing
  Human and divine?
Trismegistus! three times greatest!
  How thy name sublime
Has descended to this latest
  Progeny of time!
Happy they whose written pages
  Perish with their lives,
If amid the crumbling ages
  Still their name survives!
Thine, O priest of Egypt, lately
  Found I in the vast,
Weed-encumbered, sombre, stately,
  Graveyard of the Past;
And a presence moved before me
  On that gloomy shore,
As a waft of wind, that o'er me
  Breathed, and was no more.

THE POET'S CALENDAR.

JANUARY.
I.

JANUS am I; oldest of potentates;
  Forward I look, and backward,
    and below
I count, as god of avenues and gates,
  The years that through my
    portals come and go.

II.

I block the roads, and drift the
    fields with snow;
  I chase the wild-fowl from the
    frozen fen;
My frosts congeal the rivers in
    their flow,
  My fires light up the hearths
    and hearts of men.

FEBRUARY.

I am lustration; and the sea is
    mine!
  I wash the sands and headlands
    with my tide;
My brow is crowned with branches
    of the pine;
  Before my chariot-wheels the
    fishes glide.
By me all things unclean are puri-
    fied,
  By me the souls of men washed
    white again;
E'en the unlovely tombs of those
    who died
  Without a dirge, I cleanse from
    every stain.

MARCH.

I Martius am! Once first, and now
    the third!
  To lead the Year was my ap-
    pointed place;
A mortal dispossessed me by a word,
  And set there Janus with the
    double face.
Hence I make war on all the
    human race;
  I shake the cities with my hur-
    ricanes;
I flood the rivers and their banks
    efface,
  And drown the farms and ham-
    lets with my rains.

APRIL.

I open wide the portals of the Spring
  To welcome the procession of
    the flowers,

With their gay banners, and the
    birds that sing
    Their song of songs from their
        aerial towers.
I soften with my sunshine and my
    showers
    The heart of earth; with thoughts
        of love I glide
Into the hearts of men; and with
    the Hours
    Upon the Bull with wreathèd
        horns I ride.

MAY.

Hark! The sea-faring wild-fowl
    loud proclaim
    My coming and the swarming
        of the bees.
These are my heralds, and behold!
    my name
    Is written in blossoms on the
        hawthorn-trees.
I tell the mariner when to sail the
    seas;
    I waft o'er all the land from far
        away
The breath and bloom of the Hes-
    perides,
    My birthplace. I am Maia. I
        am May.

JUNE.

Mine is the Month of Roses; yes,
    and mine
    The Month of Marriages! All
        pleasant sights
And scents, the fragrance of the
    blossoming vine,
    The foliage of the valleys and
        the heights.
Mine are the longest days, the
    loveliest nights;
    The mower's scythe makes music
        to my ear;
I am the mother of all dear de-
    lights;
    I am the fairest daughter of the
        year.

JULY.

My emblem is the Lion, and I breathe
    The breath of Libyan deserts
        o'er the land;
My sickle as a sabre I unsheathe,
    And bent before me the pale
        harvests stand.
The lakes and rivers shrink at my
    command,
    And there is thirst and fever in
        the air;
The sky is changed to brass, the
    earth to sand;
    I am the Emperor whose name
        I bear.

AUGUST.

The Emperor Octavian, called the
    August,
    I being his favourite, bestowed
        his name
Upon me, and I hold it still in trust,
    In memory of him and of his fame.
I am the Virgin, and my vestal
    flame
    Burns less intensely than the
        Lion's rage;
Sheaves are my only garlands, and
    I claim
    The golden Harvests as my
        heritage.

SEPTEMBER.

I bear the Scales, where hang in
    equipoise
    The night and day; and when
        unto my lips
I put my trumpet, with its stress
    and noise
    Fly the white clouds like tattered
        sails of ships;
The tree-tops lash the air with
    sounding whips;
    Southward the clamorous sea-
        fowl wing their flight;
The hedges are all red with haws
    and hips,
    The Hunter's Moon reigns em-
        press of the night.

OCTOBER.

My ornaments are fruits; my gar-
ments leaves,
  Woven like cloth of gold, and
    crimson dyed;
I do not boast the harvesting of
sheaves,
  O'er orchards and o'er vineyards
    I preside.
Though on the frigid Scorpion I ride,
  The dreamy air is full, and
    overflows
With tender memories of the sum-
mertide,
  And mingled voices of the doves
    and crows.

NOVEMBER.

The Centaur, Sagittarius am I,
  Born of Ixion's and the cloud's
    embrace;
With sounding hoofs across the
earth I fly,
  A steed Thessalian with a human
    face.
Sharp winds the arrows are with
which I chase
  The leaves, half dead already
    with affright;
I shroud myself in gloom; and to
the race
  Of mortals bring nor comfort
    nor delight.

DECEMBER.

Riding upon the Goat, with snow-
white hair,
  I come, the last of all. This
    crown of mine
Is of the holly; in my hand I bear
  The thyrsus, tipped with fragrant
    cones of pine.
I celebrate the birth of the Divine,
  And the return of the Saturnian
    reign;—
My songs are carols sung at every
shrine,
  Proclaiming ' Peace on earth,
    good will to men.'

MAD RIVER,

IN THE WHITE MOUNTAINS.

TRAVELLER.

WHY dost thou wildly rush and
roar,
  Mad River, O Mad River?
Wilt thou not pause and cease to
pour
Thy hurrying, headlong waters o'er
  This rocky shelf for ever?

What secret trouble stirs thy breast?
  Why all this fret and flurry?
Dost thou not know that what is
best
In this too restless world is rest
  From over-work and worry?

THE RIVER.

What wouldst thou in these moun-
tains seek,
  O stranger from the city?
Is it perhaps some foolish freak
Of thine, to put the words I speak
  Into a plaintive ditty?

TRAVELLER.

Yes; I would learn of thee thy
song,
  With all its flowing numbers,
And in a voice as fresh and strong
As thine is, sing it all day long,
  And hear it in my slumbers.

THE RIVER.

A brooklet nameless and unknown
Was I at first, resembling
A little child, that all alone
Comes venturing down the stairs of
stone,
  Irresolute and trembling.

Later, by wayward fancies led,
  For the wide world I panted;
Out of the forest dark and dread
Across the open field I fled,
  Like one pursued and haunted.

I tossed my arms, I sang aloud,
  My voice exultant blending
With thunder from the passing
    cloud,
The wind, the forest bent and
    bowed,
  The rush of rain descending.

I heard the distant ocean call,
  Imploring and entreating ;
Drawn onward, o'er this rocky wall
I plunged, and the loud waterfall
  Made answer to the greeting.

And now, beset with many ills,
  A toilsome life I follow;
Compelled to carry from the hills
These logs to the impatient mills
  Below there in the hollow.

Yet something ever cheers and
    charms
  The rudeness of my labours ;
Daily I water with these arms
The cattle of a hundred farms,
  And have the birds for neigh-
    bours.

Men call me Mad, and well they
    may,
  When, full of rage and trouble,
I burst my banks of sand and clay,
And sweep their wooden bridge
    away,
  Like withered reeds or stubble.

Now go and write thy little rhyme,
  As of thine own creating,
Thou seest the day is past its prime;
I can no longer waste my time ;
  The mills are tired of waiting.

———◆———

AUF WIEDERSEHEN.

IN MEMORY OF J. T. F.

UNTIL we meet again ! That is the
    meaning
Of the familiar words, that men re-
    peat
  At parting in the street.

Ah yes, till then ! but when death
    intervening
Rends us asunder, with what cease-
    less pain
  We wait for the Again !

The friends who leave us do not
    feel the sorrow
Of parting as we feel it, who must
    stay
  Lamenting day by day,
And knowing, when we wake upon
    the morrow,
We shall not find in its accustomed
    place
  The one beloved face.

It were a double grief, if the departed,
Being released from earth, should
    still retain
  A sense of earthly pain;
It were a double grief, if the true-
    hearted,
Who loved us here, should on the
    farther shore
  Remember us no more.

Believing, in the midst of our afflic-
    tions,
That death is a beginning, not an
    end,
  We cry to them, and send
Farewells, that better might be
    called predictions,
Being foreshadowings of the future,
    thrown
  Into the vast Unknown.

Faith overleaps the confines of our
    reason,
And if by faith, as in old times was
    said,
  Women received their dead
Raised up to life, then only for a
    season
Our partings are, nor shall we wait
    in vain
  Until we meet again !

THE CHILDREN'S CRU-
SADE.

[A FRAGMENT.]

I.

WHAT is this I read in history,
Full of marvel, full of mystery,
Difficult to understand?
Is it fiction, is it truth?
Children in the flower of youth,
Heart in heart, and hand in hand,
Ignorant of what helps or harms,
Without armour, without arms,
Journeying to the Holy Land!

Who shall answer or divine?
Never since the world was made
Such a wonderful crusade
Started forth for Palestine.
Never while the world shall last
Will it reproduce the past;
Never will it see again
Such an army, such a band,
Over mountain, over main,
Journeying to the Holy Land.

Like a shower of blossoms blown
From the parent trees were they;
Like a flock of birds that fly
Through the unfrequented sky,
Holding nothing as their own,
Passed they into lands unknown,
Passed to suffer and to die.

O the simple, child-like trust!
O the faith that could believe
What the harnessed, iron-mailed
Knights of Christendom had failed,
By their prowess, to achieve,
They, the children, could and must!

Little thought the Hermit, preaching
Holy wars to knight and baron,
That the words dropped in his
    teaching,
His entreaty, his beseeching,
Would by children's hands be
    gleaned,
And the staff on which he leaned
Blossom like the rod of Aaron.

As a summer wind upheaves
The innumerable leaves
In the bosom of a wood,—
Not as separate leaves, but massed
All together by the blast,—
So for evil or for good
His resistless breath upheaved
All at once the many-leaved,
Many-thoughted multitude.

In the tumult of the air
Rock the boughs with all the nests
Cradled on their tossing crests;
By the fervour of his prayer
Troubled hearts were everywhere
Rocked and tossed in human
    breasts.

For a century at least
His prophetic voice had ceased;
But the air was heated still
By his lurid words and will,
As from fires in far-off woods,
In the autumn of the year,
An unwonted fever broods
In the sultry atmosphere.

II.

In Cologne the bells were ringing,
In Cologne the nuns were singing
Hymns and canticles divine;
Loud the monks sang in their stalls,
And the thronging streets were loud
With the voices of the crowd; —
Underneath the city walls
Silent flowed the river Rhine.
From the gates, that summer day,
Clad in robes of hodden gray,
With the red cross on the breast,
Azure-eyed and golden-haired,
Forth the young crusaders fared;
While above the band devoted
Consecrated banners floated,
Fluttered many a flag and streamer,
And the cross o'er all the rest!
Singing lowly, meekly, slowly,
'Give us, give us back the holy
Sepulchre of the Redeemer!'
On the vast procession pressed,
Youths and maidens. . . .

III.

Ah! what master hand shall paint
How they journeyed on their way,
How the days grew long and dreary,
How their little feet grew weary,
How their little hearts grew faint!

Ever swifter day by day
Flowed the homeward river; ever
More and more its whitening current
Broke and scattered into spray,
Till the calmly-flowing river
Changed into a mountain torrent,
Rushing from its glacier green
Down through chasm and black
        ravine.

Like a phœnix in its nest
Burned the red sun in the West,
Sinking in an ashen cloud;
In the East, above the crest
Of the sea-like mountain chain,
Like a phœnix from its shroud,
Came the red sun back again.

Now around them, white with snow,
Closed the mountain peaks. Below,
Headlong from the precipice
Down into the dark abyss,
Plunged the cataract, white with
        foam;
And it said, or seemed to say:
'Oh return, while yet you may,
Foolish children, to your home,
There the Holy City is!'

But the dauntless leader said:
'Faint not, though your bleeding
        feet
O'er these slippery paths of sleet
Move but painfully and slowly;
Other feet than yours have bled;
Other tears than yours been shed.
Courage! lose not heart or hope;
On the mountains' southern slope
Lies Jerusalem the Holy!'

As a white rose in its pride,
By the wind in summer-tide
Tossed and loosened from the
        branch,

Showers its petals o'er the ground,
From the distant mountain's side,
Scattering all its snows around,
With mysterious, muffled sound,
Loosened, fell the avalanche.
Voices, echoes far and near,
Roar of winds and waters blending,
Mists uprising, clouds impending,
Filled them with a sense of fear,
Formless, nameless, never ending.

THE CITY AND THE SEA.

THE panting City cried to the Sea,
'I am faint with heat,—O breathe
        on me!'

And the Sea said, 'Lo, I breathe!
        but my breath
To some will be life, to others death!'

As to Prometheus, bringing ease
In pain, come the Oceanides,

So to the City, hot with the flame
Of the pitiless sun, the east wind
        came.

It came from the heaving breast of
        the deep,
Silent as dreams are, and sudden
        as sleep.

Life-giving, death-giving, which
        will it be;
O breath of the merciful, merciless
        Sea?

SUNDOWN.

THE summer sun is sinking low;
Only the tree-tops redden and glow;
Only the weathercock on the spire
Of the neighbouring church is a
        flame of fire;
        All is in shadow below.

O beautiful, awful summer day,
What hast thou given, what taken
    away?
Life and death, and love and hate,
Homes made happy or desolate,
    Hearts made sad or gay!

On the road of life one mile-stone
    more!
In the book of life one leaf turned
    o'er!
Like a red seal is the setting sun
On the good and the evil men have
    done,—
    Naught can to-day restore!

——+——

PRESIDENT GARFIELD.

'E VENNI DAL MARTIRIO A
        QUESTA PACE.'

THESE words the Poet heard in
    Paradise,
    Uttered by one who, bravely
        dying here,
    In the true faith was living in
        that sphere
Where the celestial cross of sacri-
    fice
Spread its protecting arms athwart
    the skies;
    And set thereon, like jewels
        crystal clear,
    The souls magnanimous, that
        knew not fear,
Flashed their effulgence on his
    dazzled eyes.
Ah me! how dark the discipline of
    pain,
Were not the suffering followed
    by the sense
Of infinite rest and infinite release!
This is our consolation; and again
    A great soul cries to us in our
        suspense,
    'I came from martyrdom unto
        this peace!'

DECORATION DAY.

SLEEP, comrades, sleep and rest
    On this Field of the Grounded
        Arms,
Where foes no more molest,
    Nor sentry's shot alarms!

Ye have slept on the ground before,
    And started to your feet
At the cannon's sudden roar,
    Or the drum's redoubling beat.

But in this camp of Death
    No sound your slumber breaks;
Here is no fevered breath,
    No wound that bleeds and aches.

All is repose and peace;
    Untrampled lies the sod;
The shouts of battle cease,
    It is the Truce of God!

Rest, comrades, rest and sleep!
    The thoughts of men shall be
As sentinels to keep
    Your rest from danger free.

Your silent tents of green
    We deck with fragrant flowers;
Yours has the suffering been,
    The memory shall be ours.

——+——

CHIMES.

SWEET chimes! that in the loneli-
        ness of night
    Salute the passing hour, and in
        the dark
    And silent chambers of the house-
        hold mark
    The movements of the myriad
        orbs of light!
Through my closed eyelids, by the
        inner sight,
    I see the constellations in the arc
    Of their great circles moving on,
        and hark!

777

I almost hear them singing in
    their flight.
Better than sleep it is to lie awake
    O'er-canopied by the vast starry
      dome
    Of the immeasurable sky ; to feel
The slumbering world sink under
    us, and make
    Hardly an eddy,—a mere rush of
      foam
    On the great sea beneath a sink-
      ing keel.

FOUR BY THE CLOCK.

FOUR by the clock ! and yet not
    day ;
But the great world rolls and
    wheels away,
With its cities on land, and its
    ships at sea,
Into the dawn that is to be !

Only the lamp in the anchored bark
Sends its glimmer across the dark,
And the heavy breathing of the sea
Is the only sound that comes to me.

THE FOUR LAKES OF MADISON.

FOUR limpid lakes,—four Naiades
Or sylvan deities are these,
    In flowing robes of azure dressed ;
Four lovely handmaids, that uphold
Their shining mirrors, rimmed with
    gold,
    To the fair city in the West.

By day the coursers of the sun
Drink of these waters as they run
    Their swift diurnal round on
      high ;
By night the constellations glow
Far down the hollow deeps below,
    And glimmer in another sky.

Fair lakes, serene and full of light,
Fair town, arrayed in robes of white,
    How visionary ye appear !
All like a floating landscape seems
In cloudland or the land of dreams,
    Bathed in a golden atmosphere!

MOONLIGHT.

As a pale phantom with a lamp
    Ascends some ruin's haunted stair,
So glides the moon along the damp
    Mysterious chambers of the air.

Now hidden in cloud, and now re-
    vealed,
    As if this phantom, full of pain,
Were by the crumbling walls con-
    cealed,
    And at the windows seen again.

Until at last, serene and proud,
    In all the splendour of her light,
She walks the terraces of cloud,
    Supreme as Empress of the Night.

I look, but recognize no more
    Objects familiar to my view;
The very pathway to my door
    Is an enchanted avenue.

All things are changed. One mass
    of shade,
    The elm-trees drop their curtains
      down ;
By palace, park, and colonnade
    I walk as in a foreign town.

The very ground beneath my feet
    Is clothed with a diviner air ;
White marble paves the silent street
    And glimmers in the empty
      square.

Illusion ! Underneath there lies
    The common life of every day ;
Only the spirit glorifies
    With its own tints the sober gray.

In vain we look, in vain uplift
  Our eyes to heaven, if we are
    blind ;
We see but what we have the gift
  Of seeing ; what we bring we find.

TO THE AVON.

FLOW on, sweet river ! like his verse
Who lies beneath this sculptured
    hearse ;
Nor wait beside the churchyard wall
For him who cannot hear thy call.

Thy playmate once ; I see him now
A boy with sunshine on his brow,
And hear in Stratford's quiet street
The patter of his little feet.

I see him by thy shallow edge
Wading knee-deep amid the sedge;
And lost in thought, as if thy stream
Were the swift river of a dream.

He wonders whitherward it flows ;
And fain would follow where it goes,
To the wide world, that shall ere-
    long
Be filled with his melodious song.

Flow on, fair stream ! That dream
  is o'er ;
He stands upon another shore ;
A vaster river near him flows,
And still he follows where it goes.

ELEGIAC VERSE.

I.

PERADVENTURE of old, some bard
  in Ionian Islands,
  Walking alone by the sea, hearing
    the wash of the waves,
Learned the secret from them of
  the beautiful verse elegiac,
  Breathing into his song motion
  and sound of the sea.

For as the wave of the sea, upheaving in long undulations,
  Plunges loud on the sands, pauses,
    and turns, and retreats,
So the Hexameter, rising and singing, with cadence sonorous,
  Falls ; and in refluent rhythm
  back the Pentameter flows [1].

II.

Not in his youth alone, but in age,
  may the heart of the poet
  Bloom into song, as the gorse
  blossoms in autumn and spring.

III.

Not in tenderness wanting, yet
  rough are the rhymes of our
    poet ;
  Though it be Jacob's voice,
  Esau's, alas ! are the hands.

IV.

Let us be grateful to writers for
  what is left in the inkstand ;
  When to leave off is an art only
  attained by the few.

V.

How can the Three be One ? you
  ask me ; I answer by asking,
  Hail and snow and rain, are they
  not three, and yet one ?

VI.

By the mirage uplifted the land
  floats vague in the ether,
  Ships and the shadows of ships
  hang in the motionless air ;
So by the art of the poet our common life is uplifted,
  So, transfigured, the world floats
  in a luminous haze.

VII.

Like a French poem is Life ; being
  only perfect in structure
  When with the masculine rhymes
  mingled the feminine are.

---

[1] Compare Schiller :

Im Hexameter steigt des Springquells flüssige Säule;
  Im Pentameter drauf fällt sie melodisch herab.

See also Coleridge's translation.

VIII.

Down from the mountain descends
    the brooklet, rejoicing in free-
    dom ;
  Little it dreams of the mill hid
    in the valley below ;
Glad with the joy of existence, the
    child goes singing and laugh-
    ing,
  Little dreaming what toils lie in
    the future concealed.

IX.

As the ink from our pen, so flow
    our thoughts and our feelings
When we begin to write, how-
    ever sluggish before.

X.

Like the Kingdom of Heaven, the
    Fountain of Youth is within us;
  If we seek it elsewhere, old shall
    we grow in the search.

XI.

If you would hit the mark, you must
    aim a little above it ;
  Every arrow that flies feels the
    attraction of earth.

XII.

Wisely the Hebrews admit no
    Present tense in their language ;
While we are speaking the word,
    it is already the Past.

XIII.

In the twilight of age all things
    seem strange and phantasmal,
  As between daylight and dark
    ghost-like the landscape ap-
    pears.

XIV.

Great is the art of beginning, but
    greater the art of ending ;
  Many a poem is marred by a
    superfluous verse.

A FRAGMENT.

AWAKE ! arise ! the hour is late !
    Angels are knocking at thy door!
They are in haste and cannot wait,
    And once departed come no more.

Awake ! arise ! the athlete's arm
    Loses its strength by too much
    rest ;
The fallow land, the untilled farm,
    Produces only weeds at best.

Translations.

PRELUDE.

As treasures that men seek,
  Deep-buried in sea-sands,
Vanish if they but speak,
  And elude their eager hands,

So ye escape and slip,
  O songs, and fade away,
When the word is on my lip
  To interpret what ye say.

Were it not better, then,
  To let the treasures rest
Hid from the eyes of men,
  Locked in their iron chest?

I have but marked the place,
  But half the secret told,
That, following this slight trace,
  Others may find the gold.

FROM THE FRENCH.

WILL ever the dear days come
    back again,
  Those days of June, when lilacs
    were in bloom,
  And bluebirds sang their sonnets
    in the gloom
  Of leaves that roofed them in from
    sun or rain?
I know not; but a presence will
    remain
  For ever and for ever in this room,
  Formless, diffused in air, like a
    perfume,—
  A phantom of the heart, and not
    the brain.
Delicious days! when every spoken
    word

Was like a footfall nearer and
    more near,
  And a mysterious knocking at
    the gate
Of the heart's secret places, and
    we heard
  In the sweet tumult of delight
    and fear
  A voice that whispered, 'Open,
    I cannot wait!'

THE WINE OF JURANÇON.

FROM THE FRENCH OF CHARLES
    CORAN.

LITTLE sweet wine of Jurançon,
  You are dear to my memory still!
With mine host and his merry song,
  Under the rose-tree I drank my
    fill.

Twenty years after, passing that
    way,
  Under the trellis I found again
Mine host, still sitting there *au frais*,
  And singing still the same refrain.

The Jurançon, so fresh and bold,
  Treats me as one it used to know;
Souvenirs of the days of old
  Already from the bottle flow.

With glass in hand our glances met;
  We pledge, we drink. How sour
    it is!
Never Argenteuil piquette
  Was to my palate sour as this!

And yet the vintage was good, in
    sooth;
  The selfsame juice, the selfsame
    cask!
It was you, O gaiety of my youth,
  That failed in the autumnal flask!

AT LA CHAUDEAU.

FROM THE FRENCH OF XAVIER
MARMIER.

AT La Chaudeau,—'tis long since
    then :
I was young,—my years twice ten ;
All things smiled on the happy boy,
Dreams of love and songs of joy,
Azure of heaven and wave below,
    At La Chaudeau.

To La Chaudeau I come back old :
My head is gray, my blood is cold ;
Seeking along the meadow ooze,
Seeking beside the river Seymouse,
The days of my spring-time of
    long ago
    At La Chaudeau.

At La Chaudeau nor heart nor
    brain
Ever grows old with grief and
    pain ;
A sweet remembrance keeps off
    age ;
A tender friendship doth still as-
    suage
The burden of sorrow that one
    may know
    At La Chaudeau.

At La Chaudeau, had fate decreed
To limit the wandering life I lead,
Peradventure I still, forsooth,
Should have preserved my fresh
    green youth,
Under the shadows the hill-tops
    throw
    At La Chaudeau.

At La Chaudeau, live on, my friends,
Happy to be where God intends ;
And sometimes, by the evening fire,
Think of him whose sole desire
Is again to sit in the old château
    At La Chaudeau.

A QUIET LIFE.

FROM THE FRENCH.

LET him who will, by force or
    fraud innate,
    Of courtly grandeurs gain the
        slippery height ;
I, leaving not the home of my
    delight,
    Far from the world and noise
        will meditate.
Then, without pomps or perils of
    the great,
    I shall behold the day succeed
        the night ;
Behold the alternate seasons take
    their flight,
    And in serene repose old age
        await.
And so, whenever Death shall
    come to close
    The happy moments that my
        days compose,
I, full of years, shall die, ob-
    scure, alone !
How wretched is the man, with
    honours crowned,
    Who, having not the one thing
        needful found,
    Dies, known to all, but to him-
        self unknown.

Personal Poems.

LOSS AND GAIN.

WHEN I compare
What I have lost with what I have
gained,
What I have missed with what
attained,
Little room do I find for pride.

I am aware
How many days have been idly
spent;
How like an arrow the good intent
Has fallen short or been turned
aside.

But who shall dare
To measure loss and gain in this
wise?
Defeat may be victory in disguise;
The lowest ebb is the turn of the
tide.

AUTUMN WITHIN.

IT is autumn; not without,
But within me is the cold.
Youth and spring are all about;
It is I that have grown old.

Birds are darting through the air,
Singing, building without rest;
Life is stirring everywhere,
Save within my lonely breast.

There is silence : the dead leaves
Fall and rustle and are still;
Beats no flail upon the sheaves,
Comes no murmur from the mill.

VICTOR AND VANQUISHED.

As one who long hath fled with
panting breath
Before his foe, bleeding and near
to fall,
I turn and set my back against
the wall,
And look thee in the face,
triumphant Death.
I call for aid, and no one answereth;
I am alone with thee, who con-
querest all;
Yet me thy threatening form
doth not appal,
For thou art but a phantom and
a wraith.
Wounded and weak, sword broken
at the hilt,
With armour shattered, and without a shield,
I stand unmoved; do with me
what thou wilt;
I can resist no more, but will not
yield.
This is no tournament where
cowards tilt;
The vanquished here is victor
of the field.

MEMORIES.

Oft I remember those whom I
    have known
  In other days, to whom my heart
      was led
    As by a magnet, and who are
      not dead,
  But absent, and their memories
      overgrown
With other thoughts and troubles
    of my own,
  As graves with grasses are, and
      at their head
  The stone with moss and lichens
      so o'erspread,
Nothing is legible but the name
    alone.
And is it so with them? After
    long years,
  Do they remember me in the
      same way,
    And is the memory pleasant as
      to me?
I fear to ask; yet wherefore are
    my fears?
  Pleasures, like flowers, may
      wither and decay,
    And yet the root perennial may
      be.

MY BOOKS.

Sadly as some old mediaeval
    knight
  Gazed at the arms he could no
      longer wield,
    The sword two-handed and the
      shining shield
  Suspended in the hall, and full
      in sight,
While secret longings for the lost
    delight
  Of tourney or adventure in the
      field
    Came over him, and tears but
      half concealed
  Trembled and fell upon his beard
      of white,
So I behold these books upon their
    shelf,
  My ornaments and arms of other
      days;
    Not wholly useless, though no
      longer used,
For they remind me of my other
    self,
  Younger and stronger, and the
      pleasant ways
    In which I walked, now clouded
      and confused.

L'Envoi.

POSSIBILITIES.

WHERE are the Poets, unto whom belong
  The Olympian heights ; whose singing shafts were sent
  Straight to the mark, and not from bows half bent,
  But with the utmost tension of the thong ?
Where are the stately argosies of song,
  Whose rushing keels made music as they went
  Sailing in search of some new continent,
  With all sail set, and steady winds and strong ?
Perhaps there lives some dreamy boy, untaught
  In schools, some graduate of the field or street,
  Who shall become a master of the art,
An admiral sailing the high seas of thought,
  Fearless and first and steering with his fleet
  For lands not yet laid down in any chart.

Michael Angelo.

Michel, più che mortal, Angel divino.
ARIOSTO

Similamente operando all' artista
Ch' a l' abito dell' arte e man che trema.
DANTE, *Par.* xiii., st. 77.

DEDICATION.

NOTHING that is shall perish utterly,
  But perish only to revive again
  In other forms, as clouds restore in rain
  The exhalations of the land and sea.
Men build their houses from the masonry
  Of ruined tombs ; the passion and the pain
  Of hearts, that long have ceased to beat, remain
  To throb in hearts that are, or are to be.
So from old chronicles, where sleep in dust
  Names that once filled the world with trumpet tones,
  I build this verse ; and flowers of song have thrust
Their roots among the loose disjointed stones,
  Which to this end I fashion as I must.
  Quickened are they that touch the Prophet's bones.

PART I.

I.

PROLOGUE AT ISCHIA.

The Castle Terrace. VITTORIA
COLONNA *and* JULIA GONZAGA.

Vittoria. Will you then leave me,
  Julia, and so soon,
To pace alone this terrace like a
  ghost ?
Julia. To-morrow, dearest.
Vittoria. Do not say to-morrow.

A whole month of to-morrows were
  too soon.
You must not go.   You are a part
  of me.
  Julia. I must return to Fondi.
  Vittoria.   The old castle
Needs not your presence.   No one
  waits for you.
Stay one day longer with me.
  They who go
Feel not the pain of parting ; it is
  they

786

Who stay behind that suffer. I
    was thinking
But yesterday how like and how
    unlike
Have been, and are, our destinies.
    Your husband,
The good Vespasian, an old man,
    who seemed
A father to you rather than a hus-
    band,
Died in your arms; but mine, in
    all the flower
And promise of his youth, was
    taken from me
As by a rushing wind. The breath
    of battle
Breathed on him, and I saw his
    face no more,
Save as in dreams it haunts me.
    As our love
Was for these men, so is our sorrow
    for them.
Yours a child's sorrow, smiling
    through its tears;
But mine the grief of an impas-
    sioned woman,
Who drank her life up in one
    draught of love.
    Julia. Behold this locket. This
    is the white hair
Of my Vespasian. This is the
    flower-of-love,
This amaranth, and beneath it the
    device
Non moritura. Thus my heart
    remains
True to his memory; and the
    ancient castle,
Where we have lived together,
    where he died,
Is dear to me as Ischia is to you.
    Vittoria. I did not mean to
    chide you.
    Julia. Let your heart
Find, if it can, some poor apology
For one who is too young, and
    feels too keenly
The joy of life, to give up all her days

To sorrow for the dead. While I
    am true
To the remembrance of the man I
    loved
And mourn for still, I do not make
    a show
Of all the grief I feel, nor live
    secluded
And, like Veronica da Gámbara,
Drape my whole house in mourn-
    ing, and drive forth
In coach of sable drawn by sable
    horses,
As if I were a corpse. Ah, one
    to-day
Is worth for me a thousand yester-
    days.
    Vittoria. Dear Julia! Friend-
    ship has its jealousies
As well as love. Who waits for
    you at Fondi?
    Julia. A friend of mine and
    yours; a friend and friar.
You have at Naples your Fra
    Bernadino;
And I at Fondi have my Fra
    Bastiano,
The famous artist, who has come
    from Rome
To paint my portrait. That is not
    a sin.
    Vittoria. Only a vanity.
    Julia. He painted yours.
    Vittoria. Do not call up to me
    those days departed
When I was young, and all was
    bright about me,
And the vicissitudes of life were
    things
But to be read of in old histories,
Though as pertaining unto me or
    mine
Impossible. Ah, then I dreamed
    your dreams,
And now, grown older, I look back
    and see
They were illusions.
    Julia. Yet without illusions

What would our lives become, what
   we ourselves?
Dreams or illusions, call them
   what you will,
They lift us from the commonplace
   of life
To better things.

Vittoria. Are there no brighter
   dreams,
No higher aspirations, than the
   wish
To please and to be pleased?

Julia. For you there are:
I am no saint; I feel the world we
   live in
Comes before that which is to be
   hereafter,
And must be dealt with first.

Vittoria. But in what way?

Julia. Let the soft wind that
   wafts to us the odour
Of orange blossoms, let the laughing sea
And the bright sunshine bathing
   all the world,
Answer the question.

Vittoria. And for whom
   is meant
This portrait that you speak of?

Julia. For my friend
The Cardinal Ippolito.

Vittoria. For him?

Julia. Yes, for Ippolito the
   Magnificent.
'Tis always flattering to a woman's
   pride
To be admired by one whom all
   admire.

Vittoria. Ah, Julia, she that makes
   herself a dove
Is eaten by the hawk. Be on your
   guard.
He is a Cardinal; and his adoration
Should be elsewhere directed.

Julia. You forget
The horror of that night, when
   Barbarossa,

The Moorish corsair, landed on
   our coast
To seize me for the Sultan Soliman;
How in the dead of night, when all
   were sleeping,
He scaled the castle wall; how I
   escaped,
And in my night-dress, mounting
   a swift steed,
Fled to the mountains, and took
   refuge there
Among the brigands. Then of all
   my friends
The Cardinal Ippolito was first
To come with his retainers to my
   rescue.
Could I refuse the only boon he
   asked
At such a time—my portrait?

Vittoria. I have heard
Strange stories of the splendours of
   his palace,
And how, apparelled like a Spanish
   Prince,
He rides through Rome with a
   long retinue
Of Ethiopians and Numidians
And Turks and Tartars, in fantastic
   dresses,
Making a gallant show. Is this
   the way
A Cardinal should live?

Julia. He is so young;
Hardly of age, or little more than
   that;
Beautiful, generous, fond of arts
   and letters,
A poet, a musician, and a scholar;
Master of many languages, and a
   player
On many instruments. In Rome,
   his palace
Is the asylum of all men dis-
   tinguished
In art or science, and all Florentines
Escaping from the tyranny of his
   cousin,
Duke Alessandro.

Vittoria.   I have seen his portrait,
Painted by Titian. You have painted it
In brighter colours.
   Julia.   And my Cardinal,
At Itri, in the courtyard of his palace,
Keeps a tame lion !
   Vittoria.   And so counterfeits
St. Mark, the Evangelist !
   Julia.   Ah, your tame lion
Is Michael Angelo.
   Vittoria.   You speak a name
That always thrills me with a noble sound,
As of a trumpet ! Michael Angelo !
A lion all men fear and none can tame ;
A man that all men honour, and the model
That all should follow ; one who works and prays,
For work is prayer, and consecrates his life
To the sublime ideal of his art,
Till art and life are one ; a man who holds
Such place in all men's thoughts, that when they speak
Of great things done, or to be done, his name
Is ever on their lips.
   Julia.   You too can paint
The portrait of your hero, and in colours
Brighter than Titian's ; I might warn you also
Against the dangers that beset your path ;
But I forbear.
   Vittoria.   If I were made of marble,
Of Fior di Persico or Pavonazzo,
He might admire me : being but flesh and blood,
I am no more to him than other women ;
That is, am nothing.

   Julia.   Does he ride through Rome
Upon his little mule, as he was wont,
With his slouched hat, and boots of Cordovan,
As when I saw him last ?
   Vittoria.   Pray do not jest.
I cannot couple with his noble name
A trivial word ! Look, how the setting sun
Lights up Castel-a-mare and Sorrento,
And changes Capri to a purple cloud !
And there Vesuvius with its plume of smoke,
And the great city stretched upon the shore
As in a dream !
   Julia.   Parthenope the Siren !
   Vittoria. And yon long line of lights, those sunlit windows
Blaze like the torches carried in procession
To do her honour ! It is beautiful !
   Julia. I have no heart to feel the beauty of it !
My feet are weary, pacing up and down
These level flags, and wearier still my thoughts
Treading the broken pavement of the Past.
It is too sad. I will go in and rest,
And make me ready for to-morrow's journey.
   Vittoria. I will go with you ; for
I would not lose
One hour of your dear presence. 'Tis enough
Only to be in the same room with you.
I need not speak to you, nor hear you speak ;
If I but see you, I am satisfied.
                 [They go in.

II.

MONOLOGUE.

MICHAEL ANGELO'S *Studio. He is at work on the cartoon of the Last Judgment.*

Michael A. Why did the Pope
  and his ten Cardinals
Come here to lay this heavy task
  upon me?
Were not the paintings on the
  Sistine ceiling
Enough for them? They saw the
  Hebrew leader
Waiting, and clutching his tem-
  pestuous beard,
But heeded not. The bones of
  Julius
Shook in their sepulchre. I heard
  the sound;
They only heard the sound of their
  own voices.

Are there no other artists here in
  Rome
To do this work, that they must
  needs seek me?
Fra Bastian, my Fra Bastian,
  might have done it;
But he is lost to art. The Papal
  Seals,
Like leaden weights upon a dead
  man's eyes,
Press down his lids; and so the
  burden falls
On Michael Angelo, Chief Archi-
  tect
And Painter of the Apostolic
  Palace.
That is the title they cajole me with,
To make me do their work and
  leave my own;
But having once begun, I turn not
  back.
Blow, ye bright angels, on your
  golden trumpets
To the four corners of the earth,
  and wake

The dead to judgment! Ye record-
  ing angels,
Open your books and read! Ye
  dead, awake!
Rise from your graves, drowsy and
  drugged with death,
As men who suddenly aroused from
  sleep
Look round amazed, and know not
  where they are!

In happy hours, when the imagina-
  tion
Wakes like a wind at midnight, and
  the soul
Trembles in all its leaves, it is a joy
To be uplifted on its wings, and
  listen
To the prophetic voices in the air
That call us onward. Then the
  work we do
Is a delight, and the obedient hand
Never grows weary. But how
  different is it
In the disconsolate, discouraged
  hours,
When all the wisdom of the world
  appears
As trivial as the gossip of a nurse
In a sick-room, and all our work
  seems useless.

What is it guides my hand, what
  thoughts possess me,
That I have drawn her face among
  the angels,
Where she will be hereafter? O
  sweet dreams,
That through the vacant chambers
  of my heart
Walk in the silence, as familiar
  phantoms
Frequent an ancient house, what
  will ye with me?
'Tis said that Emperors write their
  names in green
When under age, but when of age
  in purple.

So Love, the greatest Emperor of
    them all,
Writes his in green at first, but
    afterwards
In the imperial purple of our blood.
First love or last love,—which of
    these two passions
Is more omnipotent? Which is
    more fair,
The star of morning or the evening
    star?
The sunrise or the sunset of the
    heart?
The hour when we look forth to the
    unknown,
And the advancing day consumes
    the shadows,
Or that when all the landscape of
    our lives
Lies stretched behind us, and
    familiar places
Gleam in the distance, and sweet
    memories
Rise like a tender haze, and
    magnify
The objects we behold, that soon
    must vanish?

What matters it to me, whose coun-
    tenance
Is like the Laocoön's, full of pain;
    whose forehead
Is a ploughed harvest-field, where
    three-score years
Have sown in sorrow and have
    reaped in anguish;
To me, the artisan, to whom all
    women
Have been as if they were not, or
    at most
A sudden rush of pigeons in the
    air,
A flutter of wings, a sound, and
    then a silence?
I am too old for love; I am too
    old
To flatter and delude myself with
    visions

Of never-ending friendship with fair
    women,
Imaginations, fantasies, illusions,
In which the things that cannot be
    take shape,
And seem to be, and for the moment
    are.   [*Convent bells ring.*

Distant and near and low and loud
    the bells,
Dominican, Benedictine, and Fran-
    ciscan,
Jangle and wrangle in their airy
    towers,
Discordant as the brotherhoods
    themselves
In their dim cloisters. The de-
    scending sun
Seems to caress the city that he
    loves,
And crowns it with the aureole of
    a saint.
I will go forth and breathe the air
    a while.

III.

SAN SILVESTRO.

*A Chapel in the Church of San
Silvestro on Monte Cavallo.*
VITTORIA COLONNA, CLAUDIO
TOLOMMEI, *and others.*

Vittoria. Here let us rest a while,
    until the crowd
Has left the church. I have already
    sent
For Michael Angelo to join us here.
Claudio. After Fra Bernardino's
    wise discourse
On the Pauline Epistles, certainly
Some words of Michael Angelo on
    Art
Were not amiss, to bring us back to
    earth.
    Michael A. (at the door). How
    like a Saint or Goddess she
    appears;

Diana or Madonna, which I know
   not !
In attitude and aspect formed
   to be
At once the artist's worship and
   despair !
  Vittoria. Welcome, Maestro.
   We were waiting for you.
  Michael A. I met your mes-
   senger upon the way,
And hastened hither.
  Vittoria. It is kind of you
To come to us, who linger here like
   gossips
Wasting the afternoon in idle talk.
These are all friends of mine and
   friends of yours.
  Michael A. If friends of yours,
   then are they friends of mine.
Pardon me, gentlemen. But when
   I entered
I saw but the Marchesa.
  Vittoria. Take this seat
Between me and Ser Claudio
   Tolommei,
Who still maintains that our Italian
   tongue
Should be called Tuscan. But for
   that offence
We will not quarrel with him.
  Michael A. Eccellenza—
  Vittoria. Ser Claudio has ban-
   ished Eccellenza
And all such titles from the Tuscan
   tongue.
  Claudio. 'Tis the abuse of them
   and not the use
I deprecate.
  Michael A. The use or the abuse
It matters not. Let them all go to-
   gether,
As empty phrases and frivolities,
And common as gold-lace upon the
   collar
Of an obsequious lackey.
  Vittoria. That may be,
But something of politeness would
   go with them ;

We should lose something of the
   stately manners
Of the old school.
  Claudio. Undoubtedly.
  Vittoria. But that
Is not what occupies my thoughts
   at present,
Nor why I sent for you, Messer
   Michele.
It was to counsel me. His Holiness
Has granted me permission, long
   desired,
To build a convent in this neigh-
   bourhood,
Where the old tower is standing,
   from whose top
Nero looked down upon the burning
   city.
  Michael A. It is an inspiration !
  Vittoria. I am doubtful
How I shall build ; how large to
   make the convent,
And which way fronting.
  Michael A. Ah, to build, to build !
That is the noblest art of all the arts.
Painting and sculpture are but
   images,
Are merely shadows cast by out-
   ward things
On stone or canvas, having in
   themselves
No separate existence. Architec-
   ture,
Existing in itself, and not in seem-
   ing
A something it is not, surpasses
   them
As substance shadow. Long, long
   years ago,
Standing one morning near the
   Baths of Titus,
I saw the statue of Laocoön
Rise from its grave of centuries,
   like a ghost
Writhing in pain ; and as it tore
   away
The knotted serpents from its
   limbs, I heard,

Or seemed to hear, the cry of agony
From its white, parted lips. And
still I marvel
At the three Rhodian artists, by
whose hands
This miracle was wrought. Yet he
beholds
Far nobler works who looks upon
the ruins
Of temples in the Forum here in
Rome.
If God should give me power in
my old age
To build for Him a temple half as
grand
As those were in their glory, I
should count
My age more excellent than youth
itself,
And all that I have hitherto accom-
plished
As only vanity.
   Vittoria.   I understand you.
Art is the gift of God, and must
be used
Unto His glory. That in Art is
highest
Which aims at this. When Saint
Hilarion blessed
The horses of Italicus, they won
The race at Gaza, for his benedic-
tion
O'erpowered all magic; and the
people shouted
That Christ had conquered Marnas.
So that art
Which bears the consecration and
the seal
Of holiness upon it will prevail
Over all others. Those few words
of yours
Inspire me with new confidence to
build.
What think you? The old walls
might serve, perhaps,
Some purpose still. The tower can
hold the bells.
   Michael A. If strong enough.

Vittoria.   If not, it can be
strengthened.
   Michael A. I see no bar nor
drawback to this building,
And on our homeward way, if it
shall please you,
We may together view the site.
   Vittoria.   I thank you.
I do not venture to request so much.
   Michael A. Let us now go to the
old walls you spake of,
Vossignoria—
   Vittoria. What, again, Maestro?
   Michael A. Pardon me, Messer
Claudio, if once more
I use the ancient courtesies of
speech.
I am too old to change.

IV.

CARDINAL IPPOLITO.

*A richly furnished apartment in
the Palace of* CARDINAL IPPO-
LITO. *Night.* JACOPO NARDI,
an old man, alone.

   Nardi. I am bewildered. These
Numidian slaves,
In strange attire; these endless
antechambers;
This lighted hall, with all its golden
splendours,
Pictures, and statues! Can this
be the dwelling
Of a disciple of that lowly Man
Who had not where to lay his head?
These statues
Are not of Saints; nor is this a
Madonna,
This lovely face, that with such
tender eyes
Looks down upon me from the
painted canvas.
My heart begins to fail me. What
can he

Who lives in boundless luxury at Rome
Care for the imperilled liberties of Florence,
Her people, her Republic? Ah, the rich
Feel not the pangs of banishment. All doors
Are open to them, and all hands extended.
The poor alone are outcasts; they who risked
All they possessed for liberty, and lost;
And wander through the world without a friend,
Sick, comfortless, distressed, unknown, uncared for.

Enter CARDINAL IPPOLITO, *in Spanish cloak and slouched hat.*

Ippolito. I pray you pardon me that I have kept you
Waiting so long alone.
Nardi. I wait to see The Cardinal.
Ippolito. I am the Cardinal; And you?
Nardi. Jacopo Nardi.
Ippolito. You are welcome. I was expecting you. Philippo Strozzi
Had told me of your coming.
Nardi. 'Twas his son That brought me to your door.
Ippolito. Pray you, be seated. You seem astonished at the garb I wear;
But at my time of life, and with my habits,
The petticoats of a Cardinal would be—
Troublesome; I could neither ride nor walk,
Nor do a thousand things, if I were dressed
Like an old dowager. It were putting wine

Young as the young Astyanax into goblets
As old as Priam.
Nardi. Oh, your Eminence Knows best what you should wear.
Ippolito. Dear Messer Nardi, You are no stranger to me. I have read
Your excellent translation of the books
Of Titus Livius, the historian Of Rome, and model of all historians
That shall come after him. It does you honour;
But greater honour still the love you bear
To Florence, our dear country, and whose annals
I hope your hand will write, in happier days
Than we now see.
Nardi. Your Eminence will pardon
The lateness of the hour.
Ippolito. The hours I count not
As a sun-dial; but am like a clock,
That tells the time as well by night as day.
So, no excuse. I know what brings you here.
You come to speak of Florence.
Nardi. And her woes.
Ippolito. The Duke, my cousin, the black Alessandro,
Whose mother was a Moorish slave, that fed
The sheep upon Lorenzo's farm, still lives
And reigns.
Nardi. Alas, that such a scourge
Should fall on such a city!
Ippolito. When he dies,
The Wild Boar in the gardens of Lorenzo,

The beast obscene, should be the monument
Of this bad man.
   Nardi.   He walks the streets at night
With revellers, insulting honest men.
No house is sacred from his lusts. The convents
Are turned by him to brothels, and the honour
Of women and all ancient pious customs
Are quite forgotten now. The offices
Of the Priori and Gonfalonieri
Have been abolished. All the magistrates
Are now his creatures. Liberty is dead.
The very memory of all honest living
Is wiped away, and even our Tuscan tongue
Corrupted to a Lombard dialect.
   Ippolito. And worst of all, his impious hand has broken
The Martinella,—our great battle bell,
That, sounding through three centuries, has led
The Florentines to victory,—lest its voice
Should waken in their souls some memory
Of far-off times of glory.
   Nardi.   What a change
Ten little years have made! We all remember
Those better days, when Niccolà Capponi,
The Gonfaloniere, from the windows
Of the Old Palace, with the blast of trumpets,
Proclaimed to the inhabitants that Christ
Was chosen King of Florence; and already

Christ is dethroned, and slain, and in his stead
Reigns Lucifer! Alas, alas, for Florence!
   Ippolito. Lilies with lilies, said Savonarola;
Florence and France! But I say Florence only,
Or only with the Emperor's hand to help us
In sweeping out the rubbish.
   Nardi.   Little hope
Of help is there from him. He has betrothed
His daughter Margaret to this shameless Duke.
What hope have we from such an Emperor?
   Ippolito. Baccio Valori and Philippo Strozzi,
Once the Duke's friends and intimates, are with us,
And Cardinals Salvati and Ridolfi.
We shall soon see, then, as Valori says,
Whether the Duke can best spare honest men,
Or honest men the Duke.
   Nardi.   We have determined
To send ambassadors to Spain, and lay
Our griefs before the Emperor, though I fear
More than I hope.
   Ippolito. The Emperor is busy
With this new war against the Algerines,
And has no time to listen to complaints
From our ambassadors; nor will I trust them,
But go myself. All is in readiness
For my departure, and to-morrow morning
I shall go down to Itri, where I meet
Dante da Castiglione and some others

Republicans and fugitives from
Florence,
And then take ship at Gaëta, and go
To join the Emperor in his new
crusade
Against the Turk. I shall have
time enough
And opportunity to plead our cause.
Nardi (*rising*). It is an inspira-
tion, and I hail it
As of good omen. May the power
that sends it
Bless our beloved country, and
restore
Its banished citizens. The soul of
Florence
Is now outside its gates. What
lies within
Is but a corpse, corrupted and
corrupting.
Heaven help us all. I will not
tarry longer,
For you have need of rest. Good-
night.
Ippolito. Good-night.

Enter FRA SEBASTIANO ; *Turkish
attendants.*

Ippolito. Fra Bastiano, how your
portly presence
Contrasts with that of the spare
Florentine
Who has just left me !
Fra Seb. As we passed
each other,
I saw that he was weeping.
Ippolito. Poor old man !
Fra Seb. Who is he ?
Ippolito. Jacopo Nardi.
A brave soul ;
One of the Fuoruseiti, and the best
And noblest of them all ; but he
has made me
Sad with his sadness. As I look
on you
My heart grows lighter. I behold
a man
Who lives in an ideal world, apart

From all the rude collisions of our
life,
In a calm atmosphere.
Fra Seb. Your Eminence
Is surely jesting. If you knew the
life
Of artists as I know it, you might
think
Far otherwise.
Ippolito. But wherefore should
I jest ?
The world of art is an ideal world,—
The world I love, and that I fain
would live in ;
So speak to me of artists and of art,
Of all the painters, sculptors, and
musicians
That now illustrate Rome.
Fra Seb. Of the musicians,
I know but Goudimel, the brave
maestro
And chapel-master of his Holiness,
Who trains the Papal choir.
Ippolito. In church this morning,
I listened to a mass of Goudimel,
Divinely chanted. In the Incar-
natus,
In lieu of Latin words, the tenor
sang
With infinite tenderness, in plain
Italian,
A Neapolitan love-song.
Fra Seb. You amaze me
Was it a wanton song ?
Ippolito. Not a divine one.
I am not over-scrupulous, as you
know,
In word or deed, yet such a song
as that,
Sung by the tenor of the Papal
choir,
And in a Papal mass, seemed out
of place ;
There 's something wrong in it.
Fra Seb. There 's
something wrong
In everything. We cannot make
the world

Go right. 'Tis not my business to reform
The Papal choir.

Ippolito. Nor mine, thank Heaven!
Then tell me of the artists.

Fra Seb. Naming one
I name them all; for there is only one:
His name is Messer Michael Angelo.
All art and artists of the present day
Centre in him.

Ippolito. You count yourself as nothing?

Fra Seb. Or less than nothing, since I am at best
Only a portrait-painter; one who draws
With greater or less skill, as best he may,
The features of a face.

Ippolito. And you have had
The honour, nay, the glory, of portraying
Julia Gonzaga! Do you count as nothing
A privilege like that? See there the portrait
Rebuking you with its divine expression.
Are you not penitent? He whose skilful hand
Painted that lovely picture has not right
To vilipend the art of portrait-painting.
But what of Michael Angelo?

Fra Seb. But lately,
Strolling together down the crowded Corso,
We stopped, well pleased, to see your Eminence
Pass on an Arab steed, a noble creature,
Which Michael Angelo, who is a lover

Of all things beautiful, especially
When they are Arab horses, much admired,
And could not praise enough.

Ippolito (to an attendant). Hassan, to-morrow,
When I am gone, but not till I am gone,—
Be careful about that,—take Barbarossa
To Messer Michael Angelo, the sculptor,
Who lives there at Macello dei Corvi,
Near to the Capitol; and take besides
Some ten mule-loads of provender, and say
Your master sends them to him as a present.

Fra Seb. A princely gift. Though Michael Angelo
Refuses presents from his Holiness,
Yours he will not refuse.

Ippolito. You think him like
Thymœtes, who received the wooden horse
Into the walls of Troy. That book of Virgil
Have I translated in Italian verse,
And shall, some day, when we have leisure for it,
Be pleased to read you. When I speak of Troy
I am reminded of another town
And of a lovelier Helen, our dear Countess
Julia Gonzaga. You remember, surely,
The adventure with the corsair Barbarossa,
And all that followed?

Fra Seb. A most strange adventure;
A tale as marvellous and full of wonder
As any in Boccaccio or Sacchetti;
Almost incredible!

Ippolito.   Were I a painter
I should not want a better theme
than that :
The lovely lady fleeing through
the night
In wild disorder ; and the brigands'
camp
With the red fire-light on their
swarthy faces.
Could you not paint it for me ?
Fra Seb.   No, not I.
It is not in my line.
Ippolito.   Then you shall paint
The portrait of the corsair, when
we bring him
A prisoner chained to Naples ; for
I feel
Something like admiration for a
man
Who dared this strange adventure.
Fra Seb.   I will do it ;
But catch the corsair first.
Ippolito.   You may begin
To-morrow with the sword.   Has-
san, come hither ;
Bring me the Turkish scimitar that
hangs
Beneath the picture yonder.   Now
unsheathe it.
'Tis a Damascus blade ; you see
the inscription
In Arabic : *La Allah illa Allah,*—
There is no God but God.
Fra Seb.   How beautiful
In fashion and in finish ! It is
perfect.
The Arsenal of Venice cannot boast
A finer sword.
Ippolito. You like it? It is yours.
Fra Seb. You do not mean it.
Ippolito.   I am not
a Spaniard
To say that it is yours and not to
mean it.
I have at Itri a whole armoury
Full of such weapons.   When you
paint the portrait
Of Barbarossa it will be of use.

You have not been rewarded as you
should be
For painting the Gonzaga.   Throw
this bauble
Into the scale, and make the
balance equal.
Till then suspend it in your studio ;
You artists like such trifles.
Fra Seb.   I will keep it
In memory of the donor.   Many
thanks.
Ippolito.   Fra Bastian, I am
growing tired of Rome,
The old dead city, with the old
dead people ;
Priests everywhere, like shadows
on a wall,
And morning, noon, and night the
ceaseless sound
Of convent bells.   I must be gone
from here ;
Though Ovid somewhere says that
Rome is worthy
To be the dwelling-place of all the
Gods,
I must be gone from here.   To-
morrow morning
I start for Itri, and go thence by sea
To join the Emperor, who is making
war
Upon the Algerines ; perhaps to
sink
Some Turkish galleys, and bring
back in chains
The famous corsair.   Thus would
I avenge
The beautiful Gonzaga.
Fra Seb.   An achievement
Worthy of Charlemagne, or of
Orlando.
Berni and Ariosto both shall add
A canto to their poems, and describe
you
As Furioso and Innamorato.
Now I must say good-night.
Ippolito.   You must not go ;
First you shall sup with me.   My
seneschal,

Giovan Andrea dal Borgo a San
    Sepolcro,—
I like to give the whole sonorous
    name,
It sounds so like a verse of the
    Æneid,—
Has brought me eels fresh from the
    Lake of Fondi,
And Lucrine oysters cradled in their
    shells :
These, with red Fondi wine, the
    Caecuban
That Horace speaks of, under a
    hundred keys
Kept safe, until the heir of Post-
    humus
Shall stain the pavement with it,
    make a feast
Fit for Lucullus, or Fra Bastian
    even ;
So we will go to supper, and be
    merry.
    Fra Seb. Beware ! Remember
    that Bolsena's eels
And Vernage wine once killed a
    Pope of Rome !
    Ippolito. 'Twas a French Pope ;
    and then so long ago ;
Who knows ?—perhaps the story
    is not true.

V.

Borgo delle Vergine at
Naples.

Room in the Palace of Julia Gon-
    zaga. *Night.* Julia Gonzaga,
    Giovanni Valdesso.

    Julia. Do not go yet.
    Valdesso. The night is
    far advanced ;
I fear to stay too late, and weary
    you
With these discussions.
    Julia. I have much to say.
I speak to you, Valdesso, with that
    frankness

Which is the greatest privilege of
    friendship,—
Speak as I hardly would to my
    confessor,
Such is my confidence in you.
    Valdesso. Dear Countess,
If loyalty to friendship be a claim
Upon your confidence, then I may
    claim it.
    Julia. Then sit again, and listen
    unto things
That nearer are to me than life
    itself.
    Valdesso. In all things I am
    happy to obey you,
And happiest then when you com-
    mand me most.
    Julia. Laying aside all useless
    rhetoric,
That is superfluous between us two,
I come at once unto the point, and
    say,
You know my outward life, my
    rank and fortune ;
Countess of Fondi, Duchess of
    Trajetto,
A widow rich and flattered, for
    whose hand
In marriage princes ask, and ask
    it only
To be rejected. All the world can
    offer
Lies at my feet. If I remind you
    of it,
It is not in the way of idle boasting,
But only to the better understanding
Of what comes after.
    Valdesso. God hath given
    you also
Beauty and intellect ; and the
    signal grace
To lead a spotless life amid tempta-
    tions
That others yield to.
    Julia. But the inward life,—
That you know not ; 'tis known
    but to myself,
And is to me a mystery and a pain.

A soul disquieted, and ill at ease,
A mind perplexed with doubts and
apprehensions,
A heart dissatisfied with all around
me,
And with myself, so that sometimes
I weep,
Discouraged and disgusted with
the world.

Valdesso. Whene'er we cross a
river at a ford,
If we would pass in safety, we
must keep
Our eyes fixed steadfast on the
shore beyond,
For if we cast them on the flowing
stream
The head swims with it; so if we
would cross
The running flood of things here
in the world,
Our souls must not look down, but
fix their sight
On the firm land beyond.

Julia.   I comprehend you.
You think I am too worldly; that
my head
Swims with the giddy whirl of
life about me.
Is that your meaning?

Valdesso. Yes; your meditations
Are more of this world and its
vanities
Than of the world to come.

Julia.   Between the two
I am confused.

Valdesso. Yet have I seen you
listen
Enraptured when Fra Bernardino
preached
Of faith and hope and charity.

Julia.   I listen,
But only as to music without
meaning.
It moves me for the moment, and
I think
How beautiful it is to be a saint,
As dear Vittoria is; but I am weak

And wayward, and I soon fall back
again
To my old ways so very easily.
There are too many week-days for
one Sunday.

Valdesso. Then take the Sunday
with you through the week,
And sweeten with it all the other
days.

Julia. In part I do so; for to put
a stop
To idle tongues, what men might
say of me
If I lived all alone here in my palace,
And not from a vocation that I feel
For the monastic life, I now am
living
With Sister Caterina at the convent
Of Santa Chiara, and I come here
only
On certain days, for my affairs, or
visits
Of ceremony, or to be with friends.
For I confess, to live among my
friends
Is Paradise to me; my Purgatory
Is living among people I dislike.
And so I pass my life in these two
worlds,
This palace and the convent.

Valdesso.   It was then
The fear of man, and not the love
of God,
That led you to this step. Why
will you not
Give all your heart to God?

Julia.   If God commands it,
Wherefore hath He not made me
capable
Of doing for Him what I wish to do
As easily as I could offer Him
This jewel from my hand, this
gown I wear,
Or aught else that is mine?

Valdesso.   The hindrance lies
In that original sin, by which all fell.

Julia. Ah me, I cannot bring my
troubled mind

To wish well to that Adam, our
first parent,
Who by his sin lost Paradise for us,
And brought such ills upon us.

Valdesso. We ourselves,
When we commit a sin, lose Para-
dise
As much as he did. Let us think
of this,
And how we may regain it.

Julia. Teach me, then,
To harmonize the discord of my
life,
And stop the painful jangle of these
wires.

Valdesso. That is a task impossible, until
You tune your heart-strings to a
higher key
Than earthly melodies.

Julia. How shall I do it?
Point out to me the way of this
perfection,
And I will follow you; for you
have made
My soul enamoured with it, and I
cannot
Rest satisfied until I find it out.
But lead me privately, so that the
world
Hear not my steps; I would not
give occasion
For talk among the people.

Valdesso. Now at last
I understand you fully. Then,
what need
Is there for us to beat about the
bush?
I know what you desire of me.

Julia. What rudeness!
If you already know it, why not
tell me?

Valdesso. Because I rather wait
for you to ask it
With your own lips.

Julia. Do me the kindness, then,
To speak without reserve; and
with all frankness,

If you divine the truth, will I confess it.

Valdesso. I am content.

Julia. Then speak.

Valdesso. You would be free
From the vexatious thoughts that
come and go
Through your imagination, and
would have me
Point out some royal road and
lady-like
Which you may walk in, and not
wound your feet;
You would attain to the divine
perfection,
And yet not turn your back upon
the world;
You would possess humility within,
But not reveal it in your outward
actions;
You would have patience, but with-
out the rude
Occasions that require its exercise;
You would despise the world, but in
such fashion
The world should not despise you
in return;
Would clothe the soul with all the
Christian graces,
Yet not despoil the body of its
gauds;
Would feed the soul with spiritual
food,
Yet not deprive the body of its
feasts;
Would seem angelic in the sight of
God,
Yet not too saint-like in the eyes of
men;
In short, would lead a holy Chris-
tian life
In such a way that even your
nearest friend
Would not detect therein one
circumstance
To show a change from what it was
before.
Have I divined your secret?

Julia. You have drawn
The portrait of my inner self as truly
As the most skilful painter ever painted
A human face.

Valdesso. This warrants me in saying
You think you can win heaven by compromise,
And not by verdict.

Julia. You have often told me
That a bad compromise was better even
Than a good verdict.

Valdesso. Yes, in suits at law;
Not in religion. With the human soul
There is no compromise. By faith alone
Can man be justified.

Julia. Hush, dear Valdesso;
That is a heresy. Do not, I pray you,
Proclaim it from the house-top, but preserve it
As something precious, hidden in your heart,
As I, who half believe and tremble at it.

Valdesso. I must proclaim the truth.

Julia. Enthusiast!
Why must you? You imperil both yourself
And friends by your imprudence. Pray, be patient.
You have occasion now to show that virtue
Which you lay stress upon. Let us return
To our lost pathway. Show me by what steps
I shall walk in it.

[*Convent bells are heard.*

Valdesso. Hark! the convent bells
Are ringing; it is midnight; I must leave you.

And yet I linger. Pardon me, dear Countess,
Since you to-night have made me your confessor,
If I so far may venture, I will warn you
Upon one point.

Julia. What is it? Speak, I pray you,
For I have no concealments in my conduct;
All is as open as the light of day.
What is it you would warn me of?

Valdesso. Your friendship
With Cardinal Ippolito.

Julia. What is there
To cause suspicion or alarm in that,
More than in friendships that I entertain
With you and others? I ne'er sat with him
Alone at night, as I am sitting now
With you, Valdesso.

Valdesso. Pardon me; the portrait
That Fra Bastiano painted was for him.
Is that quite prudent?

Julia. That is the same question
Vittoria put to me, when I last saw her.
I make you the same answer. That was not
A pledge of love, but of pure gratitude.
Recall the adventure of that dreadful night
When Barbarossa with two thousand Moors
Landed upon the coast, and in the darkness
Attacked my castle. Then, without delay,
The Cardinal came hurrying down from Rome
To rescue and protect me. Was it wrong

That in an hour like that I did not
weigh
Too nicely this or that, but granted
him
A boon that pleased him, and that
flattered me ?

Valdesso. Only beware lest, in
disguise of friendship
Another corsair, worse than Barbarossa,
Steal in and seize the castle, not
by storm
But strategy. And now I take my
leave.

Julia. Farewell; but ere you go
look forth and see
How night hath hushed the clamour and the stir
Of the tumultuous streets. The
cloudless moon
Roofs the whole city as with tiles
of silver;
The dim, mysterious sea in silence
sleeps;
And straight into the air Vesuvius
lifts
His plume of smoke. How beautiful it is ! [*Voices in the street.*

Giovan Andrea. Poisoned at
Itri.
Another Voice. Poisoned ?
Who is poisoned ?
Giovan Andrea. The Cardinal
Ippolito, my master.
Call it malaria. It was very sud-
den. [*Julia swoons.*

VI.

VITTORIA COLONNA.

A room in the Torre Argentina.
VITTORIA COLONNA *and* JULIA
GONZAGA.

Vittoria. Come to my arms and
to my heart once more;
My soul goes out to meet you and
embrace you,

For we are of the sisterhood of
sorrow.
I know what you have suffered.
Julia. Name it not.
Let me forget it.
Vittoria. I will say no more.
Let me look at you. What a joy
it is
To see your face, to hear your voice
again !
You bring with you a breath as of
the morn,
A memory of the far-off happy days
When we were young. When did
you come from Fondi ?
Julia. I have not been at Fondi
since—
Vittoria. Ah me !
You need not speak the word; I
understand you.
Julia. I came from Naples by
the lovely valley,
The Terra di Lavoro.
Vittoria. And you find me
But just returned from a long
journey northward.
I have been staying with that
noble woman
Renée of France, the Duchess of
Ferrara.
Julia. Oh, tell me of the Duchess.
I have heard
Flaminio speak her praises with
such warmth
That I am eager to hear more of
her
And of her brilliant court.
Vittoria. You shall hear all.
But first sit down and listen
patiently
While I confess myself.
Julia. What deadly sin
Have you committed ?
Vittoria. Not a sin; a folly.
I chid you once at Ischia, when
you told me
That brave Fra Bastian was to
paint your portrait.

Julia. Well I remember it.

Vittoria. Then chide me now,
For I confess to something still more strange.
Old as I am, I have at last consented
To the entreaties and the supplications
Of Michael Angelo—

Julia. To marry him?

Vittoria. I pray you, do not jest with me! You know,
Or you should know, that never such a thought
Entered my breast. I am already married.
The Marquis of Pescara is my husband,
And death has not divorced us.

Julia. Pardon me.
Have I offended you?

Vittoria. No, but have hurt me.
Unto my buried lord I give myself,
Unto my friend the shadow of myself,—
My portrait. It is not from vanity,
But for the love I bear him.

Julia. I rejoice
To hear these words. Oh, this will be a portrait
Worthy of both of you! [*A knock.*

Vittoria. Hark! he is coming.

Julia. And shall I go or stay?

Vittoria. By all means stay.
The drawing will be better for your presence;
You will enliven me.

Julia. I shall not speak;
The presence of great men doth take from me
All power of speech. I only gaze at them
In silent wonder, as if they were gods,
Or the inhabitants of some other planet.

Enter MICHAEL ANGELO.

Vittoria. Come in.

Michael A. I fear my visit is ill-timed;
I interrupt you.

Vittoria. No; this is a friend
Of yours as well as mine,—the Lady Julia,
The Duchess of Trajetto.

Michael A. (*to* JULIA). I salute you.
'Tis long since I have seen your face, my lady;
Pardon me if I say that having seen it,
One never can forget it.

Julia. You are kind
To keep me in your memory.

Michael A. It is
The privilege of age to speak with frankness.
You will not be offended when I say
That never was your beauty more divine.

Julia. When Michael Angelo condescends to flatter
Or praise me, I am proud, and not offended.

Vittoria. Now this is gallantry enough for one;
Show me a little.

Michael A. Ah, my gracious lady,
You know I have not words to speak your praise.
I think of you in silence. You conceal
Your manifold perfections from all eyes,
And make yourself more saint-like day by day,
And day by day men worship you the more.
But now your hour of martyrdom has come.
You know why I am here.

Vittoria.   Ah yes, I know it ;
And meet my fate with fortitude.
    You find me
Surrounded by the labours of your
    hands :
The Woman of Samaria at the
    Well,
The Mater Dolorosa, and the
    Christ
Upon the Cross, beneath which
    you have written
Those memorable words of Ali-
    ghieri,
' Men have forgotten how much
    blood it costs.'
    Michael A. And now I come to
    add one labour more,
If you will call that labour which is
    pleasure,
And only pleasure.
    Vittoria.   How shall I be
    seated ?
    Michael A. (*opening his port-
    folio*). Just as you are. The
    light falls well upon you.
    Vittoria. I am ashamed to steal
    the time from you
That should be given to the Sistine
    Chapel.
How does that work go on ?
    Michael A. (*drawing*).   But
    tardily.
Old men work slowly. Brain and
    hand alike
Are dull and torpid. To die young
    is best,
And not to be remembered as old
    men
Tottering about in their decrepi-
    tude.
    Vittoria. My dear Maestro !
    have you, then, forgotten
The story of Sophocles in his old
    age ?
    Michael A. What story is it ?
    Vittoria. When his
    sons accused him,
Before the Areopagus, of dotage,

For all defence he read there to his
    Judges
The Tragedy of Œdipus Colo-
    neus—
The work of his old age.
    Michael A.   'Tis an illusion,
A fabulous story, that will lead old
    men
Into a thousand follies and conceits.
    Vittoria. So you may show to
    cavillers your painting
Of the Last Judgment in the Sistine
    Chapel.
    Michael A. Now you and Lady
    Julia shall resume
The conversation that I inter-
    rupted.
    Vittoria. It was of no great im-
    port ; nothing more
Nor less than my late visit to
    Ferrara,
And what I saw there in the ducal
    palace.
Will it not interrupt you ?
    Michael A.   Not the least.
    Vittoria. Well, first, then, of
    Duke Ercole : a man
Cold in his manners, and reserved
    and silent,
And yet magnificent in all his
    ways ;
Not hospitable unto new ideas,
But from state policy, and certain
    reasons
Concerning the investiture of the
    duchy,
A partisan of Rome, and con-
    sequently
Intolerant of all the new opinions.
    Julia. I should not like the
    Duke. These silent men,
Who only look and listen, are like
    wells
That have no water in them, deep
    and empty.
How could the daughter of a king of
    France
Wed such a duke ?

Michael A. The men that women marry,
And why they marry them, will always be
A marvel and a mystery to the world.

Vittoria. And then the Duchess, —how shall I describe her,
Or tell the merits of that happy nature,
Which pleases most when least it thinks of pleasing?
Not beautiful, perhaps, in form and feature,
Yet with an inward beauty, that shines through
Each look and attitude and word and gesture;
A kindly grace of manner and behaviour,
A something in her presence and her ways
That makes her beautiful beyond the reach
Of mere external beauty; and in heart
So noble and devoted to the truth,
And so in sympathy with all who strive
After the higher life.

Julia. She draws me to her
As much as her Duke Ercole repels me.

Vittoria. Then the devout and honourable women
That grace her court, and make it good to be there;
Francesca Bucyronia, the true-hearted,
Lavinia della Rovere and the Orsini,
The Magdalena and the Cherubina,
And Anne de Parthenai, who sings so sweetly;
All lovely women, full of noble thoughts
And aspirations after noble things.

Julia. Boccaccio would have envied you such dames.

Vittoria. No; his Fiammettas and his Philomenas
Are fitter company for Ser Giovanni;
I fear he hardly would have comprehended
The women that I speak of.

Michael A. Yet he wrote
The story of Griselda. That is something
To set down in his favour.

Vittoria. With these ladies
Was a young girl, Olympia Morata,
Daughter of Fulvio, the learned scholar,
Famous in all the universities;
A marvellous child, who at the spinning-wheel,
And in the daily round of household cares,
Hath learned both Greek and Latin; and is now
A favourite of the Duchess and companion
Of Princess Anne. This beautiful young Sappho
Sometimes recited to us Grecian odes
That she had written, with a voice whose sadness
Thrilled and o'ermastered me, and made me look
Into the future time, and ask myself
What destiny will be hers.

Julia. A sad one, surely.
Frost kills the flowers that blossom out of season;
And these precocious intellects portend
A life of sorrow or an early death.

Vittoria. About the court were many learned men;
Chilian Sinapius from beyond the Alps,
And Celio Curione, and Manzolli.

The Duke's physician ; and a pale
young man,
Charles d'Espeville of Geneva,
whom the Duchess
Doth much delight to talk with
and to read,
For he hath written a book of
Institutes
The Duchess greatly praises, though
some call it
The Koran of the heretics.

Julia. And what poets
Were there to sing you madrigals,
and praise
Olympia's eyes and Cherubina's
tresses ?

Vittoria. No ; for great Ariosto
is no more.
The voice that filled those halls
with melody
Has long been hushed in death.

Julia. You should
have made
A pilgrimage unto the poet's
tomb,
And laid a wreath upon it, for the
words
He spake of you.

Vittoria. And of yourself
no less,
And of our master, Michael Angelo.

Michael A. Of me ?

Vittoria. Have you
forgotten that he calls you
Michael, less than man than angel, and
divine ?
You are ungrateful.

Michael A. A mere play on
words.
That adjective he wanted for a
rhyme,

To match with Gian Bellino and
Urbino.

Vittoria. Bernardo Tasso is no
longer there,
Nor the gay troubadour of Gas-
cony,
Clement Marot, surnamed by flat-
terers
The Prince of Poets and the Poet
of Princes,
Who, being looked upon with much
disfavour
By the Duke Ercole, has fled to
Venice.

Michael A. There let him stay
with Pietro Aretino,
The Scourge of Princes, also called
Divine.
The title is so common in our
mouths,
That even the Pifferari of Abruzzi,
Who play their bag-pipes in the
streets of Rome
At the Epiphany, will bear it soon,
And will deserve it better than
some poets.

Vittoria. What bee hath stung
you ?

Michael A. One that
makes no honey ;
One that comes buzzing in through
every window,
And stabs men with his sting. A
bitter thought
Passed through my mind, but it is
gone again ;
I spake too hastily.

Julia. I pray you, show me
What you have done.

Michael A. Not yet ; it is
not finished.

807

PART SECOND.

I.

MONOLOGUE.

A room in MICHAEL ANGELO'S
house.

Michael A. Fled to Viterbo,
the old Papal city
Where once an Emperor, humbled
in his pride,
Held the Pope's stirrup, as his
Holiness
Alighted from his mule! A fugitive
From Cardinal Caraffa's hate, who
hurls
His thunders at the house of the
Colonna,
With endless bitterness!—Among
the nuns
In Santa Catarina's convent hid-
den,
Herself in soul a nun! And now
she chides me
For my too frequent letters, that
disturb
Her meditations, and that hinder
me
And keep me from my work; now
graciously
She thanks me for the crucifix I
sent her,
And says that she will keep it:
with one hand
Inflicts a wound, and with the
other heals it.

(Reading.)

' Profoundly I believed that God
would grant you
A supernatural faith to paint this
Christ;
I wished for that which I now see
fulfilled
So marvellously, exceeding all my
wishes.

Nor more could be desired, or even
so much.
And greatly I rejoice that you
have made
The angel on the right so beautiful;
For the Archangel Michael will
place you,
You, Michael Angelo, on that new
day,
Upon the Lord's right hand! And
waiting that,
How can I better serve you than
to pray
To this sweet Christ for you, and
to beseech you
To hold me altogether yours in all
things.'

Well, I will write less often, or no
more,
But wait her coming. No one
born in Rome
Can live elsewhere; but he must
pine for Rome,
And must return to it. I, who am
born
And bred a Tuscan and a Floren-
tine,
Feel the attraction, and I linger here
As if I were a pebble in the pave-
ment
Trodden by priestly feet. This I
endure,
Because I breathe in Rome an at-
mosphere
Heavy with odours of the laurel
leaves
That crowned great heroes of the
sword and pen,
In ages past. I feel myself exalted
To walk the streets in which a
Virgil walked,
Or Trajan rode in triumph; but
far more,

And most of all, because the great Colonna
Breathes the same air I breathe, and is to me
An inspiration. Now that she is gone,
Rome is no longer Rome till she return.
This feeling overmasters me. I know not
If it be love, this strong desire to be
For ever in her presence; but I know
That I, who was the friend of solitude,
And ever was best pleased when most alone,
Now weary grow of my own company.
For the first time old age seems lonely to me.

(Opening the Divina Commedia.)

I turn for consolation to the leaves
Of the great master of our Tuscan tongue,
Whose words, like coloured garnet-shirls in lava,
Betray the heat in which they were engendered.
A mendicant, he ate the bitter bread
Of others, but repaid their meagre gifts
With immortality. In courts of princes
He was a by-word, and in streets of towns
Was mocked by children, like the Hebrew prophet,
Himself a prophet. I too know the cry,
Go up, thou bald head! from a generation
That, wanting reverence, wanteth the best food
The soul can feed on. There's not room enough
For age and youth upon this little planet.
Age must give way. There was not room enough

Even for this great poet. In his song
I hear reverberate the gates of Florence,
Closing upon him, never more to open;
But mingled with the sound are melodies
Celestial from the gates of paradise.
He came, and he is gone. The people knew not
What manner of man was passing by their doors,
Until he passed no more; but in his vision
He saw the torments and beatitudes
Of souls condemned or pardoned, and hath left
Behind him this sublime Apocalypse.

I strive in vain to draw here on the margin
The face of Beatrice. It is not hers,
But the Colonna's. Each hath his ideal,
The image of some woman excellent,
That is his guide. No Grecian art, nor Roman,
Hath yet revealed such loveliness as hers.

II.

VITERBO.

VITTORIA COLONNA *at the Convent window.*

Vittoria. Parting with friends is temporary death,
As all death is. We see no more their faces,
Nor hear their voices, save in memory;
But messages of love give us assurance
That we are not forgotten. Who shall say

That from the world of spirits comes
   no greeting,
No message of remembrance? It
   may be
The thoughts that visit us, we know
   not whence,
Sudden as inspiration, are the
   whispers
Of disembodied spirits, speaking
   to us
As friends, who wait outside a prison
   wall,
Through the barred windows speak
   to those within. [*A pause.*

As quiet as the lake that lies
   beneath me,
As quiet as the tranquil sky above
   me,
As quiet as a heart that beats no
   more,
This convent seems. Above, below,
   all peace!
Silence and solitude, the soul's best
   friends,
Are with me here, and the tumultuous world
Makes no more noise than the
   remotest planet.
O gentle spirit, unto the third circle
Of heaven among the blessed souls
   ascended,
Who, living in the faith and dying
   for it,
Have gone to their reward, I do
   not sigh
For thee as being dead, but for my-
   self
That I am still alive. Turn those
   dear eyes,
Once so benignant to me, upon
   mine,
That open to their tears such uncon-
   trolled
And such continual issue. Still
   awhile
Have patience; I will come to thee
   at last.

A few more goings in and out these
   doors,
A few more chimings of these con-
   vent bells,
A few more prayers, a few more
   sighs and tears,
And the long agony of this life will
   end,
And I shall be with thee. If I am
   wanting
To thy well-being, as thou art to
   mine,
Have patience; I will come to thee
   at last.
Ye minds that loiter in these cloister
   gardens,
Or wander far above the city walls,
Bear unto him this message, that
   I ever
Or speak or think of him, or weep
   for him.
By unseen hands uplifted in the
   light
Of sunset, yonder solitary cloud
Floats, with its white apparel
   blown abroad,
And wafted up to heaven. It fades
   away,
And melts into the air. Ah, would
   that I
Could thus be wafted unto thee,
   Francesco,
A cloud of white, an incorporeal
   spirit!

III.

MICHAEL ANGELO AND BEN-
   VENUTO CELLINI.

MICHAEL ANGELO; BENVENUTO
   CELLINI *in gay attire.*

Benvenuto. A good day and good
   year to the divine
Maestro Michael Angelo, the sculptor!
Michael A. Welcome, my Benvenuto.

Benvenuto. That is what
My father said, the first time he
beheld
This handsome face. But say
farewell, not welcome.
I come to take my leave. I start
for Florence
As fast as horse can carry me.
I long
To set once more upon its level flags
These feet, made sore by your vile
Roman pavements.
Come with me; you are wanted
there in Florence.
The Sacristy is not finished.

Michael A. Speak not of it!
How damp and cold it was! How
my bones ached
And my head reeled, when I was
working there!
I am too old. I will stay here in
Rome,
Where all is old and crumbling, like
myself,
To hopeless ruin. All roads lead
to Rome.

Benvenuto. And all lead out of it.

Michael A. There is a charm,
A certain something in the atmosphere,
That all men feel and no man can
describe.

Benvenuto. Malaria?

Michael A. Yes, malaria
of the mind,
Out of this tomb of the majestic
Past;
The fever to accomplish some great
work
That will not let us sleep. I must
go on
Until I die.

Benvenuto. Do you ne'er think
of Florence?

Michael A. Yes; whenever
I think of anything beside my work,
I think of Florence. I remember,
too,

The bitter days I passed among the
quarries
Of Seravezza and Pietrasanta;
Road-building in the marshes;
stupid people,
And cold and rain incessant, and
mad gusts
Of mountain wind, like howling
dervishes,
That spun and whirled the eddying
snow about them
As if it were a garment; aye, vexa-
tions
And troubles of all kinds, that ended
only
In loss of time and money.

Benvenuto. True, Maestro;
But that was not in Florence. You
should leave
Such work to others. Sweeter
memories
Cluster about you, in the pleasant
city
Upon the Arno.

Michael A. In my waking
dreams
I see the marvellous dome of
Brunelleschi,
Ghiberti's gates of bronze, and
Giotto's tower;
And Ghirlandajo's lovely Benci
glides
With folded hands amid my troubled
thoughts,
A splendid vision! Time rides with
the old
At a great pace. As travellers on
swift steeds
See the near landscape fly and flow
behind them,
While the remoter fields and dim
horizons
Go with them, and seem wheeling
round to meet them,
So in old age things near us slip
away,
And distant things go with us
Pleasantly

Come back to me the days when, as
   a youth,
I walked with Ghirlandajo in the
   gardens
Of Medici, and saw the antique
   statues,
The forms august of gods and godlike men,
And the great world of art revealed
   itself
To my young eyes. Then all that
   man hath done
Seemed possible to me. Alas!
   how little
Of all I dreamed of has my hand
   achieved!

Benvenuto. Nay, let the Night
And Julian in the Sacristy at Flor-
   ence,
Prophets and Sibyls in the Sistine
   Chapel,
And the Last Judgment answer.
   Is it finished?

Michael A. The work is nearly
   done. But this Last Judgment
Has been the cause of more vexation
   to me
Than it will be of honour. Ser
   Biagio,
Master of ceremonies at the Papal
   court,
A man punctilious and over nice,
Calls it improper; says that those
   nude forms,
Showing their nakedness in such
   shameless fashion,
Are better suited to a common
   bagnio,
Or wayside wine-shop, than a
   Papal Chapel.
To punish him I painted him as
   Minos,
And leave him there as master of
   ceremonies
In the Infernal Regions. What
   would you
Have done to such a man?

Benvenuto. I would have
   killed him.
When any one insults me, if I can,
I kill him, kill him.

Michael A. Oh, you gentlemen,
Who dress in silks and velvets, and
   wear swords,
Are ready with your weapons, and
   have all
A taste for homicide.

Benvenuto. I learned that lesson
Under Pope Clement at the siege
   of Rome,
Some twenty years ago. As I was
   standing
Upon the ramparts of the Campo
   Santo
With Alessandro Bene, I beheld
A sea of fog, that covered all the plain,
And hid from us the foe; when sud-
   denly,
A misty figure, like an apparition,
Rose up above the fog, as if on
   horseback.
At this I aimed my arquebus, and
   fired.
The figure vanished; and there
   rose a cry
Out of the darkness, long and fierce
   and loud,
With imprecations in all languages.
It was the Constable of France,
   the Bourbon,
That I had slain.

Michael A. Rome should be
   grateful to you.

Benvenuto. But has not been;
   you shall hear presently.
During the siege I served as bom-
   bardier,
There in Saint Angelo. His Holiness,
One day, was walking with his Cardinals
On the round bastion, while I stood
   above
Among my falconets. All thought
   and feeling,

All skill in art and all desire of fame,
Were swallowed up in the delight-
ful music
Of that artillery. I saw far off,
Within the enemy's trenches on the
Prati,
A Spanish cavalier in scarlet cloak;
And firing at him with due aim and
range,
I cut the gay Hidalgo in two pieces.
The eyes are dry that wept for him
in Spain.
His Holiness, delighted beyond
measure
With such display of gunnery, and
amazed
To see the man in scarlet cut in
two,
Gave me his benediction, and ab-
solved me
From all the homicides I had
committed
In service of the Apostolic Church,
Or should commit thereafter. From
that day
I have not held in very high esteem
The life of man.

   Michael A.   And who absolved
Pope Clement?
Now let us speak of Art.
   Benvenuto.   Of what you will.
   Michael A. Say, have you seen
our friend Fra Bastian lately,
Since by a turn of fortune he became
Friar of the Signet?
   Benvenuto. Faith, a pretty artist,
To pass his days in stamping leaden
seals
On Papal bulls!
   Michael A.   He has grown fat
and lazy,
As if the lead clung to him like a
sinker.
He paints no more, since he was
sent to Fondi
By Cardinal Ippolito to paint
The fair Gonzaga. Ah, you should
have seen him

As I did, riding through the city gate,
In his brown hood, attended by
four horsemen,
Completely armed, to frighten the
banditti.
I think he would have frightened
them alone,
For he was rounder than the O of
Giotto.
   Benvenuto. He must have looked
more like a sack of meal
Than a great painter.
   Michael A. Well, he is not great,
But still I like him greatly. Ben-
venuto,
Have faith in nothing but in in-
dustry.
Be at it late and early; persevere,
And work right on through censure
and applause,
Or else abandon Art.
   Benvenuto.   No man works
harder
Than I do. I am not a moment idle.
   Michael A. And what have you
to show me?
   Benvenuto.   This gold ring,
Made for his Holiness, — my latest
work,
And I am proud of it. A single dia-
mond,
Presented by the Emperor to the
Pope.
Targhetta of Venice set and tinted
it;
I have reset it, and retinted it
Divinely, as you see. The jewellers
Say I've surpassed Targhetta.
   Michael A.   Let me see it.
A pretty jewel!
   Benvenuto. That is not the ex-
pression.
Pretty is not a very pretty word
To be applied to such a precious
stone,
Given by an Emperor to a Pope,
and set
By Benvenuto!

Michael A. Messer Benvenuto,
I lose all patience with you; for
   the gifts
That God hath given you are of
   such a kind
They should be put to far more
   noble uses
Than setting diamonds for the Pope
   of Rome.
You can do greater things.
   Benvenuto. The God
   who made me
Knows why he made me what I
   am,—a goldsmith,
A mere artificer.
   Michael A. Oh no; an artist,
Richly endowed by nature, but who
   wraps
His talent in a napkin, and con-
   sumes
His life in vanities.
   Benvenuto. Michael Angelo
May say what Benvenuto would
   not bear
From any other man. He speaks
   the truth.
I know my life is wasted and con-
   sumed
In vanities; but I have better hours
And higher aspirations than you
   think.
Once, when a prisoner at Saint An-
   gelo,
Fasting and praying in the mid-
   night darkness,
In a celestial vision I beheld
A crucifix in the sun, of the same
   substance
As is the sun itself. And since
   that hour
There is a splendour round about
   my head,
That may be seen at sunrise and
   at sunset
Above my shadow on the grass.
   And now
I know that I am in the grace of
   God,

And none henceforth can harm me.
   Michael A. None but one,—
None but yourself, who are your
   greatest foe.
He that respects himself is safe
   from others;
He wears a coat of mail that none
   can pierce.
   Benvenuto. I always wear one.
   Michael A. O incorrigible!
At least, forget not the celestial
   vision.
Man must have something higher
   than himself
To think of.
   Benvenuto. That I know full well.
   Now listen.
I have been sent for into France,
   where grow
The Lilies that illumine heaven
   and earth,
And carry in mine equipage the
   model
Of a most marvellous golden salt-
   cellar
For the king's table; and here in
   my brain
A statue of Mars Armipotent for
   the fountain
Of Fontainebleau, colossal, wonder-
   ful.
I go a goldsmith, to return a sculptor.
And so farewell, great Master.
   Think of me
As one who, in the midst of all his
   follies,
Had also his ambition, and aspired
To better things.
   Michael A. Do not forget the
   vision.
(*Sitting down again to the Divina
   Commedia.*)
Now in what circle of his poem
   sacred
Would the great Florentine have
   placed this man?
Whether in Phlegethon, the river of
   blood,

Or in the fiery belt of Purgatory,
I know not, but most surely not
  with those
Who walk in leaden cloaks.
  Though he is one
Whose passions, like a potent
  alkahest,
Dissolve his better nature, he is not
That despicable thing, a hypocrite ;
He doth not cloak his vices, nor
  deny them.
Come back, my thoughts, from him
  to Paradise.

IV.

FRA SEBASTIANO DEL PIOMBO.

MICHAEL ANGELO ; FRA SEBAS-
TIANO DEL PIOMBO.

Michael A. (*not turning round*).
  Who is it ?
Fra Seb.   Wait, for I am out
  of breath
In climbing your steep stairs.
  Michael A.   Ah, my Bastiano,
If you went up and down as many
  stairs
As I do still, and climbed as many
  ladders,
It would be better for you. Pray
  sit down.
Your idle and luxurious way of living
Will one day take your breath away
  entirely,
And you will never find it.
  Fra Seb.   Well, what then ?
That would be better, in my appre-
  hension,
Than falling from a scaffold.
  Michael A.   That was
  nothing.
It did not kill me ; only lamed me
  slightly ;
I am quite well again.

Fra Seb.   But why, dear
  Master,
Why do you live so high up in your
  house,
When you could live below and
  have a garden,
As I do ?
  Michael A.   From this window
  I can look
On many gardens ; o'er the city
  roofs
See the Campagna and the Alban
  hills :
And all are mine.
  Fra Seb.   Can you sit down
  in them
On summer afternoons, and play
  the lute,
Or sing, or sleep the time away ?
  Michael A.   I never
Sleep in the day-time ; scarcely
  sleep at night.
I have not time. Did you meet
  Benvenuto
As you came up the stair ?
  Fra Seb.   He ran against me
On the first landing, going at full
  speed ;
Dressed like the Spanish captain in
  a play,
With his long rapier and his short
  red cloak.
Why hurry through the world at
  such a pace ?
Life will not be too long.
  Michael A.   It is his
  nature,—
A restless spirit, that consumes
  itself
With useless agitations. He o'er-
  leaps
The goal he aims at. Patience is a
  plant
That grows not in all gardens.
  You are made
Of quite another clay.
  Fra Seb.   And thank God
  for it.

And now, being somewhat rested,
  I will tell you
Why I have climbed these formid-
  able stairs.
I have a friend, Francesco Berni,
  here,
A very charming poet and com-
  panion,
Who greatly honours you and all
  your doings,
And you must sup with us.
  Michael A.   Not I, indeed.
I know too well what artists' sup-
  pers are.
You must excuse me.
  Fra Seb.   I will not ex-
  cuse you.
You need repose from your inces-
  sant work ;
Some recreation, some bright hours
  of pleasure.
  Michael A. To me, what you
  and other men call pleasure
Is only pain. Work is my recrea-
  tion,
The play of faculty ; a delight like
  that
Which a bird feels in flying, or a fish
In darting through the water,—
  nothing more.
I cannot go. The Sibylline leaves
  of life
Grow precious now, when only few
  remain.
I cannot go.
  Fra Seb. Berni, perhaps, will
  read
A canto of the Orlando Inamorato.
  Michael A. That is another
  reason for not going.
If aught is tedious and intolerable,
It is a poet reading his own verses.
  Fra Seb. Berni thinks some-
  what better of your verses
Than you of his. He says that you
  speak things,
And other poets words. So, pray
  you, come.

  Michael A. If it were now the
  Improvisatore,
Luigi Pulci, whom I used to hear
With Benvenuto, in the streets of
  Florence,
I might be tempted. I was younger
  then,
And singing in the open air was
  pleasant.
  Fra Seb. There is a Frenchman
  here, named Rabelais,
Once a Franciscan friar, and now
  a doctor,
And secretary to the embassy :
A learned man, who speaks all
  languages,
And wittiest of men ; who wrote
  a book
Of the Adventures of Gargantua,
So full of strange conceits one roars
  with laughter
At every page ; a jovial boon-com-
  panion
And lover of much wine. He too
  is coming.
  Michael A. Then you will not
  want me, who am not witty,
And have no sense of mirth, and
  love not wine.
I should be like a dead man at
  your banquet.
Why should I seek this Frenchman
  Rabelais ?
And wherefore go to hear Fran-
  cesco Berni,
When I have Dante Alighieri here,
The greatest of all poets ?
  Fra Seb.   And the dullest ;
And only to be read in episodes.
His day is past. Petrarca is our poet.
  Michael A. Petrarca is for
  women and for lovers,
And for those soft Abati, who delight
To wander down long garden walks
  in summer,
Tinkling their little sonnets all day
  long,
As lap-dogs do their bells.

Fra Seb. I love Petrarca.
How sweetly of his absent love he
    sings
When journeying in the forest of
    Ardennes!
'I seem to hear her, hearing the
    boughs and breezes
And leaves and birds lamenting,
    and the waters
Murmuring flee along the verdant
    herbage.'
    Michael A. Enough. It is all
    seeming, and no being.
If you would know how a man
    speaks in earnest,
Read here this passage, where
    Saint Peter thunders
In Paradise against degenerate
    Popes
And the corruptions of the Church,
    till all
The heaven about him blushes like
    a sunset.
I beg you to take note of what he
    says
About the Papal seals, for that
    concerns
Your office and yourself.
    Fra Seb. (*reading*). Is this the
    passage?
'Nor I be made the figure of a seal
To privileges venal and menda-
    cious;
Whereat I often redden and flash
    with fire!'—
That is not poetry.
    Michael A. What is it, then?
    Fra Seb. Vituperation; gall
    that might have spurted
From Aretino's pen.
    Michael A. Name not that
    man!
A profligate, whom your Francesco
    Berni
Describes as having one foot in
    the brothel
And the other in the hospital; who
    lives

By flattering or maligning, as best
    serves
His purpose at the time. He writes
    to me
With easy arrogance of my Last
    Judgment,
In such familiar tone that one
    would say
The great event already had oc-
    curred,
And he was present, and from
    observation
Informed me how the picture
    should be painted.
    Fra Seb. What unassuming,
    unobtrusive men
These critics are! Now, to have
    Aretino
Aiming his shafts at you brings
    back to mind
The Gascon archers in the square
    of Milan,
Shooting their arrows at Duke
    Sforza's statue,
By Leonardo, and the foolish rabble
Of envious Florentines, that at
    your David
Threw stones at night. But Are-
    tino praised you.
    Michael A. His praises were
    ironical. He knows
How to use words as weapons, and
    to wound
While seeming to defend. But
    look, Bastiano,
See how the setting sun lights up
    that picture!
    Fra Seb. My portrait of Vittoria
    Colonna.
    Michael A. It makes her look
    as she will look hereafter,
When she becomes a saint!
    Fra Seb. A noble woman!
    Michael A. Ah, these old hands
    can fashion fairer shapes
In marble, and can paint diviner
    pictures,
Since I have known her.

817

Fra Seb. And you like this picture;
And yet it is in oils, which you detest.

Michael A. When that barbarian Jan Van Eyck discovered
The use of oil in painting, he degraded
His art into a handicraft, and made it
Sign-painting, merely, for a country inn
Or wayside wine-shop. 'Tis an art for women,
Or for such leisurely and idle people
As you, Fra Bastiano. Nature paints not
In oils, but frescoes the great dome of heaven
With sunsets, and the lovely forms of clouds
And flying vapours.

Fra Seb. And how soon they fade!
Behold yon line of roofs and belfries painted
Upon the golden background of the sky,
Like a Byzantine picture, or a portrait
Of Cimabue. See how hard the outline,
Sharp-cut and clear, not rounded into shadow.
Yet that is Nature.

Michael A. She is always right.
The picture that approaches sculpture nearest
Is the best picture.

Fra Seb. Leonardo thinks
The open air too bright. We ought to paint
As if the sun were shining through a mist.
'Tis easier done in oil than in distemper.

Michael A. Do not revive again the old dispute;
I have an excellent memory for forgetting,
But I still feel the hurt. Wounds are not healed
By the unbending of the bow that made them.

Fra Seb. So say Petrarca and the ancient proverb.

Michael A. But that is past.
Now I am angry with you,
Not that you paint in oils, but that, grown fat
And indolent, you do not paint at all.

Fra Seb. Why should I paint?
Why should I toil and sweat,
Who now am rich enough to live at ease,
And take my pleasure?

Michael A. When Pope Leo died,
He who had been so lavish of the wealth
His predecessors left him, who received
A basket of gold-pieces every morning,
Which every night was empty, left behind
Hardly enough to pay his funeral.

Fra Seb. I care for banquets, not for funerals,
As did his Holiness. I have forbidden
All tapers at my burial, and procession
Of priests and friars and monks;
and have provided
The cost thereof be given to the poor!

Michael A. You have done wisely, but of that I speak not.
Ghiberti left behind him wealth and children;
But who to-day would know that he had lived,

If he had never made those gates
of bronze
In the old Baptistery,—those gates
of bronze,
Worthy to be the gates of Paradise.
His wealth is scattered to the winds;
his children
Are long since dead; but those
celestial gates
Survive, and keep his name and
memory green.

Fra Seb. But why should I
fatigue myself? I think
That all things it is possible to
paint
Have been already painted; and
if not,
Why, there are painters in the
world at present
Who can accomplish more in two
short months
Than I could in two years; so it
is well
That some one is contented to do
nothing,
And leave the field to others.

Michael A. O blasphemer!
Not without reason do the people
call you
Sebastian del Piombo, for the lead
Of all the Papal bulls is heavy
upon you,
And wraps you like a shroud.

Fra Seb. Misericordia!
Sharp is the vinegar of sweet wine,
and sharp
The words you speak, because the
heart within you
Is sweet unto the core.

Michael A. How changed
you are
From the Sebastiano I once knew,
When poor, laborious, emulous to
excel,
You strove in rivalry with Badassare
And Raphael Sanzio.

Fra Seb. Raphael is dead;
He is but dust and ashes in his
grave,
While I am living and enjoying
life,
And so am victor. One live Pope
is worth
A dozen dead ones.

Michael A. Raphael is not
dead;
He doth but sleep; for how can
he be dead
Who lives immortal in the hearts
of men?
He only drank the precious wine
of youth,
The outbreak of the grapes, before
the vintage
Was trodden to bitterness by the
feet of men.
The gods have given him sleep.
We never were
Nor could be foes, although our
followers,
Who are distorted shadows of ourselves,
Have striven to make us so; but
each one worked
Unconsciously upon the other's
thoughts,
Both giving and receiving. He
perchance
Caught strength from me, and I
some greater sweetness
And tenderness from his more
gentle nature.
I have but words of praise and admiration
For his great genius; and the
world is fairer
That he lived in it.

Fra Seb. We at least are
friends;
So come with me.

Michael A. No, no; I am
best pleased
When I 'm not asked to banquets.
I have reached

A time of life when daily walks are shortened,
And even the houses of our dearest friends,
That used to be so near, seem far away.

Fra Seb. Then we must sup without you. We shall laugh
At those who toil for fame, and make their lives
A tedious martyrdom, that they may live
A little longer in the mouths of men !
And so, good-night.

Michael A. Good-night, my Fra Bastiano.

[*Returning to his work.*

How will men speak of me when I am gone,
When all this colourless, sad life is ended,
And I am dust? They will remember only
The wrinkled forehead, the marred countenance,
The rudeness of my speech, and my rough manners,
And never dream that underneath them all
There was a woman's heart of tenderness.
They will not know the secret of my life,
Locked up in silence, or but vaguely hinted
In uncouth rhymes, that may perchance survive
Some little space in memories of men !
Each one performs his life-work, and then leaves it ;
Those that come after him will estimate
His influence on the age in which he lived.

V.

MICHAEL ANGELO AND TITIAN.

Palazzo Belvedere. TITIAN'S *studio.* A painting of Danaë *with a curtain before it.* TITIAN, MICHAEL ANGELO, *and* GIORGIO VASARI.

Michael A. So you have left at last your still lagoons,
Your City of Silence floating in the sea,
And come to us in Rome.

Titian. I come to learn,
But I have come too late. I should have seen
Rome in my youth, when all my mind was open
To new impressions. Our Vasari here
Leads me about, a blind man, groping darkly
Among the marvels of the past. I touch them,
But do not see them.

Michael A. There are things in Rome
That one might walk bare-footed here from Venice
But to see once, and then to die content.

Titian. I must confess that these majestic ruins
Oppress me with their gloom. I feel as one
Who in the twilight stumbles among tombs,
And cannot read the inscriptions carved upon them.

Michael A. I felt so once ; but I have grown familiar
With desolation, and it has become
No more a pain to me, but a delight.

Titian. I could not live here. I must have the sea,

And the sea-mist, with sunshine
    interwoven
Like cloth of gold; must have
    beneath my windows
The laughter of the waves, and at
    my door
Their pattering footsteps, or I am
    not happy.

  Michael A. Then tell me of your
    city in the sea,
Paved with red basalt of the Paduan
    hills.
Tell me of art in Venice. Three
    great names,
Giorgione, Titian, and the Tinto-
    retto,
Illustrate your Venetian school, and
    send
A challenge to the world. The
    first is dead,
But Tintoretto lives.

  Titian. And paints
    with fire,
Sudden and splendid, as the light-
    ning paints
The cloudy vault of heaven.

  Giorgio. Does he still keep
Above his door the arrogant in-
    scription
That once was painted there,—
    ' The colour of Titian,
With the design of Michael An-
    gelo'?

  Titian. Indeed, I know not.
'Twas a foolish boast,
And does no harm to any but himself.
Perhaps he has grown wiser.

  Michael A. When you two
Are gone, who is there that remains
    behind
To seize the pencil falling from
    your fingers?

  Giorgio. Oh, there are many
    hands upraised already
To clutch at such a prize, which
    hardly wait
For death to loose your grasp,—a
    hundred of them:

Schiavone, Bonifazio, Campagnola,
Moretto, and Moroni; who can
    count them,
Or measure their ambition?

  Titian. When we are gone,
The generation that comes after
    us
Will have far other thoughts than
    ours. Our ruins
Will serve to build their palaces or
    tombs.
They will posess the world that
    we think ours,
And fashion it far otherwise.

  Michael A. I hear
Your son Orazio and your nephew
    Marco
Mentioned with honour.

  Titian. Ay, brave lads,
    brave lads.
But time will show. There is a
    youth in Venice,
One Paul Cagliari, called the
    Veronese,
Still a mere stripling, but of such
    rare promise
That we must guard our laurels, or
    may lose them.

  Michael A. These are good
    tidings; for I sometimes fear
That, when we die, with us all art
    will die.
'Tis but a fancy. Nature will
    provide
Others to take our places. I rejoice
To see the young spring forward
    in the race,
Eager as we were, and as full of
    hope
And the sublime audacity of youth.

  Titian. Men die and are forgotten
    The great world
Goes on the same. Among the
    myriads
Of men that live, or have lived, or
    shall live,
What is a single life, or thine or
    mine,

That we should think all Nature
    would stand still
If we were gone? We must make
    room for others.
    Michael A. And now, Maestro,
      pray unveil your picture
Of Danaë, of which I hear such
    praise.
    Titian (drawing back the curtain).
      What think you?
    Michael A.   That Acrisius did
      well
To lock such beauty in a brazen
    tower,
And hide it from all eyes.
    Titian.   The model truly
Was beautiful.
    Michael A.   And more, that
      you were present,
And saw the showery Jove from
    high Olympus
Descend in all his splendour.
    Titian.   From your lips
Such words are full of sweetness.
    Michael A.   You have caught
These golden hues from your
    Venetian sunsets.
    Titian. Possibly.
    Michael A.   Or from sunshine
    through a shower
On the lagoons, or the broad
    Adriatic.
Nature reveals herself in all our
    arts.
The pavements and the palaces of
    cities
Hint at the nature of the neigh-
    bouring hills.
Red lavas from the Euganean
    quarries
Of Padua pave your streets; your
    palaces
Are the white stones of Istria, and
    gleam
Reflected in your waters and your
    pictures.
And thus the works of every artist
    show

Something of his surroundings and
    his habits.
The uttermost that can be reached
    by colour
Is here accomplished. Warmth
    and light and softness
Mingle together. Never yet was
    flesh
Painted by hand of artist, dead or
    living,
With such divine perfection.
    Titian.   I am grateful
For so much praise from you, who
    are a master;
While mostly those who praise and
    those who blame
Know nothing of the matter, so
    that mainly
Their censure sounds like praise,
    their praise like censure.
    Michael A. Wonderful! won-
    derful! The charm of colour
Fascinates me the more that in my-
    self
The gift is wanting. I am not a
    painter.
    Giorgio. Messer Michele, all
    the arts are yours,
Not one alone; and therefore I
    may venture
To put a question to you.
    Michael A.   Well, speak on.
    Giorgio. Two nephews of the
    Cardinal Farnese
Have made me umpire in dispute
    between them
Which is the greater of the sister
    arts,
Painting or sculpture. Solve for
    me the doubt.
    Michael A. Sculpture and paint-
    ing have a common goal,
And whosoever would attain to it,
Whichever path he take, will find
    that goal
Equally hard to reach.
    Giorgio.   No doubt, no doubt;
But you evade the question.

Michael A. When I stand
In presence of this picture, I concede
That painting has attained its uttermost;
But in the presence of my sculptured figures
I feel that my conception soars beyond
All limit I have reached.

Giorgio. You still
evade me.

Michael A. Giorgio Vasari, I
often said
That I account that painting as the best
Which most resembles sculpture.
Here before us
We have the proof. Behold those
rounded limbs!
How from the canvas they detach
themselves,
Till they deceive the eye, and one
would say,
It is a statue with a screen behind
it!

Titian. Signori, pardon me;
but all such questions
Seem to me idle.

Michael A. Idle as the wind.
And now, Maestro, I will say once
more
How admirable I esteem your
work,
And leave you, without further interruption.

Titian. Your friendly visit hath
much honoured me.

Giorgio. Farewell.

Michael A. (*to* GIORGIO, *going
out*). If the Venetian painters
knew
But half as much of drawing as of
colour,
They would indeed work miracles
in art,
And the world see what it hath
never seen.

VI.

PALAZZO CESARINI.

VITTORIA COLONNA *seated in an
arm-chair;* JULIA GONZAGA
standing near her.

Julia. It grieves me that I find
you still so weak
And suffering.

Vittoria. No, not suffering; only
dying.
Death is the chillness that precedes
the dawn;
We shudder for a moment, then
awake
In the broad sunshine of the other
life.
I am a shadow, merely, and these
hands,
These cheeks, these eyes, these
tresses that my husband
Once thought so beautiful, and I
was proud of
Because he thought them so, are
faded quite,—
All beauty gone from them.

Julia. Ah no, not that.
Paler you are, but not less beautiful.

Vittoria. Hand me the mirror.
I would fain behold
What change comes o'er our features when we die.
Thank you. And now sit down
beside me here.
How glad I am that you have come
to-day,
Above all other days, and at the
hour
When most I need you!

Julia. Do you ever need me?

Vittoria. Always, and most of
all to-day and now.
Do you remember, Julia, when we
walked,
One afternoon, upon the castle terrace

At Ischia, on the day before you
left me?

Julia. Well I remember; but
it seems to me
Something unreal, that has never
been,—
Something that I have read of in
a book,
Or heard of some one else.

Vittoria. Ten years and more
Have passed since then; and many
things have happened
In those ten years, and many
friends have died:
Marco Flaminio, whom we all ad-
mired
And loved as our Catullus; dear
Valdesso,
The noble champion of free thought
and speech;
And Cardinal Ippolito, your friend.

Julia. Oh, do not speak of him!
His sudden death
O'ercomes me now, as it o'ercame
me then.
Let me forget it; for my memory
Serves me too often as an un-
kind friend,
And I remember things I would
forget,
While I forget the things I would
remember.

Vittoria. Forgive me; I will
speak of him no more.
The good Fra Bernardino has de-
parted,
Has fled from Italy, and crossed
the Alps,
Fearing Caraffa's wrath, because
he taught
That He who made us all without
our help
Could also save us without aid of
ours.
Renée of France, the Duchess of
Ferrara,
That Lily of the Loire, is bowed by
winds

That blow from Rome; Olympia
Morata
Banished from court because of
this new doctrine.
Therefore be cautious. Keep your
secret thought
Locked in your breast.

Julia. I will be very prudent.
But speak no more, I pray; it
wearies you.

Vittoria. Yes, I am very weary.
Read to me.

Julia. Most willingly. What
shall I read?

Vittoria. Petrarca's
Triumph of Death. The book lies
on the table;
Beside the casket there. Read
where you find
The leaf turned down. 'Twas there
I left off reading.

Julia (reads).
' Not as a flame that by some force
is spent,
  But one that of itself consumeth
  quite,
    Departed hence in peace the
    soul content,
In fashion of a soft and lucent light
  Whose nutriment by slow grada-
  tion goes,
    Keeping until the end its lustre
    bright.
Not pale, but whiter than the sheet
of snows
  That without wind on some fair
  hill-top lies,
    Her weary body seemed to find
    repose.
Like a sweet slumber in her lovely eyes,
  When now the spirit was no
  longer there,
    Was what is dying called by the
    unwise.
E'en Death itself in her fair face
seemed fair.'—
Is it of Laura that he here is speak-
ing?—

She doth not answer, yet is not
  asleep ;
Her eyes are full of light and fixed
  on something
Above her in the air. I can see
  naught
Except the painted angels on the
  ceiling.
Vittoria ! speak ! What is it ?
  Answer me !—
She only smiles, and stretches out
  her hands.
  [*The mirror falls and breaks.*
Vittoria. Not disobedient to the
  heavenly vision !
Pescara ! my Pescara !   [*Dies.*
Julia.   Holy Virgin !
Her body sinks together,—she is
  dead !
  [*Kneels, and hides her face in*
  VITTORIA'S *lap.*

Enter MICHAEL ANGELO.

Julia. Hush ! make no noise.
Michael A.   How is she ?
Julia.   Never better.
Michael A. Then she is dead !
Julia.   Alas ! yes, she is
  dead !
Even death itself in her fair face
  seems fair.
Michael A. How wonderful ! The
  light upon her face
Shines from the windows of another
  world.
Saints only have such faces. Holy
  Angels !
Bear her like sainted Catherine to
  her rest !
  [*Kisses* VITTORIA'S *hand.*

PART THIRD.

I.

MONOLOGUE.

Macello de' Corvi.   A room in
  MICHAEL ANGELO'S *house.* MI-
  CHAEL ANGELO *standing before*
  a model of St. Peter's.

Michael A. Better than thou I
  cannot, Brunelleschi,
And less than thou I will not ! If
  the thought
Could, like a windlass, lift the
  ponderous stones,
And swing them to their places ; if
  a breath
Could blow this rounded dome into
  the air,
As if it were a bubble, and these
  statues
Spring at a signal to their sacred
  stations,
As sentinels mount guard upon a
  wall,

Then were my task completed.
  Now, alas !
Naught am I but a Saint Sebaldus,
  holding
Upon his hand the model of a
  church,
As German artists paint him ; and
  what years,
What weary years, must drag them-
  selves along,
Ere this be turned to stone !
  What hindrances
Must block the way ; what idle
  interferences
Of Cardinals and Canons of Saint
  Peter's,
Who nothing know of art beyond
  the colour
Of cloaks and stockings, nor of any
  building
Save that of their own fortunes !
  And what then ?
I must then the shortcoming of my
  means

Piece out by stepping forward, as
the Spartan
Was told to add a step to his short
sword.   [*A pause.*

And is Fra Bastian dead? Is all
that light
Gone out, that sunshine darkened;
all that music
And merriment, that used to make
our lives
Less melancholy, swallowed up in
silence,
Like madrigals sung in the street
at night
By passing revellers? It is strange
indeed
That he should die before me. 'Tis
against
The laws of nature that the young
should die,
And the old live; unless it be that
some
Have long been dead who think
themselves alive,
Because not buried. Well, what
matters it,
Since now that greater light, that
was my sun,
Is set, and all is darkness, all is
darkness!
Death's lightnings strike to right
and left of me,
And, like a ruined wall, the world
around me
Crumbles away, and I am left alone.
I have no friends, and want none.
My own thoughts
Are now my sole companions,—
thoughts of her,
That like a benediction from the
skies
Come to me in my solitude and
soothe me.
When men are old, the incessant
thought of Death
Follows them like their shadow;
sits with them

At every meal; sleeps with them
when they sleep;
And when they wake already is
awake,
And standing by their bedside.
Then, what folly
It is in us to make an enemy
Of this importunate follower, not
a friend!
To me a friend, and not an enemy,
Has he become since all my friends
are dead.

II.

VIGNA DI PAPA GIULIO.

POPE JULIUS III, *seated by the
Fountain of Acqua Vergine, surrounded by Cardinals.*

Julius. Tell me, why is it ye are
discontent,
You, Cardinals Salviati and Mar-
cello,
With Michael Angelo? What has
he done,
Or left undone, that ye are set
against him?
When one Pope dies, another is soon
made;
And I can make a dozen Cardinals,
But cannot make one Michael An-
gelo.
Card. Salviati. Your Holiness,
we are not set against him;
We but deplore his incapacity.
He is too old.
Julius. You, Cardinal Salviati,
Are an old man. Are you incapa-
ble?
'Tis the old ox that draws the
straightest furrow.
Card. Marcello. Your Holiness
remembers he was charged
With the repairs upon Saint Mary's
bridge;

826

Made cofferdams, and heaped up
    load on load
Of timber and travertine; and yet
    for years
The bridge remained unfinished,
    till we gave it
To Baccio Bigio.

Julius.   Always Baccio Bigio!
Is there no other architect on earth?
Was it not he that sometime had in
    charge
The harbour of Ancona?

Card. Marcello.   Ay, the same.

Julius. Then let me tell you that
    your Baccio Bigio
Did greater damage in a single day
To that fair harbour than the sea
    had done
Or would do in ten years. And
    him you think
To put in place of Michael An-
    gelo
In building the Basilica of Saint
    Peter!
The ass that thinks himself a stag
    discovers
His error when he comes to leap
    the ditch.

Card. Marcello.   He does not
    build; he but demolishes
The labours of Bramante and San
    Gallo.

Julius. Only to build more
    grandly.

Card. Marcello. But time passes:
Year after year goes by, and yet
    the work
Is not completed. Michael Angelo
Is a great sculptor, but no archi-
    tect.
His plans are faulty.

Julius. I have seen his model,
And have approved it. But here
    comes the artist.
Beware of him. He may make
    Persians of you,
To carry burdens on your backs
    for ever.

The same: MICHAEL ANGELO.

Julius. Come forward, dear
    Maestro! In these gardens
All ceremonies of our court are
    banished.
Sit down beside me here.

Michael A. (*sitting down*). How
    graciously
Your Holiness commiserates old age
And its infirmities!

Julius.   Say its privileges.
Art I respect. The building of this
    palace
And laying out these pleasant
    garden walks
Are my delight, and if I have not
    asked
Your aid in this, it is that I forbear
To lay new burdens on you at an age
When you need rest. Here I escape
    from Rome
To be at peace. The tumult of the
    city
Scarce reaches here.

Michael A. How beautiful it is,
And quiet almost as a hermitage!

Julius. We live as hermits here;
    and from these heights
O'erlook all Rome, and see the
    yellow Tiber
Cleaving in twain the city like a
    sword,
As far below there as Saint Mary's
    bridge.
What think you of that bridge?

Michael A.   I would advise
Your Holiness not to cross it, or
    not often;
It is not safe.

Julius. It was repaired of late.

Michael A. Some morning you
    will look for it in vain;
It will be gone. The current of the
    river
Is undermining it.

Julius.   But you repaired it.

Michael A. I strengthened all its
piers, and paved its road
With travertine. He who came
after me
Removed the stone, and sold it,
and filled in
The space with gravel.

Julius. Cardinal Salviati
And Cardinal Marcello, do you
listen?
This is your famous Nanni Baccio
Bigio.

Michael (*aside*). There is some
mystery here. These Cardinals
Stand lowering at me with un-
friendly eyes.

Julius. Now let us come to what
concerns us more
Than bridge or gardens. Some
complaints are made
Concerning the Three Chapels in
Saint Peter's;
Certain supposed defects or imper-
fections,
You doubtless can explain.

Michael A. This is no longer
The golden age of art. Men have
become
Iconoclasts and critics. They de-
light not
In what an artist does, but set them-
selves
To censure what they do not com-
prehend.
You will not see them bearing a
Madonna
Of Cimabue to the church in
triumph,
But tearing down the statue of a
Pope
To cast it into cannon. Who are
they
That bring complaints against me?

Julius. Deputies
Of the commissioners; and they
complain
Of insufficient light in the Three
Chapels.

Michael A. Your Holiness, the
insufficient light
Is somewhere else, and not in the
Three Chapels.
Who are the deputies that make
complaint?

Julius. The Cardinals Salviati
and Marcello,
Here present.

Michael A. (*rising*). With permission, Monsignori,
What is it ye complain of?

Card. Marcello. We regret
You have departed from Bramante's
plan,
And from San Gallo's.

Michael A. Since the
ancient time
No greater architect has lived on
earth
Than Lazzari Bramante. His de-
sign,
Without confusion, simple, clear,
well-lighted,
Merits all praise, and to depart
from it
Would be departing from the truth.
San Gallo,
Building about with columns, took
all light
Out of this plan; left in the choir
dark corners
For infinite ribaldries, and lurking
places
For rogues and robbers; so that
when the church
Was shut at night, not five and
twenty men
Could find them out. It was San
Gallo, then,
That left the church in darkness,
and not I.

Card. Marcello. Excuse me; but
in each of the Three Chapels
Is but a single window.

Michael A. Monsignore,
Perhaps you do not know that in
the vaulting

Above there are to go three other
windows.

Card. Salviati. How should we
know? You never told us of it.

Michael A. I neither am obliged,
nor will I be,
To tell your Eminence or any other
What I intend or ought to do.
Your office
Is to provide the means, and see
that thieves
Do not lay hands upon them. The
designs
Must all be left to me.

Card. Marcello. Sir architect,
You do forget yourself, to speak
thus rudely
In presence of his Holiness, and to
us
Who are his cardinals.

Michael A. (*putting on his hat*).
I do not forget
I am descended from the Counts
Conossa,
Linked with the Imperial line, and
with Matilda,
Who gave the Church Saint Peter's
Patrimony.
I, too, am proud to give unto the
Church
The labour of these hands, and what
of life
Remains to me. My father Buona-
rotti
Was Podestà of Chiusi and Caprese.
I am not used to have men speak to
me
As if I were a mason, hired to build
A garden wall, and paid on Saturdays
So much an hour.

Card. Salviati (*aside*). No wonder that Pope Clement
Never sat down in presence of this
man,
Lest he should do the same; and
always bade him
Put on his hat, lest he unasked
should do it!

Michael A. If any one could die
of grief and shame,
I should. This labour was imposed
upon me;
I did not seek it; and if I assumed
it,
'Twas not for love of fame or love
of gain,
But for the love of God. Perhaps
old age
Deceived me, or self-interest, or
ambition;
I may be doing harm instead of good.
Therefore, I pray your Holiness,
release me;
Take off from me the burden of this
work;
Let me go back to Florence.

Julius. Never, never,
While I am living.

Michael A. Doth your Holiness
Remember what the Holy Scrip-
tures say
Of the inevitable time, when those
Who look out of the windows shall
be darkened,
And the almond-tree shall flourish?

Julius. That is in
Ecclesiastes.

Michael A. And the grasshopper
Shall be a burden, and desire shall
fail,
Because man goeth unto his long
home.
Vanity of vanities, saith the
Preacher; all
Is vanity.

Julius. Ah, were to do a thing
As easy as to dream of doing it,
We should not want for artists. But
the men
Who carry out in act their great
designs
Are few in number; ay, they may
be counted
Upon the fingers of this hand.
Your place
Is at Saint Peter's.

Michael A. I have had my dream,
And cannot carry out my great conception,
And put it into act.

Julius.　　Then who can do it?
You would but leave it to some
　　Baccio Bigio
To mangle and deface.

Michael A.　　Rather than that,
I will still bear the burden on my
　　shoulders
A little longer.　If your Holiness
Will keep the world in order, and
　　will leave
The building of the church to me,
　　the work
Will go on better for it.　Holy
　　Father,
If all the labours that I have endured,
And shall endure, advantage not
　　my soul,
I am but losing time.

Julius (laying his hands on MICHAEL ANGELO'S *shoulders).*
　　　　You will be gainer
Both for your soul and body.

Michael A.　　Not events
Exasperate me, but the funest conclusions
I draw from these events; the sure
　　decline
Of art, and all the meaning of that
　　word;
All that embellishes and sweetens
　　life,
And lifts it from the level of low
　　cares
Into the purer atmosphere of
　　beauty;
The faith in the Ideal; the inspiration
That made the canons of the church
　　of Seville
Say, 'Let us build, so that all men
　　hereafter
Will say that we were madmen.'
　　Holy Father,

I beg permission to retire from
　　here.

Julius. Go; and my benediction
be upon you.

　　　　[MICHAEL ANGELO *goes out.*

My Cardinals, this Michael Angelo
Must not be dealt with as a common
　　mason.
He comes of noble blood, and for
　　his crest
Bears two bulls' horns; and he has
　　given us proof
That he can toss with them.　From
　　this day forth
Unto the end of time, let no man
　　utter
The name of Baccio Bigio in my
　　presence.
All great achievements are the
　　natural fruits
Of a great character.　As trees bear
　　not
Their fruits of the same size and
　　quality,
But each one in its kind with equal
　　ease,
So are great deeds as natural to
　　great men
As mean things are to small ones.
　　By his work
We know the master.　Let us not
　　perplex him.

III.

BINDO ALTOVITI.

A street in Rome. BINDO ALTOVITI, *standing at the door of his
house.* MICHAEL ANGELO, *passing.*

Bindo. Good-morning, Messer
　　Michael Angelo!

Michael A. Good morning, Messer Bindo Altoviti!

Bindo. What brings you forth so
　　early?

Michael A. The same reason
That keeps you standing sentinel at
  your door,—
The air of this delicious summer
  morning.
What news have you from Florence?
Bindo. Nothing new;
The same old tale of violence and
  wrong.
Since the disastrous day at Monte
  Murlo,
When in procession, through San
  Gallo's gate,
Bareheaded, clothed in rags, on
  sorry steeds,
Philippo Strozzi and the good
  Valori
Were led as prisoners down the
  streets of Florence,
Amid the shouts of an ungrateful
  people,
Hope is no more, and liberty no
  more.
Duke Cosimo, the tyrant, reigns
  supreme.
Michael A. Florence is dead:
  her houses are but tombs;
Silence and solitude are in her
  streets.
Bindo. Ah yes; and often I repeat
  the words
You wrote upon your statue of the
  Night,
There in the Sacristy of San Lorenzo:
'Grateful to me is sleep; to be of
  stone
More grateful, while the wrong and
  shame endure;
To see not, feel not, is a benediction;
Therefore awake me not; oh, speak
  in whispers.'
Michael A. Ah, Messer Bindo,
  the calamities,
The fallen fortunes, and the desolation
Of Florence are to me a tragedy
Deeper than words, and darker than
  despair.

I, who have worshipped freedom
  from my cradle,
Have loved her with the passion of
  a lover,
And clothed her with all lovely attributes
That the imagination can conceive,
Or the heart conjure up, now see
  her dead,
And trodden in the dust beneath
  the feet
Of an adventurer! It is a grief
Too great for me to bear in my
  old age.
Bindo. I say no news from
  Florence: I am wrong,
For Benvenuto writes that he is
  coming
To be my guest in Rome.
Michael A. Those are
  good tidings.
He hath been many years away
  from us.
Bindo. Pray you, come in.
Michael. A. I have
  not time to stay,
And yet I will. I see from here
  your house
Is filled with works of art. That
  bust in bronze
Is of yourself. Tell me, who is the
  master
That works in such an admirable
  way,
And with such power and feeling?
Bindo. Benvenuto.
Michael A. Ah? Benvenuto?
  'Tis a masterpiece!
It pleases me as much, and even
  more,
Than the antiques about it; and
  yet they
Are of the best one sees. But you
  have placed it
By far too high. The light comes
  from below,
And injures the expression. Were
  these windows

Above and not beneath it, then indeed
It would maintain its own among these works
Of the old masters, noble as they are.
I will go in and study it more closely
I always prophesied that Benvenuto,
With all his follies and fantastic ways,
Would show his genius in some work of art
That would amaze the world, and be a challenge
Unto all other artists of his time.

[*They go in.*]

IV.

IN THE COLISEUM.

MICHAEL ANGELO *and* TOMASO DE' CAVALIERI.

Cavalieri. What have you here alone, Messer Michele?
Michael A. I come to learn.
Cavalieri. You are already master,
And teach all other men.
Michael A. Nay, I know nothing;
Not even my own ignorance, as some
Philosopher hath said. I am a schoolboy
Who hath not learned his lesson, and who stands
Ashamed and silent in the awful presence
Of the great master of antiquity
Who built these walls cyclopean.
Cavalieri. Gaudentius
His name was, I remember. His reward
Was to be thrown alive to the wild beasts
Here where we now are standing.

Michael A. Idle tales.
Cavalieri. But you are greater than Gaudentius was,
And your work nobler.
Michael A. Silence, I beseech you.
Cavalieri. Tradition says that fifteen thousand men
Were toiling for ten years incessantly
Upon this amphitheatre.
Michael A. Behold
How wonderful it is! The queen of flowers,
The marble rose of Rome! Its petals torn
By wind and rain of thrice five hundred years;
Its mossy sheath half rent away, and sold
To ornament our palaces and churches,
Or to be trodden under feet of man
Upon the Tiber's bank; yet what remains
Still opening its fair bosom to the sun,
And to the constellations that at night
Hang poised above it like a swarm of bees.
Cavalieri. The rose of Rome, but not of Paradise;
Not the white rose our Tuscan poet saw,
With saints for petals. When this rose was perfect,
Its hundred thousand petals were not saints,
But senators in their Thessalian caps,
And all the roaring populace of Rome;
And even an Empress and the Vestal Virgins,
Who came to see the gladiators die,
Could not give sweetness to a rose like this.

Michael A. I spake not of its uses, but its beauty.

Cavalieri. The sand beneath our feet is saturate
With blood of martyrs; and these rifted stones
Are awful witnesses against a people
Whose pleasure was the pain of dying men.

Michael A. Tomaso Cavalieri, on my word,
You should have been a preacher, not a painter!
Think you that I approve such cruelties,
Because I marvel at the architects
Who built these walls, and curved these noble arches?
Oh, I am put to shame, when I consider
How mean our work is, when compared with theirs!
Look at these walls about us and above us!
They have been shaken by earthquakes, have been made
A fortress, and been battered by long sieges;
The iron clamps, that held the stones together,
Have been wrenched from them; but they stand erect
And firm, as if they had been hewn and hollowed
Out of the solid rock, and were a part
Of the foundations of the world itself.

Cavalieri. Your work, I say again, is nobler work,
In so far as its end and aim are nobler;
And this is but a ruin, like the rest.
Its vaulted passages are made the caverns
Of robbers, and are haunted by the ghosts
Of murdered men.

Michael A. A thousand wild flowers bloom
From every chink, and the birds build their nests
Among the ruined arches, and suggest
New thoughts of beauty to the architect.
Now let us climb the broken stairs that lead
Into the corridors above, and study
The marvel and the mystery of that art
In which I am a pupil, not a master.
All things must have an end; the world itself
Must have an end, as in a dream I saw it.
There came a great hand out of heaven, and touched
The earth, and stopped it in its course. The seas
Leaped, a vast cataract, into the abyss;
The forests and the fields slid off, and floated
Like wooded islands in the air. The dead
Were hurled forth from their sepulchres; the living
Were mingled with them, and themselves were dead,—
All being dead; and the fair, shining cities
Dropped out like jewels from a broken crown.
Naught but the core of the great globe remained,
A skeleton of stone. And over it
The wrack of matter drifted like a cloud,
And then recoiled upon itself, and fell
Back on the empty world, that with the weight
Reeled, staggered, righted, and then headlong plunged
Into the darkness, as a ship, when struck

833

By a great sea, throws off the waves
  at first
On either side, then settles and
  goes down
Into the dark abyss, with her dead
  crew.
  Cavalieri. But the earth does
    not move.
  Michael A. Who knows?
  who knows?
There are great truths that pitch
  their shining tents
Outside our walls, and though but
  dimly seen
In the gray dawn, they will be
  manifest
When the light widens into perfect
  day.
A certain man, Copernicus by name,
Sometime professor here in Rome,
  has whispered
It is the earth, and not the sun,
  that moves.
What I beheld was only in a dream,
Yet dreams sometimes anticipate
  events,
Being unsubstantial images of
  things
As yet unseen.

V.

BENVENUTO AGAIN.

Macello de' Corvi. MICHAEL
ANGELO, BENVENUTO CELLINI.

  Michael A. So, Benvenuto, you
    return once more
To the Eternal City. 'Tis the
  centre
To which all gravitates. One finds
  no rest
Elsewhere than here. There may
  be other cities
That please us for a while, but
  Rome alone
Completely satisfies. It becomes
  to all

A second native land by predi-
  lection,
And not by accident of birth alone.
  Benvenuto. I am but just arrived,
    and am now lodging
With Bindo Altoviti. I have been
To kiss the feet of our most Holy
  Father,
And now am come in haste to kiss
  the hands
Of my miraculous Master.
  Michael A. And to find him
Grown very old.
  Benvenuto. You know that
  precious stones
Never grow old.
  Michael A. Half sunk beneath
    the horizon,
And yet not gone. Twelve years
  are a long while.
Tell me of France.
  Benvenuto. It were too long
  a tale
To tell you all. Suffice in brief
  to say
The King received me well, and
  loved me well;
Gave me the annual pension that
  before me
Our Leonardo had, nor more nor
  less,
And for my residence the Tour de
  Nesle,
Upon the river-side.
  Michael A. A princely lodging.
  Benvenuto. What in return I did
  now matters not,
For there are other things, of
  greater moment,
I wish to speak of. First of all,
  the letter
You wrote me, not long since,
  about my bust
Of Bindo Altoviti, here in Rome.
  You said,
' My Benvenuto, I for many years
Have known you as the greatest
  of all goldsmiths,

834

And now I know you as no less a
    sculptor.'
Ah, generous Master! How shall
    I e'er thank you
For such kind language?
  Michael A.   By believing it.
I saw the bust at Messer Bindo's
    house,
And thought it worthy of the
    ancient masters,
And said so. That is all.
  Benvenuto. It is too much;
And I should stand abashed here
  in your presence,
Had I done nothing worthier of
  your praise
Than Bindo's bust.
  Michael A.   What have you
  done that's better?
  Benvenuto. When I left Rome
  for Paris, you remember
I promised you that if I went a
  goldsmith
I would return a sculptor. I have
  kept
The promise I then made.
  Michael A.   Dear Benvenuto,
I recognized the latent genius in you,
But feared your vices.
  Benvenuto.   I have turned
  them all
To virtues. My impatient, way-
  ward nature,
That made me quick in quarrel,
  now has served me
Where meekness could not, and
  where patience could not,
As you shall hear now. I have
  cast in bronze
A statue of Perseus, holding thus
  aloft
In his left hand the head of the
  Medusa,
And in his right the sword that
  severed it;
His right foot planted on the lifeless
  corse;
His face superb and pitiful, with eyes

Down-looking on the victim of his
  vengeance.
  Michael A. I see it as it should be.
  Benvenuto.   As it will be
When it is placed upon the Ducal
  Square,
Half-way between your David and
  the Judith
Of Donatello.
  Michael A. Rival of them both!
  Benvenuto. But ah, what infinite
  trouble have I had
With Bandinello, and that stupid
  beast,
The major-domo of Duke Cosimo,
Francesco Ricci, and their wretched
  agent
Gorini, who came crawling round
  about me
Like a black spider, with his
  whining voice
That sounded like the buzz of a
  mosquito!
Oh, I have wept in utter desperation,
And wished a thousand times I had
  not left
My Tour de Nesle, nor e'er re-
  turned to Florence,
Or thought of Perseus. What
  malignant falsehoods
They told the Grand Duke, to
  impede my work,
And make me desperate!
  Michael A.   The nimble lie
Is like the second-hand upon a
  clock;
We see it fly; while the hour-hand
  of truth
Seems to stand still, and yet it
  moves unseen,
And wins at last, for the clock will
  not strike
Till it has reached the goal.
  Benvenuto.   My obstinacy
Stood me in stead, and helped me
  to o'ercome
The hindrances that envy and ill-will
Put in my way.

Michael A.   When anything is done
People see not the patient doing of it,
Nor think how great would be the loss to man
If it had not been done. As in a building
Stone rests on stone, and wanting the foundation
All would be wanting, so in human life
Each action rests on the foregone event,
That made it possible, but is forgotten
And buried in the earth.

Benvenuto.   Even Bandinello,
Who never yet spake well of anything,
Speaks well of this ; and yet he told the Duke
That, though I cast small figures well enough,
I never could cast this.

Michael A.   But you have done it,
And proved Ser Bandinello a false prophet.
That is the wisest way.

Benvenuto.   And ah, that casting !
What a wild scene it was, as late at night,
A night of wind and rain, we heaped the furnace
With pine of Serristori, till the flames
Caught in the rafters over us, and threatened
To send the burning roof upon our heads ;
And from the garden side the wind and rain
Poured in upon us, and half quenched our fires.
I was beside myself with desperation.
A shudder came upon me, then a fever ;

I thought that I was dying, and was forced
To leave the workshop, and to throw myself
Upon my bed, as one who has no hope.
And as I lay there, a deformed old man
Appeared before me, and with dismal voice,
Like one who doth exhort a criminal
Led forth to death, exclaimed,
'Poor Benvenuto,
Thy work is spoiled ! There is no remedy !'
Then, with a cry so loud it might have reached
The heaven of fire, I bounded to my feet,
And rushed back to my workmen.
They all stood
Bewildered and desponding ; and I looked
Into the furnace, and beheld the mass
Half molten only, and in my despair
I fed the fire with oak, whose terrible heat
Soon made the sluggish metal shine and sparkle.
Then followed a bright flash, and an explosion,
As if a thunderbolt had fallen among us.
The covering of the furnace had been rent
Asunder, and the bronze was flowing over ;
So that I straightway opened all the sluices
To fill the mould.   The metal ran like lava,
Sluggish and heavy ; and I sent my workmen
To ransack the whole house, and bring together
My pewter plates and pans, two hundred of them,

And cast them one by one into the
  furnace
To liquefy the mass, and in a moment
The mould was filled ! I fell upon
  my knees
And thanked the Lord ; and then
  we ate and drank
And went to bed, all hearty and
  contented.
It was two hours before the break
  of day.
My fever was quite gone.

Michael A. A strange adventure,
That could have happened to no
  man alive
But you, my Benvenuto.

Benvenuto. As my workmen said
To major-domo Ricci afterward,
When he inquired of them : "'Twas
  not a man,
But an express great devil.'

Michael A. And the statue ?

Benvenuto. Perfect in every
part, save the right foot
Of Perseus, as I had foretold the
  Duke.
There was just bronze enough to
  fill the mould ;
Not a drop over, not a drop too
  little.
I looked upon it as a miracle
Wrought by the hand of God.

Michael A. And now I see
How you have turned your vices
  into virtues.

Benvenuto. But wherefore do I
  prate of this ? I came
To speak of other things. Duke
  Cosimo
Through me invites you to return
  to Florence,
And offers you great honours, even
  to make you
One of the Forty-Eight, his Sena-
  tors.

Michael A. His Senators ! That
  is enough. Since Florence

Was changed by Clement Seventh
  from a Republic
Into a Dukedom, I no longer wish
To be a Florentine. That dream
  is ended.
The Grand Duke Cosimo now
  reigns supreme ;
All liberty is dead. Ah, woe is me !
I hoped to see my country rise to
  heights
Of happiness and freedom yet un-
  reached
By other nations, but the climbing
  wave
Pauses, lets go its hold, and slides
  again
Back to the common level, with a
  hoarse
Death rattle in its throat. I am
  too old
To hope for better days. I will
  stay here
And die in Rome. The very weeds,
  that grow
Among the broken fragments of her
  ruins,
Are sweeter to me than the garden
  flowers
Of other cities ; and the desolate
  ring
Of the Campagna round about her
  walls
Fairer than all the villas that encircle
The towns of Tuscany.

Benvenuto. But your old friends!

Michael A. All dead by violence.
  Baccio Valori
Has been beheaded ; Guicciardini
  poisoned ;
Philippo Strozzi strangled in his
  prison.
Is Florence then a place for honest
  men
To flourish in ? What is there to
  prevent
My sharing the same fate ?

Benvenuto. Why, this : if all

Your friends are dead, so are your
    enemies.

Michael A. Is Aretino dead?

Benvenuto. He lives in Venice,
And not in Florence.

Michael A. 'Tis the same
    to me.

This wretched mountebank, whom
    flatterers

Call the Divine, as if to make the
    word

Unpleasant in the mouths of those
    who speak it

And in the ears of those who hear
    it, sends me

A letter written for the public eye,
And with such subtle and infernal
    malice,

I wonder at his wickedness. 'Tis he
Is the express great devil, and not
    you.

Some years ago he told me how to
    paint

The scenes of the Last Judgment.

Benvenuto. I remember.

Michael A. Well, now he writes
    to me that, as a Christian,

He is ashamed of the unbounded
    freedom

With which I represent it.

Benvenuto. Hypocrite!

Michael A. He says I show man-
    kind that I am wanting

In piety and religion, in proportion
As I profess perfection in my art.

Profess perfection? Why, 'tis only
    men

Like Bugiardini who are satisfied
With what they do. I never am con-
    tent,

But always see the labours of my
    hand

Fall short of my conception.

Benvenuto. I perceive
The malice of this creature. He
    would taint you

With heresy, and in a time like this!
'Tis infamous!

Michael A. I represent the
    angels

Without their heavenly glory, and
    the saints

Without a trace of earthly modesty.

Benvenuto. Incredible audacity!

Michael A. The heathen
Veiled their Diana with some dra-
    pery,

And when they represented Venus
    naked

They made her by her modest
    attitude,

Appear half clothed. But I, who
    am a Christian,

Do so subordinate belief to art
That I have made the very violation
Of modesty in martyrs and in vir-
    gins

A spectacle at which all men would
    gaze

With half-averted eyes even in a
    brothel.

Benvenuto. He is at home there,
    and he ought to know

What men avert their eyes from
    in such places;

From the Last Judgment chiefly,
    I imagine.

Michael A. But divine Provi-
    dence will never leave

The boldness of my marvellous
    work unpunished;

And the more marvellous it is, the
    more

'Tis sure to prove the ruin of my
    fame!

And finally, if in this composition
I had pursued the instructions that
    he gave me

Concerning heaven and hell and
    paradise,

In that same letter, known to all
    the world,

Nature would not be forced, as she
    is now,

To feel ashamed that she invested
    me

With such great talent; that I
stand myself
A very idol in the world of art.
He taunts me also with the Mauso-
leum
Of Julius, still unfinished, for the
reason
That men persuaded the inane old
man
It was of evil augury to build
His tomb while he was living; and
he speaks
Of heaps of gold this Pope be-
queathed to me,
And calls it robbery;—that is what
he says.
What prompted such a letter?

Benvenuto.   Vanity.
He is a clever writer, and he
likes
To draw his pen, and flourish it in
the face
Of every honest man, as swordsmen
do
Their rapiers on occasion, but to
show
How skilfully they do it. Had you
followed
The advice he gave, or even
thanked him for it,
You would have seen another style
of fence.
'Tis but his wounded vanity, and
the wish
To see his name in print. So give
it not
A moment's thought; it soon will
be forgotten.

Michael A. I will not think of
it, but let it pass
For a rude speech thrown at me in
the street,
As boys threw stones at Dante.

Benvenuto. And what answer
Shall I take back to Grand Duke
Cosimo?
He does not ask your labour or
your service;

Only your presence in the city of
Florence,
With such advice upon his work in
hand
As he may ask, and you may choose
to give.

Michael A. You have my an-
swer. Nothing he can offer
Shall tempt me to leave Rome.
My work is here,
And only here, the building of Saint
Peter's.
What other things I hitherto have
done
Have fallen from me, are no longer
mine;
I have passed on beyond them, and
have left them
As milestones on the way. What
lies before me,
That is still mine, and while it is
unfinished
No one shall draw me from it, or
persuade me,
By promises of ease, or wealth, or
honour,
Till I behold the finished dome
uprise
Complete, as now I see it in my
thought.

Benvenuto. And will you paint
no more?

Michael A. No more.

Benvenuto. 'Tis well.
Sculpture is more divine, and more
like Nature,
That fashions all her works in high
relief,
And that is sculpture. This vast
ball, the Earth,
Was moulded out of clay, and baked
in fire;
Men, women, and all animals that
breathe
Are statues, and not paintings.
Even the plants,
The flowers, the fruits, the grasses,
were first sculptured,

And coloured later. Painting is a lie,
A shadow merely.

Michael A. Truly, as you say,
Sculpture is more than painting. It is greater
To raise the dead to life than to create
Phantoms that seem to live. The most majestic
Of the three sister arts is that which builds;
The eldest of them all, to whom the others
Are but the handmaids and the servitors,
Being but imitation, not creation.
Henceforth I dedicate myself to her.

Benvenuto. And no more from the marble hew those forms
That fill us all with wonder?

Michael A. Many statues
Will there be room for in my work. Their station
Already is assigned them in my mind.
But things move slowly. There are hindrances,
Want of material, want of means, delays
And interruptions, endless interference
Of Cardinal Commissioners, and disputes
And jealousies of artists, that annoy me.
But I will persevere until the work
Is wholly finished, or till I sink down
Surprised by death, that unexpected guest,
Who waits for no man's leisure, but steps in,
Unasked and unannounced, to put a stop
To all our occupations and designs.
And then perhaps I may go back to Florence;
This is my answer to Duke Cosimo.

VI.

URBINO'S FORTUNE.

MICHAEL ANGELO'S *Studio*. MICHAEL ANGELO *and* URBINO.

Michael A. (*pausing in his work*). Urbino, thou and I are both old men.
My strength begins to fail me.

Urbino. Eccellenza,
That is impossible. Do I not see you
Attack the marble blocks with the same fury
As twenty years ago?

Michael A. 'Tis an old habit
I must have learned it early from my nurse
At Setignano, the stone-mason's wife:
For the first sounds I heard were of the chisel
Chipping away the stone.

Urbino. At every stroke
You strike fire with your chisel.

Michael A. Ay, because
The marble is too hard.

Urbino. It is a block
That Topolino sent you from Carrara.
He is a judge of marble.

Michael A. I remember.
With it he sent me something of his making,—
A Mercury, with long body and short legs,
As if by any possibility
A messenger of the gods could have short legs.
It was no more like Mercury than you are,
But rather like those little plaster figures
That peddlers hawk about the villages
As images of saints. But luckily

For Topolino, there are many people
Who see no difference between what is best
And what is only good, or not even good ;
So that poor artists stand in their esteem
On the same level with the best, or higher.

Urbino. How Eccellenza laughed!

Michael A. Poor Topolino !
All men are not born artists, nor will labour
E'er make them artists.

Urbino. No, no more
Than Emperors, or Popes, or Cardinals.
One must be chosen for it. I have been
Your colour-grinder six and twenty years,
And am not yet an artist.

Michael A. Some have eyes
That see not ; but in every block of marble
I see a statue,—see it as distinctly
As if it stood before me shaped and perfect
In attitude and action. I have only
To hew away the stone walls that imprison
The lovely apparition, and reveal it
To other eyes as mine already see it.
But I grow old and weak. What wilt thou do
When I am dead, Urbino ?

Urbino. Eccellenza,
I must then serve another master.

Michael A. Never !
Bitter is servitude at best. Already
So many years hast thou been serving me ;
But rather as a friend than as a servant.
We have grown old together.
Dost thou think

So meanly of this Michael Angelo
As to imagine he would let thee serve,
When he is free from service ?
Take this purse,
Two thousand crowns in gold.

Urbino. Two thousand crowns !

Michael A. Ay, it will make thee rich. Thou shalt not die
A beggar in a hospital.

Urbino. Oh, Master !

Michael A. I cannot have them with me on the journey
That I am undertaking. The last garment
That men will make for me will have no pockets.

Urbino (*kissing the hand of* MICHAEL ANGELO). My generous master !

Michael A. Hush !

Urbino. My Providence !

Michael A. Not a word more.
Go now to bed, old man.
Thou hast served Michael Angelo. Remember,
Henceforward thou shalt serve no other master.

VII.

THE OAKS OF MONTE LUCA.

MICHAEL ANGELO, *alone in the woods.*

Michael A. How still it is among these ancient oaks !
Surges and undulations of the air
Uplift the leafy boughs, and let them fall
With scarce a sound. Such sylvan quietudes
Become old age. These huge centennial oaks,
That may have heard in infancy the trumpets

Of Barbarossa's cavalry, deride
Man's brief existence, that with all
his strength
He cannot stretch beyond the
hundredth year.
This little acorn, turbaned like
the Turk,
Which with my foot I spurn, may
be an oak
Hereafter, feeding with its bitter
mast
The fierce wild boar, and tossing
in its arms
The cradled nests of birds, when all
the men
That now inhabit this vast universe,
They and their children, and their
children's children,
Shall be but dust and mould, and
nothing more.
Through openings in the trees I see
below me
The valley of Clitumnus, with its
farms
And snow-white oxen grazing in
the shade
Of the tall poplars on the river's
brink.
O Nature, gentle mother, tender
nurse!
I, who have never loved thee as I
ought,
But wasted all my years immured
in cities,
And breathed the stifling atmo-
sphere of streets,
Now come to thee for refuge.
Here is peace.
Yonder I see the little hermitages
Dotting the mountain side with
points of light,
And here St. Julian's convent, like
a nest
Of curlews, clinging to some windy
cliff.
Beyond the broad, illimitable plain
Down sinks the sun, red as Apollo's
quoit,

That, by the envious Zephyr blown
aside,
Struck Hyacinthus dead, and
stained the earth
With his young blood, that blos-
somed into flowers.
And now, instead of these fair deities,
Dread demons haunt the earth;
hermits inhabit
The leafy homes of sylvan Hama-
dryads;
And jovial friars, rotund and rubi-
cund,
Replace the old Silenus with his ass.

Here underneath these venerable
oaks,
Wrinkled and brown and gnarled
like them with age,
A brother of the monastery sits,
Lost in his meditations. What
may be
The questions that perplex, the
hopes that cheer him?
Good-evening, holy father.
 Monk. God be with you.
 Michael A. Pardon a stranger if
he interrupt
Your meditations.
 Monk. It was but a dream,—
The old, old dream, that never will
come true;
The dream that all my life I have
been dreaming,
And yet is still a dream.
 Michael A. All men have dreams.
I have had mine; but none of them
came true;
They were but vanity. Sometimes
I think
The happiness of man lies in pur-
suing,
Not in possessing; for the things
possessed
Lose half their value. Tell me of
your dream.
 Monk. The yearning of my heart,
my sole desire,

That like the sheaf of Joseph
   stands upright,
While all the others bend and bow
   to it;
The passion that torments me, and
   that breathes
New meaning into the dead forms
   of prayer,
Is that with mortal eyes I may
   behold
The Eternal City.

Michael A.   Rome?

Monk.   There is but one;
The rest are merely names.   I
   think of it
As the Celestial City, paved with
   gold,
And sentinelled with angels.

Michael A.   Would it were.
I have just fled from it.   It is
   beleagured
By Spanish troops, led by the Duke
   of Alva.

Monk. But still for me 'tis the
   Celestial City,
And I would see it once before
   I die.

Michael A. Each one must bear
   his cross.

Monk.   Were it a cross
That had been laid upon me, I
   could bear it,
Or fall with it.   It is a crucifix;
I am nailed hand and foot, and
   I am dying!

Michael A. What would you see
   in Rome?

Monk.   His Holiness.

Michael A. Him that was once
   the Cardinal Caraffa?
You would but see a man of four-
   score years,
With sunken eyes, burning like
   carbuncles,
Who sits at table with his friends
   for hours,
Cursing the Spaniards as a race of
   Jews

And miscreant Moors.   And with
   what soldiery
Think you he now defends the
   Eternal City?

Monk. With legions of bright
   angels.

Michael A. So he calls them;
And yet in fact these bright angelic
   legions
Are only German Lutherans.

Monk (crossing himself). Heaven
   protect us!

Michael A. What further would
   you see?

Monk.   The Cardinals,
Going in their gilt coaches to High
   Mass.

Michael A. Men do not go to
   Paradise in coaches.

Monk. The catacombs, the con-
   vents, and the churches;
The ceremonies of the Holy Week
In all their pomp, or, at the
   Epiphany,
The Feast of the Santissima
   Bambino
At Ara Cœli.   But I shall not see
   them.

Michael A. These pompous
   ceremonies of the Church
Are but an empty show to him who
   knows
The actors in them.   Stay here in
   your convent,
For he who goes to Rome may see
   too much.
What would you further?

Monk.   I would see
   the painting
Of the Last Judgment in the Sistine
   Chapel.

Michael A. The smoke of incense
   and of altar candles
Has blackened it already.

Monk.   Woe is me!
Then I would hear Allegri's Mi-
   serere,
Sung by the Papal choir.

Michael A. A dismal dirge!
I am an old, old man, and I have
    lived
In Rome for thirty years and more,
    and know
The jarring of the wheels of that
    great world,
Its jealousies, its discords, and its
    strife.
Therefore I say to you, remain
    content
Here in your convent, here among
    your woods,
Where only there is peace. Go
    not to Rome.
There was of old a monk of Wit-
    tenberg
Who went to Rome; you may
    have heard of him;
His name was Luther; and you
    know what followed.

        [The convent bell rings.

Monk (rising). It is the convent
    bell; it rings for vespers.
Let us go in; we both will pray for
    peace.

VIII.

The Dead Christ.

MICHAEL ANGELO's *studio.* MI-
CHAEL ANGELO, *with a light,
working upon the Dead Christ.
Midnight.*

Michael A. O Death, why is it
    I cannot portray
Thy form and features? Do I stand
    too near thee?
Or dost thou hold my hand, and
    draw me back,
As being thy disciple, not thy
    master?
Let him who knows not what old
    age is like
Have patience till it comes, and he
    will know.

I once had skill to fashion Life and
    Death
And Sleep, which is the counterfeit
    of Death;
And I remember what Giovanni
    Strozzi
Wrote underneath my statue of the
    Night
In San Lorenzo, ah, so long ago!

Grateful to me is sleep! More
    grateful now
Than it was then; for all my friends
    are dead;
And she is dead, the noblest of
    them all.
I saw her face, when the great
    sculptor Death,
Whom men should call Divine, had
    at a blow
Stricken her into marble; and I
    kissed
Her cold white hand. What was
    it held me back
From kissing her fair forehead, and
    those lips,
Those dead, dumb lips? Grateful
    to me is sleep!

      Enter GIORGIO VASARI.

Giorgio. Good-evening, or good-
    morning, for I know not
Which of the two it is.
    Michael A. How came you in?
    Giorgio. Why, by the door, as
    all men do.
    Michael A. Ascanio
Must have forgotten to bolt it.
    Giorgio. Probably.
Am I a spirit, or so like a spirit,
That I could slip through bolted
    door or window?
As I was passing down the street,
    I saw
A glimmer of light, and heard the
    well-known chink
Of chisel upon marble. So I en-
    tered,

To see what keeps you from your
bed so late.

Michael A. (*coming forward
with the lamp*). You have
been revelling with your boon
companions,
Giorgio Vasari, and you come to me
At an untimely hour.

Giorgio. The Pope hath sent me.
His Holiness desires to see again
The drawing you once showed him
of the dome
Of the Basilica.

Michael A. We will look for it.

Giorgio. What is the marble
group that glimmers there
Behind you?

Michael A. Nothing, and yet
everything,—
As one may take it. It is my own
tomb,
That I am building.

Giorgio. Do not hide it
from me.

By our long friendship and the love
I bear you,
Refuse me not!

Michael A. (*letting fall the
lamp*). Life hath become
to me
An empty theatre,—its lights extinguished,
The music silent, and the actors
gone;
And I alone sit musing on the
scenes
That once have been. I am so old
that Death
Oft plucks me by the cloak, to come
with him;
And some day, like this lamp, shall
I fall down,
And my last spark of life will be
extinguished.
Ah me! ah me! what darkness of
despair!
So near to death, and yet so far
from God!

Miscellaneous Poems.

—◆◆—

CURFEW.

I.

Solemnly, mournfully,
  Dealing its dole,
The Curfew Bell
  Is beginning to toll.

Cover the embers,
  And put out the light;
Toil comes with the morning,
  And rest with the night.

Dark grow the windows,
  And quenched is the fire;
Sound fades into silence,—
  All footsteps retire.

No voice in the chambers,
  No sound in the hall!
Sleep and oblivion
  Reign over all!

II.

The book is completed,
  And closed, like the day;
And the hand that has written it
  Lays it away.

Dim grow its fancies,
  Forgotten they lie;
Like coals in the ashes,
  They darken and die.

Song sinks into silence,
  The story is told,
The windows are darkened,
  The hearthstone is cold.

Darker and darker
  The black shadows fall;
Sleep and oblivion
  Reign over all!

—◆◆—

THE GOLDEN SUNSET.

The golden sea its mirror spreads
  Beneath the golden skies,
And but a narrow strip between
  Of land and shadow lies.

The cloud-like rocks, the rock-like
    clouds,
  Dissolved in glory float,
And midway of the radiant flood,
  Hangs silently the boat.

The sea is but another sky,
  The sky a sea as well,
And which is earth and which is
    heaven,
  The eye can scarcely tell.

So when for us life's evening hour,
  Soft fading shall descend,
May glory, born of earth and heaven,
  The earth and heaven blend.

Flooded with peace the spirits float,
  With silent rapture glow,
Till where earth ends and heaven
    begins,
  The soul shall scarcely know.

VIA SOLITARIA.

ALONE I walk the peopled city,
  Where each seems happy with
    his own;
Oh! friends, I ask not for your pity—
  I walk alone.

No more for me yon lake rejoices,
  Though moved by loving airs of
    June;
Oh! birds, your sweet and piping
    voices
  Are out of tune.

In vain for me the elm-tree arches
  Its plumes in many a feathery
    spray;
In vain the evening's starry marches
  And sunlit day.

In vain your beauty, Summer
    flowers;
Ye cannot greet these cordial eyes;
They gaze on other fields than ours,
  On other skies.

The gold is rifled from the coffer,
  The blade is stolen from the
    sheath;
Life has but one more boon to offer,
  And that is—Death.

Yet well I know the voice of Duty,
  And, therefore, life and health
    must crave,
Though she who gave the world its
    beauty
  Is in her grave.

I live, O lost one! for the living
  Who drew their earliest life from
    thee,
And wait, until with glad thanks-
    giving
  I shall be free.

For life to me is as a station
  Wherein apart a traveller stands,
One absent long from home and
    nation
  In other lands.

And I, as he who stands and listens,
  Amid the twilight's chill and
    gloom,
To hear, approaching in the dis-
    tance,
  The train for home.

For death shall bring another
    mating,
  Beyond the shadows of the tomb,
On yonder shores a bride is waiting
  Until I come.

In yonder field are children playing,
  And there—oh! vision of de-
    light!—
I see the child and mother straying
  In robes of white.

Thou, then, the longing heart that
    breakest,
  Stealing the treasures one by one,
I'll call Thee blessed when thou
    makest
  The parted—one.

THE BELLS OF SAN BLAS.

WHAT say the Bells of San Blas
To the ships that southward pass
  From the harbour of Mazatlan?
To them it is nothing more
Than the sound of surf on the
    shore,—
  Nothing more to master or man.

But to me, a dreamer of dreams,
To whom what is and what seems
　　Are often one and the same,—
The Bells of San Blas to me
Have a strange, wild melody,
　　And are something more than
　　　a name.

For bells are the voice of the Church;
They have tones that touch and
　　search
　　The hearts of young and old;
One sound to all, yet each
Lends a meaning to their speech,
　　And the meaning is manifold.

They are a voice of the Past,
Of an age that is fading fast,
　　Of a power austere and grand;
When the flag of Spain unfurled
Its folds o'er this western world,
　　And the Priest was lord of the
　　　land.

The chapel that once looked down
On the little seaport town
　　Has crumbled into the dust;
And on oaken beams below
The bells swing to and fro,
　　And are green with mould and
　　　rust.

'Is, then, the old faith dead,'
They say, 'and in its stead
　　Is some new faith proclaimed,
That we are forced to remain
Naked to sun and rain,
　　Unsheltered and ashamed?

'Once in our tower aloof
We rang over wall and roof
　　Our warnings and our complaints;
And round about us there
The white doves filled the air,
　　Like the white souls of the saints.

'The saints! Ah, have they grown
Forgetful of their own?
　　Are they asleep, or dead,
That open to the sky
Their ruined Missions lie,
　　No longer tenanted?

'Oh, bring us back once more
The vanished days of yore,
　　When the world with faith was
　　　filled;
Bring back the fervid zeal,
The hearts of fire and steel,
　　The hands that believe and build.

'Then from our tower again
We will send over land and main
　　Our voices of command,
Like exiled kings who return
To their thrones, and the people
　　learn
　　That the Priest is lord of the
　　　land!'

O Bells of San Blas, in vain
Ye call back the Past again!
　　The Past is deaf to your prayer:
Out of the shadows of night
The world rolls into light;
　　It is daybreak everywhere.

Notes.

Page 27. *Coplas de Manrique.*

This poem of Manrique is a great favourite in Spain. No less than four poetic Glosses, or running commentaries, upon it have been published, no one of which, however, possesses great poetic merit. That of the Carthusian monk, Rodrigo de Valdepeñas, is the best. It is known as the *Closa del Cartujo.* There is also a prose Commentary by Luis de Aranda.

The following stanzas of the poem were found in the author's pocket, after his death on the field of battle.

'O World ! so few the years we live,
Would that the life which thou dost give
Were life indeed !
Alas ! thy sorrows fall so fast,
Our happiest hour is when at last
The soul is freed.

Our days are covered o'er with grief,
And sorrows neither few nor brief
Veil all in gloom;
Left desolate of real good,
Within this cheerless solitude
No pleasures bloom.

Thy pilgrimage begins in tears,
And ends in bitter doubts and fears,
Or dark despair;
Midway so many toils appear,
That he who lingers longest here
Knows most of care.

Thy goods are bought with many a groan,
By the hot sweat of toil alone,
And weary hearts ;
Fleet-footed is the approach of woe,
But with a lingering step and slow
Its form departs.'

Page 40. *King Christian.*

Nils Juel was a celebrated Danish Admiral, and Peder Wessel, a Vice-Admiral, who for his great prowess re-ceived the popular title of Tordenskiold, or Thunder-shield. In childhood he was a tailor's apprentice, and rose to his high rank before the age of twenty-eight, when he was killed in a duel.

Page 46. *The Skeleton in Armour.*

This Ballad was suggested to me while riding on the sea-shore at New-port. A year or two previous a skeleton had been dug up at Fall River, clad in broken and corroded armour ; and the idea occurred to me of connecting it with the Round Tower at Newport, generally known hitherto as the Old Windmill, though now claimed by the Danes as a work of their early ancestors. Pro-fessor Rafn, in the *Mémoires de la Société Royale des Antiquaires du Nord,* for 1838–1839, says :—

' There is no mistaking in this in-stance the style in which the more ancient stone edifices of the North were constructed,—the style which belongs to the Roman or Ante-Gothic architec-ture, and which, especially after the time of Charlemagne, diffused itself from Italy over the whole of the West and North of Europe, where it continued to predominate until the close of the twelfth century,—that style which some authors have, from one of its most striking characteristics, called the round arch style, the same which in England is denominated Saxon and sometimes Norman architecture.

' On the ancient structure in Newport there are no ornaments remaining, which might possibly have served to guide us in assigning the probable date of its erection. That no vestige whatever is found of the pointed arch, nor any approximation to it, is indicative of an earlier rather than of a later period. From such characteristics as remain, however, we can scarcely form any other inference than one, in which I am persuaded that all who are familiar with Old-Northern architecture will concur, THAT THIS BUILDING WAS ERECTED AT A PERIOD DECIDEDLY NOT LATER THAN THE TWELFTH CENTURY. This remark applies, of course, to the original building only, and not to the alterations that it subsequently received; for there are several such alterations in the upper part of the building which cannot be mistaken, and which were most likely occasioned by its being adapted in modern times to various uses; for example, as the substructure of a windmill, and latterly as a hay magazine. To the same times may be referred the windows, the fireplace, and the apertures made above the columns. That this building could not have been erected for a windmill, is what an architect will easily discern.'

I will not enter into a discussion of the point. It is sufficiently well established for the purpose of a ballad; though doubtless many a citizen of Newport, who has passed his days within sight of the Round Tower, will be ready to exclaim, with Sancho: 'God bless me! did I not warn you to have a care of what you were doing, for that it was nothing but a windmill; and nobody could mistake it, but one who had the like in his head.'

Page 47. *Skoal!*

In Scandinavia, this is the customary salutation when drinking a health. I have slightly changed the orthography of the word, in order to preserve the correct pronunciation.

Page 49. *The Luck of Edenhall.*

The tradition upon which this ballad is founded, and the 'shards of the Luck of Edenhall,' still exist in England. The goblet is in the possession of Sir Christopher Musgrave, Bart., of Eden Hall, Cumberland; and is not so entirely shattered as the ballad leaves it.

Page 50. *The Elected Knight.*

This strange and somewhat mystical ballad is from Nyerup and Rahbek's *Danske Viser* of the Middle Ages. It seems to refer to the first preaching of Christianity in the North, and to the institution of Knight-Errantry. The three maidens I suppose to be Faith, Hope, and Charity. The irregularities of the original have been carefully preserved in the translation.

Page 52. *The Children of the Lord's Supper.*

There is something patriarchal still lingering about rural life in Sweden, which renders it a fit theme for song. Almost primeval simplicity reigns over that Northern land,—almost primeval solitude and stillness. You pass out from the gate of the city, and, as if by magic, the scene changes to a wild, woodland landscape. Around you are forests of fir. Overhead hang the long, fan-like branches, trailing with moss, and heavy with red and blue cones. Under foot is a carpet of yellow leaves; and the air is warm and balmy. On a wooden bridge you cross a little silver stream; and anon come forth into a pleasant and sunny land of farms. Wooden fences divide the adjoining fields. Across the road are gates, which are opened by troops of children. The peasants take off their hats as you pass; you sneeze, and they cry, 'God bless you!' The houses in the villages and smaller towns are all built of hewn timber, and for the most part painted red. The floors of the taverns are strewn with the fragrant tips of fir boughs. In many villages there are no taverns, and the peasants take turns in receiving travellers. The thrifty housewife shows you into the best chamber, the walls of which are hung round with rude pictures from the Bible; and brings you her heavy silver spoons,—an heirloom,—to dip the curdled milk from the pan. You have oaten cakes baked some months before, or bread with anise-seed and coriander in it, or perhaps a little pine bark.

Meanwhile the sturdy husband has brought his horses from the plough, and harnessed them to your carriage. Solitary travellers come and go in uncouth one-horse chaises. Most of them have pipes in their mouths, and, hanging around their necks in front, a leather wallet, in which they carry tobacco, and the great bank-notes of the country, as large as your two hands. You meet, also, groups of Dalekarlian peasant-women, travelling homeward or townward in pursuit of work. They walk barefoot, carrying in their hands their shoes, which have high heels under the hollow of the foot, and soles of birch bark.

Frequent, too, are the village churches, standing by the roadside, each in its own little Garden of Gethsemane. In the parish register great events are doubtless recorded. Some old king was christened or buried in that church; and a little sexton, with a rusty key, shows you the baptismal font, or the coffin. In the churchyard are a few flowers, and much green grass; and daily the shadow of the church spire, with its long, tapering finger, counts the tombs, representing a dial-plate of human life, on which the hours and minutes are the graves of men. The stones are flat, and large, and low, and perhaps sunken, like the roofs of old houses. On some are armorial bearings; on others only the initials of the poor tenants, with a date, as on the roofs of Dutch cottages. They all sleep with their heads to the westward. Each held a lighted taper in his hand when he died; and in his coffin were placed his little heart-treasures, and a piece of money for his last journey. Babes that came lifeless into the world were carried in the arms of gray-haired old men to the only cradle they ever slept in; and in the shroud of the dead mother were laid the little garments of the child that lived and died in her bosom. And over this scene the village pastor looks

from his window in the stillness of midnight, and says in his heart, 'How quietly they rest, all the departed!'

Near the churchyard gate stands a poor-box, fastened to a post by iron bands, and secured by a padlock, with a sloping wooden roof to keep off the rain. If it be Sunday, the peasants sit on the church steps and con their psalm-books. Others are coming down the road with their beloved pastor, who talks to them of holy things from beneath his broad-brimmed hat. He speaks of fields and harvests, and of the parable of the sower, that went forth to sow. He leads them to the Good Shepherd, and to the pleasant pastures of the spirit-land. He is their patriarch, and, like Melchizedek, both priest and king, though he has no other throne than the church pulpit. The women carry psalm-books in their hands, wrapped in silk handkerchiefs, and listen devoutly to the good man's words. But the young men, like Gallio, care for none of these things. They are busy counting the plaits in the kirtles of the peasant-girls, their number being an indication of the wearer's wealth. It may end in a wedding.

I will endeavour to describe a village wedding in Sweden. It shall be in summer-time, that there may be flowers, and in a southern province, that the bride may be fair. The early song of the lark and of chanticleer are mingling in the clear morning air, and the sun, the heavenly bridegroom with golden locks, arises in the east, just as our earthly bridegroom with yellow hair arises in the south. In the yard there is a sound of voices and trampling of hoofs, and horses are led forth and saddled. The steed that is to bear the bridegroom has a bunch of flowers upon his forehead, and a garland of corn-flowers around his neck. Friends from the neighbouring farms come riding in, their blue cloaks streaming to the wind; and finally the happy bridegroom, with a whip in his hand, and a monstrous nosegay in the breast of his black jacket, comes forth from his chamber;

and then to horse and away, towards the village where the bride already sits and waits.

Foremost rides the spokesman, followed by some half-dozen village musicians. Next comes the bridegroom between his two groomsmen, and then forty or fifty friends and wedding guests, half of them perhaps with pistols and guns in their hands. A kind of baggage-wagon brings up the rear, laden with food and drink for these merry pilgrims. At the entrance of every village stands a triumphal arch, adorned with flowers and ribbons and evergreens; and as they pass beneath it the wedding guests fire a salute, and the whole procession stops. And straight from every pocket flies a black-jack, filled with punch or brandy. It is passed from hand to hand among the crowd; provisions are brought from the wagon, and after eating and drinking and hurrahing the procession moves forward again, and at length draws near the house of the bride. Four heralds ride forward to announce that a knight and his attendants are in the neighbouring forest, and pray for hospitality. 'How many are you?' asks the bride's father. 'At least three hundred,' is the answer; and to this the host replies, 'Yes; were you seven times as many, you should all be welcome: and in token thereof receive this cup.' Whereupon each herald receives a can of ale; and soon after the whole jovial company comes storming into the farmer's yard, and, riding round the May-pole, which stands in the centre, alights amid a grand salute and flourish of music.

In the hall sits the bride, with a crown upon her head and a tear in her eye, like the Virgin Mary in old church paintings. She is dressed in a red bodice and kirtle with loose linen sleeves. There is a gilded belt around her waist; and around her neck strings of golden beads, and a golden chain. On the crown rests a wreath of wild roses, and below it another of cypress. Loose over her shoulders falls her flaxen hair; and her blue innocent eyes are fixed upon the ground. O thou good soul! thou hast hard hands, but a soft heart! Thou art poor. The very ornaments thou wearest are not thine. They have been hired for this great day. Yet art thou rich; rich in health, rich in hope, rich in thy first, young, fervent love. The blessing of Heaven be upon thee! So thinks the parish priest, as he joins together the hands of bride and bridegroom, saying in deep, solemn tones,— 'I give thee in marriage this damsel, to be thy wedded wife in all honour, and to share the half of thy bed, thy lock and key, and every third penny which you two may possess, or may inherit, and all the rights which Upland's laws provide, and the holy King Erik gave.'

The dinner is now served, and the bride sits between the bridegroom and the priest. The spokesman delivers an oration after the ancient custom of his fathers. He interlards it well with quotations from the Bible; and invites the Saviour to be present at this marriage feast, as he was at the marriage feast in Cana of Galilee. The table is not sparingly set forth. Each makes a long arm and the feast goes cheerily on. Punch and brandy pass round between the courses, and here and there a pipe is smoked while waiting for the next dish. They sit long at table; but, as all things must have an end, so must a Swedish dinner. Then the dance begins. It is led off by the bride and the priest, who perform a solemn minuet together. Not till after midnight comes the last dance. The girls form a ring around the bride, to keep her from the hands of the married women, who endeavour to break through the magic circle, and seize their new sister. After long struggling they succeed; and the crown is taken from her head and the jewels from her neck, and her bodice is unlaced and her kirtle taken off; and like a vestal virgin clad all in white she goes, but it is to her marriage chamber, not to her grave; and the wedding guests follow her with lighted candles in their hands. And this is a village bridal.

Nor must I forget the suddenly changing seasons of the Northern clime. There is no long and lingering spring, unfolding leaf and blossom one by one; no long and lingering autumn, pompous with many-coloured leaves and the glow of Indian summers. But winter and summer are wonderful, and pass into each other. The quail has hardly ceased piping in the corn, when winter from the folds of trailing clouds sows broadcast over the land snow, icicles, and rattling hail. The days wane apace. Ere long the sun hardly rises above the horizon, or does not rise at all. The moon and the stars shine through the day; only, at noon, they are pale and wan, and in the southern sky a red, fiery glow, as of sunset, burns along the horizon, and then goes out. And pleasantly under the silver moon, and under the silent, solemn stars, ring the steel shoes of the skaters on the frozen sea, and voices, and the sound of bells.

And now the Northern Lights begin to burn, faintly at first, like sunbeams playing in the waters of the blue sea. Then a soft crimson glow tinges the heavens. There is a blush on the cheek of night. The colours come and go, and change from crimson to gold, from gold to crimson. The snow is stained with rosy light. Twofold from the zenith, east and west, flames a fiery sword; and a broad band passes athwart the heavens like a summer sunset. Soft purple clouds come sailing over the sky, and through their vapoury folds the winking stars shine white as silver. With such pomp as this is Merry Christmas ushered in, though only a single star heralded the first Christmas. And in memory of that day the Swedish peasants dance on straw; and the peasant-girls throw straws at the timbered-roof of the hall, and for every one that sticks in a crack shall a groomsman come to their wedding. Merry Christmas indeed! For pious souls there shall be church songs and sermons, but for Swedish peasants, brandy and nut-brown ale in wooden bowls; and the great Yule-cake crowned with a cheese, and garlanded with apples, and upholding a three-armed candlestick over the Christmas feast. They may tell tales, too, of Jöns Lundsbracka, and Lunkenfus, and the great Riddar Finke of Pingsdaga[1].

And now the glad, leafy midsummer, full of blossoms and the song of nightingales, is come! Saint John has taken the flowers and festival of heathen Balder; and in every village there is a May-pole fifty feet high, with wreaths and roses and ribbons streaming in the wind, and a noisy weather-cock on top, to tell the village whence the wind cometh and whither it goeth. The sun does not set till ten o'clock at night; and the children are at play in the streets an hour later. The windows and doors are all open, and you may sit and read till midnight without a candle. Oh, how beautiful is the summer night, which is not night, but a sunless yet unclouded day, descending upon earth with dews and shadows and refreshing coolness! How beautiful the long, mild twilight, which like a silver clasp unites to-day with yesterday! How beautiful the silent hour, when Morning and Evening thus sit together, hand in hand, beneath the starless sky of midnight! From the church-tower in the public square the bell tolls the hour, with a soft, musical chime; and the watchman, whose watch-tower is the belfry, blows a blast on his horn, for each stroke of the hammer, and four times, to the four corners of the heavens, in a sonorous voice he chants,—

> ' Ho ! watchman, ho !
> Twelve is the clock !
> God keep our town
> From fire and brand
> And hostile hand !
> Twelve is the clock !

From his swallow's nest in the belfry he can see the sun all night long; and farther north the priest stands at his door in the warm midnight, and lights his pipe with a common burning-glass.

---

[1] Titles of Swedish popular tales.

Page 52. *The Feast of the Leafy Pavilions.*

In Swedish, *Löfhyddohögtiden*, the Leaf-huts'-high-tide.

Page 52. *Hörberg.*

The peasant-painter of Sweden. He is known chiefly by his altar-pieces in the village churches.

Page 53. *Wallin.*

A distinguished pulpit-orator and poet. He is particularly remarkable for the beauty and sublimity of his psalms.

Page 73. *As Lope says.*

'La cólera
de un Español sentado no se templa,
sino le representan en dos horas
hasta el final juicio desde el Génesis.'
Lope de Vega.

Page 75. *Abernuncio Satanas!*

'Digo, Señora, respondió Sancho, lo que tengo dicho, que de los azotes abernuncio. Abrenuncio, habeis de decir, Sancho, y no como decis, dijo el Duque.'—*Don Quixote*, Part II, ch. 35.

Page 81. *Fray Carrillo.*

The allusion here is to a Spanish epigram.

'Siempre Fray Carrillo estás
cansándonos acá fuera;
quien en tu celda estuviera
para no verte jamas!'
Böhl de Faber. Floresta, No. 611.

Page 81. *Padre Francisco.*

This is from an Italian popular song.

'"Padre Francesco,
Padre Francesco!"
—Cosa volete del Padre Francesco?—
"V' è una bella ragazzina
Che si vuole confessar!"
Fatte l' entrare, fatte l' entrare!
Che la voglio confessare.'

Kopisch. Volksthümliche Poesien aus allen Mundarten Italiens und seiner Inseln, p. 194.

Page 82. *Ave! cujus calcem clare.*

From a monkish hymn of the twelfth century, in Sir Alexander Croke's *Essay on the Origin, Progress, and Decline of Rhyming Latin Verse*, p. 109.

Page 86. *The gold of the Busné.*

Busné is the name given by the Gipsies to all who are not of their race.

Page 88. *Count of the Calés.*

The Gipsies call themselves Calés. See Borrow's valuable and extremely interesting work, *The Zincali; or an Account of the Gipsies in Spain*. London, 1841.

Page 89. *Asks if his money-bags would rise.*

'¿Y volviéndome á un lado, ví á un Avariento, que estaba preguntando á otro (que por haber sido embalsamado, y estar l xos sus tripas no hablaba, porque no habian llegado si habian de resucitar aquel dia todos los enterrados), si resucitarian unos bolsones suyos?'— *El Sueño de las Cala eras.*

Page 89. *And amen! said my Cid the Campeador.*

A line from the ancient *Poema del Cid*.

'Amen, dixo Mio Cid el Campeador.'
Line 3044.

Page 89. *The river of his thoughts.*

This expression is from Dante:

'Si che chiaro
Per essa scenda della mente il fiume.'

Byron has likewise used the expression; though I do not recollect in which of his poems.

Page 90. *Mari Franca.*

A common Spanish proverb, used to turn aside a question one does not wish to answer:

'Porque casó Mari Franca
quatro leguas de Salamanca.'

Page 90. *Ay, soft, emerald eyes.*

The Spaniards, with good reason, consider this colour of the eye as beautiful, and celebrate it in song; as, for example, in the well-known *Villaneico*:

'Ay ojuelos verdes,
ay los mis ojuelos,
ay hagan los cielos
que de mí te acuerdes!

Tengo confianza
de mis verdes ojos.'

Böhl de Faber, Floresta, No. 255.

Notes.

Dante speaks of Beatrice's eyes as emeralds : *Purgatorio*, xxxi. 116. Lami says, in his *Annotazioni*, ' Erano i suoi occhi d' un turchino verdiccio, simile a quel del mare.'

Page 91. *The Avenging Child.*

See the ancient ballads of *El Infante Venjador*, and *Calayons*.

Page 91. *All are sleeping.*

From the Spanish. *Böhl de Faber, Floresta*, No. 282.

Page 99. *Good night.*

From the Spanish; as are likewise the songs immediately following, and that which commences the first scene of Act III.

Page 107. *The evil eye.*

' In the Gitano language, casting the evil eye is called *Querelar nasula*, which simply means making sick, and which, according to the common superstition, is accomplished by casting an evil look at people, especially children, who, from the tenderness of their constitution, are supposed to be more easily blighted than those of a more mature age. After receiving the evil glance, they fall sick, and die in a few hours.

'The Spaniards have very little to say respecting the evil eye, though the belief in it is very prevalent, especially in Andalusia, amongst the lower orders. A stag's horn is considered a good safeguard, and on that account a small horn, tipped with silver, is frequently attached to the children's necks by means of a cord braided from the hair of a black mare's tail. Should the evil glance be cast, it is imagined that the horn receives it, and instantly snaps asunder. Such horns may be purchased in some of the silversmiths' shops at Seville.'—Borrow's *Zincali*, Vol. I. ch. ix.

Page 108. *On the top of a mountain I stand.*

This and the following scraps of song are from Borrow's *Zincali; or an Account of the Gipsies in Spain.*

The Gipsy words in the same scene may be thus interpreted :

John-Dorados, pieces of gold.
Pigeon, a simpleton.
In your morocco, stripped.
Doves, sheets.
Moon, a shirt.
Chirelin, a thief.
Murcigalleros, those who steal at nightfall.
Rastilleros, footpads.
Hermit, highway-robber.
Planets, candles.
Commandments, the fingers.
Saint Martin asleep, to rob a person asleep.
Lanterns, eyes.
Goblin, police-officer.
Papagayo, a spy.
Vineyards and Dancing John, to take flight.

Page 113. *If thou art sleeping, maiden.*

From the Spanish; as is likewise the song of the Contrabandista on page 114.

Page 117. *All the Foresters of Flanders.*

The title of Foresters was given to the early governors of Flanders, appointed by the kings of France. Lyderick du Bucq, in the days of Clotaire the Second, was the first of them; and Beaudoin Bras-de-Fer, who stole away the fair Judith, daughter of Charles the Bald, from the French court, and married her in Bruges, was the last. After him the title of Forester was changed to that of Count. Philippe d'Alsace, Guy de Dampierre, and Louis de Crécy, coming later in the order of time, were therefore rather Counts than Foresters. Philippe went twice to the Holy Land as a Crusader, and died of the plague at St. Jean-d'Acre, shortly after the capture of the city by the Christians. Guy de Dampierre died in the prison of Compiégne. Louis de Crécy was son and successor of Robert de Béthune, who strangled his wife, Yolande de Bourgogne, with the bridle of his horse, for

855   EE

having poisoned, at the age of eleven years, Charles, his son by his first wife, Blanche d'Anjou.

Page 117. *Stately dames, like queens attended.*

When Philippe-le-Bel, king of France, visited Flanders with his queen, she was so astonished at the magnificence of the dames of Bruges, that she exclaimed: ' Je croyais être seule reine ici, mais il paraît que ceux de Flandre qui se trouvent dans nos prisons sont tous des princes, car leurs femmes sont habilées comme des princesses, et des reines.'

When the burgomasters of Ghent, Bruges, and Ypres went to Paris to pay homage to King John, in 1351, they were received with great pomp and distinction; but, being invited to a festival, they observed that their seats at table were not furnished with cushions; whereupon, to make known their displeasure at this want of regard to their dignity, they folded their richly embroidered cloaks and seated themselves upon them. On rising from table, they left their cloaks behind them, and, being informed of their apparent forgetfulness, Simon van Eertrycke, burgomaster of Bruges, replied, ' We Flemings are not in the habit of carrying away our cushions after dinner.'

Page 117. *Knights who bore the Fleece of Gold.*

Philippe de Bourgogne, surnamed Le Bon, espoused Isabella of Portugal on the 10th of January, 1430; and on the same day instituted the famous order of the Fleece of Gold.

Page 117. *I beheld the gentle Mary.*

Marie de Valois, Duchess of Burgundy, was left by the death of her father, Charles-le-Téméraire, at the age of twenty, the richest heiress of Europe. She came to Bruges, as Countess of Flanders, in 1477, and in the same year was married by proxy to the Archduke Maximilian. According to the custom of the time, the Duke of Bavaria, Maximilian's substitute, slept with the

princess. They were both in complete dress, separated by a naked sword, and attended by four armed guards. Marie was adored by her subjects for her gentleness and her many other virtues.

Maximilian was son of the Emperor Frederick the Third, and is the same person mentioned afterwards in the poem of *Nuremberg* as the Kaiser Maximilian, and the hero of Pfinzing's poem of *Teuerdank*. Having been imprisoned by the revolted burghers of Bruges, they refused to release him, till he consented to kneel in the public square, and to swear on the Holy Evangelists and the body of Saint Donatus, that he would not take vengeance upon them for their rebellion.

Page 117. *The bloody battle of the Spurs of Gold.*

This battle, the most memorable in Flemish history, was fought under the walls of Courtray, on the 11th of July, 1302, between the French and the Flemings, the former commanded by Robert, Comte d'Artois, and the latter by Guillaume de Juliers, and Jean, Comte de Namur. The French army was completely routed, with a loss of twenty thousand infantry and seven thousand cavalry; among whom were sixty-three princes, dukes, and counts, seven hundred lords-banneret, and eleven hundred noblemen. The flower of the French nobility perished on that day; to which history has given the name of the *Journée des Eperons d'Or*, from the great number of golden spurs found on the field of battle. Seven hundred of them were hung up as a trophy in the church of Notre Dame de Courtray; and, as the cavaliers of that day wore but a single spur each, these vouched to God for the violent and bloody death of seven hundred of his creatures.

Page 117. *Saw the fight at Minnewater.*

When the inhabitants of Bruges were digging a canal at Minnewater, to bring the waters of the Lys from Deynze to their city, they were attacked and routed by the citizens of Ghent, whose commerce would have been much injured by the canal. They were led by Jean Lyons, captain of a military company at Ghent, called the *Chaperons Blancs*. He had great sway over the turbulent populace, who, in those prosperous times of the city, gained an easy livelihood by labouring two or three days in the week, and had the remaining four or five to devote to public affairs. The fight at Minnewater was followed by open rebellion against Louis de Maele, the Count of Flanders and Protector of Bruges. His superb château of Wondelghem was pillaged and burnt; and the insurgents forced the gates of Bruges, and entered in triumph, with Lyons mounted at their head. A few days afterwards he died suddenly, perhaps by poison.

Meanwhile the insurgents received a check at the village of Nevèle; and two hundred of them perished in the church, which was burned by the Count's orders. One of the chiefs, Jean de Lannoy, took refuge in the belfry. From the summit of the tower he held forth his purse filled with gold, and begged for deliverance. It was in vain. His enemies cried to him from below to save himself as best he might; and, half suffocated with smoke and flame, he threw himself from the tower and perished at their feet. Peace was soon afterwards established, and the Count retired to faithful Bruges.

Page 117. *The Golden Dragon's nest.*

The Golden Dragon, taken from the church of St. Sophia, at Constantinople, in one of the Crusades, and placed on the belfry of Bruges, was afterwards transported to Ghent by Philip van Artevelde, and still adorns the belfry of that city.

The inscription on the alarm-bell at Ghent is, '*Mynen naem is Roland; als ik klep is er brand, and als ik luy is er victorie in het land.*' 'My name is Roland; when I toll there is fire, and when I ring there is victory in the land.'

Page 120. *That their great imperial city stretched its hand through every clime.*

An old popular proverb of the town runs thus:—

'*Nürnberg's Hand
Geht durch alle Land.*'

'Nuremberg's hand
Goes through every land.'

Page 120. *Sat the poet Melchior singing Kaiser Maximilian's praise.*

Melchior Pfinzing was one of the most celebrated German poets of the sixteenth century. The hero of his *Teuerdank* was the reigning emperor, Maximilian; and the poem was to the Germans of that day what the *Orlando Furioso* was to the Italians. Maximilian is mentioned before, in the *Belfry of Bruges*. See page 117.

Page 120. *In the church of sainted Sebald sleeps enshrined his holy dust.*

The tomb of Saint Sebald, in the church which bears his name, is one of the richest works of art in Nuremberg. It is of bronze, and was cast by Peter Vischer and his sons, who laboured upon it thirteen years. It is adorned with nearly one hundred figures, among which those of the Twelve Apostles are conspicuous for size and beauty.

Page 120. *In the church of sainted Lawrence stands a pix of sculpture rare.*

This pix, or tabernacle for the vessels of the sacrament, is by the hand of Adam Kraft. It is an exquisite piece of sculpture in white stone, and rises to the height of sixty-four feet. It stands in the choir, whose richly painted windows cover it with varied colours.

Page 121. *Wisest of the Twelve Wise Masters.*

The Twelve Wise Masters was the title of the original corporation of the Mastersingers. Hans Sachs, the cobbler of Nuremberg, though not one of the original Twelve, was the most renowned of the Mastersingers, as well as the most voluminous. He flourished in the sixteenth century; and left behind him thirty-four folio volumes of manuscript, containing two hundred and eight plays, one thousand and seven hundred comic tales, and between four and five thousand lyric poems.

Page 121. *As in Adam Puschman's song.*

Adam Puschman, in his poem on the death of Hans Sachs, describes him as he appeared in a vision :—

'An old man,
Gray and white, and dove-like,
Who had, in sooth, a great beard,
And read in a fair, great book,
Beautiful with golden clasps.'

Page 129. *Who, unharmed, on his tusks once caught the bolts of the thunder.*

' A delegation of warriors from the Delaware tribe having visited the governor of Virginia, during the Revolution, on matters of business, after these had been discussed and settled in council, the governor asked them some questions relative to their country, and among others, what they knew or had heard of the animal whose bones were found at the Saltlicks on the Ohio. Their chief speaker immediately put himself into an attitude of oratory, and with a pomp suited to what he conceived the elevation of his subject, informed him that it was a tradition handed down from their fathers, " that in ancient times a herd of these tremendous animals came to the Big-bone licks, and began an universal destruction of the bear, deer, elks, buffaloes, and other animals which had been created for the use of the Indians : that the Great Man above, looking down and seeing this, was so enraged that he seized his lightning, descended on the earth, seated himself on a neighbouring mountain, on a rock of which his seat and the print of his feet are still to be seen, and hurled his bolts among them till the whole were slaughtered, except the big bull, who, presenting his forehead to the shafts, shook them off as they fell ; but missing one

at length, it wounded him in the side ; whereon, springing round, he bounded over the Ohio, over the Wabash, the Illinois, and finally over the great lakes, where he is living at this day."'—JEFFERSON's *Notes on Virginia,* Query VI.

Page 132. *Walter von der Vogelweid.*

Walter von der Vogelweid, or Bird-Meadow, was one of the principal Minnesingers of the thirteenth century. He triumphed over Heinrich von Ofterdingen in that poetic contest at Wartburg Castle, known in literary history as the War of Wartburg.

Page 136. *Like imperial Charlemagne.*

Charlemagne may be called by preeminence the monarch of farmers. According to the German tradition, in seasons of great abundance, his spirit crosses the Rhine on a golden bridge at Bingen, and blesses the cornfields and the vineyards. During his lifetime, he did not disdain, says Montesquieu, ' to sell the eggs from the farmyards of his domains, and the superfluous vegetables of his gardens ; while he distributed among his people the wealth of the Lombards and the immense treasures of the Huns.'

Page 142. The story of EVANGELINE is founded on a painful occurrence which took place in the early period of British colonization in the northern part of America.

In the year 1713, Acadia, or, as it is now named, Nova Scotia, was ceded to Great Britain by the French. The wishes of the inhabitants seem to have been little consulted in the change, and they with great difficulty were induced to take the oaths of allegiance to the British Government. Some time after this, war having again broken out between the French and British in Canada, the Acadians were accused of having assisted the French, from whom they were descended, and connected by many ties of friendship, with provisions and ammunition, at the siege of Beau Séjour. Whether the accusation was founded on fact or not, has not been satisfactorily ascertained : the result, however, was most disastrous to the primitive, simple - minded Acadians. The British Government ordered them to be removed from their homes, and dispersed throughout the other colonies, at a distance from their much-loved land. This resolution was not communicated to the inhabitants till measures had been matured to carry it into immediate effect; when the Governor of the colony, having issued a summons calling the whole people to a meeting, informed them that their lands, tenements, and cattle of all kinds were forfeited to the British crown, that he had orders to remove them in vessels to distant colonies, and they must remain in custody till their embarkation.

The poem is descriptive of the fate of some of the persons involved in these calamitous proceedings.

Page 178.

> Behold, at last,
> Each tall and tapering mast
> Is swung into its place.

I wish to anticipate a criticism on this passage by stating that sometimes, though not usually, vessels are launched fully sparred and rigged. I have availed myself of the exception as better suited to my purposes than the general rule; but the reader will see that it is neither a blunder nor a poetic license. On this subject a friend in Portland, Maine, writes me thus :—

'In this State, and also, I am told, in New York, ships are sometimes rigged upon the stocks, in order to save time, or to make a show. There was a fine large ship launched last summer at Ellsworth, fully sparred and rigged. Some years ago a ship was launched here, with her rigging, spars, sails, and cargo aboard. She sailed the next day and—was never heard of again! I hope this will not be the fate of your poem!'

Page 182. *Sir Humphrey Gilbert.*

'When the wind abated and the vessels were near enough, the Admiral was seen constantly sitting in the stern, with a book in his hand. On the 9th of September he was seen for the last time, and was heard by the people of the Hind to say, "We are as near heaven by sea as by land." In the following night, the lights of the ship suddenly disappeared. The people in the other vessel kept a good look-out for him during the remainder of the voyage. On the 22nd of September they arrived, through much tempest and peril, at Falmouth. But nothing more was seen or heard of the Admiral.'—BELKNAP'S *American Biography*, I. 203.

Page 192. *A Christmas Carol.*

The following description of Christmas in Burgundy is from M. Fertiault's *Coup d'Œil sur les Noels en Bourgogne*, prefixed to the Paris edition of *Les Noels Bourguignons de Bernard de la Monnoye (Gui Barôsai)*, 1842.

'Every year at the approach of Advent, people refresh their memories, clear their throats, and begin preluding, in the long evenings by the fireside, those carols whose invariable and eternal theme is the coming of the Messiah. They take from old closets pamphlets, little collections begrimed with dust and smoke, to which the press, and sometimes the pen, has consigned these songs; and as soon as the first Sunday of Advent sounds, they gossip, they gad about, they sit together by the fireside, sometimes at one house, sometimes at another, taking turns in paying for the chestnuts and white wine, but singing with one common voice the grotesque praises of the *Little Jesus*. There are very few villages even, which, during all the evenings of Advent, do not hear some of these curious canticles shouted in their streets, to the nasal drone of bagpipes. In this case the minstrel comes as a reinforcement to the singers at the fireside; he brings and adds his dose of joy (spontaneous or mercenary, it matters little which) to the joy which breathes around the hearth-stone; and when the voices vibrate and resound, one voice more is always welcome. There, it is not the purity of the notes which makes the concert, but the quantity, —*non qualitas, sed quantitas*; then (to finish at once with the minstrel), when the Saviour has at length been born in the manger, and the beautiful Christmas Eve is passed, the rustic piper makes his round among the houses, where every one compliments and thanks him, and, moreover, gives him in small coin the price of the shrill notes with which he has enlivened the evening entertainments.

' More or less until Christmas Eve, all goes on in this way among our devout singers, with the difference of some gallons of wine or some hundreds of chestnuts. But this famous eve once come, the scale is pitched upon a higher key; the closing evening must be a memorable one. The toilet is begun at nightfall; then comes the hour of supper, admonishing divers appetites; and groups, as numerous as possible, are formed to take together this comfortable evening repast. The supper finished, a circle gathers around the hearth, which is arranged and set in order this evening after a particular fashion, and which at a later hour of the night is to become the object of special interest to the children. On the burning brands an enormous log has been placed. This log assuredly does not change its nature, but it changes its name during this evening: it is called the *Suche* (the Yule-log). "Look you," say they to the children, "if you are good this evening, Noel" (for with children one must always personify) " will rain down sugar-plums in the night." And the children sit demurely, keeping as quiet as their turbulent little natures will permit. The groups of older persons, not always as orderly as the children, seize this good opportunity to surrender themselves with merry hearts and boisterous voices to the chanted worship of the miraculous Noel. For this final solemnity, they have kept the most powerful, the most enthusiastic, the most electrifying carols. Noel! Noel! Noel! This magic word resounds on all sides: it seasons every sauce, it is served up with every course. Of the thousands of canticles which are heard on this famous eve, ninety-nine in a hundred begin and end with this word; which is, one may say, their Alpha and Omega, their crown and footstool. This last evening, the merry-making is prolonged. Instead of retiring at ten or eleven o'clock, as is generally done on all the preceding evenings, they wait for the stroke of midnight: this word sufficiently proclaims to what ceremony they are going to repair. For ten minutes or a quarter of an hour, the bells have been calling the faithful with a triple-bob-major; and each one, furnished with a little taper streaked with various colours (the Christmas Candle), goes through the crowded streets, where the lanterns are dancing like Will-o'-the-Wisps, at the impatient summons of the multitudinous chimes. It is the Midnight Mass. Once inside the church, they hear with more or less piety the Mass, emblematic of the coming of the Messiah. Then in tumult and great haste they return homeward, always in numerous groups; they salute the Yule-log; they pay homage to the hearth; they sit down at table; and, amid songs which reverberate louder than ever, make this meal of after-Christmas, so long looked for, so cherished, so joyous, so noisy, and which it has been thought fit to call, we hardly know why, *Rossignon*. The supper eaten at nightfall is no impediment, as you may imagine, to the appetite's returning; above all, if the going to and from church has made the devout eaters feel some little shafts of the sharp and biting north-wind. *Rossignon* then goes on merrily,—sometimes far into the morning hours; but, nevertheless, gradually throats grow hoarse, stomachs are filled, the Yule-log burns out, and at last the hour arrives when each one, as best he may, regains his domicile and his bed, and puts with himself between the sheets the material for a good sore-throat or a good indigestion, for the morrow. Previous to this, care has been taken to place in the slippers, or wooden shoes of the children, the sugar-plums, which shall be for them, on their waking, the welcome fruits of the Christmas log.'

In the Glossary, the *Suche*, or Yule-log, is thus defined :—

' This is a huge log, which is placed on the fire on Christmas Eve, and which in Burgundy is called, on this account, *lai Suche de Noei*. Then the father of the family, particularly among the middle classes, sings solemnly Christmas carols with his wife and children, the smallest of whom he sends into the corner to pray that the Yule-log may bear him some sugar-plums. Meanwhile, little parcels of them are placed under each end of the log, and the children come and pick them up, believing, in good faith, that the great log has borne them.'

Page 194. *The Blind Girl of Castèl-Cuillè.*

Jasmin, the author of this beautiful poem, is to the South of France what Burns is to the South of Scotland,—the representative of the heart of the people, —one of those happy bards who are born with their mouths full of birds (*la bouco pleno d'aouzelous*). He has written his own biography in a poetic form, and the simple narrative of his poverty, his struggles, and his triumphs, is very touching. He still lives at Agen, on the Garonne; and long may he live there to delight his native land with native songs![1]

The following description of his person and way of life is taken from the graphic pages of 'Béarn and the Pyrenees,' by Louisa Stuart Costello, whose charming pen has done so much to illustrate the French provinces and their literature.

'At the entrance of the promenade, Du Gravier, is a row of small houses,— some *cafés*, others shops, the indication of which is a painted cloth placed across the way, with the owner's name in bright gold letters, in the manner of the arcades

in the streets, and their announcements. One of the most glaring of these was, we observed, a bright blue flag, bordered with gold; on which, in large gold letters, appeared the name of "Jasmin, Coiffeur." We entered, and were welcomed by a smiling, dark-eyed woman, who informed us that her husband was busy at that moment dressing a customer's hair, but he was desirous to receive us, and begged we would walk into his parlour at the back of the shop.

' She exhibited to us a laurel crown of gold, of delicate workmanship, sent from the city of Clemence Isaure, Toulouse, to the poet; who will probably one day take his place in the *capitoul*. Next came a golden cup, with an inscription in his honour, given by the citizens of Auch; a gold watch, chain, and seals, sent by the king, Louis Philippe; an emerald ring worn and presented by the lamented Duke of Orleans; a pearl pin, by the graceful Duchess, who, on the poet's visit to Paris accompanied by his son, received him in the words he puts into the mouth of Henri Quartre :—

" Brabes Gascous !
A moun amou per bous aou dibes creyre :
Benès ! benès ! ey plazé de bous beyre :
Aproucha bous !"

A fine service of linen, the offering of the town of Pau, after its citizens had given fêtes in his honour, and loaded him with caresses and praises; and knick-knacks and jewels of all descriptions offered to him by lady-ambassadresses, and great lords; English " misses " and " miladis "; and French, and foreigners of all nations who did or did not understand Gascon.

' All this, though startling, was not convincing; Jasmin, the barber, might only be a fashion, a *furore*, a caprice, after all; and it was evident that he knew how to get up a scene well. When we had become nearly tired of looking over these tributes to his genius, the door opened, and the poet himself

---
[1] Jasmin died in 1864.

appeared. His manner was free and unembarrassed, well-bred, and lively; he received our compliments naturally, and like one accustomed to homage; said he was ill, and unfortunately too hoarse to read anything to us, or should have been delighted to do so. He spoke with a broad Gascon accent, and very rapidly and eloquently; told us the story of his successes; told us that his grandfather had been a beggar, and all his family very poor; that he was now as rich as he wished to be; his son placed in a good position at Nantes; then showed us his son's picture, and spoke of his disposition; to which his brisk little wife added, that, though no fool, he had not his father's genius, to which truth Jasmin assented as a matter of course. I told him of having seen mention made of him in an English review; which he said had been sent him by Lord Durham, who had paid him a visit; and I then spoke of "Me cal mouri" as known to me. This was enough to make him forget his hoarseness and every other evil: it would never do for me to imagine that that little song was his best composition; it was merely his first; he must try to read to me a little of "L'Abuglo,"—a few verses of "Françouneto." "You will be charmed," said he; "but if I were well, and you would give me the pleasure of your company for some time, if you were not merely running through Agen, I would kill you with weeping,—I would make you die with distress for my poor Margarido,—my pretty Françouneto!"

'He caught up two copies of his book, from a pile lying on the table, and making us sit close to him, he pointed out the French translation on one side, which he told us to follow while he read in Gascon. He began in a rich, soft voice, and as he advanced, the surprise of Hamlet on hearing the player-king recite the disasters of Hecuba was but a type of ours, to find ourselves carried away by the spell of his enthusiasm. His eyes swam in tears; he became pale and red; he trembled; he re-

covered himself; his face was now joyous, now exulting, gay, jocose; in fact, he was twenty actors in one; he rang the changes from Rachel to Bouffé; and he finished by delighting us, besides beguiling us of our tears, and overwhelming us with astonishment.

'He would have been a treasure on the stage; for he is still, though his first youth is past, remarkably good-looking and striking; with black, sparkling eyes, of intense expression; a fine, ruddy complexion; a countenance of wondrous mobility; a good figure; and action full of fire and grace; he has handsome hands, which he uses with infinite effect; and, on the whole, he is the best actor of the kind I ever saw. I could now quite understand what a troubadour or *jongleur* might be, and I look upon Jasmin as a revived specimen of that extinct race. Such as he is might have been Gaucelm Faidit, of Avignon, the friend of Cœur de Lion, who lamented the death of the hero in such moving strains; such might have been Bernard de Ventadour, who sang the praises of Queen Elinore's beauty; such Geoffrey Rudel, of Blaye, on his own Garonne; such the wild Vidal: certain it is, that none of these troubadours of old could more move, by their singing or reciting, than Jasmin, in whom all their long-smothered fire and traditional magic seems re-illumined.

'We found we had stayed hours instead of minutes with the poet; but he would not hear of any apology,—only regretted that his voice was so out of tune, in consequence of a violent cold, under which he was really labouring, and hoped to see us again. He told us our countrywomen of Pau had laden him with kindness and attention, and spoke with such enthusiasm of the beauty of certain "misses," that I feared his little wife would feel somewhat piqued; but, on the contrary, she stood by, smiling and happy, and enjoying the stories of his triumphs. I remarked that he had restored the poetry of the troubadours;

asked him if he knew their songs; and said he was worthy to stand at their head. "I am, indeed, a troubadour," said he, with energy; "but I am far beyond them all: they were but beginners; they never composed a poem like my Françouneto! there are no poets in France now,—there cannot be; the language does not admit of it; where is the fire, the spirit, the expression, the tenderness, the force of the Gascon? French is but the ladder to reach to the first floor of Gascon,—how can you get up to a height except by a ladder!"

. . . . .

'I returned by Agen, after an absence in the Pyrenees of some months, and renewed my acquaintance with Jasmin and his dark-eyed wife. I did not expect that I should be recognized; but the moment I entered the little shop I was hailed as an old friend. "Ah!" cried Jasmin, "enfin la voilà encore!" I could not but be flattered by this recollection, but soon found it was less on my own account that I was thus welcomed, than because a circumstance had occurred to the poet which he thought I could perhaps explain. He produced several French newspapers, in which he pointed out to me an article headed "Jasmin à Londres"; being a translation of certain notices of himself, which had appeared in a leading English literary journal. He had, he said, been informed of the honour done him by numerous friends, and assured me his fame had been much spread by this means; and he was so delighted on the occasion, that he had resolved to learn English, in order that he might judge of the translations from his works, which, he had been told, were well done. I enjoyed his surprise, while I informed him that I knew who was the reviewer and translator; and explained the reason for the verses giving pleasure in an English dress to be the superior simplicity of the English language over Modern French, for which he has a great contempt, as unfitted for lyrical composition. He inquired of me re-

specting Burns, to whom he had been likened; and begged me to tell him something of Moore. The delight of himself and his wife was amusing, at having discovered a secret which had puzzled them so long.

'He had a thousand things to tell me; in particular, that he had only the day before received a letter from the Duchess of Orleans, informing him that she had ordered a medal of her late husband to be struck, the first of which would be sent to him: she also announced to him the agreeable news of the king having granted him a pension of a thousand francs. He smiled and wept by turns, as he told us all this; and declared, much as he was elated at the possession of a sum which made him a rich man for life, the kindness of the Duchess gratified him even more.

'He then made us sit down while he read us two new poems; both charming, and full of grace and *naïveté*; and one very affecting, being an address to the king, alluding to the death of his son. As he read, his wife stood by, and fearing we did not quite comprehend his language, she made a remark to that effect: to which he answered impatiently, "Nonsense—don't you see they are in tears?" This was unanswerable; and we were allowed to hear the poem to the end; and I certainly never listened to anything more feelingly and energetically delivered.

'We had much conversation, for he was anxious to detain us, and, in the course of it, he told me he had been by some accused of vanity. "Oh," he rejoined, "what would you have! I am a child of nature, and cannot conceal my feelings; the only difference between me and a man of refinement is, that he knows how to conceal his vanity and exultation at success, which I let everybody see."'—*Béarn and the Pyrenees,* I. 369, *et seq.*

Page 202. THE SONG OF HIAWATHA.

This Indian Edda—if I may so call it—is founded on a tradition prevalent among the North American Indians, of a personage of miraculous birth, who was sent among them to clear their rivers, forests, and fishing-grounds, and to teach them the arts of peace. He was known among different tribes by the several names of Michabou, Chiabo, Manabozo, Tarenyawagon, and Hiawatha. Mr. Schoolcraft gives an account of him in his *Algic Researches*, Vol. I. p. 134; and in his *History, Condition. and Prospects of the Indian Tribes of the United States*, Part III. p. 314, may be found the Iroquois form of the tradition, derived from the verbal narrations of an Onondaga chief.

Into this old tradition I have woven other curious Indian legends, drawn chiefly from the various and valuable writings of Mr. Schoolcraft, to whom the literary world is greatly indebted for his indefatigable zeal in rescuing from oblivion so much of the legendary lore of the Indians.

The scene of the poem is among the Ojibways on the southern shore of Lake Superior, in the region between the Pictured Rocks and the Grand Sable.

Page 202. *In the Vale of Tawasentha.*

This valley, now called Norman's Kill, is in Albany County, New York.

Page 203. *On the Mountains of the Prairie.*

Mr. Catlin, in his *Letters and Notes on the Manners, Customs, and Condition of the North American Indians*, Vol. II. p. 160, gives an interesting account of the *Côteau des Prairies*, and the Red Pipe-stone Quarry. He says :—

'Here (according to their traditions) happened the mysterious birth of the red pipe, which has blown its fumes of peace and war to the remotest corners of the continent ; which has visited every warrior, and passed through its reddened stem the irrevocable oath of war and desolation. And here, also, the peacebreathing calumet was born, and fringed with the eagle's quills, which has shed its thrilling fumes over the land, and

soothed the fury of the relentless savage.

'The Great Spirit at an ancient period here called the Indian nations together, and, standing on the precipice of the red pipe-stone rock, broke from its wall a piece, and made a huge pipe by turning it in his hand, which he smoked over them, and to the North, the South, the East, and the West, and told them that this stone was red,—that it was their flesh,—that they must use it for their pipes of peace,—that it belonged to them all, and that the war-club and scalping-knife must not be raised on its ground. At the last whiff of his pipe his head went into a great cloud, and the whole surface of the rock for several miles was melted and glazed ; two great ovens were opened beneath, and two women (guardian spirits of the place) entered them in a blaze of fire ; and they are heard there yet (Tso-mec-cos-tee and Tso-me-cos-te-won-dee`, answering to the invocations of the high-priests or medicine-men, who consult them when they are visitors to this sacred place.'

Page 206. *Hark you, Bear ! you are a coward.*

This anecdote is from Heckewelder. In his account of the *Indian Nations,* he describes an Indian hunter as addressing a bear in nearly these words. 'I was present,' he says, 'at the delivery of this curious invective ; when the hunter had despatched the bear, I asked him how he thought that poor animal could understand what he said to it. "Oh," said he in answer, "the bear understood me very well ; did you not observe how *ashamed* he looked while I was upbraiding him ?"'—*Transactions of the American Philosophical Society*, Vol. I. p. 240.

Page 211. *Hush ! the Naked Bear will hear thee !*

Heckewelder, in a letter published in the *Transactions of the American Philosophical Society*, Vol. IV. p. 260, speaks of this tradition as prevalent among the Mohicans and Delawares.

'Their reports,' he says, 'run thus : that among all animals that had been formerly in this country, this was the most ferocious ; that it was much larger than the largest of the common bears, and remarkably long-bodied; all over (except a spot of hair on its back of a white colour) naked. . . . .

'The history of this animal used to be a subject of conversation among the Indians, especially when in the woods a hunting. I have also heard them say to their children when crying : "Hush ! the naked bear will hear you, be upon you, and devour you." '

Page 216. *Where the Falls of Minnehaha*, &c.

'The scenery about Fort Snelling is rich in beauty. The Falls of St. Anthony are familiar to travellers, and to readers of Indian sketches. Between the fort and these falls are the "Little Falls," forty feet in height, on a stream that empties into the Mississippi. The Indians called them Mine-hah-hah, or "laughing waters."'—MRS. EASTMAN'S *Dacotah, or Legends of the Sioux*, Introd. p. ii.

Page 236. *Sand Hills of the Nagow Wudjoo.*

A description of the *Grand Sable*, or great sand-dunes of Lake Superior, is given in Foster and Whitney's *Report on the Geology of the Lake Superior Land District*, Part II. p. 131.

'The Grand Sable possesses a scenic interest little inferior to that of the Pictured Rocks. The explorer passes abruptly from a coast of consolidated sand to one of loose materials; and although in the one case the cliffs are less precipitous, yet in the other they attain a higher altitude. He sees before him a long reach of coast, resembling a vast sand-bank, more than three hundred and fifty feet in height, without a trace of vegetation. Ascending to the top, rounded hillocks of blown sand are observed, with occasional clumps of trees, standing out like oases in the desert.'

Page 237.

Onaway! Awake, beloved!

The original of this song may be found in Littell's *Living Age*, Vol. XXV. p. 45.

Page 238. *Or the Red Swan floating, flying.*

The fanciful tradition of the Red Swan may be found in Schoolcraft's *Algic Researches*, Vol. II. p. 9. Three brothers were hunting on a wager to see who would bring home the first game.

'They were to shoot no other animal,' so the legend says, ' but such as each was in the habit of killing. They set out different ways : Odjibwa, the youngest, had not gone far before he saw a bear, an animal he was not to kill, by the agreement. He followed him close, and drove an arrow through him, which brought him to the ground. Although contrary to the bet, he immediately commenced skinning him, when suddenly something red tinged all the air around him. He rubbed his eyes, thinking he was perhaps deceived ; but without effect, for the red hue continued. At length he heard a strange noise at a distance. It first appeared like a human voice, but after following the sound for some distance, he reached the shores of a lake, and soon saw the object he was looking for. At a distance out in the lake sat a most beautiful Red Swan, whose plumage glittered in the sun, and who would now and then make the same noise he had heard. He was within long bow-shot, and, pulling the arrow from the bowstring up to his ear, took deliberate aim and shot. The arrow took no effect; and he shot and shot again till his quiver was empty. Still the swan remained, moving round and round, stretching its long neck and dipping its bill into the water, as if heedless of the arrows shot at it. Odjibwa ran home, and got all his own and his brother's arrows, and shot them all away. He then stood and gazed at the beautiful bird. While standing, he remembered his brother's saying that in their deceased father's medicine-sack were three magic arrows. Off he started, his anxiety to kill the swan overcoming all scruples. At any other time, he would have deemed it sacrilege to open his father's medicine-sack; but now he hastily seized the three arrows and ran back, leaving the other contents of the sack scattered over the lodge. The swan was still there. He shot the first arrow with great precision, and came very near to it. The second came still closer; as he took the last arrow, he felt his arm firmer, and, drawing it up with vigour, saw it pass through the neck of the swan a little above the breast. Still it did not prevent the bird from flying off, which it did, however, at first slowly, flapping its wings and rising gradually into the air, and then flying off toward the sinking of the sun.'—pp. 10-12.

Page 242. *When I think of my beloved.*

The original of this song may be found in *Oneóta*, p. 15.

Page 243. *Sing the mysteries of Mondamin.*

The Indians hold the maize, or Indian corn, in great veneration. 'They esteem it so important and divine a grain,' says Schoolcraft, 'that their story-tellers invented various tales, in which this idea is symbolized under the form of a special gift from the Great Spirit. The Od-jibwa-Algonquins, who call it Mon-dá-min, that is, the Spirit's grain or berry, have a pretty story of this kind, in which the stalk in full tassel is represented as descending from the sky, under the guise of a handsome youth, in answer to the prayers of a young man at his fast of virility, or coming to manhood.

'It is well known that corn-planting and corn-gathering, at least among all the still *uncolonized* tribes, are left entirely to the females and children, and a few superannuated old men. It is not generally known, perhaps, that this labour is not compulsory, and that it is assumed by the females as a just equi-valent, in their view, for the onerous and continuous labour of the other sex, in providing meats, and skins for clothing, by the chase, and in defending their villages against their enemies, and keeping intruders off their territories. A good Indian housewife deems this a part of her prerogative, and prides herself to have a store of corn to exercise her hospitality, or duly honour her husband's hospitality, in the entertainment of the lodge guests.'—*Oneóta*, p. 82.

Page 243. *Thus the fields shall be more fruitful.*

'A singular proof of this belief, in both sexes, of the mysterious influence of the steps of a woman on the vegetable and insect creation, is found in an ancient custom, which was related to me, respecting corn-planting. It was the practice of the hunter's wife, when the field of corn had been planted, to choose the first dark or overclouded evening to perform a secret circuit, *sans habillement*, around the field. For this purpose she slipped out of the lodge in the evening, unobserved, to some obscure nook, where she completely disrobed. Then, taking her matchecota, or principal garment, in one hand, she dragged it around the field. This was thought to ensure a prolific crop, and to prevent the assaults of insects and worms upon the grain. It was supposed they could not creep over the charmed line.'—*Oneóta*, p. 83.

Page 245. *With his prisoner-string he bound him.*

'These cords,' says Mr. Tanner, 'are made of the bark of the elm-tree, by boiling and then immersing it in cold water. . . . . The leader of a war party commonly carries several fastened about his waist, and if, in the course of the fight, any one of his young men takes a prisoner, it is his duty to bring him immediately to the chief, to be tied, and the latter is responsible for his safe keeping.'—*Narrative of Captivity and Adventures*, p. 412.

Page 246.

Wagemin, the thief of cornfields, Paimosaid, who steals the maize-ear.

' If one of the young female huskers finds a *red* ear of corn, it is typical of a brave admirer, and is regarded as a fitting present to some young warrior. But if the ear be *crooked*, and tapering to a point, no matter what colour, the whole circle is set in a roar, and *wage-min* is the word shouted aloud. It is the symbol of a thief in the cornfield. It is considered as the image of an old man stooping as he enters the lot. Had the chisel of Praxiteles been employed to produce this image, it could not more vividly bring to the minds of the merry group the idea of a pilferer of their favourite mondámin. . . . .

' The literal meaning of the term is, a mass, or crooked ear of grain ; but the ear of corn so called is a conventional type of a little old man pilfering ears of corn in a cornfield. It is in this manner that a single word or term, in these curious languages, becomes the fruitful parent of many ideas. And we can thus perceive why it is that the word *wagemin* is alone competent to excite merriment in the husking circle.

' This term is taken as the basis of the cereal chorus, or corn song, as sung by the Northern Algonquin tribes. It is coupled with the phrase *Paimosaid,*— a permutative form of the Indian substantive, made from the verb *pim-o-sa,* to walk. Its literal meaning is, *he who walks,* or *the walker*; but the ideas conveyed by it are, he who walks by night to pilfer corn. It offers, therefore, a kind of parallelism in expression to the preceding term.'—*Oneóta,* p. 254.

Page 252. *Pugasaing, with thirteen pieces.*

This Game of the Bowl is the principal game of hazard among the Northern tribes of Indians. Mr. Schoolcraft gives a particular account of it in *Oneóta,* p. 85. ' This game,' he says, ' is very fascinating to some portions of the Indians. They stake at it their ornaments, weapons, clothing, canoes, horses, everything in fact they possess ; and have been known, it is said, to set up their wives and children, and even to forfeit their own liberty. Of such desperate stakes I have seen no examples, nor do I think the game itself in common use. It is rather confined to certain persons, who hold the relative rank of gamblers in Indian society,—men who are not noted as hunters or warriors, or steady providers for their families. Among these are persons who bear the term of *Iena-dizze-wug,* that is, wanderers about the country, braggadocios, or fops. It can hardly be classed with the popular games of amusement, by which skill and dexterity are acquired. I have generally found the chiefs and graver men of the tribes, who encouraged the young men to play ball, and are sure to be present at the customary sports, to witness, and sanction, and applaud them, speak lightly and disparagingly of this game of hazard. Yet it cannot be denied that some of the chiefs, distinguished in war and the chase, at the West, can be referred to as lending their example to its fascinating power.'

See also his *History, Condition, and Prospects of the Indian Tribes,* Part II. p. 72.

Page 259. *To the Pictured Rocks of sandstone.*

The reader will find a long description of the Pictured Rocks in Foster and Whitney's *Report on the Geology of the Lake Superior Land District,* Part II. p. 124. From this I make the following extract :—

' The Pictured Rocks may be described, in general terms, as a series of sandstone bluffs extending along the shore of Lake Superior for about five miles, and rising, in most places, vertically from the water, without any beach at the base, to a height varying from fifty to nearly two hundred feet. Were they simply a line of cliffs, they might not, so far as relates to height or extent, be worthy of a rank among great natural curiosities, although such an assemblage of rocky

Notes.

strata, washed by the waves of the great lake, would not, under any circumstances, be destitute of grandeur. To the voyager, coasting along their base in his frail canoe, they would, at all times, be an object of dread; the recoil of the surf, the rock-bound coast, affording, for miles, no place of refuge,—the lowering sky, the rising wind,—all these would excite his apprehension, and induce him to ply a vigorous oar until the dreaded wall was passed. But in the Pictured Rocks there are two features which communicate to the scenery a wonderful and almost unique character. These are, first, the curious manner in which the cliffs have been excavated and worn away by the action of the lake, which, for centuries, has dashed an ocean-like surf against their base; and, second, the equally curious manner in which large portions of the surface have been coloured by bands of brilliant hues.

'It is from the latter circumstance that the name, by which these cliffs are known to the American traveller, is derived; while that applied to them by the French voyageurs ("Les Portails") is derived from the former, and by far the most striking peculiarity.

'The term *Pictured Rocks* has been in use for a great length of time; but when it was first applied, we have been unable to discover. It would seem that the first travellers were more impressed with the novel and striking distribution of colours on the surface than with the astonishing variety of form into which the cliffs themselves have been worn...

'Our voyageurs had many legends to relate of the pranks of the *Menni-bojou* in these caverns, and, in answer to our inquiries, seemed disposed to fabricate stories, without end, of the achievements of this Indian deity.'

Page 270. *Toward the sun his hands were lifted.*

In this manner, and with such salutations, was Father Marquette received by the Illinois. See his *Voyages et Découvertes*, Section V.

Page 299. *That of our vices we can frame A ladder.*

The words of St. Augustine are,— 'De vitiis nostris scalam nobis facimus, si vitia ipsa calcamus.' Sermon III. *De Ascensione.*

Page 300. *The Phantom Ship.*

A detailed account of this 'apparition of a Ship in the Air' is given by Cotton Mather in his *Magnalia Christi*, Book I. Ch. vi. It is contained in a letter from the Rev. James Pierpont, Pastor of New Haven. To this account Mather adds these words:—

'Reader, there being yet living so many credible gentlemen that were eyewitnesses of this wonderful thing, I venture to publish it for a thing as undoubted as 'tis wonderful.'

Page 303. *And the Emperor but a Macho.*

Macho, in Spanish, signifies a mule. *Golondrina* is the feminine form of *Golondrino*, a swallow, and also a cant name for a deserter.

Page 304. *The Two Angels.*

A child was born to Longfellow the same night that his friend Mr. Lowell's wife died: he commemorates both events in this poem.

Page 306. *Oliver Basselin.*

Oliver Basselin, the '*Père joyeux du Vaudeville*,' flourished in the fifteenth century, and gave to his convivial songs the name of his native valleys, in which he sang them, Vaux-de-vire. This name was afterwards corrupted into the modern *Vaudeville*.

Page 307. *Victor Galbraith.*

This poem is founded on fact. Victor Galbraith was a bugler in a company of volunteer cavalry, and was shot in Mexico for some breach of discipline. It is a common superstition among soldiers, that no balls will kill them unless their names are written on them. The old proverb says, 'Every bullet has its billet.'

868

Page 309. *I remember the sea-fight far away.*

This was the engagement between the Enterprise and Boxer, off the harbour of Portland, in which both captains were slain. They were buried side by side, in the cemetery on Mountjoy.

Page 312. *Santa Filomena.*

'At Pisa the church of San Francisco contains a chapel dedicated lately to Santa Filomena; over the altar is a picture, by Sabatelli, representing the saint as a beautiful, nymph-like figure, floating down from heaven, attended by two angels bearing the lily, palm, and javelin, and beneath, in the foreground, the sick and maimed, who are healed by her intercession.'—MRS. JAMESON, *Sacred and Legendary Art*, II. 298.

Page 459. THE GOLDEN LEGEND.

The old *Legenda Aurea*, or Golden Legend, was originally written in Latin, in the thirteenth century, by Jacobus de Voragine, a Dominican friar, who afterwards became Archbishop of Genoa, and died in 1292.

He called his book simply 'Legends of the Saints.' The epithet of Golden was given it by his admirers; for, as Wynkin de Worde says, 'Like as passeth gold in value all other metals, so this Legend exceedeth all other books.' But Edward Leigh, in much distress of mind, calls it 'a book written by a man of a leaden heart for the basenesse of the errours, that are without wit or reason, and of a brazen forehead, for his impudent boldnesse in reporting things so fabulous and incredible.'

This work, the great text-book of the legendary lore of the Middle Ages, was translated into French in the fourteenth century by Jean de Vignay, and in the fifteenth into English by William Caxton. It has lately been made more accessible by a new French translation : *La Légende Dorée, traduite du Latin, par M. G. B.* Paris, 1850. There is a copy of the original, with the *Gesta Longobardorum* appended, in the Harvard College Library, Cambridge, printed

at Strasburg, 1496. The title-page is wanting; and the volume begins with the *Tabula Legendorum*.

I have called this poem the Golden Legend, because the story upon which it is founded seems to me to surpass all other legends in beauty and significance. It exhibits, amid the corruptions of the Middle Ages, the virtue of disinterestedness and self-sacrifice, and the power of Faith, Hope, and Charity, sufficient for all the exigencies of life and death. The story is told, and perhaps invented, by Hartmann von der Aue, a Minnesinger of the twelfth century. The original may be found in Mailáth's *Altdeutsche Gedichte*, with a modern German version. There is another in Marbach's *Volksbücher*, No. 32.

Page 459.

*For these bells have been anointed,
And baptized with holy water !*

The Consecration and Baptism of Bells is one of the most curious ceremonies of the Church in the Middle Ages. The Council of Cologne ordained as follows :—

'Let the bells be blessed, as the trumpets of the Church militant, by which the people are assembled to hear the word of God; the clergy to announce his mercy by day, and his truth in their nocturnal vigils: that by their sound the faithful may be invited to prayers, and that the spirit of devotion in them may be increased. The fathers have also maintained that demons affrighted by the sound of bells calling Christians to prayers, would flee away; and when they fled, the persons of the faithful would be secure: that the destruction of lightnings and whirlwinds would be averted, and the spirits of the storm defeated.'—*Edinburgh Encyclopaedia*, Art. *Bells*. See also Scheible's *Kloster*, VI. 776.

Page 473. *It is the malediction of Eve !*

'Nec esses plus quam femina, quae nunc etiam viros transcendis, et quae maledictionem Evae in benedictionem vertisti Mariae.'—*Epistola Abaelardi Heloissae.*

Page 483. *To come back to my text !*

In giving this sermon of Friar Cuthbert as a specimen of the *Risus Paschales,* or street-preaching of the monks at Easter, I have exaggerated nothing. This very anecdote, offensive as it is, comes from a discourse of Father Barletta, a Dominican friar of the fifteenth century, whose fame as a popular preacher was so great, that it gave rise to the proverb,

> ' *Nescit predicare*
> *Qui nescit Barlettare.*'

'Among the abuses introduced in this century,' says Tiraboschi, 'was that of exciting from the pulpit the laughter of the hearers; as if that were the same thing as converting them. We have examples of this, not only in Italy, but also in France, where the sermons of Menot and Maillard, and of others, who would make a better appearance on the stage than in the pulpit, are still celebrated for such follies.'

If the reader is curious to see how far the freedom of speech was carried in these popular sermons, he is referred to Scheible's *Kloster,* Vol. I, where he will find extracts from Abraham a Sancta Clara, Sebastian Frank, and others; and in particular an anonymous discourse called *Der Gräuel der Verwüstung,* The Abomination of Desolation, preached at Ottakring, a village west of Vienna, November 25, 1782, in which the license of language is carried to its utmost limit.

See also *Prédicatoriana, ou Révélations singulières et amusantes sur les Prédicateurs ; par G. P. Philomneste.* (Menin.) This work contains extracts from the popular sermons of St. Vincent Ferrier, Barletta, Menot, Maillard, Marini, Raulin, Valladier, De Besse, Camus, Père André, Bening, and the most eloquent of all, Jacques Brydaine.

My authority for the spiritual interpretation of bell-ringing, which follows, is Durandus, *Ration. Divin. Offic.* Lib. I. cap. 4.

Page 486. THE NATIVITY: a Miracle-Play.

A singular chapter in the history of the Middle Ages is that which gives account of the early Christian Drama, the Mysteries, Moralities, and Miracle-Plays, which were at first performed in churches, and afterwards in the streets, on fixed or movable stages. For the most part, the Mysteries were founded on the historic portions of the Old and New Testaments, and the Miracle-Plays on the lives of Saints; a distinction not always observed, however, for in Mr. Wright's *Early Mysteries and other Latin Poems of the Twelfth and Thirteenth Centuries,* the Resurrection of Lazarus is called a Miracle, and not a Mystery. The Moralities were plays in which the Virtues and Vices were personified.

The earliest religious play which has been preserved is the *Christos Paschon* of Gregory Nazianzen, written in Greek, in the fourth century. Next to this come the remarkable Latin Plays of Roswitha, the Nun of Gandersheim, in the tenth century, which, though crude and wanting in artistic construction, are marked by a good deal of dramatic power and interest. A handsome edition of these plays, with a French translation, has been lately published, entitled *Théâtre de Rotsvitha, Religieuse allemande du Xe Siècle. Par Charles Magnin.* Paris, 1845.

The most important collections of English Mysteries and Miracle-Plays are those known as the Townley, the Chester, and the Coventry Plays. The first of these collections has been published by the Surtees Society, and the other two by the Shakespeare Society. In his Introduction to the Coventry Mysteries, the editor, Mr. Halliwell, quotes the following passage from Dugdale's *Antiquities of Warwickshire* :—

' Before the suppression of the monasteries, this city was very famous for the pageants, that were played therein, upon Corpus-Christi Day ; which, occasioning very great confluence of people thither, from far and near, was of no small benefit thereto; which pageants being acted with mighty state and reverence by the friars of this house, had theaters for the severall scenes, very large and high, placed upon wheels, and drawn to all the eminent parts of the city, for the better advantage of spectators : and contain'd the story of the New Testament, composed into old English Rithme, as appeareth by an ancient MS. intituled *Ludus Corporis Christi*, or *Ludus Conventriae*. I have been told by some old people, who in their younger years were eye-witnesses of these pageants so acted, that the yearly confluence of people to see that shew was extraordinary great, and yielded no small advantage to this city.'

The representation of religious plays has not yet been wholly discontinued by the Roman Church. At Ober-Ammergau, in the Tyrol, a grand spectacle of this kind is exhibited once in ten years. A very graphic description of that which took place in the year 1850 is given by Miss Anna Mary Howitt, in her *Art-Student in Munich*, Vol. I. Chap. iv. She says :—

'We had come expecting to feel our souls revolt at so material a representation of Christ, as any representation of him we naturally imagined must be in a peasant's Miracle-Play. Yet so far, strange to confess, neither horror, disgust, nor contempt was excited in our minds. Such an earnest solemnity and simplicity breathed throughout the whole of the performance, that to me, at least, anything like anger, or a perception of the ludicrous, would have seemed more irreverent on my part than was this simple childlike rendering of the sublime Christian tragedy. We felt at times as though the figures of Cimabue's, Giotto's, and Perugino's pictures had become animated, and were moving before us ; there was the same simple arrangement and brilliant colour of drapery,—the same earnest, quiet dignity about the heads, whilst the en-

tire absence of all theatrical effect wonderfully increased the illusion. There were scenes and groups so extraordinarily like the early Italian pictures, that you could have declared they were the works of Giotto and Perugino, and not living men and women, had not the figures moved and spoken, and the breeze stirred their richly-coloured drapery, and the sun cast long, moving shadows behind them on the stage. These effects of sunshine and shadow, and of drapery fluttered by the wind, were very striking and beautiful; one could imagine how the Greeks must have availed themselves of such striking effects in their theatres open to the sky.'

Mr. Bayard Taylor, in his *Eldorado*, gives a description of a Mystery he saw performed at San Lionel, in Mexico. See Vol. II. Chap. xi.

'Against the wing-wall of the Hacienda del Mayo, which occupied one end of the plaza, was raised a platform, on which stood a table covered with scarlet cloth. A rude bower of cane-leaves, on one end of the platform, represented the manger of Bethlehem ; while a cord, stretched from its top across the plaza to a hole in the front of the church, bore a large tinsel star, suspended by a hole in its centre. There was quite a crowd in the plaza, and very soon a procession appeared, coming up from the lower part of the village. The three kings took the lead ; the Virgin, mounted on an ass that gloried in a gilded saddle and rose-besprinkled mane and tail, followed them, led by the angel ; and several women, with curious masks of paper, brought up the rear. Two characters, of the harlequin sort—one with a dog's head on his shoulders, and the other a bald-headed friar, with a huge hat hanging on his back—played all sorts of antics for the diversion of the crowd. After making the circuit of the plaza, the Virgin was taken to the platform, and entered the manger. King Herod took his seat at the scarlet table, with an attendant in blue coat and red sash, whom I took to be his Prime Minister.

The three kings remained on their horses in front of the church; but between them and the platform, under the string on which the star was to slide, walked two men in long white robes and blue hoods, with parchment folios in their hands. These were the Wise Men of the East, as one might readily know from their solemn air, and the mysterious glances which they cast towards all quarters of the heavens.

'In a little while, a company of women on the platform, concealed behind a curtain, sang an angelic chorus to the tune of "O pescator dell' onda." At the proper moment, the Magi turned towards the platform, followed by the star, to which a string was conveniently attached, that it might be slid along the line. The three kings followed the star till it reached the manger, when they dismounted, and inquired for the sovereign whom it had led them to visit. They were invited upon the platform, and introduced to Herod, as the only king; this did not seem to satisfy them, and, after some conversation, they retired. By this time the star had receded to the other end of the line, and commenced moving forward again, they following. The angel called them into the manger, where, upon their knees, they were shown a small wooden box, supposed to contain the sacred infant; they then retired, and the star brought them back no more. After this departure, King Herod declared himself greatly confused by what he had witnessed, and was very much afraid this newly-found king would weaken his power. Upon consultation with his Prime Minister, the Massacre of the Innocents was decided upon, as the only means of security.

'The angel, on hearing this, gave warning to the Virgin, who quickly got down from the platform, mounted her bespangled donkey, and hurried off. Herod's Prime Minister directed all the children to be handed up for execution. A boy, in a ragged sarape, was caught and thrust forward; the Minister took him by the heels in spite of his kicking, and held his head on the table. The little brother and sister of the boy, thinking he was really to be decapitated, yelled at the top of their voices, in an agony of terror, which threw the crowd into a roar of laughter. King Herod brought down his sword with a whack on the table, and the Prime Minister, dipping his brush into a pot of white paint which stood before him, made a flaring cross on the boy's face. Several other boys were caught and served likewise: and, finally, the two harlequins, whose kicks and struggles nearly shook down the platform. The procession then went off up the hill, followed by the whole population of the village. All the evening there were fandangos in the méson, bonfires and rockets on the plaza, ringing of bells, and high mass in the church, with the accompaniment of two guitars, tinkling to lively polkas.'

In 1852 there was a representation of this kind by Germans in Boston; and I have now before me a copy of a playbill announcing the performance, on June 10, 1852, in Cincinnati, of the 'Great Biblico-Historical Drama, the Life of Jesus Christ,' with the characters and the names of the performers.

Page 496. *The Scriptorium.*

A most interesting volume might be written on the Calligraphers and Chrysographers, the transcribers and illuminators of manuscripts in the Middle Ages. These men were for the most part monks, who laboured, sometimes for pleasure and sometimes for penance, in multiplying copies of the classics and the Scriptures.

'Of all bodily labours, which are proper for us,' says Cassiodorus, the old Calabrian monk, 'that of copying books has always been more to my taste than any other. The more so, as in this exercise the mind is instructed by the reading of the Holy Scriptures, and it is a kind of homily to the others, whom these books may reach. It is preaching with the hand, by converting the fingers into tongues; it is publishing to men in silence the words of salvation;

in fine, it is fighting against the demon with pen and ink. As many words as a transcriber writes, so many wounds the demon receives. In a word, a recluse, seated in his chair to copy books, travels into different provinces, without moving from the spot, and the labour of his hands is felt even where he is not.'

Nearly every monastery was provided with its Scriptorium. Nicolas de Clairvaux, St. Bernard's secretary, in one of his letters describes his cell, which he calls Scriptoriolum, where he copied books. And Mabillon, in his *Études Monastiques*, says that in his time were still to be seen at Citeaux 'many of those little cells, where the transcribers and bookbinders worked.'

Silvestre's *Paléographie Universelle* contains a vast number of fac-similes of the most beautifully illuminated manuscripts of all ages and all countries; and Montfaucon in his *PalaeographiaGraeca* gives the names of over three hundred calligraphers. He also gives an account of the books they copied, and the colophons, with which, as with a satisfactory flourish of the pen, they closed their long-continued labours. Many of these are very curious: expressing joy, humility, remorse; entreating the reader's prayers and pardon for the writer's sins; and sometimes pronouncing a malediction on any one who should steal the book. A few of these I subjoin:—

'As pilgrims rejoice, beholding their native land, so are transcribers made glad, beholding the end of a book.'

'Sweet is it to write the end of any book.'

'Ye who read, pray for me, who have written this book, the humble and sinful Theodulus.'

'As many therefore as shall read this book, pardon me, I beseech you, if aught I have erred in accent acute and grave, in apostrophe, in breathing soft or aspirate; and may God save you all! Amen.'

'If anything is well, praise the transcriber; if ill, pardon his unskilfulness.'

'Ye who read, pray for me, the most sinful of all men, for the Lord's sake.'

'The hand that has written this book shall decay, alas! and become dust, and go down to the grave, the corrupter of all bodies. But all ye who are of the portion of Christ, pray that I may obtain the pardon of my sins. Again and again I beseech you with tears, brothers and fathers, accept my miserable supplication, O holy choir! I am called John, woe is me! I am called Hiereus, or Sacerdos, in name only, not in unction.'

'Whoever shall carry away this book, without the permission of the Pope, may he incur the malediction of the Holy Trinity, of the Holy Mother of God, of Saint John the Baptist, of the one hundred and eighteen holy Nicene Fathers, and of all the Saints; the fate of Sodom and Gomorrah; and the halter of Judas! Anathema, amen.'

'Keep safe, O Trinity, Father, Son, and Holy Ghost, my three fingers, with which I have written this book.'

'Mathusalas Machir transcribed this divinest book in toil, infirmity, and dangers many.'

'Bacchius Barbardorius and Michael Sophianus wrote this book in sport and laughter, being the guests of their noble and common friend Vincentius Pinellus, and Petrus Nunnius, a most learned man.'

This last colophon Montfaucon does not suffer to pass without reproof. 'Other calligraphers,' he remarks, 'demand only the prayers of their readers, and the pardon of their sins: but these glory in their wantonness.'

Page 501. *Drink down to your peg!*

One of the canons of Archbishop Anselm, promulgated at the beginning of the twelfth century, ordains 'that priests go not to drinking-bouts, nor drink to pegs.' In the times of the hard-drinking Danes, King Edgar ordained that 'pins or nails should be fastened into the drinking-cups or horns at stated distances, and whosoever should drink beyond those marks at one draught should be obnoxious to a severe punishment.'

Sharpe, in his History of the Kings of England, says : 'Our ancestors were formerly famous for compotation ; their liquor was ale, and one method of amusing themselves in this way was with the peg-tankard. I had lately one of them in my hand. It had on the inside a row of eight pins, one above another, from top to bottom. It held two quarts, and was a noble piece of plate, so that there was a gill of ale, half a pint Winchester measure, between each peg. The law was, that every person that drank was to empty the space between pin and pin, so that the pins were so many measures to make the company all drink alike, and to swallow the same quantity of liquor. This was a pretty sure method of making all the company drunk, especially if it be considered that the rule was, that whoever drank short of his pin, or beyond it, was obliged to drink again, and even as deep as to the next pin.'

Page 502. *The convent of St. Gildas de Rhuys.*

Abelard, in a letter to his friend Philintus, gives a sad picture of this monastery. 'I live,' he says, 'in a barbarous country, the language of which I do not understand ; I have no conversation but with the rudest people. My walks are on the inaccessible shore of a sea, which is perpetually stormy. My monks are only known by their dissoluteness, and living without any rule or order. Could you see the abbey, Philintus, you would not call it one. The doors and walks are without any ornament, except the heads of wild boars and hinds' feet, which are nailed up against them, and the hides of frightful animals. The cells are hung with the skins of deer. The monks have not so much as a bell to wake them, the cocks and dogs supply that defect. In short, they pass their whole days in hunting ; would to heaven that were their greatest fault ; or that their pleasures terminated there ! I endeavour in vain to recall them to their duty ;

they all combine against me, and I only expose myself to continual vexations and dangers. I imagine I see every moment a naked sword hang over my head. Sometimes they surround me, and load me with infinite abuses ; sometimes they abandon me, and I am left alone to my own tormenting thoughts. I make it my endeavour to merit by my sufferings, and to appease an angry God. Sometimes I grieve for the loss of the house of the Paraclete, and wish to see it again. Ah, Philintus, does not the love of Heloise still burn in my heart ? I have not yet triumphed over that unhappy passion. In the midst of my retirement I sigh, I weep, I pine, I speak the dear name Heloise, and am pleased to hear the sound.'—*Letters of the Celebrated Abelard and Heloise. Translated by Mr. John Hughes.* Glasgow, 1751.

Page 513. *Were it not for my magic garters and staff.*

The method of making the Magic Garters and the Magic Staff is thus laid down in *Les Secrets Merveilleux du Petit Albert,* a French translation of *Alberti Parvi Lucii Libellus de Mirabilibus Naturae Arcanis* :—

'Gather some of the herb called motherwort, when the sun is entering the first degree of the sign of Capricorn ; let it dry a little in the shade, and make some garters of the skin of a young hare; that is to say, having cut the skin of the hare into strips two inches wide, double them, sew the before-mentioned herb between, and wear them on your legs. No horse can long keep up with a man on foot, who is furnished with these garters.'—p. 128.

'Gather, on the morrow of All-Saints, a strong branch of willow, of which you will make a staff, fashioned to your liking. Hollow it out, by removing the pith from within, after having furnished the lower end with an iron ferule. Put into the bottom of the staff the two eyes of a young wolf, the tongue and heart of a dog, three green lizards, and the hearts of three swallows. These must all be dried in the sun, between two papers, having been first sprinkled with finely pulverized saltpetre. Besides all these, put into the staff seven leaves of vervain, gathered on the eve of St. John the Baptist, with a stone of divers colours, which you will find in the nest of the lapwing, and stop the end of the staff with a pomel of box, or of any other material you please, and be assured, that the staff will guarantee you from the perils and mishaps which too often befall travellers, either from robbers, wild beasts, mad dogs, or venomous animals. It will also procure you the good-will of those with whom you lodge.' —p. 130.

Page 516. *Saint Elmo's Stars.*

So the Italian sailors call the phosphorescent gleams that sometimes play about the masts and rigging of ships.

Page 517. *The School of Salerno.*

For a history of the celebrated schools of Salerno and Monte - Cassino, the reader is referred to Sir Alexander Croke's Introduction to the *Regimen Sanitatis Salernitanum*; and to Kurt Sprengel's *Geschichte der Arzneikunde*, I. 463, or Jourdan's French translation of it, *Histoire de la Médicine*, II. 354.

Page 775. *The Children's Crusade.*

'The Children's Crusade' was left unfinished by Mr. Longfellow. It is founded upon an event which occurred in the year 1212. An army of twenty thousand children, mostly boys, under the lead of a boy of ten years, named Nicolas, set out from Cologne for the Holy Land. When they reached Genoa only seven thousand remained. There, as the sea did not divide to allow them to march dry-shod to the East, they broke up. Some got as far as Rome; two ship-loads sailed from Pisa, and were not heard of again; the rest straggled back to Germany.

Page 786. MICHAEL ANGELO.

Part First.

I.

Condivi, in his 'Vite di Michael Angelo Buonarotti,' describes him, when seventy-nine years old, as 'of middle height, with broad shoulders and thin legs, having a large head, a face small in proportion to the size of his skull, a square forehead, full temples, high cheek-bones, and a nose made flat by the fist of that beastly and proud man Torrigiano de' Torrigiani.' Torrigiani is said to have fled to England, and to have designed there, among other things, the tomb of Henry VIII. 'His lips,' continues Condivi, 'are thin, and the lower, being the larger, appears to protrude when the face is seen in profile. His eyebrows are sparse; his eyes gray, spotted with yellow and blue lights, and ever varying; his ears of just proportion; his hair, once black, is streaked with gray, as is his thin, forked beard, which is four or five fingers' breadth in length.' Vasari's description does not differ materially from this, so that the student is enabled to know with some certainty what the personal appearance of the great master was. These descriptions have unquestionably been of important service in the hands of artists who have studied to produce a satisfactory portrait of Michael Angelo. It is possible to find a large number of these portraits, and not easy to learn, even by a comparison of all the Lives of the artist, which are founded upon the best authority. Mr. C. D. E. Fortnum, who owns the original medallion portrait in wax by Leo Leone, which he discovered and identified, gives in an article on the portrait, published in the 'Archaeological Journal' for March, 1875, a list of the only likenesses which can be considered authentic, namely: 1. A bronze bust at the Capitol, referred to by Vasari as the work by Daniel of Volterra. 2. A bust in marble from a mask taken after death. 3. Leo Leone's medal. 4. A figure in the foreground of the Assumption of the Virgin in the church of Santa Trinita at Rome. 5. A head painted by Marcello Venusti in his copy of 'The Last Judgment.' 6. A portrait ascribed to the same painter at Casa Buonarotti. 7. The engraving (profile) by Buonasoni. Mr. C. C. Perkins, in his 'Raphael and Michael Angelo,' mentions a portrait which was reproduced in the 'Zeitschrift für Bildene Kunst,' Vol. XI. page 64, with a short article by Mr. J. E. Wessely, who claims that it was drawn and engraved by Michael Angelo, and that it is the original from which Ghisi worked.

Vittoria Colonna, Marchesa de Pescara, was born in 1490, betrothed to the Marquis de Pescara in 1495, and married to him in 1509. Pescara was killed in fighting against the French under the walls of Ravenna in 1512. It is not known when or where Vittoria Colonna first met Michael Angelo, but all authorities agree that it must have been about the year 1536, when he was over sixty years of age. She did not escape the espionage of the Inquisition, but was compelled in 1541 to fly to the convent at Viterbo. Three years later, she went to the convent of Benedictines of St. Anne in Rome, and just before her death, in 1547, she was taken to the house of Giuliano Cesarino, the husband of Giulia Colonna, her only relative in Rome. It was after she fled to the convent that she began to write sonnets to and receive them from Michael Angelo, whose love for her was not capable of being concealed.

Julia Gonzaga, Duchess of Trajetto, was known as the most beautiful woman in all Italy, and as the intimate friend of Vittoria Colonna. She also spent the last of her days in a convent.

With regard to Sebastian's portraits of Julia Gonzaga, the following, from Crowe and Cavalcaselli's 'History of Painting in North Italy,' will be interesting :—

'The real portrait of Giulia Gonzaga is supposed to exist in two different collections. In the National Gallery, we have the likeness of a lady in the character of St. Agatha, as symbolized

by a nimbus and pincers. Natural pose and posture and dignified mien indicate rank. The treatment is free and bold, but the colours are not blended with the care which Sebastian would surely have bestowed in such a case. In the Staedel Museum at Frankfort, the person represented is of a noble and elegant carriage, seated, in rich attire, and holding a fan made of feathers. A pretty landscape is seen through an opening, and a rich green hanging falls behind the figure. The handling curiously reminds us of Bronzino. It is well known that the likeness of Giulia was sent to Francis the First in Paris, and was registered in Lepicie's catalogue. The canvas of the National Gallery was purchased from the Borghese Palace, the panel at Frankfort from the heirlooms of the late King of Holland. A third female portrait by Del Piombo deserves to be recorded in connection with this inquiry,— that of Lord Radnor at Longford Castle, in which a lady with a crimson mantle and pearl head-dress stands in profile, resting her hands on the back of a chair. On a shawl which falls from the chair we read, " *Sunt laquei veneris cave.*" The shape is slender as that of Vittoria Colonna in the Santangelo palace at Naples, but the colour is too brown in light and too red in shadow to yield a pleasing effect, and were it proved that this is really Giulia Gonzaga the picture would not deserve Vasari's eulogy.'

Page 789. Brighter than Titian's.

Titian's real name was Tiziano Vecelio, called Da Cadore. He was born in 1477 and died in 1576. He studied with Gio. Bellini, and succeeded Giorgione in his commissions.

II.

Page 790.

Why did the Pope and his ten Cardinals
Come here to lay this heavy task upon
me ?

'The Last Judgment' was begun in

1534, when Paul III, Alessandro Farnese, was Pope.

Page 790. *The bones of Julius.*

This refers to Julius II, Julian della Rovere, who became Pope in 1503.

Page 790.
Fra Bastian, my Fra Bastian, might have done it.

Sebastian del Piombo, whose real name was Luciano, was born in 1485 and died in 1547. At one time he placed himself under the tutorship of Michael Angelo. He first studied with Gio. Bellini and Giorgione.

III.

Page 791. *Vittoria Colonna, Claudio Tolommei, and others.*

Among the others was Francesco D'Ollanda, a miniature-painter, who was sent to Rome by the King of Portugal that he might study with the great artists. To him we are indebted for descriptions of two Sundays which he spent with Vittoria Colonna and Michael Angelo in the chapel of San Sylvestro.

IV.

Page 794. *The Wild Boar in the gardens of Lorenzo.*

Lorenzo de' Medici.

Page 797. *And you have had the honour, nay, the glory, of portraying Julia Gonzaga!*

In 1533 Cardinal Ippolito de' Medici, being madly in love with Julia Gonzaga, sent Sebastian with an armed force to paint her portrait. It was accomplished in a month, and the portrait is said to have been one of Sebastian's best. It was sent to Francis I of France.

Part Second.

I.

Page 808. *A fugitive from Cardinal Caraffa's hate.*

Cardinal Caraffa became Pope Paul IV in 1555.

III.

Page 810. *Welcome, my Benvenuto.*

Benvenuto Cellini was born in 1500 and died in 1570. His life was full of incident. At one time he was employed by Clement VII as a musician as well as a sculptor.

Page 811. *I see the marvellous dome of Brunelleschi.*

Filippo Brunelleschi was born in 1377 and died in 1448. He is called the father of Renaissance. The dome of the cathedral at Florence, which he completed, is the one referred to in the text.

Page 811. *Ghiberti's gates of bronze.*

Lorenzo Ghiberti was born in 1370 and died in 1455. He was a goldsmith and sculptor. In 1400 he produced a design for the bronze gate to the baptistery at Florence, which was preferred to Brunelleschi's. Michael Angelo said, as Mr. Longfellow has made him say (p. 819), that these gates were ' worthy to be the gates of Paradise.'

Page 811. *Giotto's tower.*

Giotto di Bordone, born in 1276, died in 1336. He was a pupil of Cimabue, a painter as well as sculptor and architect. The bell tower of Santa Maria del Fiore in Florence is the one meant in the text. He did not live to see it completed.

Page 811. *And Ghirlandajo's lovely Benci glides.*

Domenico di Tomaso Curradi di Doffo Bigordi was born in 1449 and died in 1494. He was called Ghirlandajo from the fact that his father, a goldsmith, made beautiful garlands for the hair, so that the name signifying ' garland twister ' was given to him.

Page 812. *Under Pope Clement at the siege of Rome.*

Pope Clement VII, Giulio de' Medici, was made Pope in 1523.

Notes.

IV.

Page 818. *When Pope Leo died.*

Leo X, Giovanni de' Medici, son of Lorenzo the Magnificent, was made Pope in 1513.

Page 819. *You strove in rivalry with Baldassare and Raphael Sanzio.*

Baldassare Peruzzi was born in 1481 and died in 1537. He succeeded Raphael as architect of St. Peter's.

Raphael Sanzio was born in 1483 and died in 1520. He studied under his father, and later with Perugino.

V.

Page 820. *Our Vasari here.*

Giorgio Vasari, born in 1512 and died in 1574. His reputation rests upon his 'Vite de più eccellenti Pittori, Scultori et Architette,' published in 1555.

Page 821. *Three great names, Giorgione, Titian, and the Tintoretto.*

Giorgione di Castelfranco, whose real name was Barbarelli, was born in 1477 and died in 1511. He was the founder of the Venetian school.

The real name of Tintoretto was Jacopo Robusti. He was called Tintoretto from the fact that his father was a dyer. He was born in 1512 and died in 1594.

Page 821. *One Paul Cagliari, called the Veronese.*

Paul Cagliari was born in 1528 and died in 1588. He was the son of a sculptor.

Part Third.

II.

Page 826.

Pope Julius III, Giovanni Maria Giocci, was elected in 1550.

Page 827. *The labours of Bramante and San Gallo.*

Donato Lazzari Bramante was born in 1444 and died about 1514. He was an architect, painter, engraver, and military engineer. He was a compatriot and perhaps relative of Raphael, and was his friend and guide. It is known that he designed for Raphael the portico that surrounds the 'School of Athens.' He received from Julius II the task of rebuilding St. Peter's, and on his deathbed designated Raphael as the fit successor.

Antonio San Gallo was a nephew of Giuliano San Gallo. He was born in 1482 and died in 1546. His real name was Picconi. In 1509 he was one of the contractors for the woodwork in the Vatican and St. Peter's. He next became head carpenter at the castle, assistant to Raphael in 1516, and chief architect in 1520.

III.

Page 830.

Bindo Altoviti was a wealthy banker in Rome. He was born in 1491, and was related to Pope Innocent III through his mother. He devoted his fortune to the encouragement of art. Michael Angelo, Raphael, Cellini, Sansovino, and Vasari were his intimate friends. Michael Angelo gave him the cartoon from the Sistine Chapel called the 'Intoxication of Noah,' Raphael painted for him a Holy Family called 'Madonna dell' Impannata,' now in the Pitti palace.

Page 831. *Duke Cosimo, the tyrant, reigns supreme.*

Cosimo de' Medici, called The Great, was a son of Giovanni de' Medici. He was born in 1519, and on the death of Alexander in 1537 he was declared his successor.

Page 847. *The Bells of San Blas.*
The last poem written by Longfellow.

Index of First Lines.

879

Index of First Lines.

884

3.68